Ordnance Survey

STREET ATLAS
Surrey

Contents

III   *Key to map symbols*

IV-V   *Key to map pages*

VI   *Administrative and post code boundaries*

1   *Street maps*

219   *Town plans of Guildford and Kingston*

220   *Town plans of Dorking, Epsom, Leatherhead and Woking*

221   *Explanation of street index reference system*

221   *Key to town, village and rural locality abbreviations in index*

222   *Index of hospitals, railway stations, schools, shopping centres, street names and universities*

PHILIP'S

First colour edition published 1996
Reprinted in 1997 twice, 1998, 1999 by

Ordnance Survey® and George Philip Ltd, a division of
Romsey Road Octopus Publishing Group Ltd
Maybush 2-4 Heron Quays
Southampton London
SO16 4GU E14 4JP

ISBN 0-540-06435-1 (hardback)
ISBN 0-540-06436-X (spiral)

© Crown copyright 1996
© George Philip Ltd 1996

Printed and bound in Spain by Cayfosa

To the best of the Publishers' knowledge, the information in this
atlas was correct at the time of going to press. No responsibility
can be accepted for any errors or their consequences.

The representation in this atlas of a road, track or path is no
evidence of the existence of a right of way.

**The mapping between pages 1 and 220 (inclusive) in this atlas
is derived from Ordnance Survey® OSCAR® and Land-line® data,
and Landranger® mapping.**

Ordnance Survey, OSCAR, Land-Line and Landranger are
registered trade marks of Ordnance Survey, the national
mapping agency of Great Britain.

Also available in various formats

- Berkshire
- Bristol and Avon
- Buckinghamshire
- Birmingham and
  West Midlands
  Cannock, Lichfield
  Rugeley
- Cardiff, Swansea
  and Glamorgan
- Cheshire
- Derbyshire
  Derby and Belper
- Durham
- Edinburgh & East
  Central Scotland

- North Essex
- South Essex
- Glasgow & West
  Central Scotland
- Greater Manchester
- North Hampshire
- South Hampshire
- Hertfordshire
- East Kent
- West Kent
- Lancashire
- Merseyside
  Northwich, Winsford
  Middlewich
- Nottinghamshire

- Oxfordshire
  Peak District Towns
- Staffordshire
  Stafford, Stone
  Uttoxeter
- East Sussex
- West Sussex
- Tyne and Wear
  Warrington, Widnes
  Runcorn
- Warwickshire
- South Yorkshire
- West Yorkshire

- Colour regional atlases (hardback, spiral, wire-o, pocket) ◇ Colour local atlases (paperback)
- Black and white regional atlases (hardback, softback, pocket)

Symbol	Description
22a	Motorway (with junction number)
	Primary route (dual carriageway and single)
	A road (dual carriageway and single)
	B road (dual carriageway and single)
	Minor road (dual carriageway and single)
	Other minor road
	Road under construction
	County boundaries
	Railway
	Rural track, private road or narrow road in urban area
	Gate or obstruction to traffic (restrictions may not apply at all times or to all vehicles)
	Path, bridleway, byway open to all traffic, road used as a public path, dismantled railways, etc.

The representation in this atlas of a road, track or path is no evidence of the existence of a right of way

174 Adjoining page indicator

	British Rail station
	Underground station
	Private railway station
	Bus, coach station
	Ambulance station
	Coastguard station
	Fire station
	Police station
	Casualty entrance to hospital
	Church, place of worship
H	Hospital
i	Information centre
P	Parking
PO	Post Office
●	Public convenience
	Important buildings, schools, colleges, universities and hospitals
Guildford City Sch	
River Wey	Water name
	Stream
	River or canal (minor and major)
	Water
	Tidal water
	Woods

Abbr	Full	Abbr	Full
Acad	Academy	Mon	Monument
Cemy	Cemetery	Mus	Museum
C Ctr	Civic Centre	Obsy	Observatory
CH	Club House	Pal	Royal Palace
Coll	College	PH	Public House
Ex H	Exhibition Hall	Resr	Reservoir
Ind Est	Industrial Estate	Ret Pk	Retail Park
Inst	Institute	Sch	School
Ct	Law Court	Sh Ctr	Shopping Centre
L Ctr	Leisure Centre	Sta	Station
LC	Level Crossing	TH	Town Hall/House
Liby	Library	Trad Est	Trading Estate
Mkt	Market	Univ	University
Meml	Memorial	YH	Youth Hostel

0   ¼   ½   ¾   1 mile

0   250 m   500 m   750 m   1 Kilometre

The scale of the maps is 5.52 cm to 1 km (3½ inches to 1 mile)

The small numbers around the edges of the maps identify the 1 kilometre National Grid lines

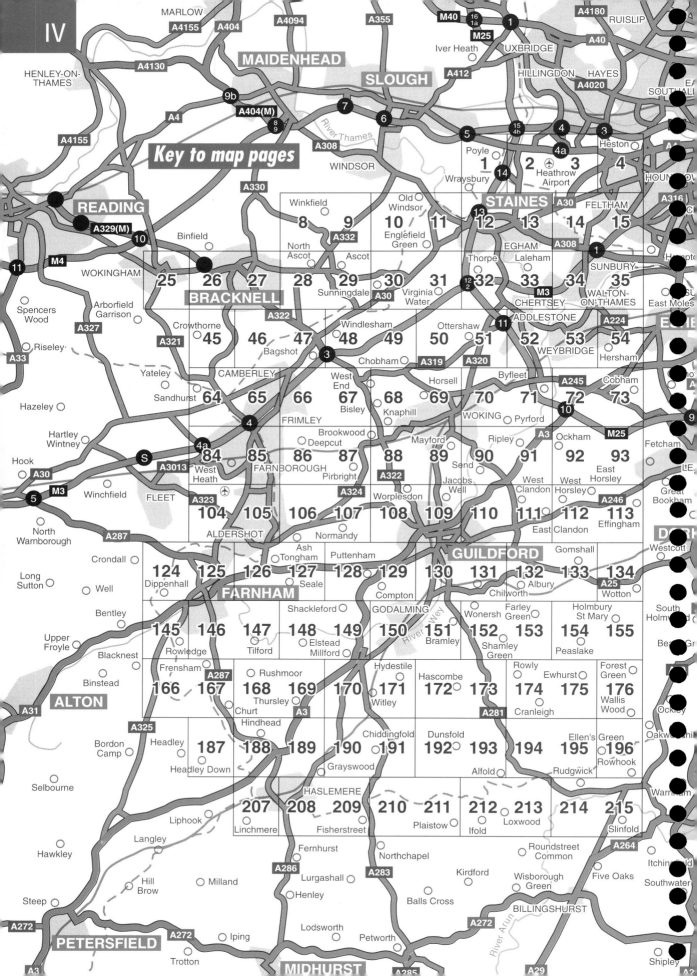

IV

Key to map pages

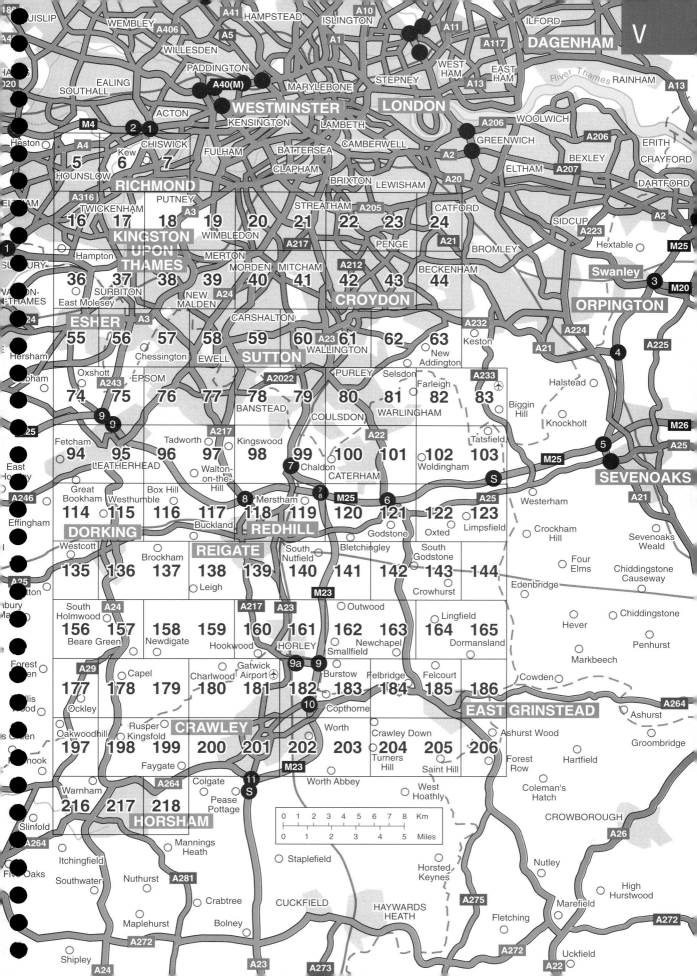

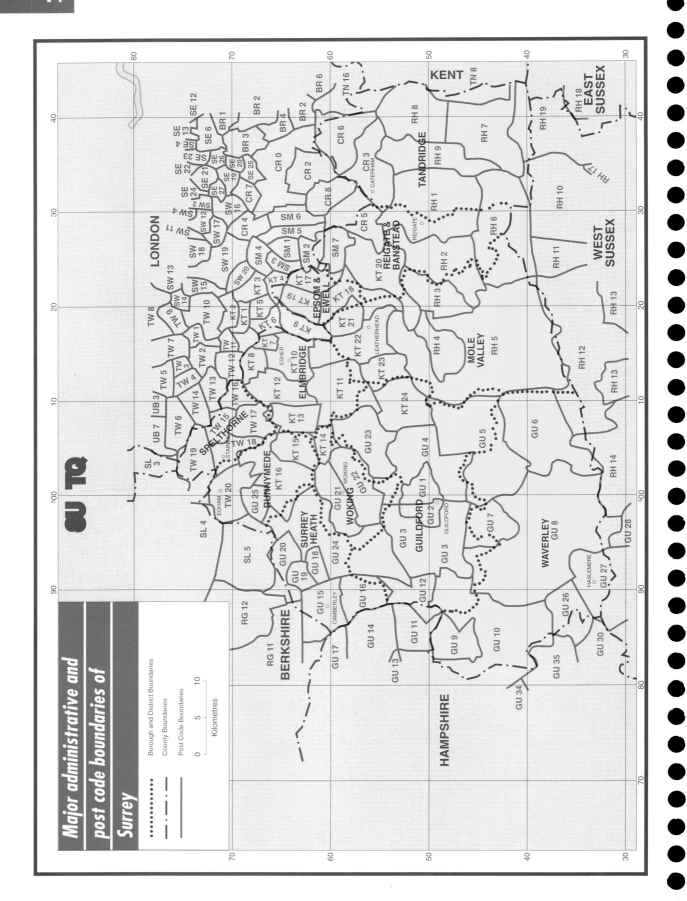

Major administrative and post code boundaries of

Surrey

Borough and District Boundaries

County Boundaries

Post Code Boundaries

0   5   10
Kilometres

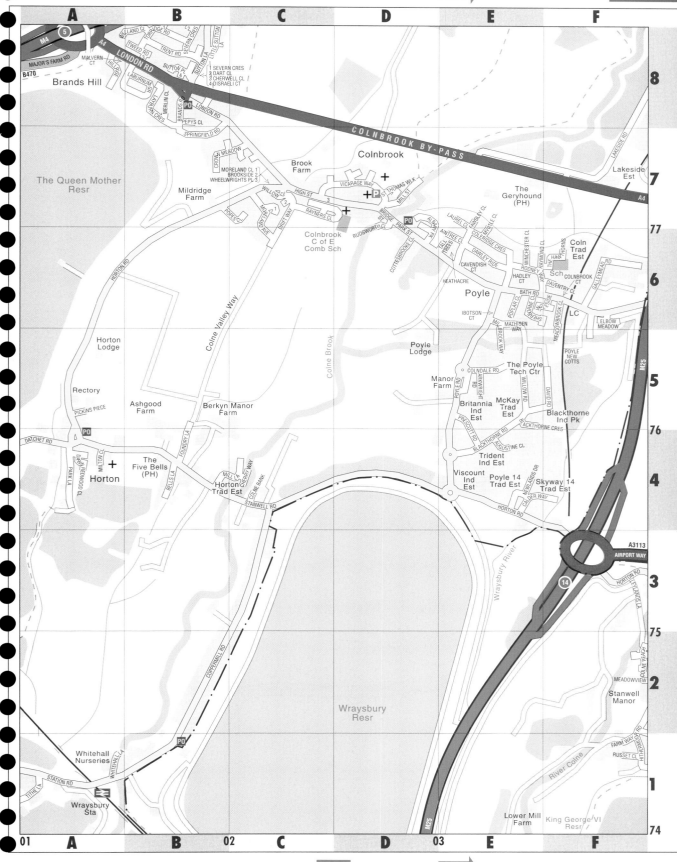

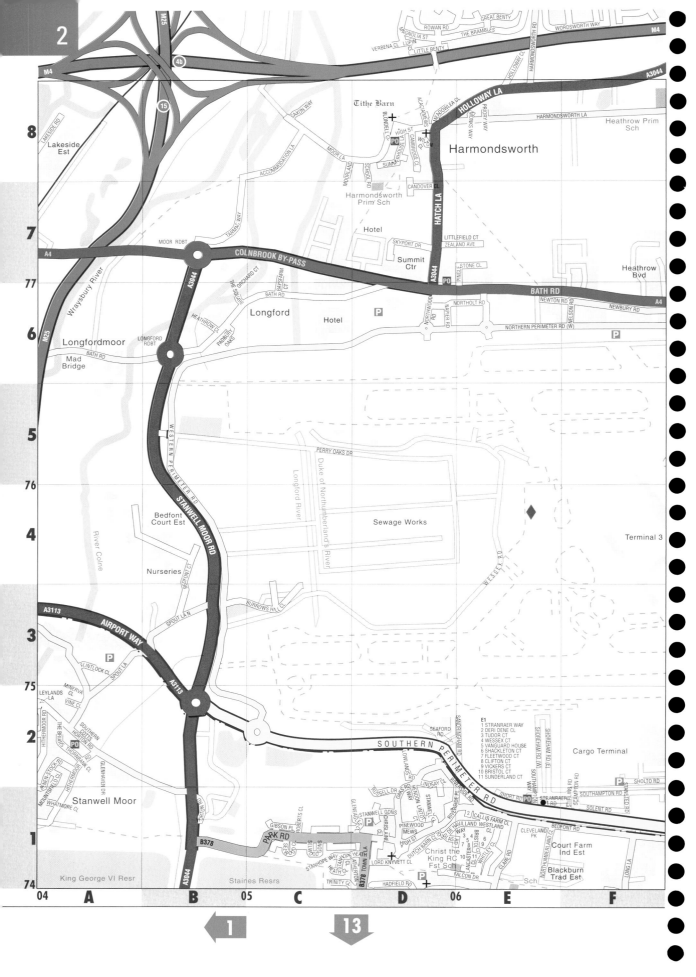

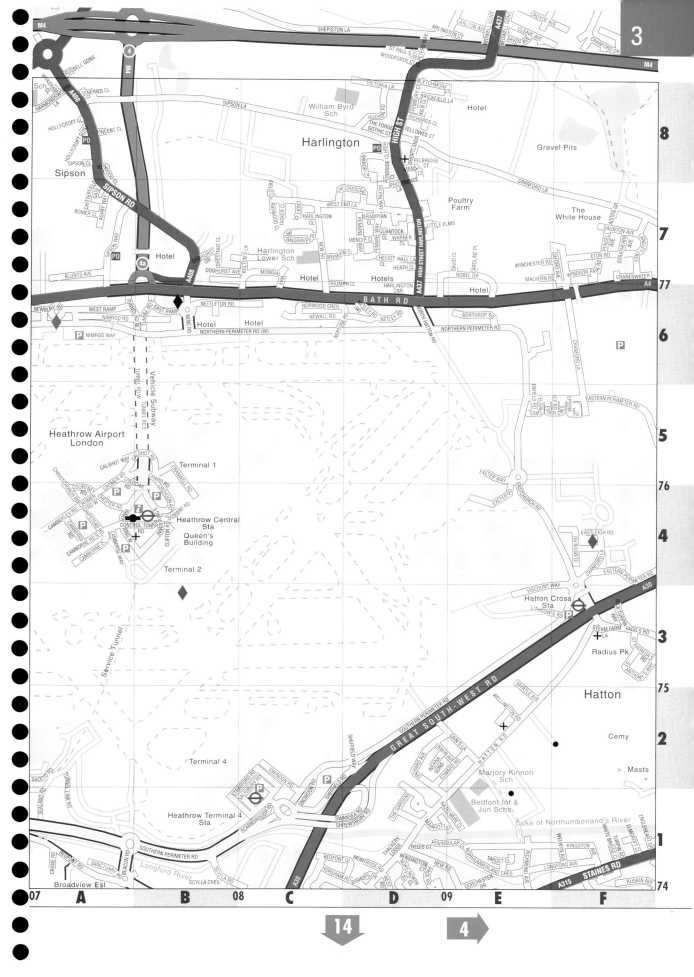

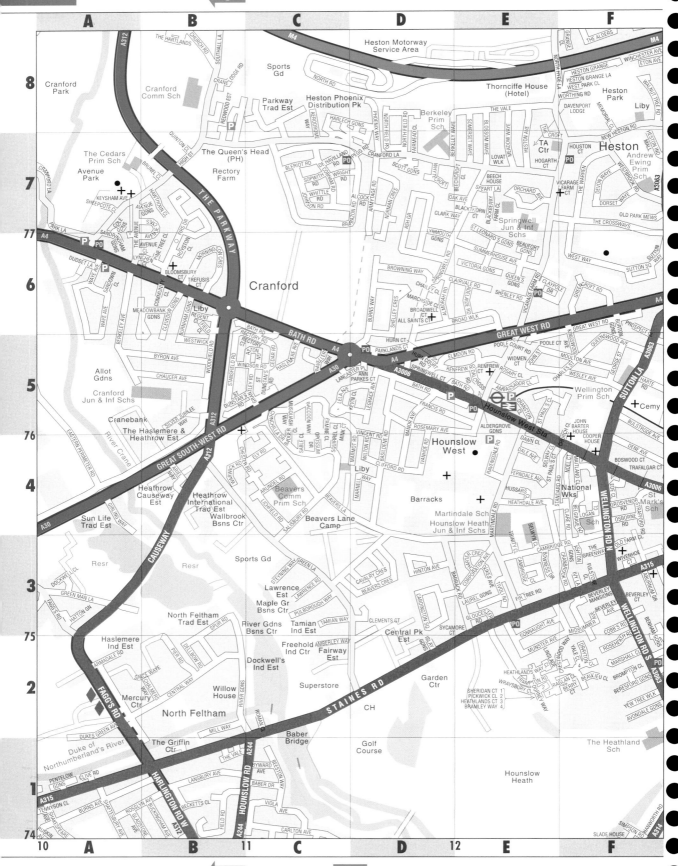

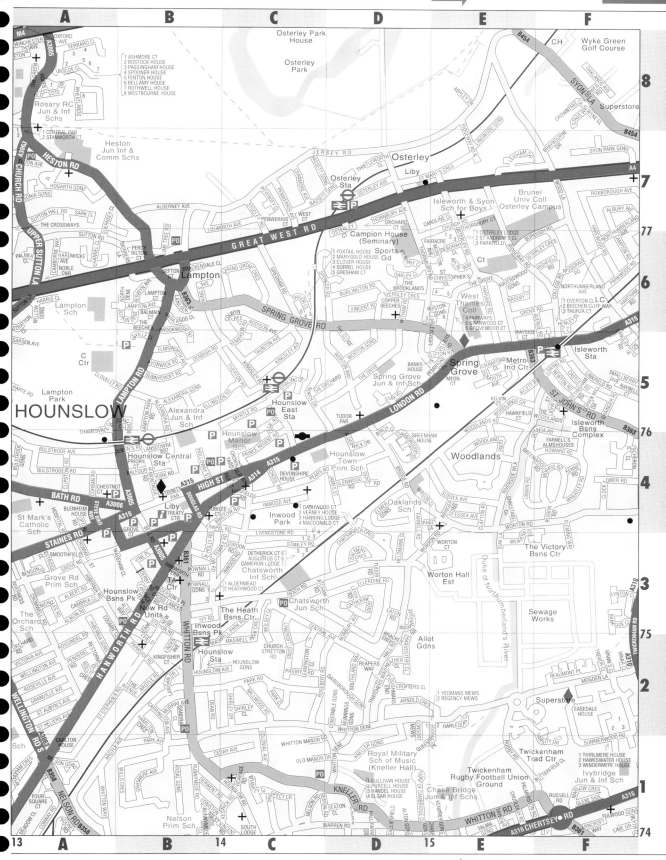

D8
1 BROCKSHOT CL
2 WESTBURY PL
3 BROOK LA N
4 BROOK LA BNS CTR
5 BREAMAR CT
6 BROOK CT
7 CLIFDEN HOUSE
8 CEDAR CT
9 CRANBROOK CT
10 ALEXANDRA RD
11 BERKELEY HOUSE
12 WATERMANS CT

E8
1 FERRY SQ
2 WATERMANS CT
3 WILKES RD
4 ALBANY PAR
5 CHARLTON HOUSE
6 ALBANY HOUSE
7 ALMA HOUSE
8 GRIFFIN CT
9 CRESSAGE HOUSE
10 TUNSTALL WLK
11 TRIMMER WLK
12 RUNNING HORSE YD
13 MISSION SQ
14 DISTILLERY WLK
15 COATES WLK
16 PERRAN WLK

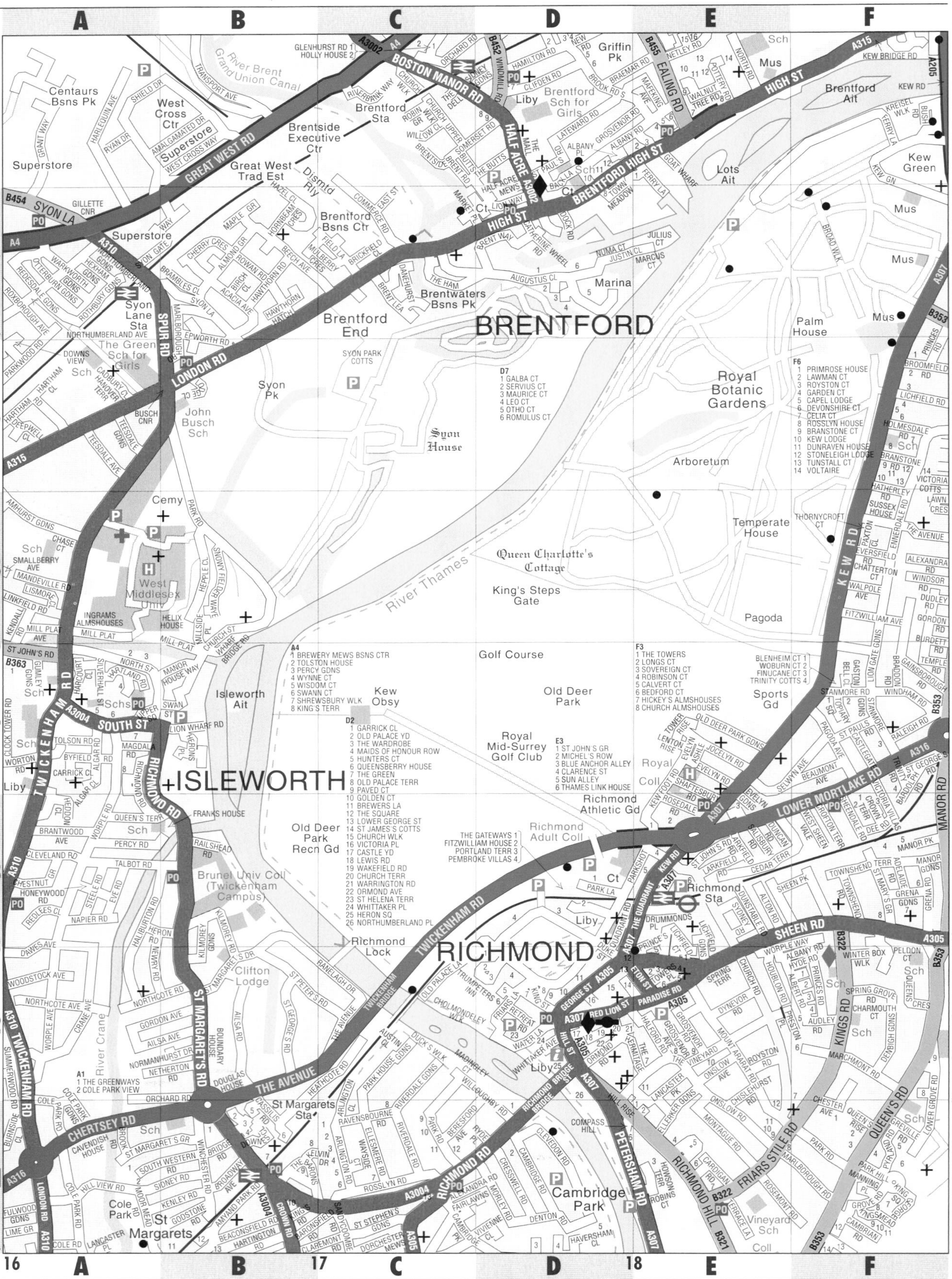
A B C D E F
8 7 77 6 5 76 4 3 75 2 1 74
16 17 18
BRENTFORD
ISLEWORTH
RICHMOND
Brentford End
Syon Pk
Syon House
Royal Botanic Gardens
Arboretum
Temperate House
Pagoda
Queen Charlotte's Cottage
King's Steps Gate
River Thames
Golf Course
Old Deer Park
Royal Mid-Surrey Golf Club
Kew Obsy
Isleworth Ait
Lots Ait
Brentford Ait
Kew Green
Richmond Sta
Richmond Lock
St Margarets
St Margarets Sta
Cambridge Park
Cole Park
West Middlesex Univ
Brunel Univ Coll (Twickenham Campus)
Syon Lane Sta
Brentford Sta
GREAT WEST RD
LONDON RD
TWICKENHAM RD
ST MARGARET'S RD
RICHMOND RD
THE AVENUE
KEW RD
LOWER MORTLAKE RD
SHEEN RD
PETERSHAM RD
RICHMOND HILL
CHERTSEY RD
HIGH ST
BRENTFORD HIGH ST
BOSTON MANOR RD
A4
A315
A310
A316
A305
A307
A3004
B353

B1
1 THE GROVE
2 CUMBERLAND CL
3 WESTMORLAND CL
4 SUSSEX CL
5 NORFOLK CL
6 NICOL CL
7 OLD LODGE PL
8 KELVIN CT
9 ST MARGARET'S CT
10 PARK COTTS
11 ST MARGARETS BSNS CTR
12 AMYAND COTTS

C1
1 HOWMIC CT
2 SEFTON LODGE
3 RAVENSBOURNE
4 ARLINGTON CT
5 GEORGINA CT
6 TREVELYAN HOUSE
7 CARADON CT
8 GREEN HEDGES
9 OLD HOUSE GDNS
10 QUEENS KEEP
11 BERESFORD CT
12 LANGHAM CT
13 POPLAR CT

D1
1 RICHMOND BRIDGE MANSIONS
2 HEATHERDENE MANSIONS
3 ROSELEIGH CL
4 BEAULIEU CL
5 RICHMOND MANSIONS
6 MALLARD CT

E1
1 LANCASTER COTTS
2 LANCASTER MEWS
3 BROMWICH HOUSE
4 PRIORS LODGE
5 RICHMOND HILL CT
6 GLENMORE HOUSE
7 HILLBROW
8 HEATHSHOT
9 FRIARS STILE PLACE
10 SPIRE CT
11 RIDGEWAY
12 MATTHIAS CT

E2
1 LICHFIELD TERR
2 UNION CT
3 CARRINGTON LODGE
4 WILTON CT
5 EGERTON CT
6 BEVERLEY LODGE
7 BISHOP DUPPA'S ALMSHOUSES
8 REGENCY WLK
9 TEMPLE CT
10 ONSLOW AVENUE MANSIONS
11 MICHELS ALMSHOUSES

F1
1 CHESTER CL
2 GROSVENOR CT
3 QUEEN S CT
4 RUSSELL WLK
5 CHARLOTTE SQ
6 JONES WLK
7 HILDITCH HOUSE
8 ISABELLA CT
9 DAMER HOUSE
10 ELIOT HOUSE
11 FITZHERBERT HOUSE
12 REYNOLDS PL
13 CHISHOLM RD
14 HOBART PL

F2
1 BEATRICE RD
2 LORNE RD
3 YORK RD
4 CONNAUGHT RD
5 ALBANY TERR
6 KINGSWOOD CT
7 SELWYN CT
8 BROADHURST CL
9 GROVE RD

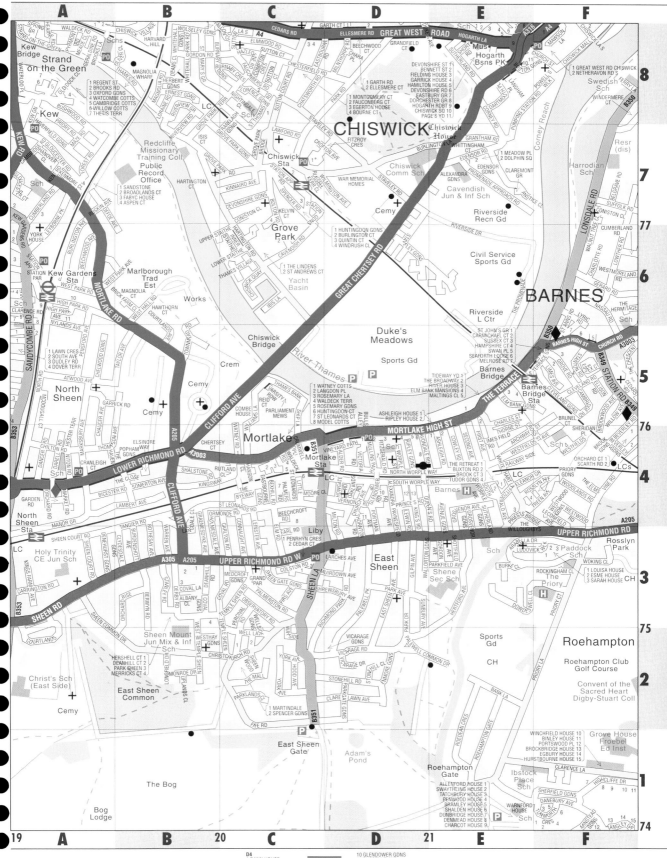

A6
1 CLARENDON CT
2 QUINTOCK HOUSE
3 BROOME CT
4 LONSDALE MEWS
5 ELIZABETH COTTS
6 SANDWAYS

7 VICTORIA COTTS
8 NORTH AVE
9 GROVEWOOD
10 HAMILTON HOUSE
11 MELVIN CT

D4
1 RANN HOUSE
2 CRAVEN HOUSE
3 JOHN DEE HOUSE
4 KINDELL HOUSE
5 MONTGOMERY HOUSE
6 AVONDALE HOUSE
7 ADDINGTON CT
8 DOVECOTE GDNS
9 FIRMSTON HOUSE

10 GLENDOWER GDNS
11 CHESTNUT AVE
12 TREHERN RD
13 ROCK AVE

18

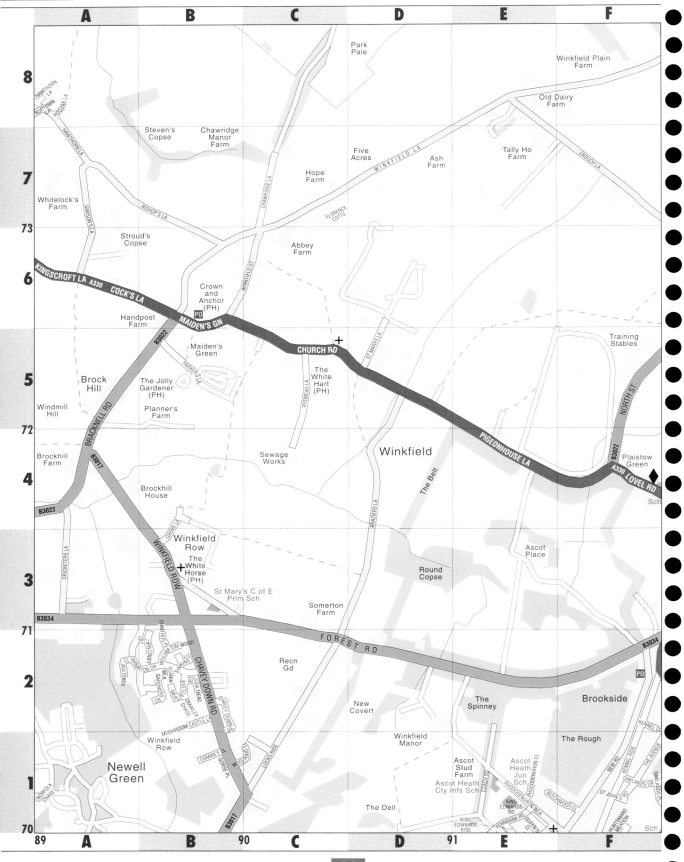

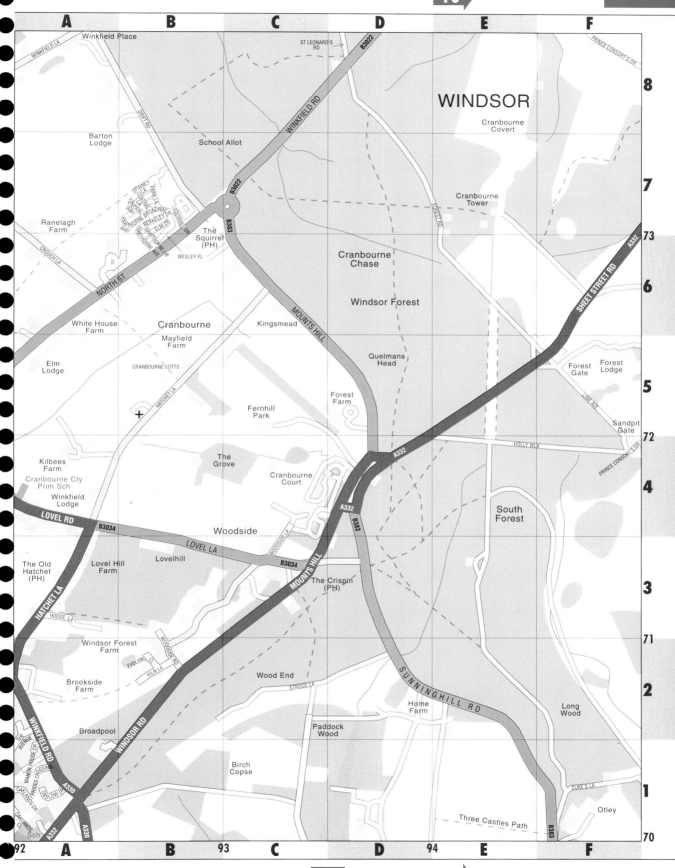

WINDSOR

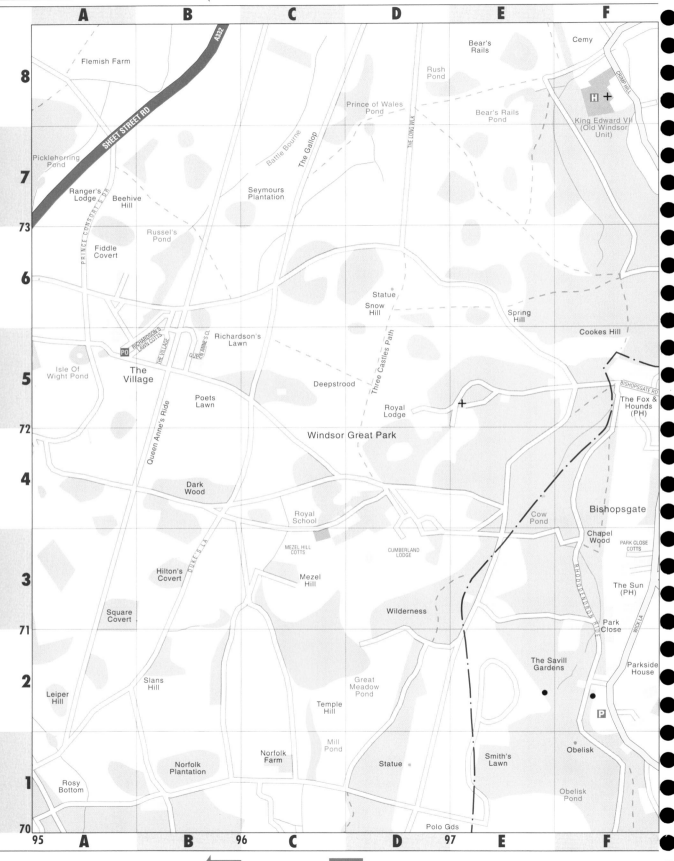

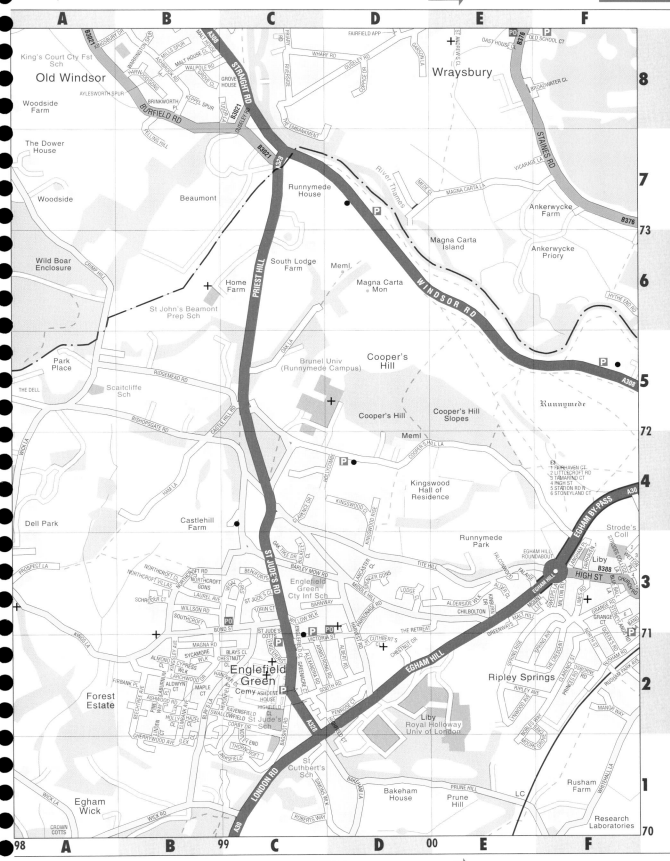

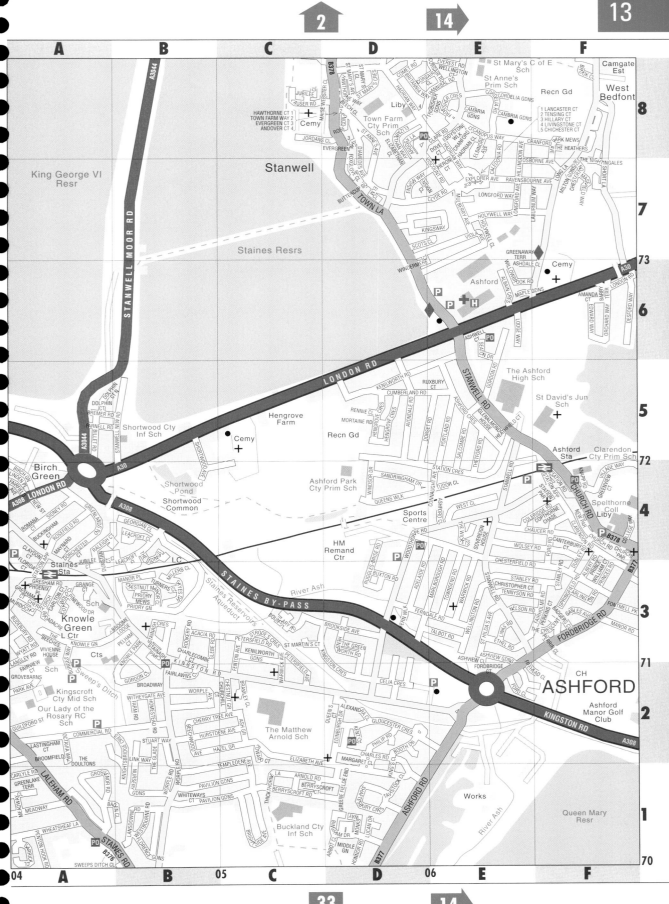

A B C D E F

8

SCYLLA CRES
STANWELL RD
Broadview Est
Wks
GREAT SOUTH-WEST RD
A30
BEDFONT CL
HATTON RD
BENEDICT DR
WEST RD
EAST RD
STAINES RD
A315
B3377
Longford Sch
CASSIOBURY AVE
BEDFONT LA
Longleat
Pates Manor Dr
Burlington Cl
Fairholme
Liby
LETCHWORTH AVE
EDWARD PAULING HOUSE

St Mary's Dr
Vicarage Ct
GROVE STILE WAY
ELM RD
CEDAR RD
Southville Jun & Inf Schs
B3377

7
The Royal Oak (PH)
B3003
A315
BEECH RD
BRIDLEPATH WAY
SOUTHVILLE CL
CHURCHILL CL
East Bedfont

73
A30
LONDON RD
HARROW RD
ASCOT RD
Cemy
BEDFONT GREEN CL
Fairholme Jun & Inf Schs

KENDAL CL 1
APPLEBY GDNS 2
DERWENT CL 3
MISSENDEN CL 4
BUTTERMERE CL 5

ROSEMEAD AVE
Grosvenor Park

6
CLOCKHOUSE LA
Bridge Farm
BEDFONT RD
Wks
Vineyard Nurseries
RECORD RD
RALEIGH RD
VERNON RD
PERCIVAL RD
PRINCES AVE
AVENUE RD
WESTBOURNE

5
HM Young Offender Institution & Remand Ctr
THE HERMITAGE 1
SPRING CNR 2
QUEENS PARK GDNS 3
Feltham Hill Jun & Inf Schs
Lower Feltham
The Sawyers Arms (PH)
A244 HIGH ST

72
REEDSFIELD CL
THE YEWS
Bedfont Ind Pk N
Ashford Ind Est
ASHFORD RD
B377
Cemy
SUNBURY CRES

4
Recn Gd
Chattern Hill
FELTHAM RD
B377
Allot Gdns
CHERTSEY RD
ELLINGTON RD
CRANLEIGH RD
Allot Gdns

B3003
B378
CHURCH RD
St-Michael's RC Prim Sch
Echelford Cty Mid Sch
Sports Gd
Meadhurst Sports Club
Felthamhill

3
Golf Course
CONVENT RD
SCHOOL RD
Ashford Sch
Ashford Common
Spelthorne Cty Inf Sch
FELTHAM HILL RD
Sunbury Common

ASHTREE CT 1
MORGAN CT 2
VAUGHAN ALMSHOUSES 3
ROWLAND HILL ALMSHOUSES 4
ROXETH CT 5
THE ELMS 6
BOURNE HOUSE 7
ST MATTHEW'S CT 8
DENCLIFFE 9

2
A308
KINGSTON RD
B378
Staines Reservoirs Aqueduct
CADBURY RD
Sunbury Common

1
Queen Mary Resr
STAINES RD W
Spelthorne Sports Club
Littleton Common
Wks
Windmill Trad Est
A244
WINDMILL RD
CEDAR HOUSE
A308
M3
Liby
THE PARADE

70

F1
1 BISHOPS CT
2 ASH LODGE
3 LIME LODGE
4 OAK LODGE
5 ELM CT
6 WILLOW LODGE
7 SYCAMORE LODGE
8 PRISCILLA HOUSE
9 SUNBURY CROSS CTR

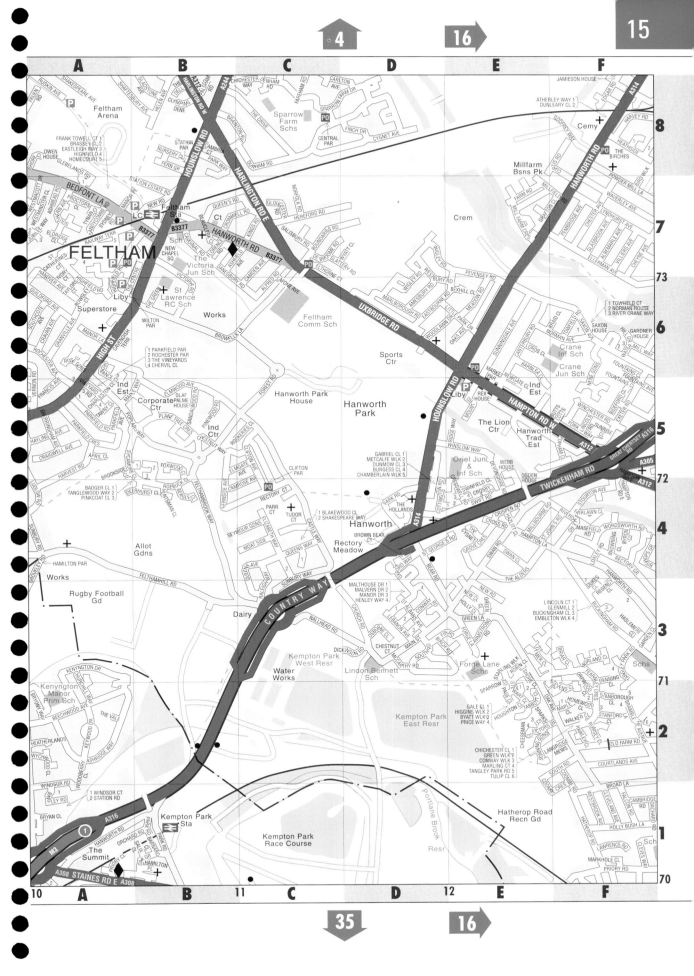

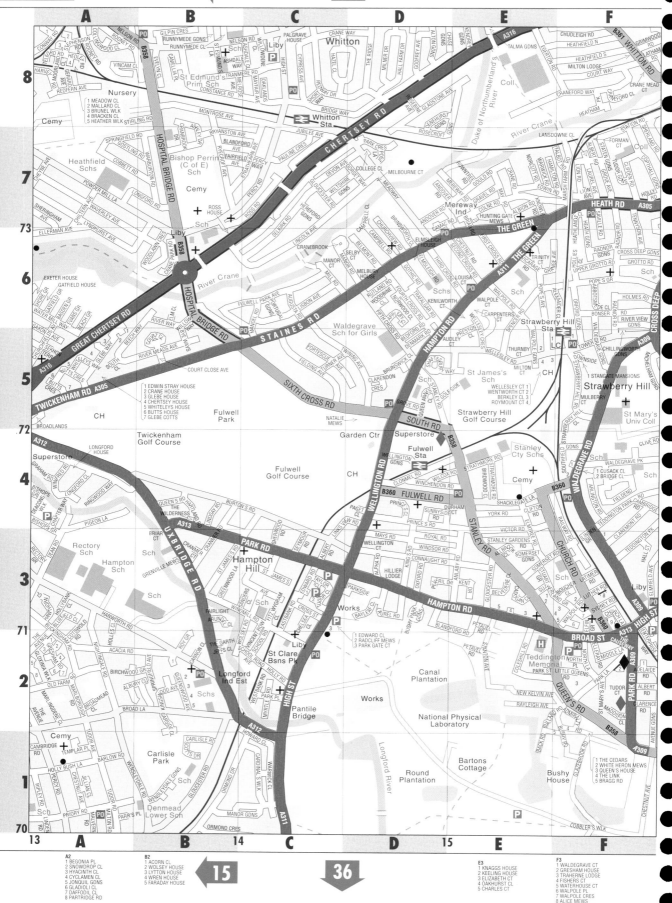

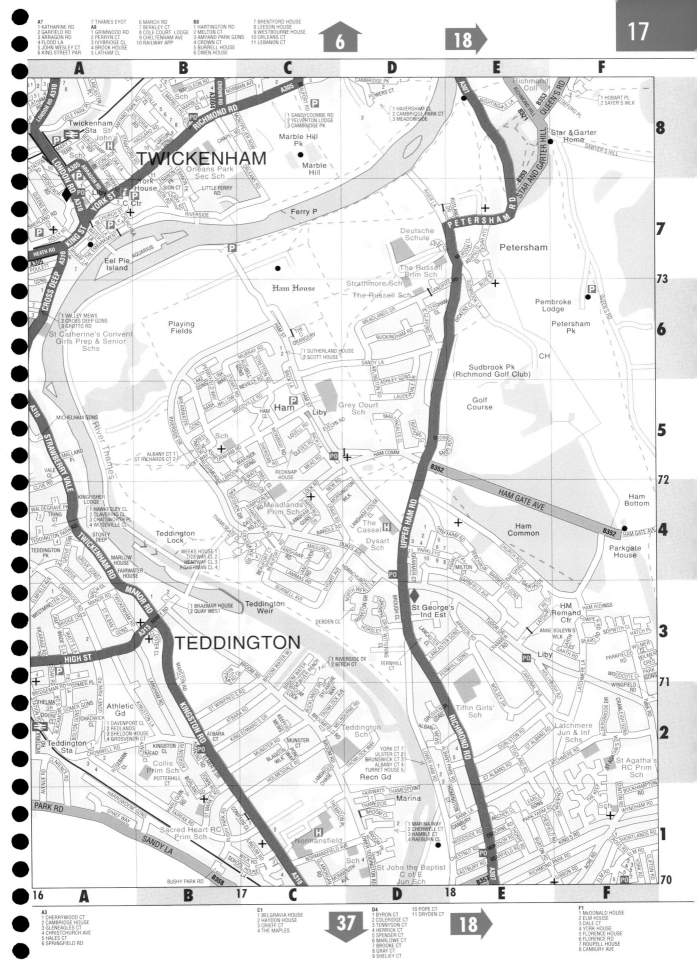

A7
1 KATHARINE RD
2 GARFIELD RD
3 ARRAGON RD
4 FLOOD LA
5 JOHN WESLEY
6 KING STREET PAR

7 THAMES EYOT

A8
1 GRIMWOOD RD
2 PERRYN CT
3 IVYBRIDGE CL
4 BROOK HOUSE
5 LATHAM CL

6 MARCH RD
7 BERKLEY CT
8 COLE COURT LODGE
9 CHELTENHAM AVE
10 RAILWAY APP

B8
1 HARTINGTON RD
2 MELTON CT
3 AMYAND PARK GDNS
4 CROWN CT
5 BURRELL HOUSE
6 OWEN HOUSE

7 BRENTFORD HOUSE
8 LEESON HOUSE
9 WESTBOURNE HOUSE
10 ORLEANS CT
11 LEBANON CT

A3
1 CHERRYWOOD CT
2 CAMBRIDGE HOUSE
3 GLENEAGLES CT
4 CHRISTCHURCH AVE
5 HALES CT
6 SPRINGFIELD RD

C1
1 BELGRAVIA HOUSE
2 HAYDON HOUSE
3 CRIEFF CT
4 THE MAPLES

D4
1 BYRON CT
2 COLERIDGE CT
3 TENNYSON CT
4 HERRICK CT
5 SPENSER CT
6 MARLOWE CT
7 BROOKE CT
8 GRAY CT
9 SHELLEY CT
10 POPE CT
11 DRYDEN CT

F1
1 McDONALD HOUSE
2 ELM HOUSE
3 DALE CT
4 YORK HOUSE
5 FLORENCE HOUSE
6 FLORENCE RD
7 ROUPELL HOUSE
8 CANBURY AVE

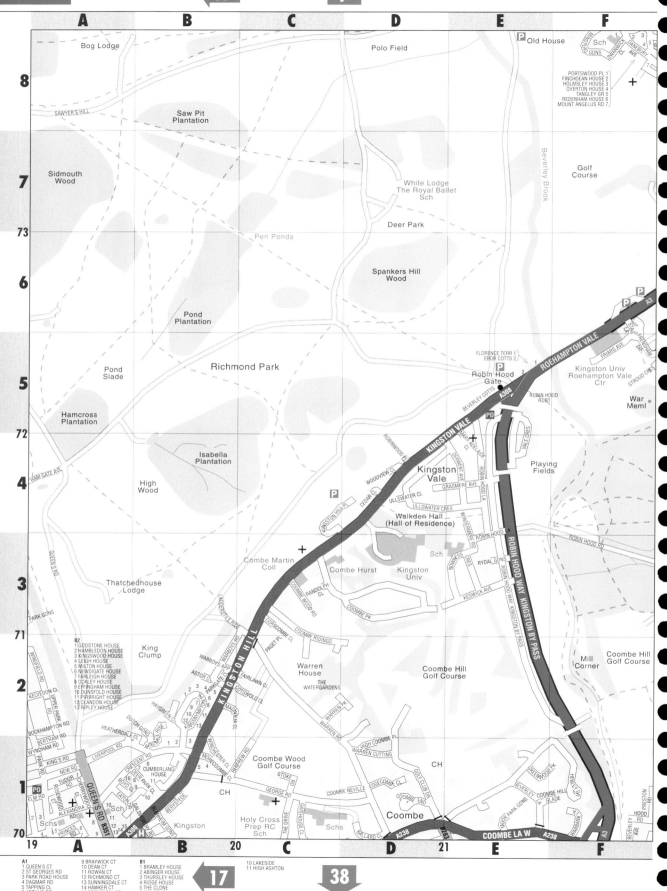

A   B   C   D   E   F

Bog Lodge

Polo Field

Old House

PORTSWOOD PL 1
FINCHDEAN HOUSE 2
HOLMSLEY HOUSE 3
OVERTON HOUSE 4
TANGLEY GR 5
REDENHAM HOUSE 6
MOUNT ANGELUS RD 7

Sch
GALSWIN GDNS
STANWICK CL
DANEBURY AVE

8

Saw Pit Plantation

Golf Course

Beverley Brook

SAWYER'S HILL

7   Sidmouth Wood

White Lodge
The Royal Ballet Sch

73

Pen Ponds

Deer Park

6

Pond Plantation

Spankers Hill Wood

P   A3

ROEHAMPTON VALE

5   Pond Slade

Richmond Park

FLORENCE TERR 1
EBOR COTTS 2

Robin Hood Gate

Kingston Univ Roehampton Vale Ctr

STAG FRESHAM DR

FRIARS AVE

STROUD CRES

War Meml

Hamcross Plantation

BEVERLEY COTTS
A308

KINGSTON VALE

ROBINWOOD CL

ROBIN HOOD RDBT

72

Isabella Plantation

WOODVIEW CL

CEDAR CL

Kingston Vale

MONT ADELAIDE CL
DERWENT AVE

ROBIN HOOD LA

GRASMERE AVE

VALE CRES

Playing Fields

4   High Wood

KINGSTON HILL PL

ULLSWATER CL

ULLSWATER CRES

WINDERMERE RD

Walkden Hall (Hall of Residence)

Sch

ROBIN HOOD LA

ROBIN HOOD RD

3   Thatchedhouse Lodge

PARK GDNS

Combe Martin Coll

Combe Hurst

Kingston Univ

RYDAL GDNS
BOLINGESS CRES
ROBIN HOOD WAY

KESWICK AVE

COOMBE WOOD RD

RANDOLPH CL

COOMBE PK

ROBIN HOOD WAY   KINGSTON BY PASS

71

QUEEN'S RD

King Clump

LAUDERDALE RIDGE

WARBOYS RD
WARBOYS APP

CODSCOMBE CL
PAGET PL

Coombe Ridings

Warren House

THE WATERGARDENS

Mill Corner

Coombe Hill Golf Course

B2
1 GODSTONE HOUSE
2 HAMBLEDON HOUSE
3 KINGSWOOD HOUSE
4 LEIGH HOUSE
5 MILTON HOUSE
6 NEWDIGATE HOUSE
7 FARLEIGH HOUSE
8 OCKLEY HOUSE
9 EFFINGHAM HOUSE
10 DUNSFOLD HOUSE
11 PIRBRIGHT HOUSE
12 CLANDON HOUSE
13 RIPLEY HOUSE

2

ASTOR CL
PARKGATE CL
KINGSNYMPTON PK
FAIRLAWN CL

MAGNOLIA CL

COTSWOLD CL

WARREN RD

KELVEDON CL
UPPER PARK

HAYGREEN CL
RISE
WYNDS

DUTCH GDNS

WARREN PK
HIGH COOMBE PL

Coombe Hill Golf Course

WARREN CUTTING

GOLF CLUB DR

CH

GREENWOOD CL

BEVERLEY

Coombe Hill Glade

HENLY DR

BOCKHAMPTON RD
BERTRAM RD
WYNDHAM RD

HEATHERDALE CL

LIVERPOOL RD

KINGSTON HILL

CUMBERLAND HOUSE

Coombe Wood Golf Course

PARK RD
KING'S RD
NEW RD

CRESCENT RD
DEER PARK CL
BOYD CL

WINCHESTER CL
MORECOMBE CL
KENFREW RD

STOKE RD

EDGECOMBE CL

MANOR PARK GDNS

A3

1

PO
ELM RD

TUDOR RD
ROSEWOOD CT
ALEXANDRA

CHERRYWOOD

EATON CL
GALSDON CL

BLENHEIM CL

BIRKDALE

GEORGE RD

THE DRIVE

COOMBE NEVILLE

COOMBE END

Coombe

COOMBE LA W   A238

BEVERLEY AVE

HOOD CL
PRESTON RD

Schs

PRINCES
QUEEN'S RD
A308
B351
H

Kingston

Holy Cross Prep RC Sch

CH

Schs

BALLARD RD

A238

A238

COOMBE LA W

70

A1
1 QUEEN'S CT
2 ST GEORGES RD
3 PARK ROAD HOUSE
4 DAGMAR RD
5 TAPPING CL
6 ARTHUR RD
7 BOROUGH RD
8 BELVEDERE CT

9 BRAYWICK CT
10 DEAN CT
11 ROWAN CT
12 RICHMOND CT
13 SUNNINGDALE CT
14 HAWKER CT
15 CROMWELL CT
16 KINGS CT

B1
1 BRAMLEY HOUSE
2 ABINGER HOUSE
3 THURSLEY HOUSE
4 RIDGE HOUSE
5 THE CLONE
6 MOUNT CT
7 HILLSIDE CT
8 HILL CT
9 ROYAL CT

10 LAKESIDE
11 HIGH ASHTON

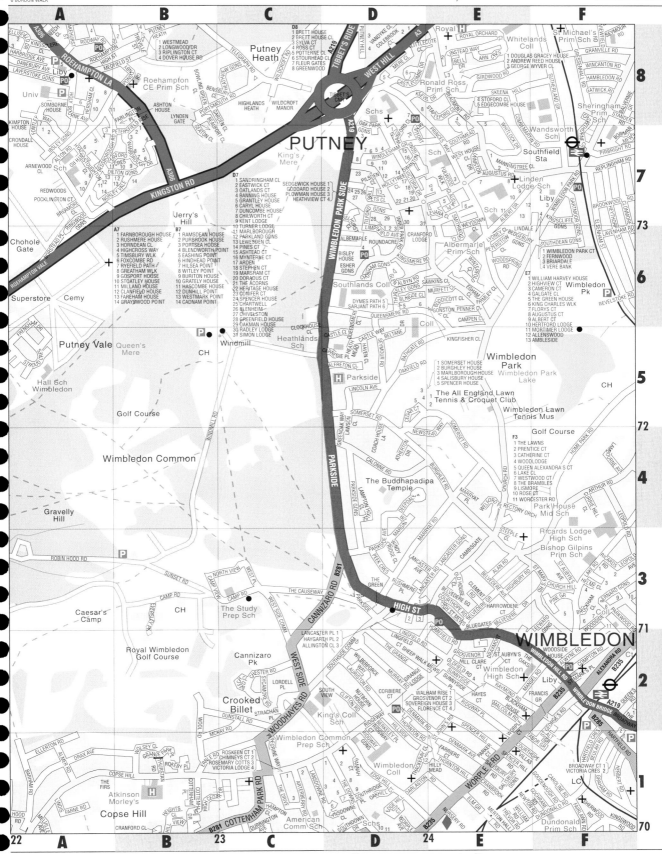

20

A8
1 WOODCOTT HOUSE
2 LYNDHURST HOUSE
3 WHEATLEY HOUSE
4 NEPEAN ST
5 ALLBROOK HOUSE
6 BORDON WALK
7 CHILCOMBE HOUSE
8 VICARAGE CT
9 SHAWFORD CT
10 EASTLEIGH WLK
11 KINGS CT

D8
1 BRETT HOUSE
2 BRETT HOUSE CL
3 SYLVA CT
4 ROSS CT
5 POTTERNE CL
6 STOURHEAD CL
7 FLEUR GATES
8 GREENWOOD

B8
1 WESTMEAD
2 LONGWOOD DR
3 RIPLINGTON CT
4 DOVER HOUSE RD

E8
1 DOUGLAS GRACEY HOUSE
2 ANDREW REED HOUSE
3 GEORGE WYVER CL

D7
1 SANDRINGHAM CL
2 EASTWICK CT
3 OATLANDS CT
4 BANNING HOUSE
5 GRANTLEY HOUSE
6 CARYL HOUSE
7 DUNCOMBE HOUSE
8 CHILWORTH CT
9 KENT LODGE
10 TURNER LODGE
11 MARLBOROUGH
12 PARKLAND GDNS
13 LEWESDEN CL
14 PINES CT
15 ASHTEAD CT
16 MYNTERNE CT
17 ARDEN
18 STEPHEN CT
19 MARSHAM CT
20 DORADUS CT
21 THE ACORNS
22 HERITAGE HOUSE
23 CONIFER CT
24 SPENCER HOUSE
25 CHARTWELL
26 BLENHEIM
27 CHIVELSTON
28 GREENFIELD HOUSE
29 OAKMAN HOUSE
30 RADLEY LODGE
31 SIMON LODGE

SEDGEWICK HOUSE 1
GODDARD HOUSE 2
PLOWMAN HOUSE 3
HEATHVIEW CT 4

A7
1 FARNBOROUGH CT
2 RUSHMERE HOUSE
3 HORNDEAN CL
4 HIGHCROSS WAY
5 TIMSBURY WLK
6 FOXCOMBE RD
7 RYEFIELD PATH
8 GREATHAM WLK
9 GOSPORT HOUSE
10 STOATLEY HOUSE
11 MILLAND HOUSE
12 CLANFIELD HOUSE
13 FAREHAM HOUSE
14 GRAYSWOOD POINT

B7
1 RAMSDEAN HOUSE
2 PURBROOK HOUSE
3 PORTSEA HOUSE
4 BLENDWORTH POINT
5 EASHING POINT
6 HINDHEAD POINT
7 HILSEA POINT
8 WITLEY POINT
9 BURITON HOUSE
10 GRATELY HOUSE
11 HASCOMBE HOUSE
12 DUNHILL POINT
13 WESTMARK POINT
14 CADNAM POINT

E7
1 WILLIAM HARVEY HOUSE
2 HIGHVIEW CT
3 CAMERON CT
4 GALGATE CL
5 THE GREEN HOUSE
6 KING CHARLES WLK
7 FLORYS CT
8 AUGUSTUS CT
9 HERTFORD LODGE
10 MORTIMER LODGE
11 MORTIMER LODGE
12 ALLENSWOOD
13 AMBLESIDE

1 WIMBLEDON PARK CT
2 FERNWOOD
3 BRIARDALE
4 VERE BANK

D5
1 SOMERSET HOUSE
2 BURGHLEY HOUSE
3 MARLBOROUGH HOUSE
4 SALISBURY HOUSE
5 SPENCER HOUSE

F3
1 THE LAWNS
2 PRENTICE CT
3 CATHERINE CT
4 WOODLODGE
5 QUEEN ALEXANDRA S CT
6 LAKE CL
7 WESTWOOD CT
8 THE BRAMBLES
9 LISMORE
10 ROSE CT
11 WORCESTER RD

ROEHAMPTON LA

KINGSTON RD

WEST HILL

WIMBLEDON PARK SIDE

PARKSIDE

CANNIZARO RD

WEST SIDE

WOODHAYES RD

COTTENHAM PARK RD

WORPLE RD

Putney Heath

PUTNEY

Jerry's Hill

Putney Vale

Wimbledon Common

Gravelly Hill

Caesar's Camp

Royal Wimbledon Golf Course

Golf Course

Crooked Billet

Copse Hill

WIMBLEDON

Wimbledon Park

Wimbledon Park Lake

The All England Lawn Tennis & Croquet Club

Wimbledon Lawn Tennis Mus

The Buddhapadipa Temple

39   20

D1
1 KINGSDOWN
2 WIMBLEDON CL
3 BERYL HARDING HOUSE
4 UPTON CL
5 LANHERNE HOUSE
6 CUMBERLAND CL
7 THAXTED PL
8 RATHBONE HOUSE
9 PRINCESS CT

D1
10 DOWNS CT
11 RAVENSCAR LODGE
12 SAVONA CL

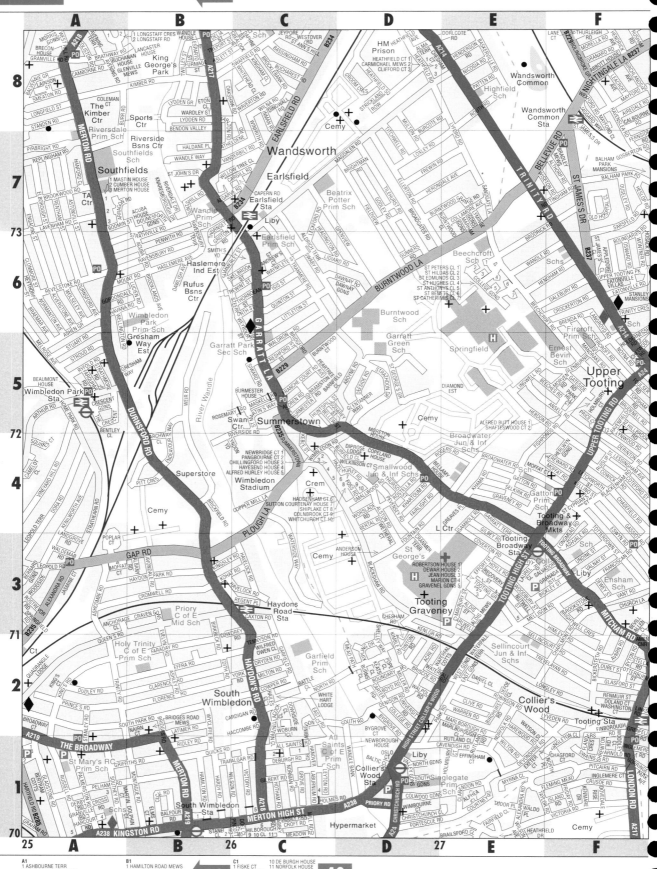

A1
1 ASHBOURNE TERR
2 SIR CYRIL BLACK WAY
3 DOWNING HOUSE
4 PALMERSTON GR
5 GLADSTONE CT

B1
1 HAMILTON ROAD MEWS
2 DOWMAN CL

C1
1 FISKE CT
2 MELLOR CT
3 OLIVE RD
4 ALLERTON HOUSE
5 VICTORY ROAD MEWS
6 WILL MILES CT
7 VANGUARD HOUSE
8 MYCHELL HOUSE
9 MERTON PL

10 DE BURGH HOUSE
11 NORFOLK HOUSE

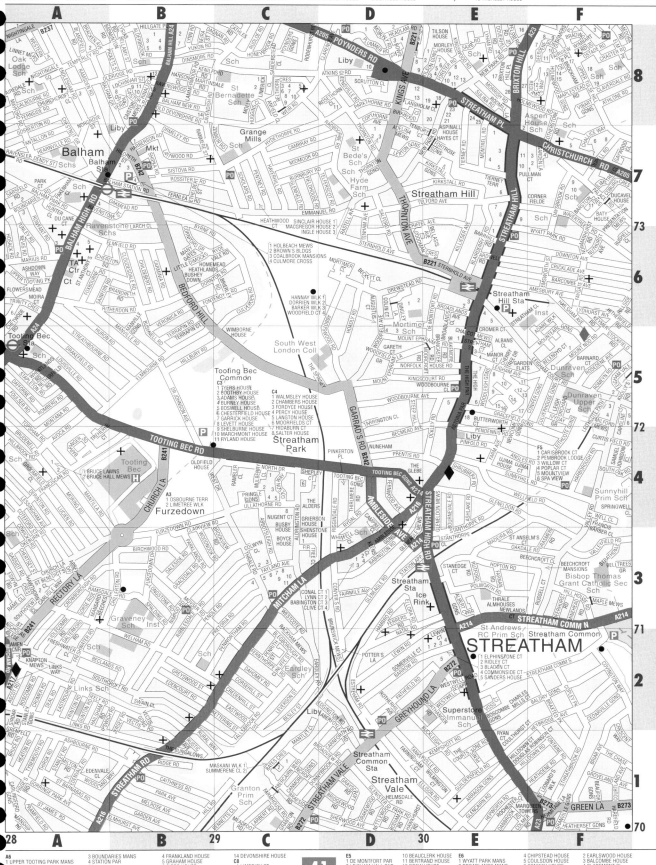

A8 / A7
1 RILEY HOUSE
2 BENNETT HOUSE
3 WHITE HOUSE
4 RODGERS HOUSE
5 DUMPHREYS HOUSE
6 HOMAN HOUSE

7 PRENDERGAST HOUSE
8 HUTCHINS HOUSE
9 WHITELEY HOUSE
10 TRESSIDER HOUSE
11 PRIMROSE CT
12 ANGUS HOUSE
13 CURRIE HOUSE

E8
1 PICTON HOUSE
2 RIGG HOUSE
3 WATSON HOUSE
4 MACARTHUR HOUSE
5 SANDON HOUSE
6 THOROLD HOUSE

7 PEARCE HOUSE
8 MUDIE HOUSE
9 MILLER HOUSE
10 LYCETT HOUSE
11 LAFONE HOUSE
12 LUCRAFT HOUSE
13 FREEMAN HOUSE

14 NEW PARK PAR
15 ARGYLL CT
16 DUMBARTON CT
17 KINTYRE CT
18 COTTON HOUSE
19 CROSSMAN HOUSES
20 CAMEFORD ST

21 PARSONS HOUSE
22 BRINDLEY HOUSE
23 ARKWRIGHT HOUSE
24 PERRY HOUSE
25 BRUNEL HOUSE
26 NEW PARK CT
27 TANHURST HOUSE

F8
1 HYPERION HOUSE
2 SOMERS RD
3 ARCHBISHOP'S PL
4 LEANDER RD
5 WITLEY HOUSE
6 OUTWOOD HOUSE

7 DUNSFOLD HOUSE
8 DEEPDENE LODGE
9 WARNHAM HOUSE
10 ALBURY LODGE
11 TILFORD HOUSE
12 ELSTEAD HOUSE
13 THURSLEY HOUSE

14 BROCKHAM HOUSE
15 CAPEL LODGE
16 LEITH HOUSE
17 FAIRVIEW HOUSE
18 WEYMOUTH CT
19 ASCALON CT

A6
1 UPPER TOOTING PARK MANS
2 CECIL MANS
3 MARIUS MANS
4 THE BOULEVARD
5 ELMFIELD MANS
6 HOLDERNESSE RD
A7
1 HESLOP CT
2 ST JAMES'S TERR

3 BOUNDARIES MANS
4 STATION PAR
A8
1 ST ANTHONY'S CT
2 HOLLIES WAY
3 ENDLESHAM CT
B8
1 MEYER HOUSE
2 FARADAY HOUSE
3 HALES HOUSE

4 FRANKLAND HOUSE
5 GRAHAM HOUSE
6 GIBBS HOUSE
7 DALTON HOUSE
8 ANSLIE WLK
9 ROKEBY HOUSE
10 CAISTER HOUSE
11 IVANHOE HOUSE
12 CATHERINE BAIRD CT
13 MARMION HOUSE

14 DEVONSHIRE HOUSE
C8
1 LIMERICK CT
2 HOMEWOODS
3 JEWELL HOUSE
4 GLANVILLE HOUSE
5 DAN BRYANT HOUSE
6 OLDING HOUSE
7 QUENNEL HOUSE
8 WEIR HOUSE

9 WEST HOUSE
10 NEVILLE CT

E5
1 DE MONTFORT PAR
2 LEIGHAM HALL PAR
3 LEIGHAM HALL
4 ENDSLEIGH MANS
5 JOHN KIRK HOUSE
6 RAEBARN CT
7 WAVEL CT
8 HOMELEIGH CT
9 HOWLAND HOUSE

10 BEAUCLERK HOUSE
11 BERTRAND HOUSE
12 DREW HOUSE
13 DOWES HOUSE
14 DUNTON HOUSE
15 RAYNALD HOUSE
16 SACKVILLE HOUSE
17 THURLOW HOUSE
18 ASTORIA MANS

E6
1 WYATT PARK MANS
2 BROADLANDS MANS
3 STONEHILL'S MANS
4 STREATFIELD PAR
5 DORCHESTER CT
E7
1 BEAUMONT HOUSE
2 CHRISTCHURCH HOUSE
3 STAPLEFIELD CL

4 CHIPSTEAD HOUSE
5 COULSDON HOUSE
6 CONWAY HOUSE
7 TELFORD AVE MANS
8 TELFORD PARK MANS
9 WAVERTREE CT
10 HARTSWOOD HOUSE
11 WRAY HOUSE
F7
1 CHARLWOOD HOUSE

2 EARLSWOOD HOUSE
3 BALCOMBE HOUSE
4 CLAREMONT CT
5 HOLBROOK HOUSE
6 GWYNNE HOUSE
7 KYNASTON HOUSE
8 TILLMAN HOUSE
9 REGENT LODGE
10 HAZELMERE CT
11 DYKES CT

A3
1 BELLTREES GR
2 ASH CT
3 ALDER CT
4 BEECH CT
5 ACACIA CT
6 BLACKTHORN CT
7 CYPRESS CT
8 HAWTHORN CT
9 HAZEL CT
10 SYCAMORE CT
11 MAPLE CT
12 LABURNAM CT
13 FERN LODGE

A4
1 JAMES BOSWELL
2 ST ALBANS HOUSE
3 SUFFOLK CT
4 ROCKHAMPTON CL
5 DELPHIAN CT

A7
1 VALENS HOUSE
2 LOVEDAY HOUSE
3 STRODE HOUSE
4 ETHELWORTH CT
6 BROOKS HOUSE
7 GODOLPHIN HOUSE
8 SHEPPARD HOUSE
9 McCORMICK HOUSE
10 TAYLOR HOUSE
11 SAUNDERS HOUSE
12 TALCOTT PATH
13 DERRICK HOUSE
14 WILLIAMS HOUSE
15 BALDWIN HOUSE
16 BERKELEY CT
17 CHURSTON CL
18 NEIL WATES CRES
19 BURNELL HOUSE
20 PORTLAND HOUSE

A8
1 ELLACOMBE HOUSE
2 BOOTH HOUSE
3 HATHERSLEY HOUSE
4 BRERETON HOUSE
5 HOLDSWORTH HOUSE
6 DEARMER HOUSE
7 CHERRY CL
8 GREENLEAF CL
9 LONGFORD WLK
10 SCARLETTE MANOR WLK
11 CHANDLERS WAY
12 UPGROVE MANOR WAY
13 ROPERS WLK
14 TEBBS HOUSE
15 BELL HOUSE
16 WORTHINGTON HOUSE
17 COURIER HOUSE
18 MACKIE HOUSE
19 HAMERS HOUSE
20 KELYWAY HOUSE

21

D6
1 COPPEDHALL
2 SHACKLETON CT
3 BULLFINCH CT
4 GANNET CT
5 FULMAR CT
6 HERON CT
7 PETREL CT
8 FALCON CT
9 EAGLE CT
10 DUNNOCK CT
11 DUNLIN CT
12 CORMORANT CT

B5
1 THANET HOUSE
2 CHAPMAN HOUSE
3 BEAUFOY HOUSE
4 EASTON HOUSE
5 ROBERTS HOUSE
6 LLOYD CT
7 KERSHAW HOUSE
8 WAKELING HOUSE
9 ELDRIDGE HOUSE
10 JESTON HOUSE
11 LANSDOWNE WOOD

C4
1 MOORE HOUSE
2 CHAUCER HOUSE
3 BUSHELL HOUSE
4 BLIGH HOUSE
5 HOBBS RD
6 HOGARTH HOUSE
7 GOODBEHERE HOUSE
8 ASTLEY HOUSE
9 ELDER GDNS
10 ELDERBERRY GR
11 THE PAVEMENT
12 DUNKIRK ST

D4
1 JOSEF PERRIN HOUSE
2 JEAN HUMBERT HOUSE
3 CHARLES STAUNTON HOUSE
4 VIOLETTE SZABO HOUSE
5 LILIAN ROLFE HOUSE
6 ODETTE HOUSE
7 ROBERT GERARD HOUSE
8 ST BERNARDS CL
9 CHAMPNESS CL
10 PENNINGTON CL
11 QUEENSWOOD CT

E2
1 NORTHWOOD WAY
2 HIGH LIMES
3 VALLEY PROSPECT
4 PLANE TREE WLK
5 CITY PROSPECT
6 BANKSIDE WAY
7 ROCHDALE
8 BARRINGTON WLK
9 GATESTONE CT
10 CHILDS LA
11 CARBERRY RD

E3
1 OAKDENE
2 THORSDEN WAY
3 OAKFIELD GDNS
4 GEORGETOWN CL
5 BRIDGETOWN CL
6 MOUNTBATTEN CL
7 BRABOURNE CL
8 ALEXANDRA WLK
9 COMPTON CT
10 BATTENBERG WLK
11 BURMA TERR
12 WISEMAN CT

E4
1 LINLEY CT
2 MELLOR HOUSE
3 WHITFIELD CT
4 MICHAELSON HOUSE
5 HOLBERRY HOUSE
6 HOVENDEN HOUSE
7 HUNTLEY HOUSE
8 MARKHAM HOUSE
9 NIGHTINGALE CT
10 MOLLIE DAVIS CT
11 PARNALL HOUSE
12 PIERSON HOUSE
13 ROPER HOUSE
14 ROUNDELL HOUSE
15 SAWYER HOUSE
16 RANSFORD HOUSE
17 CARMICHAEL HOUSE

F1
1 HETLEY GDNS
2 HIGHLAND LODGE
3 MASON CT
4 KENDALL CT
5 HIGH VIEW

E2
1 NORTHWOOD WAY

21

42

D5
1 STANDLAKE POINT	7 HEATHWOOD POINT
2 RADCOT POINT	8 ASHLEIGH POINT
3 NEWBRIDGE POINT	9 DEEPDENE POINT
4 NORTHMOOR	10 ROSEMOUNT POINT
5 KELMSCOTT	11 WOODFIELD HOUSE
6 RADNOR CT	12 CLAIRVILLE POINT
	13 TREVENNA HOUSE
	14 HYNDEWOOD

24

A5
1 TUNBRIDGE CT
2 HARROGATE CT
3 BATH CT
4 LEAMINGTON CT
5 PORLOCK HOUSE
6 CISSBURY HOUSE
7 EDDISBURY HOUSE
8 DUNDRY HOUSE
9 SILBURY HOUSE
10 HOMILDON HOUSE
11 HIGHGATE HOUSE
12 RICHMOND HOUSE
13 PENDLE HOUSE
14 TYNWALD HOUSE
15 WIRRALL HOUSE
16 GREYFRIARS

River House 1
Fordington House 2
Arbury Terr 3
Woodbury House 4
Forest Hill CT 5

Bromleigh CT 1
Parfew CT 2
Thetford CT 3
Attleborough CT 4
Dunton CT 5
Frobisher CT 6
Julian Taylor Path 7
Grizedale Terr 8
Worsley House 9

A1
1 HANOVER CT
2 BRUNSWICK CT
3 NEW CHURCH CT
4 REGENCY CT
5 OWEN WLK
6 BARGROVE CT
7 BEAVER CL

B3
1 RAGWORT CT
2 THE FIRS
3 WINGHAM HOUSE
4 SEATH HOUSE
5 RIPLEY HOUSE
6 LATHWOOD HOUSE
7 HURST HOUSE
8 GEORGE HOUSE
9 BROWNE HOUSE
10 BEACON HOUSE
11 BAILEY HOUSE
12 AGATE HOUSE

Grasmere CT 6
Torrington CT 7
Park House 8

1 SHAMROCK HOUSE
2 CAMBRIA HOUSE
3 TARQUIN HOUSE
4 PEMBERTON HOUSE
5 LONGHEDGE HOUSE

Forest Hill
Penge
Crystal Palace
Upper Sydenham
Lower Sydenham
New Beckenham
Bell Green

43

C1
1 WATERMEN'S SQ	10 GOUDHURST HOUSE
2 ST JOHN'S COTTS	11 WALMER HOUSE
3 GLADSTONE MEWS	12 STROOD HOUSE
4 BIRLING HOUSE	13 GREATSTONE HOUSE
5 SURREY TOWER	14 JOHN BAIRD HOUSE
6 MIDDLESEX HOUSE	
7 ADISHAM HOUSE	
8 BETHESDA CT	
9 OSPRINGE CL	

24

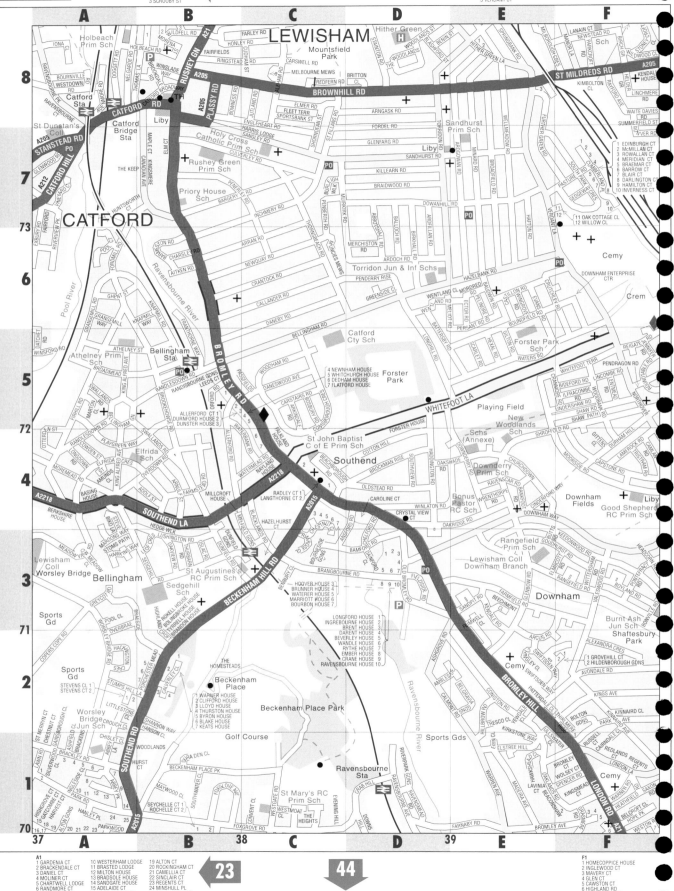

23

23
44

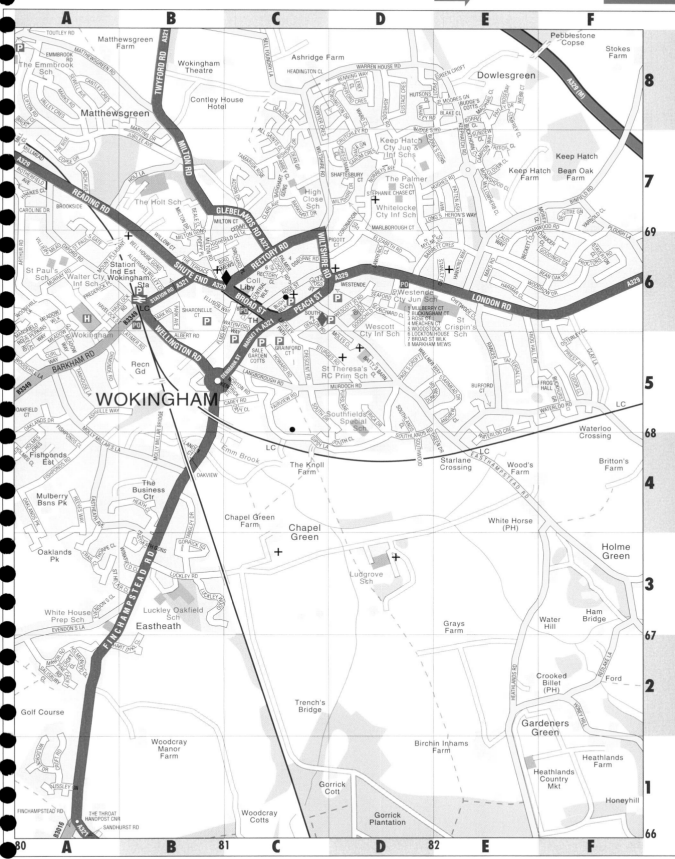

25

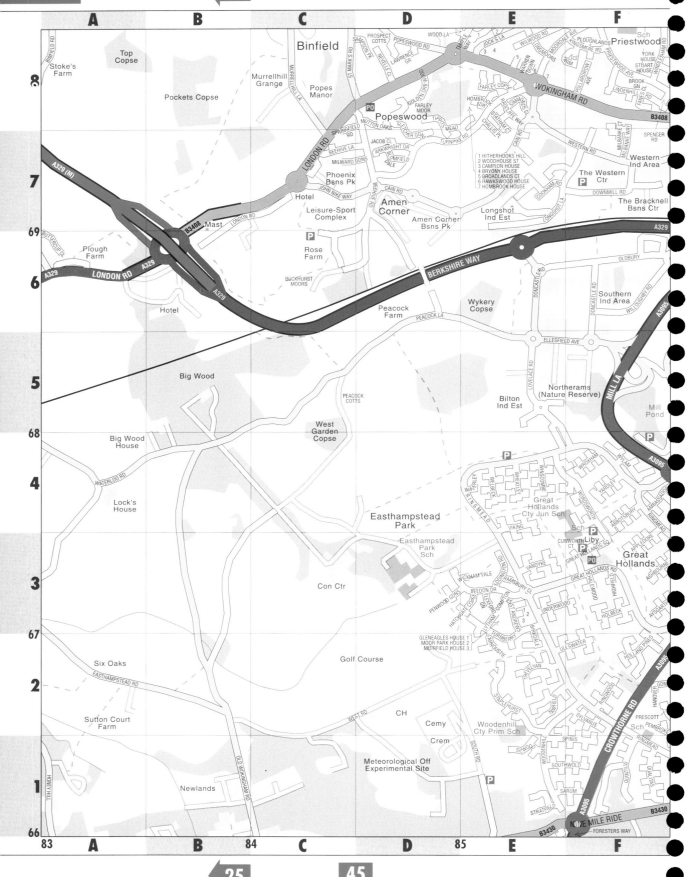

25   45

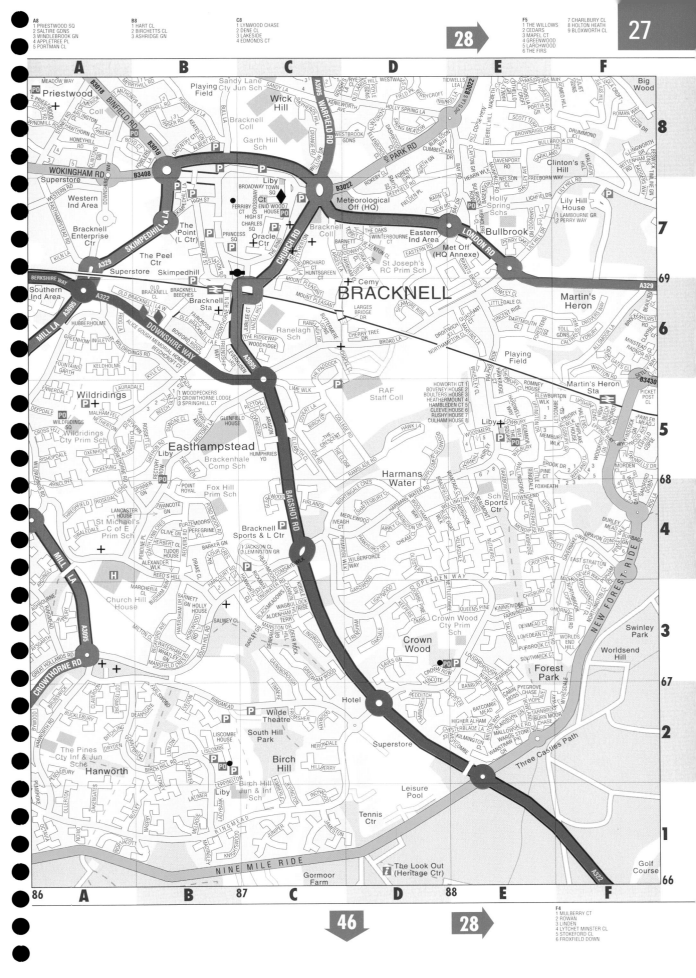

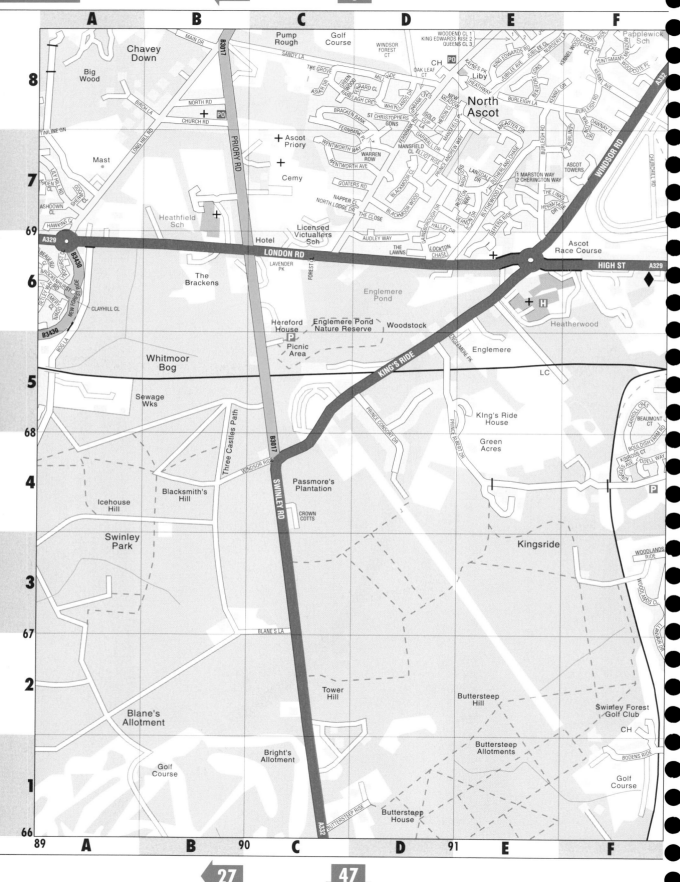

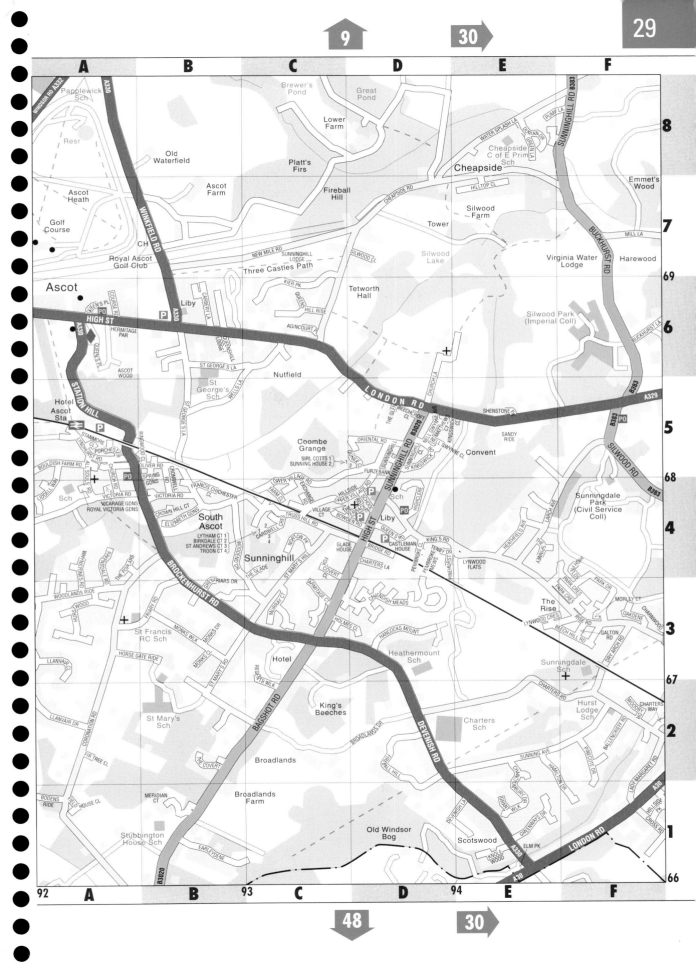

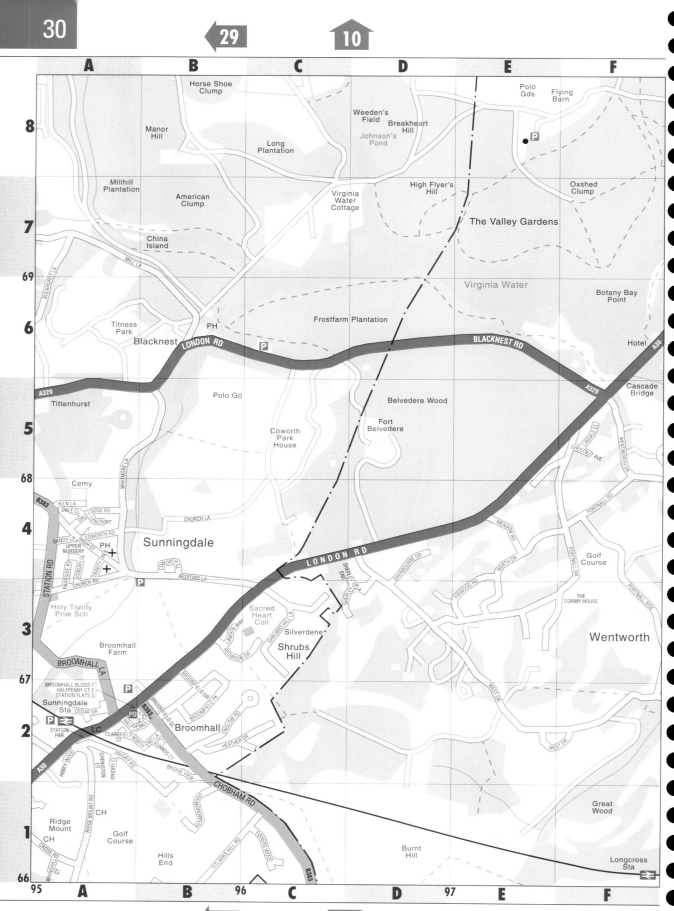

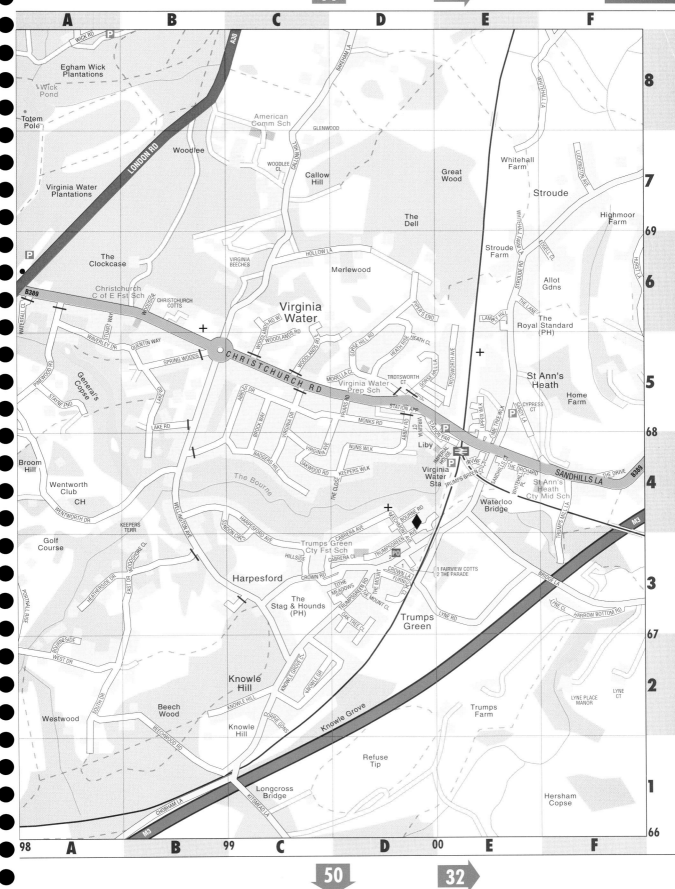

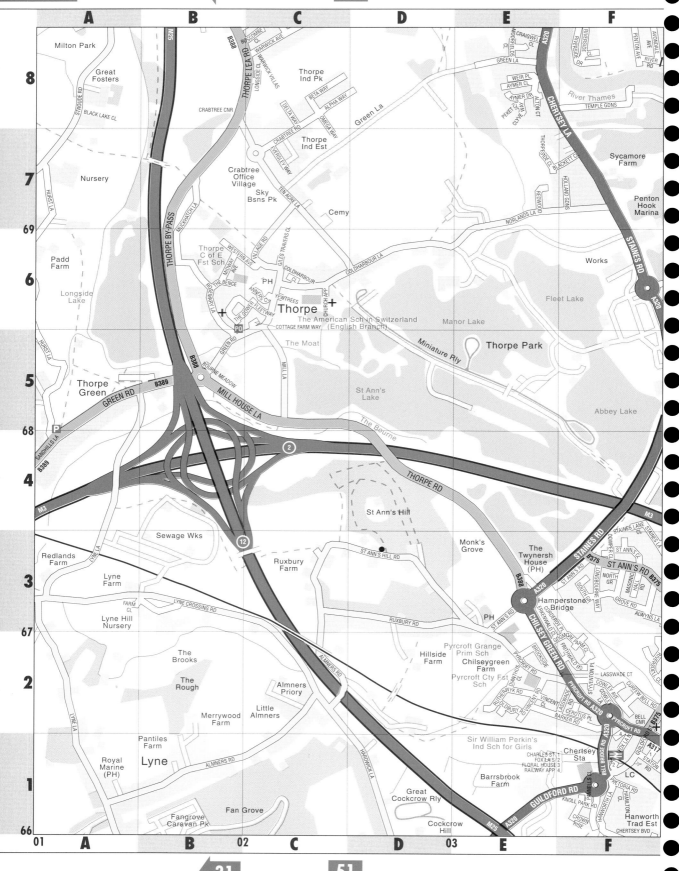

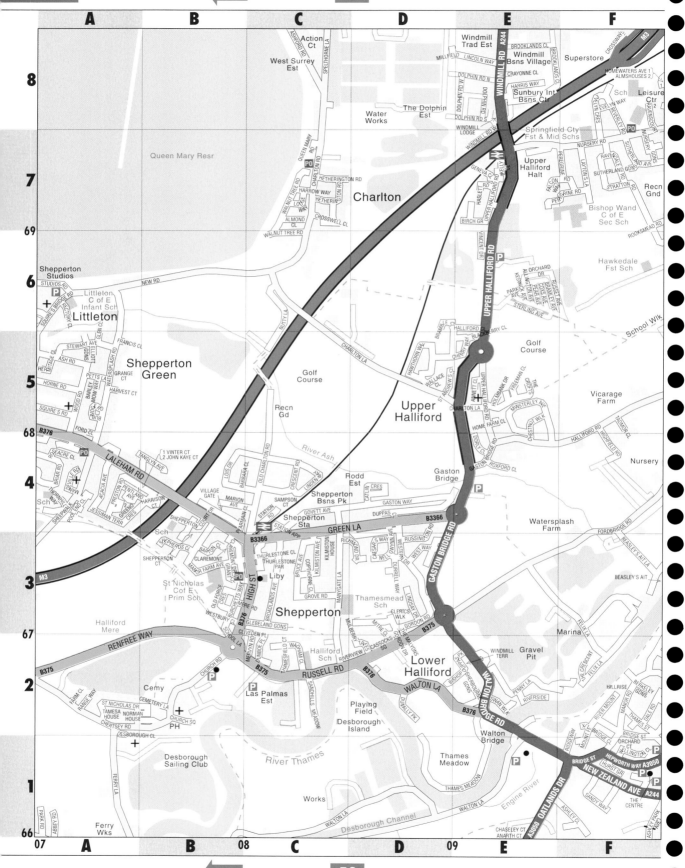

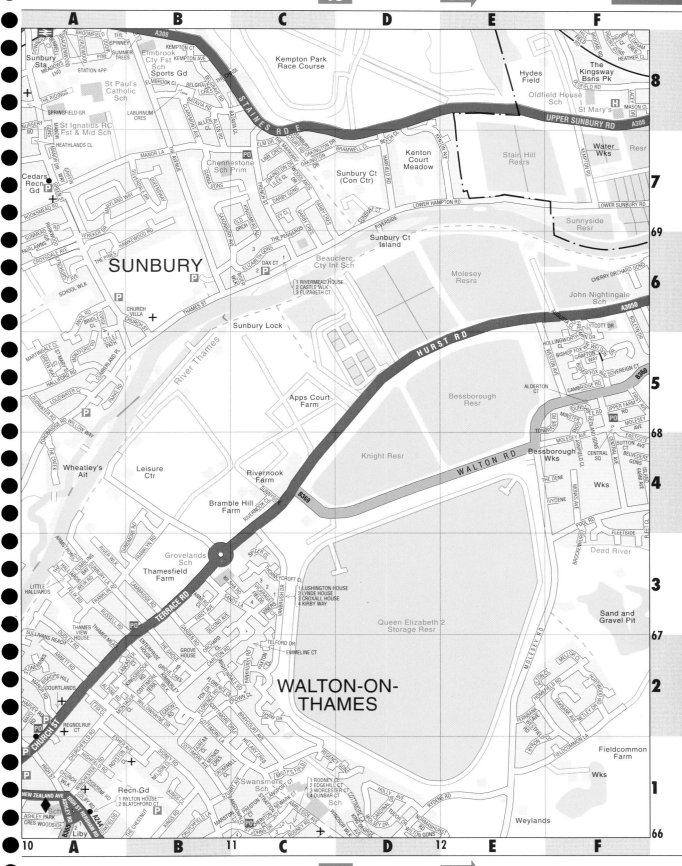

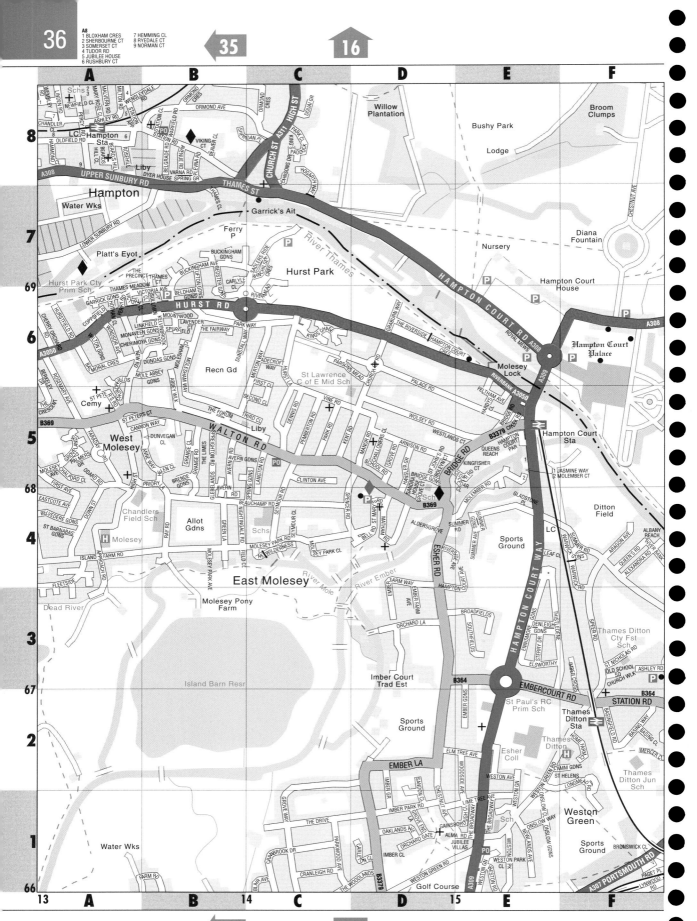

36

A8
1 BLOXHAM CRES
2 SHERBOURNE CT
3 SOMERSET CT
4 TUDOR RD
5 JUBILEE HOUSE
6 RUSHBURY CT
7 HEMMING CL
8 RYEDALE CT
9 NORMAN CT

35

16

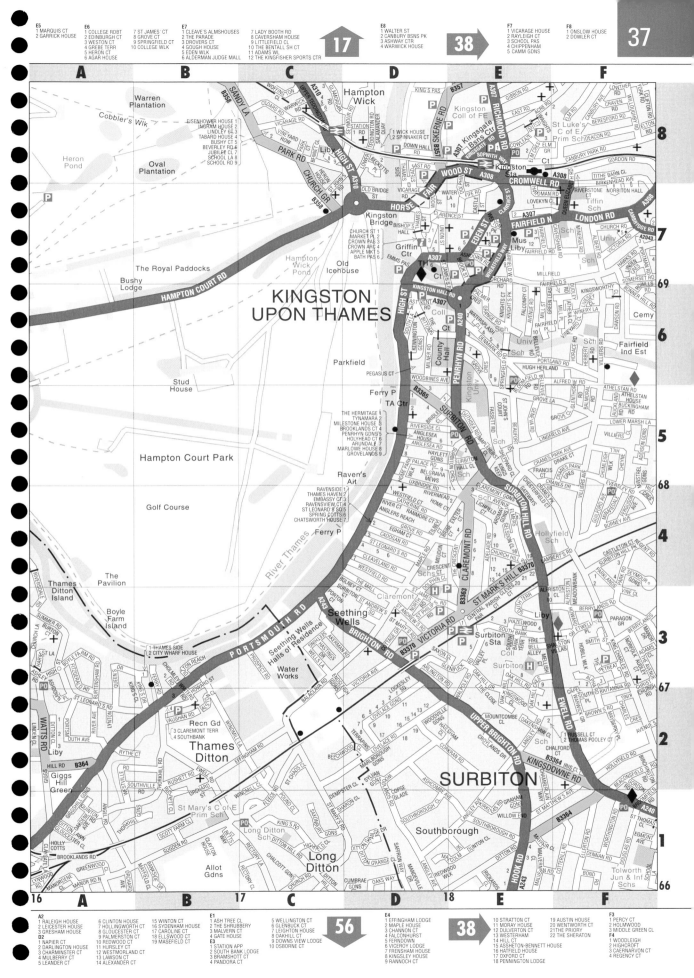

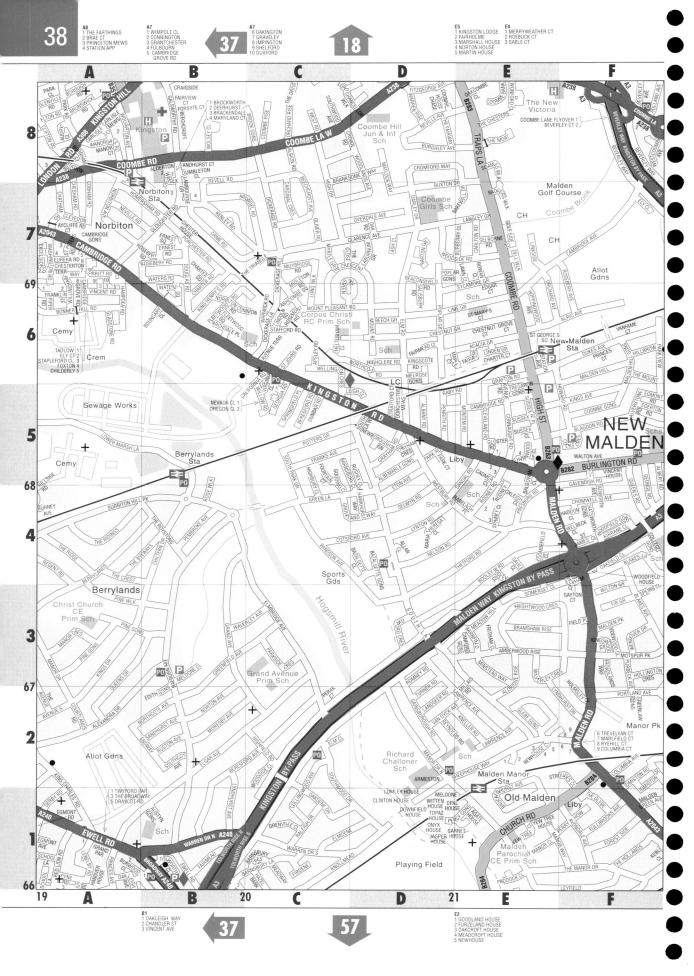

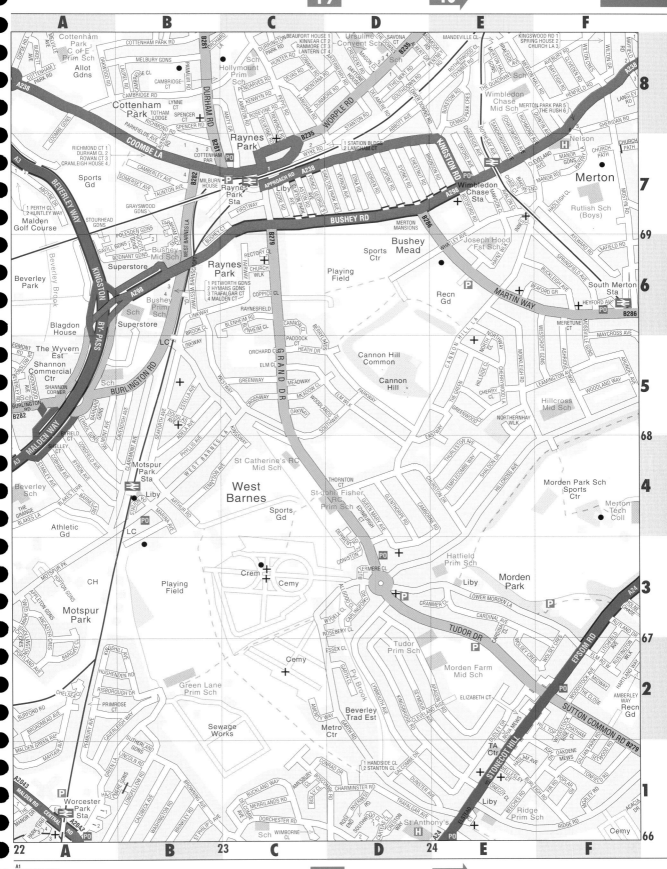

A1
1 BROOKSIDE CRES
2 BEVERLEY GDNS
3 PURDEY CT
4 THE AVENUE
5 BRIARWOOD CT
6 STATION APP
7 DOWNFIELD

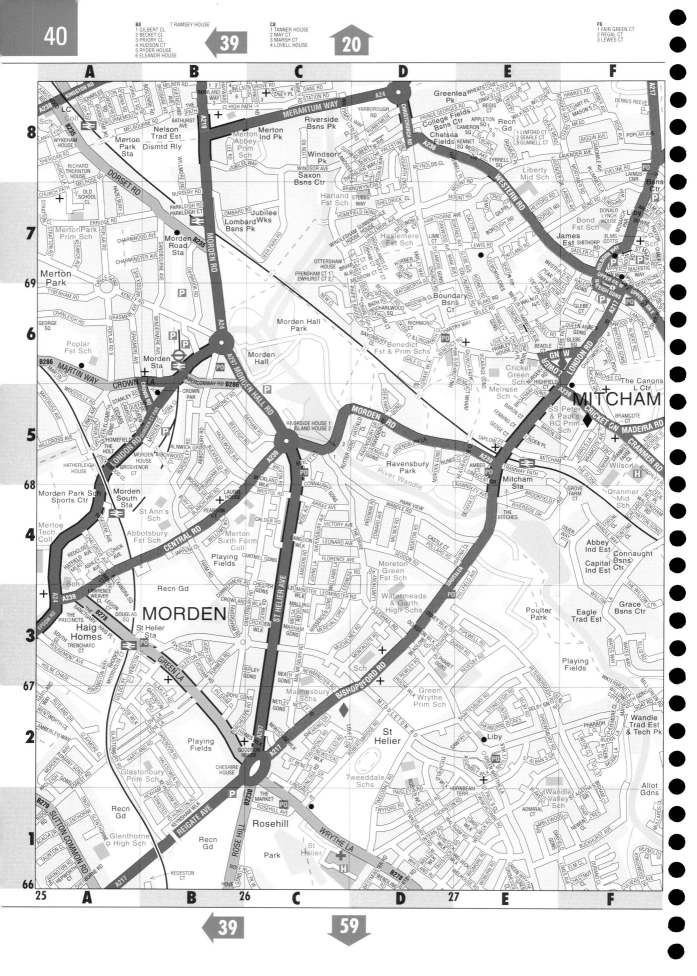

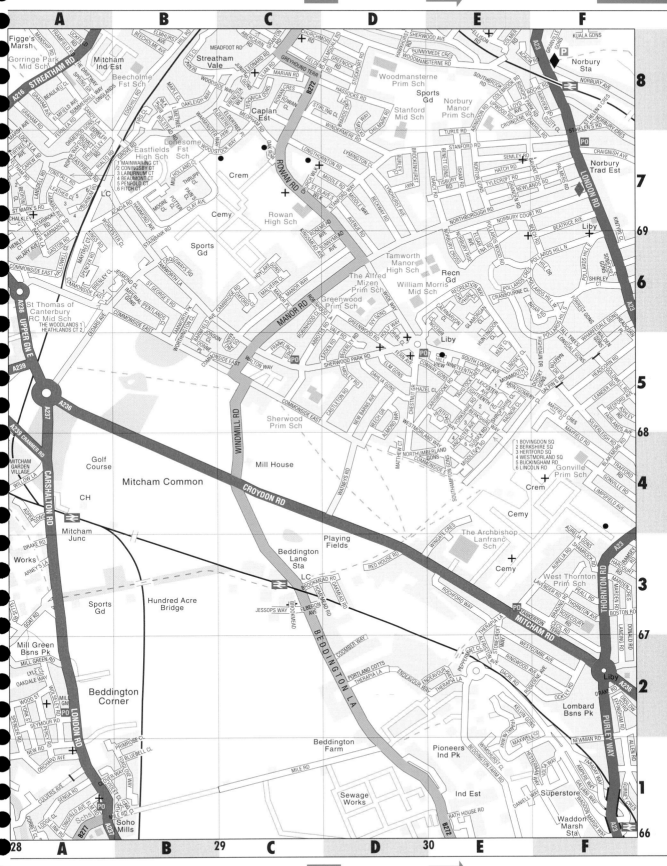

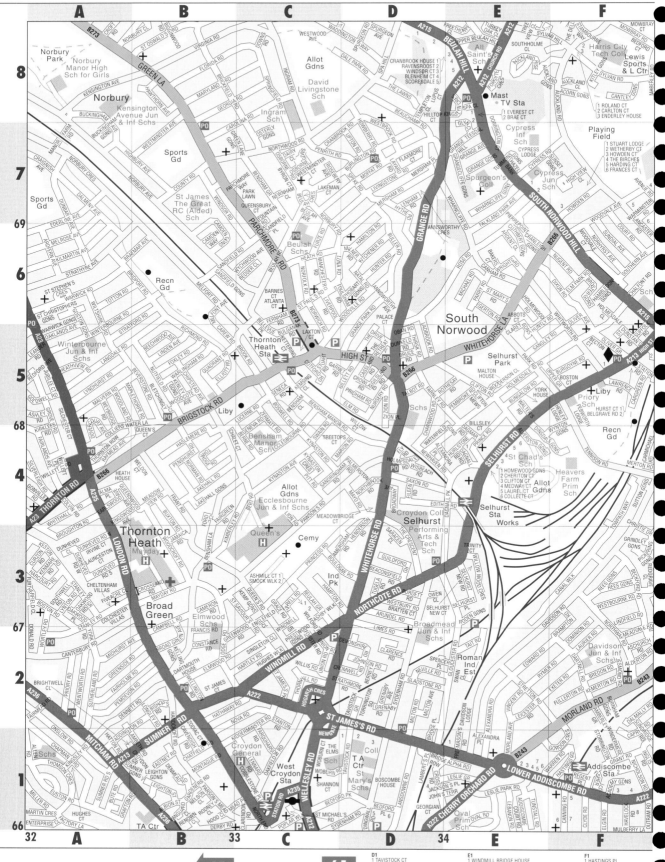

D1
1 TAVISTOCK CT
2 CHARTWELL CL
3 SPEAKER'S CT
4 CUMBERLAND CT
5 VICEROY CT
6 ORIEL CT

E1
1 WINDMILL BRIDGE HOUSE
2 SQUIRE CT
3 HOUSTON CT
4 ST JAMES'S LODGE
5 KENDAL HOUSE
6 WARREN CT
7 KENDAL CT

F1
1 HASTINGS PL
2 GRANT PL
3 CLIVE HOUSE
4 HAVELOCK HOUSE
5 BELLMORE CT
6 HEREFORD CT
7 CHEQUERS CT
8 HAVELOCK HALL

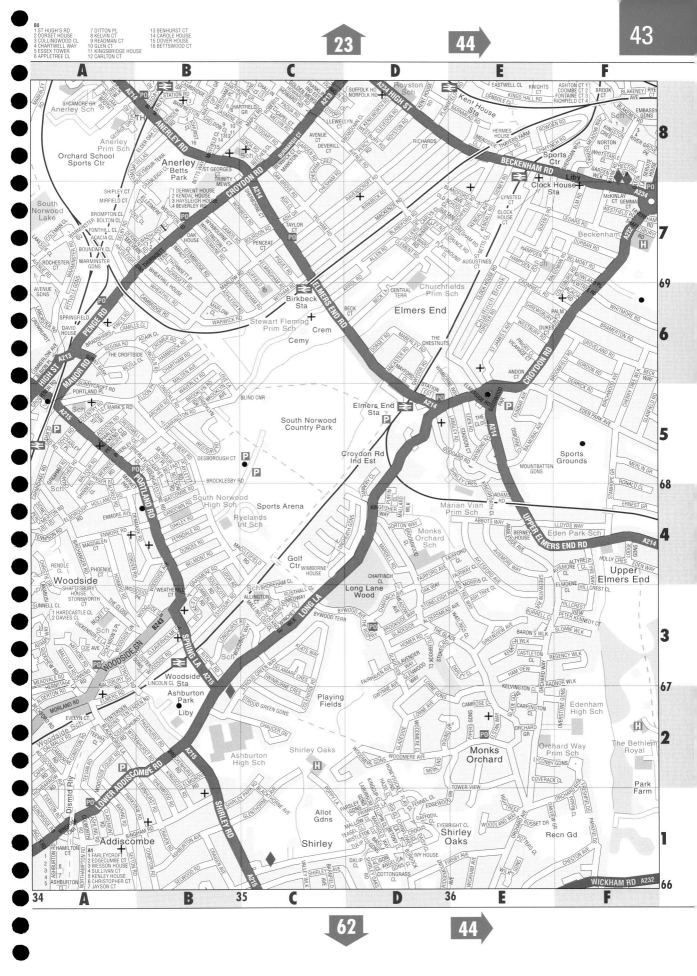

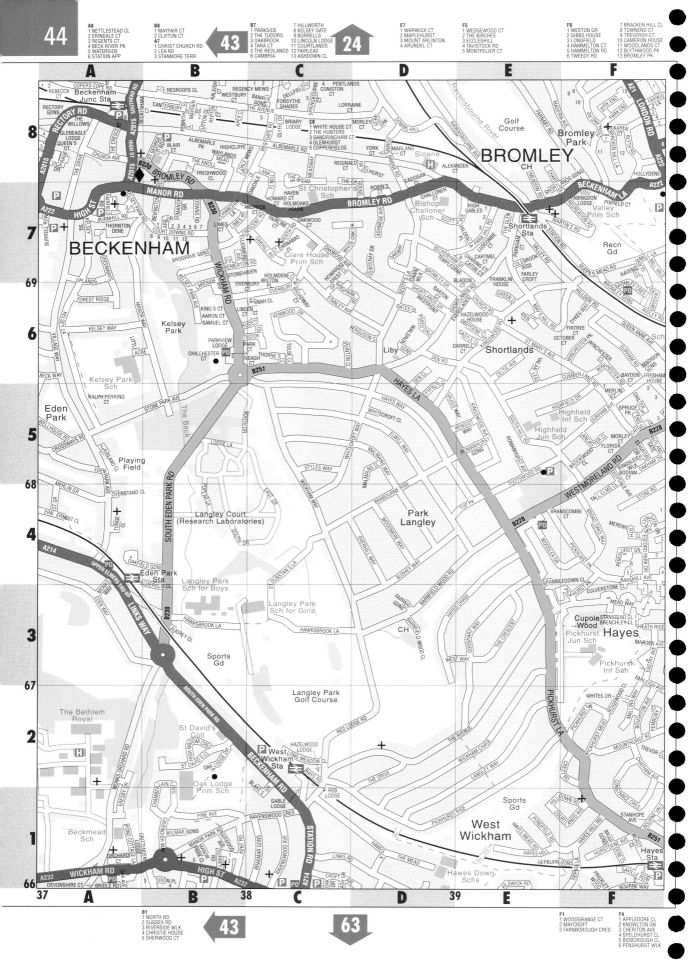

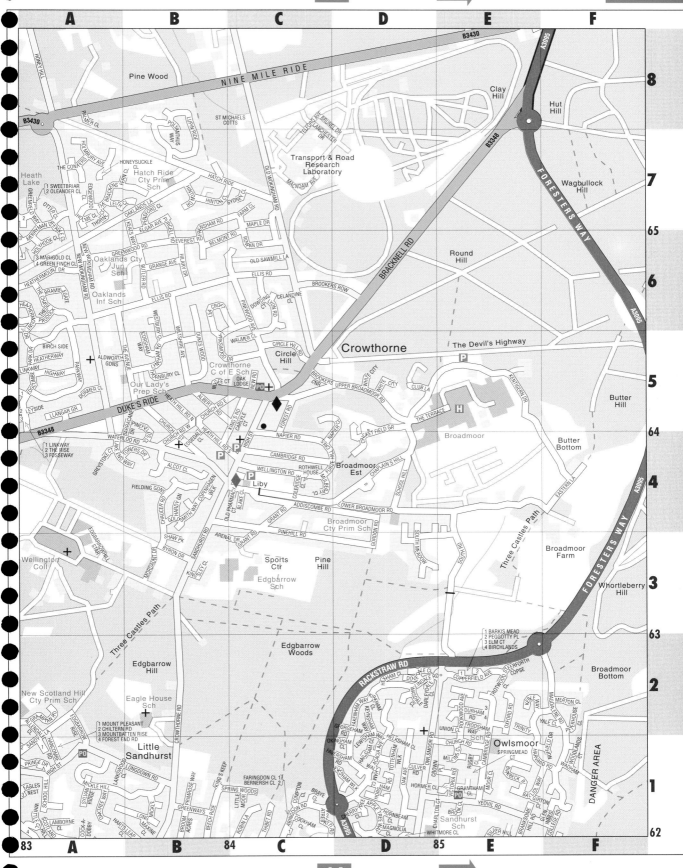

45 27

A B C D E F

Penny
Hill

A322

Gormoor
Farm

Gravel
Hill

8

Caesar's
Camp

Pudding
Hill

Mill
Pond

7

65

Wickham
Bushes

New England
Hill

6

Roman Star
or
Upper Star Post

The Devil's Highway

DANGER AREA

Windsor Ride

FORESTERS WAY

A3095

5

DANGER AREA

Lower Star
Post

64

Wishmoor
Cross

4

DANGER AREA

Deer Rock
Hill

3

Poppy
Hills

DANGER AREA

63

Paschal
Wood

2

Wishmoor Bottom

Olddean
Common

DANGER AREA

Saddleback
Hill

P

1

The Devil's
Pound

WINDSOR RIDE

HIGHVIEW CAES
WIMBLEDON CL
PEMBROKE RD
BRACKNELL CL
BERKSHIRE RD
Sch

62

86 A B 87 C D 88 E F

MATTHEWS RD
KING'S RIDE
QUEEN ELIZABETH RD
DUKE OF CORNWALL
AVE

45 65

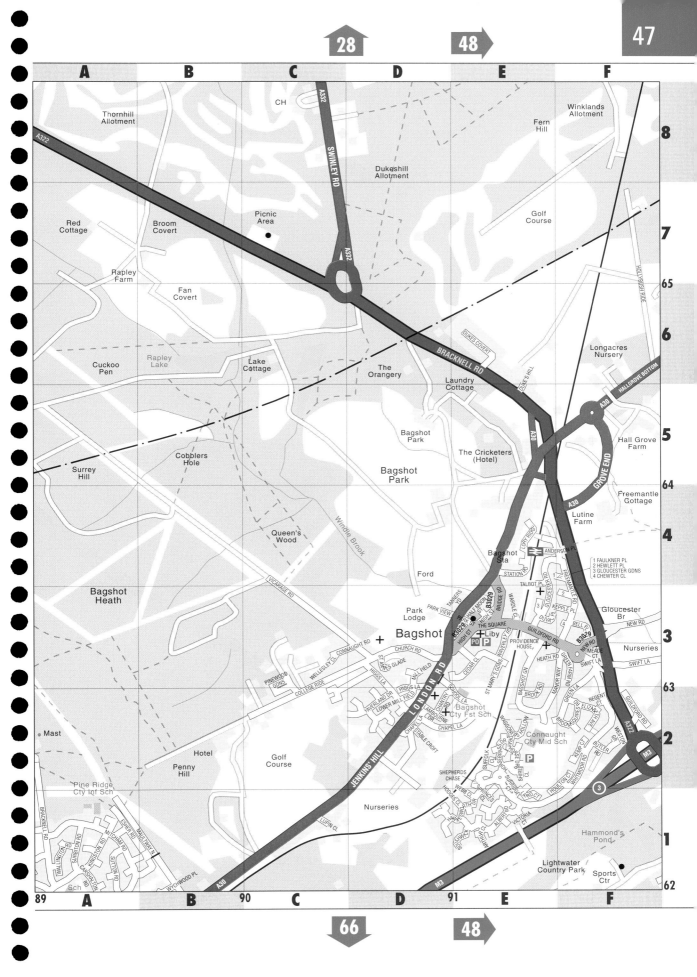

47
29

A B C D E F

8

7

65

6

5

64

4

3

63

2

Earlywood

Windlesham Moor

The Windmill (PH)

Erl Wood Manor

Hall Grove (Sch)

BAGSHOT RD
B3020
CORONATION RD
SUNNINGHILL RD
B3020
A30
B386
SCHOOL RD

Windlesham Hall Farm

Windlesham Hall

Windlesham Village Cty Inf Sch

Woodcote House (Sch)

CHEWTER LA
BOSMAN DR
NEWARK RD
POPLAR AVE
HIGHWAYMAN'S RIDGE
TURPINS RISE
MILL POND WAY
WINDSHAM CT
FOSTER GR
MOOR PL
WHITE HILL
HATTON HILL
SNOWS PADDOCK
HAWKES LEAP
LEYCESTER CL
SNOWS RIDE
WINDLES...
LONDON RD

Nursery

Hatton Hill

Camus

Freemantles Sch

KENNEL LA

Windlesham

The Half Moon (PH)

Birch Hall

RECTORY LA
CHURCH RD
NEW RD

Ashleigh Farm

Merrywood

Windlemere

WESTWOOD RD

A30

Allerton Hill

Ribsden Hall

Recn Gd

Mast

CHERTSEY RD

UPDOWN HILL
COCHRANE CT
GORE LGR
COOPER RD
FINNEY DR
7FIELD GR
BAGENTS LA
WING CL
POUND LA
HOLYMEUX RD
BURTON RD
MILL LA
SHOPS
SMITH'S LA
GRAHAM RD
HATCH LA
DEANS CL
CHS
LAWRENCE CL
WINDLESHAM CL
CROMOW
THORNDOWN CL
BROADLEY GN
HUTTON HILL
OWEN RD
KENT RD
KINGS LA
DOWELL RD
CHURCHERS LA
HERRINGTON LA
SCHOOL LA
LONE OAK DR
OAKWOOD RD
EDWARD RD
PINE GR
HEATHPARK DR
WC LEE'S RESTHOUSES
PO

ORCHARD HILL

Heathpark Wood

Oak Wood

Windlesham Park

WOODLANDS LA

Twelve Oaks

M3

Windsor Manor

King's Hill

SUNNING HOUSE

Golf Course

Lennoxwood

Ribs Down

The Brickmakers Arms (PH)

B386

WOODFORD LA
RAMSAY

SCUTLEY LA

RYE GR

3

63

2

M3
GUILDFORD RD
A322
SOUTH FARM LA
SWIFT LA

Caravan Site

South Farm

Windlesham Arboretum

Old House Farm

OLDHOUSE LA
BROADWAY RD

Windle Brook

Lee Lane Farm

1 CLEARSPRINGS
2 BIRCH TREE VIEW

HAMMOND WAY
CATENA RISE
THE CLOSE
STONEHILL RD
MONTAGUE CL
GUILDFORD RD

Broadway Green Farm

HOOK MILL LA

Manor Farm Wood

Halebourne Copse

1

Cemy

Sch

Sch

THE AVENUE
BADGER DR
APLIN WAY
MOUNT PLEASANT CL
TURNVILLE CL
MACDONALD RD
THE RIDGEWAY
WINDERMERE DR
AMBLESIDE RD
CONISTON CT
GRASMERE RD
ULLSWATER CL
COTHERINE RD
DERWENT DR
WATER RD
DENLY WAY
P
Liby
CHRISTIE CL
ALL SAINTS RD
THE SQUARE
JUNCTION RD
MICHELET CL
RIVERSIDE AV
GLEBE CL
WITHY BIRCH
MEADOWS RD
BURNT POLLARD LA

PO

Rectory Farm

THE WILLOWS

Sewage Works

A322

Hale Bourne

62

92 A 93 B C 94 D E F

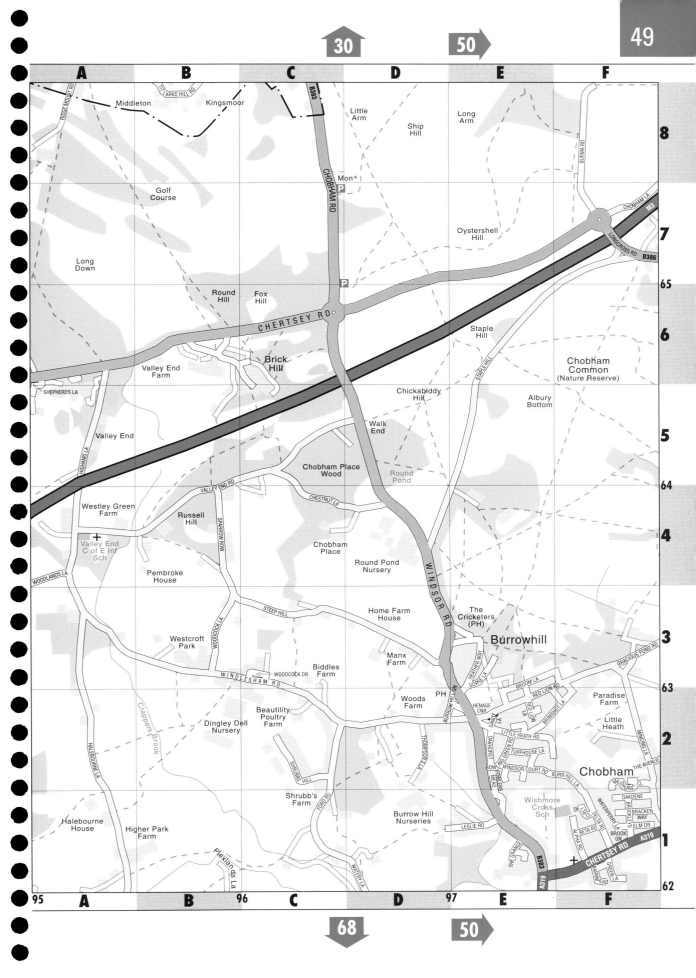

A B C D E F

8

7

65

6

5

64

4

3

63

2

1

62

M3

CHOBHAM LA

Longcross

AYBURY CL

HOLT CL

TANGLEWOOD CL

B386

KITSMEAD LA

KITSMEAD LA

LONGCROSS RD

TRYS HILL

B386

Chertsey
Common

Barrowhills

Hersham
Farm

Fan Court
Farm

Fan
Court

Poultry
Farm

Longcross
Lodge

Golf
Course

Flutters
Hill

Longcross
House

Lilypond
Farm

CH

Pipers Green
Stud

The Lodge

Childown

Fox
Hills

The
Dower
House

ACCOMMODATION RD

Budds
Cottage

Chobham
Common

Gracious
Pond

GRACIOUS POND RD

Gracious
Pond Farm

Butts
Hill

Langshot
Stud

Queenwood
Farm

STONEHILL RD

STONEHILL CRES

Stonehill

Fern Hill

Mossat
Farm

Rambridge
Farm

Stannershill
Farm

Stanners
Hill

Little Manor
Farm

A319

Stanners
Hill

THE AVENUE

CHOBHAM PARK LA

Chobham Park
Farm

Dunstall
Green

Stanyards
Farm

BONSEY'S LA

Berwin
Park

Nurseries

Larkenshaw

Larkenshaw
Farm

OLD CHERTSEY RD

CHERTSEY RD

YOUNGSTROAT LA

Fairoaks
Airport

A319

Sow Moor

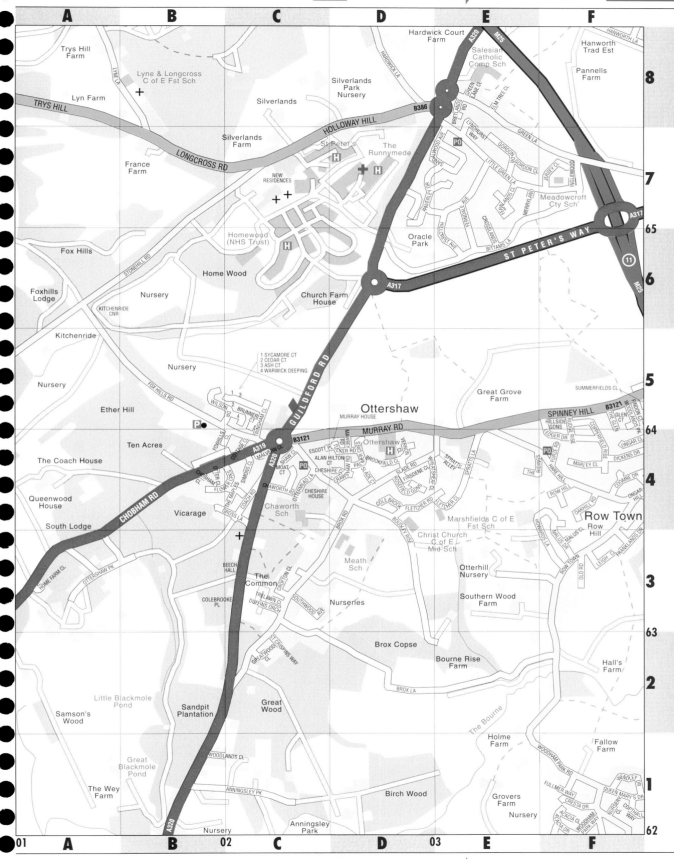

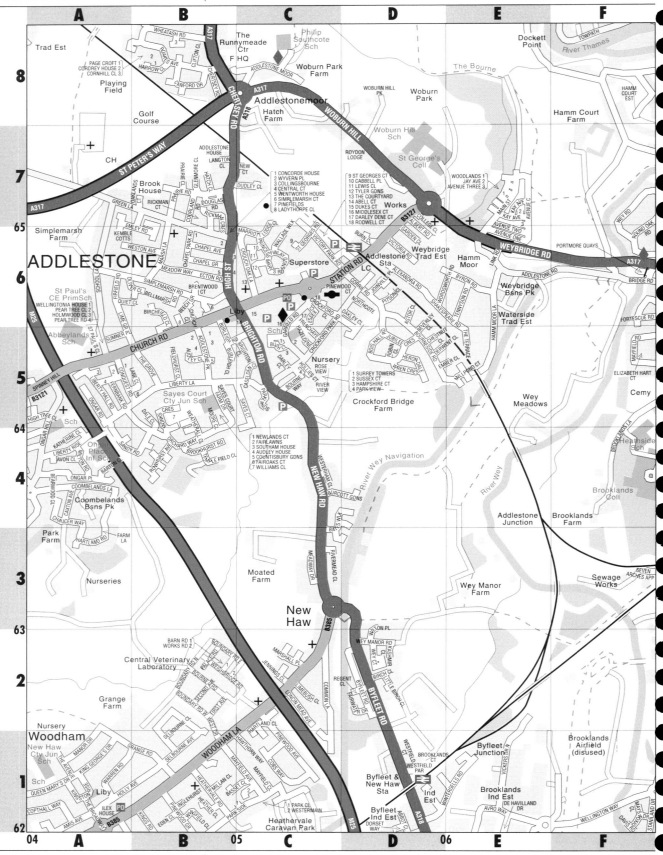

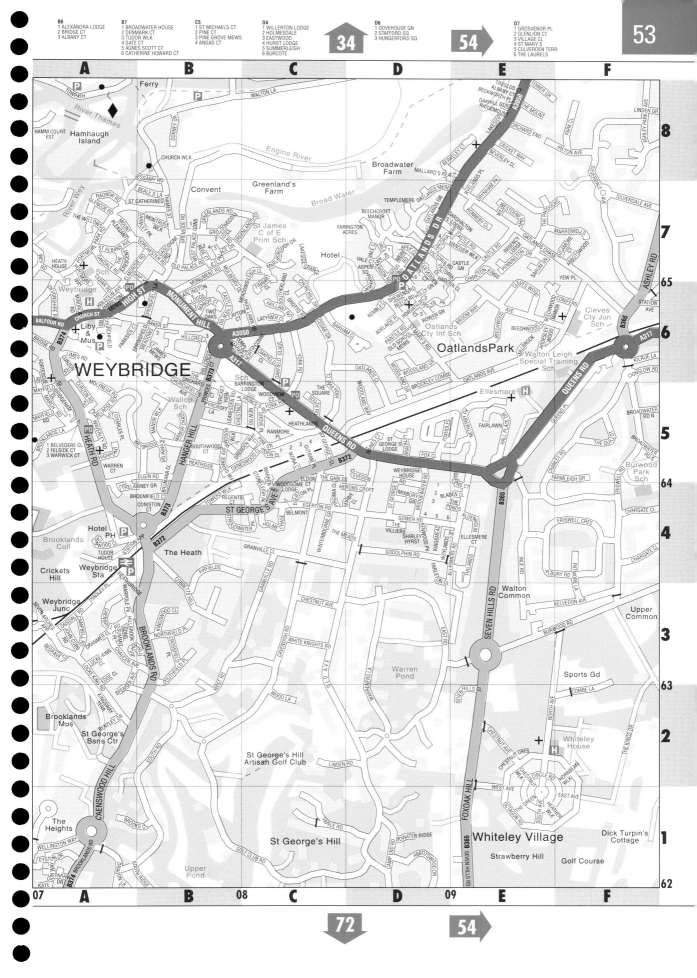

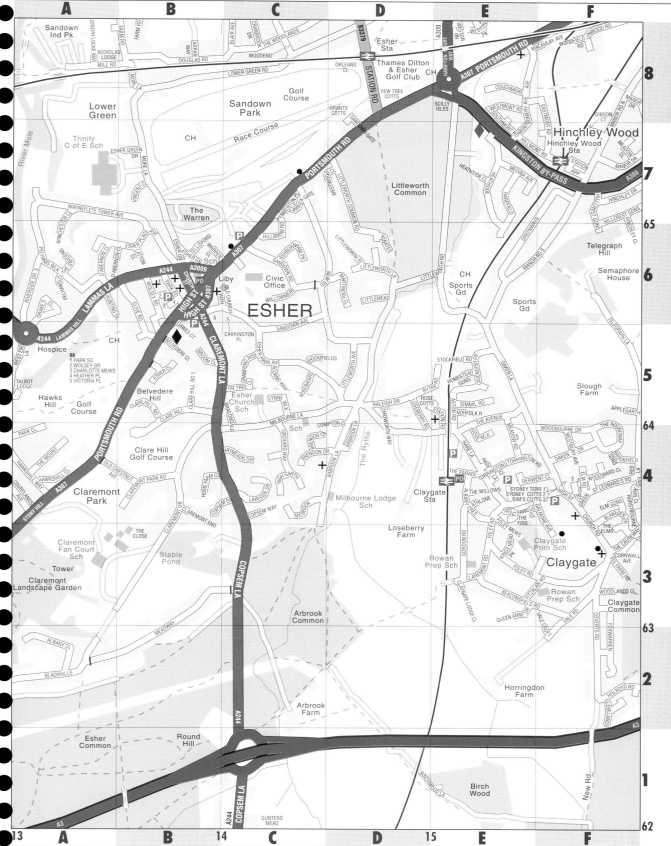

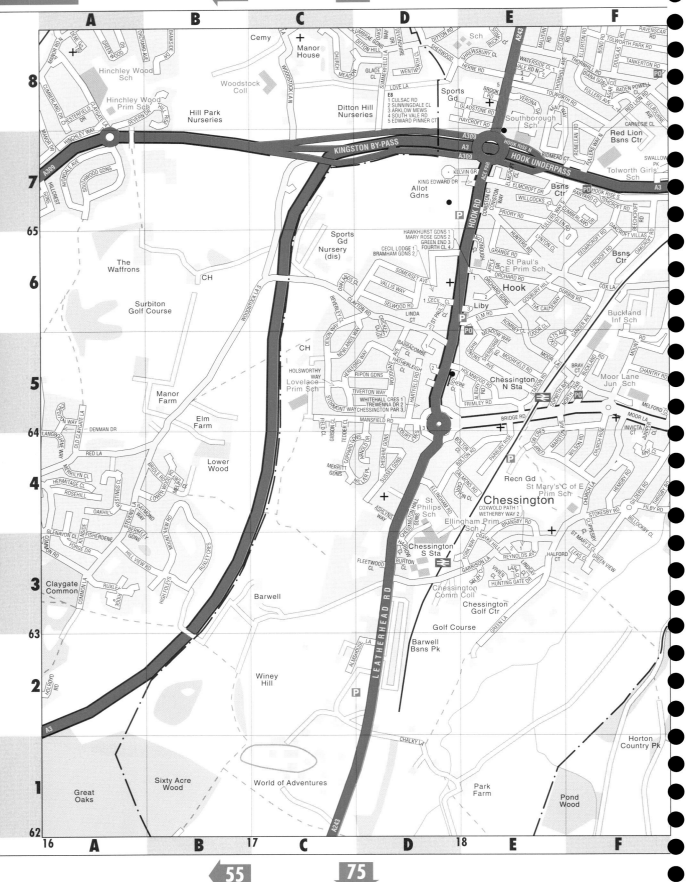

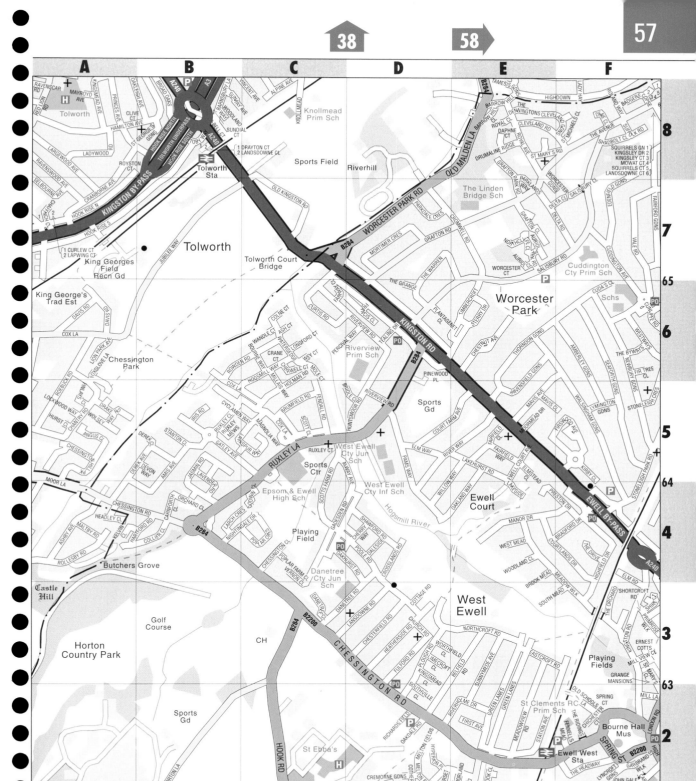

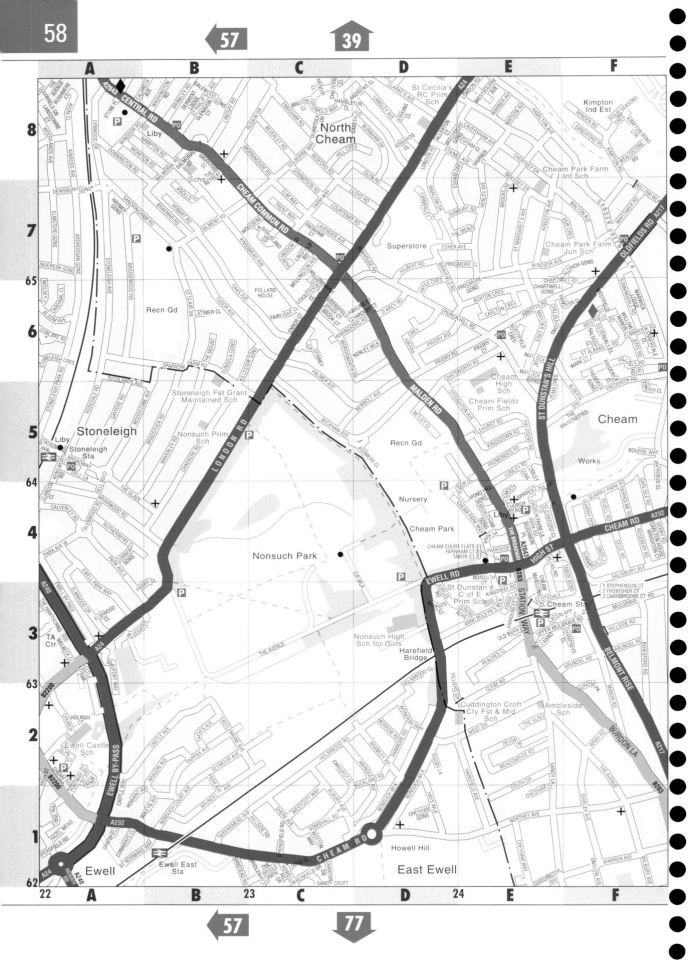

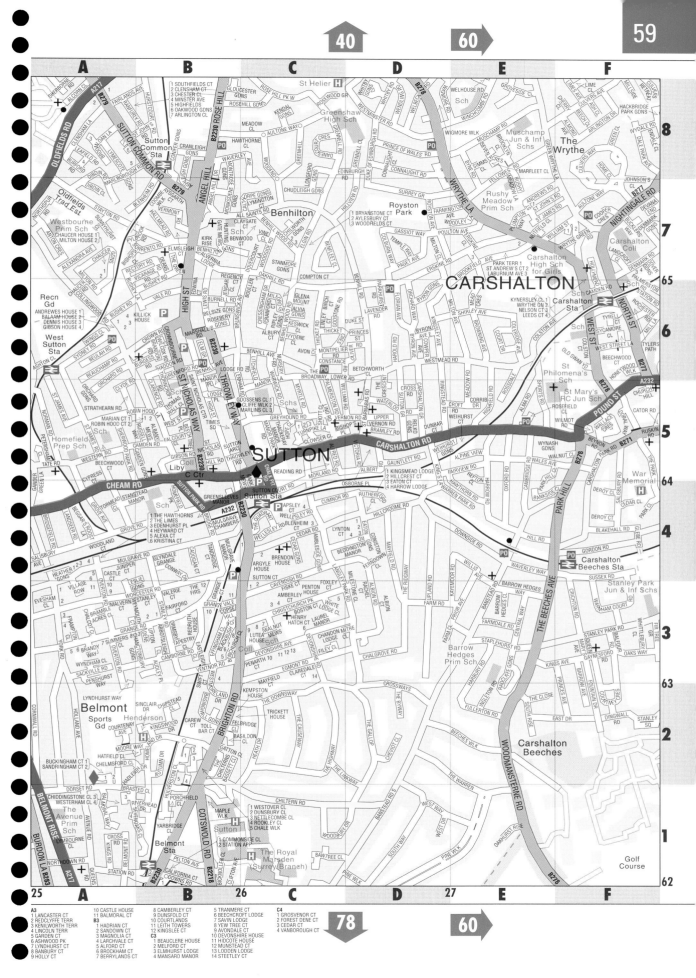

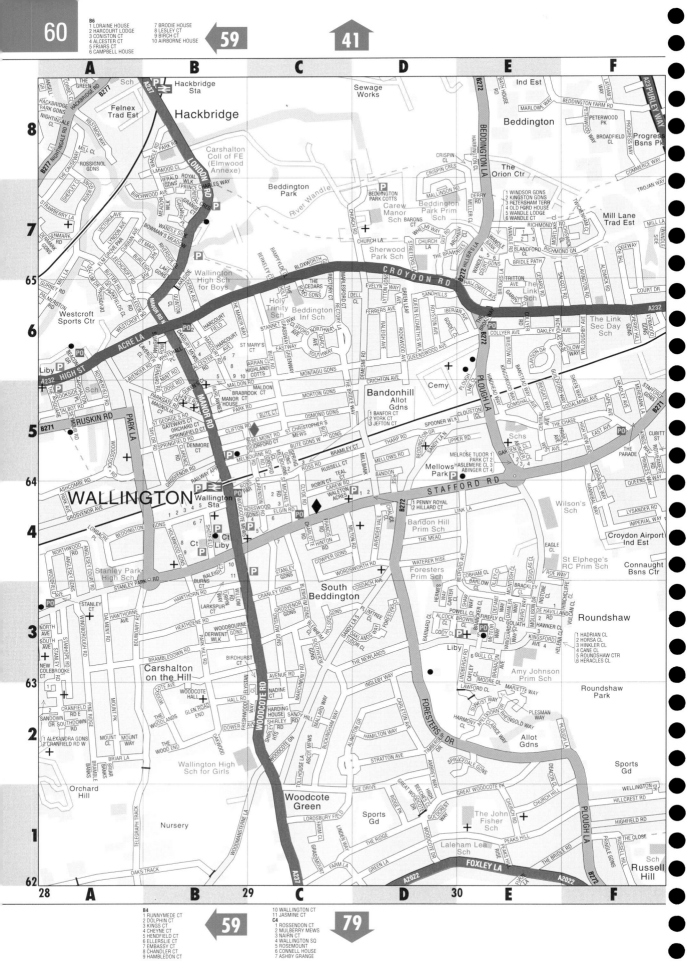

42
62
80
62

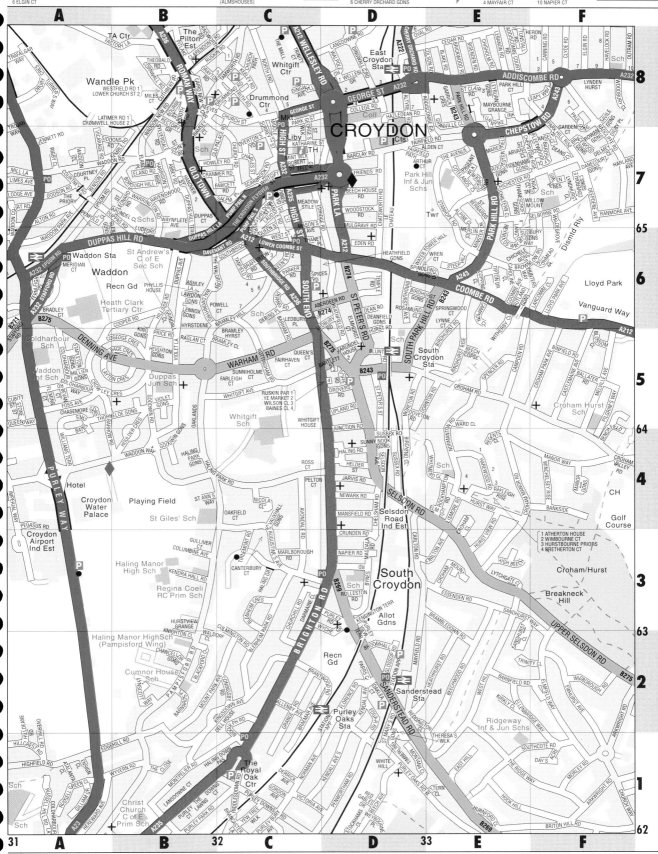

C6
1 WEST STREET PL
2 MAPLE CT
3 ST ANDREW'S RD
4 ALBURY CT
5 CHESTNUT CT
6 ELGIN CT
7 BEECHFIELD CT

C8
1 OTTERBOURNE RD
2 CHARRINGTON RD
3 TAMWORTH PL
4 PRIDDY'S YD
5 HOSPITAL OF THE HOLY TRINITY (ALMSHOUSES)

D8
1 WELLESLEY COURT RD
2 NORFOLK HOUSE
3 STATION APP
4 SUFFOLK HOUSE
5 ESSEX HOUSE
6 CHERRY ORCHARD GDNS

D8
7 HARRINGTON CT
F8
1 TIERNEY CT
2 SINCLAIR CT
3 GUINNESS CT
4 MAYFAIR CT

F8
5 GLOUCESTER LODGE
6 BISHOPSCOURT
7 BEVERLEY HYRST
8 MELTON CT
9 CECIL CT
10 NAPIER CT

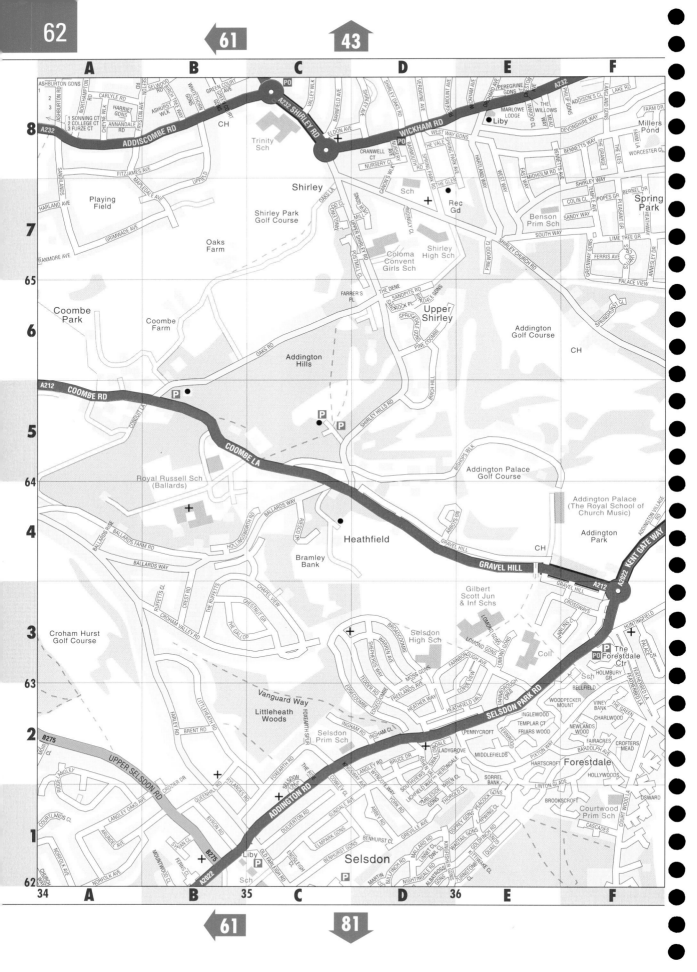

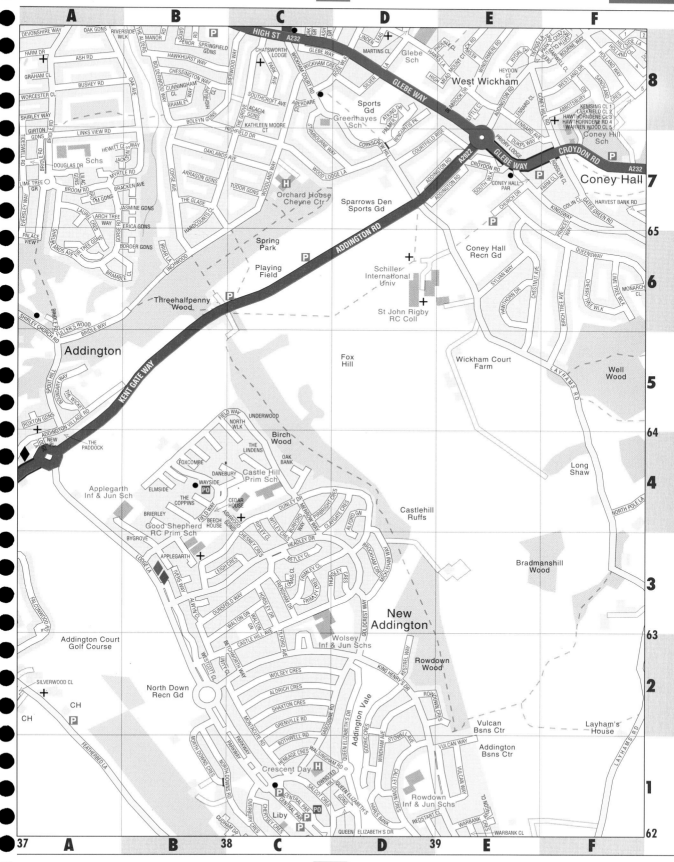

A   B   C   D   E   F

8

Devonshire Way
Oak Gdns
Riverside Wlk
The Alders
Manor Rd
Grosvenor Rd
Springfield Gdns
HIGH ST A232
Oak La
Ash Gr
Linden La
Martins Cl
Glebe Sch
Chatsworth Lodge
Glebe Way
Phoenix Cl
Chatsworth Rd
Hillside La
Holland Way

Farm Dr
Ash Rd
Hawkhurst Way
Park Ave
Wickham Cres
Glebe Way
Hawes La
Mount La
Windermere Rd
Heydon Ct
Rydal Dr
Tiepris La
Farwell Rd
Bourne Way
Holland Way

Graham Cl
Bushey Rd
Chessington Way
Boldorwood Way
Cunningham Cl
Southcroft Ave
Aberdare
Wickham Court Rd
Starbourne Way
Silver La
West Wickham
Addington Rd
Lennard Ave
Coney Hill Rd
Westland Dr
Abbotsbury
Sandland Cres

Worcester Cl
Oak Ave
Bramley Way
The Grove
Acacia Gdns
Kathleen Moore Ct
Biscurts Pk
Atkins Dr
Palmer Cl
Duke's Way
Kemsing Cl 1
Larkfield Cl 2
Hawthorndene Cl 3
Hawthorndene Rd 4
Warren Wood Cl 5

Shirley Way
Girton Gdns
Links View Rd
Highfield Dr
Oaklands Ave
Wood Lodge La
Courtfield Rise
Priory Lodge
Coney Hill Sch

Douglas Dr
Schs
Hewitt Cl
Jack
Tudor Gdns
Arragon Gdns
Orchard House Cheyne Ctr
Sparrows Den Sports Gd
A2022
Croydon Rd
Coney Hall Par
Croydon Rd A232
Coney Hill Sch
Coney Hall

7

Lime Tree Gr
Everley Way
Palace View
Lilac Gdns
Broom Rd
Elm Way
Jasmine Gdns
Larch Tree Way
Erica Gdns
Border Gdns
Briar La
The Glade
Hardcourts Cl
Spring Park
Playing Field
ADDINGTON RD
Schiller International Univ
Church Dr
South Wlk
Coney Hall Recn Gd
Kingsway
Colin Cl
Gates Green Rd
Harvest Bank Rd

Shirley Church Rd
Bridle Cl
Fuller's Wood
Bridle Way
Threehalfpenny Wood
St John Rigby RC Coll
Hawthorn Dr
Sylvan Way
Chestnut Ave
Birch Tree Ave
Cherry Tree Wlk
Lime Tree Wlk
Monarch Cl

65

6

Addington
Kent Gate Way
Fox Hill
Wickham Court Farm
Well Wood

5

The Wicket
Boundary Way
The Wicket
Roxton Gdns
Addington Village Rd
The Paddock
New PI
Field Way
Underwood
North Wlk
Birch Wood
Layhams Rd
Long Shaw

64

4

Applegarth Inf & Jun Sch
Foxcombe
Elmside
The Coppins
Danebury
Wayside
PO
Castle Hill Prim Sch
The Lindens
Oak Bank
Cedar House
Dudley Dr
Merrow Way
Pirbright Cres
Claygate Cres
Alfrid Gdn
Castlehill Ruffs
North Pole La

Brierley
Bygrove
Good Shepherd RC Prim Sch
Beech House
Ashwood Gdns
Field Way
Ripley Cl
Willey Cl
Burford Way
Headley Dr
Hetley Cl
Brackham Crescent
Bradmanshill Wood

3

Lodge La
Applegarth
Ivers Way
Always Way
Leigh Cres
Chesney Cres
Frinsham Rd
Gas Cl
Frimley Cres
Thursley Cres
Brackham Rd

Walton Gn
Walton Gn
Horsley Dr
New Addington

63

Addington Court Golf Course
Dunsfold Way
Castle Hill Ave
Tilford Ave
Wolsey Inf & Jun Schs
Goldcrest Way
Kestrel Way
King Henry's Dr
Rowdown Wood
Rowdown Cres

2

Silverwood Cl
North Down Recn Gd
Bedenworth Way
Unity Cl
Wolsey Cres
Aldrich Cres
Gascoigne Rd
Queen Elizabeth's Dr
Windham Ave
Stoney Ave
Vulcan Bsns Ctr
Layham's House

CH
CH
Shaxton Cres
Addington Vale
Vulcan Way
Addington Bsns Ctr

Featherbed La
Heneage Cres
Grenville Rd
Bothwell Rd
Monacute Rd
Parkway
Walsingham Rd
Godric Cres
Calley Down Cres
Vulcan Way
Layhams Rd

North Downs Cres
Overbury Cres
Chettsey Cres
Central Park
Crescent Day
PO
Salcot Cres
Queen Elizabeth Gdns
Hares Bank
Rowdown Inf & Jun Schs

1

Liby
Cudham La
Central Park
Queen Elizabeth's Dr
Redstart Cl
Warbank Cl
Warbank Cl

62

D8
1 MULBERRY CL
2 MAY CL
3 SHRIVENHAM CL
4 CENTURION CL
5 CHAFFINCH CL
6 TARBAT CT
7 ROCKFIELD WAY
8 BALINTORE CT

A   B   C   D   E   F

8

7

61

6

5

60

4

3

59

2

1

58

83   84   85

A   B   C   D   E   F

College Town
College Town Jun & Inf Schs
Sandhurst Sch
Rifle Ranges
Range View
Rifle Ranges

Sandhurst
Sandhurst Sta
HIGH ST
A321
YORKTOWN RD
PO
Liby
Uplands Prim Sch
1 UPLANDS CL
2 WILLOWS END

Sewage Works
Recn Gd

Frogmore
Darby Green

RACKSTRAW RD
A3095
A3095

MARSHALL RD
Blackwater River
MARSHALL RD

Royal Military Academy
Old College Sports Gd
Government House

1 MADOX BROWN END
2 THORNBURN CHASE
3 HEPWORTH CROFT

The Meadows
The Terrace
A30

Clark's Farm
Potley Hill Rd
Potley Hill Cty Prim Sch
B3272

Yateley
Frogmore Comm Sch
Heathcroft

READING RD

Leafy Oak Farm

Hayward's Cottage
Picnic Area
Picnic Area
A30

Frogmore Cty Jun & Infs Schs

Blackwater

White Hart Ind Est
LONDON RD
Blackwater Sta
PO
Sewage Works
A321

Hawley Garden Cotts
Starve Acre
HAWLEY RD
Hawley
Hawley Cty Prim Sch
L Ctr

Yateley Common (Ctry Pk)

Hawley Hill
Hawley Park
Hawley Park Farm
Hawley Lodge

Hornley Common
Hawley Common
Hawley Place Sch

Fernhill Cty Prim Sch J
Fernhill Comp Sch
B3272

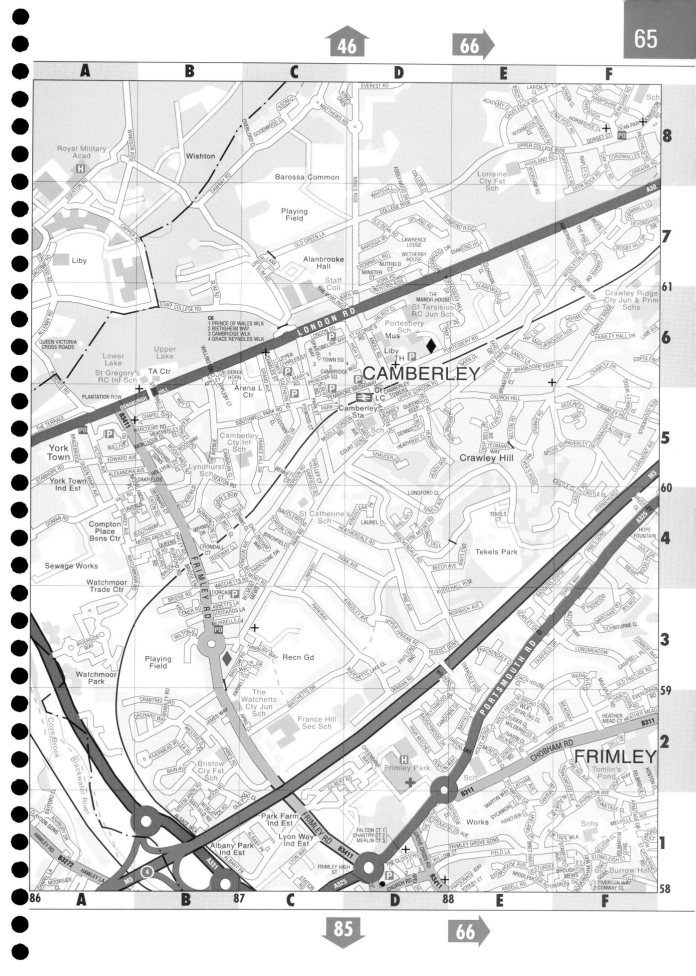

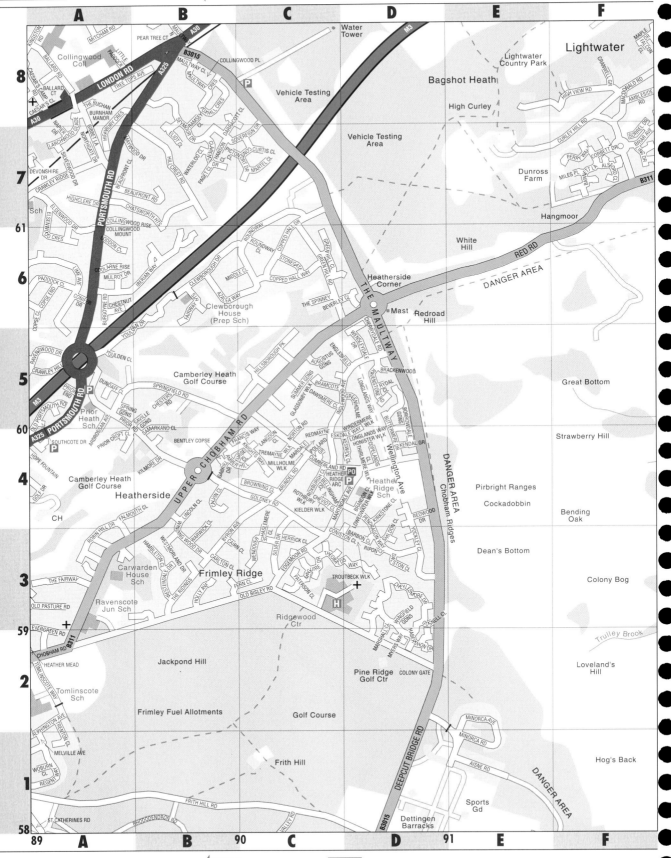

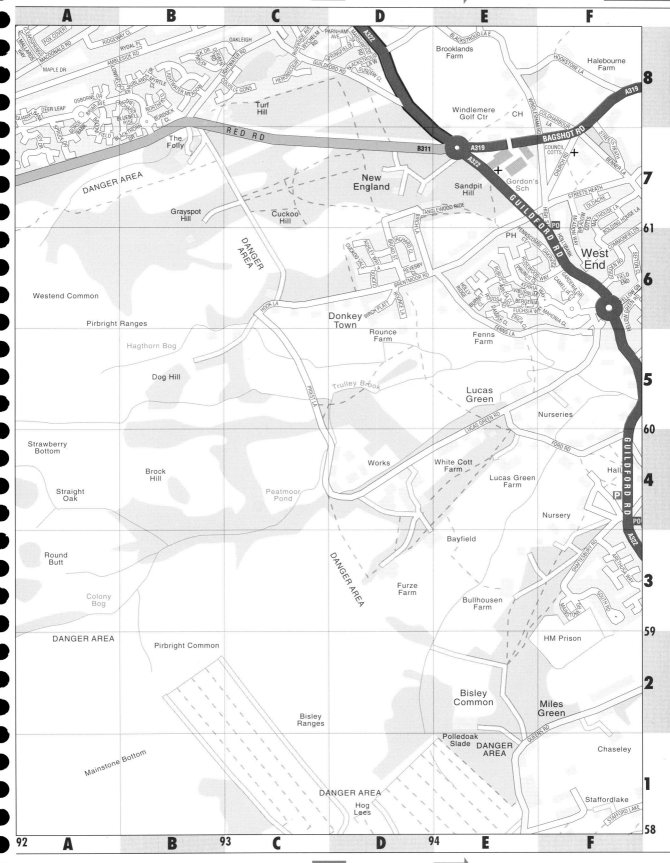

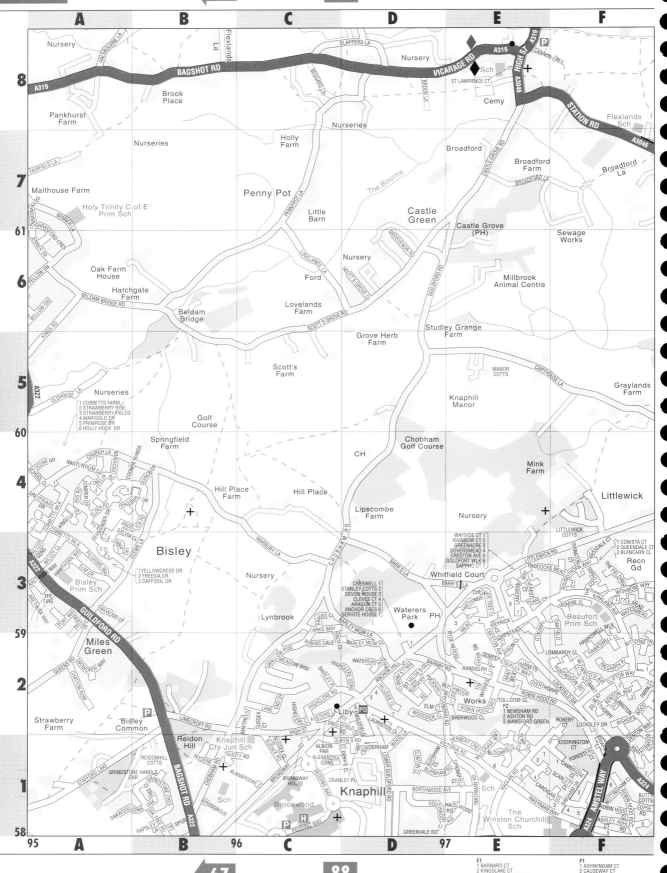

A   B   C   D   E   F

8

7

61

6

5

60

4

3

59

2

1

58

95   A   B   96   C   D   97   E   F

Nursery

HALBOURNE LA

FAIRFIELD LA

A319   BAGSHOT RD

Pankhurst Farm

Malthouse Farm

Holy Trinity C of E Prim Sch

BENNER LA

BARNSFORD CRES

JENNER DR

YELLOW GN

WILLOW GN

KINGS RD

OLDHOUSE LA

A322

Oak Farm House

Hatchgate Farm

Nurseries

Nurseries

Springfield Farm

Nurseries
1 COBBETTS FARM
2 STRAWBERRY RISE
3 STRAWBERRY FIELDS
4 MARIGOLD DR
5 PRIMROSE DR
6 HOLLY HOCK DR

Golf Course

Flexlands La

Brook Place

CLAPPERS LA

BEGGARS LA

Holly Farm

Penny Pot

Little Barn

PENNYPOT LA

LOVELAND'S LA

SCOTT'S GROVE CL

Ford

Lovelands Farm

Beldam Bridge

BELDAM BRIDGE RD

Scott's Farm

SCOTT'S GROVE RD

Grove Herb Farm

Nursery

BROOK LA

Nursery

VICARAGE RD

St LAWRENCE CT

Cemy

Broadford

CASTLE GROVE RD

GROSVENOR RD

GUILDFORD RD

Castle Green

Castle Grove (PH)

Studley Grange Farm

CH

Nursery

A319

HIGH ST

A3046

CANNON CRES.

Sch

P

STATION RD

A3046

Flexlands Sch

Broadford

Broadford Farm

BROADFORD LA

Broadford La

Sewage Works

Millbrook Animal Centre

MANOR COTTS

CARTHOUSE LA

Graylands Farm

Knaphill Manor

Chobham Golf Course

Mink Farm

Littlewick

CEDAR GR

SCHOOL CL

CHURCH LA

NASTURTIUM DR

ORCHID DR

COOMBE MANOR

QUIND RD

ROSEMARY DR

ANGEL CL

SYLVIA CL

ELGIN RD

IRIS RD

JUNIPER DR

ELDER RD

ZINNIA DR

GERANIUM DR

GLENVIS CL

Hill Place Farm

Hill Place

Lipscombe Farm

Nursery

LITTLEWICK COTTS

LITTLEWICK RD

OWING CL

WACSDALE CL

1 CONISTA CT
2 QUEENDALE CT
3 BLENCARN CL

Recn Gd

THE FIELDING'S

WISHBONE WAY

LITTLE MEAD

WATERMEAD

BITTERNE DR

GREYFRIARS DR

HAWTHORN WAY

PILGRIMS WAY

ELM GR

ARETHUSA WAY

A322

1 YELLOWCRESS DR
2 FREESIA DR
3 DAFFODIL DR

Bisley

Bisley Prim Sch

THE FIRS

Lynbrook

WARBURY LA

Nursery

CHOBHAM RD

BARR'S LA

CRESWELL 1
STANLEY COTTS 2
DEVON HOUSE 3
CLEVES CT 4
ARAGON CT 5
ANCHOR CRES 6
SERVITE HOUSE 7

WAYSIDE CT 1
RAINBOW CT 2
GREENACRE 3
DOVERSMEAD 4
CRESTON AVE 5
GOLDFORT WLK 6
SAPPHO CT 7

Whitfield Court

BARR'S LA

CHEO

PLANE TREE CL

PEARL CT

PADDOCKS MEAD

ROUNDTHORN WAY

LUCKLEY RD

Beaufort Prim Sch

JASMINE CL

KIRKLAND AV

HAWKSWELL WLK

HAWKSWELL CL

LOMBARDY CL

TREGARTH RD

CLIFTON WAY

FARN

Miles Green

GUILDFORD RD

QUEENS RD

SNOWDROP WAY

CHATTON ROW

PORT WAY

QUEENS RD

OAKWOOD CT

OAKWOOD CT

Waterers Park PH

RIKANS CL

LARKS WAY

ROBINS DALE

BARLEY MOW LA

FINCH CL

BARLEY MOW CL

SWALLOW RISE

SHIRLEY CL

LANE END DR

HIGHCLERE RD

BARLEY MOW LA

WATERERS RISE

ANCHOR HILL

St HILDA'S CL

St HILDA'S

BARNBY RD

RANDOLPH CL

BEECHWOOD

ELM CL

WOODSIDE CL

SHERWOOD CL

Works

SEMPER CL

STAVELEY WAY

CHIPSTEAD

THE WITHIES

OVERTHORPE

ROBIN HOOD RD

TOLLDENE CL

F2
1 NEWSHAM RD
2 ASHTON RD
3 WANSFORD GREEN

HUNTINGDON DR

LOCKFIELD DR

KANTON CT

LANGTON WAY

PLETHORPE

ROKEBY CT

LOCKSLEY DR

BISHOPS

DENTON WAY

BUTTS COTTS

COPSE RD

AMSTEL WAY

A324

Strawberry Farm

Bisley Common

P

LIMECROFT RD

Reidon Hill

Knaphill Cty Jun Sch

TRINITY RD

REIDONHILL COTTS

GRINDSTONE HANDLE CNR

STAFFORD LAKE

REIDONHILL CRES

GRINDSTONE CL

THE SPUR

RAPSLEY LA

OAKWOOD GDNS

BAGSHOT RD

A322

IVYDENE

ALANBROOKE CL

BIRDSGROVE

Sch

MATTHEYS CT

SUSSEX CT

SUSSEX RD

High St

FOSTERS LA

ENGLEFIELD

Liby

P O

Albion Par

ALEXANDRA GDNS

Broadway House

BROADWAY

REDDING WAY

Brookwood

P

H

REDDING WAY

Knaphill

QUEEN'S RD

DENVS CL

CRANLEY PL

POWDERHAM CT

BURNHAM CL

CLINTON CL

BURNHAM

NORTHWOOD AVE

HAZELWOOD RD

GREENVALE RD

SOU

LAURISTON CT

Victoria RD

HERBERT CRES

LOWER GUILDFORD RD

RAGLAN CL

CARDIGAN CL

INKERMAN WAY

INKERMAN RD

BLOOMFIELD

BLOOMFIELD DR

SPRINGFIELD

SCARLETT CL

ROBIN HOOD RD

CODRINGTON CT

FORESTERS

1 CAMBRIDGE CT

CARDIGAN CT

ASHLEY ASHLEY RD

The Winston Churchill Sch

Sch

NOTTINGHAM RD

RAGLAN RD

A324

E1
1 BARNARD CT
2 KINGSLAKE CT
3 WILLIAM RUSSELL CT
4 SAYER CT
5 ROBERTSON CT
6 WELLINGTON TERR

F1
1 ASHWINDAM CT
2 CAUSEWAY CT
3 NIGHTINGALE CT
4 MOYNE CT
5 GUINNESS CT
6 NOTTINGHAM CT
7 CRANFIELD CT
8 CAPSTANS WHARF
9 BARRACK PATH

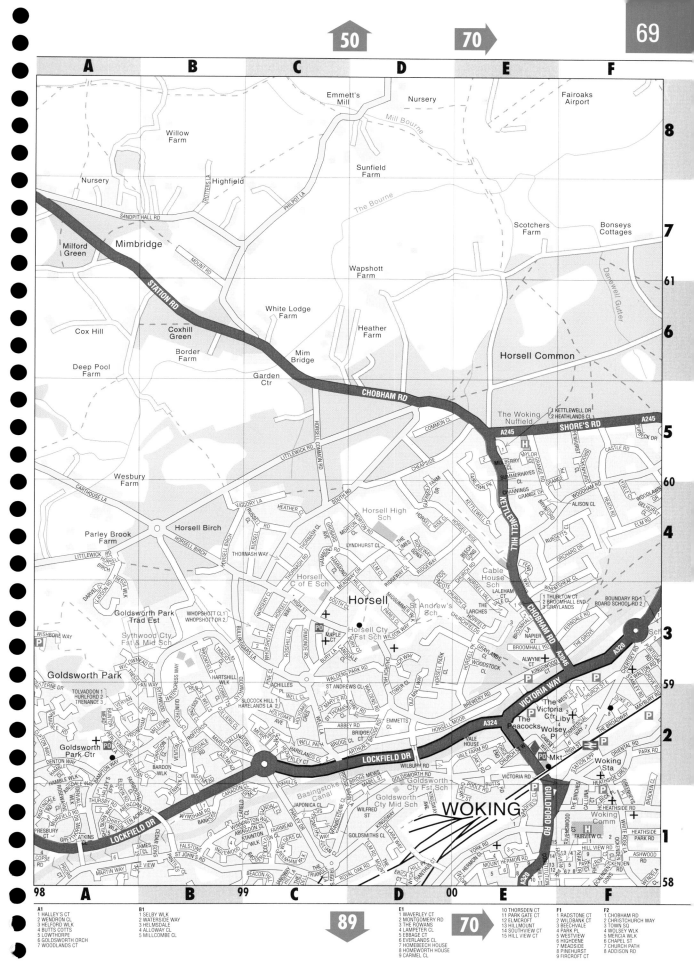

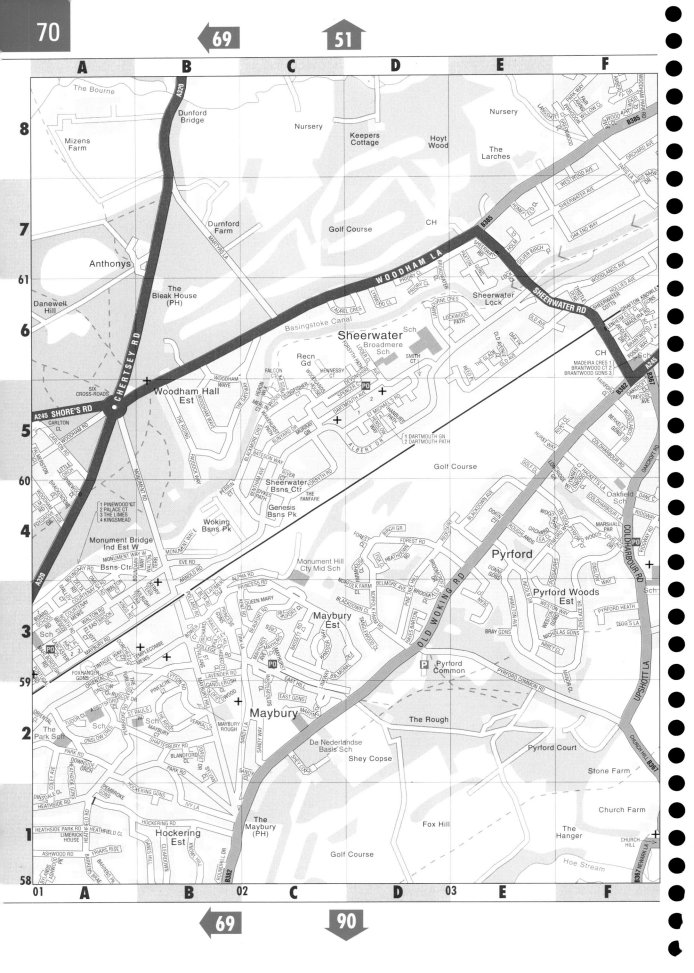

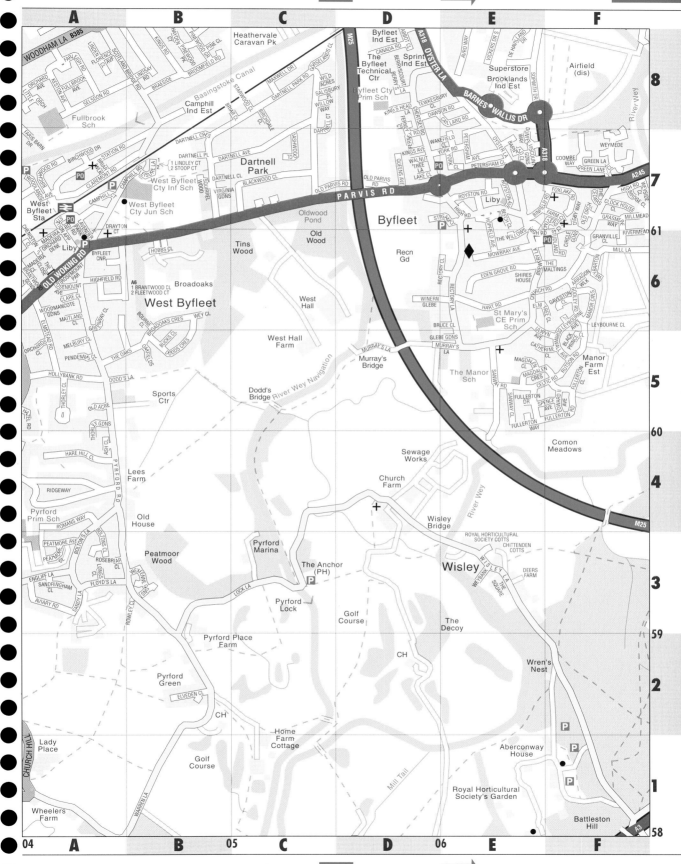

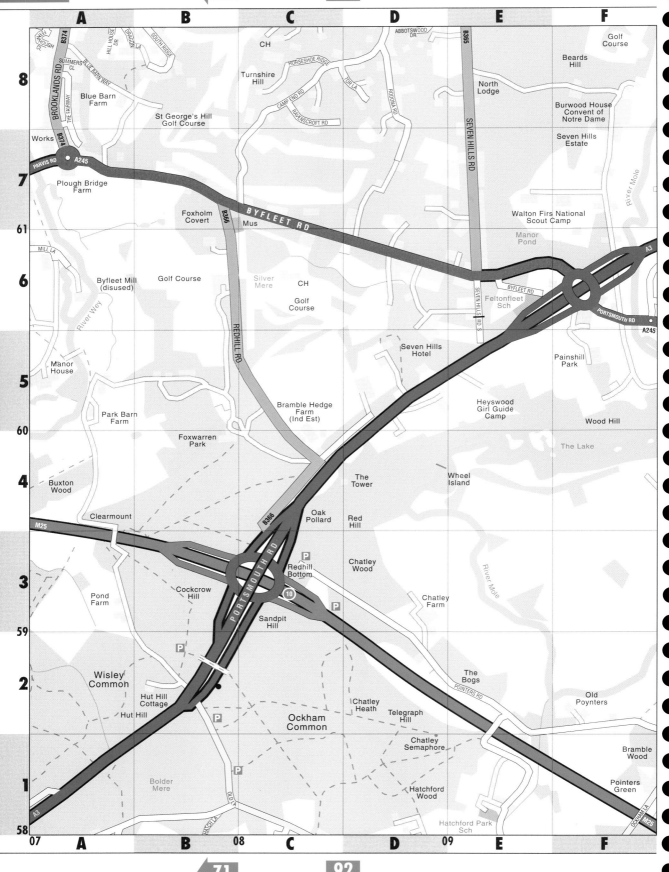

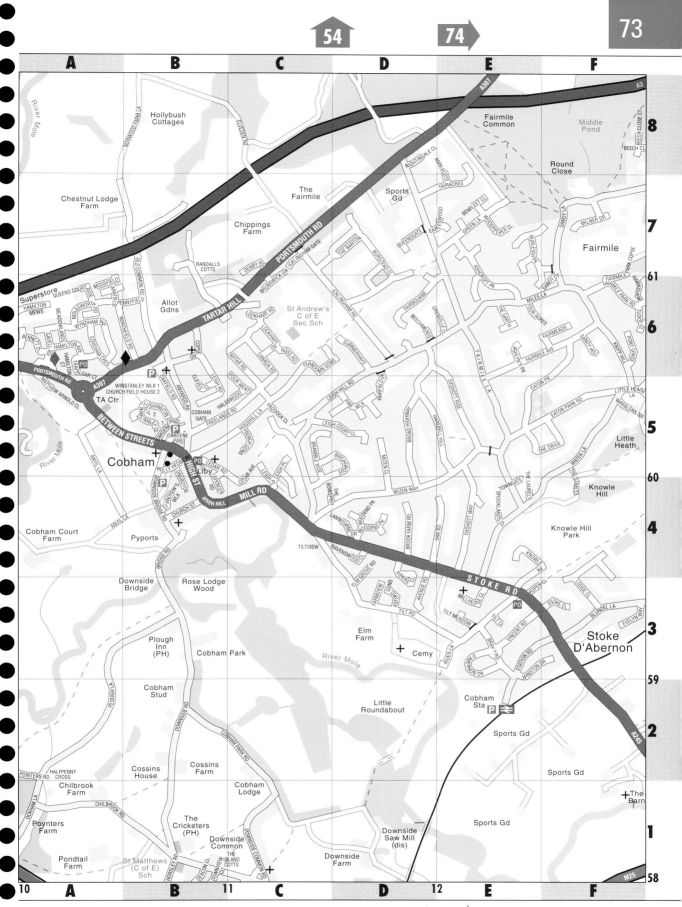

73 55

A B C D E F

8 DANESMEAD

Limekiln Wood

B280

The Heckets

FAIROAK LA

Oxshott Heath

Meml

7

WARREN LA
COPSEM LA
A244

GUNTERS MEAD
QUEENS DR
COPSEM WOOD
STOKESHEATH RD
PARKFIELDS
HIGHFIELD CL
MOLES HILL
STOKESHEATH RD

QUEENS DR
HEATH RD
THE SPINNEY
FAIR OAK CL

B280

Reed's Sch

THE RIDINGS
SANDY WAY
SANDY LA
BRACKENHILL
ROUNDHILL WAY
WINEY CL
BEECHWOOD
BEECH CL
A3

MONTROSE GDNS

LEYS RD
PRINCE'S DR

Prince's Coverts

61 Oxshott Sta

THE KNOLL
FAIRMILE PARK RD
FAIRMILE PARK COURT
FAIRMILE HTS
LEBANON DR
SANDROYD WAY
BIRCH VALE

WOODSIDE RD
KIMBERLEY RIDGE

GOLDRINGS RD

P

BIRDS HILL RD
CHATSWORTH PL
THE GABLES
THE WARREN

BROOMFIELD RIDE
SPICERS FIELD
FURZE FIELD

Stoke Wood

6 Oxshott

HOLTWOOD RD
CANTERBURY MEWS
STRATH'S CL
POND CL
PINES PIECE

HIGH ST
P
BIRDS HILL RISE
UPLANDS DR
TORLAND DR
BIRDS HILL DR

TUDOR CL
HEATH RIDGE GN
O'TWINOAKS
SOMERVILLE RD
CLOCKHOUSE MEAD
ARNEWOOD CL
STEEL'S LA

Danes Hill Jun Sch

MIDGARTH CL
OAKSHADE RD
SILVERDALE AV

BRIARS CT
HIGH DR
WOODSWAY

Cook's Crossing
LC

LINKS GREEN WAY
HEATHFIELD
HAWKHURST
LITTLE HEATH LA
RICHARDS RD
CROWE CL
KENILWORTH AVE
WATERLEY RD
LYFIELD
WEBSTER CL
RIDGEWAY CL
THE RIDGE
DANES CL

The Royal Kent Sch

DANES WAY
FERNHILL
BROOM HALL
MEADWAY

5 Fairmile Park

Little Heath

Danes Hill Sch

IRENE RD

NORTHCROFT

60 KNOTT PARK HOUSE
WREN'S HILL

BRIDLE LA

OLD FARM RD
PRIOUS DR
FALCONHURST

LEATHERHEAD RD

Horns Hill

4 Polyapes Scout Camp

RANDOLPH CL
BLUNDEL LA

The Furze

HARDWICK CL
THE CHASE
BARN CL
CHARLWOOD DR
SPINNEY CROFT

Clouds Hill Farm

Oxshott Flat

Pachesham Lake

3 Mast

MANOR WAY

MANOR WAY

Woodlands Park

OXSHOTT RD
A244

Leatherhead Common

59

Woodland Court Farm

Woodlands Farm

Tyrwhitt House

2 Manor Farm

STOKE RD
A245

WOODLANDS LA

Old Parks Cott

Woodlands Park Hotel

Woodlands Park

Queen Elizabeth's Training Coll

OAKLAWN RD

M25

Rowhurst Forge

Dorincourt

Parkside Sch

COBHAM RD

Old Parks Copse

River Mole

WOODLANDS RD
A245

1

M25

58 Stoke D'Abernon Bridge

Brook Willow Farm

13 A B 14 C D 15 E F

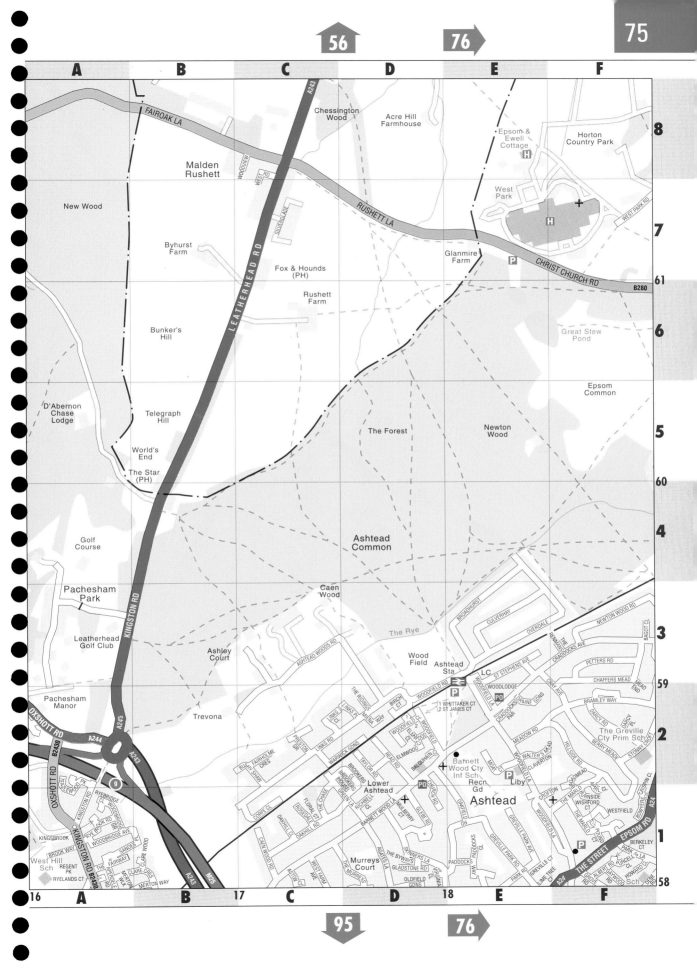

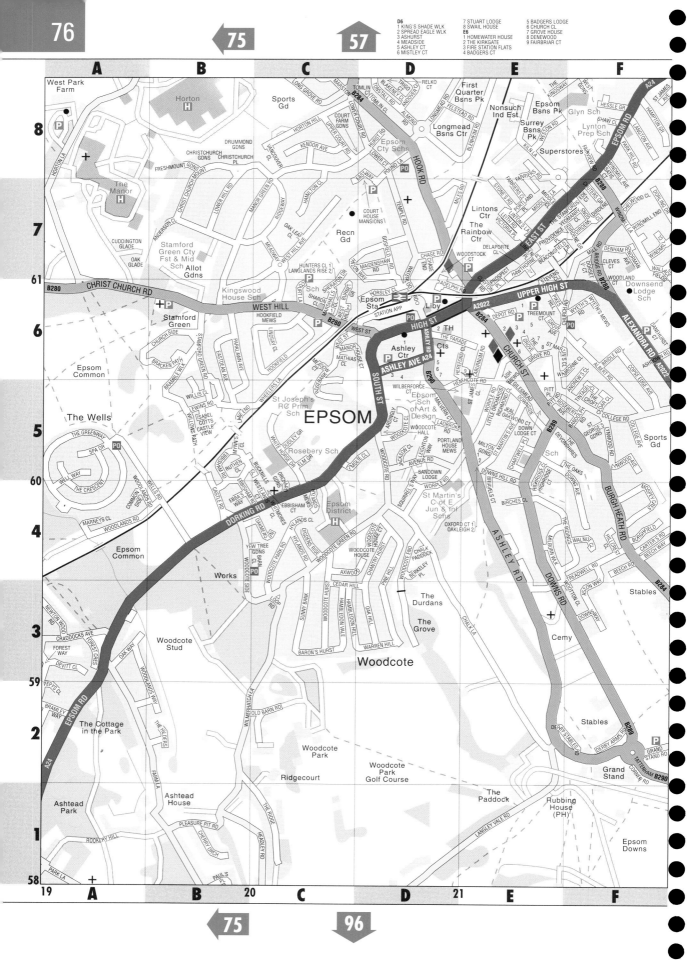

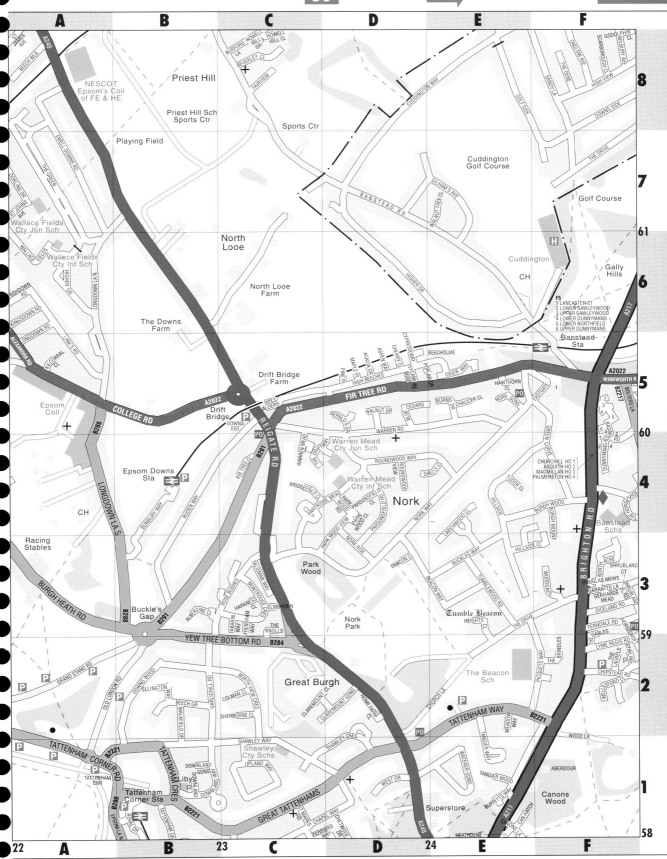

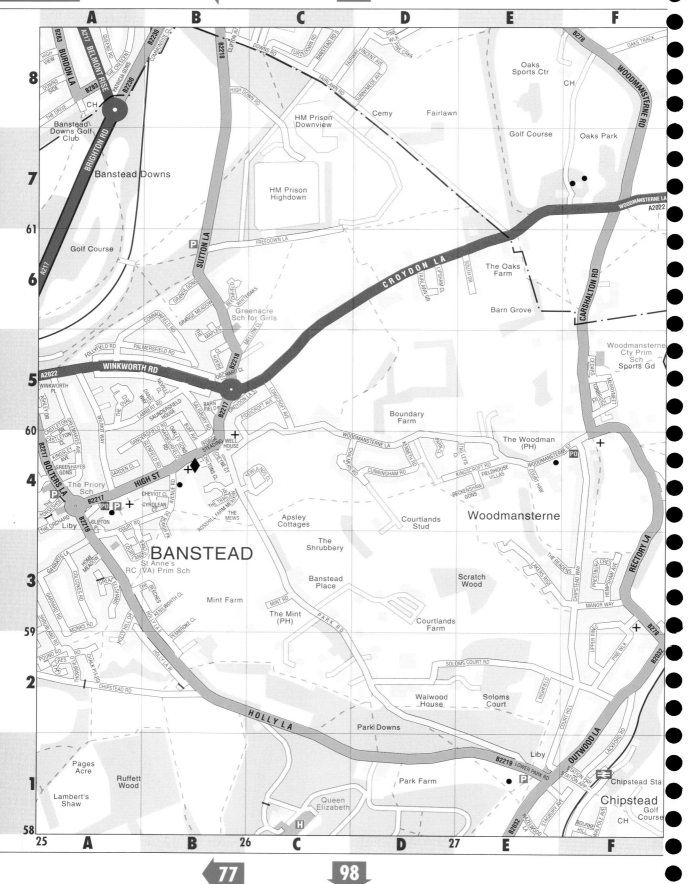

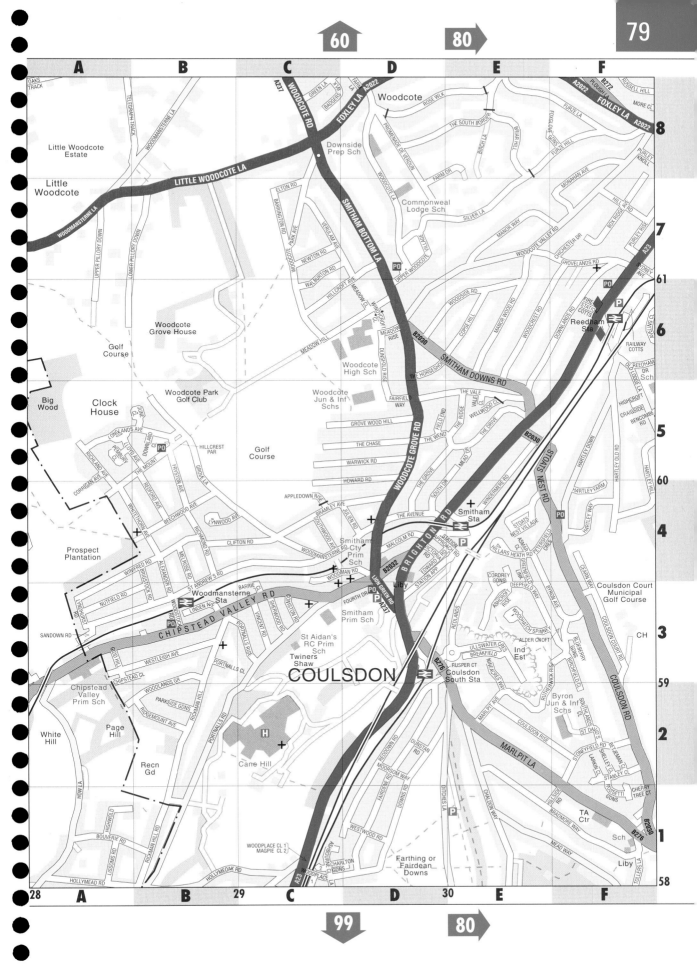

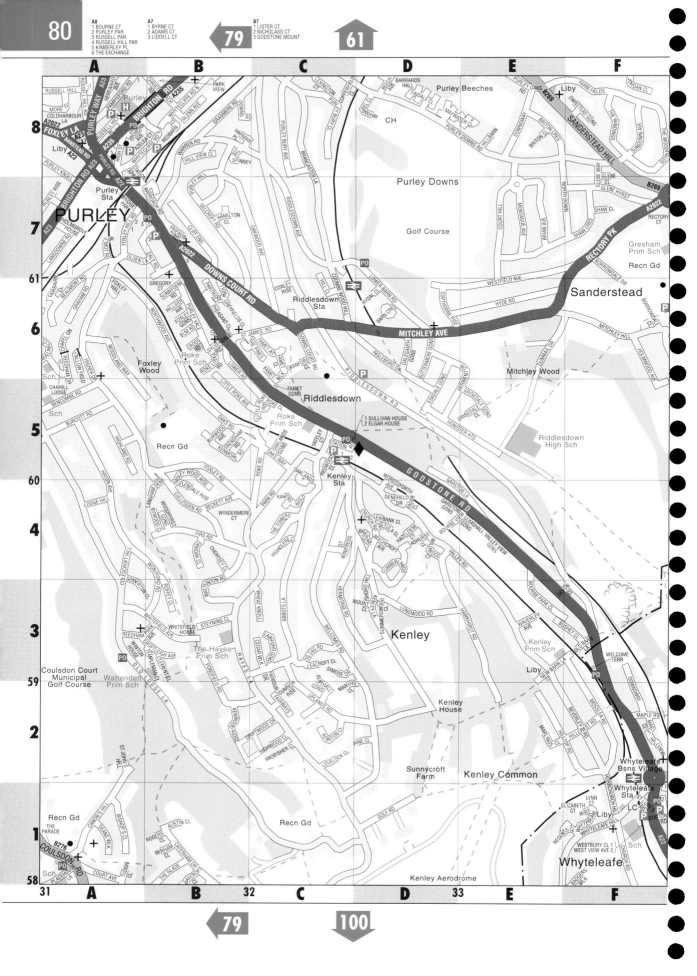

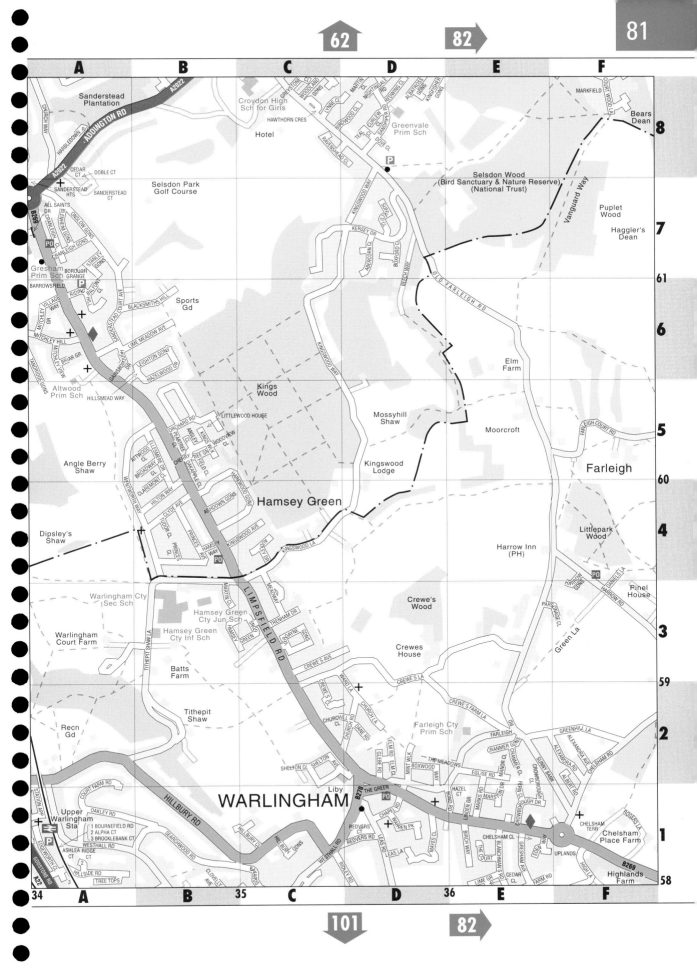

81 63

8

Bears Wood

Addington Court Golf Course

Frith Wood

FARLEIGH DEAN CRES

OVERBURY CRES

CHERTSEY CRES

CUDHAM DR

CLEVES RD

ST EDWARDS CL

MATTHEW'S GDNS

THORPE CL

FLORA GDNS

HUTCHINSONS RD

FRYLANDS CT

LEVERET CL

CALLEY DOWN

ARNHEM DR

REDSTART

REDPOLL

WARBANK

VALENTYNE CL

Kennels

MILNE PK E

UVEDALE CRES

UVEDALE CL

LEIGH CT

CATOR CL

Recn Gd

MILNE PK W

KENNEL WOOD CRES

HOMESTEAD WAY

CATOR CRES

KING HENRY'S DR

WALSH CRES

GREENWOOD

COMPORT GN

THISTLEWOOD

CORBETT CT

COMPORT GN

FAIRCHILDES AVE

LATHAMS RD

7

Farleigh Dean

Frylands Wood

Dumpsy Derry

Crab Wood

FEATHERBED LA

Fairchildes Prim Sch

Addington High Sch

SHEEPBARN LA

61

FAIRCHILDES COTTS

6

Limekiln Shaw

Coldblow Shaw

Chapel Hill

Fairchildes Farm

PARK RD

BLACKMAN'S LA

SKID HILL LA

The White Bear (PH)

Fickleshole Farm

Fickleshole

5

FARLEIGH COURT RD

Little Farleigh Green Farm

HIGH HILL RD

Greathill Shaw

Farleigh Court

60

Greatpark Wood

The Gripes

Warlingham Park

Five Acre Shaw

Midgley Shaws

FAIRCHILDES RD

Honeyoak Wood

4

H

P

SCOTSHALL LA

3

HARROW RD

CHELSHAM COMMON RD

Warlingham Park Sch

Holt Wood

HOLT WOOD

CHURCH LA

Ledgers Farm

HESIERS RD

59

CHELSHAM RD

Bull Inn (PH)

HENLEY WOOD

HESIERS HILL

2

Chelsham

Henley Wood

LEDGERS RD

WASHPOND LA

Chelsham Court

Chelsham Court Farm

CHELSHAM COURT RD

Broom Lodge Farm

BEDDLESTEAD LA

Owls Wood

1

BECCH FARM RD

Mast

Cony Crook

White Bank

58

LIMPSFIELD RD

B269

81 102

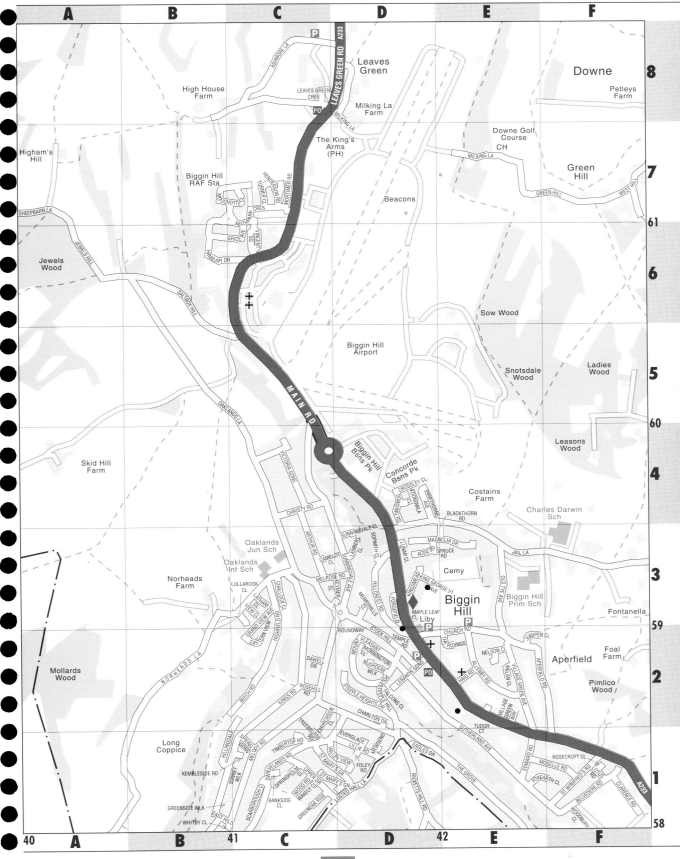

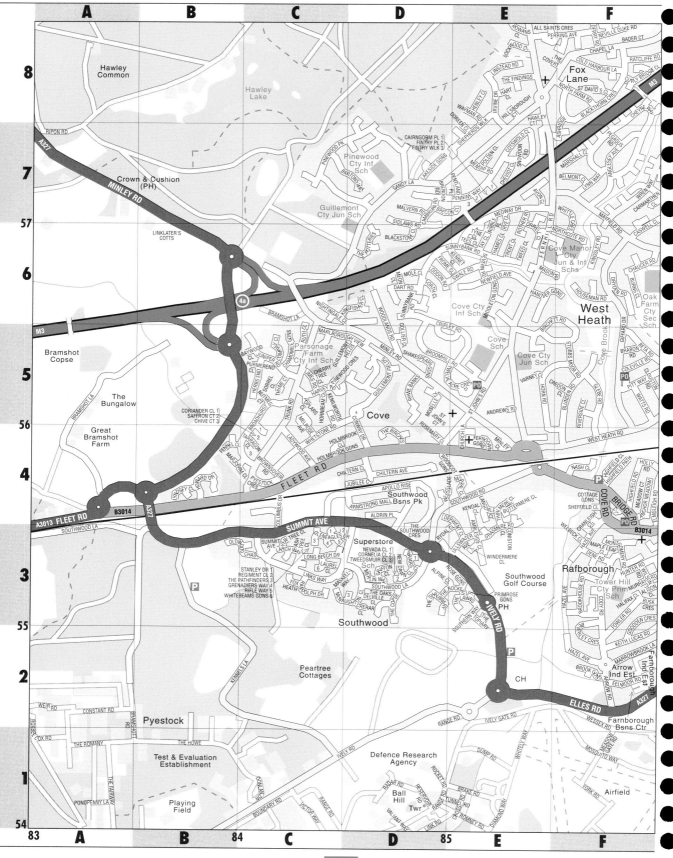

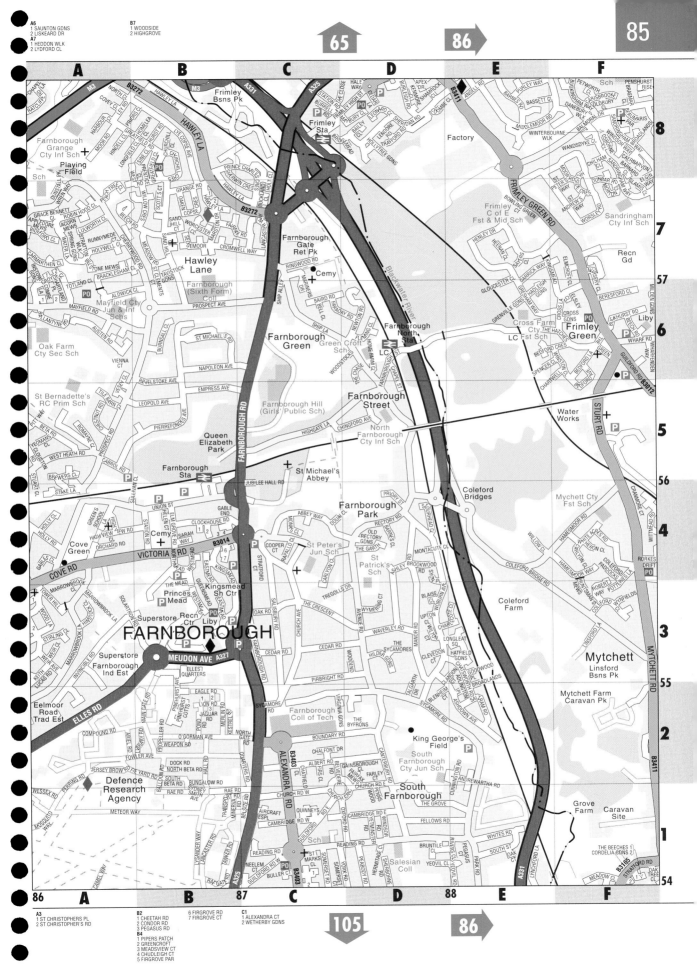

A B C D E F

8

Loen
Balmoral Dr
The Grange
Valley Rd
Blackdown Hill
Frith Hill Rd
Dettingen Barracks
B3015
Alma Barracks
Crimea Rd
Malta Rd
Cyprus Rd
Canada Rd
Union Rd
Alma Gdns
Dettingen Rd
Blackdown Prim Sch
Mainstone Hill
Pirbright Ranges

DANGER AREA

7

St Cross
Richmond Hill
St Cross Rd
Ridgemount Est
Blackdown Rd
Woodend Rd
Mainstone Cl
Alfriston Rd
P
PO
North Minden House
The Royal Way
Newfoundland Rd
Normandy Cl
The Princess Royal Barracks
Sports Gd

1 Essex Cl
2 Walmer Cl
3 Banbury Cl
4 Radcliffe Cl

Deepcut Bridge Rd
Fernleigh Rise
Bellew Rd

57

Devil's Pound
Old Windmill Hill

6

Wharfenden Lake
Wharf Way
Lake Rd
Basingstoke Canal
Frimhurst Farm
Deepcut
Blackdown Barracks
Brunswick Rd
Porridgepot Hill
Lodge Hill

(PH)
B3012
Cheswycks Prep Sch
B3015
Guildford Rd
Gapemouth Plantation
Hodge Bottom

5

The Old Mill
Deepcut Place
Gapemouth Rd
B3012

56

P
P
Four Winds
Rangelands Poultry Farm
Old Guildford Rd
Longdown Hill

4

Cramore Rd
Talbot Cl
Rorkes Drift
Loman Rd
Haining Gdns
Vine House Cl
Poplar Cl
Salisbury Gr
Nightingale Dr
Mytchett Heath
Stoney Castle Ranges

DANGER AREA

3

Salisbury Terr
Ambleside
Jubilee Rd
Tunnel Hill
Emperor's Hill

55

2

Hazel Rd
Potters (PH)
Mytchett Place
Graywsood Dr
Barnsley Cl
Keogh Cl
Mytchett Place Rd
Mytchett Gate
Bridge Hill
Pirbright Common
Hangman's Hill

Glenmount Rd
B3411
Drake Ave
Mytchett Lake Rd
Mytchett Lake
Keogh Barracks
Spur Hill
Ash Ranges
Scragley Hill

1

Playing Field
Play Hill
DANGER AREA

54

B3411
89
A
B
90
C
D
91
E
F

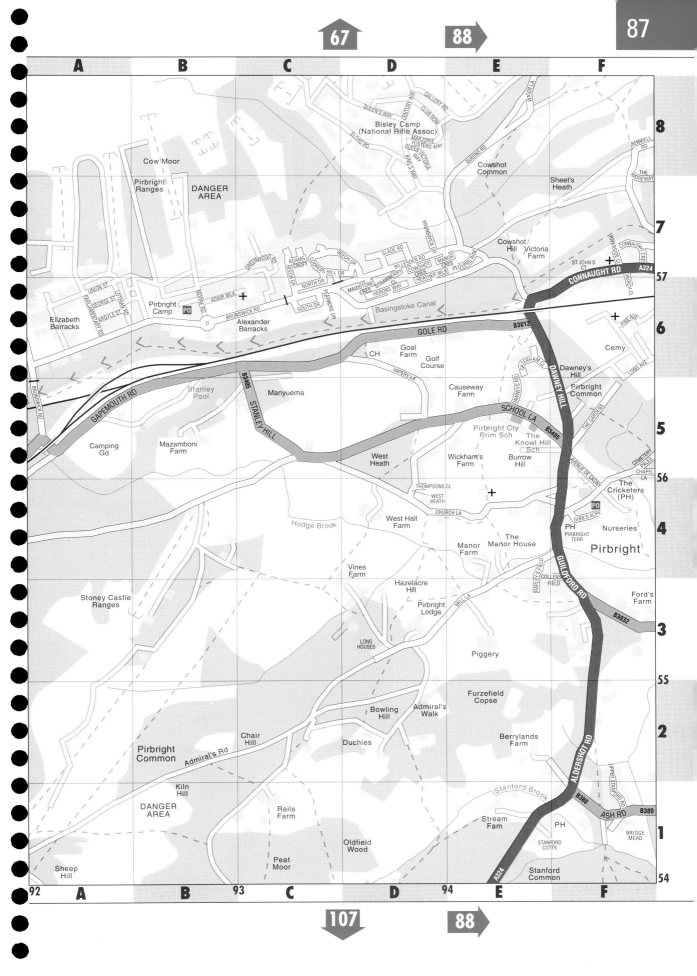

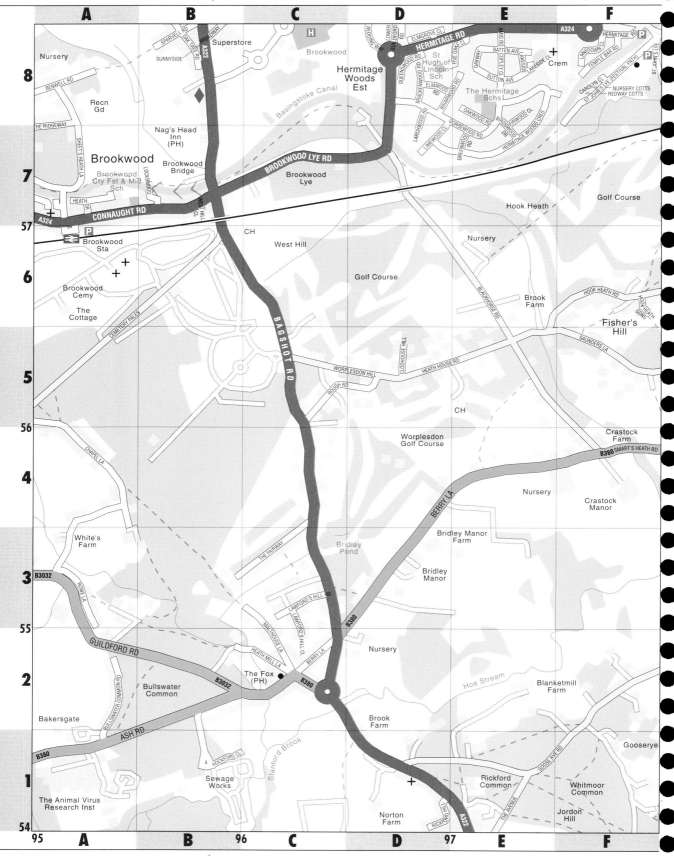

A324

Nursery

8

Benwell Rd

Recn Gd

The Ridgeway

Brookwood

Brookwood Cty Fst & Mid Sch

Sheet's Heath La

Heath Dr

Sparvel Rd

Oak Tree Rd

Broadway

Sunnyside

A322

Superstore

Nag's Head Inn (PH)

Brookwood Bridge

Locksmood

West Hill

H

Brookwood

Basingstoke Canal

Hermitage Woods Est

Redding Vale

Lower Guildford

Gun Jnford

Elmgrove Cl

HERMITAGE RD

Amis Rd

Copley Cl

Five Oaks Cl

Lakeside

Batten Ave

Oakway

St Hugh of Lincoln Sch

Sutton Ave

The Hermitage Schs

A324

Hermitage Rd

Lansdowne Cl

Temple Bar Rd

Crem

Carolyn Cl

St John's Lye (Festival Path)

St John's Lye

Nursery Cotts

Redway Cotts

P

P

P

Queenswood Rd

Brackenwood Rd

Broadwood Rd

Larchwood Rd

Elmwood Rd

Limewood Cl

Greenwood Rd

Gorsewood Rd

Oakwood Rd

Birchwood Dr

Firwood Cl

Hermitage Woods Cres

7

Brookwood Lye Rd

BROOKWOOD LYE RD

Brookwood Lye

Hook Heath

Golf Course

57

A324

CONNAUGHT RD

West Hill

West Hill

CH

Nursery

P

Brookwood Sta

Brookwood Cemy

The Cottage

6

Cemetery Pales

Golf Course

Blackhorse Rd

Brook Farm

Hook Heath Rd

Fisher's Hill

Hook Heath Gdns

Saunders La

5

Worplesdon Hill

Rough Rd

Cloudhouse Hill

Heath House Rd

CH

Bagshot Rd

BAGSHOT RD

56

Chapel La

Worplesdon Golf Course

Crastock Farm

B380

SMART'S HEATH RD

4

White's Farm

The Fairway

Bridley Pond

Berry La

Nursery

Crastock Manor

Bridley Manor Farm

3

B3032

Rowe La

Lawford's Hill Rd

Lawford's Hill Cl

Bridley Manor

55

GUILDFORD RD

Malthouse La

Heath Mill La

Berry La

B380

Nursery

2

Bullswater Common Rd

Bullswater Common

B3032

ASH RD

The Fox (PH)

B380

Hoe Stream

Blanketmill Farm

Gooserye

Bakersgate

B380

Hockford Cl

Stanford Brook

Sewage Works

Brook Farm

Rickford Common

Goose Rye Rd

The Avenue

Whitmoor Common

1

The Animal Virus Research Inst

Norton Farm

Rickford

A322

Jordon Hill

54

95

96

97

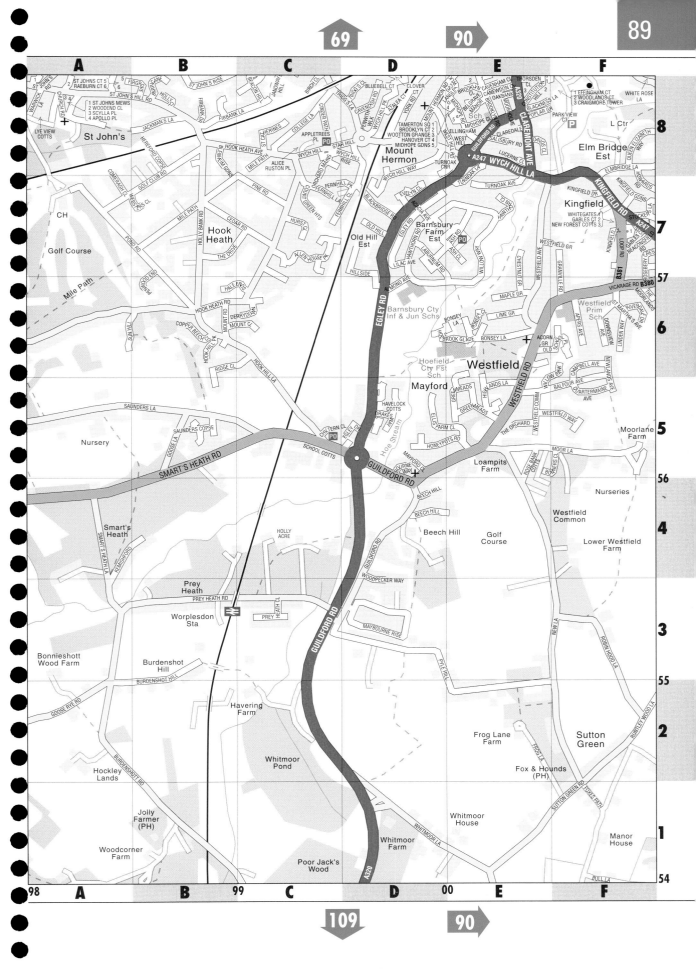

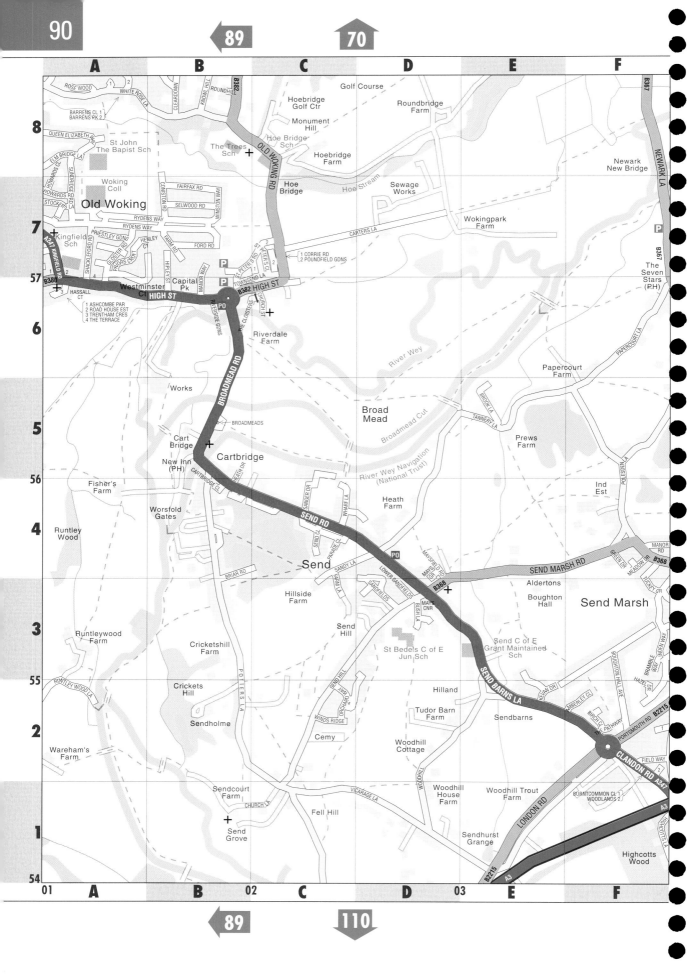

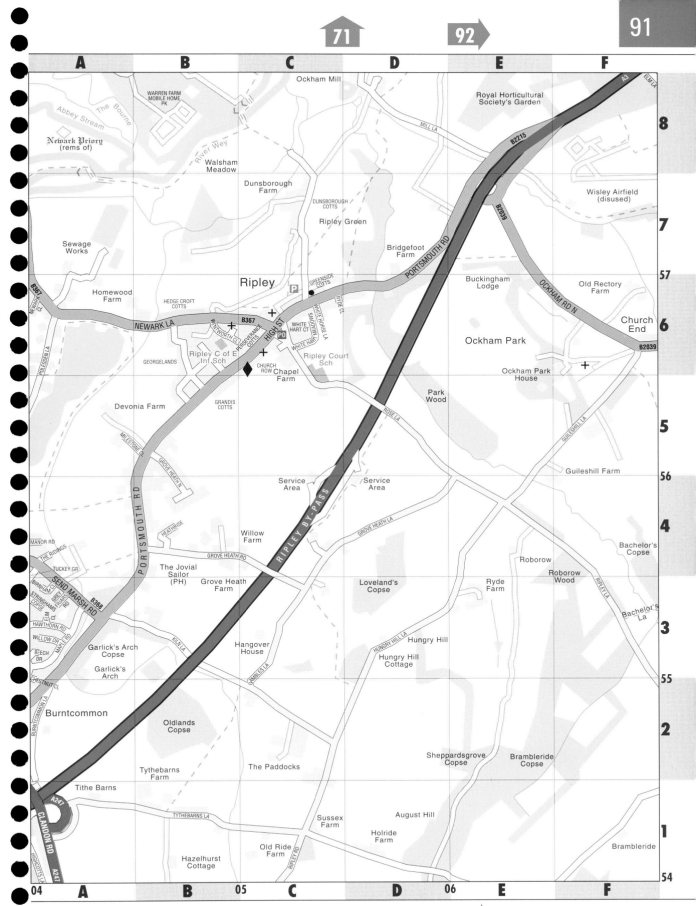

91
72

A B C D E F

8

Elm
Corner

Highfield
Farm

Hatchford
End

Cold Norton
Farm

Wisley Airfield
(dis)

Hazeldene
Farm

Black Swan
(PH)

7

Bridge End
Farm

Pound
Farm

Hyde La

HATCH LA

OCKHAM LA

OLD LA

May's
Green

Upton
Farm

Martyr's
Green

57

Bridge
End

Chestnut
Farm

Appstree
Farm

Trulliber
Copse

Chaffers
Copse

6

The Hautboy
Inn

ALMS HEATH

Ockham

B2039

PO

Hook
Wood

SCHOOL LA

Stumps
Grove

Barnsthorns

Stumps Grove
Cotts

5

Blackmoor
Farm

56

Slade
Farm

4

WHITEHILL LA

Ridings La

Barnsthorns
Wood

Rydings
Farm

CH

Blue Ridge

Golf Course

BACHELOR'S LA

Even
Wood

GREEN LA

The Drift

The
Forest

ORCHARD
CL

3

LONG REACH

Works

OCKHAM RD N

North Forest
Lodge

HEATHWAY

BERRINGTON
DRT

FALCONWOOD

Waterloo
Farm

OCKHAM DR

WILDWOOD CL

HEATHWAY

Camping
Site

PARKSIDE CL

FOREST RD

HOOK RD

55

Old
Brickyard

NORTHCOTE CRES

NIGHTINGALE CRES

PARKSIDE PL

HEATH VIEW

NIGHTINGALE AVE

The Raleigh
Sch

WESTON LEA

The Highlands

PARKSIDE

FOREST CL

Broom
House

NORTHCOTE CL

NIGHTINGALE RD

Green La W

NORTHCOTE RD

EDWIN RD

HEATHERGRENE

MEADOW WAY

Horsley
Sta

THE RIDINGS

2

EDWIN CL

NORRELLS DR

NORRELLS
RIDE

Manor
Farm

EAST LA

HOWARD CL

THE RISE

THE CHASE

COBHAM WAY

OCKHAM RD S

Ripley La

SILKMORE LA

FARLEYS CL

WOODSIDE

GREYA BANK

Station
Par

Lollesworth
Wood

KINGSTON AVE

GLENDENE AVE

THE BIRCHES

1

Jury
Farm

LOLLESWORTH LA

THE STREET

P

P

P

PO

Liby

OLD RECTORY LA

B2039

HIGH PARK AVE

Kingston La

Roundtree
Farm

54

07 A B 08 C D 09 E F

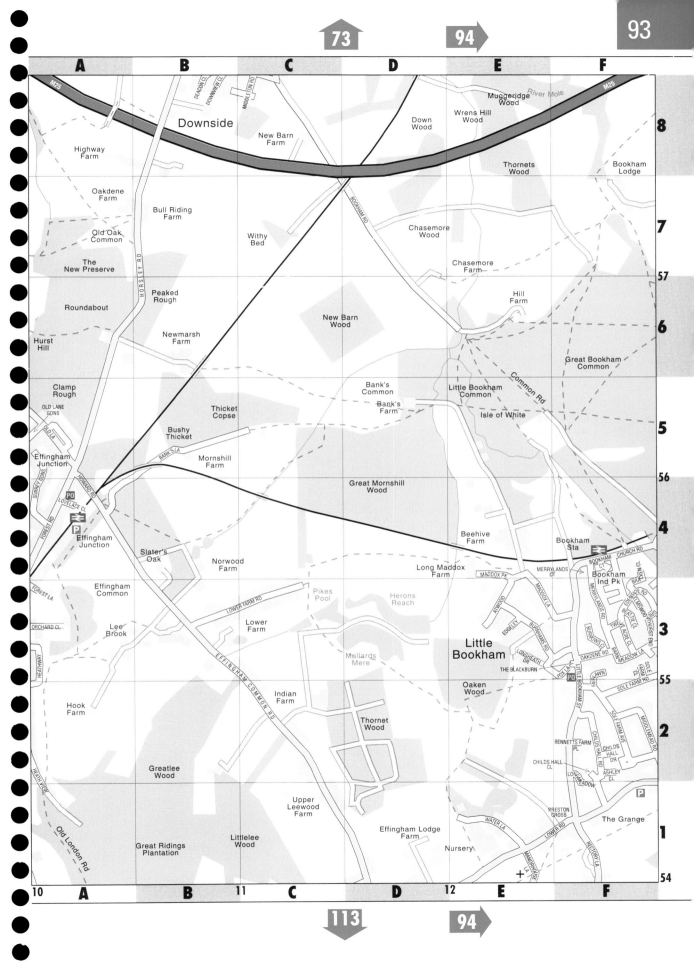

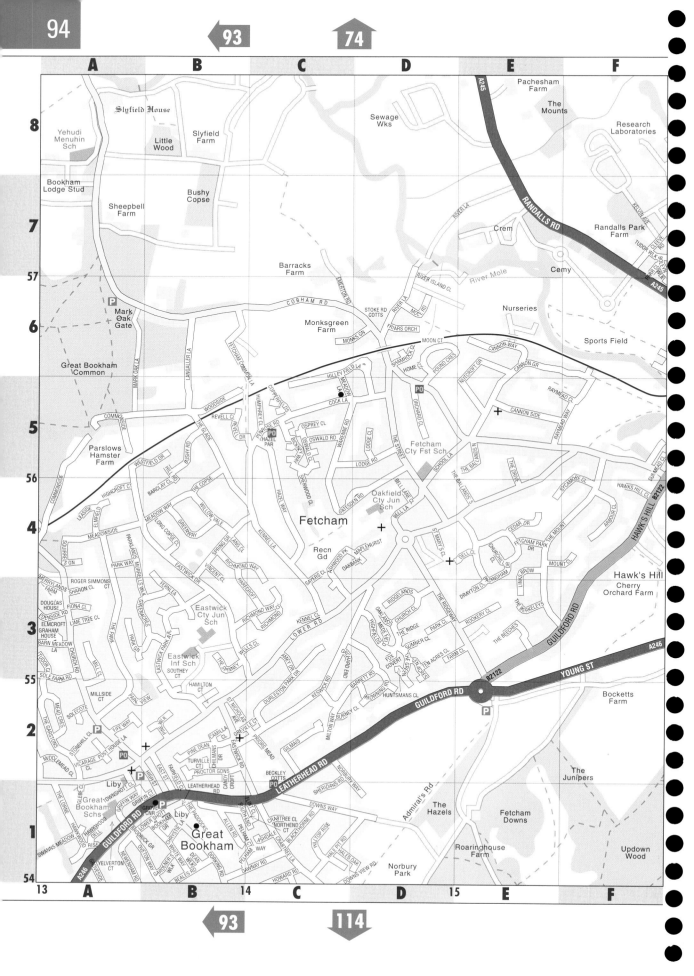

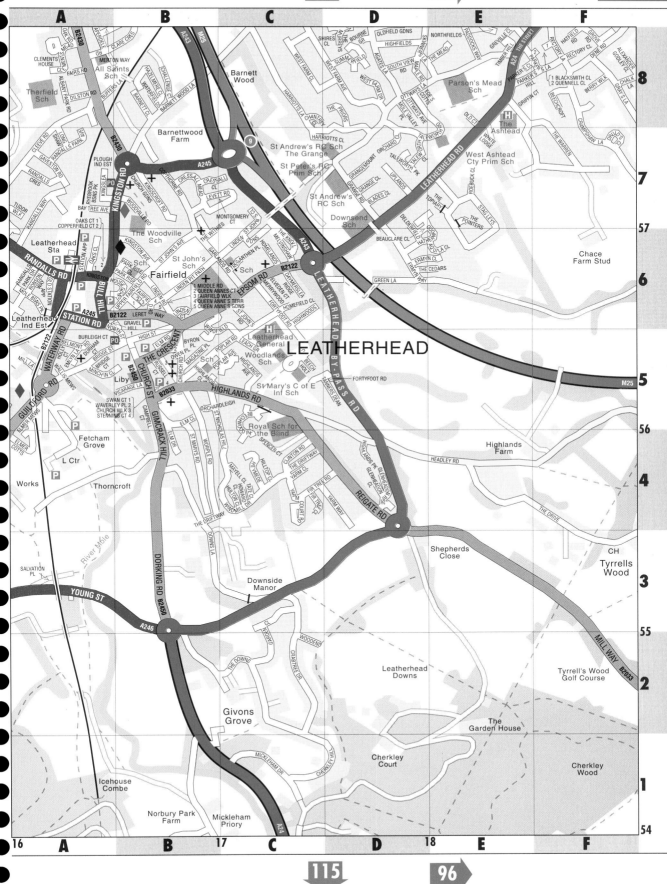

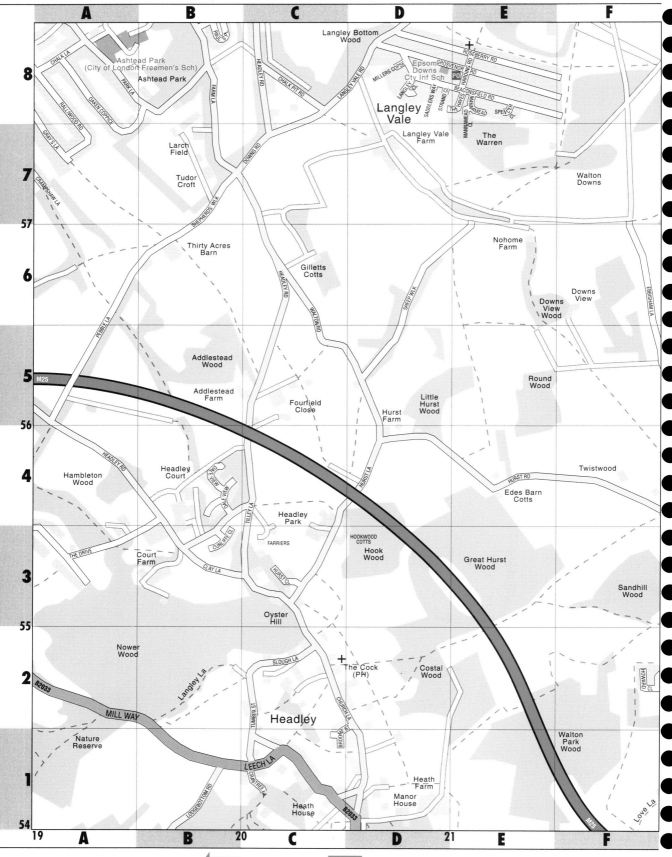

95
76

A B C D E F

8

7

57

6

5

56

4

3

55

2

1

54

19 A B 20 C D 21 E F

Langley Bottom Wood

Epsom Downs Cty Inf Sch

ROSEBERRY RD

GROSVENOR RD

HARDING RD

BEACONSFIELD RD

Langley Vale

MILLERS COPSE

LANGLEY CL

SADDLERS WAY

STRAND CL

THE HAYES

MANNAMEAD CL

MINN

PANMEAD

SPENCER CL

PO

The Warren

Langley Vale Farm

Walton Downs

CHALK LA

Ashtead Park (City of London Freemen's Sch)

Ashtead Park

PAUL'S PL

HEADLEY RD

CHALK PIT RD

LANGLEY VALE RD

PARK LA

OAKEN COPPICE

RALLWOOD RD

GRAY'S LA

CRAMPSHAW LA

FARM LA

DOWNS RD

Larch Field

Tudor Croft

SHEPHERDS WLK

Nohome Farm

Thirty Acres Barn

Gilletts Cotts

Downs View Wood

Downs View

EBBISHAM LA

HEADLEY RD

WALTON RD

SHEEP WLK

PEBBLE LA

Addlestead Wood

Addlestead Farm

Fourfield Close

Hurst Farm

Little Hurst Wood

Round Wood

M25

Hambleton Wood

HEADLEY RD

Headley Court

DALE VIEW

DALE VIEW

TILLEY LA

CUNLIFFE CL

Headley Park

FARRIERS

HURST LA

HURST RD

Edes Barn Cotts

Twistwood

THE DRIVE

Court Farm

CLAY LA

HURST CL

HOOKWOOD COTTS

Hook Wood

Great Hurst Wood

Sandhill Wood

Oyster Hill

Nower Wood

Langley La

SLOUGH LA

The Cock (PH)

Costal Wood

HOWARD CL

B2033

MILL WAY

Nature Reserve

TUMBER ST

Headley

CHURCH LA

BROOMAC

Walton Park Wood

LEECH LA

CRABTREE LA

LODGEBOTTOM RD

Heath House

B2033

Heath Farm

Manor House

Love La

M25

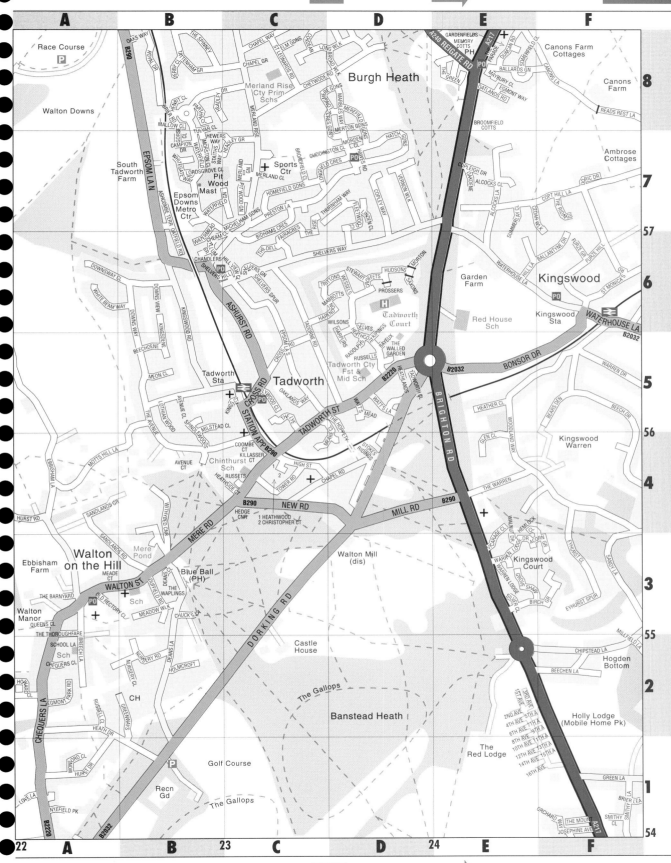

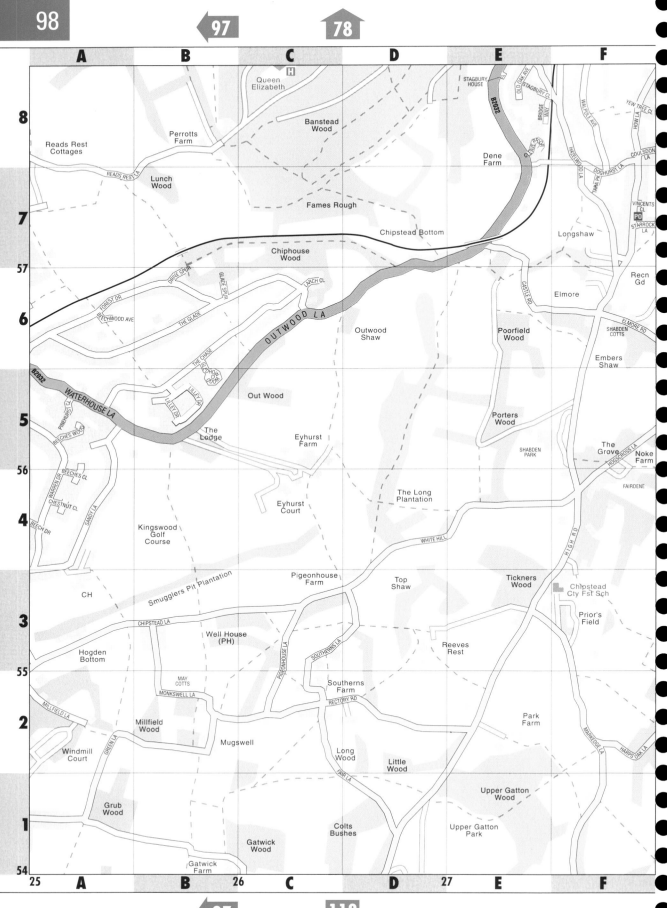

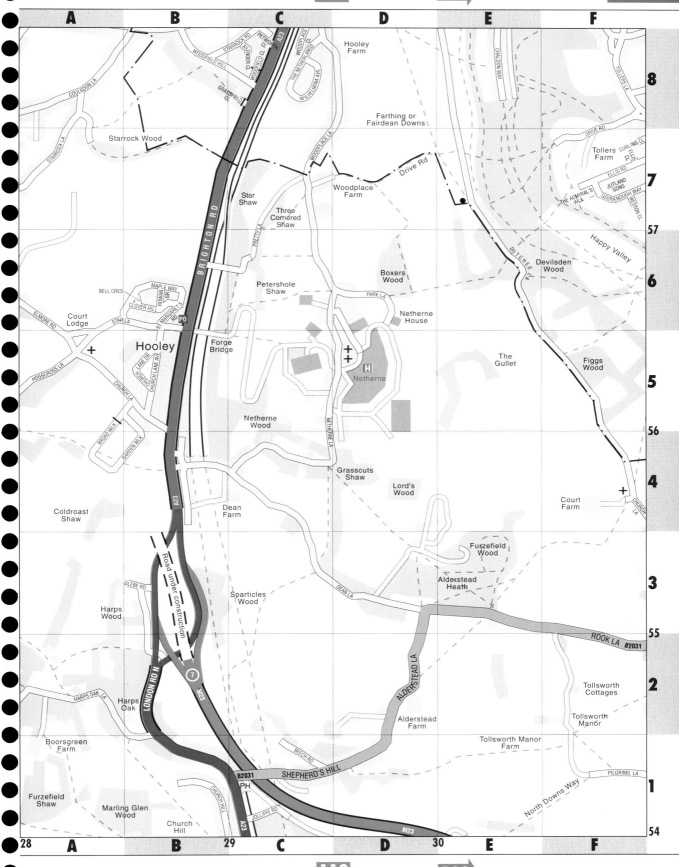

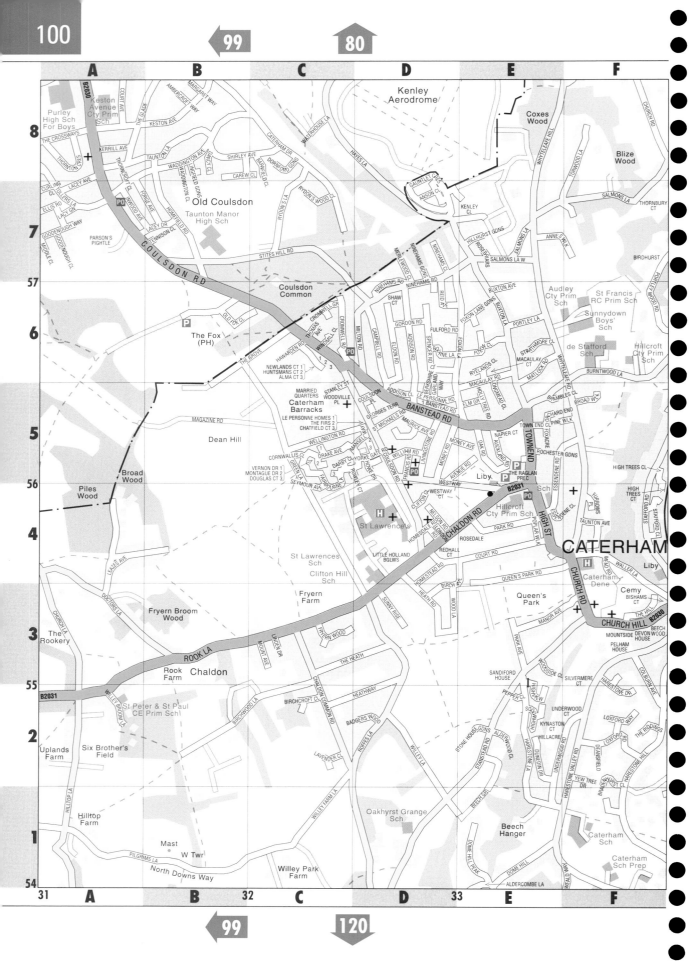

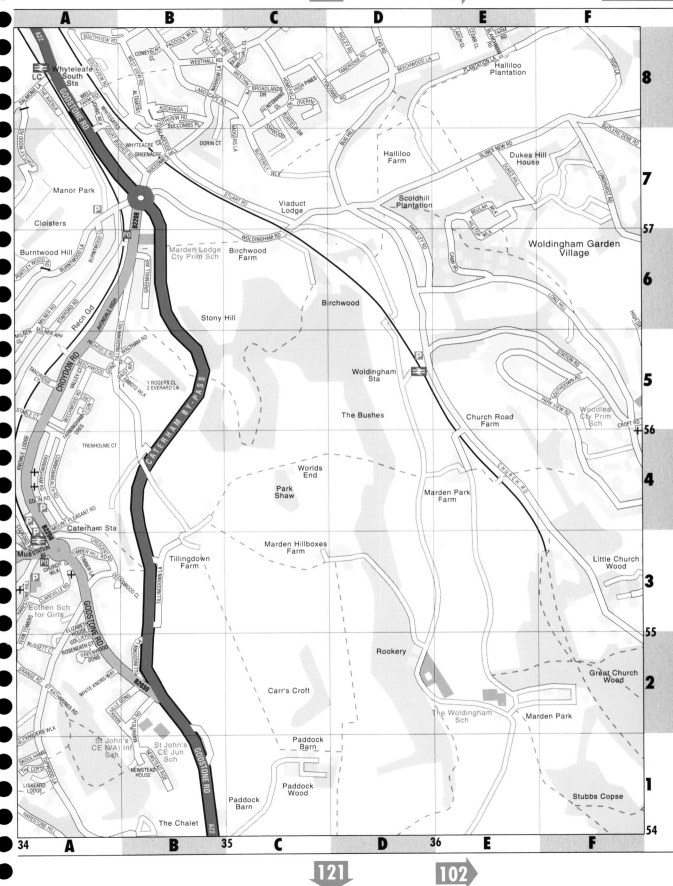

← 101
↑ 82

A B C D E F

B269
Slines Green
LEDGERS RD
Worms Heath
BROOM BANK
Mast
Milbury Cottage
LIMPSFIELD RD
8
Slines New Rd
Slines Oak
BARNARD RD
BEECH FARM RD
High Breach
Beddlestead Farm
Nore Hill
Lumberdine Wood
7
Warren Barn Farm
UPLAND RD
BUTLERS DENE RD
Hovings Hole
Beech Farm
Ashen Shaw
57
SLINES OAK RD
6
Cheverells Farm
CROYDON RD
LUNGHURST RD
Vanguard Way
5
Pitchers Wood
THE WOLD
HIGH DR
Sch
CROFT RD
56
Paygate Cottage
PO
CLARE CT
ULSTAN CT
NETHERN COURT RD
THE CRESCENT
STATION RD
4
Valleyfields
Botley Hill Farm
Botley Hill
B2024
WELCOME COTTS
PARK VIEW RD
THE GREEN
Woldingham
Greenhill Shaw
Mast
CLARKS LA
TITSEY HILL
B269
UPPER COURT RD
Whistlers Wood Farm
Warren Kennels
SOUTHFIELDS RD
3
Masts
NORTHDOWN RD
SOUTHERN RD
55
Whistlers Wood
Titsey Plantation
CHURCH RD
CH
PITCHFONT LA
2
North Downs Golf Course
Flint House
THE RIDGE
SANDERS HILL
P
CHALKPIT LA
Beech Plantation
1
Works
Greensand Way
Pilgrims' Way
North Downs Way
M25
M25
54
37 A 38 B C 39 D E F

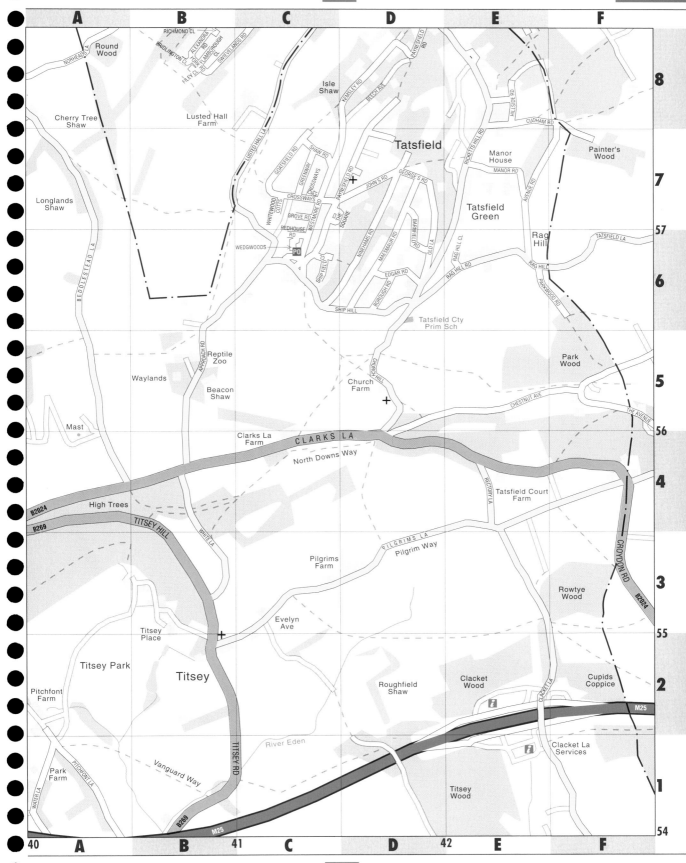

84

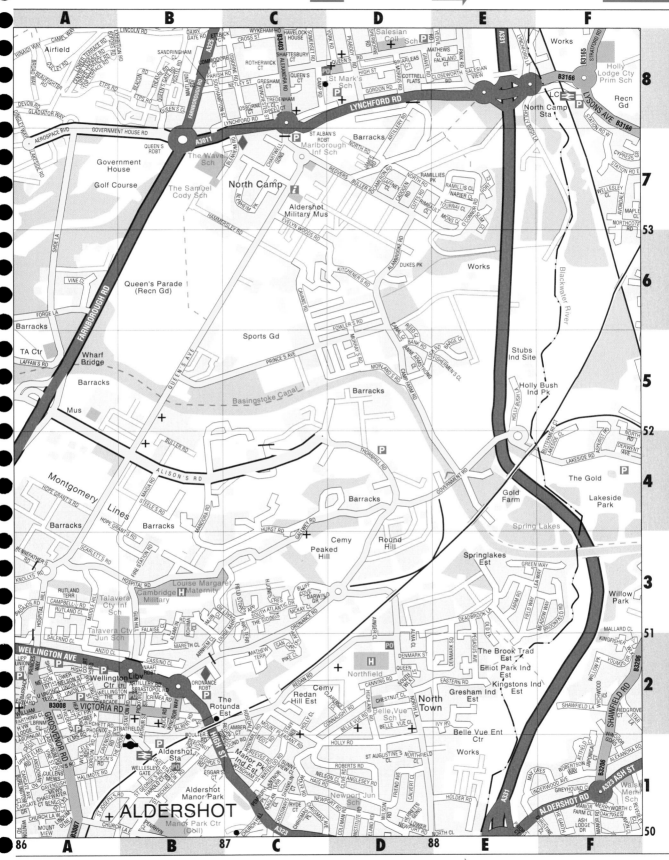

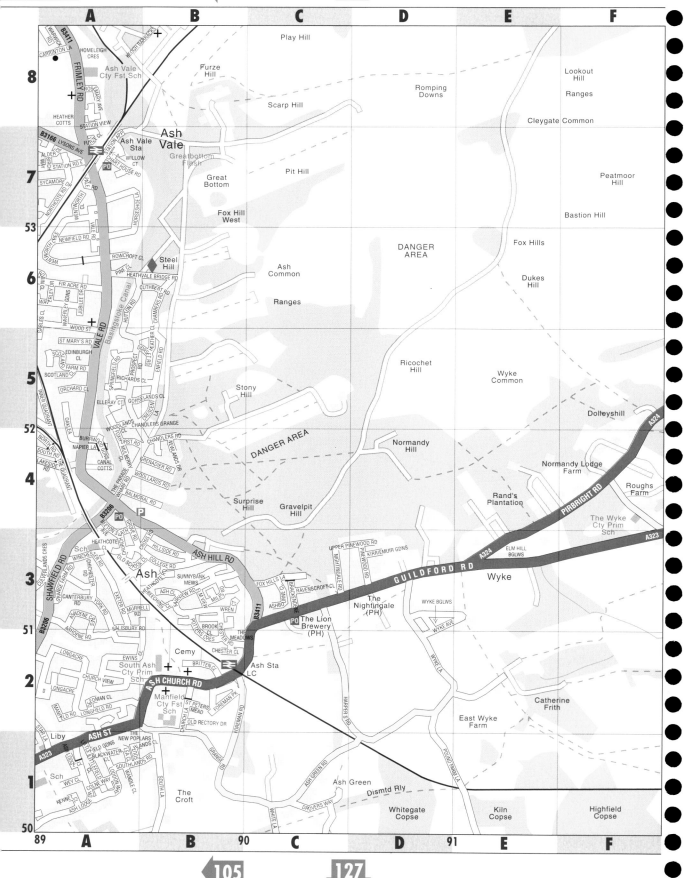

105
86
105
127

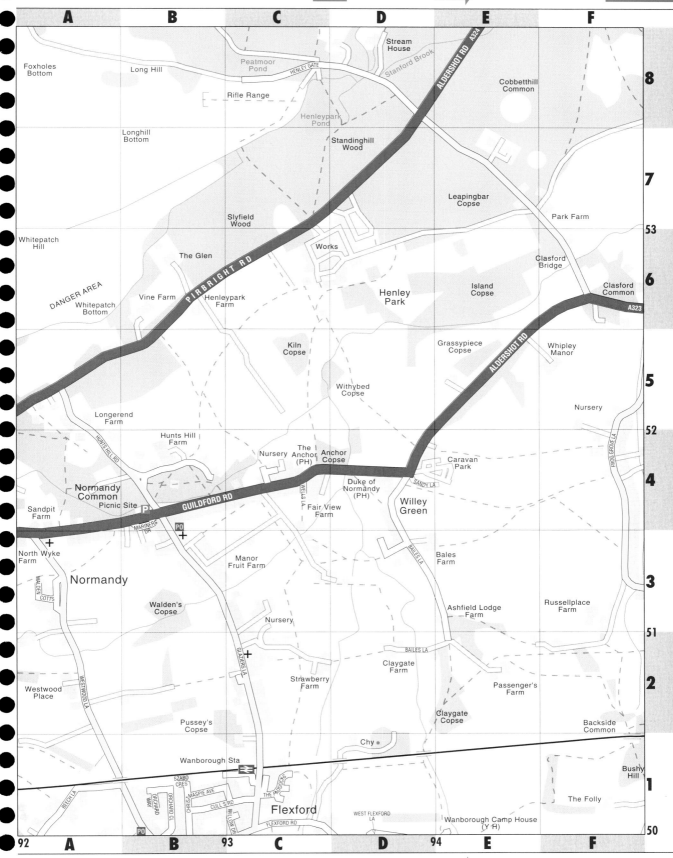

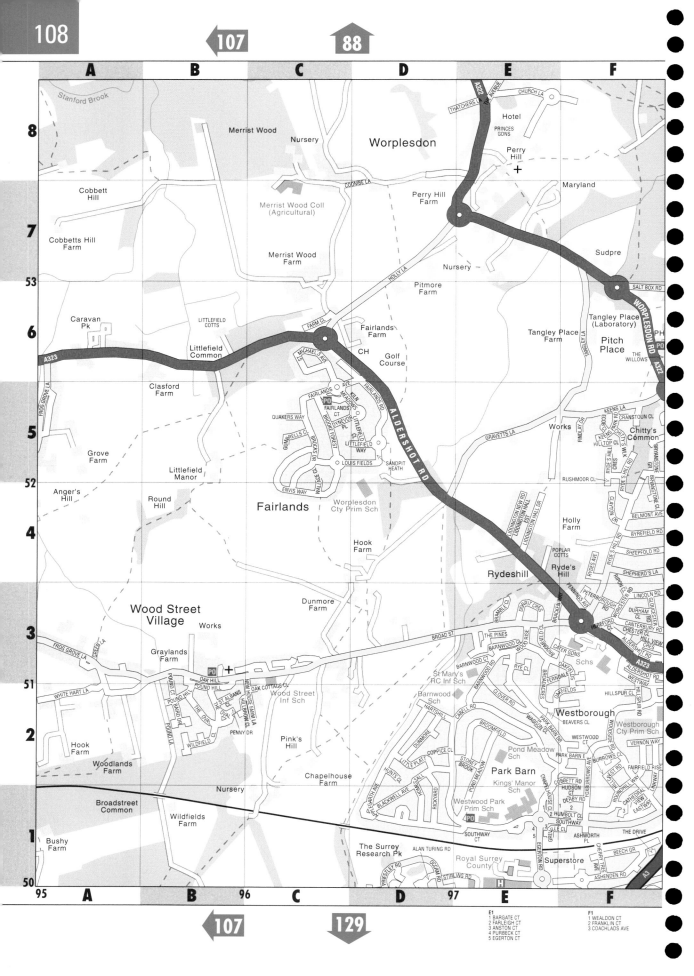

107
88

A   B   C   D   E   F

8

Stanford Brook

Merrist Wood

Nursery

Worplesdon

Hotel

PRINCES
GDNS

Perry
Hill
+

Maryland

Cobbett
Hill
Farm

7

Merrist Wood Coll
(Agricultural)

Perry Hill
Farm

COOMBE LA

Sudpre

Cobbetts Hill
Farm

Merrist Wood
Farm

Nursery

HOLLY LA

53

Pitmore
Farm

SALT BOX RD

Caravan
Pk

LITTLEFIELD
COTTS

FARM CL

Fairlands
Farm

Tangley Place
(Laboratory)

6

A323

Littlefield
Common

CH

Golf
Course

Tangley Place
Farm

Pitch
Place

PH
PO

THE
WILLOWS

Clasford
Farm

MICHAEL'S
CL

AVE

FAIRLANDS RD

Works

KEENS LA

Chitty's
Common

5

Grove
Farm

QUAKERS WAY

FAIRLANDS
MEADOWS

KILN
LA

PO

FAIRLANDS
CT

DYNEVOR
PL

LITTLEFIELD
FOREST

GUMBRELLS CL

BROOKS DR

LITTLEFIELD
WAY

Louis Fields

GRAVETTS LA

ALDERSHOT RD

Works

RUSHMOOR CL

RYDE'S HILL RD

CRANSTOUN CL

BRYANSTONE
GR

BELMONT AVE

52

Anger's
Hill

Littlefield
Manor

TALLOW
CL

ENVIS WAY

SANDPIT
HEATH

CLAYTON DR

BYREFIELD RD

4

Round
Hill

Fairlands

Worplesdon
Cty Prim Sch

LIDDINGTON NEW RD

LIDDINGTON HALL DR

Holly
Farm

Hook
Farm

POPLAR
COTTS

Ryde's
Hill

RYDES AVE

SHEEPFOLD RD

SHEPHERD'S LA

Rydeshill

RIPON CL

LINCOLN CL

3

Wood Street
Village

Works

Dunmore
Farm

BROAD ST

THE PINES

BRAMBLE CL

PENNINGS AVE

DIXON CRES

HEREFORD

CATER GDNS

Schs

DURHAM
CL

CHESTER CL

CANTERBURY CL

HILL VIEW
CRES

ALDERSHOT RD

A323

Graylands
Farm

FROG GROVE LA

GREEN LA

PO
+

OAK HILL

NEW HOUSE FARM LA

OAK COTTAGE CL

Wood Street
Inf Sch

BARNWOOD RD

RYE CL

WOOD RISE

BROADMEADS

FERNDALE

OAKFIELDS

St Mary's
RC Inf Sch

HILLSPUR CL

HILLSPUR RD

WESTWAY

51

WHITE HART LA

POUND HILL

POUND LA

POUND FIELD

THE OVAL

ST ALBANS
CL

THE OVAL

HILBROW CL

Wood Street
Sch

Barnwood
Sch

CLOVER RD

Westborough

BEAVERS CL

Westborough
Cty Prim Sch

VERNON WAY

2

Hook
Farm

WILDFIELD

PENNY DR

Pink's
Hill

DUNMORE

LITTLE PLATT

COPPICE CL

HARTSHILL

CARELL RD

BROOMFIELD

WAGGON LA

WESTWOOD

Pond Meadow
Sch

PARK BARN E

Park Barn

PARK BARN DR

BURROWS CL

FAIRFIELD RISE

KINGSWAY

Woodlands
Farm

Chapelhouse
Farm

Nursery

HUNTS CL

BLACKWELL AVE

RICKYARD

POND MEADOW

Kings' Manor
Sch

Westwood Park
Prim Sch

CHAPELHOUSE RD

COBBETT RD

HUDSON
CT

DERBY RD

FOXBURROWS AVE

CATHEDRAL
VIEW

EASTWAY

THE DRIVE

Broadstreet
Common

Wildfields
Farm

PRIESTLEY RD

OCKHAM RD

STIRLING RD

ALAN TURING RD

The Surrey
Research Pk

SOUTHWAY

HUMBOLT CT

SOUTHWAY

GREENMOUNT
LILLE CL

ASHWORTH
PL

CHERRY TREE
AVE

BEECH GR

ASHENDEN RD

A3

1

Bushy
Farm

Royal Surrey
County

H

Superstore

50

95   A   96   B   C   96   D   97   E   F

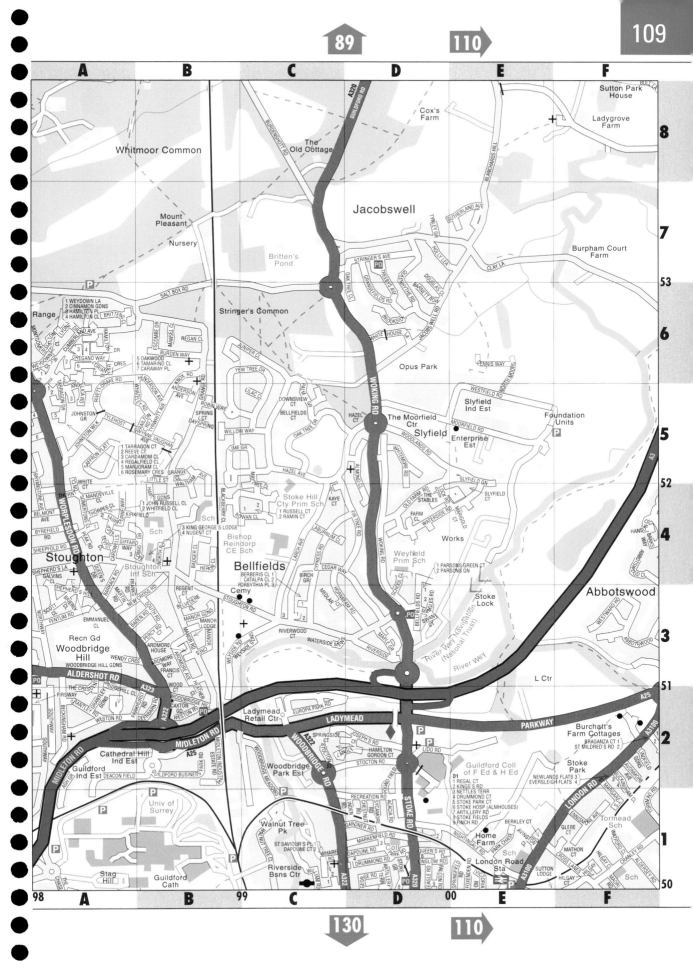

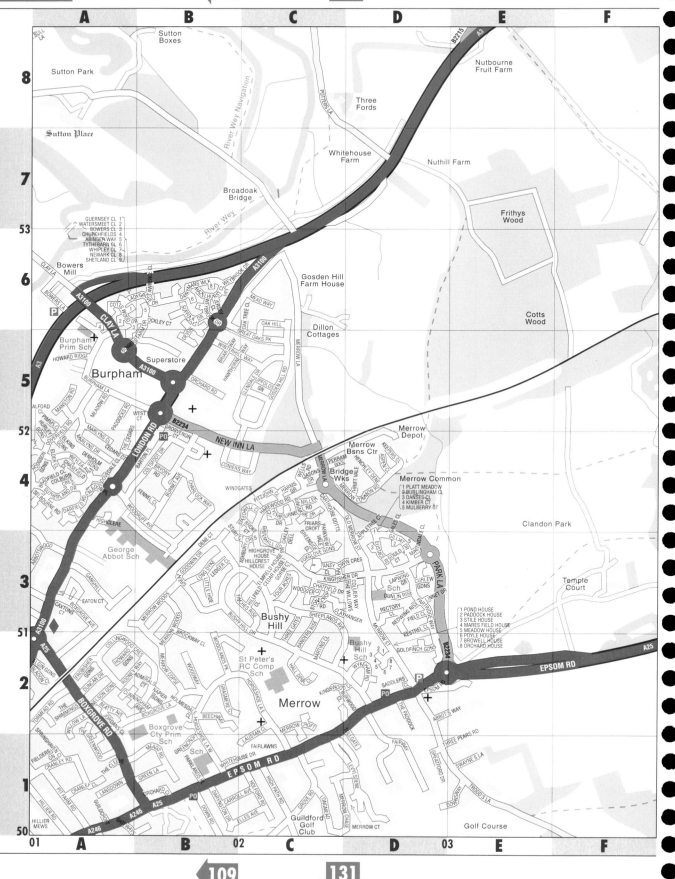

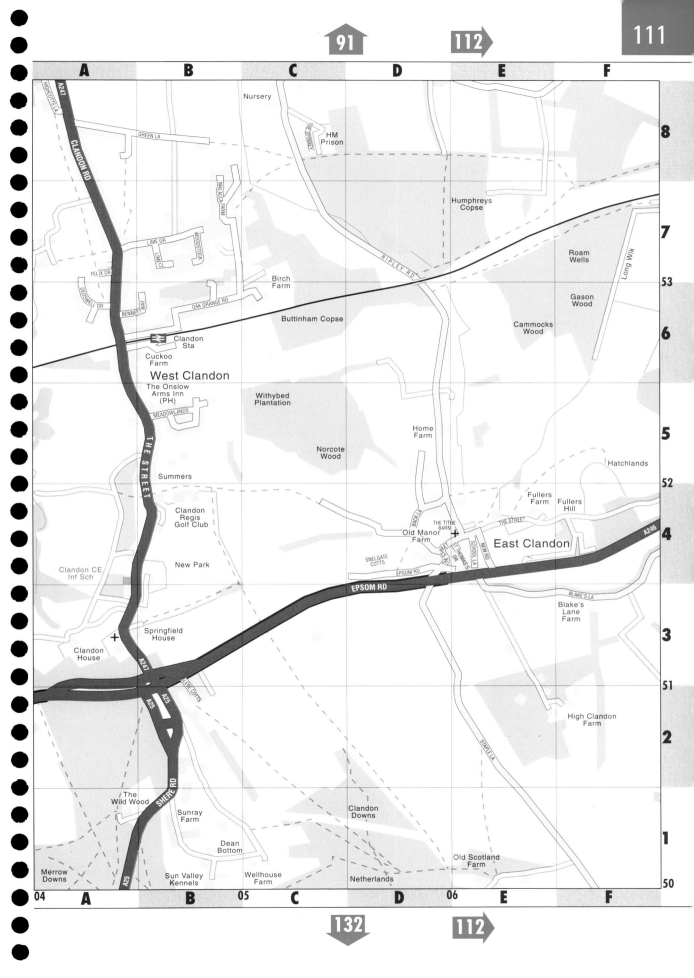

A · B · C · D · E · F

8
7
53
6
5
52
4
3
51
2
1
50

Nursery

THE SPINNEY

HM Prison

GREEN LA

Humphreys Copse

MALACCA FARM

WOODSTOCK

LIME GR
LIME CL

RIPLEY RD

Roam Wells

Long Wik

FELIX DR

Birch Farm

Gason Wood

A247

CLANDON RD

HIGHCOTTS LA

DEEPWELL DR

BENNETT WAY

OAK GRANGE RD

Buttinham Copse

Cammocks Wood

Clandon Sta

Cuckoo Farm

West Clandon

The Onslow Arms Inn (PH)

MEADOWLANDS

Withybed Plantation

Home Farm

Hatchlands

THE STREET

Norcote Wood

Summers

Fullers Farm

Fullers Hill

Clandon Regis Golf Club

BACK LA

THE TITHE BARN

THE STREET

East Clandon

A246

Old Manor Farm

ST THOMAS'S

ST THOMAS'S DR

SCHOOL LA

NEW RD

Clandon CE Inf Sch

New Park

SNELGATE COTTS

EPSOM RD

Blake's Lane Farm

BLAKE'S LA

EPSOM RD

Springfield House

Clandon House

A247

GLEBE COTTS

STABLE LA

High Clandon Farm

A25

SHERE RD

The Wild Wood

Sunray Farm

Clandon Downs

Dean Bottom

Merrow Downs

A25

Sun Valley Kennels

Wellhouse Farm

Netherlands

Old Scotland Farm

04   A · B   05   C · D   06   E · F

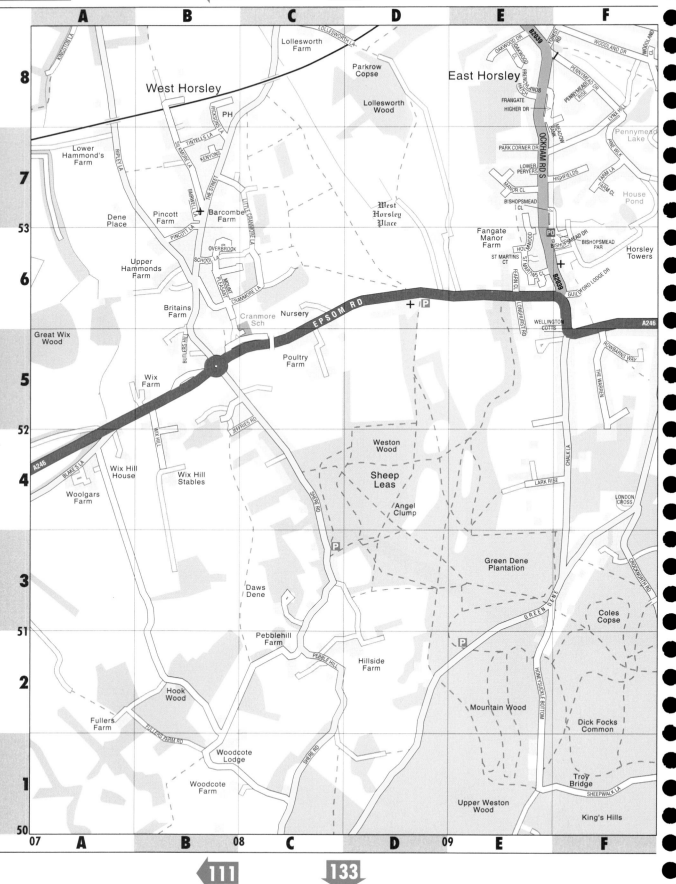

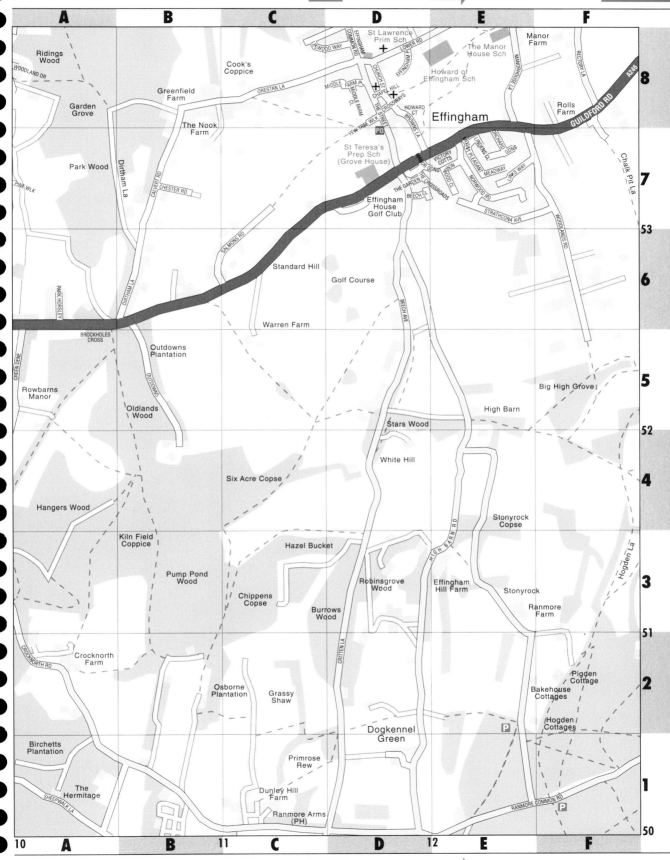

113
94

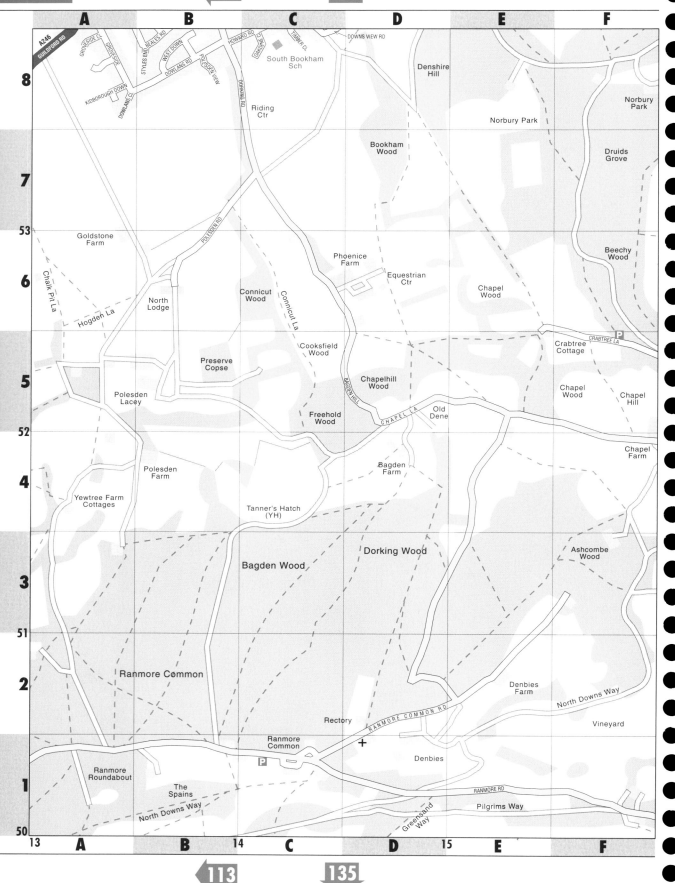

113
135

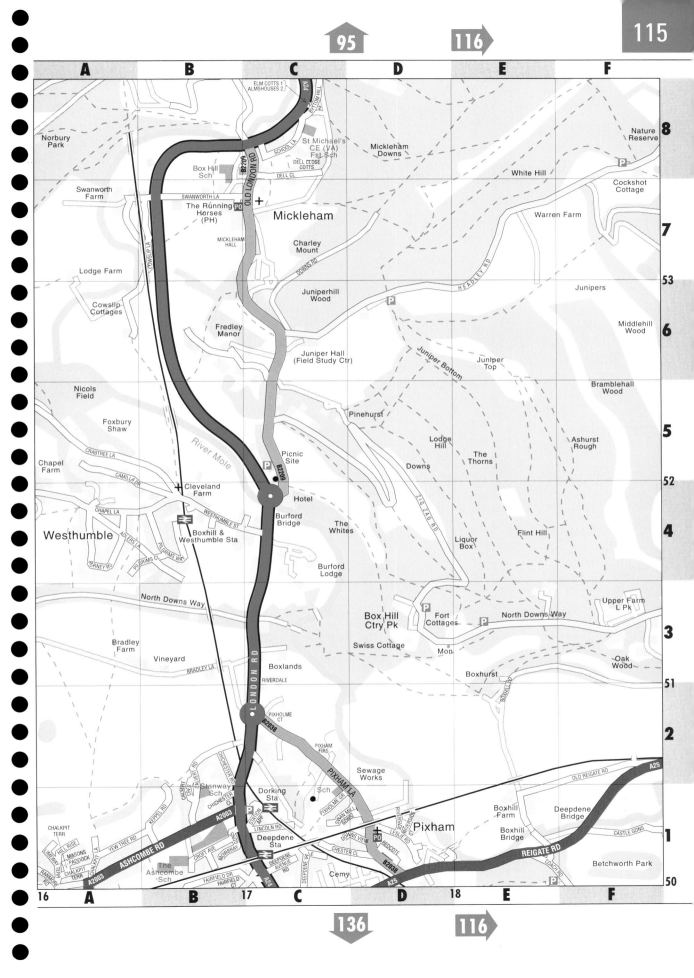

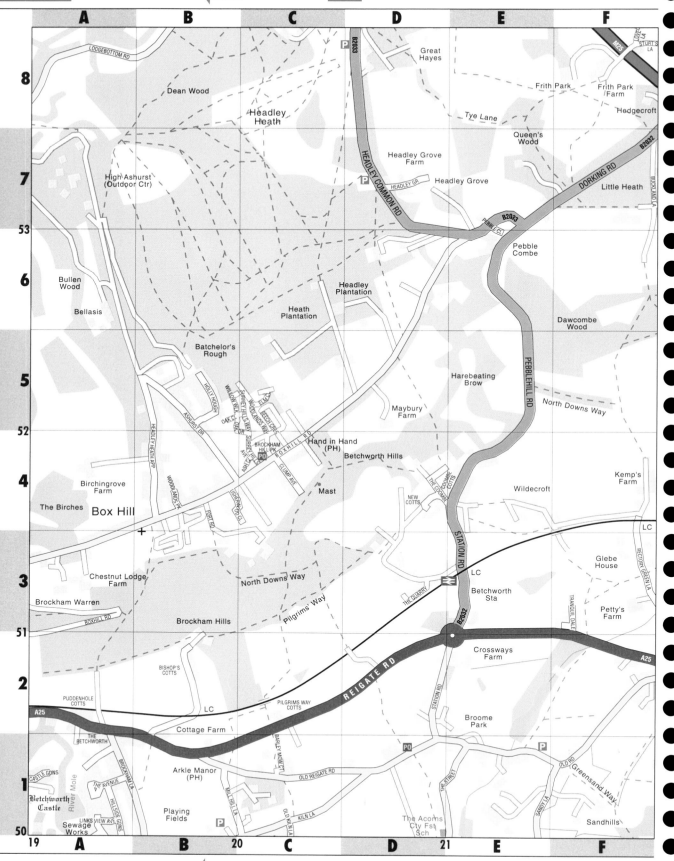

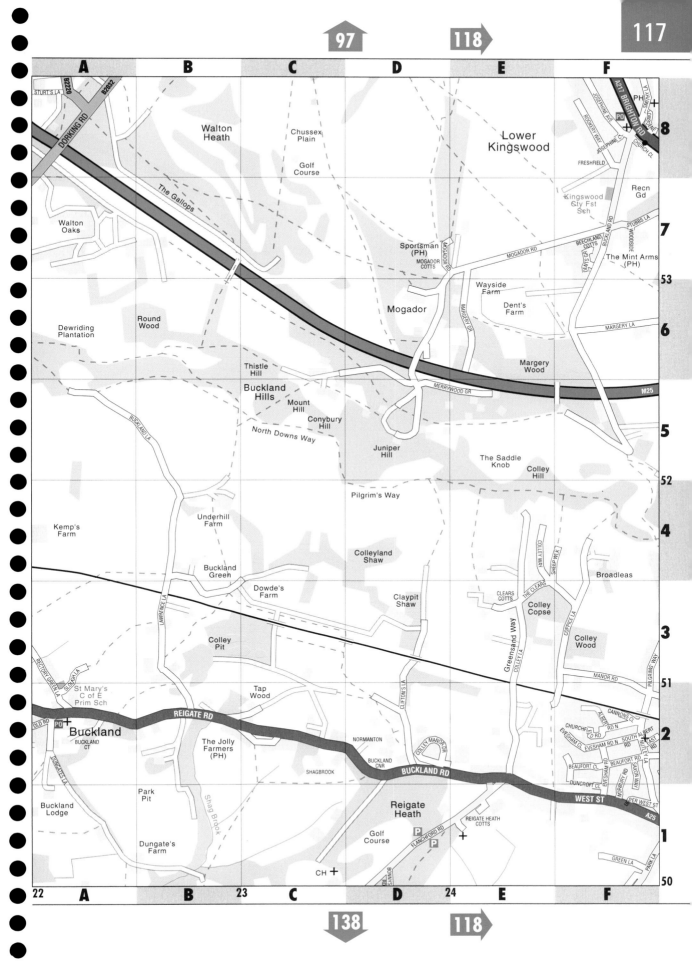

97
118
138
118

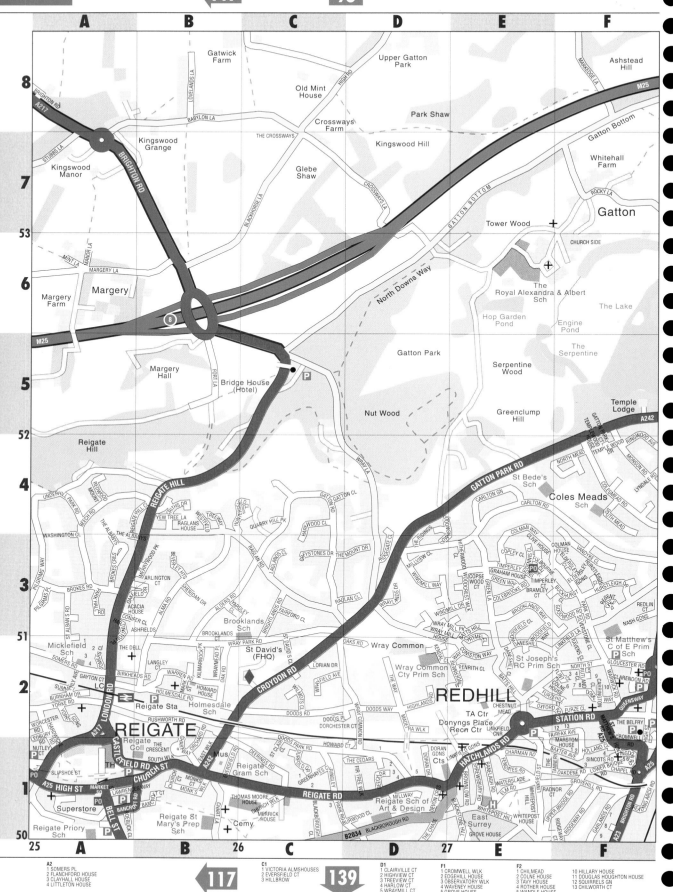

A2
1 SOMERS PL
2 FLANCHFORD HOUSE
3 CLAYHALL HOUSE
4 LITTLETON HOUSE

C1
1 VICTORIA ALMSHOUSES
2 EVERSFIELD CT
3 HILLBROW

D1
1 CLAIRVILLE CT
2 HIGHVIEW CT
3 TREEVIEW CT
4 HARLOW CT
5 WRAYMILL CT

F1
1 CROMWELL WLK
2 EDGEHILL HOUSE
3 OBSERVATORY WLK
4 WAVENEY HOUSE
5 GROVE HOUSE
6 ELY HOUSE
7 ATHOLL HOUSE
8 DUNVEGAN HOUSE
9 STIRLING HOUSE

F2
1 CHILMEAD
2 COLNE HOUSE
3 TAVY HOUSE
4 ROTHER HOUSE
5 WANDLE HOUSE
6 KENNET HOUSE
7 ORWELL HOUSE
8 WINDRUSH HOUSE
9 AVON HOUSE

10 HILLARY HOUSE
11 DOUGLAS HOUGHTON HOUSE
12 SQUIRRELS GN
13 CHILWORTH CT

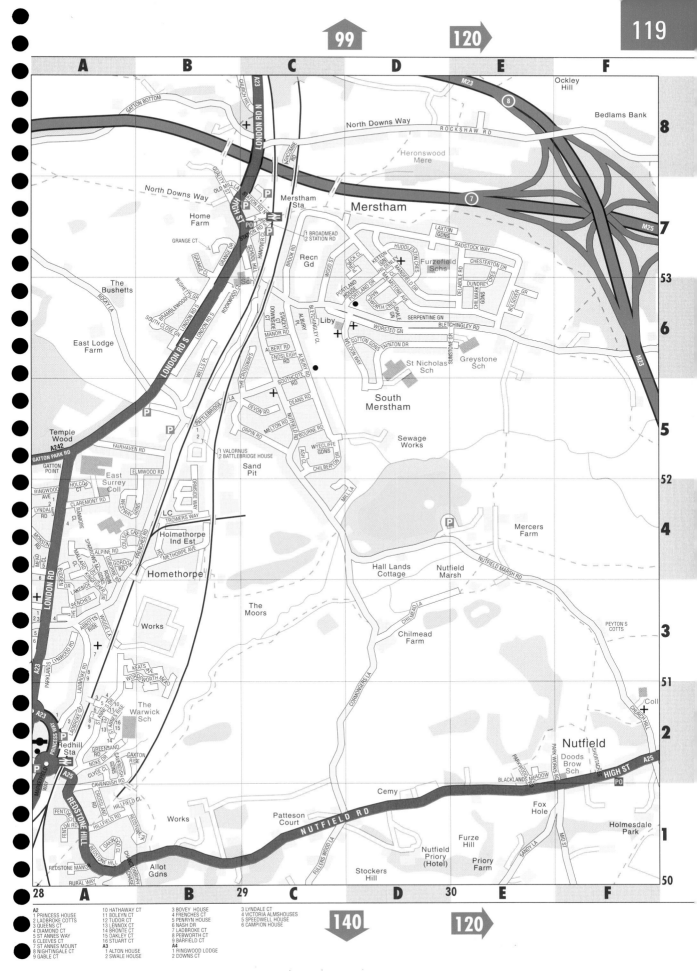

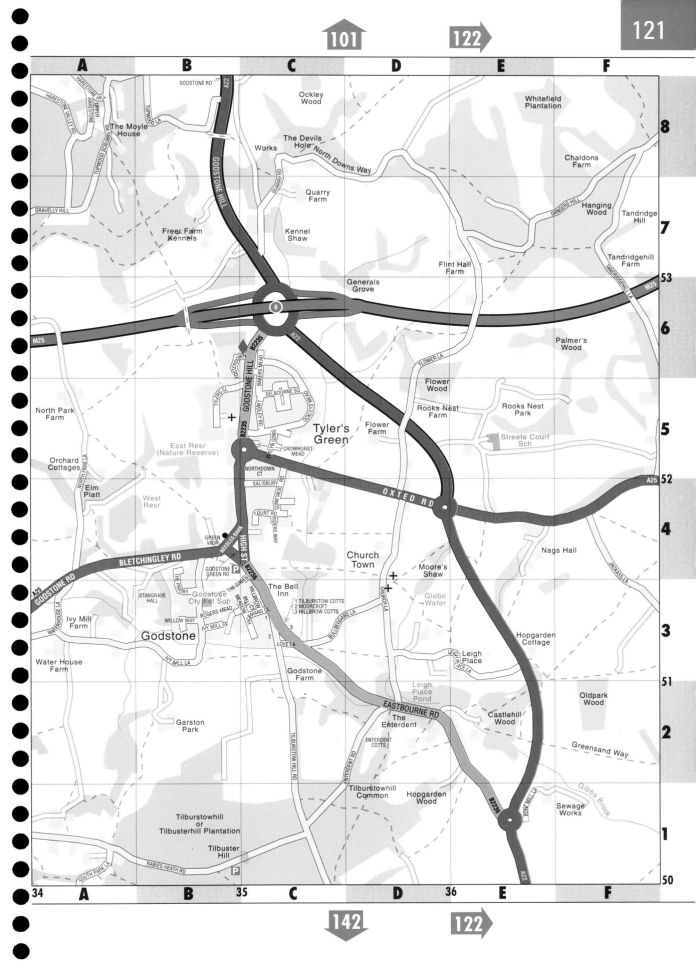

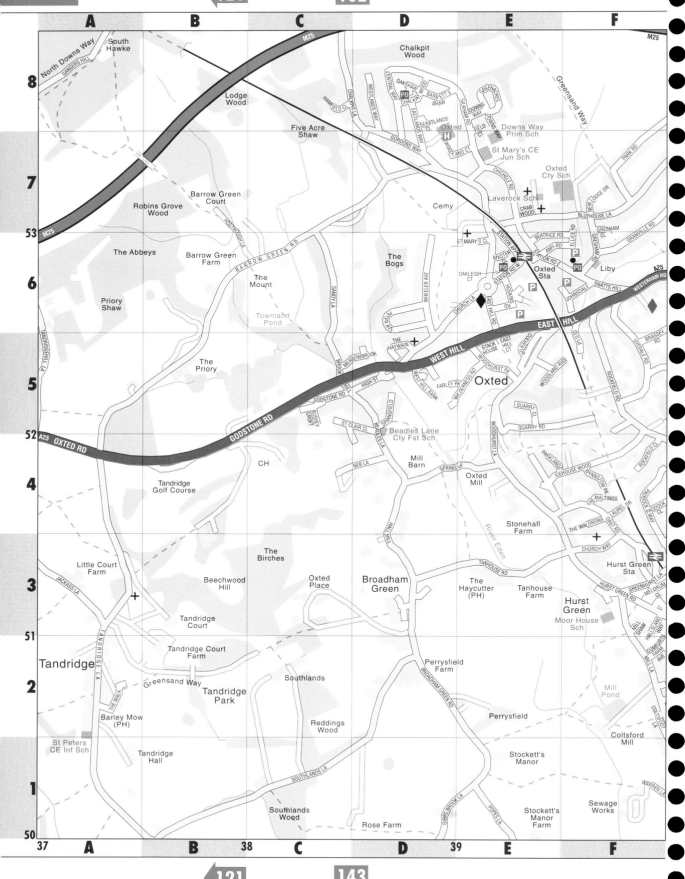

103

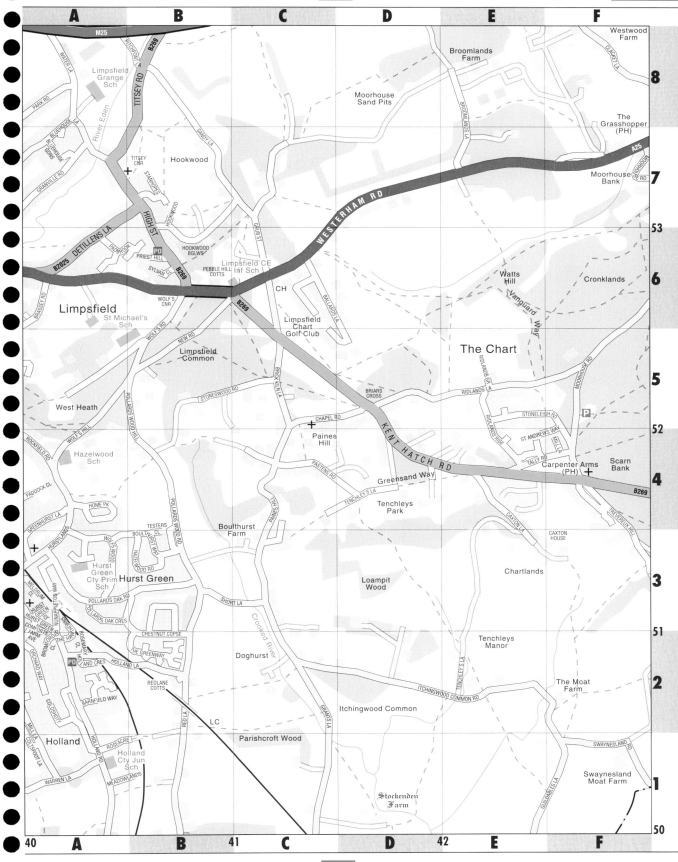

144

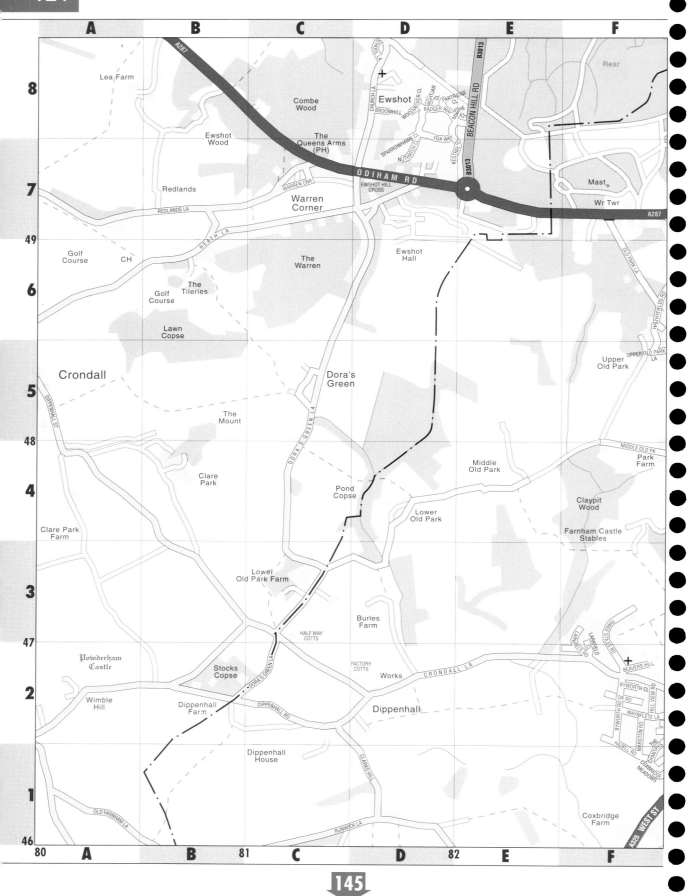

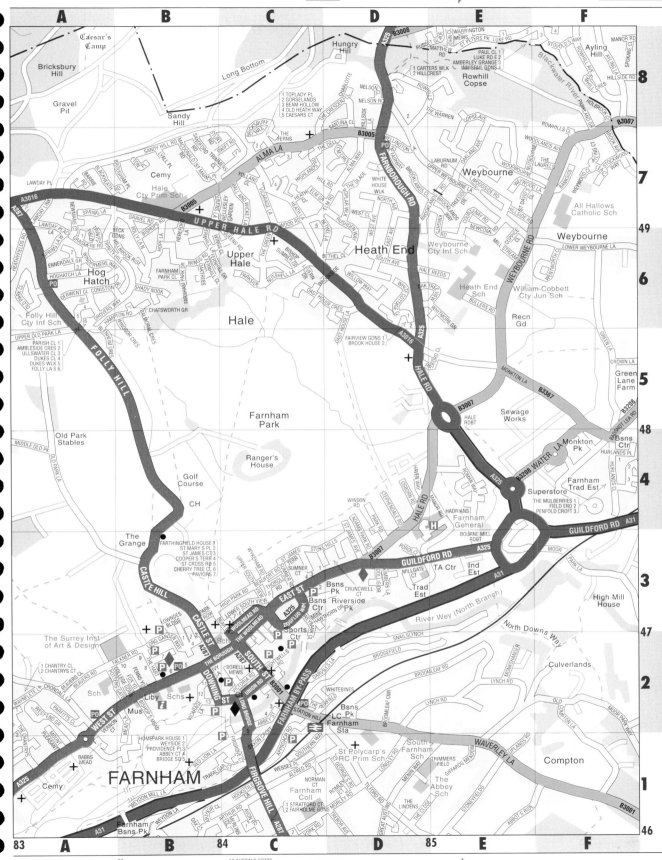

B2
1 LONG GARDEN WLK W
2 LONG GARDEN WLK E
3 LONG GARDEN MEWS
4 LONG GARDEN WLK
5 LION AND LAMB YD
6 ARUNDELL PL
7 LION AND LAMB WAY
8 WESTMEAD
9 LOVETT HOUSE
10 AUSTIN'S COTTS
11 UPPER CHURCH LA
12 MIDDLE CHURCH LA
13 LOWER CHUCH LA

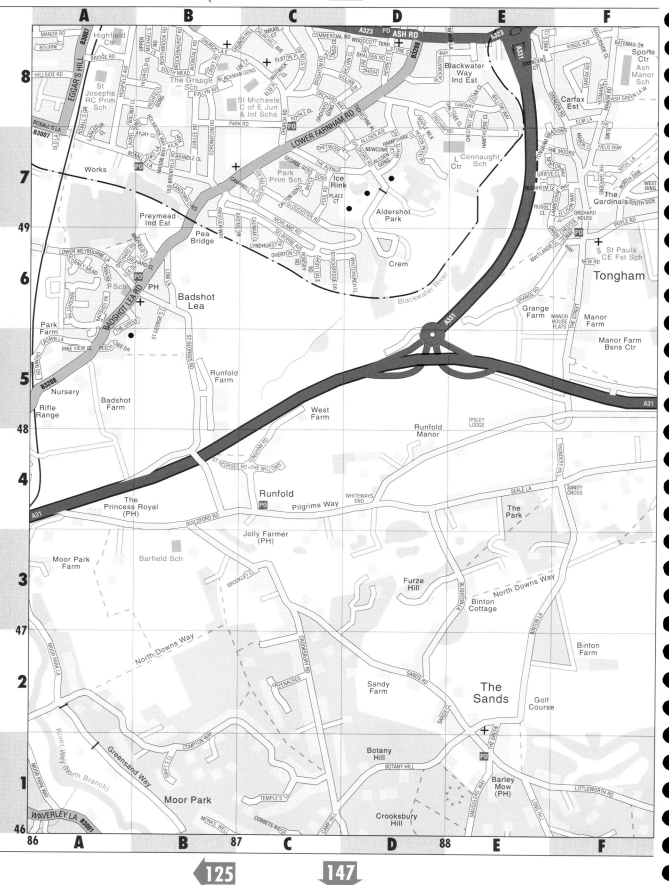

106
128

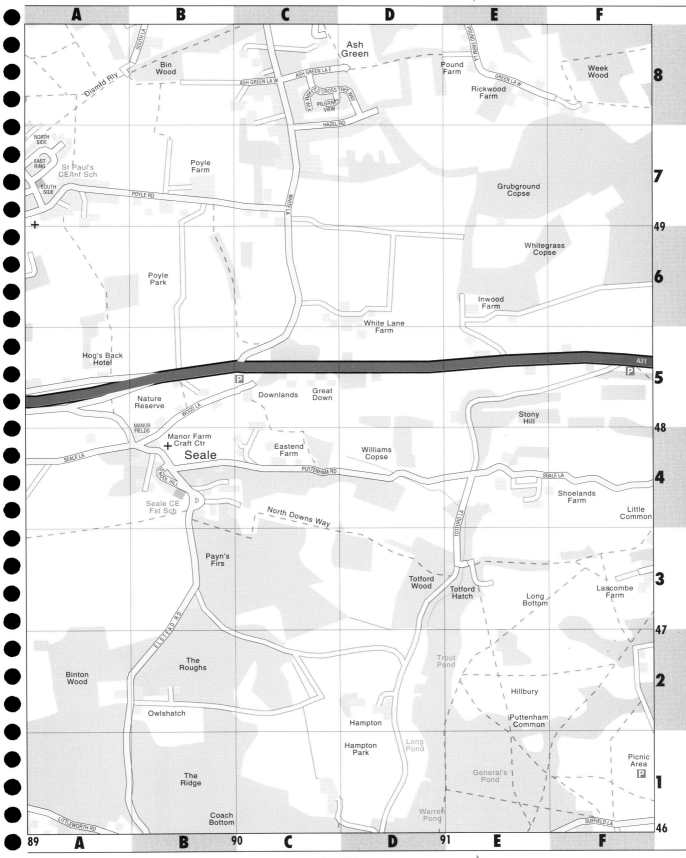

148
128

127
107

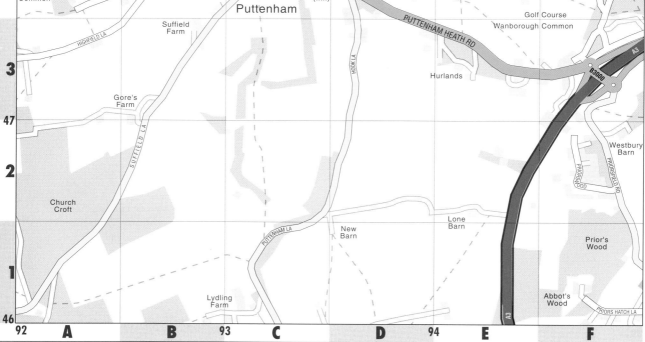

A B C D E F

8

Christmaspie

BEECH LA
FLEXFORD RD
West Flexford Farm
WEST FLEXFORD LA
Homestead Farm
Pond Hill

Long Common
GREEN LA E

7

Broadmead Row
WESTWOOD LA

Greencut Copse

Wanborough Wood

49

Wanborough Manor

EAST FLEXFORD LA

6

Wanborough

Manor Farm
WANBOROUGH HILL

Flexford House

Hog's Back

A31
A31
Greyfriars

5

P
Picnic Area

PUTTENHAM HILL B3000
Puttenham Hill

Greyfriars Farm

48

Puttenham Sch CE (VA)
SCHOOL LA
Monkgrove Copse

4

SEALE LA
Munday's Boro
DARK LA
MUNDAY'S BORO RD
LASCOMBE LA
THE STREET
Priory
P
Clear Barn
CH
P
Cemy
North Downs Way
Puttenham Heath

Little Common
Little Lascombe
PO

Jolly Farmer (Inn)

Golf Course
Wanborough Common

Puttenham
Suffield Farm

PUTTENHAM HEATH RD

A3

HIGHFIELD LA

Hurlands

B3000

3

HOOK LA

47

Gore's Farm
SUFFIELD LA

Westbury Barn
PRIORSFIELD RD
PRIORSWOOD

2

Church Croft

Lone Barn

Prior's Wood

1

New Barn

PUTTENHAM LA

A3

Lydling Farm

Abbot's Wood
PRIORS HATCH LA

46

92 A B 93 C D 94 E F

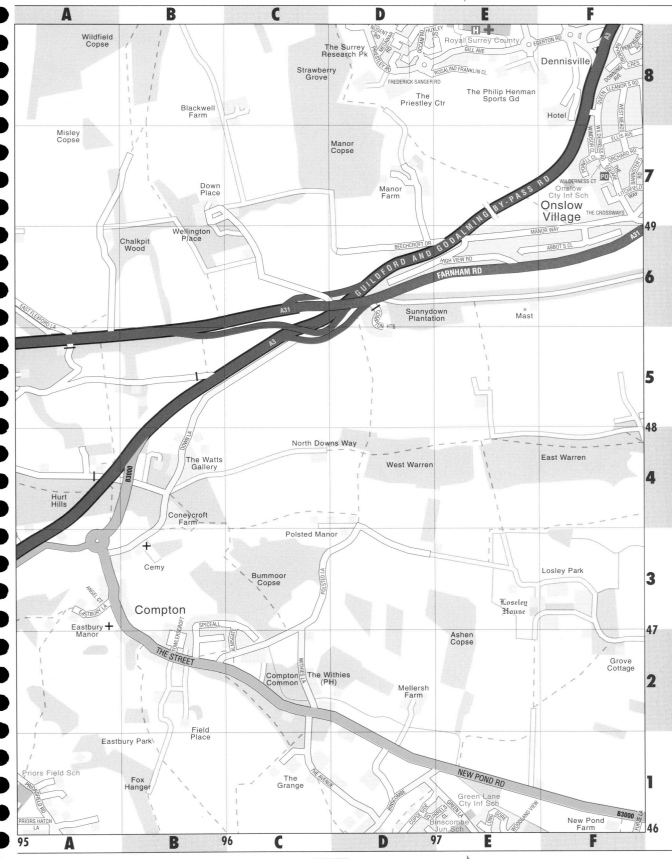

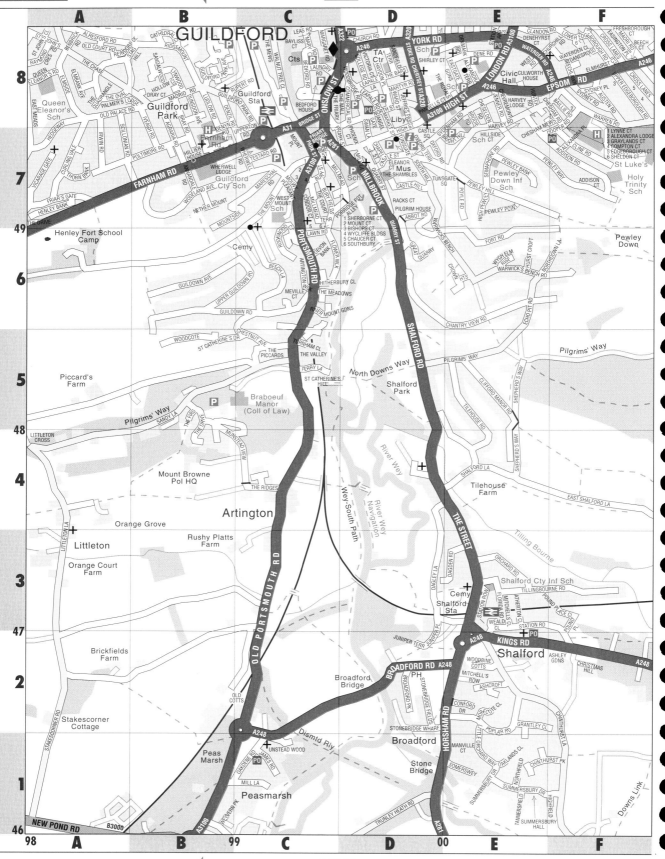

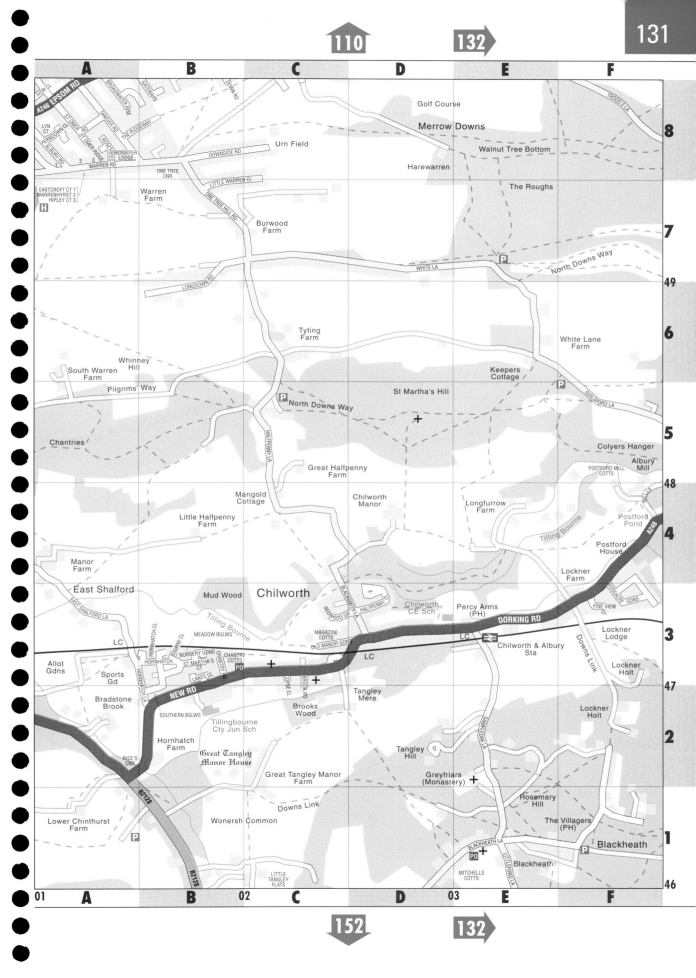

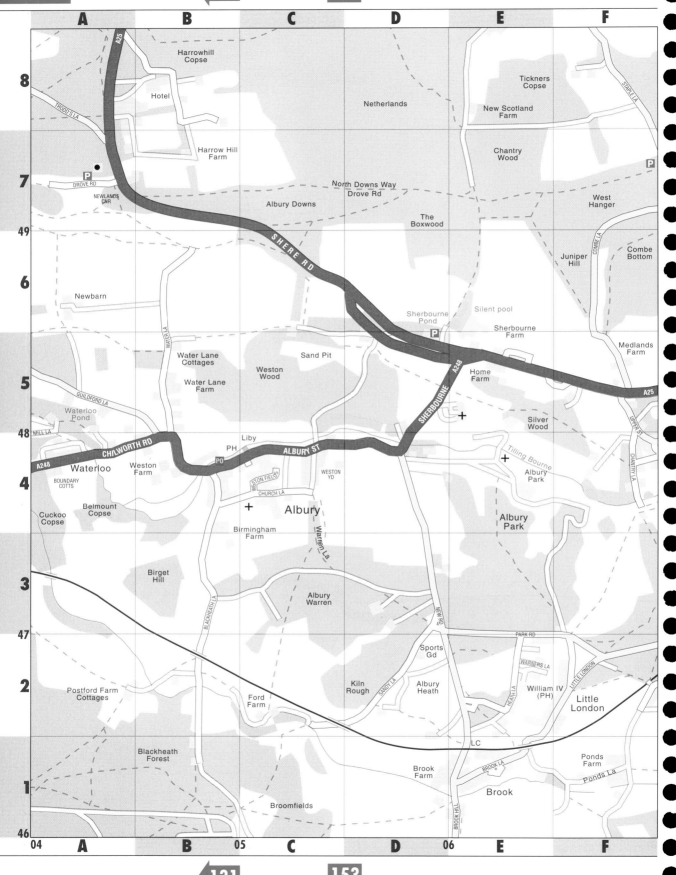

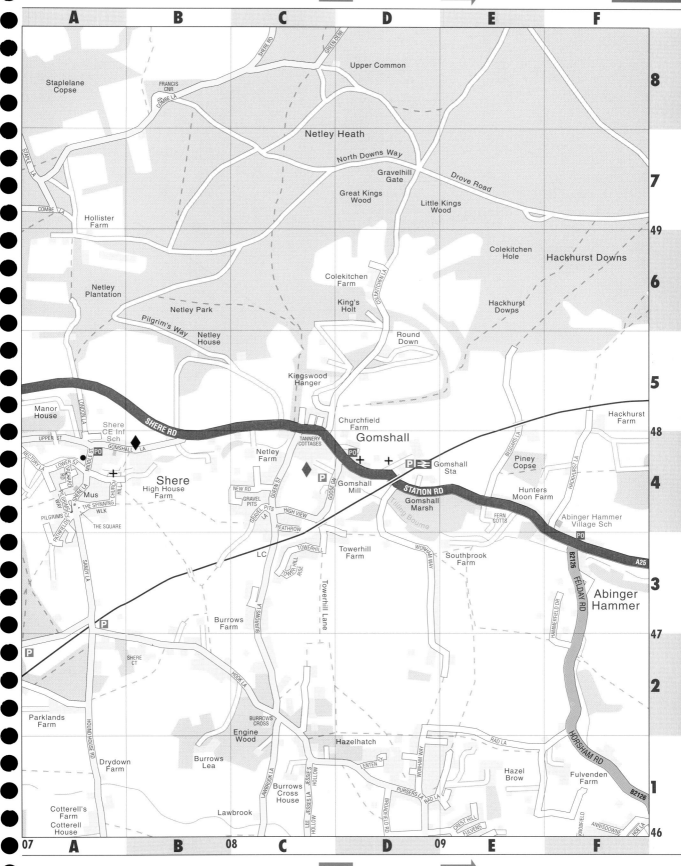

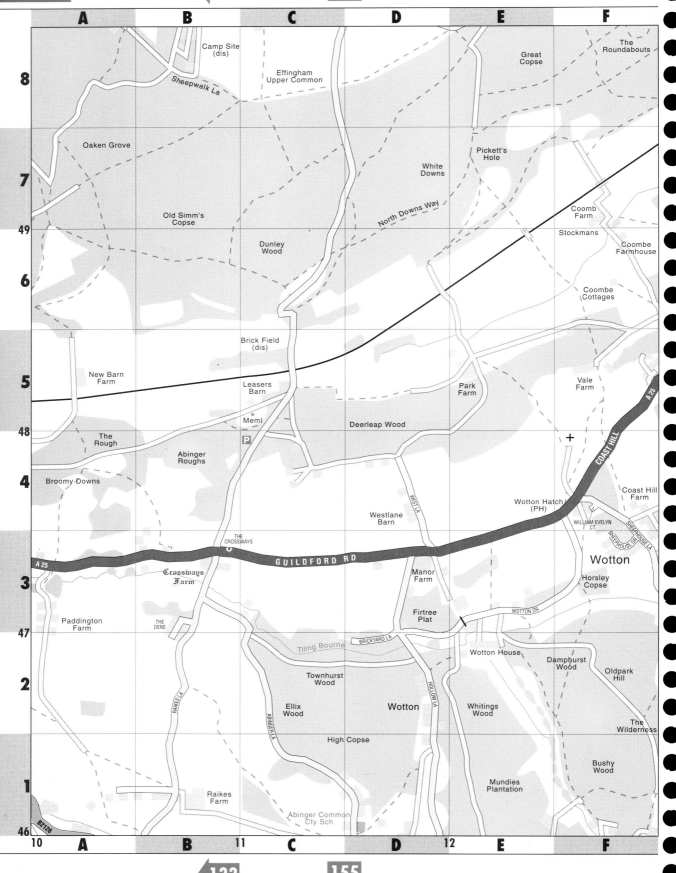

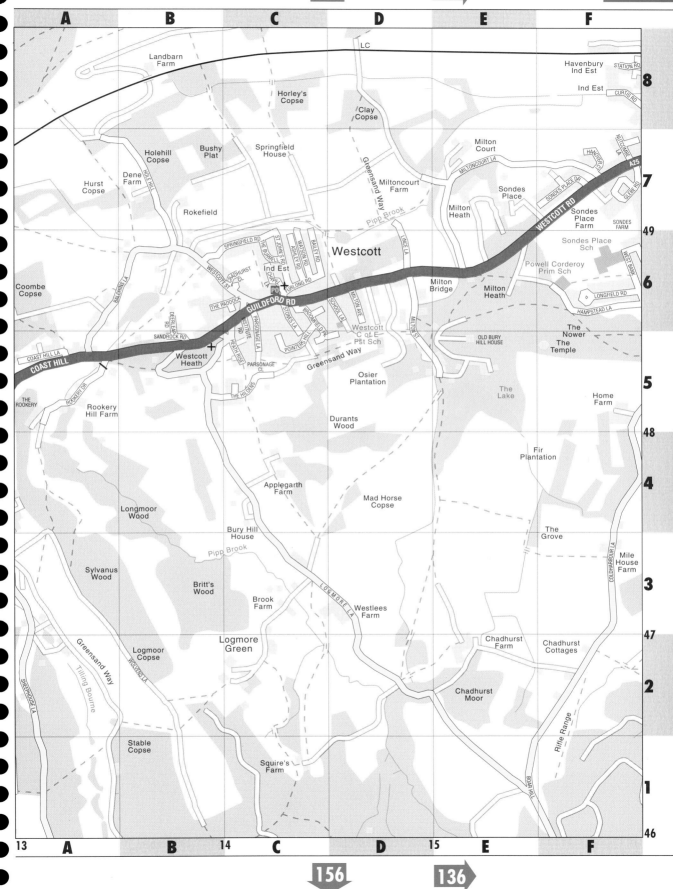

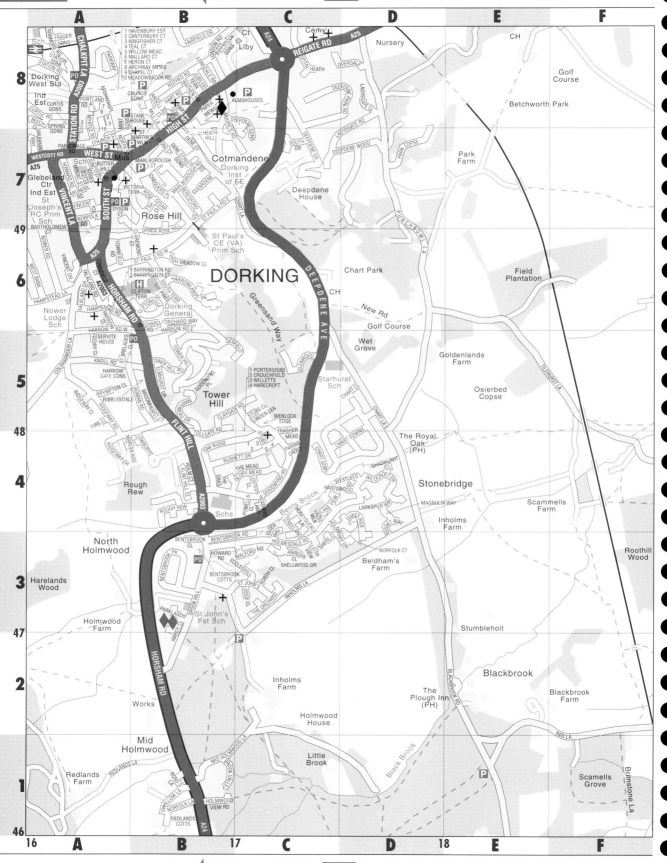

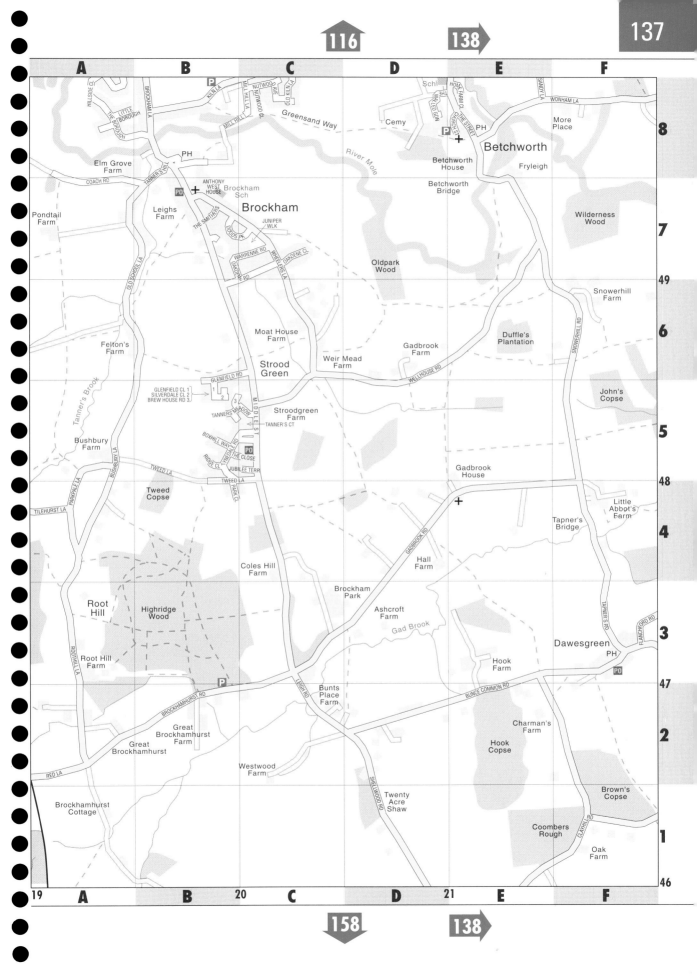

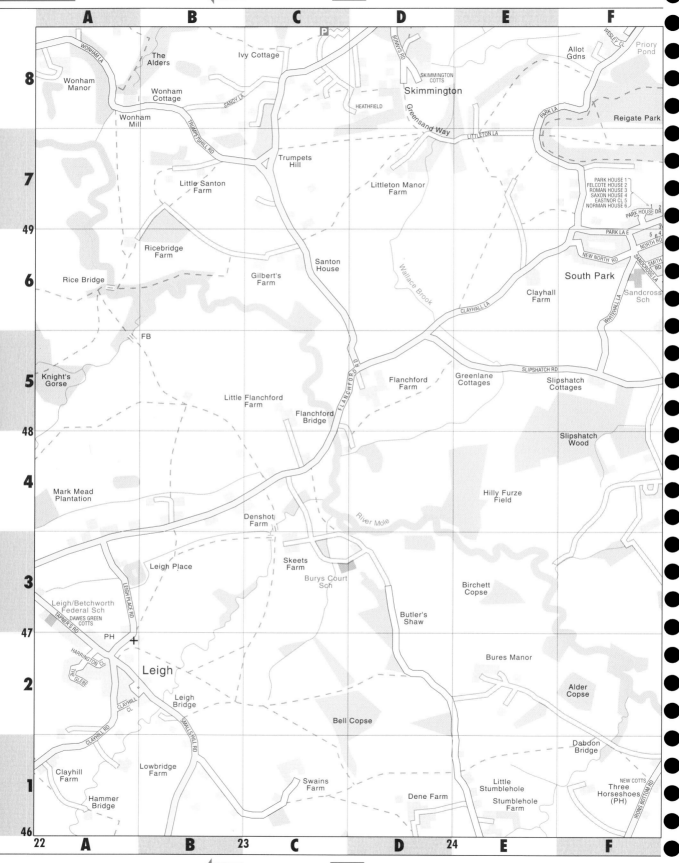

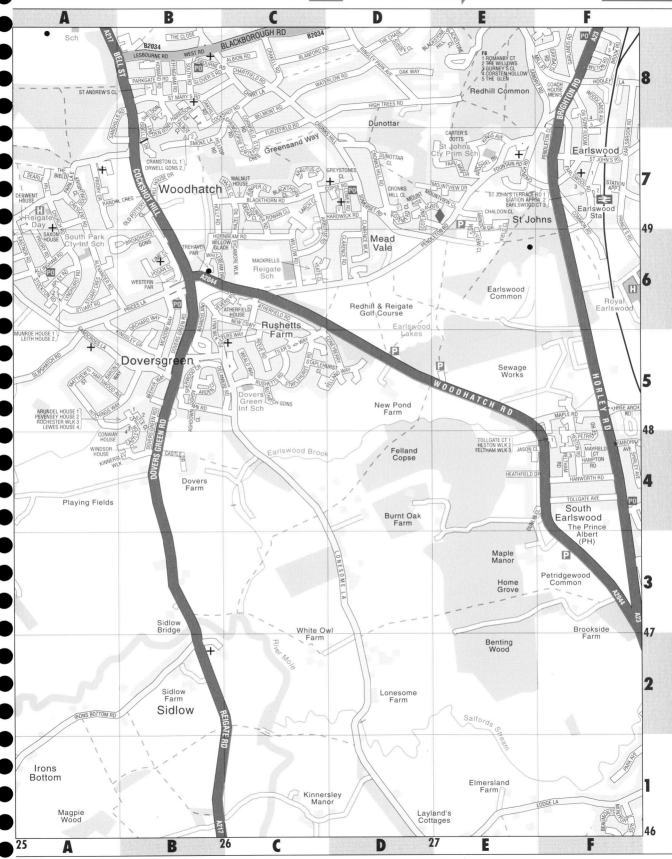

139
119

A B C D E F

8

Priory Farm
Nutfield Priory Lake
Little Cormongers Farm
Old Redstone Dr
WOODSIDE
REDSTONE HOLLOW
PALMER CL
HOOLEY LA
REDSTONE RD
SIMPSON WAY
HILLVIEW DR
PHILANTHROPIC RD
Cemy
SANDY LA
Bower Hill
Thornthrift
BYTTES MEAD
KENTWYNS RISE
Nutfield Church Prim Sch
VICTORIA RD
CHIPSTEAD CL
PO
Sch
MOSTYN TERR
RENNIE TERR
LINNELL RD
PHILANTHROPIC RD
Redhill Coll
BRAMLEY HOUSE
Bower Hill Farm
Bray's Farm
BOWER HILL LA
South Nutfield
FRINDLES RD
MID ST
HOLMESDALE RD

7
EARLSWOOD RD
VINYTHORN WAY
AFOLD RD
ALTHORNE RD
KNIGHTON RD
EARLWYN RD
CHERRY GREEN CL
HARTSPIECE RD
BRAMBLE CL
HIGH CRES
OAKLEIGH RD
BROADWAY
The Royal Philanthropic Farm
1 CHESTNUT CL
2 WILLOW WLK
CLAY LA
NORFOLK COTTS
KINGS MEAD
BOWER HILL CL
NETHERLEIGH PK
MORRIS RD
THE COPSE
Nutfield Sta
NORTH STATION APP
CRICKET HILL
PO
1 OAKWOOD CL
2 SOUTH STATION APP
TRENHAM RD
BRAMBLETYE PARK RD
Brambletye Cty Jun Sch
EASTFIELD RD
Old Gladstone's House
THE AVENUE
PH

Earlswood
Sports Gd
49
Old Garston's House
King's Mill
48

6
H
Royal Earlswood
Redhill Brook
Greensand Way
RIDGE GN
RIDGE GREEN
KINGS CROSS LA
THE PK
Ridge Green
Crab Hill Farm

5
The East Surrey
CAMULA AVE
THREE ARCH RD
H
CANADA HOUSE
CANADA DR
Robin Cooks Farm
Staplehurst Farm
Hale Farm
KINGS MILL LA

WHITE BUSHES
DENTON CL
KILN WALK
GRANTWOOD DR
HAWTHORN CL
TOOLEY
AMBLESIDE CL
Whitebushes
CRAB HILL LA
48

4
WIMBORNE AVE
EDGEFIELD CL
RATHGAR CL
BUSK FIELD DR
THE BROW
SPENCER WAY
YEOMAN WAY
VIVYEN CL
LAVENDER CL
JASMINE CL
Redhill Aerodrome

PRINCE ALBERT SQ
GREENACRE DR
JORDANS CL
GREEN LA
MOATS LA

3
BROOKFIELD CL
HILLFORD PL
MAYFIELD CL
WOODSIDE WAY
COPSLEIGH WAY
Sch
MASON'S BRIDGE RD
MOATS LA
HATCH LA
M23

WEST AVE
COPSLEIGH CL
COPSLEIGH AVE
Salfords Stream
South Hale Farm
47

2
A23
BRIGHTON RD
Salfords Bridge
PO
Dean Farm
Mason's Bridge
Dairy House Farm
Furzefield Wood

MEAD AVE
SOUTHERN AVE
HONEYCROCK LA
JUNE LA
DUNRAVEN AVE
AXES LA
Axeland Park
Caravan Park
GREEN LA
M23

1
PARK VIEW RD
WESTMEAD DR
Salfords Sta
Perrywood Bsns Pk
PICKETTS LA
Cyprus Farm
Axes Farm
NEW HOUSE LA
West View Farm

LODGE LA
WHITE LODGE GDNS
OAK LODGE DR
BONEHURST RD
SALBROOK RD
Salfords
Christmas Farm Kennels
ST GEORGE'S RD
Woolborough Hatch Farm
46

28 A B 29 C D 30 E F

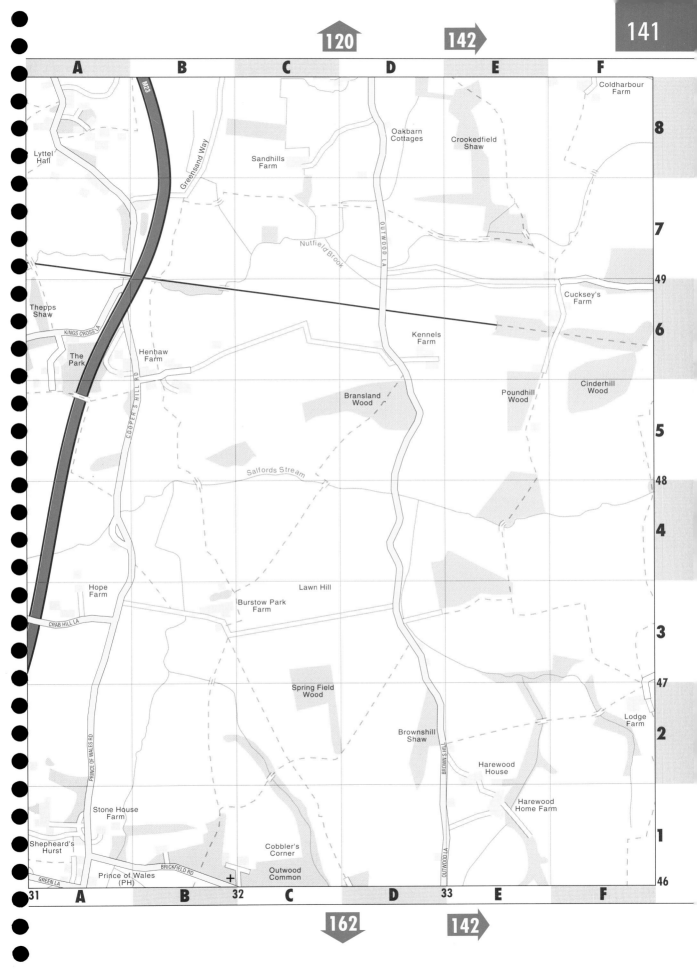

120
142
162
142

A B C D E F

8 7 49 6 5 48 4 3 47 2 1 46

31 32 33

Coldharbour Farm

Oakbarn Cottages

Crookedfield Shaw

Lyttel Hall

Sandhills Farm

Nutfield Brook

Cucksey's Farm

Thepps Shaw

Kings Cross La

Kennels Farm

The Park

Henhaw Farm

Poundhill Wood

Cinderhill Wood

Bransland Wood

Salfords Stream

Hope Farm

Lawn Hill

Burstow Park Farm

Spring Field Wood

Lodge Farm

Brownshill Shaw

Harewood House

Stone House Farm

Harewood Home Farm

Shepheard's Hurst

Cobbler's Corner

Prince of Wales (PH)

Brickfield Rd

Outwood Common

Green La

Coopers Hill Rd

Greensand Way

Crab Hill La

Prince of Wales Rd

Outwood La

Brown's Hill

M23

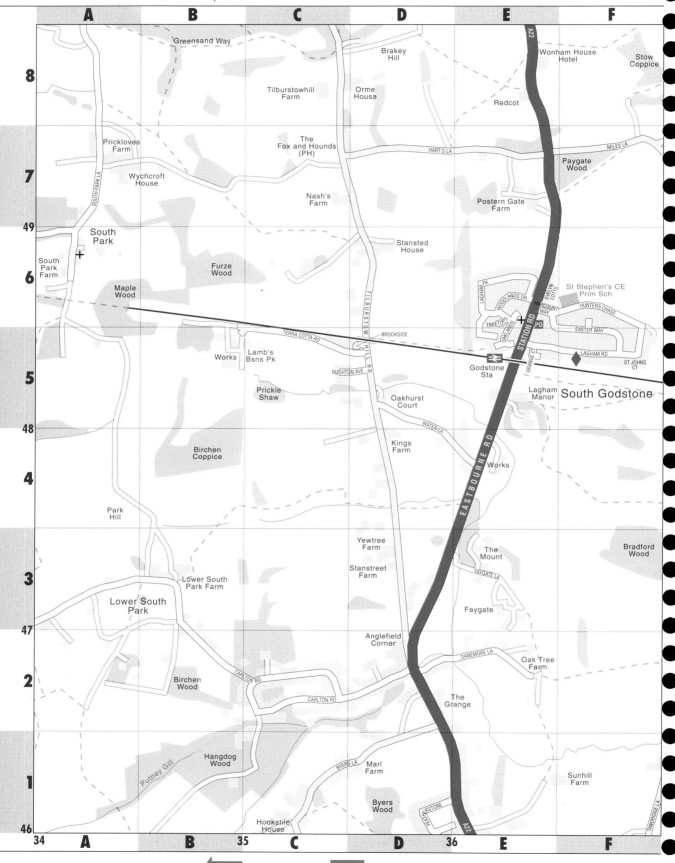

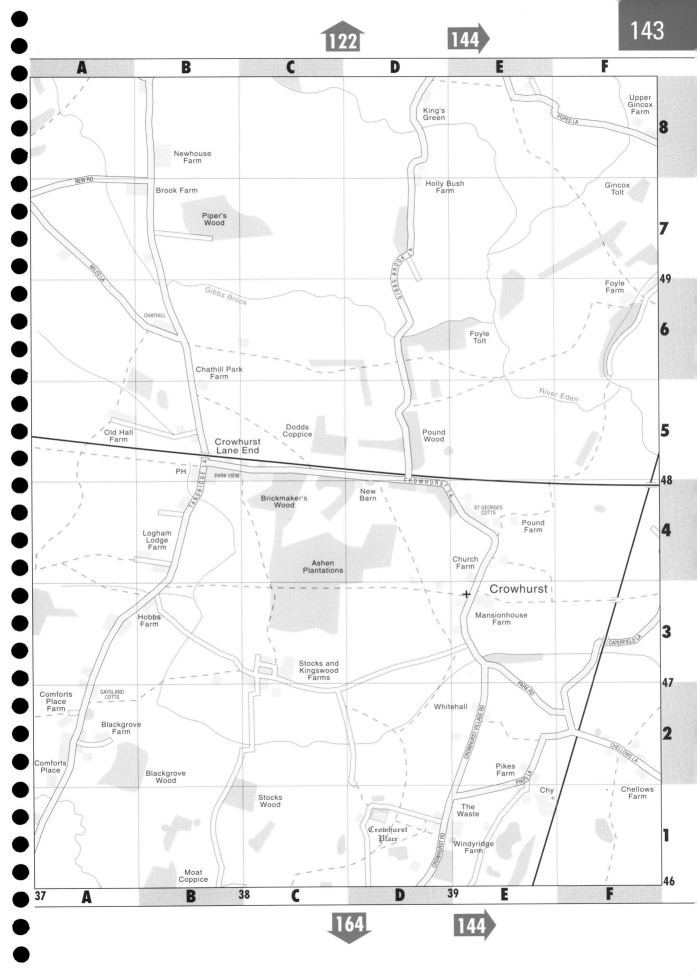

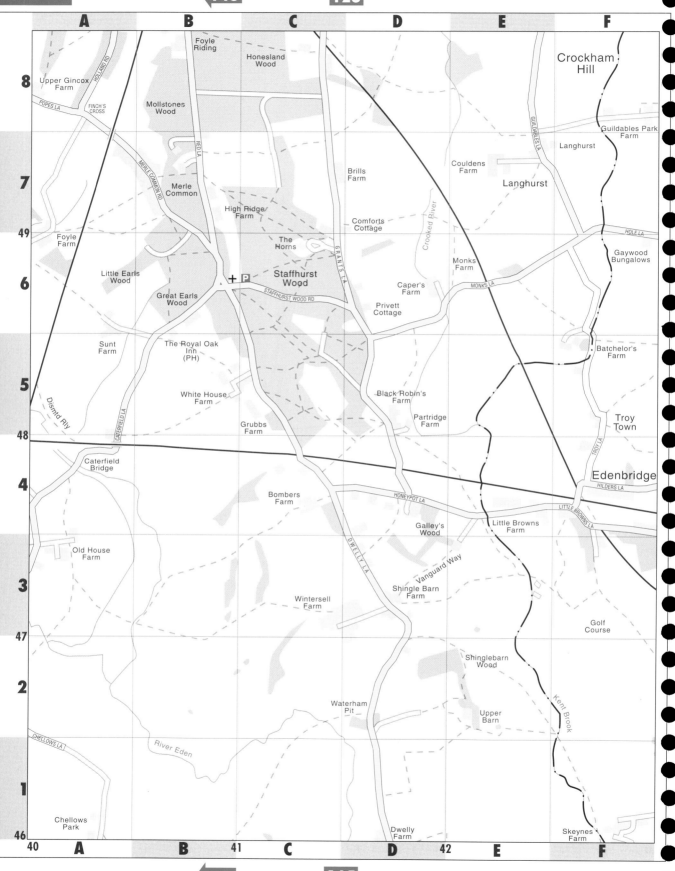

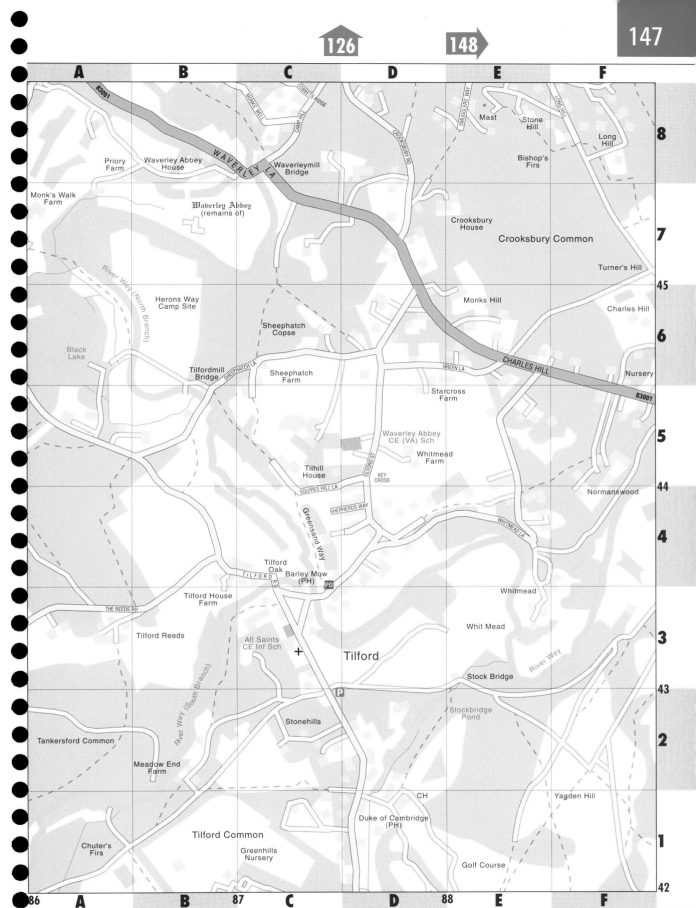

126
148

A B C D E F

8

7

45

6

5

44

4

3

43

2

1

42

86 A B 87 C D 88 E F

168
148

B3001

WAVERLEY LA

MONKS WELL

CUBBET'S RIDGE

CAMP HILL

Priory Farm

Waverley Abbey House

Waverleymill Bridge

Monk's Walk Farm

Waverley Abbey (remains of)

CROOKSBURY RD

SMUGGLERS WAY

Mast

Stone Hill

LONG HILL

Long Hill

Bishop's Firs

Crooksbury House

Crooksbury Common

Turner's Hill

Charles Hill

River Wey (North Branch)

Herons Way Camp Site

Sheephatch Copse

Monks Hill

Black Lake

Tilfordmill Bridge

SHEEPHATCH LA

Sheephatch Farm

GREEN LA

CHARLES HILL

Nursery

B3001

Starcross Farm

Waverley Abbey CE (VA) Sch

Whitmead Farm

Normanswood

Tilhill House

TILFORD ST

KEY CROSS

SQUIRES HILL LA

SHEPHERDS WAY

WHITMEAD LA

Greensand Way

Tilford Oak

Barley Mow (PH)

PO

Whitmead

TILFORD RD

Tilford House Farm

THE REEDS RD

Tilford Reeds

Whit Mead

All Saints CE Inf Sch

Tilford

River Wey

Stock Bridge

43

P

Tankersford Common

River Wey (South Branch)

Stonehills

Stockbridge Pond

Yagden Hill

Meadow End Farm

CH

Duke of Cambridge (PH)

Chuter's Firs

Tilford Common

Greenhills Nursery

Golf Course

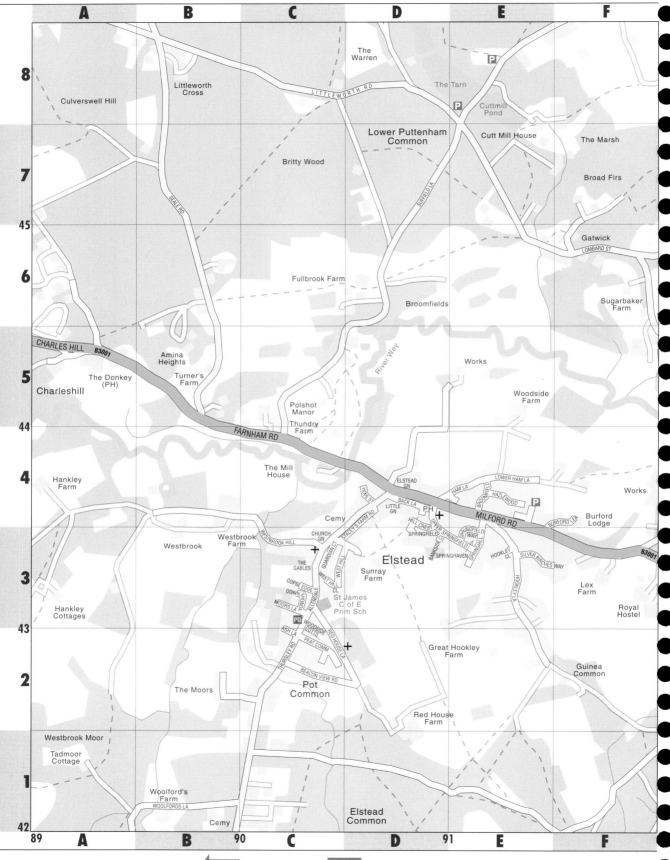

8
Culverswell Hill
Littleworth Cross
The Warren
LITTLEWORTH RD
The Tarn
P
P
Cuttmill Pond
Lower Puttenham Common
Cutt Mill House
The Marsh

7
Britty Wood
SEALE RD
SUTFIELD LA
Broad Firs

45
Gatwick
LOMBARD ST

6
Fullbrook Farm
Broomfields
Sugarbaker Farm

CHARLES HILL
B3001
Amina Heights
Turner's Farm
River Wey
Works
Woodside Farm

5
The Donkey (PH)
Charleshill
Polshot Manor

44
FARNHAM RD
Thundry Farm

4
Hankley Farm
The Mill House
ELSTEAD GN
HAM LA
LOWER HAM LA
Works
BROOMFIELD
HAZLEWOOD
P
BURFORD LEA
Burford Lodge
MILFORD RD

HORSE ST
BACK LA
LITTLE GN
PH
UPPER SPRINGFIELD
HILL CREST
SPRINGFIELD
SPRINGFIELD WAY
SPRINGHILL
HOOKLEY CL
SILVER BIRCHES WAY
B3001

Cemy
STACEY'S FARM RD
Elstead
BAINSIDE CL
SPRINGHAVEN

3
Westbrook
Westbrook Farm
WESTBROOK HILL
CHURCH GN
GUARDIAN CT
WEST HILL
Sunray Farm
HOOKLEY LA
Lex Farm

Hankley Cottages
THE GABLES
COPSE EDGE
DOWN
ALLENDALE
WEST HILL CL
St James C of E Prim Sch
Royal Hostel

43
PO
WOODSIDE COTTS
ASH LA
PEAT COMM

THURSLEY RD
RED HOUSE LA
Great Hookley Farm
Guinea Common

2
The Moors
BEACON VIEW RD
Pot Common
Red House Farm

1
Westbrook Moor
Tadmoor Cottage
Woolford's Farm
WOOLFORDS LA

42
Cemy
Elstead Common

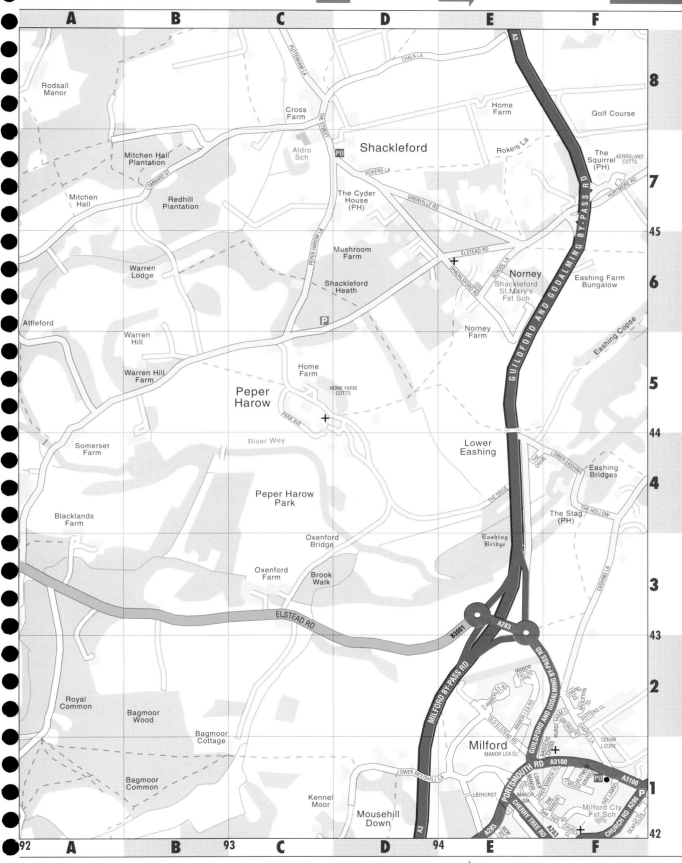

149
129

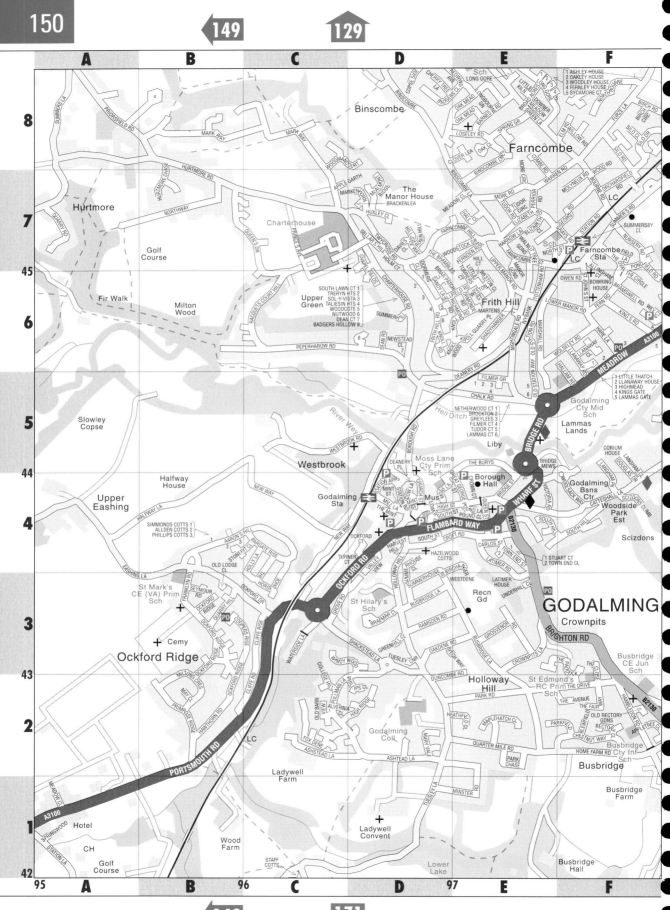

130

152

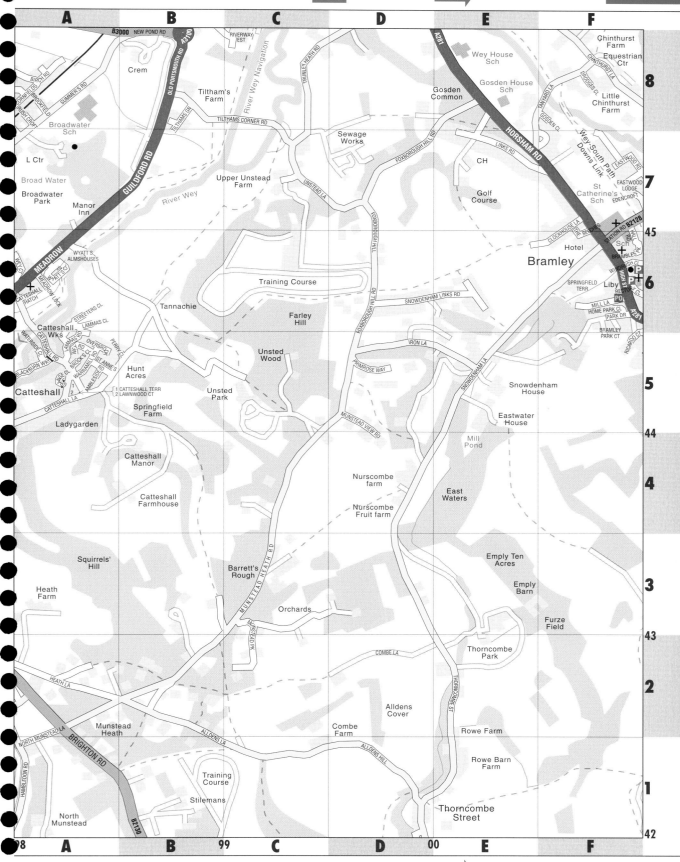

172

152

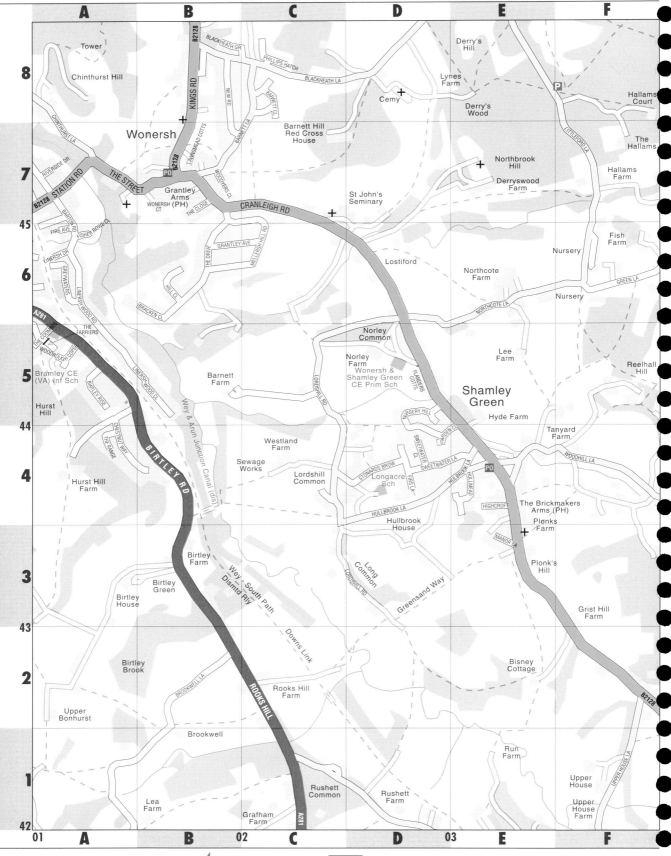

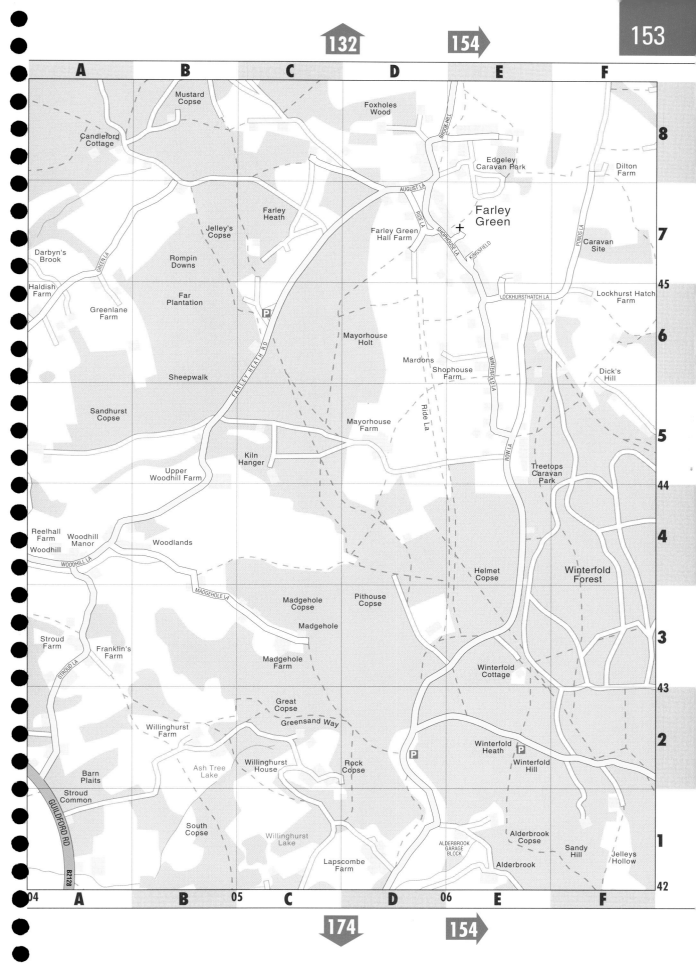

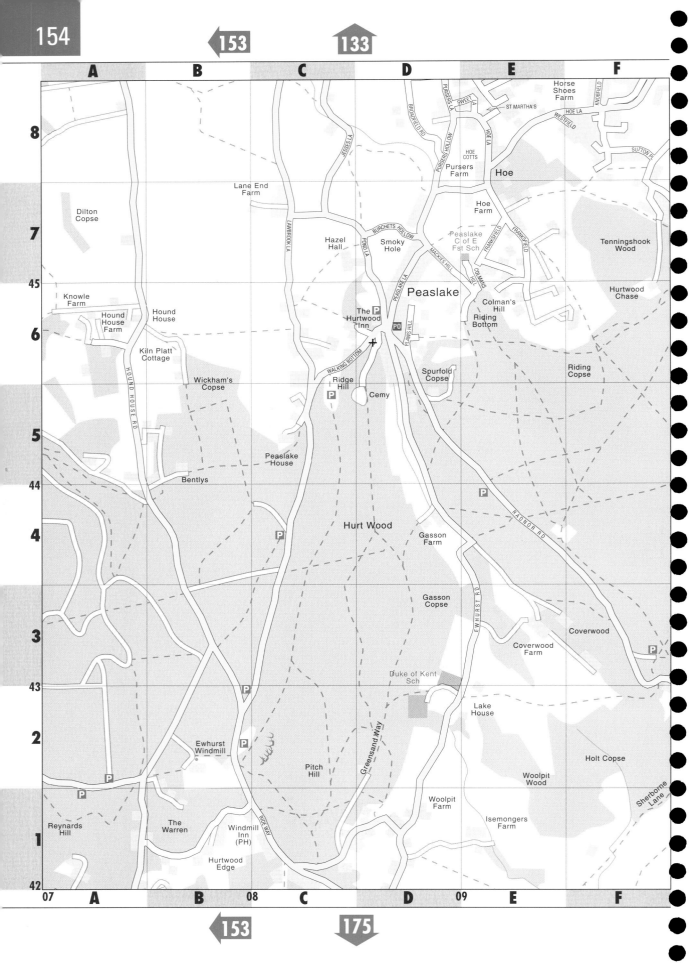

153

133

A   B   C   D   E   F

8

7

45

6

5

44

4

43

3

2

42

Dilton
Copse

Knowle
Farm

Hound
House
Farm

Hound
House

Kiln Platt
Cottage

HOUND HOUSE RD

Wickham's
Copse

Bentlys

Reynards
Hill

The
Warren

Ewhurst
Windmill

Windmill
Inn
(PH)

Hurtwood
Edge

RIDE WAY

Lane End
Farm

LAWBROOK LA

Hazel
Hall

Peaslake
House

Pitch
Hill

JESSIES LA

POND LA

BURCHETS HOLLOW

Smoky
Hole

WALKING BOTTOM

Ridge
Hill

Cemy

Hurt Wood

Greensand Way

BROADFIELD RD

PURSERS HOLLOW

SWEET

ST MARTHA'S

Hoe
Cotts

Pursers
Farm

MACKIES HILL

PEASLAKE LA

Peaslake
C of E
Fst Sch

The
Hurtwood
Inn

P

P

PO

PLAWS HILL

Peaslake

Spurfold
Copse

Gasson
Farm

Gasson
Copse

Duke of Kent
Sch

Lake
House

Woolpit
Farm

HOE LA

Hoe
Farm

FRANKSFIELD

FRANKSFIELD

COLMANS HILL

Colman's
Hill
Riding
Bottom

EWHURST RD

Coverwood
Farm

Isemongers
Farm

Horse
Shoes
Farm

WESTFIELD

HOE LA

KNOBFIELD

SUTTON PL

Hoe

Tenningshook
Wood

Hurtwood
Chase

RADNOR RD

Riding
Copse

Coverwood

Holt Copse

Woolpit
Wood

Sherborne
Lane

P

07   A   B   08   C   D   09   E   F

153

175

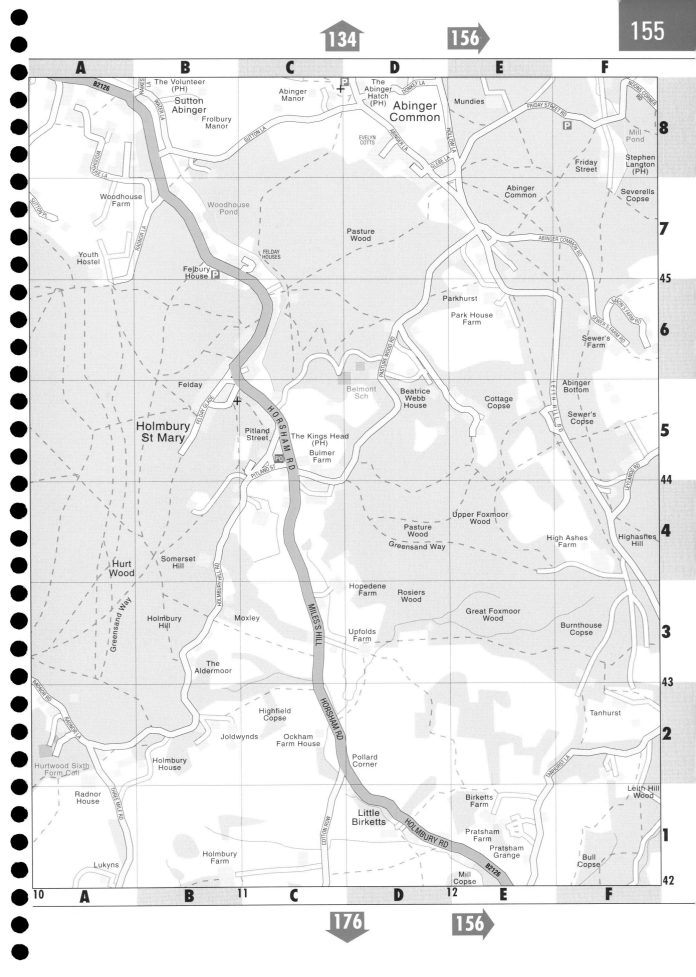

155
135

A **B** **C** **D** **E** **F**

MOONS CORNER RD
SHEEPHOUSE LA

8

Home Farm
Broadmoor
Simons Copse

High Field
Collickmoor Farm

Robbing Gate
Robin Gate Cottage

BROADMOOR COTT

Severells Copse

Pond Cottage

Pondfield Copse

WHITEBERRY RD

7

Brookwick Copse

Upper Merriden Cottage

COLDHARBOUR LA

LEYLANDS RD

45

Tilling Springs

Leylands
Shootlands Farm
Warren Farm

6

Leylands Farm

Whiteberry Rd Greensand Way

Broadmoor Bottom

Waterden Wood

5

Whiteberry Hill

Whiteberry Gate

The Duke's Warren

Coldharbour Common

WOLVENS LA

Crockers Farm

Anstiebury Farm

ANSTIE LA

Spring Copse

44

PH
Anstiebury
PO
Coldharbour

4

Wotton Common

Snakes Hill

Kitlands Farm
Kitlands

East Lodge

Gill Wood

3

P

Leith Hill

Leith Hill Tower

WEALD VIEW COTTS
The Landslip
P

Mosses Wood

LEITH HILL RD

43

ABINGER RD

Cockshot Farm

BROOMEHALL RD

Bushy Copse

East Campfield Place

2

TANHURST LA
P
LEITH HILL

Broome Hall Farm

Broome Hall

Leith Hill Place Wood

Smither's Copse

1

Leith Hill Place
Leith Hill Place Farm

Nutfold Copse

Great Copse

42

Hartshurst Farm

Fatting Hovel Copse

13 **A** **B** **14** **C** **D** **15** **E** **F**

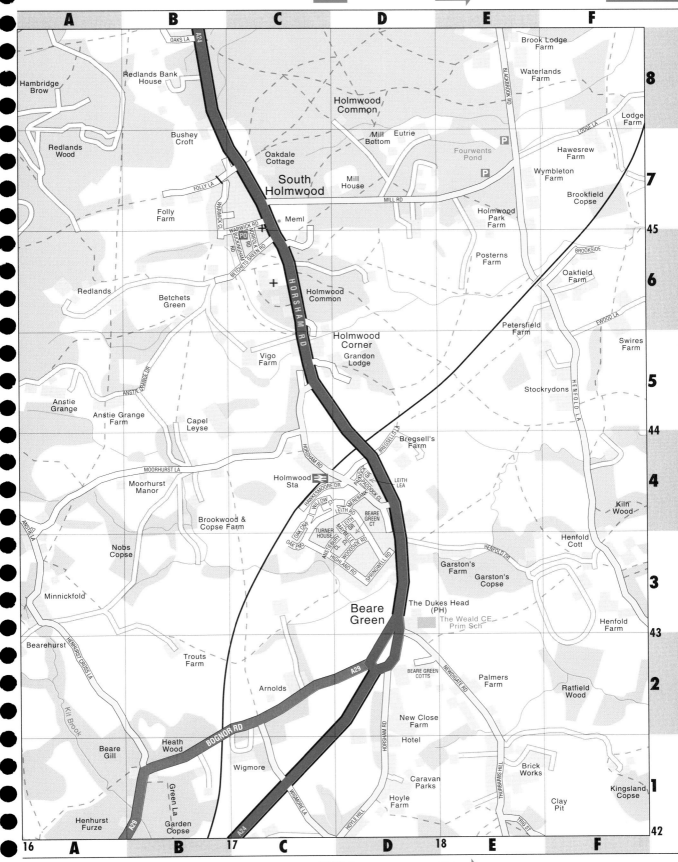

A B C D E F

8

Snellings Cottage

Shellwood Manor

GREEN LA

Little Shellwood

Profits Farm

Fettercairn

SHELLWOOD RD

CLAYHILL RD

Snelling Planted Field

Shellwood Cross

Brook Farm

Hilly Copse

7

New Barn Shaw

Birch Platts

45

Six Acre Copse

Furzefield Copse

Broadlane Rough

Parkhouse Copse

6

Ewood Cottages

EWOOD LA

Ewood Farm

EWOOD LA

EWOOD LA

Hammond's Farm

Cowroom Copse

BROAD LA

Brook Copse

Ram Field

Hammond's Copse

Parkhouse Farm

5

MILL LA

Parkgate Copse

44

BECKET WOOD

Cowless Field

Reffolds Copse

Surrey Oaks (PH)

Parkgate

PARTRIDGE LA

Collaroy Farm

4

Reffolds Copse

Well Copse

Old St John's

Springfield Farm

Curls Copse

BLANKS LA

Batts Farm

Hales Bridge

Blank's Farm

3

Broadwood's Rough

Coombers Farm

Bean Brook

43

PARKGATE RD

Mulberry Farm

Hound House Farm

The Red House

Sturtwood Farm

HENFOLD LA

Gaterounds Farm

CIDERMILL RD

2

HENFOLD COTTS

Knowle

Brooklagg Farm

WOODPECKER LA

HOSSPUDDING LA

Oak Lane Farm

Newdigate

1

Knowle Copse

VILLAGE ST

UNDERHILL RD

Newdigate Endowed CE Inf Sch

Hatchetts

PO

KINGSLAND

WINFIELD GR

WINFIELD CT

NORTHLANDS BGLWS

PH

OLD SCHOOL LA

GEORGE HORLEY PL

Horsielands Farm

42

19 A B 20 C D 21 E F

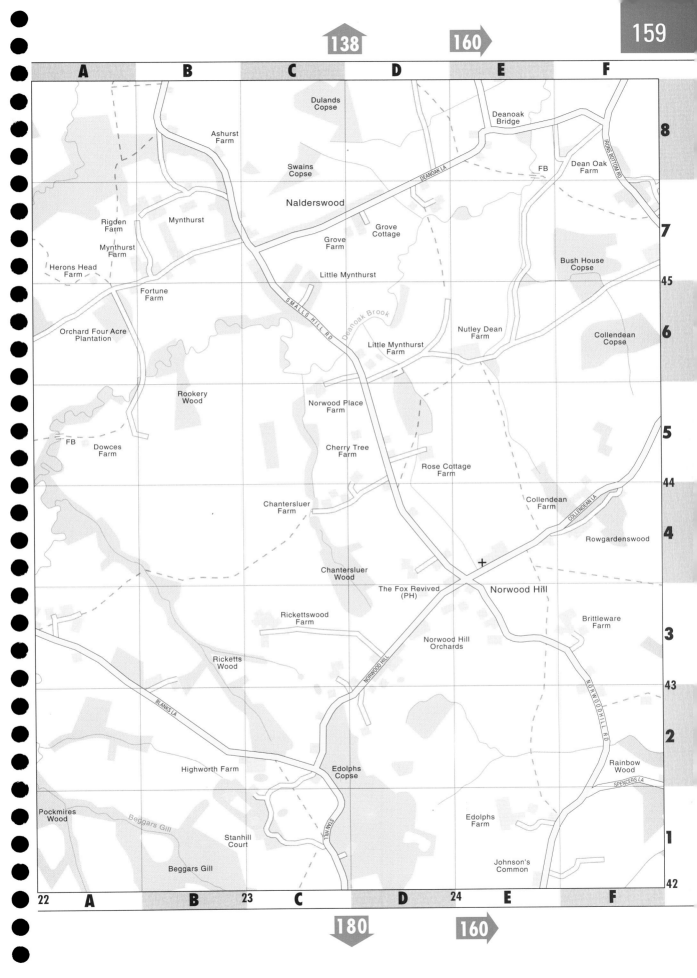

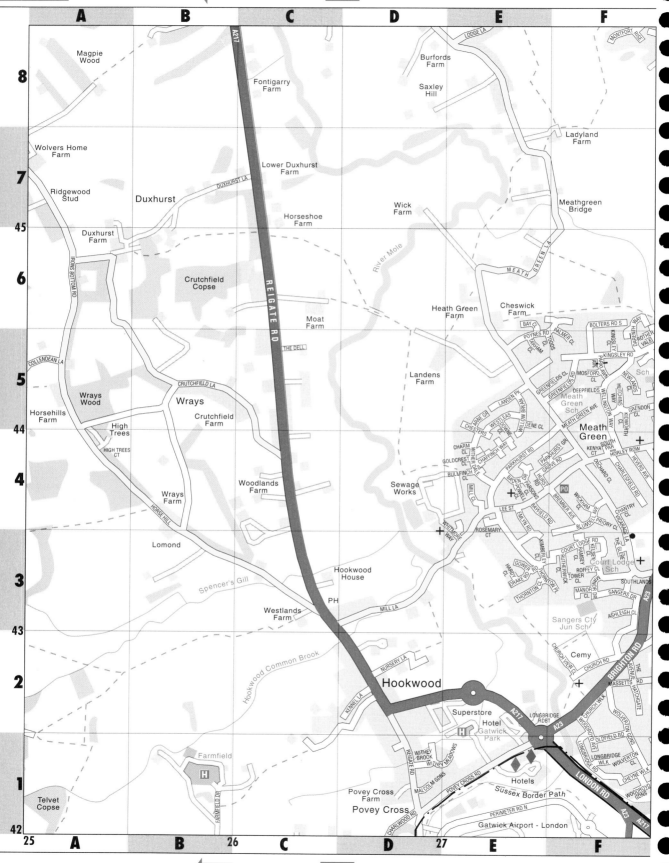

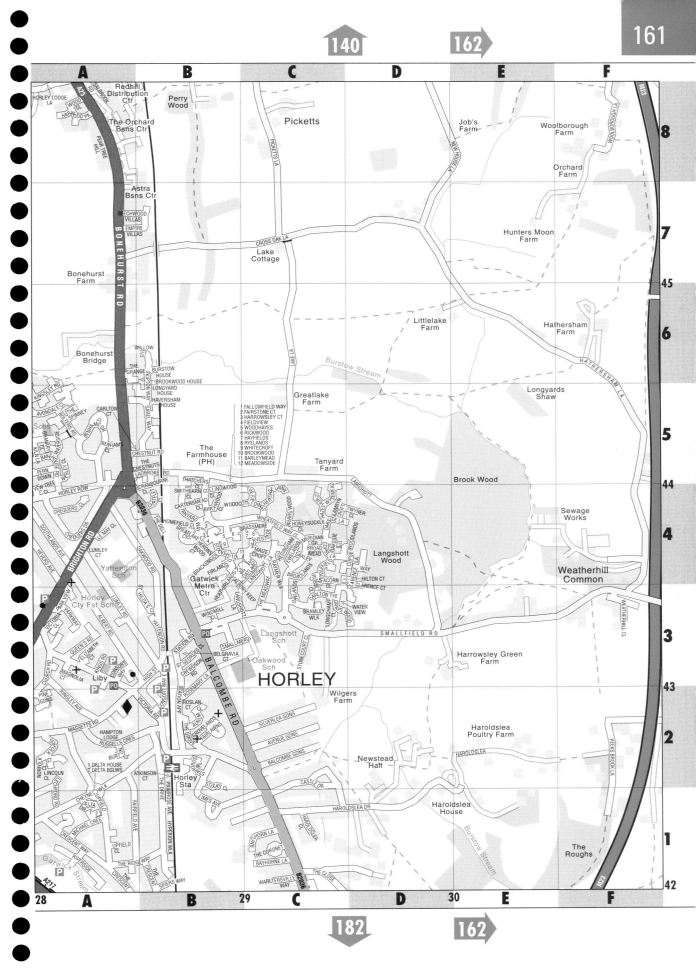

A B C D E F

8

Greenmeads Farm

BRICKFIELD RD

WASP GREEN LA

DAISEY'S HILL

BELLWELL LA

MILLERS COPSE

MILLER'S LA

The Bell Inn

OUTWOOD LA

Wasp Green Farm

Gay House

GAYHOUSE LA

HORNECOURT HILL

Windmill

The Castle (PH)

Wasp Green

Brightleigh Farm

PO

Marl House

Copsley Court

Hornecourt Wood

7

Little Collins

Outwood

Hornecourt Manor Farm

45

Rookery Farm

Drivers Green

ROOKERY HILL

Old Hall Farm

Wilmot's Farm

SCOTT'S HILL

NORMAN'S RD

WILMOT'S LA

Church Farm

Horne Grange

Maria Montessori Sch

PO

6

Horne

CHURCH RD

5

Burstow Lodge Farm

Burstow Lodge

Hollesley Farm

COSMAN'S LA

Little Abbots Farm

Horne House Farm

CROYDONBARN LA

44

Short Acre Farm

4

Weatherhill

WEATHERHILL COTTS

HAYES WLK

CHARLOTTE GR

HATHERSHAM CL

THE CRAVENS

RALEIGH DR

TUDOR CL

THE WOODLANDS

CAREY'S WOOD

CAREY'S COPSE

CHAPEL RD

FIELD VW

THISTLE WAY

CLOVER WAY

CHURCH HILL RD

ORCHARD RD

HEATHER WLK

MEADOW VIEW

Smallfield Place

SMALLFIELD RD

COOPER CL 1 LARKFIELD CL 2 GRASSLANDS 3

WEATHERHILL RD

GRANGEWAY

WOODSIDE CRES

DYER'S FIELD

NEW RD

The Plough (PH)

Bysshe Court Farm

3

ALBERTA CT VANCOUVER CL QUEBEC CL

GRANGE RD

TORONTO DR

ONTARIO CL

PLOUGH RD

Burstow Prim Sch

PO

WHEELERS LA

KINGS MEAD

BRIDGEHAM WAY

Rough Beech

Rough Beech Farm

43

PERRYLANDS LA

Smallfield

Green Farm

Triddles Farm

CHITHURST LA

2

BROADBRIDGE LA

Bridgeham Grange

RANELAGH COTTS

REDEHALL RD

Redehall/ Prep Sch

DOWLANDS LA

Broadmead Farm

Saconnex Farm

Laburnum Court (Caravan Park)

Dowlands Wood

Roughbeech Wood

1

Broadbridge Cottages

Broadbridge Farm

LONE OAK

GEARY CL

THE HOMESTEAD

Homestead Farm

PARK RD

CROSS LA

Chithurst Farm

42

31 A B 32 C D 33 E F

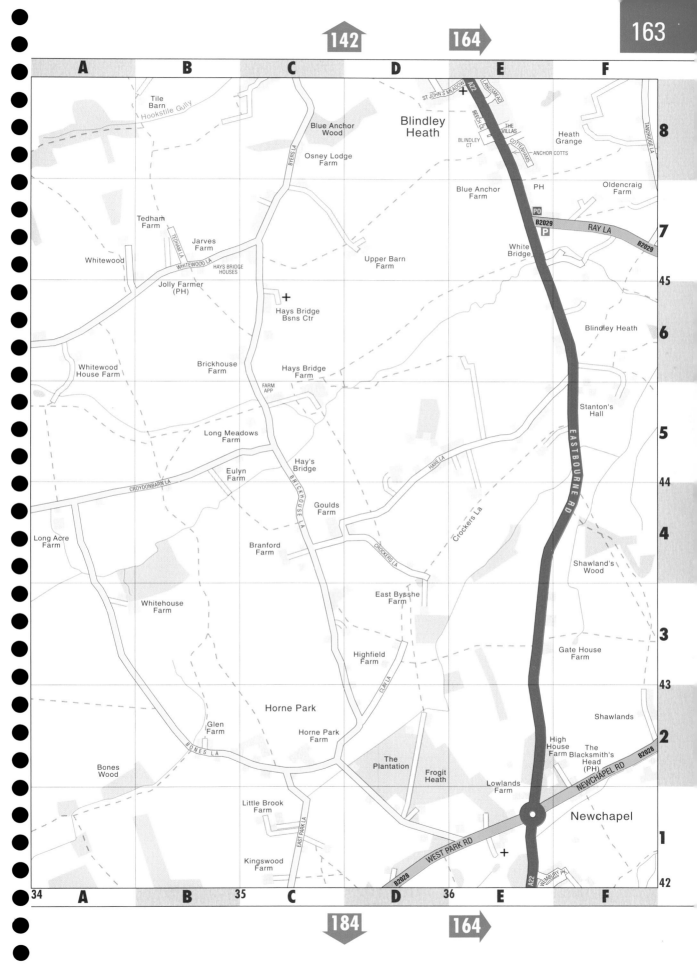

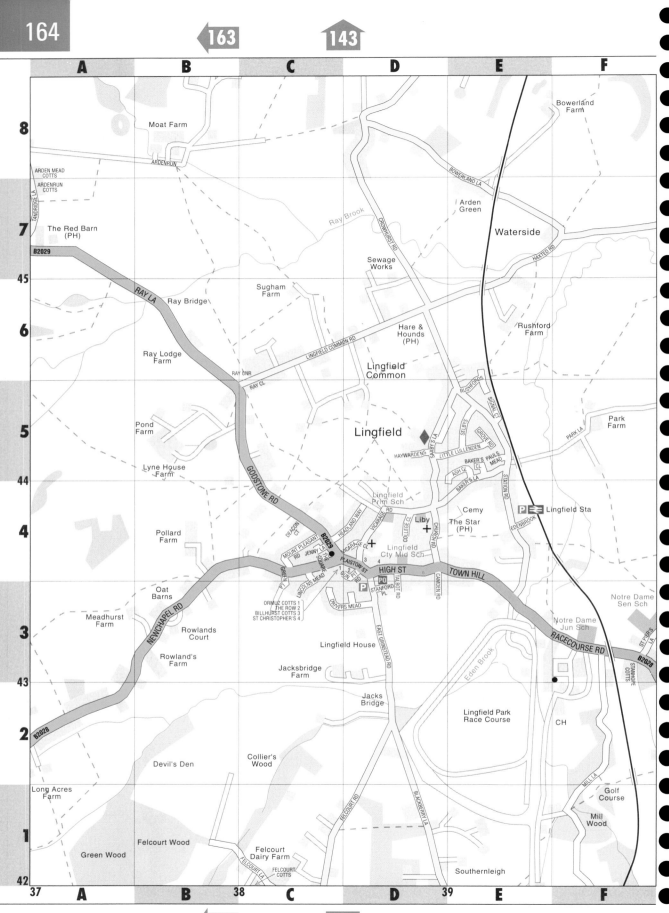

A   B   C   D   E   F

8   Moat Farm

ARDENRUN

ARDEN MEAD COTTS
ARDENRUN COTTS

Ray Brook

Bowerland Farm

BOWERLAND LA

Arden Green

Waterside

7   The Red Barn (PH)

B2029

RAY LA

Ray Bridge

Sugham Farm

CROWHURST RD

Sewage Works

HAXTED RD

45

Rushford Farm

6   Ray Lodge Farm

LINGFIELD COMMON RD

Hare & Hounds (PH)

RAY CNR

RAY CL

Lingfield Common

5   Pond Farm

Lingfield

RUSHFONDS

SELBY'S

GROVE RD

SIGNAL CT

Park Farm

HAYWARDENS

SELBY'S LA

LITTLE LULLENDEN

PARK LA

Lyne House Farm

BAKER'S LA   BAKER'S LA

ASH CL   PAULS MEAD

44   Lingfield Prim Sch

STATION RD

Pollard Farm

VICARAGE RD

College Cl

Cemy

P   Lingfield Sta

4

DEACON CT

B2029

HEADLAND WAY

CHURCH RD

Liby   +

The Star (PH)

EDENBROOK

MOUNT PLEASANT RD

VICARAGE CL

+

Lingfield Cty Mid Sch

JENNY LA   THE SQUARE

PLAISTOW ST

GREEN LA   LINCOLNS MEAD

GUN PIT RD

HIGH ST   TOWN HILL

RACECOURSE RD

Oat Barns

PO   Talbot Rd

STANFORD PL   CAMDEN RD

Notre Dame Sen Sch

Meadhurst Farm

DRIVERS MEAD

ORMUZ COTTS 1
THE ROW 2
BILLHURST COTTS 3
ST CHRISTOPHER'S 4

Notre Dame Jun Sch

ST PIER'S LA

3   Rowlands Court

Lingfield House

B2028

STANHOPE COTTS

Rowland's Farm

Jacksbridge Farm

EAST GRINSTEAD RD

43

Jacks Bridge

Eden Brook

CH

2   B2028

Devil's Den

Collier's Wood

Lingfield Park Race Course

MILL LA

Long Acres Farm

FELCOURT RD

BLACKBERRY LA

Golf Course

Mill Wood

1   Green Wood   Felcourt Wood

FELCOURT LA

Felcourt Dairy Farm

FELCOURT COTTS

Southernleigh

42

37   A   38   B   C   39   D   E   F

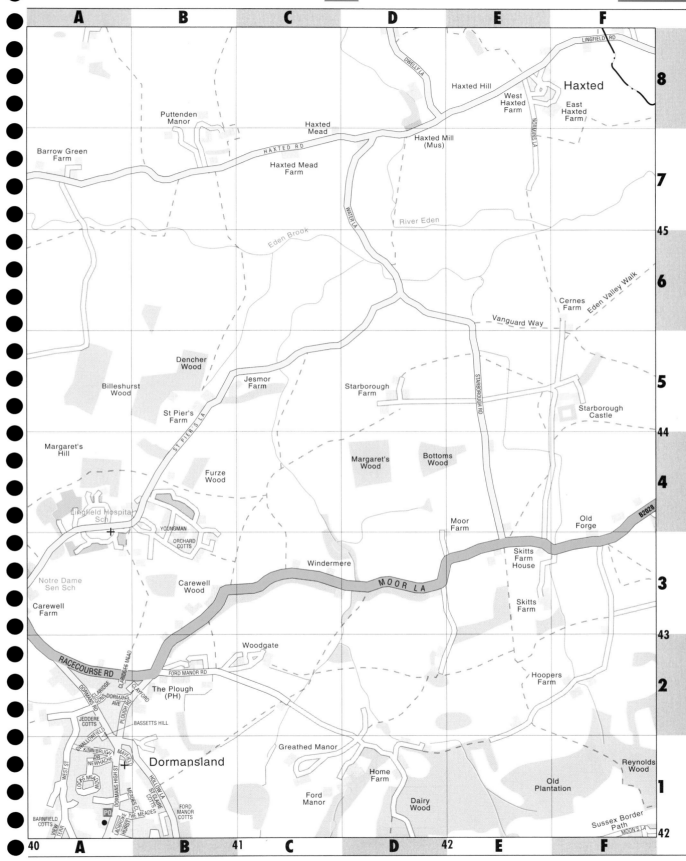

A B C D E F

8

LINGFIELD RD

Haxted

DWELLY LA

Haxted Hill

West Haxted Farm

East Haxted Farm

Puttenden Manor

Haxted Mead

Haxted Mill (Mus)

NORMANS LA

7

Barrow Green Farm

HAXTED RD

Haxted Mead Farm

WATER LA

River Eden

45

Eden Brook

6

Cernes Farm

Eden Valley Walk

Vanguard Way

5

Dencher Wood

Jesmor Farm

Starborough Farm

STARBOROUGH RD

Starborough Castle

Billeshurst Wood

St Pier's Farm

44

ST PIER'S LA

Margaret's Hill

Furze Wood

Margaret's Wood

Bottoms Wood

4

Lingfield Hospital Sch

YOUNGMAN

ORCHARD COTTS

Moor Farm

Old Forge

B2028

Notre Dame Sen Sch

Carewell Wood

Windermere

MOOR LA

Skitts Farm House

3

Carewell Farm

Skitts Farm

43

RACECOURSE RD

CLARIDGE MEAD

Woodgate

Ford Manor Rd

Hoopers Farm

2

CLARIDGE

CLAYFORD

DORMANS RD

DORMANS GDNS

DORMANS AVE

PLOUGH RD

The Plough (PH)

JEDDERE COTTS

BASSETTS HILL

SWALLOWFIELD

Greathed Manor

Reynolds Wood

Dormansland

WEST ST

KINNIBRUGH DR

MAYFIELD

NEWHACHE

DORMANS HIGH ST

MERBES CL

HOLLOW LA

ST CLAIRE COTTS

Home Farm

Old Plantation

1

LOCKS MEADOW

Ford Manor

Dairy Wood

Sussex Border Path

BARNFIELD COTTS

PO

LADBROKE HURST

THE MEADES

FORD MANOR COTTS

MOON'S LA

42

VIEW TERR

40 A B 41 C D 42 E F

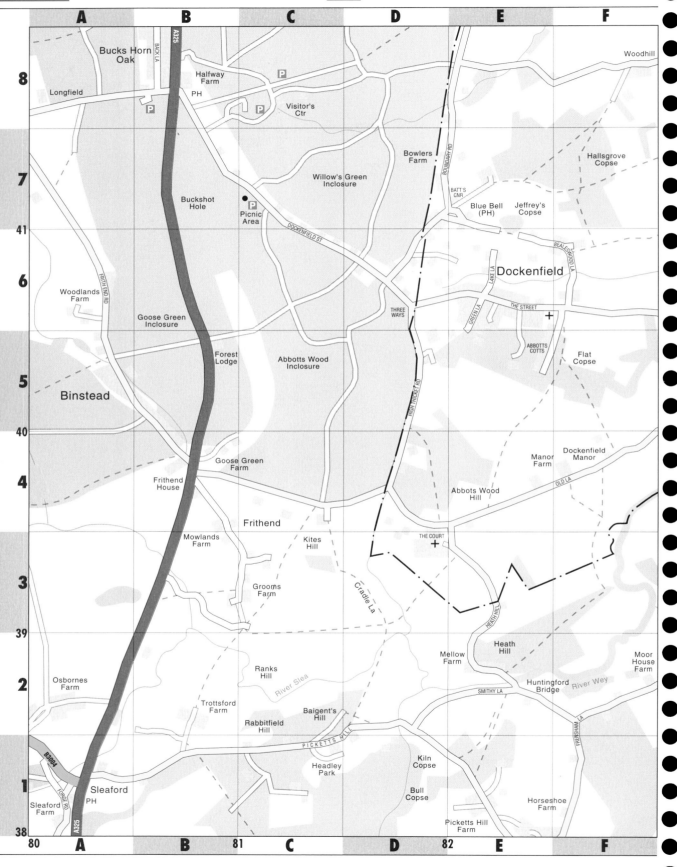

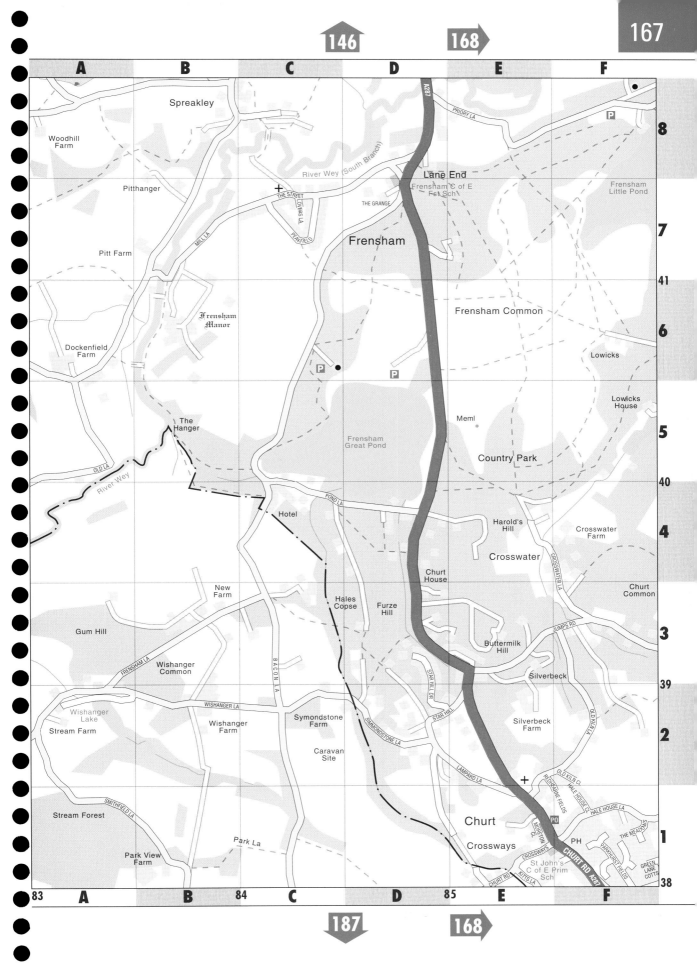

167
147

A   B   C   D   E   F

8

Chuter's
Cottage

Green Hill

Abbot's
Lodge

Greensand Way

Lion's
Mouth

Frensham
Little Pond

Greenhills
Farm

GRANGE RD

The
Grange

WINCHESTER RD

7

EGLINTON RD

41

CARLISLE RD

Hankley Common

WELLESLEY RD

6

LOWICKS RD

Grey
Walls

SANDY LA

Kettlebury Hill

GLEBE LA

Rushmoor

5

PO

40

The Flashes

TILFORD RD

Gold Hill

4

The
Devil's Jumps

Wychmoor
Copse

The
Miravalle
(PH)

THURSLEY RD

3

Kettlebury
Farm

JUMPS RD

Churt
Lea

Churt Place
Farm

Pitch
Place
Farm

39

CRABTREE LA

Old Kiln
Farm

2

HALE HOUSE LA

Hillside
Farm

Hyde
Farm

Hyde
Copse

Glenhead
Farm

Upper
Ridgeway
Farm

SAILORS LA

GREEN CROSS LA

Avalon

OLD BARN LA

HYDE LA

Fair View
Farm

1

Green
Cross
Farm

Green
Cross

Green
Farm

Stock
Farm
House

Marchants
Farm

GREEN LA

38

GREEN LA

86   A   B   87   C   D   88   E   F

167
188

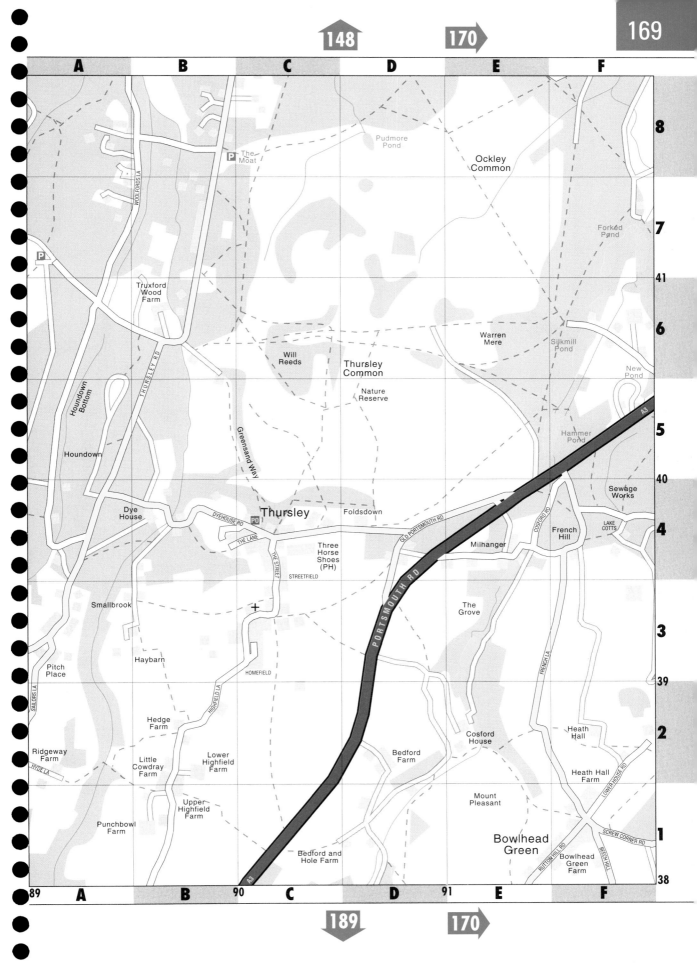

148
170

A B C D E F

8

Pudmore
Pond

Ockley
Common

7

Forked
Pond

41

Truxford
Wood
Farm

6

Warren
Mere

Silkmill
Pond

Will
Reeds

Thursley
Common

New
Pond

WOOLFORDS LA

THURSLEY RD

Houndown
Bottom

Nature
Reserve

Hammer
Pond

A3

5

Houndown

Greensand Way

40

Dye
House

DYEHOUSE LA

Thursley

Foldsdown

OLD PORTSMOUTH RD

Sewage
Works

COSFORD RD

French
Hill

LAKE
COTTS

4

THE LANE

PO

Milhanger

THE STREET

Three
Horse
Shoes
(PH)

STREETFIELD

PORTSMOUTH RD

Smallbrook

+

The
Grove

3

FRENCH LA

39

Pitch
Place

Haybarn

HOMEFIELD

SAILORS LA

Hedge
Farm

HIGHFIELD LA

Cosford
House

Heath
Hall

2

Ridgeway
Farm

HYDE LA

Little
Cowdray
Farm

Lower
Highfield
Farm

Bedford
Farm

Heath Hall
Farm

LOWER HOUSE RD

Punchbowl
Farm

Upper
Highfield
Farm

Mount
Pleasant

Bowlhead
Green

SCREW CORNER RD

1

RUTTON HILL RD

BEECH HILL

Bowlhead
Green
Farm

Bedford and
Hole Farm

A3

38

169
149

A B C D E F

8

Borough Farm

Mistlebrooks Wood

Mousehill Corner

MILFORD BY PASS RD

PORTSMOUTH RD

Mousehill

A283

A283

A3

A286

NEW RD

GREEN LA

THE CEDARS

MOUSEHILL LA

LADYCROSS

MILFORD LODGE

LADYCROSS MEWS

DOWER HOUSE

HIGHCROFT

BUSDENS WAY

BUSDENS CL

BUSDENS LA

MILFORD HEATH RD

Rodborough Hill

Cemy

Rodborough Cty Sec Sch

7

41

WEBB RD

PORTSMOUTH RD

A3

Home Pond

Witley Common

HASLEMERE RD

GASDEN DR

GASDEN LA

GASDEN COPSE

YEW TREE RD

KESWICK RD

WILDCROFT WOOD

CROFT RD

LITTLE LONDON

CRAMHURST LA

KHARTOUM RD

MERRY ACRES

HEATHVIEW RD

MARTINS

WOODPECKERS

SWALLOW CL

OXTED GN

OXTED GN

OLDWOOD

RAKE LA

Cramhurst

Wheelerstreet

PETWORTH RD

WHEELER LA

WHEELER LA

SUNNY HILL

SUNNY DOWN

BANNISTERS

OWENSWOOD

DORLCOTE

WILLOW MEAD

EASTHELDS

EASTHELDS

MIDDLEMARCH

CHESTER RD

ROKE LA

ROKE LANE COTTS

ROKE LA

Crossways

MILL LA

Enton Mill Farm

Witley

6

National Trust Information Ctr

Mare Hill

MARE HILL

MARE HILL COTTS

Chandler CE (VA) Jun Sch

Barrow Hills Sch

NEWLANDS ESTATE

GEORGE ELIOT CL

NORTHFIELD

PO

5

40

4

The Shrubbery

Stable Lake

Thursley Lake

Milford Lodge

Heath House

Hazel Copse

Chestnut Copse

Witley CE Inf Sch

PH

3

39

Witley Park

West Firs

Winkford Farm

CHURCH LA

Culmer

WATER LA

Pond Coppice

CULMER HILL

PO

2

Parsonage House

Parsonage Farm

Rockwoods

Banacle Common

GURDON S LA

King Edward's Sch

A283

Inst

1

Chocolates

SCREW CORNER RD

Furzefield Wood

Heath Hills

The Hill House

GREENSAND WAY

Sandhills

BROOK RD

COMBE LA

Wormley

Brook

A286

Birch Copse

Dog & Pheasant (PH)

38

92 A B 93 C D 94 E F

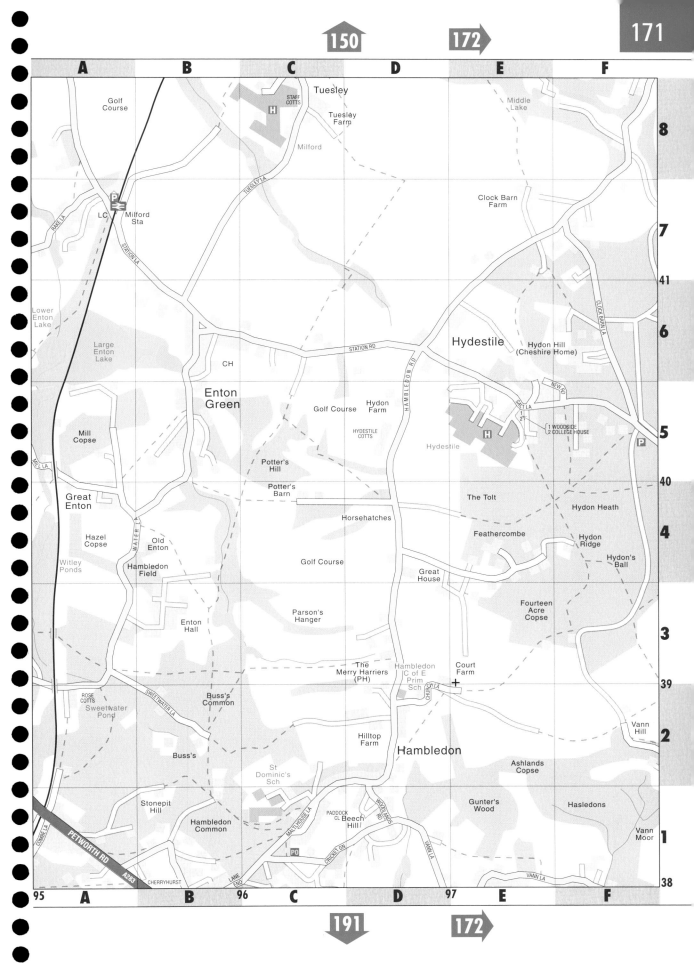

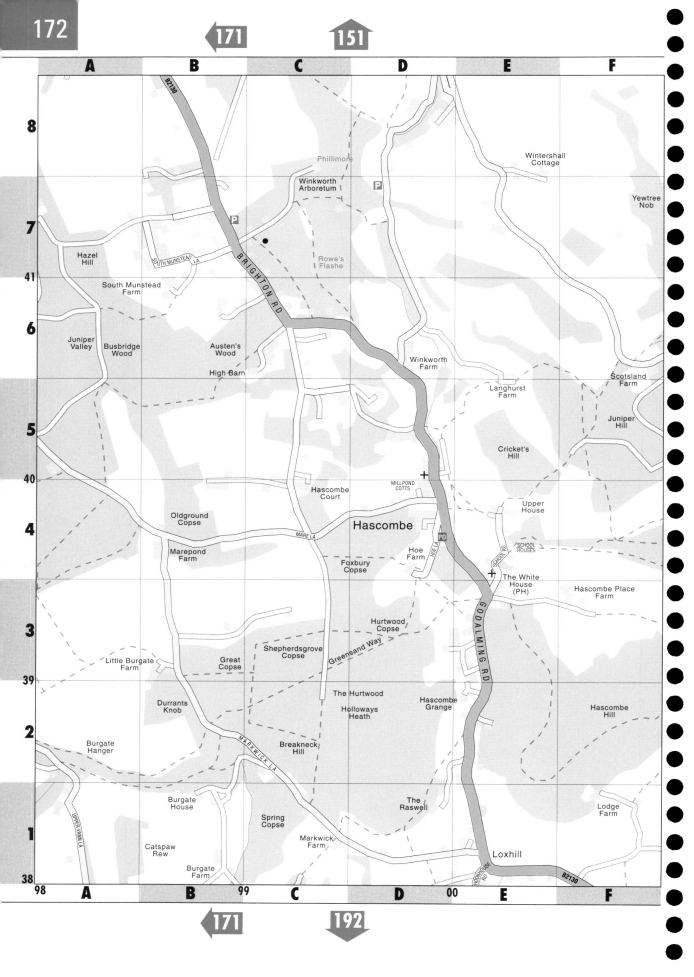

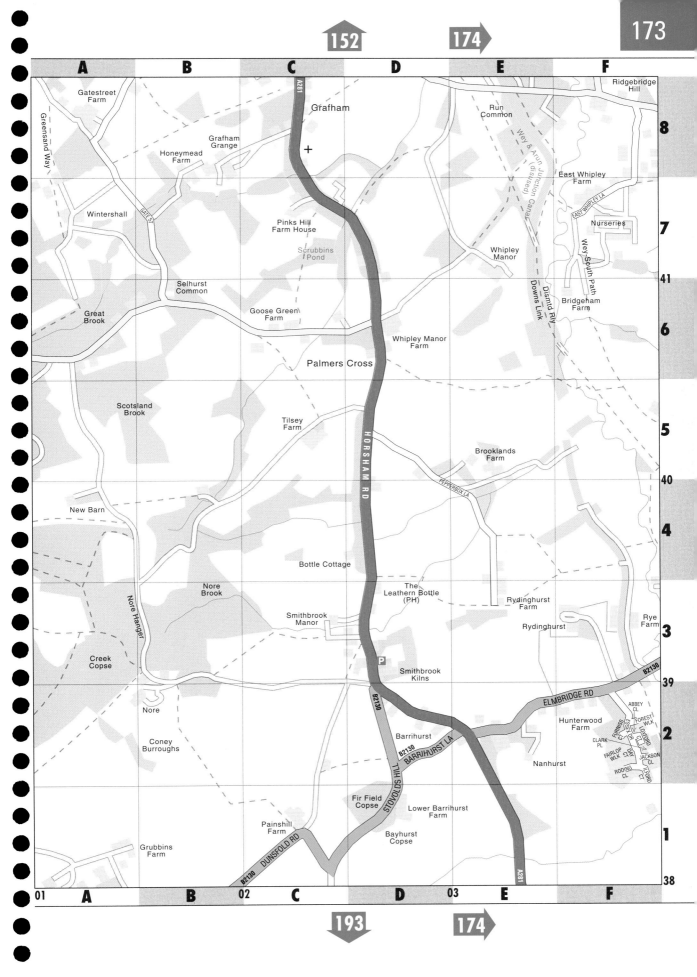

173
153

A B C D E F

8

B2128

Gaston Farm

Smithwood Farm

Pittance Farm

Alderbrook Park

Fowls Copse

Smithwood Common Rd

Brackenbrook

Smithwood Common

7

Nursery

Smithwood Ave

Strathavon Cl

Alderbrook Rd

Alderbrook Farm

Wyphurst Home Farm

41

Highland View

The Four Elms (PH)

Guildford Rd

Restwell Ave

PO

6

Rowle Edge

Rowly Dr

Cranleigh Nurseries

St Joseph's Sch

Fernfell Golf & Cntry Club

Rowly

Whitethorn Cotts

Upfold Cl

Mossy Copse

Barhatch La

Upfold La

Mannings Hill

Golf Course

Rowly Farm

High Upfold Farm

Amlets La

5

Wey-South Path

Mansfield Pk

Upfold La

Cranleigh Sch

Hilliards Barn Cottage

Coppice Edge

Barhatch Rd

Norther Farm

Horseshoe La

Waldy Rise

Slip of Wood

40

Nursery

Woodcote

Edgefield Cl

Butt Cl

Harrowerne

Barber Dr

Mower Pl

4

Wyphurst Rd

The Riding

Peregrine Cl

Ryde Lands

Strudwicks Field

Acres Plat

B2127

Ruffold Farm

Thistley La

Glebe Rd

Simmerlands

Harrier Cl

Kiln Copse

Sherriydon

Brook House

Hailey Pl

Dismtd Rly

St Andrews

Glebelands Sch

Furtherfield

Park Dr

Beaumont Sq

Cranbrook Rd

Bishops Rd

Coatham Pl

Epsom Pl

3

Sewage Works

Elmbridge Cotts

Westden Meadows

Newbridge Ct

Lashmere

Bridge Ct

Bridge Cotts

B2130

Hotel

B2128

Park Gate Cotts

Downs Link

East View

St James S

Cranleigh Cty Fst Sch

Cemy

Cranleigh City Fst Sch

St Nicolas Ct

St Nicolas Ave

The Precinct

Nuthurst

Barnfield

Kingsmead

Brockside

Ewhurst Rd

St Cuthbert Mayne RC Fst Sch

Park House Cotts

Woodland Ave

Grange Pk

The Ridgeway

Hewitts Ind Est

Elm Gr

Wykeham

Stanton Cl

Cress

Tucker's Dr

Telford

Little Mead Ind Est

Row Lane Rd

Victoria Rd

Bloggs Way

High St

St Nicholas C of E Sch

The Malthouses

Cranleigh Village

Brockhde

B2127

Redcroft Walk

Mead Cl

King St

New Park Rd

The Woodlands Cl

39

Elbridge Rd

B2130

Elmbridge Rd

Vine Cotts

PO

Liby

Libr

H

Little Manor Gdns

Char7s Cl

Bridge Mead Rd

Queensway

Gingers Cl

Seltops Cl

2

West Cranleigh Nurseries

Knowle Wood

Osier Bed

Snoxhall Field

Overford Cl

Overford Dr

Brookmead Ct

Mount Rd

Hitherwood

Wellwynds Rd

The Mount

The Drive

Fawley Cl

Cranleigh Mead

Longpoles Rd

Alfold Rd

Knowle La

Knowle

Cranleigh

Avenl Cl

Heron Shaw

Avenue Rd

Bax Cl

1

Utworth Manor

Wey-South Path

Oaklands

Coldharbour Farm

Horsham Rd

Waverleigh Rd

Brookside

Ashtrees

Nightingale Ct

Napier Pl

Thurlow Wlk

Snowdenham

Greenbush La

Ellery Cl

Broad Wlk

Grove Cl

Southwood Chase

Cromwell Pl

Woodstock Rd

Little Wildwood

B2128

38

04 A B 05 C D 06 E F

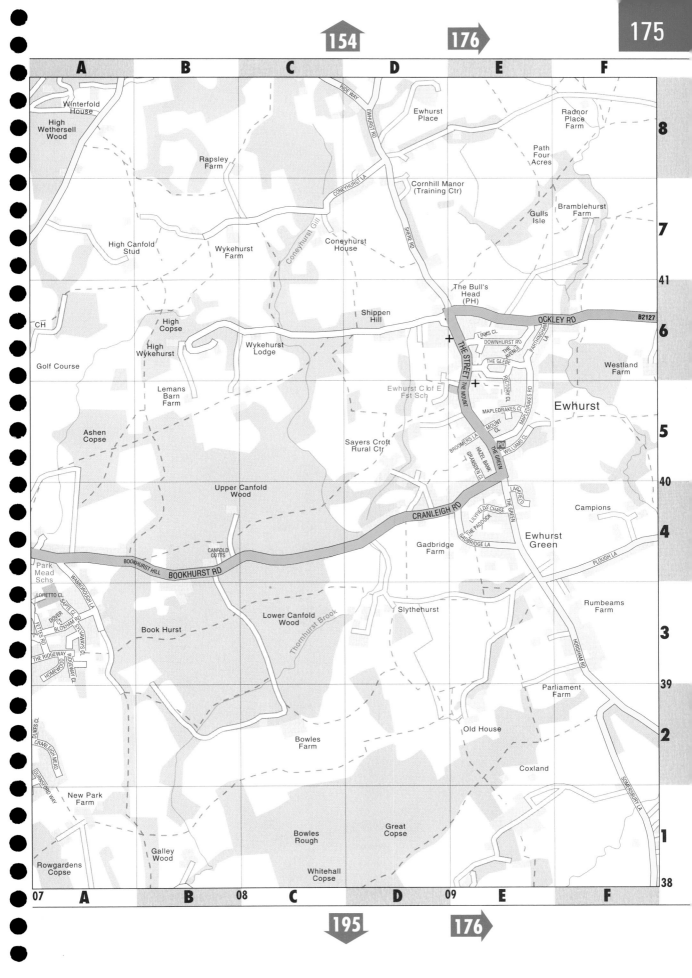

154
176
195
176

175
155

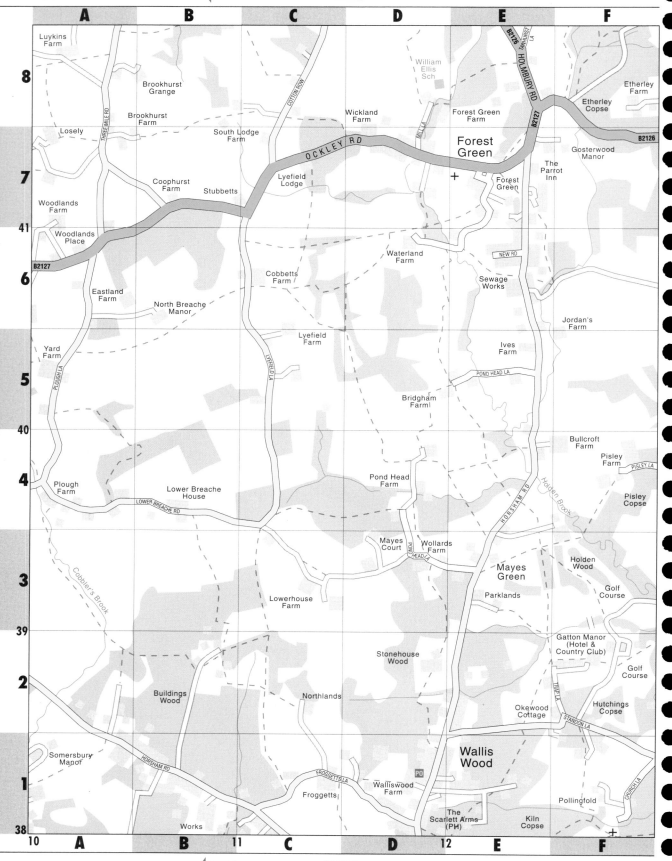

175
196

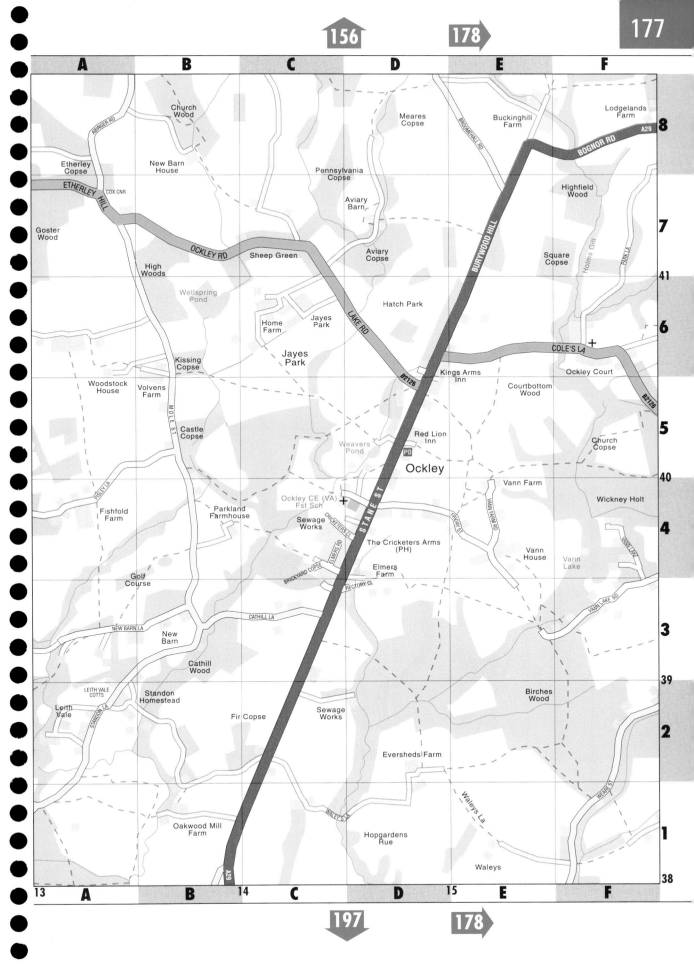

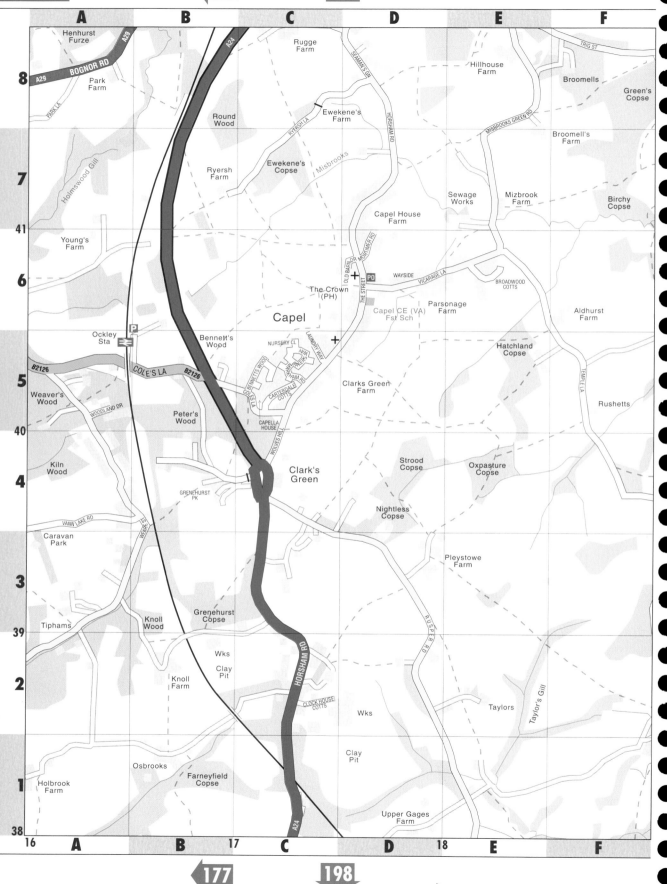

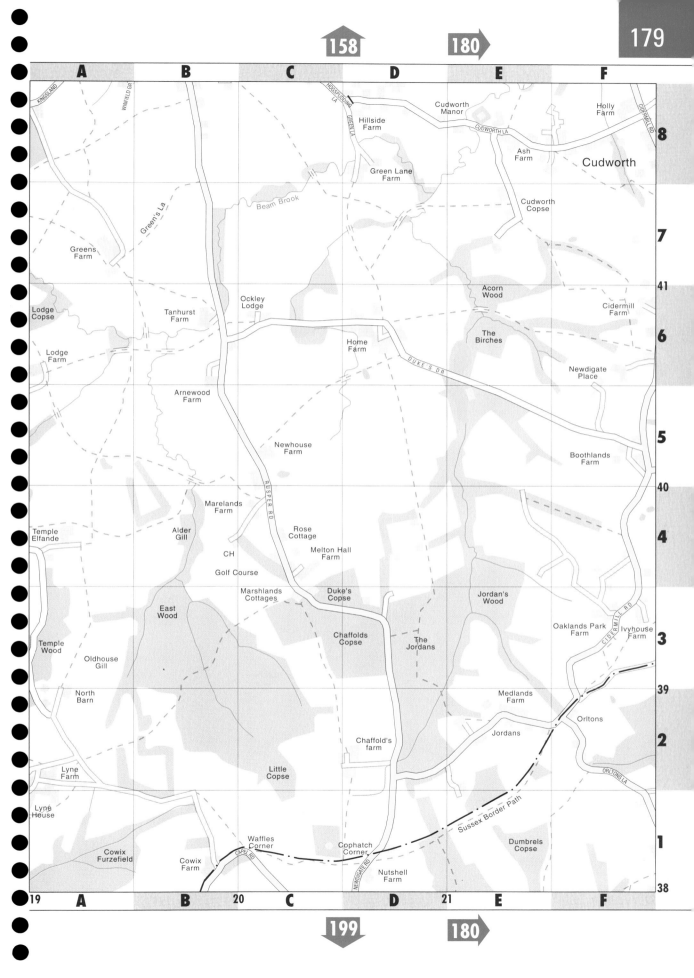

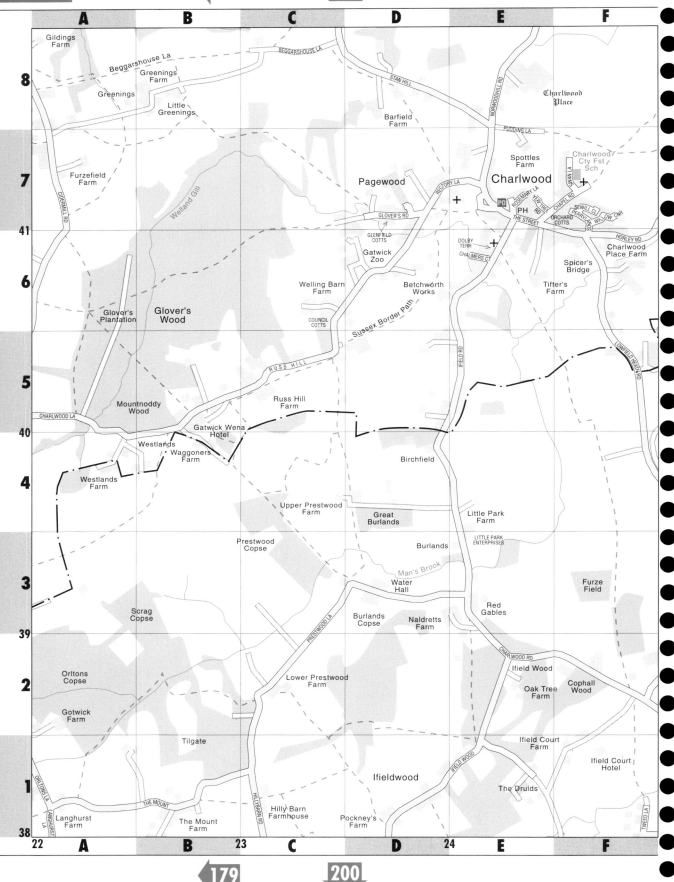

179
159

A B C D E F

8

7

41

6

5

40

4

3

39

2

1

38

22 A B 23 C D 24 E F

179
200

Gildings Farm
Beggarshouse La
Greenings Farm
Greenings
Little Greenings
BEGGARSHOUSE LA
STAN HILL
Barfield Farm
Charlwood Place
NORWOODHILL RD
PUDDING LA
Spottles Farm
Charlwood Cty Fst Sch
Charlwood
Furzefield Farm
CIDERMILL RD
Pagewood
RECTORY LA
PO
PH
THE STREET
ROSEMARY LA
YEWTREE RD
CHAPEL RD
SWAN LA
SEWILL CL
PERRY MDS
LOW CNR
ORCHARD COTTS
HORLEY RD
GLOVER'S RD
GLENFIELD COTTS
DOLBY TERR
CHALMERS CT
Charlwood Place Farm
Gatwick Zoo
Welland Gill
Welling Barn Farm
Betchworth Works
Spicer's Bridge
Glover's Plantation
Glover's Wood
COUNCIL COTTS
Sussex Border Path
Tifter's Farm
IFIELD RD
LOWFIELD HEATH RD
RUSS HILL
CHARLWOOD LA
Mountnoddy Wood
Russ Hill Farm
Gatwick Wena Hotel
Westlands
Waggoners Farm
Birchfield
Westlands Farm
Upper Prestwood Farm
Great Burlands
Little Park Farm
LITTLE PARK ENTERPRISES
Prestwood Copse
Burlands
Furze Field
Scrag Copse
Man's Brook
Water Hall
PRESTWOOD LA
Burlands Copse
Naldretts Farm
Red Gables
Orltons Copse
Lower Prestwood Farm
CHARLWOOD RD
Ifield Wood
Oak Tree Farm
Cophall Wood
Gotwick Farm
Tilgate
IFIELD WOOD
Ifield Court Farm
Ifield Court Hotel
ORLTONS LA
LANGHURST LA
THE MOUNT
HILLYBARN RD
Hilly Barn Farmhouse
Ifieldwood
Pockney's Farm
The Druids
TWEED LA
Langhurst Farm
The Mount Farm

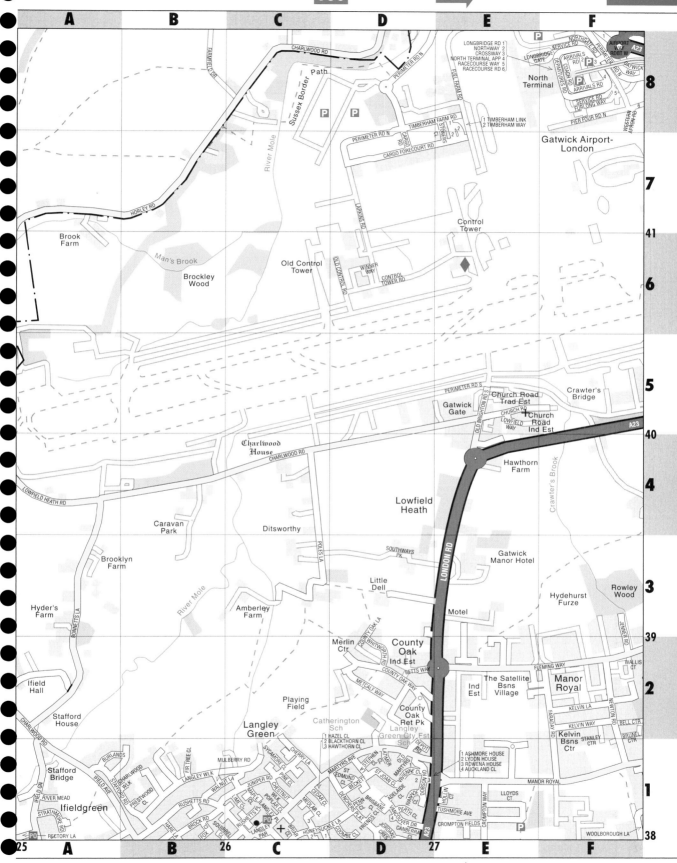

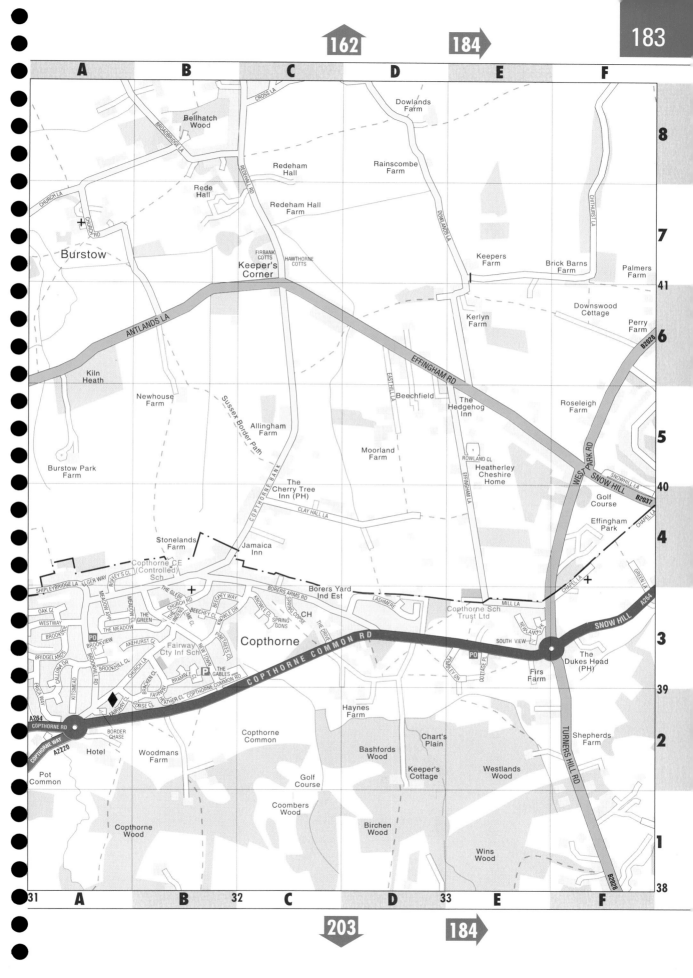

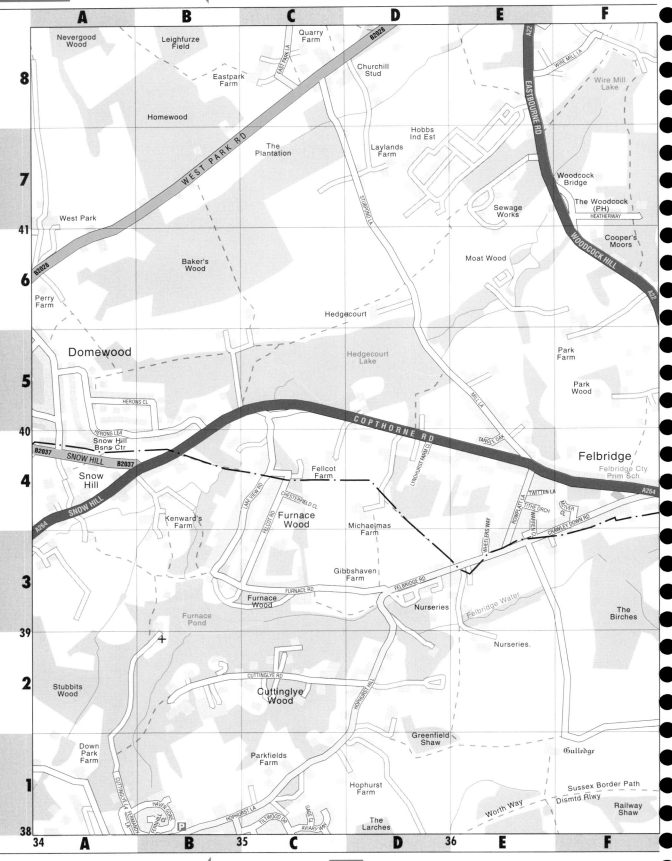

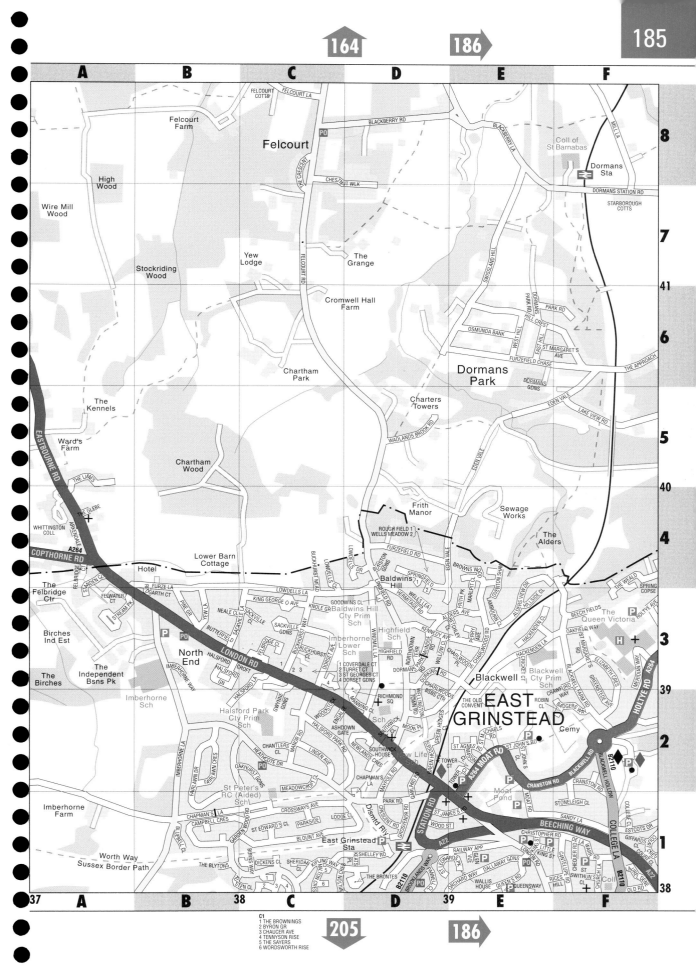

C1
1 THE BROWNINGS
2 BYRON GR
3 CHAUCER AVE
4 TENNYSON RISE
5 THE SAYERS
6 WORDSWORTH RISE

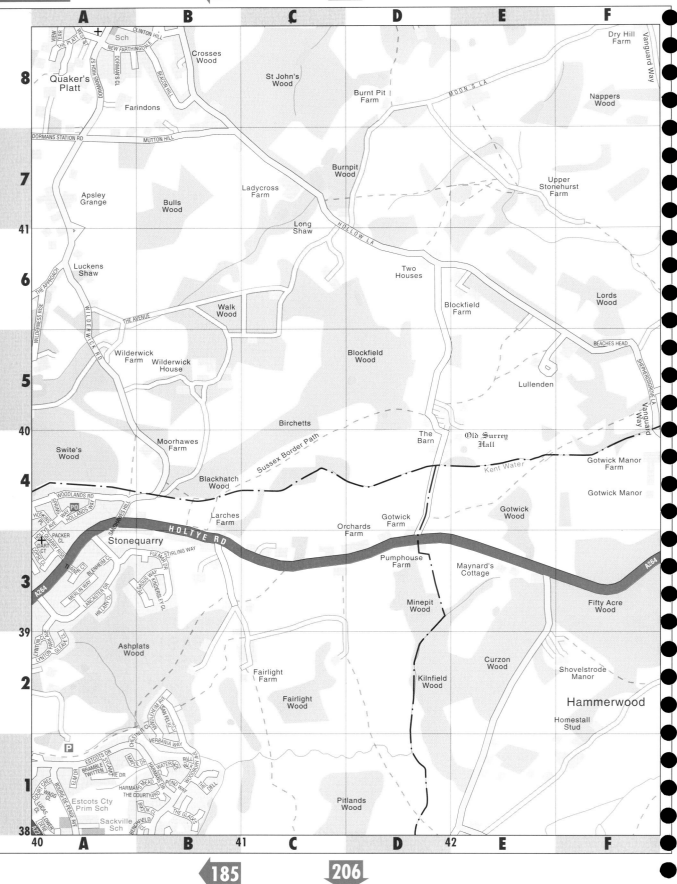

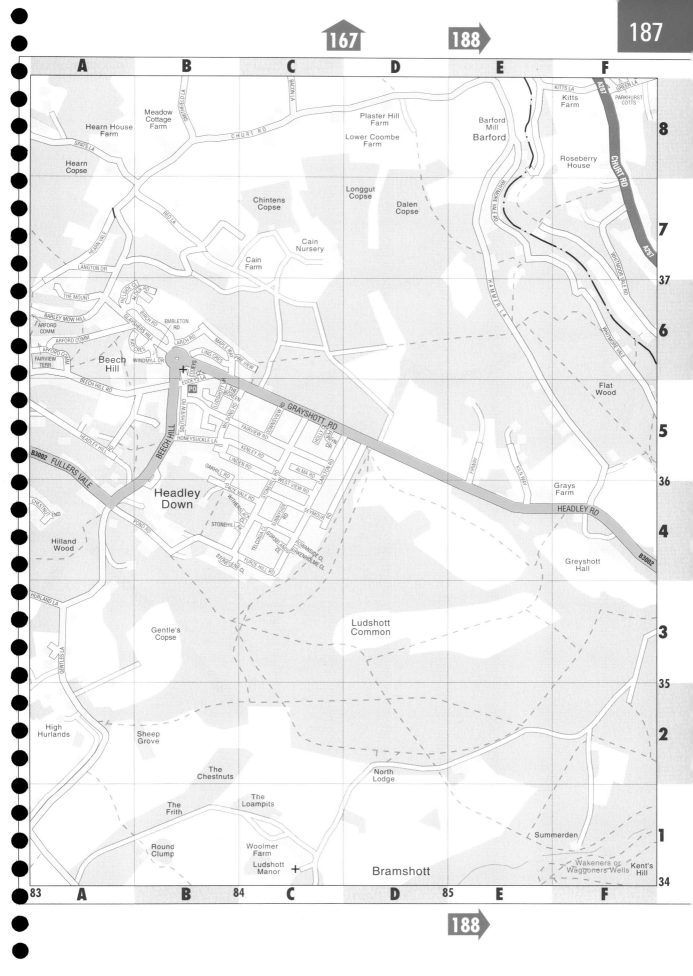

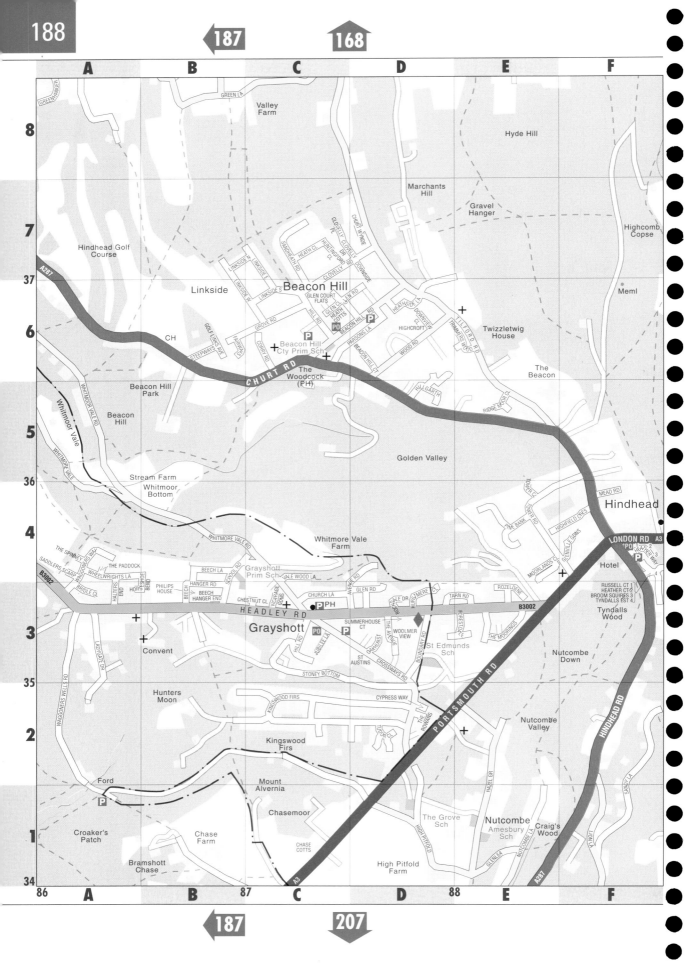

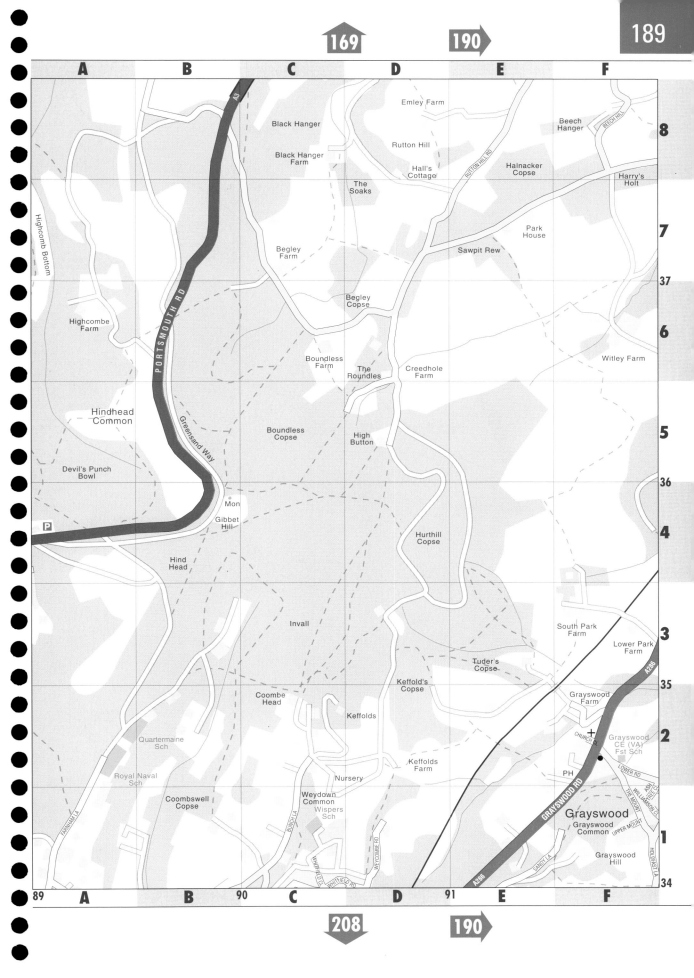

169
190

A B C D E F

8
7
37
6
5
36
4
3
35
2
1
34

Highcomb Bottom

Black Hanger

Black Hanger Farm

Emley Farm

Rutton Hill

Hall's Cottage

RUTTON HILL RD

Halnacker Copse

Beech Hanger

BEECH HILL

Harry's Holt

The Soaks

Park House

Sawpit Rew

Begley Farm

Begley Copse

Witley Farm

Highcombe Farm

Boundless Farm

The Roundles

Creedhole Farm

Hindhead Common

Boundless Copse

High Button

Devil's Punch Bowl

Greensand Way

PORTSMOUTH RD

A3

P

Mon

Gibbet Hill

Hurthill Copse

Hind Head

Invall

South Park Farm

Lower Park Farm

A286

Tuder's Copse

Keffold's Copse

Coombe Head

Keffolds

Grayswood Farm

CHURCH RD

Grayswood CE (VA) Fst Sch

Quartermaine Sch

Nursery

Keffolds Farm

PH

LOWER RD

THE MOUNT

WILLIAMSON CL

ASH

Royal Naval Sch

Coombswell Copse

FARNHAM LA

BUNCH LA

Weydown Common

Wispers Sch

WEYCOMBE RD

GRAYSWOOD RD

Grayswood

Grayswood Common

UPPER MOUNT

HOLDFAST LA

Grayswood Hill

WHITFIELD CL

WHITFIELD RD

SANDY LA

A286

89 A B 90 C D 91 E F

189
170

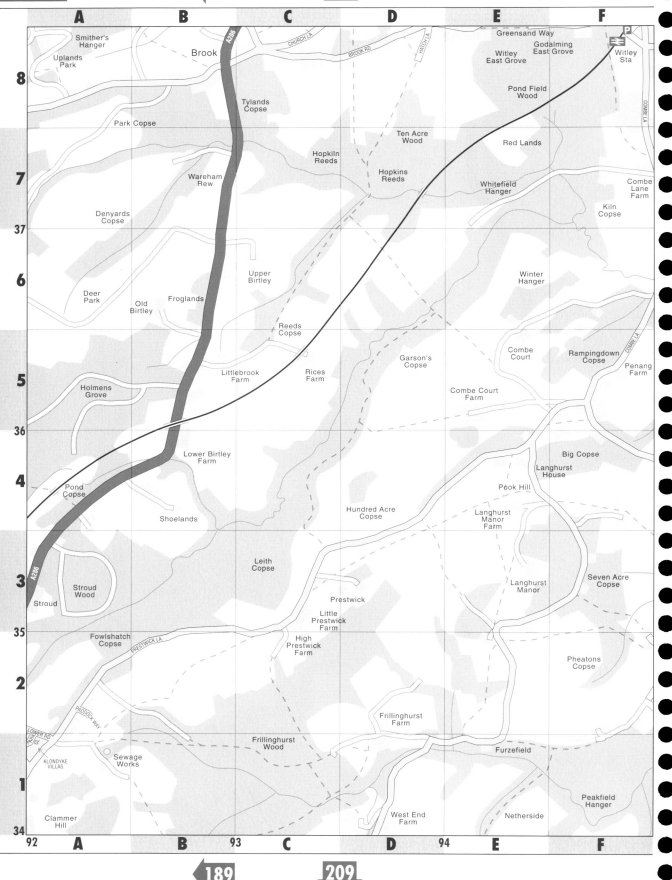

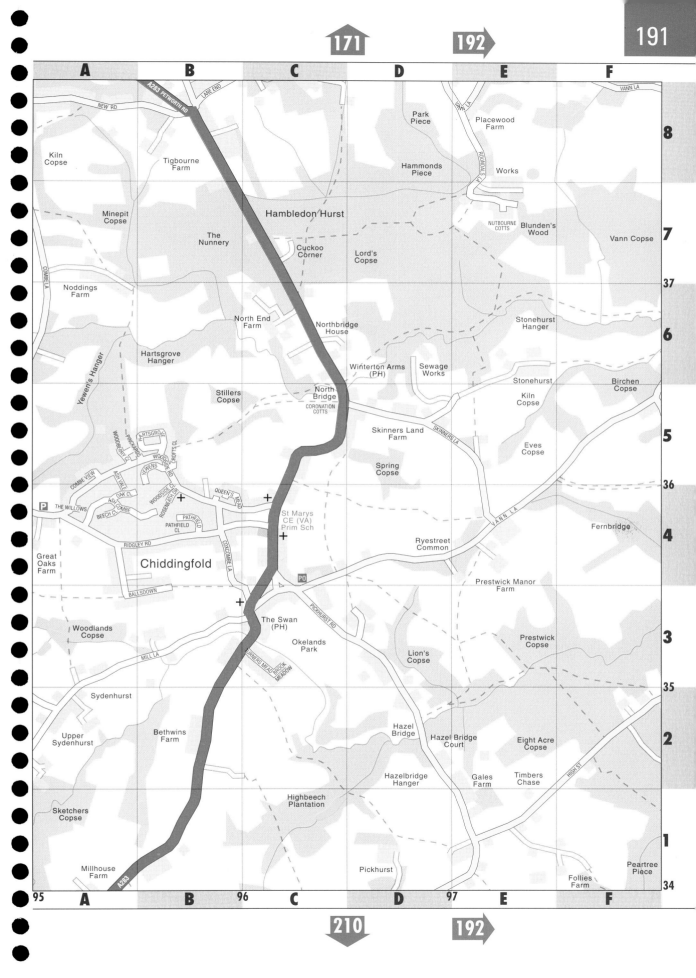

A B C D E F

8

Vann Copse
Great Godalming Copse
Enticknaps Copse
Majorland Rew
B2130 GODALMING RD
Lay Field
Vann
Standages
Hook House Farm
Ten Acre Pond
Prest Wood
Hookhouse Hanger
Park Farm

7

Woodcock Rew
Peartree Green
Six Acre Pond
DUNSFOLD RD

Little Pockford Cottage
Shernalls Pond
MEADOW CROSS
WINDWAYS

37

Dunse Copse
Farm Bottom
KING GEORGE'S COTTS
Dunsfold Green

6

Duns Farm
Field Place
HOOKHOUSE RD
Gratton Corner
Dunsfold CE Fst Sch
DUNSFOLD COMMON RD
BINHAMS LEA

Pockford Farm
Cowpasture Hanger
Church Close Farm
Dunsfold
THE MEWS
Dunsfold
BINHAMS MEADOW

Pockford Harbour
Canterbury Rew
CHURCH RD
Rumpoles (PH)
Long House
PO

5

FB
Mill Hanger
Pound Farm

White Beech
Duns Copse
Duns

36

White Beech Farm
Willards
INN RD
MILL LA
COMMON HOUSE RD

Snarham Land
Pignuts Copse
Millhanger
Dunsfold Common
Works
KINGHTONS LA

4

Wetwood Rough
Standing Wood
Blacknest Farm
WROTHAM HILL
CHAPEL HILL

Brookland Copse
HIGH ST
CHIDDINGFOLD RD
Wetwood
BLACKNEST COTTS

3

Birchen Copse
Loxley Bridge
Golf Course

Highstreet Green
Barbins

Dunsfold Ryse Farm

35

Dunsfold Ryse
Wrotham Great Copse

2

Watlands Ghyll
Lower Lagfold Copse
Hurlands
HURLANDS LA

Dunsfold Ryse
PLAISTOW RD

Botany Bay
Lagfold Copse
Burningfold Manor Stud
Howicks

1

Round Copse
Furnace Bridge

34
Peartree Piece

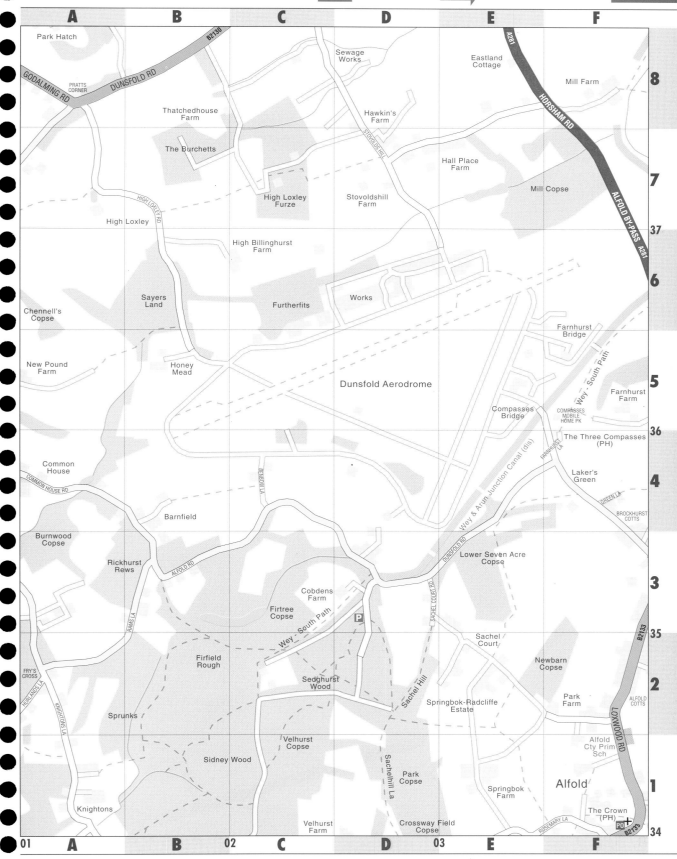

193
174

A B C D E F

B2128

8

Garson Copse
Little Garson
Sparrow Copse
Bushy Copse
Highpark

Holdhurst Farm
White Meads Copse

Great Garson
Boy & Donkey (PH)
Snoxhall Farm

7

Wey-South Path
ALFORD RD
Lion's La
Water Bridge
Dismtd Rly
VACHERY LA

37

Wey & Arun Junction Canal (disused)
Flash Bridge
Hammer Farm
Vachery Pond

Downs Link

6

A281
Waterland Farm
Waterbridge Farm
Newhouse Farm

Bridge Farm

Bookers Lee
Birch Copse
Little Withybush

5

ALFOLD BY-PASS
WILDWOOD LA
KNOWLE LA

36

Little Wildwood Farm
HAZELWOOD COTTS

4

Butcherhouse Farm
Lodge Copse

Works

CROSSWAYS COTTS
Pickenswood Copse

Alfold Crossways
CH

3

B2133
LOXWOOD RD
STONE HATCH
HATCH CL
Wildwood Copse
Shrubs Copse

Wildwood Golf Course

35

CLAPPERS MEADOW
Ivelle Farm

2

Aldermoor Copse
Furzefield Wood

HORSHAM RD
Pallinghurst Farm
Hazel Copse
BAYNARDS RD

1

White Lea
Highfield Copse
Little Birchett
HILLHOUSE LA

Alfold Farm
A281
GUILFORD RD
COOKS HILL

Hook St
Males Farm
White's Copse
Lower Hill House

34

04 A B 05 C D 06 E F

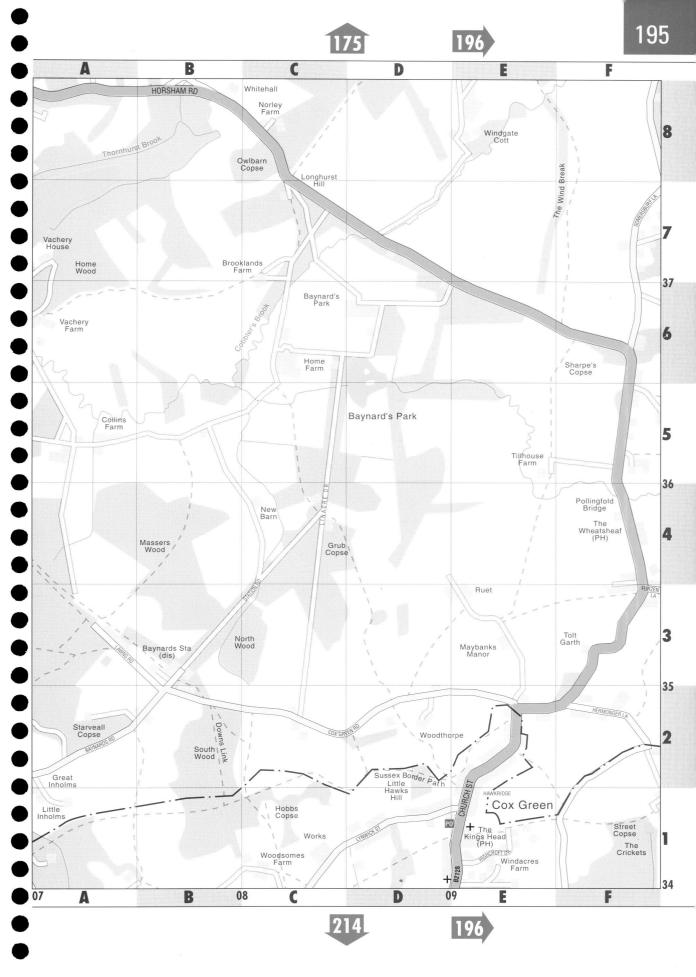

195
176

A **B** **C** **D** **E** **F**

8

Somersbury
Wood

Oakfield

Recn
Gd

Chapel
House

Oakwood
Hill

Abrahams

HORSHAM RD

Rose Hill
Farm

7

Nags Wood

Clay Pit

Works

Smokejack
Farm

SMOKEJACK HILL

Wet
Wood

37

Hillhouse
Farm

Pound
House

6

Hoopwick
Farm

Exfold Furze
Field

Broadstone
Farm

HONEYWOOD LA

Pollingfold
Copse

Monks

5

Pink
Hurst

Pinkhurst
Farm

HORSHAM RD

Honeybush
Farm

MONKS LA

36

Sansomes
Copse

Furzen
Cottage

4

FURZEN LA

Honeywood
House

Ellen's
Green

Sansomes
Farm

Ellens

Sussex Border Path

Ridge
Farm

Honeyghyll
Farm

3

Bury St Austen's
Farm

35

Old
Ockleys

White's
Copse

2

Biddenfield
Copse

Bury
St Austen's

Millfields

Rowhook

Hermongers
Farm

Germany
Field

The
Hanger

Betchetts Gill

Rowhook
Gill

Hermongers

Rowhook
Farm

1

Chequers Inn
(PH)

WATERLANDS LA

ROWHOOK RD

34

10 **A** 11 **B** **C** 12 **D** **E** **F**

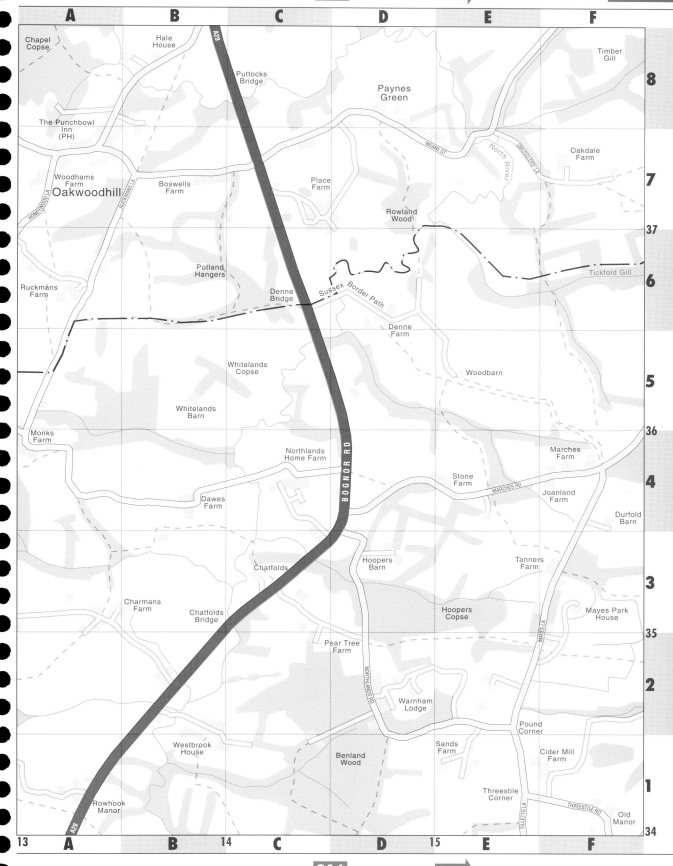

197
178

A   B   C   D   E   F

8

7

37

6

5

36

4

35

2

1

34

16   A   17   B   C   D   18   E   F

197
217

Greatwood Copse

Bonnetts

Grove Copse

Wattlehurst Farm

Shiremark Farm

Shiremark

HORSHAM RD

A24

Sussex Border Path

RISPER RD

Lower Gages Farm

Ridge Farm

MUGGERIDGE'S HILL

Lipscomb's Corner

CAPEL RD

Moat Copse

Hewells Farm

Porter's Farm

The Royal Oak (PH)

FRIDAY ST

Tickfold Farm

Boldings Brook

Cromwell (PH)

KINGSFOLD CT

Kingsfold Place

Kingsfold

Blackfriars Bridge

Great Benhams

Nunnery Farm

Ridgebrook Cottage

MARCHES RD

Blackfriars Farm

Foster's Copse

Cripplegate

Trueloves Wood

DORKING RD

LANGHURST CL

GREEN LA

Curtis's Farm

Langhurst Copse

Langhurst

Northlands Copse

Upper Chickens

Horsham Bsns Pk

Durfold

The Dog and Duck (PH)

Gunbarn Crossing

Factory

Conveyor

LANGHURSTWOOD RD

Upper Rapeland Wood

NORTHLANDS RD

Tylden House (Hotel)

Hilltop Farm

Geerings

Clay Pit

Graylands

Morris Farm

Brick Works

Lower Chickens

Slaughter Bridge

Sewage Works

Graylands Farm

Cuckmere Farm

KNOB HILL

A24

Andrew's Farm

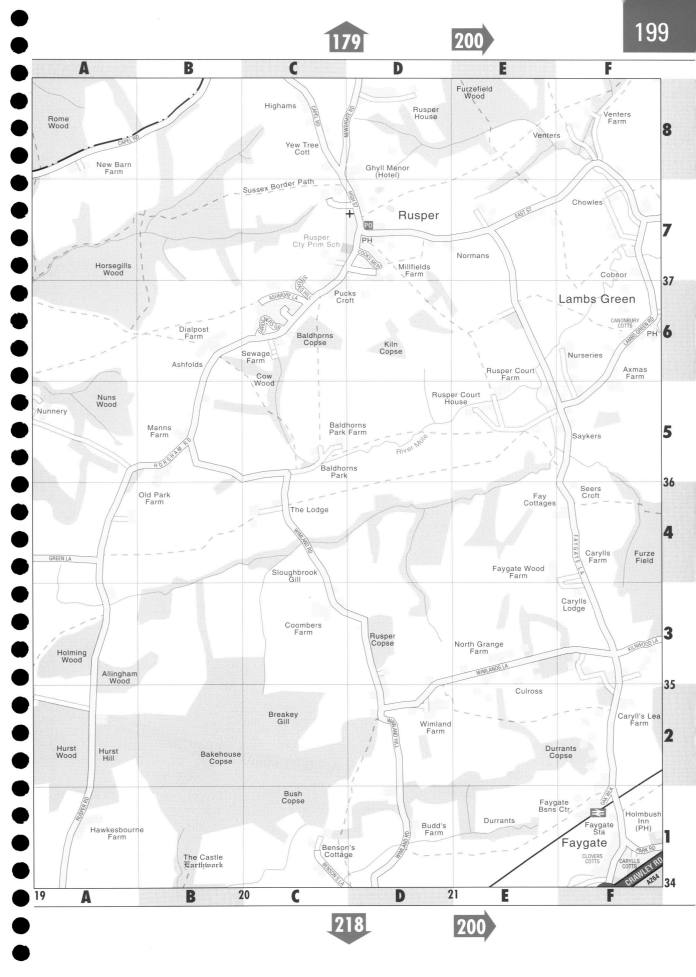

8
Martins Farm
Langhurst Hill
THE MOUNT
Kirk Farm
Bonwycks Place
River Mole
Rectory Farmhouse

7
The Gate (PH)
Broomhill House
Mount Cottages
The Grove
Works
Granthams Bridge
Lower Barn
Sandalwood
Rectory Farmhouse

37
Stumbleholm Farm
Furlong Farm
RUSPER RD
COOLHAM

6
Golf and Country Club
Golf Course
CH
Ifield Park
Ifield Mill

5
Hyde Hill
Hyde Hill Brook
D5
1 FULMAR CL
2 GUILLEMOT PATH
3 STONEYCROFT WLK
4 THE ORCHARDS
5 REDSHANK GT
6 SHEARWATER CT
7 BOWNESS CL
Moor Park Cres
Ifield Mill

36
Sandpiper Cl
Fairway
Coniston Cl
Ifield Mill Pond
Waterfield Cty Fst Sch

4
Burnt Stubbs
House Copse
Upper Bewbush
Kilwood Farm
Bewbush Brook

3
Kilnwood Copse
Kilnwood
Capon Grove
Spruce Hill Brook
Bewbush Schs
Bewbush
PO SQ

35
Pondtail Shaw
Leisure Ctr
Douster Brook

2
Fullers Shaw
HOWARD RD 1
BEWBUSH MANOR 2
SHIRLEY CL 3
WARRINGTON CL 4
PETERLEE WLK 5
CUMBERNAULD WLK 6
HATFIELD WLK 7
Manorfields
A2220   HORSHAM RD
Buchan Park

1
CRAWLEY RD
Hopper Farm
Holmbush Farm
BURNS WAY
Ind Est
Spruce Hill
Buchan Country Park
Douster Pond
Creasy's Forest
Target Hill
A264

34
Silver Hill
Island Pond
Middle Covert
Island Pond

22 A   B 23 C   D 24 E   F

F3
1 BERSTEAD WLK
2 DONNINGTON CT
3 HASSOCKS CT
4 PYECOMBE CT
5 TELHAM CT
6 WARBLETON HOUSE
7 CALDBECK HOUSE
8 HALNAKER WLK
9 ICKLESHAM HOUSE

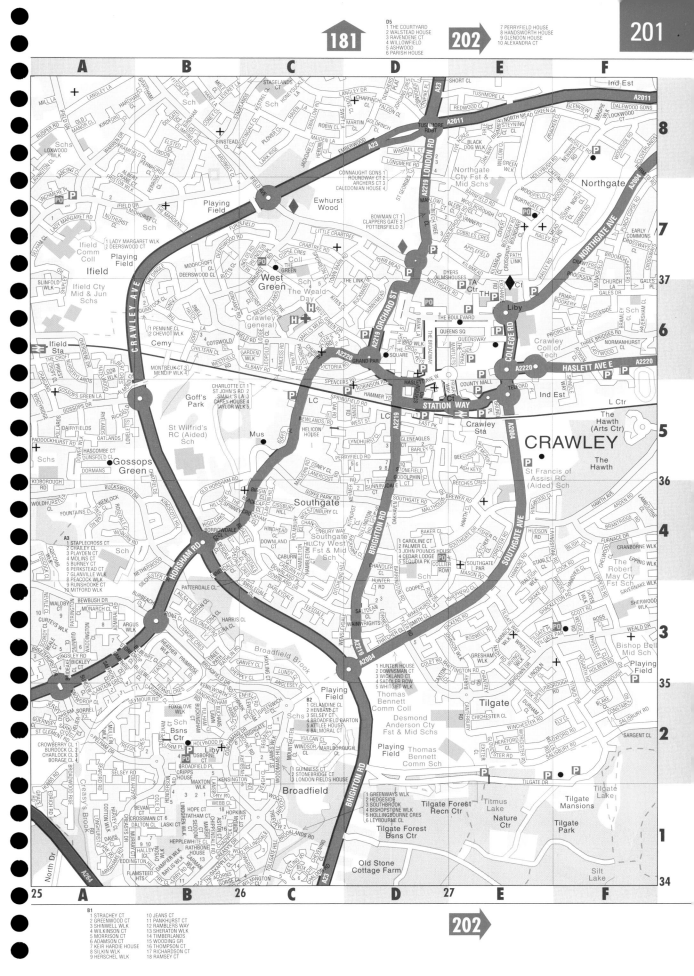

181

202

D5
1 THE COURTYARD
2 WALSTEAD HOUSE
3 RAVENDENE CT
4 WILLOWFIELD
5 ASHWOOD
6 PARISH HOUSE

7 PERRYFIELD HOUSE
8 HANDSWORTH HOUSE
9 GLENDON HOUSE
10 ALEXANDRA CT

CRAWLEY

A3
1 STAPLECROSS CT
2 CHAILEY CT
3 PLAYDEN CT
4 MOLINS CT
5 BURNEY CT
6 PERKSTEAD CT
7 GLANVILLE WLK
8 PEACOCK WLK
9 RUNSHOOKE CT
10 MITFORD WLK

B2
1 CELANDINE CL
2 HENBANE CT
3 BROADFIELD BARTON
4 ATTLEE HOUSE
5 BALMORAL CT

B1
1 STRACHEY CT
2 GREENWOOD CT
3 SHINWELL WLK
4 WILKINSON CT
5 MORRISON CT
6 ADAMSON CT
7 KEIR HARDIE HOUSE
8 SILKIN WLK
9 HERSCHEL WLK
10 JEANS CT
11 PANKHURST CT
12 RAMBLERS WAY
13 SHERATON WLK
14 TIMBERLANDS
15 WOODING GR
16 THOMPSON CT
17 RICHARDSON CT
18 RAMSEY CT

201
182

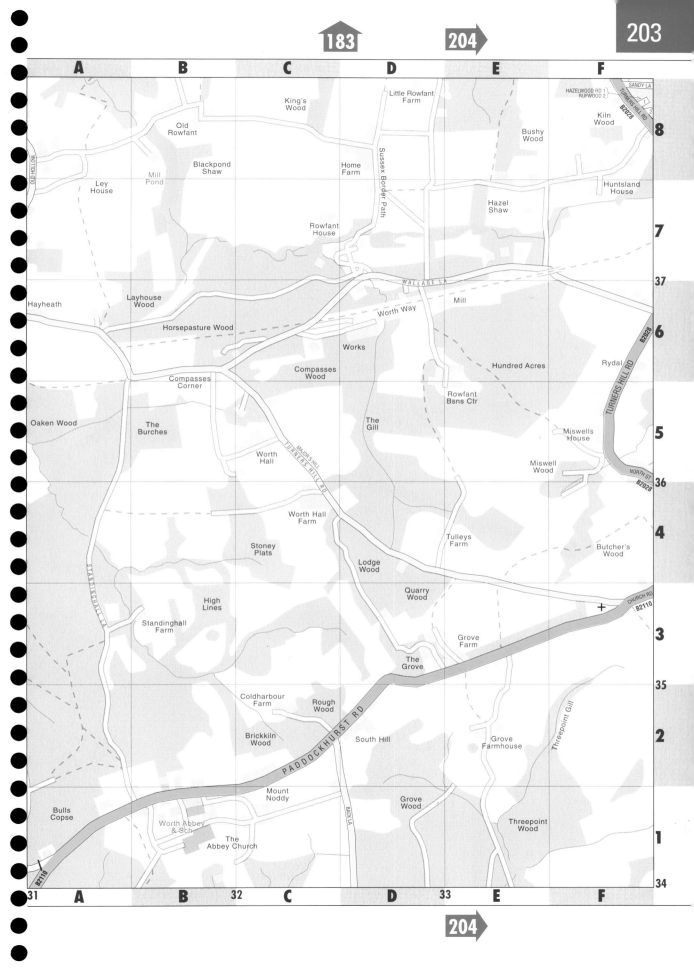

203

184

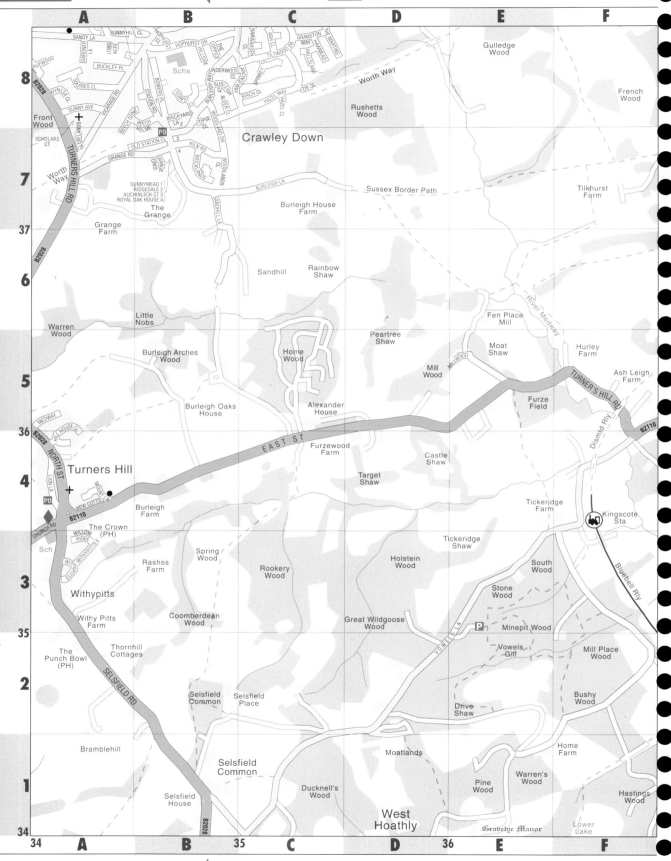

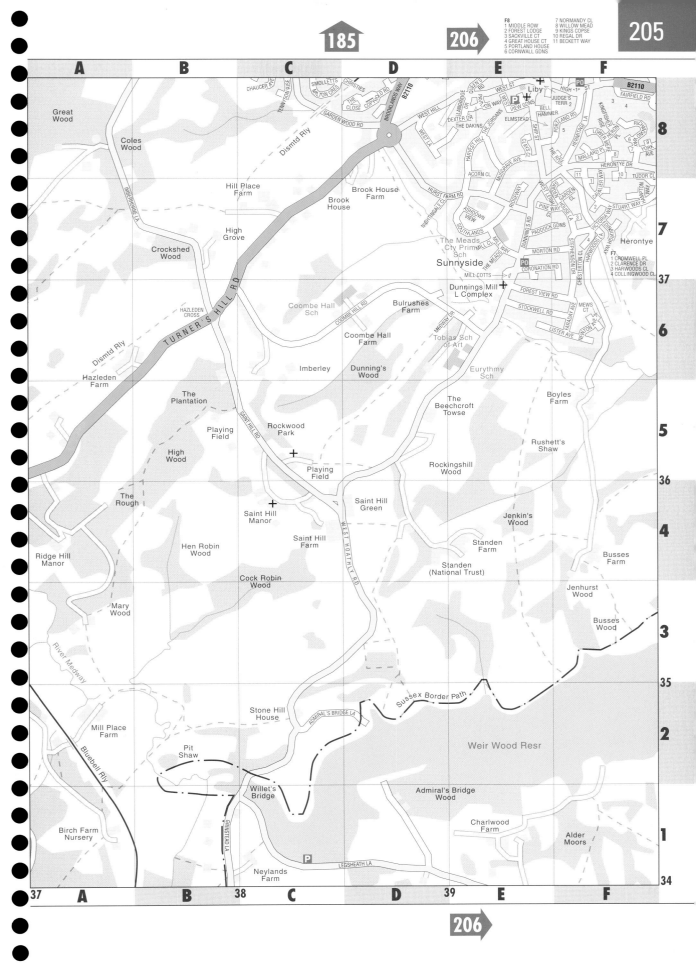

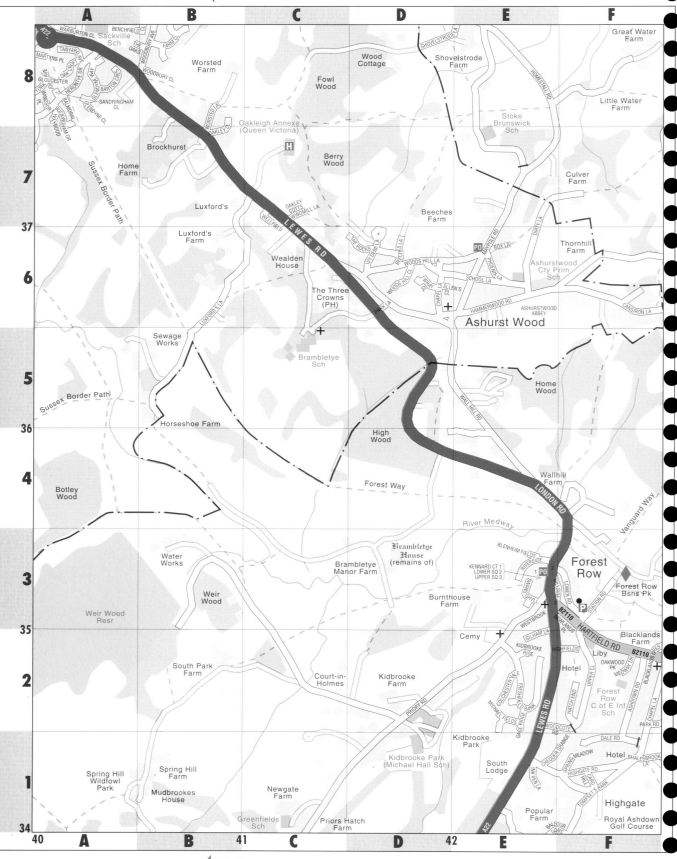

205

186

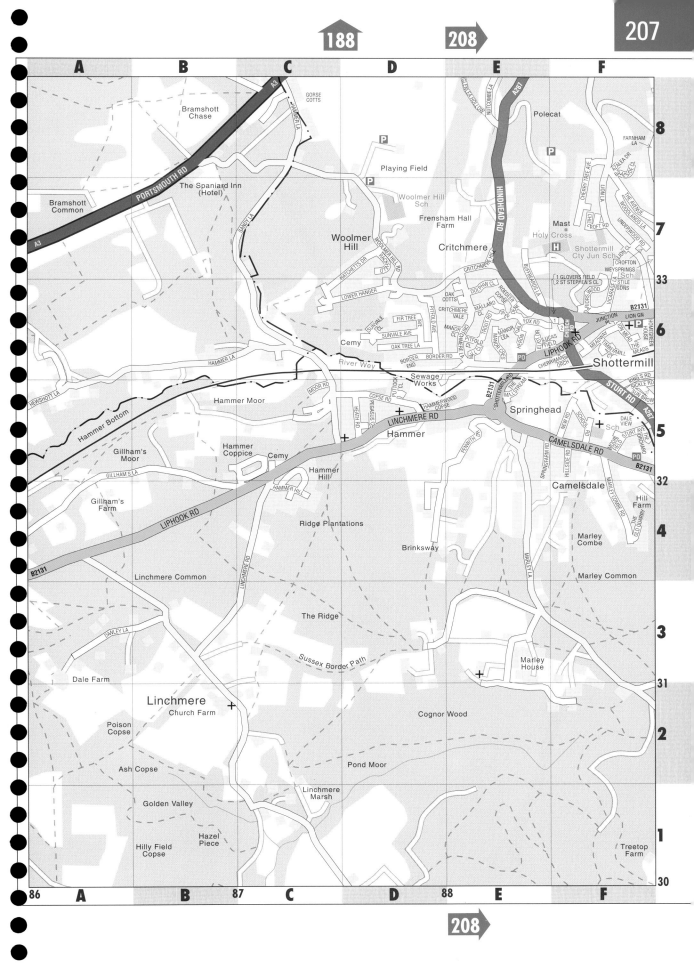

188
208
208

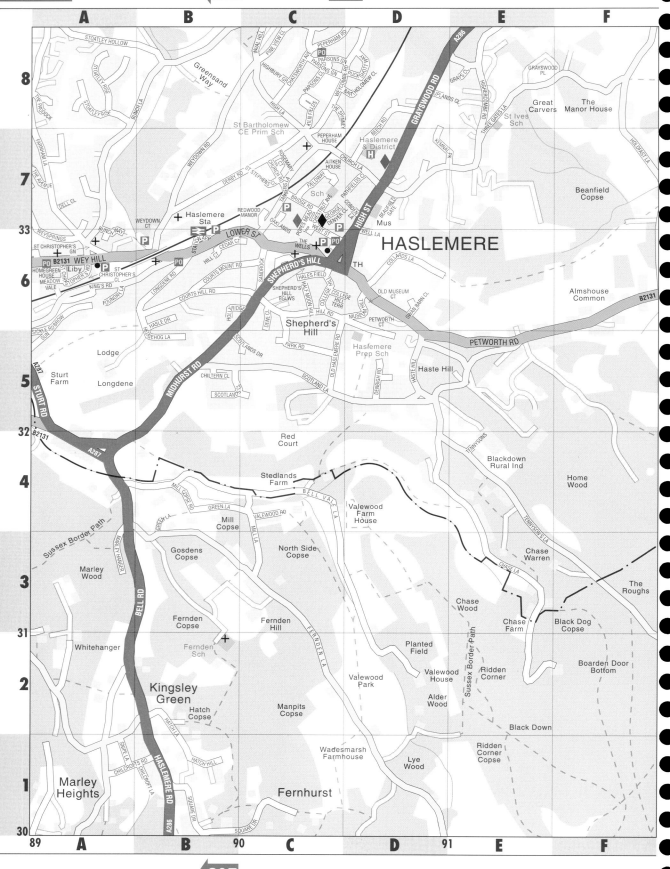

207
189

HASLEMERE

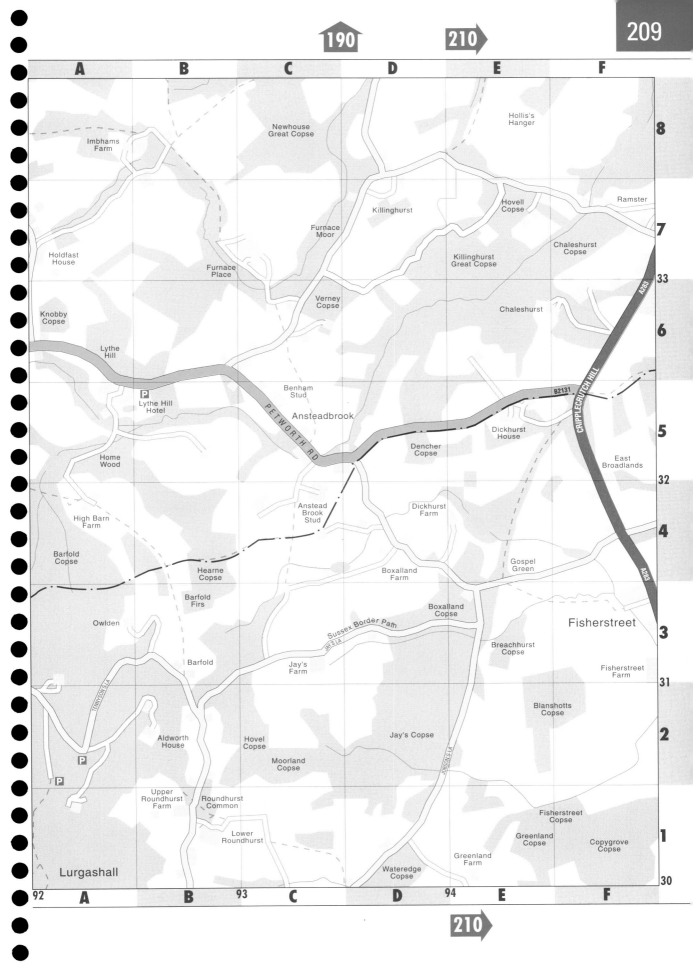

A B C D E F

8

Hollis's Hanger

Imbhams Farm

Newhouse Great Copse

Killinghurst

Hovell Copse

Ramster

7

Holdfast House

Furnace Moor

Furnace Place

Killinghurst Great Copse

Chaleshurst Copse

A283

33

Verney Copse

Chaleshurst

Knobby Copse

6

Lythe Hill

Benham Stud

B2131

CRIPPLECRUTCH HILL

PETWORTH RD

Ansteadbrook

Dickhurst House

5

East Broadlands

P
Lythe Hill Hotel

Dencher Copse

32

Home Wood

Anstead Brook Stud

Dickhurst Farm

High Barn Farm

4

Gospel Green

A283

Barfold Copse

Hearne Copse

Boxalland Farm

Barfold Firs

Boxalland Copse

Owlden

Sussex Border Path

JAY'S LA

Fisherstreet

3

Breachhurst Copse

Fisherstreet Farm

31

Barfold

Jay's Farm

TENNYSON'S LA

Blanshotts Copse

2

Aldworth House

Hovel Copse

Jay's Copse

Moorland Copse

JOBSON'S LA

P

P

Fisherstreet Copse

1

Upper Roundhurst Farm

Roundhurst Common

Greenland Copse

Copygrove Copse

Lower Roundhurst

Greenland Farm

Lurgashall

Wateredge Copse

30

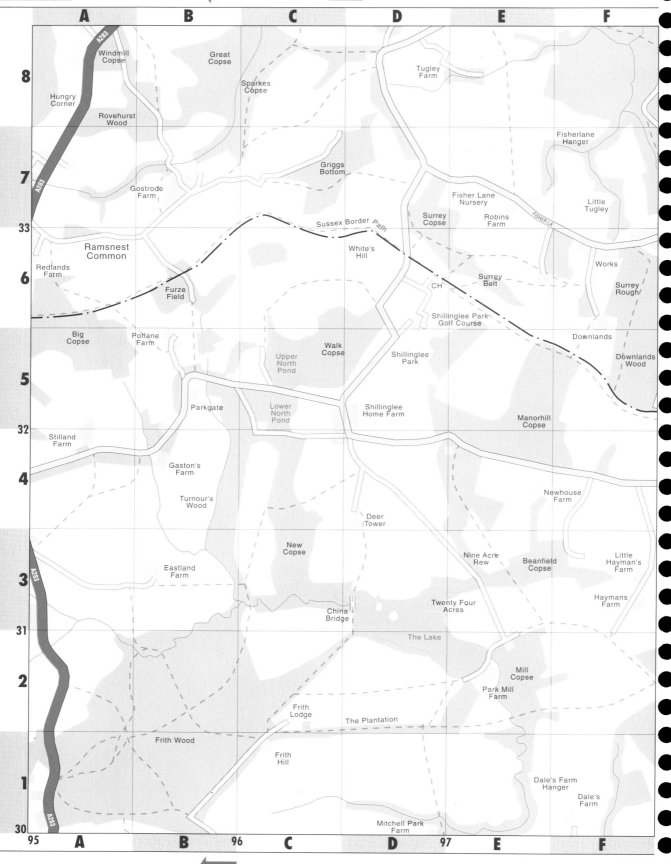

209
191
209

A B C D E F

8

Windmill Copse
Great Copse
Tugley Farm
Hungry Corner
Sparkes Copse
Rovehurst Wood
Fisherlane Hanger

7

Griggs Bottom
Gostrode Farm
Fisher Lane Nursery
Little Tugley
Robins Farm

33

Sussex Border Path
Surrey Copse

Ramsnest Common
White's Hill
Surrey Belt
Works

6

Redlands Farm
Furze Field
CH
Surrey Rough
Shillinglee Park Golf Course
Downlands

Big Copse
Potlane Farm
Walk Copse
Shillinglee Park
Downlands Wood

Upper North Pond

5

Parkgate
Lower North Pond
Shillinglee Home Farm
Manorhill Copse

Stilland Farm

32

Gaston's Farm

4

Turnour's Wood
Newhouse Farm

Deer Tower

New Copse
Nine Acre Rew
Beanfield Copse
Little Hayman's Farm

3

Eastland Farm
Twenty Four Acres
Haymans Farm

China Bridge

31

The Lake
Mill Copse

2

Park Mill Farm

Frith Lodge
The Plantation

Frith Wood

Dale's Farm Hanger

1

Frith Hill
Dale's Farm

30

Mitchell Park Farm

95 A B 96 C D 97 E F

A   B   C   D   E   F

Oaken Wood

Canterbury Copse

Ireland

Hurlands Copse

8

Burntwood Kennels

Old Lands

Peartree Hanger

The Hatchetts

Inside Copse

PLAISTOW RD

Oak Wood

Tidy's Copse

Tugley Wood

Durfold Hall

7

Durfold Hatch Cottage

Birch Copse

FISHER LA

33

Oakhurst Farm

Dungate Farm

Upper Ifold Wood

Sussex Border Path

6

Fisherlane Wood

Durfold Wood

Weald Barkfold Copse

DURFOLD WOOD

Downlands Wood

Shortland Copse

5

32

East End Farm

Barkfold Hanger

DUNSFOLD RD

Ashpark Wood

Weald Barkfold

4

Works

Short's Farm

Oakhurst

Highbridge House

Lyon's Farm

COUNCIL COTTS

3

Kingspark Wood

Plaistow Cty Inf Sch

31

THE STREET

BACK LA

NETT BALL

PO

LOXWOOD RD

Ifold Copse

2

Plaistow

Beggars Copse

Birchfold Copse

RUSHFIELD

RICKMAN'S LA

1

Sparrwood Hangar

Rumbolds Farm

Rumbold Wood

Chilsfold Farm

30

211
193

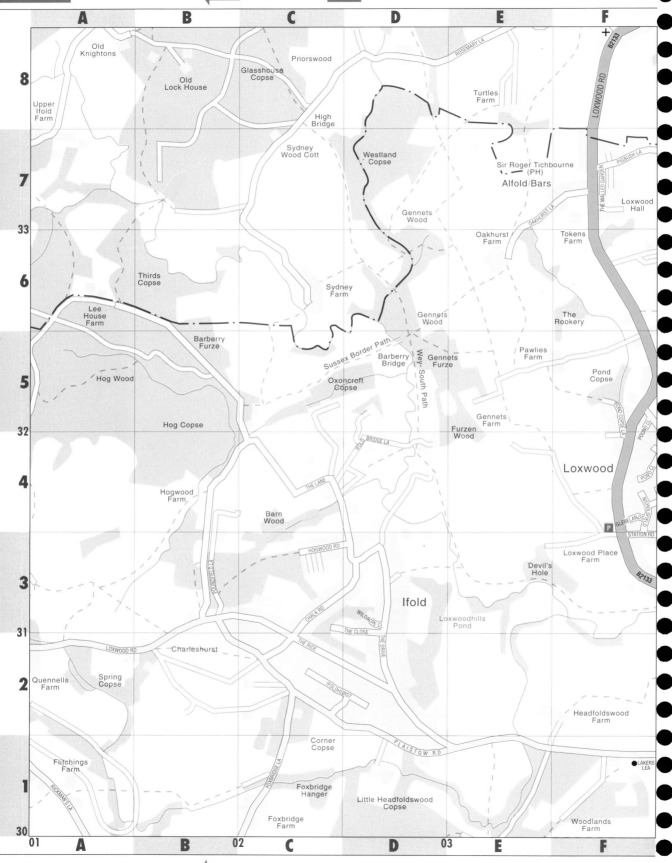

211

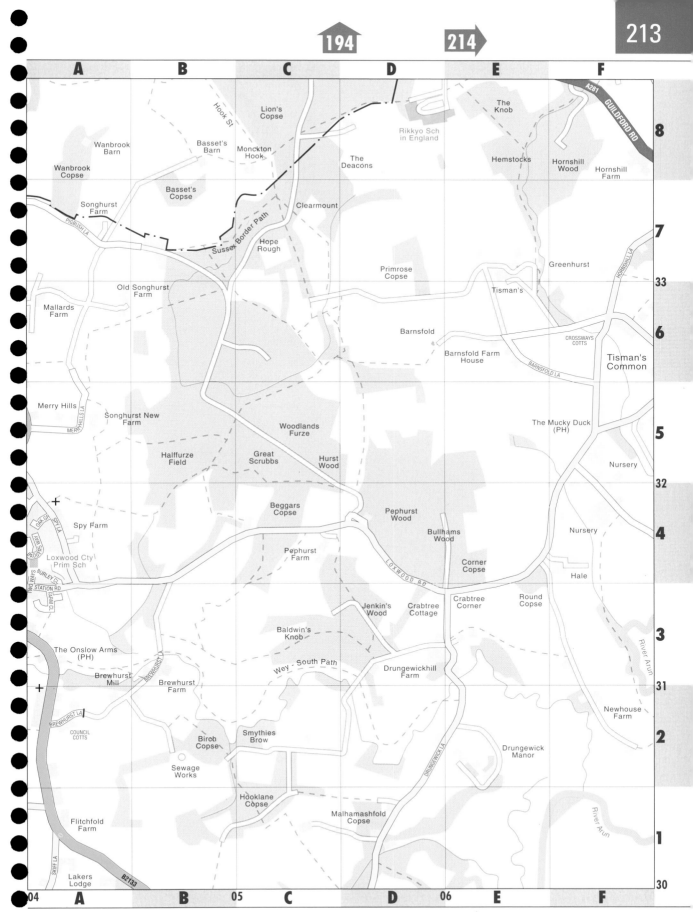

A   B   C   D   E   F

8

GUILDFORD RD
A281

The Knob

Rikkyo Sch
in England

Lion's
Copse

Hook St.

Wanbrook
Barn

Basset's
Barn

Monckton
Hook

The Deacons

Hemstocks

Hornshill
Wood

Hornshill
Farm

Wanbrook
Copse

Basset's
Copse

Songhurst
Farm

Clearmount

7

PIGBUSH LA

Sussex Border Path

Hope
Rough

Greenhurst

HORNSHILL LA

Primrose
Copse

33

Old Songhurst
Farm

Tisman's

Mallards
Farm

Barnsfold

6

Barnsfold Farm
House

CROSSWAYS
COTTS

BARNSFOLD LA

Tisman's
Common

Merry Hills

MERRY HILLS LA

Songhurst New
Farm

Woodlands
Furze

The Mucky Duck
(PH)

5

Nursery

Halffurze
Field

Great
Scrubbs

Hurst
Wood

32

Beggars
Copse

Pephurst
Wood

Nursery

4

Spy Farm

SPY LA

OAK GR
KWM
PADGES

Pephurst
Farm

Bullhams
Wood

Hale

LOXWOOD RD

Loxwood Cty
Prim Sch

BURLEY CL

STATION RD

FARM CL
KWM SWAN

Corner
Copse

Crabtree
Corner

Round
Copse

Jenkin's
Wood

Crabtree
Cottage

3

The Onslow Arms
(PH)

Baldwin's
Knob

River Arun

BREWHURST LA

Wey - South Path

Drungewickhill
Farm

Brewhurst
Mill

Brewhurst
Farm

31

BREWHURST LA

Newhouse
Farm

COUNCIL
COTTS

Birch
Copse

Smythies
Brow

2

DRUNGEWICK LA

Drungewick
Manor

Sewage
Works

Hooklane
Copse

Malhamashfold
Copse

Flitchfold
Farm

1

River Arun

SKIFF LA

Lakers
Lodge

B2133

30

A   04   B   05   C   D   06   E   F

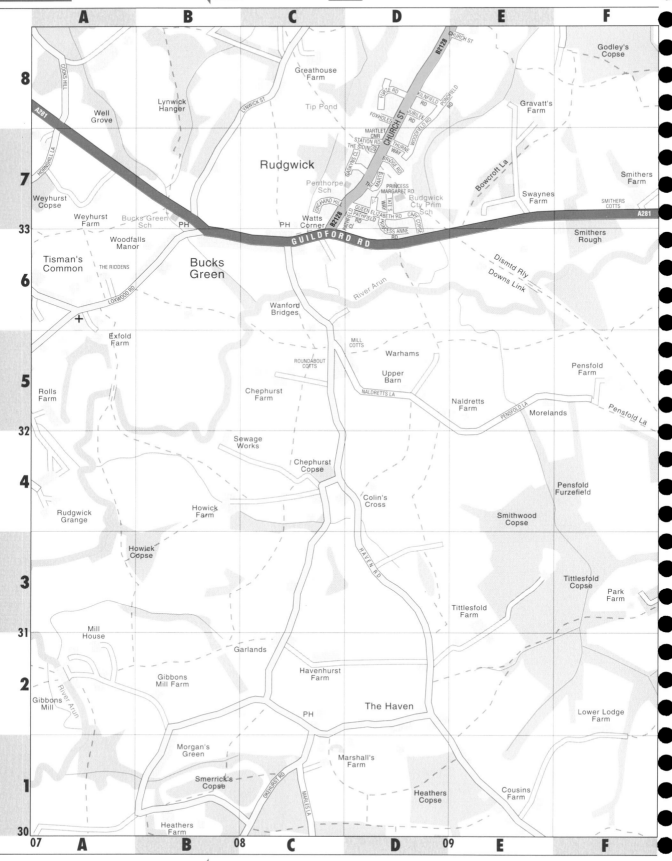

Godley's Copse

CHURCH ST

B2128

8

Greathouse Farm

Lynwick Hanger

LYNWICK ST

Tip Pond

FURZE RD

KILNFIELD RD

PONDFIELD RD

JUBILEE RD

Gravatt's Farm

Well Grove

FOXHOLES

CHURCH ST

WOODFIELD RD

THURNE WAY

A281

Rudgwick

MARTLET CNR

STATION RD

THE SIDINGS

GASKYNS CL

Smithers Farm

7

Weyhurst Copse

HORNSHILL LA

Penthorpe Sch

BRIDGE RD

PRINCESS MARGARET RD

QUEEN ELIZABETH RD

Rudgwick Cty Prim Sch

Bowcroft La

Swaynes Farm

SMITHERS COTTS

Weyhurst Farm

Bucks Green Sch

PH

Watts Corner

PH

B2128

ORCHARD HILL

PATHFIELD CL

TATE'S WAY

PRINCESS ANNE RD

CAP COPSE

33

Woodfalls Manor

PH

GUILDFORD RD

Smithers Rough

A281

Tisman's Common

THE RIDDENS

Bucks Green

Dismtd Rly

Downs Link

6

LOXWOOD RD

Wanford Bridges

River Arun

+

MILL COTTS

Exfold Farm

Warhams

Pensfold Farm

ROUNDABOUT COTTS

Upper Barn

5

Rolls Farm

Chephurst Farm

NALDRETTS LA

Naldretts Farm

PENSFOLD LA

Morelands

Pensfold La

32

Sewage Works

Chephurst Copse

Pensfold Furzefield

4

Rudgwick Grange

Howick Farm

Colin's Cross

Smithwood Copse

Howick Copse

HAVEN RD

Tittlesfold Copse

Park Farm

3

Tittlesfold Farm

31

Mill House

Garlands

Gibbons Mill Farm

Havenhurst Farm

Lower Lodge Farm

2

River Arun

Gibbons Mill

PH

The Haven

Morgan's Green

OKEHURST RD

MARLES LA

Marshall's Farm

1

Smerrick's Copse

Heathers Copse

Cousins Farm

Heathers Farm

30

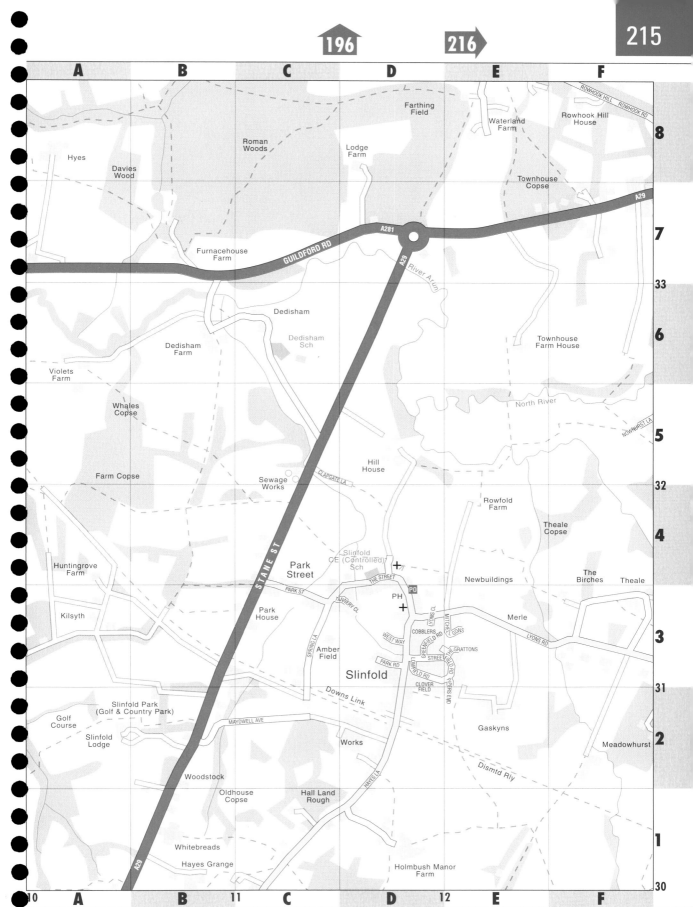

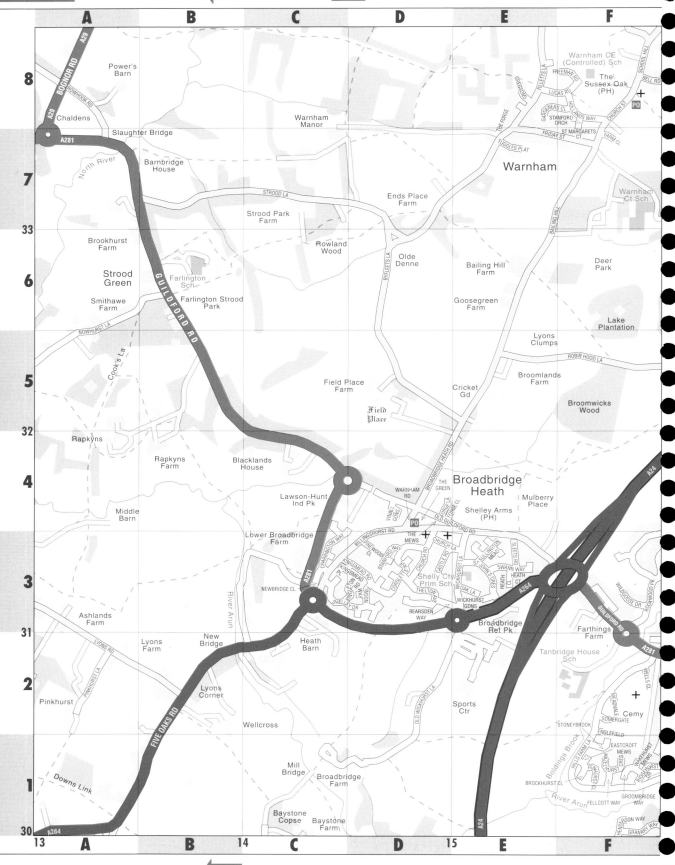

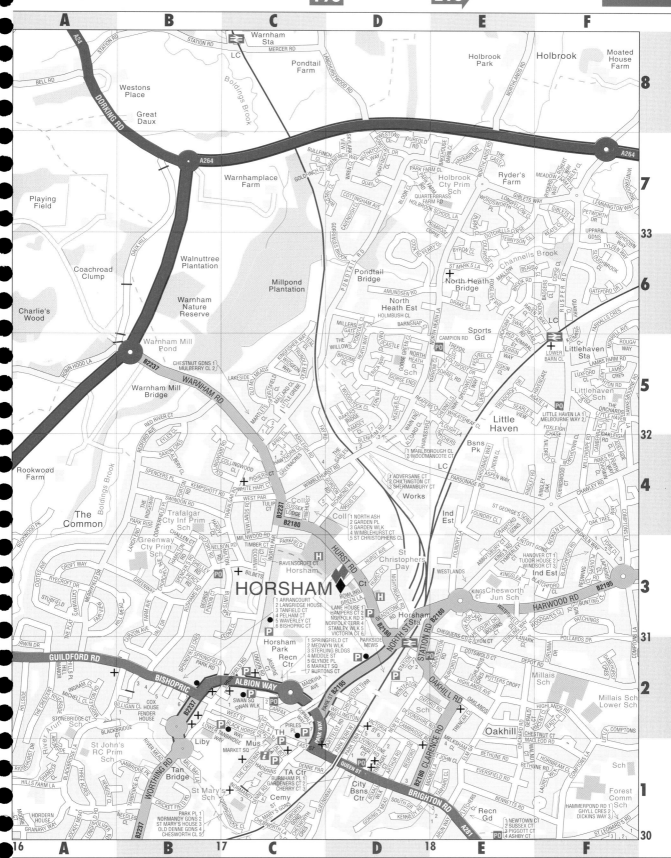

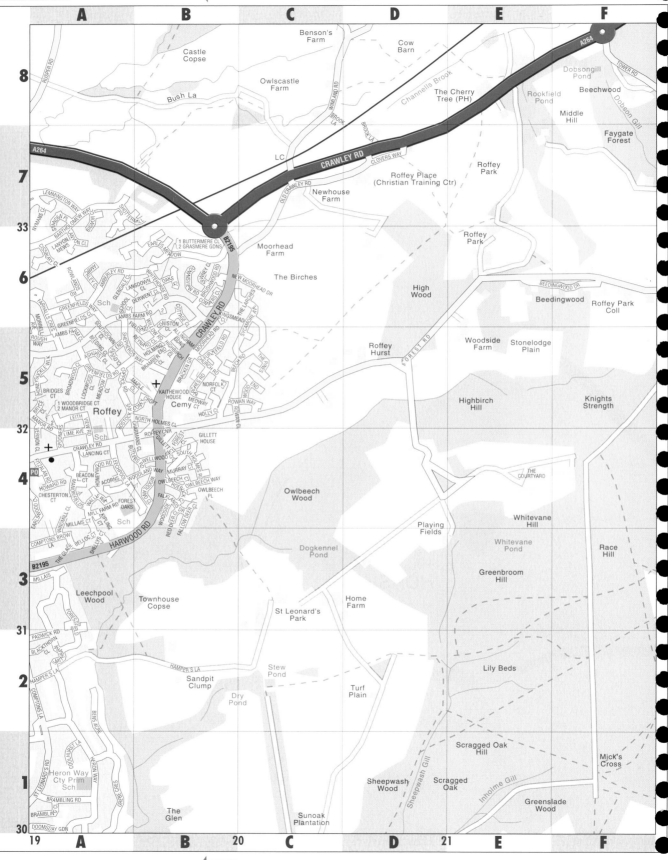

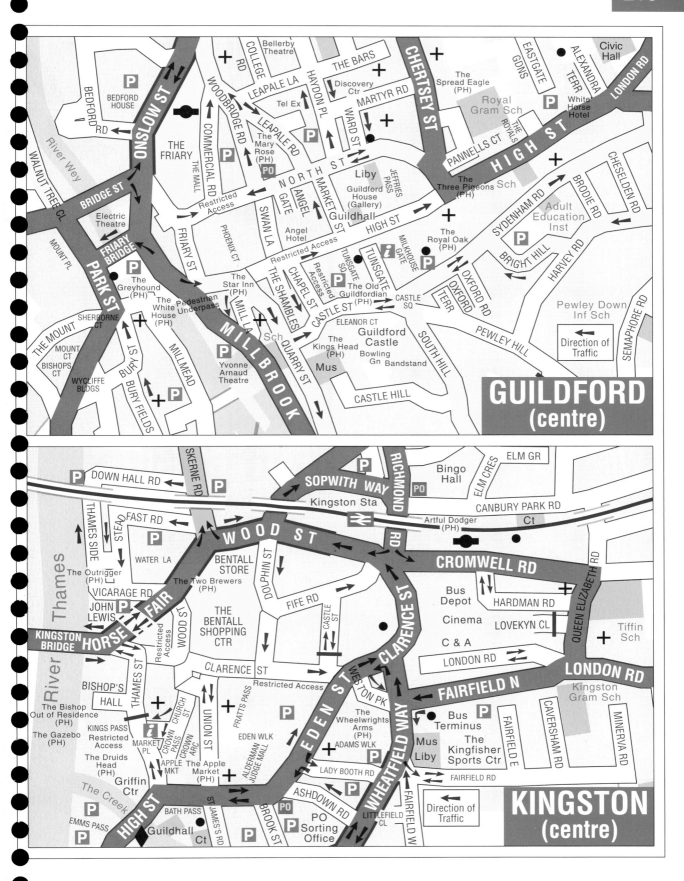

GUILDFORD (centre)

KINGSTON (centre)

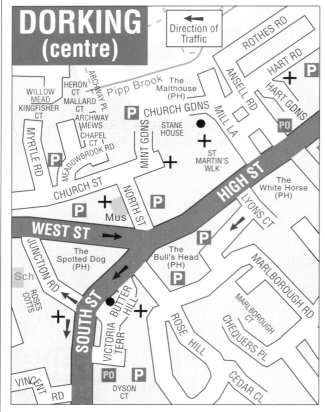

DORKING (centre)

Direction of Traffic

EPSOM (centre)

Direction of Traffic

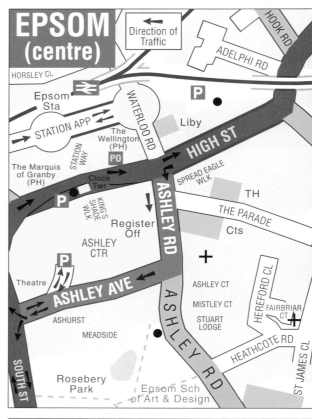

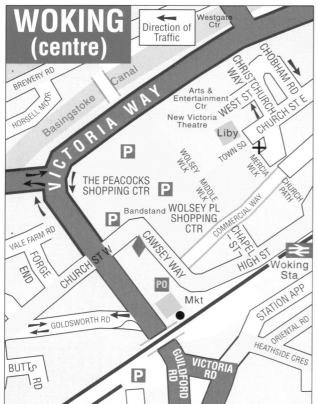

WOKING (centre)

Direction of Traffic

LEATHERHEAD (centre)

Direction of Traffic

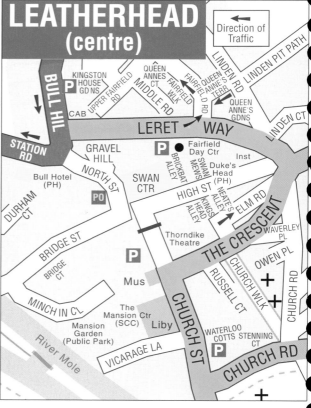

How to use the index

Street names are listed alphabetically and show the locality, the Postcode District, the page number and a reference to the square in which the name falls on the map page

Elizabeth Cotts. 5 Rich TW9 ..7 A6

- **Full street name** This may have been abbreviated on the map
- **Location Number** If present, this indicates the street's position on a congested area of the map instead of the name
- **Town, village or locality** in which the street falls. This may be indicated by one of the abbreviations listed below
- **Postcode District** for the street name
- **Page number** of the map on which the street name appears
- **Grid square** in which the centre of the street falls

Schools, hospitals, sports centres, railway stations, shopping centres, industrial estates, public amenities and other places of interest are also listed. These are highlighted in magenta

Abbreviations used in the index

App	Approach
Arc	Arcade
Ave	Avenue
Bvd	Boulevard
Bldgs	Buildings
Bsns Pk	Business Park
Bsns Ctr	Business Centre
Bglws	Bungalows
Cswy	Causeway
Ctr	Centre
Cir	Circus
Cl	Close
Comm	Common
Cnr	Corner
Cotts	Cottages
Ct	Court
Ctyd	Courtyard
Cres	Crescent
Dr	Drive
Dro	Drove
E	East
Emb	Embankment
Espl	Esplanade
Est	Estate
Gdns	Gardens
Gn	Green
Gr	Grove
Hts	Heights
Ind Est	Industrial Estate
Intc	Interchange
Junc	Junction
La	Lane
N	North
Orch	Orchard
Par	Parade
Pk	Park
Pas	Passage
Pl	Place
Prec	Precinct
Prom	Promenade
Ret Pk	Retail Park
Rd	Road
Rdbt	Roundabout
S	South
Sq	Square
Strs	Stairs
Stps	Steps
St	Street, Saint
Terr	Terrace
Trad Est	Trading Estate
Wlk	Walk
W	West
Yd	Yard

Abbreviations of town, village and rural locality names

Abbots	Abbotswood	109 F3
Abing C	Abinger Common	155 D8
Abing H	Abinger Hammer	33 F3
Add	Addington	63 A5
Addl	Addlestone	52 A6
Albury	Albury	132 C4
Alder	Aldershot	105 B1
Alf Cr	Alfold Crossways	194 A3
Alfold	Alfold	193 F1
Arting	Artington	130 C4
Ascot	Ascot	29 A6
Ash	Ash	106 B3
Ash V	Ash Vale	106 B7
Ash W	Ashurst Wood	206 E6
Ashf	Ashford	13 F2
Ashtd	Ashtead	75 E1
Bagsh	Bagshot	47 D3
Balham	Balham	21 A7
Banstd	Banstead	78 B3
Barnes	Barnes	7 F6
Beac H	Beacon Hill	188 C6
Bear Gn	Beare Green	157 D3
Beck	Beckenham	44 A7
Bellf	Bellfields	109 C4
Belm	Belmont	59 A2
Bentl	Bentley	145 A7
Betch	Betchworth	137 E8
Bigg H	Biggin Hill	83 E3
Binf	Binfield	26 C8
Binst	Binstead	166 A5
Bisley	Bisley	68 B3
Blckw	Blackwater	64 D4
Bletch	Bletchingley	120 D2
Blind H	Blindley Heath	163 D8
Bowl Gn	Bowlhead Green	169 E1
Box H	Box Hill	116 A4
Bra Hil	Brands Hill	1 A8
Brack	Bracknell	27 D6
Bramly	Bramley	151 F6
Bramsh	Bramshott	187 D1
Brent	Brentford	6 D7
Broad H	Broadbridge Heath	216 E4
Brock	Brockham	137 C7
Broml	Bromley	44 E8
Brook	Brook	170 B1
Brookw	Brookwood	88 A7
Buck Gn	Bucks Green	214 B6
Buckl	Buckland	117 A2
Burgh H	Burgh Heath	97 D8
Burph	Burpham	110 A5
Burrh	Burrowhill	49 E3
Burst	Burstow	183 A7
Byfl	Byfleet	71 D7
Camb	Camberley	65 D6
Capel	Capel	178 C6
Carsh	Carshalton	59 E6
Cater	Caterham	100 F4
Catf	Catford	24 A7
Charl	Charlwood	180 E7
Charlt	Charlton	34 D7
Cheam	Cheam	58 F5
Chelsh	Chelsham	82 A2
Chert	Chertsey	33 B2
Chess	Chessington	56 E4
Chidd	Chiddingfold	191 B4
Chil	Chilworth	131 C3
Chips	Chipstead	78 F1
Chisw	Chiswick	7 D7
Chobh	Chobham	49 F2
Chur C	Church Crookham	104 A7
Churt	Churt	167 E1
Clayg	Claygate	55 F3
Cobham	Cobham	73 B5
Coldh	Coldharbour	156 E4
Coln	Colnbrook	1 D7
Compt	Compton	129 B3
Coney H	Coney Hall	63 F7
Copth	Copthorne	183 C3
Coulsd	Coulsdon	79 D3
Cox Gn	Cox Green	195 E1
Cran	Cranleigh	174 D2
Cranf	Cranford	4 C6
Crawl	Crawley	201 F5
Crawl D	Crawley Down	204 C7
Crock H	Crockham Hill	144 F8
Crond	Crondall	124 A5
Crow	Crowhurst	143 E3
Crowth	Crowthorne	45 D5
Croy	Croydon	61 D8
Cudw	Cudworth	179 F8
Docken	Dockenfield	166 E6
Dome	Domewood	184 A5
Dork	Dorking	136 C6
Dorm Pk	Dormans Park	185 E6
Dorman	Dormansland	165 B1
Dovgn	Doversgreen	139 B5
Downe	Downe	83 F8
Downs	Downside	93 B8
Dulw	Dulwich	22 E5
Dunsf	Dunsfold	192 F5
E Bed	East Bedfont	14 E7
E Clan	East Clandon	111 E4
E Ewell	East Ewell	58 D1
E Grins	East Grinstead	185 E2
E Hors	East Horsley	112 E8
E Mole	East Molesey	36 C4
Earls	Earlswood	140 A7
Easth	Easthampstead	27 B5
Eden	Edenbridge	144 F4
Effing	Effingham	113 E8
Egham	Egham	12 A3
Ell Gn	Ellen's Green	196 A4
Elst	Elstead	148 D3
Eng Gn	Englefield Green	11 C2
Ent Gn	Enton Green	171 B5
Epsom	Epsom	76 C5
Esher	Esher	55 C6
Ewell	Ewell	58 A1
Ewh	Ewhurst	175 F5
Fairl	Fairlands	108 C4
Farl Gn	Farley Green	153 E7
Farlgh	Farleigh	81 F5
Farnb	Farnborough	85 B3
Farnc	Farncombe	150 E8
Farnh	Farnham	125 B1
Faygt	Faygate	199 F1
Felb	Felbridge	184 F4
Felct	Felcourt	185 C8
Felt	Feltham	15 A7
Fern	Fernhurst	208 C1
Fetch	Fetcham	94 C4
Fickl	Fickleshoe	82 E5
Fish	Fisherstreet	209 F3
Flexf	Flexford	107 C1
For Gn	Forest Green	176 E7
For Hil	Forest Hill	23 D7
For Row	Forest Row	206 F3
Frensh	Frensham	167 D7
Friml	Frimley	65 F2
G Book	Great Bookham	94 B1
Gatton	Gatton	118 F7
Godal	Godalming	150 F3
Godst	Godstone	121 B3
Gomsh	Gomshall	133 D4
Grays	Grayswood	189 F1
Graysh	Grayshott	188 C3
Guild	Guildford	130 B8
Hackb	Hackbridge	60 B8
Hale	Hale	125 C6
Hambl	Hambledon	171 D2
Hammer	Hammerwood	186 F2
Hampt	Hampton	36 A7
Hams Gn	Hamsey Green	81 C4
Harl	Harlington	3 C8
Harm	Harmondsworth	2 E8
Hasc	Hascombe	172 D4
Haslem	Haslemere	208 D6
Hatton	Hatton	3 F2
Hawley	Hawley	64 E3
Haxted	Haxted	165 F8
Hayes	Hayes	44 F3
Head	Headley	96 C2
Head Dn	Headley Down	157 B4
Heath E	Heath End	125 D6
Hersh	Hersham	54 D5
Heston	Heston	4 F7
Hinch W	Hinchley Wood	55 F7
Hind	Hindhead	188 F4
Hol St M	Holmbury St Mary	155 B5
Hookw	Hookwood	160 D2
Hooley	Hooley	99 B5
Horley	Horley	161 C3
Horne	Horne	162 F5
Horse	Horsell	69 D3
Horsh	Horsham	217 C3
Horton	Horton	1 A4
Hounsl	Hounslow	5 A5
Hyde	Hydestile	171 E6
Ifold	Ifold	212 D3
Islew	Isleworth	6 B4
Jacobs	Jacobswell	109 D7
Kenley	Kenley	80 D3
King Gn	Kingsley Green	208 B2
King U T	Kingston Upon Thames	37 C6
Kings	Kingswood	97 F6
Knaph	Knaphill	68 D1
L Book	Little Bookham	93 E3
L Kings	Lower Kingswood	117 E8
Laleh	Laleham	33 C6
Lamb Gn	Lambs Green	199 F6
Lang V	Langley Vale	96 D8
Leahd	Leatherhead	95 D5
Leigh	Leigh	138 B2
Lewish	Lewisham	24 C8
Lhtwat	Lightwater	66 F8
Limps	Limpsfield	123 A6
Linch	Linchmere	207 B2
Lingf	Lingfield	164 D5
Littlt	Littleton	34 A6
Lo Hall	Lower Halliford	34 D2
Long D	Long Ditton	37 C1
Longc	Longcross	50 A7
Loxwd	Loxwood	212 F4
Lurg	Lurgashall	209 A1
Lyne	Lyne	32 B1
M Bourne	Middle Bourne	146 C7
Marl Ht	Marley Heights	208 A1
Mart Gn	Martyr's Green	92 E7
Mayb	Maybury	70 C2
Merrow	Merrow	110 C2
Merst	Merstham	119 D7
Merton	Merton	39 F7
Mickle	Mickleham	115 C7
Milf	Milford	149 E1
Mitch	Mitcham	40 F5
Morden	Morden	40 B3
Mortl	Mortlake	7 C4
Mytch	Mytchett	85 F3
N Asct	North Ascot	28 E8
N Cheam	North Cheam	58 C8
New Add	New Addington	63 D3
New Gn	Newell Green	8 A1
New Haw	New Haw	52 C3
New Mal	New Malden	38 F5
Newch	Newchapel	163 F1
Newd	Newdigate	158 B1
Nork	Nork	77 D4
Normdy	Normandy	107 A3
Nutf	Nutfield	119 F2
Oakwd	Oakwoodhill	197 A7
Oat Pk	Oatlands Park	53 E6
Ock Rid	Ockford Ridge	150 B3
Ockham	Ockham	92 B6
Ockley	Ockley	177 D5
Old W	Old Windsor	11 A8
Old Wok	Old Woking	90 A7
Onsl V	Onslow Village	129 F7
Ottsh	Ottershaw	51 D5
Outw	Outwood	162 B7
Oxsh	Oxshott	74 C6
Oxted	Oxted	122 E5
P Harow	Peper Harow	149 C5
Parkg	Parkgate	158 D4
Peasl	Peaslake	154 D6
Penge	Penge	23 D2
Pirb	Pirbright	87 F4
Pixham	Pixham	115 D1
Plaist	Plaistow	211 F2
Poyle	Poyle	1 E6
Purley	Purley	80 A7
Putney	Putney	19 D7
Putt	Puttenham	128 C4
Pyrf	Pyrford	70 E4
Redh	Redhill	118 E2
Reig	Reigate	118 B2
Rhampt	Roehampton	7 F2
Rich	Richmond	6 D2
Ripley	Ripley	91 C6
Row Tn	Row Town	51 F4
Rowhk	Rowhook	196 E1
Rowl	Rowledge	145 F3
Rowly	Rowly	174 B6
Rudg	Rudgwick	214 C7
Rushm	Rushmoor	168 C5
Rusper	Rusper	199 D7
S Croy	South Croydon	61 D3
S Godst	South Godstone	14 F5
S Holm	South Holmwood	157 C7
S Norw	South Norwood	42 E5
S Nutf	South Nutfield	140 E7
Salfs	Salfords	140 B1
Sander	Sanderstead	80 F6
Sandh	Sandhurst	64 C7
Seale	Seale	127 B4
Selsd	Selsdon	62 D1
Send	Send	90 C4
Send M	Send Marsh	90 F3
Shackl	Shackleford	149 D7
Shalf	Shalford	130 E2
Sham Gn	Shamley Green	152 E5
Sheer	Sheerwater	70 D6
Shep	Shepperton	34 C3
Shep Gn	Shepperton Green	34 B5
Shere	Shere	133 B4
Shottm	Shottermill	207 F6
Sidlow	Sidlow	139 B2
Slinfd	Slinfold	215 D3
Smallf	Smallfield	162 B2
Stain	Staines	12 F4
Stan	Stanwell	13 C7
Stk D'A	Stoke D'Abernon	73 F3
Stonel	Stoneleigh	58 A5
Stough	Stoughton	109 A4
Streat	Streatham	21 E2
Sunby	Sunbury	35 B6
Sunnin	Sunningdale	30 B4
Surb	Surbiton	37 E2
Sutton	Sutton	59 C5
Tadw	Tadworth	97 C5
Tand	Tandridge	122 A2
Tats	Tatsfield	103 D7
Tedd	Teddington	17 B3
Thame D	Thames Ditton	37 B2
The Char	The Chart	123 E5
The San	The Sands	126 E2
Thor L	Thorpe Lea	12 B1
Thorn H	Thornton Heath	42 B3
Thorpe	Thorpe	32 C6
Thursl	Thursley	169 C4
Tilf	Tilford	147 D3
Titsey	Titsey	103 B2
Tolw	Tolworth	57 B7
Tongh	Tongham	126 F6
Turn H	Turners Hill	204 A4
Twick	Twickenham	17 B8
Tyl Gn	Tyler's Green	121 C5
Up Hall	Upper Halliford	34 D5
UpToot	Upper Tooting	20 F5
Vir W	Virginia Water	31 C6
W Barn	West Barnes	39 C4
W Byfl	West Byfleet	71 B6
W Clan	West Clandon	111 B6
W End	West End	67 F6
W Ewell	West Ewell	57 E3
W Heath	West Heath	84 F6
W Hoath	West Hoathly	204 D1
W Hors	West Horsley	112 B8
W Norw	West Norwood	22 C5
W Wick	West Wickham	44 E1
Wall W	Wallis Wood	176 E1
Wallin	Wallington	60 A4
Walt O T	Walton-On-Thames	35 C2
Walt o t H	Walton on the Hill	97 A3
Wanb	Wanborough	128 C6
Wands	Wandsworth	20 C7
Warlgm	Warlingham	81 C1
Warn	Warnham	216 E7
Went	Wentworth	30 F3
Westc	Westcott	135 D6
Westfd	Westfield	89 E6
Westh	Westhumble	115 A4
Weyb	Weybridge	53 A6
Whit V	Whiteley Village	53 E1
Whytlf	Whyteleafe	80 F1
Wimble	Wimbledon	19 F2
Wind	Windsor	9 E8
Windl	Windlesham	48 C4
Wink	Winkfield	8 D4
Wisley	Wisley	71 E3
Witley	Witley	170 F4
Woki	Wokingham	25 B5
Woking	Woking	69 E1
Wold	Woldingham	102 A4
Woner	Wonersh	152 B7
Wood S V	Wood Street Village	108 B3
Woodc	Woodcote	76 D3
Woodh	Woodhatch	139 B7
Woodhm	Woodham	52 A1
Woodm	Woodmansterne	78 E4
Worc Pk	Worcester Park	57 E6
Wormly	Wormley	170 F1
Worpl	Worplesdon	108 D8
Worth	Worth	202 E6
Wotton	Wotton	134 F3
Wray	Wraysbury	11 E8
Wreccl	Wrecclesham	145 E6
Yatly	Yateley	64 A5

1st Ave. L Kings KT20 ..... 97 E2
2nd Ave. L Kings KT20 ..... 97 E2
3rd Ave. L Kings KT20 ..... 97 E2
4th Ave. L Kings KT20 ..... 97 E2
5th Ave. L Kings KT20 ..... 97 E2
6th Ave. L Kings KT20 ..... 97 E2
7th Ave. L Kings KT20 ..... 97 E2
8th Ave. L Kings KT20 ..... 97 E2
9th Ave. L Kings KT20 ..... 97 E2
10th Ave. Walt o t H KT20 ..... 97 A1
11th Ave. L Kings KT20 ..... 97 F1
12th Ave. L Kings KT20 ..... 97 F1
13th Ave. L Kings KT20 ..... 97 F1
14th Ave. L Kings KT20 ..... 97 F1
15th Ave. L Kings KT20 ..... 97 F1
16th Ave. L Kings KT20 ..... 97 F1
Aaron Ct. Beck BR3 ..... 44 B6
Aaron's Hill. Ock Rid GU7 ..... 150 B4
Abbess Cl. Streat SW2 ..... 22 B7
Abbetts La. Camb GU15 ..... 65 B3
Abbey Church The.
  Worth RH10 ..... 203 B1
Abbey Cl. Brack RG12 ..... 27 D4
Abbey Cl. Crawl GU6 ..... 173 F2
Abbey Cl. Pyrf GU22 ..... 70 E3
Abbey Cl. Woki RG11 ..... 25 C7
Abbey Ct. Camb GU15 ..... 65 D5
Abbey Ct. Chert KT16 ..... 33 B2
Abbey Ct. Farnh GU9 ..... 125 C2
Abbey Dr. Laleh TW18 ..... 33 C5
Abbey Dr. Up Toot SW17 ..... 21 A3
Abbey Gdns. Chert KT16 ..... 33 A3
Abbey Gn. Chert KT16 ..... 33 A3
Abbey Ind Est. Mitch CR4 ..... 40 F4
Abbey La. Beck BR3 ..... 24 A1
Abbey Lodge. Stain TW18 ..... 12 F3
Abbey Par. Merton SW19 ..... 20 C1
Abbey Pk. Beck BR3 ..... 24 A1
Abbey Rd. Chert KT16 ..... 33 B2
Abbey Rd. Croy CR0 & CR9 ..... 61 B7
Abbey Rd. Horse GU21 ..... 69 D2
Abbey Rd. Lo Hall TW10 ..... 34 A1
Abbey Rd. Merton SW19 ..... 40 C8
Abbey Rd. Selsd CR2 ..... 62 D1
Abbey Rd. Vir W GU25 ..... 31 D5
Abbey River Cotts. Chert KT16 .. 33 C3
Abbey Sch The. M Bourn GU9 .. 125 C1
Abbey St. Farnh GU9 ..... 125 C2
Abbey Way. Farnb GU14 ..... 85 C4
Abbey Wlk. E Mole KT8 ..... 36 B5
Abbey Wood. Sunnin SL5 ..... 30 A2
Abbeylands Sch. Addl KT15 ..... 52 A5
Abbot Cl. Byfl KT14 ..... 71 D8
Abbot Cl. Stain TW18 ..... 13 D1
Abbot Rd. Guild GU1 ..... 130 D7
Abbot's Cl. Onsl V GU2 ..... 129 F6
Abbot's Way.
  Merrow GU1 & GU4 ..... 110 D2
Abbots Cl. S Norw SE25 ..... 42 E6
Abbots Dr. Vir W GU25 ..... 31 C5
Abbots Gn. S Croy CR0 & CR2 .. 62 D4
Abbots La. Kenley CR8 ..... 80 C3
Abbots Pk. Streat SW2 ..... 22 A7
Abbots Way. Beck BR3 ..... 43 E4
Abbots Wlk. Cater CR3 ..... 101 B5
Abbotsbury. Easth RG12 ..... 26 F4
Abbotsbury Ct. Horsh RH13 .. 217 E3
Abbotsbury Fst Sch.
  Morden SM4 ..... 40 B4
Abbotsbury Rd.
  Coney H BR2 ..... 63 F8
Abbotsbury Rd.
  Morden SM4 & SW19 ..... 40 B5
Abbotsfield Rd. Crawl RH11 .. 200 D4
Abbotsford Cl. Woking GU22 .. 70 A2
Abbotshall Rd. Catf SE6 ..... 24 D6
Abbotsleigh Cl. Belm SM2 ..... 59 B3
Abbotsleigh Rd. Streat SW16 .. 21 C3
Abbotsmede Cl. Twick TW1 ..... 16 F6
Abbotswood. Abbots GU1 ..... 109 F3
Abbotswood. Walt O T KT13 .. 53 F7
Abbotswood Cl. Burph GU1 .. 109 F4
Abbotswood Dr. Whit V KT13 .. 53 D1
Abbotswood Rd. Streat SW16 .. 21 D5
Abbott Ave. Wimble SW20 ..... 39 D8
Abbott Cl. Hampt TW12 ..... 15 E2
Abbott House. Balham SW12 .. 20 F8
Abbotts Cotts. Docken GU10 .. 166 E5
Abbotts Rd. Cheam SM1 & SM3 .. 58 E6
Abbotts Rd. Mitch CR4 & SW16 .. 41 C5
Abbotts Rise. Redh RH1 ..... 119 A3
Abbotts Tilt. Hersh KT12 ..... 54 E7
Abelia Cl. W End GU24 ..... 67 E6
Abercairn Rd. Streat SW16 .. 21 C1
Aberconway Rd. Morden SM4 .. 40 B5
Abercorn Cl. Selsd CR2 ..... 81 D7
Abercorn Way. Woking GU21 .. 69 A1
Aberdare Cl. W Wick BR4 ..... 63 C8
Aberdeen Rd. Croy CR0 ..... 61 D6
Aberdour. Banstd KT20 ..... 77 F1
Aberfoyle Rd. Streat SW16 .. 21 D2
Abingdon Cl. Brack RG12 ..... 27 E4
Abingdon Cl. Merton SW19 .. 20 C2
Abingdon Cl. Woking GU21 .. 69 C1
Abingdon Lodge. Broml BR2 .. 44 F7
Abingdon Rd.
  Sandh GU15 & GU47 ..... 45 C1
Abingdon Rd. Thorn H SW16 .. 41 E8
Abinger Ave. E Ewell SM2 ..... 58 D2
Abinger Cl. Dork RH5 ..... 136 C3
Abinger Cl. Wallin SM6 ..... 60 E5
Abinger Common Cty Sch.
  Abing C RH5 ..... 134 D1
Abinger Common Rd.
  Wotton RH5 ..... 155 F7
Abinger Ct. Wallin SM6 ..... 60 E5
Abinger Dr. Earls RH1 ..... 139 E7

Abinger Gdns. Islew TW7 ..... 5 E4
Abinger Hammer Village Sch.
  Abing H RH5 ..... 133 F4
Abinger House. [2] King U T KT2 .. 18 B1
Abinger La. Abing C RH5 ..... 134 C2
Abinger Rd. Wotton RH5 ..... 156 C3
Abinger Way. Burph GU4 ..... 110 B6
Aboyne Dr. Wimble SW20 ..... 39 A7
Aboyne Rd. Wands SW17 ..... 20 A5
Abrahams Rd. Crawl RH11 .. 201 A1
Acacia Ave. Brent TW8 ..... 6 B7
Acacia Ave. Sandh GU15 ..... 45 D1
Acacia Ave. Shep Gn SW17 ..... 34 A4
Acacia Ave. Woking GU22 ..... 89 D7
Acacia Cl. Penge SE20 ..... 43 A7
Acacia Cl. Woodhm KT15 ..... 51 F1
Acacia Ct. [5] W Norw SW16 .. 22 A3
Acacia Dr. Cheam SM3 ..... 40 A1
Acacia Dr. Nork KT17 ..... 77 D5
Acacia Dr. Woodhm KT15 ..... 51 F1
Acacia Gdns. W Wick BR4 ..... 63 C8
Acacia Gr. Dulw SE21 ..... 22 D6
Acacia Gr. King U T KT3 ..... 38 E6
Acacia House. Reig RH2 ..... 118 A3
Acacia Mews. Harm UB7 ..... 2 D8
Acacia Rd. Beck BR3 ..... 43 F6
Acacia Rd. Guild GU1 ..... 109 D1
Acacia Rd. Hampt TW12 ..... 16 A2
Acacia Rd. Mitch CR4 ..... 41 B7
Acacia Rd. S Norw SW16 ..... 41 E8
Acacia Rd. Stain TW18 ..... 13 B3
Academy Cl. Camb GU15 ..... 65 E8
Academy Gdns. Croy CR0 ..... 42 F1
Accommodation La. Harm UB7 .. 2 C8
Accommodation Rd. Longc KT16 .. 50 E6
Ace Par. Chess KT9 ..... 56 E7
Acer Rd. Bigg H TN16 ..... 83 D3
Acheulian Cl. M Bourn GU9 .. 146 C7
Achilles Pl. Horse GU21 ..... 69 C2
Ackroyd Rd. For Hil SE23 ..... 23 E8
Acorn Cl. E Grins RH19 ..... 205 E8
Acorn Cl. Horley RH6 ..... 161 C4
Acorn Dr. Woki RG11 ..... 25 C7
Acorn Gdns. S Norw SE19 ..... 42 F8
Acorn Gr. Harl UB3 ..... 3 F7
Acorn Gr. Kings KT20 ..... 97 F3
Acorn Gr. Westfd GU22 ..... 89 E6
Acorn Mews. W Heath GU14 .. 85 A7
Acorn Rd. Blckw GU17 ..... 64 B5
Acorn Way. For Hil SE23 ..... 23 D5
Acorns. Horsh RH13 ..... 218 A4
Acorns Cty Fst Sch The.
  Betch RH3 ..... 116 D1
Acorns The. Crawl RH11 .. 201 B1
Acorns The. [2] Putney SW19 .. 19 D7
Acorns Way. For Hil KT10 ..... 55 C5
Acre La. Wallin SM5 ..... 60 A6
Acre Rd. King U T KT2 ..... 37 E8
Acre Rd. Mitch SW19 ..... 20 D2
Acres Gdns. Burgh H KT20 .. 97 D8
Acres Platt. Cran GU6 ..... 174 F4
Action Ct. Littlt TW15 ..... 34 C8
Acuba House. Wands SW18 .. 20 B7
Acuba Rd. Wands SW18 ..... 20 B6
Adair Cl. Croy SE25 ..... 43 B6
Adair Wlk. Pirb GU24 ..... 87 B6
Adams Cl. Surb KT5 ..... 37 F3
Adams Croft. Pirb GU24 ..... 87 C7
Adams Ct. [2] Purley CR8 ..... 80 A7
Adams House. [3] Streat SW16 .. 21 C3
Adams Park Rd. Farnh GU9 .. 125 D3
Adams Rd. Beck BR3 ..... 43 E4
Adams Way. Croy SE25 & CR0 .. 43 A3
Adams Wlk. [11] King U T KT1 .. 37 E7
Adamson Ct. [6] Crawl RH11 .. 201 B1
Adamsrill Prim Sch.
  For Hil SE26 ..... 23 E5
Adamsrill Rd.
  For Hil SE23 & SE26 ..... 23 E4
Adare Wlk. Streat SW16 & SW2 .. 21 F6
Addington Bsns Ctr.
  New Add CR9 ..... 63 E1
Addington Court Golf Course.
  New Add CR0 ..... 63 A2
Addington Ct. [7] Mortl SW14 .. 7 D4
Addington Golf Course.
  S Croy CR0 & CR9 ..... 62 E6
Addington Gr. For Hil SE26 .. 23 E4
Addington High Sch.
  New Add CR0 ..... 82 E7
Addington Palace Golf Course.
  S Croy CR0 ..... 62 E5
Addington Palace (The Royal Sch
  of Church Music). S Croy CR9 .. 62 F4
Addington Rd. Sander CR2 .. 81 A8
Addington Rd. Selsd CR2 ..... 62 C1
Addington Rd. Thorn H CR0 .. 42 A1
Addington Rd.
  W Wick BR4 & CR0 ..... 63 D6
Addington Rd. W Wick BR4 ..... 63 E8
Addington Village Rd. Add CR0 .. 63 A5
Addiscombe Ave. Croy CR0 .. 43 A2
Addiscombe Court Rd.
  Croy CR0 & CR9 ..... 61 E8
Addiscombe Rd. Crowth RH11 .. 45 C4
Addiscombe Rd. Croy CR0 & CR9 .. 61 E8
Addiscombe Rd. S Croy CR0 .. 61 E8
Addiscombe Sta. Croy CR0 .. 42 F1
Addison Ave. Hounsl TW3 ..... 5 B5
Addison Cl. Cater CR3 ..... 100 D5
Addison Ct. Guild GU1 ..... 130 F7
Addison Gdns. King U T KT5 .. 37 F5
Addison Rd. Cater CR3 ..... 100 D6
Addison Rd. Croy SE25 ..... 43 A5
Addison Rd. Guild GU1 ..... 130 F7
Addison Rd. Felt TW11 ..... 17 B2
Addison Rd. [8] Woking GU21 .. 69 F2
Addison's Cl. Croy CR0 ..... 62 F8
Addlestone House. Addl KT15 .. 52 B7

Addlestone Moor. Chert KT15 .. 52 C8
Addlestone Pk. Addl KT15 ..... 52 B5
Addlestone Rd.
  Addl KT13 & KT15 ..... 52 C6
Addlestone Sta. Addl KT15 ..... 52 D6
Adecroft Way. E Mole KT8 ..... 36 C6
Adela Ave. W Barn KT3 ..... 39 B5
Adelaide Cl. Crawl RH11 ..... 181 D1
Adelaide Cl. Horsh RH12 ..... 217 E5
Adelaide Ct. Ashf TW15 ..... 13 F3
Adelaide Ct. [15] Beck BR3 ..... 24 A1
Adelaide Pl. Oat Pk KT13 ..... 53 D6
Adelaide Rd. Ashf TW15 ..... 13 D3
Adelaide Rd. Heston TW5 ..... 4 E6
Adelaide Rd. King U T KT6 ..... 37 E4
Adelaide Rd. Rich TW9 ..... 6 F3
Adelaide Rd. Tedd TW11 ..... 16 F2
Adelaide Rd. Walt O T KT12 .. 54 B7
Adelina Mews. Streat SW12 .. 21 D7
Adelphi Cl. Worth RH10 ..... 202 D4
Adelphi Rd. Ewell KT17 ..... 76 D6
Adenmore Rd. Catf SE6 ..... 24 A8
Adisham House. [7] Penge SE20 .. 23 C1
Adlers La. Westh RH5 ..... 115 A4
Adlington Pl. Farnb GU14 ..... 85 E2
Admiral Ct. Carsh SM5 ..... 40 E1
Admiral Rd. Crawl RH11 ..... 201 A3
Admiral's Bridge La.
  E Grins RH19 ..... 205 C2
Admiral's Wlk The. Coulsd CR5 .. 99 F7
Admirals Ct. Merrow GU1 ..... 110 B2
Admiralty Rd. Tedd TW11 ..... 16 F2
Admiralty Way. Camb GU15 .. 64 F4
Adolf St. Catf SE6 ..... 24 B4
Adrian Ct. Crawl RH11 ..... 201 B1
Advance Rd. W Norw SE27 ..... 22 C4
Adversane Rd. Horsh RH12 .. 217 D4
Aerodrome Way. Heston TW5 .. 4 C8
Aerospace Bvd. Farnb GU11 .. 105 A7
Agar Cl. Surb KT6 ..... 56 F8
Agar House. [6] King U T KT1 .. 37 E6
Agate House. New Mal KT4 .. 38 E1
Agate House. [12] Penge SE26 .. 23 B3
Agate La. Horsh RH12 ..... 217 F5
Agates La. Ashtd KT21 ..... 95 D8
Agincourt Pl. Ascot SL5 ..... 29 C6
Agnes Scott Ct. [5] Weyb KT13 .. 53 B7
Agnew Rd. For Hil SE23 ..... 23 D8
Agraria Rd. Guild GU2 ..... 130 B7
Ailsa Ave. Islew TW1 ..... 6 B2
Ailsa Cl. Crawl RH11 ..... 201 B3
Ailsa Rd. Islew TW1 ..... 6 B2
Ainger Cl. Alder GU12 ..... 105 D2
Ainsdale Way. Woking GU21 .. 69 A1
Ainsworth Rd.
  Thorn H CR0 & SE9 ..... 61 B8
Aintree Cl. Poyle SL3 ..... 1 E6
Aintree House. Penge SE26 .. 23 B2
Aintree Rd. Crawl RH10 ..... 202 A4
Airborne House. [10] Wallin SM6 .. 60 B6
Aircraft Espl. Farnb GU14 ..... 85 C1
Airedale Rd. Balham SW12 .. 20 F8
Airport Way. Horley RH6 ..... 182 B8
Airport Way. Stan TW19 ..... 2 A3
Airport Way Rdbt W.
  Crawl RH6 ..... 181 F8
Aisne Rd. Friml GU16 ..... 66 E1
Aitken Cl. Carsh CR4 ..... 40 F2
Aitken House. Haslem GU27 .. 208 C7
Aitken Rd. Catf SE6 ..... 24 B6
Akabusi Cl. Croy SE25 ..... 43 A3
Akehurst Cl. Copth RH10 ..... 183 B3
Akehurst St. Putney SW15 .. 19 A8
Akerman Rd. King U T KT6 ..... 37 C4
Alamein Rd. Alder GU11 ..... 105 B3
Alan Hilton Ct. Ottsh KT16 .. 51 D4
Alan Rd. Wimble SW19 ..... 19 E3
Alan Turing Rd. Onsl V GU2 .. 108 D1
Alanbrooke Cl. Knaph GU21 .. 68 C1
Alanbrooke Rd. Farnb GU11 .. 105 D6
Albain Cres. Stan TW15 ..... 13 E8
Albans Cl. Streat SW16 ..... 21 E5
Albany Cl. Esher KT10 ..... 55 A2
Albany Cl. Mortl SW14 ..... 7 B3
Albany Cres. Clayg KT10 ..... 55 E4
Albany Ct. King U T KT2 ..... 17 E2
Albany Ct. Oat Pk KT13 ..... 53 E8
Albany Ct. Rich TW10 ..... 17 B5
Albany Ct. [3] Weyb KT13 ..... 53 B6
Albany Ho. [6] Brent TW8 ..... 6 E8
Albany Mews. King U T KT2 .. 17 D2
Albany Mews. Sutton SM1 .. 59 B5
Albany Par. [4] Brent TW8 ..... 6 E8
Albany Park Ind Est. Friml GU16 65 C1
Albany Park Rd. King U T KT2 .. 17 E2
Albany Park Rd. Leahd KT22 .. 95 A8
Albany Pk. Camb GU16 ..... 65 B1
Albany Pk. Friml GU16 ..... 65 C1
Albany Pk. Poyle SL3 ..... 1 D7
Albany Pl. Brent TW8 ..... 6 E8
Albany Pl. Egham TW20 ..... 12 B4
Albany Rd. Brent TW8 ..... 6 D8
Albany Rd. Crawl RH11 ..... 201 C6
Albany Rd. Hersh KT12 ..... 54 D6
Albany Rd. New Mal KT3 ..... 38 D5
Albany Rd. Rich TW10 ..... 6 F2
Albany Rd. Wimble SW19 ..... 20 B3
Albany Reach. Thame D KT7 .. 36 F4
Albany Terr. [5] Rich TW10 ..... 6 F2
Albanys The. Reig RH2 ..... 118 A3
Albatross Gdns. Selsd CR2 .. 81 D8
Albemarle. Putney SW19 ..... 19 D6
Albemarle Ave. Twick TW2 .. 15 F7
Albemarle Gdns. New Mal KT3 .. 38 D5
Albemarle Lodge. For Hil SE26 .. 23 E3
Albemarle Pk. Beck BR3 ..... 44 B8
Albemarle Rd. Beck BR2 & BR3 .. 44 C8
Albermarle Prim Sch.
  Putney SW19 ..... 19 E6
Albermarle Prim Sch (Annexe).
  Putney SW19 ..... 19 E7
Albert Ave. Thorpe KT16 ..... 33 A6

Albert Carr Gdns. Streat SW16 .. 21 E3
Albert Crane Ct. Crawl RH11 .. 201 A8
Albert Dr. Sheer GU21 & KT14 .. 70 D5
Albert Dr. Putney SW19 ..... 19 E6
Albert Gr. Wimble SW20 ..... 39 D8
Albert Rd. Addl KT15 ..... 52 D6
Albert Rd. Alder GU11 ..... 105 B2
Albert Rd. Ashf TW15 ..... 13 F3
Albert Rd. Ashtd KT21 ..... 75 F1
Albert Rd. Bagsh GU19 ..... 47 E1
Albert Rd. Brack RG12 ..... 27 B8
Albert Rd. Camb GU15 ..... 65 C5
Albert Rd. Carsh SM1 ..... 59 D5
Albert Rd. Crowth RG11 ..... 45 B3
Albert Rd. Croy CR0 & SE25 .. 43 B5
Albert Rd. Eng Gn TW20 ..... 11 D2
Albert Rd. Epsom KT17 ..... 76 F6
Albert Rd. Farnb GU14 ..... 85 C2
Albert Rd. Hampt TW12 ..... 16 C3
Albert Rd. Horley RH6 ..... 161 A3
Albert Rd. Hounsl TW3 ..... 5 A3
Albert Rd. King U T KT1 ..... 37 F7
Albert Rd. Merst RH1 ..... 119 C6
Albert Rd. Mitch CR4 ..... 40 F6
Albert Rd. New Mal KT3 ..... 38 F5
Albert Rd. Penge SE20 ..... 23 D2
Albert Rd. Rich TW10 ..... 6 F2
Albert Rd. Sutton SM1 ..... 59 D5
Albert Rd. Tedd TW11 ..... 16 F2
Albert Rd. Twick TW1 ..... 16 F7
Albert Rd. Warlgm CR6 ..... 81 F2
Albert Rd. Woki RG11 ..... 25 B5
Albert Rd N. Reig RH2 ..... 117 F2
Alberta Ave. Cheam SM1 ..... 59 B5
Alberta Dr. Smallf RH6 ..... 162 A3
Albertine Cl. Nork KT17 ..... 77 B3
Albery Cl. Horsh RH12 ..... 217 B4
Albion Cl. Worth RH10 ..... 202 D5
Albion Ct. Sutton SM2 ..... 59 D3
Albion Par. Knaph GU21 ..... 68 C2
Albion Pl. S Norw SE25 ..... 43 A6
Albion Rd. Hounsl TW3 ..... 5 A3
Albion Rd. King U T KT2 ..... 38 C8
Albion Rd. Reig RH2 ..... 139 C8
Albion Rd. Sandh GU47 ..... 64 B8
Albion Rd. Sutton SM2 ..... 59 D3
Albion Rd. Twick TW2 ..... 16 E7
Albion St. Thorn H CR0 & CR9 .. 42 B1
Albion Track. Farnb GU14 ..... 104 F2
Albion Villas Rd.
  For Hil SE23 & SE26 ..... 23 C5
Albion Way. Horsh RH12 ..... 217 C2
Albury Ave. E Ewell SM2 ..... 58 C1
Albury Ave. Hounsl TW7 ..... 5 F7
Albury Cl. Hampt TW12 ..... 16 B2
Albury Cl. Longc KT16 ..... 50 A7
Albury Ct. [4] Croy CR0 ..... 61 C6
Albury Ct. Mitch CR4 ..... 40 D7
Albury Ct. Sutton SM1 ..... 59 C6
Albury Keep. Horley RH6 ..... 161 B4
Albury Lodge. [10] Streat SW2 .. 21 F8
Albury Pl. Merst RH1 ..... 119 C6
Albury Rd. Chess KT9 ..... 56 E5
Albury Rd. Guild GU1 ..... 131 A8
Albury Rd. Merst RH1 ..... 119 C6
Albury Rd. Whit V KT12 ..... 53 F4
Albury St. Albury GU5 ..... 132 C4
Alcester Ct. [4] Wallin SM6 .. 60 B6
Alcester Rd. Wallin SM6 ..... 60 B6
Alcock Cl. Wallin SM6 ..... 60 D3
Alcock Rd. Heston TW5 ..... 4 D7
Alcocks Cl. King U T KT2 ..... 97 E7
Alcocks La. Kings KT20 ..... 97 E7
Alcorn Cl. Cheam SM3 ..... 59 A8
Alcot Cl. Crowth RG11 ..... 45 B4
Alden Ct. S Croy CR0 ..... 61 D7
Aldenham Terr. Earls RG12 .. 27 C3
Aldenholme. Whit V KT13 ..... 53 E4
Alder Cl. Ash V GU12 ..... 106 A7
Alder Cl. Crawl D RH10 ..... 204 B8
Alder Cl. Eng Gn TW20 ..... 11 E3
Alder Croft. Coulsd CR5 ..... 79 F3
Alder Ct. [3] W Norw SW16 .. 22 A3
Alder Rd. Head Dn GU35 ..... 187 B6
Alder Rd. Mortl SW14 ..... 7 D4
Alderbrook Garage Block.
  Cran GU6 ..... 153 E1
Alderbrook Prim Sch.
  Balham SW12 ..... 21 B8
Alderbrook Rd. Balham SW12 .. 21 B8
Alderbrook Rd. Cran GU6 ..... 174 C8
Aldergrove Gdns. Hounsl TW4 .. 4 E5
Alderman Judge Mall. [6]
  King U T KT1 ..... 37 E7
Alderman Willey Cl. Woki RG11 25 B6
Aldermead. Hounsl TW3 ..... 5 B3
Aldermoor Rd. For Hil SE6 .. 23 F5
Alderney Ave. Hounsl TW5 .. 5 B7
Alders Ave. E Grins RH19 .. 185 E3
Alders Rd. Reig RH2 ..... 118 B3
Alders The. Felt TW13 ..... 15 E4
Alders The. Heston TW5 ..... 4 F8
Alders The. Streat SW16 ..... 21 C4
Alders The. W Wick BR4 ..... 63 B8
Alders View Dr. E Grins RH19 .. 185 E3
Aldersbrook Dr. King U T KT2 .. 17 F2
Aldersey Rd. Guild GU1 ..... 109 F1
Aldersgrove. E Mole KT8 ..... 36 B6
Aldershot Military Mus.
  Farnb GU11 ..... 105 C7
Aldershot Rd. Ash GU12 ..... 105 F1
Aldershot Rd. Chur C GU13 .. 104 A6
Aldershot Rd. Fairl GU3 ..... 108 D5
Aldershot Rd. Pirb GU24 & GU3 .. 87 F2
Aldershot Rd.
  Stough GU2 & GU3 ..... 108 D3
Aldershot Rd. S Word V GU3 .. 107 E5
Aldershot Sta. Alder GU11 .. 105 B1

Aldersmead Rd. Penge BR3 .. 23 E1
Alderstead La. Hooley RH1 .. 99 D2
Alderton. King U T KT2 ..... 38 B8
Alderton Ct. E Mole KT8 ..... 35 F5
Alderton Rd. Croy CR0 ..... 43 A2
Alderwick Dr. Hounsl TW3 .. 5 D4
Alderwood Cl. Cater CR3 ..... 100 E2
Aldingbourne Cl. Crawl RH11 .. 200 F3
Aldis Mews. Up Toot SW17 .. 20 E3
Aldis St. Up Toot SW17 ..... 20 E3
Aldous House. Stain TW18 .. 12 E4
Aldren Rd. Wands SW17 ..... 20 C5
Aldrich Cres. New Add CR0 .. 63 C2
Aldrich Gdns. Cheam SM3 .. 58 F7
Aldrich Terr. Wands SW18 .. 20 C6
Aldridge Rise. New Mal KT3 .. 38 E3
Aldrin Pl. Farnb GU14 ..... 84 D4
Aldrington Rd. Streat SW16 .. 21 C4
Aldro Sch. Shackl GU8 ..... 149 C7
Aldwick Cl. W Heath GU14 .. 85 A6
Aldwick Rd. Wallin CR0 ..... 60 F6
Aldworth Cl. Easth RG12 ..... 27 A3
Aldworth Gdns. Crowth RG11 .. 45 A5
Aldwych Cl. Worth RH10 ..... 202 D4
Aldwyn Ct. Eng Gn TW20 ..... 11 B2
Alexa Ct. Belm SM2 ..... 59 A4
Alexander Cl. Twick TW2 ..... 16 F6
Alexander Ct. Beck BR3 ..... 44 D8
Alexander Ct. [14] Surb KT6 .. 37 D2
Alexander Evans Mews.
  For Hil SE23 ..... 23 D6
Alexander Godley Cl.
  Ashtd KT21 ..... 95 F8
Alexander Rd. Coulsd CR5 .. 79 B4
Alexander Rd. Egham TW20 .. 12 C3
Alexander Rd. Woodh RH2 .. 139 A6
Alexanders Wlk. Cater CR3 .. 101 A1
Alexandra Ave. Camb GU15 .. 65 A5
Alexandra Ave. Sutton SM1 .. 59 A7
Alexandra Ave. Warlgm CR6 .. 81 F2
Alexandra Cl. Ashf TW15 ..... 14 D1
Alexandra Cl. Stain TW18 .. 13 D2
Alexandra Cl. Walt O T KT12 .. 54 A8
Alexandra Cotts. Penge SE20 .. 23 D2
Alexandra Cres. Broml BR1 .. 24 F2
Alexandra Ct. Ashf TW15 ..... 14 D2
Alexandra Ct. [10] Crawl RH11 .. 201 D5
Alexandra Ct. [1] Farnb GU14 .. 85 C1
Alexandra Dr. Surb KT5 ..... 38 A2
Alexandra Dr. W Norw SE19 .. 22 E3
Alexandra Gdns. Chisw W4 .. 7 E7
Alexandra Gdns. Hounsl TW3 .. 5 B5
Alexandra Gdns. Knaph GU21 .. 68 C1
Alexandra Gdns. Wallin SM5 .. 60 A2
Alexandra Inf Sch. King U T KT2 18 A1
Alexandra Inf Sch. Penge BR3 .. 23 D1
Alexandra Jun & Inf Sch.
  Hounsl TW3 ..... 5 B5
Alexandra Jun Sch. Penge SE20 23 D2
Alexandra Lodge. Guild GU1 .. 130 F8
Alexandra Lodge. [1] Weyb KT13 53 B6
Alexandra Pl. Croy CR0 ..... 42 E1
Alexandra Pl. Guild GU1 ..... 130 F7
Alexandra Pl. S Norw SE25 .. 42 D4
Alexandra Rd. Addl KT15 ..... 52 D6
Alexandra Rd. Alder GU11 .. 104 F2
Alexandra Rd. Ash GU12 ..... 105 F1
Alexandra Rd. Ashf TW15 .. 14 E2
Alexandra Rd. Bigg H TN16 .. 103 B8
Alexandra Rd. [10] Brent TW8 .. 6 D8
Alexandra Rd. Croy CR0 ..... 42 E2
Alexandra Rd. Eng Gn TW20 .. 11 C2
Alexandra Rd. Epsom KT17 .. 76 F6
Alexandra Rd.
  Farnb GU14 & GU11 ..... 85 C1
Alexandra Rd. Hounsl TW3 .. 5 B5
Alexandra Rd. King U T KT2 .. 18 A1
Alexandra Rd. Mitch SW19 .. 20 E1
Alexandra Rd. Mortl SW14 .. 7 D4
Alexandra Rd. Penge SE26 .. 23 D2
Alexandra Rd. Rich TW9 ..... 6 F5
Alexandra Rd. Thame D KT7 .. 36 F4
Alexandra Rd. Twick TW1 ..... 6 C1
Alexandra Rd. Warlgm CR6 .. 81 F2
Alexandra Rd. Wimble SW19 .. 20 A3
Alexandra Sq. Morden SM4 .. 40 A4
Alexandra Terr. Guild GU1 .. 130 E8
Alexandra Wlk. [8] W Norw SE19 22 E3
Alfold By-Pass. Alf Cr GU6 .. 194 A5
Alfold By-Pass. Alfold GU6 .. 193 F7
Alfold Cotts. Alf Cr GU6 ..... 193 F2
Alfold Cty Prim Sch.
  Alfold GU6 ..... 193 F1
Alfold La. Alf Cr GU6 ..... 194 A7
Alfold Rd. Alfold GU8 ..... 193 B3
Alfold Rd. Cran GU6 ..... 194 B7
Alfold Rd. Dunsf GU8 ..... 193 B3
Alfonso Cl. Alder GU12 ..... 126 C8
Alford Cl. Burph GU4 ..... 110 A4
Alford Ct. [5] Sutton SM2 ..... 59 B3
Alford Gn. New Add CR0 ..... 63 D4
Alfred Butt House.
  Up Toot SW17 ..... 20 F5
Alfred Cl. Worth RH10 ..... 202 E5
Alfred Hurley House.
  Up Toot SW17 ..... 20 C4
Alfred Mizen Prim Sch The.
  Mitch CR4 ..... 41 D6
Alfred Rd. Croy SE25 ..... 43 A4
Alfred Rd. Felt TW13 ..... 15 C6
Alfred Rd. King U T KT1 ..... 37 F6
Alfred Rd. M Bourn GU9 ..... 125 C1
Alfred Rd. Sutton SM1 ..... 59 C5
Alfreton Cl. Wimble SW19 .. 19 D5
Alfriston. Surb KT5 ..... 37 F3
Alfriston Ave. Thorn H CR0 .. 41 E2
Alfriston Cl. Surb KT5 ..... 37 F3
Alfriston Rd. Friml GU16 ..... 86 C7
Algar Cl. Islew TW7 ..... 6 A4
Algar Rd. Islew TW7 ..... 6 A4

Algarve Rd. Wands SW18 .... 20 B7
Alice Gough Memorial Homes.
　Easth RG12 .... 27 B6
Alice Mews. 8 Tedd TW11 .... 16 F3
Alice Rd. Alder GU11 .... 105 B2
Alice Ruston Pl. Woking GU22 ... 89 C8
Alice Way. Hounsl TW3 .... 5 B3
Alicia Ave. Crawl RH10 .... 202 C6
Alington Gr. Wallin SM6 .... 60 D2
Alison Cl. Croy CR0 .... 43 D1
Alison Cl. Farnb GU14 .... 84 F3
Alison Cl. Horse GU21 .... 69 E4
Alison Dr. Camb GU15 .... 65 F5
Alison Rd. Alder GU11 .... 104 F2
Alison's Rd. Alder GU11 .... 105 B4
All England Lawn Tennis & Croquet
　Club The. Wimble SW19 .... 19 E5
All Hallows Catholic Sch.
　Heath E GU9 .... 125 F7
All Saint's Prim Sch.
　S Norw SE19 .... 42 E8
All Saints' Benhilton C of E Prim
　Sch. Sutton SM1 .... 59 B7
All Saints C of E Inf Sch.
　Leahd KT22 .... 95 A8
All Saints C of E Prim Sch.
　Merton SW19 .... 20 C1
All Saints Carshalton CE Sch.
　Wallin SM5 .... 60 A5
All Saints CE Inf Sch.
　Tilf GU10 .... 147 C3
All Saints Cl. Woki RG11 .... 25 C7
All Saints Cres. W Heath GU14 ... 64 E1
All Saints Dr. Sander CR2 .... 81 A7
All Saints Rd. Lhtwat GU18 .... 48 C1
All Saints Rd. Merton SW19 .... 20 C1
All Saints Rd. Sutton SM1 .... 59 C7
All Souls' Rd. Ascot SL5 .... 29 A5
Allan Cl. New Mal KT3 .... 38 D4
Allbrook Cl. Tedd TW11 .... 16 E3
Allbrook House. 5
　Rhampt SW15 .... 19 A8
Allcard Cl. Horsh RH12 .... 217 D4
Allcot Cl. Crawl RH11 .... 200 E3
Allcot Cl. E Bed TW14 .... 14 F7
Allden Ave. Alder GU11 & GU12 126 D7
Allden Cotts. Ock Rid GU7 .... 150 B4
Allden Gdns. Alder GU12 .... 126 D7
Alldens Hill. Bramly GU5 & GU8 151 D1
Alldens La. Godal GU8 .... 151 B1
Allen House Pk. Woking GU22 ... 89 C7
Allen Rd. G Book KT23 .... 94 B1
Allen Rd. Penge BR3 .... 43 D7
Allen Rd. Sunby TW16 .... 35 B7
Allen Rd. Thorn H CR0 .... 42 A1
Allen's Cl. Ash W RH19 .... 206 D6
Allenby Ave. S Croy CR2 .... 61 C2
Allenby Rd. Bigg H TN16 .... 83 E2
Allenby Rd. For Hil SE23 .... 23 E5
Allenby Rd. Sandh GU15 .... 65 A6
Allendale. Elst GU8 .... 148 C3
Allendale Cl. For Hil SE26 .... 23 D3
Allendale Cl. Sandh GU17 .... 45 A2
Allenford House. Rhampt SW15 ... 7 F1
Allenswood. 12 Putney SW19 ..... 19 E7
Allerford Cl. Catf SE6 .... 24 B5
Allerford Rd. Catf SE6 .... 24 B4
Allerton Ct. N Cheam SM3 .... 58 D8
Allerton House. 4 Merton SW19 20 C1
Alleyn Cres. Dulw SE21 .... 22 D6
Alleyn Pk. Dulw SE21 .... 22 E5
Alleyn Rd. Dulw SE21 .... 22 E5
Allgood Cl. W Barn SM4 .... 39 D3
Alliance Ct. Ashf TW15 .... 14 A5
Allingham Ct. Farnc GU7 .... 150 F7
Allingham Gdns. Horsh RH12 ... 218 B5
Allingham Rd. Woodh RH12 ...... 139 A6
Allington Ave. Up Hall TW17 ..... 34 E6
Allington Cl. Wimble SW19 .... 19 D3
Allington Ct. Croy CR0 .... 43 C3
Allison Gr. Dulw SE21 .... 22 E7
Alloway Cl. 4 Woking GU21 ...... 69 B1
Allsmoor La. Brack RG12 .... 27 F6
Allum Gr. Tadw KT20 .... 97 B6
Allwood Cl. For Hil SE26 .... 23 D4
Allyington Way. Worth RH10 .... 202 D5
Allyn Cl. Stain TW18 .... 12 F2
Alma Cl. Alder GU12 .... 105 D2
Alma Cl. Knaph GU21 .... 68 E1
Alma Cres. Cheam SM1 .... 58 E5
Alma Ct. Cater CR3 .... 100 C6
Alma Gdns. Friml GU16 .... 86 E8
Alma Ho. 7 Brent TW8 .... 6 E8
Alma La. Heath E GU9 .... 125 C7
Alma Pl. Penge SE19 .... 22 F1
Alma Pl. Thorn H CR7 .... 42 A4
Alma Rd. Carsh SM5 .... 59 E5
Alma Rd. Head Do GU35 .... 187 C5
Alma Rd. Reig RH2 .... 118 B3
Alma Rd. Thame D KT10 & KT7 ... 36 E1
Alma Terr. Wands SW18 .... 20 D8
Alma Way. Heath E GU9 .... 125 D7
Almer Rd. Wimble SW20 .... 19 A1
Almners Rd. Chert KT16 .... 32 C2
Almners Rd. Lyne KT16 .... 32 B1
Almond Ave. Carsh SM5 .... 59 F8
Almond Ave. Woking GU22 .... 89 D6
Almond Cl. Belff GU1 .... 109 D5
Almond Cl. Charlt TW17 .... 34 C7
Almond Cl. Crawl RH11 .... 201 A6
Almond Cl. Eng Gn TW20 .... 11 B2
Almond Gr. Brent TW8 .... 6 B7
Almond Rd. Epsom KT19 .... 76 D8
Almond Way. Mitch CR4 .... 41 D5
Almorah Rd. Heston TW5 .... 4 D6
Alms Heath. Ockham GU23 .... 92 B6
Almsgate. Compt GU3 .... 129 C2
Almshouse La. Chess KT9 .... 56 D2
Almshouses. Dork RH4 .... 136 B8
Almshouses. Mickle RH5 .... 115 C8
Almshouses. Sunby TW16 .... 34 F8
Alnwick Gr. Morden SM4 .... 40 B5
Alpha Ct. Warlgm CR6 .... 81 A1
Alpha Rd. Chobh GU24 .... 49 F1
Alpha Rd. Crawl RH11 .... 201 C6
Alpha Rd. Croy CR0 .... 42 E1
Alpha Rd. Mayb GU22 .... 70 C4
Alpha Rd. Surb KT5 .... 37 F3
Alpha Rd. Tedd TW12 .... 16 D3
Alpha Way. Thorpe TW20 .... 32 C4
Alphabet Gdns. Carsh SM5 .... 40 D3
Alphea Cl. Mitch SW19 .... 20 E1
Alphington Ave. Friml GU16 ...... 65 F1
Alphington Gn. Friml GU16 .... 65 F1
Alpine Ave. Tolw KT5 .... 57 C8
Alpine Cl. S Croy CR0 .... 61 E7
Alpine Rd. Redh RH1 .... 119 A4
Alpine Rd. Walt O T KT12 .... 35 A2
Alpine View. Carsh SM1 .... 59 E5
Alresford Rd. Guild GU2 .... 130 A8
Alric Ave. King U T KT3 .... 38 F6
Alsace Wlk. Camb GU15 .... 65 B1
Alsford Cl. Lhtwat GU18 .... 66 F7
Alsom Ave. Worc Pk KT19 & KT4 58 A6
Alston Cl. Thame D KT7 .... 8 A8
Alston Rd. Up Toot SW17 .... 20 D4
Alt Gr. Wimble SW19 .... 19 E1
Alterton Rd. Woking GU21 .... 69 A2
Althorne Rd. Earls RH1 .... 140 A7
Althorp Rd. Up Toot SW17 .... 20 F7
Alton Cl. Islew TW7 .... 5 F5
Alton Ct. 19 Beck BR3 .... 24 A1
Alton Ct. Egham TW18 .... 32 E8
Alton Gdns. Beck BR3 .... 24 A1
Alton Gdns. Twick TW2 .... 16 D8
Alton House. 1 Redh RH1 .... 119 A3
Alton Rd. Croy CR0 & CR9 .... 61 A4
Alton Rd. Farnh GU10 & GU9 ... 145 D7
Alton Rd. Rhampt SW15 .... 19 A7
Alton Rd. Rich TW10 & TW9 .... 6 E3
Alton Ride. Blckw GU17 .... 64 C6
Altwood Prim Sch. Sander CR2 . 81 A6
Altyre Cl. Beck BR3 .... 43 F8
Altyre Rd. S Croy CR0 & CR9 ..... 61 D8
Altyre Way. Beck BR3 .... 43 F4
Alvernia Cl. Godal GU7 .... 150 C2
Alvernia Lodge. Sutton SM1 .... 59 B5
Alverstoke Gdns. Alder GU11 ... 104 E1
Alverston Gdns. S Norw SE25 .... 42 E4
Alverstone Ave.
　Wimble SW18 & SW19 .... 20 A6
Alverstone Rd. New Mal KT3 ..... 38 F5
Alvia Gdns. Sutton SM1 .... 59 C6
Alway Ave. W Ewell KT19 .... 57 D5
Alway Ave. W Ewell KT19 .... 57 D5
Alwyn Cl. New Add CR0 .... 63 B3
Alwyne Ct. Horse GU21 .... 69 E3
Alwyne Rd. Wimble SW19 .... 19 F2
Alwyns Cl. Chert KT16 .... 33 A3
Alwyns La. Chert KT16 .... 33 A3
Amalgamated Dr. Brent TW8 .... 6 B8
Amanda Ct. Ashf TW15 .... 13 F6
Ambassador. Easth RG12 .... 26 F4
Ambassador Cl. Hounsl TW3 .... 4 E5
Amber Ct. Alder GU12 .... 105 C2
Amber Ct. Mitch CR4 .... 40 E5
Amber Ct. Stain TW18 .... 12 F3
Amber Hill. Friml GU15 .... 66 B4
Ambercroft Way. Coulsd CR5 ... 100 B8
Amberley Cl. Crawl RH10 .... 202 C6
Amberley Cl. Horsh RH12 .... 218 A6
Amberley Cl. Send M GU23 .... 90 F2
Amberley Ct. Sutton SM2 .... 59 C3
Amberley Dr. Woodhm KT15 ...... 70 F8
Amberley Gdns. Worc Pk KT19 ... 57 F6
Amberley Gr. Croy CR0 .... 42 F2
Amberley Gr. For Hil SE26 .... 23 B3
Amberley Grange. Alder GU11 . 125 F8
Amberley Rd. Horsh RH12 .... 218 A6
Amberley Rd. Milf GU8 .... 149 E2
Amberley Way. Heston TW4 .... 4 C2
Amberley Way. Morden SM4 ...... 39 F2
Amberwood Dr. Camb GU15 ...... 65 F7
Amberwood Rise. New Mal KT3 .. 38 E3
Amblecote. Catf BR1 .... 24 D2
Ambleside. Godal GU7 .... 151 A6
Ambleside. 13 Putney SW19 ...... 19 E7
Ambleside Ave. Beck BR3 .... 43 E4
Ambleside Ave. Streat SW16 ..... 21 D4
Ambleside Ave. Walt O T KT12 ... 35 C1
Ambleside Cl. Crawl RH11 .... 200 D6
Ambleside Cl. Farnb GU14 .... 84 E3
Ambleside Cl. Mytch GU16 .... 86 A3
Ambleside Cres. Hale GU9 .... 125 A6
Ambleside Cty Jun Sch.
　Walt O T KT12 .... 35 C1
Ambleside Dr. E Bed TW14 .... 14 F7
Ambleside Gdns. Selsd CR2 .... 62 D1
Ambleside Gdns. Streat SW16 .... 21 D3
Ambleside Gdns. Sutton SM2 ..... 59 C4
Ambleside Rd. Lhtwat GU18 .... 67 B8
Ambleside Sch. Belm SM2 .... 58 E2
Ambleside Way. Thor L TW20 ..... 12 B1
Ambrey Way. Wallin CR8 & SM6 . 60 D2
Amen Cnr. Streat SW17 .... 21 A2
Amen Corner Bsns Pk.
　Binf RG12 .... 26 D7
Amenity Way. W Barn SM4 .... 39 C2
American Comm Sch.
　Esher KT11 .... 54 C1
American Comm Sch.
　Vir W TW20 .... 31 C7
American Comm Sch.
　Wimble SW19 .... 19 C1
American Sch in Switzerland
　(English Branch) The.
　Thorpe TW20 .... 32 C6
Amersham Rd. Thorn H CR0 ...... 42 D3
Amesbury Ave. Streat SW2 .... 21 F6
Amesbury Cl. N Cheam KT4 .... 39 C1
Amesbury Rd. Felt TW13 .... 15 D6
Amesbury Sch. Shottm GU26 ... 188 E1
Amey Dr. Fetch KT23 .... 94 C3
Amhurst Gdns. Islew TW7 .... 6 A5
Amis Ave. Chess KT19 .... 57 B5
Amis Ave. Woodhm KT15 .... 52 A1
Amis Rd. Knaph GU21 .... 88 E8
Amity Gr. Wimble SW20 .... 39 C8
Amlets La. Cran GU6 .... 174 E5
Ampere Way. Croy CR0 & CR9 ... 41 F1
Amroth Cl. For Hil SE23 .... 23 B7
Amstel Way. Knaph GU21 .... 68 F1
Amundsen Rd. Rhampt SW12 ... 217 D6
Amy Johnson Prim Sch.
　Wallin SM6 .... 60 E3
Amy Rd. Oxted RH8 .... 122 E6
Amyand Cotts. 12 Twick TW1 ..... 6 B1
Amyand Park Gdns. 3
　Twick TW1 .... 17 B8
Amyand Park Rd. Twick TW1 ..... 17 A8
Anarth Ct. Oat Pk KT13 .... 34 E1
Ancaster Cres. New Mal KT3 ..... 39 A3
Ancaster Dr. N Asct SL5 .... 28 E8
Ancaster Rd. Penge BR3 .... 43 D6
Anchor Cotts. Blind H RH7 ...... 163 E8
Anchor Cres. Knaph GU21 .... 68 D2
Anchor Hill. Knaph GU21 .... 68 D2
Anchor Meadow. Farnb GU14 .... 85 A4
Anchorage Cl. Wimble SW19 ..... 20 A3
Anderson Ave. Guild GU2 .... 109 B5
Anderson Cl. Epsom KT19 .... 76 B7
Anderson Dr. Ashf TW15 .... 14 C4
Anderson House. Up Toot SW17 20 D3
Anderson Pl. Bagsh GU19 .... 47 E4
Anderson Rd. Oat Pk KT13 .... 53 D7
Anderson's Pl. Hounsl TW3 .... 5 B3
Andhurst Ct. King U T KT2 .... 38 B8
Andon Ct. Beck BR3 .... 43 E6
Andover Cl. E Bed TW14 .... 14 F7
Andover Cl. Epsom KT19 .... 76 D8
Andover Ct. Stan TW19 .... 13 D8
Andover Rd. Blckw GU17 .... 64 C6
Andover Rd. Twick TW2 .... 16 D7
Andover Way.
　Alder GU11 & GU9 .... 126 B7
Andreck Ct. Beck BR3 .... 44 C7
Andrew Cl. Woki RG11 .... 25 E5
Andrew Ct. For Hil SE23 .... 23 D6
Andrew Ewing Prim Sch.
　Heston TW5 .... 4 F7
Andrew Reed House.
　Putney SW18 .... 19 E8
Andrewartha Rd. Farnb GU14 ... 85 E2
Andrewes House. Sutton SM1 ... 59 A6
Andrews Cl. N Cheam KT4 .... 58 D8
Andrews Rd. W Heath GU14 ...... 84 F5
Andromeda Cl. Crawl RH11 ..... 200 E4
Anerley Ct. Penge SE20 .... 23 B1
Anerley Gr. Penge SE19 .... 22 F1
Anerley Hill. Penge SE19 .... 22 F2
Anerley Park Rd. Penge SE20 ... 23 B1
Anerley Pk. Penge SE20 .... 23 B1
Anerley Prim Sch. Penge SE20 .. 43 A8
Anerley Rd. Penge SE20 & SE19 . 43 A8
Anerley Sch. Penge SE20 .... 43 A8
Anerley Sta. Penge SE20 .... 43 B8
Anerley Station Rd. Penge SE20 43 B8
Anerley Vale. Penge SE19 .... 23 A1
Anfield Cl. Streat SW12 .... 21 C8
Angas Ct. 4 Whit V KT13 .... 53 C5
Angel Ct. Compt GU3 .... 129 A3
Angel Gate. Guild GU1 .... 130 D8
Angel Hill. Sutton SM1 .... 59 B7
Angel Hill Dr. Sutton SM1 .... 59 B7
Angel Rd. Thame D KT7 .... 37 A1
Angela Ct. For Hil SE23 .... 23 C7
Angelfield. Hounsl TW3 .... 5 B2
Angelica Gdns. Croy CR0 .... 43 D1
Angelica Rd. Bisley GU21 & GU24 68 A4
Angelica Rd. Stough GU2 .... 109 A5
Anglers Reach. King U T KT6 ..... 37 D4
Angles Rd. Streat SW16 .... 21 E4
Anglesea House. King U T KT1 ... 37 D5
Anglesea Rd. King U T KT1 .... 37 D5
Anglesey Ave. W Heath GU14 .... 84 F7
Anglesey Cl. Ashf TW15 .... 14 A5
Anglesey Cl. Crawl RH11 .... 201 C2
Anglesey Court Rd. Wallin SM5 . 60 A4
Anglesey Gdns. Wallin SM5 ...... 60 A4
Anglesey Rd. Alder GU12 .... 105 D1
Angus Cl. Chess KT9 .... 57 A5
Angus Cl. Horsh RH12 .... 217 D4
Angus House. 12 Streat SW12 ... 21 D8
Anlaby Rd. Tedd TW11 .... 16 E3
Ann Parkes Ct. Hounsl TW5 .... 4 D5
Annandale Dr. M Bourn GU10 .. 146 D6
Annandale Rd. Croy CR0 .... 62 A8
Annandale Rd. Guild GU2 .... 130 B7
Anne Armstrong Cl.
　Farnb GU11 .... 105 D5
Anne Boleyn's Wlk.
　Cheam SM2 & SM3 .... 58 E3
Anne Boleyn's Wlk.
　King U T KT2 .... 17 E3
Anne Way. E Mole KT8 .... 36 B5
Anne's Wlk. Whytlf CR3 .... 100 C7
Anners Cl. Egham TW20 .... 32 C6
Annesley Dr. Croy CR0 .... 62 F7
Annett Rd. Up Hall TW17 .... 34 E5
Annett Rd. Walt O T KT12 .... 35 A2
Annie Brookes Cl. Stain TW18 ... 12 D5
Anningsley Pk. Ottsh KT16 .... 51 C1
Annisdowne. Peasl GU5 .... 133 F1
Annsworthy Ave.
　S Norw CR7 & SE25 .... 42 D6
Annsworthy Cres. S Norw CR7 .. 42 D7
Ansell Gr. Carsh SM5 .... 41 A1
Ansell Rd. Dork RH4 .... 136 B8
Ansell Rd. Friml GU16 .... 65 E1
Ansell Rd. Friml GU16 .... 85 E1
Ansell Rd. Up Toot SW17 .... 20 F5
Anselm Cl. S Croy CR0 .... 61 F7
Ansford Rd. Catf BR1 & SE6 ...... 24 D4
Ansley Cl. Hams Gn CR2 .... 81 B5
Anslie Wlk. 8 Balham SW12 ...... 21 B8
Anson Cl. Cater CR3 & CR8 ...... 100 D7
Anstice Cl. Chisw W4 .... 7 E7
Anstie Grange Dr. S Holm RH5 . 157 B3
Anstie La. Coldh RH5 .... 156 F4
Anstiebury Cl. Bear Gn RH5 .... 157 C3
Anston Ct. 3 Stough GU2 .... 108 E1
Anthony Rd. Croy CR0 & SE25 ... 43 A3
Anthony West House.
　Brock RH3 .... 137 B7
Antigua Wlk. W Norw SE19 .... 22 D3
Antlands La. Burst RH6 .... 183 B6
Antlands La. Crawl RH6 .... 182 E5
Antlands La E. Burst RH6 .... 182 F5
Antlands La W. Crawl RH6 .... 182 E6
Anton Cres. Sutton SM1 .... 59 A7
Antrobus Cl. Cheam SM1 .... 58 F5
Anvil La. Cobham KT11 .... 73 A5
Anvil Rd. Sunby TW16 .... 35 A6
Anyards Rd. Cobham KT11 .... 73 B5
Anzio Cl. Alder GU11 .... 105 A2
Apeldoorn Dr. Wallin CR8 & SM6 60 E1
Aperdele Rd. Leahd KT22 .... 75 A1
Aperfield Rd. Bigg H TN16 .... 83 E2
Apers Ave. Westfd GU22 .... 89 F6
Apex Cl. Beck BR3 .... 44 B8
Apex Cl. Oat Pk KT13 .... 53 D7
Apex Dr. Friml GU16 .... 65 D1
Apley Rd. Woodh RH2 .... 139 A6
Aplin Way. Hounsl TW7 .... 5 E6
Aplin Way. Lhtwat GU18 .... 48 A1
Apollo Pl. Woking GU21 .... 89 A8
Apollo Rise. Farnb GU14 .... 84 D4
Apple Garth. Farnc GU7 .... 150 C7
Apple Gr. Chess KT9 .... 56 E6
Apple Mkt. King U T KT1 .... 37 D7
Apple Tree Way. Sandh GU15 .... 45 D1
Appleby Cl. Twick TW2 .... 16 D6
Appleby Ct. Camb GU15 .... 65 B6
Appleby Gdns. E Bed TW14 .... 14 F7
Appledore. Easth RG12 .... 26 F3
Appledore Cl. Hayes BR2 .... 44 F4
Appledore Cl.
　Up Toot SW12 & SW17 .... 21 A6
Appledore Mews. W Heath GU14 85 A7
Appledown Rise. Coulsd CR5 ..... 79 C4
Applefield. Crawl RH10 .... 201 E7
Applegarth. Clayg KT10 .... 55 F5
Applegarth. New Add CR0 .... 63 B3
Applegarth Ave. Stough GU2 ... 108 D1
Applegarth Inf & Jun Sch.
　New Add CR0 .... 63 B4
Applelands Cl. Rowl GU10 .... 146 A4
Appleton Gdns. New Mal KT3 .... 39 A3
Appleton Sq. Mitch CR4 .... 40 E8
Appletree Cl. Godal GU7 .... 150 F2
Appletree Cl. 6 Penge SE20 ..... 43 B8
Appletree Ct. Merrow GU4 .... 110 D3
Appletree Pl. 4 Brack RG12 ...... 27 A8
Appletrees Pl. Woking GU22 ..... 89 C8
Appley Dr. Camb GU15 .... 65 B6
Approach Rd. Ashf TW15 .... 14 C2
Approach Rd. E Mole KT8 .... 36 A4
Approach Rd. Farnh GU9 .... 125 C1
Approach Rd. Merton SW20 ...... 39 C7
Approach Rd. Purley CR8 .... 80 B8
Approach Rd. Tats CR6 & TN16 103 B5
Approach The. Dorman RH19 ... 185 F6
April Cl. Ashtd KT21 .... 75 F1
April Cl. Camb GU15 .... 65 C2
April Cl. Felt TW13 .... 15 A5
April Cl. Horsh RH12 .... 217 C4
April Glen. For Hil SE23 .... 23 D5
Aprilwood Cl. Woodhm KT15 ..... 70 F8
Apsley Ct. Crawl RH11 .... 200 F4
Apsley Ct. Sutton SM2 .... 59 C4
Apsley Rd. Croy SE25 .... 43 B5
Apsley Rd. King U T KT3 .... 38 C6
Aquarius. Twick TW1 .... 17 B7
Aquarius Ct. Crawl RH11 .... 200 E4
Aquila Cl. Ashtd KT21 .... 95 E6
Arabella Dr. Rhampt SW15 .... 7 E3
Aragon Ave. Ewell KT17 .... 58 B2
Aragon Ave. Thame D KT7 .... 36 F4
Aragon Cl. Ashf TW16 .... 14 F1
Aragon Cl. New Add CR0 .... 63 E1
Aragon Ct. Easth RG12 .... 27 C5
Aragon Cl. Knaph GU21 .... 68 D2
Aragon Rd. King U T KT2 .... 17 E3
Aragon Rd. W Barn SM4 .... 39 E2
Arbor Cl. Beck BR3 .... 44 B7
Arbour Ct. Fetch KT22 .... 94 F4
Arbrook La. Esher KT10 .... 55 D4
Arbury Terr. For Hil SE26 .... 23 B5
Arbutus Cl. Woodh RH2 .... 139 C7
Arbutus Rd. Woodh RH1 & RH2 139 C6
Arcade The. Alder GU11 .... 105 A2
Arch Rd. Walt O T KT12 .... 54 D7
Archbishop Lanfranc Sch The.
　Thorn H CR0 .... 41 E3
Archbishop Tenison's Sch.
　S Croy CR0 .... 61 D5
Archbishop's Pl. 3 Streat SW2 .. 21 F8
Archdale Pl. King U T KT3 .... 38 B6
Archdeacon Cambridge's Prim Sch
　(C of E). Twick TW2 .... 16 E6
Archer Cl. King U T KT2 .... 17 E1
Archer Rd. Croy SE25 .... 43 B5
Archers Ct. Crawl RH11 .... 201 D8
Archway Cl. Wallin SM6 .... 60 E7
Archway Cl. Wimble SW19 .... 20 B4
Archway Mews. Dork RH4 .... 136 A8
Archway Pl. Dork RH4 .... 136 A8
Archway St. Mortl SW13 & SW14 .. 7 E4
Arcturus Rd. Crawl RH11 .... 200 E3
Arcus Rd. Catf BR1 .... 24 E2
Arden. 17 Putney SW19 .... 19 D7
Arden Cl. Brack RG12 .... 28 A7
Arden Cl. Dovgn RH2 .... 139 B5
Arden Mead Cotts. Tand RH7 ... 164 A8
Arden Rd. Crawl RH10 .... 201 F4
Ardenrun. Tand RH7 .... 164 B8
Ardenrun Cotts. Tand RH7 .... 164 A7
Ardent Cl. S Norw SE25 .... 42 F6
Ardesley Wood. Oat Pk KT13 ..... 53 E6
Ardfern Ave. Thorn H SW16 ...... 42 A6
Ardfillan Rd. Catf SE6 .... 24 D6
Ardgowan Rd. Catf SE6 .... 24 E7
Ardingly. Easth RG12 .... 27 A4
Ardingly Cl. Crawl RH11 .... 201 B8
Ardingly Cl. S Croy CR0 .... 62 D7
Ardingly Ct. Epsom KT18 .... 76 D5
Ardleigh Gdns. Cheam SM3 ...... 40 A2
Ardley Cl. For Hil SE23 & SE6 ... 23 E5
Ardlui Rd. W Norw SE27 .... 22 C6
Ardmay Gdns. King U T KT6 ...... 37 E4
Ardmore Ave. Stough GU2 ...... 109 B3
Ardmore House. Stough GU2 ... 109 B3
Ardmore Way. Stough GU2 ...... 109 B3
Ardoch Rd. Catf SE6 .... 24 D6
Ardrossan Ave. Friml GU15 .... 66 A5
Ardrossan Gdns. Worc Pk KT4 ... 58 A7
Ardshiel Dr. Earls RH1 .... 139 E7
Ardwell Rd. Streat SW2 .... 21 E6
Arena L Ctr. Camb GU15 .... 65 C6
Arena La. Alder GU11 .... 104 E3
Arenal Dr. Crowth RG11 .... 45 C3
Arethusa Way. Bisley GU24 .... 67 F3
Arford Comm. Head Do GU35 ... 187 A6
Argent Terr. Sandh GU15 .... 64 E8
Argosy Gdns. Stain TW18 .... 12 F2
Argosy La. Stan TW19 .... 13 D8
Argus Wlk. Crawl RH11 .... 201 A3
Argyle Ave. Islew TW2 & TW3 ..... 5 A1
Argyle Ave. Twick TW3 .... 5 A1
Argyle House. Sutton SM2 .... 59 C4
Argyle Rd. Hounsl TW3 .... 5 B2
Argyle St. Pirb GU24 .... 87 A6
Argyll Ct. 15 Streat SW2 .... 21 E8
Ariel Rd. Farnb GU14 .... 85 A2
Ariel Way. Hounsl TW4 .... 4 B4
Arkell Gr. S Norw SW16 .... 22 B1
Arkendale Rd. Felb RH19 .... 185 A4
Arkindale Rd. Catf SE6 .... 24 C5
Arklow Mews. Surb KT6 .... 56 E8
Arklow Mews. 3 Surb KT6 .... 56 E8
Arkwright Dr. Binf RG12 .... 26 D7
Arkwright House. 23
　Streat SW2 .... 21 E8
Arkwright Rd. Poyle SL3 .... 1 E5
Arkwright Rd. S Croy CR2 .... 61 F2
Arlington Cl. Brack RG12 .... 27 A8
Arlington Cl. Sutton SM1 .... 59 A8
Arlington Cl. Twick TW1 .... 6 C1
Arlington Ct. Reig RH2 .... 118 A3
Arlington Ct. 4 Twick TW1 .... 6 C1
Arlington Dr. Carsh SM5 .... 59 F8
Arlington Lodge. Weyb KT13 ..... 53 B6
Arlington Rd. Ashf TW15 .... 13 F3
Arlington Rd. Rich TW10 .... 17 D6
Arlington Rd. Surb KT6 .... 37 D3
Arlington Rd. Tedd TW11 .... 16 F4
Arlington Rd. Twick TW1 .... 6 C1
Arlington Terr. Alder GU11 ...... 104 F2
Armadale Rd. Felt TW14 .... 4 A2
Armadale Rd. Woking GU21 ...... 69 A2
Armeston. New Mal KT3 .... 38 D2
Armfield Cl. E Mole KT8 .... 35 F4
Armfield Cres. Mitch CR4 .... 40 F7
Armitage Ct. Ascot SL5 .... 29 C3
Armitage Dr. Friml GU16 .... 65 F1
Armstrong Mall. Farnb GU14 .... 84 D4
Armstrong Rd. Eng Gn TW20 ..... 11 C2
Armstrong Rd. Felt TW13 .... 15 E3
Armytage Rd. Heston TW5 .... 4 D7
Arnal Cres. Putney SW18 .... 19 E8
Arncliffe. Easth RG12 .... 27 A4
Arndale Way. Egham TW20 .... 12 A3
Arne Cl. Crawl RH11 .... 200 F3
Arne Gr. Horley RH6 .... 160 E5
Arnewood Cl. Oxsh KT22 .... 74 B5
Arnewood Cl. Rhampt SW15 ...... 19 A7
Arney's La. Mitch CR4 .... 41 A3
Arnfield Cl. Crawl RH11 .... 200 E5
Arngask Rd. Catf SE6 .... 24 D8
Arnhem Cl. Alder GU11 .... 105 B2
Arnhem Dr. New Add CR0 .... 82 D7
Arnison Rd. E Mole KT8 .... 36 D5
Arnold Cres. Islew TW7 .... 5 D2
Arnold Dr. Chess KT9 .... 56 D4
Arnold Rd. Mitch SW17 .... 20 F1
Arnold Rd. Sheer GU21 .... 70 B4
Arnold Rd. Stain TW18 .... 13 C1
Arnulf St. Catf SE6 .... 24 B4
Arnull's Rd. S Norw SW16 .... 22 B2
Arragon Gdns. Streat SW16 .... 21 E1
Arragon Gdns. W Wick BR4 .... 63 B7
Arragon Rd. 3 Twick TW1 .... 17 A7
Arragon Rd. Twick TW1 .... 17 A8
Arragon Rd. Wands SW18 .... 20 A7
Arragon Wlk. Byfl KT14 .... 71 F6
Arran Cl. Crawl RH11 .... 201 B3
Arran Cl. Wallin SM6 .... 60 C6
Arran Rd. Catf SE6 .... 24 C6
Arran Way. Thame D KT10 .... 55 B8
Arrancourt. Horsh RH12 .... 217 B2
Arras Ave. Morden SM4 .... 40 C4
Arrivals Rd. Crawl RH6 .... 181 F8
Arrol Rd. Penge BR3 .... 43 D6
Arrow Ind Est. Farnb GU14 .... 84 F2
Arrow Rd. Farnb GU14 .... 84 F2

Artel Croft. Crawl RH10 .... 202 A6
Arterberry Rd.
　Wimble SW20 & SW19 .... 39 D8
Arthur Cl. Bagsh GU19 .... 47 E1
Arthur Cl. M Bourn GU9 .... 125 B1
Arthur Ct. S Croy CR0 .... 61 D7
Arthur Rd. Bigg H TN16 .... 83 C3
Arthur Rd. Crawl RH11 .... 200 E6
Arthur Rd. Horsh RH13 .... 217 D1
Arthur Rd. 6 King U T KT2 .... 18 A1
Arthur Rd. M Bourn GU9 .... 125 C1
Arthur Rd. W Barn KT3 .... 39 B4
Arthur Rd. Wimble SW19 .... 20 A5
Arthur Rd. Woki RG11 .... 25 A6
Arthur St. Alder GU11 .... 105 B2
Arthur's Bridge Rd. Horse GU21 69 D2
Artillery Rd. Alder GU11 .... 105 B2
Artillery Rd.
　Farnb GU11 & GU14 .... 105 D8
Artillery Rd. 7 Guild GU1 .... 109 D1
Artillery Terr. Guild GU1 .... 109 D1
Artington Wlk. Guild GU2 .... 130 C6
Arun Way. Horsh RH13 .... 217 E1
Arundale. King U T KT1 .... 37 D5
Arundel Ave. Ewell KT17 .... 58 B1
Arundel Ave. Merton SM4 .... 39 F5
Arundel Ave. S Croy CR2 .... 62 A1
Arundel Cl. Crawl RH10 .... 202 C6
Arundel Cl. Croy CR0 & CR9 .... 61 B7
Arundel Cl. Hampt TW12 .... 16 B3
Arundel Ct. Beck BR2 .... 44 E7
Arundel House. Croy CR0 .... 61 D5
Arundel House. Dovgn RH2 .... 139 B5
Arundel Rd. Belm SM2 .... 58 F3
Arundel Rd. Dork RH4 .... 136 A7
Arundel Rd. Friml GU15 .... 66 C4
Arundel Rd. Hounsl TW4 .... 4 C4
Arundel Rd. King U T KT1 .... 38 C7
Arundel Rd. Thorn H CR0 .... 42 D3
Arundell Pl. 6 Farnh GU9 .... 125 B2
Arunside. Horsh RH12 .... 217 A1
Arunside Cty Prim Sch.
　Horsh RH12 .... 217 A2
Ascalon Ct. 19 Streat SW2 .... 21 F8
Aschurch Rd. Croy CR0 .... 42 F2
Ascot Heath Cty Inf Sch.
　N Asct SL5 .... 8 E1
Ascot Heath Jun Sch. N Asct SL5 8 E1
Ascot House. Penge SE26 .... 23 B2
Ascot Mews. Wallin SM6 .... 60 C2
Ascot Race Course. Ascot SL5 ... 28 F6
Ascot Rd. E Bed TW14 & TW15 ... 14 B6
Ascot Rd. Mitch SW17 .... 21 A2
Ascot Sta. Ascot SL5 .... 29 A5
Ascot Towers. N Asct SL5 .... 28 F7
Ascot Wood. Ascot SL5 .... 29 A6
Asford Gdns. Cobham KT11 .... 73 D3
Ash Church Rd. Ash GU12 .... 106 D3
Ash Cl. Ash GU12 .... 106 B3
Ash Cl. Blckw GU17 .... 64 C5
Ash Cl. Box H KT20 .... 116 C4
Ash Cl. Carsh SM5 .... 59 F8
Ash Cl. Crawl D RH10 .... 204 C8
Ash Cl. King U T KT3 .... 38 D7
Ash Cl. Lingf RH7 .... 164 C5
Ash Cl. Merst RH1 .... 119 C5
Ash Cl. Penge SE20 .... 43 C7
Ash Cl. Pyrf GU22 .... 71 A4
Ash Cl. Woking GU22 .... 89 E7
Ash Combe. Chidd GU8 .... 191 A4
Ash Ct. Ottsh KT16 .... 51 C5
Ash Ct. W Ewell KT19 .... 57 C6
Ash Ct. W Ewell KT19 .... 57 C6
Ash Ct. 2 W Norw SW16 .... 22 A3
Ash Dr. Earls RH1 .... 140 B7
Ash Gr. E Bed TW14 .... 14 E7
Ash Gr. Heston TW5 .... 4 D7
Ash Gr. Penge SE20 .... 43 C7
Ash Gr. Stain TW18 .... 13 C2
Ash Gr. Stough GU2 .... 109 A2
Ash Gr. W Wick BR4 .... 44 C1
Ash Green La E. Ash GU12 .... 127 C8
Ash Green La W. Ash GU12 .... 126 F8
Ash Green La W. Ash GU12 .... 127 C8
Ash Green Rd. Ash GU12 .... 106 C1
Ash Hill Rd. Ash GU12 .... 106 B3
Ash Keys. Crawl RH10 .... 201 E5
Ash La. Elst GU8 .... 148 C2
Ash Lodge. 2 Charlt TW16 .... 14 F1
Ash Lodge Cl. Ash GU12 .... 106 A1
Ash Lodge Dr. Ash GU12 .... 106 A1
Ash Manor Sch. Ash GU12 .... 126 F6
Ash Mews. Epsom KT18 .... 76 E6
Ash Rd. Alder GU12 .... 126 D8
Ash Rd. Cheam SM3 & SM4 .... 39 F1
Ash Rd. Crawl RH10 .... 202 A8
Ash Rd. Croy CR0 .... 63 A8
Ash Rd. Pirb GU24 & GU3 .... 88 A1
Ash Rd. Shep Gn TW17 .... 34 A5
Ash Rd. Woking GU22 .... 89 E7
Ash St. Ash GU12 .... 106 A1
Ash Sta. Ash GU12 .... 106 B2
Ash Tree Cl. Croy BR3 & CR0 ...... 43 E3
Ash Tree Cl. Farnb GU14 .... 84 C3
Ash Tree Cl. Grays GU27 .... 189 F1
Ash Tree Cl. 1 Surb KT6 .... 37 E1
Ash Tree Way. Croy CR0 .... 43 E3
Ash Vale. Chidd GU8 .... 191 A5
Ash Vale Cty Fst Sch.
　Ash V GU12 .... 106 A8
Ash Vale Sta. Ash GU12 .... 106 A7
Ashbourne. Easth RG12 .... 26 F3
Ashbourne Cl. Ash GU12 .... 106 C3
Ashbourne Cl. Coulsd CR5 .... 79 C1
Ashbourne Rd.
　Mitch CR4 & SW17 .... 21 A1
Ashbourne Terr. 1
　Merton SW19 .... 20 A1

Ashbrook Rd. Old W SL4 .... 11 B8
Ashburnham Pk. Esher KT10 .... 55 C6
Ashburnham Rd. Crawl RH10 ... 202 A4
Ashburnham Rd. Rich TW10 .... 17 B5
Ashburton Ave. Croy CR0 .... 43 B1
Ashburton Cl. Croy CR0 .... 43 A1
Ashburton Gdns. Croy CR0 .... 62 A8
Ashburton Jun & Inf Sch.
　Croy CR0 .... 43 B3
Ashburton Rd. Croy CR0 & CR9 ... 62 A8
Ashburton Sch. Croy CR0 .... 43 B2
Ashbury Cres. Merrow GU4 .... 110 C3
Ashby Dr. W Heath GU14 .... 65 A1
Ashby Ave. Chess KT19 & KT9 ..... 57 A4
Ashby Ct. Horsh RH13 .... 217 E1
Ashby Grange. 7 Wallin SM6 .... 60 C4
Ashby Way. Harm UB7 .... 3 A7
Ashby Wlk. Thorn H CR0 .... 42 C3
Ashcombe Par. Old Wok GU22 ... 90 A7
Ashcombe Rd. Surb KT6 .... 37 D2
Ashcombe Rd. Dork RH4 .... 115 B1
Ashcombe Rd. Merst RH1 .... 119 C8
Ashcombe Rd. Wallin SM5 .... 60 A4
Ashcombe Rd. Wimble SW19 .... 20 A3
Ashcombe Sch The. Dork RH4 .. 115 B1
Ashcombe Sq. King U T KT3 .... 38 C5
Ashcombe Terr. Burgh H KT20 ... 97 B7
Ashcroft. Shalf GU4 .... 130 E2
Ashcroft Pk. Cobham KT11 .... 73 E6
Ashcroft Rd. Chess KT9 .... 56 F7
Ashcroft Rise. Coulsd CR5 .... 79 E3
Ashdale. G Book KT23 .... 94 C1
Ashdale Cl. Stan TW19 .... 13 E6
Ashdale Cl. Twick TW2 .... 16 C8
Ashdale Way. Twick TW2 .... 16 B8
Ashdene Cres. Ash GU12 .... 106 A3
Ashdene House. Eng Gn TW20 ..... 11 C2
Ashdene Rd. Ash GU12 .... 106 A2
Ashdown Ave. Farnb GU14 .... 85 E2
Ashdown Cl. Beck BR3 .... 44 B7
Ashdown Cl. Brack RG12 .... 28 A7
Ashdown Cl. Dovgn RH2 .... 139 B5
Ashdown Dr. Crawl RH10 .... 201 E3
Ashdown Gate. E Grins RH19 ... 185 D2
Ashdown Gdns. Hams Gn CR2 ... 81 B4
Ashdown Pl. Thame D KT7 .... 37 A2
Ashdown Rd. Dovgn RH2 .... 139 B5
Ashdown Rd. Ewell KT17 .... 77 A6
Ashdown Rd. For Row RH18 ..... 206 F2
Ashdown Rd. King U T KT1 .... 37 E7
Ashdown View. E Grins RH19 ... 205 E7
Ashdown Way. Up Toot SW17 ..... 21 A6
Ashen Gr. Wimble SW19 .... 20 A6
Ashen Vale. Selsd CR2 .... 62 D2
Ashenden Rd. Stough GU2 .... 108 F1
Ashfield Ave. Felt TW13 .... 15 B7
Ashfield Cl. Beck BR3 .... 24 A1
Ashfield Cl. Rich TW10 .... 17 E7
Ashfields. Reig RH2 .... 118 B3
Ashford Ave. Ashf TW15 .... 14 B2
Ashford C of E Fst & Mid Sch.
　Ashf TW15 .... 14 B2
Ashford Cl. Ashf TW15 .... 13 E4
Ashford Cres. Ashf TW15 .... 13 E5
Ashford High Sch The.
　Ashf TW15 .... 13 E5
Ashford Hospl. Stan TW15 .... 13 E6
Ashford Ind Est. Felt TW15 .... 14 C4
Ashford Manor Golf Club.
　Ashf TW15 .... 13 F2
Ashford Park Cty Prim Sch.
　Ashf TW15 .... 13 D4
Ashford Rd. Felt TW13 & TW15 ... 14 E4
Ashford Rd. Littlt TW15 & TW17 .. 14 C1
Ashford Rd. Stain TW18 .... 33 D8
Ashford Rd. Stain TW18 .... 33 D8
Ashford Sta. Ashf TW15 .... 13 F5
Ashgrove Rd. Ashf TW15 .... 14 D3
Ashgrove Rd. Catf BR1 .... 24 D2
Ashlake Rd. Streat SW16 .... 21 E4
Ashlea Ct. Warlgm CR6 .... 81 A1
Ashleigh Ave. Thor L TW20 .... 12 C1
Ashleigh Rd. Horley RH6 .... 160 F3
Ashleigh Ct. Penge SE26 .... 23 B2
Ashleigh Gdns. Sutton SM1 .... 59 B8
Ashleigh House. Mortl SW14 .... 7 A4
Ashleigh Point. 8 For Hil SE26 .. 23 D5
Ashleigh Rd. Horsh RH12 .... 217 C4
Ashleigh Rd. Mortl SW14 .... 7 A4
Ashleigh Rd. Penge SE20 .... 43 B6
Ashley Ave. Epsom KT18 .... 76 D6
Ashley Ave. Morden SM4 .... 40 A4
Ashley Cl. Friml GU16 .... 86 A6
Ashley Cl. L Book KT23 .... 93 F2
Ashley Cl. Oat Pk KT12 & KT13 ... 34 F1
Ashley Cl. 5 Epsom KT18 .... 76 D6
Ashley Cl. Knaph GU21 .... 68 F1
Ashley Ctr. Epsom KT18 .... 76 D6
Ashley Dr. Banstd SM7 .... 78 A5
Ashley Dr. Blckw GU17 .... 64 C4
Ashley Dr. Hounsl TW7 .... 5 E8
Ashley Dr. Twick TW2 .... 16 B7
Ashley Dr. Walt O T KT12 .... 54 A7
Ashley Gdns. Rich TW10 .... 17 D6
Ashley Gdns. Shalf GU4 .... 130 F2
Ashley House. Farnc GU7 .... 150 E8
Ashley Inf Sch. Walt O T KT12 ... 35 A1
Ashley La. Croy CR0 .... 61 B6
Ashley Park Ave. Walt O T KT12 . 53 F8
Ashley Park Cres. Walt O T KT12 35 A1
Ashley Park Rd. Walt O T KT12 ... 54 A7
Ashley Rd. Epsom KT18 .... 76 E4
Ashley Rd. Farnb GU14 .... 85 D4
Ashley Rd. Hampt TW12 .... 36 A8
Ashley Rd. Knaph GU21 .... 68 F1
Ashley Rd. Rich TW9 .... 6 E4
Ashley Rd. Thame D KT7 .... 36 F3
Ashley Rd. Thorn H CR7 .... 41 F5
Ashley Rd. Walt O T KT12 .... 54 A8
Ashley Rd. Westc RH4 .... 135 C6

Ashley Rd. Wimble SW19 .... 20 B2
Ashley Rise. Walt O T KT12 .... 54 A7
Ashley Way. W End GU24 .... 67 D6
Ashling Rd. Croy CR0 & CR9 .... 43 A1
Ashlyn's Pk. Cobham KT11 .... 73 E6
Ashlyns Way. Chess KT9 .... 56 D4
Ashmead Rd. E Bed TW14 .... 15 A7
Ashmere Ave. Beck BR3 .... 44 D7
Ashmere Cl. Cheam SM3 .... 58 D5
Ashmill Ct. Thorn H CR0 .... 42 C3
Ashmore Ct. Heston TW5 .... 5 A8
Ashmore House. Crawl RH11 ... 181 D1
Ashmore La. Bigg H BR2 & TN16 . 83 C8
Ashmore La. Rusper RH12 .... 199 C6
Ashridge. W Heath GU14 .... 84 F7
Ashridge Gn. 3 Brack RG12 .... 27 B8
Ashridge Rd. Woki RG11 .... 25 D8
Ashridge Way. Ashf TW16 .... 15 A2
Ashridge Way.
　Merton SM4 & SW20 .... 39 F5
Ashstead La. Godal GU7 .... 150 C2
Ashstead Sta. Ashtd KT21 .... 75 E3
Ashtead Ct. 15 Putney SW19 .... 19 D7
Ashtead Hospl The. Ashtd KT21 . 95 E8
Ashtead Park (London Freemen's
　Sch). Ashtd KT21 .... 96 A3
Ashtead Woods Rd. Ashtd KT21 . 75 C3
Ashton Cl. Cheam SM1 .... 59 A6
Ashton Cl. Hersh KT12 .... 54 B4
Ashton Ct. Beck BR3 .... 43 F8
Ashton Gdns. Hounsl TW4 .... 4 F3
Ashton House. Rhampt SW15 ..... 19 B8
Ashton Rd. 2 Woking GU21 .... 68 F2
Ashtree Ave. Mitch CR4 .... 40 D7
Ashtree Ct. Stan TW15 .... 14 B3
Ashtrees. Cran GU6 .... 174 E1
Ashurst. 3 Epsom KT18 .... 76 D6
Ashurst Cl. Horsh RH12 .... 218 A5
Ashurst Cl. Kenley CR8 .... 80 D4
Ashurst Cl. Penge SE20 .... 43 B8
Ashurst Dr. Box H KT20 .... 116 B5
Ashurst Dr. Shep Gn SW17 .... 33 E5
Ashurst Dr. Worth RH10 .... 202 D6
Ashurst Rd. Ash V GU12 .... 105 F4
Ashurst Rd. Tadw KT20 .... 97 C6
Ashurst Wlk. Croy CR0 .... 62 B8
Ashurstwood Abbey.
　Ash W RH19 .... 206 E6
Ashurstwood Cty Prim Sch.
　Ash W RH19 .... 206 E6
Ashvale Rd. Up Toot SW17 .... 20 F3
Ashview Cl. Ashf TW15 .... 13 E3
Ashview Gdns. Ashf TW15 .... 13 E3
Ashville Way. Woki RG11 .... 25 A5
Ashway Ctr. 3 King U T KT2 .... 37 E8
Ashwell Ave. Camb GU15 .... 65 F6
Ashwell Ct. Ashf TW15 .... 13 E6
Ashwindam Ct. 1 Knaph GU21 ... 68 F1
Ashwood. 5 Crawl RH11 .... 201 D5
Ashwood. Warlgm CR6 .... 101 C2
Ashwood Gdns. New Add CR0 ..... 63 C4
Ashwood Pk. Belm SM2 .... 59 A3
Ashwood Pk. Fetch KT22 .... 94 C4
Ashwood Rd. Eng Gn TW20 .... 11 B2
Ashwood Rd. Woking GU22 .... 70 A1
Ashworth Pl. Stough GU2 .... 108 F1
Aslett St. Wands SW18 .... 20 C8
Asmar Cl. Coulsd CR5 .... 79 C4
Aspen Cl. Merrow GU4 .... 110 D4
Aspen Cl. Stain TW18 .... 12 F5
Aspen Cl. Stk D'A KT11 .... 73 E3
Aspen Ct. Rich TW9 .... 7 A7
Aspen Gdns. Mitch CR4 .... 41 A4
Aspen House. 14 Streat SW2 .... 21 F8
Aspen Sq. Oat Pk KT13 .... 53 D7
Aspen Way. Horsh RH12 .... 217 E6
Aspen Way. Nork KT17 .... 77 D5
Aspin Way. Blckw GU17 .... 64 B5
Aspinall House. Streat SW12 .... 21 E7
Asquith House. Banstd SM7 .... 77 F4
Assembly Wlk. Carsh SM5 .... 40 E2
Assher Rd. Hersh KT12 .... 54 E7
Assheton-Bennett House. 15
　King U T KT6 .... 37 E4
Astleham Way. Littlt TW17 .... 33 E6
Astley House. 8 W Norw SE27 ..... 22 C4
Aston Cl. Ashtd KT21 .... 75 C1
Aston Ct. Crawl RH11 .... 201 B1
Aston Gn. Cranf TW5 .... 4 C5
Aston Rd. Merton SW20 .... 39 C7
Aston Way. Epsom KT18 .... 76 F3
Astonville St. Wands SW18 .... 20 A7
Astor Cl. Addl KT15 .... 52 D6
Astor Cl. King U T KT2 .... 18 B2
Astoria Mansions. 18
　Streat SW16 .... 21 E5
Astoria Par. Streat SW16 .... 21 E5
Astra Bsns Ctr. Salfs RH1 .... 161 A7
Astra Mead. Wink RG12 .... 8 B2
Atalanta Cl. Purley CR8 .... 61 A1
Atbara Ct. Tedd TW11 .... 17 B2
Atbara Rd. Tedd TW11 .... 17 B2
Atcham Rd. Islew TW3 .... 5 C3
Atfield Gr. Windl GU20 .... 48 D4
Atheldene Rd. Wands SW18 .... 20 C7
Athelney Prim Sch. Catf SE6 .... 24 A5
Athelney St. Catf SE6 .... 24 A5
Athelstan Cl. Worth RH10 .... 202 E6
Athelstan House. King U T KT1 ... 37 F5
Athelstan House Sch.
　Hampt TW12 .... 36 A8
Athelstan Rd. King U T KT1 .... 37 F5
Athena Cl. King U T KT1 .... 37 F6
Atherfield House. Dovgn RH1 ... 139 C6
Atherfield Rd. Woodh RH1 .... 139 C6
Atherley Way. Twick TW4 .... 15 F8
Atherton Cl. Shalf GU4 .... 130 E3
Atherton Cl. Stan TW19 .... 2 D1

Atherton Dr. Wimble SW19 .... 19 D4
Atherton House. S Croy CR2 .... 61 E4
Athlone. Clayg KT10 .... 55 E4
Athlone Rd. Streat SW2 .... 22 A8
Atholl House. 7 Redh RH1 .... 118 F1
Atkins Cl. Woking GU21 .... 69 A1
Atkins Dr. W Wick BR4 .... 63 D8
Atkins Rd. Streat SW4 & SW12 ... 21 D8
Atkinson Ct. Horley RH6 .... 161 B2
Atkinson Morley's Hospl.
　Wimble SW20 .... 19 B1
Atlanta Ct. S Norw CR7 .... 42 C6
Atrebatti Rd. Sandh GU15 & GU17 45 C1
Attfield Cl. Ash GU12 .... 105 F1
Attleborough Ct. Dulw SE21 .... 23 B6
Attlee House. 5 Crawl RH11 ..... 201 B2
Attwood Cl. Hams Gn CR2 .... 81 B5
Atwater Ct. Streat SW2 .... 22 A7
Atwood. L Book KT23 .... 93 E3
Atwood Ave. Rich TW9 .... 7 A5
Atwood House. Dulw SE21 .... 22 E5
Aubyn Hill. W Norw SE27 .... 22 D4
Auchinleck Ct. Crawl D RH10 ... 204 B7
Auchinleck Way. Alder GU11 ... 104 E2
Auckland Cl. Crawl RH11 .... 181 D1
Auckland Cl. S Norw SE19 .... 42 F8
Auckland Gdns. S Norw SE19 ..... 42 F8
Auckland Hill. W Norw SE27 .... 22 C4
Auckland Rd. Cater SM3 .... 100 E5
Auckland Rd. King U T KT1 .... 37 F5
Auckland Rd. S Norw SE19 & SE25 42 F8
Auckland Rise. S Norw SE19 .... 42 F8
Audley Cl. Addl KT15 .... 52 B5
Audley Ct. Surb KT5 .... 37 F3
Audley Ct. Cheam SM3 .... 58 E5
Audley Cty Prim Sch.
　Whytf CR3 .... 100 F6
Audley Dr. Hams Gn CR2 & CR6 ... 81 C4
Audley Firs. Hersh KT12 .... 54 C6
Audley House. Addl KT15 .... 52 B5
Audley Pl. Belm SM2 .... 59 B3
Audley Rd. Rich TW10 .... 6 F2
Audley Way. N Asct SL5 .... 28 D6
Audrey Cl. W Wick BR3 .... 44 B3
Audric Cl. King U T KT2 .... 38 A8
Augur Cl. Stain TW18 .... 12 F3
August La. Farl Gn GU5 .... 153 D7
Augusta Cl. E Mole KT8 .... 35 F6
Augusta Rd. Twick TW2 .... 16 C6
Augustine Cl. Poyle SL3 .... 1 E4
Augustus Cl. Brent TW8 .... 6 D7
Augustus Cl. 8 Putney SW19 ..... 19 E7
Augustus Cl. S Norw SE19 .... 22 E1
Augustus Cl. Streat SW16 .... 21 D6
Augustus Gdns. Friml GU15 .... 66 C5
Augustus Rd. Putney SW19 .... 19 E7
Aultone Way. Carsh SM5 .... 59 F7
Aultone Way. Sutton SM1 .... 59 C8
Aurelia Gdns. Thorn H CR7 .... 41 F3
Aurelia Rd.
　Thorn H CR0 & CR7 & CR9 .... 41 F3
Auriol Cl. Worc Pk KT19 .... 57 E7
Auriol Park Rd.
　Worc Pk KT19 & KT4 .... 57 E7
Aurum Cl. Horley RH6 .... 161 B2
Austen Cl. E Grins RH19 .... 185 B1
Austen Rd. W Heath GU14 .... 85 A6
Austin Cl. Coulsd CR8 .... 80 B1
Austin Cl. For Hil SE23 & SE6 ..... 23 F8
Austin Cl. Twick TW1 .... 6 C2
Austin House. 19 King U T KT6 ... 37 E4
Austin's Cotts. Farnh GU9 .... 125 B2
Austyn Gdns. Tolw KT5 .... 38 B1
Autumn Dr. Belm SM2 .... 59 B2
Avalon Cl. Merton SW20 .... 39 E7
Avarn Rd. Up Toot SW17 .... 20 F2
Avebury. Easth RG12 .... 27 A3
Avebury Rd. Merton SW19 .... 39 F8
Aveley La. M Bourn GU10 & GU9 146 C2
Aveling Cl. Purley CR8 .... 79 F6
Aveling Cl. Worth RH10 .... 202 C4
Aven Cl. Cran GU6 .... 174 E2
Avening Rd. Wands SW18 .... 20 A8
Avening Terr. Wands SW18 .... 20 A8
Avenue C. Chert KT15 .... 52 E7
Avenue Cl. Cranf TW5 .... 4 B6
Avenue Cl. Tadw KT20 .... 97 B5
Avenue Cres. Cranf TW5 .... 4 B7
Avenue Ct. Penge SE20 .... 43 C8
Avenue Ct. Tadw KT20 .... 97 B4
Avenue De Cagny. Pirb GU24 ..... 87 F5
Avenue Elmers. King U T KT6 ..... 37 E4
Avenue Gdns. Horley RH6 .... 161 C2
Avenue Gdns. Mortl SW14 .... 7 A4
Avenue Gdns. S Norw SE25 .... 43 A7
Avenue Gdns. Tedd TW11 .... 16 F2
Avenue One. Addl KT15 .... 52 E6
Avenue Park Rd.
　W Norw SE21 & SE27 .... 22 B6
Avenue Prim Sch The.
　Belm SM2 .... 59 A1
Avenue Rd. Banstd SM7 .... 78 B4
Avenue Rd. Belm SM2 .... 59 A1
Avenue Rd. Cater CR3 .... 100 E5
Avenue Rd. Cobham KT11 .... 73 D3
Avenue Rd. Cran GU6 .... 174 F1
Avenue Rd. Egham TW18 .... 12 B8
Avenue Rd. Epsom KT18 .... 76 D5
Avenue Rd. Felt TW13 .... 14 F5
Avenue Rd. Graysh GU26 .... 188 C3
Avenue Rd. Hampt TW12 .... 36 B8
Avenue Rd. Hounsl TW7 .... 5 F6
Avenue Rd. King U T KT1 .... 37 E6
Avenue Rd. Mitch SW16 .... 41 D7
Avenue Rd. New Mal KT3 .... 38 E5
Avenue Rd. S Norw SE25 .... 43 A7
Avenue Rd. S Norw BR3 & SE20 ... 43 D8

Avenue Rd. Tats TN16 .... 103 E7
Avenue Rd. Tedd TW11 .... 17 A2
Avenue Rd. Wallin SM6 .... 60 C3
Avenue Rd. Woking GU22 .... 39 B7
Avenue South. Surb KT5 .... 38 A2
Avenue Sucy. Camb GU15 .... 65 B3
Avenue Terr. King U T KT3 .... 38 C6
Avenue The.
　Alder GU11 & GU12 .... 126 C7
Avenue The. Beck BR3 .... 44 C8
Avenue The. Belm SM2 .... 58 F2
Avenue The. Bigg H TN16 .... 103 F5
Avenue The. Brock RH3 & RH5 .. 116 A1
Avenue The. Camb GU15 .... 65 B5
Avenue The. Chobh GU24 .... 50 A2
Avenue The. Clayg KT10 .... 55 E5
Avenue The. Compt GU3 & GU7 . 129 C1
Avenue The. Coulsd CR5 .... 79 D4
Avenue The. Cranf TW5 .... 4 A6
Avenue The. Crowth RG11 .... 45 B5
Avenue The. Dorman RH19 .... 186 B6
Avenue The. Egham TW20 .... 12 B4
Avenue The. Ewh GU6 .... 175 E6
Avenue The. Godal GU7 .... 150 F2
Avenue The. Graysh GU26 .... 188 D3
Avenue The. Hampt TW12 .... 15 F2
Avenue The. Horley RH6 .... 160 F2
Avenue The. Hounsl TW3 .... 5 B2
Avenue The. Islew TW1 .... 6 A1
Avenue The. N Asct SL5 .... 8 F1
Avenue The. 4 New Mal KT4 .... 39 A1
Avenue The. Oxsh KT10 & KT22 .. 74 F8
Avenue The. Rich TW9 .... 6 F5
Avenue The. Rowl GU10 .... 145 F3
Avenue The. S Croy CR0 .... 61 E7
Avenue The. S Nutf RH1 .... 140 E5
Avenue The. Shottm GU27 .... 207 F7
Avenue The. Stain TW18 .... 33 B8
Avenue The. Stonel KT17 & SM3 . 58 C3
Avenue The. Sunby TW16 .... 35 B7
Avenue The. Surb KT5 .... 37 F3
Avenue The. Tadw KT20 .... 97 B5
Avenue The. Twick TW1 .... 6 B2
Avenue The. W Wick BR4 .... 44 E2
Avenue The. Whytf CR3 .... 101 A8
Avenue The. Woodhm KT15 .... 52 A1
Avenue The. Worc Pk KT4 .... 57 F8
Avenue The. Worpl GU3 .... 88 E1
Avenue Three. Chert KT15 .... 52 E7
Avenue Two. Addl KT15 .... 52 E6
Averil Ct. S Norw SW16 .... 22 B2
Avern Gdns. E Mole KT8 .... 36 B5
Avern Rd. E Mole KT8 .... 36 B5
Avery Ct. Penge SE20 .... 23 B1
Aviary Rd. Pyrf GU22 .... 71 A3
Aviary Way. Crawl D RH10 .... 184 C5
Aviemore Cl. Beck BR3 .... 43 F4
Aviemore Way. Beck BR3 .... 43 E4
Avington Cl. Guild GU1 .... 109 E1
Avington Gr. Penge SE20 .... 23 C1
Avoca Rd. Up Toot SW17 .... 21 A4
Avocet Cres. Sandh GU15 .... 64 E8
Avon Cl. Ash GU12 .... 105 F1
Avon Cl. Row Tn KT15 .... 52 A4
Avon Cl. Sutton SM1 .... 59 C6
Avon Cl. W Heath GU14 .... 84 E7
Avon Cl. Worc Pk KT4 .... 58 A8
Avon House. 9 Redh RH1 .... 118 F2
Avon Rd. Ashf TW16 .... 14 F1
Avon Rd. M Bourn GU9 .... 125 C1
Avon Wlk. Crawl RH11 .... 200 F5
Avondale. Ash V GU12 .... 105 F7
Avondale Ave. Hinch W KT10 ..... 56 A7
Avondale Ave. New Mal KT4 .... 38 F1
Avondale Ave. Stain TW18 .... 12 F1
Avondale Cl. Hersh KT12 .... 54 C5
Avondale Cl. Horley RH6 .... 161 A5
Avondale Ct. Sutton SM2 .... 59 C3
Avondale Gdns. Hounsl TW4 .... 4 F2
Avondale High. Cater CR3 .... 101 A6
Avondale House. 6 Mortl SW14 ... 7 D4
Avondale Rd. Alder GU11 .... 126 B8
Avondale Rd. Ashf TW15 & TW19 13 D5
Avondale Rd. Broml BR1 .... 24 F2
Avondale Rd. Catf BR1 .... 24 F2
Avondale Rd. Mortl SW14 .... 7 D4
Avondale Rd. S Croy CR2 .... 61 C4
Avondale Rd. Wimble SW19 .... 20 B3
Avonmore Ave. Guild GU1 .... 109 F2
Avonwick Rd. Hounsl TW3 .... 5 B5
Avro Way. Byfl KT13 .... 52 E1
Avro Way. Wallin SM6 .... 60 E3
Axbridge. Brack RG12 .... 27 C4
Axes La. Salfs RH1 .... 140 D2
Axford House. Streat SW2 .... 22 B7
Axwood. Woodc KT18 .... 76 C4
Aycliffe Ct. King U T KT1 .... 38 A7
Ayebridges Ave. Egham TW20 ..... 12 C1
Ayjay Cl. Alder GU11 .... 126 A7
Aylesbury Ct. Sutton SM1 .... 59 C7
Aylesford Ave. Beck BR3 .... 43 E4
Aylesworth Spur. Old W SL4 .... 11 B8
Aylett Rd. Islew TW7 .... 5 E5
Ayley Croft. Enf ... (?)
Ayling Ct. Heath E GU9 .... 125 F7
Ayling Hill. Alder GU11 .... 104 F1
Ayling La. Alder GU11 .... 125 F8
Aylward Rd. For Hil SE23 .... 23 D6
Aylward Rd. Merton SW20 .... 39 F6
Aymer Cl. Egham TW18 .... 32 E8
Aymer Dr. Egham TW18 .... 32 E8
Aysgarth. Easth RG12 .... 27 A3
Aysgarth Ct. Sutton SM1 .... 59 B7
Aysgarth Rd. Dulw SE21 .... 22 E8
Ayshe Court Dr. Horsh RH13 ... 217 E3
Azalea Ct. Woking GU22 .... 89 D8
Azalea Dr. Shottm GU27 .... 207 F8
Azalea Way. Friml GU15 .... 66 B6
Azalea Ct. Purley CR8 .... 80 B8

Babbacombe Cl. Chess KT9 56 D5
Babbs Mead. Farnh GU9 125 A1
Baber Dr. Felt TW14 4 C1
Babington Ct. Streat SW16 21 D3
Babington Rd. Streat SW16 21 D3
Babylon La. L Kings KT20 & RH2 118 B8
Bachelor's La. Ockham GU23 92 A3
Back Gn. Hersh KT12 54 C4
Back La. Binst GU10 166 B8
Back La. Brent TW8 6 D8
Back La. E Clan GU4 111 D4
Back La. Elst GU8 148 D4
Back La. Plaist RH14 211 E2
Back La. Rich TW10 17 C6
Back La. Worth RH10 203 D1
Back Rd. Tedd TW11 16 E2
Bacon Cl. Sandh GU15 64 D6
Bacon La. Head Dn GU10 167 C3
Badajos Rd. Alder GU11 104 F3
Baden Cl. Stain TW18 13 B1
Baden Dr. Horley RH6 160 E4
Baden Powell Cl. Surb KT6 56 F8
Baden Rd. Stough GU2 109 B3
Bader Cl. Kenley CR8 80 D4
Bader Ct. W Heath GU14 84 F8
Badger Cl. Felt TW13 15 B5
Badger Cl. Hounsl TW4 4 C4
Badger Cl. Stough GU2 109 B4
Badger Ct. Rowl GU10 146 A5
Badger Dr. Lhtwat GU18 48 A1
Badger Way. Crond GU10 124 D8
Badgers Cl. Ashf TW15 13 F3
Badgers Cl. Farnc GU7 150 D8
Badgers Cl. Horsh RH12 217 F6
Badgers Cl. Woking GU21 69 C1
Badgers Copse. Friml GU15 65 E4
Badgers Copse. Worc Pk KT4 57 F8
Badgers Cross. Milf GU8 149 E1
Badgers Ct. 4 Epsom KT17 76 E6
Badgers Hill. Vir W GU25 31 C4
Badgers Hollow. Farnc GU7 150 D6
Badgers La. Warlgm CR6 101 C8
Badgers Lodge. 5 Epsom KT17 76 E6
Badgers Way. Brack RG12 27 F7
Badgers Way. E Grins RH19 185 F2
Badgers Way. Loxwd RH14 213 A4
Badgers Wlk. King U T KT3 38 E7
Badgers Wlk. Purley CR8 79 C8
Badgers Wlk. Whytlf CR3 80 F1
Badgers Wood. Cater CR3 100 D2
Badgerwood Dr. Friml GU16 65 D2
Badingham Dr. Fetch KT22 94 E4
Badminton Rd. Balham SW12 21 A8
Badshot Lea Cty Inf Sch.
Farnh GU9 126 A6
Badshot Lea Rd.
Farnh GU11 & GU9 126 A6
Badshot Pk. Farnh GU9 126 A6
Bagden Hill. G Book KT23 114 D5
Bagot Cl. Ashtd KT21 75 F3
Bagshot Cty Fst Sch.
Bagsh GU19 47 E2
Bagshot Gn. Bagsh GU19 47 E3
Bagshot Rd. Ascot SL5 29 C2
Bagshot Rd. Brack GU20 & SL5 48 A8
Bagshot Rd. Brookw GU24 88 C5
Bagshot Rd. Easth RG12 27 C4
Bagshot Rd. Eng Gn TW20 11 C2
Bagshot Rd. Knaph GU21 88 C5
Bagshot Rd. Pirb GU3 88 C5
Bagshot Rd. W End GU24 68 B8
Bagshot Rd.
Woking GU22 & GU24 88 C5
Bagshot Sta. Bagsh GU19 47 E4
Bahram Rd. Epsom KT19 57 D1
Baigents La. Windl GU20 48 D4
Bailes La. Flexf GU3 107 D2
Bailes La. Normdy GU3 107 D3
Bailey Cl. Friml GU16 85 D8
Bailey Cl. Horsh RH12 217 F7
Bailey House. 11 Penge SE26 23 B3
Bailey Pl. Penge SE26 23 D2
Bailey Rd. Westc RH4 135 C6
Baileys Cl. Blckw GU17 64 C4
Bailing Hill. Warn RH12 216 E7
Baillie Rd. Guild GU1 130 F8
Bain Ave. Camb GU15 65 B2
Baines Cl. Croy CR0 61 D5
Bainton Mead. Woking GU21 69 A2
Baird Cl. Crawl RH10 182 A1
Baird Dr. Wood S V GU3 108 B2
Baird Gdns. Dulw SE19 & SE21 22 E4
Baird Rd. Farnb GU14 85 C6
Bakeham La. Eng Gn TW20 11 D1
Bakehouse Barn Cl.
Horsh RH12 217 E7
Bakehouse Rd. Horley RH6 161 A5
Baker Cl. Crawl RH10 201 D4
Baker La. Mitch CR4 41 A7
Baker St. Weyb KT13 53 B6
Baker's Cl. Lingf RH7 164 E5
Baker's La. Lingf RH7 164 E4
Bakers Ct. S Norw SE25 42 E6
Bakers End. Merton SW20 39 E7
Bakers Mead. Tyl Gn RH9 121 C6
Bakers Way. Capel RH5 178 C5
Bakewell Dr. King U T KT3 38 E7
Balaam House. Sutton SM1 59 A6
Balaclava Rd. King U T KT6 37 C2
Balchins La. Westc RH4 135 B6
Balcombe Ct. Crawl RH10 202 D7
Balcombe Gdns. Horley RH6 161 C2
Balcombe House. 3 Streat SW2 21 F7
Balcombe Rd.
Crawl RH10 & RH6 182 D5
Balcombe Rd. Horley RH6 161 B2
Balcombe Rd. Worth RH10 202 D5
Baldreys. M Bourn GU9 146 A8
Baldry Gdns. Streat SW16 21 F2
Baldwin Cres. Merrow GU4 110 C3
Baldwin House. 15 Streat SW2 22 A7
Baldwins Cty Prim Sch.
E Grins RH19 185 D3
Balfont Cl. Sander CR2 81 A6
Balfour Ave. Westfd GU22 89 F5
Balfour Cres. Easth RG12 27 B4
Balfour Gdns. For Row RH18 206 E1
Balfour Rd. Croy SE25 43 A5
Balfour Rd. Hounsl TW3 5 B4
Balfour Rd. Merton SW19 20 B1
Balfour Rd. Wallin SM5 59 F3
Balfour Rd. Weyb KT13 53 A6
Balgowan Cl. New Mal KT3 38 E5
Balgowan Prim Sch. Beck BR3 43 E7
Balgowan Rd. Beck BR3 43 F7
Balham Gr. Balham SW12 21 A8
Balham High Rd.
Balham SW12 & SW17 21 A7
Balham High Rd. Up Toot SW12 21 A7
Balham Hill. Balham SW12 21 B8
Balham New Rd. Balham SW12 21 B8
Balham Park Mansions.
Up Toot SW12 20 F7
Balham Park Rd.
Balham SW12 & SW17 21 A7
Balham Sta. Balham SW12 21 B7
Balham Station Rd.
Balham SW12 21 B7
Balintore Ct. 8 Sandh GU15 64 D8
Ball and Wicket La.
Heath E GU9 125 C7
Ballands N The. Fetch KT22 94 E5
Ballands' S The. Fetch KT22 94 E4
Ballantyne Dr. Kings KT20 97 F6
Ballantyne Rd. W Heath GU14 85 A6
Ballard Cl. King U T KT2 18 D1
Ballard Ct. Camb GU15 66 A8
Ballard Rd. Camb GU15 66 A8
Ballards Farm Rd. S Croy CR2 62 A4
Ballards Gn. Burgh H KT20 97 E8
Ballards La. Limps RH8 123 C6
Ballards Rise. S Croy CR2 62 A4
Ballards Way. S Croy CR0 & CR2 62 B4
Ballater Rd. S Croy CR2 61 F5
Ballencrieff Rd. Sunnin SL5 29 F2
Ballfield Rd. Farnc GU7 150 E6
Ballina St. For Hil SE23 23 D8
Balliol Cl. Crawl RH10 182 D1
Balliol Way. Sandh GU15 45 E1
Balloch Rd. Catf SE6 24 D6
Balloon Rd. Farnb GU14 85 B2
Ballsdown. Chidd GU8 191 A3
Balmain Ct. Hounsl TW3 5 B6
Balmoral. E Grins RH19 206 A8
Balmoral Ave. Beck BR3 43 E5
Balmoral Cres. E Mole KT8 36 A6
Balmoral Cres. Hale GU9 125 B6
Balmoral Ct. 11 Belm SM2 59 A3
Balmoral Ct. 6 Crawl RH11 201 B2
Balmoral Ct. N Cheam KT4 58 B8
Balmoral Ct. W Norw SE27 22 C4
Balmoral Dr. Friml GU16 85 F8
Balmoral Dr. Mayb GU22 70 C3
Balmoral Grange. Stain TW18 33 B7
Balmoral Rd. Ash GU12 106 B4
Balmoral Rd. King U T KT1 37 F5
Balmoral Rd. N Cheam KT4 58 B8
Balmoral Way. Belm SM2 59 A1
Balquhain Cl. Ashtd KT21 75 D2
Baltic Cl. Mitch SW19 20 D1
Balvernie Gr. Wands SW18 20 A8
Bamford Rd. Catf BR1 24 D3
Bampfylde Cl. Wallin SM6 60 C7
Bampton Rd. For Hil SE23 23 D5
Bampton Way. Woking GU21 69 A2
Banavie Gdns. Beck BR3 44 C8
Banbury. Brack RG12 27 E2
Banbury Cl. Friml GU16 86 A7
Banbury Ct. 8 Belm SM2 59 A3
Bancroft Cl. Ashf TW15 14 A3
Bancroft Ct. Reig RH2 118 B1
Bancroft Rd. Reig RH2 118 B1
Bancroft Rd. Worth RH10 202 D5
Band La. 1 Egham TW20 12 A3
Banders Rise. Merrow GU1 110 C2
Bandon Hill Prim Sch.
Wallin SM6 60 D4
Bandon Rise. Wallin SM6 60 D5
Banfor Ct. Wallin SM6 60 C4
Bank Ave. Mitch CR4 40 D7
Bank La. Crawl RH11 201 D6
Bank La. King U T KT2 17 E1
Bank La. Rhampt SW15 7 E2
Bank Mews. Sutton SM1 59 C4
Bank Rd. Farnb GU11 105 D5
Bank Willow. Rich TW10 17 B5
Bank's La. Effing KT11 & KT24 93 B5
Bankfoot Rd. Catf BR1 24 E4
Bankhurst Rd. For Hil SE4 & SE6 23 F8
Banks House. Hounsl TW7 5 E5
Banks Rd. Crawl RH10 202 C5
Banks Way. Burph GU1 109 F4
Bankside. Heath E GU9 125 F7
Bankside. S Croy CR2 61 F4
Bankside. Woking GU21 69 B1
Bankside Cl. Bigg H TN16 83 C1
Bankside Cl. Carsh SM5 59 E4
Bankside Cl. Elst GU8 148 D3
Bankside Cl. Islew TW7 5 F3
Bankside Dr. Hinch W KT7 56 B8
Bankside Way. 6 W Norw SE19 22 E2
Banning House. 4 Putney SW19 19 D7
Bannister Cl. Streat SW2 22 A7
Bannister Cl. Witley GU8 170 F6
Bannister's Rd. Onsl V GU2 129 F7
Banstead Cty Inf Sch.
Banstd SM7 77 F4
Banstead Cty Jun Sch.
Banstd SM7 77 F4
Banstead Downs Golf Club.
Belm SM2 78 A8
Banstead Rd. Belm SM7 77 D7
Banstead Rd. Carsh SM2 & SM5 59 E3
Banstead Rd. Cater CR3 100 D5
Banstead Rd. E Ewell KT17 77 D7
Banstead Rd. Nork SM7 77 D7
Banstead Rd. Purley CR8 80 A8
Banstead Rd. Sutton SM2 & SM5 59 E3
Banstead Rd S. Sutton SM2 59 D1
Banstead Sta. Banstd SM7 77 F5
Banstead Way. Wallin SM6 60 E5
Barbara Cl. Lo Hall TW17 34 B4
Barber Dr. Cran GU6 174 E4
Barberry Way. Hawley GU17 64 F2
Barbon Cl. Friml GU15 66 D3
Barclay Cl. Fetch KT23 94 B4
Barclay Rd. Croy CR0 & CR9 61 D7
Barcombe Ave. Streat SW2 21 F6
Bardney Rd. Morden SM4 40 B5
Bardolph Ave. New Add CR0 62 F2
Bardolph Rd. Rich TW9 6 F4
Bardon Wlk. Woking GU21 69 B2
Bardsley Cl. S Croy CR0 61 F7
Bardsley Dr. M Bourn GU9 146 A8
Barfield Ct. 9 Redh RH1 119 A3
Barfield Sch. Farnh GU10 126 B3
Barfields. Bletch RH1 120 C2
Barfreston Way. Penge SE20 43 B8
Bargate Cl. New Mal KT3 39 A2
Bargate Ct. 1 Stough GU2 108 E1
Bargate Rise. Ock Rid GU7 150 C4
Barge Cl. Farnb GU11 105 E5
Bargery Rd. Catf SE6 24 B7
Bargrove Cl. 8 Penge SE20 23 A1
Bargrove Cres. For Hil SE6 23 F6
Barham Cl. Weyb KT13 53 C6
Barham Rd. Croy CR0 & CR2 61 C5
Barham Rd. Wimble SW20 19 A1
Barhatch La. Cran GU6 174 F6
Barhatch Rd. Cran GU6 174 F4
Baring Rd. Croy CR0 & CR9 43 A1
Barker Gn. Easth RG12 27 B4
Barker House. Dulw SE21 22 E5
Barker Rd. Chert KT16 32 F2
Barker Wlk. Streat SW16 21 D5
Barkham Rd. Woki RG11 25 A5
Barkhart Dr. Woki RG11 25 C7
Barkhart Gdns. Woki RG11 25 C7
Barkis Mead. Sandh GU15 45 E2
Barley Cl. Crawl RH10 201 D5
Barley Mow Cl. Knaph GU21 68 D2
Barley Mow Ct. Brock RH3 116 C1
Barley Mow Hill. Head Dn GU35 187 A6
Barley Mow La. Knaph GU21 68 D3
Barley Mow Rd. Eng Gn TW20 11 C3
Barley Mow Way. Shep Gn TW17 34 A5
Barleymead. Horley RH6 161 B4
Barlow Cl. Wallin SM6 60 E3
Barlow Rd. Crawl RH11 200 E3
Barlow Rd. Hampt TW12 16 A1
Barmeston Rd. Catf SE6 24 B6
Barmouth Rd. Croy CR0 62 D8
Barn Cl. Ashf TW15 14 B3
Barn Cl. Brack RG12 27 D7
Barn Cl. Camb GU15 65 E6
Barn Cl. Oxsh KT22 74 D4
Barn Cl. Woodc KT18 76 C4
Barn Cl. Woodm SM7 78 D4
Barn Cres. Sander CR8 80 D6
Barn Field. Banstd SM7 78 B5
Barn Meadow La. L Book KT23 93 F3
Barn Rd. Woodhm KT15 52 B2
Barnard Cl. Friml GU16 85 F8
Barnard Cl. Sunby TW16 15 A1
Barnard Cl. Wallin SM6 60 D3
Barnard Ct. 1 Knaph GU21 68 E1
Barnard Ct. Streat SW16 21 F5
Barnard Gdns. W Barn KT3 39 A5
Barnard Rd. Chelsh CR6 102 B8
Barnard Rd. Mitch CR4 41 A7
Barnards Pl. S Croy CR2 61 B2
Barnato Cl. Byfl KT14 71 E7
Barnby Rd. Knaph GU21 68 D2
Barnes Bridge Sta. Barnes SW13 7 E5
Barnes Cl. Farnb GU14 85 D4
Barnes Ct. S Norw CR7 42 C6
Barnes End. W Barn KT3 39 A4
Barnes High St. Barnes SW13 7 F5
Barnes Hospl. Mortl SW14 7 E4
Barnes Rd. Farnc GU7 150 E8
Barnes Rd. Friml GU16 85 E8
Barnes Wallis Dr.
Byfl KT13 & KT14 71 E8
Barnett Cl. Leahd KT22 95 B8
Barnett Cl. Woner GU5 152 C8
Barnett Ct. Brack RG12 27 C7
Barnett Gn. Easth RG12 27 B3
Barnett La. Lhtwat GU18 66 F7
Barnett La. Woner GU5 152 C7
Barnett Row. Jacobs GU4 109 D6
Barnett Wood Cty Inf Sch.
Ashtd KT21 75 D2
Barnett Wood La.
Ashtd KT21 & KT22 75 D1
Barnett Wood La. Leahd KT22 95 B8
Barnett's Shaw. Oxted RH8 122 D8
Barnfield. Cran GU6 174 E3
Barnfield. New Mal KT3 38 E3
Barnfield Ave. Croy CR0 62 C8
Barnfield Ave. King U T KT2 17 E3
Barnfield Ave. Mitch CR4 41 B6
Barnfield Cl. Coulsd CR5 100 C8
Barnfield Cl. Wands SW17 20 C5
Barnfield Cotts. Dorman RH7 165 A1
Barnfield Gdns. King U T KT2 17 E3
Barnfield Rd.
Crawl RH10 & RH11 201 E7
Barnfield Rd. S Croy CR2 61 E2
Barnfield Rd. Tats TN16 103 D6
Barnfield Way. Oxted RH8 123 A2
Barnfield Wood Cl. W Wick BR3 44 D3
Barnfield Wood Rd. Beck BR3 44 D3
Barnhill Ave. Hayes BR2 44 F4
Barnlea Cl. Felt TW13 15 E6
Barnmead. Chobh GU24 49 F1
Barnmead Rd. Penge BR3 43 E8
Barnsbury Cl. New Mal KT3 38 C5
Barnsbury Cres. Tolw KT5 38 C1
Barnsbury Cty Inf & Jun Schs.
Woking GU22 89 D6
Barnsbury La. Tolw KT5 38 C1
Barnscroft. W Barn SW20 39 B6
Barnsfold La.
Buck Gn RH12 & RH14 213 E6
Barnsford Cres. W End GU24 68 A6
Barnsley Cl. Mytch GU16 86 B2
Barnsnap Cl. Horsh RH12 217 D6
Barnway. Eng Gn TW20 11 C3
Barnwood Cl. Crawl RH10 202 C7
Barnwood Cl. Stough GU3 108 E3
Barnwood Ct.
Stough GU2 & GU3 108 E3
Barnwood Rd.
Stough GU2 & GU3 108 E3
Barnwood Sch. Stough GU2 108 E2
Barnyard The. Walt o t H KT20 97 A3
Baron Ct. Mitch CR4 40 E5
Baron Gr. Mitch CR4 40 E5
Baron's Hurst. Woodc KT18 76 C3
Baron's Way. Dovgn RH2 139 A5
Baron's Wlk. Croy CR0 43 E3
Barons Ct. Wallin SM6 60 D7
Barons The. Twick TW1 6 B1
Barons Way. Egham TW20 12 D2
Baronsfield Rd. Twick TW1 6 B1
Barossa Rd. Camb GU15 65 D7
Barr Beacon. For Hil SE23 23 C8
Barr's La. Knaph GU21 68 D3
Barracane Dr. Crowth RG11 45 B5
Barrack Path. Knaph GU21 68 F1
Barrack Rd. Alder GU11 105 A2
Barrack Rd. Hounsl TW4 4 E3
Barrack Rd. Stough GU2 109 A4
Barrards Hall. S Croy CR2 80 D8
Barrens Brae. Mayb GU22 70 A1
Barrens Cl. Mayb GU22 90 A8
Barrens Pk. Mayb GU22 90 A8
Barrett Cres. Woki RG11 25 E6
Barrett Rd. Fetch KT22 & KT23 94 D3
Barrhill Rd. Streat SW2 21 E6
Barricane. Woking GU21 89 B8
Barrie Cl. Coulsd CR5 79 C3
Barrie Rd. Heath E GU9 125 A7
Barrihurst La. Cran GU6 173 D2
Barringer Sq. Up Toot SW17 21 A4
Barrington Ct. Dork RH4 136 A6
Barrington Ct. Stain TW18 12 F2
Barrington Lodge. Weyb KT13 53 C5
Barrington Rd. Cheam SM3 40 A1
Barrington Rd. Crawl RH10 201 D3
Barrington Rd. Dork RH4 136 A6
Barrington Rd. Horsh RH13 217 E2
Barrington Rd. Purley CR8 79 C7
Barrington Wlk. 8 S Norw SE19 22 E2
Barrow Ave. Wallin SM5 59 F3
Barrow Ct. Catf SE6 24 F7
Barrow Green Rd. Oxted RH8 122 C6
Barrow Green Rd. Tand RH9 122 C6
Barrow Hedges Cl. Sutton SM5 59 E3
Barrow Hedges Prim Sch.
Sutton SM5 59 E3
Barrow Hedges Way.
Sutton SM2 & SM5 59 E3
Barrow Hill. Worc Pk KT4 57 E8
Barrow Hill Cl. Worc Pk KT4 57 E8
Barrow Hills Sch. Witley GU8 170 E4
Barrow Rd. Croy CR0 61 A5
Barrow Rd. Streat SW16 21 D2
Barrowsfield. Sander CR2 81 A7
Barry Cl. Crawl RH10 201 E3
Barry Terr. Ashf TW15 13 F6
Bars The. Guild GU1 130 D8
Barsons Cl. Penge SE20 23 C1
Barston Rd. W Norw SE27 22 C5
Barstow Cres. Streat SW2 21 F7
Bartholomew Cl. Haslem GU27 208 D8
Bartholomew Ct. Dork RH4 136 A6
Bartholomew Way.
Horsh RH12 218 A7
Bartlett St. Croy CR0 & CR2 61 D5
Barton Cl. Alder GU11 104 E1
Barton Cl. Row Tn KT15 52 A4
Barton Cl. Shep TW17 34 B3
Barton Cres. E Grins RH19 206 A8
Barton Ct. Beck BR2 44 D6
Barton Gn. King U T KT3 38 D7
Barton Pl. Burph GU1 110 B4
Barton Rd. Bramly GU5 152 A7
Barton The. Cobham KT11 73 D7
Barton Wlk. Crawl RH10 202 B4
Bartons Way. W Heath GU14 84 D7
Barttelot Rd. Horsh RH12 217 D2
Barwell Bsns Pk. Chess KT9 56 D2
Barwood Ave. W Wick BR4 44 B1
Basden Gr. Felt TW13 16 A6
Basemoors. Brack RG12 27 E7
Bashford Way. Crawl RH10 202 D8
Basil Gdns. Croy CR0 43 E1
Basildene Rd. Hounsl TW4 & TW5 4 D4
Basildon Cl. Sutton SM2 59 B2
Basildon Way. Crawl RH11 200 E2
Basing Cl. Thame D KT7 36 F2
Basing Dr. Alder GU11 126 B7
Basing House. Catf SE6 24 A4
Basing Rd. Banstd SM7 77 F4
Basing Way. Thame D KT7 36 F2
Basingfield Rd. Thame D KT7 36 F2
Basinghall Gdns. Sutton SM2 59 B2
Baskerville Rd. Wands SW18 20 E8
Basset Cl. Woodhm KT15 52 C1
Bassett Cl. Friml GU16 85 E8
Bassett Cl. Sutton SM2 59 B2
Bassett Gdns. Hounsl TW7 5 C7
Bassett Rd. Mayb GU22 70 C3
Bassetts Hill. Dorman RH7 165 A2
Bassingham Rd. Wands SW18 20 C8
Bat and Ball La. Rowl GU10 146 A5
Bat and Ball La.
Wreccl GU10 & GU9 146 A6
Batavia Cl. Sunby TW16 35 C8
Batavia Rd. Sunby TW16 35 B8
Batcombe Mead. Brack RG12 27 E2
Bateman Gr. Ash GU12 126 F8
Batemans Ct. Crawl RH10 202 A3
Bates Cres. Croy CR0 61 A5
Bates Cres. Streat SW16 21 C1
Bates Wlk. New Haw KT15 52 C4
Bateson Way. Sheer GU21 70 C5
Bath Ct. 3 For Hil SE26 23 A5
Bath House Rd.
Wallin CR0 & CR9 41 E1
Bath Pas. King U T KT1 37 D7
Bath Rd. Camb GU15 65 D6
Bath Rd. Cranf TW3 & TW4 & TW5 4 E5
Bath Rd. Harl TW6 & UB7 & TW5 3 D6
Bath Rd. Harm TW6 & UB7 2 E6
Bath Rd. Hounsl TW3 & TW4 & TW5 4 E5
Bath Rd. Mitch CR4 40 D6
Bath Rd. Poyle SL3 & UB7 & TW6 1 E6
Bathgate Rd. Wimble SW19 19 D5
Bathurst Ave. Merton SW19 40 B8
Batsworth Rd. Mitch CR4 40 D6
Batt's Cnr. Docken GU10 166 E7
Batten Ave. Knaph GU21 88 E8
Battenberg Wlk. 10
W Norw SE19 22 E3
Battersby Rd. Catf SE6 24 D5
Battle Cl. Wimble SW19 20 C2
Battlebridge House.
Merst RH1 119 B5
Battlebridge La. Merst RH1 119 B5
Batts Hill. Redh RH1 & RH2 118 E3
Batty's Barn Cl. Woki RG11 25 D5
Baty House. Streat SW2 21 F7
Baudwin Rd. Catf SE6 24 E6
Bavant Rd. Thorn H SW16 41 F7
Bawtree Cl. Sutton SM2 59 C1
Bax Cl. Cran GU6 174 E2
Baxter Ave. Redh RH1 118 F1
Baxter Cl. Worth RH10 202 B4
Bay Cl. Horley RH6 160 E6
Bay Dr. Brack RG12 27 E7
Bay Rd. Brack RG12 27 E8
Bay Tree Ave. Leahd KT22 95 A7
Bayards. Warlgm CR6 81 C1
Baydon Ct. Beck BR2 44 F6
Bayeux. Tadw KT20 97 D5
Bayfield Ave. Friml GU15 & GU16 65 E2
Bayfield Rd. Horley RH6 160 E4
Bayford Cl. W Heath GU14 65 A1
Bayham Rd. Morden SM4 40 C5
Bayhorne La. Horley RH6 161 C1
Bayleaf Cl. Tedd TW12 16 D3
Baylis Wlk. Crawl RH11 201 B1
Bayliss Ct. Guild GU1 130 C8
Baynards Rd. Cran RH12 195 A2
Bays Cl. For Hil SE26 23 C3
Baysfarm Ct. Harm TW6 & UB7 2 C6
Baywood Cl. W Heath GU14 84 C5
Bazalgette Cl. New Mal KT3 38 D4
Bazalgette Gdns. New Mal KT3 38 D4
Beach Gr. Felt TW13 16 A6
Beachborough Rd. Catf BR1 24 C4
Beachy Rd. Crawl RH11 201 A1
Beacon Cl. Nork SM7 77 D3
Beacon Cl. Rowl GU10 146 A5
Beacon Ct. Horsh RH13 218 A4
Beacon Gr. Carsh SM5 60 A6
Beacon Hill. Dorman RH7 186 B8
Beacon Hill. Woking GU21 89 C8
Beacon Hill Ct. Beac H GU26 188 D6
Beacon Hill Cty Prim Sch.
Beac H GU26 188 C6
Beacon Hill Rd. Beac H GU26 188 D6
Beacon Hill Rd. Crond GU10 124 E8
Beacon House. 10 Penge SE26 23 B3
Beacon Rd. Farnb GU14 105 B8
Beacon Rd. Harl TW19 & TW6 3 A1
Beacon Sch The. Burgh H KT20 77 E2
Beacon View Rd. Elst GU8 148 C2
Beacon Way. Nork SM7 77 E3
Beaconsfield Pl. Ewell KT17 76 E7
Beaconsfield Rd. Clayg KT10 55 E3
Beaconsfield Rd. King U T KT3 38 D7
Beaconsfield Rd. Lang V KT18 96 E8
Beaconsfield Rd. Old Wok GU22 89 F7
Beaconsfield Rd. Surb KT5 37 F2
Beaconsfield Rd. Thorn H CR0 42 D3
Beaconsfield Rd. Twick TW1 6 B1
Beaconshaw. Broml BR1 24 E1
Beadle Ct. Mitch CR4 40 E6
Beadles La. Oxted RH8 122 D4
Beadles Lane Cty Fst Sch.
Oxted RH8 122 D5
Beadlow Cl. Carsh SM4 40 D3
Beadman Pl. W Norw SE27 22 B4
Beadman St. W Norw SE27 22 B4
Beadnell Rd. For Hil SE23 23 D7
Beaford Gr. Merton SW20 39 F6
Beagle Cl. Felt TW13 15 B4
Beale Cl. Woki RG11 25 B7
Beale Ct. Crawl RH11 201 A3
Beale's La. Weyb KT13 53 B7
Beales La. Wreccl GU10 145 F7
Beales Rd. G Book KT23 94 B1
Bealeswood La. Docken GU10 166 F6
Beam Hollow. Heath E GU9 125 C7
Bean Oak Rd. Woki RG11 25 F6
Bear La. Farnh GU9 125 C3
Bear Rd. Felt TW13 15 D4
Beard Rd. Rich TW10 17 F3
Beard's Hill. Hampt TW12 36 A8

Beard's Rd. Ashf TW15 & TW16 ... 14 E2
Beardell St. W Norw SE19 .... 22 F2
Beards Hill Cl. Hampt TW12 .... 36 A8
Beare Green Cotts.
  Bear Gn RH5 .... 157 D2
Beare Green Ct. Bear Gn RH5 . 157 D4
Bearfield Rd. King U T KT2 .... 17 E1
Bears Den. Broad H RH12 .... 216 D3
Bearsden Way. Broad H RH12 .... 216 D3
Bearwood Cl. Row Tn KT15 .... 52 A4
Bearwood Cotts. Wreccl GU10 . 145 F7
Beasley's Ait La.
  Lo Hall TW16 & TW17 .... 34 F3
Beatrice Ave. Thorn H SW16 ..... 41 F7
Beatrice Rd. Oxted RH8 .... 122 E6
Beatrice Rd. 1 Rich TW10 .... 6 F2
Beatrix Potter Prim Sch.
  Wands SW18 .... 20 C7
Beattie Cl. E Bed TW14 .... 14 F7
Beattie Cl. Book KT23 .... 93 F3
Beatty Ave. Merrow GU1 .... 110 A2
Beauchamp Rd. E Mole KT8 ...... 36 C4
Beauchamp Rd.
  S Norw CR7 & SE25 .... 42 D8
Beauchamp Rd. Sutton SM1 ..... 59 A6
Beauchamp Rd. Twick TW1 ...... 17 A8
Beauclare Cl. Ashtd GU5 .... 95 D6
Beauclerc Cty Inf Sch.
  Sunby SW16 .... 35 C6
Beauclere House. Sutton SM2 .. 59 C3
Beauclerk Cl. Felt TW13 .... 15 B7
Beauclerk House. 10
  Streat SW16 .... 21 E5
Beaufield Gate. Haslem GU27 .. 208 D7
Beaufighter Rd. Farnb GU14 .... 105 A8
Beaufort Cl. Mayb GU22 .... 70 C3
Beaufort Cl. Putney SW19 .... 19 B8
Beaufort Cl. Rich TW10 .... 17 C4
Beaufort Gdns. Heston TW5 .... 4 E6
Beaufort Gdns. N Asct SL5 .... 28 E8
Beaufort Gdns. S Norw SW16 .... 21 F1
Beaufort House. Wimble SW20 ... 39 D8
Beaufort Prim Sch. Woking GU21 68 F3
Beaufort Rd. Farnh GU21 .... 125 C3
Beaufort Rd.
  King U T KT1 & KT5 & KT6 .... 37 E5
Beaufort Rd. Mayb GU22 .... 70 C3
Beaufort Rd. Reig RH2 .... 117 F2
Beaufort Rd. Rich TW10 .... 17 C4
Beaufort Rd. Twick TW1 .... 17 C8
Beaufort Way. Stonel KT17 .... 58 A3
Beauforts. Eng Gn TW20 .... 11 C3
Beaufoy House. 3 W Norw SE27 22 B5
Beaufront Cl. Camb GU15 .... 66 A7
Beaufront Rd. Camb GU15 .... 66 B7
Beaulieu Ave. For Hil SE26 .... 23 B4
Beaulieu Cl. Brack RG12 .... 28 A6
Beaulieu Cl. Hounsl TW4 .... 4 F2
Beaulieu Cl. Mitch CR4 .... 41 A8
Beaulieu Cl. 4 Twick TW1 .... 6 D1
Beaulieu Gdns. Blckw GU17 ...... 64 C5
Beaumaris Par. Friml GU16 .... 85 F8
Beaumont Ave. Rich TW9 .... 6 F4
Beaumont Cl. Crawl RH11 .... 200 E5
Beaumont Ct. Ascot SL5 .... 28 F5
Beaumont Ct. Mitch CR4 .... 41 A7
Beaumont Cty Jun Sch.
  Alder GU11 .... 104 F2
Beaumont Dr. Ashf TW15 .... 14 D3
Beaumont Gdns. Brack RG12 ..... 27 E4
Beaumont Gr. Alder GU11 .... 104 E2
Beaumont House. 1
  Streat SW2 .... 21 E7
Beaumont House. Wimble SW19 20 A5
Beaumont Pl. Islew TW7 .... 5 F2
Beaumont Prim Sch. Purley CR8 80 A5
Beaumont Rd. Purley CR8 .... 80 A6
Beaumont Rd.
  Putney SW15 & SW19 .... 19 E8
Beaumont Rd. S Norw SE19 ...... 22 C2
Beaumont Sq. Cran GU6 .... 174 F3
Beaumont Terr. 1 Lewish SE13 24 E8
Beaumonts. Salfs RH1 .... 139 F1
Beaver Cl. Hampt TW12 .... 36 B8
Beaver Cl. Horsh RH12 .... 217 F6
Beaver Cl. 9 Penge SE20 .... 23 A1
Beavers Cl. Farnh GU9 .... 125 A2
Beavers Cl. Stough GU2 .... 108 E2
Beavers Comm Prim Sch.
  Hounsl TW4 .... 4 C4
Beavers Cres. Hounsl TW4 .... 4 D3
Beavers Hill. Farnh GU9 .... 124 F2
Beavers La. Hounsl TW4 .... 4 C4
Beavers Rd. Farnh GU9 .... 125 A2
Beck Ct. Penge BR3 .... 43 D6
Beck Gdns. Hale GU9 .... 125 A6
Beck La. Penge BR3 .... 43 D6
Beck River Pk. Beck BR3 .... 44 A8
Beck Way. Beck BR3 .... 44 A6
Beckenham Bsns Ctr.
  Penge BR3 .... 23 E2
Beckenham Ct. Beck BR3 .... 44 A8
Beckenham Gr. Beck BR2 .... 44 D7
Beckenham Hill Rd.
  Catf BR3 & SE6 .... 24 C3
Beckenham Hill Sta. Catf SE6 ... 24 C3
Beckenham Hospl. Beck BR3 ..... 43 F7
Beckenham Junction Sta.
  Beck BR3 .... 44 A8
Beckenham La. Broml BR1 & BR2 44 F7
Beckenham Place Pk. Beck BR3 24 B1
Beckenham Rd. Beck BR3 .... 43 E8
Beckenham Rd. Penge BR3 .... 43 E8
Beckenham Rd.
  W Wick BR3 & BR4 .... 44 C2
Beckenshaw Gdns. Woodm SM7 78 E4
Becket Cl. Croy SE25 .... 43 A3

Becket Cl. 2 Merton SW19 .... 40 B8
Becket Wood. Parkg RH5 .... 158 C7
Beckett Ave. Purley CR8 .... 80 B4
Beckett Cl. Streat SW16 .... 21 D6
Beckett Cl. Woki RG11 .... 25 E6
Beckett La. Crawl RH11 .... 181 D1
Beckett Wlk. Penge BR3 .... 23 E2
Becketts Cl. Felt TW14 .... 4 B1
Beckford Ave. Bracks East RG12 27 B3
Beckford Rd. Croy CR0 & SE25 .. 42 F3
Beckley Cotts. G Book KT23 ...... 94 C1
Beckmead Sch. Croy BR3 .... 44 A1
Beckway Rd. Mitch SW16 .... 41 D7
Beckworth Pl. Oat Pk KT13 .... 53 E8
Beclands Rd. Streat SW17 .... 21 A2
Becmead Ave. Streat SW16 .... 21 D4
Becondale Rd. W Norw SE19 ..... 22 E3
Bedale Cl. Crawl RH11 .... 201 C4
Beddington Farm Rd. Croy CR0 60 F8
Beddington Farm Rd.
  Wallin CR0 & CR9 .... 41 E1
Beddington Gdns.
  Wallin SM5 & SM6 .... 60 A4
Beddington Gr. Wallin SM6 .... 60 D5
Beddington Inf Sch. Wallin SM6 60 C5
Beddington Lane Sta.
  Mitch CR4 .... 41 C3
Beddington Manor. Sutton SM2 59 D4
Beddington Park Cotts.
  Wallin SM6 .... 60 D7
Beddington Park Prim Sch.
  Wallin CR0 .... 60 D7
Beddlestead La. Titsey CR6 ..... 103 A6
Bedelsford Sch. S Croy U T KT1 ... 37 E6
Bedfont Cl. E Bed TW14 .... 3 C1
Bedfont Cl. Mitch CR4 .... 41 A7
Bedfont Cl. Harm TW19 .... 2 B4
Bedfont Green Cl. E Bed TW14 .. 14 C7
Bedfont Ind Pk N. Felt TW15 .... 14 C5
Bedfont Inf Sch. Felt TW14 .... 3 E1
Bedfont Jun Sch. Felt TW14 .... 3 E1
Bedfont La. E Bed TW14 & TW13 14 F8
Bedfont Rd. E Bed TW13 & TW14 14 D6
Bedfont Rd. Felt TW13 & TW14 .. 14 D6
Bedfont Rd. Stan TW19 .... 2 F1
Bedford Ave. Friml GU16 .... 85 F5
Bedford Cres. Friml GU16 .... 85 F6
Bedford Ct. 6 Rich TW9 .... 6 F3
Bedford Ct. S Norw SE19 .... 42 F8
Bedford Hill. Balham SW12 .... 21 B6
Bedford Hill. Streat SW16 .... 21 B6
Bedford Hill.
  Up Toot SW12 & SW16 & SW17 ... 21 B6
Bedford House. Guild GU1 .... 130 C8
Bedford La. Friml GU16 .... 85 F6
Bedford La. Sunnin SL5 .... 30 B4
Bedford Pk. Croy CR0 .... 42 C1
Bedford Pl. Croy CR0 .... 42 D1
Bedford Rd. Guild GU1 .... 130 C8
Bedford Rd. Horsh RH13 .... 217 D1
Bedford Rd. N Cheam KT4 .... 58 C8
Bedford Rd. Twick TW2 .... 16 D5
Bedgebury Gdns. Putney SW19 . 19 E8
Bedlow Way. Wallin CR0 .... 60 F6
Bedser Cl. S Norw CR7 .... 42 C6
Bedster Gdns. E Mole KT8 .... 36 B6
Bedwardine Rd. S Norw SE19 .... 22 E1
Beech Ave. Brent TW8 .... 6 B7
Beech Ave. Camb GU15 .... 65 D4
Beech Ave. Effing KT24 .... 113 D6
Beech Ave. M Bourn GU10 .... 146 C5
Beech Ave. S Croy CR2 .... 61 D1
Beech Ave. Tats TN16 .... 103 D8
Beech Cl. Ashf TW15 .... 14 D3
Beech Cl. Blind H RH7 .... 163 E8
Beech Cl. Byfl KT14 .... 71 E7
Beech Cl. Carsh SM5 .... 59 F8
Beech Cl. Chidd GU8 .... 191 A4
Beech Cl. Cobham KT11 .... 74 A8
Beech Cl. Dork RH4 .... 136 A8
Beech Cl. Effing KT24 .... 113 D7
Beech Cl. Hersh KT12 .... 54 C6
Beech Cl. Putney SW15 .... 19 A8
Beech Cl. Stan TW19 .... 13 D8
Beech Cl. Sunby TW16 .... 35 D7
Beech Cl. Wimble SW19 .... 19 C2
Beech Close Ct. Cobham KT11 ... 73 F8
Beech Copse. S Croy CR2 .... 61 E5
Beech Cres. Box H KT20 .... 116 C5
Beech Dr. Beck BR3 .... 23 F1
Beech Dr. Guild GU1 .... 130 F8
Beech Dr. Tedd TW11 .... 17 C2
Beech Dr. 4 W Norw SW16 .... 22 A3
Beech Dr. Blckw GU17 .... 64 D4
Beech Dr. Kings KT20 .... 97 F5
Beech Dr. Reig RH2 .... 118 D1
Beech Dr. Send M GU23 .... 91 A3
Beech Farm Rd. Chelsh CR6 .... 102 D8
Beech Fields. E Grins RH19 ..... 185 F3
Beech Gdns. Crawl D RH10 ...... 204 A8
Beech Gdns. Horse GU21 .... 69 E4
Beech Glen. Easth RG12 .... 27 B5
Beech Gr. Addl KT15 .... 52 B6
Beech Gr. Burgh H KT18 .... 77 B2
Beech Gr. Cater CR3 .... 100 E1
Beech Gr. King U T KT3 .... 38 D6
Beech Gr. Mitch CR4 .... 41 D5
Beech Gr. Pirb GU24 .... 87 C7
Beech Gr. Pirb GU24 .... 87 D7
Beech Gr. Stough GU2 .... 108 F1
Beech Hall. Ottsh KT16 .... 51 C3
Beech Hanger End.
  Graysh GU26 .... 188 B3
Beech Hill. Bowl Gn GU8 .... 189 F8
Beech Hill. Head Dn GU35 .... 187 B5
Beech Hill. Westfd GU22 .... 89 D4
Beech Hill Rd. Head Dn GU35 .. 187 A5

Beech Hill Rd. Sunnin SL5 .... 29 F3
Beech Holme. Crawl D RH10 .... 204 B8
Beech Holt. Leahd KT22 .... 95 C5
Beech House. Heston TW5 .... 4 E7
Beech House. New Add CR0 ...... 63 B4
Beech House Rd.
  Croy CR0 & CR9 .... 61 D7
Beech La. Flexf GU3 .... 107 A1
Beech La. Graysh GU26 .... 188 B4
Beech La. Guild GU2 .... 130 C6
Beech Lodge. Egham TW18 .... 12 E3
Beech Rd. Bigg H TN16 .... 83 C2
Beech Rd. E Bed TW14 .... 14 E8
Beech Rd. Epsom KT18 .... 76 F4
Beech Rd. Friml GU16 .... 85 F6
Beech Rd. Haslem GU27 .... 208 D8
Beech Rd. Horsh RH12 .... 218 B5
Beech Rd. Merst RH1 .... 99 C1
Beech Rd. Oat Pk KT13 .... 53 D6
Beech Rd. Reig RH2 .... 118 A4
Beech Rd. Thorn H SW16 .... 41 F6
Beech Rd. W Heath GU14 .... 85 A7
Beech Ride. Sandh GU17 .... 45 B1
Beech Tree Cl. Crawl RH11 ...... 201 D7
Beech Tree Dr. Farnh GU9 ...... 126 A5
Beech Tree La. Laleh TW18 .... 33 B7
Beech Tree Pl. Sutton SM1 .... 59 B5
Beech Way. Epsom KT17 .... 76 F4
Beech Way. Godal GU7 .... 150 D3
Beech Way. Selsd CR2 .... 81 D7
Beech Way. Twick TW13 .... 16 A5
Beech Wlk. Ewell KT17 .... 77 A8
Beech Wood. Cater CR3 .... 100 F3
Beechcroft. Ashtd KT21 .... 95 F8
Beechcroft. King U T KT2 .... 38 B8
Beechcroft. Kenley CR8 .... 80 D4
Beechcroft Ave.
  King U T KT1 & KT3 .... 38 C7
Beechcroft Cl. Ascot SL5 .... 29 D5
Beechcroft Cl. Heston TW5 .... 4 D5
Beechcroft Cl. Streat SW16 .... 21 F3
Beechcroft Ct. Easth RG12 .... 27 B6
Beechcroft Dr. Onsl V GU2 ...... 129 D6
Beechcroft Lodge. Sutton SM2 . 59 C3
Beechcroft Manor. Oat Pk KT13 53 D7
Beechcroft Mansions.
  Streat SW16 .... 21 F3
Beechcroft Rd. Chess KT9 .... 56 F7
Beechcroft Rd. Mortl SW14 .... 7 C4
Beechcroft Rd. Up Toot SW17 ... 20 E6
Beechcroft Sch. Up Toot SW17 .. 20 E6
Beechdene. Tadw KT20 .... 97 B5
Beechen Cliff Way. Hounsl TW7 .. 5 F5
Beechen La. Kings KT20 .... 97 F2
Beechen Pl. For Hil SE23 .... 23 C6
Beeches Ave The. Sutton SM5 ... 59 E3
Beeches Cl. Kings KT20 .... 98 A4
Beeches Cl. Penge SE20 .... 43 C8
Beeches Cres. Crawl RH10 ...... 201 E4
Beeches Head. Dorman RH19 .. 186 F1
Beeches La. Ash W RH19 .... 206 D6
Beeches Rd. Cheam SM3 .... 39 E1
Beeches Rd. Up Toot SW17 .... 20 F5
Beeches The. Ash V GU12 .... 85 F1
Beeches The. Banstd SM7 .... 78 B3
Beeches The. Bramly GU5 .... 151 F6
Beeches The. Fetch KT22 .... 94 D4
Beeches The. Hounsl TW3 .... 5 B6
Beeches The. Mitch CR4 .... 40 E4
Beeches The. Stain TW18 .... 13 A3
Beeches Wlk. Streat SM4 & SM5 59 E2
Beeches Wood. Kings KT20 ...... 98 A5
Beechey Cl. Copth RH10 .... 183 B3
Beechey Way. Copth RH10 .... 183 B3
Beechfield. Banstd SM7 .... 78 B6
Beechfield Rd. 7 S Croy CR0 ..... 61 C6
Beechfield Rd. For Hil SE6 .... 23 F7
Beeching Cl. Ash GU12 .... 106 B5
Beeching Way. E Grins RH19 ... 185 E1
Beechland Cotts. L Kings KT20 117 F7
Beechlawn. Guild GU1 .... 130 F8
Beechmeads. Cobham KT11 ...... 73 D6
Beechmont Ave. Went GU25 ..... 31 A4
Beechmont Cl. Catf BR1 .... 24 E3
Beechmore Gdns. Cheam SM3 .. 58 D8
Beechnut Dr. Blckw GU17 .... 64 B6
Beechnut Rd. Alder GU12 .... 105 B1
Beecholme. Nork KT17 .... 77 E5
Beecholme Fst Sch. Mitch CR4 .. 41 B8
Beechrow. King U T KT2 .... 17 E4
Beechside. Crawl RH10 .... 201 E5
Beechtree Ave. Eng Gn TW20 ... 11 B2
Beechvale. 3 Woking GU22 .... 69 F1
Beechway. Merrow GU1 .... 110 B2
Beechwood Ave. Ashf TW16 ...... 14 F1
Beechwood Ave. Kings KT20 ..... 98 A6
Beechwood Ave. Oat Pk KT13 ... 53 E6
Beechwood Ave. Rich TW9 .... 7 A6
Beechwood Ave. Stain TW18 ..... 13 B2
Beechwood Ave. Thorn H CR7 ... 42 B5
Beechwood Ave. Wallin CR5 ...... 79 B4
Beechwood Cl. Knaph GU21 ...... 68 E2
Beechwood Cl. Long D KT6 .... 37 D2
Beechwood Cl. Oat Pk KT13 ...... 53 E6
Beechwood Cl. Carsh SM5 .... 59 F6
Beechwood Cl. Chisw W4 .... 7 D8
Beechwood Cl. Sutton SM1 .... 59 A5
Beechwood Dr. Cobham KT11 .... 74 A8
Beechwood Gdns. Cater CR3 ... 101 A5
Beechwood Manor. Oat Pk KT13 53 E6
Beechwood Rd. Cater CR3 .... 100 E1
Beechwood Rd. Knaph GU21 ..... 68 D2
Beechwood Rd. S Croy CR2 .... 61 E2
Beechwood Rd. Went GU25 .... 31 A6
Beechwood Villas. Salfs RH1 ... 161 A7
Beechwoods Ct. Dulw SE19 .... 22 F3

Beecot La. Walt O T KT12 .... 54 C8
Beeding Cl. Horsh RH12 .... 218 A5
Beedingwood Dr. Crawl RH12 .. 218 F6
Beedon Dr. Easth RG11 & RG12 .. 26 E3
Beehive La. Binf RG12 .... 26 C7
Beehive Rd. Binf RG12 .... 26 D7
Beehive Rd. Stain TW18 .... 12 F3
Beehive Ring Rd.
  Crawl RH10 & RH6 .... 182 B4
Beehive Way. Dovgn RH2 .... 139 B5
Beeleigh Rd. Morden SM4 .... 40 B5
Beeston Way. Felt TW14 .... 4 C1
Beeton's Ave. Ash GU12 .... 106 A4
Beggar's Roost La.
  Cheam SM1 & SM2 .... 59 A4
Beggars Cl. Chobh GU24 .... 68 C8
Beggars La. Gomsh GU5 .... 133 C4
Beggarshouse La. Charl RH6 ... 180 C8
Begonia Pl. 1 Hampt TW12 .... 16 A2
Behenna Cl. Crawl RH11 .... 200 E5
Beira St. Balham SW12 .... 21 B8
Belcroft Cl. Broml BR1 .... 24 F1
Beldam Bridge Rd. W End GU24 68 A6
Beldham Gdns. E Mole KT8 .... 36 B6
Beldham Rd.
  Wreccl GU10 & GU9 .... 145 F7
Belenoyd Ct. Streat SW16 .... 21 F5
Belfast Rd. Croy SE25 .... 43 B5
Belfield Rd. W Ewell KT19 .... 57 E3
Belfield Rd. W Ewell KT19 .... 57 E3
Belfry The. Redh RH1 .... 118 F2
Belgrade Rd. Hampt TW12 .... 36 B8
Belgrave Cl. Hersh KT12 .... 54 B6
Belgrave Cres. Sunby TW16 ...... 35 B8
Belgrave Cl. Hawley GU17 .... 64 D3
Belgrave Manor. Woking GU22 ... 89 E8
Belgrave Rd. Barnes SW13 .... 7 F7
Belgrave Rd. Hounsl TW4 .... 4 F4
Belgrave Rd. S Norw SE25 .... 42 F5
Belgrave Rd. Sunby TW16 .... 35 B8
Belgrave Wlk. Mitch CR4 .... 40 D6
Belgravia Cl. Horley RH6 .... 161 B3
Belgravia Gdns. Catf BR1 .... 24 E2
Belgravia House. 1 Tedd TW11 17 C1
Belgravia Mews. King U T KT1 ... 37 D5
Bell Bridge Rd. Chert KT16 .... 32 F1
Bell Cl. Farnb GU14 .... 85 C6
Bell Cnr. Chert KT16 .... 32 F2
Bell Cres. Hooley CR5 .... 99 B6
Bell Ct. Tolw KT5 .... 57 B8
Bell Ctr. Crawl RH10 .... 181 F2
Bell Dr. Putney SW18 .... 19 E8
Bell Farm Cty Jun Sch.
  Hersh KT12 .... 54 C6
Bell Foundry La. Woki RG11 ..... 25 C8
Bell Gn. For Hil SE6 .... 23 F4
Bell Green La.
  For Hil BR3 & SE26 & SE6 .... 23 F4
Bell Hammer. E Grins RH19 .... 205 E8
Bell House. 15 Streat SW2 .... 21 E8
Bell House Gdns. Woki RG11 ..... 25 B6
Bell La. Blckw GU17 .... 64 C5
Bell La. Fetch KT22 .... 94 D4
Bell La. Rowl GU10 .... 145 E3
Bell La. Twick TW1 .... 17 A7
Bell Lane Cl. Fetch KT22 .... 94 D4
Bell Meadow. Dulw SE19 .... 22 E4
Bell Meadow. Godst RH9 .... 121 C3
Bell Pl. Bagsh GU19 .... 47 F3
Bell Rd. E Mole KT8 .... 36 D4
Bell Rd. Hounsl TW3 .... 5 B3
Bell Rd. King Gn GU27 .... 208 B3
Bell Rd. Warn RH12 .... 217 A8
Bell St. Reig RH2 .... 139 B8
Bell Vale La. Haslem GU27 ...... 208 C4
Bell Vale La. Lurg GU27 .... 208 C4
Bell View. Beck BR3 .... 23 F1
Bell Weir Cl. Wray TW19 .... 12 B6
Bellamy House. Heston TW5 .... 5 A8
Bellamy House. Up Toot SW17 ... 20 D4
Bellamy St. Balham SW12 .... 21 B8
Belland Dr. Alder GU11 .... 104 E1
Bellasis Ave. Streat SW2 .... 21 E6
Belle Ave. Alder GU12 .... 105 D2
Belle Vue Cl. Stain TW18 .... 33 A8
Belle Vue Cty Inf Sch.
  Alder GU12 .... 105 D2
Belle Vue Ent Ctr. Alder GU12 . 105 E2
Bellever Hill. Camb GU15 .... 65 E5
Bellevue Pk. S Norw CR7 .... 42 C5
Bellevue Rd. King U T KT1 .... 37 E6
Bellevue Rd. Up Toot SW17 .... 20 F7
Bellew Rd. Friml GU16 .... 86 B7
Bellew St. Wands SW17 .... 20 C5
Bellfield. New Add CR0 .... 62 F3
Bellfields Ct. Bellf GU1 .... 109 C5
Bellfields Rd. Bellf GU1 .... 109 D3
Bellingham Cl. Friml GU15 .... 66 C4
Bellingham Gn. Catf SE6 .... 24 A5
Bellingham Rd. Catf SE6 .... 24 C5
Bellingham Sta. Catf SE6 .... 24 B6
Bellmarsh Rd. Addl KT15 .... 52 B6
Bellmore Ct. 5 Croy CR0 .... 42 F1
Bello Cl. Streat SE24 & SW2 ...... 22 B7
Belloc Cl. Crawl RH10 .... 202 C7
Belloc Ct. Horsh RH13 .... 218 A3
Bells La. Horton SL3 .... 1 B4
Belltrees Gr. 1 Streat SW16 ...... 22 A3
Bellwether La. Outw RH1 .... 162 B7
Belmont. Whit V KT13 .... 53 C4
Belmont Ave. Stough GU2 .... 108 F4
Belmont Ave. W Heath GU14 ..... 39 A5
Belmont Cl. W Heath GU14 .... 84 F7
Belmont Mews. Camb GU15 ...... 65 C3
Belmont Rd. Beck BR3 .... 43 F7
Belmont Rd. Belm SM2 .... 59 A1
Belmont Rd. Crowth RG11 .... 45 B6
Belmont Rd. Croy SE25 .... 43 B4

Belmont Rd. Leahd KT22 .... 95 A5
Belmont Rd. Reig RH2 .... 139 C8
Belmont Rd. Twick TW2 .... 16 D6
Belmont Rd. Wallin SM6 .... 60 C5
Belmont Rise. Belm SM1 & SM2 . 58 F3
Belmont Sch. Abin C RH5 .... 155 D6
Belmont Sta. Sutton SM2 .... 59 B1
Belmore Ave. Mayb GU22 .... 70 D3
Belsize Gdns. Sutton SM1 .... 59 B6
Belsize Rd. Farnb GU14 .... 85 C1
Belstone Mews. W Heath GU14 .. 85 A7
Beltane Dr. Wimble SW19 .... 19 D5
Belthorn Cres. Streat SW12 .... 21 C8
Belton Rd. Camb GU15 .... 65 C5
Belvedere Ave. Wimble SW19 .... 19 E3
Belvedere Cl. Esher KT10 .... 55 B5
Belvedere Cl. Stough GU2 .... 109 B3
Belvedere Cl. Tedd TW11 .... 16 E3
Belvedere Cl. Weyb KT13 .... 53 A5
Belvedere Ct. Crawl RH10 .... 202 B7
Belvedere Ct. 8 King U T KT2 .... 18 A1
Belvedere Ct. Hawley GU17 .... 64 D3
Belvedere Dr. Wimble SW19 ...... 19 E3
Belvedere Gdns. E Mole KT8 ..... 36 A4
Belvedere Gr. Wimble SW19 ...... 19 E3
Belvedere Rd. Bigg H TN16 .... 83 F1
Belvedere Rd. Farnb GU14 .... 85 C2
Belvedere Rd. Penge SE19 .... 22 F1
Belvedere Sq. Wimble SW19 ...... 19 E3
Belvoir Cl. Friml GU16 .... 65 F1
Belvoir Lodge. Dulw SE22 .... 23 A8
Belvoir Rd. Dulw SE22 .... 23 A8
Benbow La. Dunsf GU8 .... 193 C4
Benbrick Rd. Guild GU2 .... 130 A8
Benbury Cl. Catf BR1 .... 24 C3
Bence The. Egham TW20 .... 32 B6
Bench Field. S Croy CR2 .... 61 F5
Benchfield Cl. E Grins RH19 .... 186 B1
Bencombe Rd. Purley CR8 .... 80 A5
Bencroft Rd. Streat SW16 .... 21 C1
Bencurtis Pk. W Wick BR4 .... 63 D8
Bendon Valley. Wands SW18 ..... 20 B8
Benedict Dr. E Bed TW14 .... 14 D8
Benedict Fst Sch. Mitch CR4 .... 40 D6
Benedict Prim Sch. Mitch CR4 .. 40 D6
Benedict Rd. Mitch CR4 .... 40 D6
Benedict Wharf. Mitch CR4 .... 40 E6
Benen-Stock Rd. Stan TW19 .... 2 A2
Benett Gdns. Thorn H SW16 ...... 41 E7
Benfleet Cl. Cobham KT11 .... 73 E7
Benfleet Cl. Sutton SM1 .... 59 C7
Benham Cl. Couls CR5 & CR8 ..... 80 B1
Benham Gdns. Hounsl TW3 & TW4 4 F2
Benhams Cl. Horley RH6 .... 161 A5
Benhams Dr. Horley RH6 .... 161 A5
Benhill Ave. Sutton SM1 .... 59 B6
Benhill Ave. Sutton SM1 .... 59 C6
Benhill Rd. Sutton SM1 .... 59 C6
Benhill Wood Rd. Sutton SM1 .... 59 C6
Benhilton Gdns. Sutton SM1 ..... 59 B7
Benhurst Cl. Selsd CR2 .... 62 D1
Benhurst Ct. 13 Penge SE20 ..... 43 B8
Benhurst Ct. Streat SW16 .... 22 A3
Benhurst Gdns. Selsd CR2 .... 62 C1
Benhurst La. Streat SW16 .... 22 A3
Benin St. Lewish SE13 .... 24 D8
Benjamin Ct. Lntill GU15 .... 14 C1
Benner La. W End GU24 .... 68 A7
Bennet Cl. Tedd KT1 .... 37 C8
Bennett Cl. Cobham KT11 .... 73 A6
Bennett Cl. Crawl RH10 .... 202 B2
Bennett Ct. Camb GU15 .... 65 C5
Bennett House. 2 Streat SW4 .... 21 D8
Bennett St. Chisw W4 .... 7 E8
Bennett Way. W Clan GU4 .... 111 B6
Bennetts Ave. Croy CR0 .... 62 E8
Bennetts Cl. Mitch SW16 & SW16 41 B8
Bennetts Farm Pl. L Book KT23 . 93 F2
Bennetts Rd. Horsh RH13 .... 217 E1
Bennetts Way. Croy CR0 .... 62 F8
Bennetts Wood. Capel RH5 ...... 178 C5
Bens Acre. Horsh RH13 .... 218 A2
Bensbury Cl. Putney SW15 .... 19 C8
Bensham Cl. Thorn H CR7 .... 42 C5
Bensham Gr. S Norw CR7 .... 42 C6
Bensham La. Thorn H CR0 & CR7 42 B3
Bensham Manor Rd.
  Thorn H CR0 & CR7 .... 42 C5
Bensham Manor Sch.
  Thorn H CR7 .... 42 C4
Bensington Ct. E Bed TW14 .... 3 D1
Benson Cl. Hounsl TW3 .... 5 A3
Benson Prim Sch. Croy CR0 ...... 62 E7
Benson Rd. Croy CR0 & CR9 ...... 61 A7
Benson Rd. For Hil SE23 .... 23 C7
Benson's La. Faygt RH12 .... 199 C1
Bentall Sh Ctr The. 10
  King U T KT2 .... 37 E7
Benthall Gdns. Kenley CR8 .... 80 C2
Bentham Ave. Sheer GU21 .... 70 C4
Bentley Cl. Wimble SW19 .... 20 A5
Bentley Copse. Friml GU15 .... 66 B4
Bentley Dr. Whit V KT13 .... 53 A2
Benton's La. W Norw SE27 .... 22 C4
Benton's Rise. W Norw SE27 ..... 22 D3
Bentsbrook Cl. Dork RH5 .... 136 B3
Bentsbrook Cotts. Dork RH5 ... 136 B3
Bentsbrook Pk. Dork RH5 .... 136 B3
Bentsbrook Rd. Dork RH5 .... 136 B3
Benwell Cl. Sunby TW16 .... 35 A8
Benwell Rd. Brookw GU24 .... 88 A8
Benwick Ct. Penge SE20 .... 43 C8
Benwood Ct. Sutton SM1 .... 59 C7
Beomonds. Chert KT16 .... 33 A2
Beomonds Row. Chert KT16 ...... 33 A2
Berberis Cl. Bellf GU1 .... 109 C3
Bere Rd. Brack RG12 .... 27 E3
Beresford Ave. Tolw KT5 .... 38 C4
Beresford Ave. Twick TW1 .... 6 C1
Beresford Cl. Friml GU16 .... 85 F6
Beresford Ct. 11 Twick TW1 .... 6 C1

Beresford Gdns. Hounsl TW4 .... 4 F2
Beresford House. Dulw SE21 .... 22 E5
Beresford Rd. Belm SM2 .... 58 F3
Beresford Rd. Dork RH4 .... 136 B7
Beresford Rd. King U T KT2 .... 37 F8
Beresford Rd. King U T KT3 .... 38 C5
Bergenia Ct. W End GU24 .... 67 E6
Berkeley Ave. Cranf TW4 .... 4 A5
Berkeley Cl. Crawl RH11 .... 200 E2
Berkeley Cl. Stan TW19 .... 12 E6
Berkeley Cres. Friml GU16 .... 86 A8
Berkeley Ct. Ashtd KT21 .... 75 F1
Berkeley Ct. Oat Pk KT13 .... 53 E8
Berkeley Ct. Wallin SM6 .... 60 C6
Berkeley Dr. E Mole KT8 .... 36 A6
Berkeley Dr. Wink SL4 .... 9 B7
Berkeley Gdns. Clayg KT10 .... 56 A4
Berkeley Gdns. Pyrf KT14 .... 70 F5
Berkeley Gdns. Walt O T KT12 ... 34 F2
Berkeley House. [11] Brent TW8 ..... 6 D8
Berkeley Pl. Wimble SW19 .... 19 D2
Berkeley Pl. Woodc KT18 .... 76 D4
Berkeley Prim Sch. Heston TW5 .. 4 D7
Berkeley Waye. Heston TW5 .... 4 D7
Berkley Cl. Twick TW2 .... 16 E5
Berkley Ct. Guild GU1 .... 109 E1
Berkley Ct. [7] Twick TW1 .... 17 A8
Berkshire Cl. Cater CR3 .... 100 D5
Berkshire Copse Rd.
Farnb GU11 & GU14 .... 104 E7
Berkshire House. Catf SE6 .... 24 A4
Berkshire Rd. Camb GU15 .... 65 F8
Berkshire Sq. Mitch CR4 .... 41 E5
Berkshire Way. Binf RG12 .... 26 D6
Berkshire Way. Brack RG12 .... 26 D6
Berkshire Way. Mitch CR4 .... 41 E5
Bernard Ct. Camb GU15 .... 65 B4
Bernard Gdns. Wimble SW19 .... 19 F3
Bernard Rd. Wallin SM5 & SM6 .. 60 B6
Berne Rd. Thorn H CR7 .... 42 C4
Bernel Dr. Croy CR0 .... 62 F7
Bernersh Cl. Sandh GU15 & GU17 45 C1
Berney House. Beck BR3 .... 43 E4
Berney Rd. W Norw SE19 .... 22 E3
Berridge Rd. W Norw SE19 .... 22 E3
Berrington Dr. E Hors KT24 .... 92 F3
Berry Ct. Hounsl TW4 .... 4 F2
Berry La. Pirb GU3 .... 88 C2
Berry La. W Norw SE21 & SE27 ... 22 D4
Berry La. Woking GU22 & GU3 .... 88 D4
Berry Meade. Ashtd KT21 .... 75 F2
Berry Wlk. Ashtd KT21 .... 95 F8
Berry's La. Byfl KT14 .... 71 D8
Berrybank. Sandh GU15 .... 64 G6
Berrycroft. Wink RG12 .... 27 D8
Berrylands. Surb KT5 .... 37 F3
Berrylands. W Barn SW20 .... 39 C5
Berrylands Ct. [7] Sutton SM2 .... 59 B3
Berrylands Rd. Surb KT5 .... 37 F3
Berrylands Sta. Surb KT5 .... 38 B5
Berryman's La. For Hil SE26 .... 23 D4
Berrymeade Wlk. Crawl RH11 ... 200 E5
Berryscourt. Byfl KT14 .... 71 D8
Berryscroft Ct. Stain TW18 .... 13 C1
Berryscroft Rd. Stain TW18 .... 13 C1
Berstead Wlk. [1] Crawl RH11 ... 200 F3
Bert Rd. Thorn H CR7 .... 42 C4
Bertal Rd. Up Toot SW17 .... 20 D4
Bertie Rd. Penge SE26 .... 23 D2
Bertram Cotts. Merton SW19 .... 20 A1
Bertram Rd. King U T KT2 .... 18 A1
Bertrand House. [11]
Streat SW16 .... 21 E5
Berwyn Ave. Hounsl TW3 .... 5 B6
Berwyn Rd. Mortl SW14 & TW10 ... 7 B3
Berwyn Rd. Streat SW16 .... 22 B7
Beryl Harding House. [3]
Wimble SW19 .... 19 D1
Berystede. King U T KT2 .... 18 B1
Besley St. Streat SW16 .... 21 C2
Bessborough Rd. Rhampt SW15 19 A7
Bessborough Wks. E Mole KT8 ... 35 F4
Beswick Gdns. Brack RG12 .... 27 F8
Beta Rd. Chobh GU24 .... 49 F1
Beta Rd. Mayb GU22 .... 70 B3
Beta Rd. W Heath GU14 .... 85 A5
Beta Way. Thorpe TW20 .... 32 C8
Betchets Green Rd.
S Holm RH5 .... 157 C6
Betchley Cl. E Grins RH19 .... 185 E3
Betchworth Cl. Sutton SM1 .... 59 D5
Betchworth Sta. Betch RH5 .... 116 E3
Betchworth The. Brock RH4 .... 116 A1
Betchworth Way. New Add CR0 .. 63 C2
Betchworth Wks. Charl RH6 ..... 180 D6
Bethany Waye. E Bed TW14 .... 14 E8
Bethel Cl. Heath E GU9 .... 125 D6
Bethel La. Heath E GU9 .... 125 D6
Bethersden Cl. Beck BR3 .... 23 F1
Bethesda Ct. [8] Penge SE20 ..... 23 C1
Bethlem Royal Hospl The.
Croy BR3 .... 44 A2
Bethune Cl. Worth RH10 .... 202 D5
Bethune Rd. Horsh RH13 .... 217 E1
Betjeman Cl. Couslsd CR5 .... 79 F2
Betley Ct. Walt O T KT12 .... 54 B7
Betony Cl. Croy CR0 .... 43 D1
Betts Cl. Penge BR3 .... 43 F7
Betts Way. Crawl RH11 .... 181 D2
Betts Way. Long D KT6 .... 37 B1
Betts Way. Penge SE20 .... 43 B8
Bettswood Ct. [16] Penge SE20 .. 43 B8
Betula Ct. Kenley CR8 .... 80 D4
Between Streets. Cobham KT11 . 73 A5
Beulah Ave. S Norw CR7 .... 42 C7
Beulah Cres. S Norw CR7 .... 42 C7
Beulah Gr. Thorn H CR0 .... 42 C8
Beulah Hill. S Norw SE19 & SW16 22 C1
Beulah Inf Sch. S Norw CR7 ...... 42 C6

Beulah Jun Sch. S Norw CR7 ...... 42 C6
Beulah Rd. Merton SW19 .... 19 F1
Beulah Rd. S Norw CR7 .... 42 C6
Beulah Rd. Sutton SM1 .... 59 A6
Beulah Wlk. Wold CR3 .... 101 C2
Bevan Ct. Crawl RH11 .... 201 B1
Bevan Ct. Croy CR0 .... 61 A5
Beverley Ave. Hounsl TW4 .... 4 F3
Beverley Ave. Wimble SW20 .... 38 F8
Beverley Cl. Addl KT15 .... 52 D5
Beverley Cl. Ash Gu12 .... 105 F1
Beverley Cl. Chess KT9 .... 56 C6
Beverley Cl. E Ewell KT17 .... 77 C8
Beverley Cl. Friml GU15 .... 66 D6
Beverley Cl. Oat Pk KT13 .... 53 E8
Beverley Cotts. King U T SW15 ... 18 E5
Beverley Cres. Farnb GU14 .... 84 F2
Beverley Ct. Hounsl TW4 .... 4 F3
Beverley Ct. King U T SW20 .... 38 F8
Beverley Gdns. Barnes SW13 ..... 7 F4
Beverley Gdns. [2] N Cheam KT4 39 A1
Beverley House. Catf BR1 .... 24 D3
Beverley Hts. Reig RH2 .... 118 B3
Beverley Hyrst. [7] Croy CR0 ..... 61 F8
Beverley La. King U T KT2 .... 18 E1
Beverley Lodge. [6] Rich TW10 .. 6 E2
Beverley Mansions. Hounsl TW4 .. 4 F3
Beverley Rd. Barnes SW13 .... 7 F4
Beverley Rd. Kenley CR3 .... 80 F2
Beverley Rd. Mitch CR4 .... 41 D5
Beverley Rd. N Cheam KT4 .... 39 A1
Beverley Rd. New Mal KT3 .... 39 A5
Beverley Rd. Penge SE20 .... 43 B7
Beverley Rd. Sunby TW16 .... 34 F8
Beverley Rd. Tedd KT1 .... 37 C8
Beverley Sch. New Mal KT3 .... 39 A6
Beverley Trad Est. W Barn SM4 . 39 D2
Beverley Way.
King U T KT3 & SW20 & KT2 ... 38 F8
Beverley Way.
Wimble KT3 & SW20 .... 39 A6
Beverley Way (Kingston By Pass).
W Barn KT4 & SW20 .... 39 A6
Beverley Way Kingston Bypass.
King U T KT3 .... 38 F8
Beverstone Rd. Thorn H CR7 ..... 42 B5
Bevill Allen Cl. Up Toot SW17 .... 20 F3
Bevill Cl. Croy SE25 .... 43 A6
Bevington Rd. Beck BR3 .... 44 B7
Bew Ct. Dulw SE21 .... 23 A8
Bewbush Cl. Crawl RH11 .... 200 F3
Bewbush Fst Sch. Crawl RH11 . 200 F3
Bewbush Manor. Crawl RH11 .. 200 F3
Bewbush Mid Sch. Crawl RH11 200 F2
Bewlys Rd. W Norw SE27 .... 22 B3
Bexhill Cl. Felt TW13 .... 15 E6
Bexhill Rd. For Hil SE4 .... 23 F8
Bexhill Rd. Mortl SW14 .... 7 C4
Beynon Rd. Wallin SM5 .... 59 F5
Bicester Rd. Mortl TW9 .... 7 B4
Bickersteth Rd. Up Toot SW17 ... 20 F2
Bickley Cl. Crawl RH11 .... 201 A3
Bickley St. Up Toot SW17 .... 20 F3
Bicknell Rd. Friml GU16 .... 65 E2
Bickney Way. Fetch KT22 .... 94 C5
Bicknoller Cl. Sutton SM2 .... 59 B1
Bidborough Cl. Hayes BR2 .... 44 F4
Biddulph Rd. S Croy CR2 .... 61 C2
Bideford Cl. Felt TW13 .... 15 F6
Bideford Cl. W Heath GU14 .... 85 A7
Bideford Rd. Catf BR1 .... 24 F5
Bidhams Cres. Burgh H KT20 ..... 97 C6
Bidmead Ct. Surb KT6 .... 56 E7
Bield The. Woodh RH2 .... 139 B6
Bietigheim Way. [2] Camb GU15 65 C6
Big Common La. Bletch RH1 .... 120 B3
Biggin Ave. Mitch CR4 .... 40 F8
Biggin Cl. Crawl RH11 .... 201 C4
Biggin Hill. W Norw SE19 & SW16 22 B1
Biggin Hill Airport. Bigg H TN16 83 D5
Biggin Hill Bsns Pk.
Bigg H TN16 .... 83 D4
Biggin Hill Prim Sch.
Bigg H TN16 .... 83 E3
Biggin Way.
S Norw CR7 & SE19 & SW16 ... 22 C1
Bigginwood Rd. S Norw SW16 ... 42 B8
Bignor Cl. Horsh RH12 .... 218 A7
Bilberry Cl. Crawl RH11 .... 201 B3
Bilbets. Horsh RH12 .... 217 C3
Billesden Rd. Pirb GU24 .... 87 D7
Billet Rd. Stan TW19 & TW18 ... 13 A6
Billhurst Cotts. Lingf RH7 .... 164 D4
Billingshurst Rd. Broad H RH12 216 D3
Billinton Dr. Worth RH10 .... 202 B5
Billockby Cl. Chess KT9 .... 56 F4
Billsley Ct. S Norw SE25 .... 42 E5
Bilton Ind Est. Easth RG12 .... 26 C5
Binbury Row. Stain TW18 .... 12 E4
Binfield Rd. Bint RG11 .... 25 F7
Binfield Rd. Byfl KT14 .... 71 E7
Binfield Rd. S Croy CR2 .... 61 F5
Binfield Rd. Woki RG11 .... 25 F7
Bingham Cnr. Croy CR0 .... 43 A1
Bingham Dr. Knaph GU21 .... 68 F1
Bingham Dr. Stain TW19 .... 13 D1
Bingham Rd. Croy CR0 & CR9 ... 43 B1
Bingley Rd. Ashf TW16 .... 15 A1
Binhams Lea. Dunsf GU8 .... 192 F5
Binhams Meadow. Dunsf GU8 . 192 F5
Binley House. Rhampt SW15 ..... 7 F1
Binney Ct. Crawl RH10 .... 182 E1
Binns Rd. Chisw W4 .... 7 E8
Binscombe Cres. Farnc GU7 .. 150 E8
Binscombe Jun Sch.
Farnc GU7 .... 129 E1
Binscombe La. Farnc GU7 ..... 150 E7
Binstead Cl. Crawl RH11 .... 201 B8
Binsted Dr. Blckw GU17 .... 64 E5
Binton La. The San GU10 .... 126 E3
Birch Ave. Cater CR3 .... 100 D3

Birch Circ. Farnc GU7 .... 150 F8
Birch Cl. Brent TW8 .... 6 B7
Birch Cl. Camb GU15 .... 65 E8
Birch Cl. Crawl D RH10 .... 204 C8
Birch Cl. Hounsl TW3 .... 5 D5
Birch Cl. New Haw KT15 .... 52 D2
Birch Cl. Rowl GU10 .... 146 A4
Birch Cl. Send M GU23 .... 90 A4
Birch Cl. Tedd TW11 .... 17 A3
Birch Cl. Woking GU21 .... 89 C8
Birch Ct. Ashtd KT21 .... 75 D2
Birch Ct. Sutton SM1 .... 59 C6
Birch Ct. [9] Wallin SM6 .... 60 B6
Birch Dr. Hawley GU17 .... 64 D3
Birch Gn. Stain TW18 .... 13 A4
Birch Gr. Bellf GU1 .... 109 C4
Birch Gr. Brack RG12 .... 27 C5
Birch Gr. Kings KT20 .... 97 F3
Birch Gr. Lewish SE12 .... 24 F8
Birch Gr. Mayb GU22 .... 70 D4
Birch Gr. Up Hall W17 .... 34 E7
Birch Hill. S Croy CR0 .... 62 D5
Birch Hill Jun & Inf Sch.
Easth RG12 .... 27 B1
Birch Hill Rd. Easth RG12 .... 27 B1
Birch La. Purley CR8 .... 79 E8
Birch La. W End GU24 .... 67 E7
Birch La. Wink RG12 & SL5 .... 28 B8
Birch Lea. Crawl RH10 .... 182 A1
Birch Platt. W End GU24 .... 67 D6
Birch Rd. Farnc GU7 .... 151 A8
Birch Rd. Felt TW13 .... 15 D3
Birch Rd. Head Dn GU35 .... 187 B6
Birch Rd. Windl GU20 .... 48 A4
Birch Side. Crowth RG11 .... 45 A6
Birch Tree Ave. Coney H BR4 ... 63 F6
Birch Tree View. Lhtwat GU18 ... 48 A1
Birch Tree Way. Croy CR0 .... 62 B8
Birch Vale. Cobham KT11 .... 74 A6
Birch Way. Ash V GU12 .... 106 A7
Birch Way. Warlgm CR6 .... 81 E1
Birch Wlk. Mitch CR4 .... 41 B8
Birchanger. Godal GU7 .... 150 E4
Birchanger Rd. Croy SE25 .... 43 A4
Birchcroft Cl. Cater CR3 .... 100 C2
Birchdale Cl. W Byfl KT14 .... 71 C8
Birchend Cl. S Croy CR2 .... 61 D4
Birches Cl. Epsom KT18 .... 76 E4
Birches Cl. Mitch CR4 .... 40 F6
Birches Ind Est. E Grins RH19 .. 185 A3
Birches Rd. Horsh RH12 .... 218 B5
Birches The. Beck BR2 .... 44 F5
Birches The. Blckw GU17 .... 64 B5
Birches The. Crawl RH10 .... 202 A7
Birches The. E Hors KT24 .... 92 E1
Birches The. S Norw SE25 .... 42 F7
Birches The. Twick TW4 .... 15 F8
Birches The. W Heath GU14 ..... 84 D4
Birches The. Woking GU22 .... 69 F1
Birchett Rd. Alder GU11 .... 105 A2
Birchett Rd. W Heath GU14 ..... 84 E6
Birchetts Cl. [2] Brack RG12 ..... 27 B8
Birchfield Cl. Addl KT15 .... 52 B6
Birchfield Cl. Couslsd CR5 .... 79 F3
Birchfield Gr. E Ewell KT17 ..... 58 C2
Birchfields. Camb GU15 .... 65 C4
Birchgrove. Cobham KT11 .... 73 D5
Birchington Rd. Surb KT5 .... 37 F2
Birchlands. Sandh GU15 .... 45 E2
Birchlands Ave. Balham SW12 .. 20 F8
Birchway. Earls RH1 .... 140 B7
Birchwood Ave. Beck BR3 .... 43 F5
Birchwood Ave.
Hackb SM5 & SM6 .... 60 B7
Birchwood Cl. Horley RH6 .... 161 B4
Birchwood Cl. Morden SM4 ..... 40 B5
Birchwood Dr. Lhtwat GU18 ..... 48 C1
Birchwood Dr. W Byfl KT14 .... 71 A7
Birchwood Gr. Hampt TW12 ..... 16 A2
Birchwood La. Cater CR3 .... 100 B2
Birchwood La. S Nutk KT10 & KT22 55 E1
Birchwood Rd. Streat SW17 ..... 21 B3
Birchwood Rd.
W Byfl KT14 & KT15 .... 71 A7
Bird Mews. Woki RG11 .... 25 B6
Bird Wlk. Twick TW2 .... 15 F7
Bird-In-Hand Pas. For Hil SE23 . 23 C6
Birdham Cl. Crawl RH11 .... 201 B8
Birdhaven. Wreccl GU10 & GU9 . 146 A6
Birdhurst. Whytlf CR3 .... 100 F7
Birdhurst Ave. S Croy CR2 .... 61 D6
Birdhurst Ct. Wallin SM6 .... 60 C3
Birdhurst Gdns. S Croy CR2 ..... 61 D6
Birdhurst Rd. Mitch SW19 .... 20 E2
Birdhurst Rd. S Croy CR2 .... 61 E5
Birdhurst Rise. S Croy CR2 .... 61 E5
Birds Hill Dr. Oxsh KT22 .... 74 D6
Birds Hill Rd. Oxsh KT22 .... 74 D6
Birds Hill Rise. Oxsh KT22 .... 74 D6
Birdsgrove. Knaph GU21 .... 68 B1
Birdwood Dr. Knaph GU21 .... 88 E7
Birdwood Cl. Selsd CR2 .... 81 D8
Birdwood Cl. Tedd TW11 .... 16 E4
Birdwood Rd. Sandh GU15 .... 64 F6
Birdworld. Binst GU10 .... 145 B3
Birkbeck Hill. W Norw SE21 ..... 22 B7
Birkbeck Pl. Sandh GU15 .... 45 E1
Birkbeck Rd. W Norw SE21 .... 22 C6
Birkbeck Rd. Penge BR3 .... 43 D7
Birkbeck Rd. Wimble SW19 ..... 20 B2
Birkbeck Sta. Penge SE20 .... 43 C6
Birkdale. Easth RG12 .... 26 E2
Birkdale Dr. Crawl RH11 .... 200 D5
Birkdale Gdns. Croy CR0 .... 62 D6
Birkenhead Ave. King U T KT2 .. 37 F8
Birkenholme Cl. Head Dn GU35 187 C4
Birkhall Rd. Catf SE6 .... 24 D6
Birkheads Rd. Reig RH2 .... 118 A2
Birkwood Cl. Streat SW12 .... 21 D8
Birling House. [4] Penge SE20 .. 23 C1

Birnham Cl. Send M GU23 .... 91 A3
Birtley Rd. Bramly GU5 .... 152 B4
Birtley Rise. Bramly GU5 .... 152 A5
Biscoe Cl. Heston TW5 .... 5 A8
Bisenden Rd. Croy CR0 .... 61 E8
Bisham Cl. Carsh CR4 .... 40 F1
Bishams Ct. Cater CR3 .... 100 F3
Bishop Bell Mid Sch.
Crawl RH10 .... 201 E3
Bishop Challoner Sch.
Beck BR2 .... 44 D7
Bishop David Brown Sch.
Sheer GU21 .... 70 D6
Bishop Duppa Pk. Oat Pk TW17 34 F2
Bishop Duppa's Almshouses. [7]
Rich TW10 .... 6 E2
Bishop Fox Way. E Mole KT8 ..... 35 F5
Bishop Gilpins Prim Sch.
Wimble SW19 .... 19 F3
Bishop Perrin (C of E) Sch.
Twick TW2 .... 16 B7
Bishop Reindorp CE Sch.
Bellf GU1 .... 109 C4
Bishop Sumner Dr. Hale GU9 .. 125 C6
Bishop Thomas Grant Catholic Sec
Sch. Streat SW16 .... 21 F3
Bishop Wand C of E Sec Sch.
Sunby TW16 .... 34 F7
Bishop's Cl. Couslsd CR5 .... 80 A1
Bishop's Cotts. Box H RH3 ..... 116 B3
Bishop's Hall. King U T KT1 ..... 37 D7
Bishop's La. Wink SL4 .... 8 B7
Bishop's Mead. Farnh GU9 ..... 125 C2
Bishop's Pl. Sutton SM1 .... 59 C5
Bishop's Rd. Thorn H CR0 .... 42 B2
Bishopdale. Easth RG12 .... 27 A5
Bishops Cl. Sutton SM1 .... 59 A7
Bishops Ct. [1] Ashf TW16 .... 14 F1
Bishops Ct. Guild GU2 .... 130 C7
Bishops Dr. E Bed TW14 .... 3 D1
Bishops Dr. Woki RG11 .... 25 C7
Bishops Gr. Hampt TW12 .... 15 F4
Bishops Gr. Windl GU20 .... 48 C4
Bishops Hill. Walt O T KT12 ..... 35 A4
Bishops Park Rd. Thorn H SW16 41 E8
Bishops Rd. Hale GU9 .... 125 B7
Bishops Sq. Cran GU6 .... 174 F3
Bishops Wlk. S Croy CR0 & CR9 .. 62 E5
Bishops Wood. Woking GU21 ... 69 C2
Bishopscourt. [6] S Croy CR0 ... 61 F8
Bishopsford Rd. Morden SM4 ... 40 D3
Bishopsgate Rd.
Eng Gn SL4 & TW20 .... 11 B5
Bishopsmead C of E (Aided) Mid
Sch. Epsom KT19 .... 57 D1
Bishopsmead Cl. E Hors KT24 .. 112 F2
Bishopsmead Dr. E Hors KT24 . 112 F2
Bishopsmead Par. E Hors KT24 112 F2
Bishopsthorpe Rd. For Hil SE26 . 23 D4
Bishopsthorpe Wlk. Crawl RH11 . 201 C1
Bisley C of E Prim Sch.
Bisley GU24 .... 68 A3
Bisley Cl. N Cheam KT4 .... 39 C1
Bisley House. Putney SW19 ..... 19 D6
Bitmead Cl. Crawl RH11 .... 200 E5
Bittams La. Addl KT15 & KT16 .. 51 E6
Bittern Cl. Crawl RH11 .... 200 D5
Bittern Cl. Sandh GU15 .... 64 D8
Bitterne Dr. Woking GU21 .... 69 B2
Bittoms The. King U T KT1 .... 37 D6
Black Dog Wlk. Crawl RH10 ..... 201 E8
Black Horse Way. Horsh RH12 . 217 C2
Black Lake Dr. Thorpe TW20 ..... 32 A8
Black Pond La. M Bourn GU10 .. 146 C6
Black Prince Cl. Byfl KT14 .... 71 F5
Blackberry Cl. Stough GU1 ..... 109 B8
Blackberry Cl. Up Hall TW17 ..... 34 E5
Blackberry Farm Cl. Heston TW5 4 E7
Blackberry La. Felct RH7 .... 185 E5
Blackberry Rd. Felct RH19 & RH7 185 D8
Blackbird Cl. Sandh GU15 .... 64 D8
Blackborough Cl. Reig RH2 ..... 118 C1
Blackborough Rd. Reig RH2 .... 118 D1
Blackbridge La. Horsh RH12 ... 217 A1
Blackbridge Rd. Woking GU22 ... 89 D7
Blackbrook Rd. Dork RH5 ...... 136 C2
Blackbrook Rd. S Holm RH5 ... 157 C8
Blackburn The. E Book KT22 ... 93 F3
Blackburn Way. Godal GU7 .... 151 A5
Blackbush Cl. Sutton SM2 .... 59 B3
Blackcap Cl. Crawl RH11 .... 201 C4
Blackcap Pl. Sandh GU15 .... 64 E8
Blackdown Ave. Pyrf GU22 .... 70 E4
Blackdown Cl. Mayb GU22 .... 70 D3
Blackdown Prim Sch.
Friml GU16 .... 86 C8
Blackdown Rd. Friml GU16 .... 86 C8
Blackdown Rural Ind.
Haslem GU27 .... 208 E4
Blackenham Rd. Up Toot SW17 . 20 F4
Blackett Cl. Egham TW18 & TW20 32 F7
Blackfold Rd. Crawl RH10 ..... 202 A5
Blackford Cl. S Croy CR2 .... 61 B2
Blackham House. Wimble SW19 19 E2
Blackheath. Crawl RH10 .... 202 D8
Blackheath Gr. Woner GU5 ..... 152 B8
Blackheath La. Albury GU5 ..... 132 B3
Blackheath La.
Woner GU5 & GU4 .... 152 C8
Blackheath Rd. Heath E GU9 .. 125 C4
Blackhills. Esher KT10 .... 55 A2
Blackhorse Cl. Croy CR0 .... 43 A2
Blackhorse La. L Kings RH2 ... 118 C7
Blackhorse Rd.
Woking GU21 & GU22 .... 88 E6
Blacklands Cres. For Row RH18 206 F2

Blacklands Meadow. Nutf RH1 119 E2
Blacklands Rd. Catf SE6 .... 24 C4
Blackman Gdns. Alder GU11 ... 126 B8
Blackman's La. Fickl CR6 .... 82 F5
Blackmeadows. Easth RG12 ..... 27 C3
Blackmoor Cl. N Asct SL5 .... 28 D7
Blackmoor Wood. N Asct SL5 ... 28 D7
Blackmore Cres. Sheer GU21 ... 70 C5
Blackmore House. For Hil SE23 . 23 F7
Blackmore's Gr. Tedd TW11 ..... 17 A2
Blackness La. Woking GU22 ..... 89 B8
Blacknest Cotts. Dunsf GU8 ... 192 E3
Blacknest Rd. Went GU25 & SL5 . 30 E6
Blackshaw Rd. Up Toot SW17 ... 20 D3
Blacksmith Cl. Ashtd KT21 .... 95 F8
Blacksmith La. Chil GU4 .... 131 D3
Blacksmith's La. Laleh TW18 ... 33 C5
Blacksmiths Hill. Sander CR2 ... 81 B6
Blacksmiths La. Chert KT16 ..... 33 A2
Blackstone Cl. Reig RH2 .... 139 E8
Blackstone Cl. W Heath GU14 .. 84 D6
Blackstone Hill.
Reig RH1 & RH2 .... 118 E1
Blackstone House. Dulw SE21 .. 22 E5
Blackstroud La E.
W End GU18 & GU24 .... 67 E8
Blackstroud La W. Lhtwat GU18 67 D8
Blackthorn Cl. Crawl RH11 ..... 181 C1
Blackthorn Cl. Horsh RH13 .... 218 A2
Blackthorn Cl. Woodh RH2 .... 139 C7
Blackthorn Cres. W Heath GU14 84 F8
Blackthorn Ct. Heston TW5 .... 4 E7
Blackthorn Ct. [6] N Norw SW16 22 A2
Blackthorn Dr. Lhtwat GU18 ..... 67 B7
Blackthorn Rd. Bigg H TN16 ... 83 E3
Blackthorn Rd. Woodh RH2 .... 139 C7
Blackthorne Ave. Croy CR0 ..... 43 C1
Blackthorne Cres. Poyle SL3 ... 1 E5
Blackthorne Ind Pk. Poyle SL3 .. 1 F5
Blackthorne Rd. G Book KT23 ... 94 C1
Blackthorne Rd. Poyle SL3 .... 1 E4
Blackwater Cl. Ash GU12 .... 106 A1
Blackwater La. Crawl RH10 .... 202 D6
Blackwater Sta. Blckw GU17 ... 64 E4
Blackwater Way. Alder GU12 .. 126 D8
Blackwater Way Ind Est.
Alder GU12 .... 126 E8
Blackwell Ave. Stough GU2 .... 108 D1
Blackwell Cty Prim Sch.
E Grins RH19 .... 185 E3
Blackwell Farm Rd.
E Grins RH19 .... 185 F3
Blackwell Hollow.
E Grins RH19 .... 185 F2
Blackwell Rd. E Grins RH19 ... 185 F2
Blackwood Cl. W Byfl KT14 .... 71 C7
Bladen Cl. Whit V KT13 .... 53 E4
Blades Cl. Ashtd KT22 .... 95 D7
Bladon Cl. Guild GU1 .... 110 A2
Bladon Ct. Beck BR2 .... 44 E7
Bladon Ct. Streat SW16 .... 21 E2
Blagdon Rd. New Mal KT3 .... 38 F5
Blagdon Wlk. Tedd TW11 .... 17 C2
Blair Ave. Thame D KT10 .... 55 C8
Blair Ct. Beck BR3 .... 44 B8
Blair Ct. Carsh SM5 .... 24 F7
Blairderry Rd. Streat SW2 .... 21 E6
Blaise Cl. Farnb GU14 .... 85 D3
Blake Cl. Carsh SM5 .... 40 E1
Blake Cl. Crawl RH10 .... 201 F2
Blake Cl. Crowth RG11 .... 45 C4
Blake House. Beck BR3 .... 24 B2
Blake Rd. Croy CR0 .... 61 E8
Blake Rd. Mitch CR4 .... 40 E6
Blake's Gn. W Wick BR4 .... 44 C1
Blake's La. E Clan GU4 .... 111 F3
Blake's La. W Hors GU4 .... 111 F3
Blakeden Dr. Clayg KT10 .... 55 F4
Blakehall Rd. Wallin SM5 .... 59 F4
Blakemore Rd. Streat SW16 ..... 21 E5
Blakemore Rd. Thorn H CR7 ..... 41 F4
Blakeney Ave. Beck BR3 .... 43 F8
Blakeney Cl. Epsom KT19 .... 76 D8
Blakeney Rd. Beck BR3 .... 43 F8
Blakes Ave. New Mal KT3 .... 38 F3
Blakes La. New Mal KT3 .... 38 F3
Blakes Terr. W Barn KT3 .... 39 A4
Blakewood Cl. Felt TW13 .... 15 C4
Blakewood Ct. Penge SE20 ..... 23 B1
Blanchards Hill. Westfd GU4 ... 109 E8
Blanchland Rd. Morden SM4 ... 40 B4
Blanchman's Rd. Warlgm CR6 .. 81 E1
Blandfield Rd. Balham SW12 ... 21 A8
Blandford Ave. Penge BR3 .... 43 E7
Blandford Ave. Twick TW2 .... 16 B7
Blandford Cl. Mayb GU22 .... 70 B2
Blandford Cl. Wallin CR0 .... 60 E7
Blandford Rd. Penge BR3 .... 43 D7
Blandford Rd. Tedd TW11 .... 16 E3
Blanes La. Brack SL5 .... 28 C3
Blanford Rd. Reig RH2 .... 139 C8
Blanks La. Charl RH5 & RH6 ... 159 B2
Blanks La. Cudw RH5 & RH6 ... 159 B2
Blashford St. Lewish SE13 .... 24 D8
Blatchford Cl. Horsh RH13 ..... 217 F3
Blatchford Rd. Walt O T KT12 ... 35 A1
Blatchford Rd. Horsh RH13 .... 217 F3
Blay's La. Eng Gn TW20 .... 11 B2
Blays Cl. Eng Gn TW20 .... 11 C2
Blean Gr. Penge SE20 .... 23 C1
Blegborough Rd. Streat SW16 .. 21 C2
Blencarn Cl. Woking GU21 .... 68 F3
Blendworth Point. [4]
Rhampt SW15 .... 19 B7
Blenheim. [28] Putney SW19 ..... 19 D7
Blenheim Bsns Ctr. Mitch CR4 .. 40 F7
Blenheim Cl. Crawl RH10 ..... 182 D1

Blenheim Cl. E Grins RH19 .... 186 A3
Blenheim Cl. Tongh GU10 .... 126 E7
Blenheim Cl. W Barn SW20 .... 39 C6
Blenheim Cl. W Byfl KT14 .... 70 F6
Blenheim Cl. Wallin SM6 .... 60 C3
Blenheim Cres. Hale GU9 .... 125 A5
Blenheim Cres. S Croy CR2 .... 61 C3
Blenheim Ct. Egham TW18 .... 12 D4
Blenheim Ct. Farnb GU14 .... 85 D2
Blenheim Ct. Rich TW9 .... 6 F4
Blenheim Ct. S Norw SE19 .... 42 E8
Blenheim Ct. Sutton SM2 .... 59 C4
Blenheim Fields. For Row RH18 .... 206 E3
Blenheim Gdns. King U T KT2 .... 18 B1
Blenheim Gdns. Sander CR2 .... 81 A7
Blenheim Gdns. Wallin SM6 .... 60 C3
Blenheim Gdns. Woking GU22 .... 89 B8
Blenheim House. Hounsl TW3 .... 5 A4
Blenheim Park Rd. S Croy CR2 .... 61 C2
Blenheim Pk. Bletch RH1 .... 105 C7
Blenheim Rd. Epsom KT19 .... 76 E8
Blenheim Rd. Farnb GU11 .... 105 C7
Blenheim Rd. Horsh RH12 .... 217 D4
Blenheim Rd. Penge SE20 .... 23 C1
Blenheim Rd. Sutton SM1 .... 59 B7
Blenheim Rd. W Barn SW20 .... 39 C6
Bleriot Rd. Heston TW5 .... 4 C7
Bletchingley Cl. Merst RH1 .... 119 C6
Bletchingley Golf Course.
    Bletch RH1 .... 120 E3
Bletchingley Rd.
    Bletch RH1 & RH9 .... 121 B4
Bletchingley Rd.
    Godst RH1 & RH9 .... 121 B4
Bletchingley Rd. Merst RH1 .... 119 C6
Bletchingley Rd. Nutf RH1 .... 119 C6
Bletchingley Rd. Nutf RH1 .... 120 A2
Bletchingly Cl. Thorn H CR7 .... 42 B5
Bletchmore Cl. Harl UB3 .... 3 D8
Blewburton Wlk. Brack RG12 .... 27 E5
Blewfield. Godal GU7 .... 150 F2
Bligh Cl. Crawl RH10 .... 201 F4
Bligh House. ⁴ W Norw SE27 .... 22 C4
Blighton La. The San GU10 .... 126 E3
Blincoe Cl. Putney SW19 .... 19 D6
Blind Cnr. Croy SE25 .... 43 B5
Blindley Ct. Blind H RH7 .... 163 E8
Blindley Rd. Crawl RH10 .... 182 D1
Bloggs Way. Cran GU6 .... 174 D3
Blomfield Dale. Binf RG12 .... 26 D7
Blondell Ct. Harm UB7 .... 2 D8
Bloom Gr. W Norw SE27 .... 22 B5
Bloomfield Cl. Knaph GU21 .... 68 E1
Bloomfield Rd. King U T KT1 .... 37 E6
Bloomsbury Ct. Cranf TW5 .... 4 B6
Bloomsbury Way. Hawley GU17 ...... 64 D3
Bloor Cl. Horsh RH12 .... 217 D7
Blossom Cl. S Croy CR2 .... 61 F5
Blossom Waye. Heston TW5 .... 4 E7
Blount Ave. E Grins RH19 .... 185 C4
Bloxham Cres. Hampt TW12 .... 35 F8
Bloxham Rd. Cran GU6 .... 175 A3
Bloxworth Cl. ⁹ Brack RG12 .... 27 F5
Bloxworth Cl. Wallin SM6 .... 60 C7
Blue Anchor Alley. ³ Rich TW9 .... 6 E3
Blue Ball La. Egham TW20 .... 11 F3
Blue Barn Way. Whit V KT13 .... 72 A8
Blue Cedars. Nork SM7 .... 77 D5
Blue Coat Wlk. Brack RG12 .... 27 D4
Blue Sch The. Islew TW7 .... 6 A4
Bluebell Cl. Crawl RH11 .... 201 B3
Bluebell Cl. E Grins RH19 .... 185 B1
Bluebell Cl. For Hil SE19 & SE26 .... 22 F4
Bluebell Cl. Horsh RH12 .... 217 E5
Bluebell Cl. Wallin CR4 .... 41 B1
Bluebell Ct. Woking GU22 .... 89 D8
Bluebell Hill. Brack RG12 .... 27 E8
Bluebell Rise. Lhtwat GU18 .... 67 B8
Blueberry Gdns. Coulsd CR5 .... 79 F3
Bluefield Cl. Hampt TW12 .... 16 A3
Bluegates. Stonel K17 .... 58 A3
Bluegates. Wimble SW19 .... 19 E3
Bluehouse Gdns. Limps RH8 .... 123 A7
Bluehouse La. Limps RH8 .... 122 F7
Bluethroat Cl. Sandh GU15 .... 64 E8
Bluff Cove. Alder GU11 .... 105 C3
Blundel La. Oxsh KT11 .... 74 B4
Blundel La. Stk D'A KT11 .... 74 B4
Blundell Ave. Horley RH6 .... 160 F4
Blunden Rd. W Heath GU14 .... 84 F5
Blunt Rd. Croy CR0 .... 61 D5
Blunts Ave. Harm UB7 .... 3 A7
Blunts Way. Horsh RH12 .... 217 C5
Blyth Cl. Twick TW1 .... 5 F1
Blyth Rd. Broml BR1 & BR2 .... 44 F8
Blythe Cl. For Hil SE23 .... 23 B8
Blythe Hill. For Hil SE23 & SE6 ...... 23 B8
Blythe Hill La. For Hil SE23 & SE6 .. 23 B7
Blythe Vale. For Hil SE23 .... 23 F7
Blythewood La. N Asct SL5 .... 28 E7
Blythwood Dr.
    Friml GU15 & GU16 .... 65 D2
Blythwood Pk. Broml BR1 .... 44 F8
Blytons The. E Grins RH19 .... 185 B1
Boar Hill. Dork RH5 .... 135 C1
Board School Rd. Woking GU21 .... 69 F3
Bockhampton Rd. King U T KT2 ...... 17 F1
Boddicott Cl. Putney SW19 .... 19 E6
Bodens Ride. Brack SL5 .... 28 F1
Bodiam Cl. Crawl RH10 .... 202 C6
Bodiam Ct. Hayes BR2 .... 44 F5
Bodiam Rd. Streat SW16 .... 21 D1
Bodley Cl. New Mal KT3 .... 38 E4
Bodley Manor Way. Streat SE24 ..... 22 A8
Bodley Rd. New Mal KT3 .... 38 E4
Bodmin Gr. Morden SM4 .... 40 B4
Bodmin St. Wands SW18 .... 20 A7

Bodnant Gdns. W Barn SW20 .... 39 B6
Bofors Rd. Farnb GU14 .... 105 A8
Bog La. Brack RG12 .... 28 A5
Bognor Rd. Bear Gn RH5 .... 157 B2
Bognor Rd. Ockley RH5 .... 157 B2
Bognor Rd. Warn RH12 & RH5 ..... 197 D4
Bois Hall Rd. Addl KT15 .... 52 D5
Bolderwood Way. W Wick BR4 .... 63 B8
Bolding House La. W End GU24 ...... 67 F7
Boleyn Ave. Ewell KT17 .... 58 B1
Boleyn Cl. Egham TW18 .... 12 E3
Boleyn Ct. E Mole KT8 .... 36 D5
Boleyn Ct. ¹¹ Redh RH1 .... 119 A2
Boleyn Dr. E Mole KT8 .... 35 F6
Boleyn Gdns. W Wick BR4 .... 63 B8
Boleyn Wlk. Leahd KT22 .... 94 F7
Bolingbroke Gr. Balham SW11 .... 20 F8
Bolingbroke House. Catf BR3 .... 24 B3
Bolney Ct. Crawl RH11 .... 200 F3
Bolney Ct. King U T KT6 .... 37 C4
Bolsover Gr. Merst RH1 .... 119 E6
Bolstead Rd. Mitch CR4 .... 41 B8
Bolters La. Banstd SM7 .... 78 A4
Bolters La. Horley RH6 .... 161 A5
Bolters Rd S. Horley RH6 .... 160 F6
Bolton Cl. Chess KT9 .... 56 E4
Bolton Ct. Penge SE20 .... 43 A7
Bolton Gdns. Broml BR1 .... 24 F2
Bolton Gdns. Tedd TW11 .... 17 A2
Bolton Rd. Chess KT9 .... 56 E4
Bolton Rd. Chisw W4 .... 7 C7
Bolton Rd. Worth RH10 .... 202 C2
Bolton's La. Harl TW6 & UB7 .... 3 C7
Bolton's La. Pyrf GU22 .... 71 A3
Boltons Cl. Pyrf GU22 .... 71 A3
Bomer Cl. Harm UB7 .... 3 A7
Bonchurch Cl. Sutton SM2 .... 59 B3
Bond Fst Sch. Mitch CR4 .... 40 F7
Bond Gdns. Wallin SM6 .... 60 C6
Bond Rd. Mitch CR4 .... 40 F7
Bond Rd. Surb KT6 .... 56 F8
Bond Rd. Warlgm CR6 .... 81 E1
Bond St. Eng Gn TW20 .... 11 C3
Bond's La. Dork RH5 .... 136 B1
Bone Mill La. Godst RH9 .... 121 C5
Bonehurst Rd. Salfs RH1 & RH6 .... 161 A7
Bones La.
    Horne RH6 & RH7 & RH9 .... 163 B2
Bonner Hill Rd. King U T KT1 .... 38 A6
Bonners Cl. Westfd GU22 .... 89 F5
Bonnetts La.
    Rusper RH11 & RH6 .... 181 A3
Bonnys Rd. Reig RH2 .... 138 D8
Bonser Rd. Twick TW1 .... 16 F6
Bonsey Cl. Westfd GU22 .... 89 E6
Bonsey La. Westfd GU22 .... 89 E6
Bonsey's La. Chobh GU24 & KT16 .. 50 F2
Bonsor Dr. Kings KT20 .... 97 E5
Bonus Pastor RC Sch. Catf BR1 ..... 24 E4
Bonville Rd. Broml BR1 .... 24 F2
Bookham Cl. L Book KT23 .... 93 F4
Bookham Ct. Mitch CR4 .... 40 D6
Bookham Gr. G Book KT23 .... 94 B1
Bookham Ind Pk. L Book KT23 .... 93 F4
Bookham Rd. Downs KT11 .... 93 D7
Bookham Sta. L Book KT23 .... 93 F4
Bookhurst Hill. Cran GU6 .... 175 A4
Bookhurst Rd. Cran GU6 .... 175 A4
Booth Dr. Stain TW18 .... 13 D2
Booth House. ² Streat SW2 .... 22 A8
Booth Rd. Crawl RH11 .... 200 E3
Booth Rd. Croy CR0 & CR9 .... 61 B8
Boothby House. ² Streat SW16 ...... 21 C3
Borage Cl. Crawl RH11 .... 201 A3
Borland Rd. Tedd TW11 .... 17 B1
Borough Grange. Sander CR2 .... 81 A7
Borough Hill. Croy CR0 & CR9 .... 61 B7
Borough Rd. Farnc GU7 .... 150 D5
Borough Rd. Godal GU7 .... 150 D5
Borough Rd. Hounsl TW7 .... 5 F6
Borough Rd. ⁷ King U T KT2 .... 18 A1
Borough Rd. Mitch CR4 .... 40 E7
Borough Rd. Tats TN16 .... 103 D6
Borough The. Brock RH3 & RH5 .... 137 A8
Borough The. Farnh GU9 .... 125 B2
Borrowdale Cl. Crawl RH11 .... 201 B4
Borrowdale Cl. Sander CR2 .... 80 F6
Borrowdale Cl. Thor L TW20 .... 12 B1
Borrowdale Dr. Sander CR2 .... 80 F7
Borrowdale Gdns. Friml GU15 .... 66 D4
Bosbury Rd. Catf SE6 .... 24 C5
Boscombe Cl. Thor L TW20 .... 32 C8
Boscombe Gdns. Streat SW16 .... 21 E2
Boscombe House. Croy CR0 .... 42 D1
Boscombe Rd. Merton SW19 .... 40 B8
Boscombe Rd. Mitch CR4 .... 41 A2
Boscombe Rd. N Cheam KT4 .... 39 D1
Bosman Dr. Windl GU20 .... 48 A6
Bostock Ave. Horsh RH12 .... 218 A5
Bostock House. Heston TW5 .... 5 A8
Boston Ct. S Norw SE25 .... 42 F5
Boston Ct. Sutton SM2 .... 59 C3
Boston Gdns. Chisw W4 .... 7 E8
Boston Manor Rd. Brent TW8 .... 6 C8
Boston Park Rd. Brent TW8 .... 6 D8
Boston Rd. Croy CR0 .... 42 A3
Boswell House. ⁵ Streat SW16 .... 21 C3
Boswell Rd. Crawl RH10 .... 201 E3

Boswood Ct. Hounsl TW4 .... 4 F4
Boswood Ct. Hounsl TW4 .... 4 F4
Botany Hill. The San GU10 .... 126 D1
Botery's Cross. Bletch RH1 .... 120 B2
Bothwell Rd. New Add CR0 .... 63 C1
Botsford Rd. Merton SW20 .... 39 E7
Boucher Cl. Tedd TW11 .... 16 F3
Boughton Ave. Hayes BR2 .... 44 F2
Boughton Hall Ave.Send M GU23 .... 90 F3
Bouldish Farm Rd. Ascot SL5 .... 29 A5
Boulevard The.
    Crawl RH10 & RH11 .... 201 E6
Boulevard The. ⁴ Up Toot SW17 .... 21 A6
Boullen Ct. Sutton SM1 .... 59 C6
Boulogne Rd. Thorn H CR0 .... 42 C3
Boulter's Rd.
    Alder GU11 & GU12 .... 105 B2
Boulters House. Brack RG12 .... 27 E3
Boulthurst Way. Oxted RH8 .... 123 B3
Boundaries Mansions. ⁴
    .... 21 A7
Boundaries Rd. Balham SW12 .... 21 A7
Boundaries Rd. Felt TW13 .... 15 C7
Boundaries Rd.
    Up Toot SW12 & SW17 .... 21 A7
Boundary Bsns Ct. Mitch CR4 .... 40 D6
Boundary Bsns Ctr.Woking GU21 70 A4
Boundary Cl. Crawl RH10 .... 201 E7
Boundary Cl. King U T KT1 .... 38 B6
Boundary Cl. Penge SE20 .... 43 A7
Boundary Cotts. Albury GU4 .... 132 A4
Boundary House. Twick TW1 .... 6 B2
Boundary Rd. Binst GU10 .... 145 E2
Boundary Rd. Crawl RH10 .... 201 E7
Boundary Rd. Docken GU10 .... 166 D7
Boundary Rd. Farnb GU14 .... 84 C1
Boundary Rd. Farnb GU14 .... 85 C2
Boundary Rd. Frensh GU10 .... 145 E2
Boundary Rd. Graysh GU26 .... 188 D3
Boundary Rd. Mitch SW19 .... 20 D2
Boundary Rd. Stain TW15 .... 13 C3
Boundary Rd. Wallin SM5 & SM6 .... 60 A3
Boundary Rd. Woking GU21 .... 69 F3
Boundary Rd. Woking GU21 .... 70 A4
Boundary Rd E. Woodhm KT15 .... 52 B2
Boundary Rd N. Woodhm KT15 .... 52 B2
Boundary Rd W. Woodhm KT15 ...... 52 B2
Boundary Way. Add CR0 .... 63 A5
Boundary Way. Woking GU21 .... 70 A4
Boundfield Rd. Catf SE6 .... 24 E6
Boundstone Cl. Rowl GU10 .... 146 B5
Boundstone Rd. Rowl GU10 .... 146 A4
Bourbon House. Catf SE6 .... 24 C4
Bourdon Rd. Penge SE20 .... 43 C7
Bourg-De-Peage Ave.
    E Grins RH19 .... 186 A1
Bourke Hill. Chips CR5 .... 78 F1
Bourley La. Crond GU10 .... 104 A2
Bourley Rd. Alder GU11 .... 104 C2
Bourley Rd. Crond GU10 .... 104 C2
Bourne Ave. Thorpe KT16 .... 33 A6
Bourne Cl. Chil GU4 .... 131 B3
Bourne Cl. W Byfl KT14 .... 71 B6
Bourne Cl. Alder GU11 .... 126 A8
Bourne Ct. Chisw W4 .... 7 C8
Bourne Ct. ¹ Purley CR8 .... 80 A8
Bourne Dene. Rowl GU10 .... 146 A5
Bourne Dr. Mitch CR4 .... 40 D7
Bourne Firs. M Bourn GU9 .... 146 D5
Bourne Gr. Ashtd KT21 .... 95 D8
Bourne Gr.
    M Bourn GU10 & GU9 .... 146 E7
Bourne Grove Cl.
    M Bourn GU10 & GU9 .... 146 E7
Bourne Grove Dr.
    M Bourn GU10 .... 146 E7
Bourne Hall. Ewell KT17 .... 57 F2
Bourne House. Asht SW15 .... 14 A3
Bourne Hts. M Bourn GU9 .... 146 C8
Bourne La. Cater CR3 .... 100 D6
Bourne Meadow.
    Egham KT16 & TW20 .... 32 B5
Bourne Mill Ind Est.
    Farnh GU9 .... 125 E3
Bourne Mill Rdbt.
    Farnh GU9 .... 125 E3
Bourne Park Cl. Kenley CR8 .... 80 E3
Bourne Rd. Farnc GU7 .... 150 F7
Bourne Rd. Merst RH1 .... 119 C5
Bourne Rd. Went GU25 .... 31 D4
Bourne Rd. Woodhm KT15 .... 52 B2
Bourne Sch The. M Bourn GU10146 D6
Bourne St. S Croy CR0 & CR9 .... 61 B8
Bourne Vale. Hayes BR2 .... 44 F1
Bourne View. Kenley CR8 .... 80 D4
Bourne Way. Addl KT15 .... 52 C5
Bourne Way. Cheam SM1 .... 58 F5
Bourne Way. Coney H BR2 & BR4 ... 63 F8
Bourne Way. W Ewell KT19 .... 57 C6
Bourne Way. W Ewell KT19 .... 57 C6
Bourne Way. Westfd GU22 .... 89 D5
Bournefield Rd. Whytif CR3 .... 81 A1
Bournemouth Rd. Merton SW19 ..... 40 A8
Bourneside. Went GU25 .... 31 A2
Bourneside Gdns. Catf SE6 .... 24 C5
Bourneside Rd. Addl KT15 .... 52 D5
Bournevale Rd. Streat SW16 .... 21 E4
Bourns Ct. Horsh RH13 .... 217 F1
Bournville Rd. For Hil SE13 & SE6 .. 24 A8
Bousley Rise. Ottsh KT16 .... 51 D4
Bouverie Rd. Chips CR5 .... 79 A1
Boveney House. Brack RG12 .... 27 E5
Boveney Rd. For Hil SE23 .... 23 D8
Bovey House. ³ Redh RH1 .... 119 A3
Bovill Rd. For Hil SE23 .... 23 D8
Bovingdon Sq. Mitch CR4 .... 41 E5
Bowater Rd. Worth RH10 .... 202 C3
Bowater Ridge. Whit V KT13 .... 53 D1
Bowden Cl. E Bed TW14 .... 14 D7
Bowden Rd. Ascot SL5 .... 29 D4
Bowen Dr. Dulw SE19 & SE21 .... 22 E5

Bower Ct. Mayb GU22 .... 70 B3
Bower Hill Cl. S Nutf RH1 .... 140 E6
Bower Hill La. Nutf RH1 .... 140 D7
Bower Rd. Rowl GU10 .... 146 A5
Bowerland La. Crow RH7 .... 164 E7
Bowers Cl. Burph GU4 .... 110 A5
Bowers Farm Dr. Burph GU4 .... 110 B5
Bowers La. Burph GU4 .... 110 A6
Bowers Pl. Crawl D RH10 .... 204 B8
Bowes Rd. Egham TW18 .... 12 E2
Bowes Rd. Walt-T KT12 .... 54 B8
Bowie Cl. Streat SW4 .... 21 D8
Bowland Dr. Brack RG12 .... 27 E2
Bowley Cl. Dulw SE19 .... 22 F2
Bowley La. Dulw SE19 .... 22 F3
Bowling Green Cl. Putney SW19 ..... 19 B8
Bowling Green Cl. Friml GU16 .... 85 E7
Bowling Green La. Horsh RH12 ..... 217 D3
Bowling Green Rd. Burrh GU24 ...... 49 E2
Bowlings The. Camb GU15 .... 65 C6
Bowman Ct. Crawl RH11 .... 201 D6
Bowman Mews. Wands SW18 .... 19 F7
Bowman's Meadow. Hackb SM6 ...... 60 B7
Bowmans Lea. For Hil SE23 .... 23 C8
Bowness Cl. ⁷ Crawl RH11 .... 200 D5
Bowness Cres.
    King U T KT2 & SW15 .... 18 E3
Bowness Dr. Hounsl TW4 .... 4 E3
Bowness Rd. Catf SE6 .... 24 B8
Bowring House. Farnc GU7 .... 150 F6
Bowsley Ct. Felt TW13 .... 15 A6
Bowsprit The. Cobham KT11 .... 73 C4
Bowyer Cres. Woki RG11 .... 25 C8
Bowyers Cl. Ashtd KT21 .... 75 F1
Box Cl. Crawl RH11 .... 201 C1
Box Hill Ctry Pk. Mickle RH4 .... 115 D3
Box Hill Sch. Mickle RH5 .... 115 B8
Box La. Ash W RH19 .... 206 E6
Box Ridge Ave. Purley CR8 .... 79 F7
Boxall Rd. Dulw SE21 .... 22 E8
Boxall Wlk. Horsh RH13 .... 217 D1
Boxall's Gr. Alder GU11 .... 126 A8
Boxall's La. Alder GU11 .... 126 B7
Boxford Cl. Selsd CR2 .... 81 D7
Boxford Ridge. Brack RG12 .... 27 B6
Boxgrove Ave. Abbots GU1 .... 110 A3
Boxgrove Cty Prim Sch.
    .... 110 B2
Boxgrove La. Merrow GU1 .... 110 B2
Boxgrove Rd. Abbots GU1 .... 110 A2
Boxgrove Rd. Merrow GU1 .... 110 A2
Boxhill Rd. Box H RH4 .... 115 E3
Boxhill Way. Brock RH3 .... 137 B5
Boxhill & Westhumble Sta.
    Westh RH5 .... 115 B4
Boxley Rd. Morden SM4 & SW19 .... 40 C5
Boxwood Way. Warlgm CR6 .... 81 D2
Boyce House. Streat SW16 .... 21 C4
Boyd Cl. King U T KT2 .... 18 A1
Boyd Ct. Brack RG12 .... 27 A8
Boyd Rd. Mitch SW19 .... 20 D2
Boyland Rd. Broml BR1 .... 24 F3
Boyle Farm Rd. Thames D KT7 .... 37 A3
Brabazon Ave. Wallin SM6 .... 60 E3
Brabazon Rd. Heston TW5 .... 4 D7
Braboeuf Manor (Coll of Law).
    Arting GU2 .... 130 C5
Brabon Rd. W Heath GU14 .... 84 F5
Brabourne Cl. ⁷ W Norw SE19 .... 22 E3
Brabourne Rise. Beck BR3 .... 44 D4
Brabrook Ct. Wallin SM6 .... 60 B5
Bracebridge. Camb GU15 .... 65 A3
Bracewood Gdns. S Croy CR0 .... 61 F7
Bracken Ave. Balham SW12 .... 21 A8
Bracken Ave. W Wick CR0 .... 63 B7
Bracken Bank. N Asct SL5 .... 28 C8
Bracken Cl. Ashf TW16 .... 14 F2
Bracken Cl. Copth RH10 .... 183 B2
Bracken Cl. Crawl RH10 .... 201 F8
Bracken Cl. Twick TW4 .... 16 A8
Bracken Cl. Woking GU22 .... 69 F1
Bracken Cl. Woner GU5 .... 152 B6
Bracken End. Islew TW7 .... 5 D2
Bracken Gr. Horsh RH12 .... 218 B5
Bracken Hill Cl. Broml BR1 .... 44 F8
Bracken Hill La. Broml BR1 .... 44 F8
Bracken Path. Epsom KT18 .... 76 B6
Bracken Way. Chobh GU24 .... 49 F1
Bracken Way. Stough GU3 .... 108 E3
Brackendale. King U T KT2 .... 38 B7
Brackendale Cl. Friml GU15 .... 65 E3
Brackendale Cl. Hounsl TW5 .... 5 B6
Brackendale Ct. ² Beck BR3 .... 44 A7
Brackendale Rd. Camb GU15 .... 65 D4
Brackendene. Ash GU12 .... 106 C3
Brackendene Cl. Horse GU21 .... 70 A4
Brackenham Comp Sch.
    Easth RG12 .... 27 B5
Brackenhill. Oxsh KT11 .... 74 B7
Brackenlea. Farnc GU7 .... 150 D7
Brackens. Beck BR3 .... 24 A1
Brackens The. Crowth RG11 .... 45 A7
Brackenside. Horley RH6 .... 161 B4
Brackenwood. For Hil SE26 .... 66 D5
Brackenwood. Sunby TW16 .... 35 A8
Brackenwood Rd. Knaph GU21 .... 88 D8
Bracklesham Cl. W Heath GU14 ...... 85 A7
Brackley. Whit V KT13 .... 53 D5
Brackley Cl. Wallin SM6 .... 60 E3
Brackley Rd. Beck BR3 .... 24 A1
Bracknell Beeches. Brack RG12 ...... 27 B6
Bracknell Bsns Ctr The.
    Brack RG12 .... 26 E7
Bracknell Cl. Camb GU15 .... 46 F1
Bracknell Coll. Brack RG12 .... 27 C7
Bracknell Coll. Brack RG12 .... 27 C8
Bracknell Coll (Annexe).
    Brack RG12 .... 27 A8
Bracknell Enterprise Ctr.
    Brack RG12 .... 27 A7

Bracknell Rd. Brack RG19 .... 47 E5
Bracknell Rd. Camb GU15 .... 47 A1
Bracknell Rd. Crowth RG11 .... 45 D6
Bracknell Rd. Wink RG12 & SL4 .... 8 A5
Bracknell Sports & L Ctr.
    Easth RG12 .... 27 C4
Bracknell Sta. Easth RG12 .... 27 B6
Bracknell Wlk. Crawl RH11 .... 200 E3
Bracondale. Esher KT10 .... 55 C5
Bradbury Rd. Worth RH10 .... 202 C3
Braddon Rd. Rich TW9 .... 6 F4
Bradenhurst. Cater CR3 .... 100 F4
Bradfield Cl. Burph GU1 .... 110 A4
Bradfield Cl. Woking GU22 .... 69 E1
Bradfields. Brack RG12 .... 27 D4
Bradford Cl. For Hil SE26 .... 23 B4
Bradford Dr. W Ewell KT19 .... 57 F4
Bradford Dr. W Ewell KT19 .... 57 F4
Brading Rd. Streat SW2 .... 21 F8
Brading Rd. Thorn H CR0 .... 41 F3
Bradley Ct. Croy CR0 .... 61 A6
Bradley La. Westh RH4 & RH5 .... 115 B3
Bradley Mews. Up Toot SW12 .... 20 F7
Bradley Rd. S Norw SE19 .... 22 C2
Bradlord House. Dulw SE21 .... 22 E5
Bradmore Way. Coulsd CR5 .... 79 F1
Bradshaws Cl. Croy SE25 .... 43 A6
Bradsole House. ¹³ Beck BR3 .... 24 A1
Bradstock Rd. Stonel K17 .... 58 B5
Brae Ct. ² King U T KT2 .... 38 A8
Brae Ct. S Norw SE25 .... 42 E8
Braemar Ave. S Croy CR2 .... 61 C2
Braemar Ave. Thorn H CR7 .... 42 B6
Braemar Ave.
    Wimble SW18 & SW19 .... 20 A6
Braemar Cl. Friml GU16 .... 85 F8
Braemar Cl. Godal GU7 .... 150 D3
Braemar Ct. ⁵ Brent TW8 .... 6 D8
Braemar Ct. Catf SE6 .... 24 F7
Braemar Gdns. W Wick BR4 .... 44 C1
Braemar House. Rich TW11 .... 17 B3
Braemar Rd. Brent TW8 .... 6 D8
Braemar Rd. N Cheam KT4 .... 58 B7
Braes Mead. S Nutf RH1 .... 140 E8
Braeside. Beck BR3 .... 24 B3
Braeside. Woodhm KT15 .... 71 B8
Braeside Ave. Merton SW19 .... 39 E8
Braeside Rd. Shottm GU27 .... 207 F8
Braeside Rd. Streat SW16 .... 21 C1
Brafferton Rd. Croy CR0 .... 61 C6
Braganza Ct. Guild GU1 .... 109 F2
Bragg Rd. Tedd TW11 .... 16 F1
Braid Cl. Felt TW13 .... 15 F6
Braidwood Rd. Catf SE6 .... 24 D7
Brailsford Cl. Mitch SW19 .... 20 E1
Brainton Ave. Felt TW14 .... 15 C8
Brake Rd. Farnb GU14 .... 84 E1
Brakey Hill. Bletch RH1 .... 120 E1
Bramber Cl. Crawl RH10 .... 201 E8
Bramber Cl. Horsh RH12 .... 218 B5
Bramble Acres Cl. Belm SM2 .... 59 A3
Bramble Bank. Friml GU16 .... 86 A6
Bramble Banks. Wallin SM5 .... 60 A2
Bramble Cl. Copth RH10 .... 183 B3
Bramble Cl. Croy CR0 .... 63 B6
Bramble Cl. Earls RH1 .... 140 A7
Bramble Cl. Stough GU3 .... 108 E3
Bramble Cl. Up Hall TW17 .... 34 D6
Bramble Hedge Farm (Ind Est).
    Whit V KT11 .... 72 C5
Bramble La. Hampt TW12 .... 15 F2
Bramble Rise. Cobham KT11 .... 73 C5
Bramble Twitten. E Grins RH19 ..... 186 A1
Bramble Way. Send M GU23 .... 90 F3
Bramble Wlk. Epsom KT18 .... 76 B6
Brambledene Cl. Woking GU21 .... 69 C1
Brambledown. Stain TW18 .... 33 B8
Brambledown Cl.
    Hayes BR2 & BR4 .... 44 E4
Brambledown Rd. S Croy CR2 .... 61 E3
Brambledown Rd.
    Wallin SM5 & SM6 .... 60 B3
Bramblegate. Crowth RG11 .... 45 A6
Brambles Cl. Brent TW7 & TW8 .... 6 B7
Brambles Cl. Cater CR3 .... 100 E5
Brambles Pk. Bramly GU5 .... 151 F6
Brambles The. Farnc GU7 .... 150 D7
Brambles The. ⁸ Wimble SW19 .... 19 F3
Brambletye Ave. M Bourn GU9 ...... 146 B7
Brambletye Cty Jun Sch.
    Earls RH1 .... 140 A7
Brambletye Park Rd.
    Earls RH1 .... 140 A7
Brambletye Rd. Crawl RH10 .... 202 A5
Brambletye Sch. Ash W RH19 .... 206 C2
Bramblewood. Merst RH2 .... 119 B6
Bramblewood Cl. Carsh SM5 .... 40 E1
Brambling Cl. Horsh RH13 .... 218 A1
Brambling Rd. Horsh RH13 .... 218 A1
Bramcote. Friml GU15 .... 66 C5
Bramcote Ave. Mitch CR4 .... 40 F5
Bramcote Ct. Mitch CR4 .... 40 F5
Bramerton Rd. Beck BR3 .... 43 F6
Bramham Gdns. Chess KT9 .... 56 D6
Bramley Ave. Coulsd CR5 .... 79 C4
Bramley Ave. Sunby TW17 .... 34 E6
Bramley CE (VA) Inf Sch.
    Bramly GU5 .... 152 A5
Bramley Cl. Chert KT16 .... 33 B1
Bramley Cl. Crawl RH10 .... 201 F6
Bramley Cl. Croy CR2 .... 61 C5
Bramley Cl. S Croy CR2 .... 61 C5
Bramley Cl. Stain TW18 .... 13 C2
Bramley Cl. Twick TW2 .... 5 C1
Bramley Ct. Mitch CR4 .... 40 D7
Bramley Ct. Redh RH1 .... 118 E3
Bramley Ct. Wallin SM6 .... 60 C5
Bramley Hill. S Croy CR0 & CR2 ..... 61 C5
Bramley House. Earls RH1 .... 140 A7
Bramley House. ¹ King U T KT2 ...... 18 B1
Bramley House. Rhampt SW15 .... 7 F1
Bramley La. Blckw GU17 .... 64 B5

Bramley Park Ct. Bramly GU5 .. 151 F6
Bramley Rd. Camb GU15 .... 65 B2
Bramley Rd. Carsh SM1 .... 59 D5
Bramley Rd. E Ewell SM2 .... 58 D2
Bramley Way. Ashtd KT21 .... 75 F2
Bramley Way. Hounsl TW4 .... 4 F2
Bramley Way. W Wick BR4 .... 63 B8
Bramley Wlk. Horley RH6 .... 161 C3
Bramleyhyrst. Croy CR2 .... 61 C5
Brampton Gdns. Hersh KT12 .... 54 C5
Brampton Rd. Croy CR0 .... 42 F3
Bramshaw Rise. New Mal KT3 .... 38 E3
Bramshot La. Hawley GU14 .... 84 A5
Bramshot La. W Heath GU14 .... 84 C6
Bramshott Ct. 3 Surb KT6 .... 37 E3
Bramshott Rd. Farnb GU14 .... 84 A2
Bramston Rd. Wands SW17 .... 20 C5
Bramswell Rd. Farnc GU7 .... 150 F6
Bramwell Cl. Sunby TW16 .... 35 D7
Brancaster La. Purley CR8 .... 80 C8
Brancaster Rd. Streat SW16 .... 21 E5
Brancker Cl. Wallin SM6 .... 60 E3
Brandon Cl. Friml GU15 .... 66 D4
Brandon House. Catf BR3 .... 24 B3
Brandon Rd. Sutton SM1 .... 59 B6
Brandreth Rd. Up Toot SW17 .... 21 B6
Brandries The. Wallin SM6 .... 60 D7
Brands Rd. Bra Hil SL3 .... 1 B8
Brandsland. Dovgn RH2 .... 139 B6
Brandy Way. Belm SM2 .... 59 A3
Brangbourne Rd. Catf BR1 .... 24 C3
Brangwyn Cres. Mitch SW19 .... 40 D7
Branksome Cl. Camb GU15 .... 65 E6
Branksome Cl. Walt O T KT12 .... 54 D8
Branksome Hill Rd. Sandh GU15 64 E8
Branksome Park Rd.
Camb GU15 .... 65 E6
Branksome Rd. Merton SW19 .... 40 A8
Branksome Way. King U T KT3 .... 38 D8
Bransby Rd. Chess KT9 .... 56 E4
Branscombe Ct. Hayes BR2 .... 44 E4
Branstone Ct. 9 Rich TW9 .... 6 F6
Branstone Rd. Rich TW9 .... 6 F6
Brantridge Rd. Crawl RH10 .... 201 F4
Brants Bridge. Brack RG12 .... 27 E7
Brantwood Ave. Islew TW7 .... 6 A3
Brantwood Cl. 1 W Byfl KT14 .... 71 A6
Brantwood Ct. W Byfl KT14 .... 70 F6
Brantwood Dr. W Byfl KT14 .... 70 F6
Brantwood Gdns. W Byfl KT14 .... 71 A6
Brantwood Rd. S Croy CR2 .... 61 D2
Brassey Cl. E Bed TW14 .... 15 A7
Brassey Rd. Limps RH8 .... 123 A6
Brasted Cl. Belm SM2 .... 59 A1
Brasted Cl. For Hil SE26 .... 23 C4
Brasted Lodge. 11 Beck BR3 .... 24 A1
Brathway Rd. Wands SW18 .... 20 A8
Bratten Ct. Thorn H CR0 .... 42 D3
Bravington Cl. Shep Gn TW17 .... 33 F4
Braxted Pk. Streat SW16 .... 21 F2
Bray Ct. Chess KT9 .... 56 F5
Bray Gdns. Pyrf GU22 .... 70 E3
Bray Rd. Guild GU2 .... 130 B8
Bray Rd. Stk D'A KT11 .... 73 E3
Braybourne Dr. Hounsl TW7 .... 5 F7
Braybrooke Gdns. S Norw SE19 . 22 E1
Braycourt Ave. Walt O T KT12 ...... 35 C2
Braye Cl. Sandh GU17 .... 45 C1
Braywick Ct. 9 King U T KT2 ...... 18 A1
Braywood Ave. Egham TW20 .... 12 A2
Braziers La. Wink SL4 & SL5 .... 8 D4
Breakfield. Coulsd CR5 .... 79 E3
Breakspeare. Dulw SE21 .... 22 F5
Breamore Cl. Rhampt SW15 .... 19 A7
Breamwater Gdns. Rich TW10 ...... 17 B5
Brecon Cl. Mitch CR4 .... 41 E6
Brecon Cl. N Cheam KT4 .... 58 C8
Brecon Cl. W Heath GU14 .... 84 D7
Brecon House. Wands SW18 .... 20 A8
Bredhurst Cl. Penge SE20 .... 23 C2
Bredinghurst. Dulw SE22 .... 23 A8
Bredon Rd. Croy CR0 .... 42 F2
Bredune. Kenley CR8 .... 80 D4
Breech La. Walt o t H KT20 .... 97 A2
Breech The. Sandh GU15 .... 64 E7
Breezehurst Dr. Crawl RH11 ...... 200 F3
Bregsells La. Bear Gn RH5 .... 157 D4
Bremer Rd. Stan TW18 & TW19 .... 13 A5
Bremner Ave. Horley RH6 .... 160 F4
Brenchley Cl. Hayes BR2 .... 44 F3
Brenda Rd. Up Toot SW17 .... 20 F6
Brende Gdns. E Mole KT8 .... 36 B5
Brendon Cl. Esher KT10 .... 55 C4
Brendon Cl. Harl UB7 .... 3 C7
Brendon Dr. Esher KT10 .... 55 C4
Brendon House. Sutton SM2 .... 59 C4
Brendon Rd. W Heath GU14 .... 84 D7
Brenley Cl. Mitch CR4 .... 41 A6
Brent House. Catf BR1 .... 24 D3
Brent Knoll Spec Sch.
For Hil SE26 .... 23 D5
Brent Lea. Brent TW8 .... 6 C7
Brent Rd. Brent TW8 .... 6 C8
Brent Rd. S Croy CR2 .... 62 B2
Brent Way. Brent TW8 .... 6 D7
Brentford Bsns Ctr. Brent TW8 ...... 6 C7
Brentford High St. Brent TW8 ...... 6 D8
Brentford House. 7 Twick TW1 17 B8
Brentford Sch for Girls.
Brent TW8 .... 6 D8
Brentford Sta. Brent TW8 .... 6 C8
Brentmoor Rd. W End GU24 .... 67 D6
Brentside. Brent TW8 .... 6 C8
Brentside Executive Ctr.
Brent TW8 .... 6 B8
Brentwaters Bsns Pk. Brent TW8 6 C7
Brentwood Ct. Addl KT15 .... 52 B6
Brereton House. 4 Streat SW2 ..... 22 A8
Breston Cross. G Book KT23 .... 93 F1
Bret Harte Rd. Friml GU16 .... 65 E1
Bretherton Ct. S Croy CR2 .... 61 E4
Bretlands Rd. Addl KT16 .... 51 E8
Brett House. 1 Putney SW15 ...... 19 D8
Brett House Cl. 2 Putney SW15 19 D8
Brettgrave. Epsom KT19 .... 57 C1
Brettingham Cl. Crawl RH11 .... 200 E3
Brew House Rd. Brock RH3 ...... 137 B5
Brewer Rd. Crawl RH10 .... 201 E4
Brewer St. Bletch RH1 .... 120 C4
Brewers Cl. W Heath GU14 .... 85 A5
Brewers La. 11 Rich TW9 .... 6 D2
Brewery La. Byfl KT14 .... 71 E6
Brewery Mews Bsns Ctr. 1
Islew TW7 .... 6 A4
Brewery Rd. Horse GU21 .... 69 E2
Brewhurst La. Loxwd RH14 .... 213 A2
Breydon Wlk. Crawl RH10 .... 202 B4
Brian Ave. Sander CR2 .... 80 E7
Briane Rd. Epsom KT19 .... 57 C1
Briar Ave. Lhtwat GU18 .... 67 A8
Briar Ave. S Norw SW16 .... 21 F1
Briar Banks. Wallin SM5 .... 60 A2
Briar Cl. Crawl RH11 .... 181 C1
Briar Cl. Hampt TW12 .... 15 F3
Briar Cl. Islew TW7 .... 5 F2
Briar Cl. W Byfl KT14 .... 71 C8
Briar Ct. Cheam SM3 .... 58 C6
Briar Ct. Hampt TW12 .... 16 B3
Briar Gdns. Hayes BR2 .... 44 F1
Briar Gr. Sander CR2 .... 81 A6
Briar Hill. Purley CR8 .... 79 E8
Briar La. Croy CR0 .... 63 B6
Briar La. Wallin SM5 .... 60 A2
Briar Patch. Farnc GU7 .... 150 D6
Briar Rd. Send GU23 .... 90 B4
Briar Rd. Shep Gn TW17 .... 34 A4
Briar Rd. Thorn H SW16 .... 41 F6
Briar Rd. Twick TW2 .... 16 E7
Briar Way. Burph GU4 .... 110 B5
Briar Wlk. W Byfl KT14 .... 71 A7
Briardale. Wands SW19 .... 19 F7
Briarleas Ct. Farnb GU14 .... 105 D8
Briars Cl. Farnb GU14 .... 84 D3
Briars Cross. The Char RH8 .... 123 D5
Briars Ct. Oxsh KT22 .... 74 D5
Briars The. Stan TW19 .... 2 A2
Briars Wood. Horley RH6 .... 161 C4
Briarswood Cl. Crawl RH10 .... 202 D8
Briarwood Cl. Felt TW13 .... 14 E5
Briarwood Ct. 5 Worc Pk KT4 .... 39 A1
Briarwood Rd. Knaph GU21 .... 88 D8
Briarwood Rd. Stonel KT17 .... 58 A4
Briary Lodge. Beck BR3 .... 44 C8
Briavels Ct. Epsom KT18 .... 76 E4
Brick Farm Cl. Rich TW9 .... 7 B6
Brick Kiln La. Limps RH8 .... 123 C5
Brickfield Cl. Brent TW8 .... 6 C7
Brickfield La. Harl UB3 .... 3 D8
Brickfield Rd. Outw RH1 .... 162 C8
Brickfield Rd.
S Norw CR7 & SW16 .... 42 B8
Brickfield Rd. Wimble SW19 .... 20 B4
Brickhouse La.
Horne RH7 & RH9 .... 163 C4
Bricklands. Crawl D RH10 .... 204 B7
Bricksbury Hill. Heath E GU9 ..... 125 C7
Brickwood Cl. For Hil SE26 .... 23 B5
Brickwood Rd. Croy CR0 .... 61 E8
Brickyard Copse. Ockley RH5 ..... 177 C4
Brickyard La. Crawl D RH10 .... 204 B8
Brickyard La. Wotton RH5 .... 134 D2
Brideake Cl. Crawl RH11 .... 201 A3
Bridge Barn La. Woking GU21 .... 69 D1
Bridge Cl. Byfl KT14 .... 71 F7
Bridge Cl. Horse GU21 .... 69 C2
Bridge Cl. Lo Hall KT12 .... 34 F1
Bridge Cl. Stain TW18 .... 12 E4
Bridge Cl. Tedd TW11 .... 16 F4
Bridge Cotts. Cran GU6 .... 174 B3
Bridge Ct. Cran GU6 .... 174 B3
Bridge Ct. Horse GU21 .... 69 D2
Bridge Ct. Leahd KT22 .... 95 A5
Bridge Ct. 2 Weyb KT13 .... 53 B6
Bridge End. Camb GU15 .... 65 B4
Bridge Gdns. E Mole KT8 .... 36 D5
Bridge Gdns. Littlt TW15 .... 14 C1
Bridge La. Longc GU25 & KT16 ..... 31 F3
Bridge Mead. Pirb GU24 .... 87 F1
Bridge Mews. Godal GU7 .... 150 E4
Bridge Mews. Woking GU21 .... 69 D2
Bridge Par. Purley CR8 .... 80 A7
Bridge Pl. Croy CR0 .... 42 D1
Bridge Rd. Alder GU11 .... 126 A8
Bridge Rd. Ascot SL5 .... 29 D4
Bridge Rd. Bagsh GU19 .... 47 E3
Bridge Rd. Beck BR3 .... 23 F1
Bridge Rd. Camb GU15 .... 65 B3
Bridge Rd. Chert KT16 .... 33 B2
Bridge Rd. Chess KT9 .... 56 E5
Bridge Rd. Cobham KT11 .... 73 B4
Bridge Rd. Cran GU6 .... 174 E3
Bridge Rd. E Mole KT8 .... 36 E5
Bridge Rd. Epsom KT17 .... 76 F7
Bridge Rd. Farnb GU14 .... 84 F4
Bridge Rd. Farnc GU7 .... 150 E5
Bridge Rd. Haslem GU27 .... 208 C7
Bridge Rd. Hounsl TW3 .... 5 D4
Bridge Rd. Islew TW3 & TW7 .... 5 D4
Bridge Rd. Penge BR3 .... 23 F1
Bridge Rd. Rudg RH12 .... 214 D7
Bridge Rd. Sutton SM2 .... 59 B4
Bridge Rd. Twick TW1 .... 6 B1
Bridge Rd. Wallin SM6 .... 60 C5
Bridge Rd. Weyb KT13 .... 52 F6
Bridge Row. Croy CR0 .... 42 D1
Bridge Sq. Farnh GU9 .... 125 C2
Bridge St. Coln SL3 .... 1 D7
Bridge St. Godal GU7 .... 150 E4
Bridge St. Guild GU1 .... 130 C8
Bridge St. Leahd KT22 .... 95 A5
Bridge St. Rich TW10 .... 6 D2
Bridge St. Stain TW18 .... 12 E4
Bridge St. Walt O T KT12 .... 34 F2
Bridge View. Sunnin SL5 .... 30 B2
Bridge Way. Chips CR5 .... 98 E8
Bridge Way. Twick TW2 .... 16 C8
Bridge Wks. Merrow GU4 .... 110 C4
Bridgefield. Farnh GU9 .... 125 D2
Bridgefield Cl. Nork SM7 .... 77 C4
Bridgefield Rd.
Cheam SM1 & SM2 .... 59 A4
Bridgeham Cl. Weyb KT13 .... 53 A5
Bridgeham Way. Smallf RH6 .... 162 B2
Bridgehill Cl. Stough GU2 .... 109 A3
Bridgelands. Copth RH10 .... 183 A3
Bridgeman Rd. Tedd TW11 .... 17 A2
Bridgemead. Friml GU16 .... 85 D8
Bridges Ct. Horsh RH12 .... 218 A5
Bridges La. Wallin CR0 .... 60 E6
Bridges Rd. Wimble SW19 .... 20 B2
Bridges Road Mews.
Wimble SW19 .... 20 B2
Bridgetown Cl. 5 W Norw SE19 ..... 22 E3
Bridgewater Rd. Whit V KT13 ...... 53 D4
Bridgewood Cl. Penge SE20 .... 23 B1
Bridgewood Rd.
N Cheam KT17 & KT4 .... 58 A6
Bridgewood Rd. Streat SW16 .... 21 D1
Bridgford St.
Wands SW17 & SW18 .... 20 C5
Bridle Cl. Graysh GU26 .... 188 A3
Bridle Cl. King U T KT1 .... 37 D5
Bridle Cl. Sunby TW16 .... 35 A6
Bridle Cl. W Ewell KT19 .... 57 D5
Bridle Cl. W Ewell KT19 .... 57 D5
Bridle Ct. Alder GU11 .... 104 E2
Bridle La. Oxsh KT11 & KT22 .... 74 B4
Bridle Path. Wallin CR0 .... 60 E7
Bridle Path The. E Ewell KT17 ...... 58 C1
Bridle Rd. Clayg KT10 .... 56 B4
Bridle Rd. Croy CR0 .... 63 A6
Bridle Rd. Croy CR0 .... 63 A7
Bridle Rd. Epsom KT17 .... 76 F6
Bridle Rd The. Purley CR8 .... 60 E1
Bridle Way. Crawl RH10 .... 202 D7
Bridle Way. Croy CR0 .... 63 A6
Bridle Way The. Wallin SM6 .... 60 C5
Bridlepath Way. E Bed TW14 .... 14 E8
Bridleway Cl. E Ewell KT17 .... 58 C1
Bridlington Cl. Bigg H TN16 ...... 103 B8
Bridport Rd. Thorn H CR7 .... 42 B6
Brier Lea. L Kings KT20 .... 97 F1
Brier Rd. Burgh H KT20 .... 97 B8
Brierley. New Add CR0 .... 63 B4
Brierley Cl. Croy SE25 .... 43 A5
Brierley Rd. Up Toot SW12 .... 21 C6
Brierly Cl. Stough GU2 .... 109 A3
Bright Hill. Guild GU1 .... 130 E7
Brightlands Rd. Reig RH2 .... 118 C3
Brightman Rd. Wands SW18 .... 20 D7
Brighton Cl. Addl KT15 .... 52 C5
Brighton Rd. Addl KT15 .... 52 C5
Brighton Rd.
Alder GU11 & GU12 .... 126 C8
Brighton Rd. Banstd SM2 .... 78 A7
Brighton Rd.
Burgh H KT20 & SM2 & SM7 .... 77 F3
Brighton Rd. Coulsd CR5 & CR8 .. 79 D4
Brighton Rd. Crawl RH11 .... 201 D4
Brighton Rd. Croy CR2 & CR8 .... 61 C3
Brighton Rd. Earls RH1 .... 139 F8
Brighton Rd. Hooley CR5 & RH1 .. 99 B6
Brighton Rd. Horley RH6 .... 160 F2
Brighton Rd. Horsh RH13 .... 217 E1
Brighton Rd. King U T KT6 .... 37 D3
Brighton Rd. Kings KT20 .... 97 E5
Brighton Rd. L Kings KT20 .... 117 F8
Brighton Rd. Purley CR8 .... 80 B8
Brighton Rd. Redh RH1 .... 139 F8
Brighton Rd. S Croy CR2 .... 61 C3
Brighton Rd. Salfs RH1 .... 140 A2
Brighton Rd. Sutton SM2 .... 59 B2
Brightside Ave. Stain TW18 .... 13 C1
Brightwell Cl. Thorn H CR0 .... 42 A1
Brightwell Cres. Up Toot SW17 .. 20 F6
Brightwells Rd. Farnh GU9 .... 125 C2
Brigstock Rd. Coulsd CR5 .... 79 B3
Brigstock Rd. Thorn H CR7 .... 42 B5
Brimshot La. Burrh GU24 .... 49 E2
Brindle Cl. Alder GU11 .... 126 B7
Brindles The. Burgh H SM7 .... 77 F2
Brindley House. 22
Streat SW12 .... 21 E8
Brine Ct. King U T KT6 .... 37 D4
Brinkley Rd. N Cheam KT4 .... 58 B8
Brinkworth Pl. Old W SL4 .... 11 B8
Brinn's La. Blckw GU17 .... 64 C5
Brinsworth Cl. Twick TW2 .... 16 D6
Brisbane Ave. Merton SW19 .... 40 B8
Brisbane Cl. Crawl RH11 .... 181 D1
Briscoe Rd. Mitch SW19 .... 20 D2
Brisson Cl. Esher KT10 .... 54 F4
Bristol Cl. Crawl RH10 .... 182 D1
Bristol Cl. Stan TW19 .... 2 E1
Bristol Ct. 10 Stan TW19 .... 2 E1
Bristol Rd. Morden SM4 .... 40 C4
Bristow Cty Fst Sch. Camb GU15 65 B2
Bristow Rd. Camb GU15 .... 65 B3
Bristow Rd. Hounsl TW3 .... 5 C4
Bristow Rd. W Norw SE19 .... 22 E3
Bristow Rd. Wallin CR0 .... 60 E6
Britannia Ind Est. Poyle SL3 .... 1 E5
Britannia Rd. Surb KT5 .... 37 F2
Britannia Way. Stan TW19 .... 13 D8
British Home and Hospl for Incurables. W Norw SE27 .... 22 B3
Briton Cl. S Croy CR2 .... 80 E8
Briton Cres. S Croy CR2 .... 80 E8
Briton Hill Rd. S Croy CR2 .... 61 F1
Brittain Ct. Sandh GU17 .... 64 C7
Brittain Rd. Hersh KT12 .... 54 D5
Britten Cl. Ash GU12 .... 106 B2
Britten Cl. Crawl RH11 .... 200 F3
Brittens Cl. Stough GU2 & GU3 .. 109 A6
Britton Cl. Lewish SE6 .... 24 D8
Brixton Hill. Streat SW2 .... 21 E8
Brixton Hill Pl. Streat SW2 .... 21 E8
Broad Acres. Farnc GU7 .... 150 E8
Broad Cl. Hersh KT12 .... 54 E7
Broad Green Ave. Thorn H CR0 .. 42 B2
Broad Ha'penny. Rowl GU10 .... 146 A5
Broad Highway. Cobham KT11 .... 73 D5
Broad La. Brack RG12 .... 27 D6
Broad La. Hampt TW12 .... 16 A2
Broad La. Parkg RH2 & RH5 .... 158 E6
Broad Oak. Ashf TW16 .... 14 F2
Broad Oaks. Tolw KT6 .... 57 B8
Broad Oaks Way. Hayes BR2 .... 44 F4
Broad St. Stough GU3 .... 108 D3
Broad St. Tedd TW11 .... 16 F2
Broad St. W End GU24 .... 67 D6
Broad St. Woki RG11 .... 25 C6
Broad St. Wood S V GU3 .... 108 D3
Broad St Wlk. Woki RG11 .... 25 C6
Broad Way. Farnb GU14 .... 105 A8
Broad Wlk. Burgh H KT20 .... 97 D8
Broad Wlk. Cater CR3 .... 100 F5
Broad Wlk. Cran GU6 .... 174 F1
Broad Wlk. Crawl RH10 & RH11 201 D6
Broad Wlk. Friml GU16 .... 65 E2
Broad Wlk. Heston TW5 .... 4 D6
Broad Wlk. Heston TW5 .... 4 E6
Broad Wlk. L Kings CR5 .... 99 A4
Broad Wlk. Rich TW9 .... 6 F7
Broadacre. Stain TW18 .... 13 A3
Broadacres. Stough GU2 & GU3 108 E2
Broadbridge Heath Rd.
Broad H RH12 .... 216 D4
Broadbridge La. Burst RH6 .... 183 B8
Broadbridge La. Smallf RH6 ...... 162 A2
Broadbridge Ret Pk.
Broad H RH12 .... 216 E3
Broadcoombe. S Croy CR2 .... 62 D3
Broadfield Barton. 4
Crawl RH11 .... 201 B2
Broadfield Cl. Burgh H KT20 .... 97 C7
Broadfield Cl. Croy CR0 .... 60 F8
Broadfield Dr. Crawl RH11 .... 201 B3
Broadfield East Cty Fst Sch.
Crawl RH11 .... 201 C2
Broadfield East Cty Mid Sch.
Crawl RH11 .... 201 C2
Broadfield North Cty Fst & Mid Sch.
Crawl RH11 .... 201 B2
Broadfield Pl. Crawl RH11 .... 201 B2
Broadfield Rd. Catf SE6 .... 24 E7
Broadfield Rd. Peasl GU5 .... 154 D8
Broadfields. Thame D KT8 .... 36 E3
Broadford La. Chobh GU24 .... 68 E7
Broadford Pk. Shalf GU4 .... 130 D2
Broadford Rd. Shalf GU4 .... 130 D2
Broadgates Rd. Wands SW18 .... 20 D7
Broadham Green Rd.
Oxted RH8 .... 122 D2
Broadhurst. Ashtd KT21 .... 75 E3
Broadhurst. W Heath GU14 .... 84 C5
Broadhurst Cl. 8 Rich TW10 .... 6 F2
Broadhurst Gdns. Woodh RH2 . 139 B6
Broadlands. Farnb GU14 .... 85 E2
Broadlands. Felt TW13 .... 16 A5
Broadlands. Friml GU16 .... 85 F8
Broadlands. Horley RH6 .... 161 C4
Broadlands Ave. Shep TW17 .... 34 C3
Broadlands Ave. Streat SW16 .... 21 E6
Broadlands Cl. Streat SW16 .... 21 E6
Broadlands Ct. Brack RG12 .... 26 E8
Broadlands Ct. Rich TW9 .... 7 A7
Broadlands Dr. Sunnin SL5 .... 29 D2
Broadlands Dr. Warlgm CR6 .... 101 C8
Broadlands Mansions. 2
Streat SW16 .... 21 E6
Broadlands Way. New Mal KT3 .. 38 F3
Broadley Gn. Windl GU20 .... 48 D4
Broadmead. Ashtd KT21 .... 75 F2
Broadmead. Catf SE6 .... 24 A5
Broadmead. Horley RH6 .... 161 C4
Broadmead. Merst RH1 .... 119 C7
Broadmead Ave. New Mal KT4 .... 39 A2
Broadmead Cl. Hampt TW12 .... 16 A2
Broadmead Inf Sch.
Thorn H CR0 .... 42 D2
Broadmead Jun Sch.
Thorn H CR0 .... 42 D3
Broadmead Rd.
Send GU22 & GU23 .... 90 B5
Broadmeads. Send GU23 .... 90 B5
Broadmere Sch. Sheer GU21 .... 70 D6
Broadmoor Cott. Wotton RH5 .. 156 A8
Broadmoor Cty Prim Sch.
Crowth RG11 .... 45 D4
Broadmoor Hospl. Crowth RG11 45 E5
Broadoaks Cres. W Byfl KT14 .... 71 B6
Broadview Est. E Bed TW19 .... 14 A8
Broadview Rd. Streat SW16 .... 21 D1
Broadwater Cl. Sheer GU21 .... 70 D7
Broadwater Cl. Whit V KT12 .... 54 A5
Broadwater Cl. Wray TW19 .... 11 E8
Broadwater House. 1
Weyb KT13 .... 53 B7
Broadwater Inf Sch.
Up Toot SW17 .... 20 E4
Broadwater Jun Sch.
Up Toot SW17 .... 20 E4
Broadwater Rd. Up Toot SW17 ...... 20 E4
Broadwater Rd N. Whit V KT12 .. 54 A5
Broadwater Rd S. Whit V KT12 .. 54 A5
Broadwater Rise. Guild GU1 ...... 131 A8
Broadwater Sch. Farnc GU7 .... 151 A8
Broadway. Brack RG12 .... 27 C7
Broadway. Knaph GU21 .... 68 C1
Broadway. Stain TW18 .... 13 B2
Broadway. Stonel KT17 .... 58 A5
Broadway. Tolw KT6 .... 38 B1
Broadway. Wink SL4 .... 9 B7
Broadway Ave. Thorn H CR0 .... 42 D4
Broadway Ave. Twick TW1 .... 6 B1
Broadway Cl. Hams Gn CR2 .... 81 B5
Broadway Ct. Beck BR3 .... 44 C6
Broadway Ct. Wimble SW19 .... 19 F2
Broadway Gdns. Mitch CR4 .... 40 E5
Broadway House. Knaph GU21 .. 68 C1
Broadway Mkt. Up Toot SW17 ...... 20 F4
Broadway Rd. Lhtwat GU18 .... 48 C2
Broadway Rd.
Windl GU18 & GU20 & GU24 .... 48 C2
Broadway The. Cheam SM3 .... 58 E4
Broadway The. Crawl RH10 .... 201 D6
Broadway The. Laleh TW18 .... 33 C7
Broadway The. Mortl SW13 .... 7 E5
Broadway The. Sandh GU17 .... 64 B8
Broadway The. Sutton SM1 .... 59 C6
Broadway The. Thame D KT10 ...... 36 E1
Broadway The. Tolw KT6 .... 38 A1
Broadway The. Wallin SM6 .... 60 E6
Broadway The. Wimble SW19 .... 19 F2
Broadway The. Woking GU21 .... 69 F2
Broadway The. Woodhm KT15 .... 52 A1
Broadwell Ct. Heston TW5 .... 4 D6
Broadwell Rd. Wreccl GU10 .... 145 F6
Broadwood Cl. Horsh RH12 .... 218 A5
Broadwood Cotts. Capel RH5 .... 178 E6
Broadwood Rise. Crawl RH11 .. 201 A2
Brock Rd. Crawl RH11 .... 181 B1
Brock Way. Vir W GU25 .... 31 C5
Brock's Cl. Godal GU7 .... 151 A5
Brockbridge House.
Rhampt SW15 .... 7 F1
Brockenhurst. E Mole KT8 .... 35 F3
Brockenhurst Ave. New Mal KT4 38 E1
Brockenhurst Cl. Horse GU21 ...... 69 F5
Brockenhurst Rd. Alder GU11 .... 126 B8
Brockenhurst Rd. Ascot SL5 .... 29 B3
Brockenhurst Rd. Brack RG12 ...... 28 A6
Brockenhurst Rd. Croy CR0 .... 43 B2
Brockenhurst Way. Mitch SW16 41 D7
Brockham Cl. Wimble SW19 .... 19 F3
Brockham Cres. New Add CR0 ... 63 D3
Brockham Ct. 6 Sutton SM2 .... 59 B3
Brockham Dr. Streat SW2 .... 21 F8
Brockham Hill Pk. Box H KT20 116 C4
Brockham House. 14
Streat SW2 .... 21 F8
Brockham La. Brock RH3 & RH4 116 A1
Brockham Sch. Brock RH3 .... 137 B7
Brockhamhurst Rd. Betch RH3 137 B2
Brockholes Cross. E Hors KT24 113 A6
Brockhurst Cl. Horsh RH12 .... 216 F1
Brockhurst Cotts. Alf Cr GU6 .. 193 F4
Brockhurst Lodge.
M Bourn GU9 .... 146 B7
Brocklebank Ct. Whytlf CR6 .... 81 A1
Brocklebank Rd. Wands SW18 .. 20 C8
Brocklesby Rd. Croy SE25 .... 43 B5
Brockley Combe. Oat Pk KT13 .... 53 D6
Brockley Pk. For Hil SE23 .... 23 E8
Brockley Rise. For Hil SE23 .... 23 E8
Brockley View. For Hil SE23 .... 23 E8
Brockman Rise. Catf BR1 .... 24 D4
Brocks Dr. Cheam SM3 .... 58 E7
Brocks Dr. Fairl GU3 .... 108 C5
Brockshot Cl. 1 Brent TW8 .... 6 D8
Brockton. Farnc GU7 .... 150 E5
Brockway Cl. Merrow GU1 .... 110 B2
Brockwell Park Gdns.
Streat SE24 .... 22 B8
Brockworth. King U T KT2 .... 38 B8
Broderick House. Dulw SE21 .... 22 E5
Brodie House. 7 Wallin SM6 .... 60 B6
Brodie Rd. Guild GU1 .... 130 E8
Brodrick Gr. G Book KT23 .... 94 A1
Brodrick Rd. Up Toot SW17 .... 20 E6
Brograve Gdns. Beck BR3 .... 44 B7
Broke Ct. Merrow GU4 .... 110 C4
Brokes Cres. Reig RH2 .... 118 A3
Brokes Rd. Reig RH2 .... 118 A3
Bromford Cl. Oxted RH8 .... 123 A2
Bromleigh Ct. Dulw SE21 & SE22 23 B6
Bromley Ave. Broml BR1 .... 24 E1
Bromley Cres. Broml BR2 .... 44 F6
Bromley Ct. Broml BR1 .... 24 F1
Bromley Gdns. Broml BR2 .... 44 F6
Bromley Gr. Beck BR2 .... 44 D7
Bromley Hill. Catf BR1 .... 24 E2
Bromley Pk. Broml BR1 .... 44 F8
Bromley Rd. Beck BR3 .... 44 B8
Bromley Rd. Beck BR2 & BR3 .... 44 D7
Bromley Rd. Catf SE6 & BR1 .... 24 B5
Bromley Road Infs Sch.
Beck BR3 .... 44 B8
Brompton Cl. Hounsl TW4 .... 4 F2
Brompton Cl. Penge SE20 .... 43 A7
Bromwich House. 3 Rich TW10 .... 6 E1
Bronson Rd. Merton SW20 .... 39 E7
Bronte Ct. 14 Redh RH1 .... 119 A2
Brontes The. E Grins RH19 .... 185 D1
Brook Ave. Heath E GU9 .... 125 F7
Brook Cl. Ash GU12 .... 106 B3
Brook Cl. E Grins RH19 .... 186 B1
Brook Cl. Epsom KT19 .... 57 E2
Brook Cl. Sandh GU15 .... 45 E1
Brook Cl. Stan TW19 .... 13 F8
Brook Cl. W Barn SW20 .... 39 B6
Brook Cl. Woki RG11 .... 25 A8
Brook Ct. Beck BR3 .... 43 F8
Brook Ct. 6 Brent TW8 .... 6 D8
Brook Ct. Cheam SM3 .... 58 C6
Brook Ct. Mortl SW14 .... 7 E4
Brook Dr. Ashf TW16 .... 14 E2
Brook Dr. Brack RG12 .... 27 E5
Brook Farm Rd. Cobham KT11 ...... 73 D4
Brook Gdns. Barnes SW13 .... 7 F4
Brook Gdns. Farnb GU14 .... 84 F2

Brook Gdns. King U T KT2 ...... 38 C8
Brook Gn. Brack RG12 ...... 26 F8
Brook Gn. Chobh GU24 ...... 49 F1
Brook Hill. Farl Gn GU5 ...... 153 D8
Brook Hill. Oxted RH8 ...... 122 C5
Brook House. Cran GU6 ...... 174 F4
Brook House. Heath E GU9 ...... 125 D6
Brook House. **4** Twick TW1 ...... 17 A8
Brook La. Farl Gn GU5 ...... 68 D8
Brook La. Farl Gn GU5 ...... 132 E1
Brook La. Faygt RH12 ...... 218 C3
Brook La. Send GU23 ...... 90 E5
Brook La Bns Ctr. **4** Brent TW8 ...... 6 D8
Brook La N. **3** Brent TW8 ...... 6 D8
Brook Mead. W Ewell KT19 ...... 57 E4
Brook Mead. W Ewell KT19 ...... 57 E4
Brook Meadow. Chidd GU8 ...... 191 C3
Brook Rd. Bagsh GU19 ...... 47 E2
Brook Rd. Brook GU8 ...... 190 D8
Brook Rd. Camb GU15 ...... 65 B4
Brook Rd. Chil GU4 ...... 131 C3
Brook Rd. Horsh RH12 ...... 217 E6
Brook Rd. Merst RH1 ...... 119 C7
Brook Rd. Redh RH1 ...... 139 �
Brook Rd. Surb KT6 ...... 56 E8
Brook Rd. Thorn H CR7 ...... 42 C5
Brook Rd. Twick TW1 ...... 6 A1
Brook Rd. Wormly GU8 ...... 170 E1
Brook Rd S. Brent TW8 ...... 6 D8
Brook St. King U T KT1 ...... 37 E7
Brook Trad Est The. Alder GU12 ...... 105 E2
Brook Valley. Dork RH5 ...... 136 B1
Brook Way. Leahd KT22 ...... 75 A1
Brookdale Rd. Catf SE6 ...... 24 B8
Brookdale Rd. **2** Lewish SE6 ...... 24 B8
Brooke Ct. **7** King U T KT2 ...... 17 D4
Brooke Forest. Fairl GU3 ...... 108 C5
Brookehowse Rd. Catf SE6 ...... 24 B5
Brookers. Ashtd KT21 ...... 75 D2
Brookers Cnr. Crowth RG11 ...... 45 C5
Brookers House. Ashtd KT21 ...... 75 D2
Brookers Row. Crowth RG11 ...... 45 C6
Brookfield. Farnc GU7 ...... 151 A8
Brookfield Ave.
  Carsh SM1 & SM5 ...... 59 E7
Brookfield Cl. Earls RH1 ...... 140 A3
Brookfield Cl. Ottsh KT16 ...... 51 D4
Brookfield Gdns. Clayg KT10 ...... 55 F4
Brookfield Rd. Alder GU12 ...... 105 F3
Brookfields Ave. Mitch CR4 ...... 40 E4
Brookhill Cl. Copth RH10 ...... 183 A3
Brookhill Rd. Copth RH10 ...... 183 A3
Brookhouse Rd. Farnb GU14 ...... 84 F3
Brookhurst Rd. Addl KT15 ...... 52 B4
Brooklands. Alder GU11 ...... 104 E1
Brooklands Ave. Wimble SW19 ...... 20 B6
Brooklands Cl. Charlt TW16 ...... 34 E8
Brooklands Cl. Cobham KT11 ...... 73 E4
Brooklands Cl. Heath E GU9 ...... 125 D7
Brooklands Coll. Weyb KT13 ...... 52 F4
Brooklands Ct. King U T KT1 ...... 37 D5
Brooklands Ct. Mitch CR4 ...... 40 D7
Brooklands Ct. New Haw KT15 ...... 52 D1
Brooklands Ct. Reig RH2 ...... 118 B3
Brooklands Ind Est. Byfl KT13 ...... 52 E1
Brooklands La. Weyb KT13 ...... 52 F4
Brooklands Mus. Whit V KT13 ...... 53 A2
Brooklands Rd. Crawl RH11 ...... 201 C1
Brooklands Rd. Heath E GU9 ...... 125 D7
Brooklands Rd. Thame D KT7 ...... 37 A1
Brooklands Rd. Whit V KT13 ...... 53 B3
Brooklands Rd.
  Whit V KT13 & KT14 ...... 72 A8
Brooklands Sch. Reig RH2 ...... 118 B3
Brooklands The. Hounsl TW7 ...... 5 D6
Brooklands Way. E Grins RH19 ...... 205 D8
Brooklands Way. Heath E GU9 ...... 125 E7
Brooklands Way. Redh RH1 ...... 118 B3
Brookley Cl. Farnh GU10 ...... 126 C3
Brookleys. Chobh GU24 ...... 49 F1
Brooklyn. Penge SE20 ...... 23 A1
Brooklyn Ave. Croy SE25 ...... 43 B5
Brooklyn Cl. Carsh SM5 ...... 59 E8
Brooklyn Cl. Woking GU22 ...... 89 E8
Brooklyn Ct. Woking GU22 ...... 89 E8
Brooklyn Gr. Croy SE25 ...... 43 B5
Brooklyn Rd. Croy SE25 ...... 43 B5
Brooklyn Rd. Woking GU22 ...... 89 E8
Brookmead. Mitch CR4 ...... 41 C3
Brookmead Ct. Cran GU6 ...... 174 E2
Brookmead Rd. Wallin CR0 ...... 41 C3
Brooks Cl. Whit V KT13 ...... 53 A1
Brooks House. **6** Streat SW2 ...... 22 A7
Brooks La. Brent W4 ...... 7 A8
Brooks Rd. Brent W4 ...... 7 A8
Brooksby Cl. Blckw GU17 ...... 64 B5
Brookscroft. New Add CR0 ...... 62 E1
Brookside. Bear Gn RH5 ...... 157 F6
Brookside. Chert KT16 ...... 32 C6
Brookside. Coln SL3 ...... 1 C7
Brookside. Copth RH10 ...... 183 A3
Brookside. Cran GU6 ...... 174 E1
Brookside. Cran GU6 ...... 174 E3
Brookside. Crawl RH10 ...... 201 F7
Brookside. Hale GU9 ...... 125 D6
Brookside. Jacobs GU4 ...... 109 D6
Brookside. S Godst RH9 ...... 142 D5
Brookside. Sandh GU17 ...... 64 C8
Brookside. Wallin SM5 ...... 60 A5
Brookside. Woki RG11 ...... 25 A7
Brookside Ave. Stain TW15 ...... 13 D3
Brookside Cl. Felt TW13 ...... 15 A5
Brookside Cres. **1**
  N Cheam KT4 ...... 39 A1
Brookside Way. Croy CR0 ...... 43 D3
Brookview. Copth RH10 ...... 183 A3

Brookview Rd.
  Streat SW16 & SW17 ...... 21 C3
Brookwell La. Bramly GU5 ...... 152 B2
Brookwood. Horley RH6 ...... 161 B4
Brookwood Ave. Barnes SW13 ...... 7 F5
Brookwood Cl. Beck BR2 ...... 44 F5
Brookwood Cty Fst & Mid Sch.
  Brookw GU24 ...... 88 A7
Brookwood Hospl. Knaph GU21 ...... 68 C1
Brookwood Hospl. Knaph GU21 ...... 88 C8
Brookwood House. Horley RH6 ...... 161 B6
Brookwood Lye Rd.
  Brookw GU21 & GU22 ...... 88 C7
Brookwood Rd. Farnb GU14 ...... 85 D4
Brookwood Rd. Hounsl TW3 ...... 5 B6
Brookwood Rd. Wands SW18 ...... 20 A7
Brookwood Sta. Brookw GU24 ...... 88 A6
Broom Acres. Sandh GU17 ...... 45 B1
Broom Bank. Chelsh CR6 ...... 102 C8
Broom Cl. Esher KT10 ...... 55 B5
Broom Cl. Hawley GU17 ...... 64 E4
Broom Cl. Tedd KT1 & TW11 ...... 17 D1
Broom Field. Lhtwat GU18 ...... 67 A7
Broom Gdns. Croy CR0 ...... 63 A7
Broom Hall. Oxsh KT22 ...... 74 D5
Broom La. Burrh GU24 ...... 49 E3
Broom Lock. Tedd TW11 ...... 17 C2
Broom Pk. Tedd KT1 ...... 17 D1
Broom Rd. Croy CR0 ...... 63 A7
Broom Rd. Rich TW11 ...... 17 C3
Broom Rd. Tedd KT1 & TW11 ...... 17 C2
Broom Squires. Hind GU26 ...... 188 F4
Broom Water. Tedd TW11 ...... 17 C3
Broom Water W. Tedd TW11 ...... 17 C3
Broom Way. Oat Pk KT13 ...... 53 E6
Broomcroft Dr. Mayb GU22 ...... 70 D3
Broomdashers Rd. Crawl RH10 ...... 201 F7
Broome Cl. Horsh RH12 ...... 217 D5
Broome Cl. **3** Rich TW9 ...... 7 A6
Broome Lodge. Stain TW18 ...... 13 B3
Broome Rd. Hampt TW12 ...... 35 F8
Broome St. Head KT18 ...... 96 C1
Broomehall Rd. Coldh RH5 ...... 156 D2
Broomehall Rd. Ockley RH5 ...... 177 E8
Broomers La. Ewh GU6 ...... 175 E5
Broomfield. Elst GU8 ...... 148 E4
Broomfield. Stain TW18 ...... 13 A2
Broomfield. Stough GU2 ...... 108 E2
Broomfield. Sunby TW16 ...... 35 A8
Broomfield Cl. Mayb GU22 ...... 70 D3
Broomfield Cl. Stough GU2 ...... 108 E3
Broomfield Cotts. Burgh H KT20 ...... 97 E8
Broomfield Ct. Weyb KT13 ...... 53 B4
Broomfield Dr. Sunnin SL5 ...... 30 B3
Broomfield La. Frensh GU10 ...... 146 B1
Broomfield Pk. Sunnin SL5 ...... 30 B2
Broomfield Pk. Westc RH4 ...... 135 C6
Broomfield Rd. Beck BR3 ...... 43 F6
Broomfield Rd. Rich TW9 ...... 6 F6
Broomfield Rd. Surb KT5 ...... 37 F1
Broomfield Rd. Tedd TW11 ...... 17 C2
Broomfield Rd. Woodhm KT15 ...... 71 B8
Broomfield Ride. Oxsh KT22 ...... 74 D7
Broomfields. Esher KT10 ...... 55 C5
Broomhall Bldgs. Sunnin SL5 ...... 30 B2
Broomhall End. Horse GU21 ...... 69 E3
Broomhall La. Horse GU21 ...... 69 E3
Broomhall Rd. Sunnin SL5 ...... 30 A3
Broomhall Rd. Horse GU21 ...... 69 E3
Broomhall Rd. S Croy CR2 ...... 61 D2
Broomhill. Crond GU10 ...... 124 D8
Broomhill Rd. W Heath GU14 ...... 84 D5
Broomhurst Ct. Dork RH4 ...... 136 B5
Broomlands La. Titsey RH8 ...... 123 E8
Broomleaf Cnr. M Bourn GU9 ...... 125 D2
Broomleaf Rd. M Bourn GU9 ...... 125 E2
Broomleaf Bsns Pk. Beck SE6 ...... 23 F3
Broomloan La. Sutton SM1 ...... 59 A8
Broomsquires Rd. Bagsh GU19 ...... 47 F2
Broomwood Cl. Croy CR0 ...... 43 D4
Broomwood Way.
  M Bourn GU10 ...... 146 C6
Broseley Gr. For Hil SE26 ...... 23 E3
Broster Gdns. S Norw SE25 ...... 42 F6
Brough Cl. King U T KT2 ...... 17 D3
Brougham Pl. Heath E GU9 ...... 125 B7
Broughton Ave. Rich TW10 ...... 17 C4
Broughton Mews. Friml GU16 ...... 65 F1
Broughton Rd. Thorn H CR7 ...... 42 A3
Brow The. Earls RH1 ...... 140 A4
Browell House. Merrow GU4 ...... 110 D2
Browells La. Felt TW13 ...... 15 B6
Brown Bear Ct. Felt TW13 ...... 15 D4
Brown Cl. Wallin SM6 ...... 60 E3
Brown's Bldgs. Balham SW12 ...... 21 B7
Brown's Hill. Outw RH1 ...... 141 D2
Brown's Rd. Surb KT5 & KT6 ...... 37 F2
Browne House. **9** Penge SE26 ...... 23 B3
Browngraves Rd. Harl UB7 ...... 3 C7
Brownhill Rd. Catf SE6 ...... 24 C8
Browning Ave. Carsh SM1 ...... 59 E6
Browning Ave. N Cheam KT4 ...... 39 B1
Browning Cl. Crawl RH10 ...... 202 C7
Browning Cl. Friml GU15 ...... 66 C4
Browning Cl. Hampt TW12 ...... 15 F4
Browning Rd. Fetch KT22 ...... 94 D2
Browning Way. Heston TW5 ...... 4 D6
Brownings The. **1**
  E Grins RH19 ...... 185 C1
Brownlow Rd. Redh RH1 ...... 118 E1
Brownlow Rd. S Croy CR0 ...... 61 F6
Brownrigg Cres. Brack RG12 ...... 27 E8
Brownrigg Rd. Ashf TW15 ...... 14 A4
Browns La. Effing KT24 ...... 113 D8
Browns Wlk. Rowl GU10 ...... 145 F5
Browns Wood. E Grins RH19 ...... 185 A4
Brownsover Rd. W Heath GU14 ...... 84 C4
Brox La. Ottsh KT15 & KT16 ...... 51 D2
Brox La. Row Tn KT15 & KT16 ...... 51 D2
Brox La. Woodhm KT15 & KT16 ...... 51 D2

Broxholm Rd.
  W Norw SE27 & SW16 ...... 22 A5
Broxted Rd. For Hil SE23 & SE6 ...... 23 F6
Bruce Ave. Shep TW17 ...... 34 C3
Bruce Cl. Byfl KT14 ...... 71 E6
Bruce Dr. Selsd CR2 ...... 62 D2
Bruce Hall Mews. Up Toot SW17 ...... 21 A4
Bruce Lawns. Up Toot SW17 ...... 21 A4
Bruce Rd. Mitch CR4 ...... 21 A1
Bruce Rd. S Norw SE25 ...... 42 D5
Brudenell Rd. Up Toot SW17 ...... 21 A4
Brumana Cl. Weyb KT13 ...... 53 B4
Brumfield Rd. W Ewell KT19 ...... 57 C5
Brumfield Rd. W Ewell KT19 ...... 57 C5
Brunel Cl. Cranf TW5 ...... 4 B7
Brunel Cl. S Norw SE19 ...... 22 F2
Brunel Cl. Mortl SW13 ...... 7 F5
Brunel Ctr. Crawl RH10 ...... 181 F2
Brunel Dr. Crowth RG11 ...... 45 C8
Brunel House. **25** Redh RH1 ...... 119 A3
Brunel Pl. Crawl RH10 ...... 201 E5
Brunel Univ Coll Osterley Campus.
  Hounsl TW7 ...... 5 F7
Brunel Univ Coll (Twickenham
  Campus). Islew TW1 ...... 6 B3
Brunel Univ Coll (Runnymede Campus).
  Eng Gn TW20 ...... 11 C5
Brunel Wlk. **3** Twick TW4 ...... 16 A8
Brunner Ct. Ottsh KT16 ...... 51 C5
Brunner House. Catf SE6 ...... 24 C4
Brunswick. Easth RG12 ...... 27 A2
Brunswick Cl. Crawl RH10 ...... 202 A4
Brunswick Cl. Thame D KT7 ...... 36 F1
Brunswick Cl. Twick TW2 ...... 16 D5
Brunswick Cl. Walt O T KT12 ...... 54 C8
Brunswick Cl. Crawl RH10 ...... 202 A4
Brunswick Ct. **2** Penge SE19 ...... 23 A1
Brunswick Ct. Pirb GU24 ...... 87 D7
Brunswick Gr. Cobham KT11 ...... 73 C6
Brunswick Mews. Streat SW16 ...... 21 D2
Brunswick Pl. Penge SE19 ...... 23 A1
Brunswick Rd. King U T KT2 ...... 38 A8
Brunswick Rd. Pirb GU16 & GU24 ...... 86 E6
Brunswick Rd. Sutton SM1 ...... 59 B6
Bruntile Cl. Farnb GU14 ...... 85 D1
Brushwood Rd. Horsh RH12 ...... 218 B6
Bruton Cl. Morden SM4 ...... 40 C5
Bruton Way. Brack RG12 ...... 27 E2
Bryan Cl. Ashf TW16 ...... 15 A1
Bryanston Ave. Twick TW2 ...... 16 B7
Bryanstone Ave. Stough GU2 ...... 109 A4
Bryanstone Cl. Stough GU2 ...... 108 F4
Bryanstone Ct. Sutton SM1 ...... 59 C7
Bryanstone Gr. Stough GU2 ...... 108 F5
Bryce Cl. Horsh RH12 ...... 218 A5
Bryce Gdns. Alder GU11 ...... 126 C7
Bryden Cl. For Hil SE26 ...... 23 E3
Brympton Cl. Dork RH4 ...... 136 A5
Bryn Rd. Wreccl GU10 ...... 145 F7
Brynford Cl. Horse GU21 ...... 69 E4
Bryony House. Brack RG12 ...... 26 E8
Bryony Rd. Burph GU1 ...... 110 B4
Bryony Way. Ashf TW16 ...... 15 A2
Buchan The. Camb GU15 ...... 66 A8
Buchanan House. Dulw SE21 ...... 22 E5
Buchanan House. Wands SW18 ...... 20 A8
Buchans Lawn. Crawl RH11 ...... 201 B2
Bucharest Rd. Wands SW18 ...... 20 C8
Buckfast Rd. Morden SM4 ...... 40 B5
Buckhurst Ave. Carsh CR4 & SM5 ...... 40 F1
Buckhurst Cl. E Grins RH19 ...... 185 C3
Buckhurst Cl. Redh RH1 ...... 118 F3
Buckhurst Gr. Woki RG11 ...... 25 F5
Buckhurst Hill. Brack RG12 ...... 27 F5
Buckhurst La. Ascot SL5 ...... 30 A6
Buckhurst Mead. E Grins RH19 ...... 185 C4
Buckhurst Moors. Binf RG12 ...... 26 C6
Buckhurst Rd. Ascot SL5 ...... 29 F7
Buckhurst Rd. Friml GU16 ...... 85 F6
Buckhurst Way. E Grins RH19 ...... 185 C3
Buckingham Ave. E Mole KT8 ...... 36 B7
Buckingham Ave. S Norw CR7 ...... 42 A8
Buckingham Ave. Guild GU1 ...... 109 F2
Buckingham Cl. Hampt TW12 ...... 15 F3
Buckingham Ct. Belm SM2 ...... 59 A2
Buckingham Ct. Crawl RH11 ...... 201 B2
Buckingham Ct. Stain TW18 ...... 13 A4
Buckingham Ct. Woki RG11 ...... 25 C6
Buckingham Dr. E Grins RH19 ...... 206 A8
Buckingham Gate. Crawl RH6 ...... 182 C7
Buckingham Gdns. Hampt KT8 ...... 36 B7
Buckingham Gdns. S Norw CR7 ...... 42 A7
Buckingham La. For Hil SE23 ...... 23 E8
Buckingham Prim Sch.
  Hampt TW12 ...... 15 F3
Buckingham Rd.
  Hampt TW12 & TW13 ...... 15 F3
Buckingham Rd. King U T KT1 ...... 37 F5
Buckingham Rd. Mitch CR4 ...... 41 E4
Buckingham Rd. Rich TW10 ...... 17 D6
Buckingham Rd. S Holm RH5 ...... 157 C6
Buckingham Way. Wallin SM6 ...... 60 C2
Buckland Cl. Farnb GU14 ...... 85 C7
Buckland Cnr. Reig RH2 ...... 117 D2
Buckland Ct. Buckl RH3 ...... 117 A2
Buckland Cty Inf Sch.
  Stain TW18 ...... 13 C1
Buckland Inf Sch. Chess KT9 ...... 56 F6
Buckland La. Buckl RH3 ...... 117 B5
Buckland Rd. Chess KT9 ...... 56 F5
Buckland Rd. E Ewell SM2 ...... 58 D2
Buckland Rd. L Kings KT20 ...... 117 F7
Buckland Rd. Reig RH2 ...... 117 D2
Buckland Way. N Cheam KT4 ...... 39 C1
Buckland Wlk. Morden SM4 ...... 40 C5
Bucklands Rd. Tedd TW11 ...... 17 C2
Bucklebury. Easth RG12 ...... 27 A2

Buckleigh Ave. Merton SW20 ...... 39 E6
Buckleigh Rd. Streat SW16 ...... 21 E1
Buckleigh Way. S Norw SE19 ...... 22 F1
Bucklers' Way. Carsh SM5 ...... 59 F7
Buckles Way. Nork SM7 ...... 77 E3
Buckley Pl. Crawl D RH10 ...... 204 A8
Buckmans Rd. Crawl RH11 ...... 201 D6
Bucknills Cl. Epsom KT18 ...... 76 C5
Bucks Cl. W Byfl KT14 ...... 71 B5
Bucks Green Sch.
  Buck Gn RH12 ...... 214 B7
Buckswood Dr. Crawl RH11 ...... 201 A4
Buckthorn Cl. Woki RG11 ...... 25 E7
Buddhapadipa Temple The.
  Wimble SW19 ...... 19 D4
Budebury Rd. Stain TW18 ...... 13 A3
Budge La. Carsh CR4 ...... 40 F2
Budge's Cotts. Woki RG11 ...... 25 E8
Budge's Gdns. Woki RG11 ...... 25 E7
Budge's Rd. Woki RG11 ...... 25 D7
Budgen Cl. Crawl RH10 ...... 182 D1
Budgen Dr. Redh RH1 ...... 119 A3
Budham Way. Easth RG12 ...... 27 B3
Buff Ave. Banstd SM7 ...... 78 B4
Buffbeards La. Shottm GU27 ...... 207 E6
Buffers La. Leahd KT22 ...... 95 A8
Bug Hill. Warlgm CR6 ...... 101 D7
Bugkingham Way. Friml GU16 ...... 65 F1
Bulbrook Row. Brack RG12 ...... 27 E2
Bulganak Rd. S Norw SE27 ...... 42 C5
Bulkeley Cl. Eng Gn TW20 ...... 11 C3
Bull Hill. Leahd KT22 ...... 95 A6
Bull La. Brack RG12 ...... 27 B8
Bull La. Westfd GU4 ...... 89 F1
Bullard Rd. Tedd TW11 ...... 16 F2
Bullbeggars La. Godst RH9 ...... 121 C3
Bullbeggars La. Horse GU21 ...... 69 B3
Bullbrook Dr. Brack RG12 ...... 27 F8
Buller Ct. Farnb GU14 ...... 85 C1
Buller Rd. Alder GU11 ...... 105 B4
Buller Rd. S Norw CR7 ...... 42 D6
Bullers Rd. Heath E GU9 ...... 125 E6
Bullfinch Cl. Horley RH6 ...... 160 E1
Bullfinch Cl. Horsh RH12 ...... 217 C7
Bullfinch Cl. Sandh GU15 ...... 64 E8
Bullfinch **3** W Norw SE21 ...... 22 B6
Bullfinch Rd. Selsd CR2 ...... 62 D1
Bulls Alley. Mortl SW14 ...... 7 D5
Bullswater Common Rd.
  Pirb GU3 & GU3 ...... 88 A2
Bulstrode Ave. Hounsl TW3 ...... 5 A4
Bulstrode Gdns. Hounsl TW3 ...... 5 A4
Bulstrode Rd. Hounsl TW3 ...... 5 A4
Bunbury Way. Nork KT17 ...... 77 B4
Bunce Common Rd.
  Leigh RH2 & RH3 ...... 137 E2
Bunch La. Haslem GU27 ...... 208 B8
Bunch La. Shottm GU27 ...... 208 B8
Bunch Way. Shottm GU27 ...... 208 A6
Bundy's Way. Egham TW18 ...... 12 F2
Bungalow Rd. Farnb GU14 ...... 85 B2
Bungalow Rd. S Norw SE25 ...... 42 E5
Bungalows The. Mitch SW16 ...... 21 B1
Bunting Cl. Horsh RH13 ...... 217 F3
Bunting Cl. Mitch CR4 ...... 40 F4
Buntings The. Wreccl GU9 ...... 145 E8
Bunyan Cl. Crawl RH11 ...... 200 E3
Bunyard Dr. Sheer GU21 ...... 70 C5
Burbage Gn. Brack RG12 ...... 27 F4
Burbage Rd. Dulw SE21 & SE24 ...... 22 D8
Burbeach Cl. Crawl RH11 ...... 201 B3
Burberry Cl. King U T KT3 ...... 38 E7
Burbidge Rd. Shep Gn TW17 ...... 34 A5
Burchets Hollow. Peasl GU5 ...... 154 D7
Burchetts Way. Shep TW17 ...... 34 A3
Burcote. **6** Weyb KT13 ...... 53 D4
Burcote Rd. Wands SW18 ...... 20 D8
Burcott Gdns. New Haw KT15 ...... 52 D4
Burcott Rd. Purley CR8 ...... 80 A5
Burden Way. Stough GU2 ...... 109 A5
Burdenshot Hill.
  Woking GU22 & GU3 ...... 89 B3
Burdenshott Ave. Mortl TW10 ...... 7 B3
Burdenshott Rd. Jacobs GU4 ...... 109 C8
Burdenshott Rd.
  Woking GU22 & GU3 & GU4 ...... 89 A2
Burdett Ave. Wimble SW20 ...... 39 A8
Burdett Cl. Worth RH10 ...... 202 D5
Burdett Rd. Rich TW9 ...... 6 F4
Burdett Rd. Thorn H CR0 ...... 42 D3
Burdock Cl. Crawl RH11 ...... 201 A2
Burdock Cl. Croy CR0 ...... 43 D1
Burdock Cl. Lhtwat GU18 ...... 67 B8
Burdon La. Belm SM2 ...... 58 F2
Burdon Pk. Belm SM2 ...... 58 F2
Burfield Cl. Up Toot SW17 ...... 20 C4
Burfield Rd. Old W SL4 & TW19 ...... 11 B8
Burford Ct. Woki RG11 ...... 25 E5
Burford La. E Ewell KT17 ...... 77 C8
Burford Lea. Elst GU8 ...... 148 E4
Burford Rd. For Hil SE6 ...... 23 F6
Burford Rd. Horsh RH13 ...... 217 E2
Burford Rd. New Mal KT4 ...... 39 A2
Burford Rd. Sutton SM1 ...... 59 A8
Burford Way. New Add CR0 ...... 63 C4
Burges Way. Stain TW18 ...... 13 A3
Burgess Cl. Felt TW13 ...... 15 E4
Burgess Rd. Sutton SM1 ...... 59 B6
Burgh Cl. Crawl RH10 ...... 182 D1
Burgh Heath Rd.
  Epsom KT17 & KT18 ...... 76 F4
Burgh Mount. Nork SM7 ...... 77 F4
Burgh Wood. Nork SM7 ...... 77 F4
Burghead Cl. Sandh GU15 ...... 64 D7
Burghfield. Epsom KT17 ...... 76 F4
Burghill Rd. For Hil SE26 ...... 23 E4
Burghley Ave. King U T KT3 ...... 38 D8
Burghley House. Wimble SW19 ...... 19 E5
Burghley Pl. Mitch CR4 ...... 40 F5

Burghley Rd. Wimble SW19 ...... 19 E4
Burgoyne Rd. Ashf TW16 ...... 14 F2
Burgoyne Rd. Camb GU15 ...... 66 A6
Burgoyne Rd. S Norw SE25 ...... 42 F5
Burham Cl. Penge SE20 ...... 23 C1
Burhill Cty Inf Sch. Hersh KT12 ...... 54 D4
Burhill Rd. Hersh KT12 ...... 54 C3
Buriton House. **9** Rhampt SW15 ...... 19 B7
Burke Cl. Rhampt SW15 ...... 7 E3
Burlands. Crawl RH11 ...... 181 A1
Burlea Cl. Hersh KT12 ...... 54 B5
Burleigh Ave. Hackb SM6 ...... 60 B7
Burleigh Cl. Addl KT15 ...... 52 B5
Burleigh Cl. Crawl D RH10 ...... 204 B8
Burleigh Ct. Leahd KT22 ...... 95 A5
Burleigh Cty Inf Sch.
  Crawl D RH10 ...... 204 B8
Burleigh Gdns. Ashf TW15 ...... 14 C3
Burleigh La. Crawl D RH10 ...... 204 C1
Burleigh La. N Asct SL5 ...... 28 E8
Burleigh Pk. Cobham KT11 ...... 73 E7
Burleigh Rd. Addl KT15 ...... 52 B5
Burleigh Rd. Frlml GU16 ...... 85 D8
Burleigh Rd. N Asct SL5 ...... 28 E7
Burleigh Rd. Cheam SM3 & SM4 ...... 39 E1
Burleigh Wlk. Catf SE6 ...... 24 C7
Burleigh Way. Crawl D RH10 ...... 204 B8
Burley Cl. Loxwd RH14 ...... 213 A4
Burley Cl. Mitch SW16 ...... 41 D7
Burley Orchard. Chert KT16 ...... 33 A3
Burley Way. Blckw GU17 ...... 64 C6
Burleys Rd. Crawl RH10 ...... 202 C6
Burlingham Cl. Merrow GU4 ...... 110 D3
Burlington Ave. Rich TW9 ...... 7 A6
Burlington Cl. E Bed TW14 ...... 14 D8
Burlington Cl. Alder GU11 ...... 105 A1
Burlington Ct. Chisw W4 ...... 7 C7
Burlington Ct. Chisw W4 ...... 7 C8
Burlington Ct. Hawley GU17 ...... 64 D3
Burlington Jun Sch.
  New Mal KT3 ...... 38 F5
Burlington La. Chisw W4 ...... 7 B8
Burlington Rd. Hounsl TW7 ...... 5 D6
Burlington Rd. New Mal KT3 ...... 38 F5
Burlington Rd. S Norw CR7 ...... 42 D7
Burlsdon Way. Brack RG12 ...... 27 E8
Burma Rd. Burph GU24 ...... 49 F8
Burma Terr. **11** S Norw SE19 ...... 22 E3
Burmarsh Ct. Penge SE20 ...... 43 C8
Burmester House. Wands SW17 ...... 20 C5
Burmester Rd. Wands SW17 ...... 20 C5
Burn Cl. Addl KT15 ...... 52 D6
Burn Moor Chase. Brack RG12 ...... 27 E2
Burnaby Cres. Chisw W4 ...... 7 C8
Burnaby Gdns. Chisw W4 ...... 7 B8
Burnbury Rd. Streat SW12 ...... 21 C7
Burne-Jones Dr. Sandh GU15 ...... 64 D6
Burnell Ave. Rich TW10 ...... 17 C3
Burnell House. **19** Streat SW2 ...... 22 A7
Burnell Rd. Sutton SM1 ...... 59 B6
Burnet Ave. Burph GU1 & GU4 ...... 110 B4
Burnet Gr. Epsom KT19 ...... 76 C6
Burney Ave. King U T KT5 ...... 37 F4
Burney Cl. Fetch KT23 ...... 94 C2
Burney Ct. **6** Crawl RH11 ...... 201 A3
Burney House. **4** Streat SW16 ...... 21 C3
Burney Rd. Westh RH5 ...... 115 A4
Burnham Cl. Knaph GU21 ...... 68 D1
Burnham Dr. N Cheam KT4 ...... 58 D8
Burnham Dr. Reig RH2 ...... 118 A2
Burnham Gdns. Cranf TW5 ...... 4 B6
Burnham Gdns. Croy CR0 ...... 42 F2
Burnham Manor. Camb GU15 ...... 66 A8
Burnham Pl. Horsh RH13 ...... 217 D1
Burnham Rd. Knaph GU21 ...... 68 D1
Burnham Rd. Morden SM4 ...... 40 B5
Burnham St. King U T KT2 ...... 38 A8
Burnhams Rd. L Book KT23 ...... 93 E3
Burnhill Rd. Beck BR3 ...... 44 A7
Burns Ave. Felt TW14 ...... 4 A1
Burns Cl. Horsh RH12 ...... 217 E2
Burns Cl. Mitch SW17 ...... 20 D2
Burns Cl. W Heath GU14 ...... 84 F6
Burns Ct. Wallin SM6 ...... 60 B3
Burns Dr. Nork SM7 ...... 77 E5
Burns Rd. Crawl RH10 ...... 202 C8
Burns Rd. Crawl RH11 ...... 200 C1
Burns Way. E Grins RH19 ...... 185 C1
Burns Way. Heston TW5 ...... 4 D6
Burnsall Cl. Farnb GU14 ...... 85 B6
Burnside. Ashtd KT21 ...... 75 F1
Burnside Cl. Twick TW1 ...... 6 A1
Burnt Ash Jun Sch. Broml BR1 ...... 24 F3
Burnt Hill Rd. Rowl GU10 & GU9 ...... 146 B6
Burnt Hill Way. Rowl GU10 ...... 146 B5
Burnt House La. Rowl RH12 ...... 200 A7
Burnt Pollard La. Windl GU24 ...... 48 L1
Burntcommon Cl. Send M GU23 ...... 90 F2
Burntcommon La. Send M GU23 ...... 91 A2
Burntwood Cl. Cater CR3 ...... 101 A6
Burntwood Cl. Wands SW18 ...... 20 E7
Burntwood Ct. Wands SW17 ...... 20 C5
Burntwood Grange Rd.
  Wands SW18 ...... 20 E7
Burntwood La. Cater CR3 ...... 101 A6
Burntwood La. Wands SW17 ...... 20 D6
Burntwood Sch. Wands SW17 ...... 20 D6
Burntwood View. Dulw SE19 ...... 22 F3
Burnwood Park Rd. Hersh KT12 ...... 54 B6
Burpham La. Burph GU4 ...... 110 A5
Burpham Prim Sch. Burph GU4 ...... 110 A5
Burr Hill La. Burrh GU24 ...... 49 F2
Burr Rd. Wands SW18 ...... 20 A8
Burrell Cl. Croy CR0 ...... 43 E3
Burrell Ct. Crawl RH11 ...... 200 F4
Burrell House. **5** Twick TW1 ...... 17 B8
Burrell Rd. Friml GU16 ...... 85 C8
Burrell Row. Beck BR3 ...... 44 A7
Burrell The. Westc RH4 ...... 135 C6
Burrells. Beck BR3 ...... 44 B7
Burritt Rd. King U T KT1 ...... 38 A7

Bur – Car 231

Burrow Hill Gn. Burrh GU24 49 E2
Burrow Hill Sch. Friml GU16 65 F1
Burrow Wlk. W Norw SE21 22 C8
Burrows Cl. L Book KT23 93 F3
Burrows Cl. Stough GU2 108 F2
Burrows Cross. Gomsh GU5 133 C2
Burrows Hill Cl.Harm TW19 & TW6 2 C3
Burrows La. Gomsh GU5 133 C3
Burrwood Gdns. Ash V GU12 106 A4
Burstead Cl. Cobham KT11 73 D7
Burston Gdns. E Grins RH19 185 D8
Burstow House. Horley RH6 161 B6
Burstow Prim Sch. Smallf RH6 162 B3
Burstow Rd. Wimble SW20 39 E8
Burtenshaw Rd. Thame D KT7 37 A3
Burton Cl. Chess KT9 56 D3
Burton Cl. Horley RH6 161 A2
Burton Cl. Windl GU20 48 D4
Burton Ct. Thame D KT7 37 A3
Burton Gdns. Hounsl TW5 4 F6
Burton House. Penge SE26 23 B3
Burton Rd. King U T KT2 17 E1
Burton's Rd. Hampt TW12 16 C4
Burtons Ct. Horsh RH12 217 C2
Burtwell La.
W Norw SE21 & SE27 22 D4
Burwash Rd. Crawl RH10 202 A5
Burway Cres. Thorpe KT16 33 A5
Burwood Ave. Purley CR8 80 B5
Burwood Cl. Hersh KT12 54 C4
Burwood Cl. Merrow GU1 110 D2
Burwood Cl. Reig RH2 118 D1
Burwood Cl. Tolw KT6 38 A1
Burwood Ct. For Hil SE23 23 C8
Burwood Park Sch. Whit V KT12 53 F5
Burwood Rd. Hersh KT12 & KT13 54 B4
Burwood Rd. Hersh KT12 54 D5
Bury Cl. Horse GU21 69 D3
Bury Fields. Guild GU2 130 C7
Bury Gr. Morden SM4 40 B4
Bury La. Horse GU21 69 C3
Bury St. Guild GU2 130 C7
Burys Court Sch. Leigh RH2 138 C3
Burys The. Godal GU7 150 E5
Burywood Hill. Ockley RH5 177 E7
Busbridge CE Jun Sch.
Godal GU7 150 F2
Busbridge Cty Inf Sch.
Godal GU7 150 F2
Busbridge La. Godal GU7 150 E3
Busby House. Streat SW16 21 C4
Busch Cnr. Brent TW7 6 B6
Busdens Cl. Milf GU8 170 F8
Busdens La. Milf GU8 170 F8
Busdens Way. Milf GU8 170 F8
Bush Cl. Addl KT15 52 C5
Bush La. Send GU23 90 D3
Bush Rd. Rich TW9 6 F8
Bush Rd. Shep Gn TW17 33 F4
Bush Wlk. Woki RG11 25 C6
Bushbury La. Brock RH3 137 A5
Bushell Cl. Streat SW2 21 F6
Bushell House. 3 W Norw SE27 22 C4
Bushetts Gr. Merst RH1 & RH2 119 B6
Bushey Cl. Kenley CR3 & CR8 80 F3
Bushey Croft. Oxted RH8 122 C5
Bushey Ct. W Barn SW20 39 B7
Bushey Down. Up Toot SW12 21 B6
Bushey La. Sutton SM1 59 A6
Bushey Mid Sch. W Barn SW20 39 B6
Bushey Prim Sch. W Barn KT3 39 B6
Bushey Rd. Croy CR0 63 A8
Bushey Rd. Merton SW20 39 D7
Bushey Rd. Sutton SM1 59 A6
Bushey Rd. Sutton SM1 59 B6
Bushey Rd. W Barn SW20 39 D7
Bushey Way. Beck BR3 44 D4
Bushfield. Plaist RH14 211 F2
Bushfield Dr. Earls RH1 140 A4
Bushnell Rd. Up Toot SW17 21 B5
Bushwood Rd. Rich TW9 7 A8
Bushy Ct. Tedd KT1 37 C8
Bushy Hill Dr. Merrow GU1 110 C3
Bushy Hill Sch. Merrow GU1 110 D2
Bushy Park Gdns. Tedd TW12 16 D3
Bushy Park Rd. Tedd TW11 17 B1
Bushy Rd. Fetch KT22 & KT23 94 B5
Bushy Rd. Tedd TW11 16 F1
Bushy Shaw. Ashtd KT21 75 C2
Business Ctr The. Woki RG11 25 B4
Busk Cres. Farnb GU14 84 F3
Bute Ave. Rich TW10 17 E6
Bute Ct. Wallin SM6 60 C5
Bute Gdns. Wallin SM6 60 C5
Bute Gdns W. Wallin SM6 60 C5
Bute Rd. Thorn H CR0 42 A1
Bute Rd. Wallin SM6 60 C6
Butler Rd. Bagsh GU19 47 F2
Butler Rd. Crowth RG11 45 B6
Butlers Dene Rd. Wold CR3 102 A7
Butlers Hill. W Hors KT24 112 B5
Butlers Rd. Horsh RH13 218 B4
Butt Cl. Cran GU6 174 E4
Butter Hill. Dork RH4 136 A7
Butter Hill. Hackb SM5 & SM6 60 A6
Buttercup Cl. Woki RG11 26 A6
Buttercup Sq. Stan TW19 13 D7
Butterfield. Camb GU15 65 B4
Butterfield. E Grins RH19 185 B3
Butterfield Cl. Twick TW1 5 F1
Butterfly Wlk. Warlgm CR6 101 C7
Buttermer Cl. Wreccl GU10 145 F7
Buttermere Cl. E Bed TW14 14 F7
Buttermere Cl. Farnb GU14 84 E4
Buttermere Cl. Horsh RH12 218 B6
Buttermere Cl. W Barn SM4 39 D3
Buttermere Ct. Ash V GU12 105 F4
Buttermere Dr. Friml GU15 66 D4
Buttermere Gdns. Brack RG12 27 C6
Buttermere Gdns. Sander CR8 80 D6
Buttermere Way. Thor L TW20 12 B1
Buttersteep Rise.
Brack GU20 & SL5 28 C1
Butterworth Ct. Streat SW16 21 E5
Butts Cl. Crawl RH11 201 B7
Butts Cotts. 4 Woking GU21 69 A1
Butts Cres. Felt TW13 16 A5
Butts House. Felt TW13 16 A5
Butts Rd. Catf BR1 24 E3
Butts Rd. Woking GU21 69 E2
Butts The. Brent TW8 6 D8
Buxton Ave. Cater CR3 100 E6
Buxton Cres. Cheam SM3 58 E6
Buxton Dr. King U T KT3 38 D7
Buxton La. Cater CR3 100 E6
Buxton Rd. Ashf TW15 13 D3
Buxton Rd. Mortl SW14 7 E4
Buxton Rd. Thorn H CR7 42 B4
Byards Croft. Mitch SW16 41 D8
Byatt Wlk. Hampt TW12 15 E2
Bychurch End. 9 Tedd TW11 16 F3
Bycroft St. Penge SE20 23 D1
Bycroft Way. Crawl RH10 202 B8
Bye Ways. Twick TW2 16 B5
Byerley Way. Crawl RH10 202 E7
Byers La. Blind H RH7 & RH9 142 C1
Byeway The. Mortl SW14 7 C4
Byeways The. Surb KT5 38 B4
Byfield Ct. W Barn KT3 39 A5
Byfield Rd. Islew TW7 6 A4
Byfleet Cnr. W Byfl KT14 71 A6
Byfleet Cty Prim Sch. Byfl KT14 71 D8
Byfleet Ind Est. Byfl KT14 71 D8
Byfleet & New Haw Sta.
New Haw KT15 52 D1
Byfleet Rd.
New Haw KT14 & KT15 52 D2
Byfleet Rd.
Whit V KT11 & KT13 & KT14 72 C7
Byfleet Tech Ctr The. Byfl KT14 71 D8
Byfleets La. Warn RH12 216 D6
Byfrons The. Farnb GU14 85 D2
Bygrove. New Add CR0 63 B3
Bygrove Ct. Mitch SW19 20 D2
Bygrove Rd. Mitch SW19 20 D2
Bylands. Woking GU22 70 A1
Byne Rd. Carsh SM5 59 E8
Byne Rd. Penge SE20 & SE26 23 C3
Bynes Rd. S Croy CR2 61 D3
Byrd Rd. Crawl RH11 200 F3
Byrefield Rd. Stough GU2 108 F4
Byrne Ct. 1 Purley CR8 80 A7
Byrne Rd. Up Toot SW12 21 B6
Byron Ave. Carsh SM1 59 D6
Byron Ave. Coulsd CR5 79 F3
Byron Ave. Cranf TW4 4 B5
Byron Ave. Friml GU15 & GU16 66 B3
Byron Ave. W Barn KT3 39 A4
Byron Ave E. Carsh SM1 59 D6
Byron Cl. Crawl RH10 202 B7
Byron Cl. For Hil SE26 23 E4
Byron Cl. Hampt TW12 15 F4
Byron Cl. Horsh RH12 217 E6
Byron Cl. Knaph GU21 68 E2
Byron Cl. Walt O T KT12 35 E1
Byron Ct. Dulw SE21 23 A7
Byron Ct. 1 Rich TW10 17 D4
Byron Ct. S Norw CR7 42 C7
Byron Dr. Crowth RG11 45 B3
Byron Gdns. Carsh SM1 59 D6
Byron Gr. 2 E Grins RH19 185 C1
Byron House. Beck BR3 24 B2
Byron Inf Sch. Coulsd CR5 79 F2
Byron Jun Sch. Coulsd CR5 79 F2
Byron Pl. Leahd KT22 95 B5
Byron Rd. Addl KT15 52 E6
Byron Rd. S Croy CR2 62 B1
Byton Rd. Up Toot SW17 20 F2
Byttom Hill. Mickle RH5 115 C8
Byward Ave. Felt TW14 4 C1
Byway The. Sutton SM2 59 D2
Byways The. Ashtd KT21 75 D1
Byways The. Worc Pk KT19 57 F6
Bywood. Easth RG12 27 A2
Bywood Ave. Croy CR0 43 D3
Bywood Cl. Purley CR8 80 B4
Bywood Terr. Croy CR0 43 C3
Byworth Cl. Farnh GU9 124 F2
Byworth Rd. Farnh GU9 124 F2

Cabbell Pl. Addl KT15 52 C6
Cabell Rd. Stough GU2 108 E2
Cabin Moss. Brack RG12 27 E2
Cable House Sch. Horse GU21 69 E4
Cabrera Ave. Went GU25 31 D3
Cabrera Cl. Went GU25 31 D3
Cabrol Rd. Farnb GU14 85 A5
Caburn Ct. Crawl RH11 201 C4
Caburn Hts. Crawl RH11 201 C4
Cackstones The. Crawl RH10 202 D7
Cadbury Cl. Ashf TW16 14 E1
Cadbury Cl. Islew TW7 6 A6
Cadbury Rd. Ashf TW16 14 E2
Caddy Cl. 4 Egham TW20 12 A3
Cadley Terr. For Hil SE23 23 C6
Cadmer Cl. New Mal KT3 38 E5
Cadnam Cl. Alder GU11 126 C6
Cadnam Point. 14
Rhampt SW15 19 B7
Cadogan Cl. Beck BR3 44 D7
Cadogan Cl. Tedd TW11 16 E3
Cadogan Ct. Sutton SM2 59 B4
Cadogan Rd. King U T KT6 37 D4
Cadogen Rd. Farnb GU11 105 D7
Caen Wood Rd. Ashtd KT21 75 C1
Caenshill Rd. Whit V KT13 53 A3
Caenswood Hill. Whit V KT13 53 A1
Caenwood Cl. Weyb KT13 53 A4
Caernarvon. Friml GU16 85 F8
Caernarvon Cl. Mitch CR4 41 E6
Caernarvon Ct. 3 Surb KT5 37 F4
Caesar Ct. Alder GU11 104 E2
Caesar's Camp Rd. Camb GU15 66 A8
Caesar's Cl. Camb GU15 43 B6
Caesar's Way. Shep TW17 34 D3
Caesars Ct. Heath E GU9 125 C7
Caesars Wlk. Mitch CR4 40 F4
Caffins Cl. Crawl RH10 201 E8
Caillard Rd. Byfl KT14 71 E8
Cain Rd. Binf RG12 26 E7
Cain's La. Hatton TW14 3 E2
Cairn Cl. Friml GU15 & GU16 66 B3
Cairndale Cl. Broml BR1 24 F1
Cairngorm Pl. W Heath GU14 84 E7
Cairo New Rd. Croy CR0 & CR9 61 B8
Caister House. 10
Balham SW12 21 B8
Caistor Mews. Balham SW12 21 B8
Caistor Rd. Balham SW12 21 B8
Caithness Rd. Mitch CR4 21 B1
Calbourne Rd. Balham SW12 21 A8
Caldbeck Ave. N Cheam KT4 39 B1
Caldbeck House. 7
Crawl RH11 200 F3
Calder Rd. Morden SM4 40 C4
Calder Way. Poyle SL3 1 E4
Calderdale Cl. Crawl RH11 201 B4
Caldwell Rd. Windl GU20 48 D5
Caledon Pl. Burph GU1 110 A4
Caledon Rd. Hackb SM5 & SM6 60 A6
Caledonia Rd. Stan TW19 13 E7
Caledonian House.
Crawl RH11 201 D8
Caledonian Way. Horley RH6 182 B8
Calfridus Way. Brack RG12 27 F6
California Ct. Sutton SM2 59 B1
California Rd. King U T KT3 38 C6
Callander Rd. Catf SE6 24 C6
Calley Down Cres.
New Add CR0 & CR9 63 D1
Callis Farm Cl. Stan TW19 2 E1
Callisto Cl. Crawl RH11 200 E3
Callow Field. Purley CR8 80 A6
Callow Hill. Vir W GU25 & TW20 31 C7
Calluna Ct. Woking GU22 69 F1
Calluna Dr. Copth RH10 183 A3
Calmont Rd. Catf BR1 24 E2
Calonne Rd. Wimble SW19 19 D4
Calshot Rd. Harl TW6 3 A5
Calshot Way. Friml GU16 86 A7
Calshot Way. Harl TW6 3 A5
Calthorpe Gdns. Sutton SM1 59 C7
Calton Gdns. Alder GU11 126 C7
Calverley Cl. Beck BR3 24 B2
Calverley Rd. Stonel KT17 58 A4
Calvert Cl. Alder GU12 105 D1
Calvert Cres. Dork RH4 115 B1
Calvert Ct. 5 Rich TW9 6 F3
Calvert Rd. Dork RH4 115 B2
Calvert Rd. Effing KT24 113 B7
Calvin Cl. Friml GU15 66 B4
Calvin Wlk. Crawl RH11 200 E3
Camac Rd. Twick TW2 16 D7
Camber Cl. Crawl RH10 202 C6
Camberley Ave. Wimble SW20 39 B7
Camberley Cl. Cheam SM3 58 D7
Camberley Ct. 8 Sutton SM2 59 B3
Camberley Cty Inf Sch.
Camb GU15 65 C5
Camberley Heath Golf Course.
Friml GU15 66 B5
Camberley Rd. Harl TW6 3 A4
Camberley Sta. Camb GU15 65 D5
Camberley Towers. Camb GU15 65 D5
Cambisgate. Wimble SW19 19 E3
Camborne Cl. Harm TW6 3 A4
Camborne Rd. Belm SM2 59 A3
Camborne Rd. Croy CR0 43 A2
Camborne Rd. Sutton SM2 59 B3
Camborne Rd. W Barn SM4 39 D4
Camborne Rd. Wands SW18 20 A8
Camborne Rd S. Harm TW6 3 A4
Camborne Way. Harm TW6 3 A4
Camborne Way. Heston TW5 5 A6
Cambray Rd. Streat SW12 21 C7
Cambria. Beck BR3 44 B7
Cambria Cl. Hounsl TW3 5 A3
Cambria Ct. Felt TW14 15 B8
Cambria Ct. Stain TW18 12 E4
Cambria Gdns. Stan TW19 13 E8
Cambria House. For Hil SE26 23 A4
Cambrian Cl. Camb GU15 65 B5
Cambrian Cl. W Norw SE27 22 B5
Cambrian Rd. Rich TW10 6 F1
Cambrian Way. W Heath GU14 84 D7
Cambridge Ave.
King U T KT3 & SW20 38 F7
Cambridge Cl. Harm UB7 2 D8
Cambridge Cl. Hounsl TW4 4 E3
Cambridge Cl. Knaph GU21 68 F1
Cambridge Cl. Wimble SW20 39 B8
Cambridge Cotts. Rich TW9 7 A8
Cambridge Cres. Tedd TW11 17 A3
Cambridge Ct. Wimble SW20 39 B8
Cambridge Gdns. King U T KT1 38 A7
Cambridge Gr. Penge SE20 43 B8
Cambridge Grove Rd.
King U T KT1 38 A6
Cambridge Grove Rd. 5
King U T KT1 38 A7
Cambridge House. 2
Tedd TW11 17 A3
Cambridge House Sch.
Wimble SW20 39 C8
Cambridge Meadows.
Farnh GU9 125 A1
Cambridge Military Hospl.
Alder GU11 105 B3
Cambridge Park Ct. Twick TW1 17 D8
Cambridge Pk. Twick TW1 6 C1
Cambridge Rd. Alder GU11 104 F2
Cambridge Rd. Barnes SW13 7 F5
Cambridge Rd. Carsh SM5 59 E5
Cambridge Rd. Crowth RG11 45 C4
Cambridge Rd. Croy SE20 & SE25 43 B6
Cambridge Rd. E Mole KT8 35 F5
Cambridge Rd. Hampt TW12 15 F1
Cambridge Rd. Horsh RH13 217 D2
Cambridge Rd. Hounsl TW4 4 E3
Cambridge Rd. King U T KT1 38 A7
Cambridge Rd.
Littlt TW15 & TW17 14 C1
Cambridge Rd. Mitch CR4 41 C6
Cambridge Rd. New Mal KT3 38 E5
Cambridge Rd. Rich TW9 7 A7
Cambridge Rd. Sandh GU15 45 E1
Cambridge Rd. Tedd TW11 17 A3
Cambridge Rd. Twick TW1 6 D1
Cambridge Rd. Walt O T KT12 35 B3
Cambridge Rd. Wimble SW20 39 B8
Cambridge Rd E. Farnb GU14 85 D1
Cambridge Rd W. Farnb GU14 85 C1
Cambridge Sq. Camb GU15 65 C6
Cambridge Wlk. 3 Camb GU15 65 C6
Camden Ave. Felt TW13 15 C7
Camden Gdns. S Norw CR7 42 B6
Camden Gdns. Sutton SM1 59 B5
Camden Hill Rd. W Norw SE19 22 E2
Camden Jun Sch. Carsh SM5 59 F6
Camden Rd. Carsh SM5 59 F6
Camden Rd. Lingf RH7 164 D4
Camden Rd. Sutton SM1 59 B5
Camden Way. S Norw CR7 42 B6
Cameford Ct. 20 Streat SW12 21 E8
Camel Way. Farnb GU14 105 A8
Camellia Ct. 21 Beck BR3 24 A1
Camellia Ct. W End GU24 67 F6
Camellia Pl. Twick TW2 16 B8
Camelot Cl. Bigg H TN16 83 C3
Camelot Cl. Wimble SW19 20 A4
Camelot Ct. Crawl RH11 200 E6
Camelsdale Cty Fst Sch.
King Gn GU27 207 F5
Camelsdale Rd. King Gn GU27 207 F5
Camelsdale Rd. Linch GU27 207 F5
Cameron Cl. Cran GU6 174 E1
Cameron Ct. 3 Putney SW19 19 E7
Cameron House. Broml BR1 44 F8
Cameron Lodge. Hounsl TW3 5 C3
Cameron Rd. Farnb GU11 105 D7
Cameron Rd. For Hil SE6 23 F6
Cameron Rd. Thorn H CR0 42 B3
Cameron Sq. Mitch CR4 40 E8
Camgate Est. Stan TW19 13 F8
Camilla Cl. Ashf TW16 14 F2
Camilla Cl. G Book KT23 94 B2
Camilla Dr. Westh RH5 115 A5
Camille Cl. Croy SE25 43 A6
Camlan Rd. Catf BR1 24 F4
Camm Gdns. 5 King U T KT1 37 F7
Camm Gdns. Thame D KT7 36 F2
Camomile Ave. Mitch CR4 40 F8
Camp End Rd.
Whit V KT11 & KT13 72 C8
Camp Farm Rd. Farnb GU11 105 D5
Camp Hill. Farnh GU10 & GU9 147 C8
Camp Rd. Farnb GU14 105 C8
Camp Rd. Wimble SW19 19 C3
Camp Rd. Wold CR3 101 E6
Camp View. Wimble SW19 19 B3
Campbell Ave. Westfd GU22 89 F6
Campbell Cl. Alder GU11 126 C7
Campbell Cl. Streat SW16 21 D4
Campbell Cl. Twick TW2 16 D7
Campbell Cres. E Grins RH19 185 B1
Campbell Ct. Dulw SE21 23 A7
Campbell Ct. Leahd KT22 95 B5
Campbell House. 6 Wallin SM6 60 B6
Campbell Pl. Friml GU16 65 F3
Campbell Rd. Alder GU11 105 A3
Campbell Rd. Cater CR3 100 D6
Campbell Rd. Thorn H CR0 42 B3
Campbell Rd. Twick TW2 16 D6
Campbell Rd. Whit V KT13 53 A3
Campbell Rd. Worth RH10 202 C5
Campden Rd. S Croy CR0 & CR2 61 E5
Campen Cl. Putney SW19 19 E6
Camphill Ct. W Byfl KT14 71 A7
Camphill Ind Est. W Byfl KT14 71 B8
Camphill Rd. W Byfl KT14 & KT15 71 B7
Campion Cl. Hawley GU17 64 F3
Campion Cl. S Croy CR2 61 E6
Campion Dr. Burgh H KT20 97 B7
Campion House. Brack RG12 26 E8
Campion House. 6 Redh RH1 119 A4
Campion House (Seminary).
Hounsl TW7 5 D6
Campion Rd. Horsh RH12 217 E5
Campion Rd. Hounsl TW7 5 F6
Campion Way. Woki RG11 25 E7
Camrose Ave. Felt TW13 15 C4
Camrose Cl. Croy CR0 43 E2
Camrose Cl. Morden SM4 40 A5
Can Hatch. Burgh H KT20 77 E1
Canada Ave. Earls RH1 140 A5
Canada Dr. Earls RH1 140 A5
Canada House. Earls RH1 140 A5
Canada Rd. Byfl KT14 71 D8
Canada Rd. Cobham KT11 73 C6
Canada Rd. Friml GU16 86 E8
Canadian Ave. Catf SE6 24 B7
Canal Cl. Farnb GU11 105 D5
Canal Cotts. Ash V GU12 106 A4
Canal Wlk. Croy CR0 42 F3
Canal Wlk. For Hil SE26 23 C3
Canberra Cl. Crawl RH11 181 D1
Canberra Cl. Horsh RH12 217 F4
Canberra Pl. Horsh RH12 217 F5
Canberra Rd. Harl TW6 3 A4
Canberra Way. Farnb GU14 104 F8
Canbury Ave. King U T KT2 37 F8
Canbury Ct. King U T KT2 17 E1
Canbury Mews. Dulw SE26 23 A5
Canbury Park Rd. King U T KT2 37 F8
Candlerush Cl. Mayb GU22 70 B2
Candover Cl. Harm UB7 2 D7
Candy Croft. G Book KT23 94 B2
Cane Cl. Wallin SM6 60 E3
Cane Hill Hospl. Coulsd CR5 79 C2
Canewdon Cl. Woking GU22 89 E8
Canford Dr. Chert KT15 52 B8
Canford Gdns. New Mal KT3 38 E3
Canham Rd. S Norw SE25 42 E6
Canmore Gdns. Streat SW16 21 C1
Canning Rd. Alder GU12 105 D2
Canning Rd. Croy CR0 & CR9 61 F8
Cannizaro Rd. Wimble SW19 19 D3
Cannon Cl. Hampt TW12 16 B2
Cannon Cl. Sandh GU15 64 F8
Cannon Cl. W Barn SW20 39 C6
Cannon Cres. Chobh GU24 68 E8
Cannon Gr. Fetch KT22 94 E6
Cannon Hill. Easth RG12 27 C3
Cannon Hill La.
Merton KT3 & SM4 & SW20 39 E5
Cannon Hill La.
W Barn KT3 & SM4 & SW20 39 E5
Cannon House. Penge SE26 23 B2
Cannon Side. Fetch KT22 94 E5
Cannon Way. E Mole KT8 36 B5
Cannon Way. Fetch KT22 94 E6
Cannons Cl. Reig RH2 117 F2
Canon's Hill. Coulsd CR5 & CR8 80 A1
Canon's Wlk. Croy CR0 62 D7
Canonbie Rd. For Hil SE23 23 C8
Canonbury Cotts.
Lamb Gn RH12 199 F6
Canons L Ctr The. Mitch CR4 40 F5
Canons La. Burgh H KT20 97 F8
Canopus Way. Stan TW19 13 E8
Cansiron La. Ash W RH19 206 F6
Cantelupe Rd. E Grins RH19 185 F1
Canter The. Crawl RH10 202 E7
Canterbury Cl. Beck BR3 44 B8
Canterbury Ct. Ashf TW15 13 F4
Canterbury Ct. Dork RH4 136 A8
Canterbury Ct. S Croy CR2 61 C3
Canterbury Gr.
W Norw SE27 & SW16 22 A5
Canterbury Mews. Oxsh KT22 74 C6
Canterbury Rd. Ash GU12 106 A3
Canterbury Rd. Crawl RH10 201 E2
Canterbury Rd. Farnb GU14 85 D2
Canterbury Rd. Felt TW13 15 E6
Canterbury Rd. Morden SM4 40 C3
Canterbury Rd. Stough GU2 108 F3
Canterbury Rd.
Thorn H CR0 & CR7 42 A2
Cantley Cres. Woki RG11 25 A8
Cantley Gdns. S Norw SE19 42 F8
Canute Ct. W Norw SW16 22 A5
Canvey Cl. Crawl RH11 201 C3
Cape Copse. Rudg RH12 214 D7
Capel. Surb KT5 37 F2
Capel Ave. Wallin SM6 60 F5
Capel CE (VA) Fst Sch.
Capel RH5 178 D6
Capel Ct. Penge SE20 43 C8
Capel La. Crawl RH11 200 F5
Capel Lodge. 5 Rich TW9 6 F6
Capel Lodge. 15 Streat SW2 21 F8
Capel Rd. Rusper RH12 199 A8
Capella House. Capel RH5 178 C5
Capern Rd. Wands SW18 20 C7
Capital Ind Est. Mitch CR4 40 F4
Capital Pk. Old Wok GU22 90 B6
Caplan Est. Mitch CR4 41 C8
Capper Rd. Sandh GU15 65 A7
Capri Rd. Croy CR0 42 F2
Capricorn Cl. Crawl RH11 200 E4
Capsey Rd. Crawl RH11 200 E6
Capstans Wharf. Knaph GU21 68 F1
Capstone Rd. Catf BR1 24 F4
Caradon Cl. Woking GU21 69 B1
Caradon Ct. 7 Twick TW1 6 C1
Caraway Cl. Crawl RH11 201 B2
Caraway Pl. Hackb SM6 60 B7
Caraway Pl. Stough GU2 109 A6
Carberry Rd. 11 S Norw SE19 22 E2
Carbery La. Ascot SL5 29 B6
Card Hill. For Row RH18 206 F1
Cardamom Cl. Stough GU2 109 A5
Cardigan Cl. Knaph GU21 68 F1
Cardigan Rd. Rich TW10 6 E1
Cardigan Rd. Wimble SW19 20 C2
Cardinal Ave. King U T KT2 17 E2
Cardinal Ave. W Barn SM4 39 E3
Cardinal Cl. W Barn SM4 39 E3
Cardinal Cl. Worc Pk KT19 & KT4 58 A6
Cardinal Cres. King U T KT3 38 C7
Cardinal Dr. Walt O T KT12 35 D1
Cardinal Newman RC Sch.
Hersh KT12 54 D7
Cardinal Rd. Felt TW13 15 B7
Cardinal Road Inf Sch.
Felt TW13 15 B7
Cardinal's Wlk. Ashf TW16 14 E2
Cardinal's Wlk. Hampt TW12 16 C1
Cardingham. Woking GU21 69 B2
Cardington Sq. Hounsl TW4 4 D3
Cardwell Cres. Ascot SL5 29 C4
Cardwells Keep. Stough GU2 109 A4
Carew Cl. Coulsd CR5 100 B8
Carew Ct. Sutton SM2 59 B2
Carew House. Streat SW16 22 A5
Carew Manor Sch. Wallin SM6 60 D7
Carew Rd. Ashf TW15 14 C2
Carew Rd. Mitch CR4 41 A7
Carew Rd. Thorn H CR7 42 B5

Carew Rd. Wallin SM6 .... 60 C4
Carey House. Crawl RH11 .... 201 C6
Carey Rd. Woki RG11 .... 25 C5
Carey's Copse. Smallf RH6 ...... 162 B3
Carey's Wood. Smallf RH6 .... 162 B3
Carfax. Horsh RH12 .... 217 C2
Carfax Ave. Ash GU10 .... 126 F8
Cargate Ave. Alder GU11 .... 105 A1
Cargate Gr. Alder GU11 .... 105 A1
Cargate Hill. Alder GU11 .... 104 F1
Cargate Terr. Alder GU11 .... 104 F1
Cargill Rd. Wands SW18 .... 20 C7
Cargo Forecourt Rd.
  Crawl RH6 .... 181 D7
Cargo Rd. Crawl RH6 .... 181 D7
Cargreen Rd. S Norw SE25 .... 42 F5
Carholme Rd. For Hil SE23 .... 23 F7
Carisbrook Ct. 1 Streat SW16 .... 21 F5
Carisbrooke. Friml GU16 .... 85 F8
Carisbrooke Ct. Belm SM2 .... 58 F3
Carisbrooke Rd. Mitch CR4 .... 41 E5
Carleton Ave. Wallin SM6 .... 60 D2
Carleton Cl. Thame KT10 .... 36 F1
Carlingford Gdns. Mitch CR4 ..... 21 A1
Carlingford Rd. W Barn SM4 ...... 39 D3
Carlinwark Dr. Camb GU15 .... 65 F7
Carlisle Rd. Rushm GU10 .... 168 C5
Carlisle Way. For Toot SW17 ...... 21 A3
Carlos St. Godal GU7 .... 150 E4
Carlton Ave. Felt TW14 .... 4 C1
Carlton Ave. S Croy CR2 .... 61 E3
Carlton Cl. Chess KT9 .... 56 D4
Carlton Cl. Friml GU15 & GU16 .... 66 B3
Carlton Cl. Horse GU21 .... 70 A5
Carlton Cres. Cheam SM3 .... 58 E6
Carlton Ct. Horley RH6 .... 161 A5
Carlton Ct. 12 Penge SE20 .... 43 B8
Carlton Ct. S Norw SE19 .... 42 F8
Carlton Ct. Stain TW18 .... 13 A3
Carlton Gn. Redh RH1 .... 118 C4
Carlton House. Cheam SM1 .... 58 F4
Carlton House. Hounsl TW4 .... 5 A1
Carlton Park Ave.
  Merton SW20 .... 39 D7
Carlton Rd. Ashf TW16 .... 14 F1
Carlton Rd. Blind H RH9 .... 142 C2
Carlton Rd. Head Dn GU35 .... 187 C5
Carlton Rd. Horse GU21 .... 70 A5
Carlton Rd. King U T KT3 .... 38 E7
Carlton Rd. Mortl SW14 .... 7 C3
Carlton Rd. Redh RH1 .... 118 E4
Carlton Rd. S Croy CR2 .... 61 D3
Carlton Rd. Walt O T KT12 .... 35 B2
Carlton Terr. For Hil SE26 .... 23 C5
Carlton Tye. Horley RH6 .... 161 C3
Carlwell St. Up Toot SW17 .... 20 E3
Carlyle Cl. E Mole KT8 .... 36 B7
Carlyle Cl. Crowth RG11 .... 45 C5
Carlyle Rd. Croy CR0 .... 62 A8
Carlyle Rd. Stain TW18 .... 13 A1
Carlyon Cl. Farnb GU14 .... 85 C4
Carlyon Rd. Mytch GU16 .... 85 F3
Carlys Cl. Penge BR3 .... 43 D7
Carmalt Gdns. Hersh KT12 .... 54 C5
Carman Wlk. Crawl RH11 .... 201 B1
Carmarthen Cl. W Heath GU14 .... 85 A7
Carmel Cl. 9 Woking GU22 .... 69 E1
Carmichael Ct. Barnes SW13 .... 7 F5
Carmichael House. 17
  Dulw SE21 .... 22 E4
Carmichael Mews. Wands SW18 20 D8
Carmichael Rd. Croy SE25 .... 43 A5
Carminia Rd. Up Toot SW17 .... 21 B6
Carnac St. W Norw SE21 & SE27 .. 22 D5
Carnation Dr. Wink RG12 .... 8 B2
Carnegie Cl. Surb KT6 .... 56 F8
Carnegie Pl. Wimble SW19 .... 19 D5
Carnforth Cl. W Ewell KT19 .... 57 B4
Carnforth Rd. Streat SW16 .... 21 D1
Carnoustie. Easth RG12 .... 26 E2
Carole House. 14 Penge SE20 ...... 43 B8
Carolina Rd. S Norw CR7 .... 42 C8
Caroline Cl. Hounsl TW7 .... 5 E7
Caroline Cl. S Croy CR0 .... 61 E6
Caroline Cl. Streat SW16 .... 21 F5
Caroline Ct. Ashf TW15 .... 14 B2
Caroline Ct. Catf SE6 .... 24 D4
Caroline Ct. Crawl RH11 .... 201 D4
Caroline Ct. 17 Surb KT6 .... 37 D2
Caroline Dr. Woki RG11 .... 25 A7
Caroline Pl. Harl UB3 .... 3 E7
Caroline Rd. Merton SW19 .... 19 F1
Carolyn Cl. Woking GU21 .... 88 F8
Carpenter Cl. Ewell KT17 .... 57 F2
Carpenters Cl. Twick TW2 .... 16 E6
Carrick Cl. Islew TW7 .... 6 A4
Carrick Gate. Esher KT10 .... 55 C7
Carrington Ave. Islew TW3 .... 5 B2
Carrington Cl. Croy CR0 .... 43 E2
Carrington Cl. Redh RH1 .... 118 F2
Carrington Lodge. 3 Rich TW10 .. 6 E2
Carrington Pl. Esher KT10 .... 55 C6
Carrington Rd. Rich TW10 .... 7 A3
Carrinton La. Ash V GU12 .... 106 A8
Carroll Ave. Merrow GU1 .... 110 B1
Carroll Cres. Ascot SL5 .... 28 F5
Carrow Rd. Walt O T KT12 .... 54 D7
Carshalton Beeches Sta.
  Wallin SM5 .... 59 F4
Carshalton Coll. Carsh SM5 .... 59 F7
Carshalton Coll of FE
  (Elmwood Annexe). Hackb SM6 60 B8
Carshalton Gr. Carsh SM1 .... 59 D5

Carshalton High Sch for Boys.
  Carsh SM5 .... 59 E8
Carshalton High Sch for Girls.
  Carsh SM5 .... 59 E7
Carshalton Lodge. Oat Pk KT13 .. 53 E7
Carshalton Park Rd. Wallin SM5 . 59 F5
Carshalton Pl. Wallin SM5 .... 60 A5
Carshalton Rd. Camb GU15 .... 47 A1
Carshalton Rd. Carsh SM1 & SM5 59 D5
Carshalton Rd. Mitch CR4 .... 41 A4
Carshalton Rd.
  Sutton SM1 & SM5 .... 59 D5
Carshalton Rd. Wallin SM7 .... 78 F6
Carshalton Rd. Woodm SM7 ...... 78 F6
Carshalton Sta. Carsh SM5 .... 59 F6
Carson Rd. W Norw SE21 .... 22 B6
Carstairs Rd. Catf SE6 .... 24 C5
Carswell Rd. Lewish SE6 .... 24 C8
Cartbridge Cl. Send GU23 .... 90 B4
Carter Cl. Wallin SM6 .... 60 D3
Carter Rd. Mitch SW19 .... 20 D2
Carter's Cotts. Earls RH1 .... 139 E7
Carter's Rd. Epsom KT17 .... 76 F4
Carterdale Cotts. Capel RH5 .... 178 C5
Carters Cl. N Cheam KT4 .... 39 D1
Carters La. Mayb GU22 .... 90 D7
Carters Wlk. Heath E GU9 .... 125 D8
Cartersmead Cl. Horley RH6 ..... 161 B4
Carthouse Cotts. Merrow GU4 .. 110 C4
Carthouse La. Woking GU21 .... 68 E5
Cartmel Cl. Redh RH1 .... 118 C3
Cartmel Rd. Beck BR2 .... 44 E7
Cartmel Gdns. Morden SM4 .... 40 C4
Carwarden House Sch.
  Friml GU15 .... 66 A3
Caryl House. 3 Putney SW19 ...... 19 D7
Carylls Cotts. Faygt RH12 .... 199 F1
Cascades. New Add CR0 .... 62 F1
Caselden Rd. Addl KT15 .... 52 C5
Casewick Rd. W Norw SE27 .... 22 B4
Cassel Hospl The. Rich TW10 .... 17 D4
Cassilis Rd. Twick TW1 .... 6 B1
Cassino Cl. Alder GU11 .... 105 B2
Cassiobury Ave. E Bed TW14 ...... 14 F8
Cassland Rd. S Norw CR7 .... 42 D5
Casslee Rd. For Hil SE6 .... 23 F8
Cassocks Sq. Shep TW17 .... 34 D2
Castillon Rd. Catf SE6 .... 24 E6
Castlands Rd. For Hil SE6 .... 23 F6
Castle Ave. Ewell KT17 .... 58 B2
Castle Cl. Beck BR2 .... 44 E6
Castle Cl. Bletch RH1 .... 120 C2
Castle Cl. Charlt TW16 .... 14 E1
Castle Cl. Dovgn RH2 .... 139 B5
Castle Cl. Friml GU15 .... 65 F4
Castle Cl. Belm SM2 .... 59 A4
Castle Cl. For Hil SE26 .... 23 E4
Castle Cl. Morden SM4 .... 40 D4
Castle Dr. Dovgn RH2 .... 139 B4
Castle Dr. Horley RH6 .... 161 C2
Castle Gdns. Brock RH4 .... 115 F1
Castle Gn. Oat Pk KT13 .... 53 E7
Castle Grove Rd. Chobh GU24 .... 68 E7
Castle Hill. Farnh GU9 .... 125 B3
Castle Hill. Guild GU1 .... 130 D7
Castle Hill Ave. New Add CR0 .... 63 C2
Castle Hill Prim Sch.
  New Add CR0 .... 63 C4
Castle Hill Rd. Eng Gn TW20 ...... 11 C5
Castle House. 10 Belm SM2 .... 59 A3
Castle Par. Stonel KT17 .... 58 A3
Castle Rd. Alder GU11 .... 104 E4
Castle Rd. Broad R RH12 .... 216 D3
Castle Rd. Camb GU15 .... 65 F4
Castle Rd. Epsom KT18 .... 76 B4
Castle Rd. Horse GU21 .... 69 F5
Castle Rd. Islew TW7 .... 5 F5
Castle Rd. Kings CR5 .... 98 E6
Castle Rd. Oat Pk KT13 .... 53 E7
Castle Sq. Bletch RH1 .... 120 C2
Castle Sq. Guild GU1 .... 130 D7
Castle St. Bletch RH1 .... 120 C2
Castle St. Farnh GU9 .... 125 B3
Castle St. Guild GU1 .... 130 D7
Castle St. King U T KT1 .... 37 E7
Castlemaine Ave. Ewell KT17 ..... 58 B2
Castlemaine Ave.
  S Croy CR0 & CR2 .... 61 F5
Castleman House. Ascot SL5 ...... 29 D4
Castleton Cl. Banstd SM7 .... 78 A4
Castleton Cl. Croy CR0 .... 43 E3
Castleton Ct. Surb KT5 .... 37 F4
Castleton Dr. Banstd SM7 .... 78 A5
Castleton Rd. Mitch CR4 .... 41 D5
Caswell Cl. W Heath GU14 .... 84 F6
Catalpa Cl. Bellf GU1 .... 109 C3
Catena Rise. Lightw GU18 .... 48 B1
Caterfield La. Crow RH7 .... 143 F3
Caterfield La. Oxted RH7 & RH8 144 A5
Caterham By-Pass. Cater CR3 .. 101 B4
Caterham Cl. Pirb GU24 .... 87 C6
Caterham Dene Hospl.
  Cater CR3 .... 100 F4
Caterham Dr.
  Coulsd CR3 & CR5 & CR8 .... 100 C8

Caterham Sch. Cater CR3 .... 100 F1
Caterham Sch Prep. Cater CR3 100 F1
Caterham Sta. Cater CR3 .... 101 A3
Caterways. Horsh RH12 .... 217 A3
Catford Bridge Sta. Catf SE6 ..... 24 A8
Catford Broadway. Catf SE6 ...... 24 B8
Catford Cty Sch. Catf SE6 .... 24 C5
Catford Cty Sch (Annexe).
  Catf BR1 .... 24 A4
Catford Hill. For Hil SE6 .... 24 A7
Catford Rd. Catf SE6 .... 24 B8
Catford Sta. Catf SE6 .... 24 B8
Cathedral View. Stough GU2 .... 108 F1
Cathedral Hill Ind Est.
  Stough GU2 .... 109 A2
Cathedral View. Guild GU2 ...... 108 F1
Catherine Baird Ct. 12
  Balham SW12 .... 21 B8
Catherine Cl. Byfl KT14 .... 71 F5
Catherine Ct. 3 Wimble SW19 .... 19 F3
Catherine Dr. Ashf TW16 .... 14 F2
Catherine Ct. Islew TW3 .... 5 D3
Catherine Howard Ct. 6
  Weyb KT13 .... 53 B7
Catherine Rd. King U T KT6 .... 37 D4
Catherine Wheel Rd. Brent TW8 .. 6 D7
Catheringtons Sch. Crawl RH11 177 C1
Cathill La. Ockley RH5 .... 177 C3
Cathles Rd. Balham SW12 .... 21 C8
Catlin Cres. Shep TW17 .... 34 D4
Catling Cl. For Hil SE23 .... 23 D5
Caton Ct. Beck BR2 .... 44 E7
Cator Cl. New Add CR0 .... 82 E8
Cator Cres. New Add CR0 .... 82 E8
Cator La. Beck BR3 .... 43 F8
Cator Park Girls Sch.
  Penge BR3 .... 23 E1
Cator Rd. Penge SE20 & SE26 ..... 23 D2
Cator Rd. Wallin SM5 .... 59 F5
Catteshall Hatch. Farnc GU7 .... 151 A6
Catteshall La. Godal GU7 .... 150 F4
Catteshall Rd. Farnc GU7 .... 151 A5
Catteshall Terr. Godal GU7 ...... 151 A5
Causeway. Felt TW14 & TW4 .... 4 B3
Causeway Cl. 3 Knaph GU21 ...... 68 F1
Causeway Est. Egham TW20 ...... 12 C4
Causeway The. Carsh SM5 .... 60 A8
Causeway The. Clayg KT10 .... 55 F3
Causeway The.
  Egham TW18 & TW20 .... 12 D4
Causeway The. Horsh RH12 ..... 217 C1
Causeway The. Sutton SM2 .... 59 C2
Causeway The. Tedd TW11 .... 16 F2
Causeway The. Wimble SW19 .... 19 C3
Cavalier Way. E Grins RH19 ...... 205 F7
Cavalry Cres. Hounsl TW4 .... 4 D3
Cavalry Ct. Alder GU11 .... 104 E2
Cavans Rd. Farnb GU11 .... 105 C6
Cave Rd. Rich TW10 .... 17 C4
Cavell Rd. Worth RH10 .... 202 C5
Cavendish Ave. W Barn KT3 .... 39 B5
Cavendish Cl. Ashf TW16 .... 14 F2
Cavendish Cl. Horsh RH12 .... 217 D7
Cavendish Ct. Ashf TW16 .... 14 F2
Cavendish Ct. Hawley GU17 ...... 64 D3
Cavendish Ct. Poyle SL3 .... 1 E6
Cavendish Dr. Clayg KT10 .... 55 E5
Cavendish Gdns. Earls RH1 ...... 119 A2
Cavendish House. Twick TW1 ...... 6 A1
Cavendish Jun & Inf Sch.
  Chisw W4 .... 7 E7
Cavendish Meads. Ascot SL5 ..... 29 D3
Cavendish Mews. Alder GU11 ... 105 A1
Cavendish Rd. Alder GU11 .... 105 A1
Cavendish Rd. Ashf TW16 .... 14 F2
Cavendish Rd. Balham SW12 ...... 21 B8
Cavendish Rd. Chisw W4 .... 7 C5
Cavendish Rd. Mitch SW19 .... 20 E1
Cavendish Rd. New Mal KT3 ...... 38 F5
Cavendish Rd. Sutton SM2 .... 59 C3
Cavendish Rd. Thorn H CR0 .... 42 B1
Cavendish Rd. Whit V KT13 .... 53 D2
Cavendish Rd. Woking GU22 ..... 89 D8
Cavendish Terr. Felt TW13 .... 15 A6
Cavendish Way. W Wick BR4 ...... 44 B1
Cavenham Cl. Woking GU22 .... 89 E8
Caverleigh Way. New Mal KT4 .... 39 B2
Caversham Ave. Cheam SM3 ...... 58 E8
Caversham House. 8
  King U T KT1 .... 37 E7
Caversham Rd. King U T KT1 ...... 37 F7
Caves Farm Cl. Sandh GU17 ...... 64 A8
Cawnpore St. W Norw SE19 .... 22 E3
Cawsey Way. Woking GU21 .... 69 E2
Cawston Ct. Broml BR1 .... 24 F1
Caxton Ave. Row Tn KT15 .... 52 A4
Caxton Cl. Crawl RH10 .... 201 E3
Caxton Gdns. Stough GU2 .... 109 B2
Caxton House. The Char RH8 .... 123 F3
Caxton La. The Char RH8 .... 123 E4
Caxton Rd. Wimble SW19 .... 20 C3
Caxton Rise. Earls RH1 .... 119 A2
Caxtons Ct. Abbots GU1 .... 110 A3
Caygill Cl. Beck BR2 .... 44 F5
Cayley Cl. Wallin SM6 .... 60 E3
Cearn Way. Coulsd CR5 .... 79 F4
Cecil Ave. Ashf TW15 .... 14 C1
Cecil Cl. Chess KT9 .... 56 D6
Cecil Ct. 9 Croy CR0 .... 61 F8
Cecil Lodge. Chess KT9 .... 56 D6
Cecil Mansions. 2
  Up Toot SW17 .... 21 A6
Cecil Pl. Mitch CR4 .... 40 F4
Cecil Rd. Ashf TW15 .... 14 C2
Cecil Rd. Cheam SM1 & SM2 ...... 58 F4
Cecil Rd. Hounsl TW3 .... 5 C5
Cecil Rd. Merton SW19 .... 20 B1
Cecil Rd. Thorn H CR0 .... 41 F3
Cedar Ave. Blckw GU17 .... 64 D5
Cedar Ave. Cobham KT11 .... 73 C4

Cedar Ave. Twick TW2 .... 5 C1
Cedar Cl. Alder GU12 .... 126 E8
Cedar Cl. Bagsh GU19 .... 47 E3
Cedar Cl. Crawl RH11 .... 181 C1
Cedar Cl. Dork RH4 .... 136 B7
Cedar Cl. E Mole KT8 .... 36 E5
Cedar Cl. Epsom KT17 .... 76 F5
Cedar Cl. Esher KT10 .... 54 F3
Cedar Cl. Horsh RH12 .... 217 C3
Cedar Cl. King U T KT2 .... 18 D4
Cedar Cl. Laleh TW18 .... 33 C6
Cedar Cl. W Norw SE21 .... 22 C6
Cedar Cl. Wallin SM5 .... 59 F4
Cedar Cl. Warlgm CR6 .... 81 E1
Cedar Cl. Warlgm CR6 .... 101 E8
Cedar Cl. Woki RG11 .... 25 C6
Cedar Cl. Woodh RH2 .... 139 C7
Cedar Ct. 8 Brent TW8 .... 6 D8
Cedar Ct. Egham TW20 .... 12 A4
Cedar Ct. Haslem GU27 .... 208 B6
Cedar Ct. Mortl SW14 .... 7 C3
Cedar Ct. Ottsh KT16 .... 51 C5
Cedar Ct. Sander CR2 .... 81 A8
Cedar Ct. W Norw SE19 .... 19 D5
Cedar Dr. Fetch KT22 .... 94 E4
Cedar Dr. Sunnin SL5 .... 30 A2
Cedar Gdns. Bisley GU24 .... 68 A4
Cedar Gr. Weyb KT13 .... 53 C6
Cedar Gdns. Sutton SM2 .... 59 C4
Cedar Gdns. Woking GU21 .... 69 B1
Cedar Hill. Woodc KT18 .... 76 C3
Cedar Hts. Rich TW10 .... 17 E7
Cedar La. Friml GU16 .... 85 D8
Cedar Lodge. Crawl RH11 .... 201 D4
Cedar Lodge. Milf GU8 .... 149 F2
Cedar Rd. Cobham KT11 .... 73 B5
Cedar Rd. Cranf TW5 .... 4 C5
Cedar Rd. Croy CR0 & CR9 .... 61 E8
Cedar Rd. E Bed TW14 .... 14 D7
Cedar Rd. E Mole KT8 .... 36 E5
Cedar Rd. Farnb GU14 .... 85 C3
Cedar Rd. Sutton SM2 .... 59 C4
Cedar Rd. Tedd TW11 .... 17 A3
Cedar Rd. Weyb KT13 .... 53 A6
Cedar Rd. Woking GU22 .... 89 C7
Cedar Terr. W Norw SE19 .... 6 E3
Cedar Tree Gr. W Norw SE27 ...... 22 B3
Cedar Way. Bellf GU1 .... 109 C4
Cedar Way. Charlt TW16 .... 14 E1
Cedar Way. Sutton SM2 .... 59 E3
Cedar Wlk. Kenley CR8 .... 80 C3
Cedar Wlk. Kings KT20 .... 97 E7
Cedarcroft Rd. Chess KT9 .... 56 F6
Cedars. 2 Brack RG12 .... 27 F5
Cedars. Woodm SM7 .... 78 F5
Cedars Ave. Mitch CR4 .... 41 A6
Cedars Rd. Burph GU1 .... 110 A4
Cedars Rd. Barnes SW13 .... 7 F5
Cedars Rd. Beck BR3 .... 43 F7
Cedars Rd. Morden SM4 .... 40 A5
Cedars Rd. Hawley GU17 .... 64 D3
Cedars The. Ashtd KT21 & KT22 .. 95 D6
Cedars The. Burph GU1 .... 110 A4
Cedars The. Milf GU8 .... 170 E8
Cedars The. Reig RH2 .... 118 D1
Cedars The. Tedd TW11 .... 16 F2
Cedars The. Wallin SM6 .... 60 C6
Cedarville Gdns. Streat SW16 ..... 21 F2
Cedarways. M Bourn GU9 .... 146 B7
Celandine Cl. 1 Crawl RH11 .... 201 B2
Celandine Cl. Crowth RG11 .... 45 C6
Celandine Rd. Hersh KT12 .... 54 E8
Celia Cres. Stain TW15 .... 13 D2
Celia Ct. 7 Rich TW9 .... 6 F6
Celtic Ave. Beck BR2 .... 44 E6
Celtic Rd. Byfl KT14 .... 71 F5
Cemetery La. Lo Hall TW17 .... 34 B2
Cemetery Pales. Brookw GU24 ... 88 A6
Cemetery Pales. Pirb GU24 .... 87 F5
Centaurs Bsns Pk. Brent TW7 ...... 6 A8
Central Ave. E Mole KT8 .... 35 F4
Central Ave. Islew TW3 & TW7 ..... 5 C3
Central Ave. Wallin SM6 .... 60 E5
Central Ct. Addl KT15 .... 52 B6
Central Hill. S Norw SE19 & SE27 22 D2
Central La. Wink SL4 .... 9 B7
Central Par. Felt TW14 .... 15 C8
Central Par. Heston TW5 .... 5 A8
Central Par. King U T KT6 .... 37 E3
Central Par. New Add CR0 & CR9 63 C1
Central Par. Penge SE20 .... 23 D1
Central Pk Est. Hounsl TW4 .... 4 D3
Central Rd. Morden SM4 .... 40 B4
Central Rd. N Cheam KT4 .... 58 A8
Central Sq. E Mole KT8 .... 35 F5
Central Terr. Penge BR3 .... 43 D6
Central Veterinary Laboratory.
  Woodhm KT15 .... 52 B2
Central Way. Felt TW14 .... 15 C8
Central Way. Oxted RH8 .... 122 D8
Central Way. Sutton SM5 .... 59 E3
Central Way. Wink SL4 .... 9 B7
Central Wlk. Woki RG11 .... 25 C6
Centre Terrace Rd.
  Farnb GU14 .... 105 A8
Centre The. Felt TW13 .... 15 B6
Centre The. Felt TW13 .... 15 B7
Centre The. Walt O T KT12 .... 35 A6
Centurion Cl. 4 Sandh GU15 ...... 64 D8
Century Rd. Egham TW20 .... 11 D3
Century Way. Pirb GU24 .... 87 D8
Cerne Rd. Morden SM4 .... 40 C3
Cerotus Pl. Chert KT16 .... 32 F2
Chadacre Rd. Stonel KT17 .... 58 B5
Chadhurst Cl. Dork RH5 .... 136 D4

Chadwick Cl. Crawl RH11 .... 201 B1
Chadwick Cl. Tedd TW11 .... 17 A2
Chadworth Way. Esher KT10 ...... 55 D5
Chaffers Mead. Ashtd KT21 .... 75 F3
Chaffinch Ave. Croy CR0 .... 43 D3
Chaffinch Cl. Crawl RH11 .... 201 D8
Chaffinch Cl. Croy CR0 .... 43 D3
Chaffinch Cl. Horsh RH12 .... 217 D7
Chaffinch Cl. 5 Guild GU15 .... 64 D8
Chaffinch Cl. Tolw KT6 .... 57 A7
Chaffinch Rd. Beck BR3 .... 43 E7
Chaffinch Way. Horley RH6 ...... 160 E4
Chagford Ct. Mitch SW19 .... 20 E1
Chailey Cl. 3 Crawl RH11 .... 201 A3
Chailey Cl. Heston TW5 .... 4 D6
Chailey Pl. Hersh KT12 .... 54 E6
Chalcot Cl. Belm SM2 .... 59 A3
Chalcot Mews. Streat SW16 ...... 21 E5
Chalcott Gdns. Long D KT6 .... 37 C1
Chaldon Ct. Earls RH1 .... 139 E7
Chaldon Common Rd.
  Cater CR3 .... 100 C2
Chaldon Rd. Crawl RH11 .... 201 C1
Chaldon Way. Coulsd CR5 .... 79 F1
Chale Wlk. Sutton SM2 .... 59 B2
Chalet Ct. Thorn H CR7 .... 42 B4
Chalfont Dr. Farnb GU14 .... 85 C2
Chalfont Rd. S Norw SE25 .... 42 F6
Chalford Cl. E Mole KT8 .... 36 A5
Chalford Ct. Surb KT6 .... 37 F2
Chalford Rd. W Norw SE21 .... 22 D4
Chalgrove Ave. Morden SM4 ...... 40 A4
Chalgrove Rd. Sutton SM2 .... 59 D3
Chalice Cl. Wallin SM6 .... 60 D4
Chalk La. Ashtd KT21 .... 96 A8
Chalk La. E Hors KT24 .... 112 F4
Chalk La. Shackl GU8 .... 149 D8
Chalk La. Woodc KT18 .... 76 E3
Chalk Paddock. Woodc KT18 ..... 76 D4
Chalk Pit Rd. Banstd SM7 .... 78 A2
Chalk Pit Rd. Lang V KT18 & KT21 96 C8
Chalk Pit Rd. Sutton SM1 .... 59 C5
Chalk Rd. Farnc GU14 .... 150 E5
Chalk Rd. Ifold RH14 .... 212 C3
Chalkenden Cl. Penge SE20 .... 23 B1
Chalkley Cl. Mitch CR4 .... 41 A7
Chalkpit La. Dork RH4 .... 136 A8
Chalkpit La. Oxted RH8 .... 122 D8
Chalkpit La. Wold CR3 & RH8 ... 102 C1
Chalkpit Terr. Dork RH4 .... 115 A1
Chalkpit Wood. Oxted RH8 ...... 122 D8
Chalky La. Chess KT9 .... 56 D1
Challen Ct. Horsh RH12 .... 217 B3
Challenge Ct. Leahd KT22 .... 95 B8
Challenge Rd. Felt TW15 .... 14 D4
Challice Way. Streat SW2 .... 21 F7
Challin St. Penge SE20 .... 43 C8
Challis Pl. Binf RG12 .... 26 E8
Challock Cl. Bigg H TN16 .... 83 C3
Challoner Ct. Beck BR2 .... 44 D7
Challoners Cl. E Mole KT8 .... 36 D5
Chalmers Ct. Charl RH6 .... 180 E6
Chalmers Rd. Ashf TW15 .... 14 B3
Chalmers Rd. Banstd SM7 .... 78 C4
Chalmers Rd E. Ashf TW15 .... 14 C3
Chalmers Way. Felt TW14 .... 4 B2
Chalner House. 21 Streat SW2 .... 22 A7
Chamber La. Farnh GU10 .... 145 C7
Chamberlain Cres. W Wick BR4 .. 44 B2
Chamberlain Way. Surb KT6 ...... 37 E2
Chamberlain Wlk. Felt TW13 ..... 15 E4
Chambers House. 2
  Streat SW16 .... 21 C4
Chambers Rd. Ash GU12 .... 106 B6
Chamomile Gdns.
  W Heath GU14 .... 84 C5
Champion Cres. For Hil SE26 ..... 23 E4
Champion Rd. For Hil SE26 .... 23 E4
Champness Cl. 9 W Norw SE27 .. 22 D4
Champneys Cl. Belm SM2 .... 58 F3
Chancellor Gdns. Croy CR2 .... 61 B2
Chancellor Gr. W Norw SE21 ..... 22 C5
Chancery La. Beck BR3 .... 44 B7
Chanctonbury Chase.
  Earls RH1 .... 119 A1
Chanctonbury Dr. Sunnin SL5 .... 29 E1
Chanctonbury Gdns. Belm SM2 . 59 B3
Chanctonbury Way.
  Crawl RH11 .... 201 C4
Chandler CE (VA) Jun Sch.
  Witley GU8 .... 170 F5
Chandler Cl.
  Crawl RH10 & RH11 .... 201 D4
Chandler Cl. Hampt TW12 .... 36 A8
Chandler Ct. 2 Tolw KT5 .... 38 B1
Chandler Ct. 8 Wallin SM6 .... 60 B4
Chandlers. Tadw KT20 .... 97 B6
Chandlers Cl. E Bed TW14 .... 14 F8
Chandlers Field Sch.
  E Mole KT8 .... 36 A4
Chandlers Grange. Ash GU12 ... 106 A5
Chandlers Rd. Ash GU12 .... 106 B4
Chandlers Way. 11 Streat SE24 .. 22 A8
Chandon Lodge. Sutton SM2 ..... 59 C3
Chandos Rd. Egham TW18 .... 12 D3
Channel Cl. Heston TW5 .... 5 A6
Channings. Horse GU21 .... 69 E4
Channon Ct. 3 King U T KT6 ...... 37 E4
Chantlers Cl. E Grins RH19 ...... 185 C2
Chanton Dr. E Ewell SM2 .... 58 C1
Chantrey Cl. Ashtd KT21 .... 95 C8
Chantrey Rd. Crawl RH10 .... 201 E3
Chantry Cl. Farnh GU9 .... 125 A2
Chantry Cl. Horley RH6 .... 160 F4
Chantry Cotts. Chil GU4 .... 131 B3
Chantry Ct. Friml GU16 .... 65 D1
Chantry Hurst. Woodc KT18 .... 76 D4
Chantry La. Shere GU5 .... 132 F4
Chantry Rd. Bagsh GU19 .... 47 D2
Chantry Rd. Chert KT16 .... 33 C2

Chantry Rd. Chess KT9 .... 57 A5
Chantry Rd. Chil GU4 .... 131 B3
Chantry View Rd.
  Guild GU1 & GU4 .... 130 E6
Chantry Way. Mitch CR4 .... 40 D6
Chantrys Ct. Farnh GU9 .... 125 A2
Chantrys The. Farnh GU9 .... 125 A1
Chapel La. Addl KT15 .... 52 B6
Chapel Cl. Brack RG12 .... 27 D6
Chapel Cl. Milf GU8 .... 149 F2
Chapel Ct. Dork RH4 .... 136 A7
Chapel Fields. Farnc GU7 ...... 150 D7
Chapel La. Purley CR8 .... 80 A6
Chapel Gr. Addl KT15 .... 52 B6
Chapel Gr. Burgh H KT20 .... 97 C8
Chapel Hill. Dunsf GU8 .... 192 F3
Chapel Hill. Effing KT24 .... 113 D8
Chapel La. Ash W RH19 .... 206 D6
Chapel La. Bagsh GU19 .... 47 D2
Chapel La. Copth RH10 .... 183 F4
Chapel La. For Row RH18 ...... 206 C3
Chapel La. G Book KT23 .... 114 D5
Chapel La. Milf GU8 .... 149 F2
Chapel La. Pirb GU24 .... 88 A4
Chapel La. W Heath GU14 ...... 84 F8
Chapel La. Westc RH4 .... 135 C6
Chapel La. Smallf RH5 .... 114 D5
Chapel Park Rd. Addl KT15 .... 52 B6
Chapel Rd. Camb GU15 .... 65 B5
Chapel Rd. Charl RH6 .... 180 F7
Chapel Rd. Hounsl TW3 .... 5 B4
Chapel Rd. Limps RH8 .... 123 C5
Chapel Rd. Redh RH1 .... 118 F1
Chapel Rd. Rowl GU10 .... 145 E3
Chapel Rd. Smallf RH6 .... 162 B4
Chapel Rd. Tadw KT20 .... 97 D4
Chapel Rd. Twick TW1 .... 17 B8
Chapel Rd. W Norw SE27 .... 22 B4
Chapel Sq. Sandh GU15 .... 64 F6
Chapel St. Farnb GU14 .... 85 D6
Chapel St. Guild GU1 .... 130 D7
Chapel St. 6 Woking GU21 ...... 69 F2
Chapel View. S Croy CR2 .... 62 C3
Chapel Way.
  Burgh H KT18 & KT20 .... 77 C1
Chapelhouse Cl. Stough GU2 .. 108 E1
Chaplain's Hill. Crowth RG11 .... 45 D4
Chaplin Cres. Ashf TW16 .... 14 E2
Chapman House. 2
  W Norw SE27 .... 22 B5
Chapman Rd. Thorn H CR0 ...... 42 A1
Chapman Rd. Worth RH10 ...... 202 C2
Chapman's La. E Grins RH19 .. 185 E1
Chapman's La. E Grins RH19 .. 185 D1
Chapter Way. Hampt TW12 ...... 16 A4
Chara Pl. Chisw W4 .... 7 D8
Charcot House. Rhampt SW15 .... 7 F1
Chard Rd. Harl TW6 .... 3 B5
Chargate Cl. Whit V KT12 .... 54 A4
Charing Ct. Beck BR2 .... 44 E7
Charlbury Cl. 7 Brack RG12 .... 27 F5
Charlecombe Cl. Stain TW18 .. 13 B3
Charlecote Cl. Farnb GU14 ...... 85 D3
Charlecote Gr. For Hil SE26 .... 23 B5
Charles Ct. 5 Tedd TW11 .... 16 E3
Charles Darwin Sch.
  Big H TN16 .... 83 F3
Charles Dickens Ct. Croy SE25 .. 43 A5
Charles Hill. Tilf GU10 .... 147 E6
Charles Mills Ct. Streat SW16 .. 21 E2
Charles Rd. Merton SW19 .... 40 A8
Charles Rd. Stain TW18 .... 13 D2
Charles Sq. Brack RG12 .... 27 C7
Charles St. Chert KT16 .... 32 F1
Charles St. Croy CR0 & CR9 .... 61 C7
Charles St. Hounsl TW3 .... 4 F5
Charles St. Mortl SW13 & SW14 .. 7 E5
Charles Staunton House. 3
  W Norw SE27 .... 22 A4
Charlesfield Rd. Horley RH6 .. 160 F4
Charleston Cl. Felt TW13 .... 15 A5
Charleston Ct. Crawl RH10 .... 202 B3
Charleville Cir.
  Penge SE19 & SE26 .... 23 A3
Charlmont Rd. Up Toot SW17 .. 20 F2
Charlock Cl. Crawl RH11 .... 201 A2
Charlock Way. Burph GU1 ...... 110 B4
Charlotte Cl. Heath E GU9 ...... 125 D8
Charlotte Ct. Crawl RH11 .... 201 C6
Charlotte Gr. Smallf RH6 .... 162 A4
Charlotte Mews. 3 Esher KT10 .. 55 B6
Charlotte Rd. Barnes SW13 .... 7 F6
Charlotte Rd. Wallin SM6 .... 60 C4
Charlotte Sq. 5 Rich TW10 ...... 6 F1
Charlton Ave. Hersh KT12 .... 54 B6
Charlton Ct. Sandh GU15 .... 45 D1
Charlton Dr. Bigg H TN16 .... 83 D2
Charlton Ho. 5 Brent TW8 .... 6 E8
Charlton Kings. Oat Pk KT13 .... 53 E7
Charlton La. Up Hall TW17 ...... 34 D5
Charlton Rd. Charlt SW17 .... 34 C7
Charlwood. New Add CR0 .... 62 F2
Charlwood Cty Fst Sch.
  Charl RH6 .... 180 F7
Charlwood Dr. Oxsh KT22 .... 74 D4
Charlwood House. 1
  Streat SW2 .... 21 F7
Charlwood La. Charl RH5 ...... 180 A5
Charlwood Rd. Crawl RH6 ...... 181 C4
Charlwood Rd. Hookw RH6 .... 181 C8
Charlwood Rd.
  Rusper RH11 & RH6 .... 180 E2
Charlwood Sq. Mitch CR4 .... 40 D6
Charlwood Wlk. Crawl RH11 .. 181 B1
Charlwoods Bsns Ctr.
  E Grins RH19 .... 185 D2
Charlwoods Pl. E Grins RH19 .. 185 E3
Charlwoods Rd. E Grins RH19 .. 185 E3
Charm Cl. Horley RH6 .... 160 E4

Charman Rd. Redh RH1 .... 118 E1
Charmans Cl. Horsh RH12 ...... 218 B5
Charminster Ave. Merton SW19 .. 40 B7
Charminster Ct. 3 Surb KT6 .... 37 D2
Charminster Rd. N Cheam KT4 .. 39 D1
Charmouth Ct. Rich TW10 .... 6 F2
Charnwood. Sunnin SL5 .... 29 F2
Charnwood Ave. Merton SW19 .. 40 B7
Charnwood Cl. New Mal KT3 .... 38 E5
Charnwood Rd. S Norw SE25 .. 42 D5
Charrington Rd. 2
  Croy CR0 & CR9 .... 61 C8
Charrington Way.
  Broad H RH12 .... 216 C3
Charsley Rd. Catf SE6 .... 24 B6
Chart Cl. Broml BR2 .... 44 E8
Chart Cl. Croy CR0 .... 43 C3
Chart Ct. Dork RH5 .... 136 D5
Chart Downs. Dork RH5 .... 136 D4
Chart Gdns. Dork RH5 .... 136 D4
Chart House Rd. Ash V GU12 .. 106 A7
Chart La. Dork RH4 & RH5 .... 136 C7
Chart La. Reig RH2 .... 139 C8
Chart La S. Dork RH5 .... 136 D5
Charta Rd E. Egham TW20 .... 12 C2
Charta Rd S. Egham TW20 .... 12 C2
Charta Rd W. Egham TW20 ...... 12 C2
Charter Cres. Hounsl TW4 .... 4 E3
Charter Ct. King U T KT3 .... 38 E6
Charter Rd. King U T KT1 .... 38 B6
Charter Sq. King U T KT1 .... 38 B7
Charterhouse. Farnc GU7 ...... 150 C7
Charterhouse Cl. Brack RG12 .. 27 E4
Charterhouse Rd. Farnc GU7 .. 150 D6
Charters Cl. W Norw SE19 .... 22 E3
Charters La. Ascot SL5 .... 29 D4
Charters Rd. Sunnin SL5 .... 29 E2
Charters Sch. Sunnin SL5 .... 29 D2
Chartfield Rd. Reig RH2 .... 139 C8
Chartham Gr. W Norw SE27 ...... 22 B5
Chartham Rd. Croy SE25 .... 43 B6
Charts Cl. Cran GU6 .... 174 E2
Chartway. Reig RH2 .... 118 B1
Chartwell. Friml GU16 .... 85 F6
Chartwell. 25 Putney SW19 ...... 19 D7
Chartwell. Wreccl GU9 .... 145 F6
Chartwell Cl. 2 Croy CR0 .... 42 D1
Chartwell Gdns. Cheam SM3 .... 58 E6
Chartwell Gdns. Farnb GU11 .. 105 C2
Chartwell Lodge. 8 Beck BR3 .. 24 A1
Chartwell Pl. Cheam SM3 .... 58 F6
Chartwell Pl. Epsom KT18 .... 76 E5
Chartwell Way. 4 Penge SE20 .. 43 B8
Charwood Rd. Woki RG11 .... 25 F7
Chase Bridge Inf Sch. Twick TW2 .. 5 E1
Chase Bridge Jun Sch.
  Twick TW2 .... 5 E1
Chase Cotts. Shottm GU26 .... 188 C1
Chase Cl. Islew TW7 .... 6 A5
Chase Cl. Merton SW20 .... 39 E7
Chase End. Epsom KT19 .... 76 D7
Chase Gdns. Twick TW2 .... 16 D8
Chase La. Haslem GU27 .... 208 E3
Chase Rd. Epsom KT17 & KT19 .. 76 D7
Chase The. Ashtd KT21 .... 75 C1
Chase The. Coulsd CR5 .... 79 D5
Chase The. Crawl RH10 .... 202 A5
Chase The. Crowth RG11 .... 45 A6
Chase The. E Hors KT24 .... 92 F1
Chase The. Farnb GU14 .... 85 D6
Chase The. Guild GU2 .... 130 A8
Chase The. Kings SL5 .... 98 B6
Chase The. Oxsh KT22 .... 74 C4
Chase The. Reig RH2 .... 139 D8
Chase The. S Norw SW16 .... 22 A1
Chase The. Sunby TW16 .... 35 B8
Chase The. Wallin CR0 & SM6 .. 60 F5
Chasefield Cl.
  Burgh GU1 & GU4 .... 110 A4
Chasefield Rd. Up Toot SW17 .. 20 F4
Chaseley Cl. Oat Pk KT13 .... 34 E1
Chasemore Cl. Carsh CR4 .... 40 F2
Chasemore Gdns. Croy CR0 .... 61 A5
Chaseside Ave. Merton SW20 .. 39 E7
Chaseside Gdns. Chert KT16 .... 33 B2
Chasewater Ct. Alder GU11 .... 105 A1
Chatelet Cl. Horley RH6 .... 161 B4
Chatfield Cl. Farnb GU14 .... 85 C2
Chatfield Ct. Cater CR3 .... 100 D5
Chatfield Dr. Merrow GU4 ...... 110 C3
Chatfield Rd. Thorn H CR0 ...... 42 B1
Chatfields. Crawl RH11 .... 201 B4
Chatham Ave. Hayes BR2 .... 44 F2
Chatham Cl. Cheam SM3 .... 39 F2
Chatham Rd. King U T KT1 & KT2 .. 38 A7
Chathill. Tand RH8 .... 143 B6
Chatsfield. Ewell KT17 .... 58 A1
Chatsworth Ave. Haslem GU27 .. 208 C7
Chatsworth Ave. Merton SW20 .. 39 E7
Chatsworth Cl.
  Coney H BR2 & BR4 .... 63 F8
Chatsworth Cres.
  Islew TW3 & TW7 .... 5 D4
Chatsworth Gdns. New Mal KT3 .. 38 F4
Chatsworth Gr. Hale GU9 ...... 125 B6
Chatsworth Hts. King U T K18 .. 18 E2
Chatsworth Hts. Camb GU15 .... 66 B7
Chatsworth Inf Sch. Islew TW3 .. 5 C3
Chatsworth Jun Sch. Islew TW3 .. 5 C3
Chatsworth Lodge. W Wick BR4 .. 63 C8
Chatsworth Pl. Mitch CR4 .... 40 E6
Chatsworth Pl. Oxsh KT22 .... 74 D6
Chatsworth Rd. 7 Tedd TW11 .. 17 A8
Chatsworth Rd. Cheam SM3 .... 58 E6
Chatsworth Rd. Chisw W4 .... 7 C8
Chatsworth Rd. Croy CR0 & CR9 .. 61 D7
Chatsworth Rd. Farnb GU14 .... 85 E3
Chatsworth Way. W Norw SE27 .. 22 C5
Chattern Hill. Ashf TW15 .... 14 B4
Chattern Rd. Ashf TW15 .... 14 C4

Chatterton Ct. Rich TW9 .... 6 F5
Chatton Row. Bisley GU24 .... 68 A2
Chaucer Ave. Cranf TW4 .... 4 B5
Chaucer Ave. 3 E Grins RH19 .. 185 C1
Chaucer Ave. Rich TW9 .... 7 A5
Chaucer Ave. Whit V KT13 .... 53 A3
Chaucer Cl. Banst SM7 .... 77 E5
Chaucer Cl. Woki RG11 .... 25 F6
Chaucer Ct. Guild GU2 .... 130 C7
Chaucer Gdns. Sutton SM1 ...... 59 A7
Chaucer Gn. Croy CR0 .... 43 C2
Chaucer Gr. Camb GU15 .... 65 D5
Chaucer Gn. Hams Gn CR2 ...... 81 B5
Chaucer La. Farnc GU7 .... 150 D8
Chaucer House. 2
  W Norw SE27 .... 22 C4
Chaucer Rd. Ashf TW15 .... 13 F4
Chaucer Rd. Crawl RH10 ...... 202 C8
Chaucer Rd. Crowth RG11 .... 45 B4
Chaucer Rd. Sutton SM1 .... 59 A6
Chaucer Rd. W Heath GU14 .... 84 F6
Chaucer Way. Row Tn KT15 .... 52 A4
Chavey Down Rd.
  Wink RG12 & SL5 .... 8 B2
Chaworth Rd. Ottsh KT16 .... 51 C4
Chaworth Sch. Ottsh KT16 ...... 51 C4
Chawridge La. Wink SL4 .... 8 C7
Cheam Cl. Brack RG12 .... 27 D4
Cheam Cl. Burgh H KT20 .... 97 B6
Cheam Common Inf Sch.
  N Cheam KT4 .... 58 B8
Cheam Common Jun Sch.
  N Cheam KT4 .... 58 B8
Cheam Common Rd.
  N Cheam KT4 .... 58 C7
Cheam Court Flats. Cheam SM3 .. 58 E4
Cheam Fields Prim Sch.
  Cheam SM3 .... 58 E5
Cheam High Sch. Cheam SM3 .. 58 E6
Cheam Mansions. Belm SM2 .. 58 E3
Cheam Park Farm Inf Sch.
  Cheam SM3 .... 58 E7
Cheam Park Farm Jun Sch.
  Cheam SM3 .... 58 E7
Cheam Park Way. Cheam SM3 .. 58 E4
Cheam Rd. Belm SM2 .... 58 C1
Cheam Rd. Cheam SM1 .... 59 A4
Cheam Rd. E Ewell KT17 & SM2 .. 58 C1
Cheam Rd. Ewell SM2 .... 58 C1
Cheam Sta. Belm SM2 .... 58 E3
Cheapside. Horse GU21 .... 69 D5
Cheapside C of E Prim Sch.
  Ascot SL5 .... 29 E8
Cheapside Rd. Ascot SL5 .... 29 D7
Cheddar Rd. Harl TW6 .... 3 A5
Cheeseman Cl. Hampt TW12 .... 15 E2
Cheeseman Cl. Woki RG11 ...... 25 D7
Cheetah Rd. 1 Farnb GU14 ...... 85 B2
Chelford Rd. Catf BR1 & SE6 .... 24 D3
Chellows La. Crow RH7 .... 143 F2
Chelmsford Cl. Belm SM2 .... 59 A2
Chelsea Cl. Hampt TW12 .... 16 C3
Chelsea Cl. New Mal KT3 .... 39 A2
Chelsea Fields. Mitch SW19 .... 40 D8
Chelsea Gdns. Cheam SM3 ...... 58 E6
Chelsfield Gdns. For Hil SE26 .. 23 C5
Chelsham Common Rd.
  Chelsh CR6 .... 82 A3
Chelsham Court Rd. Chelsh CR6 .. 82 E2
Chelsham Rd. Croy CR2 .... 61 D4
Chelsham Rd. Warlgm CR6 ...... 81 F2
Chelsham Terr. Warlgm CR6 .... 81 F1
Cheltenham Ave. 9 Twick TW1 .. 17 A8
Cheltenham Cl. King U T KT3 .. 38 C6
Cheltenham Villas. Thorn H CR7 .. 42 A3
Cheney Ct. For Hil SE23 .... 23 D7
Cheniston Cl. W Byfl KT14 .... 71 A6
Cheniston Ct. Sunningh SL5 ...... 30 A2
Chennells Way. Horsh RH12 .. 217 E5
Chennestone Cty Prim Sch.
  Sunby TW16 .... 35 B7
Chepstow Cl. Crawl RH10 ...... 202 E6
Chepstow Rd. S Croy CR0 .... 61 F8
Chequer Grange.
  For Row RH18 .... 206 D1
Chequer Rd. E Grins RH19 .... 185 F1
Chequer Tree Cl. Woking GU21 .. 68 E3
Chequers Cl. Horley RH6 .... 161 A4
Chequers Cl. Walt o t H KT20 .. 97 A2
Chequers Ct. 7 Croy CR0 .... 42 E1
Chequers Dr. Horley RH6 .... 161 A4
Chequers La. Walt o t H KT20 .. 97 A2
Chequers Pl. Dork RH4 .... 136 B7
Cherbury Cl. Brack RG12 .... 27 E5
Cherimoya Gdns. E Mole KT8 .. 36 B6
Cherington Way. N Asct SL5 .... 28 E7
Cheriton Ave. Hayes BR2 .... 44 F4
Cheriton Ct. S Norw SE25 .... 42 E4
Cheriton Sq. Up Toot SW17 ...... 21 A6
Cheriton Way. Blckw GU17 ...... 64 D5
Cherkley Hill. Leahd KT22 & RH5 .. 95 F8
Cherrimans Orch. Shottm GU27 207 F6
Cherry Cl. Carsh SM5 .... 59 F8
Cherry Cl. Merton SM4 .... 39 E5
Cherry Cl. Worth RH11 .... 77 D5
Cherry Cl. 7 Streat SW2 .... 22 A8
Cherry Cres. Brent TW8 .... 6 B7
Cherry Ct. Horsh RH13 .... 217 D1
Cherry Green Cl. Earls RH1 .... 140 B7
Cherry Hill Gdns. Croy CR0 ...... 60 F6
Cherry La. Crawl RH11 .... 181 C1
Cherry Orch. Ashtd KT21 .... 76 B1
Cherry Orch. Stain TW18 .... 13 A3
Cherry Orchard Gdns. 6
  Croy CR0 .... 61 D8
Cherry Orchard Gdns.
  E Mole KT8 .... 35 F6

Cherry Orchard Rd. Croy CR0 .. 42 E1
Cherry Orchard Rd. E Mole KT8 .. 36 A6
Cherry St. Woking GU21 .... 69 E1
Cherry Tree Ave. Shottm GU27 207 F7
Cherry Tree Ave. Stain TW18 .... 13 B2
Cherry Tree Ave. Stough GU2 .. 108 F1
Cherry Tree Cl. Farnh GU9 .... 125 C5
Cherry Tree Cl. Sandh GU15 .... 45 D1
Cherry Tree Cl. W Heath GU14 .. 84 C5
Cherry Tree Ct. Coulsd CR5 ...... 79 F1
Cherry Tree Dr. Brack RG12 ...... 27 D6
Cherry Tree Dr. Streat SW16 .... 21 E5
Cherry Tree Gn. Hams Gn CR2 .. 81 B5
Cherry Tree La. Farnc GU7 .... 150 D8
Cherry Tree Rd. Rowl GU10 .... 145 E3
Cherry Tree Wlk. Beck BR3 ...... 43 F5
Cherry Tree Wlk. Coney H BR4 .. 63 F6
Cherry Way. Horton SL3 .... 1 C4
Cherry Way. Up Hall TW17 ...... 34 C5
Cherry Way. W Ewell KT19 ...... 57 D4
Cherry Way. W Ewell KT19 ...... 57 D4
Cherrydale Rd. Friml GU15 ...... 66 D5
Cherryhill Gr. Alder GU11 ...... 104 F1
Cherryhurst. Hambl GU8 ...... 171 B1
Cherrywood Ave. Eng Gn TW20 .. 11 B1
Cherrywood Cl. King U T KT2 .. 18 A1
Cherrywood Ct. 1 Tedd TW11 .. 17 A3
Cherrywood La.
  Merton SM4 & SW20 .... 39 E5
Cherrywood Rd. Farnb GU14 .... 85 B7
Chertsey Bridge Rd.
  Laleh KT16 & TW18 .... 33 D2
Chertsey Bvd. Chert KT16 .... 32 F1
Chertsey Cl. Purley CR8 .... 80 B4
Chertsey Cres. New Add CR0 .... 63 C1
Chertsey Ct. Mortl SW14 .... 7 B4
Chertsey Dr. Cheam SM3 .... 58 E8
Chertsey House. Felt TW13 ...... 16 A5
Chertsey Rd. Egham TW18 ...... 12 F2
Chertsey Rd. Addl KT15 .... 52 B8
Chertsey Rd.
  Ashf TW15 &TW16 TW16 .... 14 D2
Chertsey Rd. Burrh GU20 & GU24 49 C6
Chertsey Rd. Byfl KT14 .... 71 D8
Chertsey Rd. Chert KT15 .... 52 B8
Chertsey Rd.
  Chobh GU24 & KT16 & GU21 .. 50 D1
Chertsey Rd. Felt TW13 & TW16 .. 14 D2
Chertsey Rd.
  Felt TW13 &TW16 TW16 ...... 14 E4
Chertsey Rd. Lo Hall TW17 ...... 34 A2
Chertsey Rd. Shep TW17 .... 33 F2
Chertsey Rd. Twick TW2 .... 16 D7
Chertsey Rd. Windl GU20 .... 48 E5
Chertsey Rd. Woking GU21 ...... 69 F3
Chertsey St. Guild GU1 .... 130 D8
Chertsey St. Up Toot SW17 ...... 21 A3
Chertsey Sta. Chert KT16 .... 32 F1
Chertsey Wlk. Chert KT16 .... 33 A2
Chervil Cl. Felt TW13 .... 15 A5
Cherwell Cl. Bra Hil SL3 .... 1 B8
Cherwell Cl. Tedd KT1 .... 17 D1
Cherwell Ct. W Ewell KT19 ...... 57 C6
Cherwell Ct. W Ewell KT19 ...... 57 C6
Cherwell Wlk. Crawl RH11 ...... 200 F5
Cheselden Rd. Guild GU1 ...... 130 E8
Cheseman St. For Hil SE26 ...... 23 B5
Chesfield Rd. King U T KT2 ...... 17 E1
Chesham Cl. Belm SM2 .... 58 E1
Chesham Cres. Penge SE20 ...... 43 C8
Chesham Ct. Wands SW18 .... 20 D8
Chesham Mews. Guild GU1 .... 130 E8
Chesham Rd. Guild GU1 .... 130 E8
Chesham Rd. King U T KT1 & KT2 38 A7
Chesham Rd. Penge SE20 .... 43 C8
Cheshire Cl. Mitch CR4 & SW16 .. 41 D6
Cheshire Gdns. Chess KT9 ...... 56 D4
Cheshire House. Cheam SM4 .... 40 B2
Cheshire House. Ottsh KT16 .... 51 D4
Chesney Cres. New Add CR0 .... 63 C3
Chessholme Ct. Ashf TW16 ...... 14 E1
Chessholme Rd. Ashf TW15 ...... 14 C2
Chessington Cl. W Ewell KT19 .. 57 C4
Chessington Cl. W Ewell KT19 .. 57 C4
Chessington Comm Coll.
  Chess KT9 .... 56 D3
Chessington Hall Gdns.
  Chess KT9 .... 56 D4
Chessington Hill Pk. Chess KT9 57 A5
Chessington North Sta.
  Chess KT9 .... 56 E5
Chessington Par. Chess KT9 .... 56 D5
Chessington Park. Chess KT9 .... 57 A6
Chessington Rd. Ewell KT19 .... 57 D3
Chessington Rd. W Ewell KT19 .. 57 D3
Chessington South Sta.
  Chess KT9 .... 56 D3
Chessington Way. W Wick BR4 .. 63 B8
Chester Ave. Rich TW10 .... 6 F1
Chester Ave. Twick TW2 .... 15 F7
Chester Cl. Ash GU12 .... 106 B2
Chester Cl. Ashf TW15 .... 14 D3
Chester Cl. Pixham RH4 .... 115 C1
Chester Cl. 1 Rich TW10 .... 6 F1
Chester Cl. Stough GU2 .... 108 F3
Chester Cl. Sutton SM1 .... 59 A8
Chester Gdns. Morden SM4 ...... 40 C3
Chester House. King U T KT1 .... 38 B7
Chester Rd. Ash GU12 .... 106 B2
Chester Rd. Effing KT24 .... 113 B7
Chester Rd. Harl TW6 .... 3 A4
Chester Rd. Hounsl TW4 .... 4 B4
Chester Rd.
  Wimble SW19 & SW20 .... 19 C2
Chester Way. Tongh GU10 ...... 126 F6
Chesterblade La. Brack RG12 .. 27 E2
Chesterfield Cl. Copth RH10 .. 184 C1

Chesterfield Ct. King U T KT6 .... 37 E4
Chesterfield Dr. Hinch W KT10 .. 56 A8
Chesterfield House. 6
  Streat SW16 .... 21 C3
Chesterfield Rd. Ashf TW15 ...... 13 E3
Chesterfield Rd. Chisw W4 .... 7 C8
Chesterfield Rd. W Ewell KT19 .. 57 D3
Chesterfield Rd. W Ewell KT19 .. 57 D3
Chesters. Horley RH6 .... 160 E5
Chesters Rd. Friml GU15 .... 66 B5
Chesters The. King U T KT3 ...... 38 E8
Chesterton Cl. E Grins RH19 .. 205 F1
Chesterton Ct. Horsh RH13 .... 218 A4
Chesterton Dr. Merst RH1 ...... 119 E7
Chesterton Dr. Stan TW19 ...... 13 F1
Chesterton Terr. King U T KT1 .. 38 A7
Chestnut Ave. Alder GU12 ...... 126 E8
Chestnut Ave. Camb GU15 ...... 66 A6
Chestnut Ave. Coney H BR4 ...... 63 E6
Chestnut Ave. Esher KT10 ...... 130 C5
Chestnut Ave. Hampt TW12 ...... 16 A1
Chestnut Ave. Hampt KT8 &KT11 36 F7
Chestnut Ave. Haslem GU27 .... 208 C7
Chestnut Ave. M Bourn GU9 .... 146 A8
Chestnut Ave. 11 Mortl SW14 .... 7 D4
Chestnut Ave. Tats TN16 .... 103 E5
Chestnut Ave. Thame D KT10 .... 36 D1
Chestnut Ave. Went GU25 .... 30 F5
Chestnut Ave. Whit V KT13 ...... 53 C3
Chestnut Ave. Whit V KT13 ...... 53 E2
Chestnut Ave. Worc Pk KT19 .... 57 E6
Chestnut Cl. Addl KT15 .... 52 D5
Chestnut Cl. Alder GU12 .... 105 D2
Chestnut Cl. Ashf TW15 .... 14 B4
Chestnut Cl. Ashf TW16 .... 14 F2
Chestnut Cl. Blckw GU17 .... 64 E4
Chestnut Cl. Carsh SM5 .... 40 F1
Chestnut Cl. Catf SE6 .... 24 C4
Chestnut Cl. E Grins RH19 .... 186 A1
Chestnut Cl. Earls RH1 .... 140 B7
Chestnut Cl. Eng Gn TW20 ...... 11 C2
Chestnut Cl. Graysh GU26 ...... 188 C3
Chestnut Cl. Harl UB7 .... 3 B7
Chestnut Cl. Kings KT20 .... 98 A4
Chestnut Cl. Send M GU23 ...... 91 A3
Chestnut Copse.
  W Norw SE27 & SW16 .... 22 A4
Chestnut Copse. Oxted RH8 .... 123 B2
Chestnut Cl. Beck BR3 .... 24 A1
Chestnut Cl. 5 S Croy CR0 ...... 61 C6
Chestnut Ct. Felt TW13 .... 15 D3
Chestnut Ct. Horsh RH13 .... 217 E2
Chestnut Ct. Hounsl TW3 .... 5 A4
Chestnut Ct. King U T KT3 .... 38 E6
Chestnut Dr. Eng Gn TW20 ...... 11 D2
Chestnut End. Head Dn GU35 .. 187 A4
Chestnut Gdns. Horsh RH12 .... 217 C5
Chestnut Gr. Balham SW12 ...... 21 A7
Chestnut Gr. Islew TW7 .... 6 A3
Chestnut Gr. King U T KT3 ...... 38 D6
Chestnut Gr. Mitch CR4 .... 41 D5
Chestnut Gr. S Croy CR2 .... 62 C3
Chestnut Gr. Stain TW18 .... 13 C2
Chestnut Gr. Westfd GU22 ...... 89 E7
Chestnut Grove Sch.
  Balham SW12 .... 21 A7
Chestnut House. W Norw SE27 .. 22 C5
Chestnut La. Burrh GU24 .... 49 C4
Chestnut La. Weyb KT13 .... 53 B5
Chestnut Manor Cl. Stain TW18 .. 13 B3
Chestnut Mead. Redh RH1 ...... 118 E2
Chestnut Rd. Ashf TW15 .... 14 B4
Chestnut Rd. Guild GU1 .... 109 D1
Chestnut Rd. Horsh RH13 ...... 161 B5
Chestnut Rd. King U T KT2 ...... 17 E1
Chestnut Rd. Merton SW20 ...... 39 D7
Chestnut Rd. Twick TW2 .... 16 E6
Chestnut Rd. W Heath GU14 .... 85 A5
Chestnut Rd.
  W Norw SE21 & SE27 .... 22 C5
Chestnut Way. Bramly GU5 .... 152 A4
Chestnut Way. Felt TW13 .... 15 B5
Chestnut Way. Godal GU2 ...... 150 F2
Chestnut Wlk. Crawl RH11 ...... 181 C1
Chestnut Wlk. Felct RH19 ...... 185 C8
Chestnut Wlk. Up Hall TW17 .... 34 E5
Chestnut Wlk. Whit V KT13 ...... 53 E2
Chestnuts The. Horley RH6 .... 161 A5
Chestnuts The. Penge BR3 ...... 43 D6
Chestnuts The. Walt O T KT12 .. 54 A8
Cheston Ave. Croy CR0 .... 43 F1
Chesworth Cl. Horsh RH13 .... 217 C1
Chesworth Cres. Horsh RH13 .. 217 C1
Chesworth Gdns. Horsh RH13 .. 217 C1
Chesworth Jun Sch.
  Horsh RH13 .... 217 E3
Chesworth La.
  Horsh RH12 & RH13 .... 217 C1
Cheswycks Prep Sch.
  Mytch GU16 .... 86 B5
Chetwode Cl. Woki RG11 .... 25 E6
Chetwode Dr. Burgh H KT20 .... 77 D1
Chetwode Pl. Alder GU11 ...... 126 C7
Chetwode Rd. Burgh H KT20 .... 97 C8
Chetwode Rd. Up Toot SW17 .... 20 F5
Chetwode Terr. Alder GU11 .... 104 E1
Chetwood Rd. Crawl RH11 ...... 200 D2
Chevening Cl. Crawl RH11 ...... 201 C1
Chevening Rd. S Norw SE19 .... 22 D2
Chevington Villas. Bletch RH1 . 120 F3
Cheviot Cl. Banstd SM7 .... 78 B4
Cheviot Cl. Friml GU15 .... 66 C4
Cheviot Cl. Harl UB3 .... 3 D7
Cheviot Cl. Sutton SM2 .... 59 D2
Cheviot Cl. W Heath GU14 .... 84 F1
Cheviot Gdns. W Norw SE27 .... 22 B4
Cheviot Rd. W Norw SE27 .... 22 B3

Cheviot Wlk. Crawl RH11 .... **201** B6
Chevremont. Guild GU1 .... **130** E8
Chewter Cl. Bagsh GU19 .... **47** F3
Chewter La. Windl GU20 .... **48** B6
Cheyham Gdns. E Ewell SM2 .... **58** D1
Cheyham Way. Belm SM2 .... **58** E1
Cheylesmore Dr. Friml GU16 .... **66** D3
Cheyne Ave. Twick TW2 .... **15** F7
Cheyne Ct. Banstd SM7 .... **78** B4
Cheyne Ct. **4** Wallin SM6 .... **60** B4
Cheyne Hill. King U T KT5 .... **37** F5
Cheyne Rd. Ashf TW15 .... **14** D2
Cheyne Way. W Heath GU14 ..... **84** F8
Cheyne Wlk. Croy CR0 .... **62** A8
Cheyne Wlk. Horley RH6 .... **161** A1
Cheynell Wlk. Crawl RH11 .... **200** F4
Chichele Gdns. S Croy CR0 .... **61** E6
Chichele Rd. Oxted RH8 .... **122** E7
Chichester Cl. Crawl RH10 .... **201** E2
Chichester Cl. Dork RH4 .... **115** B1
Chichester Cl. Hampt TW12 ..... **15** F2
Chichester Cl. Witley GU8 .... **170** E5
Chichester Ct. Ewell KT17 .... **57** F2
Chichester Ct. Stan TW19 .... **13** E2
Chichester Dr. Purley CR8 .... **79** F7
Chichester Rd. Ash GU12 .... **106** A3
Chichester Rd. Dork RH4 .... **115** B2
Chichester Rd. S Croy CR0 .... **61** E7
Chichester Terr. Horsh RH12 ... **217** D2
Chichester Way. Felt TW14 .... **15** C8
Chiddingfold Rd. Dunsf GU8 ... **192** C3
Chiddingly Cl. Crawl RH10 ...... **202** B5
Chiddingstone Cl. Belm SM2 .... **59** A1
Chilberton Dr. Merst RH1 .... **119** C5
Chilbolton. Eng Gn TW20 .... **11** E3
Chilbrook Rd. Downs KT11 .... **73** A1
Chilchester Ct. Beck BR3 .... **44** B6
Chilcombe House. **7**
　 Rhampt SW15 .... **19** A8
Chilcroft La. Marl Ht GU27 ..... **208** B1
Chilcroft Rd. Shottm GU27 ..... **207** F7
Chilcrofts Rd. Marl Ht GU27 ... **208** A1
Childebert Rd. Up Toot SW17 .... **21** B6
Childerly. King U T KT1 .... **38** A6
Childs Hall Cl. L Book KT23 ...... **93** F2
Childs Hall Dr. L Book KT23 ...... **93** F2
Childs Hall Rd. L Book KT23 ..... **93** F2
Childs La. **10** S Norw SE19 .... **22** E2
Chilham Cl. Friml GU16 .... **85** F8
Chillerton Rd. Streat SW17 .... **21** B3
Chillingford House.
　 Up Toot SW17 .... **20** C4
Chillingham Way. Camb GU15 ... **65** C4
Chillingworth Gdns. Twick TW1 **16** F5
Chilmans Dr. G Book KT23 .... **94** B2
Chilmark Gdns. Merst RH1 ...... **119** C6
Chilmark Gdns. New Mal KT3 ... **39** A3
Chilmark Rd. Mitch SW16 .... **41** D8
Chilmead. **1** Redh RH1 .... **118** F2
Chilmead La. Nutf RH1 .... **119** D3
Chilsey Green Rd. Chert KT16 ... **32** E2
Chiltern. Woking GU22 .... **89** C5
Chiltern Ave. Twick TW2 .... **16** A7
Chiltern Ave. W Heath GU14 .... **84** D4
Chiltern Cl. Crawl RH11 .... **201** B6
Chiltern Cl. Haslem GU27 .... **208** B5
Chiltern Cl. N Cheam KT4 .... **58** C8
Chiltern Cl. S Croy CR0 .... **61** E7
Chiltern Cl. W Heath GU14 ...... **84** D4
Chiltern Dr. Surb KT5 .... **38** B4
Chiltern Gdns. Beck BR2 .... **44** F5
Chiltern Rd. Sandh GU17 .... **45** A1
Chiltern Rd. Sutton SM2 .... **59** C1
Chilterns The. Sutton SM2 .... **59** B2
Chilthorne Cl. For Hil SE6 .... **23** F8
Chiltington Ct. Horsh RH12 .... **217** D4
Chilton Cl. Walt O T KT12 .... **54** A6
Chilton Rd. Rich TW9 .... **7** A4
Chiltons Cl. Banstd SM7 .... **78** B4
Chilworth & Albury Sta.
　 Chil GU4 .... **131** C3
Chimneys Cl. Wimble SW19 ..... **19** C1
Chinchilla Dr. Hounsl TW4 .... **4** C5
Chine The. Wreccl GU10 .... **145** F5
Chingford Ave. Farnb GU14 ..... **85** D5
Chingley Cl. Catf BR1 .... **24** E2
Chinthurst La. Shalf GU4 & GU5 **130** F2
Chinthurst La. Woner GU5 ...... **152** A7
Chinthurst Pk. Shalf GU4 .... **130** E1
Chinthurst Sch. Tadw KT20 ...... **97** C4
Chippendale Cl. Hawley GU17 ... **64** E4
Chippendale Rd. Crawl RH11 .. **201** B1
Chippenham. **4** King U T KT1 .... **37** F7
Chipstead Ave. Thorn H CR7 .... **42** B5
Chipstead Cl. Belm SM2 .... **59** B2
Chipstead Cl. Coulsd CR5 .... **79** A3
Chipstead Cl. Earls RH1 .... **140** A7
Chipstead Cl. Penge SE19 .... **22** F1
Chipstead Ct. Knaph GU21 .... **68** C2
Chipstead Cty Fst Sch.
　 L Kings CR5 .... **98** F3
Chipstead House. **4** Streat SW2 **21** E7
Chipstead La. Kings CR5 & KT20 **98** B3
Chipstead Rd. Harl TW6 .... **3** A4
Chipstead Sta. Chips CR5 .... **78** F1
Chipstead Valley Prim Sch.
　 Chips CR5 .... **79** A3
Chipstead Valley Rd. Chips CR5 **79** B3
Chipstead Valley Rd.
　 Coulsd CR5 .... **79** B3
Chipstead Way.
　 Woodm CR5 & SM7 .... **78** F3

Chirton Wlk. Woking GU21 .... **69** A1
Chisbury Cl. Brack RG12 .... **27** E3
Chisholm Rd. Croy CR0 .... **61** E8
Chisholm Rd. **13** Rich TW10 .... **6** F1
Chislehurst Rd. Rich TW10 .... **6** E2
Chislet Cl. Beck BR3 .... **24** A1
Chiswick Cl. Wallin CR0 .... **60** F7
Chiswick Comm Sch. Chisw W4 . **7** D7
Chiswick La S. Chisw W4 .... **7** F8
Chiswick Mall. Chisw W4 .... **7** F8
Chiswick Quay. Chisw W4 .... **7** C6
Chiswick Sq. Chisw W4 .... **7** F8
Chiswick Sta. Chisw W4 .... **7** C7
Chiswick Village. Brent W4 .... **7** B8
Chithurst La. Horne RH6 & RH7 **162** F2
Chittenden Cotts.
　 Wisley GU23 & KT14 .... **71** E3
Chitterfield Gate. Harlm UB7 ..... **3** A7
Chitty's Wlk. Stough GU3 .... **108** F5
Chive Ct. W Heath GU14 .... **84** C4
Chivelston. **27** Putney SW19 ..... **19** D7
Chobham Cl. Ottsh KT16 .... **51** B4
Chobham Gdns. Putney SW19 ... **19** D6
Chobham Golf Course.
　 Knaph GU21 .... **68** C5
Chobham La. Went KT16 & GU24 **50** A8
Chobham Park La. Chobh GU24 . **50** B2
Chobham Rd. Chobh GU21 .... **69** E3
Chobham Rd. Friml GU16 .... **66** A2
Chobham Rd.
　 Horse GU21 & GU24 .... **69** D5
Chobham Rd. Knaph GU21 .... **68** B1
Chobham Rd. Knaph GU21 .... **68** D3
Chobham Rd. Ottsh KT16 .... **51** B4
Chobham Rd. **1** Woking GU21 ... **69** E2
Choir Gn. Knaph GU21 .... **68** E2
Cholmley Rd. Thame D KT7 ...... **37** B3
Cholmondeley Wlk. Rich TW9 ..... **6** C2
Chrislaine Cl. Stan TW19 .... **2** E1
Chrismas Ave. Alder GU12 ...... **105** C1
Chrismas Pl. Alder GU12 .... **105** C1
Christ Church C of E Mid Sch.
　 Ottsh KT16 .... **51** D4
Christ Church C of E Prim Sch.
　 Purley CR8 .... **61** B1
Christ Church C of E Prim Sch.
　 Streat SW2 .... **21** F7
Christ Church CE Inf Sch.
　 King U T KT3 .... **38** E6
Christ Church CE Jun Sch.
　 King U T KT3 .... **38** D6
Christ Church CE Prim Sch.
　 Surb KT5 .... **38** A3
Christ Church Mount.
　 Epsom KT19 .... **76** B7
Christ Church　Prim Sch.
　 For Hil SE23 .... **23** D6
Christ Church Rd. Beck BR3 ...... **44** B7
Christ Church Rd. Epsom KT18 . **76** A6
Christ Church Rd. Surb KT5 ...... **37** F3
Christ the King RC Fst Sch.
　 Stan TW19 .... **2** E1
Christ's Sch (East Side).
　 Mortl SW14 .... **7** D4
Christ's Sch (West Side).
　 Rich TW10 .... **6** F2
Christabel Cl. Islew TW7 .... **5** E4
Christchurch Ave. **4**
　 Tedd TW11 .... **17** A3
Christchurch C of E Fst Sch.
　 Vir W GU25 .... **31** B6
Christchurch Cl. Mitch SW19 .... **20** D1
Christchurch Cotts. Vir W GU25 **31** B6
Christchurch Dr. Blckw GU17 ... **64** D6
Christchurch Gdns. Epsom KT19 **76** B8
Christchurch House. **2**
　 Streat SW2 .... **21** E7
Christchurch Pk. Sutton SM2 .... **59** C3
Christchurch Pl. Epsom KT19 ... **76** B8
Christchurch Rd. Harl TW6 .... **3** A4
Christchurch Rd. Mitch SW19 ... **20** D1
Christchurch Rd. Mortl SW14 ..... **7** C2
Christchurch Rd. Purley CR8 .... **80** B8
Christchurch Rd. Streat SW2 .... **21** F7
Christchurch Rd. Vir W GU25 ... **31** C5
Christchurch Way. **2**
　 Woking GU21 .... **69** F2
Christian Fields. S Norw SW16 .. **22** A1
Christie Cl. Lhtwat GU18 .... **48** C1
Christie Dr. Croy SE25 .... **43** A4
Christie House. W Wick BR4 ..... **44** B1
Christies. E Grins RH19 .... **205** D8
Christine Cl. Ash GU12 .... **105** F1
Christmas Hill. Shalf GU4 .... **130** F2
Christmaspie Ave. Flexf GU3 ... **107** B1
Christopher Cl. Ashf TW15 .... **13** E3
Christopher Ct. **6** Croy CR0 .... **43** A1
Christopher Ct. Tadw KT20 .... **97** C4
Christopher Rd. E Grins RH19 .. **185** C1
Christy Rd. Bigg H TN16 .... **83** C4
Chrystie La. G Book KT23 .... **94** B1
Chuck's La. Walt o t h KT20 ...... **97** B3
Chudleigh Ct. **4** Farnb GU14 .... **85** B4
Chudleigh Gdns. Sutton SM1 ... **59** C7
Chudleigh Rd. Twick TW1 & TW2 **16** F8
Chulsa Rd. For Hil SE26 .... **23** B3
Chumleigh Wlk. King U T KT5 ... **37** F5
Church Almshouses. **8** Rich TW9 **6** F3
Church App. Dulw SE21 .... **22** D5
Church App. Egham TW20 .... **32** C6
Church Ave. Beck BR3 .... **44** A8
Church Ave. Farnb GU14 .... **85** C3
Church Ave. Mortl SW14 .... **7** D4
Church Circ. Farnb GU14 .... **85** C1
Church Cl. Addl KT15 .... **52** B6
Church Cl. **6** Epsom KT17 .... **76** E6
Church Cl. Fetch KT22 .... **94** D3
Church Cl. Grays GU27 .... **189** F2
Church Cl. Horse GU21 .... **69** E3
Church Cl. Hounsl TW4 .... **4** F5
Church Cl. L Kings KT20 .... **117** F8

Church Cl. Laleh TW18 .... **33** C6
Church Cl. Milf GU8 .... **149** F1
Church Cl. Pirb GU24 .... **87** F6
Church Cl. For Hil SE26 .... **23** E3
Church Cl. Reig RH2 .... **118** B1
Church Dr. Coney H BR4 .... **63** E7
Church Farm La. Cheam SM3 ... **58** E4
Church Field House.
　 Cobham KT11 .... **73** B5
Church Gdns. Dork RH4 .... **136** B8
Church Gdns. Leahd KT22 .... **95** B7
Church Gn. Elst GU8 .... **148** C3
Church Gn. Hersh KT12 .... **54** C4
Church Gr. Tedd KT1 .... **37** C7
Church Hill. Alder GU11 & GU12 **126** C8
Church Hill. Camb GU15 .... **65** E5
Church Hill. Cater CR3 .... **100** F3
Church Hill. Horse GU21 .... **69** D3
Church Hill. Merst RH1 .... **99** B1
Church Hill. Nutf RH1 .... **119** F2
Church Hill. Purley CR8 .... **60** E1
Church Hill. Shere GU5 .... **133** A4
Church Hill. Tats TN16 .... **103** D5
Church Hill. Wallin SM5 .... **59** F5
Church Hill. Wimble SW19 .... **19** F3
Church Hill House Hospl.
　 Easth RG12 .... **27** A3
Church Hill Rd.
　 Cheam SM1 & SM3 .... **58** E6
Church Hill Rd. King U T KT6 .... **37** E4
Church La. Albury GU5 .... **132** C4
Church La. Ascot SL5 .... **29** D5
Church La. Ash GU12 .... **106** B2
Church La. Binst GU10 .... **145** E3
Church La. Bisley GU21 & GU24 .. **68** A4
Church La. Bletch RH1 .... **120** D3
Church La. Broad H RH12 .... **216** D3
Church La. Brook GU8 .... **190** C8
Church La. Burgh H KT18 & SM7 . **77** E2
Church La. Burst RH6 .... **182** F7
Church La. Cater CR3 .... **100** A3
Church La. Chelsh CR6 .... **82** C3
Church La. Chess KT9 .... **56** F4
Church La. Copth RH10 .... **183** B3
Church La. Crawl RH11 .... **201** F6
Church La. Crond GU10 .... **124** D8
Church La. E Grins RH19 .... **185** F1
Church La. Godst RH9 .... **121** D3
Church La. Graysh GU26 .... **188** C3
Church La. Hambl GU8 .... **171** D2
Church La. Haslem GU27 .... **208** D7
Church La. Head KT18 .... **96** C2
Church La. Hooley CR5 .... **99** B5
Church La. Merton SW19 .... **39** F8
Church La. Oxted RH8 .... **122** E6
Church La. Pirb GU24 .... **87** D4
Church La. Send GU23 .... **90** C1
Church La. Sunnin SL5 .... **30** B4
Church La. Tedd TW11 .... **16** F3
Church La. Thame D KT7 .... **37** A3
Church La. Twick TW1 .... **17** A7
Church La. Up Toot SW17 .... **21** A3
Church La. Up Toot SW17 .... **21** B4
Church La. W Heath GU14 .... **84** E4
Church La. Wall W RH5 .... **176** F1
Church La. Wallin SM6 .... **60** D7
Church La. Warlgm CR6 .... **81** D2
Church La. Witley GU8 .... **170** E2
Church La. Wormly GU8 .... **170** E2
Church La. Worpl GU3 .... **108** E8
Church La. Wreccl GU10 .... **145** F7
Church La E. Alder GU11 .... **126** B8
Church La W. Alder GU11 .... **105** A1
Church Lane Ave. Hooley CR5 .. **99** B5
Church Lane Dr. Hooley CR5 .... **99** B5
Church Meadow. Long D KT6 ... **56** C8
Church Par. Ashf TW15 .... **13** F4
Church Path. Ash GU12 .... **106** A3
Church Path. Croy CR0 & CR9 ... **61** C8
Church Path. Merton SW19 ...... **40** A7
Church Path. Mitch CR4 .... **40** E6
Church Path. **7** Woking GU21 ... **69** F2
Church Pl. Mitch CR4 .... **40** E6
Church Rd. Addl KT15 .... **52** B6
Church Rd. Alder GU11 .... **126** C8
Church Rd. Ascot SL5 .... **29** A5
Church Rd. Ashf TW15 .... **13** F4
Church Rd. Ashf TW15 .... **14** A3
Church Rd. Ashtd KT21 .... **75** D1
Church Rd. Bagsh GU19 .... **47** D3
Church Rd. Barnes SW13 .... **7** F5
Church Rd. Beck BR2 .... **44** E6
Church Rd. Bigg H TN16 .... **83** E2
Church Rd. Broad H RH12 ...... **183** A4
Church Rd. Byfl KT14 .... **71** E6
Church Rd. Cater CR3 .... **100** F3
Church Rd. Cheam SM3 .... **58** E4
Church Rd. Clayg KT10 .... **55** F3
Church Rd. Copth RH10 .... **183** B3
Church Rd. Croy CR0 & CR9 ..... **61** C7
Church Rd. Dunsf GU8 .... **192** D5
Church Rd. E Mole KT8 .... **36** D6
Church Rd. Egham TW20 .... **12** A3
Church Rd. Epsom KT17 .... **76** E6
Church Rd. Felt TW13 .... **15** D3
Church Rd. Fetch KT23 .... **94** A3
Church Rd. Friml GU16 .... **65** D1
Church Rd. Guild GU1 .... **130** D8
Church Rd. Haslem GU27 .... **208** C7
Church Rd. Heston TW5 .... **4** B8
Church Rd. Heston TW5 .... **5** A7
Church Rd. Horley RH6 .... **160** F2
Church Rd. Horley RH6 .... **161** A3
Church Rd. Horne RH6 .... **162** F5
Church Rd. Horse GU21 .... **69** E4
Church Rd. Horsh RH12 .... **218** A5
Church Rd. Hounsl TW7 .... **5** E7

Church Rd. Kenley CR8 .... **80** D4
Church Rd. King U T KT1 .... **37** F7
Church Rd. Leahd KT22 .... **95** B5
Church Rd. Lingf RH7 .... **164** D4
Church Rd. Lo Hall TW17 .... **34** B2
Church Rd. Long D KT6 .... **37** C1
Church Rd. Milf GU8 .... **149** F1
Church Rd. Mitch CR4 & SW19 .. **40** D7
Church Rd. New Mal KT4 .... **38** E1
Church Rd. Purley CR8 .... **60** E1
Church Rd. Rich TW10 & TW9 ..... **6** E2
Church Rd. Rich TW10 .... **17** E4
Church Rd. S Norw SE19 .... **22** E1
Church Rd. Sandh GU15 .... **45** E1
Church Rd. Sandh GU15 .... **64** F7
Church Rd. Shottm GU27 .... **207** F6
Church Rd. Sunnin SL5 .... **30** A3
Church Rd. Tedd TW11 .... **16** F3
Church Rd. Turn H RH10 .... **204** A3
Church Rd. W End GU24 .... **67** F7
Church Rd. W Ewell KT19 .... **57** D3
Church Rd. W Ewell KT19 .... **57** D3
Church Rd. Wallin SM6 .... **60** D7
Church Rd. Warlgm CR6 .... **81** D2
Church Rd. Whytlf CR3 .... **100** F8
Church Rd. Wimble SW19 .... **19** E4
Church Rd. Windl GU20 .... **48** C4
Church Rd. Wink SL4 .... **8** C5
Church Rd. Wink SL5 .... **28** B8
Church Rd. Woking GU21 .... **89** A8
Church Rd. Wold CR3 & RH9 ... **101** E4
Church Rd. Woodh RH2 .... **139** A7
Church Rd. Wrth RH10 .... **202** E6
Church Rd E. Crowth RG11 ...... **45** B5
Church Rd E. Farnb GU14 .... **85** D2
Church Rd W. Crowth RG11 ...... **45** B4
Church Rd W. Farnb GU14 .... **85** C1
Church Rise. Chess KT9 .... **56** F4
Church Rise. For Hil SE23 .... **23** D6
Church Road Ind Est.
　 Crawl RH6 .... **181** E5
Church Road Trad Est.
　 Crawl RH6 .... **181** E5
Church Row. Ripley GU23 .... **91** C6
Church Side. Epsom KT18 .... **76** B6
Church Side. Gatton RH2 .... **118** F6
Church Sq. Lo Hall TW17 .... **34** B2
Church St. Alder GU11 .... **104** F2
Church St. Betch RH3 .... **137** E8
Church St. Chisw W4 .... **7** F8
Church St. Cobham KT11 .... **73** B4
Church St. Cox Gn RH12 .... **195** E1
Church St. Crawl RH11 .... **201** C6
Church St. Crowth RG11 .... **45** B4
Church St. Croy CR0 & CR9 ...... **61** C8
Church St. Dork RH4 .... **136** A7
Church St. Effing KT24 .... **113** D8
Church St. Epsom KT17 & KT18 .. **76** E6
Church St. Esher KT10 .... **55** B6
Church St. Ewell KT17 .... **58** A2
Church St. Godal GU7 .... **150** D4
Church St. Hampt TW12 .... **36** C8
Church St. Islew TW7 .... **6** B5
Church St. King U T KT1 .... **37** D7
Church St. Leahd KT22 .... **95** B5
Church St. Old Wok GU22 .... **90** C6
Church St. Reig RH2 .... **118** B1
Church St. Rudg RH12 .... **214** E8
Church St. Stain TW18 .... **12** E4
Church St. Sunby TW16 .... **35** B6
Church St. Twick TW1 .... **17** A7
Church St. Walt O T KT12 .... **35** A2
Church St. Warn RH12 .... **216** F8
Church St. Weyb KT13 .... **53** A6
Church St E. Woking GU21 .... **69** F2
Church St W. Woking GU21 ...... **69** E2
Church Stretton Rd. Hounsl TW3 . **5** C2
Church Terr. **20** Rich TW10 .... **6** D2
Church Vale. For Hil SE23 .... **23** D6
Church View. Ash GU12 .... **106** A2
Church View Cl. Horley RH6 ... **160** F2
Church Villa. Sunby TW16 .... **35** B6
Church Way. Oxted RH8 .... **122** F3
Church Way. S Croy CR2 .... **81** A8
Church Wlk. Brent TW8 .... **6** C8
Church Wlk. Cater CR3 .... **101** A3
Church Wlk. Cher KT16 .... **33** A3
Church Wlk. Horley RH6 .... **160** F2
Church Wlk. Leahd KT22 .... **95** B5
Church Wlk. Mitch SW16 .... **41** C7
Church Wlk. Reig RH2 .... **118** C1
Church Wlk. **15** Rich TW10 .... **6** D2
Church Wlk. Thame D KT7 .... **36** F3
Church Wlk. W Barn SW20 .... **39** C6
Church Wlk. Walt O T KT12 ...... **35** A1
Church Wlk. Weyb KT13 .... **53** B8
Churchcroft Cl. Balham SW12 .. **21** A8
Churchdown. Catf BR1 .... **24** E4
Churchfield Rd. Reig RH2 .... **117** F2
Churchfield Rd. Walt O T KT12 .. **35** A1
Churchfield Rd. Weyb KT13 ...... **53** A6
Churchfields. Burgh GU4 .... **110** A6
Churchfields. E Mole KT8 .... **36** A6
Churchfields. Horse GU21 .... **69** E3
Churchfields Ave. Felt TW13 .... **16** A5
Churchfields Ave. Weyb KT13 ... **53** B6
Churchfields Prim Sch.
　 Penge BR3 .... **43** D6
Churchfields Rd. Penge BR3 .... **43** E7
Churchill Ave. Alder GU12 ...... **126** C8
Churchill Ave. Horsh RH12 ..... **217** B3
Churchill Cl. E Bed TW14 .... **14** F7
Churchill Cl. Farnb GU14 .... **85** B8
Churchill Cl. Fetch KT22 .... **94** E4
Churchill Cl. Warlgm CR6 .... **81** D7
Churchill Cres. Farnb GU14 ..... **85** B8
Churchill Ct. Stain TW18 .... **13** C2
Churchill Dr. Weyb KT13 .... **53** C6
Churchill House. Banstd SM7 ... **77** F4
Churchill Rd. Guild GU1 .... **130** F8

Churchill Rd. N Asct SL5 .... **28** F7
Churchill Rd. S Croy CR2 .... **61** C3
Churchill Rd. Smallf RH6 .... **162** B3
Churchill Way. Ashf TW16 .... **15** A2
Churchley Rd. For Hil SE26 ...... **23** B4
Churchley Villas. Twick TW2 ..... **16** D6
Churchmore Rd. Streat SW16 .. **41** D8
Churchside Cl. Bigg H TN16 .... **83** C2
Churchview Rd. Twick TW2 ...... **16** D6
Churston Cl. **17** Streat SW2 ..... **22** A7
Churston Dr. W Barn SM4 .... **39** E4
Churt Rd. Beac H GU26 .... **188** C6
Churt Rd. Head Dn GU10 & GU5 **187** C8
Churt Wynde. Beac H GU26 .... **188** D7
Chuters Cl. Byfl KT14 .... **71** F7
Chuters Gr. Ewell KT17 .... **76** F7
Cibber Rd. For Hil SE23 .... **23** D6
Cidermill Rd. Cudw RH12 & RH5 **179** F3
Cidermill Rd. Newd RH5 & RH12 **179** F3
Cinder Path. Woking GU22 .... **89** C8
Cinderford Way. Catf BR1 .... **24** E4
Cinnamon Gdns. Stough GU2 . **109** A6
Cintra Ct. Penge SE19 .... **22** F2
Cintra Pk. Penge SE19 .... **22** F1
Circle Gdns. Byfl KT14 .... **71** F6
Circle Gdns. Merton SW19 .... **40** A7
Circle Hill Rd. Crowth RG11 ..... **45** C5
Circle Rd. Whit V KT12 .... **53** E2
Circle The. Farnc GU7 .... **150** F6
Cissbury Cl. Horsh RH12 .... **218** A6
Cissbury Hill. Crawl RH11 ...... **201** C4
Cissbury House. **6** For Hil SE26 **23** A5
City Bsns Ctr. Horsh RH13 ..... **217** D1
City Prospect. **5** W Norw SE19 . **22** E2
City Wharf House. Thame D KT7 **37** B3
Clacket La. Tats TN16 .... **103** E2
Clairvale Rd. Heston TW5 .... **4** E6
Clairview Rd.
　 Streat SW16 & SW17 .... **21** B4
Clairville Point. **12**
　 For Hil SE23 .... **23** D5
Clandon Ave. Thor L TW20 .... **12** C1
Clandon CE Inf Sch.
　 W Clan GU4 .... **111** A4
Clandon Cl. Stonel KT17 .... **58** A4
Clandon Ct. Farnb GU14 .... **85** D3
Clandon House. **12**
　 King U T KT2 .... **18** B2
Clandon Rd. Guild GU1 .... **130** D8
Clandon Rd. Send M GU4 & GU23 **91** A1
Clandon Rd.
　 W Clan GU4 & GU23 .... **111** A8
Clandon Regis Golf Club.
　 W Clan GU4 .... **111** B4
Clandon Sta. W Clan GU4 .... **111** B6
Clanfield House. **12**
　 Rhampt SW15 .... **19** A7
Clanfield Ride. Blckw GU17 ...... **64** D5
Clapgate La. Slinfd RH13 .... **215** C5
Clappers Gate.
　 Crawl RH10 & RH11 .... **201** D7
Clappers La. Chobh GU24 .... **68** D8
Clappers Meadow. Alf Cr GU6 . **194** A3
Clare Ave. Woki RG11 .... **25** C7
Clare Cl. Crawl RH10 .... **182** C1
Clare Cl. W Byfl KT14 .... **71** A6
Clare Cotts. Bletch RH1 .... **120** B3
Clare Cres. Leahd KT22 .... **75** B1
Clare Ct. Wimble SW19 .... **19** E2
Clare Ct. Wold CR3 .... **102** A4
Clare Gdns. Egham TW20 .... **12** A3
Clare Hill. Esher KT10 .... **55** B5
Clare Hill Golf Course.
　 Esher KT10 .... **55** B4
Clare Hill (No 1). Esher KT10 .... **55** B5
Clare Hill (No 2). Esher KT10 .... **55** B5
Clare House Prim Sch.
　 Beck BR3 .... **44** C7
Clare Lawn Ave. Mortl SW14 ..... **7** D2
Clare Mead. Rowl GU10 .... **145** F4
Clare Rd. Hounsl TW4 .... **4** F4
Clare Rd. Stan TW19 .... **13** E8
Clare Wood. Leahd KT22 .... **75** B1
Claredale. Woking GU22 .... **89** E8
Claredale Ct. Sutton SM2 .... **59** C3
Clarefield Ct. Sunnin SL5 .... **30** A2
Claremont. Shep TW17 .... **34** B3
Claremont Ave. Camb GU15 .... **65** F5
Claremont Ave. Esher KT10 ...... **54** F4
Claremont Ave. Hersh KT12 ..... **54** D6
Claremont Ave. Sunby TW16 .... **35** B8
Claremont Ave. W Barn KT3 ..... **39** B4
Claremont Ave. Woking GU22 ... **89** E8
Claremont Cl. Hams Gn CR2 .... **81** B4
Claremont Cl. Hersh KT12 .... **54** D5
Claremont Cl. **4** Streat SW2 .... **21** F7
Claremont Ct. Dork RH4 .... **136** B6
Claremont Dr. Esher KT10 .... **55** B4
Claremont Dr. Shep TW17 .... **34** B3
Claremont End. Esher KT10 ..... **55** B4
Claremont Fan Court Sch.
　 Esher KT10 .... **55** A3
Claremont Gdns. King U T KT6 . **37** E4
Claremont Gr. Chisw W4 .... **7** E7
Claremont Hospl. King U T KT6 . **37** D3
Claremont Park Rd. Esher KT10 **55** B4
Claremont Rd. Clayg KT10 .... **55** E3
Claremont Rd. Croy CR0 .... **43** A1
Claremont Rd. Egham TW20 .... **12** D3
Claremont Rd. King U T KT6 ..... **37** E4
Claremont Rd. Redh RH1 .... **119** A4
Claremont Rd. Tedd TW11 .... **16** F4
Claremont Rd. Twick TW1 .... **6** C1
Claremont Rd. W Byfl KT14 ...... **71** A7
Claremont Terr. Thame D KT7 ... **37** B2
Claremount Cl. Burgh H KT18 ... **77** C2
Claremount Gdns. Burgh H KT18 **77** D2
Clarence Ave. King U T KT3 ...... **38** D7
Clarence Ave. Streat SW4 .... **21** D8

Clarence Cl. Alder GU12 .... 105 D2
Clarence Cl. Hersh KT12 .... 54 B6
Clarence Cl. Horley RH6 .... 161 D4
Clarence Dr. ☑ Camb GU15 .... 66 B7
Clarence Dr. ☑ E Grins RH19 .... 205 F7
Clarence Dr. Eng Gn TW20 .... 11 C4
Clarence House. Hersh KT12 .... 54 B5
Clarence La. Rhampt SW15 .... 7 F1
Clarence Rd. Bigg H TN16 .... 83 F1
Clarence Rd. Hersh KT12 .... 54 B6
Clarence Rd. Horsh RH13 .... 217 E1
Clarence Rd. Rich TW9 .... 7 A6
Clarence Rd. Sutton SM1 .... 59 B5
Clarence Rd. Tedd TW11 .... 17 A2
Clarence Rd. Thorn H CR0 .... 42 D2
Clarence Rd. Wallin SM6 .... 60 B5
Clarence Rd. Wimble SW19 .... 20 B2
Clarence Rd. Woodh RH1 .... 139 D6
Clarence St. Egham TW20 .... 11 F2
Clarence St. King U T KT1 & KT2 ... 37 E7
Clarence St. ☑ Rich TW9 .... 6 E3
Clarence St. Stain TW18 .... 12 E4
Clarence Terr. Hounsl TW3 .... 5 B3
Clarence Way. Horley RH6 .... 161 D4
Clarence Wlk. Woodh RH1 .... 139 D6
Clarendon Cres. Twick TW2 .... 16 D5
Clarendon Ct. Hawley GU17 .... 64 D3
Clarendon Ct. ☑ Rich TW9 .... 7 A6
Clarendon Cty Prim Sch.
 Ashf TW15 .... 13 F5
Clarendon Gr. Mitch CR4 .... 40 F6
Clarendon Rd. Ashf TW15 .... 13 F4
Clarendon Rd. Croy CR0 & CR9 ... 61 B8
Clarendon Rd. Mitch SW19 .... 20 E1
Clarendon Rd. Redh RH1 .... 118 F2
Clarendon Rd. Wallin SM6 .... 60 C4
Clarendon Sch. Hampt TW12 .... 16 B2
Clarens St. For Hil SE6 .... 23 F6
Claret Gdns. S Norw SE25 .... 42 E5
Clareville Rd. Cater CR3 .... 101 A3
Clarewood Dr. Camb GU15 .... 65 E6
Clarice Way. Wallin SM6 .... 60 E2
Claridge Gdns. Dorman RH7 ... 165 A2
Claridges Mead. Dorman RH7 ... 165 A2
Clark Pl. Crawl GU6 .... 173 F2
Clark Rd. Crawl RH11 .... 201 A1
Clark Way. Heston TW5 .... 4 D7
Clarke Cres. Sandh GU15 .... 64 E7
Clarke's Ave.
 N Cheam KT4 & SM3 .... 58 D8
Clarks Hill. Farnh GU10 .... 124 D1
Clarks La. Titsey CR6 & TN16 ... 103 C4
Claudia Pl. Putney SW19 .... 19 E7
Claverdale Rd. Streat SW2 .... 22 A8
Claverdon. Easth RG12 .... 27 A2
Clavering Ct. Tedd TW1 .... 17 A4
Claverton. Ashtd KT21 .... 75 E2
Clay Ave. Mitch CR4 .... 41 B7
Clay Hall La. Burst RH10 .... 183 C4
Clay La. Burph GU4 .... 110 A5
Clay La. Head KT18 .... 96 B3
Clay La. Horne RH7 .... 163 D3
Clay La. Jacobs GU4 .... 109 E2
Clay La. Nutf RH1 .... 140 D7
Clay La. S Nutf RH1 .... 140 D7
Clay La. Woki RG11 .... 25 F5
Claycart Rd. Alder GU11 .... 104 D4
Claycart Rd. Alder GU11 .... 104 E3
Claydon Ct. Stain TW18 .... 13 A4
Claydon Dr. Wallin CR0 .... 60 E6
Claydon Gdns. W Heath GU14 ... 65 A1
Claydon Rd. Woking GU21 .... 69 A3
Clayford. Dorman RH7 .... 165 B2
Claygate Cres. New Add CR0 ... 63 D4
Claygate La. Hinch W KT10 .... 56 A8
Claygate La. Thame D KT7 .... 37 A1
Claygate Lodge Cl. Clayg KT10 ... 55 E3
Claygate Prim Sch. Clayg KT10 ... 55 E3
Claygate Sta. Clayg KT10 .... 55 E4
Clayhall House. ☑ Reig RH2 ... 118 A2
Clayhall La. Woodh RH2 .... 138 E6
Clayhanger. Merrow GU4 & GU4 110 C3
Clayhill Cl. Brack RG12 .... 28 A6
Clayhill Cl. Leigh RH2 .... 138 A2
Clayhill Rd. Leigh RH2 .... 137 F1
Claylands Ct. S Norw SE19 .... 22 D3
Claymore Cl. Morden SM3 & SM4 40 A2
Claypole Dr. Heston TW5 .... 4 E6
Clays Cl. E Grins RH19 .... 205 E8
Clayton Dr. Stough GU2 .... 108 F4
Clayton Gr. Brack RG12 .... 27 E8
Clayton Hill. Crawl RH11 .... 201 C4
Clayton House. Long D KT7 .... 37 B1
Clayton Rd. Chess KT10 & KT9 ... 56 D6
Clayton Rd. Ewell KT17 .... 76 E6
Clayton Rd. Islew TW7 .... 5 E4
Clayton Rd. W Heath GU14 .... 64 F1
Cleardene. Dork RH4 .... 136 B7
Cleardown. Mayb GU22 .... 70 B1
Clears Cotts. Reig RH2 .... 117 E3
Clears The. Reig RH2 .... 117 E3
Clearsprings. Lhtwat GU18 .... 67 A8
Cleave Prior. Chips CR5 .... 98 E8
Cleave's Almshouses. ☑
 King U T KT2 .... 37 E7
Cleaveland Rd. King U T KT6 ... 37 D4
Cleaverholme Cl. Croy SE25 ... 43 B3
Cleeve Ct. E Bed TW14 .... 14 E7
Cleeve Hill. For Hil SE23 .... 23 B7
Cleeve House. Brack RG12 .... 27 E5
Cleeve Rd. Leahd KT22 .... 95 A7
Cleeve The. Guild GU1 .... 110 A1
Cleeves Ct. ☑ Redh RH1 .... 119 A2
Clement Cl. Purley CR8 .... 80 B3
Clement Rd. Penge BR3 .... 43 D7
Clement Rd. Wimble SW19 .... 19 E3
Clements Ct. Hounsl TW4 .... 4 D3
Clements House. Leahd KT22 ... 95 A8
Clements Mead. Leahd KT22 ... 95 A8
Clements Rd. Walt O T KT12 ... 54 B8

Clensham Ct. Sutton SM3 .... 59 A8
Clensham La. Sutton SM1 .... 59 A8
Clerics Wlk. Shep TW17 .... 34 D3
Clerks Croft. Bletch RH1 .... 120 D2
Clevedon. Whit V KT13 .... 53 D5
Clevedon Ct. Farnb GU14 .... 85 D3
Clevedon Ct. Friml GU16 .... 86 A8
Clevedon Ct. King U T KT1 .... 38 A7
Clevedon Ct. W Norw SE21 .... 22 D5
Clevedon Gdns. Cranf TW5 .... 4 B6
Clevedon Rd. King U T KT1 .... 38 A7
Clevedon Rd. Penge SE20 .... 43 D8
Clevedon Rd. Twick TW1 .... 6 D1
Cleveland Ave. Hampt TW12 ... 15 F1
Cleveland Ave. Merton SW20 ... 39 F7
Cleveland Cl. Walt O T KT12 ... 54 B7
Cleveland Dr. Stain TW18 .... 33 B8
Cleveland Gdns. Barnes SW13 ... 7 F5
Cleveland Gdns. Worc Pk KT4 ... 57 F8
Cleveland Pk. Stan TW19 .... 2 E1
Cleveland Rd. Barnes SW13 .... 7 F5
Cleveland Rd. Islew TW7 .... 6 A3
Cleveland Rd. New Mal KT3 ... 38 E5
Cleveland Rd. Worc Pk KT4 ... 57 E8
Cleveland Rise. W Barn SM4 ... 39 D2
Cleves Ave. Ewell KT17 .... 58 B2
Cleves Cl. Cobham KT11 .... 73 B5
Cleves Cres. New Add CR0 .... 82 C8
Cleves Ct. Epsom KT17 .... 76 F7
Cleves Ct. King U T KT6 .... 37 E3
Cleves Ct. Knaph GU21 .... 68 C3
Cleves Cty Jun Sch.
 Walt O T KT13 .... 53 F6
Cleves Rd. Rich TW10 .... 17 C5
Cleves Way. Ashf TW16 .... 14 F2
Cleves Way. Hampt TW12 .... 15 F1
Cleves Wood. Oat Pk KT13 .... 53 E6
Clewborough Dr. Friml GU15 ... 66 B6
Clewborough House (Prep Sch).
 Friml GU15 .... 66 B6
Clews La. Bisley GU21 & GU24 ... 68 B3
Clifden Centre (Richmond Adult &
 Comm Coll). Twick TW1 .... 16 F7
Clifden House. ☑ Brent TW8 ... 6 D8
Clifden Rd. Brent TW8 .... 6 D8
Clifden Rd. Twick TW1 .... 16 F7
Cliff End. Purley CR8 .... 80 B7
Cliffe Rd. Croy CR2 .... 61 D5
Cliffe Rise. Ock Rid GU7 .... 150 C2
Cliffe Rise. Ock Rid GU7 .... 150 C3
Cliffe Wlk. Sutton SM1 .... 59 C5
Clifford Ave.
 Mortl SW14 & TW10 & TW9 ... 7 B4
Clifford Ave. Wallin SM6 .... 60 C6
Clifford Ct. Wands SW18 .... 20 D8
Clifford Gr. Ashf TW15 .... 14 A4
Clifford House. Beck BR3 .... 24 B2
Clifford Manor Rd. Guild GU4 . 130 E5
Clifford Rd. Croy SE25 .... 43 A5
Clifford Rd. Hounsl TW4 .... 4 D4
Clifford Rd. Rich TW10 .... 17 D7
Clifton Av. Sutton SM2 .... 78 B8
Clifton Ave. Felt TW13 .... 15 C5
Clifton Cl. Cater CR3 .... 100 D4
Clifton Cl. Chert KT15 .... 52 B8
Clifton Cl. Rowl GU10 .... 146 A4
Clifton Ct. Beck BR3 .... 44 B8
Clifton Ct. S Norw SE25 .... 42 E4
Clifton Ct. ☑ Stan TW19 .... 2 E1
Clifton Hill Sch. Cater CR3 .... 100 D4
Clifton Lodge (Brunel Univ Coll
 Twickenham Campus).
 Islew TW1 .... 6 B2
Clifton Mews. S Norw SE25 ... 42 E5
Clifton Parr. Felt TW13 .... 15 C4
Clifton Park Ave. Merton SW20 . 39 C7
Clifton Pl. Banstd SM7 .... 78 A4
Clifton Rd. Coulsd CR5 .... 79 C4
Clifton Rd. Harl TW6 .... 3 B4
Clifton Rd. Hounsl TW7 .... 5 E5
Clifton Rd. King U T KT2 .... 37 F8
Clifton Rd. S Norw SE25 .... 42 E5
Clifton Rd. Tedd TW11 .... 16 E4
Clifton Rd. Wallin SM6 .... 60 B5
Clifton Rd. Wimble SW19 .... 19 D2
Clifton Rd. Woki RG11 .... 25 A8
Clifton Rd. Worth RH10 .... 202 C5
Clifton Terr. Dork RH4 .... 136 B6
Clifton Way. Woking GU21 .... 68 F2
Clifton Way. Woking GU22 .... 69 A2
Clifton's La. Reig RH2 .... 117 D2
Cliftonville. Dork RH4 .... 136 B6
Climping Rd. Crawl RH11 .... 201 B8
Cline Rd. Guild GU1 .... 130 F7
Clinton Ave. E Mole KT8 .... 36 C5
Clinton Cl. Knaph GU21 .... 68 D1
Clinton Hill. Dorman RH7 .... 186 A8
Clinton House. New Mal KT3 ... 38 D1
Clinton House. ☑ Surb KT6 ... 37 D2
Clinton Rd. Leahd KT22 .... 95 C4
Clintons Gn. Brack RG12 .... 27 A8
Clippesby Cl. Chess KT9 .... 56 F4
Clipstone Rd. Hounsl TW3 .... 5 A4
Clive Ct. Streat SW16 .... 21 D3
Clive Ct. Tolw KT6 .... 57 A8
Clive Gn. Easth RG12 .... 27 B4
Clive House. Redh RH1 .... 118 E3
Clive House. ☑ Croy CR0 .... 42 F1
Clive Rd. Alder GU12 .... 105 D1
Clive Rd. Esher KT10 .... 55 B6
Clive Rd. Felt TW14 .... 4 A1
Clive Rd. Mitch SW19 .... 20 E2
Clive Rd. Tedd TW11 .... 17 A4
Clive Rd. W Norw SE21 & SE27 ... 22 D5
Clive Way. Crawl RH10 .... 202 C6
Cliveden Rd. Shep TW17 .... 34 C3
Cliveden Rd. Merton SW19 .... 39 F8
Clock Barn La. Hyde GU8 .... 171 F6
Clock House Cl. Byfl KT14 .... 71 F7
Clock House Cotts. Leahd RH5 . 178 C2
Clock House Ct. Beck BR3 .... 43 E7
Clock House Mead. Oxsh KT11 . 74 B5

Clock House Rd. Beck BR3 .... 43 E7
Clock House Sta. Penge BR3 ... 43 E8
Clock Tower Rd. Islew TW7 .... 5 F4
Clockhouse Cl. Putney SW19 ... 19 C6
Clockhouse La.
 Ashf TW14 & TW15 .... 14 B5
Clockhouse La. Bramly GU5 ... 151 F7
Clockhouse La.
 E Bed TW14 & TW15 .... 14 B5
Clockhouse La E. Thor L TW20 ... 12 B1
Clockhouse La W. Thor L TW20 . 12 A1
Clockhouse Rd. Farnb GU14 ... 85 B4
Clodhouse Hill. Woking GU22 ... 88 D5
Cloister Cl. Rich TW11 .... 17 B3
Cloister Gdns. Croy SE25 .... 43 B3
Cloisters The. Friml GU16 .... 65 D3
Cloisters The. Old Wok GU22 ... 90 B6
Clone The. ☑ King U T KT2 ... 18 B1
Clonmel Rd.
 Tedd TW11 & TW12 & TW2 ... 16 D4
Clonmore St. Wands SW18 .... 19 F7
Close The. Beck BR3 .... 43 E5
Close The. Brack RG12 .... 27 C5
Close The. Brock RH3 .... 137 B5
Close The. Cheam SM3 .... 39 F2
Close The. Croy SE25 .... 43 A3
Close The. E Grins RH19 .... 205 D8
Close The. Esher KT10 .... 55 B3
Close The. Friml GU16 .... 85 C8
Close The. Godal GU7 .... 150 F3
Close The. Horley RH6 .... 161 C1
Close The. Hounsl TW7 .... 5 D5
Close The. Ifold RH14 .... 212 D3
Close The. King U T KT3 .... 38 C7
Close The. Lhtwat GU18 .... 48 A1
Close The. M Bourn GU9 .... 125 D1
Close The. Mitch CR4 .... 40 F5
Close The. Mortl TW4 .... 7 B4
Close The. N Asct SL5 .... 28 D7
Close The. Purley CR8 .... 58 C3
Close The. Purley CR8 .... 61 B1
Close The. Reig RH2 .... 139 B8
Close The. Sandh GU15 .... 64 E8
Close The. Surb KT6 .... 37 E3
Close The. Vir W GU25 .... 31 D4
Close The. W Byfl KT14 .... 71 A6
Close The. Wallin SM5 .... 59 E2
Close The. Woner GU5 .... 152 B7
Closeworth Rd. Farnb GU14 ... 105 E8
Cloudesdale Rd. Up Toot SW17 . 21 B6
Clouston Cl. Wallin SM6 .... 60 E5
Clouston Rd. W Heath GU14 ... 84 F5
Clovelly Ave. Warlgm CR6 .... 101 B8
Clovelly Dr. Beac H GU26 .... 188 D7
Clovelly Pl. Beac H GU26 .... 188 C7
Clovelly Rd. Beac H GU26 .... 188 C7
Clovelly Rd. Hounsl TW3 .... 5 B5
Clover Cl. Woki RG11 .... 25 C7
Clover Ct. Woking GU22 .... 89 D8
Clover Hill. Hooley CR5 .... 99 B6
Clover House. Hounsl TW3 .... 5 C6
Clover Lea. Farnc GU7 .... 150 E8
Clover Rd. Stough GU2 .... 108 E2
Clover Way. Carsh CR4 .... 41 A1
Clover Way. Smallf RH6 .... 162 C3
Cloverlands. Crawl RH10 .... 201 F8
Clovers Cotts. Faygt RH12 .... 199 F1
Clovers End. Horsh RH12 .... 218 A5
Clovers Way. Horsh RH12 .... 218 D7
Clowders Rd. For Hil SE6 .... 23 F5
Clowser Cl. Sutton SM1 .... 59 C5
Club La. Crowth RG11 .... 45 D5
Club Row. Pirb GU24 .... 87 D8
Clubhouse Rd. Alder GU11 ... 104 F5
Clump Ave. Box H KT20 .... 116 C4
Clumps Rd. M Bourn GU10 ... 146 E4
Clumps The. Felt TW15 .... 14 D4
Clyde Ave. Hams Gn CR2 .... 81 B4
Clyde Cl. Earls RH1 .... 119 A2
Clyde Rd. Croy CR0 .... 61 F8
Clyde Rd. Stan TW19 .... 13 E7
Clyde Rd. Sutton SM1 .... 59 A5
Clyde Rd. Wallin SM6 .... 60 C4
Clyde Terr. For Hil SE23 .... 23 C6
Clyde Vale. For Hil SE23 .... 23 C6
Clydesdale Gdns. Mortl TW10 ... 7 B3
Clymping Dene. Felt TW1 & 15 B8
Clytha C. W Norw SE27 .... 22 C4
Clyve Way. Egham TW18 .... 32 E8
Coach House Cl.
 Friml GU15 & GU16 .... 65 E3
Coach House La. Wimble SW19 . 19 D5
Coach Rd. Brock RH4 & RH5 ... 115 E1
Coach Rd. Brock RH3 & RH5 ... 137 A7
Coach Rd. Crawl RH6 .... 181 F8
Coach Rd. Crawl RH6 .... 182 B7
Coach Rd. N Asct SL5 .... 8 E1
Coach Rd. Ottsh KT16 .... 51 C4
Coachlads Ave. ☑ Stough GU2 108 F1
Coachmans Dr. Crawl RH11 ... 201 B2
Coalbrook Mansions.
 Balham SW12 .... 21 B7
Coaldale Wlk. W Norw SE21 ... 22 C8
Coast Hill. Wotton RH4 & RH5 . 134 F4
Coast Hill La. Westc RH4 .... 135 A5
Coates Wlk. ☑ Brent TW8 .... 6 E8
Coatham Pl. Cran GU6 .... 174 F3
Cob Cl. Crawl D RH10 .... 204 C8
Cob Wlk. Crawl RH11 .... 201 A6
Cobb's Rd. Hounsl TW4 .... 4 F3
Cobbets Ridge. Farnh GU10 ... 147 C8
Cobbett Cl. Crawl RH10 .... 202 C8
Cobbett Rd. Guild GU2 .... 108 F2
Cobbett Rd. Twick TW2 .... 16 A7
Cobbetts Cl. Woking GU21 .... 69 B2
Cobbetts Farm. Bisley GU24 ... 68 A4
Cobbetts Hill. Whit V KT13 ... 53 B3
Cobbetts Way.
 Wreccl GU10 & GU9 .... 145 F6
Cobbetts Wlk. Bisley GU24 ... 68 A4

Cobbler's Wlk. Tedd TW11 .... 16 F1
Cobblers. Slinfd RH13 .... 215 D4
Cobbles The. Crawl RH10 .... 201 E7
Cobden La. Haslem GU27 .... 208 D7
Cobden Rd. Croy SE25 .... 43 A4
Cobham Ave. W Barn KT3 .... 39 A4
Cobham Cl. Wallin SM6 .... 60 E4
Cobham Ct. Mitch CR4 .... 40 D7
Cobham Gate. Cobham KT11 ... 73 B6
Cobham Park Rd. Downs KT11 . 73 C2
Cobham Rd.
 Fetch KT11 & KT22 & KT23 ... 94 C6
Cobham Rd. Heston TW5 .... 4 C7
Cobham Rd. King U T KT1 & KT2 . 38 A7
Cobham Sta. Stk D'A KT11 .... 73 E2
Cobham Way. Crawl RH10 .... 182 B4
Cobham Way. E Hors KT24 .... 92 E1
Cobnor Cl. Crawl RH11 .... 200 F4
Cobs Way. Woodhm KT15 .... 52 C1
Coburg Cres. Streat SW2 .... 22 A7
Cochrane Pl. Windl GU20 .... 48 D5
Cochrane Rd. Merton SW19 ... 19 F1
Cock La. Fetch KT22 .... 94 C5
Cock's La. New Gn SL4 .... 8 A6
Cock's La. Wink RG12 .... 8 A6
Cock-A-Dobby. Sandh GU17 ... 45 A1
Cocks Cres. New Mal KT3 .... 38 F5
Cockshot Hill. Woodh RH2 ... 139 B5
Cockshot Rd. Reig RH2 .... 139 C8
Codrington Ct. Knaph GU21 ... 68 F1
Codrington Hill.
 For Hil SE23 & SE4 .... 23 E8
Cody Cl. Wallin SM6 .... 60 D3
Cody Rd. Farnb GU14 .... 84 F3
Coe Ave. Croy SE25 .... 43 A3
Coe Cl. Alder GU11 .... 105 A1
Cogman's La. Smallf RH6 .... 162 D4
Cokenor Wood. Wreccl GU10 . 145 F6
Cokers La. Dulw SE21 .... 22 D7
Colborne Way. N Cheam KT4 ... 58 C8
Colburn Ave. Cater CR3 .... 100 F3
Colburn Cres. Burph GU1 .... 110 A4
Colburn Way. Carsh SM1 .... 59 D7
Colby Rd. Dulw SE19 .... 22 E3
Colby Rd. Walt O T KT12 .... 35 A1
Colchester Vale. For Row RH18 206 E2
Colchester Villas. Thorn H CR7 ... 42 A3
Colcokes Rd. Banstd SM7 .... 78 A3
Cold Harbour La. W Heath GU14 84 F8
Coldharbour Cl. Egham TW20 ... 32 C6
Coldharbour La. Bletch RH1 ... 120 F1
Coldharbour La.
 Dork RH4 & RH5 .... 135 F3
Coldharbour La. Egham TW20 ... 32 D6
Coldharbour La. Purley CR8 ... 61 A1
Coldharbour La. Pyrf GU22 ... 70 F4
Coldharbour La. S Holm RH5 ... 156 F6
Coldharbour La. W End GU24 ... 67 F8
Coldharbour Rd. Croy CR0 .... 61 A5
Coldharbour Sch. Croy CR0 ... 61 A5
Coldharbour Way.
 Pyrf GU22 & KT14 .... 70 F4
Coldshott. Oxted RH8 .... 123 A2
Cole Cl. Crawl RH11 .... 201 B1
Cole Court Lodge. ☑
 Twick TW1 .... 17 A8
Cole Gdns. Cranf TW5 .... 4 A7
Cole Park Gdns. Twick TW1 .... 6 A1
Cole Park Rd. Twick TW1 .... 6 A1
Cole Park View. ☑ Twick TW1 ... 6 A1
Cole Rd. Twick TW1 .... 6 A1
Cole's La. Ockley RH5 .... 178 B5
Colebrook. Ottsh KT16 .... 51 D4
Colebrook Cl. Putney SW19 ... 19 D8
Colebrook Rd. Thorn H SW16 ... 41 E8
Colebrook Rise. Beck BR2 .... 44 E7
Colebrook Pl. Ottsh KT16 .... 51 C2
Colebrooke Rd. Redh RH1 ... 118 E3
Coleford Bridge Rd.
 Farnb GU16 .... 85 D4
Coleford Bridge Rd.
 Mytch GU4 & GU16 .... 85 E4
Coleford Cl. Mytch GU16 .... 85 F3
Coleford Paddocks. Mytch GU16 85 F4
Colekitchen La. Gomsh GU5 ... 133 D6
Coleman Cl. S Norw SE25 .... 43 A7
Coleman Rd. Wands SW18 .... 20 A8
Coleman Rd. Alder GU12 .... 105 D1
Coleridge Ave. Carsh SM1 .... 59 E6
Coleridge Cl. Crowth RG11 ... 45 C4
Coleridge Cl. Horsh RH12 .... 217 E6
Coleridge Cres. Poyle SL3 .... 1 E6
Coleridge Ct. ☑ Rich TW10 ... 17 D4
Coleridge Rd. Ashf TW15 .... 13 F4
Coleridge Rd. Croy CR0 .... 43 C2
Coles La. Capel RH5 .... 178 C5
Colesburg Rd. Beck BR3 .... 43 F7
Colescroft Hill. Purley CR8 ... 80 A4
Coleshill Rd. Tedd TW11 .... 16 E2
Colesmead Rd. Redh RH1 .... 118 E4
Coleson Hill Rd. Wreccl GU10 . 145 F5
Colet Rd. Crawl RH10 .... 201 D3
Coleville Rd. W Heath GU14 ... 84 F5
Coley Ave. Woking GU22 .... 70 A2
Colfe Rd. For Hil SE23 .... 23 E7
Colgate Cl. Crawl RH11 .... 201 B8
Colin Cl. Coney H BR4 .... 63 F7
Colin Cl. Croy CR0 .... 63 A7
Colin Rd. Streat SW16 .... 21 D6
Colin Rd. Cater CR3 .... 101 A4
Coliston Rd. Wands SW18 .... 20 A8
Coll of Liberal Arts. Sutton SM1 59 B5
Coll of St Barnabas. Felt RH7 . 185 F8
Coll of Tech Three Bridges
 Outpost. Crawl RH10 .... 202 A7
Collamore Ave. Wands SW18 ... 20 E7
Collards La. Haslem GU27 .... 208 D6
College Ave. Egham TW20 .... 12 B2
College Ave. Epsom KT17 .... 76 F5
College Cl. Addl KT15 .... 52 D7

College Cl. Camb GU15 .... 65 D7
College Cl. E Grins RH19 .... 185 F1
College Cl. Lingf RH7 .... 164 D4
College Cl. Twick TW2 .... 16 D7
College Cres. Redh RH1 .... 119 A4
College Cres. Sandh GU15 .... 64 E8
College Ct. Croy CR0 .... 62 A8
College Fields Bsns Ctr.
 Mitch SW19 .... 40 E8
College Gdns. Dulw SE21 .... 22 E7
College Gdns. Farnh GU9 ... 125 B2
College Gdns. New Mal KT3 ... 38 F4
College Gdns. Up Toot SW17 ... 20 E6
College Gn. S Norw SE19 .... 22 E1
College Hill. Godal GU7 .... 150 C2
College Hill. Haslem GU27 ... 208 C6
College Hill Terr.
 Haslem GU27 .... 208 C6
College House. Hyde GU8 .... 171 E5
College La. E Grins RH19 .... 185 F1
College La. Woking GU22 .... 89 C8
College Rd. Ash GU12 .... 106 B3
College Rd. Brack RG12 .... 27 D5
College Rd. Crawl RH10 .... 201 E4
College Rd. Croy CR0 & CR9 ... 61 D8
College Rd. Dulw SE19 & SE21 . 22 E4
College Rd. Dulw SE19 .... 22 F3
College Rd. Epsom KT17 .... 76 F5
College Rd. Guild GU1 .... 130 D8
College Rd. Hounsl TW7 .... 5 F6
College Rd. Mayb GU22 .... 70 B3
College Rd. Mitch SW19 .... 20 D2
College Rd. Sandh GU15 .... 64 E8
College Rdbt. ☑ King U T KT1 . 37 E6
College Ride. Bagsh GU19 .... 47 C2
College Ride. Camb GU15 .... 65 D7
College Town Inf Sch.
 Sandh GU15 .... 64 E8
College Town Jun Sch.
 Sandh GU15 .... 64 E8
College Way. Ashf TW15 .... 13 F4
College Wlk. King U T KT1 .... 37 E6
Collendean La. Sidlow RH6 ... 159 F4
Collens Field. Pirb GU24 .... 87 F4
Collette Ct. S Norw SE25 .... 42 E4
Colley La. Reig RH2 .... 117 E3
Colley Manor Dr. Reig RH2 ... 117 D2
Colley Way. Reig RH2 .... 117 E4
Collier Cl. W Ewell KT19 .... 57 B4
Collier Cl. W Ewell KT19 .... 57 B4
Collier Cl. W Heath GU14 .... 84 D5
Collier Row. Crawl RH10 .... 201 D4
Collier Way. Merrow GU4 .... 110 D3
Collier's Wood Sta. Mitch SW19 20 D1
Colliers. Cater CR3 .... 101 A4
Colliers Cl. Woking GU21 .... 69 B2
Colliers Water La. Thorn H CR7 . 42 A4
Collingdon. Cran GU6 .... 174 F1
Collingbourne. Addl KT15 .... 52 B6
Collingtree Rd. For Hil SE26 ... 23 C4
Collingwood Ave. Tolw KT5 ... 38 C1
Collingwood Cl. ☑
 E Grins RH19 .... 205 F7
Collingwood Cl. Horley RH6 ... 161 B4
Collingwood Cl. Horsh RH12 ... 217 B4
Collingwood Cl. ☑ Penge SE20 . 43 B8
Collingwood Cl.
 Twick TW2 & TW4 .... 16 A8
Collingwood Coll. Camb GU15 ... 66 A8
Collingwood Cres.
 Merrow GU1 .... 110 A2
Collingwood Mount.
 Camb GU15 .... 66 A7
Collingwood Pl. Camb GU15 ... 66 A7
Collingwood Pl. Walt O T KT12 . 54 B7
Collingwood Rd. Horsh RH12 ... 217 B4
Collingwood Rd. Mitch CR4 ... 40 E6
Collingwood Rd. Sutton SM1 ... 59 A6
Collingwood Rd. Worth RH10 . 202 D5
Collingwood Rise. Camb GU15 . 66 A7
Collins Rd. Crawl RH11 .... 200 E4
Collis Prim Sch. Tedd TW11 ... 17 B2
Collyer Ave. Wallin CR0 .... 60 E6
Collyer Rd. Wallin CR0 .... 60 E6
Collyer's Sixth Form Coll.
 Horsh RH12 .... 217 D4
Colman Cl. Burgh H KT18 .... 77 C2
Colman House. Redh RH1 .... 118 F3
Colman Way. Redh RH1 .... 118 E4
Colmans Hill. Peasl GU5 .... 154 E7
Colmer Rd. Streat SW16 .... 21 E1
Coln Trad Est. Poyle SL3 .... 1 F6
Colnbrook By-Pass.
 Bra Hil SL3 & UB7 .... 1 D7
Colnbrook By-Pass.
 Coln SL3 & UB7 .... 1 D7
Colnbrook By-Pass. Harm UB7 . 2 C7
Colnbrook C of E Comb Sch.
 Coln SL3 .... 1 D7
Colnbrook Ct. Poyle SL3 .... 1 F6
Colnbrook Ct. Up Toot SW17 ... 20 D4
Colndale Rd. Poyle SL3 .... 1 E5
Colne Bank. Horton SL3 & TW19 ... 1 C4
Colne Ct. W Ewell KT19 .... 57 C6
Colne Ct. W Ewell KT19 .... 57 C6
Colne Dr. Walt O T KT12 .... 54 D7
Colne House. ☑ Redh RH1 ... 118 F2
Colne Lodge. Walt O T KT12 ... 54 D7
Colne Rd. Twick TW1 & TW2 ... 16 E7
Colne Reach. Stan TW19 .... 1 F2
Colne Way. Ash GU12 .... 106 A1
Colne Way. Wray TW19 .... 12 B6
Colne Wlk. Crawl RH11 .... 200 F5
Colnebridge Cl. Stain TW18 ... 12 E3
Coloma Convent Girls Sch.
 S Croy CR9 .... 62 D7
Colonel's La. Chert KT16 .... 33 A3

Colonial Ave. Twick TW2 5 C1
Colonial Rd. E Bed TW14 14 E8
Colonsay Rd. Crawl RH11 201 B3
Colony Gate. Friml GU16 66 D2
Colson Rd. Croy CR0 & CR9 61 E8
Colson Way. Streat SW16 21 C4
Colston Ave. Carsh SM1 & SM5 59 E6
Colston Ct. Carsh SM5 59 F6
Colston Rd. Mortl SW14 7 C3
Coltash Rd. Crawl RH10 202 A5
Coltsfoot Dr. Burph GU1 & GU4 110 B4
Coltsfoot Dr. Horsh RH12 217 E5
Coltsfoot La. Oxted RH8 123 A2
Columbia Ave. New Mal KT4 38 F2
Columbia Ct. New Mal KT3 38 F2
Columbine Ave. Croy CR2 61 B3
Columbus Dr. Farnb GU14 84 C4
Colville Gdns. Lhtwat GU18 67 C8
Colvin Cl. For Hil SE26 23 C3
Colvin Rd. Thorn H CR7 42 A4
Colwood Gdns. Mitch SW19 20 D1
Colworth Rd. Croy CR0 43 A1
Colwyn Cl. Crawl RH11 200 F4
Colwyn Cl. Streat SW16 21 C3
Colwyn Cres. Hounsl TW3 5 C6
Colyton Cl. Woking GU21 69 C1
Combe House. Mortl SW14 7 C5
Combe Hurst. King U T KT2 18 C3
Combe La. Bramly GU5 & GU8 151 D2
Combe La. Chidd GU8 191 A7
Combe La. Shere KT24 & GU4 133 B8
Combe La. W Heath GU14 85 A6
Combe La. Whit V KT12 53 F2
Combe La. Wormly GU8 170 F1
Combe Martin Coll. King U T KT2 18 C3
Combe Rd. Farnc GU7 150 E8
Combe Rise. M Bourn GU10 146 D5
Combe View. Chidd GU8 191 A5
Combemartin Rd. Putney SW18 19 E7
Combermere Rd. Morden SM4 40 B4
Comeragh Cl. Woking GU22 89 A7
Comet Rd. Stan TW19 13 D8
Comforts Farm Ave. Oxted RH8 123 A3
Comfrey Cl. W Heath GU14 84 C5
Comfrey Cl. Woki RG11 25 E8
Commerce Track. Farnb GU14 104 C7
Commerce Rd. Brent TW8 6 C7
Commerce Way. Croy CR0 60 F8
Commercial Rd. Alder GU12 126 C8
Commercial Rd. Guild GU1 130 D8
Commercial Rd. Stain TW18 13 A2
Commercial Way. Woking GU21 69 F2
Commodore Ct. Farnb GU14 105 B8
Common Cl. Horse GU21 69 D5
Common House Rd. Dunsf GU8 192 F4
Common La. Clayg KT10 56 A3
Common La. New Haw KT15 52 C2
Common Rd. Clayg KT10 56 A3
Common Rd. Earls RH1 139 F7
Common Side. Epsom KT18 76 A4
Commonfield Rd. Banstd SM7 78 B6
Commonfields. W End GU24 67 F6
Commonfields. W End GU24 68 A7
Commonside. Fetch KT22 & KT23 94 A5
Commonside Cl. Sutton SM2 78 B8
Commonside Ct. Streat SW16 21 E2
Commonside E. Mitch CR4 41 B6
Commonweal Lodge Sch. Purley CR8 79 D7
Commonwealth Rd. Cater CR3 101 A4
Community Cl. Cranf TW5 4 B6
Como Rd. For Hil SE23 23 E6
Compass Hill. Rich TW10 6 D1
Compasses Mobile Home Pk. Alf Cr GU8 193 F5
Compassion Cl. Crawl RH11 200 E5
Comper Cl. Crawl RH11 200 E4
Comport Gn. New Add CR0 82 E7
Compound Rd. Farnb GU14 85 A2
Compton Cl. Easth RG12 26 E3
Compton Cl. Esher KT10 55 D5
Compton Cl. Sandh GU17 45 C1
Compton Cres. Chess KT9 56 E4
Compton Cres. Chisw W4 7 C8
Compton Ct. Guild GU1 130 F8
Compton Ct. Sutton SM1 59 C6
Compton Ct. 9 W Norw SE19 22 E3
Compton Hts. Compt GU3 129 D6
Compton Place Bsns Ctr. Camb GU15 65 A4
Compton Rd. Croy CR0 43 B1
Compton Rd. Wimble SW19 19 F2
Compton Way. Farnh GU10 126 B1
Comptons Brow La. Horsh RH13 218 A3
Comptons La. Horsh RH12 & RH13 217 F3
Comsaye Wlk. Easth RG12 27 C4
Conal Ct. Streat SW16 21 D3
Conaways Cl. Ewell KT17 58 A1
Concorde Bsns Pk. Bigg H TN16 83 D4
Concorde Cl. Hounsl TW3 5 B5
Concorde House. Addl KT15 52 B6
Condor Ct. Guild GU2 130 C7
Condor Rd. 2 Farnb GU14 85 B2
Condor Rd. Laleh TW18 33 C6
Conduit La. S Croy CR0 62 A5
Conduit The. Bletch RH1 120 D6
Coney Acre. W Norw SE21 22 C7
Coney Cl. Crawl RH11 201 B8
Coney Croft. Horsh RH12 218 B5
Coney Hall Par. Coney H BR4 63 E7
Coney Hill Rd. Coney H BR4 63 F8
Coney Hill Sch. Coney H BR2 63 F7
Coneyberry. Dovgn RH1 139 D5
Coneybury. Bletch RH1 120 E1
Coneybury Cl. Warlgm CR6 101 B8
Coneyhurst La. Ewh GU6 175 D7
Conford Dr. Shalf GU4 130 E2
Coniers Way. Burph GU1 & GU4 110 B4
Conifer Cl. Reig RH2 118 A3
Conifer Ct. 23 Putney SW19 19 D7
Conifer Dr. Camb GU15 66 A6
Conifer Gdns. Streat SW16 21 F5
Conifer Gdns. Sutton SM1 59 B8
Conifer La. Egham TW20 12 C3
Conifers. Oat Pk KT13 53 F6
Conifers Cl. Horsh RH12 218 B6
Conifers Cl. Tedd TW11 17 C1
Conifers The. Crowth RG11 45 A7
Coningsby. Easth RG12 27 C5
Coningsby Ct. Mitch CR4 41 A7
Coningsby Rd. S Croy CR2 61 C2
Conisborough Cres. Catf SE6 24 C5
Conista Ct. Woking GU21 68 F3
Coniston Cl. Barnes SW13 7 F7
Coniston Cl. Chisw W4 7 C7
Coniston Cl. Crawl RH11 200 D4
Coniston Cl. Farnb GU14 84 E3
Coniston Cl. Friml GU15 66 C3
Coniston Cl. Horsh RH12 218 B6
Coniston Cl. W Barn SM4 39 D3
Coniston Ct. Beck BR3 44 C8
Coniston Ct. Chess KT9 56 E7
Coniston Ct. Lhtwat GU18 48 B1
Coniston Ct. Penge SE26 23 B2
Coniston Ct. 3 Wallin SM6 60 B6
Coniston Ct. Whit V KT13 53 B4
Coniston Dr. Hale GU9 125 A6
Coniston Gdns. Sutton SM2 59 D4
Coniston Rd. Catf BR1 24 E2
Coniston Rd. Coulsd CR5 79 C3
Coniston Rd. Croy CR0 43 A2
Coniston Rd. Old Wok GU22 90 B7
Coniston Rd. Twick TW2 5 B1
Coniston Way. Chess KT9 56 E7
Coniston Way. Redh RH1 118 E2
Coniston Way. Thor L TW20 12 B1
Connaught Ave. Ashf TW15 13 E4
Connaught Ave. Hounsl TW4 4 E3
Connaught Ave. Mortl SW14 7 C3
Connaught Bsns Ctr. Mitch CR4 40 F4
Connaught Bsns Ctr. Wallin CR9 60 F4
Connaught Cl. Carsh SM1 59 D8
Connaught Cres. Brookw GU24 87 F7
Connaught Gdns. Crawl RH11 201 D8
Connaught Gdns. Morden SM4 40 C5
Connaught Rd. Alder GU12 105 D2
Connaught Rd. Bagsh GU19 47 C3
Connaught Rd. Brookw GU24 87 F7
Connaught Rd. Camb GU15 65 F5
Connaught Rd. Carsh SM1 59 D8
Connaught Rd. New Mal KT3 38 E5
Connaught Rd. 4 Rich TW10 6 F2
Connaught Rd. Tedd TW11 & TW12 16 D3
Connaught Sch. Alder GU12 126 E7
Connell House. 6 Wallin SM6 60 C5
Connington. 2 King U T KT1 38 A7
Connop Way. Friml GU16 65 F3
Conquest Rd. Addl KT15 52 A5
Conrad Dr. N Cheam KT4 39 D1
Consfield Ave. W Barn KT3 39 A4
Consort Dr. Camb GU15 66 C7
Consort Mews. Islew TW7 5 D2
Consort Way. Horley RH6 161 A3
Consort Way E. Horley RH6 161 B2
Constable Gdns. Islew TW7 5 D2
Constable Rd. Crawl RH10 201 F2
Constable Way. Sandh GU15 64 E6
Constable Wlk. Dulw SE21 22 E5
Constance Cres. Hayes BR2 44 F1
Constance Rd. Sutton SM1 59 C6
Constance Rd. Thorn H CR0 42 B2
Constance Rd. Twick TW2 16 B8
Constant Rd. Farnb GU14 84 A2
Constantine House. Streat SW2 22 B7
Constitution Hill. Woking GU22 89 E8
Contley House Hotel. Woki RG11 25 B8
Control Tower Rd. Crawl RH6 181 D6
Control Tower Rd. Harl TW6 3 B4
Convent Cl. Beck BR3 24 C1
Convent Hill. S Norw SE19 22 C2
Convent of the Sacred Heart Digby-Stuart Coll. Rhampt SW15 7 F2
Convent Rd. Ashf TW15 14 B3
Conway Cl. Friml GU16 65 F1
Conway Dr. Ashf TW15 14 C2
Conway Dr. Sutton SM2 59 B4
Conway Dr. W Heath GU14 84 D4
Conway Gdns. Mitch CR4 41 E5
Conway House. Dovgn RH2 139 A4
Conway House. 6 Streat SW2 21 E7
Conway Rd. Felt TW13 15 D3
Conway Rd. Harl TW6 3 B4
Conway Rd. Twick TW4 16 A8
Conway Rd. Wimble SW20 39 C8
Conway Wlk. Hampt TW12 15 F2
Conyer's Rd. Streat SW16 21 D3
Conyers Cl. Hersh KT12 54 D5
Cook Rd. Crawl RH10 201 F4
Cook Rd. Horsh RH12 217 D6
Cookes La. Cheam SM3 58 E4
Cookham Cl. Sandh GU17 45 C1
Cookham Rd. Binf RG12 26 E7
Cooks Hill. Buck Gn RH12 214 A8
Cooks Mead. Rusper RH12 199 D7
Coolarne Rise. Camb GU15 66 A6
Coolgardie Rd. Ashf TW15 14 C3
Coolham Ct. Crawl RH11 200 F6
Coolhurst La. Horsh RH13 218 A1
Coombe Ave. S Croy CR0 61 E6
Coombe Bank. King U T KT2 & KT3 38 E8
Coombe Cl. Crawl RH11 181 D1
Coombe Cl. Friml GU16 85 D8
Coombe Cl. Hounsl TW3 5 A3
Coombe Cotts. Betch RH3 116 D4
Coombe Cres. Hampt TW12 15 E1
Coombe Ct. Beck BR3 43 F8
Coombe Ct. Tadw KT20 97 C4
Coombe Dr. Row Tn KT15 51 F4
Coombe End. King U T KT2 18 D1
Coombe Gdns. New Mal KT3 38 F5
Coombe Gdns. Wimble SW20 39 A8
Coombe Girls Sch. King U T KT3 38 D7
Coombe Hall Sch. E Grins RH19 205 D6
Coombe Hill Glade. King U T KT2 18 E1
Coombe Hill Golf Course. King U T KT2 18 C1
Coombe Hill Inf Sch. King U T KT3 38 D8
Coombe Hill Jun Sch. King U T KT3 38 D8
Coombe Hill Rd. E Grins RH19 205 D6
Coombe Hill Rd. King U T KT2 18 E1
Coombe House Chase. King U T KT3 38 D8
Coombe La. S Croy CR0 62 B5
Coombe La. Wimble SW20 39 B7
Coombe La. Worpl GU3 108 D7
Coombe La W. King U T KT2 18 E1
Coombe Lane Flyover. King U T SW20 38 F8
Coombe Manor. Bisley GU24 68 B4
Coombe Neville. King U T KT2 18 D1
Coombe Pine. Brack RG12 27 D3
Coombe Pk. King U T KT2 18 D3
Coombe Rd. Croy CR0 61 E6
Coombe Rd. For Hil SE26 23 B4
Coombe Rd. Hampt TW12 15 F2
Coombe Rd. King U T KT2 38 A8
Coombe Rd. King U T KT3 38 E6
Coombe Rd. S Croy CR0 & CR2 61 E6
Coombe Ridings. King U T KT2 18 C3
Coombe Rise. King U T KT2 38 C8
Coombe The. Betch RH3 116 D4
Coombe Way. Byfl KT14 71 F7
Coombe Wlk. Sutton SM1 59 B7
Coombe Wood Golf Course. King U T KT2 18 C1
Coombe Wood Hill. Purley CR8 80 C6
Coombe Wood Rd. King U T KT2 18 C3
Coombefield Cl. New Mal KT3 38 E4
Coombelands Bsns Pk. Row Tn KT15 52 A4
Coombelands La. Row Tn KT15 52 A4
Coomber Way. Wallin CR0 & CR4 41 D2
Coombes The. Bramly GU5 152 A5
Cooper Cl. Smallf RH6 162 A3
Cooper Cres. Carsh SM5 59 F7
Cooper Ct. Farnb GU14 85 C4
Cooper House. Hounsl TW4 4 F4
Cooper House. 7 W Norw SW27 22 B3
Cooper Rd. Croy CR0 & CR9 61 B6
Cooper Rd. Guild GU1 130 F8
Cooper Rd. Windl GU20 48 D4
Cooper Row. Crawl RH10 201 D3
Cooper's Hill La. Eng Gn TW20 11 D4
Cooper's Hill Rd. Nutf RH1 120 A1
Cooper's Hill Rd. S Nutf RH1 120 A1
Cooper's Hill Rd. S Nutf RH1 141 B5
Cooper's Terr. Farnh GU9 125 C3
Cooper's Yd. W Norw SE19 22 E2
Coopers Cl. Egham TW18 12 E3
Coopers Hill Dr. Pirb GU24 87 C7
Coopers Rise. Ock Rid GU7 150 C3
Cootes Ave. Horsh RH12 217 A3
Copeland House. Up Toot SW17 20 D4
Copelands. Beck BR3 23 F1
Copelands Cl. Friml GU15 66 D4
Copeman Cl. For Hil SE26 23 C3
Copenhagen Way. Walt O T KT12 54 B7
Copenhagen Wlk. Crowth RG11 45 B4
Copers Cope Rd. Beck BR3 23 F1
Copleigh Dr. Kings KT20 97 E7
Copley Cl. Knaph GU21 88 E8
Copley Cl. Redh RH1 118 E3
Copley Pk. Streat SW16 21 F2
Copley Way. Tadw KT20 97 D7
Copnall Way. Horsh RH12 217 C2
Coppard Gdns. Chess KT9 56 C4
Copped Hall Dr. Friml GU15 66 C6
Copped Hall Way. Friml GU15 66 C6
Coppedhall. 1 Dulw SE21 22 D6
Copper Beech Cl. Woking GU22 89 B6
Copper Beeches. Hounsl TW7 5 D6
Copper Cl. S Norw SE19 22 F1
Copper Mill Dr. Islew TW7 5 F5
Copper Mill La. Wimble SW17 20 C4
Copperfield Ave. Sandh GU15 45 E2
Copperfield Cl. Purley CR2 & CR8 80 C8
Copperfield Ct. Leahd KT22 95 A6
Copperfield Pl. Horsh RH12 217 B4
Copperfield Rise. Row Tn KT15 51 F4
Copperfields. Beck BR3 44 C8
Copperfields. Fetch KT22 94 C5
Coppermill Rd. Horton TW19 1 B2
Coppice Cl. Heath E GU9 125 E6
Coppice Cl. Stough GU2 108 D2
Coppice Cl. W Barn SW20 39 C6
Coppice Dr. Wray TW19 11 D8
Coppice La. Reig RH2 117 F3
Coppice Rd. Horsh RH12 218 A5
Coppice The. Ashf TW15 14 B2
Coppice The. Crawl D RH10 204 B8
Coppice Wlk. Crawl RH10 202 A7
Coppin House. Streat SW2 22 B7
Coppins Cl. S Croy CR0 61 E6
Coppins The. New Add CR0 63 B4
Coppsfield. E Mole KT8 36 A6
Copse Ave. Heath E GU9 125 E8
Copse Ave. W Wick BR4 63 B7
Copse Cl. Camb GU15 66 A6
Copse Cl. Chil GU4 131 C3
Copse Cl. Crawl D RH10 204 B8
Copse Cl. E Grins RH19 186 A3
Copse Cl. Horsh RH12 217 F6
Copse Cres. Crawl RH11 201 C7
Copse Dr. Woki RG11 25 A7
Copse Edge. Cran GU6 174 F4
Copse Edge. Elst GU8 148 C3
Copse Edge Ave. Epsom KT17 76 F6
Copse End. Camb GU15 66 A6
Copse Glade. Surb KT6 37 D1
Copse Hill. Purley CR8 79 E6
Copse Hill. Sutton SM2 59 B3
Copse Hill. Wimble SW20 19 B1
Copse La. Horley RH6 161 D4
Copse Rd. Cobham KT11 73 B6
Copse Rd. Knaph GU21 68 F1
Copse Rd. Linch GU27 207 D5
Copse Rd. Woodh RH2 139 D7
Copse Side. Farnc GU7 129 D1
Copse The. Cater CR3 101 A1
Copse The. Farnb GU14 84 D3
Copse The. Fetch KT22 & KT23 94 B4
Copse The. Rowl GU10 145 F4
Copse The. S Nutf RH1 140 E7
Copse View. S Croy CR2 62 E2
Copse Way. Wreccl GU10 145 F6
Copse Wood Ct. Redh RH1 118 E3
Copsem Dr. Esher KT10 55 B4
Copsem La. Esher KT10 55 C3
Copsem La. Oxsh KT22 55 C1
Copsem Way. Esher KT10 55 C4
Copsen Wood. Oxsh KT22 74 C8
Copsleigh Ave. Earls RH1 140 A3
Copsleigh Cl. Earls RH1 140 A3
Copsleigh Way. Earls RH1 140 A3
Copt Hill La. Kings KT20 97 F7
Copthall Gdns. Twick TW1 16 F7
Copthall Way. Woodhm KT15 52 A1
Copthorne Ave. Streat SW12 21 D8
Copthorne Bank. Burst RH10 & RH6 183 C4
Copthorne CE (Controlled) Sch. Copth RH10 183 B3
Copthorne Chase. Ashf TW15 13 F4
Copthorne Cl. Shep TW17 34 C3
Copthorne Common Rd. Copth RH10 183 C3
Copthorne Dr. Lhtwat GU18 48 B1
Copthorne Rd. Copth RH10 182 F1
Copthorne Rd. Crawl RH10 202 E8
Copthorne Rd. Dome RH10 & RH19 184 D4
Copthorne Rd. Felb RH10 & RH19 184 D4
Copthorne Rd. Leahd KT22 95 B7
Copthorne Rise. Sander CR8 80 D6
Copthorne Sch Trust Ltd. Copth RH10 183 E3
Copthorne Way. Copth RH10 182 F2
Copyhold Rd. E Grins RH19 205 D8
Corban Rd. Hounsl TW3 5 A4
Corbet Cl. Carsh CR4 & SM6 60 A8
Corbet Rd. Ewell KT17 57 E1
Corbett Cl. New Add CR0 82 D7
Corbett Ct. Catf SE6 23 F4
Corbett Dr. Lhtwat GU18 66 F7
Corbiere Ct. Wimble SW19 19 D2
Corby Cl. Crawl RH11 200 E3
Corby Dr. Eng Gn TW20 11 C2
Cordelia Croft. Wink RG12 27 E8
Cordelia Gdns. Ash V GU12 85 F1
Cordelia Gdns. Stan TW19 13 E8
Cordelia Rd. Stan TW19 13 E8
Corderoy Pl. Chert KT16 32 F3
Cordrey Gdns. Coulsd CR5 79 E4
Cordrey House. Chert KT15 52 B8
Cordwalles Cty Mid Sch. Camb GU15 65 F8
Cordwalles Rd. Camb GU15 65 F8
Corfe Cl. Ashtd KT21 75 C1
Corfe Gdns. Friml GU16 65 F1
Coriander Cl. W Heath GU14 84 C4
Coriander Cres. Stough GU2 109 A6
Corium House. Godal GU7 150 F5
Cork Tree House. 3 W Norw SW27 22 B3
Corkran Rd. Surb KT6 37 E2
Corkscrew Hill. W Wick BR4 63 D7
Cormongers La. Redh RH1 119 D2
Cormorant Ct. 12 W Norw SE21 22 D6
Cormorant Pl. Sandh GU15 64 E7
Cornbunting Cl. Sandh GU15 64 D8
Cornelia Cl. Farnb GU14 84 D3
Corner Fielde. Streat SW2 21 F7
Cornerside. Littlt TW15 14 C1
Cornerstone Sch The. Epsom KT18 76 C6
Corney Rd. Chisw W4 7 E8
Cornfield Rd. Reig RH2 139 C8
Cornfields. Farnc GU7 151 A8
Cornflower La. Croy CR0 43 D1
Cornford Gr. Up Toot SW12 21 B6
Cornhill Cl. Chert KT15 52 B8
Cornish Gr. Penge SE20 43 B8
Cornwall Ave. Byfl KT14 71 F5
Cornwall Ave. Clayg KT10 55 F3
Cornwall Cl. Camb GU15 65 F7
Cornwall Gdns. 6 E Grins RH19 205 F8
Cornwall Rd. Belm SM2 59 A2
Cornwall Rd. Thorn H CR0 & CR9 61 B8
Cornwall Rd. Twick TW1 17 A7
Cornwall Way. Egham TW18 12 E2
Cornwallis Cl. Cater CR3 100 C5
Coronation Cotts. Chidd GU8 191 C5
Coronation Rd. Alder GU11 126 B7
Coronation Rd. Ascot SL5 29 A2
Coronation Rd. Brack SL5 29 A2
Coronation Rd. E Grins RH19 205 E7
Coronation Sq. Woki RG11 25 D7
Coronet Cl. Crawl RH10 202 E7
Coronet The. Horley RH6 161 C1
Corporation Ave. Hounsl TW4 4 E3
Corpus Christi RC Prim Sch. King U T KT3 38 C6
Corrib Dr. Carsh SM1 59 E5
Corrie Gdns. Went GU25 31 C2
Corrie Rd. Addl KT15 52 D6
Corrie Rd. Old Wok GU22 90 C7
Corrigan Ave. Wallin CR5 79 A5
Corry Rd. Beac H GU26 188 C6
Corsair Cl. Stan TW19 13 E8
Corsair Rd. Stan TW19 13 E8
Corscombe Cl. King U T KT2 18 C3
Corsehill St. Streat SW16 21 C2
Corsham Way. Crowth RG11 45 B5
Corsletts Ave. Broad H RH12 216 D3
Corsten Hollow. 4 Earls RH1 139 F8
Corunna Dr. Horsh RH13 217 F2
Cosdach Ave. Wallin SM6 60 D3
Cosedge Cres. Croy CR0 & CR9 61 B5
Cosford Rd. Bowl Gn GU8 169 E4
Coteford St. Up Toot SW17 21 A4
Cotelands. S Croy CR0 61 E7
Cotford Rd. S Norw CR7 42 C5
Cotherstone. Epsom KT19 57 D2
Cotherstone Rd. Streat SW2 21 F7
Cotland Acres. Woodh RH1 139 D7
Cotsford Ave. New Mal KT3 38 D4
Cotswold Cl. Crawl RH11 201 B6
Cotswold Cl. King U T KT2 18 C2
Cotswold Cl. Stain TW18 13 A3
Cotswold Cl. W Heath GU14 84 E7
Cotswold Ct. Horsh RH13 217 E2
Cotswold Rd. Hampt TW12 16 A2
Cotswold Rd. Sutton SM2 59 B1
Cotswold St. W Norw SE27 22 B4
Cotswold Way. N Cheam KT4 58 C8
Cottage Cl. Horsh RH12 218 B6
Cottage Cl. Ottsh KT16 51 C4
Cottage Farm Way. Egham TW20 32 C6
Cottage Gdns. Farnb GU14 84 F4
Cottage Gr. King U T KT6 37 D3
Cottage Pl. Copth RH10 183 E3
Cottage Rd. W Ewell KT19 57 D3
Cottage Rd. W Ewell KT19 57 D3
Cottenham Dr. Wimble SW20 19 B1
Cottenham Par. Wimble SW20 39 B7
Cottenham Park C of E Prim Sch. Wimble SW20 39 A8
Cottenham Park Rd. Wimble SW20 39 B8
Cottenham Pl. Wimble SW20 19 B1
Cottenhams. Blind H RH7 163 E8
Cotterill Rd. Surb KT6 37 F1
Cottesbrooke Cl. Poyle SL3 1 D6
Cottesmore. Easth RG12 27 A2
Cottimore Ave. Walt O T KT12 35 B1
Cottimore Cres. Walt O T KT12 35 B2
Cottimore La. Walt O T KT12 35 B2
Cottimore La. Walt O T KT12 35 D1
Cottimore Terr. Walt O T KT12 35 B2
Cottingham Ave. Horsh RH12 217 D7
Cottingham Rd. Penge SE20 23 D1
Cottington Rd. Felt TW13 15 D4
Cotton Hill. Catf BR1 24 D4
Cotton House. 18 Streat SW12 21 E8
Cotton Row. For Gn RH5 176 C8
Cotton Wlk. Crawl RH11 201 A1
Cottongrass Cl. Croy CR0 43 D1
Cottrell Flats. Farnb GU14 105 D8
Cotts Wood Dr. Burph GU4 110 A6
Couchmore Ave. Hinch W KT10 55 E8
Coulsdon C of E Prim Sch. Coulsd CR5 79 F1
Coulsdon Court Municipal Golf Course. Purley CR5 79 F3
Coulsdon Court Rd. Coulsd CR5 79 F3
Coulsdon House. 5 Streat SW2 21 E7
Coulsdon La. Chips CR5 99 A8
Coulsdon Pl. Cater CR3 100 D5
Coulsdon Rd. Cater CR3 & CR5 100 B7
Coulsdon Rd. Coulsd CR3 & CR5 100 B7
Coulsdon Rise. Coulsd CR5 79 E2
Coulsdon South Sta. Coulsd CR5 79 D3
Coulthurst Ct. Streat SW16 21 E1
Council Cotts. Charl RH6 180 C6
Council Cotts. Loxwd RH14 213 A2
Council Cotts. Plaist RH14 211 D3
Council Cotts. W End GU24 67 F7
Countisbury Gdns. Addl KT15 52 B5
Countisbury House. Dulw SE26 23 A5
Country Way. Felt TW13 & TW16 15 C3
County Mall. Crawl RH10 201 E5
County Oak La. Crawl RH11 181 D3
County Oak Ret Pk. Crawl RH11 181 D2
County Oak Way. Crawl RH11 181 D3
County Rd. S Norw CR7 42 B7
Courier House. 17 Streat SW2 22 A8
Courland Rd. Addl KT15 52 B7
Course Rd. Ascot SL5 29 A6
Court Ave. Coulsd CR5 100 A8
Court Bushes Rd. Whytlf CR3 101 B7
Court Cl. E Grins RH19 185 F1
Court Cl. Twick TW13 & TW2 16 B5
Court Close Ave. Twick TW13 & TW2 16 B5
Court Cres. Chess KT9 56 D4
Court Cres. E Grins RH19 185 F1
Court Downs Rd. Beck BR3 44 B7
Court Dr. Carsh SM1 59 E6
Court Dr. Croy CR0 60 F6
Court Farm Ave. W Ewell KT19 57 D5
Court Farm Ave. W Ewell KT19 57 D5
Court Farm Gdns. Epsom KT19 76 C8
Court Farm Ind Est. Stan TW19 2 F1

Court Farm Rd. Warlgm CR6 ..... 81 A2
Court Gdns. Camb GU15 ..... 65 D5
Court Green Hts. Woking GU22.. 89 C7
Court Haw. Woodm SM7 ..... 78 E4
Court Hill. Sander CR2 ..... 80 E7
Court Hill. Woodm CR5 ..... 78 F2
Court House Mansions.
  Epsom KT19 ..... 76 D7
Court La. Dulw SE21 ..... 22 E8
Court La. Epsom KT19 ..... 76 C6
Court Lane Gdns. Dulw SE21 ..... 22 E8
Court Lodge Cty Fst Sch.
  Horley RH6 ..... 160 F3
Court Lodge Rd. Horley RH6 ..... 160 F3
Court Rd. Alder GU11 ..... 105 A2
Court Rd. Banstd SM7 ..... 78 A4
Court Rd. Cater CR3 ..... 100 E4
Court Rd. S Norw SE25 ..... 42 F6
Court Rd. Tyl Gn RH9 ..... 121 C4
Court The. Docken GU10 ..... 166 D3
Court The. Guild GU2 ..... 130 C7
Court The. Warlgm CR6 ..... 81 E1
Court Way. Twick TW1 & TW2 ..... 16 F8
Court Wood La. New Add CR0 ..... 62 F1
Courtenay Ave. Belm SM2 ..... 59 A2
Courtenay Dr. Beck BR3 ..... 44 D7
Courtenay Rd. Heath E GU9 ..... 125 E7
Courtenay Rd.
  N Cheam KT4 & SM3 ..... 58 C7
Courtenay Rd. Penge BR3 & SE20 23 D2
Courtenay Rd. Woking GU21 ..... 70 A3
Courtfield Rd. Ashf TW15 ..... 14 B2
Courtfield Rise. Wimble SW19 ..... 19 E3
Courthope Rd. Wimble SW19 ..... 19 E1
Courthope Villas. Wimble SW19 19 E1
Courtland Ave. S Norw SW16 ..... 21 F1
Courtlands. Rich TW10 ..... 7 A2
Courtlands. 10 Sutton SM2 ..... 59 B3
Courtlands. Walt O T KT12 ..... 35 A2
Courtlands Ave. Esher KT10 ..... 55 A4
Courtlands Ave. Hampt TW12 ..... 15 F2
Courtlands Ave. Rich TW9 ..... 7 B5
Courtlands Ave. W Wick BR2 ..... 44 F1
Courtlands Cl. S Croy CR2 ..... 62 A1
Courtlands Cres. Banstd SM7 ..... 78 A3
Courtlands Dr. W Ewell KT19 ..... 57 F4
Courtlands Dr. W Ewell KT19 ..... 57 F4
Courtlands Rd. Surb KT5 ..... 38 A2
Courtleas. Cobham KT11 ..... 74 A6
Courtney Cl. S Norw SE19 ..... 22 E2
Courtney Cres. Wallin SM5 ..... 59 F2
Courtney Pl. Croy CR0 ..... 61 A7
Courtney Rd. Croy CR0 & CR9 ..... 61 A7
Courtney Rd. Harl TW6 ..... 3 A4
Courtney Rd. Mitch SW19 ..... 20 E1
Courts Hill Rd. Haslem GU27 ..... 208 B6
Courts Mount Rd.
  Haslem GU27 ..... 208 B6
Courts The. Streat SW16 ..... 21 E1
Courtside. For Hil SE23 ..... 23 C5
Courtwood Prim Sch.
  New Add CR0 ..... 62 F1
Courtyard The. Addl KT15 ..... 52 C6
Courtyard The. 1 Crawl RH10 201 D5
Courtyard The. Crawl RH13 ..... 218 E4
Courtyard The. E Grins RH19 ..... 186 B1
Coutts Ave. Chess KT9 ..... 56 E5
Coval Gdns. Mortl SW14 ..... 7 B3
Coval La. Mortl SW14 ..... 7 B3
Coval Rd. Mortl SW14 ..... 7 C3
Cove Cty Inf Sch. W Heath GU14 84 E6
Cove Cty Jun Sch.
  W Heath GU14 ..... 84 E5
Cove Manor Cty Inf Sch.
  W Heath GU14 ..... 84 E6
Cove Manor Cty Jun Sch.
  W Heath GU14 ..... 84 F6
Cove Rd. Farnb GU14 ..... 84 F4
Cove Sch. W Heath GU14 ..... 84 E5
Coveham Cres. Cobham KT11 ..... 73 A6
Coventry Rd. Croy SE25 ..... 43 A5
Coverack Cl. Croy CR0 ..... 43 E2
Coverdale Cl. E Grins RH19 ..... 185 C3
Coverdale Gdns. S Croy CR0 ..... 61 F7
Covert Cl. Crawl RH10 ..... 201 E7
Covert La. Brack RG12 ..... 27 C5
Covert The. Ascot SL5 ..... 29 B2
Covert The. W Heath GU14 ..... 84 E8
Coverton Rd. Up Toot SW17 ..... 20 E3
Coverts Rd. Clayg KT10 ..... 55 F3
Covey Cl. Farnb GU14 ..... 85 A8
Covey The. Crawl RH10 ..... 202 E8
Covington Gdns. S Norw SW16 ..... 22 B1
Covington Way. S Norw SW16 ..... 22 A1
Covington Way. S Norw SW16 ..... 22 B1
Covington Way. Streat SW16 ..... 21 F2
Cow La. Godal GU7 ..... 150 D4
Cowden St. Catf SE6 ..... 24 A4
Cowdray Cl. Crawl RH10 ..... 202 C5
Cowdrey Rd. Wimble SW19 ..... 20 C3
Cowfold Cl. Crawl RH11 ..... 200 F3
Cowick Rd. Up Toot SW17 ..... 20 F4
Cowleaze Rd. King U T KT2 ..... 37 E8
Cowley Ave. Chert KT16 ..... 32 F2
Cowley Cl. Selsd CR2 ..... 62 C2
Cowley Cres. Hersh KT12 ..... 54 C6
Cowley La. Chert KT16 ..... 32 F2
Cowley Rd. Mortl SW14 ..... 7 E4
Coworth Cl. Sunnin SL5 ..... 30 B4
Coworth Rd. Sunnin SL5 ..... 30 A4
Cowper Ave. Carsh SM1 ..... 59 D6
Cowper Cl. Chert KT16 ..... 32 F3
Cowper Gdns. Wallin SM6 ..... 60 C4
Cowper Rd. Rich TW10 ..... 17 D3
Cowper Rd. Wimble SW19 ..... 20 C2
Cowshot Cres. Pirb GU24 ..... 87 D7
Cowslip La. Mickle RH5 ..... 115 B7
Cox Cnr. Ockley RH5 ..... 177 A7
Cox Green Rd. Cran RH12 ..... 195 C2

Cox Green Rd. Ewh RH12 ..... 195 C2
Cox House. Horsh RH12 ..... 217 B2
Cox La. Chess KT9 ..... 56 F6
Cox La. W Ewell KT19 ..... 57 C5
Cox La. W Ewell KT19 ..... 57 C5
Coxbridge. Farnh GU9 ..... 124 F1
Coxcomb Wlk. Crawl RH11 ..... 201 A4
Coxcombe La. Chidd GU8 ..... 191 B4
Coxdean. Burgh H KT20 ..... 97 C8
Coxgreen. Sandh GU15 ..... 64 D6
Coxley Rise. Purley CR8 ..... 80 C6
Coxs Ave. Sunby TW17 ..... 34 E6
Coxwell Rd. S Norw SE19 ..... 22 E1
Crab Hill. Beck BR3 ..... 24 D1
Crab Hill La. S Nutf RH1 ..... 140 F4
Crabbet Rd. Crawl RH10 ..... 202 B7
Crabtree Cl. G Book KT23 ..... 94 C1
Crabtree Cnr. Thorpe TW20 ..... 32 B8
Crabtree Dr. Leahd KT22 ..... 95 C2
Crabtree La. Churt GU10 ..... 168 A2
Crabtree La. G Book KT23 ..... 94 C1
Crabtree La. Head KT22 ..... 96 C1
Crabtree La. Westh RH5 ..... 115 A5
Crabtree Office Village.
  Thorpe TW20 ..... 32 C8
Crabtree Rd. Camb GU15 ..... 65 B2
Crabtree Rd. Crawl RH11 ..... 201 C5
Crabtree Rd. Thorpe TW20 ..... 32 C7
Crabwood. Oxted RH8 ..... 122 E7
Craddocks Ave. Ashtd KT21 ..... 75 F3
Craddocks Par. Ashtd KT21 ..... 75 F2
Cradhurst Cl. Westc RH4 ..... 135 C6
Craig Rd. Rich TW10 ..... 17 C4
Craigans. Crawl RH11 ..... 201 A5
Craigen Ave. Croy CR0 ..... 43 B1
Craigmore Tower. Woking GU22 89 E8
Craignair Rd. Streat SW2 ..... 22 A8
Craignish Ave. Thorn H SW16 ..... 41 F7
Craigside. King U T KT2 ..... 38 B8
Craigside. Purley CR8 ..... 79 F5
Craigwell Ave. Felt TW13 ..... 15 A5
Craigwell Cl. Egham TW18 ..... 32 E8
Crail Cl. Woki RG11 ..... 25 A3
Crake Pl. Sandh GU15 ..... 64 D8
Crakell Rd. Reig RH2 ..... 139 C8
Cramhurst La. Witley GU8 ..... 170 E6
Cramond Ct. Bed TW14 ..... 14 F7
Crampshaw La. Ashtd KT21 ..... 95 F7
Crampton Rd. Penge SE20 ..... 23 C2
Cranborne Ave. Tolw KT6 & KT9 . 57 A7
Cranborne Wlk. Crawl RH10 ..... 201 F4
Cranbourne Cl. Horley RH6 ..... 161 B5
Cranbourne Cotts. Wink SL4 ..... 9 B5
Cranbourne Cty Prim Sch.
  Wink SL5 ..... 9 A4
Cranbrook Ct. 9 Brent TW8 ..... 6 D8
Cranbrook Dr. Thame D KT10 ..... 36 C1
Cranbrook Dr. Twick TW2 ..... 16 B7
Cranbrook House. S Norw SE19 42 D8
Cranbrook Rd. Hounsl TW4 ..... 4 F3
Cranbrook Rd. S Norw CR7 ..... 42 C7
Cranbrook Rd. Wimble SW19 ..... 19 E1
Cranbrook Terr. Cran GU6 ..... 174 F3
Crane Ave. Islew TW7 ..... 6 A2
Crane Ct. Sandh GU15 ..... 64 D8
Crane Ct. W Ewell KT19 ..... 57 C6
Crane Ct. W Ewell KT19 ..... 57 C6
Crane House. Catf BR1 ..... 24 D3
Crane House. Felt TW13 ..... 16 A5
Crane Inf Sch. Felt TW13 ..... 15 F6
Crane Jun Sch. Felt TW13 ..... 15 F6
Crane Lodge Rd. Heston TW5 ..... 4 B8
Crane Mead Ct. Twick TW1 ..... 16 F8
Crane Park Rd. Twick TW2 ..... 16 B6
Crane Rd. Stan TW19 ..... 3 A1
Crane Rd. Twick TW2 ..... 16 E7
Crane Way. Twick TW2 ..... 16 C8
Cranebrook. Twick TW2 ..... 16 C6
Craneford Cl. Twick TW2 ..... 16 F8
Craneford Way. Twick TW2 ..... 16 F8
Cranes Dr. King U T KT5 ..... 37 F5
Cranes Park Ave.
  King U T KT5 & KT6 ..... 37 F5
Cranes Park Cres. King U T KT5. 37 F5
Cranes Pk. King U T KT5 & KT6 ..... 37 E4
Cranewater. Harl TW6 ..... 3 F7
Cranfield Ct. 7 Woking GU21 ..... 68 F1
Cranfield Rd E. Wallin SM5 ..... 60 A2
Cranfield Rd W. Wallin SM5 ..... 60 A2
Cranford Ave. Stan TW19 ..... 13 E8
Cranford Cl. Purley CR8 ..... 80 C6
Cranford Cl. Stan TW19 ..... 13 E8
Cranford Cl. Wimble SW20 ..... 19 B1
Cranford Comm Sch. Cranf TW5 . 4 B8
Cranford Ct. Sutton SM1 ..... 59 C6
Cranford Jun & Inf Schs.
  Cranf TW4 ..... 4 B5
Cranford La. Cranf UB3 ..... 4 A7
Cranford La. Harl UB3 ..... 3 D4
Cranford La. Hatton TW6 ..... 3 F4
Cranford La. Hatton TW6 ..... 3 F6
Cranford La. Heston TW5 ..... 4 D7
Cranford Lodge. Putney SW19 ..... 19 E6
Cranford Rise. Esher KT10 ..... 55 C5
Cranleigh Cl. Penge SE20 ..... 43 B7
Cranleigh Cl. Sander CR2 ..... 81 A7
Cranleigh Cl. Farnb GU14 ..... 84 F4
Cranleigh Cl. Rich TW9 ..... 7 A4
Cranleigh Cty Fst Sch.
  Cran GU6 ..... 174 E3
Cranleigh Gdns. King U T KT2 ..... 17 F2
Cranleigh Gdns. S Norw SE25 ..... 42 E6
Cranleigh Gdns. Sander CR2 ..... 81 A7
Cranleigh Gdns. Sutton SM1 ..... 59 B8
Cranleigh House. Wimble SW20 39 B7
Cranleigh Mead. Cran GU6 ..... 174 F2
Cranleigh Rd. Ewh GU6 ..... 175 D4
Cranleigh Rd. Felt TW13 ..... 14 F4
Cranleigh Rd. Merton SW19 ..... 40 A6

Cranleigh Rd. Thame D KT10 ..... 36 C1
Cranleigh Rd. Woner GU5 ..... 152 C2
Cranleigh Sch. Cran GU6 ..... 174 C5
Cranleigh Village Hospl.
  Cran GU6 ..... 174 D3
Cranley Cl. Guild GU1 ..... 110 A1
Cranley Gdns. Wallin SM6 ..... 60 C3
Cranley Pl. Knaph GU21 ..... 68 D1
Cranley Rd. Guild GU1 ..... 109 F1
Cranley Rd. Whit V KT12 ..... 53 F5
Cranmer Cl. W Barn SM4 ..... 39 E3
Cranmer Cl. Warlgm CR6 ..... 81 C2
Cranmer Cl. Whit V KT13 ..... 53 A3
Cranmer Ct. Hampt TW12 ..... 16 B3
Cranmer Ct. King U T KT2 ..... 17 E3
Cranmer Farm Cl. Mitch CR4 ..... 40 F5
Cranmer Gdns. Warlgm CR6 ..... 81 C2
Cranmer Rd. Croy CR0 & CR9 ..... 61 C7
Cranmer Rd. Hampt TW12 ..... 16 B3
Cranmer Rd. King U T KT2 ..... 17 E3
Cranmer Rd. Mitch CR4 ..... 40 F5
Cranmer Terr. Up Toot SW17 ..... 20 D3
Cranmer Wlk. Worth RH10 ..... 202 C5
Cranmore Ave. Hounsl TW7 ..... 5 C7
Cranmore Cl. Alder GU11 ..... 104 C1
Cranmore Cl. Mytch GU16 ..... 85 F4
Cranmore Gdns. Alder GU11 ..... 104 C1
Cranmore La. Alder GU11 ..... 104 C1
Cranmore La. W Hors KT24 ..... 112 C6
Cranmore Rd. Catf BR1 ..... 24 F5
Cranmore Rd. Mytch GU16 ..... 86 A4
Cranmore Sch. W Hors KT24 ..... 112 C6
Cranston Cl. Hounsl TW3 & TW4 ..... 4 E5
Cranston Cl. Reig RH2 ..... 139 B8
Cranston Rd. E Grins RH19 ..... 185 F2
Cranston Rd. For Hil SE23 ..... 23 E6
Cranstoun Cl. Stough GU3 ..... 108 F5
Crantock Rd. Catf SE6 ..... 24 C6
Cranwell Cl. Croy CR0 ..... 62 D8
Cranwell Gr. Lhtwat GU18 ..... 66 F8
Cranwell Gr. Shep Gn TW17 ..... 33 F5
Cranwell Rd. Harl TW6 ..... 3 B5
Craster Rd. Streat SW2 ..... 21 F8
Cravan Ave. Felt TW13 ..... 15 A6
Craven Ave. M Bourn GU10 ..... 146 C6
Craven Gdns. Wimble SW19 ..... 20 B3
Craven House. 2 Mortl SW14 ..... 7 D4
Craven Rd. Croy CR0 ..... 43 B1
Craven Rd. King U T KT2 ..... 37 F8
Craven Rd. Worth RH10 ..... 202 B5
Cravens The. Smallf RH6 ..... 162 A3
Crawford Cl. Hounsl TW7 ..... 5 E5
Crawford Gdns. Camb GU15 ..... 65 B5
Crawford Gdns. Horsh RH13 ..... 217 E4
Crawford Way. E Grins RH19 ..... 185 F3
Crawley Ave. Crawl RH10 ..... 182 C1
Crawley Ave.
  Crawl RH10 & RH11 ..... 201 A6
Crawley Chase. Wink RG12 ..... 8 B2
Crawley Coll of Tech.
  Crawl RH10 ..... 201 E6
Crawley Coll (West Green Annexe).
  Crawl RH11 ..... 201 C7
Crawley Down CE (Controlled) Sch.
  Craw D RH10 ..... 204 B8
Crawley Down Rd.
  E Grins RH19 ..... 184 F4
Crawley Down Rd. Felb RH19 ..... 184 F4
Crawley Dr. Camb GU15 ..... 65 F6
Crawley Hill. Camb GU15 ..... 65 F5
Crawley Hospl (General).
  Crawl RH10 ..... 201 C6
Crawley La. Crawl RH10 ..... 202 C7
Crawley Rd. Crawl RH12 ..... 200 B1
Crawley Rd. Faygt RH12 ..... 218 D7
Crawley Rd. Horsh RH12 ..... 218 B5
Crawley Ridge. Camb GU15 ..... 65 F6
Crawley Ridge Cty Fst Sch.
  Camb GU15 ..... 65 F6
Crawley Ridge Cty Mid Sch.
  Camb GU15 ..... 65 F7
Crawley Sta. Crawl RH10 ..... 201 E5
Crawley Wood Cl. Camb GU15 ..... 65 F5
Crawshaw Rd. Ottsh KT16 ..... 51 D4
Crawters Cl. Crawl RH10 ..... 201 F7
Cray Ave. Ashtd KT21 ..... 75 F2
Crayke Hill. Chess KT9 ..... 56 E3
Crayonne Cl. Charlt TW16 ..... 34 E8
Crealock St. Wands SW18 ..... 20 B8
Creasys Dr. Crawl RH11 ..... 201 B1
Credenhill St. Streat SW16 ..... 21 C2
Crediton Way. Clayg KT10 ..... 56 A5
Credon Cl. W Heath GU14 ..... 84 F5
Cree's Meadow. Windl GU20 ..... 48 D3
Creek Rd. E Mole KT8 ..... 36 E5
Creek The. Sunby TW16 ..... 35 A4
Creeland Gr. For Hil SE6 ..... 23 F7
Cremorne Gdns. Epsom KT19 ..... 57 D2
Crerar Cl. Farnb GU14 ..... 84 D3
Crescent Ct. King U T KT6 ..... 37 D4
Crescent Day Hospl.
  New Add CR0 ..... 63 C1
Crescent Gr. Mitch CR4 ..... 40 E5
Crescent La. Ash GU12 ..... 106 B5
Crescent Rd. Beck BR3 ..... 44 B7
Crescent Rd. Bletch RH1 ..... 120 C2
Crescent Rd. Cater CR3 ..... 101 A3
Crescent Rd. E Grins RH19 ..... 185 D1
Crescent Rd. King U T KT2 ..... 18 B1
Crescent Rd. Shep TW17 ..... 34 C4
Crescent Rd. Wimble SW20 ..... 39 D8
Crescent Rd. Woki RG11 ..... 25 C5
Crescent Rd. Woodh RH2 ..... 139 A7
Crescent The. Ashf TW15 ..... 13 F3
Crescent The. Barnes SW13 ..... 7 F5
Crescent The. Beck BR3 ..... 44 A8
Crescent The. Belm SM2 ..... 78 A8
Crescent The. Brack RG12 ..... 27 C5
Crescent The. Carsh SM1 ..... 59 D5

Crescent The. E Mole KT8 ..... 36 A5
Crescent The. Egham TW20 ..... 11 F2
Crescent The. Epsom KT18 ..... 76 A4
Crescent The. Felct RH19 ..... 185 C8
Crescent The. Farnb GU14 ..... 85 C3
Crescent The. Harl UB7 ..... 3 D7
Crescent The. Heath E GU9 ..... 125 D8
Crescent The. Horley RH6 ..... 182 B8
Crescent The. Horsh RH12 ..... 217 A2
Crescent The. King U T KT6 ..... 37 E4
Crescent The. King U T KT5 ..... 38 C7
Crescent The. Lo Hall TW7 ..... 34 F2
Crescent The. Leahd KT22 ..... 95 B5
Crescent The. Reig RH2 ..... 118 B1
Crescent The. Stough GU2 ..... 109 A3
Crescent The.
  Thorn H CR0 & SE25 ..... 42 D3
Crescent The. Thorpe RH10 ..... 33 A6
Crescent The. W Wick BR4 ..... 44 E3
Crescent The. Weyb KT13 ..... 53 A7
Crescent The. Wimble SW19 ..... 20 A5
Crescent The. Wold CR3 ..... 102 A4
Crescent Way. Horley RH6 ..... 161 A1
Crescent Way. S Norw SW16 ..... 22 A1
Crescent Wood Rd.
  Dulw SE21 & SE26 ..... 23 A5
Cressage Ho. 9 Brent TW8 ..... 6 E8
Cressall Cl. Leahd KT22 ..... 95 B7
Cressall Mead. Leahd KT22 ..... 95 B7
Cressingham Gr. Sutton SM1 ..... 59 C6
Cresswell Rd. Croy SE25 ..... 43 A5
Cresswell Rd. Felt TW13 ..... 15 E4
Cresswell Rd. Felt TW13 ..... 15 E4
Cresswell Rd. Twick TW1 ..... 6 D1
Crest Hill. Peasl GU5 ..... 133 E1
Crest Rd. S Croy CR2 ..... 62 B3
Crest Rd. W Wick BR2 ..... 44 F2
Crest The. Surb KT5 ..... 38 A4
Crest The. 10 W Norw SW27 ..... 22 B3
Cresta Dr. Woodhm KT15 ..... 51 F1
Creston Ave. Knaph GU21 ..... 68 E3
Creston Way. N Cheam KT4 ..... 39 D1
Crestwood Way. Hounsl TW4 ..... 4 E2
Creswell. Knaph GU21 ..... 68 D2
Crewdson Rd. Horley RH6 ..... 161 B3
Crewe's Ave. Warlgm CR6 ..... 81 C3
Crewe's Cl. Warlgm CR6 ..... 81 C2
Crewe's Farm La. Warlgm CR6 . 81 E2
Crewe's La. Warlgm CR6 ..... 81 D3
Crichton Ave. Wallin SM6 ..... 60 D6
Crichton Rd. Wallin SM5 ..... 59 F3
Cricket Ct. E Grins RH19 ..... 185 C1
Cricket Field Gr. Crowth RG11 ..... 45 D4
Cricket Field Rd. Horsh RH12 ..... 217 B1
Cricket Gn. Hambl GU8 ..... 171 C1
Cricket Gn. Mitch CR4 ..... 40 F5
Cricket Green Sch. Mitch CR4 . 40 E6
Cricket Hill. S Nutf RH1 ..... 140 F7
Cricket La. M Bourn GU10 ..... 146 D6
Cricket La. Penge BR3 ..... 23 E3
Cricket View. Weyb KT13 ..... 53 B5
Cricket Way. Oat Pk KT13 ..... 53 E8
Cricketers Cl. Chess KT9 ..... 56 D6
Cricketers Cl. Ockley RH5 ..... 177 C4
Cricketers La. Windl GU20 ..... 48 D4
Cricketers La. Wink RG12 ..... 8 A3
Cricklade Ave. Streat SW2 ..... 21 F6
Crieff Ct. 3 Tedd TW11 & KT8 ..... 17 C1
Criffel Ave. Streat SW2 ..... 21 D7
Crimea Rd. Alder GU11 ..... 105 B2
Crimea Rd. Friml GU16 ..... 86 D8
Crimp Hill. Eng Gn SL4 & TW20 ..... 11 A6
Crimp Hill. Old W SL4 & TW20 ..... 11 A6
Cripley Rd. W Heath GU14 ..... 84 A6
Cripplecrutch Hill. Chidd GU8 ..... 209 F5
Cripplecrutch Hill. Fish GU8 ..... 209 F5
Cripps House. Crawl RH11 ..... 201 B2
Crispen Rd. Felt TW13 ..... 15 E4
Crispin Cl. Ashtd KT21 ..... 75 F1
Crispin Cl. Wallin SM6 ..... 60 E8
Crispin Cres. Wallin SM6 ..... 60 D8
Critchmere Hill. Shottm GU27 ..... 207 F7
Critchmere La. Shottm GU27 ..... 207 E6
Critchmere Vale. Shottm GU27 207 E6
Critten La. Effing KT24 & RH5 ..... 113 D2
Crittenden Lodge. W Wick BR4 . 44 A1
Crocker Cl. N Asct SL5 ..... 28 F8
Crockers La. Horne RH7 ..... 163 D4
Crockford Cl. Addl KT15 ..... 52 C6
Crockford Park Rd. Addl KT15 ..... 52 C5
Crockham Cl. Crawl RH11 ..... 201 C4
Crocknorth Rd. E Hors KT24 ..... 113 A2
Crocus Cl. Croy CR0 ..... 43 D1
Croffets. Tadw KT20 ..... 97 D6
Croft Ave. Dork RH4 ..... 115 B1
Croft Ave. W Wick BR4 ..... 44 C1
Croft Cl. Harl UB7 ..... 3 C7
Croft Cl. Woki RG11 ..... 25 A2
Croft Rd. Alder GU11 ..... 126 B8
Croft Rd. Carsh SM1 ..... 59 E5
Croft Rd. Godal GU7 ..... 150 E6
Croft Rd. Merton SW19 ..... 20 C1
Croft Rd. S Norw SW16 ..... 22 A1
Croft Rd. Witley GU8 ..... 170 E5
Croft Rd. Woki RG11 ..... 25 A1
Croft Rd. Wold CR3 ..... 102 A5
Croft The. Crawl RH11 ..... 201 A6
Croft The. Epsom KT17 ..... 76 F5
Croft The. Heston TW5 ..... 4 E7
Croft Way. Friml GU16 ..... 65 F2
Croft Way. Horsh RH12 ..... 217 A3
Croft Way. Rich TW10 ..... 17 B5
Crofter's Cl. Sandh GU17 ..... 64 A8
Crofters Cl. Islew TW7 ..... 5 D2
Crofters Mead. New Add CR0 ..... 62 F2
Croftleigh Ave. Purley CR8 ..... 80 B3
Crofton. Ashtd KT21 ..... 75 E1
Crofton Ave. Chisw W4 ..... 7 D6
Crofton Ave. Walt O T KT12 ..... 54 C7
Crofton Cl. Brack RG12 ..... 27 E4
Crofton Cl. Ottsh KT16 ..... 51 C1

Crofton Terr. Rich TW9 ..... 6 F3
Crofts Cl. Chidd GU8 ..... 191 B5
Crofts The. Up Hall TW17 ..... 34 E5
Croftside The. S Norw SE25 ..... 43 A6
Croham Cl. S Croy CR2 ..... 61 E4
Croham Hurst Golf Course.
  S Croy CR2 ..... 62 A3
Croham Hurst Sch. S Croy CR2 ..... 61 F4
Croham Manor Rd. S Croy CR2 ..... 61 E4
Croham Mount. S Croy CR2 ..... 61 E3
Croham Park Ave.
  S Croy CR0 & CR2 ..... 61 F5
Croham Rd. Croy CR0 & CR2 ..... 61 F5
Croham Rd. S Croy CR2 ..... 61 E5
Croham Valley Rd. S Croy CR2 . 62 B3
Croindene Rd. Thorn H SW16 ..... 41 E8
Cromer Ct. Streat SW16 ..... 21 E5
Cromer Rd. Croy SE25 ..... 43 B6
Cromer Rd. Harl TW6 ..... 3 A5
Cromer Rd. Mitch SW17 ..... 21 A2
Cromer Rd W. Harl TW6 ..... 3 A4
Cromford Way. King U T KT3 ..... 38 D8
Crompton Fields. Crawl RH10 ..... 181 E1
Crompton Way. Crawl RH10 ..... 181 E1
Cromwell Ave. New Mal KT3 ..... 38 F4
Cromwell Cl. Walt O T KT12 ..... 35 B1
Cromwell Ct. 15 King U T KT2 ..... 18 A1
Cromwell Gr. Cater CR3 ..... 100 C6
Cromwell House. Croy CR0 ..... 61 B7
Cromwell Pl. Cran GU6 ..... 174 F1
Cromwell Pl. 1 E Grins RH19 ..... 205 F7
Cromwell Pl. Mortl SW14 ..... 7 C4
Cromwell Rd. Ascot SL5 ..... 29 B4
Cromwell Rd. Beck BR3 ..... 43 E6
Cromwell Rd. Camb GU15 ..... 65 D7
Cromwell Rd. Cater CR3 ..... 100 C6
Cromwell Rd. Hounsl TW3 ..... 5 A3
Cromwell Rd. King U T KT2 ..... 37 E8
Cromwell Rd. Redh RH1 ..... 118 F1
Cromwell Rd. Tedd TW11 ..... 17 A2
Cromwell Rd. Thorn H CR0 ..... 42 D2
Cromwell Rd. Wimble SW19 ..... 20 B3
Cromwell Rd.
  Worc Pk KT19 & KT4 ..... 57 E7
Cromwell St. Hounsl TW3 ..... 5 A3
Cromwell Way. Farnb GU14 ..... 85 C7
Cromwell Wlk. 1 Redh RH1 ..... 118 F1
Crondall Ct. Camb GU15 ..... 65 B4
Crondall House. Rhampt SW15 ..... 19 A7
Crondall La. Farnh GU10 & GU9 124 D2
Crondall Rd. Bentl GU10 ..... 145 A6
Cronks Hill. Woodh RH2 ..... 139 D7
Cronks Hill Cl. Woodh RH1 ..... 139 D7
Cronks Hill Rd.
  Woodh RH1 & RH2 ..... 139 D7
Crooksbury Rd. Farnh GU10 ..... 126 C2
Crooksbury Rd. Tilf GU10 ..... 147 D8
Crosby Cl. Felt TW13 ..... 15 E4
Crosby Hill Dr. Camb GU15 ..... 65 F7
Crosby Wlk. Streat SE24 ..... 22 A8
Cross Deep. Twick TW1 ..... 17 A6
Cross Deep Gdns. Twick TW1 ..... 16 F6
Cross Farm Cty Fst Sch.
  Friml GU16 ..... 85 E6
Cross Fell. Easth RG12 ..... 27 A5
Cross Gates Cl. Brack RG12 ..... 27 F6
Cross Gdns. Friml GU16 ..... 85 E6
Cross Keys. Crawl RH10 & RH11 201 D6
Cross La. Burst RH6 ..... 162 C1
Cross La. Friml GU16 ..... 85 E6
Cross La. Ottsh KT16 ..... 51 C4
Cross Lances Rd. Hounsl TW3 ..... 5 B3
Cross Lanes. Guild GU1 ..... 130 F8
Cross Oak La. Salfs RH1 & RH6 . 161 C7
Cross Rd. Ash GU12 ..... 106 B3
Cross Rd. Belm SM2 ..... 59 A1
Cross Rd. Croy CR0 ..... 42 D1
Cross Rd. Farnb GU14 ..... 84 C1
Cross Rd. Felt TW13 ..... 15 E4
Cross Rd. King U T KT2 ..... 17 F1
Cross Rd. Merton SW19 ..... 20 A1
Cross Rd. Oat Pk KT13 ..... 53 D7
Cross Rd. Purley CR8 ..... 80 B6
Cross Rd. Tadw KT20 ..... 97 C5
Cross Rd. Went SL5 ..... 30 A1
Cross St. Alder GU11 ..... 105 A2
Cross St. Farnb GU14 ..... 105 C8
Cross St. Hampt TW12 ..... 16 C3
Cross St. Mortl SW13 ..... 7 E4
Cross St. Woki RG11 ..... 25 C6
Crossacres. Pyrf GU22 ..... 70 E4
Crossfield Pl. Whit V KT13 ..... 53 B3
Crossland Rd. Earls RH1 ..... 119 A1
Crossland Rd. Thorn H CR7 ..... 42 B3
Crosslands. Addl KT16 ..... 51 E6
Crosslands Rd. W Ewell KT19 ..... 57 D4
Crosslands Rd. W Ewell KT19 ..... 57 D4
Crossley Cl. Bigg H TN16 ..... 83 D4
Crossman Ct. Crawl RH11 ..... 201 B1
Crossman Houses. 19
  Streat SW12 ..... 21 E8
Crosspath. Crawl RH10 ..... 201 E7
Crossroads The. Effing KT24 ..... 113 D7
Crosswater La. Frensh GU10 ..... 167 F4
Crossway. Brack RG12 ..... 27 C7
Crossway. Crawl RH6 ..... 181 F8
Crossway. W Barn KT3 & SW20 ..... 39 C5
Crossways. Alder GU12 ..... 105 C1
Crossways. Charlt TW16 ..... 14 F1
Crossways. Churt GU10 ..... 167 E1
Crossways. Crawl RH10 ..... 202 A7
Crossways. Effing KT24 ..... 113 D8
Crossways. Egham TW20 ..... 12 D2
Crossways. S Croy CR0 & CR2 ..... 62 F3
Crossways. Sutton SM2 ..... 59 D2

Crossways. Tats TN16 .... 103 C7
Crossways Ave. E Grins RH19 .. 185 C1
Crossways Cl. Crawl RH10 .... 201 F7
Crossways Cotts. Alf Cr GU6 .... 194 A3
Crossways Cotts. Buck Gn RH12 213 F6
Crossways Ct. Tats TN16 .... 103 C7
Crossways La. L Kings RH2 ...... 118 D7
Crossways Rd. Beck BR3 .... 44 A5
Crossways Rd. Graysh GU26 ...... 188 D3
Crossways Rd. Mitch CR4 .... 41 B6
Crossways The. Abing H RH5 .... 134 B3
Crossways The. Coulsd CR5 ..... 100 A8
Crossways The. Heston TW5 ...... 4 F7
Crossways The. L Kings RH2 .... 118 C7
Crossways The. Merst RH1 ...... 119 C6
Crossways The. Onsl V GU2 ..... 129 F7
Crosswell Cl. Charlt TW17 ...... 34 C7
Crouch La. Wink SL4 .... 8 F7
Crouch Oak La. Addl KT15 .... 52 C6
Crouchfield. Dork RH4 .... 136 C4
Crouchmans Cl.
  Dulw SE21 & SE26 .... 23 A5
Crowberry Cl. Crawl RH11 .... 201 A2
Crowborough Cl. Warlgm CR6 .... 81 E1
Crowborough Dr. Warlgm CR6 .... 81 E1
Crowborough Rd. Streat SW17 ... 21 A3
Crowhurst. S Norw SE25 .... 43 A6
Crowhurst Cl. Worth RH10 .... 202 E6
Crowhurst Keep. Worth RH10 .... 202 E6
Crowhurst La. Crow RH7 .... 143 D5
Crowhurst La. Tand RH7 .... 143 D5
Crowhurst Mead. Tyl Gn RH9 .... 121 C5
Crowhurst Rd. Crow RH7 .... 164 D7
Crowhurst Rd. Lingf RH7 .... 164 D7
Crowhurst Village Rd.
  Crow RH7 .... 143 E2
Crowland Rd. S Norw CR7 .... 42 D5
Crowland Wlk. Morden SM4 ...... 40 C3
Crowley Cres. Croy CR0 .... 61 A5
Crowmarsh Gdns. For Hil SE23 .. 23 C8
Crown Arc. King U T KT1 .... 37 D7
Crown Cl. Walt O T KT12 .... 35 C2
Crown Cotts. Brack SL5 .... 28 C4
Crown Cotts. Eng Gn TW20 ...... 11 A1
Crown Ct. Godal GU7 .... 150 E4
Crown Ct. Twick TW1 .... 17 B8
Crown Dale.
  W Norw SE19 & SE27 .... 22 C3
Crown Dr. Farnh GU9 .... 126 A5
Crown Hill Ct. Ascot SL5 .... 29 B4
Crown Hts. Guild GU1 .... 130 E6
Crown La. Farnh GU9 .... 126 A5
Crown La. Merton SM4 & SW19 ... 40 A6
Crown La. S Norw SE19 & SW16 .. 22 A3
Crown La. Went GU25 .... 31 D3
Crown Lane Gdns. S Norw SE27 22 A3
Crown Lane Prim Sch.
  W Norw SE27 .... 22 B3
Crown Meadow. Coln SL3 .... 1 B7
Crown Par. Morden SM4 .... 40 A5
Crown Par. S Norw SE19 .... 22 B2
Crown Pas. King U T KT1 .... 37 D7
Crown Pl. Sandh GU15 .... 45 E1
Crown Point. S Norw SE19 .... 22 B2
Crown Rd. King U T KT3 .... 38 C8
Crown Rd. Morden SM4 & SW19 . 40 B5
Crown Rd. Sutton SM1 .... 59 B6
Crown Rd. Twick TW1 .... 6 B1
Crown Rd. Went GU25 .... 31 C3
Crown Rise. Chert KT16 .... 32 F1
Crown Row. Brack RG12 .... 27 D3
Crown St. Egham TW20 .... 12 A4
Crown Terr. Rich TW9 .... 6 F3
Crown Wood Cty Prim Sch.
  Brack RG12 .... 27 E3
Crown Yard. Hounsl TW3 .... 5 C4
Crownbourne Ct. Sutton SM1 .... 59 B6
Crownpits La. Godal GU7 .... 150 E3
Crowntree Cl. Hounsl TW7 .... 5 F8
Crowther Rd. S Norw SE25 ...... 43 A5
Crowthorne C of E Sch.
  Crowth RG11 .... 45 C5
Crowthorne Cl. Wands SW18 ..... 19 F7
Crowthorne Lodge. Easth RG12 27 B5
Crowthorne Rd.
  Easth RG11 & RG12 .... 26 F2
Crowthorne Rd. Easth RG12 ..... 27 A5
Crowthorne Rd.
  Sandh GU17 & RG11 .... 45 B2
Crowthorne Rd N. Easth RG12 ... 27 B6
Croxall House. Walt O T KT12 ... 35 C3
Croxden Wlk. Morden SM4 .... 40 C3
Croxted Cl. W Norw SE21 .... 22 C8
Croyde Cl. W Heath GU14 .... 85 A7
Croydon Airport Ind Est.
  Wallin CR9 .... 60 F4
Croydon Coll. Croy CR9 .... 61 D8
Croydon Coll Annexe. Croy CR0 42 D1
Croydon Coll (Selhurst
  Tertiary Ctr). Thorn H SE25 .. 42 D4
Croydon Flyover The.
  Croy CR0 & CR9 .... 61 C7
Croydon General Hospl.
  Thorn H CR9 .... 42 C1
Croydon Gr. Thorn H CR0 .... 42 B1
Croydon High Sch for Girls.
  Selsd CR2 .... 62 C1
Croydon La. Banstd SM7 .... 78 D6
Croydon La. Wallin SM7 .... 78 D6
Croydon La S. Banstd SM7 .... 78 B5
Croydon Rd. Beck BR3 .... 43 E6
Croydon Rd. Cater CR3 .... 101 A5
Croydon Rd. Chelsh CR6 .... 102 D5
Croydon Rd.
  Coney H BR2 & BR4 .... 63 F7
Croydon Rd. Croy CR0 .... 60 D7
Croydon Rd. Harl TW6 .... 3 B4

Croydon Rd.
  Mitch CR0 & CR4 & CR9 ...... 41 C4
Croydon Rd. Penge SE20 .... 43 C8
Croydon Rd. Reig RH2 .... 118 C2
Croydon Rd. Tats TN16 .... 103 C7
Croydon Rd. Titsey CR6 .... 102 D5
Croydon Rd.
  Wallin CR0 & SM5 & SM6 ..... 60 D7
Croydon Rd Ind Est. Beck BR3 ... 43 D5
Croydon Water Palace.
  Croy CR9 .... 61 A4
Croydonbarn La.
  Horne RH6 & RH9 .... 163 B4
Croylands Dr. Surb KT6 .... 37 E2
Croysdale Ave. Sunby TW16 ..... 35 A6
Crozier Dr. S Croy CR2 .... 62 B1
Cruikshank Lea. Sandh GU15 .... 64 E6
Crunden Rd. S Croy CR2 .... 61 D3
Crundwell Ct. Farnh GU9 .... 125 D3
Crusader Gdns. S Croy CR0 ...... 61 E7
Crusoe Rd. Mitch CR4 .... 20 F1
Crutchfield La. Sidlow RH6 ..... 160 B5
Crutchfield La. Walt O T KT12 .. 54 B8
Crutchley Rd. Catf SE6 .... 24 E6
Crutchley Rd. Woki RG11 .... 25 D7
Crystal Palace National Sports Ctr.
  Penge SE19 .... 23 A2
Crystal Palace Par. Dulw SE19 .. 22 F3
Crystal Palace Park Rd.
  Penge SE19 & SE26 .... 23 B3
Crystal Palace Sta. Penge SE19 . 23 A2
Crystal Palace Station Rd.
  Penge SE19 .... 23 A2
Crystal Terr. S Norw SE19 ...... 22 D2
Crystal View Ct. Catf BR1 ...... 24 D4
Cty Inf Sch. Stain TW18 .... 13 A3
Cubitt St. Croy CR0 .... 60 F5
Cuckfield Cl. Crawl RH11 .... 200 F3
Cuckmere Cres. Crawl RH11 ..... 200 F5
Cuckoo La. W End GU24 .... 67 D6
Cuckoo Vale. W End GU24 .... 67 D6
Cuda's Cl. Worc Pk KT19 .... 57 F6
Cuddington Ave.
  Worc Pk KT19 & KT4 .... 57 F7
Cuddington Cl. Burgh H KT20 ... 97 D7
Cuddington Croft Cty Fst & Mid
  Sch. E Ewell SM2 .... 58 D2
Cuddington Cty Prim Sch.
  Worc Pk KT4 .... 57 F7
Cuddington Glade. Epsom KT19 76 A7
Cuddington Golf Course.
  Belm SM2 .... 77 E7
Cuddington Hospl. Belm SM7 ... 77 F6
Cuddington Way.
  Belm SM2 & SM7 .... 77 D8
Cudham Dr. New Add CR0 .... 82 C8
Cudham Rd. Tats TN16 .... 103 E8
Cudham St. Lewish SE6 .... 24 C8
Cudworth La. Cudw RH5 .... 179 E8
Cuffs Hill. Worth RH10 .... 202 E2
Culham House. Brack RG12 ...... 27 E5
Cull's Rd. Flexf GU3 .... 107 B1
Cullens Mews. Alder GU11 ...... 105 A1
Cullerne Cl. Ewell KT17 .... 57 F1
Cullesden Rd. Purley CR8 .... 80 B4
Culmer Hill. Wormly GU8 .... 170 F2
Culmington Rd. S Croy CR2 ..... 61 C2
Culmore Cross. Balham SW12 ... 21 B7
Culsac Rd. Surb KT6 .... 56 E8
Culver Dr. Oxted RH8 .... 122 E5
Culver Rd. Sandh GU15 .... 45 D1
Culverden Ct. Oat Pk KT13 ..... 53 D7
Culverden Rd. Up Toot SW12 ... 21 C6
Culverden Terr. Oat Pk KT13 ... 53 D7
Culverhay. Ashtd KT21 .... 75 E3
Culverhouse Gdns. Streat SW16 21 F5
Culverlands Cres. Ash GU12 .... 106 A3
Culverley Rd. Catf SE6 .... 24 C7
Culvers Ave. Carsh SM5 & CR4 .. 59 F8
Culvers Retreat. Carsh SM5 .... 59 F8
Culvers Way. Carsh SM5 .... 59 F8
Culverstone Cl. Hayes BR2 ...... 44 F4
Culworth House. Guild GU1 ..... 130 E8
Cumber House. Wands SW18 ..... 20 A7
Cumberland Ave.
  Stough GU2 & GU3 .... 109 A6
Cumberland Cl. Epsom KT19 .... 57 E1
Cumberland Cl. Twick TW1 ...... 6 B1
Cumberland Cl.
  Wimble SW20 .... 19 D1
Cumberland Ct. S Croy CR0 ..... 42 D1
Cumberland Dr. Brack RG12 .... 27 E5
Cumberland Dr. Chess KT9 ...... 56 F7
Cumberland Dr. Hinch W KT10 .. 56 A8
Cumberland House.
  King U T KT2 .... 18 B1
Cumberland Lodge. Old W SL4 . 10 D4
Cumberland Pl. Catf SE6 .... 24 F7
Cumberland Pl. Sunby TW16 .... 35 A5
Cumberland Rd. Ashf TW15 ..... 13 D5
Cumberland Rd. Barnes SW13 ... 7 F6
Cumberland Rd. Beck BR2 .... 44 F6
Cumberland Rd. Croy SE25 ...... 43 B3
Cumberland Rd. Friml GU15 .... 66 C4
Cumberland Rd. Rich TW9 .... 7 A7
Cumberland St. Egham TW18 .... 12 D3
Cumberlands. Kenley CR8 .... 80 D4
Cumberlow Ave. S Norw SE25 ... 43 A6
Cumbernauld Gdns. Ashf TW16 14 F3
Cumbernauld Wlk. Crawl RH11 200 F3
Cumbrae Gdns. Long D KT6 ...... 56 D8
Cumnor Gdns. Stonel KT17 ...... 58 A4
Cumnor House Sch. S Croy CR2 61 B2
Cumnor Rise. Kenley CR8 .... 80 C2
Cumnor Rd. Sutton SM2 .... 59 C4
Cumnor Way. Brack RG12 .... 27 E5
Cunliffe Rd. Sandh GU15 .... 64 D7
Cunliffe Rd. Worc Pk KT19 ..... 57 F6
Cunliffe St. Streat SW16 .... 21 C2
Cunningham Ave. Merrow GU1 110 D3
Cunningham Cl. W Wick BR4 .... 63 B8

Cunningham Rd. Woodm SM7 ... 78 D4
Cunnington Rd. Farnb GU14 .... 85 E2
Cunworth Ct. Easth RG12 .... 26 F3
Curfew Bell Rd. Chert KT16 .... 32 F2
Curl Way. Woki RG11 .... 25 A5
Curlew Cl. Selsd CR2 .... 81 D8
Curlew Ct. Tolw KT6 .... 57 A7
Curlew Gdns. Merrow GU4 ...... 110 D3
Curley Hill Rd. Windl GU18 .... 66 F7
Curling Cl. Coulsd CR5 .... 100 A7
Curling Vale. Onsl V GU2 .... 130 A7
Curly Bridge Cl. W Heath GU14 . 84 F8
Curnick's La. W Norw SE27 ..... 22 C4
Curran Ave. Hackb SM6 .... 60 A7
Currie House. Streat SW12 ..... 21 D8
Curteys Wlk. Crawl RH11 .... 201 A3
Curtis Cl. Guild GU1 .... 66 C7
Curtis Field Rd. Streat SW16 .. 22 A4
Curtis Gdns. Dork RH4 .... 136 A8
Curtis Rd. Dork RH4 .... 136 A8
Curtis Rd. Twick TW4 .... 15 F8
Curtis Rd. Ewell KT19 .... 57 C6
Curtis Rd. Ewell KT19 .... 57 C6
Curvan Cl. Ewell KT17 .... 57 F1
Curzon Ave. Horsh RH12 .... 217 B3
Curzon Cl. Weyb KT13 .... 53 A6
Curzon Rd. Thorn H CR7 .... 42 A3
Curzon Rd. Weyb KT13 .... 53 A5
Cusack Cl. Tedd TW1 .... 16 F4
Cuthbert Gdns. S Norw SE25 ... 42 E6
Cuthbert Rd. Ash GU12 .... 106 B6
Cuthbert Rd. Thorn H CR0 & CR9 61 B8
Cutting La. Crawl D RH10 ...... 184 A1
Cuttinglye Rd. Crawl D RH10 ... 184 C2
Cutts Rd. Farnb GU11 .... 105 D2
Cyclamen Cl. Hampt TW12 ...... 16 A2
Cyclamen Way. W Ewell KT19 ... 57 C5
Cyclamen Way. W Ewell KT19 ... 57 C5
Cygnet Ave. Felt TW14 .... 15 D8
Cygnets The. Felt TW13 .... 15 E4
Cypress Ave. Twick TW2 .... 16 C8
Cypress Ct. Sutton SM1 .... 59 A4
Cypress Ct. Thorpe GU25 .... 31 E5
Cypress Ct. S Norw SW16 .... 22 A3
Cypress Gr. Ash V GU12 .... 105 F7
Cypress Inf Sch. S Norw SE25 .. 42 E7
Cypress Jun Sch. S Norw SE25 . 42 E7
Cypress Lodge. S Norw SE25 ... 42 E7
Cypress Rd. S Norw SE25 .... 42 E7
Cypress Way. Bellf GU1 .... 109 C4
Cypress Way. Blckw GU17 ...... 64 B5
Cypress Way. Graysh GU26 ..... 188 D2
Cypress Way. Nork KT17 .... 77 D5
Cypress Wlk. Eng Gn TW20 ..... 11 B2
Cyprus Rd. Friml GU16 .... 86 D8

D'abernon Cl. Esher KT10 ...... 55 A6
D'Abernon Dr. Stk D'A KT11 .... 73 E3
D'arcy Rd. Cheam SM3 .... 58 D6
Dacre Rd. Thorn H CR0 .... 41 E2
Dacres Rd. For Hil SE23 .... 23 D5
Daffodil Cl. Croy CR0 .... 43 D1
Daffodil Cl. Hampt TW12 .... 16 A2
Daffodil Dr. Bisley GU24 .... 68 A3
Dafforne Rd. Up Toot SW17 .... 21 A5
Dagden Rd. Shalf GU4 .... 130 E3
Dagley La. Shalf GU4 .... 130 D3
Dagmar Rd. King U T KT2 .... 18 A1
Dagmar Rd. S Norw SE25 .... 42 E4
Dagnall Pk. Thorn H CR0 & SE25 . 42 E4
Dagnall Rd. S Norw SE25 .... 42 E4
Dagnan Rd. Balham SW12 .... 21 C8
Dahlia Gdns. Mitch CR4 .... 41 D5
Dahomey Rd. Streat SW16 ...... 21 C2
Daimler Way. Wallin SM6 .... 60 E3
Dainford Cl. Catf BR1 .... 24 D3
Dairy Cl. S Norw CR7 .... 42 C7
Dairy Gate Rd. Farnb GU14 .... 105 B8
Dairyfields. Crawl RH11 .... 201 A5
Dairymans Wlk. Burgh GU4 ..... 110 B6
Daisy Cl. Croy CR0 .... 43 D1
Dakin Cl. Worth RH10 .... 202 C2
Dakins The. E Grins RH19 ...... 205 E8
Dalcross. Brack RG12 .... 27 E3
Dalcross Rd. Hounsl TW4 & TW5 ... 4 E5
Dale Ave. Hounsl TW4 .... 4 E4
Dale Cl. Addl KT15 .... 52 B5
Dale Cl. Horsh RH12 .... 217 F5
Dale Cl. Sunnin SL5 .... 30 A4
Dale Cl. Wreccl GU10 .... 145 F7
Dale Ct. King U T KT2 .... 17 F1
Dale Gdns. Sandh GU17 .... 64 A8
Dale Lodge Rd. Sunnin SL5 .... 30 A4
Dale Park Ave. Carsh SM5 ...... 59 F8
Dale Park Rd. S Norw SE19 ..... 42 D8
Dale Rd. Ashf TW16 .... 14 F1
Dale Rd. Cheam SM1 .... 58 F6
Dale Rd. For Row RH18 .... 206 F1
Dale Rd. Purley CR8 .... 80 B7
Dale Rd. Walt O T KT12 .... 34 F2
Dale View. Haslem GU27 .... 207 F5
Dale View. Head KT18 .... 96 B4
Dale View. Woking GU21 .... 69 B1
Dalebury Rd. Up Toot SW17 .... 20 F6
Dalegarth Gdns. Sander CR8 ... 80 D6
Daleham Ave. Egham TW20 ...... 12 A2
Daleside Rd. Streat SW17 ...... 21 B3
Daleside Rd. W Ewell KT19 ..... 57 D4
Daleside Rd. W Ewell KT19 ..... 57 D4
Dalewood Gdns. Crawl RH10 ... 201 F8
Dalewood Gdns. N Cheam KT4 ... 58 B8
Dalkeith Rd. W Norw SE21 ..... 22 C8
Dallas Rd. Cheam SM3 .... 58 E4
Dallas Rd. For Hil SE26 .... 23 B5
Dallaway Gdns. E Grins RH19 .. 185 E1
Dalley Ct. Sandh GU15 .... 64 D7
Dallington Cl. Hersh KT12 ..... 54 C4
Dalmain Prim Sch. For Hil SE23 23 E7
Dalmain Rd. For Hil SE23 ...... 23 D7
Dalmally Rd. Croy CR0 .... 43 A2

Dalmeny Ave. Thorn H SW16 ... 42 A7
Dalmeny Cres. Islew TW3 .... 5 D3
Dalmeny Rd. N Cheam KT4 ...... 58 B7
Dalmeny Rd. Wallin SM5 .... 60 A3
Dalmore Rd. Clayg KT10 .... 55 F4
Dalmore Rd. W Norw SE21 ...... 22 C6
Dalston Cl. Friml GU15 .... 66 D3
Dalton Ave. Mitch CR4 .... 40 E7
Dalton Cl. Crawl RH11 .... 201 B1
Dalton House. Balham SW12 .. 21 B8
Dalton St. W Norw SE27 .... 22 B5
Damascene Wlk. W Norw SE21 .. 22 C7
Damask Cl. W End GU24 .... 67 E6
Damer House. Rich TW10 .... 6 F1
Damer Park Rd. Crawl RH11 ... 201 B1
Dan Bryant House.
  Streat SW12 .... 21 C8
Danbrook Rd. Streat SW16 ..... 21 E1
Danbury Mews.
  Wallin SM5 & SM6 .... 60 B6
Dancer Rd. Rich TW9 .... 7 A4
Dane Ct. Pyrf GU22 .... 70 F4
Dane Rd. Ashf TW15 .... 14 D2
Dane Rd. Merton SW19 .... 40 C8
Dane Rd. Warlgm CR6 .... 81 D2
Danebury. New Add CR0 .... 63 B4
Danebury Prim Sch.
  Rhampt SW15 .... 18 F8
Danebury Wlk. Friml GU16 ..... 85 F8
Daneby Rd. Catf SE6 .... 24 C6
Danecourt Gdns. S Croy CR0 ... 61 F7
Danehurst. Brent TW8 .... 6 C7
Danehurst Cres. Horsh RH13 ... 217 F2
Danemere La. Blind H RH9 ..... 142 E2
Danemore St. Wands SW18 ..... 20 C8
Danes Cl. Oxsh KT22 .... 74 C5
Danes Hill. Mayb GU22 .... 70 B1
Danes Hill Jun Sch. Oxsh KT22 . 74 C6
Danes Hill Sch. Oxsh KT22 .... 74 D6
Danes Way. Oxsh KT22 .... 74 D5
Danesbury Rd. Felt TW13 ...... 15 B7
Danescourt Cres. Sutton SM1 . 59 C8
Danesfield. Redh RH1 .... 118 E2
Daneshill. Redh RH1 .... 118 E2
Danesmead. Cobham KT11 ...... 74 A8
Danesrood. Guild GU1 .... 130 F8
Daneswood Ave. Catf SE6 ...... 24 C5
Daneswood Cl. Weyb KT13 ..... 53 C5
Danetree Cl. W Ewell KT19 .... 57 C3
Danetree Cty Mid Sch.
  W Ewell KT19 .... 57 C4
Danetree Cty Mid Sch.
  .... 57 C4
Danetree Rd. W Ewell KT19 .... 57 D3
Danetree Rd. W Ewell KT19 .... 57 D3
Daniel Cl. Mitch SW17 & SW19 .. 20 E2
Daniel Ct. Beck BR3 .... 24 A1
Daniel Way. Banstd SM7 .... 78 B5
Daniell Way. Croy CR0 & CR9 .. 41 F1
Daniels La. Warlgm CR6 .... 81 F4
Danley La. Linch GU27 .... 207 A3
Danses Cl. Merrow GU4 .... 110 D3
Dapdune Ct. Guild GU1 .... 109 C1
Dapdune Rd. Guild GU1 .... 109 D1
Daphne Ct. Worc Pk KT4 .... 57 E8
Daphne St. Wands SW18 .... 20 C8
Darby Cl. Cater CR3 .... 100 C5
Darby Gdns. Sunby TW16 ...... 35 C7
Darby Green La. Blckw GU17 ... 64 B5
Darby Green Rd. Blckw GU17 .. 64 B5
Darcy Ave. Wallin SM6 .... 60 C6
Darcy Cl. Coulsd CR5 .... 100 B8
Darcy Pl. Ashtd KT21 .... 75 E2
Darcy Rd. Ashtd KT21 .... 75 F2
Darcy Rd. Thorn H SW16 .... 41 E7
Darell Prim Sch. Rich TW9 .... 7 A4
Darell Rd. Rich TW9 .... 7 A4
Darent House. Catf BR1 .... 24 D3
Darenth Way. Horley RH6 ...... 160 F6
Darfield Rd. Burgh GU4 .... 110 A4
Dargate Cl. Penge SE19 .... 22 F1
Dark La. Putt GU3 .... 128 B4
Darlaston Rd. Wimble SW19 ... 19 E1
Darley Cl. Addl KT15 .... 52 C5
Darley Cl. Croy CR0 .... 43 E3
Darley Dene Inf Sch. Addl KT15 52 C5
Darley Dr. King U T KT3 ...... 38 D7
Darley Gdns. Morden SM4 ..... 40 B3
Darleydale. Crawl RH11 .... 201 C3
Darleydale Cl. Sandh GU15 .... 45 D2
Darlington Ct. Catf SE6 ...... 24 F7
Darlington House. Surb KT6 . 37 D2
Darlington Rd. W Norw SE27 ... 22 B3
Darmaine Cl. S Croy CR2 ...... 61 C3
Darnley Pk. Weyb KT13 .... 53 B7
Darracott Cl. Camb GU15 ..... 66 B8
Dart Cl. Bra Hil SL3 .... 1 B8
Dart Rd. W Heath GU14 .... 84 D6
Dartmouth Ave. Sheer GU21 ... 70 D5
Dartmouth Cl. Brack RG12 .... 27 E6
Dartmouth Gn. Sheer GU21 .... 70 D5
Dartmouth House. Thorn H CR0 42 B2
Dartmouth Path. Sheer GU21 .. 70 D5
Dartmouth Pl. For Hil SE23 ... 23 C6
Dartmouth Rd.
  For Hil SE23 & SE26 .... 23 C5
Dartnell Ave. W Byfl KT14 .... 71 C7
Dartnell Cl. W Byfl KT14 ..... 71 B7
Dartnell Cres. W Byfl KT14 ... 71 B7
Dartnell Ct. W Byfl KT14 ..... 71 C7
Dartnell Park Rd. W Byfl KT14 . 71 C8
Dartnell Pl. W Byfl KT14 ..... 71 B7
Dartnell Rd. Croy CR0 .... 42 F2
Darvel Cl. Woking GU21 .... 69 A3

Darvills La. Farnh GU9 .... 125 C2
Darwall Dr. N Asct SL5 .... 28 D7
Darwin Dr. Horsh RH12 .... 217 F4
Darwin Gr. Alder GU11 .... 105 C3
Daryngton Dr. Merrow GU1 .... 110 B1
Dashwood Cl. Brack RG12 ..... 27 D8
Dashwood Cl. W Byfl KT14 .... 71 C7
Dashwood Ct. Hounsl TW3 ..... 5 C3
Dashwood House. Dulw SE27 ... 22 F5
Dassett Rd. W Norw SE27 ...... 22 B3
Datchet Rd. For Hil SE6 .... 23 F6
Datchet Rd. Horton SL3 .... 1 A4
Daux Hill. Warn RH12 .... 217 B6
Davenant Rd. Croy CR0 & CR9 . 61 B6
Davenport Cl. Tedd TW11 ...... 17 A2
Davenport Lodge. Heston TW5 . 4 E7
Davenport Rd. Brack RG12 ..... 27 E8
Daventry Cl. Poyle SL3 .... 1 F6
Daventry Rd. Brack RG12 ...... 27 B8
David Cl. Harl UB3 .... 3 E7
David House. S Norw SE25 ..... 43 A6
David Livingstone Prim Sch.
  S Norw SE27 .... 42 C8
David Rd. Poyle SL3 .... 1 F5
David's Rd. For Hil SE23 ...... 23 C7
Davidson Inf Sch. Croy CR0 ... 42 F2
Davidson Jun Sch. Croy CR0 .. 42 F2
Davidson Lodge. Croy CR0 .... 42 F3
Davidson Rd. Croy CR0 & SE25 . 42 F3
Davies Cl. Croy CR0 & SE25 ... 43 A3
Davies Cl. Farnc GU7 .... 150 D7
Davis Gdns. Sandh GU15 ...... 65 C8
Davis Rd. Chess KT9 .... 57 A6
Davis Rd. Whit V KT13 .... 52 F1
Davos Cl. Woking GU22 .... 89 E8
Davy Cl. Woki RG11 .... 25 C5
Dawell Dr. Bigg H TN16 .... 83 C2
Dawes Ave. Islew TW7 .... 6 A3
Dawes Ct. Esher KT10 .... 55 B5
Dawes Green Cotts. Leigh RH2 138 A3
Dawley Ride. Poyle SL3 .... 1 E6
Dawlish Ave. Wimble SW18 .... 20 B6
Dawn Cl. Hounsl TW4 .... 4 E4
Dawn Redwood Cl. Horton SL3 . 1 A4
Dawn Wlk. Beck BR2 .... 44 D7
Dawnay Cl. N Asct SL5 .... 28 F8
Dawnay Gdns. Wands SW18 .... 20 D6
Dawnay Rd. Camb GU15 .... 65 B7
Dawnay Rd. G Book KT23 ...... 94 C1
Dawnay Rd.
  Wands SW17 & SW18 .... 20 D6
Dawney Hill. Pirb GU24 .... 87 F5
Dawneys Rd. Pirb GU24 .... 87 E5
Dawsmere Cl. Friml GU15 ..... 66 C5
Dawson Rd. Byfl KT14 .... 71 E7
Dawson Rd. King U T KT1 ...... 37 F6
Dax Ct. Sunby TW16 .... 35 C6
Day Ct. Crawl GU6 .... 173 F2
Day's Acre. S Croy CR2 .... 61 F1
Daybrook Rd. Merton SW19 .... 40 B6
Daymerslea Ridge. Leahd KT22 . 95 C6
Daysbrook Rd. Streat SW2 ..... 21 F7
Dayseys Hill. Outw RH1 .... 162 A8
Dayspring. Stough GU2 .... 109 B5
Daytone House. Wimble SW20 .. 39 D8
De Broome Rd. Felt TW13 ...... 15 C7
De Burgh House.
  Merton SW19 .... 20 C1
De Burgh Pk. Banstd SM7 ...... 78 B4
De Frene Rd. For Hil SE23 & SE26 23 E5
De Havilland Dr. Byfl KT13 ... 52 E1
De Havilland Dr. Byfl KT13 ... 71 E8
De Havilland Rd. Heston TW5 .. 4 C7
De Havilland Rd. Wallin SM6 .. 60 E3
De Havilland Way. Stan TW19 .. 2 E1
De La Warr Rd. E Grins RH19 .. 185 F1
De Lara Way. Woking GU21 .... 69 D1
De Montfort Par.
  Streat SW16 .... 21 E5
De Montfort Rd. Streat SW16 .. 21 E5
De Nederlandse Basis Sch.
  Mayb GU22 .... 70 C2
De Ros Pl. Egham TW20 .... 12 A2
De Stafford Sch. Whytlf CR3 .. 100 F6
De'arn Gdns. Mitch CR4 .... 40 E6
De-Vitre Gn. Woki RG11 .... 25 F7
Deacon Cl. Downs KT11 .... 93 B8
Deacon Cl. Wallin CR8 .... 60 B2
Deacon Cl. Woki RG11 .... 25 C8
Deacon Ct. Lingf RH7 .... 164 C4
Deacon Field. Stough GU2 ..... 109 A2
Deacon Rd. King U T KT2 ...... 37 F8
Deacons Wlk. Hampt TW12 ..... 16 A4
Deadbrook La. Alder GU12 ..... 105 E3
Deal Rd. Mitch SW17 .... 21 A2
Dean Cl. Pyrf GU22 .... 70 E4
Dean Ct. Farnc GU7 .... 150 D6
Dean Ct. King U T KT2 .... 18 A1
Dean Gr. Woki RG11 .... 25 C7
Dean La. Hooley CR3 & CR5 & RH1 99 D3
Dean Par. Camb GU15 .... 65 F8
Dean Rd. Croy CR0 .... 61 D6
Dean Rd. Farnc GU7 .... 150 D6
Dean Rd. Hampt TW12 .... 16 A4
Dean Rd. Hampt TW12 .... 16 A4
Dean Rd. Islew TW7 .... 5 B2
Dean Wlk. G Book KT23 .... 94 C1
Deanery Pl. Godal GU7 .... 150 D4
Deanery Rd. Farnc GU7 .... 150 E6
Deanfield Gdns. Croy CR0 ..... 61 D6
Deanhill Ct. Mortl SW14 ...... 7 B3
Deanhill Rd. Mortl SW14 ...... 7 B3
Deanoak La. Leigh RH2 .... 159 D8
Deanoak La. Sidlow RH2 .... 159 D8
Deans Cl. Chisw W4 .... 7 B8
Deans Cl. Croy CR0 .... 61 F7
Deans Cl. Walt o t H KT20 .... 97 B3
Deans Ct. Windl GU20 .... 48 D4
Deans Gate Cl. For Hil SE23 .. 23 D5
Deans La. Nutf RH1 .... 120 A2

Deans La. Walt o t H KT20 97 B2
Deans Rd. Merst RH1 119 C5
Deans Rd. Sutton SM1 59 B7
Deans Wlk. Coulsd CR5 80 A1
Deansfield. Cater CR3 100 F2
Deansgate. Easth RG12 27 B2
Dearmer House. 6 Streat SW2 22 A8
Debden Cl. King U T KT2 17 D3
Deborah Cl. Hounsl TW7 5 E6
Deburgh Rd. Merton SW19 20 C1
Dedham House. Catf SE6 24 C4
Dedisham Cl. Crawl RH10 202 A3
Dedisham Sch. Slinfd RH12 215 C6
Dedswell Dr. W Clan GU4 111 A6
Dee Rd. Rich TW9 6 F3
Dee Way. Epsom KT19 57 E1
Deedman Cl. Ash GU12 106 A2
Deep Dene. Shottm GU27 207 E6
Deep Well Dr. Camb GU15 65 E5
Deepcut Bridge Rd. Friml GU16 86 C7
Deepdale. Easth RG12 27 A5
Deepdale. Wimble SW19 19 D4
Deepdale Ave. Hayes BR2 44 F5
Deepdene. M Bourn GU10 146 D7
Deepdene Ave.
Dork RH4 & RH5 136 C6
Deepdene Ave. S Croy CR0 61 F7
Deepdene Avenue Rd.
Dork RH4 115 C1
Deepdene Ct. Beck BR2 44 E6
Deepdene Dr. Dork RH5 136 C7
Deepdene Gdns.
Dork RH4 & RH5 136 C8
Deepdene Gdns. Streat SW2 21 F8
Deepdene Lodge. 8 Streat SW2 21 F8
Deepdene Park Rd. Dork RH5 136 D8
Deepdene Point. 9 For Hil SE26 23 D5
Deepdene Sta. Dork RH4 115 C1
Deepdene Vale. Dork RH4 115 C1
Deepdene Wood. Dork RH5 136 D7
Deepfield Rd. Brack RG12 27 D7
Deepfield Way. Coulsd CR5 79 E3
Deepfields. Horley RH6 160 F5
Deepwell Cl. Islew TW7 6 A6
Deer Leap. Lhtwat GU18 67 A8
Deer Park Cl. King U T KT2 18 B1
Deer Park Gdns. Mitch CR4 40 D5
Deer Park Rd. Merton SW19 40 C7
Deer Park Way. Coney H BR4 63 F8
Deer Rock Hill. Easth RG12 27 C3
Deer Rock Rd. Camb GU15 65 F8
Deerbarn Rd. Stough GU2 109 B2
Deerbrook Rd.
Streat SE24 & SW2 22 B7
Deerhurst. King U T KT2 38 B8
Deerhurst Cl. Felt TW13 15 B4
Deerhurst Rd. Streat SW16 21 F3
Deerings Rd. Reig RH2 118 C1
Deerleap Rd. Westc RH4 135 B6
Deers Farm. Wisley GU23 & KT14 71 E3
Deerswood Cl. Cater CR3 101 A3
Deerswood Cl. Crawl RH11 201 B7
Deerswood Ct. Crawl RH11 201 A7
Deerswood Lower Sch.
Crawl RH11 201 A8
Deerswood Rd. Crawl RH11 201 B7
Deerswood Upper Sch.
Crawl RH11 201 A8
Deeside Rd. Wands SW17 20 D5
Defiant Rd. Farnb GU14 104 F8
Defiant Way. Wallin SM6 60 E3
Defoe Ave. Rich TW9 7 A7
Defoe Cl. Mitch SW17 & SW19 20 E2
Delabole Rd. Merst RH1 119 E6
Delamare Cres. Croy CR0 43 C3
Delamere Rd. Dovgn RH2 139 C5
Delamere Rd. Wimble SW20 39 D8
Delaporte Cl. Ewell KT17 76 E7
Delcombe Ave. N Cheam KT4 39 C1
Delderfield. Ashtd KT21 95 D6
Delia St. Wands SW18 20 B8
Dell Cl. Fetch KT22 94 E4
Dell Cl. Mickle RH5 115 C8
Dell Cl. Shottm GU27 208 A7
Dell Cl. Wallin SM6 60 D6
Dell Close Cotts. Mickle RH5 115 C8
Dell Gr. Friml GU16 65 F2
Dell House. S Croy CR2 61 C2
Dell La. Stonel KT17 58 A5
Dell Rd. Stonel KT17 58 A4
Dell The. Brent TW8 6 C8
Dell The. Burgh H KT20 97 C6
Dell The. E Grins RH19 186 B1
Dell The. Eng Gn SL4 11 A5
Dell The. Felt TW14 15 B8
Dell The. Heath E GU9 125 D7
Dell The. Horley RH6 161 B4
Dell The. Reig RH2 118 A2
Dell The. S Norw SE19 42 F8
Dell The. Sidlow RH6 160 C5
Dell The. Woking GU21 69 C1
Dell Wlk. King U T KT3 38 E7
Dellbow Rd. Felt TW14 4 B2
Dellfield Cl. Beck BR3 44 C8
Delmey Cl. S Croy CR0 61 F7
Delphian Ct. 5 Streat SW16 22 A4
Delta Bglws. Horley RH6 161 A1
Delta Cl. Chobh GU24 49 F1
Delta Cl. Worc Pk KT4 57 F7
Delta Dr. Horley RH6 161 A1
Delta House. Horley RH6 161 A1
Delta Rd. Chobh GU24 49 F1
Delta Rd. Woking GU21 70 A3
Delta Rd. Worc Pk KT19 & KT4 57 E7
Delta Way. Thorpe TW20 32 C8
Delves. Tadw KT20 97 D6
Delville Cl. Farnb GU14 84 D3
Demesne Rd. Wallin SM6 60 D6
Dempster Cl. Long D KT6 37 C1
Den Cl. Beck BR2 & BR3 44 D6
Den Rd. Beck BR2 44 D6
Denbigh Cl. Cheam SM1 58 F5
Denbigh Gdns. Rich TW10 6 F2
Denbigh Rd. Haslem GU27 208 D5
Denbigh Rd. Hounsl TW3 5 B5
Denby Rd. Cobham KT11 73 C7
Denchers Plat. Crawl RH11 181 D1
Dencliffe. Ashf TW15 14 A3
Dendy St. Balham SW12 21 A7
Dene Ave. Hounsl TW3 4 F4
Dene Cl. 2 Brack RG12 27 C8
Dene Cl. Haslem GU27 208 C6
Dene Cl. Hayes BR2 44 F1
Dene Cl. Horley RH6 160 E5
Dene Cl. M Bourn GU10 146 E6
Dene Cl. Worc Pk KT4 57 F8
Dene Ct. Merrow GU1 110 B3
Dene Gdns. Hinch W KT7 56 A8
Dene La. M Bourn GU10 146 E6
Dene La W. M Bourn GU10 146 E5
Dene Pl. Woking GU21 69 C1
Dene Rd. Ashtd KT21 95 F8
Dene Rd. Farnb GU14 84 F3
Dene Rd. Guild GU1 130 E8
Dene St. Dork RH4 136 B7
Dene Street Gdns. Dork RH4 136 B7
Dene The. Abing H RH5 134 B3
Dene The. Belm SM2 77 F8
Dene The. E Mole KT12 & KT8 35 F4
Dene The. S Croy CR0 62 D6
Dene Tye. Crawl RH10 202 D7
Dene Wlk. M Bourn GU10 146 E6
Denefield Dr. Kenley CR8 80 D4
Denehurst Gdns. Mortl TW10 7 A3
Denehurst Gdns. Twick TW2 16 D8
Denehyrst Ct. Guild GU1 130 E8
Denewood. 8 Epsom KT17 76 E6
Denfield. Dork RH4 136 C5
Denham Cres. Mitch CR4 40 F5
Denham Ct. For Hil SE26 23 B5
Denham Gr. Easth RG12 27 C3
Denham Rd. Egham TW20 12 A4
Denham Rd. Ewell KT17 76 F7
Denham Rd. Felt TW14 15 C8
Denholm Gdns.
Burph GU1 & GU4 110 A4
Denison Rd. Felt TW13 14 F4
Denison Rd. Mitch SW19 20 D2
Denleigh Gdns. Thame D KT7 36 E3
Denly Way. Lhtwat GU18 48 C1
Denman Dr. Ashf TW15 14 B2
Denman Dr. Clayg KT10 56 A5
Denmans. Crawl RH10 202 D7
Denmark Ave. Wimble SW19 19 E1
Denmark Ct. Morden SM4 40 A4
Denmark Ct. 2 Weyb KT13 53 B7
Denmark Gdns. Carsh SM5 59 F7
Denmark Rd. Carsh SM5 59 F7
Denmark Rd. Croy SE25 43 B4
Denmark Rd. Guild GU1 130 E8
Denmark Rd. King U T KT1 37 E6
Denmark Rd. Twick TW2 16 D5
Denmark Rd. Wimble SW19 19 D2
Denmark Sq. Alder GU12 105 E2
Denmark St. Alder GU12 105 D2
Denmark St. Woki RG11 25 C5
Denmead Ct. Brack RG12 27 E3
Denmead House. Rhampt SW15 7 F1
Denmead Lower Sch.
Hampt TW12 16 B1
Denmead Rd. Thorn H CR0 42 B1
Denmead Upper Sch.
Hampt TW12 16 B1
Denmore Ct. Wallin SM6 60 B5
Dennan Rd. Surb KT6 37 F1
Denne Par. Horsh RH12 & RH13 217 C1
Denne Rd. Crawl RH11 201 D5
Denne Rd. Horsh RH12 217 C1
Dennett Rd. Thorn H CR0 42 A2
Denning Ave. Croy CR0 61 A5
Denning Cl. Hampt TW12 15 F3
Denningtons The. Worc Pk KT4 57 E8
Dennis Cl. Ashf TW15 14 D1
Dennis Cl. Redh RH1 118 E3
Dennis House. Sutton SM1 59 A6
Dennis Park Cres. Wimble SW20 39 E8
Dennis Rd. E Mole KT8 36 C5
Dennis Reeve Cl. Mitch CR4 40 F8
Dennis Track. Farnb GU14 104 C7
Dennis Way. Jacobs GU1 109 E6
Dennistoun Cl. Camb GU15 65 D5
Densole Cl. Penge BR3 43 E8
Denton Cl. Earls RH1 140 A4
Denton Gr. Walt O T KT12 54 E8
Denton Rd. Twick TW1 6 D1
Denton Rd. Woki RG11 25 C6
Denton Way. Friml GU16 65 D2
Denton Way. Woking GU21 69 A2
Dents Gr. L Kings KT20 117 F7
Denvale Wlk. Woking GU21 69 A1
Denwood. For Hil SE23 23 D5
Denzil Rd. Guild GU2 130 B8
Departures Rd. Crawl RH6 181 F8
Depot Rd. Crawl RH11 181 D1
Depot Rd. Epsom KT17 76 E6
Depot Rd. Horsh RH13 217 E2
Depot Rd. Hounsl TW3 & TW7 5 D4
Derby Arms Rd. Epsom KT18 76 F2
Derby Cl. Burgh H KT18 & KT20 97 B8
Derby Hill. For Hil SE23 23 C6
Derby Hill Cres. For Hil SE23 23 C6
Derby Rd. Cheam SM1 & SM2 58 F4
Derby Rd. Haslem GU27 208 B7
Derby Rd. Hounsl TW3 5 B3
Derby Rd. Merton SW19 20 A1
Derby Rd. Mortl SW14 7 B3
Derby Rd. Stough GU2 108 F1
Derby Rd. Surb KT5 & KT6 38 A1
Derby Rd. Thorn H CR0 42 B1
Derby Stables Rd. Epsom KT18 76 F2
Derek Ave. Hackb SM6 60 B6
Derek Ave. W Ewell KT19 57 B5
Derek Ave. W Ewell KT19 57 B5
Derek Cl. W Ewell KT19 57 B5
Derek Cl. W Ewell KT19 57 B5
Derek Horn Ct. Camb GU15 65 B6
Deri Dene Cl. 2 Stan TW19 2 E1
Dering Pl. Croy CR0 61 C6
Dering Rd. Croy CR0 & CR9 61 C6
Derinton Rd. Up Toot SW17 21 A4
Deronda Rd. Streat SE24 & SW2 22 B7
Deroy Cl. Wallin SM5 59 F4
Deroy Ct. Wallin SM5 59 F4
Derrick Ave. S Croy CR2 61 C1
Derrick House. 13 Streat SW2 22 A7
Derrick Rd. Beck BR3 43 F5
Derry Rd. W Heath GU14 84 F8
Derry Rd. Wallin CR0 & SM6 60 E7
Derrydown. Woking GU22 89 C6
Derwent Ave. Ash V GU12 105 F4
Derwent Ave. King U T SW15 18 E4
Derwent Cl. Addl KT15 52 D5
Derwent Cl. Clayg KT10 55 F4
Derwent Cl. Crawl RH11 200 F5
Derwent Cl. E Bed TW14 14 F7
Derwent Cl. Farnb GU14 84 E4
Derwent Cl. Hale GU9 125 A6
Derwent Cl. Horsh RH12 218 B6
Derwent Dr. Sander CR8 80 E6
Derwent House. Penge SE20 43 B7
Derwent House. Woodh RH2 139 A7
Derwent Lodge. N Cheam KT4 58 B8
Derwent Rd. Lhtwat GU18 67 B8
Derwent Rd. Penge SE20 43 B7
Derwent Rd. Thor L TW20 12 B1
Derwent Rd. Twick TW2 5 B1
Derwent Rd. W Barn SM4 39 D3
Derwent Wlk. Wallin SM6 60 B3
Desborough Cl. Lo Hall TW17 34 A2
Desborough Ct. Croy SE25 43 B5
Desford Way. Ashf TW15 13 F6
Desmond Anderson Cty Fst Sch.
Crawl RH10 201 E2
Desmond Anderson Cty Mid Sch.
Crawl RH10 201 E2
Despard House. Streat SW2 22 A6
Detherick Ct. Hounsl TW3 5 C3
Detillens La. Limps RH8 123 A6
Detling Rd. Crawl RH11 201 C1
Dettingen Rd. Friml GU16 86 E8
Deutsche Schule. Rich TW10 17 D7
Devana End. Carsh SM5 59 F7
Devas Rd. Wimble SW20 39 C8
Devenish La. Sunnin GU20 & SL5 29 D1
Devenish Rd. Ascot GU20 & SL5 29 D2
Devenish Rd. Sunnin GU20 & SL5 29 D2
Deverill Ct. Penge SE20 43 C8
Devil's La. Egham TW20 12 C2
Devitt Cl. Ashtd KT21 76 A3
Devoil Cl. Burph GU4 110 B5
Devoke Way. Walt O T KT12 54 D8
Devon Ave. Twick TW2 16 C7
Devon Bank. Guild GU2 130 C6
Devon Cl. Kenley CR8 80 E3
Devon Cl. Sandh GU15 64 D7
Devon Cres. Reig RH1 & RH2 118 D1
Devon House. Cater CR3 100 F3
Devon House. Knaph GU21 68 D2
Devon House. Penge SE20 23 B1
Devon Rd. Belm SM2 58 E2
Devon Rd. Farnb GU11 & GU14 104 F7
Devon Rd. Hersh KT12 54 C6
Devon Rd. Merst RH1 119 C5
Devon Way. Chess KT9 56 C6
Devon Way. W Ewell KT19 57 B5
Devon Way. W Ewell KT19 57 B5
Devon Waye. Heston TW5 4 F7
Devoncroft Gdns. Twick TW1 17 A8
Devonshire Ave. Sheer GU21 70 D6
Devonshire Ave. Sutton SM2 59 C3
Devonshire Ct. Croy CR0 44 A1
Devonshire Ct. 6 Rich TW9 6 F6
Devonshire Dr. Camb GU15 65 F7
Devonshire Dr. Camb GU15 66 A7
Devonshire Dr. Long D KT6 56 D8
Devonshire Gdns. Chisw W4 7 C7
Devonshire House. 14
Balham SW12 21 B8
Devonshire House. Hounsl TW3 5 C4
Devonshire House. Sutton SM2 59 C3
Devonshire Pl. Alder GU11 104 F1
Devonshire Prim Sch.
Sutton SM2 59 C3
Devonshire Rd. Chisw W4 7 E8
Devonshire Rd. Felt TW13 15 E4
Devonshire Rd. For Hil SE23 23 C8
Devonshire Rd.
Hackb SM5 & SM6 60 A6
Devonshire Rd. Horsh RH13 217 D2
Devonshire Rd.
Mitch SW17 & SW19 20 E1
Devonshire Rd. Sutton SM2 59 C3
Devonshire Rd. Thorn H CR0 42 D2
Devonshire Rd. Weyb KT13 53 A6
Devonshire St. Chisw W4 7 E8
Devonshire Way.
Croy CR0 & CR9 62 F8
Devonshires The. Epsom KT18 76 F5
Dewar Cl. Crawl RH11 200 E5
Dewar House. Up Toot SW17 20 E3
Dewey St. Up Toot SW17 20 F3
Dewlands. Tyl Gn RH9 121 C4
Dewlands Cl. Cran GU6 174 E3
Dewlands La. Cran GU6 174 E3
Dewsbury Gdns. Worc Pk KT4 58 A7
Dexter Dr. E Grins RH19 205 E8
Diamedes Ave. Stan TW19 13 D7
Diamond Ct. 4 Redh RH1 119 A2
Diamond Est. Up Toot SW17 20 E5
Diamond Hill. Camb GU15 65 E7
Diamond Ridge. Camb GU15 65 E7
Diamond Way. Farnb GU14 104 E8
Diana Gdns. Surb KT6 56 F8
Dianthus Cl. Chert KT16 32 E2
Dianthus Ct. Woking GU22 69 D1
Dianthus Pl. Wink RG12 8 B2
Dibdin Cl. Sutton SM1 59 A7
Dibdin Rd. Sutton SM1 59 A8
Diceland Rd. Banstd SM7 77 F3
Dick Sheppard Sch. Streat SE24 22 A8
Dick Turpin Way. Hatton TW14 3 F3
Dickens Cl. E Grins RH19 185 C1
Dickens Cl. Rich TW10 17 E6
Dickens Dr. Row Tn KT15 51 F4
Dickens Rd. Crawl RH10 201 E3
Dickenson's La. Croy SE25 43 A3
Dickenson's Pl. Croy SE25 43 A3
Dickerage Hill. King U T KT3 38 C6
Dickerage La. King U T KT3 38 C6
Dickerage Rd.
King U T KT1 & KT2 & KT3 38 C7
Dickins Way. Horsh RH13 217 F1
Dickinson Rd. Felt TW13 15 D3
Digby Pl. S Croy CR0 61 F7
Digby Way. Byfl KT14 71 F7
Digdens Rise. Woodc KT18 76 C4
Dillwyn Cl. For Hil SE26 23 E4
Dilston Rd. Leahd KT22 95 A8
Dilton Gdns. Rhampt SW15 19 B7
Dingle Rd. Ashf TW15 14 B3
Dingle The. Crawl RH11 201 B6
Dingley La. Streat SW16 21 D6
Dingley Way. Farnb GU14 104 F8
Dingwall Ave. Croy CR0 & CR9 61 C8
Dingwall Rd. Croy CR0 & CR9 61 D8
Dingwall Rd. Wallin SM5 59 F2
Dingwall Rd. Wands SW18 20 C8
Dinsdale Cl. Woking GU22 70 A1
Dinsdale Gdns. S Norw SE25 42 E4
Dinsmore Rd. Balham SW12 21 B8
Dinton Rd. King U T KT2 17 F1
Dinton Rd. Mitch SW17 & SW19 20 D2
Dione Wlk. Crawl RH11 200 E4
Dippenhall Rd. Farnh GU10 124 C2
Dippenhall St. Crond GU10 124 A5
Dirdene Cl. Ewell KT17 76 F7
Dirdene Gdns. Ewell KT17 76 F7
Dirdene Gr. Ewell KT17 76 F7
Dirtham La. Effing KT24 113 B6
Dirty La. Ash W RH19 206 E7
Discovery Pk. Crawl RH10 182 A2
Disraeli Ct. Bra Hil SL3 1 B8
Distillery Wlk. 14 Brent TW8 6 E8
Ditches La. Coulsd CR3 & CR5 99 E6
Ditchling. Easth RG12 27 A2
Ditchling Hill. Crawl RH11 201 C4
Ditton Cl. Thame D KT7 37 A2
Ditton Grange Cl. Long D KT6 37 D1
Ditton Grange Dr. Long D KT6 37 D1
Ditton Hill. Long D KT6 56 D8
Ditton Hill Rd. Long D KT6 37 C1
Ditton Lawn. Thame D KT7 37 A1
Ditton Pl. 7 Penge SE20 43 B8
Ditton Rd. Surb KT6 37 E1
Ditton Reach. Thame D KT7 37 B3
Dixon Dr. Whit V KT13 52 F1
Dixon Pl. W Wick BR4 44 B1
Dixon Rd. S Norw SE25 42 F6
Dobbins Pl. Crawl RH11 200 E5
Doble Ct. Sander CR2 81 A8
Dobson Rd. Crawl RH11 181 D1
Dock Rd. Brent TW8 6 D7
Dock Rd. Farnb GU14 85 B2
Dockenfield St. Binst GU10 166 C6
Dockett Eddy La. Lo Hall TW17 33 F1
Dockett Moorings. Chert KT16 33 F1
Dockwell Cl. Hatton TW14 4 A3
Dockwell's Ind Est. Felt TW14 4 C2
Doctors Cl. For Hil SE26 23 C3
Doctors La. Cater CR3 100 A3
Dodbrooke Rd. W Norw SE27 22 B5
Dodd's La. W Byfl KT14 71 A5
Dodds Cres. W Byfl KT14 71 B5
Dodds Pk. Brock RH3 137 B7
Doel Cl. Merton SW19 20 C1
Dogflud Way. Farnh GU9 125 C3
Doggett Rd. Catf SE6 24 A8
Doggett Rd. Lewish SE6 24 A8
Doghurst Ave. Harl UB7 3 B7
Doghurst Dr. Harl UB7 3 B7
Doghurst La. Chips CR5 98 F7
Doland Ct. Up Toot SW17 20 F2
Dolby Terr. Charl RH6 180 E6
Dollis Cl. Worth RH10 202 C5
Dollis Dr. Farnh GU9 125 D3
Dolphin Cl. King U T KT6 37 D4
Dolphin Cl. Shottm GU27 207 E6
Dolphin Ct. Merton SW19 20 A1
Dolphin Ct. Stan TW19 13 A5
Dolphin Ct. 2 Wallin SM6 60 B4
Dolphin Ct N. Stan TW19 13 A5
Dolphin Rd. Charlt TW16 34 E8
Dolphin Rd N. Charlt TW16 34 E8
Dolphin Rd S. Charlt TW16 34 E8
Dolphin Rd W. Charlt TW16 34 E8
Dolphin Sq. Chisw W4 7 E7
Dolphin St. King U T KT2 37 E8
Doman Rd. Camb GU15 65 A4
Dome Hill. Cater CR3 120 E8
Dome Hill Peak. Cater CR3 100 E1
Dome Hill Pk. For Hil SE26 22 F4
Dome Way. Redh RH1 118 F2
Dominion Rd. Croy CR0 42 F2
Donald Lynch House. Mitch CR4 40 F7
Donald Rd. Thorn H CR0 & CR9 41 F2
Doncaster Wlk. Crawl RH10 202 A4
Doncastle Rd. Easth RG12 26 F6
Donkey La. Abin C RH5 155 D8
Donkey La. Crawl RH6 182 D7
Donlan Dr. Farnb GU14 84 C1
Donne Cl. Crawl RH10 202 B8
Donne Gdns. Pyrf GU22 70 E4
Donne Pl. Mitch CR4 41 B5
Donnington Cl. Camb GU15 65 B4
Donnington Ct. 2 Crawl RH11 200 F3
Donnington Rd. N Cheam KT4 58 A8
Donnybrook. Easth RG12 27 A2
Donnybrook Rd. Streat SW16 21 D1
Donovan Cl. Epsom KT19 57 D1
Donyngs Place Recn Ctr.
Redh RH1 118 E2
Doods Brow Sch. Nutf RH1 119 F2
Doods Park Rd. Reig RH2 118 C1
Doods Pl. Reig RH2 118 D2
Doods Rd. Reig RH2 118 C2
Doods Way. Reig RH2 118 D2
Doomsday Garden.
Horsh RH13 218 A1
Doone Cl. Tedd TW11 17 A2
Dora Rd. Wimble SW19 20 A4
Dora's Green La. Crond GU10 124 C5
Doradus Ct. 20 Putney SW19 19 D7
Doral Way. Wallin SM5 59 F5
Doran Dr. Reig RH2 118 D1
Doran Gdns. Reig RH2 118 D1
Dorcas Ct. Camb GU15 65 B3
Dorchester Ct. Mayb GU22 70 A3
Dorchester Ct. Reig RH2 118 C2
Dorchester Ct. Stain TW18 13 A4
Dorchester Ct. 5 Streat SW16 21 E6
Dorchester Dr. Felt TW14 3 E1
Dorchester Gr. Chisw W4 7 E8
Dorchester Mews. New Mal KT3 38 D5
Dorchester Mews. Twick TW1 6 C1
Dorchester Prim Sch.
N Cheam KT4 39 C1
Dorchester Rd. Cheam SM4 40 C2
Dorchester Rd. Morden CR4 40 C2
Dorchester Rd. N Cheam KT4 39 C1
Dorchester Rd. Weyb KT13 53 B7
Dore Gdns. Morden SM4 40 B2
Doreen Cl. W Heath GU14 84 E7
Dorian Dr. Ascot SL5 29 E8
Doric Dr. Kings KT20 97 F7
Dorien Rd. Merton SW20 39 D7
Dorin Ct. Pyrf GU22 70 E4
Dorin Ct. Warlgm CR6 101 B7
Doris Rd. Ashf TW15 14 D2
Dorking Cl. N Cheam KT4 58 D8
Dorking General Hospl.
Dork RH4 136 B6
Dorking Inst of FE. Dork RH4 136 B7
Dorking Rd. Chil GU4 131 E3
Dorking Rd. Epsom KT18 76 B4
Dorking Rd. G Book KT23 114 C8
Dorking Rd. L Kings KT20 116 F7
Dorking Rd. Leahd KT22 95 B3
Dorking Rd. Tadw KT20 97 C3
Dorking Rd. Walt o t H KT20 97 C3
Dorking Rd. Warn RH12 & RH5 198 B4
Dorking Sta. Dork RH4 115 C1
Dorking West Sta. Dork RH4 136 A8
Dorlcote. Witley GU8 170 E5
Dorlcote Rd. Wands SW18 20 E8
Dorling Dr. Ewell KT17 76 F7
Dorly Cl. Up Hall TW17 34 E4
Dorman's Cl. Dorman RH7 186 A8
Dormans. Crawl RH11 201 A5
Dormans Ave. Dorman RH7 165 A2
Dormans Gdns. Dorm Pk RH19 185 E6
Dormans High St. Dorman RH7 186 A8
Dormans Park Rd.
Dorm Pk RH19 185 E6
Dormans Park Rd.
E Grins RH19 185 D3
Dormans Rd. Dorman RH7 165 A2
Dormans Sta. Felct RH7 185 F8
Dormans Station Rd.
Dorman RH7 185 F7
Dormans Station Rd.
Felct RH7 185 F7
Dormansland Prim Sch.
Dorman RH7 186 A8
Dormer Cl. Crowth RG11 45 A5
Dormers Cl. Farnc GU7 150 D7
Dormy House The. Went GU25 30 F3
Dorney Gr. Weyb KT13 53 B8
Dorney Way. Hounsl TW4 4 E2
Dornford Gdns. Coulsd CR5 100 C8
Dornton Rd. S Croy CR2 61 D5
Dornton Rd.
Up Toot SW12 & SW17 21 C6
Dorrien Wlk. Streat SW16 21 D6
Dorrington Ct. S Norw SE25 42 E7
Dorrit Cres. Stough GU3 108 E3
Dorryn Ct. For Hil SE26 23 D3
Dorset Ave. E Grins RH19 185 C3
Dorset Ct. Camb GU15 65 F8
Dorset Ct. Epsom KT17 76 F7
Dorset Dr. Mayb GU22 70 B2
Dorset Gdns. E Grins RH19 185 C3
Dorset Gdns. Thorn H SW16 41 F5
Dorset House. 2 Penge SE20 43 B8
Dorset Rd. Ash GU12 106 B5
Dorset Rd. Ashf TW15 13 D5
Dorset Rd. Belm SM2 59 A1
Dorset Rd. Merton SW19 40 A7
Dorset Rd. Mitch CR4 40 E7
Dorset Rd. Penge BR3 43 D6
Dorset Sq. Epsom KT19 57 D1
Dorset Way. Byfl KT14 52 D1
Dorset Way. Twick TW2 16 D7
Dorset Waye. Heston TW5 4 F7
Dorsten Sq. Crawl RH11 200 F3
Douai Cl. Farnb GU14 85 C4
Douai Gr. Hampt TW12 36 C8
Douglas Ave. W Barn KT3 39 B5
Douglas Cl. Jacobs GU4 109 D6
Douglas Cl. Wallin SM6 60 E4
Douglas Ct. Cater CR3 100 D5
Douglas Dr. Croy CR0 63 A7
Douglas Dr. Godal GU7 150 F5

Douglas Gr. M Bourn GU10 .... 146 C5
Douglas Gracey House.
 Putney SW18 .... 19 E8
Douglas Houghton House. 11
 Redh RH1 .... 118 F2
Douglas House. L Book KT23 .... 94 A3
Douglas House. Twick TW1 .... 6 B2
Douglas Mews. Banstd SM7 .... 77 F3
Douglas Rd. Addl KT15 .... 52 B7
Douglas Rd. Farnb GU14 .... 104 B8
Douglas Rd. Hounsl TW3 .... 5 B4
Douglas Rd. King U T KT1 .... 38 B7
Douglas Rd. Stan TW19 .... 2 D1
Douglas Rd. Surb KT6 .... 37 F1
Douglas Rd. Thame D KT10 .... 55 B8
Douglas Robinson Ct.
 Streat SW16 .... 21 E1
Douglas Sq. Morden SM4 .... 40 A3
Doultons The. Stain TW18 .... 13 A2
Dounesforth Gdns.
 Wands SW18 .... 20 B7
Dove Cl. Crawl RH11 .... 201 D8
Dove Cl. Selsd CR2 .... 81 D8
Dove Ct. Stan TW19 .... 13 E8
Dovecote Cl. Weyb KT13 .... 53 B7
Dovecote Gdns. 8 Mortl SW14 .... 7 D4
Dovedale Cl. Burph GU4 .... 110 A4
Dovedale Cl. Sandh GU15 .... 45 D2
Dovedale Cres. Crawl RH11 .... 201 B4
Dovedale Rise. Mitch CR4 .... 20 F1
Dovehouse Gn. 1 Oat Pk KT13 .... 53 D6
Dover Ct. Cran GU6 .... 175 A3
Dover Gdns. Carsh SM5 .... 59 F7
Dover House. 7 Beck BR3 .... 24 A1
Dover House. 15 Penge SE20 .... 43 B8
Dover House Rd. Putney SW15 .... 19 B8
Dover Rd. S Norw SE19 .... 22 D2
Dover Terr. Rich TW9 .... 7 A5
Dovercourt Ave. Thorn H CR7 .... 42 A5
Dovercourt La. Sutton SM1 .... 59 C7
Dovercourt Rd.
 Dulw SE21 & SE22 .... 22 E8
Doverfield Rd. Burph GU4 .... 110 A4
Doverfield Rd. Streat SW2 .... 21 E8
Dovers Green Inf Sch.
 Dovgn RH1 .... 139 C5
Dovers Green Rd. Dovgn RH2 ...... 139 B4
Doversmead. Knaph GU21 .... 68 E3
Doveton Rd. S Croy CR2 .... 61 D5
Dowanhill Rd. Catf SE6 .... 24 D7
Dowdeswell Cl. Rhampt SW15 .... 7 E3
Dowding Ct. Crowth RG11 .... 45 C6
Dowding Rd. Bigg H TN16 .... 83 D4
Dowell House. Dulw SE21 .... 22 F5
Dower Ave. Wallin SM6 .... 60 B2
Dower House. Milf GU8 .... 170 F8
Dower Wlk. Crawl RH11 .... 201 A5
Dowes House. 13 Streat SW16 .... 21 E5
Dowlands La.
 Burst RH10 & RH6 .... 183 D7
Dowlans Cl. G Book KT23 .... 114 A8
Dowlans Rd. G Book KT23 .... 114 B8
Dowler Ct. 2 King U T KT2 .... 37 F8
Dowman Cl. 2 Merton SW19 .... 20 B1
Down Hall Rd. King U T KT2 .... 37 D8
Down La. Compt GU3 .... 129 B4
Down Lodge Ct. Epsom KT18 .... 76 E5
Down Rd. Merrow GU1 .... 110 B1
Down Rd. Tedd TW11 .... 17 B2
Down St. E Mole KT8 .... 36 A4
Down Yhonda. Elst GU8 .... 148 C3
Downderry Prim Sch. Catf BR1 .... 24 E4
Downderry Rd. Catf BR1 .... 24 E4
Downe Cl. Horley RH6 .... 160 E5
Downe Golf Course. Downe BR6 ..... 83 E7
Downe Rd. Mitch CR4 .... 40 F7
Downer Meadow. Farnc GU7 .... 150 E8
Downes Cl. Twick TW1 .... 6 B1
Downfield. 7 New Mal KT3 .... 39 A1
Downfield House. New Mal KT3 ...... 38 D1
Downham Enterprise Ctr.
 Catf SE6 .... 24 F6
Downham Way. Catf BR1 .... 24 E4
Downhurst Rd. Ewh GU6 .... 175 E6
Downing Ave. Onsl V GU2 .... 129 F8
Downing House. 3
 Merton SW19 .... 20 A1
Downing St. Farnh GU9 .... 125 B2
Downland Cl. Burgh H KT18 .... 77 B1
Downland Cl. Wallin CR5 .... 79 B5
Downland Ct. Crawl RH11 .... 201 C4
Downland Dr. Crawl RH11 .... 201 C3
Downland Gdns. Burgh H KT18 ...... 77 B1
Downland Pl. Crawl RH11 .... 201 C4
Downland Way. Burgh H KT18 .... 77 B1
Downlands Rd. Purley CR8 .... 79 F6
Downmill Rd. Brack RG12 .... 26 F7
Downs Ave. Epsom KT18 .... 76 F4
Downs Bridge Rd.
 Beck BR2 & BR3 .... 44 D8
Downs Court Rd. Purley CR8 .... 80 B6
Downs Ct. Purley CR8 .... 61 B1
Downs Ct. 2 Redh RH1 .... 119 A4
Downs Ct. 10 Wimble SW19 .... 19 D1
Downs Est. Ashtd KT17 .... 77 C5
Downs Hill. Beck BR2 & BR3 .... 44 D8
Downs Hill Rd. Epsom KT18 .... 76 E5
Downs La. Leahd KT22 .... 95 B3
Downs Rd. Ashtd KT18 & KT21 ...... 96 C7
Downs Rd. Beck BR3 .... 44 B7
Downs Rd. Coulsd CR5 .... 79 D1
Downs Rd. Epsom KT17 & KT18 ..... 76 E3
Downs Rd. Mickle RH5 .... 115 C7
Downs Rd. Purley CR8 .... 80 B8
Downs Rd. S Norw SE25 .... 43 B4
Downs Rd. Sutton SM2 .... 78 C8
Downs Side. Belm SM2 .... 77 F8
Downs The. Leahd KT22 .... 95 C2

Downs The.
 Wimble SW19 & SW20 .... 19 D1
Downs View. Hounsl TW7 .... 6 A6
Downs View. Pixham RH4 .... 115 D1
Downs View. Tadw KT20 .... 97 B6
Downs View Lodge. 9
 Surb KT6 .... 37 E3
Downs View Rd. G Book KT23 ..... 114 C8
Downs Way. Epsom KT18 .... 76 F3
Downs Way. G Book KT23 .... 94 C1
Downs Way. Oxted RH8 .... 122 E8
Downs Way. Tadw KT20 .... 97 B6
Downs Way Prim Sch.
 Oxted RH8 .... 122 E8
Downs Wood. Burgh H KT18 .... 77 B2
Downsend Lodge Pre Prep Sch.
 Leahd KT22 .... 95 B6
Downsend Lodge Sch.
 Ewell KT17 .... 76 F7
Downsend Sch. Ashtd KT22 .... 95 D7
Downshire Way. Easth RG12 .... 27 B6
Downside. Beac H GU26 .... 188 D7
Downside. Epsom KT18 .... 76 E5
Downside. Twick TW1 .... 16 F5
Downside Bridge Rd.
 Cobham KT11 .... 73 B4
Downside Cl. Wimble SW19 .... 20 C2
Downside Common Rd.
 Downs KT11 .... 73 C1
Downside Ct. Merst RH1 .... 119 C6
Downside Orch. Downs KT11 .... 70 A2
Downside Prep Sch. Purley CR8 ..... 79 D8
Downside Rd. Downs KT11 .... 73 B2
Downside Rd. Merrow GU4 .... 131 B8
Downsman Ct. Crawl RH10 .... 201 D3
Downsview Ave. Westfd GU22 .... 89 F6
Downsview Ct. Bellf GU1 .... 109 C5
Downsview Gdns. S Norw SE19 ..... 22 C1
Downsview Prim Sch.
 S Norw SE19 .... 22 C1
Downsview Rd. Head Dn GU35 .... 187 C5
Downsview Rd. Horsh RH12 .... 218 B6
Downsview Rd.
 S Norw CR7 & SE19 .... 22 C1
Downsway. Merrow GU1 .... 110 E1
Downsway. S Croy CR2 .... 80 E8
Downsway. Whytlf CR3 .... 80 F6
Downsway Cl. Tadw KT20 .... 97 A6
Downsway The. Sutton SM2 .... 59 C2
Downswood. Redh RH1 .... 118 D4
Downton Ave. Streat SW2 .... 21 F6
Downview Cl. Beac H GU26 .... 188 D6
Downview Cl. Downs KT11 .... 93 B8
Doyle Rd. Croy SE25 .... 43 A5
Dr Johnson Ave. Up Toot SW17 ..... 21 B5
Dragon La. Whit V KT13 .... 53 A1
Dragoon Ct. Alder GU11 .... 104 E2
Drake Ave. Cater CR3 .... 100 C5
Drake Ave. Mytch GU16 .... 86 A1
Drake Ave. Stain TW18 .... 12 F3
Drake Cl. Easth RG12 .... 27 B4
Drake Cl. Horsh RH12 .... 217 E6
Drake Cl. Dulw SE19 .... 22 F3
Drake Ct. King U T KT5 .... 37 F5
Drake Rd. Chess KT9 .... 57 A5
Drake Rd. Crawl RH10 .... 201 E3
Drake Rd. Horley RH6 .... 160 E3
Drake Rd. Mitch CR4 .... 41 A3
Drake Rd. Thorn H CR0 & CR9 .... 41 F2
Drake's Cl. Esher KT10 .... 55 A6
Drakefield Rd. Up Toot SW17 .... 21 A5
Drakes Cl. For Hil SE23 .... 23 C7
Drakes Way. Woking GU22 .... 89 D5
Drakewood Rd. Streat SW16 .... 21 D1
Drax Ave. Wimble SW20 .... 19 A1
Draxmont. Wimble SW19 .... 19 E2
Dray Ct. Guild GU2 .... 130 B8
Draycot Rd. Tolw KT6 .... 38 A1
Draycott. Brack RG12 .... 27 E4
Drayhorse Dr. Bagsh GU19 .... 47 E2
Drayton Cl. Brack RG12 .... 27 D7
Drayton Cl. Fetch KT22 .... 94 E3
Drayton Cl. Hounsl TW4 .... 4 F2
Drayton Ct. Tolw KT5 .... 37 F4
Drayton Ct. W Byfl KT14 .... 71 A6
Drayton Rd. Croy CR0 & CR9 .... 61 B8
Dresden Way. Weyb KT13 .... 53 C5
Drew House. 12 Streat SW16 .... 21 E5
Drewstead Rd. Streat SW16 .... 21 D6
Drift The. E Hors KT11 & KT24 ...... 92 E3
Drift The. Mart Gn KT11 & KT24 .... 92 E3
Drift Way. Coln SL3 .... 1 C7
Driftway The. Leahd KT22 .... 95 C4
Driftway The. Mitch CR4 .... 41 A8
Driftway The. Nork SM7 .... 77 C4
Driftway (Worple Road) The.
 Leahd KT22 .... 95 B4
Driftwood Dr. Kenley CR8 .... 80 C2
Drill Hall Rd. Chert KT16 .... 33 A2
Drive Rd. Coulsd CR5 .... 99 F7
Drive Spur. Kings KT20 .... 98 B6
Drive The. Arting GU3 .... 130 B5
Drive The. Ashf TW15 .... 14 D1
Drive The. Beck BR3 .... 44 A8
Drive The. Belm SM2 .... 77 F7
Drive The. Cobham KT11 .... 73 F5
Drive The. Copth RH10 .... 183 C3
Drive The. Coulsd CR5 & CR8 .... 79 E5
Drive The. Cran GU6 .... 174 F2
Drive The. Felt TW14 .... 15 C8
Drive The. Fetch KT22 .... 94 E5
Drive The. Godal GU7 .... 150 F2
Drive The. Head KT18 & KT22 .... 96 A3
Drive The. Horley RH6 .... 161 B1
Drive The. Hounsl TW3 & TW7 .... 5 D5
Drive The. Ifold RH14 .... 212 D2
Drive The. King U T KT2 .... 18 C1
Drive The. Leahd KT22 & KT18 ...... 95 F4
Drive The. M Bourn GU9 .... 146 B7
Drive The. Morden SM4 .... 40 D4
Drive The. Nork SM7 .... 77 E3

Drive The. Onsl V GU2 .... 108 F1
Drive The. S Norw CR7 & SW16 ..... 42 A7
Drive The. S Norw CR7 .... 42 D5
Drive The. Shackl GU7 & GU8 ...... 149 E4
Drive The. Thame D KT10 .... 36 C1
Drive The. Thorpe GU25 .... 31 F4
Drive The. W Ewell KT19 .... 57 F4
Drive The. W Ewell KT19 .... 57 F4
Drive The. W Wick BR4 .... 44 D2
Drive The. Wallin SM4 & SM6 .... 60 D1
Drive The. Wimble SW19 & SW20 .. 19 C1
Drive The. Woking GU22 .... 89 B7
Drive The. Woner GU5 .... 152 B6
Drivers Mead. Lingf RH7 .... 164 D3
Drodges Cl. Shalf GU5 .... 151 F8
Droitwich Cl. Brack RG12 .... 27 E6
Droitwich Cl. For Hil SE26 .... 23 A5
Drove Rd. Albury GU4 .... 132 A7
Drovers Ct. 3 King U T KT1 .... 37 E7
Drovers Rd. Croy CR2 .... 61 D5
Drovers Way. Ash GU12 .... 106 C1
Drovers Way. Brack RG12 .... 27 F6
Drovers Way. Hale GU9 .... 125 A6
Druid's Cl. Ashtd KT21 .... 95 F7
Druids Way. Beck BR2 .... 44 D5
Drumaline Ridge. Worc Pk KT4 ...... 57 E8
Drummond Cl. Brack RG12 .... 27 F8
Drummond Cl. 4 Guild GU1 .... 109 D1
Drummond Ctr. Croy CR9 .... 61 C8
Drummond Gdns. Epsom KT19 ...... 76 B8
Drummond Rd. Crawl RH11 .... 200 E5
Drummond Rd. Croy CR0 & CR9 .... 61 C8
Drummond Rd. Guild GU1 .... 109 D1
Drummonds Pl. Rich TW9 .... 6 E3
Drungewick La. Loxwd RH14 .... 213 D2
Drury Cl. Worth RH10 .... 202 D4
Drury Cres. Croy CR0 & CR9 .... 61 A8
Dry Arch Rd. Sunnin SL5 .... 29 F3
Dryden. Easth RG12 .... 27 A2
Dryden Ct. 5 Thorn H CR10 .... 17 F8
Dryden Rd. W Heath GU14 .... 84 F6
Dryden Rd. Wimble SW19 .... 20 C2
Drynham Pk. Oat Pk KT13 .... 53 E7
Du Cane Ct. Up Toot SW12 .... 21 A7
Ducavel House. Streat SW2 .... 21 F7
Duck's Wlk. Twick TW1 .... 6 C2
Dudley Cl. Addl KT15 .... 52 C7
Dudley Dr. W Barn SM4 .... 39 E2
Dudley Gr. Epsom KT18 .... 76 C5
Dudley Rd. Ashf TW15 .... 13 F4
Dudley Rd. E Bed TW14 .... 14 D7
Dudley Rd. King U T KT1 .... 37 F6
Dudley Rd. Rich TW9 .... 7 A5
Dudley Rd. Walt O T KT12 .... 35 A2
Dudley Rd. Wimble SW19 .... 20 A2
Dudset La. Cranf TW5 .... 4 A6
Duffield Rd. Walt o t H KT20 .... 97 B3
Duffins Orch. Ottsh KT16 .... 51 C3
Duke Of Cambridge Cl.
 Twick TW2 .... 5 D1
Duke Of Cornwall Ave.
 Camb GU15 .... 46 D1
Duke St. Rich TW10 & TW9 .... 6 D2
Duke St. Sutton SM1 .... 59 D6
Duke St. Woking GU21 .... 69 F2
Duke's Ave. Chisw W4 .... 7 D8
Duke's Hill. Wodd CR3 & CR6 ...... 101 E7
Duke's La. Old W SL4 & SL5 .... 10 B3
Duke's La. Wink SL5 .... 9 F1
Duke's Ride. Crowth RG11 .... 45 B5
Dukes Ave. Hounsl TW4 .... 4 F2
Dukes Ave. King U T KT2 & TW10 .. 17 D4
Dukes Ave. King U T KT3 .... 38 F6
Dukes Ave. Rich KT2 & TW10 .... 17 D4
Dukes Cl. Ashf TW15 .... 14 C4
Dukes Cl. Cran GU6 .... 175 A2
Dukes Cl. Hale GU9 .... 125 A6
Dukes Cl. Hampt TW12 .... 15 F3
Dukes Covert. Brack GU19 .... 47 E6
Dukes Ct. Addl KT15 .... 52 C5
Dukes Ct. Beck BR3 .... 43 E6
Dukes Green Ave. Felt TW14 .... 4 A2
Dukes Hill. Wodd CR3 & CR6 ...... 101 E7
Dukes Pk. Farnb GU11 .... 105 D6
Dukes Rd. Hersh KT12 .... 54 D5
Dukes Ride. Dork RH5 .... 136 D4
Dukes Way. Coney H BR4 .... 63 E7
Dukes Wlk. Hale GU9 .... 125 A6
Dukes Wood. Crowth RG11 .... 45 B5
Dukeshill Rd. Brack RG12 .... 27 B8
Dulverton Ct. 12 King U T KT6 .... 37 E4
Dulverton Rd. Selsd CR2 .... 62 C1
Dulwich and Sydenham Hill Golf
 Course. Dulw SE21 .... 22 F6
Dulwich Bsns Ctr. For Hil SE23 ...... 23 D7
Dulwich Coll (Endowed).
 Dulw SE21 .... 22 F6
Dulwich Coll Picture Gal.
 Dulw SE21 .... 22 E8
Dulwich Coll Prep Sch.
 Dulw SE21 .... 22 E5
Dulwich Comm. Dulw SE21 .... 22 E7
Dulwich Ct. Dulw SE22 .... 23 B7
Dulwich Oaks The. Dulw SE21 ...... 22 F5
Dulwich Village. Dulw SE21 .... 22 E8
Dulwich Wood Ave.
 Dulw SE19 .... 22 E3
Dulwich Wood Pk.
 Dulw SE21 & SE19 .... 22 E4
Dumbarton Ct. 16 Streat SW2 .... 21 E8
Dumbleton Cl. King U T KT2 .... 38 B8
Dump Rd. Farnb GU14 .... 84 E1
Dumphreys House. 5
 Streat SW4 .... 21 D8
Dunally Pk. Lo Hall TW17 .... 34 D2
Dunbar Ave. Beck BR3 .... 43 E5

Dunbar Ave.
 Thorn H CR7 & SW16 .... 42 A7
Dunbar Ct. Carsh SM1 .... 59 D5
Dunbar Ct. Walt O T KT12 .... 35 C1
Dunbar Rd. Friml GU16 .... 85 F7
Dunbar Rd. King U T KT3 .... 38 C5
Dunbar St. W Norw SE27 .... 22 C5
Dunboe Pl. Shep TW17 .... 34 C2
Dunbridge House. Rhampt SW15 ..... 7 F1
Duncan Dr. Merrow GU1 .... 110 A2
Duncan Dr. Woki RG11 .... 25 E5
Duncan Rd. Burgh H KT20 .... 97 E8
Duncan Rd. Rich TW9 .... 6 E3
Duncombe Ct. Stain TW18 .... 12 F1
Duncombe House. For Hil SE23 ...... 23 E8
Duncombe House. 7
 Putney SW19 .... 19 D7
Duncombe Rd. Godal GU7 .... 150 D2
Duncroft Cl. Reig RH2 .... 117 F1
Dundaff Cl. Friml GU15 .... 66 A5
Dundas Cl. Easth RG12 .... 27 B5
Dundas Gdns. E Mole KT8 .... 36 B6
Dundee Rd. Croy SE25 .... 43 B4
Dundela Gdns.
 N Cheam KT17 & KT4 .... 58 B6
Dundonald Prim Sch.
 Merton SW19 .... 19 F1
Dundonald Rd. Merton SW19 .... 19 F1
Dundrey Cres. Merst RH1 .... 119 E6
Dundry House. 8 For Hil SE26 .... 23 A5
Dunedin Dr. Cater CR3 .... 100 E2
Dunelm Gr. W Norw SE27 .... 22 C5
Dunfee Way. Byfl KT14 .... 71 E7
Dunfield Gdns. Catf SE6 .... 24 B3
Dunfield Rd. Catf SE6 .... 24 B3
Dungates La. Buckl RH3 .... 117 A2
Dunheved Cl. Thorn H CR7 .... 42 A3
Dunheved Rd N. Thorn H CR7 .... 42 A3
Dunheved Rd S. Thorn H CR7 .... 42 A3
Dunheved Rd W. Thorn H CR7 .... 42 A3
Dunhill Point. 12 Rhampt SW15 ..... 19 B7
Dunkeld Rd. S Norw SE25 .... 42 D5
Dunkirk St. 12 W Norw SE27 .... 22 C4
Dunleary Cl. Twick TW4 .... 15 F8
Dunley Dr. New Add CR0 .... 63 C4
Dunlin Cl. Earls RH1 .... 139 F4
Dunlin Ct. 11 W Norw SE21 .... 22 D6
Dunlin Rise. Merrow GU4 .... 110 D3
Dunmail Dr. Sander CR2 & CR8 ..... 80 E6
Dunmore. Stough GU2 .... 108 D2
Dunmore Rd. Wimble SW20 .... 39 D8
Dunmow Cl. Felt TW13 .... 15 E4
Dunnets. Knaph GU21 .... 68 E2
Dunning's Rd. E Grins RH19 .... 205 E7
Dunnings Mill L Complex.
 E Grins RH19 .... 205 E6
Dunnock Ct. 10 W Norw SE21 .... 22 D6
Dunnymans Rd. Banstd SM7 .... 77 F4
Dunoon Gdns. For Hil SE23 .... 23 D8
Dunoon Rd. For Hil SE23 .... 23 C8
Dunottar Cl. Woodh RH2 .... 139 C7
Dunraven Ave. Salfs RH1 .... 140 B2
Dunraven House. 11 Rich TW9 .... 6 F6
Dunraven Lower Sch.
 Streat SW16 .... 21 F5
Dunraven Upper Sch.
 Streat SW16 .... 21 F5
Dunsborough Cotts.
 Ripley GU23 .... 91 C7
Dunsbury Cl. Sutton SM2 .... 59 B3
Dunsdon Ave. Guild GU2 .... 130 B8
Dunsfold CE Fst Sch.
 Dunsf GU8 .... 192 F6
Dunsfold Cl. Crawl RH11 .... 201 A5
Dunsfold Common Rd.
 Dunsf GU8 .... 192 F6
Dunsfold Ct. 9 Sutton SM2 .... 59 B3
Dunsfold House. 10
 King U T KT2 .... 18 B2
Dunsfold House. 7 Streat SW2 .... 21 F8
Dunsfold Rd. Alf Cr GU6 & GU8 ... 193 E8
Dunsfold Rd. Alfold GU6 & GU8 ... 193 E3
Dunsfold Rise. Coulsd CR5 .... 79 D6
Dunsfold Way. New Add CR0 .... 63 C3
Dunsfold Rd.
 Bramly GU5 & GU8 .... 173 C1
Dunsfold Rd. Dunsf GU6 & GU8 ... 193 B8
Dunsfold Rd. Plaist GU8 & RH14 .. 211 D4
Dunsmore Rd. Walt O T KT12 .... 35 B5
Dunstable Rd. E Mole KT8 .... 35 F5
Dunstable Rd. Rich TW10 & TW9 .... 6 E3
Dunstall Pk. W Heath GU14 .... 85 A7
Dunstall Rd.
 Wimble SW19 & SW20 .... 19 C2
Dunstall Way. E Mole KT8 .... 36 B6
Dunstan Ct. Stain TW18 .... 13 A4
Dunstan Rd. Coulsd CR5 .... 79 D2
Dunstan's Rd. Dulw SE22 .... 23 A8
Dunster Ave. W Barn SM4 .... 39 D1
Dunster House. Catf SE6 .... 24 B5
Dunton Cl. Surb KT6 .... 37 E1
Dunton Ct. Dulw SE26 .... 23 B6
Dunton House. 14 Streat SW16 ...... 21 E5
Duntshill Rd. Wands SW18 .... 20 B7
Dunvegan Cl. E Mole KT8 .... 36 B6
Dunvegan House. 8 Redh RH1 ..... 118 F1
Dupont Rd. Merton SW20 .... 39 D7
Duppas Ave. Croy CR0 .... 61 B6
Duppas Cl. Shep TW17 .... 34 D4
Duppas Ct. Croy CR0 .... 61 B7
Duppas Hill La. Croy CR0 .... 61 B6
Duppas Hill Rd. Croy CR0 .... 61 B6
Duppas Hill Terr.
 Croy CR0 & SE19 .... 61 B7
Duppas Jun Sch. Croy CR0 .... 61 B5
Duppas Rd. Croy CR0 & CR9 .... 61 B7
Dura Den Cl. Beck BR3 .... 24 B1
Durand Cl. Carsh SM5 .... 40 F1
Durban Rd. Beck BR3 .... 43 F7
Durban Rd. W Norw SE27 .... 22 C4
Durbin Rd. Chess KT9 .... 56 F6

Durfold Dr. Reig RH2 .... 118 C1
Durfold Rd. Horsh RH12 .... 217 D7
Durfold Wood. Plaist RH14 .... 211 D5
Durford Cres. Rhampt SW15 .... 19 B7
Durham Ave. Beck BR2 .... 44 F5
Durham Cl. Crawl RH10 .... 201 E2
Durham Cl. Stough GU2 .... 108 F3
Durham Cl. Wimble SW20 .... 39 B7
Durham Ct. Leahd KT22 .... 95 A5
Durham Ct. Tedd TW11 .... 16 E4
Durham Hill. Catf BR1 .... 24 F4
Durham Rd. Beck BR2 .... 44 F6
Durham Rd. Felt TW14 .... 15 C8
Durham Rd. Sandh GU15 .... 45 A2
Durham Rd. Wimble SW20 .... 39 B8
Durkins Rd. E Grins RH19 .... 185 D3
Durleston Park Dr. Fetch KT23 ...... 94 C2
Durley Mead. Brack RG12 .... 27 F4
Durlston Rd. King U T KT2 .... 17 E2
Durnford House. Catf SE6 .... 24 B5
Durning Rd. W Norw SE19 .... 22 D3
Durnsford Ave.
 Wimble SW18 & SW19 .... 20 A6
Durnsford Rd.
 Wimble SW18 & SW19 .... 20 B5
Durnsford Way. Cran GU6 .... 175 A2
Durrell Way. Shep TW17 .... 34 D3
Durrington Ave. Wimble SW20 ...... 19 C1
Durrington Park Rd.
 Wimble SW20 .... 39 C8
Dutch Barn Cl. Stan TW19 .... 2 D1
Dutch Gdns. King U T KT2 .... 18 B2
Dutchells Copse. Horsh RH12 ...... 217 F7
Dutton House. Streat SW2 .... 22 B7
Duval Pl. Bagsh GU19 .... 47 E3
Duxford. 10 King U T KT1 .... 38 A7
Duxhurst La. Sidlow RH6 .... 160 B7
Dwelly La. Haxted TN8 .... 165 D8
Dwelly La.
 Limps RH7 & RH8 & TN8 .... 144 D3
Dyehouse Rd. Thursl GU8 .... 169 C4
Dyer House. Hampt TW12 .... 36 B8
Dyer's Field. Smallf RH6 .... 162 B3
Dyers Almshouses.
 Crawl RH10 .... 201 D7
Dykes Ct. 11 Streat SW2 .... 21 F7
Dykes Path. Sheer GU22 .... 70 C4
Dykes Way. Beck BR2 .... 44 F6
Dymes Path. Putney SW19 .... 19 D6
Dynevor Pl. Fairl GU3 .... 108 C5
Dynevor Rd. Rich TW10 .... 6 E2
Dysart Ave. King U T KT2 & TW10 . 17 C4
Dysart Sch. King U T KT2 .... 17 D4
Dyson Cl. Dork RH4 .... 136 A7
Dyson Wlk. Crawl RH11 .... 201 B1

Eady Cl. Horsh RH13 .... 217 F2
Eagle Cl. Crowth RG11 .... 45 A7
Eagle Cl. Wallin SM6 .... 60 E4
Eagle Ct. 9 W Norw SE21 .... 22 D6
Eagle Hill. S Norw SE19 .... 22 D2
Eagle House Sch. Sandh GU17 ...... 45 B2
Eagle Rd. Farnb GU14 .... 85 B2
Eagle Rd. Guild GU1 .... 109 D1
Eagle Trad Est. Mitch CR4 .... 40 F3
Eagles Dr. Bigg H TN16 .... 83 D1
Eagles Nest. Sandh GU17 .... 45 A1
Ealing Rd. Brent TW8 .... 6 E8
Eardley Prim Sch. Streat SW16 ...... 21 C2
Eardley Rd. Streat SW16 .... 21 C2
Earl Rd. Mortl SW14 .... 7 C3
Earle Gdns. King U T KT2 .... 17 E1
Earles Meadow. Horsh RH12 .... 218 A6
Earles Meadow. Horsh RH12 .... 218 B6
Earlswood. Cobham KT11 .... 73 E7
Earlsbrook Rd. Earls RH1 .... 139 F7
Earlsdene. Sunnin SL5 .... 29 B1
Earls Gr. Camb GU15 .... 65 E6
Earlsbrook Rd. Earls RH1 .... 139 F7
Earlsfield Prim Sch.
 Wands SW18 .... 20 C6
Earlsfield Rd. Wands SW18 .... 20 C8
Earlsfield Sta. Wands SW18 .... 20 C7
Earlsthorpe Rd. For Hil SE26 .... 23 D4
Earlswood. Easth RG12 .... 27 B2
Earlswood Ave. Thorn H CR7 .... 42 A4
Earlswood Cl. Horsh RH13 .... 218 A4
Earlswood Ct. Earls RH1 .... 139 F7
Earlswood Cty Inf Sch.
 Earls RH1 .... 140 A8
Earlswood House. 2
 Streat SW2 .... 21 F7
Earlswood Rd. Earls RH1 .... 139 F7
Earlswood Sta. Earls RH1 .... 139 F7
Early Commons. Crawl RH10 .... 201 F7
Easby Cres. Morden SM4 .... 40 B3
Easedale House. Islew TW7 .... 5 F2
Eashing La. Ock Rid GU7 & GU8 .. 150 A3
Eashing La. Shackl GU7 & GU8 .... 149 F3
Eashing Point. 5 Rhampt SW15 ..... 19 B7
Easington Pl. Guild GU1 .... 130 F8
East Ave. Heath E GU9 .... 125 D6
East Ave. Wallin CR0 .... 60 F5
East Ave. Whit V KT12 .... 53 F1
East Croydon Sta. Croy CR9 .... 61 D8
East Dr. Beck BR3 .... 44 C4
East Dr. Wallin SM5 .... 59 F2
East Dr. Went GU25 .... 31 B3
East Flexford La. Wanb GU3 .... 128 F6
East Gdns. Mayb GU22 .... 70 F1
East Gdns. Mitch SW17 & SW19 ... 20 C2
East Gn. Blckw GU17 .... 64 C4
East Grinstead Sta.
 E Grins RH19 .... 185 D1
East Hill. Bigg H TN16 .... 83 B1
East Hill. Dorm Pk RH19 .... 185 E6
East Hill. Mayb GU22 .... 70 C2
East Hill. Oxted RH8 .... 122 E6
East Hill. S Croy CR2 .... 61 E1
East Hill Ct. Oxted RH8 .... 122 E5
East Hill La. Burst RH10 .... 183 D5

East Hill Rd. Oxted RH8 .... 122 E6
East La. King U T KT1 .... 37 D6
East La. W Hors KT24 .... 92 D2
East Meads. Onsl V GU2 .... 130 A8
East Park La. Horne RH7 .... 163 C1
East Pk. Crawl RH10 & RH11 .... 201 D5
East Pl. W Norw SE27 .... 22 C4
East Ramp. Harl TW6 .... 3 B6
East Rd. E Bed TW14 .... 14 D8
East Rd. King U T KT2 .... 37 E8
East Rd. Merton SW19 .... 20 C2
East Rd. Reig RH2 .... 117 F2
East Rd. Whit V KT13 .... 53 D3
East Rd. Wimble SW19 .... 20 C2
East Resr (Nature Reserve).
 Tyl Gn RH9 .... 121 B5
East Ring. Tongh GU10 .... 127 A7
East Shalford La. Chil GU4 .... 131 A3
East Sheen Ave. Mortl SW14 .... 7 D3
East Sheen Prim Sch.
 Mortl SW14 .... 7 E3
East St. Brent TW8 .... 6 C7
East St. Ewell KT17 .... 76 E7
East St. Farnh GU9 .... 125 C3
East St. G Book KT23 .... 94 B2
East St. Horsh RH12 .... 217 C1
East St. Rusper RH12 .... 199 E7
East St. Turn H RH10 & RH19 ..... 204 C4
East Station Rd. Alder GU12 ...... 105 B1
East Stratton Cl. Brack RG12 ...... 27 F4
East Surrey Coll. Redh RH1 .... 119 A4
East Surrey Hospl. Redh RH1 .... 118 C1
East Surrey Hospl The.
 Earls RH1 .... 140 A5
East View La. Cran GU6 .... 174 C3
East Way. Croy CR0 .... 62 E7
East Whipley La. Rowly GU5 ...... 173 F1
East Whipley La. Sham Gn GU5 .. 173 F8
East Wlk. Reig RH2 .... 118 B1
Eastbank Rd. Hampt TW12 .... 16 C3
Eastbourne Gdns. Mortl SW14 .... 7 C4
Eastbourne Rd. Blind H RH9 .... 142 E4
Eastbourne Rd. Chisw W4 .... 7 C3
Eastbourne Rd. Felb RH6 .... 184 E8
Eastbourne Rd. Felt TW13 .... 15 D6
Eastbourne Rd. Godst RH9 .... 121 D2
Eastbourne Rd. Mitch SW17 ...... 21 A2
Eastbourne Rd.
 Newch RH7 & RH9 .... 163 F5
Eastbourne Rd. S Godst RH9 .... 142 E4
Eastbrook Cl. Woking GU21 .... 70 A3
Eastbury Gr. Chisw W4 .... 7 E8
Eastbury La. Compt GU3 .... 129 A3
Eastbury Rd. King U T KT2 .... 17 E1
Eastchurch Rd. Hatton TW6 .... 3 E4
Eastcote Ave. E Mole KT8 .... 36 A4
Eastcroft Ct. Guild GU1 .... 131 A8
Eastcroft Mews. Horsh RH12 ... 216 F1
Eastcroft Rd. W Ewell KT19 ...... 57 E3
Eastcroft Rd. W Ewell KT19 ...... 57 E3
Eastdean Ave. Epsom KT18 .... 76 B6
Easter Way. S Godst RH9 .... 142 F5
Eastern Ave. Thorpe KT16 .... 33 A6
Eastern Ind Area. Brack RG12 .... 27 D7
Eastern La. Crowth RG11 .... 45 F4
Eastern Perimeter Rd.
 Hatton TW14 .... 3 F5
Eastern Rd. Alder GU12 .... 105 E2
Eastern Rd. Brack RG12 .... 27 D7
Eastern View. Bigg H TN16 .... 83 C2
Eastfield Rd. Nutf RH1 .... 140 C8
Eastfields. Witley GU8 .... 170 F5
Eastfields High Sch. Mitch CR4 . 41 B7
Eastfields Rd. Mitch CR4 .... 41 A7
Eastgate. Nork SM7 .... 77 F5
Eastgate Gdns. Guild GU1 .... 130 E8
Easthampstead Park Sch.
 Easth RG12 .... 26 D3
Easthampstead Rd. Brack RG12 . 27 A7
Easthampstead Rd. Woki RG11 .. 25 E4
Eastheath Ave. Woki RG11 .... 25 A4
Eastheath Gdns. Woki RG11 ...... 25 B3
Eastlands Cl. Oxted RH8 .... 122 D8
Eastlands Cres.
 Dulw SE21 & SE22 .... 22 F5
Eastlands Way. Oxted RH8 .... 122 D8
Eastleigh Cl. Sutton SM2 .... 59 B3
Eastleigh Rd. Hatton TW6 .... 3 F4
Eastleigh Way. E Bed TW14 .... 15 A7
Eastleigh Wlk. [10]
 Rhampt SW15 .... 19 A8
Eastmead. Farnb GU14 .... 85 B3
Eastmead. Woking GU21 .... 69 B2
Eastmearn Rd.
 W Norw SE21 & SE27 .... 22 C6
Eastmont Rd. Hinch W KT10 ...... 55 F8
Eastney Rd. Thorn H CR0 .... 42 B1
Eastnor Cl. Woodh RH2 .... 138 F6
Eastnor Rd. Woodh RH2 .... 139 A6
Easton House. [4] W Norw SE27 . 22 B5
Eastry Ave. Hayes BR2 .... 44 F3
Eastway. Crawl RH6 .... 182 B7
Eastway. Epsom KT19 .... 76 D8
Eastway. Merton SM4 & SW20 ... 39 E5
Eastway. Stough GU2 .... 108 F1
Eastway. Wallin SM6 .... 60 C6
Eastwell Cl. Penge BR3 .... 23 E1
Eastwick Ct. [5] Putney SW19 ... 19 D7
Eastwick Cty Jun Sch.
 Fetch KT23 .... 94 B3
Eastwick Dr. Fetch KT23 .... 94 B4
Eastwick Inf Sch. Fetch KT23 .... 94 B3
Eastwick Park Ave. Fetch KT23 .. 94 B3
Eastwick Rd. G Book KT23 .... 94 B2
Eastwick Rd. Whit V KT13 .... 54 B5
Eastwood. Crawl RH10 .... 201 F6
Eastwood. [3] Whit V KT13 .... 53 D4
Eastwood Lodge. Bramly GU5 .. 151 F7
Eastwood Rd. Bramly GU5 .... 151 F7
Eastwood St. Streat SW16 .... 21 C2
Eastworth Rd. Chert KT15 & KT16 33 A1

Eaton Ct. Abbots GU1 .... 110 A3
Eaton Ct. Sutton SM2 .... 59 D4
Eaton Dr. King U T KT2 .... 18 A1
Eaton Park Rd. Cobham KT11 .... 73 F5
Eaton Pk. Cobham KT11 .... 73 E5
Eaton Rd. Islew TW3 & TW7 .... 5 D3
Eaton Rd. Sutton SM2 .... 59 D4
Eatonville Rd. Up Toot SW17 ...... 20 F6
Eatonville Villas. Up Toot SW17 . 20 F6
Ebba's Way. Epsom KT18 .... 76 B4
Ebbage Ct. [5] Woking GU22 ...... 69 E1
Ebbisham Ct. Epsom KT18 .... 76 C4
Ebbisham La.
 Walt o t H KT20 & KT18 .... 97 A4
Ebbisham Rd. Epsom KT18 .... 76 B5
Ebbisham Rd. N Cheam KT4 .... 58 C8
Ebenezer Wlk. Mitch CR4 .... 41 C8
Ebor Cotts. King U T SW15 .... 18 E5
Ebsworth St. For Hil SE23 .... 23 D8
Ecclesbourne Inf Sch.
 Thorn H CR7 .... 42 C4
Ecclesbourne Jun Sch.
 Thorn H CR7 .... 42 C4
Ecclesbourne Rd. Thorn H CR7 . 42 C4
Eccleshill. Beck BR2 .... 44 F5
Eccleshill. Dorkh RH5 .... 136 C3
Echelford Cty Mid Sch.
 Ashf TW15 .... 14 B3
Echelford Dr. Ashf TW15 .... 14 A4
Echo Barn La. Wreccl GU10 ...... 145 F5
Echo Pit Rd. Guild GU1 & GU4 .. 130 E6
Ecob Cl. Stough GU3 .... 108 F5
Ecton Rd. Addl KT15 .... 52 B6
Eddeys Cl. Head Dn GU35 .... 187 B6
Eddeys La. Head Dn GU35 .... 187 B6
Eddington Hill. Crawl RH11 ...... 201 B1
Eddington Rd. Easth RG12 .... 26 E3
Eddisbury House. [7]
 For Hil SE26 .... 23 A5
Eddy Rd. Alder GU12 .... 105 C1
Eddystone Wlk. Stan TW19 .... 13 E8
Ede Cl. Hounsl TW4 .... 4 F4
Ede Ct. Epsom KT17 .... 76 F7
Ede's Cotts. Ashtd KT21 .... 95 D8
Eden Cl. Woodhm KT15 .... 52 B1
Eden Grove Rd. Byfl KT14 .... 71 E6
Eden Park Ave. Beck BR3 .... 44 A4
Eden Park Sch. Beck BR3 .... 43 F4
Eden Park Sta. Beck BR3 .... 44 A4
Eden Rd. Crawl RH11 .... 200 F4
Eden Rd. Croy CR0 .... 61 D6
Eden Rd. Penge BR3 .... 43 E8
Eden Rd. W Norw SE27 .... 22 B3
Eden St. King U T KT1 & KT2 ...... 37 E7
Eden Vale. Dorm Pk RH19 .... 185 E5
Eden Vale. E Grins RH19 .... 185 E5
Eden Way. Beck BR3 .... 44 A3
Eden Way. Warlgm CR6 .... 81 E1
Eden Wlk. [5] King U T KT1 .... 37 E7
Edenbrook. Lingf RH7 .... 164 E4
Edencourt Rd. Streat SW16 .... 21 B2
Edencroft. Bramly GU5 .... 151 F7
Edenfield Gdns. Worc Pk KT4 .... 57 F7
Edenham High Sch. Croy CR0 ... 43 F2
Edenhurst Pl. Belm SM2 .... 59 A4
Edensor Gdns. Chisw W4 .... 7 E7
Edenside Rd. L Book KT23 .... 93 F3
Edensor Rd. Chisw W4 .... 7 E7
Edenvale Cl. Mitch CR4 .... 21 A1
Edenvale Rd. Mitch CR4 .... 21 A1
Edgar Cl. Worth RH10 .... 202 E5
Edgar Ct. King U T KT1 .... 38 E6
Edgar Rd. S Croy CR2 .... 61 D2
Edgar Rd. Tats TN16 .... 103 D6
Edgar Rd. Twick TW4 .... 15 F8
Edgarley Terr. Fulh SW6 .... 6 C7 (?)
Edgbarrow Rise. Sandh GU47 .... 45 A2
Edgbarrow Sch. Crowth RG11 .... 45 C3
Edgbarrowhill Star.
 Crowth RG11 .... 45 A3
Edgcumbe Park Dr. Crowth RG11 45 A5
Edge Cl. Whit V KT13 .... 53 A3
Edge Hill. Wimble SW19 .... 19 D1
Edge Hill Ct. Wimble SW19 .... 19 D1
Edgeborough. M Bourn GU10 .. 146 F2
Edgeborough Ct. Guild GU1 ..... 130 F8
Edgecombe Cl. King U T KT2 ...... 18 D1
Edgecombe House.
 Putney SW19 .... 19 E8
Edgecoombe. S Croy CR2 .... 62 D2
Edgecumbe Ct. [2] Croy CR0 ...... 43 A1
Edgedale Cl. Crowth RG11 .... 45 B5
Edgefield Cl. Cran GU6 .... 174 C4
Edgefield Cl. Earls RH1 .... 140 A4
Edgehill Ct. Walt O T KT12 .... 35 C1
Edgehill House. [3] Redh RH1 .. 118 F1
Edgehill Rd. Mitch CR4 .... 41 B8
Edgehill Rd. Purley CR2 & CR8 .. 61 B1
Edgeley. L Book KT23 .... 93 E3
Edgell Cl. Stain TW18 .... 13 C6
Edgemoor Rd. Friml GU15 & GU16 66 C3
Edgewood Cl. Crowth RG11 .... 45 A7
Edgewood Gn. Croy CR0 .... 43 D1
Edgeworth Cl. Whytf CR3 .... 81 A1
Edgington Rd. Streat SW16 .... 21 D2
Edinburgh Cl. Ash V GU12 .... 106 A5
Edinburgh Ct. Catf SE6 .... 24 F7
Edinburgh Ct. [2] King U T KT1 .. 37 E6
Edinburgh Ct. W Barn SM4 .... 39 D4
Edinburgh Dr.
 Stain TW15 & TW18 .... 13 D3
Edinburgh Rd. Sutton SM1 .... 59 D8
Edinburgh Way. E Grins RH19 .. 205 F7
Edith Gdns. Tolw KT5 .... 38 B2
Edith Rd. Thorn H SE25 .... 42 D4
Edith Rd. Wimble SW19 .... 20 B2
Edmonds Ct. [4] Brack RG12 ...... 27 C8
Edmund Rd. Mitch CR4 .... 40 E6

Edna Rd. Merton SW20 .... 39 D7
Edrich Rd. Crawl RH11 .... 201 A1
Edridge House. [9] W Norw SE27 22 B5
Edridge Rd. Croy CR0 & CR9 ...... 61 D7
Edward Alleyn House.
 Dulw SE21 .... 22 E8
Edward Ave. Camb GU15 .... 65 A5
Edward Ave. Morden CR4 & SM4 . 40 D4
Edward Cl. Hampt TW12 .... 16 C3
Edward Cl. Stain TW18 .... 13 C2
Edward II Ave. Byfl KT14 .... 71 F5
Edward Pauling House.
 E Bed TW14 .... 14 F8
Edward Pinner Ct. [5] Surb KT6 . 56 E8
Edward Rd. Bigg H TN16 .... 83 E1
Edward Rd. Coulsd CR5 .... 79 D4
Edward Rd. Croy CR0 .... 42 E2
Edward Rd. Hampt TW12 .... 16 C3
Edward Rd. Hatton TW14 .... 3 C2
Edward Rd. M Bourn GU10 .... 146 C7
Edward Rd. Penge SE20 .... 23 D2
Edward Rd. Windl GU20 .... 48 D4
Edward St. Alder GU11 .... 105 A2
Edward Way. Ashf TW15 .... 13 F6
Edwards Cl. N Cheam KT4 .... 58 D8
Edwin Rd. W Hors KT24 .... 92 D2
Edwin Rd. Twick TW1 & TW2 .... 16 E7
Edwin Rd. W Hors KT24 .... 92 D2
Edwin Stray House. Felt TW13 .... 16 A5
Edwina Ct. Sutton SM1 .... 59 B6
Eelmoor Plain Rd. Alder GU11 .. 104 D5
Eelmoor Rd. Alder GU11 .... 104 D5
Eelmoor Rd. Farnb GU14 .... 84 F2
Eelmoor Road Trad Est.
 Farnb GU14 .... 85 A2
Effingham Cl. Sutton SM2 .... 59 B3
Effingham Common Rd.
 Effing KT24 .... 93 C2
Effingham Ct. Mitch SW19 .... 20 C1
Effingham Ct. Woking GU22 ...... 89 E8
Effingham House. [9]
 King U T KT2 .... 18 B2
Effingham House Golf Club.
 Effing KT24 .... 113 D7
Effingham Junction.
 E Hors KT24 .... 93 A4
Effingham La. Burst RH10 .... 183 E4
Effingham Lodge. [1]
 King U T KT6 .... 37 E4
Effingham Pl. Effing KT24 .... 113 D8
Effingham Rd.
 Burst RH10 & RH6 .... 183 D6
Effingham Rd.
 Dome RH10 & RH6 .... 183 D6
Effingham Rd. Reig RH2 .... 139 B8
Effingham Rd.
 Thame D KT6 & KT7 .... 37 C2
Effingham Rd. Thorn H CR0 .... 41 F2
Effort St. Up Toot SW17 .... 20 E3
Effra Ct. S Norw SE19 .... 22 E1
Effra Rd. Wimble SW19 .... 20 B2
Egbury House. Rhampt SW15 .... 7 F1
Egerton Ct. [5] Rich TW10 .... 6 E2
Egerton Ct. [5] Stough GU2 .... 108 E1
Egerton House. Chisw W4 .... 7 C8
Egerton Pl. Whit V KT13 .... 53 C4
Egerton Rd. New Mal KT3 .... 38 F5
Egerton Rd. Onsl V GU2 .... 129 F8
Egerton Rd. Sandh GU15 .... 64 F7
Egerton Rd. Sandh GU15 .... 65 A7
Egerton Rd. Twick TW2 .... 16 E8
Egerton Rd. Whit V KT13 .... 53 C4
Eggar's Ct. Alder GU11 .... 105 B1
Eggar's Hill. Alder GU11 .... 126 A8
Egham By-Pass. Egham TW20 ... 12 A4
Egham Cl. Cheam SM3 .... 58 E8
Egham Cl. Putney SW19 .... 19 E6
Egham Cres. Cheam SM3 .... 58 D8
Egham Ct. King U T KT6 .... 37 D4
Egham Hill. Egham TW20 .... 11 F3
Egham Hill. Eng Gn TW20 .... 11 D2
Egham Hill Rdbt. Egham TW20 .. 11 F3
Egham Sta. Egham TW20 .... 12 A3
Egleston Rd. Morden SM4 .... 40 B3
Egley Dr. Woking GU22 .... 89 D5
Egley Rd. Woking GU22 .... 89 D6
Eglinton Rd. Rushm GU10 .... 168 B3
Eglise Rd. Warlgm CR6 .... 81 E2
Egmont Ave. Surb KT6 .... 37 F1
Egmont Park Rd.
 Walt o t H KT20 .... 97 A2
Egmont Rd. New Mal KT3 .... 38 F5
Egmont Rd. Surb KT6 .... 37 F1
Egmont Rd. Sutton SM2 .... 59 C3
Egmont Rd. Walt O T KT12 .... 35 B2
Egmont Way. Burgh H KT20 .... 97 E8
Egremont Rd. W Norw SE27 .... 22 B5
Eighteenth Rd. Mitch CR4 .... 41 E5
Eileen Rd. Thorn H SE25 .... 42 D4
Eisenhower House. Tedd KT8 ..... 37 E8
Eland Pl. Croy CR9 .... 61 B7
Eland Rd. Alder GU12 .... 105 D1
Eland Rd. Croy CR0 & CR9 .... 61 B7
Elberon Ave. Croy CR0 .... 41 C3
Elborough Rd. Croy SE25 .... 43 A4
Elborough St. Wands SW18 .... 20 A7
Elbow Meadow. Poyle SL3 .... 1 F6
Elcho Rd. Pirb GU24 .... 87 D8
Elder Cl. Burgh GU1 & GU4 ...... 110 A4
Elder Gdns. [9] W Norw SE27 ..... 22 C4
Elder Oak Cl. Penge SE20 .... 43 B8
Elder Rd. Bisley GU24 .... 68 A4
Elder Rd. W Norw SE27 .... 22 C3
Elder Way. Dork RH5 .... 136 C3
Elderberry Gr. [10] W Norw SE27 22 C4
Eldersley Cl. Redh RH1 .... 118 F3
Eldersley Gdns. Redh RH1 .... 118 F3
Elderslie Cl. Beck BR3 .... 44 B3
Elderton Rd. For Hil SE26 .... 23 E4
Eldertree Pl. Mitch CR4 .... 41 C8

Eldertree Way. Mitch CR4 .... 41 C8
Elderwood. W Norw SE27 .... 22 C3
Eldon Ave. Croy CR0 .... 62 C8
Eldon Ave. Heston TW5 .... 5 A7
Eldon Ct. Whit V KT13 .... 53 C5
Eldon Dr. M Bourn GU10 .... 146 D5
Eldon Pk. Croy SE25 .... 43 B5
Eldon Rd. Cater CR3 .... 100 D6
Eldrick Ct. Felt TW14 .... 14 D7
Eldridge Cl. E Bed TW14 .... 15 A7
Eleanor Ave. Epsom KT19 .... 57 D1
Eleanor Ct. Guild GU1 .... 130 D7
Eleanor Gr. Mortl SW13 & SW14 .. 7 E4
Eleanor House. [6] Merton SW19 40 B8
Elfin Gr. Tedd TW11 .... 16 F3
Elfrida Cres. Catf SE6 .... 24 A4
Elfrida Inf & Jun Sch. Catf SE6 .. 24 A4
Elgar Ave. Crowth RG11 .... 45 B7
Elgar Ave. Thorn H SW16 .... 41 E6
Elgar Ave. Tolw KT5 & KT6 .... 38 B2
Elgar House. Kenley CR8 .... 80 C5
Elgar House. Twick TW2 .... 5 D1
Elger Way. Copth RH10 .... 183 A4
Elgin Ave. Ashf TW15 .... 14 C2
Elgin Cl. Horsh RH13 .... 217 E3
Elgin Cres. Cater CR3 .... 101 A5
Elgin Cres. Harl TW6 .... 3 E5
Elgin Ct. [6] Croy CR0 .... 61 C6
Elgin Gdns. Guild GU1 .... 110 A2
Elgin Rd. Croy CR0 .... 61 F8
Elgin Rd. Sutton SM1 .... 59 C7
Elgin Rd. Wallin SM6 .... 60 C4
Elgin Rd. Weyb KT13 .... 53 B5
Elgin Way. Friml GU16 .... 85 F3
Eliot Bank. For Hil SE23 & SE26 . 23 B6
Eliot Bank Prim Sch.
 For Hil SE23 .... 23 B6
Eliot Cl. Camb GU15 .... 66 B7
Eliot Dr. Shottm GU27 .... 207 E6
Eliot House. [10] Rich TW10 .... 6 F1
Eliot Cl. Worth RH10 .... 202 C4
Eliot Park Ind Est. Alder GU12 .. 105 E2
Eliot Rise. N Asct SL5 .... 28 D7
Eliott Cl. Woking GU21 .... 70 A3
Eliott Gdns. Shep Gn TW17 .... 34 A5
Eliott Rd. Thorn H CR7 .... 42 A5
Ellis Ave. Onsl V GU2 .... 129 F7
Ellis Cl. Coulsd CR5 .... 99 F7
Ellis Farm Cl. Westfd GU22 .... 89 D5
Ellis Rd. Coulsd CR5 .... 99 F7
Ellis Rd. Crowth RG11 .... 45 B6
Ellis Rd. Mitch CR4 .... 40 F3
Ellisfield Dr. Rhampt SW15 .... 18 F8
Ellisfield Dr. Rhampt SW15 .... 19 A8
Ellison Rd. Barnes SW13 .... 7 F5
Ellison Rd. Streat SW16 .... 21 E1
Ellison Way. Tongh GU10 .... 126 F7
Ellison Way. Woki RG11 .... 25 B6
Ellman Rd. Crawl RH11 .... 200 F4
Ellora Rd. Streat SW16 .... 21 D3
Ellson Cl. Worth RH10 .... 202 C4

Ellswood Ct. [18] Surb KT6 .... 37 D2
Elm Bank Gdns. Mortl SW13 .... 7 E5
Elm Bank Mansions. Mortl SW13 . 7 E5
Elm Bridge La. Old Wok GU22 ... 90 A8
Elm Cl. Box H KT20 .... 116 C5
Elm Cl. Carsh SM5 .... 40 F1
Elm Cl. Horse GU21 .... 69 D4
Elm Cl. Leahd KT22 .... 95 B5
Elm Cl. S Croy CR2 .... 61 E4
Elm Cl. Send M GU23 .... 91 A3
Elm Cl. Stan TW19 .... 13 D7
Elm Cl. Tolw KT5 .... 38 C2
Elm Cl. Twick TW13 & TW2 .... 16 B6
Elm Cl. W Barn SW20 .... 39 C5
Elm Cl. Warlgm CR6 .... 81 D2
Elm Court Sch. W Norw SE27 ..... 22 C6
Elm Cotts. Mickle RH5 .... 115 C8
Elm Cres. Heath E GU9 .... 125 D7
Elm Cres. King U T KT2 .... 37 E8
Elm Ct. Catf SE6 .... 24 B7
Elm Ct. [5] Charlt TW16 .... 14 F1
Elm Ct. Knaph GU21 .... 68 D2
Elm Ct. Mitch CR4 .... 40 F7
Elm Ct. Sandh GU15 .... 45 E2
Elm Dr. Chobh GU24 .... 49 F1
Elm Dr. E Grins RH19 .... 186 A1
Elm Dr. Leahd KT22 .... 95 B4
Elm Dr. Sunby TW16 .... 35 C7
Elm Dr. Wink SL4 .... 9 B7
Elm Gdns. Burgh H KT20 .... 97 C8
Elm Gdns. Clayg KT10 .... 55 F4
Elm Gdns. Mitch CR4 .... 41 D5
Elm Gr. Bisley GU24 .... 68 A3
Elm Gr. Cater CR3 .... 100 E5
Elm Gr. Cran GU6 .... 174 A3
Elm Gr. Epsom KT18 .... 76 C5
Elm Gr. Heath E GU9 .... 125 C7
Elm Gr. Horsh RH13 .... 217 E1
Elm Gr. King U T KT2 .... 37 E8
Elm Gr. Sutton SM1 .... 59 B6
Elm Gr. Wimble SW19 .... 19 E1
Elm Grove Par. Hackb SM6 .... 60 A7
Elm Grove Rd. Cobham KT11 ..... 73 D3
Elm Grove Rd. Farnb GU14 .... 85 B4
Elm Hill Bglws. Normdy GU3 .... 106 E3
Elm House. [2] King U T KT2 .... 17 F1
Elm La. Ash GU10 .... 126 F8
Elm La. For Hil SE6 .... 23 F6
Elm La. Ockham GU23 .... 92 A8
Elm Park Rd. S Norw SE25 .... 42 F6
Elm Pk. Streat SW2 .... 21 F8
Elm Pk. Sunnin GU20 & SL5 .... 29 E1
Elm Pl. Alder GU11 .... 126 C8
Elm Rd. Beck BR3 .... 43 F7
Elm Rd. Carsh CR4 & SM6 .... 41 A1
Elm Rd. Chess KT9 .... 56 E6
Elm Rd. Clayg KT10 .... 55 F4
Elm Rd. E Bed TW14 .... 14 D8
Elm Rd. Farnc GU7 .... 150 F8
Elm Rd. Heath E GU9 .... 125 D7
Elm Rd. Horse GU21 .... 69 F4
Elm Rd. King U T KT2 .... 37 F8
Elm Rd. King U T KT3 .... 38 D6
Elm Rd. Leahd KT22 .... 95 B5
Elm Rd. Mortl SW14 .... 7 C3
Elm Rd. Purley CR8 .... 80 B6
Elm Rd. Redh RH1 .... 118 E1
Elm Rd. S Norw CR7 .... 42 D5
Elm Rd. Stonel KT17 .... 57 F4
Elm Rd. Warlgm CR6 .... 81 D2
Elm Rd. Woking GU21 .... 69 D1
Elm Rd W. Cheam SM4 .... 39 F2
Elm Tree Ave. Thame D KT10 ...... 36 E2
Elm Tree Cl. Addl KT16 .... 51 E8
Elm Tree Cl. Ashf TW15 .... 14 B3
Elm View. Ash GU12 .... 106 B3
Elm Way. N Cheam KT4 .... 58 C7
Elm Way. W Ewell KT19 .... 57 C5
Elm Way. W Ewell KT19 .... 57 D5
Elm Wlk. W Barn SW20 .... 39 D5
Elm Wood Prim Sch.
 W Norw SE27 .... 22 D5
Elmbank Ave. Eng Gn TW20 .... 11 B2
Elmbank Ave. Guild GU2 .... 130 A8
Elmbourne Rd. Up Toot SW17 .... 21 B5
Elmbridge Ave. Tolw KT5 .... 38 C3
Elmbridge Cotts. Cran GU6 ...... 174 B3
Elmbridge La. Old Wok GU22 ..... 89 F8
Elmbridge Rd. Crawl GU6 .... 173 F2
Elmbrook Cl. Sunby TW16 .... 35 B8
Elmbrook Cty Fst Sch.
 Sunby TW16 .... 35 B8
Elmbrook Rd. Cheam SM1 .... 58 F6
Elmcourt Rd.
 W Norw SE21 & SE27 .... 22 B6
Elmcroft. L Book KT23 .... 94 A3
Elmcroft. [12] Woking GU21 .... 69 E1
Elmcroft Cl. Chess KT9 .... 56 E7
Elmcroft Cl. Felt TW14 .... 3 F1
Elmcroft Cl. Friml GU16 .... 85 F7
Elmcroft Dr. Ashf TW15 .... 14 A3
Elmcroft Dr. Chess KT9 .... 56 E7
Elmdene. Tolw KT5 .... 38 C1
Elmdene Cl. Beck BR3 .... 43 F4
Elmdon Rd. Hatton TW6 .... 3 F4
Elmdon Rd. Hounsl TW5 .... 4 E5
Elmer Cotts. Fetch KT22 .... 95 A4
Elmer Gdns. Islew TW7 .... 5 D4
Elmer Mews. Fetch KT22 .... 95 A5
Elmer Rd. Catf SE6 .... 24 C8
Elmer's Dr. Tedd TW11 .... 17 B2
Elmers End Rd. Beck BR3 .... 43 D5
Elmers End Rd.
 Penge BR3 & SE20 .... 43 C6
Elmers End Sta. Beck BR3 .... 43 D4
Elmers Rd. Croy CR0 & SE25 ...... 43 A2
Elmers Rd. Ockley RH5 .... 177 C4
Elmerside Rd. Beck BR3 .... 43 E5

Elmfield. Fetch KT23 .... 94 A4
Elmfield Ave. Mitch CR4 .... 41 A8
Elmfield Ave. Tedd TW11 .... 16 F3
Elmfield House. Merrow GU4 .... 110 C3
Elmfield Mansions. **5**
Up Toot SW17 .... 21 A4
Elmfield Rd. Up Toot SW17 ...... 21 B6
Elmfield Way. S Croy CR2 .... 61 F2
Elmgate Ave. Felt TW13 .... 15 C5
Elmgrove Cl. Knaph GU21 .... 88 D8
Elmgrove Rd. Croy CR0 .... 43 B2
Elmgrove Rd. Weyb KT13 .... 53 A7
Elmhurst Ave. Mitch CR4 .... 21 B1
Elmhurst Ballet Sch.
Camb GU15 .... 65 D5
Elmhurst Cl. Croy CR0 .... 61 D5
Elmhurst Cl. Guild GU1 .... 130 F8
Elmhurst Dr. Dork RH4 .... 136 B5
Elmhurst Lodge. Sutton SM2 .... 59 C3
Elmhurst Sch for Boys.
S Croy CR2 .... 61 D5
Elmore Rd. Chips CR5 .... 99 A6
Elmpark Gdns. Selsd CR2 .... 62 C1
Elsinore Ave. Mitch CR4 .... 40 F7
Elms Cotts. Merton SW19 .... 20 B1
Elms Rd. Alder GU11 .... 105 A2
Elms Rd. Woki RG11 .... 25 B5
Elms The. Ash GU10 .... 126 F8
Elms The. Ashf TW15 .... 14 A3
Elms The. Clayg KT10 .... 55 F3
Elms The. Croy CR0 .... 42 C1
Elms The. Mortl SW13 .... 7 F4
Elmscott Rd. Catf BR1 .... 24 F3
Elmshorn. Nork KT17 .... 77 C3
Elmside. Guild GU2 .... 130 A8
Elmside. Milf GU8 .... 149 F1
Elmside. New Add CR0 .... 63 B4
Elmsleigh Ctr The. Stain TW18 .. 12 F4
Elmsleigh House. Twick TW2 .... 16 D6
Elmsleigh Rd. Farnb GU14 ...... 84 F4
Elmsleigh Rd. Stain TW18 .... 12 F3
Elmsleigh Rd. Twick TW2 .... 16 D6
Elmslie Cl. Epsom KT18 .... 76 C5
Elmstead. E Grins RH19 .... 205 E8
Elmstead Cl. W Ewell KT19 ...... 57 E5
Elmstead Cl. W Ewell KT19 ...... 57 E5
Elmstead Gdns. Worc Pk KT4 .... 58 A7
Elmstead Rd. W Byfl KT14 .... 71 A5
Elmsway. Ashf TW15 .... 14 A3
Elmswood. L Book KT23 .... 93 F3
Elmsworth Ave. Hounsl TW3 ...... 5 B5
Elmtree Cl. Byfl KT14 .... 71 E6
Elmtree Rd. Tedd TW11 .... 16 E3
Elmwood Ave. Felt TW13 .... 15 B5
Elmwood Cl. Ashtd KT21 .... 75 D5
Elmwood Cl. Hackb SM6 .... 60 B8
Elmwood Cl. Stonel KT17 .... 58 A3
Elmwood Cl. Stonel KT17 .... 58 A3
Elmwood Dr. Stonel KT17 .... 58 A3
Elmwood Inf Sch. Thorn H CR0 .. 42 B3
Elmwood Jun Sch. Thorn H CR0 .. 42 B3
Elmwood Rd. Chisw W4 .... 7 C8
Elmwood Rd. Knaph GU21 .... 88 D8
Elmwood Rd. Mitch CR4 .... 40 F6
Elmwood Rd. Redh RH1 .... 119 B5
Elmwood Rd. Thorn H CR0 .... 42 B2
Elmworth Gr. W Norw SE21 ...... 22 D6
Elphinstone Ct. Streat SW16 .... 21 E2
Elsdon Rd. Woking GU21 .... 69 A1
Elsenham St.
Wands SW18 & SW19 .... 19 F6
Elsenwood Cres. Camb GU15 .... 66 A6
Elsenwood Dr. Camb GU15 .... 66 A7
Elsinore Ave. Stan TW19 .... 13 E8
Elsinore For Hil SE23 .... 23 E7
Elsinore Way. Mortl TW9 .... 7 B4
Elsley Cl. Friml GU16 .... 85 F6
Elsrick Ave. Morden SM4 .... 40 A4
Elstan Way. Croy CR0 .... 43 E2
Elstead Ct. Cheam SM4 .... 39 E1
Elstead House. Elst GU8 .... 148 D4
Elstead House. **12** Streat SW2 .. 21 F8
Elstead Rd. Milf GU8 .... 149 C3
Elstead Rd. Seale GU10 .... 127 B3
Elstead Rd. Shackl GU7 & GU8 .. 149 E6
Elstead Rd. The San GU10 ...... 127 A2
Elsted Cl. Crawl RH11 .... 201 B8
Elston Pl. Alder GU12 .... 126 C8
Elston Rd. Alder GU11 & GU12 .. 126 C8
Elstree Hill. Catf BR1 .... 24 E1
Elsworth Cl. E Bed TW14 .... 14 E7
Elsworthy. Thame D KT7 .... 36 E3
Elthorne Ct. Felt TW13 .... 15 C7
Elton Rd. King U T KT2 .... 38 A8
Elton Rd. Purley CR8 .... 79 C7
Elveden Cl. Mayb GU22 .... 71 B2
Elveden Ct. Leahd KT22 .... 95 C6
Elveden Rd. Esher KT11 .... 73 C8
Elvington Gn. Hayes BR2 .... 44 F4
Elvino Rd. For Hil SE26 .... 23 E3
Elwell Cl. Egham TW20 .... 12 A2
Elwill Way. Beck BR3 .... 44 D5
Ely Cl. Crawl RH10 .... 201 F2
Ely Cl. Friml GU16 .... 86 A7
Ely Cl. King U T SW20 .... 38 F7
Ely Ct. King U T KT1 .... 38 A1
Ely House. **6** Redh RH1 .... 118 F1
Ely Rd. Hatton TW6 .... 3 F5
Ely Rd. Hounsl TW4 .... 4 C4
Ely Rd. Thorn H CR0 .... 42 D3
Elystan Cl. Wallin SM6 .... 60 C2
Embankment The. Twick TW1 .... 17 A7
Embankment The. Wray TW19 .... 11 C7
Embassy Cl. King U T KT6 .... 37 D4
Embassy Ct. **7** Wallin SM6 ..... 60 B4
Embassy Gdns. Beck BR3 .... 43 F8
Ember Cl. Addl KT15 .... 52 D5

Ember Ctr. Walt O T KT12 .... 54 E8
Ember Farm Ave. Thame D KT8 .. 36 D3
Ember Farm Way. E Mole KT8 .... 36 D4
Ember Gdns.
Thame D KT10 & KT8 .... 36 E2
Ember House. Catf BR1 .... 24 D3
Ember La.
Thame D KT10 & KT8 .... 36 E3
Embercourt Rd.
Thame D KT10 & KT7 & KT8 ..... 36 E3
Emberwood. Crawl RH11 .... 201 B8
Embleton Rd. Head Dn GU35 ... 187 B6
Embleton Wlk. Hampt TW12 ..... 15 F3
Emerton Rd. Fetch KT22 .... 94 C6
Emery Down Cl. Brack RG12 ..... 28 A6
Emley Rd. Addl KT15 .... 52 B6
Emlyn La. Leahd KT22 .... 95 A5
Emlyn Rd. Earls RH1 .... 140 A7
Emlyn Rd. Horley RH6 .... 160 E4
Emmanuel Cl. Stough GU2 ...... 109 A6
Emmanuel House. W Norw SE21 22 D5
Emmanuel Rd. Streat SW12 ...... 21 D7
Emmbrook Rd. Woki RG11 ...... 25 A8
Emmbrook Sch The. Woki RG11 25 A8
Emmeline Ct. Walt O T KT12 .... 35 C2
Emmetts Cl. Horse GU21 .... 69 D2
Empire Villas. Salfs RH1 .... 161 B7
Empress Ave. Farnb GU14 .... 85 B5
Emsworth St. Streat SW2 .... 21 F6
Ena Rd. Thorn H SW16 .... 41 E6
Endale Cl. Carsh SM5 .... 59 F8
Endeavour Way. Wallin CR0 ..... 41 E2
Endeavour Way. S Norw SE19 .. 42 F8
Enderley House. S Norw SE19 .. 42 F8
Endlesham Cl. **3** Balham SW12 21 A8
Endlesham Rd. Balham SW12 ... 21 A8
Endsleigh Cl. Selsd CR2 .... 62 C1
Endsleigh Gdns. Hersh KT12 .... 54 C5
Endsleigh Gdns. King U T KT6 .. 37 C3
Endsleigh Mansions. **4**
Streat SW16 .... 21 E5
Endsleigh Rd. Merst RH1 .... 119 C6
Endway. Tolw KT5 .... 38 B2
Enfield Rd. Ash GU12 .... 106 B5
Enfield Rd. Crawl RH11 .... 201 C2
Enfield Rd. Harl TW6 .... 3 E5
Engadine Cl. S Croy CR0 .... 61 F7
Engadine St. Wands SW18 .... 20 A7
Engalee. E Grins RH19 .... 185 C2
Englefield. Horsh RH12 .... 216 F2
Englefield Cl. Eng Gn TW20 ..... 11 C2
Englefield Cl. Thorn H CR0 ...... 42 C3
Englefield Green Cty Inf Sch.
Eng Gn TW20 .... 11 C3
Englefield Rd. Knaph GU21 ..... 68 D2
Engleheart Dr. Felt TW14 .... 3 F1
Engleheart Rd. Catf SE6 .... 24 C8
Englehurst. Eng Gn TW20 .... 11 C2
Englemere Pk. Ascot SL5 .... 28 D5
Englemere Pond Nature Reserve.
Ascot SL5 .... 28 F6
Englesfield. Friml GU15 .... 66 D5
Engliff La. Pyrf GU22 .... 71 A3
Enid Wood House. Brack RG12 .. 27 C7
Enmore Ave. Croy SE25 .... 43 A4
Enmore Gdns. Mortl SW14 .... 7 D2
Enmore Rd. Croy SE25 .... 43 A4
Ennerdale. Easth RG12 .... 27 A5
Ennerdale Cl. Cheam SM1 .... 58 F6
Ennerdale Cl. Crawl RH11 ..... 201 B4
Ennerdale Cl. E Bed TW14 .... 14 F7
Ennerdale Gr. Hale GU9 .... 125 A6
Ennerdale Rd. Rich TW9 .... 6 F5
Ennismore Ave. Guild GU1 ..... 109 F1
Ennismore Gdns. Thame D KT7 36 E3
Ennor Ct. Cheam KT4 .... 58 C6
Ensham Sec Sch (Annexe).
Up Toot SW17 .... 20 F3
Ensign Cl. Purley CR8 .... 61 A1
Ensign Cl. Stan TW19 .... 13 D7
Ensign Way. Stan TW19 .... 13 D7
Enterdent Cotts. Godst RH9 ... 121 D2
Enterdent Rd. Godst RH9 ...... 121 D2
Enterprise Cl. Thorn H CR0 ...... 42 A1
Enterprise Est. Stough GU1 .... 109 E5
Enterprise House.
Walt O T KT12 .... 35 B2
Enterprise Way. Tedd TW11 ..... 16 F2
Envis Way. Fairl GU3 .... 108 C4
Eothen Sch for Girls. Cater CR3 101 A3
Epping Way. Brack RG12 .... 27 F5
Epping Wlk. Crawl RH10 .... 201 F4
Epsom Cl. Camb GU15 .... 65 C8
Epsom Coll. Epsom KT17 .... 77 A5
Epsom Cty Jun & Inf Schs.
Epsom KT19 .... 76 D8
Epsom District Hospl.
Epsom KT18 .... 76 C4
Epsom Downs Cty Inf Sch.
Lang V KT20 .... 96 D8
Epsom Downs Metro Ctr.
Burgh H KT18 .... 97 B7
Epsom Downs Sta. Epsom KT17 77 B4
Epsom & Ewell Cottage Hospl.
Epsom KT19 .... 75 E8

Epsom La N.
Burgh H KT18 & KT20 .... 97 B7
Epsom La S. Tadw KT20 .... 97 C5
Epsom Pl. Cran GU6 .... 174 F3
Epsom Rd. Ashtd KT18 & KT21 .. 76 A2
Epsom Rd. Cheam SM4 .... 39 F2
Epsom Rd. Crawl RH10 .... 202 A4
Epsom Rd. Croy CR0 .... 61 A6
Epsom Rd. E Clan GU4 .... 111 D3
Epsom Rd. Guild GU1 .... 130 D8
Epsom Rd. Leahd KT22 .... 95 C6
Epsom Rd. Merrow GU1 & GU4 . 110 C1

Epsom Rd. Merrow GU4 .... 110 F2
Epsom Rd. Morden SM4 .... 39 F2
Epsom Rd. W Clan GU4 .... 111 D3
Epsom Rd. W Hors GU4 & KT24 . 112 C6
Epsom Sch of Art & Design.
Epsom KT18 .... 76 D5
Epsom Sq. Hatton TW6 .... 3 F5
Epsom Sta. Epsom KT18 .... 76 D6
Epworth Rd. Brent TW7 & TW8 .. 6 B7
Eresby Dr. Croy BR3 .... 44 A1
Erica Cl. W End GU24 .... 67 E6
Erica Cl. Woking GU22 .... 69 D1
Erica Dr. Woki RG11 .... 25 D5
Erica Gdns. Croy CR0 .... 63 B7
Erica Way. Copth RH10 .... 183 A2
Erica Way. W Wick CR0 .... 63 B7
Eridge Cl. Crawl RH10 .... 202 C6
Erin Cl. Catf BR1 .... 24 E1
Erindale Ct. Beck BR3 .... 44 A8
Eriswell Cres. Whit V KT12 ...... 53 F4
Eriswell Rd. Whit V KT12 .... 53 F5
Erkenwald Cl. Chert KT16 .... 32 E3
Ermine Rd. Hounsl TW4 .... 4 C5
Ermyn Cl. Ashtd KT21 .... 95 D6
Ermyn Way. Ashtd KT21 & KT22 95 D6
Erncroft Way. Twick TW1 .... 5 F1
Ernest Ave. W Norw SE27 .... 22 B4
Ernest Cl. Woking GU22 .... 68 E3
Ernest Cl. M Bourn GU10 & GU9 146 B6
Ernest Cotts. Ewell KT17 .... 57 F3
Ernest Gdns. Chisw W4 .... 7 B8
Ernest Gr. Beck BR3 .... 43 F4
Ernest Rd. King U T KT1 .... 38 B7
Ernest Sq. King U T KT1 .... 38 B7
Ernle Rd. Wimble SW20 .... 19 C1
Erridge Rd. Merton SW19 .... 40 A7
Errol Gdns. Barn KT3 .... 39 A5
Erskine Cl. Carsh SM1 .... 59 E7
Erskine Cl. Crawl RH11 .... 200 E2
Erskine Rd. Carsh SM1 & SM5 .. 59 D7
Esam Way. W Norw SE27 & SW16 22 A3
Escombe Dr. Stough GU2 & GU3 109 B6
Escot Rd. Charlt TW16 .... 14 E1
Escott Pl. Ottsh KT16 .... 51 D4
Esher Ave. Cheam SM3 .... 58 D7
Esher Ave. Walt O T KT12 .... 35 A1
Esher C of E Fst & Mid Sch.
Esher KT10 .... 55 B6
Esher Church Sch. Esher KT10 .. 55 C5
Esher Cl. Esher KT10 .... 55 B5
Esher Coll. Thame D KT7 .... 36 E2
Esher Cres. Hatton TW6 .... 3 F5
Esher Gdns. Putney SW19 .... 19 D6
Esher Gn. Esher KT10 .... 55 B6
Esher Green Dr. Esher KT10 ..... 55 B7
Esher Mews. Mitch CR4 .... 40 F6
Esher Park Ave. Esher KT10 ..... 55 C5
Esher Place Ave. Esher KT10 .... 55 B6
Esher Rd. E Mole KT8 .... 36 D4
Esher Rd. Hersh KT10 & KT12 .. 54 E6
Esher Sta. Esher KT10 .... 55 D8
Eskdale Gdns. Sander CR8 ...... 80 D5
Eskdale Rd. Friml GU15 .... 66 D4
Eskmont Ridge. S Norw SE19 .. 22 E1
Esme House. Rhampt SW15 .... 7 F3
Esparto St. Wands SW18 .... 20 B8
Essenden Rd. S Croy CR2 .... 61 E3
Essendene Cl. Cater CR3 .... 100 E4
Essendene Lodge Sch.
Cater CR3 .... 100 E4
Essendene Rd. Cater CR3 ...... 100 E5
Essex Ave. Islew TW7 .... 5 E4
Essex Cl. Addl KT15 .... 52 C6
Essex Cl. Friml GU16 .... 86 A7
Essex Cl. W Barn SM4 .... 39 D2
Essex Ct. Barnes SW13 .... 7 F5
Essex Ct. S Norw SE19 .... 22 D2
Essex Dr. Crawl GU6 .... 173 F2
Essex Gr. S Norw SE19 .... 22 D2
Essex House. **5** Croy CR0 ..... 61 D8
Essex Tower. **5** Penge SE20 .. 43 B8
Estcots Cty Prim Sch.
E Grins RH19 .... 186 A1
Estcots Dr. E Grins RH19 .... 186 A1
Estcourt Rd. Croy CR0 & SE25 .. 43 B3
Estella Ave. W Barn KT3 & SW20 39 B5
Estreham Rd. Streat SW16 ...... 21 D2
Estridge Cl. Hounsl TW3 .... 5 A3
Eswyn Rd. Up Toot SW17 .... 20 F3
Ethel Rd. Ashf TW15 .... 13 E3
Ethelbert Rd. Wimble SW20 ..... 39 D8
Ethelbert St. Balham SW12 ...... 21 B7
Ethelworth Ct. **4** Streat SW2 .. 22 A7
Etherley Hill. Wotton RH5 ...... 177 A7
Etherstone Gn. Streat SW16 .... 22 A4
Etherstone Rd. Streat SW16 .... 22 A4
Eton Ave. Heston TW5 .... 5 A8
Eton Ave. New Mal KT3 .... 38 D5
Eton Cl. Wands SW18 .... 20 B8
Eton Ct. Stain TW18 .... 12 F3
Eton Pl. Heath E GU9 .... 125 B7
Eton Rd. Harl UB3 .... 3 F7
Eton St. Rich TW10 .... 6 E2
Etps Rd. Farnb GU14 .... 105 B8
Ettrick Ct. Farnb GU14 .... 105 B8
Etwell Pl. Surb KT5 .... 37 F3
Eureka Rd. King U T KT1 .... 38 A7
Europa Park Rd. Guild GU1 .... 109 C2
Eurythmy Sch. E Grins RH19 ... 205 D1
Eustace Cres. Woki RG11 .... 25 D8
Eustace Rd. Merrow GU4 ...... 110 D3
Euston Rd. Thorn H CR0 .... 42 A1
Evans Cl. Worth RH10 .... 202 D5
Evans Gr. Felt TW13 .... 16 A6
Evans Rd. Catf SE6 .... 24 F6
Eve Rd. Islew TW7 .... 6 A3
Eve Rd. Sheer GU21 .... 70 B4
Evedon. Easth RG12 .... 27 B2

Evelina Rd. Penge SE20 .... 23 D1
Eveline Rd. Mitch CR4 .... 40 F8
Evelyn Ave. Alder GU11 .... 126 B8
Evelyn Cl. Twick TW2 .... 16 B8
Evelyn Cl. Woking GU22 .... 89 D7
Evelyn Cotts. Abin C RH5 ...... 155 D8
Evelyn Cotts. S Godst RH9 .... 142 E6
Evelyn Cres. Sunby TW16 .... 34 F8
Evelyn Ct. Croy CR0 .... 43 A2
Evelyn Gdns. Rich TW9 .... 6 E3
Evelyn Gdns. Tyl Gn RH9 ...... 121 C5
Evelyn Rd. Rich TW9 .... 6 E4
Evelyn Rd. Rich TW10 .... 17 C5
Evelyn Rd. Wimble SW19 .... 20 B2
Evelyn Terr. Rich TW9 .... 6 E4
Evelyn Way. Stk D'A KT11 .... 73 F3
Evelyn Way. Sunby TW16 .... 34 F8
Evelyn Way. Wallin SM6 .... 60 D6
Evelyn Woods Rd. Farnb GU11 105 C7
Evendon's Cl. Woki RG11 .... 25 A3
Evendon's La. Woki RG11 .... 25 A3
Evening Hill. Beck BR3 .... 24 C1
Evenlode Way.
Sandh GU15 & GU17 .... 64 D8
Everard La. Cater CR3 .... 101 B5
Everest Ct. S Norw SE19 .... 42 E8
Everest Ct. Woking GU21 .... 68 E3
Everest Rd. Camb GU15 .... 65 D8
Everest Rd. Crowth RG11 .... 45 B6
Everest Rd. Stan TW19 .... 13 E8
Everglade. Bigg H TN16 .... 83 D1
Evergreen Ct. Stan TW19 .... 13 D8
Evergreen Rd. Friml GU16 .... 66 A3
Evergreen Way. Stan TW19 ..... 13 D8
Everlands Cl. **2** Woking GU22 69 E1
Eversfield Rd. Horsh RH13 .... 217 E1
Eversfield Rd. Reig RH2 .... 118 B1
Eversfield Rd. Richm TW9 .... 6 F5
Eversley Cres. Hounsl TW7 .... 5 D6
Eversley Pk. Wimble SW19 ...... 19 B3
Eversley Rd. King U T KT5 .... 37 F4
Eversley Rd. S Norw SE19 .... 22 D1
Eversley Way. Croy CR0 .... 63 A7
Eversley Way. Thorpe TW20 .... 32 C7
Everton Rd. Croy CR0 .... 43 A1
Evesham Cl. Belm SM2 .... 59 A3
Evesham Cl. Reig RH2 .... 117 F2
Evesham Gn. Morden SM4 .... 40 B3
Evesham Rd. Morden SM4 .... 40 B3
Evesham Rd. Reig RH2 .... 117 F2
Evesham Rd N. Reig RH2 .... 117 F2
Evesham Wlk. Sandh GU15 ...... 45 D1
Ewart Rd. For Hil SE23 .... 23 D8
Ewelands. Horley RH6 .... 161 C4
Ewell By-Pass. Ewell KT17 ...... 58 A2
Ewell Castle Sch. Ewell KT17 ... 58 A2
Ewell Court Ave. W Ewell KT19 .. 57 E5
Ewell Court Ave. W Ewell KT19 .. 57 E5
Ewell Downs Rd. Ewell KT17 ... 77 A7
Ewell East Sta. Ewell KT17 ...... 58 B1
Ewell Grove Cty Inf Sch.
Ewell KT17 .... 57 F1
Ewell House. Ewell KT17 .... 57 F1
Ewell House Gr. Ewell KT17 ..... 57 F1
Ewell Park Way. Stonel KT17 ... 58 A3
Ewell Rd. Cheam SM2 & SM3 ... 58 D4
Ewell Rd. Surb KT5 & KT6 .... 37 F2
Ewell Rd. Thame D KT6 & KT7 .. 37 B2
Ewell Rd. Tolw KT6 .... 38 B1
Ewell West Sta. W Ewell KT19 .. 57 E2
Ewell West Sta. W Ewell KT19 .. 57 E2
Ewelme Rd. For Hil SE23 .... 23 C7
Ewen Cres. Streat SW2 .... 22 A8
Ewhurst Ave. S Croy CR2 .... 61 F2
Ewhurst C of E Fst Sch.
Ewh GU6 .... 175 E5
Ewhurst Cl. Crawl RH11 .... 201 C6
Ewhurst Cl. E Ewell SM2 .... 58 C2
Ewhurst Rd. Cran GU6 .... 174 E3
Ewhurst Rd. Crawl RH11 .... 201 C7
Ewhurst Rd. Ewh GU5 & GU6 .. 154 C3
Ewins Cl. Ash GU12 .... 106 A2
Ewood La. Bear Gn RH5 .... 157 F6
Ewood La. Parkg RH5 .... 158 C5
Eworth Hill Cross. Crond GU10 124 D7
Exbury Rd. For Hil SE6 .... 24 A6
Excalibur Cl. Crawl RH11 ...... 200 E5
Excelsior Cl. King U T KT1 .... 38 A7
Exchange Rd. Ascot SL5 .... 29 C4
Exchange Rd. Crawl RH10 ..... 201 E6
Exchange The. **6** Purley CR8 .. 80 A8
Exeforde Ave. Ashf TW15 .... 14 A4
Exeter Cl. Crawl RH10 .... 201 E2
Exeter Ct. King U T KT6 .... 37 E4
Exeter Ct. Mitch SW19 .... 20 E1
Exeter House. Felt TW13 .... 16 A6
Exeter Rd. Ash GU12 .... 106 A3
Exeter Rd. Croy CR0 .... 42 F2
Exeter Rd. Felt TW13 .... 15 F5
Exeter Rd. Harl TW6 .... 3 E5
Exeter Way. Harl TW6 .... 3 E5
Exhibition Rd. Farnb GU14 ..... 105 A8
Explorer Ave. Stan TW19 .... 13 E7
Eyebright Cl. Croy CR0 .... 43 D1
Eyhurst Cl. Kings KT20 .... 97 F3
Eyhurst Spur. Kings KT20 .... 97 F3
Eyles Cl. Horsh RH12 .... 217 B4
Eylewood Rd. W Norw SE27 ..... 22 C3
Eynella Rd. Dulw SE21 .... 22 D8
Eyston Dr. Whit V KT13 .... 53 A1

Fabyc House. Rich TW9 .... 7 A7
Factory Cotts. Farnb GU10 .... 124 D2
Factory La. Thorn H CR0 & CR9 .. 61 B8
Fagg's Rd. Felt TW14 .... 4 A2
Fagg's Rd. Hatton TW6 .... 4 A2
Fair Green Ct. **1** Mitch CR4 .. 40 F6
Fair La. L Kings CR5 & RH2 ...... 98 D1

Fair Oak Cl. Oxsh KT22 .... 74 D7
Fair St. Hounsl TW3 .... 5 C4
Fair View. Horsh RH12 .... 217 A3
Fairacre. Hounsl TW7 .... 5 D6
Fairacre. King U T KT5 .... 38 E6
Fairacres. Burgh H KT20 .... 97 C6
Fairacres. Cobham KT11 .... 73 E7
Fairacres. New Add CR0 .... 62 F2
Fairbairn Cl. Purley CR8 .... 80 A6
Fairbourne. Cobham KT11 .... 73 D6
Fairbourne Cl. Woking GU21 .... 69 A1
Fairbourne La. Cater CR3 ...... 100 C3
Fairbriar Ct. **9** Epsom KT18 ... 76 E6
Fairchildes Ave. New Add CR0 .. 82 D7
Fairchildes Cotts. W Wick CR6 .. 82 F6
Fairchildes PrimSch.
New Add CR9 .... 82 E7
Fairchildes Rd. Fickl CR6 .... 82 E4
Faircroft. For Hil SE26 .... 23 C4
Faircross. Easth RG12 .... 27 B6
Fairdene. Kings CR5 .... 98 F6
Fairdene Rd. Coulsd CR5 .... 79 D2
Fairfax. Brack RG12 .... 27 A8
Fairfax Ave. Ewell KT17 .... 58 B2
Fairfax Ave. Redh RH1 .... 118 F2
Fairfax Cl. Walt O T KT12 .... 35 B1
Fairfax Mews. Farnb GU14 ..... 85 D2
Fairfax Rd. Farnb GU14 .... 85 C7
Fairfax Rd. Old Wok GU22 .... 90 B7
Fairfax Rd. Tedd TW11 .... 17 B1
Fairfield App. Wray TW19 .... 11 D8
Fairfield Ave. Horley RH6 ...... 161 A1
Fairfield Ave. Stain TW18 .... 12 F4
Fairfield Ave. Twick TW2 .... 16 B7
Fairfield Cl. G Book KT23 .... 94 B1
Fairfield Cl. Mitch SW19 .... 20 E1
Fairfield Cl. W Ewell KT19 .... 57 E5
Fairfield Cl. W Ewell KT19 .... 57 E5
Fairfield Ct. Dork RH4 .... 115 B1
Fairfield Dr. Dork RH4 .... 136 B8
Fairfield Dr. Friml GU16 .... 65 E3
Fairfield E. King U T KT1 .... 37 E7
Fairfield Ind Est. King U T KT1 .. 37 F6
Fairfield La. W End GU24 .... 68 A7
Fairfield N. King U T KT1 & KT2 .. 37 E7
Fairfield Path. S Croy CR0 & CR9 61 D7
Fairfield Pk. Cobham KT11 .... 73 D5
Fairfield Pl. King U T KT1 .... 37 E6
Fairfield Rd. Beck BR3 .... 44 A7
Fairfield Rd. E Grins RH19 ..... 205 F8
Fairfield Rd. King U T KT1 .... 37 E7
Fairfield Rd. Leahd KT22 .... 95 B6
Fairfield Rd. S Croy CR0 & CR9 . 61 E7
Fairfield Rise. Stough GU2 .... 108 F2
Fairfield S. King U T KT1 .... 37 F7
Fairfield The. Farnh GU9 .... 125 C2
Fairfield W. King U T KT1 .... 37 E7
Fairfield Way. Coulsd CR5 .... 79 D5
Fairfield Way. W Ewell KT19 .... 57 E5
Fairfield Way. W Ewell KT19 .... 57 E5
Fairfield Wlk. Leahd KT22 .... 95 B6
Fairfields. Lewish SE6 .... 24 B8
Fairfields Rd. Hounsl TW3 .... 5 C4
Fairford. For Hil SE6 .... 24 A7
Fairford Ave. Croy CR0 .... 43 D4
Fairford Cl. Croy CR0 .... 43 E4
Fairford Cl. Pyrf KT14 .... 70 F5
Fairford Cl. Reig RH2 .... 118 C3
Fairford Ct. Sutton SM2 .... 59 B3
Fairford Gdns. Worc Pk KT4 ..... 57 F7
Fairgreen Rd. Thorn H CR7 ...... 42 B4
Fairhaven. Egham TW20 .... 11 F3
Fairhaven Ave. Croy CR0 .... 43 D3
Fairhaven Ct. S Croy CR2 .... 61 C5
Fairhaven Ct. **1** Egham TW20 . 11 F3
Fairhaven Rd. Redh RH1 .... 119 A5
Fairholme. E Bed TW14 .... 14 E8
Fairholme. **2** New Mal KT3 ... 38 E5
Fairholme Cres. Ashtd KT21 .... 75 C2
Fairholme Gdns. M Bourn GU9 125 C1
Fairholme Jun & Inf Schs.
E Bed TW14 .... 14 D7
Fairholme Rd. Ashf TW15 .... 13 F3
Fairholme Rd. Cheam SM1 ...... 58 F4
Fairholme Rd. Thorn H CR0 ..... 42 A2
Fairings The. Hersh KT12 .... 54 B6
Fairlands Ave. Fairl GU3 .... 108 C5
Fairlands Ave. Sutton SM1 ...... 59 A8
Fairlands Ave. Thorn H CR7 ..... 42 A4
Fairlands Ct. Fairl GU3 .... 108 C5
Fairlands Rd. Fairl GU3 .... 108 D5
Fairlawn. L Book KT23 .... 93 F3
Fairlawn. Whit V KT13 .... 53 E5
Fairlawn Cl. Clayg KT10 .... 55 F4
Fairlawn Cl. Felt TW13 .... 15 F4
Fairlawn Cl. King U T KT2 .... 18 C2
Fairlawn Cres. E Grins RH19 ... 185 B2
Fairlawn Dr. E Grins RH19 ..... 185 B2
Fairlawn Dr. Earls RH1 .... 139 E7
Fairlawn Dr. Woodh RH1 ...... 139 E7
Fairlawn Gr. Banstd SM7 .... 78 D6
Fairlawn Pk. For Hil SE26 .... 23 E3
Fairlawn Pk. Horse GU21 .... 69 E4
Fairlawn Prim Sch. Hersh SE23 23 C8
Fairlawn Prim Sch Annexe.
For Hil SE23 .... 23 C7
Fairlawn Rd. Merton SW19 ...... 19 F1
Fairlawn Rd. Sutton SM2 & SM5 78 C8
Fairlawnes. Wallin SM6 .... 60 B5
Fairlawns. Addl KT15 .... 52 B5
Fairlawns. Horley RH6 .... 161 B2
Fairlawns. Merrow GU1 .... 110 C1
Fairlawns. Sunby TW16 .... 35 A6
Fairlawns. Twick TW1 .... 6 C1
Fairlawns. Woodhm KT15 .... 70 F8
Fairlawns Cl. Stain TW18 .... 13 B2
Fairleas. Beck BR3 .... 44 B7
Fairlie Gdns. For Hil SE23 .... 23 C8
Fairlight. Hampt TW12 .... 16 B3
Fairlight Cl. N Cheam KT4 .... 58 C6

Fairlight Rd. Up Toot SW17 .... 20 D4
Fairline Ct. Beck BR3 .... 44 C7
Fairlop Wlk. Crawl GU6 .... 173 F2
Fairmead. Woking GU21 .... 69 C1
Fairmead Cl. Heston TW5 .... 4 D7
Fairmead Cl. King U T KT3 .... 38 D6
Fairmead Cl. Sandh GU15 .... 64 E7
Fairmead Rd. Thorn H CR0 .... 42 A2
Fairmeads. Cobham KT11 .... 73 F6
Fairmile Ave. Cobham KT11 .... 73 F6
Fairmile Ave. Streat SW16 .... 21 D3
Fairmile Hts. Cobham KT11 .... 74 A6
Fairmile La. Cobham KT11 .... 73 E5
Fairmile Park Copse.
  Cobham KT11 .... 73 F6
Fairmile Park Rd. Cobham KT11 ... 73 F6
Fairoak Cl. Purley CR8 .... 80 B4
Fairoak La.
  Chess KT9 & KT22 & KT10 .... 75 B8
Fairoak La.
  Oxsh KT10 & KT22 & KT10 .... 74 E8
Fairoaks Airport. Chobh GU24 ...... 50 E1
Fairoaks Ct. Addl KT15 .... 52 B5
Fairs Rd. Leahd KT22 .... 95 A8
Fairstone Ct. Horley RH6 .... 161 B4
Fairview. E Ewell KT17 .... 77 C8
Fairview Ave. Woking GU22 .... 69 F1
Fairview Cl. Woking GU22 .... 69 F1
Fairview Cotts. Went GU25 .... 31 D3
Fairview Ct. Ashf TW15 .... 14 A3
Fairview Ct. King U T KT2 .... 38 B8
Fairview Ct. Stain TW18 .... 13 A2
Fairview Dr. Shep Gn TW17 .... 33 F4
Fairview Gdns. Heath E GU9 .... 125 D6
Fairview House. ☑ Streat SW2 .... 21 F8
Fairview Pl. Streat SW2 .... 21 F8
Fairview Rd. Ash GU12 .... 106 B3
Fairview Rd. Carsh SM1 & SM5 .... 59 E5
Fairview Rd. Ewell KT17 .... 76 F8
Fairview Rd. Head Dn GU35 .... 187 C5
Fairview Rd. Thorn H SW16 .... 41 F8
Fairview Rd. Woki RG11 .... 25 C5
Fairview Terr. Head Dn GU35 .... 187 A6
Fairwater Dr. New Haw KT15 .... 52 D2
Fairwater House. Tedd TW11 .... 17 A4
Fairway. Chert KT16 .... 33 B1
Fairway. Copth RH10 .... 183 B2
Fairway. Crawl RH11 .... 200 D4
Fairway. Merrow GU4 .... 110 D1
Fairway. Sutton SM5 .... 78 C8
Fairway. W Barn SW20 .... 39 C6
Fairway Cl. Copth RH10 .... 183 A2
Fairway Cl. Croy BR3 & CR0 .... 43 E4
Fairway Cl. W Ewell KT19 .... 57 C6
Fairway Cl. W Ewell KT19 .... 57 C6
Fairway Cty Inf Sch.
  Copth RH10 .... 183 B3
Fairway Est. Hounsl TW4 .... 4 C2
Fairway Gdns. Beck BR3 .... 44 D3
Fairway Hts. Friml GU15 .... 66 B6
Fairway The. E Mole KT8 .... 36 B6
Fairway The. Farnb GU14 .... 84 A1
Fairway The. Friml GU15 & GU16 . 66 A3
Fairway The. Godal GU7 .... 150 F2
Fairway The. Heath E GU9 .... 125 D7
Fairway The. King U T KT3 .... 38 D8
Fairway The. Leahd KT22 .... 75 A1
Fairway The. Pirb GU22 & GU24 ... 88 C3
Fairway The. Whit V KT13 .... 72 A8
Fairways. Ashf TW15 .... 14 B2
Fairways. Beac H GU26 .... 188 B6
Fairways. ⚍ Hounsl TW7 .... 5 E6
Fairways. Kenley CR8 .... 80 C2
Fairways. Tedd TW11 .... 17 C1
Fairwell La. W Hors KT24 .... 112 B7
Fairwyn Rd. For Hil SE26 .... 23 E4
Fakenham Way. Sandh GU15 ...... 45 D2
Falaise. Egham TW20 .... 11 F3
Falaise Cl. Alder GU11 .... 105 B3
Falcon Cl. Chisw W4 .... 7 C8
Falcon Cl. Crawl RH11 .... 201 D8
Falcon Cl. Lhtwat GU18 .... 66 F8
Falcon Ct. Friml GU16 .... 65 D1
Falcon Ct. Sheer GU21 .... 70 C6
Falcon Ct. ⚍ N Worw SE21 .... 22 D6
Falcon Dr. Stan TW19 .... 2 E1
Falcon Rd. Guild GU1 .... 109 D1
Falcon Rd. Hampt TW12 .... 15 F1
Falcon Way. Sunby TW16 .... 34 E7
Falconhurst. ⚍ King U T KT6 ...... 37 E4
Falconhurst. Oxsh KT22 .... 57 E4
Falconry Ct. King U T KT1 .... 37 E6
Falcons Cl. Bigg H TN16 .... 83 D2
Falconwood. E Hors KT24 .... 92 F3
Falconwood. Eng Gn TW20 .... 11 E3
Falconwood Rd. New Add CR0 ..... 63 A3
Falcourt Cl. Sutton SM1 .... 59 B5
Falkland Ct. Farnb GU14 .... 105 E8
Falkland Gr. Dork RH4 .... 136 A6
Falkland House. Catf SE6 .... 24 E4
Falkland Park Ave. S Norw SE25 . 42 E7
Falkland Rd. Dork RH4 .... 136 A6
Falklands Dr. Horsh RH13 .... 218 B4
Falkner Rd. Farnh GU9 .... 125 B2
Fallow Deer Cl. Horsh RH13 .... 218 B4
Fallowfield Way. Horley RH6 .... 161 B4
Fallsbrook Rd. Streat SW16 .... 21 C2
Falmer Cl. Crawl RH11 .... 201 D4
Falmouth Cl. Friml GU16 .... 66 A4
Falmouth Cl. Hersh KT12 .... 54 C6
Falstone. Woking GU21 .... 69 B1
Fambridge Cl. For Hil SE26 .... 23 F4
Famet Ave. Purley CR8 .... 80 C6
Famet Cl. Purley CR8 .... 80 C6
Famet Gdns. Purley CR8 .... 80 C6
Famet Wlk. Purley CR8 .... 80 C6
Fanchford Rd. Reig RH2 .... 117 E1
Fanes Cl. Brack RG12 .... 26 F8
Fanfare The. Sheer GU22 .... 70 C4
Fanshawe Rd. Rich TW10 .... 17 C4

Faraday Ave. E Grins RH19 .... 205 F6
Faraday House. ☑ Balham SW12 21 B8
Faraday House. ⚍ Hampt TW12 ... 16 B1
Faraday Rd. Crawl RH10 .... 181 F2
Faraday Rd. E Mole KT8 .... 36 A5
Faraday Rd. Farnb GU14 .... 85 C6
Faraday Rd. Wimble SW19 .... 20 B2
Faraday Way. Croy CR0 & CR9 .... 41 F1
Farcrosse Cl. Sandh GU17 .... 64 C8
Fareham House. ⓭
  Rhampt SW15 .... 19 A7
Fareham Rd. Felt TW14 .... 15 C4
Farewell Pl. Mitch CR4 .... 40 E8
Farhalls Cres. Horsh RH12 .... 217 F6
Faringdon Cl. Sandh GU17 .... 45 C1
Faringdon Dr. Brack RG12 .... 27 C4
Farington Acres. Oat Pk KT13 ...... 53 D7
Faris Barn Dr. Woodhm KT15 ...... 70 F8
Faris La. Woodhm KT15 .... 70 F8
Farleigh Ave. Hayes BR2 .... 44 F7
Farleigh Court Rd. Farlgh CR6 ..... 82 B5
Farleigh Ct. Croy CR2 .... 61 C5
Farleigh Ct. ⓶ Stough GU2 .... 108 E1
Farleigh Cty Prim Sch.
  Warlgm CR6 .... 81 E2
Farleigh Dean Cres.
  New Add CR0 .... 82 B8
Farleigh House. �7 King U T KT2 . 18 B2
Farleigh Rd. Warlgm CR6 .... 81 E2
Farleigh Rd. Woodhm KT15 .... 71 A8
Farleton Cl. Whit V KT13 .... 53 D4
Farley Copse. Binf RG12 .... 26 E8
Farley Croft. Beck BR2 .... 44 E7
Farley Ct. Farnb GU14 .... 85 D2
Farley Heath Rd. Farl Gn GU5 ..... 153 C6
Farley House. For Hil SE26 .... 23 B5
Farley Moor. Binf RG12 .... 26 D8
Farley Pk. Oxted RH8 .... 122 D5
Farley Pl. Croy SE25 .... 43 A5
Farley Rd. Lewish SE6 .... 24 C8
Farley Rd. S Croy CR2 .... 62 B2
Farleycroft. ⓵ Croy CR0 .... 43 A1
Farleys Cl. W Hors KT24 .... 92 C1
Farlington Pl. Rhampt SW15 .... 19 B8
Farlington Sch. Slinfd RH12 .... 216 B6
Farlton Rd. Wands SW18 .... 20 B8
Farm App. Blind H RH9 .... 163 C5
Farm Ave. Horsh RH12 .... 217 B3
Farm Ave. Streat SW16 .... 21 E4
Farm Cl. Ascot SL5 .... 29 C4
Farm Cl. Bellf GU1 .... 109 D4
Farm Cl. Brack RG12 .... 26 F8
Farm Cl. Byfl KT14 .... 71 F7
Farm Cl. Chert KT16 .... 32 A3
Farm Cl. Coney H BR4 .... 63 F7
Farm Cl. Crawl RH10 .... 202 A7
Farm Cl. E Grins RH19 .... 206 B8
Farm Cl. E Hors KT24 .... 112 F7
Farm Cl. Egham TW18 .... 12 E3
Farm Cl. Fairl GU3 .... 108 C6
Farm Cl. Fetch KT22 .... 94 E3
Farm Cl. Lo Hall TW17 .... 34 A2
Farm Cl. Loxwd RH14 .... 213 A3
Farm Cl. Sutton SM2 .... 59 D3
Farm Cl. Wallin SM6 .... 60 C1
Farm Cl. Warn RH12 .... 216 F7
Farm Dr. Croy CR0 .... 62 F8
Farm Dr. Purley CR8 .... 79 D8
Farm Fields. S Croy CR2 .... 80 F8
Farm La. Ashtd KT21 & KT18 ...... 76 B2
Farm La. Croy CR0 .... 62 F8
Farm La. E Hors KT24 .... 112 F7
Farm La. Purley CR8 .... 60 C1
Farm La. Row Tn KT15 .... 52 A3
Farm La. Send GU23 .... 90 C3
Farm La. Wallin CR8 .... 60 C1
Farm Rd. Alder GU12 .... 105 C3
Farm Rd. Friml GU16 .... 65 F2
Farm Rd. Morden SM4 .... 40 B4
Farm Rd. Old Wok GU22 .... 90 B7
Farm Rd. Stain TW18 .... 13 B2
Farm Rd. Sutton SM2 .... 59 D3
Farm Rd. Thame D KT10 .... 55 B8
Farm Rd. Twick TW4 .... 15 E7
Farm Rd. Warlgm CR6 .... 101 E8
Farm Way. N Cheam KT4 .... 58 C7
Farm Way. Stan TW19 .... 1 F1
Farm Wlk. Ash GU12 .... 107 F8
Farmdale Rd. Sutton SM2 & SM5 59 E3
Farmer's Rd. Egham TW18 .... 12 E3
Farmfield Dr. Hookw RH6 .... 160 B1
Farmfield Dr. Hookw RH6 .... 181 B8
Farmfield Hospl. Hookw RH6 ...... 160 B1
Farmhouse Cl. Mayb GU22 .... 70 D4
Farmhouse Rd. Streat SW16 .... 21 C1
Farmington Ave. Carsh SM1 .... 59 D7
Farmleigh Cl. Crawl RH10 .... 202 C3
Farmleigh Gr. Whit V KT12 .... 53 F5
Farmstead Rd. Catf SE6 .... 24 B4
Farmview. Cobham KT11 .... 73 D3
Farnaby Rd. Broml BR1 & BR2 .... 44 E8
Farnan Rd. Streat SW16 .... 21 E3
Farnborough Ave. S Croy CR2 .... 62 E3
Farnborough Bsns Ctr.
  Farnb GU14 .... 84 F2
Farnborough Coll of Tech.
  Farnb GU14 .... 85 C2
Farnborough Cres. Coney H BR2 44 F1
Farnborough Cres. S Croy CR2 ... 62 E2
Farnborough Gate Ret Pk.
  Farnb GU14 .... 85 C7
Farnborough Grange Cty Inf Sch.
  Farnb GU14 .... 85 A8
Farnborough Grange Cty Jun Sch.
  W Heath GU14 .... 85 A7
Farnborough Hill (Girls' Public
  Sch). Farnb GU14 .... 85 C5
Farnborough House. ⓵
  Rhampt SW15 .... 19 A7

Farnborough Ind Est.
  Farnb GU14 .... 85 A3
Farnborough North Sta.
  Farnb GU14 .... 85 D6
Farnborough Rd. Alder GU11 ...... 104 E3
Farnborough Rd. Farnb GU14 ..... 85 C5
Farnborough Rd.
  Heath E GU11 & GU9 .... 125 D7
Farnborough (Sixth Form) Coll.
  W Heath GU14 .... 85 B6
Farnborough St. Farnb GU14 ...... 85 E7
Farnborough St. Mytch GU14 ..... 85 B5
Farncombe C of E Inf Sch.
  Farnc GU7 .... 150 E7
Farncombe Hill. Farnc GU7 .... 150 E7
Farncombe St. Farnc GU7 .... 150 E7
Farncombe Sta. Farnc GU7 .... 150 F7
Farnell Rd. Islew TW7 .... 5 D4
Farnell Rd. Stan TW18 .... 13 A5
Farnell's Almshouses. Islew TW7 5 F5
Farnham Bsns Ctr. Farnh GU9 .... 125 C3
Farnham Bsns Pk. Farnh GU9 .... 125 C1
Farnham By-Pass.
  Farnh GU10 & GU9 .... 125 C2
Farnham Cl. Brack RG12 .... 27 D7
Farnham Coll. M Bourn GU9 .... 125 C1
Farnham Ct. Cheam SM3 .... 58 E4
Farnham Gdns. W Barn SW20 ..... 39 B7
Farnham General Hospl.
  Farnh GU9 .... 125 E4
Farnham La. Shottm GU27 .... 208 A7
Farnham Park Cl. Hale GU9 .... 125 B6
Farnham Park Dr. Hale GU9 .... 125 B6
Farnham Rd. Elst GU10 & GU8 .... 148 C4
Farnham Rd.
  Guild GU1 & GU2 & GU3 .... 130 B7
Farnham Rd. Onsl V GU2 & GU3 . 129 E6
Farnham Rd Hospl. Guild GU2 ..... 130 B7
Farnham Sch of Art.
  Farnh GU9 .... 125 B2
Farnham Sta. Farnh GU9 .... 125 C2
Farnham Trad Est. Farnh GU9 ..... 125 C3
Farnhurst La. All Cr GU6 & GU8 .. 193 F4
Farningham. Brack RG12 .... 27 E3
Farningham Cres. Cater CR3 ...... 101 A4
Farningham St. Streat SW16 .... 21 D1
Farningham Rd. Cater CR3 .... 101 A4
Farnley. Woking GU21 .... 68 F2
Farnley Rd. S Norw CR7 & SE25 . 42 D5
Farnsworth House. ⓼
  W Norw SW27 .... 22 B3
Farquhar Rd. Dulw SE19 .... 22 F3
Farquhar Rd. Wimble SW19 .... 20 A5
Farquharson Rd. Thorn H CR0 .... 42 C1
Farrell Cl. Camb GU15 .... 65 C3
Farren Rd. For Hil SE23 .... 23 E6
Farrer's Pl. S Croy CR0 .... 62 D6
Farriers. Head KT18 .... 96 C3
Farriers Cl. Ewell KT17 .... 76 E7
Farriers Ct. Balham SM2 .... 58 E3
Farriers Ct. Wimble SW19 .... 19 E1
Farriers Rd. Ewell KT17 .... 76 E8
Farriers The. Bramly GU5 .... 152 A5
Farthingfield House.
  Farnh GU9 .... 125 C3
Farthingham La. Ewh GU6 .... 175 E6
Farthings. Woking GU21 .... 69 B1
Farthings The. ⓵ King U T KT2 .. 38 A8
Farwig La. Broml BR1 .... 44 F8
Fassett Rd. King U T KT1 .... 37 E5
Fauconberg Ct. Chisw W4 .... 7 C8
Fauconberg Rd. Chisw W4 .... 7 C8
Faulkner Pl. Bagsh GU19 .... 47 F4
Faulkner's Rd. Hersh KT12 .... 54 C6
Faversham Rd. Beck BR3 .... 43 F7
Faversham Rd. For Hil SE6 .... 23 F7
Faversham Rd. Morden SM4 .... 40 B3
Faversham Rd. Sandh GU15 .... 45 D1
Fawcett Rd. Croy CR0 & CR9 ...... 61 C7
Fawcus Cl. Clayg KT10 .... 55 E4
Fawler Mead. Brack RG12 .... 27 F5
Fawley Cl. Cran GU6 .... 174 F2
Fawns Manor Cl. E Bed TW14 ..... 14 D7
Fawns Manor Rd. E Bed TW14 .... 14 D7
Fawsley Cl. Poyle SL3 .... 1 E7
Fay Rd. Horsh RH12 .... 217 C5
Faygate Bsns Ctr. Faygt RH12 .... 199 F1
Faygate La. Blind H RH9 .... 142 E3
Faygate La. Faygt RH12 .... 199 F4
Faygate La. Rusper RH12 .... 199 C5
Faygate Rd. Streat SW2 .... 21 F6
Faygate Sta. Faygt RH12 .... 199 F1
Fayland Ave. Streat SW16 .... 21 C3
Fearn Cl. E Hors KT24 .... 112 E6
Fearnley Cres. Hampt TW12 .... 15 F2
Featherbed La. New Add CR0 ...... 63 A1
Feathers La. Wray TW19 .... 12 A6
Featherstone. Blind H RH7 .... 142 D1
Featherstone Ave. For Hil SE23 .. 23 C6
Fee Farm Rd. Clayg KT10 .... 55 F3
Felbridge Ave. Crawl RH10 .... 202 D7
Felbridge Cl. E Grins RH19 .... 185 C3
Felbridge Cl. Friml GU16 .... 65 F1
Felbridge Cl. Streat SW16 .... 22 A4
Felbridge Ct. Sutton SM2 .... 59 B2
Felbridge Ct. E Grins RH19 .... 185 A4
Felbridge Ct. Harl UB3 .... 3 D8
Felbridge Ctr The.
  E Grins RH19 .... 185 A3
Felbridge Cty Prim Sch.
  Felb RH19 .... 184 F4
Felbridge Rd. Copth RH19 .... 184 D3
Felcot Rd. Copth RH10 .... 184 D4
Felcote House. Woodh RH2 .... 138 F7
Felcott Cl. Hersh KT12 .... 54 C7
Felcott Rd. Hersh KT12 .... 54 C7
Felcourt Cotts. Felct RH19 .... 185 C8
Felcourt Rd. Felct RH19 & RH7 ... 164 C1
Felcourt Rd.
  Dorm Pk RH19 & RH7 .... 185 C4
Felcourt Rd. Felct RH19 & RH7 ... 185 C7

Felday Glade. Hol St M RH5 .... 155 B5
Felday Houses. Hol St M RH5 ..... 155 C7
Felday Rd. Abing H RH5 .... 133 F3
Felix Dr. W Clan GU4 .... 111 A7
Felix La. Lo Hall TW17 .... 34 E3
Felix Rd. Walt O T KT12 .... 35 A3
Fell Rd. Croy CR0 & CR9 .... 61 C7
Felland Way. Dovgn RH1 .... 139 D5
Fellbrook. Rich TW10 .... 17 B5
Fellcott Way. Horsh RH12 .... 216 F1
Fellow Gn. W End GU24 .... 67 F6
Fellow Green Rd. W End GU24 .... 67 F6
Fellowes Ct. Harl UB3 .... 3 D8
Fellowes Rd. Carsh SM1 & SM5 . 59 E8
Fellows Rd. Farnb GU14 .... 85 D1
Felmingham Rd. Penge SE20 ...... 43 C7
Felnex Trad Est. Hackb SM6 .... 60 A8
Felsberg Rd. Streat SW2 .... 21 E8
Felside Ct. Weyb KT13 .... 53 A5
Felstead Rd. Epsom KT19 .... 76 D8
Feltham Arena. Felt TW14 .... 15 A8
Feltham Ave. E Mole KT8 .... 36 E5
Feltham Comm Sch. Felt TW13 ... 15 C6
Feltham Corporate Ctr.
  Felt TW13 .... 15 B5
Feltham Hill Jun & Inf Schs.
  Felt TW13 .... 14 F5
Feltham Hill Rd. Ashf TW15 .... 14 C2
Feltham Rd. Ashf TW15 .... 14 C4
Feltham Rd. Mitch CR4 .... 41 A7
Feltham Sta. Felt TW13 .... 15 B7
Feltham Wlk. Earls RH1 .... 139 F4
Felthambrook Ind Ctr.
  Felt TW13 .... 15 B5
Felthambrook Way. Felt TW13 .... 15 B3
Felthamhill Rd. Felt TW13 .... 15 B4
Feltonfleet Sch. Whit V KT11 ...... 72 E6
Felwater Ct. E Grins RH19 .... 185 A3
Fenchurch Rd. Worth RH10 .... 202 B4
Fencote. Brack RG12 .... 27 D3
Fendall Rd. W Ewell KT19 .... 57 C5
Fendall Rd. W Ewell KT19 .... 57 C5
Fender House. Horsh RH12 .... 217 B2
Fengates Rd. Redh RH1 .... 118 C1
Fenhurst Cl. Horsh RH12 .... 216 F1
Fenn's Way. Woking GU21 .... 69 E4
Fennel Cl. Burph GU1 .... 110 B4
Fennel Cl. Croy CR0 .... 43 D1
Fennel Cl. W Heath GU14 .... 84 B4
Fennel Cres. Crawl RH11 .... 201 B2
Fennells Mead. Ewell KT17 .... 57 F2
Fenner House. Hersh KT12 .... 54 A6
Fenning Ct. Mitch CR4 .... 40 E5
Fenns La. W End GU24 .... 67 E5
Fenns Yd. Farnh GU9 .... 125 B2
Fennscombe Ct. W End GU24 ..... 67 F6
Fenstanton Prim Sch.
  Streat SW2 .... 22 A7
Fenton Ave. Stain TW18 .... 13 C3
Fenton Cl. Earls RH1 .... 119 A1
Fenton House. Heston TW5 .... 5 A8
Fenton Rd. Earls RH1 .... 119 A1
Fentum Rd. Stough GU2 .... 109 A3
Fenwick Cl. Woking GU21 .... 69 B1
Ferguson Ave. King U T KT5 .... 37 F4
Ferguson Cl. Beck BR2 & BR3 .... 44 D6
Fermandy La. Crawl D RH10 .... 184 A1
Fermor Rd. For Hil SE23 .... 23 E7
Fern Ave. Mitch CR4 .... 41 D5
Fern Cl. Crowth RG11 .... 45 A7
Fern Cl. Friml GU16 .... 66 C3
Fern Cl. Gomsh GU5 .... 133 E4
Fern Gr. Felt TW14 .... 15 B8
Fern Lodge. ⓭ N Worw SE16 ..... 22 D7
Fern Rd. Farnc GU7 .... 150 F6
Fern Towers. Cater CR3 .... 101 A2
Fern Way. Horsh RH12 .... 217 D5
Fern Wlk. Ashf TW15 .... 13 D3
Fernbank Ave. Walt O T KT12 ..... 35 E2
Fernbank Cres. N Asct SL5 .... 28 D8
Fernbank Pl. N Asct SL5 .... 28 D7
Fernbank Rd. Addl KT15 .... 52 A5
Fernbank Rd. N Asct SL5 .... 28 D8
Fernbrae Cl. Rowl GU10 .... 146 B3
Ferndale. Stough GU2 .... 108 E3
Ferndale Ave. Addl KT16 .... 51 E7
Ferndale Ave. Hounsl TW4 .... 4 D4
Ferndale Rd. Ashf TW15 .... 13 E3
Ferndale Rd. Banstd SM7 .... 77 F3
Ferndale Rd. Croy SE25 .... 43 B4
Ferndale Rd. Woking GU21 .... 69 F3
Fernden La. Fern GU27 .... 208 C2
Ferndon Rise. Farnc GU7 .... 150 E7
Ferndon Sch. Fern GU27 .... 208 B2
Ferndown. Crawl RH10 .... 182 C2
Ferndown. Horley RH6 .... 161 A5
Ferndown. ⓵ King U T KT6 .... 37 E4
Ferndown Cl. Guild GU1 .... 131 A8
Ferndown Cl. Sutton SM2 .... 59 D4
Ferndown Gdns. Cobham KT11 ... 73 C6
Ferndown Gdns. W Heath GU14 . 84 F4
Fernery The. Egham TW18 .... 12 E3
Ferney Ct. Byfl KT14 .... 71 D8
Ferney Rd. Byfl KT14 .... 71 D7
Fernfell Golf & Ctry Club.
  Cran GU6 .... 174 F6
Fernham Rd. S Norw CR7 .... 42 C6
Fernhill. Oxsh KT22 .... 74 D7
Fernhill Cl. Crawl D RH10 .... 184 B1
Fernhill Cl. Hale GU9 .... 125 B6
Fernhill Cl. W Heath GU14 .... 64 F1
Fernhill Cl. Woking GU22 .... 89 D7
Fernhill Comp Sch.
  W Heath GU14 .... 64 F1
Fernhill Ct. King U T KT2 .... 17 D3
Fernhill Cty Prim Sch.
  W Heath GU14 .... 64 F1
Fernhill Dr. Hale GU9 .... 125 B6
Fernhill Gdns. King U T KT2 .... 17 E2

Fernhill La. Hale GU9 .... 125 B6
Fernhill La. W Heath GU14 .... 64 F1
Fernhill La. Woking GU22 .... 89 C7
Fernhill Pk. Woking GU22 .... 89 D7
Fernhill Rd. Crawl RH6 .... 182 D7
Fernhill Rd. Hawley GU14 & GU17 64 E2
Fernhill Rd.
  W Heath GU14 & GU17 .... 64 E2
Fernhill Rd.
  W Heath GU14 & GU17 .... 84 E6
Fernhill Wlk. W Heath GU14 .... 64 F1
Fernhurst Cl. Crawl RH11 .... 201 B8
Fernhurst Rd. Ashf TW15 .... 14 C4
Fernhurst Rd. Croy CR0 .... 43 B1
Ferniehurst. Camb GU15 .... 65 F4
Fernihough Cl. Whit V KT13 .... 72 A8
Fernlands Cl. Addl KT16 .... 51 E7
Fernlea. Fetch KT23 .... 94 B3
Fernlea Rd. Balham SW12 .... 21 B7
Fernlea Rd. Mitch CR4 .... 41 A8
Fernleigh Cl. Croy CR0 .... 61 A6
Fernleigh Cl. Walt O T KT12 .... 54 B7
Fernleigh Rise. Friml GU16 .... 86 C7
Fernley House. Farnc GU7 .... 150 E8
Ferns Cl. S Croy CR2 .... 62 B1
Ferns The. Heath E GU9 .... 125 C7
Fernside Ave. Felt TW13 .... 15 B4
Fernside Rd. Balham SW12 .... 21 A8
Fernthorpe Rd. Streat SW16 ...... 21 C2
Fernwood. New Add CR0 & CR2 .. 62 E2
Fernwood. Putney SW19 .... 19 F7
Fernwood Ave. Streat SW16 .... 21 D4
Feroners Cl. Crawl RH10 .... 202 A4
Ferrard Cl. N Asct SL5 .... 28 D8
Ferraro Cl. Heston TW5 .... 5 A8
Ferrers Ave. Wallin SM6 .... 60 D6
Ferrers Rd. Streat SW16 .... 21 D3
Ferriby Ct. Brack RG12 .... 27 C7
Ferring Cl. Crawl RH11 .... 201 B8
Ferrings. Dulw SE21 .... 22 E5
Ferris Ave. Croy CR0 .... 62 F7
Ferroners Ct. Crawl RH10 .... 202 A4
Ferry Ave. Egham TW18 .... 12 E1
Ferry La. Barnes SW13 .... 7 F8
Ferry La. Brent TW8 .... 6 E8
Ferry La. Chert KT16 .... 33 A3
Ferry La. Guild GU2 & GU3 .... 130 C5
Ferry La. Laleh TW18 .... 33 C6
Ferry La. Lo Hall TW17 .... 34 A1
Ferry La. Rich TW9 .... 6 F8
Ferry La. Wray TW19 .... 12 B5
Ferry Rd. E Mole KT8 .... 36 A4
Ferry Rd. Rich TW11 .... 17 B3
Ferry Rd. Thame D KT7 .... 37 B3
Ferry Rd. Twick TW1 .... 17 B7
Ferry Sq. ⓵ Brent TW8 .... 6 E8
Ferry Wks. Lo Hall TW17 .... 34 A1
Ferrymoor. Rich TW10 .... 17 B5
Fetcham Common La.
  Fetch KT22 .... 94 B6
Fetcham Cty Fst Sch.
  Fetch KT22 .... 94 D5
Fetcham Park Dr. Fetch KT22 ..... 94 E4
Fettes Rd. Cran GU6 .... 175 A3
Fiddicroft Ave. Banstd SM7 .... 78 C5
Fie Yard Rd. Farnb GU14 .... 85 B2
Field Cl. Chess KT9 .... 56 C5
Field Cl. Cranf TW4 .... 4 B6
Field Cl. E Mole KT8 .... 36 B4
Field Cl. Hams Gn CR2 .... 81 B5
Field Cl. Harl UB7 .... 3 C7
Field Cl. Merrow GU4 .... 110 D3
Field Cl. Oxted RH8 .... 122 E8
Field End. Coulsd CR5 .... 79 D5
Field End. Farnb GU14 .... 125 F4
Field End. W End GU24 .... 67 F6
Field House Cl. Brack SL5 .... 29 A1
Field La. Brent TW8 .... 6 C7
Field La. Farnc GU7 .... 150 F7
Field La. Friml GU16 .... 65 E1
Field La. Tedd TW11 .... 17 A3
Field Pl. New Mal KT3 .... 38 F3
Field Rd. Felt TW14 .... 4 B1
Field Rd. W Heath GU14 .... 64 F1
Field Stores App. Alder GU11 ..... 105 C3
Field View. Egham TW20 .... 12 C3
Field View. Felt TW13 .... 14 D5
Field Way. Alder GU12 .... 105 C3
Field Way. New Add CR0 .... 63 B4
Field Way. Send M GU23 .... 90 F2
Field Way. Tongh GU10 .... 126 F7
Field Wlk. Smallf RH6 .... 162 A3
Fieldcommon La. Walt O T KT12 . 35 F1
Fielden Pl. Brack RG12 .... 27 D7
Fieldend. Horsh RH12 .... 218 B5
Fieldend. Tedd TW11 .... 16 F4
Fieldend Rd. Streat SW16 .... 41 C8
Fielders Gn. Guild GU1 .... 110 A1
Fieldhouse Rd. Streat SW12 ...... 21 C7
Fieldhouse Villas. Woodm SM7 .. 78 E4
Fieldhurst Cl. Addl KT15 .... 52 B5
Fielding Ave. Twick TW2 .... 16 C5
Fielding Gdns. Crowth RG11 .... 45 A4
Fielding House. Chisw W4 .... 7 E8
Fielding Rd. Sandh GU15 .... 64 E6
Fieldings The. For Hil SE23 .... 23 C7
Fieldings The. Horley RH6 .... 161 C4
Fieldings The. Woking GU21 .... 68 F3
Fieldsend Rd. Cheam SM3 .... 58 E5
Fieldside Rd. Catf BR1 .... 24 D3
Fieldview. Horley RH6 .... 161 B4
Fieldview. Wands SW17 & SW18 . 20 D7
Fieldway. Haslem GU27 .... 208 C7
Fife Rd. King U T KT1 .... 37 E7
Fife Rd. Mortl SW14 .... 7 C2
Fife Way. Fetch KT23 .... 94 A2
Fifehead Cl. Ashf TW15 .... 13 E2

Fifield La. Frensh GU10 .... 146 C2
Fifield Path. For Hil SE23 .... 23 D5
Fifth Cross Rd. Twick TW2 ...... 16 D6
Figge's Rd. Mitch CR4 .... 21 A1
Filber Cres. Crawl RH11 .... 201 A6
Filby Rd. Chess KT9 .... 56 F4
Filey Cl. Bigg H TN16 .... 103 B8
Filey Cl. Crawl RH11 .... 200 F4
Filey Cl. Sutton SM2 .... 59 C3
Filmer Ct. Farnc GU7 .... 150 E5
Filmer Gr. Farnc GU7 .... 150 E5
Finborough Rd. Mitch SW17 ...... 20 F2
Finch Ave. W Norw SE27 .... 22 D4
Finch Cl. Knaph GU21 .... 68 C2
Finch Dr. Felt TW14 .... 15 D8
Finch Rd. ⑨ Guild GU1 .... 109 D1
Finch's Cross. Oxted RH8 .... 144 A8
Finchampstead Rd. Woki RG11 .. 25 C3
Finchdean House. Rhampt SW15 18 F8
Finches Rise. Merrow GU1 .... 110 C3
Findhorn Cl. Sandh GU15 .... 64 D7
Findings The. W Heath GU14 ..... 84 E8
Findlay Dr. Stough GU3 .... 108 F5
Findon Ct. Row Tn KT15 .... 51 F5
Findon Rd. Crawl RH11 .... 201 B8
Findon Way. Broad H RH12 ...... 216 D3
Finlay Gdns. Addl KT15 .... 52 C6
Finlays Cl. Chess KT9 .... 57 A5
Finmere. Easth RG12 .... 27 C2
Finnart Cl. Weyb KT13 .... 53 C6
Finney Dr. Windl GU20 .... 48 D4
Finsbury Cl. Crawl RH11 .... 201 C2
Finstock Gn. Brack RG12 .... 27 F5
Finton House Sch.

  Up Toot SW17 .... 20 F6
Fintry Pl. W Heath GU14 .... 84 E7
Fintry Wlk. W Heath GU14 .... 84 E7
Finucane Ct. Rich TW9 .... 6 F4
Fiona Cl. Fetch KT23 .... 94 A3
Fir Acre Rd. Ash V GU12 .... 106 A6
Fir Cl. Walt O T KT12 .... 35 A2
Fir Dr. Hawley GU17 .... 64 D3
Fir Gr. New Mal KT3 .... 38 F3
Fir Grange Ave. Weyb KT13 ...... 53 B5
Fir Rd. Cheam SM3 .... 39 F1
Fir Rd. Felt TW13 .... 15 D3
Fir Tree Alley. Alder GU11 .... 105 A2
Fir Tree Ave. Shottm GU27 ...... 207 D6
Fir Tree Cl. Ascot SL5 .... 29 A2
Fir Tree Cl. Crawl RH11 .... 181 B1
Fir Tree Cl. Esher KT10 .... 55 C5
Fir Tree Cl. Leahd KT22 .... 95 C4
Fir Tree Cl. Nork KT17 .... 77 C4
Fir Tree Cl. Streat SW16 .... 21 C3
Fir Tree Cl. Worc Pk KT19 .... 57 F6
Fir Tree Gdns. Croy CR0 .... 63 A6
Fir Tree Gr. Wallin SM5 .... 59 F3
Fir Tree Rd. Bellf GU1 .... 109 D4
Fir Tree Rd. Hounsl TW4 .... 4 E3
Fir Tree Rd. Leahd KT22 .... 95 C4
Fir Tree Rd. Nork KT17 & SM7 .. 77 D5
Fir Tree Wlk. Reig RH2 .... 118 D1
Fir Wlk. Cheam KT17 & SM3 ..... 58 C4
Firbank Cotts. Burst RH6 .... 183 C7
Firbank Dr. Woking GU21 .... 89 B8
Firbank La. Woking GU21 .... 89 B8
Firbank Pl. Eng Gn TW20 .... 11 B2
Fircroft Cl. Woking GU21 .... 69 F1
Fircroft Ct. ⑨ Woking GU22 ..... 69 F1
Fircroft Prim Sch. Up Toot SW17 20 F5
Fircroft Rd. Chess KT9 .... 56 F6
Fircroft Rd. Up Toot SW17 .... 20 F5
Firdene. Tolw KT5 .... 38 C1
Fire Bell Alley. Surb KT6 .... 37 E3
Fire Station Cotts. Purley CR8 ... 79 F6
Fire Station Flats. ③

  Epsom KT17 .... 76 E6
Fire Station Rd. Alder GU11 ..... 105 B3
Fireball Hill. Sunnin SL5 .... 29 D2
Firefly Cl. Wallin SM6 .... 60 E3
Firfield Rd. Addl KT15 .... 52 A6
Firfield Rd. M Bourn GU9 .... 146 A7
Firfields. Whit V KT13 .... 53 B4
Firgrove. Woking GU21 .... 89 B8
Firgrove Ct. ⑦ Farnb GU14 ..... 85 B4
Firgrove Ct. Farnh GU9 .... 125 C1
Firgrove Hill. Farnh GU9 .... 125 C1
Firgrove Hill. M Bourn GU9 ..... 125 C1
Firgrove Par. ⑤ Farnb GU14 ... 85 B4
Firgrove Rd. ⑥ Farnb GU14 .... 85 B4
Firhill Rd. Catf SE6 .... 24 A5
Firlands. Brack RG12 .... 27 C4
Firlands. Horley RH6 .... 161 B4
Firlands. Whit V KT13 .... 53 E4
Firlands Ave. Camb GU15 .... 65 D5
Firle Cl. Crawl RH10 .... 201 E8
Firmston House. ⑨ Mortl SW14 .. 7 D4
Firs Ave. Bramly GU5 .... 152 A6
Firs Ave. Mortl SW14 .... 7 C3
Firs Cl. Clayg KT10 .... 55 E4
Firs Cl. Dork RH4 .... 136 A5
Firs Cl. Farnb GU14 .... 85 C2
Firs Cl. For Hil SE23 .... 23 E8
Firs Cl. Mitch CR4 .... 41 B8
Firs Dr. Cranf TW5 .... 4 B7
Firs La. Sham Gn GU5 .... 152 D4
Firs Rd. Purley CR8 .... 80 B4
Firs The. Arting GU3 .... 130 B5
Firs The. Bisley GU24 .... 68 A3
Firs The. ⑧ Brack RG12 .... 27 F5
Firs The. Cater CR3 .... 100 D5
Firs The. Clayg KT10 .... 55 E4
Firs The. ② For Hil SE26 .... 23 B3
Firs The. For Hil SE26 .... 23 C3
Firs The. Sutton SM2 .... 59 B3
Firs The. Wimble SW20 .... 19 A1
Firsby Ave. Croy CR0 .... 43 E1
Firsdene Cl. Ottsh KT16 .... 51 D4

First Ave. E Mole KT8 .... 36 A5
First Ave. Mortl SW14 .... 7 E4
First Ave. W Ewell KT19 .... 57 E2
First Ave. W Ewell KT19 .... 57 E2
First Ave. Walt O T KT12 .... 35 B3
First Ave. Woodhm KT15 .... 52 B2
First Cl. E Mole KT8 .... 36 C6
First Cross Rd. Twick TW2 .... 16 E6
First Quarter Bsns Pk.

  Epsom KT19 .... 76 E8
Firstway. W Barn SW20 .... 39 C7
Firsway. Stough GU2 .... 109 A2
Firswood Ave. Worc Pk KT19 .... 57 F5
Firtree Ave. Mitch CR4 .... 41 A7
Firway. Graysh GU26 .... 187 E5
Firwood Cl. Knaph GU21 .... 88 E8
Firwood Ct. Camb GU15 .... 65 C5
Firwood Dr. Camb GU15 .... 65 C5
Firwood Rd. Went GU25 .... 30 E3
Fisher Cl. Crawl RH10 .... 201 E4
Fisher Cl. Croy CR0 .... 42 F1
Fisher Cl. Hersh KT12 .... 54 B6
Fisher La. Chidd GU8 .... 210 E7
Fisher La. Dunsf GU8 .... 211 B7
Fisher Rowe Cl. Bramly GU5 .... 152 A6
Fisherdene. Clayg KT10 .... 56 A3
Fisherman Cl. Rich TW10 .... 17 C4
Fishermen's Cl. Farnb GU11 ..... 105 E5
Fishers Ct. Horsh RH12 .... 217 C4
Fishers Ct. ④ Tedd TW11 .... 16 F3
Fishers Wood. Sunnin SL5 .... 30 C1
Fishponds Cl. Woki RG11 .... 25 A4
Fishponds Est. Woki RG11 .... 25 A4
Fishponds Rd. Up Toot SW17 .... 20 F4
Fishponds Rd. Woki RG11 .... 25 A4
Fiske Ct. ① Merton SW19 .... 20 C1
Fiske Ct. Sutton SM2 .... 59 C3
Fitch Ct. Mitch CR4 .... 41 A7
Fitchet Cl. Crawl RH11 .... 201 B8
Fitz Wygram Cl. Hampt TW12 ... 16 C3
Fitzalan Rd. Clayg KT10 .... 55 E3
Fitzalan Rd.

  Horsh RH12 & RH13 .... 218 A4
Fitzgeorge Ave.

  King U T KT2 & KT3 .... 38 D8
Fitzgerald Ave. Mortl SW14 .... 7 E4
Fitzgerald Rd. Mortl SW14 .... 7 E4
Fitzgerald Rd. Thame D K7 .... 37 A3
Fitzherbert House. ⑪

  Rich TW10 .... 6 F1
Fitzjames Ave. S Croy CR0 .... 62 A8
Fitzjohn Cl. Merrow GU4 .... 110 C4
Fitzrobert Pl. Egham TW20 .... 12 A2
Fitzroy Cres. Chisw W4 .... 7 D7
Fitzroy Gdns. S Norw SE19 .... 22 E1
Fitzwilliam Ave. Rich TW9 .... 6 F5
Fitzwilliam House. Rich TW9 ...... 6 D3
Fitzwilliam Hts. For Hil SE23 ..... 23 C6
Five Acres. Crawl RH10 .... 201 E8
Five Oaks Cl. Knaph GU21 .... 88 E8
Five Oaks Rd.

  Broad H RH12 & RH13 .... 216 B2
Five Oaks Rd.

  Slinfd RH12 & RH13 .... 216 B2
Fiveacre Cl. Thorn H CR7 .... 42 A3
Flag Cl. Croy CR0 .... 43 D1
Flambard Way. Godal GU7 .... 150 D4
Flamborough Cl. Bigg H TN16 .. 103 B8
Flamsteed Hts. Crawl RH11 ..... 201 B1
Flanchford House. ②

  Reig RH2 .... 118 A2
Flanchford Rd. Dovgn RH2 ...... 138 D5
Flanchford Rd. Leigh RH2 .... 138 D5
Flanchford Rd. Reig RH2 .... 138 D5
Flanders Cotts. Sham Gn GU5 .. 152 D5
Flanders Cres.

  Mitch SW17 & SW19 .... 20 F2
Flanders Ct. Egham TW20 .... 12 C3
Flatford House. Catf SE6 .... 24 C4
Flats The. Blckw GU17 .... 64 C4
Flaxley Rd. Morden SM4 .... 40 B2
Flaxmore Ct. S Norw CR7 .... 42 D7
Fleece Rd. Long D KT6 .... 37 C1
Fleet Cl. E Mole KT8 .... 35 F4
Fleet Rd. Alder GU11 .... 104 D6
Fleet Rd. Chur C GU13 & GU14 .. 104 D6
Fleet Rd. Hawley GU14 .... 84 A4
Fleet Rd. W Heath GU14 .... 84 C4
Fleetside. E Mole KT8 .... 36 A4
Fleetway. Egham TW20 .... 32 C6
Fleetwood Cl. Chess KT9 .... 56 D3
Fleetwood Cl. S Croy CR0 .... 61 F7
Fleetwood Cl. Tadw KT20 .... 97 D7
Fleetwood Ct. ⑦ Stan TW19 ..... 13 D7
Fleetwood Ct. ② W Byfl KT14 ... 71 A6
Fleetwood Rd. King U T KT3 ...... 38 B6
Fleetwood Sq. King U T KT3 ...... 38 B6
Fleming Cl. Farnb GU14 .... 85 D6
Fleming Ct. Croy CR0 .... 61 A5
Fleming Mead.

  Mitch CR4 & SW19 .... 20 F1
Fleming Way.

  Crawl RH10 & RH11 .... 181 F2
Fleming Way. Islew TW7 .... 5 F3
Flemish Fields. Chert KT16 .... 33 A2
Fletcher Cl. Crawl RH10 .... 201 E4
Fletcher Cl. Ottsh KT15 & KT16 .. 51 E4
Fletcher Gdns. Binf RG12 .... 26 D8
Fletcher Rd. Ottsh KT16 .... 51 D4
Fletchers Cl. Horsh RH13 .... 217 E1
Fleur Gates. ⑦ Putney SW19 ... 19 D8
Flexford Gn. Easth RG12 .... 26 E3
Flexford Rd. Flexf GU3 .... 107 C1
Flimwell Cl. Catf BR1 .... 24 E3
Flint Cl. ⑧ Book KT23 .... 94 C1
Flint Cl. Redh RH1 .... 118 F2
Flint Cl. Worth RH10 .... 202 A4
Flint Hill. Dork RH4 & RH5 ...... 136 B5

Flint Hill Cl. Dork RH4 .... 136 B4
Flintgrove. Brack RG12 .... 27 D8
Flintlock Cl. Stan TW19 .... 2 A3
Flitwick Grange. Milf GU8 .... 149 F1
Flood La. ④ Twick TW1 .... 17 A7
Flora Gdns. New Add CR0 .... 82 C8
Floral Cl. Ashtd KT21 .... 75 C1
Floral House. Chert KT16 .... 32 F1
Florence Ave. Morden SM4 .... 40 C4
Florence Ave. Woodhm KT15 ..... 71 A8
Florence Cl. Walt O T KT12 .... 35 B2
Florence Cotts. King U T SW15 .. 18 E5
Florence Cotts. Wink SL4 .... 8 C7
Florence Gdns. Chisw W4 .... 7 C8
Florence Gdns. Stain TW18 .... 13 B1
Florence House. ⑤ King U T KT2 17 F1
Florence Rd. Felt TW13 .... 15 B7
Florence Rd. ⑥ King U T KT2 ... 17 F1
Florence Rd. Penge BR2 .... 43 E7
Florence Rd. S Croy CR2 .... 61 D2
Florence Rd. Sandh GU15 .... 64 F7
Florence Rd. Walt O T KT12 ...... 35 B2
Florence Rd. Wimble SW19 .... 20 B2
Florence Terr. King U T SW15 .... 18 E5
Florian Ave. Carsh SM1 .... 59 D6
Florida Ct. Beck BR2 .... 44 F5
Florida Rd. Stain TW18 .... 13 A3
Florida Rd. S Norw CR7 .... 42 B8
Florida Rd. Shalf GU4 .... 130 E3
Florys Ct. ⑦ Putney SW19 .... 19 E7
Flower Cres. Ottsh KT16 .... 51 C4
Flower La. Tyl Gn RH9 .... 121 D6
Flower La. Wold RH9 .... 121 D6
Flower Wlk. Guild GU2 .... 130 C6
Flowersmead. Up Toot SW17 ..... 21 A6
Floyd's La. Pyrf GU22 .... 71 A3
Foden Track. Farnb GU14 .... 104 C8
Foley Mews. Clayg KT10 .... 55 E4
Foley Rd. Bigg H TN16 .... 83 D1
Foley Rd. Clayg KT10 .... 55 E3
Folly Hill. Farnb GU9 .... 125 A5
Folly Hill. Hale GU9 .... 125 A5
Folly Hill Cty Inf Sch.

  Hale GU9 .... 125 A6
Folly La. S Holm RH5 .... 157 B7
Folly La N. Hale GU9 .... 125 B6
Folly La S. Hale GU9 .... 125 A5
Follyfield Rd. Banstd SM7 .... 78 A5
Fontaine Ct. Beck BR3 .... 43 F8
Fontaine Rd. Streat SW16 .... 21 F1
Fontenoy Rd.

  Up Toot SW12 & SW17 .... 21 C6
Fonthill Cl. Penge SE20 .... 43 A7
Fonthill Ct. For Hil SE23 .... 23 C8
Fontley Way. Rhampt SW15 ...... 19 A8
Fontmell Cl. Ashf TW15 .... 14 A3
Fontmell Pk. Ashf TW15 .... 14 A3
Fontwell Rd. Crawl RH10 .... 202 A3
Forbes Chase. Sandh GU15 .... 64 D7
Forbes Ct. Dulw SE19 .... 22 E3
Forburys. M Bourn GU9 .... 146 B8
Ford Cl. Ashf TW15 .... 13 E2
Ford Cl. Shep Gn TW17 .... 34 A4
Ford Cl. Thorn H CR7 .... 42 B4
Ford La. M Bourn GU10 & GU9 .. 146 B6
Ford Manor Cotts.

  Dorman RH7 .... 165 B1
Ford Manor Rd. Dorman RH7 ... 165 B2
Ford Rd. Ashf TW15 .... 13 F4
Ford Rd. Bisley GU24 .... 67 F4
Ford Rd. Burrh GU24 .... 49 C1
Ford Rd. Chert KT16 .... 33 B1
Ford Rd. Old Wok GU22 .... 90 B7
Fordbridge Ct. Ashf TW15 .... 13 E2
Fordbridge Rd. Ashf TW15 .... 13 F3
Fordbridge Rd. Sunby TW16 ..... 35 A5
Fordbridge Rd.

  Up Hall TW16 & TW17 .... 34 F3
Fordel Rd. Catf SE6 .... 24 D7
Fordingbridge Cl. Chert KT16 ... 33 B1
Fordingbridge Cl. Horsh RH12 217 C1
Fordington House. For Hil SE26 .. 23 B5
Fordmill Rd. Catf SE6 .... 24 A6
Fordwater Rd.

  Chert KT15 & KT16 .... 33 B1
Fordwater Trad Est. Chert KT16 33 C1
Fordwells Dr. Brack RG12 .... 27 F5
Fordyce House. ③ Streat SW16 . 21 C4
Foreman Rd. Ash GU12 .... 106 B2
Foreman Rd. Ash GU12 .... 106 B2
Forest Cl. Brack SL5 .... 28 C6
Forest Cl. Crawl D RH10 .... 204 B8
Forest Cl. E Hors KT24 .... 92 F2
Forest Cl. Horsh RH12 .... 218 B4
Forest Cl. Mayb GU22 .... 70 D4
Forest Comm Sch. Horsh RH13 217 F1
Forest Cres. Ashtd KT21 .... 76 A3
Forest Croft. For Hil SE23 .... 23 B6
Forest Dene Ct. Sutton SM2 ...... 59 C4
Forest Dr. Charlt TW16 .... 14 F1
Forest Dr. Kings KT20 .... 98 A6
Forest End Rd. Sandh GU17 ...... 64 A8
Forest Glade. Binst GU10 .... 145 D3
Forest Gn. Brack RG12 .... 27 D7
Forest Hill Bsns Ctr.

  For Hil SE23 .... 23 C6
Forest Hill Ct. For Hil SE26 .... 23 C5
Forest Hill Ind Est. For Hil SE23 23 C5
Forest Hill Rd. For Hil SE23 ...... 23 C8
Forest Hill Sec Sch.

  For Hil SE23 .... 23 D5
Forest Hill Sta. For Hil SE23 ..... 23 C6
Forest Hills. Camb GU15 .... 65 B4
Forest La. E Hors KT24 .... 92 E2
Forest Lodge. ② E Grins RH19 . 205 F8
Forest Lodge. For Hil SE23 .... 23 C5
Forest Oaks. Horsh RH13 .... 218 B4
Forest Rd. Cheam SM3 & SM4 ... 40 A2
Forest Rd. Crawl RH12 .... 218 D5

Forest Rd. Crowth RG11 .... 45 C5
Forest Rd. E Hors KT24 .... 92 F2
Forest Rd. Felt TW13 .... 15 C6
Forest Rd. Mayb GU22 .... 70 D4
Forest Rd. N Asct RG12 .... 8 D2
Forest Rd. Rich TW9 .... 7 A7
Forest Rd. Wind SL4 .... 9 E7
Forest Rd. Wink RG12 & SL5 .... 8 D2
Forest Ridge. Beck BR3 .... 44 A6
Forest Row Bsns Pk.

  For Row RH18 .... 206 E4
Forest Row C of E Inf Sch.

  For Row RH18 .... 206 E2
Forest Side. New Mal KT4 .... 38 F1
Forest View. Crawl RH10 .... 202 A3
Forest View Rd. E Grins RH19 .. 205 E6
Forest Wlk. Guild GU6 .... 173 F2
Forestdale Ctr The.

  New Add CR0 .... 62 D7
Forestdale Prim Sch.

  New Add CR0 .... 62 D7
Forester Rd. Crawl RH10 .... 201 E4
Foresters Cl. Knaph GU21 .... 68 F1
Foresters Cl. Wallin SM6 .... 60 D3
Foresters Dr. Wallin CR8 & SM6 . 60 D3
Foresters Prim Sch. Wallin SM6 60 D4
Foresters Sq. Brack RG12 .... 27 E6
Foresters Way. Crowth RG11 ..... 45 E8
Forestfield. Crawl RH10 .... 202 B3
Forestfield. Horsh RH13 .... 218 A3
Forestholme Cl. For Hil SE23 .... 23 C6
Forge Ave. Coulsd CR5 .... 100 B7
Forge Cl. Broad H RH12 .... 216 D4
Forge Cl. Farnh GU9 .... 125 D3
Forge Dr. Clayg KT10 .... 56 A3
Forge End. Woking GU21 .... 69 E2
Forge La. Broad H RH12 .... 216 D4
Forge La. Cheam SM2 & SM3 .... 58 E3
Forge La. Crawl RH10 .... 202 A3
Forge La. Felt TW13 .... 15 E3
Forge La. Sunby TW16 .... 35 A6
Forge Lane Inf Sch. Felt TW13 .. 15 E3
Forge Lane Jun Sch. Felt TW13 15 E3
Forge Rd. Crawl RH10 .... 202 A7
Forge Rd. Headly GU35 .... 166 A1
Forge Steading. Banstd SM7 ..... 78 B4
Forge The. Harl UB3 .... 3 D8
Forge The. Streat SW16 .... 216 E7
Forge Wood. Crawl RH10 .... 182 D3
Forge Wood Ind Est.

  Crawl RH10 .... 182 B3
Forgefield. Bigg H TN16 .... 83 D3
Forman Ct. Twick TW1 .... 16 F7
Forrest Gdns. Thorn H SW16 ..... 41 F6
Forrester Path. For Hil SE26 ..... 23 C4
Forster House. Catf SE6 .... 24 D5
Forster Park Sch. Catf SE6 .... 24 E5
Forster Rd. Beck BR3 .... 43 E6
Forster Rd. Streat SW2 .... 21 E8
Forster Rd. Thorn H CR0 .... 42 C7
Forsyte Cres. S Norw SE19 .... 42 E8
Forsyte Ct. King U T KT2 .... 38 B8
Forsyth Path. Sheer GU21 .... 70 C5
Forsyth Rd. Sheer GU21 .... 70 C5
Forsythe Shades. Beck BR3 .... 44 C8
Forsythia Pl. Bellf GU1 .... 109 C3
Fort La. Reig RH2 .... 118 B5
Fort Narrien. Sandh GU15 .... 64 F7
Fort Rd. Box H KT20 .... 116 B4
Fort Rd. Guild GU1 .... 130 E6
Fortescue Ave. Twick TW2 .... 16 C5
Fortescue Rd. Mitch SW19 .... 20 D1
Fortescue Rd. Weyb KT13 .... 52 F6
Forth Cl. W Heath GU14 .... 84 D6
Fortrose Cl. Sandh GU15 .... 64 D7
Fortrose Gdns.

  Streat SW12 & SW2 .... 21 E7
Fortune Dr. Cran GU6 .... 174 E1
Fortyfoot Rd. Leahd KT22 .... 95 C6
Forum The. E Mole KT8 .... 36 B5
Forval Cl. Mitch CR4 .... 40 F4
Foss Ave. Croy CR0 & CR9 .... 61 A5
Foss Rd. Up Toot SW17 .... 20 D4
Fosse Way. W Byfl KT14 .... 70 F6
Fosseway Cl. Crowth RG11 .... 45 D7
Fossewood Dr. Camb GU15 .... 65 D7
Fosterdown. Tyl Gn RH9 .... 121 B6
Fosters Gr. Windl GU20 .... 48 B6
Fosters La. Knaph GU21 .... 68 C2
Foulser Rd. Up Toot SW17 .... 21 A5
Foulsham Rd. S Norw CR7 .... 42 D6
Foundation Units. Bellf GU1 .... 109 F5
Founders Gdns. S Norw SE19 ... 22 C1
Foundry Cl. Horsh RH13 .... 217 E4
Foundry Ct. Chert KT16 .... 33 A2
Foundry La. Haslem GU27 .... 208 A6
Foundry La. Horsh RH12 & RH13 217 E3
Foundry La. Horton SL3 .... 1 B4
Foundry Mews. Chert KT16 .... 33 A2
Fountain Ct. New Mal KT3 .... 38 C5
Fountain Ct. Penge SE26 .... 23 C2
Fountain Dr. Dulw SE19 .... 22 F4
Fountain Dr. Wallin SM5 .... 59 F2
Fountain Rd. Earls RH1 .... 139 E7
Fountain Rd. S Norw CR7 .... 42 C7
Fountain Rd. Up Toot SW17 ...... 20 D4
Fountains Ave. Felt TW13 .... 15 F5
Fountains Cl. Crawl RH11 .... 201 A4
Fountains Cl. Felt TW13 .... 15 F5
Fountains Garth. Easth RG12 .... 27 A6
Four Acres. Cobham KT11 .... 73 E6
Four Acres. Merrow GU1 & GU4 110 C3
Four Seasons Cres. Cheam SM3 58 F8
Four Square Ct. Twick TW4 .... 5 A1
Four Wents. Cobham KT11 .... 73 C5
Fourth Cross Rd. Twick TW2 ..... 16 D6
Fourth Dr. Coulsd CR5 .... 79 D3
Fowler Ave. Farnb GU14 .... 85 B2

Fowler Cl. Worth RH10 .... 202 C4
Fowler Rd. Farnb GU14 .... 84 F3
Fowler Rd. Mitch CR4 .... 41 A7
Fowler's Rd. Farnb GU11 .... 105 D6
Fowlers La. Brack RG12 .... 27 B8
Fowlers Mead. Burrh GU24 .... 49 E2
Fowlerscroft. Compt GU3 .... 129 B2
Fox Cl. Crawl RH11 .... 181 B1
Fox Cl. Mayb GU22 .... 70 D4
Fox Cl. Whit V KT13 .... 53 D5
Fox Covert. Fetch KT22 .... 94 D3
Fox Covert. Lhtwat GU18 .... 67 A8
Fox Covert Cl. Ascot SL5 .... 29 C4
Fox Gr. Walt O T KT12 .... 35 B2
Fox Heath. Farnb GU14 .... 84 C3
Fox Hill. S Norw SE19 .... 22 F1
Fox Hill Gdns. S Norw SE19 ...... 22 F1
Fox Hill Prim Sch. Easth RG12 .. 27 B4
Fox Hills La. Ash GU12 .... 106 C3
Fox Hills Rd. Ottsh KT16 .... 51 B5
Fox La. L Book KT23 .... 93 F3
Fox La N. Chert KT16 .... 32 F1
Fox La S. Chert KT16 .... 32 F1
Fox Rd. Brack RG12 .... 27 C5
Fox Rd. M Bourn GU10 .... 146 C7
Fox Rd. Shottm GU27 .... 207 E6
Fox Way. Crond GU10 .... 124 D8
Fox Yd. Farnh GU9 .... 125 B2
Foxacre. Cater CR3 .... 100 E5
Foxborough Hill. Bramly GU5 .. 151 D6
Foxborough Hill Rd.

  Bramly GU5 .... 151 D6
Foxbourne Rd. Up Toot SW17 ... 21 A6
Foxbridge La. Ifold RH14 .... 212 C1
Foxburrows Ave. Stough GU2 .. 108 F2
Foxcombe. New Add CR0 .... 63 B4
Foxcombe Rd. ⑥ Rhampt SW15 19 A7
Foxdown Cl. Camb GU15 .... 65 C5
Foxearth Cl. Bigg H TN16 .... 83 E1
Foxearth Rd. S Croy CR2 .... 62 C2
Foxearth Spur. S Croy CR2 .... 62 C2
Foxenden Rd. Guild GU1 .... 109 E1
Foxes Dale. Beck BR2 .... 44 D6
Foxes Path. Westfd GU4 .... 89 F1
Foxglove Ave. Beck BR3 .... 24 B1
Foxglove Ave. Horsh RH12 .... 217 E6
Foxglove Cl. Stan TW19 .... 13 D7
Foxglove Gdns. Merrow GU4 ... 110 C3
Foxglove Gdns. Purley CR8 .... 79 F8
Foxglove La. Chess KT9 .... 57 A6
Foxglove Way. Carsh CR4 .... 41 B8
Foxglove Wlk. Crawl RH11 .... 201 B3
Foxgrove Dr. Horse GU21 .... 70 A4
Foxgrove Rd. Beck BR3 .... 24 C1
Foxhanger Gdns. Woking GU22 . 70 A3
Foxheath. Brack RG12 .... 27 E4
Foxhill Cres. Camb GU15 .... 66 B8
Foxhills. Woking GU21 .... 69 C2
Foxhills Cl. Ottsh KT16 .... 51 C4
Foxholes. Rudg RH12 .... 214 D8
Foxholes. Whit V KT13 .... 53 D5
Foxhurst Rd. Ash GU12 .... 106 A4
Foxlake Rd. Byfl KT14 .... 71 F7
Foxleigh Chase. Horsh RH12 ... 217 F5
Foxley Cl. Earls RH1 .... 140 A4
Foxley Ct. Sutton SM2 .... 59 C3
Foxley Gdns. Purley CR8 .... 80 B6
Foxley Hall. Purley CR8 .... 80 A6
Foxley Hill Rd. Purley CR8 .... 80 A7
Foxley La. Purley CR8 .... 60 E1
Foxley Rd. Purley CR8 .... 80 B5
Foxley Rd. Thorn H CR7 .... 42 B5
Foxoak Hill. Whit V KT12 & KT13 . 53 E1
Foxon Cl. Cater CR3 .... 100 E6
Foxon La. Cater CR3 .... 100 E6
Foxon Lane Gdns. Cater CR3 ... 100 E6
Foxtail House. Hounsl TW3 .... 5 C6
Foxton. King U T KT1 .... 38 A6
Foxwarren. Clayg KT10 .... 55 F2
Foxwood Cl. Felt TW13 .... 15 B5
Frailey Cl. Mayb GU22 .... 70 B3
Frailey Hill. Mayb GU22 .... 70 B3
Framfield Cl. Crawl RH11 .... 201 A8
Framfield Ct. Mitch CR4 .... 21 A1
Frampton Cl. Belm SM2 .... 59 A3
Frampton Rd. Hounsl TW4 .... 4 E2
France Hill Dr. Camb GU15 .... 65 C5
France Hill Sch. Camb GU15 ..... 65 C2
Frances Ct. S Norw SE25 .... 42 F7
Franche Court Rd. Wands SW17 20 C5
Francis Ave. Felt TW13 .... 15 A5
Francis Barber Cl. Streat SW16 . 21 F4
Francis Chichester Cl.Ascot SL5 29 B4
Francis Cl. Shep Gn TW17 .... 34 A5
Francis Cl. W Ewell KT19 .... 57 D6
Francis Cl. W Ewell KT19 .... 57 D6
Francis Cnr. Shere KT24 .... 133 B8
Francis Ct. King U T KT5 .... 37 E5
Francis Ct. Stough GU2 .... 109 B3
Francis Edwards Way.

  Crawl RH11 .... 200 E2
Francis Gr. Wimble SW19 .... 19 F2
Francis Rd. Cater CR3 .... 100 D5
Francis Rd. Hounsl TW4 .... 4 D5
Francis Rd. Thorn H CR0 .... 42 B2
Francis Rd. Wallin SM6 .... 60 C4
Francis Way. Friml GU15 .... 66 C3
Franciscan Prim Sch.

  Up Toot SW17 .... 21 A3
Franciscan Rd. Up Toot SW17 ... 21 A4
Frangate. E Hors KT24 .... 112 E8
Frank Dixon Cl. Dulw SE21 .... 22 E7
Frank Dixon Way. Dulw SE21 ... 22 E7
Frank Towell Ct. E Bed TW14 .... 15 A7
Frankland House. ④

  Balham SW12 .... 21 B8
Franklands Dr. Row Tn KT15 ..... 51 F3
Franklin Cl. King U T KT1 .... 38 A6
Franklin Cl. W Norw SE27 .... 22 B5

Franklin Cres. Mitch CR4 .... 41 C5
Franklin Ct. 2 Stough GU2 .... 108 F1
Franklin House. Beck BR2 .... 44 E7
Franklin Ind Est. Penge SE20 .... 43 C8
Franklin Rd. Penge SE20 .... 23 C1
Franklin Rd. Penge SE20 .... 43 C8
Franklin Rd. Walt O T KT12 .... 35 A3
Franklin Way. Croy CR0 & CR9 ... 41 E2
Franklyn Rd. Ock Rid GU7 .... 150 B3
Franklyn Rd. Walt O T KT12 .... 35 B3
Franks Ave. New Mal KT3 .... 38 C5
Franks House. Islew TW7 .... 6 B3
Franks Rd. Stough GU2 .... 109 A3
Franksfield. Peasl GU5 .... 154 E7
Fransfield Gr. For Hil SE26 .... 23 B5
Frant Cl. Penge SE20 .... 23 C1
Frant Rd. Thorn H CR0 & CR7 ..... 42 A3
Franthorne Way. Catf SE6 .... 24 B5
Fraser Gdns. Dork RH4 .... 136 A8
Fraser Mead. Sandh GU15 .... 64 E6
Fraser Rd. Brack RG12 .... 27 B8
Frederick Cl. Cheam SM1 .... 58 F5
Frederick Gdns. Cheam SM1 ...... 58 F5
Frederick Pl. Woki RG11 .... 25 A6
Frederick Rd. Cheam SM1 .... 58 F5
Frederick Sanger Rd.
  Onsl V GU2 .... 129 D8
Frederick St. Alder GU11 .... 105 A2
Free Prae Rd. Chert KT16 .... 33 A1
Freeborn Way. Brack RG12 .... 27 E7
Freedown La. Banstd SM2 .... 78 C6
Freehold Ind Ctr. Hounsl TW4 .... 4 C2
Freelands Ave. S Croy CR2 .... 62 D2
Freelands Rd. Cobham KT11 ...... 73 B5
Freeman Cl. Up Hall TW17 .... 34 E5
Freeman Dr. E Mole KT8 .... 35 F5
Freeman House. 13
  Streat SW2 .... 21 E8
Freeman Rd. Morden CR4 & SM4 . 40 D4
Freeman Rd. Warn RH12 .... 216 F8
Freemantle Rd. Bagsh GU19 ...... 47 F4
Freemantles Sch. Windl GU20 .... 48 C5
Freemason's Rd. Croy CR0 .... 42 E1
Freesia Dr. Bisley GU24 .... 68 A3
Freethorpe Cl. S Norw SE19 ...... 42 E8
French Gdns. Cobham KT11 .... 73 C5
French Gdns. Hawley GU17 .... 64 D4
French La. Bowl Gn GU8 .... 169 E3
French St. Sunby TW16 .... 35 C7
Frenchaye. Addl KT15 .... 52 C5
Frenches Ct. 4 Redh RH1 .... 119 A3
Frenches Rd. Redh RH1 .... 119 B4
Frenches The. Redh RH1 .... 119 A3
Frenchlands Hatch.
  E Hors KT24 .... 112 E8
Frensham. Brack RG12 .... 27 D3
Frensham C of E Fst Sch.
  Frensh GU10 .... 167 D7
Frensham Ct. Mitch CR4 .... 40 D6
Frensham Dr. New Add CR0 .... 63 C3
Frensham Dr. Rhampt SW15 ...... 19 A6
Frensham Heights Rd.
  Rowl GU10 .... 146 A2
Frensham Heights Sch.
  Rowl GU10 .... 146 A2
Frensham House. 7
  King U T KT6 .... 37 E4
Frensham La. Head Dn GU35 ...... 166 F2
Frensham Rd. Crowth RG11 .... 45 B7
Frensham Rd.
  M Bourn GU10 & GU9 .... 146 D6
Frensham Rd. Purley CR8 .... 80 B5
Frensham Vale. M Bourn GU10 146 C4
Frensham Way. Nork KT17 .... 77 C3
Fresham House. Beck BR2 .... 44 F6
Freshborough Ct. Guild GU1 ...... 130 F8
Freshfield. 1 Kings KT20 .... 117 E8
Freshfield Bank. For Row RH18 206 E2
Freshfield Cl. Crawl RH10 .... 40 D1
Freshfields. Croy CR0 .... 43 F1
Freshford St.
  Wands SW17 & SW18 .... 20 C5
Freshmount Gdns. Epsom KT19 . 76 B8
Freshwater Cl. Streat SW17 .... 21 A2
Freshwater Rd. Streat SW17 ...... 21 A2
Freshwood Cl. Beck BR3 .... 44 B8
Freshwood Way. Wallin SM6 ...... 60 C2
Frewin Rd. Wands SW18 .... 20 D1
Friar Mews. W Norw SE27 .... 22 B5
Friar's Gate. Onsl V GU2 .... 130 A7
Friars Ave. Rhampt SW15 .... 18 F5
Friars Croft. Merrow GU4 .... 110 C4
Friars Ct. 5 Wallin SM6 .... 60 B6
Friars Keep. Easth RG12 .... 27 B5
Friars La. Rich TW9 .... 6 D2
Friars Orch. Fetch KT22 .... 94 D6
Friars Rd. Vir W GU25 .... 31 D5
Friars Rise. Mayb GU22 .... 70 A1
Friars Rookery. Crawl RH10 ...... 201 F6
Friars Stile Pl. 9 Rich TW10 ...... 6 E1
Friars Stile Rd. Rich TW10 .... 6 E1
Friars Way. Chert KT16 .... 33 A3
Friars Wood. New Add CR0 .... 62 E2
Friary Bridge. Guild GU1 .... 130 C7
Friary Ct. Knaph GU21 .... 68 F1
Friary Pas. Guild GU1 .... 130 C7
Friary Rd. Ascot SL5 .... 29 B3
Friary Rd. Wray TW19 .... 11 C8
Friary St. Guild GU1 & GU2 .... 130 C7
Friary The. Guild GU1 .... 130 C8
Friary Way. Crawl RH10 .... 201 E5
Friday Rd. Mitch CR4 .... 20 F1
Friday St. Faygt RH12 .... 198 E6
Friday St. Ockley RH5 .... 177 E4
Friday St. Rusper RH12 .... 198 E6
Friday St. Warn RH12 .... 216 E7
Friday Street Rd. Abin CR H5 .... 155 E8
Friend Ave. Alder GU12 .... 105 D1
Friends Cl. Crawl RH11 .... 181 D1
Friends' Rd. Croy CR0 & CR9 ..... 61 D7

Friends Rd. Purley CR8 .... 80 B7
Friendship Way. Easth RG12 ...... 27 B6
Friern Rd. Dulw SE22 .... 23 A8
Frimley Ave. Wallin SM6 .... 60 F5
Frimley Bsns Pk. Farnb GU16 .... 85 B8
Frimley C of E Fst & Mid Sch.
  .... 85 E7
Frimley Cl. New Add CR0 .... 63 C3
Frimley Cl. Putney SW15 .... 19 E6
Frimley Cres. New Add CR0 .... 63 C3
Frimley Gdns. Mitch CR4 .... 40 E6
Frimley Green Rd. Friml GU16 ... 85 E7
Frimley Grove Gdns. Friml GU16 65 E1
Frimley Hall Dr. Camb GU15 ...... 65 F6
Frimley High St. Friml GU16 ...... 85 D8
Frimley House. Mitch CR4 .... 40 E6
Frimley Park Hospl.
  Friml GU16 .... 65 D2
Frimley Rd. Ash V GU12 .... 106 A8
Frimley Rd. Camb GU15 .... 65 E3
Frimley Rd. Chess KT9 .... 56 E5
Frimley Rd. Friml GU15 & GU16 .. 65 C1
Frinton Rd. Mitch SW17 .... 21 A2
Friston Wlk. Crawl RH11 .... 201 A7
Frith End Rd.
  Binst GU34 & GU35 .... 166 A6
Frith Hill Rd. Farnc GU7 .... 150 D6
Frith Hill Rd. Friml GU16 .... 66 B1
Frith Knowle. Hersh KT12 .... 54 B5
Frith Pk. E Grins RH19 .... 185 E3
Frith Rd. Croy CR0 & CR9 .... 61 C8
Fritham Cl. New Mal KT3 .... 38 E3
Friths Dr. Reig RH2 .... 118 B4
Frithwald Rd. Chert KT16 .... 32 F2
Frobisher. Easth RG12 .... 27 C2
Frobisher Cl. Kenley CR8 .... 80 C2
Frobisher Cres. Stan TW19 .... 13 E8
Frobisher Ct. Belm SM2 .... 58 F3
Frobisher Ct. For Hil SE23 .... 23 B6
Frobisher Gdns. Merrow GU1 .... 110 A2
Frobisher Gdns. Stan TW19 ...... 13 E8
Frodsham Way. Sandh GU15 ..... 45 E2
Frog Grove La. Wood S V GU3 .. 107 F4
Frog Hall. Woki RG11 .... 25 F5
Frog Hall Dr. Woki RG11 .... 25 E5
Frog La. Easth RG12 .... 27 A6
Frog La. Westfd GU4 .... 89 E2
Froggetts La.
  Wall W GU6 & RH5 .... 176 C1
Frogmore Cl. Cheam SM3 .... 58 E1
Frogmore Comm Sch.
  Yatly GU17 .... 64 A5
Frogmore Ct. Blckw GU17 .... 64 C4
Frogmore Cty Inf Sch.
  Blckw GU17 .... 64 B5
Frogmore Cty Jun Sch.
  Blckw GU17 .... 64 B5
Frogmore Gdns. Cheam SM3 .... 58 E6
Frogmore Gr. Blckw GU17 .... 64 C4
Frogmore Park Dr. Blckw GU17 . 64 C3
Frogmore Rd. Blckw GU17 .... 64 C5
Frome Cl. W Heath GU14 .... 84 D6
Fromondes Rd. Cheam SM3 ...... 58 E5
Fromow Gdns. Windl GU20 .... 48 B6
Froxfield Down. 6 Brack RG12 .. 27 F4
Fruen Rd. E Bed TW14 .... 14 F8
Fry Cl. Crawl RH11 .... 201 B1
Fry's Cross. Dunsf GU8 .... 193 A2
Frylands Ct. New Add CR0 .... 82 C8
Fryern Wood. Cater CR3 .... 100 C3
Fryston Ave. Croy CR0 .... 62 A8
Fryston Ave. Wallin CR5 .... 79 B5
Fuchsia Way. W End GU24 .... 67 E6
Fuel Farm Rd. Crawl RH6 .... 181 E8
Fulbourn. 4 King U T KT1 .... 38 A7
Fulbourne Cl. Redh RH1 .... 118 E3
Fulford Rd. W Ewell KT19 .... 57 D3
Fulford Rd. W Ewell KT19 .... 57 D3
Fulham Cl. Crawl RH11 .... 200 E7
Fullbrook Ave. Woodhm KT15 ... 71 A8
Fullbrook Sch. Woodhm KT15 ... 71 A8
Fullbrooks Ave. New Mal KT4 .... 38 F1
Fuller's Wood. Croy CR0 .... 63 A6
Fullers Ave. Surb KT6 .... 56 F8
Fullers Farm Rd. Shere KT24 .... 112 B1
Fullers Rd. Binst GU10 .... 145 D3
Fullers Rd. Rowl GU10 .... 145 D3
Fullers Vale. Head Dn GU35 ...... 187 A5
Fullers Way N. Surb KT6 .... 56 F7
Fullers Way S. Chess KT9 .... 56 E7
Fullers Wood La. Earls RH1 ...... 119 C1
Fullerton Cl. Byfl KT14 .... 71 A5
Fullerton Dr. Byfl KT14 .... 71 E5
Fullerton Rd. Byfl KT14 .... 71 E5
Fullerton Rd. Croy CR0 .... 42 F2
Fullerton Rd. Sutton SM5 .... 59 E2
Fullerton Way. Byfl KT14 .... 71 E5
Fullmer Way. Woodhm KT15 ..... 51 F1
Fulmar Cl. 1 Crawl RH11 .... 200 D5
Fulmar Ct. 5 N Norw SE21 .... 22 D6
Fulmar Dr. E Grins RH19 .... 186 B3
Fulmer Cl. Hampt TW12 .... 15 E3
Fulstone Cl. Hounsl TW4 .... 4 F3
Fulvens. Peasl GU5 .... 133 E1
Fulwell Golf Course.
  Hampt TW12 .... 16 C4
Fulwell Park Ave. Twick TW2 ..... 16 C6
Fulwell Rd. Tedd TW11 & TW12 .. 16 D4
Fulwell Sta. Tedd TW11 .... 16 D4
Fulwood Gdns. Twick TW1 .... 6 A1
Fulwood Wlk. Putney SW19 .... 19 E7
Furlong Cl. Carsh CR4 .... 41 B1
Furlong Rd. Westc RH4 .... 135 C6
Furlong Way. Crawl RH6 .... 181 F8
Furlough The. Woking GU22 ...... 70 A2
Furmage St. Wands SW18 .... 20 B8
Furnace Dr. Crawl RH10 .... 201 E4
Furnace Farm Rd. Crawl RH10 .. 202 A4
Furnace Par. Crawl RH10 .... 202 A4
Furnace Pl. Crawl RH10 .... 202 A4

Furnace Rd.
  Copth RH10 & RH19 .... 184 C3
Furneaux Ave. W Norw SE27 ..... 22 B3
Furness Rd. Morden SM4 .... 40 B3
Furniss Ct. Crawl RH10 .... 173 F2
Furnival Cl. Went GU25 .... 31 D3
Furrows Pl. Cater CR3 .... 100 D5
Furrows The. Walt O T KT12 ...... 54 C8
Furse Cl. Ash V GU12 .... 106 A7
Furse Cl. Redh RH1 .... 118 F2
Furze Cl. Ash V GU12 .... 106 A7
Furze Cl. Redh RH1 .... 118 F2
Furze Field. Oxsh KT22 .... 74 E6
Furze Gr. Kings KT20 .... 97 F6
Furze Hill. Kings KT20 .... 97 F6
Furze Hill. Purley CR8 .... 79 F8
Furze Hill Cres. Crowth RG11 ... 45 C4
Furze Hill Rd. Head Dn GU35 .... 187 C4
Furze La. E Grins RH19 .... 185 B4
Furze La. Farnc GU7 & GU3 ...... 150 F4
Furze La. Purley CR8 .... 79 F8
Furze La. Row Tn KT15 .... 51 F4
Furze Rd. Rudg RH12 .... 214 D8
Furze Rd. S Norw SE25 .... 42 C6
Furze Vale Rd. Head Dn GU35 .. 187 B4
Furzebank. Ascot SL5 .... 29 D5
Furzedown Dr. Streat SW17 ...... 21 B3
Furzedown Prim Sch.
  Mitch SW17 .... 21 A2
Furzedown Rd. Streat SW17 ..... 21 B3
Furzedown Rd. Sutton SM2 ...... 78 C8
Furzefield. Crawl RH11 .... 201 C7
Furzefield Chase.
  Dorm Pk RH19 .... 185 E6
Furzefield Cres. Reig RH2 .... 139 C7
Furzefield Cty Fst Sch.
  Merst RH1 .... 119 D7
Furzefield Cty Mid Sch.
  Merst RH1 .... 119 D7
Furzefield Rd. E Grins RH19 .... 185 D4
Furzefield Rd. Horsh RH12 ...... 218 B5
Furzefield Rd. Reig RH2 .... 139 C7
Furzehill. Redh RH1 .... 118 E2
Furzeland House. 2
  New Mal KT3 .... 38 E2
Furzemoors. Brack RG12 .... 27 B4
Furzen La. Ell Gn RH12 & RH5 .. 196 B4
Furzen La. Wall W RH12 & RH5 . 196 B4
Furzewood. Sunby TW16 .... 35 A8
Fyfield Cl. Beck BR2 & BR3 ...... 44 D5
Fyfield Cl. Blckw GU17 .... 64 D5

Gable Ct. For Hil SE26 .... 23 B4
Gable Ct. 9 Redh RH1 .... 119 A2
Gable End. Farnb GU14 .... 85 B4
Gable Lodge. W Wick BR4 .... 44 C1
Gables Ave. Ashf TW15 .... 13 F3
Gables Cl. Ash V GU12 .... 106 A5
Gables Cl. Farnb GU14 .... 85 A4
Gables Cl. Old Wok GU22 .... 89 F7
Gables Ct. Old Wok GU22 .... 89 F7
Gables The. Banstd SM7 .... 77 F2
Gables The. Copth RH10 .... 183 B3
Gables The. Elst GU8 .... 148 C3
Gables The. Horsh RH12 .... 217 D4
Gables The. Oxsh KT22 .... 74 C7
Gables The. Whit V KT13 .... 53 C5
Gabriel Cl. Felt TW13 .... 15 D4
Gabriel Dr. Friml GU15 .... 66 B4
Gabriel St. For Hil SE23 .... 23 E8
Gadbridge La. Ewh GU6 .... 175 E4
Gadbrook Rd. Betch RH3 .... 137 D4
Gadesden Rd. W Ewell KT19 .... 57 C4
Gadesden Rd. W Ewell KT19 .... 57 C4
Gaffney Cl. Farnb GU11 .... 105 D7
Gage Cl. Crawl D RH10 .... 184 C1
Gage Ridge. For Row RH18 ...... 206 E2
Gainsborough Cl. Beck BR3 ..... 24 A1
Gainsborough Cl. Camb GU15 .. 65 F3
Gainsborough Cl. Thame D KT10 36 E1
Gainsborough Cl. Dulw SE21 ... 22 E6
Gainsborough Dr. Walt O T KT12 54 A6
Gainsborough Dr. Sander CR2 .. 81 A6
Gainsborough Gdns. Islew TW7 . 5 D2
Gainsborough Rd. Crawl RH10 201 F3
Gainsborough Rd. Epsom KT19 . 57 C1
Gainsborough Rd. New Mal KT3 38 D2
Gainsborough Rd. Rich TW9 ..... 6 F4
Gaist Ave. Cater CR3 .... 101 B5
Galahad Rd. Crawl RH11 .... 200 E6
Galba Ct. 1 Brent TW8 .... 6 D7
Gale Cl. Hampt TW12 .... 15 E2
Gale Cl. Mitch CR4 .... 40 D6
Gale Cres. Banstd SM7 .... 78 A2
Gale Dr. Lhtwat GU18 .... 48 A1
Gales Cl. Merrow GU4 .... 110 D3
Gales Dr. Crawl RH10 .... 201 F6
Gales Pl. Crawl RH10 .... 201 F6
Galgate Cl. 4 Putney SW19 ..... 19 E7
Gallery Rd. Dulw SE21 .... 22 D7
Gallery Rd. Pirb GU24 .... 87 D8
Galleymead Rd. Poyle SL3 ...... 1 F6
Gallop The. S Croy CR2 .... 62 B3
Gallop The. Sutton SM2 .... 59 D2
Gallwey Rd. Alder GU11 .... 105 C3
Galpin's Rd. Thorn H CR4 & CR7 . 41 F5
Galsworthy Rd. Chert KT16 ..... 33 A2
Galsworthy Rd. King U T KT2 ... 38 B8
Galton Rd. Sunnin SL5 .... 29 F3
Galvani Way. Croy CR0 & CR9 .. 41 F1
Galvins Cl. Stough GU2 .... 109 A4
Gambles La. Ripley GU23 .... 91 C2
Gambol Rd. Up Toot SW17 ...... 20 E4
Gander Green La.
  Cheam KT4 & SM1 & SM3 .... 58 F7

Gangers Hill. Wold RH9 .... 121 F7
Ganghill. Stough GU1 .... 110 A3
Gannet Ct. 4 W Norw SE21 ...... 22 D6
Ganymede Ct. Crawl RH11 .... 200 E3
Gap Rd. Wimble SW19 .... 20 B3
Gapemouth Rd.
  Pirb GU16 & GU24 .... 86 E5
Garbetts Way. Tongh GU10 ...... 126 F6
Garbrand Wlk. Ewell KT17 .... 57 F2
Garden Ave. Mitch CR4 .... 21 B1
Garden Cl. Addl KT15 .... 52 D6
Garden Cl. Ashf TW15 .... 14 C2
Garden Cl. Banstd SM7 .... 78 A4
Garden Cl. E Grins RH19 .... 205 F7
Garden Cl. Hampt TW12 .... 15 F3
Garden Cl. Leahd KT22 .... 95 C3
Garden Cl. Putney SW15 .... 19 B8
Garden Cl. Sham Gn GU5 .... 152 D6
Garden Cl. Wallin SM6 .... 60 E5
Garden Ct. 5 Belm SM2 .... 59 A3
Garden Ct. 4 Rich TW9 .... 6 F6
Garden Ct. S Croy CR0 .... 61 F7
Garden Flats. Streat SW16 .... 21 E5
Garden House La. E Grins RH19 205 F7
Garden La. Streat SW2 .... 21 F7
Garden Pl. Horsh RH12 .... 217 C4
Garden Rd. Mortl TW9 .... 7 A4
Garden Rd. Penge SE20 .... 43 C8
Garden Rd. Walt O T KT12 .... 35 B2
Garden The. Effing KT24 .... 113 D7
Garden Wlk. Beck BR3 .... 43 F8
Garden Wlk. Crawl RH11 .... 201 C6
Garden Wlk. Hooley CR5 .... 99 B4
Garden Wlk. Horsh RH12 .... 217 C4
Garden Wood Rd.
  E Grins RH19 .... 205 C8
Gardener's Hill Rd. Rowl GU10 146 B4
Gardener's Wlk. G Book KT23 ... 94 B1
Gardeners Cl. Warn RH12 .... 216 E8
Gardeners Ct. Horsh RH13 ...... 217 D1
Gardeners Gn. Rusper RH12 .... 199 C6
Gardeners Rd. Thorn H CR0 ..... 42 B1
Gardenfields. Burgh H KT20 .... 97 E8
Gardenia Ct. 1 Beck BR3 .... 24 A1
Gardenia Dr. W End GU24 .... 67 F6
Gardens The. Beck BR3 .... 44 D7
Gardens The. Esher KT10 .... 55 A6
Gardens The. Hatton TW14 ...... 3 D1
Gardens The. Pirb GU24 .... 87 F5
Gardens The. Tongh GU10 .... 126 F7
Gardner House. Felt TW13 .... 16 A6
Gardner Ind Est. Penge SE26 ... 23 F3
Gardner La. Crawl D RH10 .... 204 A8
Gardner Rd. Guild GU1 .... 109 D1
Gareth Cl. N Cheam KT4 .... 58 D8
Gareth Ct. Streat SW16 .... 21 D5
Garfield Prim Sch.
  Wimble SW19 .... 20 C2
Garfield Rd. Addl KT15 .... 52 C6
Garfield Rd. Camb GU15 .... 65 C5
Garfield Rd. 2 Twick TW1 .... 17 A7
Garfield Rd. Wimble SW19 .... 20 C2
Garibaldi Rd. Redh RH1 .... 139 F8
Garland Rd. E Grins RH19 .... 185 D2
Garland Way. Cater CR3 .... 100 D5
Garlands Rd. Leahd KT22 .... 95 C6
Garlands Rd. Redh RH1 .... 118 F1
Garlichill Rd.
  Burgh H KT17 & KT18 .... 77 B2
Garlies Rd. For Hil SE23 .... 23 E5
Garnet House. New Mal KT4 ..... 38 D1
Garnet Rd. S Norw CR7 .... 42 D5
Garrad's Rd. Streat SW16 .... 21 D4
Garrard Rd. Banstd SM7 .... 78 A3
Garrat La. Up Toot SW17 & SW18 20 C5
Garratt Cl. Wallin CR0 .... 60 E6
Garratt Green Sch.
  Wands SW17 .... 20 D5
Garratt La. Wands SW17 & SW18 20 C5
Garratt Park Sec Sch.
  Wands SW17 .... 20 C5
Garratt Terr. Up Toot SW17 ...... 20 E4
Garratts La. Banstd SM7 .... 78 A3
Garraway House. Dulw SE21 .... 22 F5
Garrett Cl. Worth RH10 .... 202 C4
Garrick Cl. Hersh KT12 .... 54 B6
Garrick Cl. 1 Rich TW9 .... 6 D2
Garrick Cl. Stain TW18 .... 13 A1
Garrick Cres. S Croy CR0 .... 61 E8
Garrick Gdns. E Mole KT8 .... 36 A6
Garrick House. 2 King U T KT1 . 37 E5
Garrick House. 7 Streat SW16 . 21 C3
Garrick Rd. Rich TW9 .... 7 A5
Garrick Wlk. Crawl RH10 .... 201 E3
Garrison Cl. Hounsl TW4 .... 4 F3
Garrison La. Chess KT9 .... 56 E3
Garrones The. Crawl RH10 .... 202 F7
Garside Cl. Hampt TW12 .... 16 B2
Garson La. Wray TW19 .... 11 D8
Garson Rd. Esher KT10 .... 54 F4
Garson's La. New Gn SL4 .... 8 A7
Garston Gdns. Kenley CR8 .... 80 D4
Garston La. Kenley CR8 .... 80 D4
Garstons The. L Book KT23 ...... 94 A2
Garswood. Brack RG12 .... 27 D3
Garth Cl. King U T KT2 .... 17 F3
Garth Cl. M Bourn GU9 .... 146 A7
Garth Cl. W Barn SM4 .... 39 D2
Garth Ct. Chisw W4 .... 7 D8
Garth High Sch. Morden SM4 .... 40 D3
Garth Hill Sch. Brack RG12 ...... 27 C8
Garth Rd. Chisw W4 .... 7 D8
Garth Rd. King U T KT2 .... 17 F3
Garth Rd. W Barn SM4 .... 39 D2
Garth The. Ash GU10 & GU12 .. 105 F1
Garth The. Cobham KT11 .... 73 E6
Garth The. Farnb GU14 .... 85 D4

Garth The. Hampt TW12 .... 16 B2
Garthorne Rd. For Hil SE23 .... 23 D8
Garthside. Rich TW10 .... 17 E3
Gartmoor Gdns. Wands SW19 ... 19 F7
Garton Cl. Crawl RH11 .... 200 E5
Garvens. Dulw SE19 .... 22 E3
Gascoigne Rd. New Add CR0 ..... 63 C2
Gascoigne Rd. Weyb KT13 .... 53 B7
Gasden Copse. Witley GU8 .... 170 D5
Gasden Dr. Witley GU8 .... 170 D6
Gasden La. Witley GU8 .... 170 D6
Gaskyns Cl. Rudg RH12 .... 214 D7
Gassiot Rd. Up Toot SW17 .... 20 F4
Gassiot Way. Carsh SM1 .... 59 D7
Gasson Wood Rd. Crawl RH11 .. 200 E4
Gaston Bell Cl. Rich TW9 .... 6 F4
Gaston Bridge Rd. Shep TW17 .. 34 D3
Gaston Bridge Rd. Up Hall TW17 34 E4
Gaston Rd. Mitch CR4 .... 41 A6
Gaston Way. Shep TW17 .... 34 A4
Gatcombe Ct. Beck BR3 .... 24 A1
Gate Cl. 4 Weyb KT13 .... 53 B7
Gate House. 4 Surb KT6 .... 37 E1
Gate St. Bramly GU5 .... 173 B7
Gateford Dr. Horsh RH12 .... 217 F6
Gatehouse Cl. King U T KT2 ..... 18 C1
Gates Green Rd. Coney H BR4 ... 63 F7
Gatesden Rd. Fetch KT22 .... 94 C4
Gateside Rd. Up Toot SW17 ...... 20 F5
Gatestone Ct. 9 S Norw SE19 ... 22 E2
Gatestone Rd. S Norw SE19 ..... 22 E2
Gateway The. Sheer GU21 .... 70 C5
Gateways. Guild GU1 .... 131 B8
Gateways. King U T KT6 .... 37 E4
Gateways Ct. Wallin SM6 .... 60 B5
Gateways The. Rich TW9 .... 6 D3
Gatfield Gr. Felt TW13 .... 16 A6
Gatfield House. Felt TW13 .... 16 A6
Gatley Ave. W Ewell KT19 .... 57 B5
Gatley Ave. W Ewell KT19 .... 57 B5
Gatton Bottom.
  Gatton RH2 & RH1 .... 118 E7
Gatton Bottom.
  L Kings RH1 & RH2 .... 119 D8
Gatton Bottom.
  Merst RH1 & RH2 .... 119 B8
Gatton Cl. Reig RH2 .... 118 C4
Gatton Cl. Sutton SM2 .... 59 B2
Gatton Park Ct. Redh RH1 .... 118 F4
Gatton Park Rd.
  Redh RH1 & RH2 .... 118 E4
Gatton Point. Redh RH1 .... 119 A5
Gatton Prim Sch. Up Toot SW17 . 20 F4
Gatton Rd. Reig RH2 .... 118 C4
Gatton Rd. Up Toot SW17 .... 20 E4
Gatwick Airport Sta.
  Crawl RH6 .... 182 B7
Gatwick Airport-London.
  Crawl RH6 .... 181 F7
Gatwick Gate. Crawl RH6 .... 181 E5
Gatwick Metro Ctr. Horley RH6 161 B4
Gatwick Park Hospl.
  Hookw RH6 .... 160 E2
Gatwick Rd. Crawl RH10 & RH6 . 182 A3
Gatwick Way. Crawl RH6 .... 181 E8
Gatwick Zoo. Charl RH6 .... 180 D6
Gauntlet Cres. Cater CR3 & CR8 100 D7
Gauntlett Rd. Carsh SM1 .... 59 D5
Gavell Rd. Cobham KT11 .... 73 A6
Gaveston Cl. Byfl KT14 .... 71 F6
Gaveston Rd. Leahd KT22 .... 95 A7
Gavina Cl. Morden SM4 .... 40 E4
Gayfere Rd. Stonel KT17 .... 58 A5
Gayhouse La. Horne RH1 .... 162 E8
Gayler Cl. Bletch RH1 .... 120 F2
Gaynesford Rd. For Hil SE23 .... 23 D6
Gaynesford Rd. Wallin SM5 ...... 59 F3
Gaysland Cotts. Tand RH7 .... 143 A2
Gayton Ct. New Mal KT3 .... 38 F4
Gayton Ct. Reig RH2 .... 118 A2
Gaywood Ct. Streat SW2 .... 22 A7
Gaywood Rd. Ashtd KT21 .... 75 F1
Geary Cl. Burst RH6 .... 162 B1
Gedge Ct. Mitch CR4 .... 40 E5
Geffers Ride. N Asct SL5 .... 28 E7
Gemini Cl. Crawl RH11 .... 200 E4
Gemma Ct. Beck BR3 .... 43 F7
Genesis Bsns Pk. Sheer GU21 .. 70 C4
Geneva Cl. Up Hall TW17 .... 34 E7
Geneva Rd. King U T KT1 .... 37 E5
Geneva Rd. Thorn H CR7 .... 42 C4
Genoa Rd. Penge SE20 .... 43 C8
Gentles La.
  Head Dn GU30 & GU35 .... 187 A3
Genyn Rd. Guild GU2 .... 130 B8
George Abbot Sch.
  Abbots GU1 .... 110 A3
George Denyer Cl.
  Haslem GU27 .... 208 C7
George Eliot Cl. Witley GU8 .... 170 F5
George Gdns. Alder GU11 .... 126 C7
George Groves Rd. Penge SE20 . 43 A8
George Horley Pl. Newd RH5 .... 158 B1
George House. 8 Penge SE26 ... 23 B3
George Pinion Ct. Horsh RH12 217 B3
George Rd. Farnc GU7 .... 150 F7
George Rd. Guild GU1 .... 109 D1
George Rd. King U T KT2 .... 18 C1
George Rd. Milf GU8 .... 149 F2
George Rd. New Mal KT3 .... 38 F4
George Sq. Merton SW19 .... 40 A6
George St. Croy CR0 & CR9 ...... 61 D8
George St. Hounsl TW3 & TW5 ... 4 F5
George St. Pirb GU24 .... 87 A6
George St. Rich TW10 .... 6 D2
George St. Stain TW18 .... 12 F4
George Wyver Cl. Putney SW18 . 19 E8

George's Rd. Tats TN16 .... 103 D7
Georgeham Rd. Sandh GU15 ..... 45 D2
Georgelands. Ripley GU23 .... 91 B6
Georges Terr. Cater CR3 .... 100 D5
Georgetown Cl. 4 W Norw SE19 22 E3
Georgia Rd. N T KT3 .... 38 C5
Georgia Rd. S Norw CR7 .... 42 B8
Georgian Cl. Camb GU15 .... 65 E7
Georgian Cl. Stain TW18 .... 13 B4
Georgian Cl. Worth RH10 .... 202 D5
Georgian Ct. Croy CR0 & CR9 .... 42 D1
Georgina Ct. 5 Twick TW1 .... 6 C1
Gerald Ct. Horsh RH13 .... 217 E2
Gerald's Gr. Nork SM7 .... 77 D5
Geraldine Rd. Brent W4 .... 7 A8
Gerard Ave. Twick TW4 .... 16 A8
Gerard Rd. Barnes SW13 .... 7 F6
Germander Dr. Bisley GU24 .... 68 A4
Gerrards Mead. Banstd SM7 .... 77 F3
Ghent St. Catf SE6 .... 24 A6
Ghyll Cres. Horsh RH13 .... 217 E1
Gibb's Acre. Pirb GU24 .... 87 F4
Gibbet La. Camb GU15 .... 66 A7
Gibbon Rd. King U T KT1 .... 17 F1
Gibbons Cl. Sandh GU17 .... 64 C8
Gibbs Ave. W Norw SE19 .... 22 D3
Gibbs Brook La.
  Crow RH7 & RH8 .... 143 D7
Gibbs Brook La.
  Oxted RH7 & RH8 .... 143 D7
Gibbs Cl. W Norw SE19 .... 22 D3
Gibbs House. 6 Balham SW12 ..... 21 B8
Gibbs House. Broml BR1 .... 44 F8
Gibbs Sq. W Norw SE19 .... 22 D3
Giblets La. Horsh RH12 .... 217 F7
Giblets Way. Horsh RH12 .... 217 E7
Gibraltar Cres. Epsom KT19 .... 57 E1
Gibson Cl. Chess KT9 .... 56 C5
Gibson Cl. Islew TW7 .... 5 D4
Gibson Ct. Hinch W KT10 .... 55 F7
Gibson House. Sutton SM1 .... 59 A6
Gibson Pl. Stan TW19 .... 2 C1
Gibson Rd. Sutton SM1 .... 59 B5
Gibson's Hill. S Norw SW16 .... 22 A1
Gibson's Hill. S Norw SW16 .... 22 A2
Gidd Hill. Coulsd CR5 .... 79 A3
Giffard Dr. W Heath GU14 .... 84 F5
Giffard Way. Stough GU2 .... 109 A4
Giffards Cl. E Grins RH19 .... 185 F1
Giffards Meadow.
  M Bourn GU9 .... 125 E1
Giggs Hill Rd. Thame D KT7 .... 37 A2
Giggshill Gdns. Thame D KT7 ...... 37 A1
Gilbert Cl. 1 Merton SW19 .... 40 B8
Gilbert Rd. Friml GU16 .... 65 C2
Gilbert Rd. Merton SW19 .... 20 C1
Gilbert Scott Jun & Inf Sch.
  S Croy CR2 .... 62 E3
Gilbert St. Hounsl TW3 .... 5 C4
Gilbey Rd. Up Toot SW17 .... 20 E3
Gilders Rd. Chess KT9 .... 56 F4
Giles Coppice. Dulw SE19 .... 22 F4
Giles Travers Cl. Egham TW20 .... 32 C6
Gilesmead. Epsom KT18 .... 76 E5
Gilham La. For Row RH18 .... 206 E2
Gilham's Ave. Belm SM7 .... 77 E7
Gill Ave. Onsl V GU2 .... 129 E8
Gillett Ct. Horsh RH13 .... 218 B4
Gillett House. Horsh RH13 .... 218 B4
Gillett Rd. S Norw CR7 .... 42 D5
Gillette Cnr. Brent TW7 .... 6 A7
Gillham's La. Linch GU27 .... 207 A5
Gilliam Gr. Purley CR8 .... 61 A1
Gillian Ave. Alder GU11 & GU12 126 D8
Gillian Cl. Alder GU12 .... 126 D8
Gillian Park Rd. Cheam SM3 .... 39 F1
Gilliat Dr. Merrow GU4 .... 110 D3
Gilligan Cl. Horsh RH12 .... 217 B2
Gilmais. Fetch KT23 .... 94 C2
Gilmore Cres. Ashf TW15 .... 14 A2
Gilpin Ave. Mortl SW14 .... 7 D3
Gilpin Cl. Mitch CR4 .... 40 E7
Gilpin Cres. Twick TW2 .... 16 B8
Gilpin Way. Harl UB3 .... 3 D7
Gilsland Rd. S Norw CR7 .... 42 D5
Gilton Rd. Catf SE6 .... 24 E5
Gimcrack Hill. Leahd KT22 .... 95 B5
Gingers Cl. Cran GU6 .... 174 F2
Ginhams Rd. Crawl RH11 .... 201 B6
Gipsy Hill. W Norw SE19 & SE27 .. 22 E3
Gipsy Hill Sta. W Norw SE19 .... 22 E3
Gipsy La. Brack RG12 .... 27 D7
Gipsy La. Woki RG11 .... 25 C4
Gipsy Rd. W Norw SE21 & SE27 .. 22 D4
Gipsy Road Gdns. W Norw SE27 .. 22 C4
Girdwood Rd.
  Putney SW18 & SW19 .... 19 E8
Girling Way. Hatton TW14 .... 4 A4
Girton Cl. Sandh GU15 .... 45 E1
Girton Gdns. Croy CR0 .... 63 A7
Girton Rd. For Hil SE26 .... 23 D7
Gittens Cl. Catf BR1 .... 24 F4
Glade Cl. Long D KT6 .... 56 D8
Glade Gdns. Croy CR0 .... 43 E2
Glade House. Ascot SL5 .... 29 D4
Glade Spur. Kings KT20 .... 98 B6
Glade The. Ascot SL5 .... 29 C4
Glade The. Belm SM2 .... 58 E2
Glade The. Binst GU10 .... 145 B1
Glade The. Coulsd CR5 & CR8 .. 100 A8
Glade The. Crawl RH10 .... 202 A4
Glade The. Croy CR0 .... 43 D3
Glade The. Fetch KT22 .... 94 B5
Glade The. Heath E GU9 .... 125 D7
Glade The. Horsh RH13 .... 218 A4
Glade The. Kings KT20 .... 98 B6
Glade The. Sheer KT14 .... 70 E6
Glade The. Stain TW18 .... 13 B2

Glade The. Stonel KT17 .... 58 A4
Glade The. W Wick BR4 .... 63 B7
Glades The. E Grins RH19 .... 186 B1
Gladeside. Croy CR0 .... 43 D3
Gladeside Cl. Warlgm CR6 .... 101 B7
Gladiator Way.
  Farnb GU11 & GU14 .... 105 A8
Gladioli Cl. 6 Hampt TW12 .... 16 A2
Gladsmuir Cl. Walt O T KT12 ...... 54 C8
Gladstone Ave. Felt TW14 .... 4 B1
Gladstone Ave. Felt TW14 .... 15 B8
Gladstone Ave. Twick TW2 .... 16 D8
Gladstone Mews. 5 Merton SW19 20 A1
Gladstone Mews. 3 Penge SE20 23 C1
Gladstone Pl. Thame D KT8 .... 36 E4
Gladstone Rd. Ashtd KT21 .... 75 D1
Gladstone Rd. Croy CR0 .... 42 D2
Gladstone Rd. Horsh RH12 .... 217 D3
Gladstone Rd. King U T KT1 .... 38 A6
Gladstone Rd. Merton SW19 .... 20 A1
Gladstone Rd. Surb KT6 .... 56 E8
Glamis Cl. Friml GU16 .... 85 F7
Glamorgan Cl.
  Mitch CR4 & SW16 .... 41 E6
Glamorgan Rd. Tedd KT1 .... 17 C1
Glanfield Rd. Beck BR3 .... 43 F5
Glanty The. Egham TW20 .... 12 B4
Glanville House. 4 Streat SW12 21 C8
Glanville Wlk. 8 Crawl RH11 .... 201 A3
Glasbrook Ave. Twick TW2 .... 15 F7
Glasford St. Up Toot SW17 .... 20 F2
Glassmill La. Broml BR2 .... 44 F7
Glassonby Wlk. Friml GU16 .... 66 C5
Glastonbury Prim Sch.
  Cheam SM4 .... 40 B2
Glastonbury Rd. Cheam CR4 .... 40 A1
Glastonbury Rd. Morden SM4 ...... 40 A2
Glayshers Hill. Head Dn GU35 .. 187 B6
Glazebrook Cl. Dulw SE21 .... 22 D6
Glazebrook Rd. Tedd TW11 .... 16 F1
Glaziers La. Flexf GU3 .... 107 C2
Gleave Cl. E Grins RH19 .... 186 A2
Glebe Ave. Mitch CR4 .... 40 E7
Glebe Cl. Crawl RH10 .... 201 E7
Glebe Cl. G Book KT23 .... 94 A1
Glebe Cl. Lthwat GU18 .... 48 C1
Glebe Cl. Sander CR2 .... 80 F8
Glebe Cotts. Felt TW13 .... 16 A5
Glebe Cotts. W Clan GU4 .... 111 B3
Glebe Ct. Mitch CR4 .... 40 F6
Glebe Gdns. Byfl KT14 .... 71 E5
Glebe Gdns. New Mal KT3 .... 38 E2
Glebe House. Felt TW13 .... 16 A5
Glebe Hyrst. Sander CR2 .... 80 F7
Glebe La. Abin C RH5 .... 155 D8
Glebe La. Rushm GU10 .... 168 C5
Glebe Path. Mitch CR4 .... 40 F6
Glebe Rd. Ashtd KT21 .... 75 D1
Glebe Rd. Belm SM2 .... 58 E2
Glebe Rd. Cran GU6 .... 174 E4
Glebe Rd. Dork RH4 .... 135 F7
Glebe Rd. Egham TW20 .... 12 C2
Glebe Rd. Merst CR5 .... 99 B3
Glebe Rd. Stain TW18 .... 13 B3
Glebe Rd. W Heath GU14 .... 84 F5
Glebe Rd. Wallin SM5 .... 59 F4
Glebe Rd. Warlgm CR6 .... 81 D2
Glebe Sch. W Wick BR4 .... 63 D8
Glebe Side. Twick TW1 .... 5 F1
Glebe Sq. Mitch CR4 .... 40 F6
Glebe The. Copth RH10 .... 183 B3
Glebe The. Ewh GU6 .... 175 E6
Glebe The. Felb RH19 .... 185 A4
Glebe The. Hawley GU17 .... 64 E3
Glebe The. Hawley GU17 .... 64 E4
Glebe The. Horley RH6 .... 160 F3
Glebe The. Leigh RH2 .... 138 A2
Glebe The. New Mal KT4 .... 38 F1
Glebe The. Streat SW16 .... 21 D4
Glebe Way. Coney H BR4 .... 63 E7
Glebe Way. Felt TW13 .... 16 A5
Glebe Way. Sander CR2 .... 80 F8
Glebe Way. W Wick BR4 .... 63 D8
Glebeland Ctr. Dork RH4 .... 136 A7
Glebeland Gdns. Shep TW17 .... 34 C3
Glebeland Rd. Camb GU15 .... 64 F4
Glebelands. Clayg KT10 .... 55 F2
Glebelands. Crawl D RH10 .... 204 A7
Glebelands. E Mole KT8 .... 36 B5
Glebelands. Loxwd RH14 .... 212 F4
Glebelands Rd. E Bed TW14 .... 15 A8
Glebelands Rd. Woki RG11 .... 25 C7
Glebelands Sch. Cran GU6 .... 174 D3
Glebewood. Easth RG12 .... 27 C4
Gledhow Wood. Kings KT20 .... 98 B5
Glen Albyn Rd. Putney SW19 ...... 19 D6
Glen Ave. Ashf TW15 .... 14 A4
Glen Cl. Beac H GU26 .... 188 C6
Glen Cl. Kings KT20 .... 97 E4
Glen Cl. Shep Gn TW17 .... 34 A5
Glen Court Flats. Beac H GU26 188 C6
Glen Ct. Broml BR1 .... 24 F1
Glen Ct. 10 Penge SE20 .... 43 B8
Glen Ct. Row Tn KT15 .... 51 F5
Glen Ct. Stain TW18 .... 12 F1
Glen Dale Mews. Beck BR3 .... 44 B8
Glen Gdns. Croy CR0 & CR9 .... 61 A6
Glen Innes. Sandh GU15 .... 45 E1
Glen Rd. Beac H GU26 .... 188 D6
Glen Rd. Chess KT9 .... 56 F7
Glen Rd. Graysh GU26 .... 188 D3
Glen Road End. Wallin SM6 .... 60 B2
Glen The. Ascot SL5 .... 29 D5
Glen The. Beck BR2 .... 44 E7
Glen The. Croy CR0 .... 62 D7
Glen The. Earls RH1 .... 139 F8
Glen The. Row Tn KT15 .... 51 F5
Glen Vue. E Grins RH19 .... 185 E1
Glena Mount. Sutton SM1 .... 59 C6

Glenalmond House. Ashf TW15 ... 13 E5
Glenavon Cl. Clayg KT10 .... 56 A4
Glenavon Cl. N Cheam KT4 .... 58 B8
Glenbow Rd. Catf BR1 .... 24 E3
Glenbuck Ct. 5 Surb KT6 .... 37 E3
Glenbuck Rd. Surb KT6 .... 37 E3
Glenburnie Rd. Up Toot SW17 .... 20 F5
Glencairn Rd. Streat SW16 .... 21 E1
Glencoe Cl. Friml GU16 .... 86 A8
Glencoe Rd. Weyb KT13 .... 53 A7
Glendale Cl. Horsh RH12 .... 218 A6
Glendale Cl. Woking GU21 .... 69 C1
Glendale Dr. Burph GU4 .... 110 C5
Glendale Rise. Purley CR8 .... 80 B4
Glendene Ave. E Hors KT24 .... 92 E1
Glendon House. 9
  Crawl RH11 .... 201 D5
Glendower Gdns. 10
  Mortl SW14 .... 7 D4
Glendower Rd. Mortl SW14 .... 7 D4
Glendyne Cl. E Grins RH19 .... 206 A8
Glendyne Way. E Grins RH19 .... 206 A8
Gleneagle Lodge. Beck BR3 .... 44 A8
Gleneagle Mews. Streat SW16 .... 21 D3
Gleneagle Rd. Streat SW16 .... 21 D3
Gleneagles Cl. Stan TW19 .... 2 D1
Gleneagles Cl.
  Crawl RH10 & RH11 .... 201 D5
Gleneagles Cl. 3 Tedd TW11 .... 17 A3
Gleneagles Dr. Farnb GU14 .... 84 C3
Gleneagles House. Easth RG12 ... 26 E3
Gleneldon Mews. Streat SW16 .... 21 E4
Gleneldon Rd. Streat SW16 .... 21 E4
Glenfarg Rd. Catf SE6 .... 24 D7
Glenfield Cl. Brock RH3 .... 137 B5
Glenfield House. Easth RG12 ...... 27 C5
Glenfield Rd. Ashf TW15 .... 14 C2
Glenfield Rd. Banstd SM7 .... 78 B4
Glenfield Rd. Brock RH3 .... 137 B6
Glenfield Rd. Streat SW12 .... 21 C7
Glenhaven Dr. Stan TW19 .... 2 A2
Glenheadon Cl. Leahd KT22 .... 95 D4
Glenheadon Rise. Leahd KT22 ... 95 D4
Glenhurst. Beck BR3 .... 44 C8
Glenhurst Cl. Hawley GU17 .... 64 E4
Glenhurst Rd. Brent TW8 .... 6 C8
Glenhurst Rise. W Norw SE19 ..... 22 C1
Glenister Park Rd. Streat SW16 .. 21 D1
Glenlea. Shottm GU26 .... 188 E1
Glenlea Hollow.
  Shottm GU26 & GU27 .... 207 E8
Glenlion Ct. 2 Oat Pk KT13 .... 53 D7
Glenmill. Hampt TW12 .... 15 F3
Glenmore Cl. Addl KT15 .... 52 B7
Glenmore House. 6 Rich TW10 .... 6 E1
Glenmount Rd. Mytch GU16 .... 86 A2
Glenn Ave. Purley CR8 .... 80 B8
Glennie Cl. Dulw SE21 .... 23 A7
Glennie Rd.
  W Norw SE27 & SW16 .... 22 A5
Glentanner Way. Wands SW17 .... 20 D5
Glenthorne Ave. Croy CR0 & CR9 43 C1
Glenthorne Cl. Cheam SM3 .... 40 A1
Glenthorne Gdns. Cheam SM3 .... 40 A1
Glenthorne High Sch.
  Cheam SM3 .... 40 A1
Glenthorne Rd. King U T KT1 ...... 37 F5
Glenthorpe Rd. W Barn SM4 .... 39 D4
Glenview Cl. Crawl RH10 .... 201 F8
Glenville Gdns. Hind GU26 .... 188 F4
Glenville Mews. Wands SW18 ..... 20 A8
Glenville Rd. King U T KT2 .... 38 A8
Glenwood. Brack RG12 .... 27 D5
Glenwood. Dork RH4 & RH5 ..... 136 C5
Glenwood. Vir W GU25 .... 31 C8
Glenwood Rd. For Hil SE6 .... 24 A7
Glenwood Rd. Hounsl TW3 .... 5 D4
Glenwood Rd. Stonel SE14 .... 58 A4
Glenwood Way. Croy CR0 .... 43 D3
Globe Farm La. Blckw GU17 .... 64 B5
Glorney Mead. Farnh GU9 .... 126 A6
Glory Mead. Dork RH4 & RH5 ... 136 C4
Glossop Rd. S Croy CR2 .... 61 D2
Gloster Rd. New Mal KT3 .... 38 E5
Gloster Rd. Old Wok GU22 .... 90 A7
Gloucester Cl. E Grins RH19 ..... 206 A6
Gloucester Cl. Friml GU16 .... 85 E6
Gloucester Cl. Thame D KT7 .... 37 A1
Gloucester Cres. Stain TW18 ...... 13 D2
Gloucester Ct. Croy CR0 .... 42 E2
Gloucester Ct. 8 Surb KT6 .... 37 D2
Gloucester Dr.
  Wray TW18 & TW19 .... 12 D5
Gloucester Gdns. Bagsh GU19 .... 47 E3
Gloucester Gdns. Sutton SM1 ..... 59 B8
Gloucester Lodge. 5 Croy CR0 ... 61 F8
Gloucester Rd. Alder GU11 .... 126 C7
Gloucester Rd. Bagsh GU19 .... 47 E3
Gloucester Rd. Croy CR0 .... 42 E2
Gloucester Rd. Felt TW13 .... 15 C7
Gloucester Rd. Hampt TW12 .... 16 B1
Gloucester Rd. Hounsl TW4 .... 4 E3
Gloucester Rd.
  King U T KT1 & KT2 .... 38 B7
Gloucester Rd. Redh RH1 .... 118 F2
Gloucester Rd. Rich TW9 .... 7 A7
Gloucester Rd. Stough GU2 .... 108 F3
Gloucester Rd. Tedd TW11 .... 16 E3
Gloucester Rd. Thorn H CR7 .... 42 E2
Gloucester Rd. Twick TW2 .... 16 C7
Glover's Rd. Charl RH6 .... 180 D7
Glover's Rd. Reig RH2 .... 139 B8
Glovers Field. Shottm GU27 ...... 207 F6
Gloxinia Wlk. Hampt TW12 .... 16 A2
Glyn Cl. Ewell KT17 .... 58 A2
Glyn Cl. S Norw SE19 & SE25 ..... 42 E8
Glyn Ct. W Norw SE27 .... 22 A5
Glyn Rd. N Cheam KT4 & SM3 ..... 58 D8

Glyn Sch. Ewell KT17 .... 76 F8
Glyndale Grange. Sutton SM2 ..... 59 B4
Glynde Pl. Horsh RH12 .... 217 C2
Glynswood. Friml GU15 .... 65 F3
Glynswood. Rowl GU10 .... 146 A4
Glynwood Ct. For Hil SE23 .... 23 C6
Goat Rd. Carsh CR4 .... 40 F2
Goat Wharf. Brent TW8 .... 6 E8
Goaters Rd. N Ascot SL5 .... 28 C7
Goatsfield Rd. Tats TN16 .... 103 C7
Godalming Ave. Wallin SM6 .... 60 F5
Godalming Bsns Ctr.
  Godal GU7 .... 150 D3
Godalming Coll. Godal GU7 .... 150 D2
Godalming Cty Mid Sch.
  Farnc GU7 .... 150 F5
Godalming Rd. Dunsf GU8 .... 193 A8
Godalming Rd. Hasc GU8 .... 172 E3
Godalming Sta. Godal GU7 .... 150 D4
Goddard Cl. Littlt TW17 .... 33 F6
Goddard Cl. Worth RH10 .... 200 F3
Goddard House. Putney SW19 ..... 19 D6
Goddard Rd. Beck BR3 .... 43 E5
Goddards La. Camb GU15 .... 65 B3
Godfrey Ave. Twick TW2 .... 16 D8
Godfrey Way. Twick TW4 .... 15 F8
Godley Rd. Byfl KT14 .... 71 G6
Godley Rd. Wands SW18 .... 20 D7
Godolphin Cl. Belm SM2 .... 77 F8
Godolphin Ct.
  Crawl RH10 & RH11 .... 201 D5
Godolphin House. 7
  Streat SW2 .... 22 A7
Godolphin Rd. Whit V KT13 .... 53 D4
Godric Cres. New Add CR0 .... 63 D1
Godson Rd. Croy CR0 & CR9 ...... 61 A7
Godstone Cty Fst Sch.
  Godst RH9 .... 121 B3
Godstone Green Rd.
  Godst RH9 .... 121 B4
Godstone Hill. Tyl Gn RH9 .... 121 C5
Godstone Hill. Wold CR3 & RH9 121 B7
Godstone House. 1
  King U T KT2 .... 18 B2
Godstone Mount. 3 Purley CR8 .. 80 B7
Godstone Rd. Bletch RH1 .... 120 F2
Godstone Rd. Cater CR3 .... 101 A3
Godstone Rd. Kenley CR3 & CR8 80 D4
Godstone Rd. Lingf RH7 .... 164 C4
Godstone Rd. Oxted RH8 & RH9 122 C5
Godstone Rd. Purley CR8 .... 80 D4
Godstone Rd. Sutton SM1 .... 59 C6
Godstone Rd. Twick TW1 .... 6 B1
Godstone Rd. Whytlf CR3 .... 80 D4
Godstone Rd. Whytlf CR3 .... 101 A3
Godstone Sta. 5 Godst RH9 ...... 142 E5
Godwin Cl. W Ewell KT19 .... 57 C4
Godwin Cl. W Ewell KT19 .... 57 C4
Goffs Cl. Crawl RH11 .... 201 B5
Goffs La. Crawl RH11 .... 201 B6
Goffs Park Rd. Crawl RH11 .... 201 C4
Goffs Rd. Ashf TW15 .... 14 D2
Gogmore Farm Cl. Chert KT16 .... 32 F2
Gogmore La. Chert KT16 .... 33 A2
Goidel Cl. Wallin SM6 .... 60 D6
Gold Cup La. N Ascot SL5 .... 28 C8
Goldcliff Cl. Morden SM4 .... 40 A2
Goldcrest Cl. Horley RH6 .... 160 E4
Goldcrest Way. New Add CR0 ...... 63 D3
Goldcrest Way. Wallin CR8 .... 60 D1
Golden Ct. 10 Rich TW9 .... 6 D2
Golden Mews. Penge SE20 .... 43 C8
Golden Orb Wood. Binf RG12 .... 26 D8
Goldfinch Cl. Crawl RH11 .... 201 D8
Goldfinch Cl. Horsh RH12 .... 217 C7
Goldfinch Gdns. Merrow GU4 ... 110 D2
Goldfinch Rd. Selsd CR0 & CR2 . 62 E1
Goldfort Wlk. Woking GU21 .... 68 E2
Goldhill. M Bourn GU10 .... 146 C6
Goldings The. Woking GU21 .... 68 F3
Goldrings Rd. Oxsh KT22 .... 74 C6
Goldsmith Way. Crowth RG11 ..... 45 B4
Goldsmiths Cl. Woking GU21 ...... 69 C1
Goldsworth Cty Fst Sch.
  Woking GU21 .... 69 D2
Goldsworth Cty Mid Sch.
  Woking GU21 .... 69 D2
Goldsworth Orch. 6
  Woking GU21 .... 69 A1
Goldsworth Park Ctr.
  Woking GU21 .... 69 A2
Goldsworth Park Trad Est.
  Woking GU21 .... 69 B3
Goldsworth Rd. Woking GU21 ..... 69 D2
Goldwell Rd. Thorn H CR7 .... 41 F5
Gole Rd. Pirb GU24 .... 87 D6
Golf Cl. Pyrf GU22 .... 70 E5
Golf Club Dr. King U T KT2 .... 18 D1
Golf Club Rd. Whit V KT13 .... 53 C1
Golf Club Rd. Woking GU22 .... 89 B7
Golf Dr. Friml GU15 .... 65 F4
Golf Links Ave. Beac H GU26 .... 188 B6
Golf Rd. Kenley CR8 .... 80 D1
Golf Side. Belm SM2 .... 77 E8
Golf Side. Twick TW2 .... 16 D5
Golf Side Cl. Wallin SM6 .... 60 D3
Goliath Cl. Wallin SM6 .... 60 D3
Gomer Gdns. Tedd TW11 .... 17 A2
Gomer Pl. Tedd TW11 .... 17 A2
Gomshall Ave. Wallin SM6 .... 60 E5
Gomshall Gdns. Kenley CR8 .... 80 E4
Gomshall La. Shere GU5 .... 133 B4
Gomshall Rd.
  E Ewell KT17 & SM2 .... 58 C1
Gomshall Sta. Gomsh GU5 .... 133 E4
Gong Hill. Frensham Rd.
  M Bourn GU10 .... 146 D4
Gong Hill Dr. M Bourn GU10 ..... 146 D4
Gonston Cl. Putney SW19 .... 19 E6
Gonville Prim Sch. Thorn H CR7 41 F4
Gonville Rd. Thorn H CR7 .... 41 F4

Good Shepherd RC Prim Sch.
  Catf BR1 .... 24 F4
Good Shepherd RC Prim Sch.
  New Add CR0 .... 63 B3
Goodbehere House. 7
  W Norw SE27 .... 22 C4
Goodchild Rd. Woki RG11 .... 25 D6
Goodden Cres. Farnb GU14 .... 84 F3
Goodenough Rd. Merton SW19 . 19 F1
Goodenough Way. Coulsd CR5 .... 99 F7
Goodhart Way. W Wick BR4 .... 44 E3
Goodhew Rd. Croy CR0 & SE25 .. 43 A3
Gooding Cl. New Mal KT3 .... 38 C4
Goodings Gn. Woki RG11 .... 25 F6
Goodland House. 1
  New Mal KT3 .... 38 E2
Goodman Cres. Streat SW2 .... 21 D6
Goodman Pl. Stain TW18 .... 12 F4
Goodson House. Morden SM4 ..... 40 C2
Goodways Dr. Brack RG12 .... 27 D7
Goodwin Cl. Crawl RH11 .... 200 F3
Goodwin Cl. Mitch CR4 .... 40 D6
Goodwin Gdns. Croy CR0 & CR2 . 61 B4
Goodwin Rd. Croy CR0 .... 61 B5
Goodwins Cl. E Grins RH19 ...... 185 D3
Goodwood Cl. Camb GU15 .... 65 C8
Goodwood Cl. Crawl RH10 .... 202 A3
Goodwood Cl. Morden SM4 .... 40 A5
Goodwood House. Penge SE26 .. 23 B2
Goodwood Par. Beck BR3 .... 43 E5
Goodwood Rd. Redh RH1 .... 118 F3
Goodwyns Pl. Dork RH4 .... 136 C5
Goodwyns Rd. Dork RH4 & RH5 136 C4
Goose Gn. Gomsh GU5 .... 133 C4
Goose Green Cl. Horsh RH12 .... 217 D6
Goose La. Woking GU22 .... 89 B5
Goose Rye Rd. Woking GU3 .... 89 A3
Goose Rye Rd. Worpl GU3 .... 88 E1
Goossens Cl. Sutton SM1 .... 59 C5
Gordon Ave. Camb GU15 .... 65 C4
Gordon Ave. Islew TW1 .... 6 B2
Gordon Ave. Mortl SW14 .... 7 E3
Gordon Ave. S Croy CR2 & CR8 ... 61 C1
Gordon Cl. Addl KT16 .... 51 E7
Gordon Cl. Stain TW18 .... 13 B2
Gordon Cres. Camb GU15 .... 65 C4
Gordon Cres. Croy CR0 .... 42 F1
Gordon Dr. Addl KT16 .... 51 E7
Gordon Dr. Shep TW17 .... 34 D2
Gordon Rd. Alder GU11 .... 105 A1
Gordon Rd. Ashf TW15 .... 13 E5
Gordon Rd. Beck BR3 .... 43 F6
Gordon Rd. Camb GU15 .... 65 C5
Gordon Rd. Cater CR3 .... 100 D6
Gordon Rd. Chisw W4 .... 7 B8
Gordon Rd. Clayg KT10 .... 55 E3
Gordon Rd. Farnb GU14 .... 105 D8
Gordon Rd. Horsh RH12 .... 217 D4
Gordon Rd. Hounsl TW3 .... 5 C3
Gordon Rd. King U T KT2 .... 37 F8
Gordon Rd. Redh RH1 .... 119 A4
Gordon Rd. Rich TW9 .... 6 F5
Gordon Rd. Shep TW17 .... 34 D3
Gordon Rd. Surb KT5 .... 37 F2
Gordon Rd. Wallin SM5 .... 59 F4
Gordon's Sch. W End GU24 .... 67 E7
Gordondale Rd.
  Wimble SW18 & SW19 .... 20 A6
Gordons Way. Oxted RH8 .... 122 D7
Gore Rd. Merton SW20 .... 39 C7
Goring Rd. Egham TW18 .... 12 E3
Goring's Mead. Horsh RH13 ...... 217 D1
Gorling Cl. Crawl RH11 .... 200 E5
Gorrick Sq. Woki RG11 .... 25 B3
Gorringe Park Ave.
  Mitch CR4 & SW17 .... 21 A1
Gorringe Park Mid Sch.
  Mitch CR4 .... 41 A8
Gorringes Brook. Horsh RH12 ... 217 D6
Gorse Bank. Lhtwat GU18 .... 67 A8
Gorse Cl. Burgh H KT20 .... 97 B7
Gorse Cl. Copth RH10 .... 183 B2
Gorse Cl. Crawl RH11 .... 201 B1
Gorse Cl. Wreccl GU10 .... 146 B6
Gorse Cotts. Bramsh GU27 .... 207 C8
Gorse Ct. Merrow GU4 .... 110 C3
Gorse Dr. Smallf RH6 .... 162 C3
Gorse End. Horsh RH12 .... 217 D5
Gorse Hill La. Vir W GU25 .... 31 D5
Gorse Hill Rd. Vir W GU25 .... 31 D5
Gorse La. Burrh GU24 .... 49 E3
Gorse La. Wreccl GU10 .... 146 B6
Gorse Pl. Winkf RG12 .... 8 B1
Gorse Rd. Croy CR0 .... 63 A7
Gorse Rd. Friml GU16 .... 65 E2
Gorse Rise. Streat SW17 .... 21 A3
Gorselands. Heath E GU9 .... 125 C7
Gorselands Cl. Ash GU12 .... 106 A5
Gorselands Cl. Head Dn GU35 .. 187 C4
Gorselands Cl. W Byfl KT14 .... 71 C8
Gorsewood Rd. Knaph GU21 .... 88 E7
Gort Cl. Farnb GU11 .... 105 E2
Gosberton Rd. Balham SW12 ...... 21 A7
Gosbury Hill. Chess KT9 .... 56 E6
Gosden Cl. Crawl RH10 .... 202 A5
Gosden Cl. Shalf GU5 .... 151 F8
Gosden Hill Rd. Burph GU4 ...... 110 C5
Gosden House Sch. Shalf GU5 .. 151 E8
Gosden Rd. W End GU24 .... 67 F6
Gosfield Rd. Epsom KT19 .... 76 D7
Gosnell Cl. Friml GU16 .... 66 D3
Gosport House. 9
  Rhampt SW15 .... 19 A7
Gossops Dr. Crawl RH11 .... 201 A5
Gossops Green Cty Fst Sch.
  Crawl RH11 .... 201 A5
Gossops Green Cty Mid Sch.
  Crawl RH11 .... 201 A5

Gossops Green La. Crawl RH11 201 A5
Gossops Par. Crawl RH11 200 F5
Gostling Rd. Twick TW2 16 A7
Goston Gdns. Thorn H CR7 42 A6
Gothic Ct. Harl UB3 3 D8
Gothic Ct. Sandh GU17 64 B7
Gothic Rd. Twick TW2 16 D6
Goudhurst Cl. Worth RH10 202 E6
Goudhurst House. 10
Penge SE20 23 C1
Goudhurst Keep. Worth RH10 202 E6
Goudhurst Rd. Catf BR1 24 F3
Gough House. 4 King U T KT1 37 E7
Gough's La. Brack RG12 27 D8
Gough's Meadow. Sandh GU17 64 B7
Gould Ct. Dulw SE19 22 E3
Gould Ct. Merrow GU4 110 D3
Gould Rd. E Bed TW14 14 E8
Gould Rd. Twick TW2 16 E7
Government House Rd.
Farnb GU11 105 B7
Government Rd. Alder GU11 105 E4
Government Rd. Farnb GU11 105 E4
Governor's Rd. Sandh GU15 64 F6
Govett Ave. Shep TW17 34 C4
Govett Gr. Windl GU20 48 D5
Gower Pk. Sandh GU15 64 D7
Gower Rd. Horley RH6 160 E3
Gower Rd. Hounsl TW7 5 F8
Gower Rd. Whit V KT13 53 D4
Gower The. Egham TW20 32 C6
Gowland Pl. Beck BR3 43 F7
Graburn Way. E Mole KT8 36 D6
Grace Bennett Cl.
W Heath GU14 85 A7
Grace Bsns Ctr. Mitch CR4 40 F3
Grace House. Penge SE26 23 B3
Grace Path. For Hil SE26 23 C4
Grace Rd. Crawl RH11 201 A1
Grace Rd. Thorn H CR0 42 C3
Grace Reynolds Wlk. 4
Camb GU15 65 C6
Gracedale Rd.
Streat SW16 & SW17 21 B3
Gracefield Gdns. Streat SW16 21 E5
Gracious Pond Rd. Burrh GU24 50 B4
Gradient The. For Hil SE26 23 A4
Graemesdyke Ave. Mortl SW14 7 B3
Graffham Cl. Crawl RH11 201 B8
Grafton Cl. Twick TW4 15 F7
Grafton Cl. W Byfl KT14 70 F6
Grafton Cl. Worc Pk KT4 57 E7
Grafton Ct. E Bed TW14 14 D7
Grafton Park Rd. Worc Pk KT4 57 E8
Grafton Rd. King U T KT3 38 E6
Grafton Rd. Thorn H CR0 42 A1
Grafton Rd. Worc Pk KT19 & KT4 57 E7
Grafton Way. E Mole KT8 35 F5
Graham Ave. Mitch CR4 41 A8
Graham Cl. Croy CR0 63 A8
Graham Gdns. Surb KT6 37 E1
Graham House. 5 Balham SW12 21 B8
Graham House. L Book KT23 94 A3
Graham House. Redh RH1 118 E3
Graham Rd. Hampt TW12 16 A4
Graham Rd. Merton SW19 19 F1
Graham Rd. Mitch CR4 41 A8
Graham Rd. Purley CR8 80 A6
Graham Rd. Windl GU20 48 C4
Grainford Ct. Woki RG11 25 C5
Grainger Rd. Islew TW7 5 F5
Grampian Cl. Harl UB3 3 D7
Grampian Rd. Sandh GU17 45 A2
Granada St. Up Toot SW17 20 F3
Granard Rd.
Balham SW11 & SW12 20 F8
Granary Cl. Horley RH6 161 A5
Granary Way. Horsh RH12 217 A1
Grand Ave. Camb GU15 65 C6
Grand Ave. Tolw KT5 38 B3
Grand Avenue Prim Sch.
Tolw KT5 38 C3
Grand Avenue Prim Sch
(Upper Sch). Tolw KT5 38 C3
Grand Dr.
W Barn KT3 & SM4 & SW20 39 C5
Grand Par. Crawl RH11 201 D6
Grand Par. Mortl SW14 7 C3
Grand Par. Tolw KT6 38 A1
Grand Stand Rd.
Epsom KT17 & KT18 77 A2
Grand View Ave. Bigg H TN16 83 C3
Granden Rd. Thorn H SW16 41 E7
Grandfield Ct. Chisw W4 7 D8
Grandis Cotts. Ripley GU23 91 B5
Grandison Rd. N Cheam KT4 58 C7
Grange Ave. Crowth RG11 45 B6
Grange Ave. S Norw SE25 42 E7
Grange Ave. Twick TW2 16 E6
Grange Cl. Ashtd KT22 95 D7
Grange Cl. Bletch RH1 120 D2
Grange Cl. Crawl RH10 202 A8
Grange Cl. E Mole KT8 36 B5
Grange Cl. Godal GU7 151 A5
Grange Cl. Heston TW5 4 F8
Grange Cl. Merst RH1 & RH2 119 B7
Grange Cl. Stough GU2 109 B5
Grange Cres. Crawl D RH10 204 B7
Grange Ct. Egham TW20 11 F3
Grange Ct. Hackb SM6 60 B7
Grange Ct. Merst RH2 119 B7
Grange Ct. S Godst RH9 142 E5
Grange Ct. Shep Gn TW17 34 A5
Grange Ct. Stain TW18 13 A3
Grange Ct. Sutton SM2 59 B3
Grange Ct. Walt O T KT12 54 A8
Grange Cty Inf Sch The.
Woodhm KT15 52 A1
Grange Dr. Horse GU21 69 E4
Grange Dr. Merst RH1 119 B7
Grange End. Smallf RH6 162 A3
Grange Farm Rd. Ash GU12 106 A3
Grange Gdns. Banstd SM7 78 B6
Grange Gdns. S Norw SE25 42 E7
Grange Hill. S Norw SE25 42 E7
Grange La. Dulw SE21 22 F6
Grange Lodge. Wimble SW19 19 D2
Grange Mansions. Ewell KT17 57 F3
Grange Meadow. Banstd SM7 78 B6
Grange Mills. Streat SW12 21 C7
Grange Park Pl. Wimble SW20 19 B1
Grange Park Rd. S Norw CR7 42 D6
Grange Pk. Cran GU6 174 F3
Grange Pk. Horse GU21 69 F5
Grange Pl. Laleh TW18 33 C7
Grange Rd. Ash GU12 106 B1
Grange Rd. Ashtd KT21 & KT22 95 D7
Grange Rd. Belm SM2 59 A3
Grange Rd. Brack RG12 27 C8
Grange Rd. Camb GU15 65 E5
Grange Rd. Cater CR3 101 A2
Grange Rd. Chess KT9 56 E6
Grange Rd. Crawl D RH10 204 A7
Grange Rd. E Mole KT8 36 B5
Grange Rd. Egham TW20 11 F3
Grange Rd. Farnb GU14 85 B7
Grange Rd. Hersh KT12 54 E6
Grange Rd. Horse GU21 69 E5
Grange Rd. King U T KT1 37 E6
Grange Rd. Rushm GU10 168 C7
Grange Rd. S Croy CR2 61 C2
Grange Rd. S Norw SE19 & SE25 42 D7
Grange Rd. Stough GU2 & GU3 109 B5
Grange Rd. Sutton SM2 59 A3
Grange Rd. Tongh GU10 126 E6
Grange Rd. Woodhm KT15 52 B1
Grange Sch The. Alder GU11 126 B8
Grange The. Chobh GU24 49 E1
Grange The. Croy CR0 62 F8
Grange The. Frensh GU10 167 D7
Grange The. Horley RH6 161 A6
Grange The. New Mal KT3 39 A4
Grange The. Walt O T KT12 54 B8
Grange The. Wimble SW19 19 D2
Grange The. Worc Pk KT19 57 D6
Grange Vale. Sutton SM2 59 B3
Grangecliffe Gdns. S Norw SE25 42 E7
Grangefields Rd. Jacobs GU4 109 D6
Grangemill Rd. Catf SE6 24 A6
Grangemill Way. Catf SE6 24 A6
Grangemount. Ashtd KT22 95 D7
Grangeway. Smallf RH6 162 A3
Grangewood La. Beck BR3 23 F2
Gransden Cl. Ewh GU6 175 E5
Granston Way. Crawl D RH10 204 C8
Grant Cl. Shep TW17 34 B3
Grant Pl. 2 Croy CR0 42 F1
Grant Rd. Crowth RG11 45 C4
Grant Rd. Croy CR0 42 F1
Grant Way. Brent TW7 & TW8 6 A8
Grant Wlk. Sunnin SL5 29 E1
Grantchester. 3 King U T KT1 38 A7
Grantham Cl. Sandh GU15 45 E1
Grantham House. Charlt TW16 14 E1
Grantham Rd. Chisw W4 7 E7
Grantley Ave. Woner GU5 152 B6
Grantley Cl. Shalf GU4 130 E2
Grantley House. Putney SW19 19 D7
Grantley Rd. Cranf TW4 & TW5 4 C5
Grantley Rd. Stough GU2 109 A2
Granton Rd. Streat SW16 41 C8
Grants Cotts. Esher KT10 55 D8
Grants La. Limps RH7 & RH8 144 C6
Grantwood Cl. Earls RH1 140 B4
Granville Ave. Felt TW13 15 A6
Granville Ave. Hounsl TW3 & TW4 5 A2
Granville Cl. Byfl KT14 71 F6
Granville Cl. S Croy CR0 61 E8
Granville Cl. Whit V KT13 53 C4
Granville Gdns. S Norw SW16 21 F1
Granville Rd. Limps RH8 123 A7
Granville Rd. Merton SW19 20 A1
Granville Rd. Wands SW18 19 F8
Granville Rd. Westfd GU22 89 F7
Granville Rd. Whit V KT13 53 C4
Granwood Ct. 5 Hounsl TW7 5 E6
Grasmere Ave. King U T SW15 18 E4
Grasmere Ave. Merton SW19 40 A6
Grasmere Ave. Twick TW3 5 B1
Grasmere Cl. E Bed TW14 14 F7
Grasmere Cl. Merrow GU1 110 B2
Grasmere Cl. Thor L TW20 12 B1
Grasmere Ct. For Hil SE26 23 A3
Grasmere Gdns. Horsh RH12 218 B6
Grasmere Rd. Broml BR1 24 F1
Grasmere Rd. Croy SE25 43 B4
Grasmere Rd. Farnb GU14 84 E4
Grasmere Rd. Hale GU9 125 A6
Grasmere Rd. Lhtwat GU18 48 B1
Grasmere Rd. Purley CR8 80 B8
Grasmere Rd. Streat SW16 21 F3
Grasmere Way. Byfl KT14 71 F7
Grassfield Cl. Coulsd CR5 99 C8
Grasslands. Smallf RH6 162 A3
Grassmere. Horley RH6 161 C4
Grassmount. For Hil SE23 23 B6
Grassmount. Wallin CR8 60 C1
Grassway. Wallin SM6 60 C6
Grately House. 10
Rhampt SW15 19 B7
Grattons Dr. Crawl RH10 182 C1
Grattons The. Slinfd RH13 215 E3
Gravel Hill. Leahd KT22 95 B6
Gravel Hill. S Croy CR0 & CR2 62 E4
Gravel Hill Rd. Binst GU10 145 A3
Gravel Pits. Gomsh GU5 133 C4
Gravel Pits La. Gomsh GU5 133 C4
Gravel Rd. Farnb GU14 105 D8
Gravel Rd. Hale GU9 125 B7
Gravel Rd. Twick TW2 16 E7
Graveley. 7 King U T KT1 38 A7
Gravelly Hill. Cater RH1 & RH9 120 F7
Gravenel Gdns. Up Toot SW17 20 E3
Graveney Gr. Penge SE20 23 C1
Graveney Rd. Up Toot SW17 20 E4
Graveney Rd. Worth RH10 202 C5
Graveney Sch. Streat SW17 21 B3
Gravetts La. Worpl GU3 108 E5
Gravetye Cl. Crawl RH10 202 A4
Gray Ct. 8 King U T KT2 17 D4
Gray's La. Ashtd KT21 95 F8
Grayham Cres. New Mal KT3 38 D5
Grayham Rd. New Mal KT3 38 D5
Graylands. Horse GU21 69 E3
Graylands Cl. Horse GU21 69 E3
Graylands Ct. Guild GU1 130 F8
Grays Cl. Haslem GU27 208 E8
Grays La. Ashf TW15 14 B4
Grays Rd. Farnc GU7 150 F7
Grays Wood. Horley RH6 161 C3
Grayscroft Rd. Streat SW16 21 D1
Grayshot Dr. Blckw GU17 64 C5
Grayshott Prim Sch.
Graysh GU26 188 D3
Grayshott Rd.
Head Dn GU26 & GU35 187 C5
Grayswood CE (VA) Fst Sch.
Grays GU27 189 F2
Grayswood Dr. Mytch GU16 86 A2
Grayswood Gdns. W Barn SW20 39 B7
Grayswood Pl. Haslem GU27 208 E8
Grayswood Point. 14
Rhampt SW15 19 A7
Grayswood Rd. Grays GU27 189 F1
Grayswood Rd. Haslem GU27 189 F1
Grazely Ct. W Norw SE19 22 E3
Great Austins. M Bourn GU9 146 D8
Great Bookham Cty Inf Sch.
G Book KT23 94 A1
Great Bookham Cty Mid Sch.
G Book KT23 94 A1
Great Brownings. Dulw SE21 22 F4
Great Chertsey Rd.
Chisw SW14 & W4 7 D6
Great Chertsey Rd.
Felt TW13 & TW2 16 A5
Great Elshams. Banstd SM7 78 A3
Great George St. Godal GU7 150 E4
Great Goodwin Dr.
Merrow GU1 110 B3
Great Hollands Cty Inf Sch.
Easth RG12 26 F4
Great Hollands Cty Jun Sch.
Easth RG12 26 E4
Great Hollands Rd. Easth RG12 26 F3
Great Hollands Sq. Easth RG12 26 F3
Great House Ct. 4
E Grins RH19 205 F8
Great Oaks Pk. Burph GU4 110 C5
Great Quarry. Guild GU1 130 D6
Great South-West Rd.
E Bed TW14 & TW6 3 D2
Great South-West Rd.
Felt TW6 & TW14 3 D2
Great South-West Rd.
Hatton TW4 & TW14 3 D2
Great South-West Rd.
Hounsl TW5 4 B4
Great Tattenhams. Burgh H KT18 77 C1
Great West Rd. Brent TW8 6 B8
Great West Rd. Cranf TW5 4 F6
Great West Rd. Heston TW5 4 F6
Great West Rd.
Hounsl TW5 & TW7 5 C6
Great West Road Cedars Rd.
Chisw W4 7 C8
Great West Road Chiswick.
Chisw W4 7 F8
Great West Road Ellesmere Rd.
Chisw W4 7 D8
Great West Road Hogarth La.
Chisw W4 7 E8
Great West Trad Est. Brent TW8 6 B8
Great Woodcote Dr. Wallin CR8 60 D1
Great Woodcote Pk.
Wallin CR8 & SM6 60 E1
Greatfield Cl. Farnb GU14 85 B8
Greatfield Rd. Farnb GU14 85 B8
Greatford Dr. Merrow GU1 110 D1
Greatham Wlk. 8 Rhampt SW15 19 A7
Greathurst End. L Book KT23 93 F3
Greatlake Ct. Horley RH6 161 B4
Greatstone House. 13
Penge SE20 23 C1
Greatwood Cl. Ottsh KT16 51 C2
Greaves Pl. Up Toot SW17 20 E4
Grebe Cres. Horsh RH13 218 A1
Grebe Terr. 4 King U T KT1 37 E6
Grecian Cres.
S Norw SE19 & SW16 22 B2
Green Acre. Alder GU11 104 F1
Green Acres. S Croy CR0 61 F7
Green Bsns Ctr The.
Egham TW20 12 C4
Green Cl. Beck BR2 44 E6
Green Cl. Carsh SM5 59 F8
Green Cl. Felt TW13 15 E3
Green Court Ave. Croy CR0 62 B8
Green Court Gdns. Croy CR0 62 B8
Green Croft. Woki RG11 25 E8
Green Croft Sch. Farnb GU14 85 D6
Green Cross La. Churt GU10 168 A1
Green Ct. Ashf TW16 14 F2
Green Curve. Nork SM7 77 F4
Green Dene. E Hors KT24 112 E3
Green Dene. W Hors KT24 112 E3
Green Dr. Send M GU23 90 F4
Green Dr. Woki RG11 25 E4
Green Dragon Jun & Inf Sch.
Brent TW8 6 E8
Green End. Chess KT9 56 E6
Green Farm Rd. Bagsh GU19 47 F3
Green Finch Cl. Crowth RG11 45 A6
Green Hedges. 8 Twick TW1 6 C1
Green Hedges Ave.
E Grins RH19 185 D2
Green Hedges Cl. E Grins RH19 185 D2
Green Hill. Downe BR6 83 F7
Green Hill Cl. Friml GU15 66 C6
Green Hill Rd. Friml GU15 66 C6
Green House The. 5
Putney SW19 19 E7
Green La. Addl KT15 & KT16 51 E7
Green La. Alf Cr GU6 193 F4
Green La. Ascot SL5 29 E8
Green La. Ashf TW16 14 F2
Green La. Ashtd KT21 75 D1
Green La. Ashtd KT22 95 D6
Green La. Bagsh GU19 47 F2
Green La. Blckw GU17 64 B4
Green La. Burst RH6 182 F6
Green La. Byfl KT14 71 F7
Green La. Cater CR3 100 C5
Green La. Cheam SM4 40 B3
Green La. Chert KT15 & KT16 51 E7
Green La. Chess KT9 56 E3
Green La. Chobh GU24 49 F1
Green La. Churt GU10 168 A1
Green La. Cobham KT11 73 E7
Green La. Copth RH10 183 F4
Green La. Crawl RH10 201 E8
Green La. Cudw RH5 179 D8
Green La. Docken GU10 166 E6
Green La. E Mole KT8 36 B4
Green La. Earls RH1 140 A4
Green La. Egham TW20 12 B3
Green La. Egham TW18 32 E8
Green La. Farnc GU7 & GU3 150 E8
Green La. Farnh GU9 125 F5
Green La. Faygt RH12 198 F4
Green La. Felt TW13 15 E3
Green La. Fern GU27 208 B4
Green La. Hawley GU17 64 E4
Green La. Heath E GU9 125 F5
Green La. Hersh KT12 54 B5
Green La. Hounsl TW4 4 C3
Green La. L Kings KT20 97 F1
Green La. Leahd KT22 95 D6
Green La. Leigh RH2 158 E8
Green La. Lingf RH7 164 C4
Green La. M Bourn GU9 146 A7
Green La. Merrow GU1 110 B1
Green La. Milf GU8 170 E8
Green La. Morden SM4 40 B3
Green La. N Cheam KT4 39 A1
Green La. New Mal KT3 38 C4
Green La. Penge SE20 23 D1
Green La. Purley CR8 60 D1
Green La. Redh RH1 118 E3
Green La. Reig RH2 117 F1
Green La. S Norw CR7 & SW16 42 B8
Green La. S Nutf RH1 140 F1
Green La. Sandh GU17 64 C7
Green La. Sham Gn GU4 & GU5 153 A7
Green La. Shep TW17 34 C4
Green La. Streat SW16 21 F1
Green La. Tilf GU10 147 E6
Green La. W Clan GU4 111 B8
Green La. W Hors GU23 & KT24 92 B3
Green La. Wood S V GU3 108 A3
Green La. Worth RH10 202 D6
Green La E. Flexf GU3 128 B8
Green La W. Normdy GU12 127 E8
Green Lane Ave. Hersh KT12 54 C5
Green Lane Cl. Addl KT16 51 E8
Green Lane Cl. Byfl KT14 71 F7
Green Lane Cl. Camb GU15 65 C7
Green Lane Cotts. Churt GU10 167 F1
Green Lane Cty Inf Sch.
Farnc GU7 129 E1
Green Lane Gdns. S Norw CR7 42 C7
Green Lane Prim Sch.
N Cheam KT4 39 B2
Green Lanes. W Ewell KT19 57 E2
Green Lanes. W Ewell KT19 57 E2
Green Leaf Ave. Wallin SM6 60 D6
Green Leas. Ashf TW16 14 F2
Green Leas. King U T KT1 37 E6
Green Leas Cl. Ashf TW16 14 F2
Green Man La. Hatton TW14 4 A3
Green Mead. Esher KT10 54 F4
Green Pk. Stain TW18 12 E5
Green Rd. Egham KT16 & TW20 32 B5
Green Sch for Girls The.
Islew TW7 6 A6
Green St. Sunby TW16 35 A7
Green The. Broad H RH12 216 D4
Green The. Burgh H KT20 97 E8
Green The. Carsh SM6 60 A8
Green The. Clayg KT10 55 F4
Green The. Copth RH10 183 B3
Green The. Crawl RH11 201 C7
Green The. Easth RG12 27 B5
Green The. Ewell KT17 77 A7
Green The. Ewh GU6 175 E4
Green The. Farnh GU9 126 A6
Green The. Felt TW13 15 B6
Green The. Fetch KT22 94 D3
Green The. Friml GU16 85 F6
Green The. Hale GU9 125 C6
Green The. Heston TW5 5 A8
Green The. King U T KT3 38 C7
Green The. Merton SM4 39 E5
Green The. New Add CR0 62 F2
Green The. 7 Rich TW9 6 D2
Green The. Stain TW18 13 D3
Green The. Sutton SM1 59 B7
Green The. The San GU10 126 E1
Green The. Twick TW2 16 E6
Green The. Tyl Gn RH9 121 C4
Green The. Warlgm CR6 81 D1
Green The. Whit V KT12 53 E1
Green The. Wimble SW19 19 D3
Green The. Wold CR3 102 A4
Green View. Chess KT9 56 F3
Green View. Godst RH9 121 B4
Green Way. Alder GU12 105 E3
Green Way. Redh RH1 118 E3
Green Way. Sunby TW16 35 A5
Green Wlk. Crawl RH10 201 E8
Green Wlk. Hampt TW12 15 F2
Green Wood. N Asct SL5 28 C8
Green Wrythe Cres. Carsh SM5 40 E1
Green Wrythe La.
Carsh SM4 & SM5 40 E2
Green Wrythe Prim Sch.
Carsh SM5 40 D3
Green's School La. Farnb GU14 85 A4
Greenacre. Knaph GU21 68 E3
Greenacre. Whytlf CR3 101 B7
Greenacre Ct. Eng Gn TW20 11 C2
Greenacre Sch for Girls.
Banstd SM7 78 B6
Greenacres. Crawl RH10 202 A5
Greenacres. Farnh GU10 126 C2
Greenacres. Fetch KT23 94 A3
Greenacres. Horsh RH12 217 C4
Greenacres. Oxted RH8 122 E8
Greenaway Terr. Stan TW19 13 E7
Greenbank Way. Friml GU16 65 D2
Greenbush La. Cran GU6 174 F1
Greencroft. 2 Farnb GU14 85 B4
Greencroft. Merrow GU1 110 B1
Greencroft Rd. Heston TW5 4 F6
Greene Fielde End. Stain TW18 13 D1
Greenfield Ave. Tolw KT5 38 B3
Greenfield House. 28
Putney SW19 19 D7
Greenfield Link. Coulsd CR5 79 E4
Greenfield Rd.
M Bourn GU9 & GU10 146 A7
Greenfield Rd. Slinfd RH13 215 D3
Greenfield Rd. Wreccl GU9 145 F7
Greenfield Sch. Woking GU22 89 E8
Greenfield Way. Crowth RG11 45 A7
Greenfields Cl. Horley RH6 160 E5
Greenfields Cl. Horsh RH12 218 A6
Greenfields Rd. Horley RH6 160 F5
Greenfields Rd. Horsh RH12 218 A5
Greenfields Sch.
For Row RH18 206 C1
Greenfields Way. Horsh RH12 218 A6
Greenfinch Way. Horsh RH12 217 D7
Greenford Rd. Sutton SM1 59 B6
Greenham House. Hounsl TW7 5 D4
Greenham Wlk. Woking GU21 69 C1
Greenham Wood. Easth RG12 27 C3
Greenhanger. Churt GU10 188 A8
Greenhayes Ave. Banstd SM7 78 A4
Greenhayes Cl. Reig RH2 118 C1
Greenhayes Gdns. Banstd SM7 78 A4
Greenhayes Sch. W Wick BR4 63 C8
Greenheys Pl. Woking GU22 69 F1
Greenhill. Sutton SM1 59 C8
Greenhill Ave. Cater CR3 101 B6
Greenhill Cl. Godal GU7 150 D3
Greenhill Cl. Wreccl GU9 146 A7
Greenhill Gdns. Merrow GU4 110 C3
Greenhill La. Warlgm CR6 81 F2
Greenhill Rd. M Bourn GU9 146 D8
Greenhill Way. M Bourn GU9 146 A7
Greenhill Way. Wreccl GU9 146 A7
Greenhills. M Bourn GU9 146 E8
Greenholme. Friml GU15 66 D5
Greenhow. Easth RG12 27 A6
Greenhurst La. Oxted RH8 123 A3
Greenhurst Rd. W Norw SE27 22 A3
Greenlake Terr. Stain TW18 13 A1
Greenlands Rd. Camb GU15 65 B1
Greenlands Rd. Stain TW18 13 A4
Greenlands Rd. Weyb KT13 53 C7
Greenlaw Gdns. New Mal KT3 38 F2
Greenlea Pk. Mitch SW19 40 E8
Greenleaf Cl. 8 Streat SW2 22 A8
Greenleas. Friml GU16 65 E2
Greenleaves Ct. Ashf TW15 14 B2
Greenmeads. Westfd GU22 89 E5
Greeno Cres. Shep Gn TW17 34 A4
Greenoak Rise. Bigg H TN16 83 C1
Greenoak Way. Wimble SW19 19 D4
Greenock Rd. Streat SW16 41 D8
Greensand Rd. Earls RH1 119 A2
Greenside Cl. Catf SE6 24 D6
Greenside Cl. Merrow GU4 110 C3
Greenside Cotts. Ripley GU23 91 C6
Greenside Rd. Thorn H CR0 42 A2
Greenside Wlk. Bigg H TN16 83 B1
Greensleeves Manor.
Sutton SM2 59 B4
Greenstede Ave. E Grins RH19 185 F2
Greenvale Prim Sch. Selsd CR2 81 D8
Greenvale Rd. Knaph GU21 68 D1
Greenvale Spec Sch.
For Hil SE23 23 E5
Greenview Ave. Beck CR0 43 E3
Greenview Ct. Ashf TW15 13 F4
Greenway. Fetch KT23 94 B4
Greenway. Horsh RH12 217 B3
Greenway. Tats TN16 103 C7
Greenway. W Barn SW20 39 C5
Greenway. Wallin SM6 60 C6
Greenway Cl. W Byfl KT14 71 A6
Greenway Cty Prim Sch.
Horsh RH12 217 B3
Greenway Dr. Stain TW18 33 D8
Greenway Gdns. Croy CR0 62 F7
Greenway The. Epsom KT18 76 A5
Greenway The. Hounsl TW4 4 F3
Greenway The. Oxted RH8 123 B2
Greenways. Beck BR3 44 A7
Greenways. Egham TW20 11 E3
Greenways. For Hil SE26 23 C4

Greenways. Hinch W KT10 ... 55 E6
Greenways. Sandh GU17 ... 45 B1
Greenways. Walt o t H KT20 ... 97 B2
Greenways Dr. Sunnin SL5 ... 29 E1
Greenways The. 1 Twick TW1 ... 6 A1
Greenways Wlk. Crawl RH11 ... 201 C1
Greenwich Cl. Crawl RH11 ... 201 C2
Greenwood. 4 Brack RG12 ... 27 F5
Greenwood. 8 Putney SW19 ... 19 D8
Greenwood Cl. Hinch W KT7 ... 37 A1
Greenwood Cl. Merton SM4 ... 39 E5
Greenwood Cl. Woodhm KT15 ... 70 F8
Greenwood Ct. 2 Crawl RH11 . 201 B1
Greenwood Dr. Earls RH1 ... 140 A4
Greenwood Gdns. Cater CR3 ... 101 A2
Greenwood La. Hampt TW12 ... 16 B3
Greenwood Pk. King U T KT2 ... 18 E1
Greenwood Prim Sch.
Mitch CR4 ... 41 D6
Greenwood Rd. Crowth RG11 ... 45 B6
Greenwood Rd. Hinch W KT7 ... 56 A8
Greenwood Rd. Islew TW7 ... 5 F4
Greenwood Rd. Knaph GU21 ... 88 E7
Greenwood Rd. Mitch CR4 ... 41 D6
Greenwood Rd. Pirb GU24 ... 87 C7
Greenwood Rd.
Thorn H CR0 & CR9 ... 42 C2
Greenwood The. Guild GU1 ... 110 A1
Gregan Ct. Alder GU11 ... 104 F1
Gregory Cl. Worth RH10 ... 202 C2
Gregory Ct. Purley CR8 ... 80 B6
Gregsons. Warn RH12 ... 216 E8
Grena Gdns. Rich TW9 ... 6 F3
Grena Rd. Rich TW10 & TW9 ... 6 F3
Grenaby Ave. Croy CR0 ... 42 D2
Grenaby Rd. Croy CR0 ... 42 D2
Grenadier Rd. Ash GU12 ... 106 B4
Grenadiers Way. Farnb GU14 ... 84 C3
Grendon Cl. Horley RH6 ... 160 F5
Grenehurst Pk. Capel RH5 ... 178 B4
Grenfell Rd. Mitch CR4 & SW17 ... 20 F2
Grennell Cl. Sutton SM1 ... 59 D8
Grennell Rd. Sutton SM1 ... 59 C8
Grenside Rd. Weyb KT13 ... 53 B7
Grenville Cl. Cobham KT11 ... 73 E6
Grenville Cl. Tolw KT5 ... 38 C1
Grenville Ct. Dulw SE19 ... 22 F3
Grenville Gdns. Friml GU16 ... 85 E6
Grenville Mews. Hampt TW12 ... 16 B3
Grenville Rd. New Add CR0 ... 63 C2
Grenville Rd. Shackl GU8 ... 149 D7
Gresham Ave. Warlgm CR6 ... 81 E1
Gresham Cl. Limps RH8 ... 122 F7
Gresham Ct. Farnb GU14 ... 105 C8
Gresham Ct. Hounsl TW3 ... 5 C6
Gresham Ct. Stain TW18 ... 13 A3
Gresham House. 2 Tedd TW11 16 F3
Gresham House. 3
Thame D KT7 ... 37 A2
Gresham Ind Est. Alder GU12 ... 105 E2
Gresham Prim Sch. Sander CR2 81 A8
Gresham Rd. Croy SE25 ... 43 A5
Gresham Rd. Hampt TW12 ... 16 A2
Gresham Rd. Hounsl TW3 & TW5 ... 5 C6
Gresham Rd. Limps RH8 ... 122 F6
Gresham Rd. Penge BR3 ... 43 E7
Gresham Rd. Stain TW18 ... 13 A3
Gresham Way. Friml GU16 ... 85 E6
Gresham Way. Wimble SW19 ... 20 A5
Gresham Way Est. Wimble SW19 20 B5
Gresham Wlk. Crawl RH10 ... 201 E3
Gressenhall Rd. Wands SW18 ... 19 F8
Greta Bank. W Hors KT24 ... 92 C1
Greville Ave. Selsd CR2 ... 62 D1
Greville Cl. Ashtd KT21 ... 95 E8
Greville Cl. Stough GU2 ... 108 E1
Greville Cl. Twick TW1 ... 17 B8
Greville Ct. Ashtd KT21 ... 75 E1
Greville Ct. Fetch KT23 ... 94 C2
Greville Cty Prim Sch The.
Ashtd KT21 ... 75 F2
Greville Park Ave. Ashtd KT21 ... 75 E1
Greville Park Rd. Ashtd KT21 ... 75 E1
Greville Rd. Rich TW10 ... 6 F1
Grey Alders. Nork KT17 ... 77 C5
Grey Court Sch. Rich TW10 ... 17 C5
Greycot Rd. Beck BR3 ... 24 A3
Greyfields Cl. Purley CR8 ... 80 B6
Greyfriars. 16 For Hil SE26 ... 23 A5
Greyfriars Dr. Ascot SL5 ... 29 B3
Greyfriars Dr. Bisley GU24 ... 68 A4
Greyfriars Rd. Send M GU23 ... 91 A3
Greyhound Cl. Ash GU12 ... 105 F1
Greyhound La. Streat SW16 ... 21 D2
Greyhound Rd. Sutton SM1 ... 59 C5
Greyhound Slip. Crawl RH10 ... 202 D7
Greyhound Terr. Mitch SW16 ... 41 C8
Greylees. Farnc GU7 ... 150 E5
Greys Ct. Alder GU11 ... 104 E2
Greystead Pk. Wreccl GU10 ... 145 E5
Greystead Rd. For Hil SE23 ... 23 C8
Greystoke Ct. Crowth RG11 ... 45 A4
Greystone Cl. Selsd CR2 ... 81 C8
Greystone Sch. Merst RH1 ... 119 E6
Greystones Cl.
Woodh RH1 & RH2 ... 139 D7
Greystones Dr. Reig RH2 ... 118 C3
Greyswood St. Streat SW16 ... 21 B2
Greythorne Rd. Woking GU21 ... 69 A1
Greywaters. Bramly GU5 ... 152 A6
Grice Ave. Bigg H TN16 ... 83 C6
Grier Cl. Crawl RH11 ... 200 E5
Grierson House. Streat SW16 ... 21 C4
Grierson Rd. For Hil SE23 ... 23 D8
Grieve Cl. Tongh GU10 ... 126 E7
Griffin Ct. Ashtd KT21 ... 95 E8
Griffin Ct. 8 Brent TW8 ... 6 E8
Griffin Ct. G Book KT23 ... 94 B1
Griffin Ctr. King U T KT1 ... 37 D7
Griffin Ctr The. Felt TW14 ... 4 B1
Griffin Pk (Brentford FC).
Brent TW8 ... 6 D8
Griffin Way. G Book KT23 ... 94 A1
Griffin Way. Sunby TW16 ... 35 A7
Griffiths Cl. N Cheam KT4 ... 58 B8
Griffiths Rd. Merton SW19 ... 20 B1
Griffon Cl. Farnb GU14 ... 84 D3
Griggs Meadow. Dunsf GU8 ... 192 F7
Grimwade Ave. S Croy CR0 ... 62 A7
Grimwood Rd. Twick TW1 ... 16 F8
Grindall Cl. Croy CR0 ... 61 B6
Grindley Gdns. Croy CR0 ... 42 F3
Grindstone Cres. Knaph GU21 ... 68 B1
Grindstone Handle Cnr.
Knaph GU21 ... 68 C1
Grinstead La. E Grins RH19 ... 205 B1
Grisedale Cl. Crawl RH11 ... 201 C4
Grisedale Cl. Sander CR8 ... 80 E5
Grisedale Gdns. Sander CR8 ... 80 E5
Grizedale Terr. For Hil SE23 ... 23 B6
Grobars Ave. Horse GU21 ... 69 C4
Groom Cres. Wands SW18 ... 20 D8
Groombridge Cl. Hersh KT12 ... 54 B5
Groombridge House.
Penge SE20 ... 23 D1
Groombridge Way.
Horsh RH12 ... 216 F1
Groomfield Cl. Up Toot SW17 ... 21 A4
Grooms The. Crawl RH10 ... 202 D8
Grosslea. Morden SM4 ... 40 D4
Grosvenor Ave. Mortl SW14 ... 7 E4
Grosvenor Ave. Rich TW10 ... 6 E2
Grosvenor Ave.
Wallin SM5 & SM6 ... 60 A4
Grosvenor Ct. Burph GU4 ... 110 B4
Grosvenor Ct. Hawley GU17 ... 64 D3
Grosvenor Ct. Morden SM4 ... 40 A5
Grosvenor Ct. Penge SE19 ... 22 F2
Grosvenor Ct. 2 Rich TW10 ... 6 F1
Grosvenor Ct. 1 Sutton SM2 ... 59 C4
Grosvenor Ct. Tedd TW11 ... 17 A2
Grosvenor Ct. Wimble SW19 ... 19 E2
Grosvenor Gdns. King U T KT2 ... 17 D2
Grosvenor Gdns. Mortl SW14 ... 7 E4
Grosvenor Gdns. Wallin SM6 ... 60 C3
Grosvenor Hill. Wimble SW19 ... 19 E2
Grosvenor Pl. 1 Oat Pk KT13 ... 53 D7
Grosvenor Rd. Alder GU11 ... 105 A1
Grosvenor Rd. Brent TW8 ... 6 D8
Grosvenor Rd. Croy SE25 ... 43 A5
Grosvenor Rd. E Grins RH19 ... 185 D1
Grosvenor Rd. Godal GU7 ... 150 E3
Grosvenor Rd. Hounsl TW3 & TW4 4 F4
Grosvenor Rd.
Lang V KT18 & KT21 ... 96 E8
Grosvenor Rd. Rich TW10 ... 6 E2
Grosvenor Rd. Stain TW18 ... 13 A1
Grosvenor Rd. Twick TW1 ... 17 A7
Grosvenor Rd. W End GU24 ... 68 D6
Grosvenor Rd. W Wick BR4 ... 63 B8
Grosvenor Rd. Wallin SM6 ... 60 B5
Groton Rd. Wands SW18 ... 20 B6
Grotto Rd. Twick TW1 ... 16 F6
Grotto Rd. Weyb KT13 ... 53 B7
Grove Ave. Epsom KT17 ... 76 E6
Grove Ave. Sutton SM1 & SM2 ... 59 A4
Grove Ave. Twick TW1 ... 16 F7
Grove Cl. Cran GU6 ... 174 F1
Grove Cl. For Hil SE23 ... 23 E7
Grove Cl. 8 King U T KT1 ... 37 F5
Grove Cl. Old W SL4 ... 11 B8
Grove Cnr. G Book KT23 ... 94 B1
Grove Cres. Felt TW13 ... 15 E4
Grove Cres. King U T KT1 ... 37 E6
Grove Cres. Walt O T KT12 ... 35 B2
Grove Cross Rd. Friml GU16 ... 65 D1
Grove Ct. E Mole KT8 ... 36 D4
Grove Ct. Egham TW20 ... 12 A3
Grove Ct. For Hil SE26 ... 23 E4
Grove Ct. Hounsl TW3 ... 5 B4
Grove Ct. 8 King U T KT1 ... 37 E6
Grove Ct. King U T KT3 ... 38 E6
Grove Ct. Penge SE20 ... 23 B1
Grove Cty Prim Sch The.
Friml GU16 ... 65 E2
Grove End. Windl GU19 ... 47 F5
Grove End La. Thame D KT10 ... 36 D1
Grove End Rd. M Bourn GU9 ... 146 B8
Grove Farm Ct. Mitch CR4 ... 40 F4
Grove Gdns. Tedd TW11 ... 17 A4
Grove Heath La. Ripley GU23 ... 91 D4
Grove Heath N. Ripley GU23 ... 91 B5
Grove Heath Rd. Ripley GU23 ... 91 B4
Grove House. 7 Epsom KT17 ... 76 E6
Grove House. Old W SL4 ... 11 C8
Grove House. 5 Redh RH1 ... 118 F1
Grove House. Walt O T KT12 ... 35 B2
Grove House Froebel Ed Inst.
Rhampt SW15 ... 7 F1
Grove House Prim Sch.
W Norw SE27 ... 22 B6
Grove Jun & Inf Sch. Chisw W4 ... 7 C8
Grove La. King U T KT1 ... 37 E5
Grove La. Wallin CR5 ... 79 B5
Grove La. Wink RG12 ... 8 B4
Grove Park Bridge. Chisw W4 ... 7 C7
Grove Park Gdns. Chisw W4 ... 7 C7
Grove Park Rd. Chisw W4 ... 7 B7
Grove Park Terr. Chisw W4 ... 7 B8
Grove Pl. Weyb KT13 ... 53 C5
Grove Rd. Ash GU12 ... 106 A3
Grove Rd. Ashtd KT21 ... 95 F8
Grove Rd. Barnes SW13 ... 7 F5
Grove Rd. Beac H GU26 ... 188 C6
Grove Rd. Camb GU15 ... 65 F5
Grove Rd. Cheam SM2 ... 59 A4
Grove Rd. Chert KT16 ... 32 F3
Grove Rd. Cran GU6 ... 174 F1
Grove Rd. E Mole KT8 ... 36 D5
Grove Rd. Epsom KT17 & KT18 ... 76 E6
Grove Rd. Godal GU7 ... 150 C3
Grove Rd. Horley RH6 ... 160 F4
Grove Rd. Hounsl TW3 ... 5 A3
Grove Rd. Hounsl TW7 ... 5 E6
Grove Rd. King U T KT6 ... 37 D4
Grove Rd. Lingf RH7 ... 164 E5
Grove Rd. Merrow GU1 ... 110 C1
Grove Rd. Merton SW19 ... 20 C1
Grove Rd. Mitch CR4 ... 41 B7
Grove Rd. Rich TW10 ... 6 F1
Grove Rd. 9 Rich TW10 ... 6 F2
Grove Rd. Shep TW17 ... 34 C3
Grove Rd. Sutton SM2 ... 59 A4
Grove Rd. Tats TN16 ... 103 C7
Grove Rd. Thorn H CR7 ... 42 A5
Grove Rd. Twick TW2 ... 16 D5
Grove Rd. Woking GU21 ... 69 F3
Grove Rd Prim Sch. Hounsl TW3 . 5 A3
Grove Sch The. Shottm GU26 ... 188 D1
Grove Shaw. Kings KT20 ... 97 E3
Grove Terr. Tedd TW11 ... 17 A4
Grove The. Addl KT15 ... 52 B5
Grove The. Alder GU11 ... 105 A1
Grove The. Bigg H TN16 ... 83 E1
Grove The. Cater CR3 ... 100 C6
Grove The. Coulsd CR5 ... 79 D5
Grove The. Crawl RH11 ... 201 C6
Grove The. Egham TW20 ... 12 A3
Grove The. Epsom KT17 ... 76 E6
Grove The. Farnb GU14 ... 85 D1
Grove The. Friml GU16 ... 65 D1
Grove The. Horley RH6 ... 161 B2
Grove The. Hounsl TW7 ... 5 E6
Grove The. N Asct SL5 ... 28 C8
Grove The. Tedd TW11 ... 17 A4
Grove The. 1 Twick TW1 ... 6 B1
Grove The. W Wick BR4 ... 63 C7
Grove The. Walt O T KT12 ... 35 B2
Grove The. Woking GU21 ... 69 F3
Grove Way. Thame D KT10 ... 36 C1
Grove Wood Hill. Coulsd CR5 ... 79 D5
Grovebarns. Stain TW18 ... 13 A2
Grovebell Ind Est. Wreccl GU9 . 145 F7
Grovefields Ave. Friml GU16 ... 65 D1
Grovehill Ct. Catf BR1 ... 24 F2
Grovehill Rd. Redh RH1 ... 118 F1
Groveland Ave. S Norw SW16 ... 21 F1
Groveland Rd. Beck BR3 ... 43 F6
Groveland Way. New Mal KT3 ... 38 D4
Grovelands. E Mole KT8 ... 36 A5
Grovelands. Horley RH6 ... 161 B2
Grovelands. King U T KT1 ... 37 D5
Grovelands. M Bourn GU10 ... 146 E7
Grovelands Rd. Purley CR8 ... 79 F7
Grovelands Sch. Walt O T KT12 . 35 B3
Groveley Rd. Ashf TW13 & TW16 14 F3
Groveside. G Book KT23 ... 114 A8
Groveside Cl. Carsh SM5 ... 59 E8
Groveside Cl. G Book KT23 ... 114 A8
Grovestile Waye. E Bed TW14 ... 14 D8
Grovewood. 9 Rich TW9 ... 7 A6
Grovewood Ct. 6 Hounsl TW7 ... 5 E6
Grub St. Limps RH8 ... 123 C6
Guardian Ct. Elst GU8 ... 148 C3
Guards Ct. Sunnin SL5 ... 30 B2
Guernsey Cl. Burph GU4 ... 110 A6
Guernsey Cl. Crawl RH11 ... 201 A2
Guernsey Cl. Heston TW5 ... 5 A7
Guernsey Farm Dr. Horse GU21 69 D4
Guernsey Gr. Streat SE24 ... 22 C8
Guildables La. Limps RH8 & TN8 144 E7
Guildcroft. Guild GU1 ... 110 A1
Guildersfield Rd. Streat SW16 ... 21 E1
Guildford Ave. Felt TW13 ... 15 A6
Guildford Business Park Rd.
Stough GU2 ... 109 B2
Guildford Cath. Guild GU2 ... 109 B1
Guildford Coll Markenfield House.
Guild GU1 ... 109 D1
Guildford Cty Sch. Guild GU2 ... 130 B7
Guildford & Godalming By-Pass Rd.
Compt GU3 ... 129 E6
Guildford & Godalming By-Pass Rd.
Onsl V GU2 ... 129 E6
Guildford & Godalming By-Pass Rd.
Shackl GU7 ... 149 F6
Guildford Golf Club.
Merrow GU1 ... 110 C1
Guildford High Sch for Girls.
Guild GU1 ... 109 E1
Guildford Ind Est. Stough GU2 . 109 A2
Guildford Lodge Dr.
E Hors KT24 ... 112 F6
Guildford Park Ave. Guild GU2 130 B8
Guildford Park Rd. Guild GU2 .. 130 C8
Guildford Rd. Abing H RH5 ... 134 C3
Guildford Rd. Addl KT16 ... 51 C5
Guildford Rd.
Alder GU11 & GU12 ... 126 D7
Guildford Rd. Ash GU12 & GU3 106 D3
Guildford Rd. Bagsh GU19 ... 47 E3
Guildford Rd. Bisley GU24 ... 67 F7
Guildford Rd. Broad H RH12 ... 216 B6
Guildford Rd. Buck Gn RH12 ... 214 C6
Guildford Rd. Chert KT16 ... 32 F1
Guildford Rd. Cran GU6 ... 174 B6
Guildford Rd. Farnc GU7 ... 151 B7
Guildford Rd.
Farnh GU10 & GU9 ... 125 F4
Guildford Rd. Farnh GU10 ... 126 B4
Guildford Rd. Fetch KT22 ... 94 F3
Guildford Rd. Friml GU16 ... 85 F6
Guildford Rd. G Book KT23 ... 94 A1
Guildford Rd. Horsh RH12 ... 217 A2
Guildford Rd.
Lhtwat GU18 & GU19 ... 48 B1
Guildford Rd. Mytch GU16 ... 86 B5
Guildford Rd. Normdy GU3 ... 107 B4
Guildford Rd. Ottsh KT16 ... 51 C5
Guildford Rd. Pirb GU3 ... 88 C2
Guildford Rd. Rowhk RH12 ... 215 C7
Guildford Rd. Rowly GU6 ... 174 B6
Guildford Rd. Rudg RH12 ... 214 C6
Guildford Rd. Sham Gn GU5 ... 153 A1
Guildford Rd. Slinfd RH12 ... 215 C7
Guildford Rd. Thorn H CR0 ... 42 D3
Guildford Rd. W End GU24 ... 67 F7
Guildford Rd.
W End GU21 & GU24 ... 68 D6
Guildford Rd. Westc RH4 ... 135 C6
Guildford Rd.
Westfd GU22 & GU4 ... 89 D4
Guildford Rd. Windl GU19 ... 47 F2
Guildford Rd.
Woking GU22 & GU4 ... 89 E8
Guildford Rd. Wotton RH5 ... 134 C3
Guildford Rd E. Farnb GU14 ... 85 C1
Guildford Rd W. Farnb GU14 ... 85 C1
Guildford Road Trad Est.
Farnh GU9 ... 125 D3
Guildford Sch of Acting.
Guild GU2 ... 130 D7
Guildford St. Chert KT16 ... 33 A2
Guildford St. Stain TW18 ... 13 A2
Guildford Sta. Guild GU1 ... 130 C8
Guildford Way. Wallin SM6 ... 60 E5
Guildown Ave. Guild GU2 ... 130 B6
Guildown Rd. Guild GU2 ... 130 C6
Guileshill La. Ockham GU23 ... 91 F5
Guilford Ave. King U T KT5 ... 37 F4
Guillemont Cty Jun Sch.
W Heath GU14 ... 84 D7
Guillemont Fields.
W Heath GU14 ... 84 D5
Guillemot Path. 2 Crawl RH11 200 D5
Guinevere Rd. Crawl RH11 ... 200 E6
Guinness Ct. Crawl RH11 ... 201 C2
Guinness Ct. 5 Knaph GU21 ... 68 F1
Guinness Ct. 3 S Croy CR0 ... 61 F8
Gull Cl. Wallin SM6 ... 60 E3
Gulley Rd. Farnb GU14 ... 105 A8
Gulliver Ct. Croy CR0 ... 61 B3
Gumbrells Cl. Fairl GU3 ... 108 C5
Gumley Gdns. Islew TW7 ... 6 A4
Gumley House Convent Sch for
Girls. Islew TW7 ... 6 A4
Gun Hill. Alder GU11 ... 105 B3
Gun Pit Rd. Lingf RH7 ... 164 D4
Gunnell Cl. Croy SE25 ... 43 A3
Gunnell Ct. Mitch CR4 ... 40 E8
Gunners Rd. Wands SW18 ... 20 D6
Gunning Ct. Crawl RH11 ... 201 A3
Gunters Mead. Oxsh KT22 ... 74 C8
Gunton Rd. Mitch SW17 ... 21 A2
Gurdon's La. Wormly GU8 ... 170 F2
Gurney Cres. Thorn H CR0 ... 41 F1
Gurney Rd. Carsh SM5 ... 60 A6
Gurney's Cl. 3 Redh RH1 ... 139 F8
Guy Rd. Wallin CR0 & SM6 ... 60 D7
Guy Track. Farnb GU14 ... 104 D8
Guyatt Gdns. Mitch CR4 ... 41 A7
Gwydor Rd. Penge BR3 ... 43 D6
Gwydyr Rd. Broml BR2 ... 44 F6
Gwynne Ave. Croy CR0 ... 43 D2
Gwynne Gdns. E Grins RH19 ... 185 C2
Gwynne House. 6 Streat SW2 ... 21 F7
Gwynne Vaughan Ave.
Stough GU2 ... 109 B5

H. Jones Cres. Alder GU11 ... 105 C3
Habershon Dr. Friml GU16 ... 66 D2
Haccombe Rd. Wimble SW19 ... 20 C2
Hackbridge Inf Sch. Hackb SM6 41 A1
Hackbridge Jun Sch.
Hackb SM5 ... 41 A1
Hackbridge Park Gdns.
Carsh SM5 ... 59 F8
Hackbridge Rd.
Hackb SM5 & SM6 ... 60 A8
Hackbridge Sta. Hackb SM6 ... 60 B8
Hackenden Cl. E Grins RH19 ... 185 E3
Hackenden La. E Grins RH19 ... 185 E3
Hacketts La. Pyrf GU22 ... 70 F4
Hackhurst La. Abing H RH5 ... 133 F4
Hackington Cres. Beck BR3 ... 24 A2
Haddenham Ct. Up Toot SW17 ... 20 D4
Haddington Rd. Catf BR1 ... 24 D4
Haddon Cl. New Mal KT3 ... 38 F4
Haddon Cl. Oat Pk KT13 ... 53 D6
Haddon Rd. Sutton SM1 ... 59 B6
Hadfield Rd. Stan TW19 ... 2 D1
Hadleigh Cl. Merton SW20 ... 39 F7
Hadleigh Dr. Belm SM2 ... 59 B2
Hadleigh Gdns. Friml GU16 ... 85 E6
Hadley Ct. Poyle SL3 ... 1 E6
Hadley Pl. Whit V KT13 ... 53 A3
Hadley Rd. Mitch CR4 ... 41 D5
Hadley Wood Rise. Purley CR8 ... 80 B5
Hadleys. Rowl GU10 ... 145 E3
Hadlow Pl. Penge SE19 ... 23 A1
Hadmans Cl. Horsh RH12 ... 217 C1
Hadrian Cl. Stan TW19 ... 13 E8
Hadrian Cl. Wallin SM6 ... 60 E3
Hadrian Ct. 1 Belm SM2 ... 59 B3
Hadrian Way. Stan TW19 ... 13 D8
Hadrian Way. Stan TW19 ... 13 E8
Hadrians. Farnh GU9 ... 125 E4
Hafton Rd. Catf SE6 ... 24 E6
Haggard Rd. Twick TW1 ... 17 B8
Haig Pl. Morden SM4 ... 40 A3
Haig Rd. Alder GU12 ... 105 C1
Haig Rd. Bigg H TN16 ... 83 E2
Haig Rd. Sandh GU15 ... 64 F6
Haigh Cres. Earls RH1 ... 140 B7
Hailes Cl. Wimble SW19 ... 20 C2
Hailey Pl. Cran GU6 ... 174 F4
Hailsham Ave. Streat SW2 ... 21 F6
Hailsham Cl. Sandh GU15 ... 45 D1
Hailsham Cl. Surb KT6 ... 37 D2
Hailsham Rd. Mitch SW17 ... 21 A2
Haines Ct. Whit V KT13 ... 53 D5
Haines Wlk. Cheam SM4 ... 40 B2
Haining Gdns. Mytch GU16 ... 86 A3
Hainthorpe Rd. W Norw SE27 ... 22 B4
Halcyon Ct. Stain TW18 ... 33 B7
Haldane Pl. Wands SW18 ... 20 B7
Hale Cty Prim Sch.
Heath E GU9 ... 125 B7
Hale End. Brack RG12 ... 27 F5
Hale Ends. Woking GU22 ... 89 B6
Hale House Cl. Churt GU10 ... 167 F1
Hale House La. Churt GU10 ... 168 B2
Hale Pit Rd. G Book KT23 ... 94 C1
Hale Rd. Farnh GU9 ... 125 D4
Hale Rd. Hale GU9 ... 125 D5
Hale Rdbt. Hale GU9 ... 125 E5
Hale Reeds. Heath E GU9 ... 125 E6
Hale St. Stain TW18 ... 12 E4
Hale Way. Friml GU16 ... 85 D8
Halebourne La. W End GU24 ... 49 A2
Hales Ct. 5 Tedd TW11 ... 17 A3
Hales Field. Haslem GU27 ... 208 C6
Hales House. 3 Balham SW12 ... 21 B8
Hales Oak. G Book KT23 ... 94 C1
Halesowen Rd. Cheam SM4 ... 40 B2
Haleswood. Cobham KT11 ... 73 C5
Halewood. Easth RG12 ... 26 F3
Half Acre. Brent TW8 ... 6 D8
Half Acre Mews. Brent TW8 ... 6 D8
Half Moon Hill. Haslem GU27 ... 208 C6
Half Moon St. Bagsh GU19 ... 47 E3
Half Way Cotts. Farnh GU10 ... 124 C3
Halford Rd. Rich TW10 ... 6 E2
Halfpenny Cl. Chil GU4 ... 131 D3
Halfpenny Cross. Downs KT11 ... 73 A2
Halfpenny Ct. Sunnin SL5 ... 30 B2
Halfpenny La. Merrow GU4 ... 131 C5
Halfpenny La. Sunnin SL5 ... 30 A2
Halfway La. Shackl GU7 ... 150 B4
Haliburton Rd. Islew TW1 & TW7 . 6 A3
Halifax Cl. Crawl RH10 ... 182 E1
Halifax Cl. Farnb GU14 ... 84 F3
Halifax St. For Hil SE26 ... 23 B5
Halifax Way. Farnb GU14 ... 104 F7
Halimote Rd. Alder GU11 ... 105 A1
Haling Down Pas. Purley CR8 ... 61 C1
Haling Gr. S Croy CR2 ... 61 C3
Haling Manor High Sch.
Croy CR2 ... 61 B3
Haling Manor High Sch
(Pampisford Wing). Croy CR2 . 61 B2
Haling Park Gdns. Croy CR2 ... 61 B4
Haling Park Rd. Croy CR2 ... 61 C4
Haling Rd. Croy CR2 ... 61 D4
Hall Cl. Camb GU15 ... 65 E6
Hall Cl. Farnc GU7 ... 150 E7
Hall Ct. Tedd TW11 ... 16 F3
Hall Dene Cl. Merrow GU1 ... 110 C2
Hall Dr. For Hil SE26 ... 23 C3
Hall Farm Dr. Twick TW2 ... 16 D8
Hall Grove (Sch). Windl GU19 ... 48 A5
Hall Hill. Oxted RH8 ... 122 D4
Hall La. Harl UB3 ... 3 D7
Hall Pl. Woking GU21 ... 70 A3
Hall Place Dr. Whit V KT13 ... 53 E5
Hall Rd. Bramly GU5 ... 151 F6
Hall Rd. Farnb GU14 ... 85 B2
Hall Rd. Islew TW7 ... 5 D2
Hall Rd. Wallin SM6 ... 60 B2
Hall Sch Wimbledon.
Rhampt SW15 ... 19 A5
Hallam Rd. Farnc GU7 ... 150 F5
Halland Cl. Crawl RH10 ... 202 A7
Hallane House. W Norw SE27 ... 22 C3
Halley Cl. Crawl RH11 ... 201 B1
Halley Dr. N Asct SL5 ... 28 D7
Halley's App. Woking GU21 ... 69 A1
Halley's Ct. 1 Woking GU21 ... 69 A1
Halley's Wlk. New Haw KT15 ... 52 C3
Hallgrove Bottom. Windl GU19 ... 47 F5
Halliards The. Walt O T KT12 ... 35 A3
Halliford Cl. Up Hall TW17 ... 34 E6
Halliford Rd. Sunby TW16 ... 35 A5
Halliford Rd.
Up Hall TW16 & TW17 ... 34 F5
Halliford Sch. Shep TW17 ... 34 C2
Hallington Cl. Woking GU21 ... 69 B2
Hallmark Cl. Sandh GU15 ... 64 E8
Hallmead Rd. Sutton SM1 ... 59 B7
Hallowell Ave. Wallin CR0 ... 60 E6
Hallowell Cl. Mitch CR4 ... 41 A6
Hallowfield Way. Mitch CR4 ... 40 E6
Halls Farm Cl. Knaph GU21 ... 68 D2
Hallsland. Crawl D RH10 ... 204 C8
Hallsland Way. Oxted RH8 ... 122 F3
Halnaker Wlk. 9 Crawl RH11 ... 200 F3
Halsford Croft. E Grins RH19 ... 185 B3
Halsford Gn. E Grins RH19 ... 185 B3
Halsford La. E Grins RH19 ... 185 C3
Halsford Park Cty Prim Sch.
E Grins RH19 ... 185 C2
Halsford Park Rd. E Grins RH19 185 C2
Halters End. Graysh GU26 ... 188 A3
Ham Cl. Rich TW10 ... 17 C5
Ham Comm. Rich TW10 ... 17 D5
Ham Farm Rd. Rich KT2 & TW10 17 E4
Ham Gate Ave. Rich TW10 ... 17 E4
Ham Gate Ave. Rich TW10 ... 18 A4
Ham La. Elst GU8 ... 148 E4
Ham La. Eng Gn TW20 ... 11 B4
Ham Ridings. Rich TW10 ... 17 F3
Ham St. Rich TW10 ... 17 C5
Ham St. Rich TW10 ... 17 C6
Ham The. Brent TW8 ... 6 C7
Ham View. Croy CR0 ... 43 E3
Hamble Ave. Blckw GU17 ... 64 D5
Hamble Cl. Woking GU21 ... 69 A2
Hamble Ct. Tedd KT1 ... 17 D1
Hamble Wlk. Woking GU21 ... 69 A2
Hambleden Ct. Brack RG12 ... 27 E5
Hambledon C of E Prim Sch.
Hambl GU8 ... 171 D2

Hambledon Ct. **9** Wallin SM6 ... 60 B4
Hambledon Gdns. S Norw SE25 .. 42 F6
Hambledon Hill. Woodc KT18 .. 76 C3
Hambledon House. **2**
  King U T KT2 .... 18 B2
Hambledon Pl. Dulw SE21 ...... 22 F7
Hambledon Rd.
  Godal GU8 & GU7 .... 171 D5
Hambledon Rd.
  Hambl GU8 & GU7 .... 171 D5
Hambledon Rd.
  Hyde GU8 & GU7 .... 171 D5
Hambledon Rd. Wands SW18 .... 19 F8
Hambledon Vale. Woodc KT18 .. 76 C3
Hamblelon Cl.
  Friml GU15 & GU16 .... 66 B3
Hamblelon Cl. N Cheam KT4 .... 58 C8
Hamblelon Cl. Crawl RH11 ...... 201 C4
Hamblelon Hill. Crawl RH11 ... 201 C4
Hambridge Way. Streat SW2 .... 22 A8
Hambro Rd. Streat SW16 .... 21 D3
Hambrook Rd. Croy SE25 .... 43 B6
Hamers House. **19** Streat SW2 .. 22 A8
Hamesmoor Rd. Mytch GU16 .... 85 F4
Hamesmoor Way. Mytch GU16 .. 85 F4
Hamfield. Oxted RH8 .... 122 C8
Hamhaugh Island. Lo Hall TW17 53 A8
Hamilton Ave. Cheam SM3 ...... 58 E8
Hamilton Ave. Cobham KT11 .... 73 A6
Hamilton Ave. Pyrf GU22 .... 70 E3
Hamilton Ave. Tolw KT6 & SM3 .. 57 A8
Hamilton Cl. Ashf TW13 .... 14 F3
Hamilton Cl. Chert KT16 .... 32 F1
Hamilton Cl. Epsom KT19 .... 76 C7
Hamilton Cl. Purley CR8 .... 80 B7
Hamilton Cl. Stough GU2 ...... 109 A6
Hamilton Cres. Hounsl TW3 ..... 5 B2
Hamilton Ct. Catf SE6 .... 24 F7
Hamilton Ct. Cobham KT11 ..... 73 A6
Hamilton Ct. Croy CR0 .... 43 A1
Hamilton Ct. Fetch KT23 .... 94 B2
Hamilton Ct. W Heath GU14 .... 64 E1
Hamilton Dr. Stough GU2 ...... 109 A6
Hamilton Dr. Sunnin SL5 .... 29 E2
Hamilton House. Chisw W4 ...... 7 B8
Hamilton House. **13** Rich TW9 ... 7 A6
Hamilton Mews. Cobham KT11 .. 73 A6
Hamilton Mews. Weyb KT13 .... 53 A6
Hamilton Par. Felt TW13 .... 15 A4
Hamilton Pl. Stough GU2 ...... 109 A6
Hamilton Pl. Sunby TW16 .... 15 B2
Hamilton Pl. Brent TW8 .... 6 D8
Hamilton Pl. Felt TW13 .... 15 A4
Hamilton Rd. Horsh RH12 ...... 217 B3
Hamilton Rd. Merton SW19 ..... 20 B1
Hamilton Rd. S Norw CR7 .... 42 D6
Hamilton Rd. Twick TW2 .... 16 E7
Hamilton Rd. W Norw SE27 ..... 22 D4
Hamilton Road Ind Est.
  W Norw SE27 .... 22 D4
Hamilton Road Mews. **1**
  Merton SW19 .... 20 B1
Hamilton Way. Wallin SM6 ...... 60 D2
Hamlash Cotts. Frensh GU10 .. 146 C2
Hamlash La. Frensh GU10 ..... 146 C1
Hamlet Rd. Penge SE19 .... 23 A1
Hamlet St. Wink RG12 .... 27 E8
Hamlyn Gdns. S Norw SE19 ..... 22 E1
Hamm Court Est. Lo Hall KT13 .. 52 F8
Hamm Moor La. Addl KT15 ...... 52 E6
Hammelton Ct. Broml BR1 .... 44 F8
Hammelton Rd. Broml BR1 ...... 44 F8
Hammer Hill. Linch GU27 ...... 207 C4
Hammer La.
  Bramsh GU27 & GU30 .... 207 B6
Hammer La. Bramsh GU30 ...... 207 A6
Hammer La.
  Graysh GU10 & GU26 & GU35 .. 187 E6
Hammer Yd. Crawl RH11 .... 201 D5
Hammerfield Dr. Abing H RH5 .. 133 F3
Hammerpond Rd. Horsh RH13 .. 217 F1
Hammersley Rd. Farnb GU11 ... 105 C7
Hammerwood Copse.
  Linch GU27 .... 207 C4
Hammerwood Rd. Ash W RH19 206 E6
Hammond Ave. Mitch CR4 ...... 41 B7
Hammond Cl. Hampt TW12 ...... 36 A8
Hammond Cl. Horse GU21 ...... 69 C4
Hammond Cty Mid Sch.
  Lhtwat GU18 .... 48 A1
Hammond Rd. Horse GU21 ...... 69 C4
Hammond Way. Lhtwat GU18 .... 48 B1
Hampden Ave. Beck BR3 .... 43 E7
Hampden Cl. Crawl RH10 ...... 182 C1
Hampden Rd. Beck BR3 .... 43 E7
Hampden Rd. King U T KT1 ..... 38 A6
Hamper's La. Horsh RH13 ...... 218 A2
Hampers Ct. Horsh RH13 ...... 217 D2
Hampshire Cl. Alder GU12 ..... 126 D7
Hampshire Cl. Addl KT15 .... 52 C5
Hampshire Ct. Barnes SW13 ..... 7 F5
Hampshire Rd. Camb GU15 ..... 65 F8
Hampstead Cl. Dork RH4 ...... 135 F6
Hampstead La. Dork RH4 ...... 136 A6
Hampstead Rd. Dork RH4 ...... 136 A6
Hampton Cl. Wimble SW20 ...... 19 C1
Hampton Court Ave.
  Thame D KT8 .... 36 E3
Hampton Court Cres.
  E Mole KT8 .... 36 D6
Hampton Court Palace.
  Hampt KT8 .... 36 F6
Hampton Court Par. E Mole KT8 36 E5
Hampton Court Rd.
  Hampt KT1 & KT8 .... 37 B6
Hampton Court Sta. E Mole KT8 36 E5
Hampton Court Way.
  Thame D KT10 & KT7 & KT8 .... 36 E5
Hampton Farm Ind Est.
  Felt TW13 .... 15 E5
Hampton Gr. Ewell KT17 .... 76 F8

Hampton Hill Jun Mix Sch.
  Felt TW12 .... 16 C3
Hampton Inf Sch. Hampt TW12 . 16 A1
Hampton Jun Sch. Hampt TW12 36 A8
Hampton La. Felt TW13 .... 15 E4
Hampton Lodge. Horley RH6 ... 161 A2
Hampton Rd. Earls RH5 .... 139 F4
Hampton Rd. Hale GU9 .... 125 B6
Hampton Rd. N Cheam KT4 ..... 58 B8
Hampton Rd. Tedd TW11 & TW12 16 E3
Hampton Rd. Thorn H CR0 ...... 42 C3
Hampton Rd E. Felt TW13 .... 15 F5
Hampton Rd W. Felt TW13 ...... 15 E5
Hampton Road Ind Pk.
  Thorn H CR0 .... 42 C3
Hampton Sch. Hampt TW12 ..... 16 A3
Hampton Sta. Hampt TW12 ..... 16 A1
Hampton Way. E Grins RH19 ... 205 F7
Hampton Wick Inf Sch.
  Tedd KT1 .... 17 D1
Hampton Wick Sta. Tedd KT1 ... 37 C8
Hamsey Green Cty Inf Sch.
  Warlgm CR6 .... 81 B3
Hamsey Green Cty Jun Sch.
  Warlgm CR6 .... 81 B3
Hamsey Green Gdns.
  Warlgm CR6 .... 81 C3
Hamsey Way. Hams Gn CR2 ..... 81 B4
Hanbury Dr. Bigg H TN16 ...... 83 B6
Hanbury Path. Sheer GU21 ..... 70 D5
Hanbury Rd. Crawl RH11 ...... 200 D5
Hanbury Way. Camb GU15* 65 C3
Hancock Rd. S Norw SE19 ...... 22 D2
Hancocks Mount. Ascot SL5 .... 29 D3
Hancombe Rd. Sandh GU17 ..... 45 A1
Handcroft Rd. Thorn H CR0 ..... 42 B1
Handel House. Twick TW2 .... 5 D1
Handside Cl. N Cheam KT4 ..... 39 D1
Handsworth House. **8**
  Crawl RH11 .... 201 D5
Hanford Cl. Wands SW18 .... 20 A7
Hanger Hill. Weyb KT13 .... 53 A5
Hanley Pl. Beck BR3 .... 24 A1
Hannah Cl. Beck BR3 .... 44 C6
Hannah Ct. Wimble SW19 .... 19 D1
Hannay Wlk. Streat SW16 ...... 21 D6
Hannen Rd. W Norw SE27 ...... 22 B5
Hannibal Rd. Stan TW19 .... 13 E8
Hannibal Way. Wallin CR0 ...... 60 F4
Hanning Lodge. Hounsl TW3 ..... 5 C3
Hanover Ave. Felt TW13 .... 15 A4
Hanover Cl. Cheam SM3 .... 58 F6
Hanover Cl. Crawl RH10 .... 201 F3
Hanover Cl. Eng Gn TW20 ...... 11 B2
Hanover Cl. Friml GU16 .... 65 E1
Hanover Cl. Merst RH1 .... 119 C7
Hanover Cl. Rich TW9 .... 7 A7
Hanover Cl. Dork RH4 .... 135 C7
Hanover Cl. Horsh RH13 ...... 217 F3
Hanover Cl. **1** Penge SE19 ..... 23 A1
Hanover Cl. Woking GU22 .... 89 E8
Hanover Gdns. Easth RG12 ..... 26 F2
Hanover Gdns. W Heath GU14 .. 84 E6
Hanover House. Tolw KT6 .... 38 A1
Hanover Rd. Merton SW19 ...... 20 C1
Hanover St. Croy CR0 & CR9 ... 61 B7
Hanover Terr. Islew TW7 .... 6 A6
Hanover Wlk. Oat Pk KT13 ...... 53 F7
Hansler Gr. E Mole KT8 .... 36 D5
Hanson Cl. Balham SW12 .... 21 B8
Hanson Cl. Beck BR3 .... 24 B2
Hanson Cl. Burph GU1 .... 109 F4
Hanson Cl. Camb GU15 .... 66 B7
Hanson Cl. Mortl SW14 .... 7 C4
Hanworth Cl. Redh RH1 .... 27 C3
Hanworth La. Chert KT16 ...... 32 F1
Hanworth Rd. Earls RH1 ...... 139 F4
Hanworth Rd. Felt TW13 .... 15 B3
Hanworth Rd. Hampt TW12 ..... 16 A3
Hanworth Rd. Hounsl TW3 & TW4 . 5 B2
Hanworth Rd. Sunby TW16 ..... 15 A1
Hanworth Rd. Twick TW4 .... 15 F8
Hanworth Terr. Hounsl TW3 ...... 5 B3
Hanworth Trad Est. Chert KT16 . 32 F1
Hanworth Trad Est. Felt TW13 .. 15 E5
Harberson Rd. Balham SW12 ... 21 B7
Harbin House. **5** Streat SW2 ... 22 A7
Harbledown Rd. S Croy CR2 .... 81 A8
Harborough Rd. Streat SW16 ... 21 F4
Harbour Cl. Farnb GU14 .... 85 A8
Harbourfield Rd. Banstd SM7 .. 78 B4
Harbridge Ave. Rhampt SW15 .. 19 A8
Harbury Rd. Sutton SM5 .... 59 E3
Harcourt Ave. Wallin SM6 ...... 60 B6
Harcourt Cl. Egham TW20 ...... 12 C2
Harcourt Cl. Islew TW7 .... 6 A4
Harcourt Field. Wallin SM6 ..... 60 B6
Harcourt Lodge. **2** Wallin SM6 . 60 B6
Harcourt Rd. Camb GU15 .... 65 B5
Harcourt Rd. Easth RG12 .... 27 B4
Harcourt Rd. Merton SW19 ..... 20 A1
Harcourt Rd. Thorn H CR7 ...... 42 A3
Harcourt Rd. Wallin SM6 .... 60 B6
Harcourt Way. S Godst RH9 ... 142 E6
Hardcastle Cl. Croy SE25 .... 43 A3
Hardcourts Cl. W Wick BR4 ..... 63 B7
Hardel Rise. Streat SW2 .... 22 B7
Hardel Wlk. Streat SE24 & SW2 . 22 A8
Hardham Cl. Crawl RH11 ...... 201 A8
Harding Cl. S Norw SE25 .... 42 F7
Harding House. Wallin SM6 ..... 60 E2
Harding Pl. For Hil SE23 .... 23 E8
Harding Rd. Lang V KT18 .... 96 E8
Hardings La. Penge SE20 .... 23 D2
Hardman Rd. King U T KT2 ...... 37 E7
Hardwell Way. Brack RG12 ..... 27 E5
Hardwick Cl. Oxsh KT22 .... 74 C4
Hardwick La. Lyne KT16 .... 32 D1

Hardwick Rd.
  Woodh RH1 & RH2 .... 139 D7
Hardwicke Ave. Heston TW5 ..... 5 A6
Hardwicke Rd. Reig RH2 ...... 118 A2
Hardwicke Rd. Rich TW10 ...... 17 C4
Hardy Cl. Crawl RH10 .... 202 C7
Hardy Cl. Dork RH5 .... 136 B3
Hardy Cl. Horley RH6 .... 160 E3
Hardy Cl. Horsh RH12 .... 217 B4
Hardy Gn. Crowth RG11 .... 45 B4
Hardy Rd. Merton SW19 .... 20 B1
Hardys Cl. E Mole KT8 .... 36 E5
Hare Hill. Row Tn KT15 .... 51 F4
Hare Hill Cl. Pyrf GU22 .... 71 A4
Hare La. Clayg KT10 .... 55 E4
Hare La. Crawl RH11 .... 201 B8
Hare La. Farnc GU7 .... 150 F6
Hare La. Horne RH7 .... 163 D5
Harebell Hill. Cobham KT11 .... 73 E5
Harecroft. Dork RH4 & RH5 ... 136 C4
Harecroft. Fetch KT23 .... 94 C3
Haredon Cl. For Hil SE23 .... 23 D8
Harefield. Hinch W KT10 .... 55 E7
Harefield Ave. E Ewell SM2 ..... 58 E2
Harefield Rd. S Norw SW16 .... 21 F1
Harelands Cl. Horse GU21 ...... 69 C2
Harelands La. Horse GU21 ...... 69 C2
Harendon. Tadw KT20 .... 97 D6
Hares Bank. New add CR0 ...... 63 D1
Harestone Dr. Cater CR3 ...... 100 F1
Harestone Hill. Cater CR3 ..... 100 F2
Harestone La. Cater CR3 ...... 100 E2
Harestone Valley Rd. Cater CR3 100 F2
Harewood Cl. Crawl RH10 ...... 182 A1
Harewood Cl. Reig RH2 .... 118 C4
Harewood Gdns. Hams Gn CR2 .. 81 C4
Harewood Rd. Hounsl TW7 ...... 5 F6
Harewood Rd. Merrow GU4 .... 110 D2
Harewood Rd. Mitch SW19 ..... 20 E2
Harewood Rd. S Croy CR2 ...... 61 E4
Harfield Rd. Sunby TW16 .... 35 D7
Harkness Cl. Nork KT17 .... 77 C3
Harland Ave. S Croy CR2 .... 62 A7
Harland Fst Sch. Mitch CR4 .... 40 D7
Harlech Ct. For Hil SE23 .... 23 C7
Harlech Gdns. Heston TW5 ...... 4 C7
Harlech Rd. Hawley GU17 ...... 64 B5
Harlequin Ave. Brent TW8 .... 6 A8
Harlequin Cl. Islew TW7 .... 5 E2
Harlequin Rd. Tedd TW11 ...... 17 B1
Harlington Cl. Harl UB7 .... 3 C6
Harlington Cnr. Harl UB3 .... 3 D6
Harlington Lower Sch. Harl UB7 . 3 C7
Harlington Rd E.
  Felt TW13 & TW14 .... 15 C7
Harlington Rd W. Felt TW14 .... 4 A1
Harlow Ct. **4** Reig RH2 .... 118 D1
Harman Pl. Purley CR8 .... 80 B8
Harmans Dr. E Grins RH19 ..... 186 B1
Harmans Mead. E Grins RH19 .. 186 B1
Harmans Water Cty Jun Sch.
  Brack RG12 .... 27 D4
Harmans Water Rd. Brack RG12 27 D4
Harmar Cl. Woki RG11 .... 25 E6
Harmondsworth La. Harm UB7 .. 2 E8
Harmondsworth Prim Sch.
  Harm UB7 .... 2 D8
Harmony Cl. Crawl RH11 ...... 200 E4
Harmony Cl. Wallin SM6 .... 60 E2
Harms Gr. Merrow GU4 .... 110 C4
Harold Cl. Alder GU12 .... 105 B1
Harold Rd. Carsh SM1 .... 59 D6
Harold Rd. S Norw SE19 .... 22 D1
Harold Rd. Worth RH10 .... 202 E5
Haroldslea. Horley RH6 .... 161 E2
Haroldslea Cl. Horley RH6 ..... 161 C1
Haroldslea Dr. Horley RH6 .... 161 D1
Harpenden Rd.
  W Norw SE27 & SW16 .... 22 B6
Harper Dr. Worth RH10 .... 202 C2
Harper's Rd. Ash GU12 .... 106 C2
Harpesford Ave. Vir W GU25 ... 31 C4
Harps Oak La. L Kings RH1 & RH2 99 A2
Harpurs. Tadw KT20 .... 97 D5
Harrier Cl. Cran GU6 .... 174 E4
Harrier Ct. Crawl RH10 .... 182 D1
Harriet Gdns. Croy CR0 .... 62 A8
Harrington Cl. Leigh RH2 ...... 138 A2
Harrington Cl. Wallin CR0 ...... 60 E8
Harrington Ct. **7** Croy CR0 .... 61 D8
Harrington Rd. Croy SE25 ...... 43 B5
Harriotts Cl. Ashtd KT22 .... 95 C7
Harriotts La. Ashtd KT21 & KT22 95 C8
Harris City Tech Coll.
  S Norw SE19 .... 42 F8
Harris Cl. Crawl RH11 .... 201 B3
Harris Cl. Hounsl TW5 .... 5 A6
Harris Lodge. Catf SE6 .... 24 C7
Harris Way. Charlt TW16 .... 34 E8
Harrison Cl. Reig RH2 .... 139 B8
Harrison Ct. Shep Gn TW17 .... 34 B4
Harrison's Rise. Croy CR0 & CR9 61 B7
Harrodian Sch. Barnes SW13 ... 7 F7
Harrogate Ct. **2** For Hil SE26 .. 23 A5
Harrow Bottom Rd. Longc GU25 31 F3
Harrow Cl. Chert KT15 .... 52 B8
Harrow Cl. Chess KT9 .... 56 D3
Harrow Cl. Dork RH4 .... 136 A5
Harrow Gate Gdns. Dork RH4 .. 136 A5
Harrow Gdns. Warlgm CR6 ..... 81 F3
Harrow La. Farnc GU7 .... 150 E7
Harrow Lodge. Sutton SM2 ..... 59 D4
Harrow Rd. Ashf TW15 .... 14 A4
Harrow Rd.
  Carsh SM1 & SM2 & SM5 ..... 59 E4
Harrow Rd. Warlgm CR6 .... 81 F3
Harrow Rd E. Dork RH4 .... 136 B6
Harrow Rd W. Dork RH4 ...... 136 A6
Harrow Way. Charlt TW17 ...... 34 C7
Harrowdene. Cran GU6 .... 174 E4
Harrowdene Ct. Wimble SW19 .. 19 E3

Harrowdene Gdns. Tedd TW11 .. 17 A1
Harrowlands Pk. Dork RH4 .... 136 B6
Harrowsley Ct. Horley RH6 .... 161 B4
Hart Cl. Bletch RH1 .... 120 E2
Hart Cl. **1** Brack RG12 .... 27 B8
Hart Cl. W Heath GU14 .... 84 E8
Hart Dyke Cl. Woki RG11 .... 25 B2
Hart Gdns. Dork RH4 .... 136 B8
Hart House. Streat SW2 .... 22 A7
Hart Rd. Byfl KT14 .... 71 E6
Hart Rd. Dork RH4 .... 136 B8
Hart The. Farnh GU9 .... 125 B2
Hart's La. S Godst RH9 .... 142 D7
Harte Rd. Hounsl TW3 .... 4 F5
Hartfield Cres. Merton SW19 ... 19 F1
Hartfield Gr. Penge SE20 .... 43 C8
Hartfield Rd. Chess KT9 .... 56 D5
Hartfield Rd. For Row RH18 ... 206 F2
Hartfield Rd. Merton SW19 ..... 20 A1
Hartford Rd. W Ewell KT19 ..... 57 B4
Hartford Rd. W Ewell KT19 ..... 57 B4
Hartford Rise. Camb GU15 ..... 65 D6
Hartham Cl. Islew TW7 .... 6 A6
Hartham Rd. Islew TW7 .... 6 A6
Harting Ct. Crawl RH11 .... 200 F3
Hartington Ct. Chisw W4 .... 7 B7
Hartington Pl. Reig RH2 ...... 118 A3
Hartington Rd. Chisw W4 .... 7 C6
Hartington Rd. Twick TW1 ...... 6 B1
Hartland Cl. Woodhm WK15 .... 52 C2
Hartland Pl. W Heath GU14 .... 85 A7
Hartland Rd. Cheam SM4 .... 40 B2
Hartland Rd. Hampt TW12 ..... 16 B4
Hartland Rd. Islew TW7 .... 6 A4
Hartland Way. Croy CR0 .... 62 E8
Hartland Way. Morden SM4 .... 39 F2
Hartlands. The. Heston TW5 ..... 4 B7
Hartley Cl. Blckw GU17 .... 64 B5
Hartley Down. Coulsd CR5 & CR8 79 F5
Hartley Farm. Coulsd CR8 ...... 79 F4
Hartley Hill. Coulsd CR8 .... 79 F4
Hartley Old Rd. Coulsd CR8 .... 79 F5
Hartley Rd. Thorn H CR0 .... 42 C2
Hartley Way. Coulsd CR5 & CR8 . 79 F4
Harts Gdns. Stough GU2 ...... 109 B4
Harts Leap Cl. Sandh GU17 .... 45 B1
Harts Leap Rd. Sandh GU17 ... 64 A8
Hartscroft. New add CR0 .... 62 E2
Hartsgrove. Chidd GU8 .... 191 B5
Hartshill. Stough GU2 .... 108 D2
Hartshill Wlk. Woking GU21 .... 69 B3
Hartspiece Rd. Earls RH1 ..... 140 B7
Hartswood Ave. Dovgn RH2 ... 139 A5
Hartswood House. **10**
  Streat SW2 .... 21 E7
Harvard Hill. Chisw W4 .... 7 B7
Harvard Rd. Hounsl TW7 .... 5 E6
Harvard Rd. Sandh GU15 .... 45 E1
Harvest Bank Rd. Coney H BR4 . 63 F7
Harvest Ct. Beck BR3 .... 24 A1
Harvest Ct. Shep Gn TW17 ..... 34 A5
Harvest Hill. E Grins RH19 .... 205 E8
Harvest Hill. Godal GU7 .... 150 D4
Harvest La. Thame D KT7 .... 37 A3
Harvest Rd. Eng Gn TW20 ...... 11 D2
Harvest Rd. Felt TW13 .... 15 A5
Harvest Rd. Worth RH10 ...... 202 C4
Harvester Rd. Epsom KT19 ..... 57 D1
Harvesters. Horsh RH12 ...... 217 D5
Harvesters Cl. Islew TW7 .... 5 D2
Harvestside. Horley RH6 ...... 161 C4
Harvey Cl. Crawl RH11 .... 201 A1
Harvey Lodge. Guild GU1 ...... 130 E8
Harvey Rd. Guild GU1 .... 130 E8
Harvey Rd. Twick TW4 .... 15 F8
Harvey Rd. W Heath GU14 ..... 84 C5
Harvey Rd. Walt O T KT12 ...... 35 A2
Harwarden Cl. Crawl D RH10 .. 204 C8
Harwood Ave. Mitch CR4 .... 40 E6
Harwood Gdns. Old W SL4 ..... 11 B8
Harwood Pk. Salfs RH1 .... 161 A8
Harwood Rd. Horsh RH13 ..... 217 F3
Harwood Rd.
  Horsh RH12 & RH13 .... 218 A3
Harwoods Cl. **3** E Grins RH19 . 205 F7
Harwoods La. E Grins RH19 ... 205 F7
Hascombe Ct. Crawl RH11 .... 201 A5
Hascombe House. **11**
  Rhampt SW15 .... 19 B7
Haseley End. For Hil SE23 ...... 23 C8
Haseltine Prim Sch. For Hil SE6 23 F4
Haseltine Rd. For Hil SE26 ..... 23 F4
Haslam Ave. Cheam SM3 & SM4 39 E1
Hasle Dr. Haslem GU27 .... 208 B6
Haslemere Ave. Cranf TW5 ...... 4 C5
Haslemere Ave.
  Mitch CR4 & SW19 .... 40 D7
Haslemere Ave. Wimble SW18 .. 20 B6
Haslemere Cl. Friml GU16 ...... 66 C3
Haslemere Cl. Hampt TW12 .... 15 F3
Haslemere Cl. Wallin SM6 ...... 60 E5
Haslemere & District Hospl.
  Haslem GU27 .... 208 D7
Haslemere Fst Sch. Mitch CR4 . 40 D7
Haslemere & Heathrow Est The.
  Cranf TW4 .... 4 B4
Haslemere Ind Est. Felt TW14 .. 4 A2
Haslemere Ind Est.
  Wimble SW18 .... 20 B6
Haslemere Prep Sch.
  Haslem GU27 .... 208 B7
Haslemere Rd. Brook GU8 ..... 170 C5
Haslemere Rd. Marl Ht GU27 . 208 B1
Haslemere Rd. Thorn H CR7 .... 42 B5
Haslemere Rd. Witley GU8 .... 170 C5
Haslemere Rd. Wimble SW19 ... 20 B8
Haslett Ave E. Crawl RH10 .... 202 A6
Haslett Ave W.
  Crawl RH10 & RH11 .... 201 D5

Haslett Rd. Up Hall TW17 ...... 34 E7
Hassall Ct. Old Wok GU22 ...... 90 A6
Hassocks Cl. For Hil SE23 & SE26 23 B5
Hassocks Ct. **3** Crawl RH11 .. 200 F3
Hassocks Rd. Mitch SW16 ...... 41 D8
Haste Hill. Haslem GU27 ...... 208 D5
Hastings Cl. Friml GU16 .... 86 A7
Hastings Dr. King U T KT6 ...... 37 C3
Hastings Pl. **1** Croy CR0 .... 42 F1
Hastings Rd. Crawl RH10 ..... 202 C6
Hastings Rd. Croy CR0 .... 42 F1
Hatch Cl. Addl KT15 .... 52 B7
Hatch Cl. Alf Cr GU6 .... 194 A3
Hatch End. For Row RH18 ..... 206 F2
Hatch End. Windl GU20 .... 48 C4
Hatch Gdns. Burgh H KT20 ..... 97 D7
Hatch Hill. Marl Ht GU27 ...... 208 B1
Hatch La. Harm TW6 & UB7 ..... 2 D7
Hatch La. Marl Ht GU27 ...... 208 B2
Hatch La. Ockham GU23 .... 72 B1
Hatch La. Ockham GU23 .... 92 B1
Hatch La. S Nutf RH1 .... 140 F3
Hatch La. Wormly GU8 .... 190 D8
Hatch Pl. Rich TW10 .... 17 F3
Hatch Rd. Thorn H SW16 .... 41 E7
Hatch Ride. Crowth RG11 .... 45 B7
Hatch Ride Cty Prim Sch.
  Crowth RG11 .... 45 B7
Hatches The. Farnh GU9 ...... 145 F8
Hatches The. Friml GU16 .... 85 F6
Hatchet La. Wink SL4 & SL5 ..... 9 B5
Hatchett Rd. E Bed TW14 ...... 14 C7
Hatchetts Dr. Shottm GU27 ... 207 D7
Hatchford Park Sch.
  Downs RH5 .... 72 E1
Hatchgate. Horley RH6 .... 160 F2
Hatchgate Copse. Easth RG12 .. 26 E3
Hatchlands Rd. Redh RH1 ..... 118 E1
Hatfield Cl. Belm SM2 .... 59 B2
Hatfield Gdns. Farnb GU14 .... 85 E3
Hatfield House. **16**
  King U T KT6 .... 37 E4
Hatfield Mead. Morden SM4 .... 40 A4
Hatfield Prim Sch. W Barn SM4 . 39 E3
Hatfield Rd. Ashtd KT21 .... 95 F8
Hatfield Wlk. Crawl RH11 ..... 200 D5
Hathaway Ct. **10** Redh RH1 ... 119 A2
Hathaway Rd. Thorn H CR0 .... 42 B2
Hatherleigh Cl. Chess KT9 ..... 56 D5
Hatherleigh Cl. Morden SM4 ... 40 A5
Hatherleigh House.
  Morden SM4 .... 40 A5
Hatherley Rd. Rich TW9 .... 6 F6
Hatherop Rd. Hampt TW12 ..... 15 F1
Hathersham Cl. Smallf RH6 ... 162 A4
Hathersham La.
  S Nutf RH1 & RH6 .... 161 F6
Hathersley House. **3**
  Streat SW2 .... 22 A8
Hatherwood. Ashtd KT21 .... 95 E6
Hatton Cross Sta. Hatton TW6 ... 3 F3
Hatton Gdns. Mitch CR4 .... 40 F4
Hatton Gn. Hatton TW14 .... 4 A3
Hatton Hill. Windl GU20 .... 48 C5
Hatton Rd. E Bed TW14 .... 14 D8
Hatton Rd. Hatton TW14 & TW6 .. 3 E2
Hatton Rd. Thorn H CR0 .... 42 A1
Havana Rd.
  Wimble SW19 & SW20 .... 20 A6
Havelock Cotts. Woking GU22 .. 89 D5
Havelock Hall. **8** Croy CR0 .... 42 F1
Havelock House. **4** Croy CR0 .. 42 F1
Havelock House. For Hil SE23 ... 23 C7
Havelock Rd. Croy CR0 .... 61 F8
Havelock Rd. Wimble SW19 .... 20 C3
Havelock St. Woki RG11 .... 25 A6
Havelock Wlk. For Hil SE23 .... 23 C6
Haven Cl. Wimble SW19 .... 19 D5
Haven Ct. Beck BR3 .... 44 C7
Haven Gdns. Crawl D RH10 ... 184 B1
Haven Rd. Ashf TW15 .... 14 B5
Haven Rd. Rudg RH12 & RH14 . 214 D3
Haven The. Rich TW9 .... 7 A4
Haven Way. Farnh GU9 .... 125 D4
Havenbury Est. Dork RH4 ..... 136 A8
Havenbury Ind Est. Dork RH4 . 135 F8
Havengate. Horsh RH12 .... 217 F5
Haverfield Gdns. Rich TW9 ...... 7 A7
Haverhill Rd. Streat SW12 ...... 21 C7
Havers Ave. Hersh KT12 .... 54 D5
Haves Down Schs. W Wick BR4 44 D1
Hawes La. W Wick BR4 .... 63 E8
Hawes Rd. Burgh H KT20 .... 97 D7
Haweswater House. Islew TW1 ... 5 F2
Hawk Cl. Brack RG12 .... 27 D5
Hawk's Hill. Fetch KT22 .... 94 F4
Hawke Rd. S Norw SE19 .... 22 E2
Hawkedale Fst Sch.
  Sunby TW16 .... 34 F6
Hawker Cl. Wallin SM6 .... 60 E3
Hawker Ct. **14** King U T KT2 .... 18 A1
Hawkes Cl. Woki RG11 .... 25 A7
Hawkes Leap. Windl GU20 ..... 48 B6
Hawkes Rd. Mitch CR4 .... 40 F8
Hawkesbourne Rd.
  Horsh RH12 .... 217 F5
Hawkesfield Rd.
  For Hil SE23 & SE6 .... 23 F6

Hawkesley Cl. Tedd TW1 .... 17 A4
Hawkesmoor Rd. Crawl RH11 .. 200 E4
Hawkesmoore Dr.
Bear Gn RH5 .... 157 C4
Hawksworth Dr. Bagsh GU19 ..... 47 E1
Hawkewood Rd. Sunby TW16 ...... 35 A6
Hawkfield Ct. Islew TW7 .... 5 E5
Hawkhirst Rd. Kenley CR8 .... 80 E3
Hawkhurst. Cobham KT11 .... 74 A5
Hawkhurst Gdns. Chess KT9 .... 56 E6
Hawkhurst Rd. Streat SW16 .... 41 D8
Hawkhurst Way. New Mal KT3 ..... 38 D4
Hawkhurst Way. W Wick BR4 .... 63 B8
Hawkhurst Wlk. Crawl RH10 ...... 202 B4
Hawkins Cl. Brack RG12 .... 28 A7
Hawkins Rd. Crawl RH10 .... 201 E4
Hawkins Rd. Tedd TW11 .... 17 B2
Hawkins Way. Catf SE6 .... 24 A3
Hawkins Way. Woki RG11 .... 25 E6
Hawkley Gdns. N Norw SE27 .... 22 B6
Hawkridge. Cox Gn RH12 .... 195 E1
Hawkridge Ct. Brack RG12 .... 27 E6
Hawks Hill Ct. Fetch KT22 .... 94 F4
Hawks Rd. King U T KT1 .... 37 F7
Hawksbrook La. Beck BR3 .... 44 C3
Hawkshead Cl. Broml BR1 .... 24 E1
Hawkshill Cl. Esher KT10 .... 55 A4
Hawkshill Way. Esher KT10 .... 55 A4
Hawksview. Cobham KT11 .... 73 F6
Hawksway. Stain TW18 .... 12 F5
Hawkswell Cl. Woking GU21 .... 68 F2
Hawkswell Wlk. Woking GU21 ..... 68 F3
Hawkswood Ave. Friml GU16 .... 65 F2
Hawkswood Dell. G Book KT23 .... 94 A1
Hawkswood Rise. G Book KT23 ... 94 A1
Hawley Cl. Hampt TW12 .... 15 F2
Hawley Ct. W Heath GU14 .... 84 E8
Hawley City Prim Sch.
Hawley GU17 .... 64 E3
Hawley Garden Cotts.
Hawley GU17 .... 64 D4
Hawley La. Farnb GU14 .... 85 B8
Hawley Lodge. Hawley GU17 .... 64 F2
Hawley Place Sch. Hawley GU17 64 E1
Hawley Rd. Hawley GU14 & GU17 64 F3
Hawley Way. Ashf TW15 .... 14 B3
Hawmead. Crawl D RH10 .... 204 C8
Hawth (Arts Ctr) The.
Crawl RH10 .... 201 F5
Hawth Ave. Crawl RH10 .... 201 F4
Hawth Cl. Crawl RH10 .... 201 E4
Hawthorn Ave. S Norw CR7 .... 42 B8
Hawthorn Cl. Brack RG12 .... 27 A8
Hawthorn Cl. Crawl TW5 .... 4 B7
Hawthorn Cl. Crawl RH11 .... 181 C1
Hawthorn Cl. Earls RH1 .... 140 A4
Hawthorn Cl. Hampt TW12 .... 16 A3
Hawthorn Cl. Horsh RH12 .... 217 C4
Hawthorn Cl. Nork SM7 .... 77 E5
Hawthorn Cl. Woking GU22 .... 89 E7
Hawthorn Cres. Selsd CR2 .... 81 C8
Hawthorn Cres. Up Toot SW17 ... 21 A3
Hawthorn Ct. Rich TW9 .... 7 B6
Hawthorn Ct. 8 W Norw SW16 ... 22 A3
Hawthorn Dr. Coney H BR4 .... 63 E6
Hawthorn Gr. Penge SE20 .... 43 B8
Hawthorn Hatch. Brent TW8 .... 6 B7
Hawthorn La. New Gn SL4 .... 8 A7
Hawthorn La. Rowl GU10 .... 145 F3
Hawthorn Rd. Brent TW8 .... 6 B7
Hawthorn Rd.
Carsh SM1 & SM2 & SM5 .... 59 E4
Hawthorn Rd. Friml GU16 .... 65 F2
Hawthorn Rd. Ock Rid GU7 .... 150 B2
Hawthorn Rd. Send M GU23 .... 91 A3
Hawthorn Rd. Wallin SM5 & SM6 60 B3
Hawthorn Rd. Woking GU22 .... 89 D7
Hawthorn Way. Bisley GU24 .... 68 A3
Hawthorn Way. Earls RH1 .... 140 B8
Hawthorn Way. Up Hall TW17 ...... 34 D5
Hawthornedene Cl. Coney H BR2 63 F8
Hawthornedene Rd. Coney H BR2 63 F8
Hawthorne Ave. Bigg H TN16 .... 83 D4
Hawthorne Ave. Mitch CR4 .... 40 D7
Hawthorne Ave. Wallin SM5 .... 60 A3
Hawthorne Ave. Wink SL4 .... 9 B6
Hawthorne Cl. Alder GU12 .... 126 E7
Hawthorne Cl. Sutton SM1 .... 59 C8
Hawthorne Cotts. Burst RH6 ...... 183 C7
Hawthorne Cres. Hawley GU17 .... 64 E4
Hawthorne Ct. Stan TW19 .... 13 D8
Hawthorne Dr. Wink SL4 .... 9 B7
Hawthorne Pl. Ewell KT17 .... 76 E7
Hawthorne Rd. Egham TW20 .... 12 C4
Hawthorne Way. Burph GU4 .... 110 B5
Hawthorne Way. Stan TW19 .... 13 D8
Hawthorne Way. Wink SL4 .... 9 B7
Hawthorns Sch (Pendell
Court) The. Bletch RH1 .... 120 B4
Hawthorns The. Belm SM2 .... 59 A4
Hawthorns The. Ewell KT17 .... 58 A3
Hawthorns The. Oxted RH8 .... 123 A2
Hawthorns The. Poyle SL3 .... 1 F6
Haxted Mill (Mus). Haxted TN8 165 D8
Haxted Rd. Haxted RH7 & TN8 ... 165 C7
Haxted Rd. Lingf RH7 & TN8 ...... 165 C7
Haybarn Dr. Horsh RH12 .... 217 E7
Haycroft Cl. Coulsd CR8 .... 80 E1
Haycroft Rd. Surb KT6 .... 56 E7
Hayden Ct. Woodhm KT15 .... 71 B8
Haydn Ave. Purley CR8 .... 80 A4
Haydn House. 2 Tedd TW1 .... 17 C1
Haydon Park Rd. Wimble SW19 .. 20 B3
Haydon Pl. Guild GU1 .... 130 D8
Haydon's Rd. Merton SW19 .... 20 C2
Haydon's Rd. Wimble SW19 .... 20 C2

Haydons Road Sta.
Wimble SW19 .... 20 C3
Hayes Barton. Mayb GU22 .... 70 D3
Hayes Chase. W Wick BR4 .... 44 E3
Hayes Cres. Cheam SM3 .... 58 D6
Hayes Ct. Streat SW12 .... 21 E7
Hayes Ct. Wimble SW19 .... 19 E2
Hayes Hill. W Wick BR2 .... 44 E1
Hayes Hill Rd. Hayes BR2 .... 44 F1
Hayes La. Beck BR2 & BR3 .... 44 D5
Hayes La. Kenley CR8 & CR3 .... 80 B3
Hayes La. Purley CR8 .... 80 B3
Hayes La. Slinfd RH13 .... 215 D2
Hayes Mead Rd. W Wick BR2 ...... 44 E1
Hayes Prim Sch The. Purley CR8 80 B3
Hayes Sta. Coney H BR2 .... 44 F1
Hayes The. Lang V KT18 .... 96 E8
Hayes Way. Beck BR3 .... 44 D5
Hayes Wlk. Smallf RH6 .... 162 A4
Hayesend House. Up Toot SW17 . 20 C4
Hayesford Park Dr. Hayes BR2 ... 44 F4
Hayfields. Horley RH6 .... 161 C4
Haygarth Pl. Wimble SW19 .... 19 D3
Haygreen Cl. King U T KT2 .... 18 B2
Haylett Gdns. King U T KT1 .... 37 D5
Hayling Ave. Felt TW13 .... 15 A5
Hayling Ct. Cheam SM3 .... 58 C6
Hayling Ct. Crawl RH11 .... 201 C3
Haymeads Dr. Esher KT10 .... 55 C4
Haymer Gdns. N Cheam KT4 .... 58 A7
Hayne Rd. Beck BR3 .... 43 F8
Haynes La. S Norw SE19 .... 22 E2
Haynt Wlk. Merton SW20 .... 39 E6
Hays Bridge Bsns Ctr.
Blind H RH9 .... 163 C6
Hays Bridge Bsns Ctr.
Horne RH9 .... 163 B7
Hays Bridge Houses.
Horne RH9 .... 163 B7
Hays Wlk. E Ewell SM2 .... 58 D1
Haysleigh Gdns. Penge SE20 ...... 43 A7
Haysleigh House. Penge SE20 ..... 43 B7
Haywain The. Oxted RH8 .... 122 D5
Hayward Cl. Merton SW19 .... 40 B8
Haywardens. Lingf RH7 .... 164 D5
Haywards. Crawl RH10 .... 182 D1
Haywood. Easth RG12 .... 27 C2
Hayworth Rd. Crawl RH10 .... 182 D1
Hazel Ave. Bellf GU1 .... 109 C5
Hazel Ave. Farnb GU14 .... 84 F3
Hazel Bank. Ewh GU6 .... 175 E5
Hazel Bank. S Norw SE25 .... 42 E7
Hazel Bank. Tolw KT5 .... 38 C1
Hazel Cl. Brent TW8 .... 6 B7
Hazel Cl. Crawl RH11 .... 181 C1
Hazel Cl. Crawl RH10 .... 204 C8
Hazel Cl. Croy CR0 .... 43 D1
Hazel Cl. Eng Gn TW20 .... 11 B2
Hazel Cl. Mitch CR4 .... 41 D5
Hazel Cl. Twick TW2 .... 16 C8
Hazel Cl. Woodh RH2 .... 139 C7
Hazel Cl. Bellf GU1 .... 109 D5
Hazel Ct. 9 N Norw SW16 .... 22 A3
Hazel Ct. Warlgm CR6 .... 81 E1
Hazel Dr. Send M GU23 .... 90 F2
Hazel Gr. For Hil SE26 .... 23 D4
Hazel Gr. Shottm GU26 .... 188 E2
Hazel Gr. Stain TW18 .... 13 C2
Hazel Mead. Ewell KT17 .... 58 A1
Hazel Par. Fetch KT22 .... 94 C5
Hazel Rd. Ash GU12 .... 127 C8
Hazel Rd. Mytch GU16 .... 86 A2
Hazel Rd. Woodh RH2 .... 139 C7
Hazel Way. Crawl D RH10 .... 204 C8
Hazel Way. Fetch KT22 .... 94 C4
Hazel Wlk. Dork RH5 .... 136 C4
Hazelbank Ct. Chert KT16 .... 33 C1
Hazelbank Rd. Catf SE6 .... 24 E6
Hazelbank Rd. Chert KT16 .... 33 C2
Hazelbury Cl. Merton SW19 .... 40 A7
Hazeldene. Addl KT15 .... 52 C5
Hazeldene Rd. Kenley CR8 .... 80 D4
Hazelhurst. Beck BR3 .... 44 D8
Hazelhurst Cl. Burph GU4 .... 110 B6
Hazelhurst Cres. Horsh RH12 ... 216 F1
Hazelhurst Ct. Catf SE6 .... 24 C3
Hazelhurst Dr. Worth RH10 .... 202 E6
Hazelhurst Rd. Up Toot SW17 .... 20 D4
Hazelhurst Sch. Wimble SW20 .. 39 D8
Hazell Hill. Brack RG12 .... 27 C6
Hazell Rd. Farnh GU9 .... 124 F1
Hazelmere Cl. Hatton TW14 .... 3 E1
Hazelmere Cl. Leahd KT22 .... 95 B8
Hazelmere Ct. 10 Streat SW2 ...... 21 F7
Hazelwick Ave. Crawl RH10 ...... 202 B8
Hazelwick Mill La. Crawl RH10 202 A8
Hazelwick Rd. Crawl RH10 .... 202 A7
Hazelwick Sch. Crawl RH10 ...... 202 A8
Hazelwood. Crawl RH11 .... 201 A5
Hazelwood Ave. Morden SM4 ...... 40 B5
Hazelwood Cl. Crawl D RH10 .... 203 F8
Hazelwood Cotts. Cran GU6 ..... 194 D4
Hazelwood Cotts. Godal GU5 .... 150 D4
Hazelwood Ct. Surb KT6 .... 37 E3
Hazelwood Gr. Sander CR2 .... 81 B6
Hazelwood House. Beck BR2 .... 44 E6
Hazelwood La. Chips CR5 .... 98 F8
Hazelwood Lodge. W Wick BR4 .. 44 C2
Hazelwood Rd. Knaph GU21 .... 68 E1
Hazelwood Rd. Oxted RH8 .... 123 B3
Hazledean Rd. Croy CR0 & CR9 ... 61 D8
Hazleden Cross. E Grins RH19 .. 205 B6
Hazledene Rd. Chisw W4 .... 7 C8
Hazlemere Gdns. N Cheam KT4 . 39 A1
Hazlewood. Elst GU8 .... 148 E4
Hazlitt Cl. Felt TW13 .... 15 E4
Hazon Way. Epsom KT19 .... 76 C7
Headcorn Pl. Thorn H CR7 .... 41 F5
Headcorn Rd. Broml BR1 .... 24 F3
Headcorn Rd. Thorn H CR7 .... 41 F5
Headington Cl. Woki RG11 .... 25 D8
Headington Dr. Woki RG11 .... 25 D8

Headington Rd. Wands SW18 ...... 20 C6
Headland Way. Lingf RH7 .... 164 D4
Headley Ave. Wallin CR0 & SM6 .. 60 F5
Headley Cl. Chess KT19 .... 57 A4
Headley Cl. Crawl RH10 .... 182 D1
Headley Common Rd.
Head KT18 & KT20 .... 116 D7
Headley Ct. For Hil SE26 .... 23 C3
Headley Dr. Burgh H KT20 .... 97 B8
Headley Dr. New Add CR0 .... 63 C3
Headley Dr. Burgh H KT20 .... 97 C7
Headley Gr. Burgh H KT20 .... 116 D7
Headley Heath App.
Box H KT20 .... 116 B4
Headley Hill Rd. Head Dn GU35 187 A5
Headley Rd. Ashtd KT18 .... 96 C6
Headley Rd. Graysh GU26 .... 188 C3
Headley Rd. Head KT18 .... 96 A4
Headley Rd. Hind GU26 .... 188 C3
Headley Rd. Lang V KT21 .... 96 C8
Headley Rd. Leahd KT18 & KT22 .. 95 E4
Headley Rd. Mickle RH5 .... 115 E7
Headway Cl. Rich TW10 .... 17 C4
Headway The. Ewell KT17 .... 57 F2
Hearn Vale. Head Dn GU35 .... 187 A7
Hearn Wlk. Brack RG12 .... 27 E8
Hearne Rd. Brent W4 .... 7 A8
Hearnville Prim Sch.
Balham SW12 .... 21 A7
Hearnville Rd. Balham SW12 .... 21 A7
Hearsey Gdns. Blckw GU17 .... 64 B6
Hearsey Gdns. Blckw GU17 .... 64 C6
Heath Bsns Ctr Rd. Hounsl TW3 .. 5 C3
Heath Cl. Banstd SM7 .... 78 B5
Heath Cl. Beac H GU26 .... 188 C7
Heath Cl. Broad H RH12 .... 216 E3
Heath Cl. Harl UB3 .... 3 D7
Heath Cl. Heath E GU9 .... 125 C7
Heath Cl. Stan TW19 .... 2 C1
Heath Cl. Vir W GU25 .... 31 D5
Heath Cl. Woki RG11 .... 25 B4
Heath Clark Tertiary Ctr.
Croy CR9 .... 61 A6
Heath Cotts. Beac H GU26 .... 188 C6
Heath Ct. Broad H RH12 .... 216 E3
Heath Dr. Brookw GU24 .... 88 A7
Heath Dr. Send GU23 .... 90 B5
Heath Dr. Sutton SM2 .... 59 C2
Heath Dr. W Barn SW20 .... 39 C5
Heath Dr. Walt o't H KT20 .... 97 A2
Heath End Sch. Heath E GU9 ..... 125 E6
Heath Gdns. Twick TW1 .... 16 F6
Heath Gr. Ashf TW16 .... 14 F1
Heath Gr. Penge SE20 .... 23 C1
Heath Hill. Docken GU10 .... 166 E3
Heath Hill. Dork RH4 .... 136 B7
Heath Hill Rd N. Crowth RG11 ..... 45 B5
Heath Hill Rd S. Crowth RG11 ..... 45 B4
Heath House. Thorn H CR7 .... 42 A4
Heath House. Weyb KT13 .... 53 A6
Heath House. Woking GU22 .... 88 D5
Heath La. Albury GU5 .... 132 E2
Heath La. Crond GU10 .... 124 B7
Heath La. Godal GU7 & GU8 .... 151 A2
Heath La. Heath E GU9 .... 125 C7
Heath Mead. Wimble SW19 .... 19 D5
Heath Mill La. Pirb GU24 .... 88 C2
Heath Rd. Bagsh GU19 .... 47 D3
Heath Rd. Cater CR3 .... 100 D3
Heath Rd. Horse GU21 .... 69 F4
Heath Rd. Islew TW3 & TW7 .... 5 C3
Heath Rd. Linch GU7 .... 207 D5
Heath Rd. Oxsh KT22 .... 74 C7
Heath Rd. S Norw CR7 .... 42 C6
Heath Rd. Twick TW1 .... 16 F7
Heath Rd. Weyb KT13 .... 53 A5
Heath Ridge Gn. Cobham KT11 ... 74 A6
Heath Rise. Camb GU15 .... 65 D5
Heath Rise. Hayes BR2 .... 44 F3
Heath Rise. Vir W GU25 .... 31 D5
Heath The. Cater CR3 .... 100 C5
Heath View. E Hors KT24 .... 92 F2
Heath Way. Horsh RH12 .... 217 D5
Heathacre. Poyle SL3 .... 1 E6
Heatham Pk. Twick TW2 .... 16 F8
Heathbridge. Whit V KT13 .... 53 A4
Heathcote. Tadw KT20 .... 97 D5
Heathcote Dr. E Grins RH19 ...... 185 C2
Heathcote Rd. Ash GU12 .... 106 A3
Heathcote Rd. Camb GU15 .... 65 D5
Heathcote Rd. Epsom KT18 .... 76 E6
Heathcote Rd. Twick TW1 .... 6 B2
Heathcroft Ave. Ashf TW16 .... 14 F1
Heathdale Ave. Hounsl TW4 .... 4 E4
Heathdene. Burgh H KT20 .... 77 E1
Heathdene Rd. Streat SW16 .... 21 F1
Heathdene Rd. Wallin SM5 & SM6 60 B3
Heathdown Rd. Mayb GU22 .... 70 D4
Heathedge. For Hil SE23 & SE26 .. 23 B6
Heather Cl. Ash GU12 .... 106 B5
Heather Cl. Copth RH10 .... 183 B2
Heather Cl. Hampt TW12 .... 35 F8
Heather Cl. Horse GU21 .... 69 C4
Heather Cl. Horsh RH12 .... 217 D5
Heather Cl. Islew TW7 .... 5 D2
Heather Cl. Kings KT20 .... 97 E5
Heather Cl. Stough GU2 .... 109 B3
Heather Cl. Woodhm KT15 .... 52 B1
Heather Cl. Wreccl GU9 .... 145 F6
Heather Cotts. Ash V GU12 .... 106 A8
Heather Dr. Sunn SL5 .... 30 B2
Heather Gdns. Belm SM2 .... 59 A4
Heather Mead. Friml GU16 .... 65 F2
Heather Mead Ct. Friml GU16 ..... 65 F2
Heather Ridge Arc. Friml GU15 .. 66 C4

Heather Ridge Fst Sch.
Friml GU15 .... 66 D4
Heather Way. Burrh GU24 .... 49 E3
Heather Way. Hind GU26 .... 188 F4
Heather Way. S Croy CR2 .... 62 D2
Heather Wlk. Crawl RH11 .... 201 B3
Heather Wlk. Pirb GU24 .... 87 D7
Heather Wlk. Smallf RH6 .... 162 C3
Heather Wlk. Twick TW4 .... 16 A8
Heather Wlk. Whit V GU12 .... 53 F1
Heatherdale Cl. King U T KT2 ..... 18 B1
Heatherdale Rd. Camb GU15 ...... 65 D4
Heatherdene. W Hors KT24 .... 92 D2
Heatherdene Cl. Mitch CR4 .... 40 E5
Heatherdene Mansions. 2
Twick TW1 .... 6 D1
Heatherlands. Ashf TW16 .... 15 A2
Heatherlands. Horley RH6 .... 161 B4
Heatherley Cl. Camb GU15 .... 65 B5
Heatherley Rd. Camb GU15 .... 65 B5
Heathermount. Brack RG12 .... 27 E5
Heathermount Dr. Crowth RG11 . 45 A6
Heathermount Sch. Ascot SL5 ... 29 D3
Heathers Land. Dork RH5 .... 136 C4
Heatherset Gdns. S Norw SW16 21 F1
Heatherside Dr. Went GU25 .... 31 A3
Heatherside Rd. W Ewell KT19 ... 57 D3
Heatherside Rd. W Ewell KT19 ... 57 D3
Heathervale Rd. Woodhm KT15 .. 52 B1
Heatherway. Crowth RG11 .... 45 A5
Heatherway. Felb RH19 & RH7 .. 184 F7
Heatherwood Hospl. Ascot SL5 .. 28 E6
Heathfield. Cobham KT11 .... 74 A5
Heathfield. Crawl RH10 .... 202 D8
Heathfield. Reig RH2 .... 138 D8
Heathfield Ave. Ascot SL5 .... 29 E4
Heathfield Ave. Wands SW18 ...... 20 D8
Heathfield Cl. Godal GU7 .... 150 E2
Heathfield Cl. Woking GU22 .... 70 A1
Heathfield Ct. Ashf TW15 .... 13 E5
Heathfield Ct. Penge SE20 .... 23 C1
Heathfield Ct. Wands SW18 .... 20 D8
Heathfield Dr. Earls RH1 .... 139 E4
Heathfield Dr. Mitch SW19 .... 20 E1
Heathfield Gdns. Croy CR0 .... 61 D6
Heathfield Inf Sch. Twick TW2 ... 16 A7
Heathfield Jun Sch. Twick TW2 .. 16 A7
Heathfield N. Twick TW1 & TW2 .. 16 F8
Heathfield Rd. Broml BR1 .... 24 F1
Heathfield Rd. Croy CR0 .... 61 D6
Heathfield Rd. Hersh KT12 .... 54 E6
Heathfield Rd. Wands SW18 .... 20 D8
Heathfield Rd. Woking GU21 .... 70 A1
Heathfield S. Twick TW1 & TW2 .. 16 F8
Heathfield Sq. Wands SW18 .... 20 D8
Heathfield Vale. S Croy CR2 .... 62 E2
Heathhurst Rd. S Croy CR2 .... 61 E2
Heathland Sch The. Hounsl TW4 .. 4 F1
Heathland St. Alder GU11 .... 105 A2
Heathlands. Tadw KT20 .... 97 D5
Heathlands. Up Toot SW12 .... 21 B6
Heathlands. Weyb KT13 .... 53 C5
Heathlands Cl. Horse GU21 .... 69 E5
Heathlands Cl. Sunby TW16 .... 35 A7
Heathlands Cl. Twick TW1 .... 16 F6
Heathlands Ct. Hounsl TW4 .... 4 A6
Heathlands Ct. Mitch CR4 .... 41 A6
Heathlands Ct. Woki RG11 .... 25 E2
Heathlands Ctry Mkt.Woki RG11 25 E1
Heathlands Sch. Wimble SW19 ... 19 C5
Heathlands Way. Hounsl TW4 .... 4 E2
Heathmere Prim Sch.
Rhampt SW15 .... 19 A7
Heathmoors. Easth RG12 .... 27 C4
Heathpark Dr. Windl GU20 .... 48 E4
Heathrise. Ruish KT13 .... 91 B4
Heathrow. Gomsh GU5 .... 133 C4
Heathrow Airport London.
Harm TW6 .... 3 A5
Heathrow Bvd. Harm UB7 .... 2 F7
Heathrow Causeway Est.
Hounsl TW4 .... 4 B4
Heathrow Central Sta. Harl TW6 .. 3 B4
Heathrow Cl. Harm TW6 .... 2 B6
Heathrow International Trad Est.
Hounsl TW4 .... 4 B4
Heathrow Prim Sch. Harm UB7 ... 2 F8
Heathrow Terminal 4 Sta.
E Bed TW6 .... 3 C1
Heathshot. 8 Rich TW10 .... 6 E1
Heathside. Hinch W KT10 .... 55 E7
Heathside. Twick TW4 .... 15 F8
Heathside. Weyb KT13 .... 53 B5
Heathside. Hinch W KT10 .... 55 E7
Heathside Cres. Woking GU22 .... 69 F2
Heathside Gdns. Woking GU22 ... 70 A2
Heathside La. Beac H GU26 .... 188 D6
Heathside Park Rd.
Woking GU22 .... 70 A1
Heathside Rd. Woking GU22 .... 69 F1
Heathside Sch. Weyb KT13 .... 52 F4
Heathvale Bridge Rd.
Ash V GU12 .... 106 A6
Heathview. Putney SW19 .... 19 D6
Heathview Gdns. Putney SW15 ... 19 C8
Heathview Rd. Thorn H CR7 .... 42 A5
Heathview Rd. Witley GU8 .... 170 E2
Heathway. Camb GU15 .... 65 D5
Heathway. Cater CR3 .... 100 D2
Heathway. Croy CR0 .... 62 F7
Heathway. E Hors KT24 .... 93 A3
Heathway. N Asct SL5 .... 28 E8
Heathway Cl. Camb GU15 .... 65 D5
Heathwood Ct. Hounsl TW3 .... 5 B3
Heathwood Ct. Streat SW12 .... 21 C7
Heathwood Point. 7
For Hil SE26 .... 23 D5

Heathyfields Rd. Hale GU9 .... 125 A6
Heaton Rd. Mitch CR4 .... 21 A1
Heavers Farm Prim Sch.
S Norw SE25 .... 42 F4
Hebdon Rd. Up Toot SW17 .... 20 F5
Heddon Cl. Islew TW7 .... 6 A3
Heddon Wlk. 1 W Heath GU14 .... 85 A7
Hedge Cnr. Tadw KT20 .... 97 C4
Hedge Croft Cotts. Ripley GU23 .. 91 B6
Hedge Wlk. Catf SE6 .... 24 B4
Hedgehog La. Haslem GU27 ...... 208 B5
Hedgerley Ct. Horse GU21 .... 69 C2
Hedgeside. Crawl RH11 .... 201 C1
Hedgeway. Onsl V GU2 .... 130 A7
Hedingham Cl. Horley RH6 .... 161 C4
Hedley Rd. Twick TW4 .... 16 A8
Heelas Rd. Woki RG11 .... 25 A5
Heenan Cl. Friml GU16 .... 65 F3
Heighton Gdns. Croy CR0 .... 61 B5
Heights Cl. Nork SM7 .... 77 E3
Heights Cl. Wimble SW20 .... 19 B1
Heights The. Beck BR3 .... 24 C1
Helder Gr. Lewish SE12 .... 24 F8
Helder St. S Croy CR2 .... 61 D4
Heldmann Cl. Islew TW7 .... 5 D3
Helen Ave. Felt TW14 .... 15 B8
Helen Cl. E Mole KT8 .... 36 B5
Helen Ct. Farnb GU14 .... 85 B4
Helena Cl. Wallin SM6 .... 60 E1
Helford Wlk. 3 Woking GU21 .... 69 A1
Helgiford Gdns. Ashf TW16 .... 14 E1
Helicon House. Crawl RH11 .... 201 C5
Helix Ho. Twick TW7 .... 6 B5
Helksham Cl. Sandh GU15 .... 45 D3
Helme Cl. Wimble SW19 .... 19 F3
Helmsdale. Brack RG12 .... 27 E4
Helmsdale. 8 Woking GU21 .... 69 B1
Helmsdale Rd. Streat SW16 .... 21 D1
Helston Cl. Friml GU16 .... 86 A7
Helvellyn Cl. Thor L TW20 .... 12 C1
Helvetia St. For Hil SE6 .... 23 F6
Hemingford Rd. Cheam SM3 ...... 58 C6
Hemlock Cl. Kings KT20 .... 97 E4
Hemming Cl. 7 Hampt TW12 .... 36 A8
Hempshaw Ave. Woodm SM7 ..... 78 F3
Hemsby Rd. Chess KT9 .... 56 F4
Hemsby Wlk. Crawl RH10 .... 202 B4
Henage Cnr. Burrh GU24 .... 49 E2
Henbane Ct. 2 Crawl RH11 .... 201 B2
Henbit Cl. Burgh H KT20 .... 97 B8
Henchley Dene. Merrow GU4 ..... 110 D3
Henderson Ave. Stough GU2 ..... 109 B5
Henderson Hospl. Belm SM2 ...... 59 B2
Henderson Rd. Bigg H TN16 .... 83 C7
Henderson Rd. Crawl RH11 .... 201 B1
Henderson Rd. Thorn H CR0 .... 42 D3
Henderson Rd. Wands SW18 ...... 20 E8
Henderson Way. Horsh RH12 .... 216 F1
Hendfield Ct. 5 Wallin SM6 .... 60 B4
Hendham Rd. Up Toot SW17 .... 20 F6
Hendon Terr. Ashf TW15 .... 14 D2
Hendon Way. Stan TW19 .... 2 D1
Hendrick Ave. Balham SW12 .... 20 F8
Heneage Cres. New Add CR0 ...... 63 C1
Henfield Rd.
Merton SW19 & SW20 .... 39 F8
Henfold Cotts. Bear Gn RH5 ...... 158 A2
Henfold La. Bear Gn RH5 .... 157 F5
Hengelo Gdns. Mitch CR4 .... 40 D5
Hengist Cl. Horsh RH12 .... 217 A1
Hengist Way. Beck BR2 & BR3 .... 44 E5
Hengrave Rd. For Hil SE23 .... 23 D8
Hengrove Cres. Ashf TW15 .... 13 D5
Henhurst Cross La. Coldh RH5 .. 157 A2
Henley Ave. Cheam SM3 .... 58 E7
Henley Bank. Onsl V GU2 .... 130 A7
Henley Cl. Hounsl TW7 .... 5 F6
Henley Cl. W Heath GU14 .... 84 E8
Henley Cl. Mitch CR4 .... 41 A6
Henley Ct. Old Wok GU22 .... 90 A7
Henley Dr. Friml GU16 .... 85 E7
Henley Dr. King U T KT2 .... 18 F1
Henley Gate. Pirb GU24 & GU3 .. 107 C8
Henley Lodge. S Norw SE25 .... 42 F5
Henley Way. Felt TW13 .... 15 D3
Henley Wood. Chelsh CR6 .... 82 A2
Hennel Cl. For Hil SE23 .... 23 C5
Hennessy Ct. Sheer GU21 .... 70 C6
Henry Cavendish Prim Sch.
Streat SW12 .... 21 C7
Henry Hatch Ct. Sutton SM2 .... 59 C3
Hensford Gdns. For Hil SE26 ...... 23 B4
Henshaw Cl. Crawl RH11 .... 200 F4
Henslow Way. Sheer GU21 .... 70 D5
Henson Rd. Crawl RH10 .... 202 B7
Hensworth Rd. Stain TW15 .... 13 D3
Henty Cl. Crawl RH11 .... 200 E3
Hepburn Gdns. W Wick BR2 .... 44 F1
Hepple Cl. Islew TW7 .... 6 B5
Hepplewhite Cl. Crawl RH11 ..... 201 B3
Hepworth Croft. Sandh GU15 ..... 64 E6
Hepworth Ct. Cheam SM3 .... 40 A1
Hepworth Rd. Streat SW16 .... 21 E1
Hepworth Way. Walt O T KT12 .... 34 F1
Heracles Cl. Wallin SM6 .... 60 E3
Herald Gdns. Hackb SM6 .... 60 B7
Herbert Cl. Easth RG12 .... 27 B4
Herbert Cres. Knaph GU21 .... 68 E1
Herbert Gdns. Chisw W4 .... 7 B8
Herbert Rd. King U T KT1 .... 37 F6
Herbert Rd. Merton SW19 .... 19 F1
Herbs End. W Heath GU14 .... 84 C5
Hereford Cl. Crawl RH10 .... 201 E2
Hereford Cl. Epsom KT18 .... 76 D6
Hereford Cl. Stain TW18 .... 33 B8
Hereford Cl. Stough GU2 .... 108 F3
Hereford Copse. Woking GU22 ... 89 B8
Hereford Ct. 6 Croy CR0 .... 42 F1
Hereford Gdns. Twick TW2 .... 16 C7
Hereford La. Hale GU9 .... 125 B7

Hereford Rd. Felt TW13 .... 15 C7
Hereford Way. Chess KT9 .... 56 D5
Hereward Ave. Purley CR8 .... 61 A1
Hereward Rd. Up Toot SW17 ...... 20 F4
Heriot Rd. Chert KT16 .... 33 A2
Heritage Ct. 2 Egham TW20 ..... 12 A3
Heritage House. 22
   Putney SW19 .... 19 D7
Heritage Lawn. Horley RH6 ...... 161 C4
Herlwyn Gdns. Up Toot SW17 ..... 20 F4
Herm Cl. Crawl RH11 .... 201 A2
Hermes House. Penge BR3 .... 43 E8
Hermes Way. Wallin SM6 .... 60 D3
Hermitage Cl. Clayg KT10 .... 56 A4
Hermitage Cl. Farnb GU14 .... 85 D1
Hermitage Cl. Friml GU16 .... 65 F1
Hermitage Cl. Shep Gn SW17 ..... 34 A5
Hermitage Cl. Stain TW18 .... 12 F3
Hermitage Cty Fst Sch The.
   Knaph GU21 .... 88 E8
Hermitage Cty Jun Sch The.
   Knaph GU21 .... 88 E8
Hermitage Dr. N Asct SL5 .... 28 E7
Hermitage Gdns. S Norw SE19 ..... 22 C1
Hermitage La. Croy CR0 .... 43 A3
Hermitage La. E Grins RH19 ..... 205 F8
Hermitage La. Streat SW16 .... 21 F1
Hermitage Par. Ascot SL5 .... 29 A6
Hermitage Rd. E Grins RH19 ..... 185 D3
Hermitage Rd. Kenley CR8 .... 80 C3
Hermitage Rd. Knaph GU21 .... 88 D8
Hermitage Rd. Knaph GU21 .... 88 E8
Hermitage Rd. S Norw SE19 .... 22 D2
Hermitage The. Barnes SW13 ...... 7 F6
Hermitage The. Felt TW13 .... 14 F5
Hermitage The. For Hil SE23 .... 23 C7
Hermitage The. King U T KT1 ...... 37 D5
Hermitage The. Rich TW10 .... 6 E2
Hermitage Woods Cres.
   Knaph GU21 .... 88 E7
Hermits Rd. Crawl RH10 .... 201 F7
Hermonger La. Ell Gn RH12 ..... 195 F2
Herndon Cl. Egham TW20 .... 12 A4
Herne Rd. Surb KT6 .... 56 E8
Heron Cl. Crawl RH11 .... 201 C8
Heron Cl. Mytch GU16 .... 85 F4
Heron Cl. N Asct SL5 .... 28 D8
Heron Cl. Stough GU2 .... 109 B4
Heron Cl. Dork RH4 .... 136 A8
Heron Ct. 5 King U T KT1 .... 37 E6
Heron Ct. Stan TW19 .... 13 E7
Heron Ct. 6 W Norw SE21 .... 22 D6
Heron Dale. Addl KT15 .... 52 D5
Heron House. Tedd KT1 .... 37 C8
Heron Pl. E Grins RH19 .... 205 F8
Heron Rd. Croy CR0 .... 61 E8
Heron Rd. Islew TW1 .... 6 B3
Heron Shaw. Cran GU6 .... 174 E1
Heron Sq. 25 Rich TW10 .... 6 D2
Heron Way. Horsh RH13 .... 218 A1
Heron Way Cty Prim Sch.
   Horsh RH13 .... 218 A1
Heron Wlk. Sheer GU21 .... 70 C5
Heron Wood Rd. Alder GU12 ..... 126 D7
Heron's Way. Woki RG11 .... 25 E7
Herondale. Easth RG12 .... 27 C2
Herondale. Selsd CR2 .... 62 D2
Herondale. Shottm GU27 .... 207 E6
Herondale Ave. Wands SW18 ..... 20 E7
Heronfield. Eng Gn TW20 .... 11 C2
Heronry The. Whit V KT12 .... 54 A4
Herons Cl. Dome RH10 .... 184 B5
Herons Croft. Whit V KT13 .... 53 D3
Herons Lea. Dome RH10 .... 184 A4
Herons Pl. Islew TW7 .... 6 B4
Herons Way. Pirb GU24 .... 87 D6
Herons Wood Ct. Horley RH6 ... 161 B4
Heronscourt. Lhtwat GU18 .... 67 C8
Herontye Dr. E Grins RH19 ..... 206 A8
Herrett St. Alder GU12 .... 126 D8
Herretts Gdns. Alder GU12 .... 105 D1
Herrick Cl. Crawl RH10 .... 202 C8
Herrick Cl. Friml GU16 .... 66 C3
Herrick Ct. 4 Rich TW10 .... 17 D4
Herrings La. Windl GU20 .... 48 D4
Herschel Wlk. 9 Crawl RH11 .... 201 B1
Herschell Rd. For Hil SE23 .... 23 E8
Hersham Cl. Rhampt SW15 .... 19 A8
Hersham Gdns. Hersh KT12 .... 54 D6
Hersham Rd. Hersh KT12 .... 54 D6
Hersham Rd. Walt O T KT12 .... 54 E7
Hersham Sta. Hersh KT12 .... 54 E7
Hersham Trad Est.
   Walt O T KT12 .... 54 E8
Hershell Ct. Mortl SW14 .... 7 B3
Hertford Ave. Mortl SW14 .... 7 E3
Hertford Lodge. 10
   Putney SW19 .... 19 C7
Hertford Sq. Mitch CR4 .... 41 E5
Hertford Way. Mitch CR4 .... 41 E5
Hesiers Hill. Chelsh CR6 .... 82 E2
Hesiers Rd. Chelsh CR6 .... 82 F3
Hesketh Cl. Cran GU6 .... 174 E3
Heslop Ct. 2 Up Toot SW12 .... 21 A7
Heslop Rd. Up Toot SW12 .... 20 F7
Hessle Gr. Ewell KT17 .... 76 F8
Hester Terr. Rich TW9 .... 7 A4
Hesterman Way. Croy CR0 & CR9 41 F1
Heston Ave. Heston TW5 .... 4 E7
Heston Comm Sch. Heston TW5 .. 5 A7
Heston Grange. Heston TW5 .... 4 F8
Heston Grange La. Heston TW5 .... 4 F8
Heston Ind Mall. Heston TW5 .... 4 F7
Heston Inf Sch. Heston TW5 .... 5 A7
Heston Jun Sch. Heston TW5 .... 5 A7
Heston Phoenix Distribution Pk.
   Heston TW5 .... 4 C8
Heston Rd. Earls RH1 .... 139 F4
Heston Rd. Heston TW5 .... 5 A7
Heston Wlk. Earls RH1 .... 139 F4
Hetherington Rd. Charlt TW17 ..... 34 C7

Hetley Gdns. 1 S Norw SE19 ..... 22 F1
Hevers Ave. Horley RH6 .... 161 A4
Hewers Way. Burgh H RH12 .... 97 C7
Hewitt Cl. Croy CR0 .... 63 A7
Hewitts Ind Est. Cran GU6 .... 174 B3
Hewlett Pl. Bagsh GU19 .... 47 F3
Hewshott La. Linch GU30 .... 207 A5
Hexal Rd. Catf SE6 .... 24 E5
Hexham Cl. Crawl RH10 .... 202 E6
Hexham Cl. Sandh GU15 .... 45 D2
Hexham Gdns. Hounsl TW7 .... 6 A7
Hexham Rd. Cheam SM4 .... 40 B1
Hexham Rd. W Norw SE27 .... 22 C6
Hextalls La. Bletch RH1 .... 120 E6
Heybridge Ave. Streat SW16 ...... 21 F2
Heydon Ct. W Wick BR4 .... 63 E8
Heyford Ave. Merton SW20 .... 39 F6
Heyford Rd. Mitch CR4 .... 40 E7
Heymede. Leahd KT22 .... 95 C4
Heythorp St. Wands SW18 .... 19 F6
Heythorpe Cl. Woking GU21 .... 68 F2
Heyward Ct. Belm SM2 .... 59 A4
Hibernia Gdns. Hounsl TW3 .... 5 A2
Hibernia Rd. Hounsl TW3 .... 5 A3
Hickey's Almshouses. 7
   Rich TW9 .... 6 F3
Hickling Wlk. Crawl RH10 .... 202 B4
Hickmans Cl. Godst RH9 .... 121 C3
Hicks La. Blckw GU17 .... 64 B5
Hidaburn Ct. 7 Streat SW16 ...... 21 C4
Hidcote Gdns. W Barn SW20 ...... 39 B6
Hidcote House. Sutton SM2 .... 59 C3
Hidecote Cl. Mayb GU22 .... 70 B3
Higgins Wlk. Hampt TW12 .... 15 E2
Higgs La. Bagsh GU19 .... 47 E4
High Ashton. 11 King U T KT2 ... 18 B1
High Ashurst (Outdoor Ctr).
   Head RH5 .... 116 A7
High Barn Rd.
   Wotton KT24 & RH5 .... 113 E3
High Beech. Brack RG12 .... 27 F5
High Beech. S Croy CR2 .... 61 E3
High Beeches. Friml GU16 .... 65 D2
High Beeches. Nork KT17 & SM7 77 D5
High Beeches Cl. Wallin CR8 ..... 60 D1
High Broom Cres. W Wick BR4 ... 44 B2
High Cedar Dr. Wimble SW20 ..... 19 B1
High Close Sch. Woki RG11 ...... 25 C7
High Coombe Pl. King U T KT2 .. 18 D1
High Down Rd. Sutton SM2 .... 78 B8
High Dr. King U T KT2 & KT3 ...... 38 C7
High Dr. Oxsh KT22 .... 74 D5
High Dr. Wold CR3 .... 102 A5
High Fields. Sunnin SL5 .... 29 F4
High Foleys. Clayg KT10 .... 56 B3
High Gables. Beck BR2 .... 44 E7
High Garth. Esher KT10 .... 55 C4
High Hill Rd. Farlgh CR6 .... 82 C5
High Hill Rd. Fickl CR6 .... 82 C5
High La. Haslem GU27 .... 208 C8
High La. Warlgm CR3 & CR6 ..... 101 F8
High Level Dr. For Hil SE26 .... 23 A4
High Limes. 2 W Norw SE19 ...... 22 E2
High Loxley Rd. Dunsf GU8 ...... 193 B7
High Mead. W Wick BR4 .... 63 E8
High Meadow Cl. Dork RH4 ...... 136 B6
High Oaks. Crawl RH11 .... 201 B4
High Par The. Streat SW16 .... 21 E5
High Park Ave. E Hors KT24 .... 92 F1
High Park Ave. Rich TW9 .... 7 A6
High Park Rd. Farnh GU9 .... 125 C3
High Park Rd. Rich TW9 .... 7 A6
High Path. Merton SW19 .... 40 C8
High Path Rd. Merrow GU1 .... 110 C1
High Pewley. Guild GU1 .... 130 E7
High Pine Cl. Weyb KT13 .... 53 C5
High Pines. Warlgm CR6 .... 101 C8
High Pitfold. Shottm GU26 .... 188 D1
High Rd. Byfl KT14 .... 71 E6
High Rd. Chips CR5 & RH2 .... 98 F4
High Rd. Kings CR5 & RH2 .... 98 F4
High Rd. L Kings CR5 & RH2 ...... 98 F4
High Ridge. Godal GU7 .... 150 D2
High St. Addl KT15 .... 52 B6
High St. Alder GU11 .... 105 A2
High St. Alder GU11 & GU12 ..... 105 B1
High St. Ascot SL5 .... 29 A6
High St. Ascot SL5 .... 29 D4
High St. Bagsh GU19 .... 47 E3
High St. Banstd SM7 .... 78 B4
High St. Beck BR3 .... 44 A7
High St. Bletch RH1 .... 120 D2
High St. Brack RG12 .... 27 B7
High St. Brack RG12 .... 27 C7
High St. Bramly GU5 .... 151 F6
High St. Brent TW8 .... 6 D7
High St. Brent TW8 .... 6 E8
High St. Camb GU15 .... 65 D6
High St. Carsh SM5 .... 60 A6
High St. Cater CR3 .... 100 E4
High St. Cheam SM1 & SM3 .... 58 E4
High St. Chidd GU8 .... 191 F2
High St. Chobh GU24 .... 68 E8
High St. Clayg KT10 .... 55 F4
High St. Cobham KT11 .... 73 B4
High St. Coln SL3 .... 1 C7
High St. Cran GU6 .... 174 D3
High St. Cranf TW5 .... 4 B7
High St. Crawl RH11 .... 201 D6
High St. Crowth RG11 .... 45 C4
High St. Croy SE25 .... 43 A5
High St. Croy CR0 & CR9 .... 61 C7
High St. Dork RH4 .... 136 B8
High St. E Grins RH19 .... 205 F8
High St. E Mole KT8 .... 36 A5
High St. Egham TW20 .... 11 F3
High St. Epsom KT17 & KT18 ..... 76 D6
High St. Esher KT10 .... 55 B6
High St. Esher KT10 .... 55 C6
High St. Ewell KT17 .... 58 A2
High St. Farnb GU14 .... 105 D8

High St. Felt TW13 .... 15 A6
High St. G Book KT23 .... 94 B2
High St. Godal GU7 .... 150 D4
High St. Godst RH9 .... 121 C4
High St. Guild GU1 & GU2 .... 130 D7
High St. Hampt TW12 .... 16 C2
High St. Harl UB3 .... 3 D8
High St. Harm UB7 .... 2 D8
High St. Haslem GU27 .... 208 D7
High St. Heston TW5 .... 4 B7
High St. Horley RH6 .... 161 B3
High St. Horse GU21 .... 69 C3
High St. Hounsl TW3 .... 5 B4
High St. King U T KT1 .... 37 D6
High St. Knaph GU21 .... 68 C2
High St. Leahd KT22 .... 95 B5
High St. Limps RH8 .... 123 B7
High St. Lingf RH7 .... 164 D4
High St. Merst RH1 .... 119 B7
High St. New Mal KT3 .... 38 E5
High St. Old Wok GU22 .... 90 B6
High St. Oxsh KT22 .... 74 D5
High St. Oxted RH8 .... 122 D5
High St.
   Penge SE19 & SE20 & BR3 ..... 23 C1
High St. Purley CR8 .... 80 A8
High St. Redh RH1 .... 118 F2
High St. Reig RH2 .... 118 A1
High St. Ripley GU23 .... 91 C6
High St. Rowl GU10 .... 145 E4
High St. Rusper RH12 .... 199 D7
High St. S Norw CR7 & SE25 ...... 42 D5
High St. S Norw SE25 .... 43 A6
High St. Sandh GU17 .... 45 A1
High St. Sandh GU17 .... 64 A8
High St. Shep TW17 .... 34 C3
High St. Stain TW18 .... 12 F4
High St. Stan TW19 .... 2 D1
High St. Sunnin SL5 .... 30 A4
High St. Sutton SM1 & SM2 .... 59 B5
High St. Sutton SM1 .... 59 B6
High St. Tadw KT20 .... 97 C4
High St. Tedd TW12 .... 16 C2
High St. Tedd TW11 .... 17 A3
High St. Tedd KT1 .... 37 D8
High St. Thame D KT7 .... 37 A3
High St. Twick TW2 .... 16 C8
High St. Tyl Gn RH9 .... 121 C4
High St. W End GU24 .... 67 F7
High St. Walt O T KT12 .... 44 B1
High St. Walt O T KT12 .... 35 A1
High St. Weyb KT13 .... 53 A6
High St. Wimble SW19 .... 19 D3
High St. Woking GU21 .... 69 F2
High St Mews. Wimble SW19 ..... 19 E3
High Street Collier's Wood.
   Mitch SW17 & SW19 .... 20 D2
High Street Harlington.
   Harl TW6 .... 3 D7
High The. Streat SW16 .... 21 E5
High Thicket Rd. Docken GU10 166 D5
High Tree Cl. Row Tn KT15 .... 52 A5
High Trees. Croy CR0 .... 43 E1
High Trees. Streat SW2 .... 22 A7
High Trees Cl. Cater CR3 .... 100 F5
High Trees Ct. Cater CR3 .... 100 F4
High Trees Ct. Sidlow RH6 .... 160 A4
High Trees Rd. Reig RH2 .... 139 D8
High View. Belm SM2 .... 77 F8
High View. Gomsh GU5 .... 133 C4
High View. 5 Penge SE19 .... 22 F1
High View Ave.
   Wallin CR0 & SM6 .... 60 F5
High View Cl. Farnb GU14 .... 85 A4
High View Cl.
   S Norw SE19 & SE25 .... 42 F7
High View Lodge. Alder GU11 .. 105 A2
High View Prim Sch.
   Wallin SM6 .... 60 E5
High View Rd. Farnb GU14 .... 85 A4
High View Rd. Lhtwat GU18 .... 66 F8
High View Rd. Onsl V GU2 .... 129 E6
High View Rd. S Norw SE19 .... 22 D2
Highams Hill. Crawl RH11 .... 200 F5
Highams La. Burrh GU20 & GU24 49 A5
Highbarrow Rd. Croy CR0 .... 43 A4
Highbirch Cl. Horsh RH12 .... 218 B5
Highbury Ave. S Norw CR7 .... 42 B7
Highbury Cl. New Mal KT3 .... 38 C4
Highbury Cl. W Wick BR4 .... 63 B8
Highbury Cres. Camb GU15 .... 66 A8
Highbury Rd. Wimble SW19 .... 19 E3
Highclere. Ascot SL5 .... 29 D4
Highclere. Burph GU1 .... 110 A4
Highclere Cl. Brack RG12 .... 27 E7
Highclere Cl. Kenley CR8 .... 80 C4
Highclere Ct. Knaph GU21 .... 68 C2
Highclere Dr. Camb GU15 .... 66 A2
Highclere Gdns. Knaph GU21 ..... 68 D2
Highclere Rd. Alder GU12 .... 126 D8
Highclere Rd. King U T KT3 .... 38 D6
Highclere Rd. Knaph GU21 .... 68 C2
Highclere St. For Hil SE26 .... 23 E4
Highcliffe. Beck BR3 .... 44 B8
Highcliffe Dr. Rhampt SW15 .... 7 F1
Highcotts La.
   Send GU4 & GU23 .... 91 A1
Highcroft. Beac H GU26 .... 188 D6
Highcroft. Milf GU8 .... 170 F8
Highcroft. Purley CR8 .... 79 F5
Highcroft. Sham Gn GU5 .... 152 E4
Highcroft. 2 Surb KT6 .... 37 F4
Highcroft Ct. Fetch KT23 .... 94 A4
Highcroft Dr. Burgh RH12 .... 195 E1
Highcross Way. 4
   Rhampt SW15 .... 19 A7
Highdaun Dr. Thorn H SW16 ...... 41 F5
Highdene. 6 Woking GU22 .... 69 F1
Highdown. New Mal KT4 .... 57 F8

Highdown Ct. Crawl RH10 .... 202 B3
Highdown Way. Horsh RH12 ..... 217 F1
Higher Alham. Brack RG12 .... 27 E2
Higher Dr. Belm KT17 & SM7 ...... 78 D7
Higher Dr. E Hors KT24 .... 112 E8
Higher Dr. Purley CR8 .... 80 A6
Higher Gn. Ewell KT17 .... 77 A6
Highercombe Rd.
   Haslem GU27 .... 208 B6
Highfield. Easth RG12 .... 26 F3
Highfield. Felt TW14 .... 15 A7
Highfield. Shalf GU4 .... 130 F1
Highfield. Woodm SM7 .... 78 E2
Highfield Ave. Alder GU11 .... 126 A8
Highfield Cl. Alder GU11 .... 126 B8
Highfield Cl. Eng Gn TW20 .... 11 C2
Highfield Cl. Farnb GU14 .... 84 F4
Highfield Cl. Long D KT6 .... 37 C1
Highfield Cl. M Bourn GU9 .... 146 B7
Highfield Cl. Oxsh KT22 .... 74 D8
Highfield Cl. Woki RG11 .... 25 B6
Highfield Cres. Hind GU26 .... 188 F4
Highfield Cres. Eng Gn TW20 ..... 11 C2
Highfield Ct. Mitch CR4 .... 40 E5
Highfield Ctr (Farnborough Coll
   of Tech Annexe. Alder GU11 .. 126 A8
Highfield Dr. Beck BR2 .... 44 F5
Highfield Dr. W Ewell KT19 .... 57 F4
Highfield Dr. W Ewell KT19 .... 57 F4
Highfield Dr. W Wick BR4 .... 63 C7
Highfield Gdns. Alder GU11 ..... 126 B8
Highfield Hill. S Norw SE19 .... 22 E1
Highfield Inf Sch. Beck BR2 .... 44 F5
Highfield Jun Sch. Beck BR2 ...... 44 F5
Highfield La. Putt GU3 .... 128 A3
Highfield La. Thursl GU8 .... 169 B2
Highfield Path. Farnb GU14 .... 84 F4
Highfield Rd. Bigg H TN16 .... 83 C3
Highfield Rd. Carsh SM1 .... 59 E5
Highfield Rd. Cater CR3 .... 101 A5
Highfield Rd. Chert KT16 .... 33 A1
Highfield Rd. E Grins RH19 ..... 185 D3
Highfield Rd. Farnb GU14 .... 84 F4
Highfield Rd. Felt TW13 .... 15 A7
Highfield Rd. Hounsl TW7 .... 5 F6
Highfield Rd. Purley CR8 .... 61 A1
Highfield Rd. Tolw KT5 .... 38 C7
Highfield Rd. Up Hall TW16 .... 34 F4
Highfield Rd. W Byfl KT14 .... 71 A6
Highfield Rd. Walt O T KT12 .... 35 A1
Highfield Sch. E Grins RH19 .... 185 D3
Highfield Sch. Wands SW18 ...... 20 E8
Highfields. Ashtd KT21 .... 95 D8
Highfields. E Hors KT24 .... 112 F7
Highfields. Fetch KT22 .... 94 D3
Highfields. For Row RH18 .... 206 F2
Highfields. Sutton SM1 .... 59 A8
Highgate Ct. Crawl RH11 .... 201 C2
Highgate House. 11
   For Hil SE23 .... 23 A5
Highgate La. Farnb GU14 .... 85 C5
Highgate Rd. For Hil SE23 .... 206 F1
Highgrove. 2 Farnb GU14 .... 85 B7
Highgrove Ct. Beck BR3 .... 24 A1
Highgrove House.
   Merrow GU4 .... 110 C3
Highland Cotts. Wallin SM6 .... 60 C6
Highland Croft. Catf BR3 .... 24 B2
Highland Lodge. 2 S Norw SE19 22 F1
Highland Pk. Felt TW13 .... 14 F4
Highland Rd. Alder GU11 .... 105 D2
Highland Rd. Bear Gn RH5 .... 157 D3
Highland Rd. Broml BR1 & BR2 .. 44 F8
Highland Rd. Camb GU15 .... 65 E8
Highland Rd. Purley CR8 .... 80 A5
Highland Rd. W Norw SE19 .... 22 E2
Highland View. Cran GU6 .... 174 C7
Highlands Ave. Horsh RH13 ..... 217 E2
Highlands Ave. Leahd KT22 .... 95 C5
Highlands Cl. Hounsl TW3 .... 5 B6
Highlands Cl. Leahd KT22 .... 95 B5
Highlands Cres. Horsh RH13 ..... 217 E2
Highlands Ct. W Norw SE19 .... 22 E2
Highlands Heath. Putney SW15 .. 19 C8
Highlands La. Westfd GU22 .... 89 E5
Highlands Pk. Leahd KT22 .... 95 D4
Highlands Rd. Heath E GU9 ...... 125 C7
Highlands Rd. Horsh RH13 .... 217 F2
Highlands Rd. Leahd KT22 .... 95 C5
Highlands Rd. Reig RH1 & RH2 . 118 D2
Highlands The. W Hors KT24 ...... 92 E2
Highmead. Cranf GU7 .... 150 F6
Highpoint. Weyb KT13 .... 53 A5
Highridge Cl. Epsom KT18 .... 76 E5
Highridge Ct. Epsom KT18 .... 76 E5
Highview. Cater CR3 .... 100 E2
Highview Cres. Camb GU15 .... 46 F1
Highview Ct. 2 Putney SW19 ..... 19 E7
Highview Ct. 2 Reig RH2 .... 118 D1
Highview High Sch. Wallin SM6 60 E5
Highway. Crowth RG11 .... 45 A5
Highway The. Sutton SM2 .... 59 C2
Highwayman's Ridge.
   Windl GU20 .... 48 B6
Highwold. Chips CR5 .... 79 A1
Highwood Cl. Kenley CR8 .... 80 C2
Highwoods. Cater CR3 .... 100 E2
Highwoods. Leahd KT22 .... 95 C6
Hilary Ave. Mitch CR4 .... 41 A6
Hilary Dr. Crowth RG11 .... 45 B6
Hilbert Rd. Cheam SM3 .... 58 D7
Hilborough Cl. Wimble SW19 ..... 20 B1
Hildenborough Gdns. Catf BR1 .. 24 F7
Hildenbrough House. Beck BR3 23 F1
Hildenlea Pl. Beck BR2 .... 44 E7
Hildenley Cl. Merst RH1 .... 119 D7
Hildens The. Westc RH4 .... 135 C5
Hilder Gdns. Farnb GU14 .... 85 D3
Hilders La. Eden TN8 .... 144 F4
Hilders The. Ashtd KT21 .... 76 B2

Hilditch House. 7 Rich TW10 ...... 6 F1
Hildreth St. Balham SW12 .... 21 B7
Hilgay. Guild GU1 .... 109 F1
Hilgay Cl. Guild GU1 .... 109 F1
Hilgay Ct. Guild GU1 .... 109 F1
Hill Cl. Horse GU21 .... 69 D3
Hill Cl. Purley CR8 .... 80 C6
Hill Cl. Woner GU5 .... 152 B6
Hill Copse View. Brack RG12 ...... 27 E8
Hill Cres. King U T KT5 .... 37 F4
Hill Cres. N Cheam KT4 .... 58 C8
Hill Crest. Dorm Pk RH19 .... 185 E6
Hill Crest. Elst GU8 .... 148 D4
Hill Crest Dr. Wreccl GU10 ...... 145 F6
Hill Ct. Farnc GU7 .... 150 E6
Hill Ct. Haslem GU27 .... 208 B6
Hill Ct. 8 King U T KT2 .... 18 B1
Hill Ct. 14 King U T KT6 .... 37 E4
Hill Dr. Thorn H SW16 .... 41 F6
Hill Gr. Felt TW13 .... 15 F6
Hill House Cl. Turn H RH10 ...... 204 A5
Hill House Dr. Whit V KT13 .... 72 A8
Hill House Dr. Woodh RH2 .... 139 B7
Hill House Rd. Streat SW16 .... 21 F3
Hill La. Kings KT20 .... 97 E6
Hill Manor. Horsh RH12 .... 217 A2
Hill Mead. Horsh RH12 .... 217 B3
Hill Rd. Beac H GU26 .... 188 C6
Hill Rd. Carsh SM5 .... 59 E4
Hill Rd. Fetch KT23 .... 94 B5
Hill Rd. Graysh GU26 .... 188 C3
Hill Rd. Haslem GU27 .... 208 C6
Hill Rd. Heath E GU9 .... 125 D7
Hill Rd. Mitch CR4 .... 21 B3
Hill Rd. Purley CR8 .... 79 F7
Hill Rd. Sutton SM1 .... 59 B5
Hill Rise. Dork RH4 .... 115 A1
Hill Rise. Hinch W KT10 .... 56 B8
Hill Rise. Rich TW10 .... 6 D2
Hill St. Rich TW10 .... 6 D2
Hill The. Cater CR3 .... 100 F3
Hill Top. Cheam SM3 & SM4 ...... 39 F2
Hill View. Mitch CR4 .... 41 E5
Hill View Cl. Purley CR8 .... 80 B8
Hill View Cl. Tadw KT20 .... 97 C6
Hill View Cres. Stough GU2 ...... 108 F3
Hill View Ct. 15 Woking GU22 .... 69 E1
Hill View Rd. Clayg KT10 .... 56 A3
Hill View Rd. Farnh GU9 .... 124 F2
Hill View Rd. Twick TW1 .... 6 A1
Hill View Rd. Woking GU22 .... 69 F1
Hillacre. Cater CR3 .... 100 E2
Hillard Ct. Wallin SM6 .... 60 D4
Hillars Heath Rd. Coulsd CR5 .... 79 E4
Hillary Cl. E Grins RH19 .... 186 A3
Hillary Cl. M Bourn GU9 .... 146 B7
Hillary Cres. Walt O T KT12 .... 35 C1
Hillary Dr. Crowth RG11 .... 13 E7
Hillary House. 10 Redh RH1 ..... 118 F2
Hillary Rd. M Bourn GU9 .... 146 B7
Hillbarn. S Croy CR2 .... 80 E8
Hillberry. Easth RG12 .... 27 C2
Hillbrook Gdns. Whit V KT13 ..... 53 A3
Hillbrook Prim Sch & Hillcroft
   Sch Annexe. Up Toot SW17 ..... 21 A4
Hillbrook Rd. Up Toot SW17 ...... 21 A4
Hillbrook Rise. Hale GU9 .... 125 B6
Hillbrow. New Mal KT3 .... 38 F6
Hillbrow. 3 Reig RH2 .... 118 C1
Hillbrow. 7 Rich TW10 .... 6 E1
Hillbrow Cl. Wood S V GU3 ...... 108 B2
Hillbrow Ct. Godst RH9 .... 121 C3
Hillbrow Cotts. Godst RH9 .... 121 C3
Hillbrow Rd. Catf BR1 .... 24 C2
Hillbrow Rd. Esher KT10 .... 55 C6
Hillbury Cl. Warlgm CR6 .... 81 C1
Hillbury Gdns. Warlgm CR6 .... 81 C1
Hillbury Rd. Up Toot SW17 .... 21 B1
Hillbury Rd. Warlgm CR3 & CR6 . 81 B1
Hillcote Ave. S Norw SW16 .... 22 A1
Hillcrest. Heath E GU9 .... 125 D8
Hillcrest. Weyb KT13 .... 53 B6
Hillcrest Ave. Addl KT16 .... 51 E6
Hillcrest Cl. Beck BR3 .... 43 F3
Hillcrest Cl. Crawl RH10 .... 202 D6
Hillcrest Cl. Epsom KT18 .... 76 F4
Hillcrest Cl. For Hil SE26 .... 23 A4
Hillcrest Ct. Sutton SM2 .... 59 D4
Hillcrest Ct. Weyb KT13 .... 53 B6
Hillcrest Gdns. Hinch W KT10 .... 55 F7
Hillcrest House. Merrow GU4 ... 110 C3
Hillcrest Par. Wallin CR5 .... 79 B5
Hillcrest Rd. Bigg H TN16 .... 83 D3
Hillcrest Rd. Camb GU15 .... 66 B7
Hillcrest Rd. Kenley CR8 .... 80 F2
Hillcrest Rd. Stough GU2 .... 108 F2
Hillcrest Rd. Wallin CR8 .... 60 F1
Hillcrest View. Beck BR3 .... 43 F3
Hillcroft Ave. Purley CR5 & CR8 . 79 D6
Hillcroft Coll. Surb KT6 .... 37 E3
Hillcroft Cty Prim Sch.
   Cater CR3 .... 100 E4
Hillcroft Cty Prim Sch.
   Whytlf CR3 .... 100 F6
Hillcroome Rd. Sutton SM2 .... 59 D4
Hillcross Ave. Merton SM4 .... 39 E4
Hillcross Ave. W Barn SM4 .... 39 E4
Hillcross Mid Sch. Merton SM4 .. 39 F5
Hilldale Rd. Cheam SM1 .... 58 F6
Hilldeane Rd. Wallin CR8 .... 61 A1
Hilldown Ct. Streat SW16 .... 21 E1
Hilldown Rd. Streat SW16 .... 21 E1
Hilldown Rd. W Wick BR2 .... 44 F1
Hilley Field La. Fetch KT22 .... 94 C6
Hillfield Ave. Carsh SM4 .... 40 E4
Hillfield Cl. Earls RH1 .... 119 A1
Hillfield Cl. Merrow GU1 .... 110 C3

Hillfield Rd. Earls RH1 .... 119 A1
Hillford Pl. Earls RH1 .... 140 A3
Hillgarth. Beac H GU26 .... 188 D5
Hillgate Pl. Balham SW12 ...... 21 B8
Hillhouse La. Cran RH12 & RH14 194 F1
Hillhurst Gdns. Cater CR3 ...... 100 F7
Hillier Gdns. Croy CR0 .... 61 A5
Hillier House. Guild GU2 .... 130 B7
Hillier Lodge. Tedd TW12 ...... 16 D3
Hillier Mews. Guild GU1 .... 110 A1
Hillier Pl. Chess KT9 .... 56 C4
Hillier Rd. Guild GU1 .... 110 A1
Hillier's La. Wallin CR0 & SM6 .... 60 E7
Hillingdale. Bigg H TN16 .... 83 B1
Hillingdale. Crawl RH11 .... 201 C1
Hillingdon Ave. Stan TW19 ...... 13 E7
Hillmead. Crawl RH11 .... 200 F6
Hillmont Rd. Hinch KT10 .... 55 E7
Hillmore Gr. For Hil SE26 ...... 23 E3
Hillmount. 13 Woking GU22 .... 69 E1
Hillrise. Bra Hil SL3 .... 1 A8
Hillrise. Walt O T KT12 .... 34 F2
Hills Farm La. Horsh RH12 .... 216 F1
Hills Pl. Horsh RH12 .... 217 A2
Hillsborough Ct. W Heath GU14 84 E8
Hillsborough Pk. Friml GU15 .... 66 C5
Hillside. Ascot SL5 .... 29 C4
Hillside. Crawl D RH10 .... 204 B8
Hillside. For Row RH18 .... 206 E3
Hillside. Horsh RH12 .... 217 A2
Hillside. Nork SM7 .... 77 E4
Hillside. Sandh GU15 .... 64 F7
Hillside. Went GU25 .... 31 C3
Hillside. Wimble SW19 .... 19 D2
Hillside. Woking GU22 .... 89 D7
Hillside Ave. Purley CR8 ...... 80 B6
Hillside Cl. Brock RH3 & RH5 .... 137 A8
Hillside Cl. Crawl RH11 .... 201 B4
Hillside Cl. E Grins RH19 ...... 185 C3
Hillside Cl. Head Dn GU35 .... 187 A6
Hillside Cl. Knaph GU21 .... 68 D2
Hillside Cl. Merton SM4 ...... 39 E5
Hillside Cl. Nork SM7 .... 77 E3
Hillside Cres. Friml GU16 ...... 85 F7
Hillside Ct. Guild GU1 .... 130 E8
Hillside Ct. 7 King U T KT2 .... 18 B1
Hillside Gdns. Brock RH3 & RH5 116 A1
Hillside Gdns. Row Tn RH15 .... 51 F5
Hillside Gdns. Streat SW2 ...... 22 A6
Hillside Gdns. Wallin SM6 ...... 60 C3
Hillside La. Coney H BR2 ...... 63 F8
Hillside La. Heath E GU9 ...... 125 D8
Hillside Pk. Sunnin SL5 .... 29 F1
Hillside Rd. Alder GU11 .... 126 A8
Hillside Rd. Ash GU12 .... 106 B3
Hillside Rd. Ashtd KT21 .... 75 F2
Hillside Rd. Beck BR2 .... 44 F6
Hillside Rd. Belm SM2 .... 58 F3
Hillside Rd. Coulsd CR5 .... 79 F1
Hillside Rd. Croy CR0 .... 61 B6
Hillside Rd. E Ewell KT17 ...... 58 C1
Hillside Rd. Heath E GU9 ...... 125 E7
Hillside Rd. King U T KT5 ...... 38 A4
Hillside Rd. Linch GU7 .... 207 F5
Hillside Rd. M Bourn GU10 .... 146 C3
Hillside Rd. Streat SW2 .... 22 A6
Hillside Rd. Tats TN16 .... 103 E8
Hillside Rd. Warlgm CR3 & CR6 .. 81 A1
Hillside Rd. Whytif CR3 & CR6 .. 81 A1
Hillside Way. Farnc GU7 ...... 150 D7
Hillsmead Way. Sander CR2 .... 81 B6
Hillspur Cl. Stough GU2 ...... 108 F2
Hillspur Rd. Stough GU2 ...... 108 F2
Hilltop Cl. Ascot SL5 .... 29 E7
Hilltop Cl. Leahd KT22 .... 95 C4
Hilltop Cl. Stough GU3 .... 108 F5
Hilltop Ct. S Norw SE19 ...... 42 D8
Hilltop La. Cater CR3 & RH1 .... 100 A1
Hilltop Rd. Kenley CR3 .... 80 F2
Hilltop Rd. Reig RH2 .... 139 B7
Hilltop Rise. G Book KT23 .... 94 C1
Hilltop Wlk. Wold CR3 .... 101 E6
Hillview. Whytlf CR3 .... 80 F2
Hillview. Wimble SW20 .... 19 B1
Hillview Ct. W Norw SE19 .... 22 E4
Hillview Dr. Earls RH1 .... 140 A8
Hillview Rd. Sutton SM1 ...... 59 D7
Hillworth. Beck BR3 .... 44 B7
Hillworth Rd. Streat SW2 ...... 22 A8
Hilly Mead. Wimble SW19 .... 19 E1
Hillybarn Rd. Rusper RH11 .... 180 C1
Hilsea Point. 7 Rhampt SW15 .. 19 B7
Hilton Ct. Horley RH6 .... 161 C4
Hilton Way. Hams Gn CR2 .... 81 B4
Himley Rd. Up Toot SW17 ...... 20 F2
Hinchcliffe Cl. Wallin SM6 .... 60 F3
Hinchley Cl. Hinch W KT10 .... 55 F7
Hinchley Dr. Hinch W KT10 .... 55 F7
Hinchley Way. Hinch W KT10 .. 56 A7
Hinchley Wood Prim Sch.
  Hinch W KT10 .... 56 A8
Hinchley Wood Sch.
  Hinch W KT10 .... 56 A8
Hinchley Wood Sta.
  Hinch W KT10 .... 55 F7
Hindell Cl. Farnb GU14 .... 85 A8
Hindhead Point. 6
  Rhampt SW15 .... 19 B7
Hindhead Rd.
  Shottm GU26 & GU27 ...... 188 F2
Hindhead Way. Wallin SM6 .... 60 E5
Hindsley's Pl. For Hil SE23 .... 23 C6
Hinkler Cl. Wallin SM6 .... 60 E3
Hinstock Ct. Farnb GU14 ...... 85 A3
Hinton Ave. Hounsl TW4 ...... 4 D3
Hinton Cl. Crowth RG11 ...... 45 B7
Hinton Dr. Crowth RG11 ...... 45 B7

Hinton Rd. Wallin SM6 .... 60 C4
Hipley Cl. Guild GU1 .... 131 A8
Hipley St. Old Wok GU22 ...... 90 B7
Hitchcock Cl. Littlt TW17 ...... 33 F6
Hitchings Way. Dovgn RH2 .... 139 A5
Hither Green Hospl.
  Lewish SE13 .... 24 D8
Hither Green La. Lewish SE13 .. 24 F8
Hitherbury Cl. Guild GU2 ...... 130 C6
Hitherfield Prim Sch.
  Streat SW2 .... 22 A6
Hitherfield Rd.
  Streat SW16 & SW27 ...... 22 A5
Hithermoor Rd. Stan TW19 .... 2 A2
Hitherhooks Hill. Binf RG12 .... 26 E8
Hithermoor Rd. Cran GU6 ...... 174 E2
Hitherwood Cl. Redh RH1 ...... 118 E3
Hitherwood Ct. Dulw SE21 .... 22 F4
Hitherwood Dr.
  Dulw SE19 & SE21 .... 22 F4
Hoadly Rd. Streat SW16 ...... 21 D6
Hobart Gdns. S Norw CR7 ...... 42 D6
Hobart Pl. 14 Rich TW10 ...... 6 F1
Hobart Rd. N Cheam KT4 ...... 58 B7
Hobbs Cl. W Byfl KT14 .... 71 B6
Hobbs Ind Est. Felb RH7 ...... 184 D7
Hobbs Rd. Crawl RH11 .... 201 A1
Hobbs Rd. 5 W Norw SE27 .... 22 C4
Hobill Wlk. Surb KT5 .... 37 F3
Hocken Mead. Crawl RH10 .... 202 D8
Hockering Gdns. Mayb GU22 .. 70 B1
Hockering Rd. Mayb GU22 .... 70 B1
Hockford Cl. Pirb GU3 .... 88 B1
Hodge La. Wink SL5 .... 9 A3
Hodges Cl. Bagsh GU19 ...... 47 E1
Hodgson Gdns.
  Burph GU1 & GU4 .... 110 A4
Hoe Bridge Sch. Mayb GU22 .. 90 C8
Hoe Cotts. Peasl GU5 .... 154 E8
Hoe La. Hasc GU8 .... 172 D4
Hoe La. Peasl GU5 .... 154 F8
Hoebridge Golf Ctr. Mayb GU22 90 C8
Hoebrook Glade. Westfd GU22 .. 89 E6
Hoebrook Glade. Woking GU22 .. 89 D6
Hoefield Cty Fst Sch.
  Westfd GU22 .... 89 E6
Hogarth Ave. Ashf TW15 ...... 14 C2
Hogarth Bsns Pk. Chisw W4 .. 7 E8
Hogarth Cl. Sandh GU15 ...... 64 E6
Hogarth Cres. Mitch CR4 & SW19 40 D8
Hogarth Cres. Thorn H CR0 .... 42 C2
Hogarth Ct. Dulw SE21 .... 22 F4
Hogarth Ct. Heston TW5 ...... 4 E7
Hogarth Gdns. Heston TW5 .... 5 A7
Hogarth House. 6
  W Norw SW2 .... 22 C4
Hogarth La. Chisw W4 .... 7 E8
Hogarth Rd. Crawl RH10 ...... 201 F3
Hogarth Roundabout. Chisw W4 . 7 E8
Hogarth Way. Hampt TW12 .... 36 C8
Hogbatch La. Hale GU9 .... 125 A6
Hogoak La. New Gn SL4 ...... 8 A8
Hogscross La. Kings CR5 ...... 98 F5
Hogshill La. Cobham KT11 .... 73 C5
Hogsmill Way. E Ewell KT19 .. 57 C6
Hogsmill Way. E Ewell KT19 .. 57 C6
Hogspudding La. Newd RH5 .. 158 C1
Hogtrough La. Nutf RH1 ...... 140 D8
Hogtrough La. Oxted RH8 .... 122 B6
Hogwood Rd. Ifold RH14 ...... 212 C3
Holbeach Mews. Balham SW12 .. 21 B7
Holbeach Prim Sch. Lewish SE6 24 A8
Holbeach Rd. Lewish SE6 .... 24 B8
Holbeck. Easth RG12 .... 26 F3
Holbeck Pl. Woking GU22 ...... 69 F1
Holbein Rd. Crawl RH10 ...... 201 F3
Holberry House. 5 Dulw SE21 .. 22 E4
Holborn Way. Mitch CR4 ...... 40 F7
Holbrook Cl. Heath E GU9 .... 125 F8
Holbrook Cl. Redh RH1 .... 118 F1
Holbrook Cty Prim Sch.
  Horsh RH12 .... 217 E7
Holbrook House. 5 Streat SW2 21 F7
Holbrook School La.
  Horsh RH12 .... 217 E7
Holbrook Way. Alder GU11 .... 126 B7
Holcon Ct. Redh RH1 .... 119 A4
Holder Rd. Alder GU12 .... 105 E1
Holder Rd. Worth RH10 .... 202 B3
Holdernesse Rd. 6
  Up Toot SW17 .... 21 A6
Holdsworth House. 5
  Streat SW2 .... 22 A8
Hole Hill. Westc RH4 .... 135 B7
Holford Rd. Merrow GU1 ...... 110 C1
Holland Ave. Belm SM2 ...... 59 A2
Holland Ave. Wimble SW20 .... 38 F8
Holland Cl. Coney H GU9 ...... 63 F8
Holland Cl. M Bourn GU9 ...... 146 E8
Holland Cl. Redh RH1 .... 118 F1
Holland Cres. Oxted RH8 ...... 123 A2
Holland Cty Jun Sch.
  Oxted RH8 .... 123 A1
Holland Dr. For Hil SE23 ...... 23 E5
Holland Gdns. Egham TW20 .. 32 F7
Holland La. Oxted RH8 .... 123 A2
Holland Pines. Easth RG12 .... 26 F2
Holland Rd. Croy SE25 .... 43 A4
Holland Rd. Oxted RH8 .... 123 A1
Holland Way. Coney H BR2 .... 63 F8
Hollands The. Felt TW13 ...... 15 D4
Hollands The. New Mal KT4 .. 38 F1
Hollands Way. E Grins RH19 .. 186 A4
Hollands Way. Warn RH12 .... 216 F8
Holles Cl. Hampt TW12 .... 16 A3
Hollies Ave. W Byfl KT14 ...... 70 F6
Hollies Cl. S Norw SW16 ...... 22 A2
Hollies Cl. Twick TW1 .... 16 F5
Hollies Ct. Addl KT15 .... 52 C5
Hollies Way. 2 Balham SW12 .. 21 A8

Hollin Ct. Crawl RH10 & RH11 .. 181 E1
Hollingbourne Cres.
  Crawl RH11 .... 201 C1
Hollingsworth Rd.
  S Croy CR0 & CR2 .... 62 B4
Hollingworth Cl. E Mole KT8 .. 35 F5
Hollingworth Ct. 7 Surb KT6 .. 37 D2
Hollis Wood Dr. Wreccl GU10 .. 145 E5
Hollman Gdns. S Norw SW16 .. 22 B2
Hollow Cl. Guild GU2 .... 130 A8
Hollow La. Dorman RH19 & RH7 186 D6
Hollow La. Vir W GU25 .... 31 C6
Hollow La. Wotton RH5 .... 134 D2
Hollow The. Crawl RH11 ...... 200 F5
Hollow The. Shackl GU7 ...... 149 F4
Holloway Hill. Godal GU7 .... 150 D4
Holloway Hill. Lyne KT16 ...... 51 D8
Holloway La. Harm U B7 ...... 2 E8
Holloway St. Hounsl TW3 ...... 5 B4
Holly Acre. Woking GU22 ...... 89 C4
Holly Ave. Friml GU16 .... 66 B3
Holly Ave. Walt O T KT12 .... 35 D1
Holly Ave. Woodhm KT15 .... 52 A1
Holly Bank Rd. Woking GU22 .. 89 B7
Holly Bush Ind Pk. Farnb GU12 105 E5
Holly Bush La. Farnb GU11 .... 105 E5
Holly Bush La. Farnb GU11 .... 105 E7
Holly Bush La. Hampt TW12 .. 15 F1
Holly Cl. Alder GU12 .... 105 C2
Holly Cl. Crawl RH10 .... 202 A8
Holly Cl. Eng Gn TW20 .... 11 B2
Holly Cl. Farnb GU14 .... 85 A4
Holly Cl. Felt TW13 .... 15 E3
Holly Cl. Head Dn GU35 ...... 187 C5
Holly Cl. Longc KT16 .... 50 A7
Holly Cl. Woking GU21 .... 89 B8
Holly Cott. Thame D KT7 ...... 37 A1
Holly Cres. 9 Belm SM2 ...... 59 A3
Holly Cres. Beck BR3 .... 43 F4
Holly Ct. 9 Belm SM2 .... 59 A3
Holly Gn. Oat Pk KT13 .... 53 D6
Holly Hedge Cl. Friml GU16 .. 65 E2
Holly Hedge Rd. Cobham KT11 73 B5
Holly Hedge Rd. Friml GU16 .. 65 E2
Holly Hill Dr. Banstd SM7 .... 78 A3
Holly Hock. Shalg GU24 ...... 68 A4
Holly Hough. Box H KT20 .... 116 B5
Holly House. Brent TW8 ...... 6 C8
Holly House. Easth RG12 ...... 27 B3
Holly La. Banstd SM7 .... 78 C2
Holly La. Ock Rid GU7 .... 150 C4
Holly La. Woodm SM7 .... 78 C2
Holly La. Worpl GU3 .... 108 D7
Holly La E. Banstd SM7 ...... 78 B3
Holly La W. Banstd SM7 ...... 78 B2
Holly Lea. Jacobs GU4 .... 109 D7
Holly Lodge Cty Prim Sch.
  Ash V GU12 .... 105 F8
Holly Rd. Alder GU12 .... 105 D1
Holly Rd. Farnb GU14 .... 85 A4
Holly Rd. Hampt TW12 .... 16 C2
Holly Rd. Hounsl TW3 .... 5 B3
Holly Rd. Twick TW1 .... 17 A7
Holly Rd. Woodh RH2 .... 139 B7
Holly Ridge. W End GU24 ...... 67 E6
Holly Spring Cty Inf Sch.
  Brack RG12 .... 27 E7
Holly Spring Cty Jun Sch.
  Brack RG12 .... 27 E7
Holly Spring La. Brack RG12 .. 27 D8
Holly Tree Rd. Cater CR3 .... 100 E5
Holly Way. Blckw GU17 ...... 64 D4
Holly Way. Mitch CR4 .... 41 D6
Holly Wlk. Wink SL4 .... 9 A4
Hollybank. W End GU24 ...... 67 F6
Hollybank Cl. Hampt TW12 .. 16 A3
Hollybank Rd. Pyrf KT14 ...... 71 A5
Hollybush Rd. Crawl RH10 .... 201 E8
Hollybush Rd. King U T KT2 .. 17 E2
Hollybush Ride.
  Windl GU19 & GU20 ...... 47 F6
Hollycombe. Eng Gn TW20 .... 11 D4
Hollycroft Cl. Harm UB7 ...... 3 A8
Hollycroft Gdns. Harm UB7 .. 3 A8
Hollydene. Broml BR1 .... 44 F8
Hollyfield Rd. Surb KT5 ...... 37 F2
Hollyfield Sch. King U T KT6 .. 37 E4
Hollyfields Cl. Camb GU15 .... 65 B5
Hollymead. Carsh SM5 .... 59 F7
Hollymead Rd. Chips CR5 .... 79 A1
Hollyoak Rd. Coulsd CR5 .... 79 B1
Hollymoor La. Epsom KT19 .. 57 D1
Hollymount Prim Sch.
  Wimble SW20 .... 39 C8
Hollyridge. Haslem GU27 ...... 208 B6
Hollytree Cl. Putney SW19 .... 19 D7
Hollytree Gdns. Friml GU16 .. 85 D7
Hollywoods. New Add CR0 .... 62 F2
Holm Cl. Woodhm KT15 ...... 70 E7
Holm Ct. Dork RH4 .... 136 B4
Holm Ct. Farnc GU7 .... 150 D7
Holman Rd. E Ewell KT19 .... 57 A2
Holman Rd. W Ewell KT19 .... 57 C5
Holmbank Dr. Up Hall TW17 .. 34 E5
Holmbrook Cl. W Heath GU14 .. 84 C4
Holmbrook Gdns. W Heath GU14 84 C4
Holmbury Ave. Crowth RG11 .. 45 A7
Holmbury Cl. Crawl RH11 .... 201 C4
Holmbury Ct. Mitch SW19 .... 20 E1
Holmbury Ct. S Croy CR2 .... 61 D5
Holmbury Dr. Dork RH5 ...... 136 C4
Holmbury Gr. New Add CR0 .. 62 F3
Holmbury Hill Rd.
  Hol St M RH5 .... 155 B3
Holmbury Rd. For Gn RH5 .... 155 D1
Holmbush Cl. Horsh RH12 .... 217 D6
Holmcroft. Crawl RH10 ...... 201 E5
Holmcroft. Walt o t H KT20 .. 97 B2

Holmdene Cl. Beck BR3 ...... 44 C7
Holme Chase. Whit V KT13 .. 53 C4
Holme Cl. Crowth RG11 ...... 45 A7
Holmes Cl. Ascot SL5 .... 29 C3
Holmes Cl. Woki RG11 .... 25 A5
Holmes Cres. Woki RG11 .... 25 A4
Holmes Rd. Merton SW19 .... 20 C1
Holmes Rd. Twick TW1 ...... 16 F6
Holmesdale. 2 Whit V KT13 .. 53 D4
Holmesdale Ave. Mortl SW14 .. 7 B3
Holmesdale Cl. Merrow GU1 .. 110 B2
Holmesdale Cl. S Norw SE25 .. 42 F6
Holmesdale Rd. Dork RH5 .... 136 C3
Holmesdale Rd. Reig RH2 .... 118 B2
Holmesdale Rd. Rich TW9 .... 6 F6
Holmesdale Rd. S Norw SE25 .. 42 F5
Holmesdale Rd. S Nutf RH1 .. 140 F7
Holmesdale Rd. Tedd TW11 .. 17 C2
Holmesdale Rd. Thorn H CR0 .. 42 D4
Holmesdale Sch. Reig RH2 .. 118 B2
Holmethorpe Ave. Redh RH1 .. 119 B4
Holmethorpe Ind Est.
  Redh RH1 .... 119 B4
Holmewood Cl. Woki RG11 .... 25 A2
Holmewood Gdns. Streat SW2 .. 21 F8
Holmewood Rd. S Norw SE25 .. 42 E6
Holmewood Rd. Streat SW2 .. 21 F8
Holmgrove House. Purley CR8 .. 80 A7
Holming End. Horsh RH12 .... 218 B5
Holmoaks House. Beck BR3 .. 44 C7
Holmshaw Cl. For Hil SE26 & SE6 23 E4
Holmsley Cl. New Mal KT3 .. 38 F2
Holmwood. 2 Surb KT5 ...... 37 F3
Holmwood Ave. Sander CR2 .. 80 F6
Holmwood Cl. Addl KT15 .... 52 A5
Holmwood Cl. E Hors KT24 .. 112 E6
Holmwood Gdns. Wallin SM6 .. 60 B4
Holmwood Rd. Chess KT9 .... 56 E5
Holmwood Rd.
  E Ewell KT17 & SM2 ...... 58 C2
Holmwood Sta. Bear Gn RH5 .. 157 C4
Holmwood View Rd. Dork RH5 136 B1
Holne Chase. Morden SM4 .... 40 A3
Holroyd Rd. Clayg KT10 ...... 55 F2
Holstein Ave. Weyb KT13 .... 53 A6
Holsworthy Way. Chess KT9 .. 56 C5
Holt Cl. Farnb GU14 .... 85 C7
Holt La. Woki RG11 .... 25 B7
Holt Pound La. Binst GU10 .. 145 C5
Holt Sch The. Woki RG11 .... 25 B7
Holt The. Morden SM4 .... 40 A5
Holt The. Wallin SM6 .... 60 C6
Holt Wood. Chelsh CR6 ...... 82 A3
Holton Heath. 8 Brack RG12 .. 27 F5
Holtwood Rd. Ashtd KT22 .... 74 C6
Holtye Ave. E Grins RH19 .... 186 A3
Holtye Rd. E Grins RH19 .... 186 B3
Holtye Wlk. Crawl RH10 ...... 202 A4
Holy Cross Catholic Prim Sch.
  Catf SE6 .... 24 C7
Holy Cross Hospl. Shottm GU27 207 F2
Holy Cross RC Convent Sch.
  New Mal KT3 .... 38 E4
Holy Cross RC Prep Sch.
  King U T KT2 .... 18 C1
Holy Family RC Prim Sch The.
  Row Tn KT15 .... 52 A5
Holy Ghost RC Prim Sch.
  Balham SW12 .... 21 A8
Holy Trinity C of E Inf Sch.
  Up Toot SW17 .... 20 F6
Holy Trinity C of E Prim Sch.
  For Hil SE23 .... 23 C6
Holy Trinity C of E Prim Sch.
  Streat SW2 .... 21 F8
Holy Trinity C of E Prim Sch.
  W End GU24 .... 68 A7
Holy Trinity C of E Prim Sch.
  Wimble SW19 .... 20 B2
Holy Trinity CE (Aided) Sch The.
  Crawl RH11 .... 201 A4
Holy Trinity CE Jun Sch.
  Mortl TW10 .... 7 A3
Holy Trinity C of E Jun Sch.
  Wallin SM6 .... 60 C6
Holy Trinity Prim Sch.
  Sunnin SL5 .... 30 A3
Holy Trinity Sch. Guild GU1 .. 130 F7
Holybourne Ave. Rhampt SW15 . 19 A8
Holyhead Ct. King U T KT1 .. 37 D5
Holyhook Cl. Crowth RG11 .. 45 A6
Holyoake Ave. Horse GU21 .. 69 C2
Holyoake Cres. Horse GU21 .. 69 C2
Holyrood. E Grins RH19 ...... 206 A8
Holyrood Pl. Crawl RH11 .... 201 B2
Holywell Cl. Stan TW19 ...... 13 E7
Holywell Cl. W Heath GU14 .. 85 A7
Holywell Way. Stan TW19 .... 13 E7
Homan House. 6 Streat SW4 .. 21 D8
Hombrook Dr. Binf RG12 ...... 26 E8
Hombrook House. Brack RG12 .. 26 E8
Home Cl. Carsh SM5 .... 59 F8
Home Cl. Crawl RH10 .... 202 C8
Home Cl. Fetch KT22 .... 94 D6
Home Ct. King U T KT6 ...... 37 D4
Home Farm Cl. Betch RH3 .... 137 E8
Home Farm Cl. Burgh H KT18 .. 77 D2
Home Farm Cl. Esher KT10 .. 55 B4
Home Farm Cl. Farnb GU14 .. 85 D6
Home Farm Cl. Ottsh KT16 .. 51 A3
Home Farm Cl. Thame D KT7 .. 36 F2
Home Farm Cl. Up Hall TW17 .. 34 C5
Home Farm Cotts.
  P Harow GU8 .... 149 C5
Home Farm Gdns.
  Walt O T KT12 .... 54 C8
Home Farm Rd. Godal GU7 .. 150 F2
Home Meadow. Banstd SM7 .. 78 A3
Home Park Cl. Bramly GU5 .. 151 F6

Home Park Rd. Wimble SW19 .. 19 F4
Home Park Wlk. King U T KT1 .. 37 D5
Home Pk. Oxted RH8 .... 123 A4
Homebeech House. 7
  Woking GU22 .... 69 E1
Homecoppice House. 1
  Broml BR1 .... 24 F1
Homecourt. Felt TW14 .... 15 A7
Homecroft Rd. For Hil SE26 .. 23 C3
Homefield. Morden SM4 ...... 40 A5
Homefield. Thursl GU8 .... 169 C3
Homefield Cl. Horley RH6 .... 161 B4
Homefield Cl. Leahd KT22 .... 95 C6
Homefield Cl. Woodhm KT15 .. 70 E7
Homefield Gdns. Burgh H KT20 . 97 C7
Homefield Gdns.
  Mitch CR4 & SW19 .... 40 D7
Homefield House. For Hil SE23 . 23 D5
Homefield Pk. Sutton SM1 & SM2 59 B4
Homefield Prep Sch.
  Sutton SM1 .... 59 A5
Homefield Rd.
  Coulsd CR3 & CR5 .... 100 B7
Homefield Rd. Walt O T KT12 .. 35 E2
Homefield Rd. Warlgm CR6 .. 101 C8
Homefield Rd. Wimble SW19 .. 19 E3
Homegreen House.
  Shottm GU27 .... 208 A6
Homeland Dr. Belm SM2 ...... 59 B2
Homelands. Leahd KT22 ...... 95 C6
Homelands Dr. S Norw SE19 .. 22 E1
Homelea Cl. Farnb GU14 ...... 85 B8
Homeleigh Cres. Ash V GU12 .. 106 A8
Homeleigh Ct. 8 Streat SW16 .. 21 E5
Homemead. Up Toot SW17 ... 21 B6
Homemead Rd. Wallin CR0 .. 41 C3
Homepark House. Farnh GU9 . 125 C2
Homer Rd. Croy CR0 .... 43 D3
Homersham Rd. King U T KT1 .. 38 B7
Homesdale Rd. Cater CR3 .... 100 D4
Homestall. Stough GU2 ...... 108 D2
Homestall Rd. Hammer RH19 .. 206 E8
Homestead. Cran GU6 .... 174 F4
Homestead Gdns. Clayg KT10 .. 55 E5
Homestead Rd. Cater CR3 .... 100 D4
Homestead Rd. Stain TW18 .. 13 A3
Homestead Way. New Add CR0 . 82 D7
Homesteads The. Catf BR3 .. 24 B2
Homewalk House. For Hil SE26 . 23 C4
Homewater House. 1
  Epsom KT17 .... 76 E6
Homewaters Ave. Sunby TW16 .. 34 F8
Homewood. Cran GU6 .... 175 A3
Homewood Cl. Hampt TW12 .. 15 F2
Homewood Ct. S Norw SE25 .. 42 E4
Homewood (NHS Trust) Hospl.
  Addl KT16 .... 51 C6
Homewoods. 2 Streat SW12 .. 21 C8
Homeworth House. 8
  Woking GU22 .... 69 E1
Homildon House. 10
  For Hil SE26 .... 23 A5
Homington Ct. King U T KT2 .. 17 E1
Homstead The. Burst RH6 .. 162 B1
Hone Hill. Sandh GU17 .... 64 B8
Hones Yard Bsns Pk.
  M Bourn GU9 .... 125 D2
Honey Hill. Woki RG11 ...... 26 A1
Honeybrook Rd.
  Streat SW12 & SW4 ...... 21 C8
Honeycrock La. Salfs RH1 .... 140 B2
Honeyhill Rd. Brack RG12 .... 27 A8
Honeypot La. Limps RH7 & TN8 144 D4
Honeypots Rd. Westfd GU22 .. 89 D5
Honeysuckle Bottom.
  E Hors KT24 .... 112 E2
Honeysuckle Cl. Crowth RG11 . 45 A7
Honeysuckle Cl. Horley RH6 .. 161 C4
Honeysuckle Gdns. Croy CR0 .. 43 D1
Honeysuckle La. Crawl RH11 .. 181 C1
Honeysuckle La. Dork RH5 .. 136 C4
Honeysuckle La. Head Dn GU35 187 B5
Honeysuckle Wlk. Horsh RH12 218 A5
Honeywood La. Oakwd RH5 .. 196 F5
Honeywood La. Rowhk RH5 .. 196 F5
Honeywood Rd. Horsh RH12 .. 218 A4
Honeywood Rd. Islew TW7 .. 6 A3
Honeywood Wlk. Carsh SM5 .. 59 F6
Honister Hts. Sander CR8 .... 80 E5
Honister Wlk. Friml GU15 .... 66 D4
Honley Rd. Lewish SE6 ...... 24 B8
Honnor Rd. Stain TW18 ...... 13 D1
Honor Oak Rd. For Hil SE23 .. 23 C8
Hood Ave. Mortl SW14 ...... 7 C2
Hood Cl. Thorn H CR0 & CR9 .. 42 B1
Hood Rd. Wimble SW20 ...... 18 F1
Hook Heath Ave. Woking GU22 . 89 C6
Hook Heath Gdns. Woking GU22 88 F6
Hook Heath Rd. Woking GU22 . 89 B6
Hook Hill. S Croy CR2 .... 61 E1
Hook Hill La. Woking GU22 .. 89 C6
Hook Hill Pk. Woking GU22 .. 89 B6
Hook House. 9 W Norw SW27 .. 22 B3
Hook La. Gomsh GU5 .... 133 C2
Hook La. Putt GU3 .... 128 D3
Hook La. W End GU24 .... 67 C6
Hook Mill La. Windl GU24 .... 48 D2
Hook Rd. Chess KT6 .... 56 E7
Hook Rd. Epsom KT19 & KT17 . 57 C2
Hook Rd. Surb KT6 & KT9 .... 56 E7
Hook Rd. Ewell KT19 .... 76 E8
Hook Rise N. Tolw KT6 & KT9 .. 57 B8
Hook Rise North. Surb KT6 .. 56 E7
Hook Rise S. Tolw KT6 & KT9 .. 57 B8
Hook Rise South. Chess KT6 .. 56 E7
Hook Underpass. Surb KT6 .. 56 E7
Hooke Rd. E Hors KT24 ...... 92 F2
Hookfield. Epsom KT18 & KT19 . 76 C6
Hookfield Mews. Epsom KT19 . 76 C6
Hookhouse Rd. Dunsf GU8 .. 192 D6
Hookley Cl. Elst GU8 .... 148 E3

Hookley La. Elst GU8 .... 148 E3
Hookstile La. M Bourn GU9 ..... 125 C1
Hookstone La. W End GU24 ..... 67 F8
Hookwood Bglws. Limps RH8 .. 123 B6
Hookwood Cnr. Limps RH8 ...... 123 B7
Hookwood Cotts. Head KT18 .... 96 C3
Hooley La. Earls RH1 .... 139 F8
Hoover House. Catf SE6 .... 24 C4
Hope Ave. Brack RG12 .... 27 E2
Hope Cl. Sutton SM1 .... 59 C5
Hope Ct. Crawl RH11 .... 201 B1
Hope Fountain. Friml GU15 ...... 65 F4
Hope Grant's Rd. Alder GU11 .. 105 A4
Hope La. Hale GU9 .... 125 B6
Hope Pk. Brom BR1 .... 24 F1
Hope St. Elst GU8 .... 148 D4
Hopeman Cl. Sandh GU15 .... 64 D7
Hopes Cl. Heston TW5 .... 5 A8
Hopfield. Horse GU21 .... 69 E3
Hopfield Ave. Byfl KT14 .... 71 E6
Hophurst Cl. Crawl D RH10 ..... 204 B8
Hophurst Dr. Crawl D RH10 ..... 204 B8
Hophurst Hill.
  Crawl D RH10 & RH19 .... 184 D2
Hophurst La. Crawl D RH10 .... 184 B1
Hopkins Ct. Crawl RH11 .... 201 B1
Hoppety The. Tadw KT20 .... 97 D5
Hoppingwood Ave. King U T KT3 38 E6
Hopton Gdns. New Mal KT3 ..... 39 A3
Hopton Rd. Street SW16 .... 21 E3
Horace Rd. King U T KT1 .... 37 F6
Horatio Ave. Wink RG12 .... 27 E8
Horatius Way. Wallin CR0 .... 60 F2
Hordern House. Horsh RH12 .... 217 A1
Horewood Rd. Easth RG12 .... 27 B3
Horley Cty Fst Sch. Horley RH6 161 A3
Horley Lodge La. Salfs RH1 .... 161 A8
Horley Rd. Crawl RH6 .... 181 B7
Horley Rd. Hookw RH6 .... 181 B7
Horley Row. Horley RH6 .... 161 A4
Horley Sta. Horley RH6 .... 161 B2
Hormer Cl. Sandh GU15 .... 45 D1
Horn Rd. W Heath GU14 .... 84 E5
Hornbeam Cl. Sandh GU15 ...... 45 D1
Hornbeam Cl. W Heath GU14 ... 84 C5
Hornbeam Cres. Brent TW8 ..... 6 B7
Hornbeam Rd. Bellf GU1 .... 109 C3
Hornbeam Rd. Woodh RH2 ..... 139 C6
Hornbeam Terr. Carsh SM5 ..... 40 E1
Hornbeam Wlk. Whit V KT12 ... 53 F2
Hornchurch Cl. King U T KT2 ... 17 D3
Hornchurch Hill. Whytlf CR3 ... 80 F1
Horndean Cl. Crawl RH10 .... 182 D2
Horndean Ct. Rhampt SW15 .... 19 A7
Horndean Rd. Brack RG12 .... 27 F3
Horne Rd. Shep Gn TW17 .... 34 A5
Hornecourt Hill.
  Horne RH1 & RH6 & RH9 ...... 162 F7
Hornhatch. Chil GU4 .... 131 B3
Hornhatch Cl. Chil GU4 .... 131 B3
Hornhatch La. Chil GU4 .... 131 B2
Horniman Dr. For Hil SE23 ...... 23 C8
Horniman Prim Sch.
  For Hil SE23 .... 23 B7
Hornshill La. Buck Gn RH12 .... 213 F7
Horsa Cl. Wallin SM6 .... 60 E3
Horse Fair. King U T KT1 .... 37 D7
Horse Gate Ride. Ascot SL5 ..... 29 A3
Horse Hill. Horley RH6 .... 160 B4
Horsebrass Dr. Bagsh GU19 .... 47 E2
Horsecroft. Banstd SM7 .... 77 F2
Horsell Birch. Horse GU21 ...... 69 A4
Horsell Birch. Woking GU21 .... 69 A4
Horsell C of E Sch. Horse GU21 69 C3
Horsell Common Rd.
  Horse GU21 .... 69 C5
Horsell Ct. Cher KT16 .... 33 B2
Horsell Cty Fst Sch. Horse GU21 69 D4
Horsell High Sch. Horse GU21 .. 69 D4
Horsell Moor. Horse GU21 .... 69 D4
Horsell Park Cl. Horse GU21 .... 69 E3
Horsell Pk. Horse GU21 .... 69 E3
Horsell Rise. Horse GU21 .... 69 E4
Horsell Rise Cl. Horse GU21 .... 69 D4
Horsell Vale. Horse GU21 .... 69 E4
Horsell Way. Horse GU21 .... 69 C4
Horseshoe Bend. Graysh GU26 188 B3
Horseshoe Cl. Camb GU15 ...... 65 F8
Horseshoe Cl. Crawl RH10 ..... 202 D7
Horseshoe Cres. Camb GU15 ... 65 F8
Horseshoe La. Ash V GU12 ..... 106 A7
Horseshoe La. Cran GU6 .... 174 D4
Horseshoe La E. Merrow GU1 .. 110 C2
Horseshoe La W. Merrow GU1 . 110 B1
Horseshoe Ridge. Whit V KT13 . 72 C8
Horseshoe The. Banstd SM7 ... 77 F4
Horseshoe The.
  Coulsd CR5 & CR8 .... 79 D6
Horseshoe The. Ock Rid GU7 .. 150 C3
Horsham Bsns Pk. Faygt RH12 198 C4
Horsham Hospl. Horsh RH12 .. 217 C3
Horsham Rd. Alfold GU6 .... 193 F8
Horsham Rd. Bear Gn RH5 ..... 157 C4
Horsham Rd. Bear Gn RH5 ..... 157 C6
Horsham Rd. Bramly GU5 & GU4 151 E7
Horsham Rd.
  Bramly GU5 & GU6 .... 173 D5
Horsham Rd. Capel RH5 .... 178 C2
Horsham Rd. Capel RH5 .... 178 D8
Horsham Rd. Cran GU6 .... 174 E1
Horsham Rd. Cran GU6 & RH5 194 C1
Horsham Rd. Crawl GU5 & GU6 173 D5
Horsham Rd. Crawl RH11 .... 201 B4
Horsham Rd. Dork RH4 .... 136 A6
Horsham Rd. Dork RH5 .... 136 B2
Horsham Rd. E Bed TW14 .... 3 C1
Horsham Rd. Ell Gn GU6 .... 176 B1
Horsham Rd. Ewh GU6 .... 175 F3
Horsham Rd.
  Hol St M GU5 & RH5 & GU6 .. 155 C5
Horsham Rd.
  Rowhk RH5 & RH12 .... 196 D5
Horsham Rd. Rusper RH12 ..... 199 B5
Horsham Rd. S Holm RH5 ...... 157 C6
Horsham Rd. Sandh GU15 ...... 45 D1
Horsham Rd. Shalf GU4 .... 130 C3
Horsham Rd.
  Wall W RH5 & GU6 .... 176 E4
Horsham Rd.
  Wall W RH12 & RH5 .... 196 D5
Horsham Sta. Horsh RH13 ..... 217 D2
Horsley Cl. Epsom KT19 .... 76 D6
Horsley Dr. King U T KT2 .... 17 D3
Horsley Dr. New Add CR0 .... 63 C3
Horsley Rd. Downs KT11 & KT24 . 93 B7
Horsley Sta. W Hors KT24 ...... 92 E2
Horsneile La. Brack RG12 .... 27 B8
Horton Hill. Epsom KT19 .... 76 C8
Horton Hospl. Epsom KT19 .... 76 B8
Horton La. Epsom KT19 & KT18 . 57 B2
Horton Rd. Coln SL3 .... 1 A6
Horton Rd. Horton SL3 .... 1 A6
Horton Rd. Poyle SL3 & TW19 . 1 E4
Horton Rd. Stan TW19 .... 2 A2
Horton Trad Est. Horton SL3 ... 1 C4
Horton Way. Croy CR0 .... 43 D4
Horvath Cl. Oat Pk KT13 .... 53 D6
Hosack Rd.
  Up Toot SW12 & SW17 .... 21 A6
Hoskins Pl. E Grins RH19 .... 186 A4
Hoskins Rd. Oxted RH8 .... 122 E6
Hospital Bridge Rd. Twick TW2 . 16 B7
Hospital Hill. Alder GU11 ...... 105 A3
Hospital of the Holy Trinity
  (Almshouses). Croy CR9 ...... 61 C8
Hospital Rd. Alder GU11 .... 105 B3
Hospital Rd. Hounsl TW3 .... 5 A4
Hostel Rd. Farnb GU14 .... 105 B8
Hotham Cl. E Mole KT8 .... 36 A6
Hotham Rd. Merton SW19 ...... 20 C1
Houblon Rd. Rich TW10 .... 6 E2
Houghton Cl. Hampt TW12 ..... 15 E2
Houlder Cres. Croy CR0 .... 61 B4
Houlton Cl. Bagsh GU19 .... 47 F2
Hound House Rd. Shere GU5 .. 154 A5
Hounslow Ave. Islew TW3 .... 5 B2
Hounslow Bsns Pk. Hounsl TW3 . 5 B3
Hounslow Central Sta.
  Hounsl TW3 .... 5 B3
Hounslow East Sta. Hounsl TW3 . 5 C5
Hounslow Gdns. Islew TW3 ..... 5 B2
Hounslow Heath Jun & Inf Schs.
  Hounsl TW4 .... 4 E4
Hounslow Manor Sch.
  Hounsl TW3 .... 5 B3
Hounslow Rd. Felt TW14 .... 4 B1
Hounslow Rd. Felt TW13 & TW14 15 B8
Hounslow Rd. Felt TW13 .... 15 C4
Hounslow Rd. Twick TW2 & TW3 . 5 C1
Hounslow Sta. Islew TW3 .... 5 B2
Hounslow Town Prim Sch.
  Hounsl TW3 .... 5 B3
Hounslow West Sta. Hounsl TW3 . 4 E5
Houseman Rd. W Heath GU14 .. 84 F6
Houston Ct. Croy CR0 .... 42 E1
Houston Ct. Heston TW5 .... 4 F7
Houston Rd. For Hil SE23 & SE6 . 23 E5
Hove Gdns. Cheam SM1 .... 40 B1
Hovenden House. Dulw SE21 .. 22 E4
How La. Chips CR5 .... 79 A1
Howard Ave. Ewell KT17 .... 58 A1
Howard Cl. Ashf TW15 .... 14 F2
Howard Cl. Ashtd KT21 .... 75 F1
Howard Cl. Hampt TW12 .... 16 C2
Howard Cl. Leahd KT22 .... 95 C4
Howard Cl. W Hors KT24 .... 92 D2
Howard Cl. Walt o t h KT20 .... 97 A2
Howard Cole Way. Alder GU11 104 E2
Howard Ct. Beck BR3 .... 44 C7
Howard Ct. Effing KT24 .... 113 D8
Howard Ct. Reig RH2 .... 118 B2
Howard Dr. W Heath GU14 ..... 84 B4
Howard Gdns. Merrow GU1 ... 110 A2
Howard House. Penge SE20 .... 43 C8
Howard House. Reig RH2 ...... 118 B2
Howard of Effingham Sch.
  Effing KT24 .... 113 E8
Howard Prim Sch. Croy CR0 ... 61 C6
Howard Rd. Coulsd CR5 .... 79 D5
Howard Rd. Crawl RH11 .... 200 D2
Howard Rd. Croy SE25 .... 43 A3
Howard Rd. Dork RH4 .... 136 A7
Howard Rd. Dork RH5 .... 136 C3
Howard Rd. E Hors KT24 .... 93 A4
Howard Rd. G Book KT23 ...... 114 C8
Howard Rd. Horsh RH13 .... 218 A4
Howard Rd. Islew TW7 .... 5 F4
Howard Rd. New Mal KT3 .... 38 F5
Howard Rd. Penge SE20 .... 43 C8
Howard Rd. Reig RH2 .... 139 B8
Howarth Rd. Surb KT5 .... 37 F3
Howard Rd. Woki RG11 .... 25 C5
Howard Ridge. Burph GU4 .... 110 A5
Howards Cl. Old Wok GU22 .... 90 A1
Howards Crest Cl. Beck BR3 ... 44 C7
Howards La. Row Tn KT15 .... 51 F3
Howards Rd. Old Wok GU22 .... 89 F7
Howberry Rd. S Norw SE25 .... 42 D7
Howden Cl. S Norw SE25 .... 42 F7
Howden Rd. S Norw SE25 ...... 42 F7
Howe Dr. Cater CR3 .... 100 D5
Howe The. Farnb GU14 .... 84 B1
Howell Hill Cl. Ewell KT17 .... 77 C8
Howell Hill Gr. E Ewell KT17 .. 58 C1
Howgate Rd. Mortl SW14 .... 7 D4
Howland House. Street SW16 .. 21 E5
Howley Rd. Croy CR0 & CR9 ... 61 C7
Howmic Ct. Twick TW1 .... 6 C1
Howorth Ct. Brack RG12 .... 27 E5
Howson Terr. Rich TW10 .... 6 E1
Hoylake Cl. Crawl RH11 .... 200 D5
Hoylake Gdns. Mitch CR4 ...... 41 C6
Hoyle Hill. Bear Gn RH5 .... 157 D1
Hoyle Rd. Up Toot SW17 .... 20 E3
Hubbard Rd. W Norw SE27 .... 22 C4
Hubberholme. Easth RG12 ..... 27 A6
Huddleston Cres. Merst RH1 . 119 D7
Hudson Ct. ◢ Merton SW19 ... 40 B8
Hudson Ct. Stough GU2 .... 108 F1
Hudson Rd. Crawl RH10 .... 201 E4
Hudson Rd. Harl UB7 .... 3 D8
Hudsons. Tadw KT20 .... 97 D6
Hugh Herland. Merst RH1 ..... 119 D7
Hughenden Rd. New Mal KT4 .. 39 A2
Hughes Ct. Thorn H CR0 .... 42 A1
Hughes Rd. Ashf TW15 .... 14 C2
Hughes Wlk. Thorn H CR0 ...... 42 C2
Hullbrook La. Sham Gn GU5 .. 152 D4
Hullmead. Sham Gn GU5 ...... 152 E4
Hulton Cl. Leahd KT22 .... 95 C4
Hulverston Cl. Sutton SM2 ..... 59 B2
Humber Way. Sandh GU15 ...... 64 D8
Humbolt Cl. Stough GU2 .... 108 F1
Humphrey Cl. Fetch KT22 .... 94 C5
Humphries Yd. Easth GU15 .... 27 C5
Hungerford Cl. Sandh GU17 .... 64 C8
Hungerford Sq. ◢ Oat Pk KT13 . 53 D6
Hungry Hill La. Ripley GU23 .... 91 D3
Hunstanton Cl. Crawl RH11 .. 200 D5
Hunston Rd. Cheam SM4 .... 40 B1
Hunter Cl. Up Toot SW12 .... 21 A7
Hunter House. Crawl RH10 .... 201 D3
Hunter Rd. Crawl RH10 & RH11 201 D4
Hunter Rd. Farnb GU14 .... 84 F3
Hunter Rd. Guild GU1 .... 130 E8
Hunter Rd. S Norw CR7 .... 42 D6
Hunter Rd. Wimble SW20 .... 39 C8
Hunters Chase. S Godst RH9 .. 142 F6
Hunters Cl. Epsom KT19 .... 76 C6
Hunters Cl. ◢ Rich TW9 .... 6 D2
Hunters Meadow. Dulw SE19 .. 22 E4
Hunters Rd. Chess KT9 .... 56 E6
Hunters The. Beck BR3 .... 44 C8
Hunters Way. S Croy CR0 .... 61 E6
Huntersfield Cl. Reig RH2 ..... 118 B4
Hunting Cl. Esher KT10 .... 55 A6
Hunting Gate Dr. Chess KT9 ... 56 F3
Hunting Gate Mews. Sutton SM1 59 B7
Hunting Gate Mews. Twick TW2 16 E7
Huntingdon Cl.
  Mitch CR4 & SW16 .... 41 D6
Huntingdon Gdns. Mortl SW14 . 7 C4
Huntingdon Gdns. Chisw W4 .. 7 C7
Huntingdon Gdns. N Cheam KT4 58 D7
Huntingdon Rd. Redh RH1 .... 118 F1
Huntingdon Rd. Woking GU21 . 68 F2
Huntingfield. New Add CR0 ..... 62 F3
Huntingfield Way. Egham TW20 12 D2
Huntingford Dr. Beac H GU26 . 188 C7
Huntley House. ◢ Dulw SE21 .. 22 E4
Huntley Way. Wimble SW20 .... 39 A7
Huntly Rd. S Norw SE25 .... 42 E5
Hunts Cl. Stough GU2 .... 108 D2
Hunts Hill Rd. Normdy GU3 ... 107 A4
Hunts Slip Rd. Dulw SE21 ...... 22 E6
Huntsgreen Ct. Brack RG12 ... 27 C7
Huntsman Cl. Felt TW13 .... 15 B4
Huntsman's Mews. Mytch GU16 85 F3
Huntsmans Cl. Fetch KT22 ..... 94 D3
Huntsmans Cl. Warlgm CR6 .. 101 C8
Huntsmans Ct. Cater CR3 ..... 100 C6
Huntsmans Meadow. N Asct SL5 28 F8
Huntsmoor Rd. W Ewell KT19 . 57 D5
Huntsmoor Rd. W Ewell KT19 . 57 D5
Huntspill Rd. Wands SW17 ..... 20 C5
Huntsworth Ct. Catf SE6 .... 24 D6
Hurlands Bsns Ctr. Farnh GU9 125 F5
Hurlands Cl. Farnh GU10 & GU9 125 F4
Hurlands La. Dunsf GU8 .... 192 F2
Hurlands Pl. Farnh GU9 .... 125 F4
Hurley Cl. Walt O T KT12 .... 54 B8
Hurley Ct. Brack RG12 .... 27 E5
Hurley Gdns. Burph GU4 ...... 110 A4
Hurlford. Woking GU21 .... 69 A2
Hurlstone Rd. S Norw SE25 .... 42 E4
Hurn Court Rd. Hounsl TW5 .... 4 D5
Hurn Ct. Hounsl TW5 .... 4 D5
Hurnford Cl. S Croy CR2 .... 61 E1
Huron Rd. Up Toot SW17 .... 21 A5
Hurricane Way. Farnb GU14 .. 104 F7
Hursley Ct. ◢ Surb KT6 .... 37 D2
Hurst Ave. Horsh RH12 .... 217 D3
Hurst Cl. Chess KT9 .... 57 A5
Hurst Cl. Crawl RH11 .... 200 F4
Hurst Cl. Hayes BR2 .... 44 F1
Hurst Cl. Head KT18 .... 96 C3
Hurst Cl. Woking GU22 .... 89 C7
Hurst Croft. Guild GU1 .... 130 E6
Hurst Ct. Beck BR3 .... 24 A1
Hurst Ct. Horsh RH12 .... 217 D3
Hurst Ct. S Norw SE25 .... 42 F5
Hurst Dr. Walt o t H KT20 .... 97 A1
Hurst Farm Cl. Milf GU8 .... 149 F2
Hurst Farm Rd. E Grins RH19 205 D7
Hurst Gr. Walt O T KT12 .... 34 F1
Hurst Green Cl. Oxted RH8 ... 123 A3
Hurst Green Cty Prim Sch.
  Oxted RH8 .... 123 A3
Hurst Green Rd. Oxted RH8 .. 122 F3
Hurst Green Sta. Oxted RH8 .. 122 F3
Hurst Hill Cotts. Bramly GU5 . 152 B4
Hurst House. ◢ Penge SE26 .... 23 B3
Hurst La. E Mole KT8 .... 36 C6
Hurst La. Head KT18 .... 96 D4
Hurst La. Thorpe TW20 .... 32 A7
Hurst Lodge. ◢ Whit V KT13 .... 53 D4
Hurst Lodge Sch. Sunnin SL5 . 29 F2
Howorth Ct. Brack RG12 .... 27 E5

Hurst Park Cty Prim Sch.
  E Mole KT8 .... 36 A6
Hurst Rd. Alder GU11 .... 105 C4
Hurst Rd. Croy CR0 .... 61 D5
Hurst Rd. E Mole KT8 & KT12 .. 36 C6
Hurst Rd. Epsom KT19 .... 76 D8
Hurst Rd. Farnb GU14 .... 85 B8
Hurst Rd. Horley RH6 .... 160 E4
Hurst Rd. Horsh RH12 .... 217 D3
Hurst Rd. Walt O T KT8&KT12 . 35 C5
Hurst View Rd. S Croy CR2 ..... 61 E3
Hurst Way. Pyrf GU22 .... 70 E5
Hurst Way. S Croy CR2 .... 61 E4
Hurstbourne. Clayg KT10 .... 55 F4
Hurstbourne House.
  Rhampt SW15 .... 7 F1
Hurstbourne Priors. S Croy CR2 61 E4
Hurstbourne Rd. For Hil SE23 . 23 E7
Hurstcourt Rd. Sutton SM1 .... 59 B8
Hurstdene Ave. Hayes BR2 ...... 44 F1
Hurstdene Ave. Stain TW18 .... 13 B2
Hurstfield Rd. E Mole KT8 ...... 36 A6
Hurstlands. Oxted RH8 .... 123 A3
Hurstleigh Cl. Redh RH1 .... 118 F3
Hurstleigh Dr. Redh RH1 ...... 118 F3
Hurstmere Cl. Graysh GU26 .. 188 D3
Hurstview Grange. Croy CR0 ... 61 B3
Hurstwood. Ascot SL5 .... 29 A3
Hurtmore Chase. Farnc GU7 . 150 B7
Hurtmore Rd. Farnc GU7 ...... 150 B7
Hurtmore Rd. Shackl GU7 ..... 150 B7
Hurtwood Rd. Walt O T KT12 .. 35 F2
Hurtwood Sixth Form Coll.
  Ewh GU6 .... 155 A2
Hussar Cl. Alder GU11 .... 104 E2
Hussars Cl. Hounsl TW4 .... 4 E4
Hutchinson's Rd. New Add CR0 82 C8
Hutchins House. ◢ Street SW4 . 21 D8
Hutchins Way. Horley RH6 .... 160 F5
Hutsons Cl. Woki RG11 .... 25 D8
Hutton Cl. Windl GU20 .... 48 D3
Hutton Rd. Ash V GU12 .... 106 A6
Huxley Cl. Farnc GU7 .... 150 D7
Huxley Cl. Onsl V GU2 .... 129 D8
Hyacinth Cl. ◢ Hampt TW12 ... 16 A2
Hyacinth Rd. Rhampt SW15 .... 19 A7
Hyde Cl. Ashf TW16 .... 14 E2
Hyde Dr. Crawl RH11 .... 200 E5
Hyde Farm Sch. Street SW12 .. 21 D7
Hyde Heath Ct. Crawl RH10 .. 202 D8
Hyde La. Beac H GU10 & GU8 . 168 E1
Hyde La. Thursl GU8 .... 169 A2
Hyde Rd. Rich TW10 .... 6 F2
Hyde Rd. Sander CR2 & CR8 .... 80 E6
Hyde Terr. Ashf TW15 & TW16 . 14 E2
Hyde Wlk. Morden SM4 .... 40 A2
Hydestile Cotts. Hyde GU8 .... 171 D5
Hydestile Hospl. Hyde GU8 ... 171 E5
Hydethorpe Rd. Street SW12 .. 21 C7
Hylands Cl. Crawl RH10 .... 202 A5
Hylands Cl. Woodc KT18 .... 76 C4
Hylands Mews. Woodc KT18 ... 76 C4
Hylands Rd. Woodc KT18 .... 76 C4
Hylton Lodge. Mert KT12 .... 54 C5
Hyndewood. ◢ For Hil SE23 ... 23 D5
Hyperion Ct. Crawl RH11 ...... 200 E5
Hyperion House. ◢ Street SW2 21 F8
Hyperion Pl. Epsom KT19 .... 57 D2
Hyperion Wlk. Horley RH6 .... 161 B1
Hyrstdene. Croy CR0 .... 61 B6
Hythe Cl. Brack RG12 .... 27 E4
Hythe End Rd. Wray TW19 ...... 12 A5
Hythe Field Ave. Egham TW20 . 12 D2
Hythe Park Rd. Egham TW20 .. 12 D2
Hythe Rd. Egham TW20 .... 12 D3
Hythe Rd. S Norw CR7 & SE25 . 42 D7
Hythe Sch The. Egham TW18 .. 12 D3
Hythe The. Egham TW18 .... 12 D2

Ian Ct. For Hil SE23 .... 23 C6
Iberian Ave. Wallin CR0 & SM6 60 E6
Iberian Way. Camb GU15 .... 66 B6
Ibis La. Chisw W4 .... 7 C6
Ibotson Ct. Poyle SL3 .... 1 E6
Ibsley Gdns. Rhampt SW15 ..... 19 A7
Ibstock Place Sch. Rhampt SW15 7 E1
Icehouse Wood. Oxted RH8 ... 122 F4
Icklesham House. ◢
  Crawl RH11 .... 200 D3
Icklingham Gate. Cobham KT11 . 73 C7
Icklingham Rd. Cobham KT11 . 73 D6
Iden Cl. Beck BR2 .... 44 E6
Idlecombe Rd. Street SW17 ..... 21 A2
Idmiston Rd. New Mal KT4 ..... 38 F2
Idmiston Rd.
  W Norw SE21 & SE27 .... 22 C6
Idmiston Sq. New Mal KT4 ..... 38 F2
Ifield Ave. Crawl RH11 .... 201 C7
Ifield Cl. Earls RH1 .... 139 E7
Ifield Comm Sch. Crawl RH11 201 A6
Ifield Cty Jun Sch. Crawl RH11 201 A6
Ifield Cty Mid Sch. Crawl RH11 201 A6
Ifield Fst Sch. Crawl RH11 .... 201 A6
Ifield Gn. Crawl RH11 .... 181 A1
Ifield Rd. Charl RH6 .... 180 E5
Ifield Rd. Crawl RH11 .... 201 C6
Ifield Rd. Crawl RH11 .... 200 F8
Ifield Sta. Crawl RH11 .... 201 A6
Ifield Wood. Rusper RH11 .... 180 E1
Ifold Bridge La. Ifold RH14 .. 212 D4
Ifold Rd. Earls RH1 .... 140 A7
Ifoldhurst. Ifold RH14 .... 212 C2
Ightham House. Beck BR3 ...... 23 F1
Ikona Ct. Whit V KT13 .... 53 C5
Ildersly Gr. Dulw SE21 .... 22 C6
Ilex Cl. Eng Gn TW20 .... 11 B1
Ilex Cl. Sunby TW16 .... 35 C7
Ilex House. Woodhm KT15 ...... 52 A1
Ilex Way. W Norw SW16 .... 22 A3
Ilford Cl. Crawl GU6 .... 173 F2
Ilfracombe Rd. Catf BR1 .... 24 F5

Ilkley Rd. S Norw SE19 .... 22 D2
Illingworth Cl. Mitch CR4 ...... 40 D6
Illingworth Gr. Brack RG12 .... 27 F8
Imber Cl. Thame D KT7 .... 36 D1
Imber Court Trad Est.
  Thame D KT8 .... 36 D3
Imber Cross. Thame D KT7 ..... 36 F3
Imber Gr. Thame D KT10 .... 36 D3
Imber Park Rd. Thame D KT10 . 36 D1
Imberhorne La. E Grins RH19 185 B2
Imberhorne Lower Sch.
  E Grins RH19 .... 185 B3
Imberhorne Sch. E Grins RH19 185 B3
Imberhorne Way. E Grins RH19 185 B3
Imjin Cl. Alder GU11 .... 105 B3
Immanuel & St Andrew C of E
  Prim Sch. Street SW16 .... 21 E2
Impact Ct. Penge SE20 .... 43 B7
Imperial Gdns. Mitch CR4 ...... 41 B6
Imperial House. Vir W GU25 .... 31 E4
Imperial Rd. E Bed TW14 .... 14 C8
Imperial Way. Croy CR0 & CR9 61 A4
Impington. ◢ King U T KT1 ..... 38 A7
Imran Ct. Alder GU12 .... 126 C8
Ince Rd. Whit V KT12 .... 53 E4
Inchmery Rd. Catf SE6 .... 24 C7
Inchwood. Croy BR4 & CR0 .... 63 B6
Inchwood. Easth RG12 .... 27 C1
Independent Bsns Pk The.
  E Grins RH19 .... 185 A3
Ingatestone Rd. Croy SE25 ..... 43 B5
Ingham Cl. S Croy CR2 .... 62 D2
Ingham Rd. S Croy CR2 .... 62 D2
Ingle Dell. Camb GU15 .... 65 D4
Ingle House. Street SW12 .... 21 D7
Ingleboro Dr. Sander CR8 .... 80 D6
Ingleby Way. Wallin SM6 .... 60 D3
Inglehurst. Woodhm KT15 ...... 52 B1
Inglemere Ct. Mitch CR4 & SW17 20 F1
Inglemere Rd. For Hil SE23 .... 23 D5
Inglemere Rd. Mitch CR4 & SW17 20 F1
Ingleside. Poyle SL3 .... 1 F6
Ingleside Cl. Beck BR3 .... 24 A1
Ingleton. Easth RG12 .... 27 A6
Ingleton Rd. Sutton SM5 .... 59 C8
Inglewood. Addl KT16 .... 51 F7
Inglewood. New Add CR0 .... 62 E2
Inglewood. Woking GU21 .... 69 B1
Inglewood Ave. Friml GU15 .... 66 D5
Inglewood Ct. ◢ Broml BR1 .... 24 F1
Inglis Rd. Croy CR0 .... 42 F1
Ingram Cl. Horsh RH12 .... 217 A2
Ingram High Sch for Boys.
  S Norw CR7 .... 42 C8
Ingram House. Tedd KT8 .... 37 C8
Ingram Rd. S Norw CR7 .... 42 C8
Ingrams Almshouses. Islew TW7 6 A5
Ingrams Cl. Hersh KT12 .... 54 C5
Ingrebourne House. Catf BR1 .. 24 D3
Inholms La. Dork RH5 .... 136 C3
Ink Pen La. For Row RH18 ..... 206 E1
Inkerman Rd. Knaph GU21 ..... 68 E1
Inkerman Way. Knaph GU21 ... 68 E1
Inman Rd. Wands SW18 .... 20 C8
Inner Park Rd. Putney SW19 ... 19 D6
Inner Quadrant. Ash V GU12 . 106 A5
Inner Ring E. Harl TW6 .... 3 B4
Inner Ring W. Harl TW6 .... 3 A4
Inner Staithe. Chisw W4 .... 7 C6
Innes Cl. Merton SW20 .... 39 E7
Innes Lodge. For Hil SE23 ...... 23 C5
Innes Rd. Horsh RH12 .... 217 F4
Innes Yd. Croy CR0 & CR9 .... 61 C7
Innings La. Wink RG12 .... 27 E8
Innisfail Gdns. Alder GU11 ... 125 F8
Inst of Oceanographic Sciences.
  Wormly GU8 .... 170 F1
Institute Rd. Alder GU11 ...... 105 D1
Institute Rd. Westc RH4 .... 135 C6
Instone Cl. Wallin SM6 .... 60 E3
Instow Gdns. W Heath GU14 ... 85 A7
Inval Hill. Haslem GU27 .... 208 C8
Inveresk Gdns. Worc Pk KT4 ... 58 A7
Inverness Ct. Catf SE6 .... 24 F7
Inverness Rd. Hounsl TW3 .... 5 A3
Inverness Rd. N Cheam KT4 .... 39 D1
Inverness Way. Sandh GU15 .... 64 D7
Invicta Cl. E Bed TW14 .... 14 F7
Invicta Ct. Chess KT9 .... 56 F5
Invincible Rd. Farnb GU14 ...... 85 A3
Inwood Ave. Coulsd CR5 .... 100 A4
Inwood Ave. Hounsl TW3 .... 5 C4
Inwood Bsns Pk. Hounsl TW3 ... 5 B3
Inwood Cl. Croy CR0 .... 62 E8
Inwood Cl. ◢ Walt O T KT12 .... 54 C8
Inwood Rd. Hounsl TW3 .... 5 C3
Iona Cl. Crawl RH11 .... 201 B3
Iona Cl. For Hil SE3 & SE4 & SE6 . 24 A8
Ipsley Lodge. Tongh GU10 .... 126 E5
Ipswich Rd. Mitch SW17 .... 21 A2
Irene Rd. Oxsh KT11 .... 74 B5
Ireton Ave. Oat Pk KT13 .... 53 F8
Iris Cl. Croy CR0 .... 43 D1
Iris Cl. Surb KT6 .... 37 F2
Iris Rd. Bisley GU24 .... 68 A4
Iris Rd. W Ewell KT19 .... 57 B5
Iris Rd. W Ewell KT19 .... 57 B5
Iron La. Bramly GU5 .... 151 D5
Irons Bottom Rd. Sidlow RH2 159 F8
Irvine Ct. Thorn H CR7 .... 42 A3
Irvine Dr. W Heath GU14 .... 84 E8
Irvine Pl. Thorpe GU25 .... 31 E4
Irving Wlk. Crawl RH10 .... 201 E3
Irwin Dr. Horsh RH12 .... 217 A2
Irwin Rd. Guild GU2 .... 130 A7
Isabel Cotts. Epsom KT18 .... 76 B5
Isabella Ct. ◢ Rich TW10 .... 6 F1
Isbells Dr. Reig RH2 .... 139 B7

Isham Rd. Thorn H SW16 .... 41 E7
Isis Ct. Chisw W4 .... 7 B7
Isis St. Wands SW18 .... 20 C6
Isis Way. Sandh GU15 & GU17 .... 64 D8
Island Cl. Stain TW18 .... 12 E4
Island Cotts The. Downs KT11 .... 73 B1
Island Farm Ave. E Mole KT8 .... 35 F4
Island Farm Rd. E Mole KT8 .... 36 A4
Island House. Morden SW19 .... 40 C5
Island Rd. Mitch CR4 & SW19 .... 20 F1
Islay Gdns. Hounsl TW4 .... 4 D2
Isleworth Bsns Complex.
  Islew TW7 .... 5 F5
Isleworth Sta. Hounsl TW7 .... 5 F5
Isleworth & Syon Sch for Boys.
  Hounsl TW7 .... 5 E7
Isleworth Town Sch. Islew TW7 .... 6 A5
Itchingwood Common Rd.
  Limps RH8 .... 123 C2
Ivanhoe Ct. Crawl RH11 .... 181 D1
Ivanhoe House. [11]
  Balham SW12 .... 21 B8
Ivanhoe Rd. Hounsl TW4 .... 4 D4
Iveagh Cl. Crawl RH11 .... 201 C1
Iveagh Ct. Beck BR3 .... 44 B6
Iveagh Ct. Brack RG12 .... 27 C4
Iveagh Rd. Guild GU2 .... 130 B7
Ively Gate Rd. Farnb GU14 .... 84 E2
Ively Rd. Farnb GU14 .... 84 D1
Iverna Gdns. Hatton TW14 .... 3 D2
Ivers Way. New Add CR0 .... 63 B3
Ivestor Terr. For Hil SE23 .... 23 C8
Ivor Cl. Guild GU1 .... 131 A8
Ivory Ct. Felt TW13 .... 15 A7
Ivory Wlk. Crawl RH11 .... 200 E3
Ivy Cl. Sunby TW16 .... 35 C7
Ivy Dene La. Ash W RH19 .... 206 D6
Ivy Dr. Lhtwat GU18 .... 67 A7
Ivy Gdns. Mitch CR4 .... 41 D6
Ivy House. Croy CR0 .... 43 D1
Ivy La. Farnb GU9 .... 125 B2
Ivy La. Hounsl TW4 .... 4 F3
Ivy La. Mayb GU22 .... 70 B1
Ivy Mill Cl. Godst RH9 .... 121 B3
Ivy Mill La. Bletch RH1 & RH9 .... 121 B3
Ivy Mill La. Godst RH1 & RH9 .... 121 B3
Ivy Rd. Alder GU12 .... 105 C2
Ivy Rd. Hounsl TW3 .... 5 B3
Ivy Rd. Tolw KT6 .... 38 A1
Ivy Rd. Up Toot SW17 .... 20 E3
Ivybank. Farnc GU7 .... 150 E6
Ivybridge Cl. [3] Twick TW1 .... 17 A8
Ivybridge Jun & Inf Sch.
  Islew TW1 .... 5 F1
Ivychurch Cl. Penge SE20 .... 23 C1
Ivydale Rd. Carsh SM5 .... 59 F8
Ivyday Gr. Streat SW16 .... 21 F5
Ivydene. E Mole KT12 & KT8 .... 35 F4
Ivydene. Knaph GU21 .... 68 B1
Ivydene Cl. Earls RH1 .... 140 B4
Ivydene Cl. Sutton SM1 .... 59 C6
Ivymount Rd. W Norw SE27 .... 22 A5

Jackass La. Tand RH9 .... 121 F4
Jackdaw Cl. Crawl RH11 .... 201 C8
Jackdaw La. Horsh RH12 .... 217 E6
Jackman's La. Woking GU21 .... 89 B8
Jackson Cl. Crawl RH10 .... 173 F2
Jackson Cl. Easth RG12 .... 27 B4
Jackson Cl. Crawl KT18 .... 76 D5
Jackson's Pl. Croy CR0 .... 42 E1
Jackson's Way. W Wick CR0 .... 63 B7
Jacob Cl. Binf RG12 .... 26 D7
Jacob Rd. Sandh GU15 .... 65 A7
Jacobean Cl. Worth RH10 .... 202 C5
Jacobs Well Rd. Jacobs GU4 .... 109 D6
Jaggard Way. Balham SW12 .... 20 F8
Jaguar Rd. Farnb GU14 .... 85 B2
Jail La. Bigg H TN16 .... 83 E3
Jamaica Rd. Thorn H CR7 .... 42 B3
James Boswell. [1] Streat SW16 .... 22 A4
James Dixon Prim Sch.
  Penge SE20 .... 23 B1
James Est. Mitch CR4 .... 40 F7
James Rd. Camb GU15 .... 65 B2
James Rd. Farnb GU11 .... 105 D7
James Rd. Shalf GU3 .... 130 C1
James St. Hounsl TW3 .... 5 D4
James Watt Way. Crawl RH10 .... 182 A4
James Way. Camb GU15 .... 65 B2
Jameston. Easth RG12 .... 27 C1
Jamieson House. Twick TW4 .... 15 F8
Jamnagar Cl. Stain TW18 .... 12 F2
Janoway Hill. Woking GU21 .... 89 C8
Japonica Cl. Woking GU21 .... 69 C1
Japonica Cl. Ash GU12 .... 105 F1
Jarrett Cl. Streat SW2 .... 22 B7
Jarrow Rd. Morden SM4 .... 40 B4
Jarvis Rd. S Croy CR2 .... 61 D4
Jasmin Rd. W Ewell KT19 .... 57 B5
Jasmin Rd. W Ewell KT19 .... 57 B5
Jasmine Cl. Earls RH1 .... 140 A4
Jasmine Cl. Woking GU21 .... 68 F3
Jasmine Cl. Horsh RH12 .... 217 C2
Jasmine Cl. [11] Wallin SM6 .... 60 B4
Jasmine Gdns. W Wick CR0 .... 63 B7
Jasmine Gr. Penge SE20 .... 43 B8
Jasmine Way. Thame D KT7 .... 36 F5
Jason Cl. Earls RH1 .... 139 E4
Jason Cl. Weyb KT13 .... 53 C5
Jasons Dr. Guild GU4 .... 110 C4
Jasper House. New Mal KT4 .... 38 D1
Jasper Rd. Dulw SE19 .... 22 F2
Jasper Rd. Dulw SE19 .... 22 F2
Javelin Ct. Crawl RH10 .... 182 D1
Jawahar Bagh. S Norw SW16 .... 22 B5
Jay Ave. Chert KT15 .... 52 E2
Jay's La. Fish GU27 .... 209 C3

Jay's La. Lurg GU27 .... 209 C3
Jays Nest Cl. Blckw GU17 .... 64 D4
Jayson Ct. [7] Croy CR0 .... 43 A1
Jeal Oakwood Ct. Epsom KT18 .... 76 E5
Jean House. Up Toot SW17 .... 20 E3
Jean Humbert House. [2]
  W Norw SE27 .... 22 D4
Jeans Ct. [10] Crawl RH11 .... 201 B1
Jeddere Cotts. Dorman RH7 .... 165 A2
Jeffries Pas. Guild GU1 .... 130 D8
Jeffries Rd. W Hors KT24 .... 112 C5
Jeffs Cl. Hampt TW12 .... 16 B2
Jeffs Rd. Cheam SM1 .... 58 F6
Jefton Cl. Wallin SM6 .... 60 C4
Jengar Cl. Sutton SM1 .... 59 B6
Jenkins' Hill London Rd.
  Bagsh GU19 .... 47 D2
Jenner Dr. W End GU24 .... 68 A6
Jenner Rd. Crawl RH10 .... 181 F3
Jenner Rd. Guild GU1 .... 130 E8
Jennett Rd. Croy CR0 & CR9 .... 61 A7
Jennifer Rd. Catf BR1 .... 24 F5
Jennings Cl. New Haw KT15 .... 52 C2
Jenny La. Lingf R... .... 164 C4
Jenson Way. S Norw SE19 .... 22 F1
Jeppo's La. Mitch CR4 .... 40 F5
Jersey Brow Rd. Farnb GU14 .... 85 A2
Jersey Cl. Addl KT16 .... 51 F7
Jersey Cl. Burph GU4 .... 110 B6
Jersey Cl. Crawl RH11 .... 201 B1
Jersey Rd. Hounsl TW5 & TW7 .... 5 D7
Jersey Rd. Mitch SW17 .... 21 B2
Jerviston Gdns. S Norw SW16 .... 22 A2
Jesmond Cl. Mitch CR4 .... 41 B6
Jesmond Rd. Croy CR0 .... 42 F2
Jessamy Rd. Weyb KT13 .... 53 B8
Jesses La. Gomsh GU5 .... 154 C8
Jessie's Hollow. Gomsh GU5 .... 133 C1
Jessiman Terr. Shep Gn SW17 .... 34 A4
Jessops Way. Mitch CR0 & CR4 .... 41 C3
Jeston House. [10] W Norw SE.. .... 22 B5
Jevington. Easth RG12 .... 27 C1
Jewell House. [3] Streat SW12 .... 21 C8
Jewels Hill. Bigg H TN16 .... 83 A6
Jewels Wlk. W Wick CR6 .... 83 A6
Jews Wlk. For Hil SE26 .... 23 B4
Jeypore Rd. Wands SW18 .... 20 C8
Jig's La S. Wink RG12 .... 27 E8
Jillian Cl. Hampt TW12 .... 16 A1
Jobson's La. Fish GU27 .... 209 D2
Jobson's La. Lurg GU27 .... 209 D1
Jocelyn Rd. Rich TW9 .... 6 E4
Jock's La. Brack RG12 .... 26 E8
Jockey Mead. Horsh RH12 .... 217 A1
Joe Hunte Ct. [2] W Norw SE27 .... 22 D3
John Baird Ct. For Hil SE26 .... 23 D4
John Baird House. [14]
  Penge SE26 .... 23 C1
John Barter House. Hounsl TW3 .... 4 F5
John Busch Sch. Brent TW7 .... 6 B6
John Cl. Alder GU11 & GU9 .... 125 E8
John Cobb Rd. Whit V KT13 .... 53 A3
John Dee House. [3] Mortl SW14 .... 7 D4
John Fisher Sch The.
  Purley CR8 .... 60 E1
John Gale Ct. Ewell KT17 .... 57 F2
John Kaye Ct. Shep Gn SW17 .... 34 A4
John Kirk House. [5]
  Streat SW16 .... 21 E5
John Nightingale Sch.
  E Mole KT8 .... 35 F6
John Nike Way. Binf RG12 .... 26 C7
John Paul II RC Sec Sch.
  Putney SW19 .... 19 D8
John Pounds House.
  Crawl RH11 .... 201 D4
John Ruskin Sixth Form Coll.
  S Croy CR2 .... 62 E3
John Russell Cl. Stough GU2 .... 109 A4
John St. Croy SE25 .... 43 A5
John St. Hounsl TW3 & TW5 .... 4 E5
John Wesley Ct. [1] Twick TW1 .... 17 A7
John Wiskar Dr. Cran GU6 .... 174 D2
John's Cl. Ashf TW15 .... 14 C4
John's Rd. Tats TN16 .... 103 D7
John's Terr. Croy CR0 .... 42 E1
Johns La. Morden SM4 .... 40 C4
Johns Wlk. Whytlf CR3 .... 101 A8
Johnsdale. Oxted RH8 .... 122 F6
Johnson Rd. Heston TW5 .... 4 C7
Johnson Rd. Thorn H CR0 .... 42 D2
Johnson Wlk. Crawl RH10 .... 201 B3
Johnson's Cl. Carsh SM5 .... 59 F7
Johnsons Dr. Hampt TW12 .... 36 C8
Johnston Gr. Stough GU2 .... 109 A5
Johnston Wlk. Stough GU2 .... 109 A5
Joinville Pl. Addl KT15 .... 52 D5
Jolesfield. Crawl RH11 .... 200 F3
Jolliffe Rd. Merst RH1 .... 99 C1
Jones Wlk. [6] Rich TW10 .... 6 F1
Jonquil Gdns. [5] Hampt TW12 .... 16 A2
Jonson Cl. Mitch CR4 .... 41 B6
Jordan Cl. S Croy CR2 .... 80 F8
Jordans Cl. Crawl RH11 .... 201 D8
Jordans Cl. Earls RH1 .... 140 A4
Jordans Cl. Merrow GU1 .... 110 A2
Jordans Cl. Stan TW19 .... 13 C8
Jordans Cres. Crawl RH11 .... 181 D1
Jordans The. E Grins RH19 .... 205 E8
Josef Perrin House. [1]
  W Norw SE27 .... 22 D4
Joseph Hood Fst Sch.
  Merton SW20 .... 39 E6
Joseph Locke Way.
  Thame D KT7 .... 55 A8
Joseph's Rd. Guild GU1 .... 109 D2
Josephine Ave. L Kings KT20 .... 117 F8
Josephine Cl. L Kings KT20 .... 117 F8
Jubilee Ave. N Asct SL5 .... 28 E8
Jubilee Ave. Twick TW2 .... 16 C7
Jubilee Ave. Woki RG11 .... 25 B7

Jubilee Cl. N Asct SL5 .... 28 E8
Jubilee Cl. Stan TW19 .... 13 C8
Jubilee Cl. Tedd KT1 .... 37 C8
Jubilee Cl. W Heath GU14 .... 84 D4
Jubilee Cres. Addl KT15 .... 52 D5
Jubilee Ct. Brack RG12 .... 27 C6
Jubilee Ct. Hounsl TW3 .... 5 B4
Jubilee Ct. Stain TW18 .... 13 A4
Jubilee Ct. Thorn H CR7 .... 42 A5
Jubilee Dr. Ash V GU12 .... 106 A6
Jubilee Hall Rd. Farnb GU14 .... 85 C4
Jubilee House. [5] Hampt TW12 .... 36 A8
Jubilee La. Graysh GU26 .... 188 C3
Jubilee La. Rowl GU10 .... 146 A5
Jubilee Rd. Alder GU11 .... 126 B7
Jubilee Rd. Cheam SM3 .... 58 D3
Jubilee Rd. Mytch GU16 .... 86 A2
Jubilee Rd. Rudg RH12 .... 214 D8
Jubilee Terr. Brock RH3 .... 137 C5
Jubilee Terr. Dork RH4 .... 136 B8
Jubilee Villas. Thame D KT10 .... 36 E1
Jubilee Way. E Bed TW14 .... 15 A7
Jubilee Way. Chess KT4 & KT9 .... 57 B7
Jubilee Way. Merton SW19 .... 40 B8
Jubilee Way. Tolw KT4 & KT9 .... 57 B7
Jubilee Wks. Merton SW19 .... 40 C7
Jubilee Wlk. Crawl RH10 .... 202 A6
Judge Wlk. Clayg KT10 .... 55 E4
Judge's Terr. E Grins RH19 .... 205 E7
Julian Cl. Woking GU21 .... 69 C1
Julian Hill. Whit V KT13 .... 53 B3
Julian House. Dulw SE21 .... 22 E4
Julian Taylor Path. For Hil SE23 .... 23 D5
Julians Prim Sch. Streat SW16 .... 22 A4
Julien Rd. Coulsd CR5 .... 79 D4
Juliet Gdns. Wink RG12 .... 27 F8
Julius Ct. Brent TW8 .... 6 F7
Julius Hill. Wink RG12 .... 27 F8
Jumps Rd. Churt GU10 .... 168 B3
Junction Pl. Shottm GU27 .... 207 F6
Junction Rd. Ashf TW15 .... 14 D3
Junction Rd. Croy CR2 .... 61 D5
Junction Rd. Dork RH4 .... 136 A7
Junction Rd. Lhtwat GU18 .... 48 B1
June Cl. Wallin CR5 .... 79 B5
June La. Salfs RH1 .... 140 B2
Junewood Cl. Woodhm KT15 .... 70 F8
Juniper. Easth RG12 .... 27 C1
Juniper Cl. Bellf GU1 .... 109 C6
Juniper Cl. Bigg H TN16 .... 83 E2
Juniper Cl. Chess KT9 .... 56 F5
Juniper Cl. Woodh RH2 .... 139 C7
Juniper Cl. Belm SM2 .... 59 A4
Juniper Dr. Bisley GU24 .... 68 A4
Juniper Gdns. Ashf TW16 .... 14 F2
Juniper Gdns. Mitch CR4 .... 41 C8
Juniper Hall (Field Study Ctr).
  Mickle RH5 .... 115 C6
Juniper Pl. Shalf GU4 .... 130 D2
Juniper Rd. Crawl RH11 .... 181 C1
Juniper Rd. W Heath GU14 .... 84 C5
Juniper Rd. Woodh RH2 .... 139 C7
Juniper Terr. Shalf GU4 .... 130 D2
Juniper Wlk. Brock RH3 .... 137 C7
Jura Cl. Crawl RH11 .... 201 B3
Justin Cl. Brent TW8 .... 6 D7
Jutland Gdns. Coulsd CR5 .... 99 F7
Jutland Pl. Egham TW20 .... 12 C3
Jutland Rd. Catf SE6 .... 24 C8
Juxon Cl. Crawl RH11 .... 200 F4

Kaithwood House. Horsh RH12 .... 218 B5
Kangley Bridge Ctr. Penge SE26 .... 23 F3
Kangley Bridge Rd. For Hil SE26 .... 23 F3
Kangley Bridge Rd. Penge SE26 .... 23 F3
Karen Ct. Broml BR1 .... 44 F8
Kashmir Cl. New Haw KT15 .... 52 D2
Katharine Cl. [1] Twick TW1 .... 17 A7
Katharine St. Croy CR0 & CR9 .... 61 C7
Katherine Cl. Row Tn KT15 .... 52 A4
Katherine Ct. For Hil SE23 .... 23 C7
Kathleen Moore Ct. W Wick BR4 .... 63 C8
Kay Ave. Chert KT15 .... 52 E7
Kay Cres. Head Dn GU35 .... 187 B6
Kaye Ct. Bellf GU1 .... 109 C5
Kaye Don Way. Whit V KT13 .... 53 A1
Kayemoor Rd. Sutton SM2 .... 59 E4
Kaynes Pk. N Asct SL5 .... 28 E8
Keable Rd. Wreccl GU10 .... 145 E7
Kearton Cl. Kenley CR8 .... 80 C2
Keates Gn. Brack RG12 .... 27 B8
Keats Ave. Redh RH1 .... 119 B3
Keats Cl. Horsh RH12 .... 217 F7
Keats Cl. Mitch SW17 & SW19 .... 20 D2
Keats House. Beck BR3 .... 24 B2
Keats Pl. E Grins RH19 .... 185 D1
Keats Way. Crowth RG11 .... 45 B6
Keats Way. Croy CR0 .... 43 C3
Keble Cl. Crawl RH10 .... 182 D1
Keble Cl. New Mal KT4 .... 38 F1
Keble St. Wands SW17 .... 20 C4
Keble Way. Sandh GU15 .... 45 E2
Kedeston Ct. Sutton SM3 .... 40 B1
Keedonwood Rd. Broml BR1 .... 24 F3
Keedonwood Rd. Catf BR1 .... 24 F3
Keeley Rd. Croy CR0 & CR9 .... 61 C8
Keeling House. [2] Tedd TW11 .... 16 E3
Keen's Rd. Croy CR0 .... 61 C6
Keens Cl. Streat SW16 .... 21 D3
Keens La. Stough GU2 & GU3 .... 108 F5
Keens Park Rd. Stough GU3 .... 108 F5
Keep Hatch Cty Inf Sch.
  Woki RG11 .... 25 D7
Keep Hatch Cty Jun Sch.
  Woki RG11 .... 25 D7
Keep The. Catf SE6 .... 24 B7
Keep The. King U T KT2 .... 17 F1
Keepers Cl. Merrow GU4 .... 110 D4
Keepers Combe. Brack RG12 .... 27 D3
Keepers Mews. Tedd TW11 .... 17 C2
Keepers Terr. Went GU25 .... 31 B4

Keepers Wlk. Vir W GU25 .... 31 D4
Keephatch Rd. Woki RG11 .... 25 E7
Keevil Dr. Putney SW19 .... 19 E8
Keir Hardie House. [7]
  Crawl RH11 .... 201 B1
Keith Lucas Rd. Farnb GU14 .... 84 F2
Keith Park Cres. Bigg H TN16 .... 83 C7
Keldholme. Easth RG12 .... 27 A6
Kelling Gdns. Thorn H CR0 .... 42 B2
Kellino St. Up Toot SW17 .... 20 F4
Kelly Cl. Up Hall TW17 .... 34 E7
Kelmscott. [5] For Hil SE23 .... 23 D5
Kelsey Cl. Horley RH6 .... 160 F3
Kelsey Gate. Beck BR3 .... 44 A6
Kelsey La. Beck BR3 .... 44 A6
Kelsey Park Ave. Beck BR3 .... 44 B7
Kelsey Park Rd. Beck BR3 .... 44 A6
Kelsey Park Sch. Beck BR3 .... 44 A6
Kelsey Sq. Beck BR3 .... 44 A7
Kelsey Way. Beck BR3 .... 44 A6
Kelso Cl. Crawl RH10 .... 202 E7
Kelso Ct. Penge SE20 .... 23 B1
Kelso Rd. Carsh SM5 .... 40 C2
Kelvedon Ave. Whit V KT12 .... 53 F3
Kelvedon Cl. King U T KT2 .... 18 A2
Kelvin Ave. Leahd KT22 .... 94 F7
Kelvin Bsns Ctr. Crawl RH10 .... 181 F2
Kelvin Cl. Chess KT19 .... 57 A4
Kelvin Cl. Chisw W4 .... 7 C7
Kelvin Cl. Islew TW7 .... 5 E5
Kelvin Cl. [8] Penge SE20 .... 43 B8
Kelvin Cl. [8] Twick TW1 .... 6 B1
Kelvin Dr. Twick TW1 .... 6 B1
Kelvin Gdns. Croy CR0 .... 41 E2
Kelvin Gr. Chess KT6 .... 56 E7
Kelvin Gr. For Hil SE26 .... 23 B5
Kelvin Grove Prim Sch.
  For Hil SE26 .... 23 B5
Kelvin Grove Prim Sch.
  For Hil SE26 .... 23 E7
Kelvin La. Crawl RH10 .... 181 F2
Kelvin Way. Crawl RH10 .... 181 F2
Kelvinbrook. E Mole KT8 .... 36 B6
Kelvington Cl. Croy CR0 .... 43 E2
Kelway House. [20] Streat SW2 .... 22 A8
Kemble Cl. Oat Pk KT13 .... 53 D6
Kemble Cotts. Addl KT15 .... 52 A6
Kemble Rd. Croy CR0 & CR9 .... 61 B7
Kemble Rd. For Hil SE23 .... 23 D7
Kembleside Rd. Bigg H TN16 .... 83 C1
Kemerton Rd. Beck BR3 .... 44 B7
Kemerton Rd. Croy CR0 .... 42 F2
Kemishford. Woking GU22 .... 89 A4
Kemnal Pk. Haslem GU27 .... 208 D7
Kemp Ct. Bagsh GU19 .... 47 D3
Kemp Gdns. Thorn H CR0 .... 42 C3
Kempe Rd. Belm SM2 .... 59 B2
Kempshott Rd. Horsh RH12 .... 217 B4
Kempshott Rd. Streat SW16 .... 21 E1
Kempston House. Sutton SM2 .... 59 B2
Kempton Ave. Sunby TW16 .... 35 B8
Kempton Ct. Sunby TW16 .... 35 B8
Kempton Park Race Course.
  Sunby TW16 .... 15 C1
Kempton Park Sta. Sunby TW16 .... 15 B1
Kempton Rd. Hampt TW12 .... 35 F7
Kempton Wlk. Croy CR0 .... 43 E3
Kemsing Cl. Coney H BR2 .... 63 F8
Kemsing Cl. Thorn H CR7 .... 42 C5
Kemsley Rd. Tats TN16 .... 103 D8
Kendal Cl. E Bed TW14 .... 14 F7
Kendal Cl. Farnb GU14 .... 84 E4
Kendal Cl. Redh RH1 .... 118 D2
Kendal Ct. [7] Croy CR0 .... 42 E1
Kendal Gdns. Sutton SM1 .... 59 C8
Kendal Gr. Friml GU15 .... 66 D4
Kendal House. [5] Croy CR0 .... 42 E1
Kendal House. Penge SE20 .... 43 B7
Kendale Rd. Lewish BR1 .... 24 E3
Kendall Ave. Penge BR3 .... 43 E7
Kendall Ave. S Croy CR2 .... 61 D2
Kendall Ave S. S Croy CR2 .... 61 D1
Kendall Ct. [8] Penge SE19 .... 22 F1
Kendall House. Lewish SE12 .... 24 F8
Kendall Rd. Islew TW7 .... 6 A5
Kendall Rd. Penge BR3 .... 43 E7
Kendor Ave. Epsom KT19 .... 76 C8
Kendra Hall Rd. Croy CR2 .... 61 B3
Kendrey Gdns. Twick TW2 .... 16 E8
Kendrick Cl. Woki RG11 .... 25 C5
Kenilford Rd. Balham SW12 .... 21 B8
Kenilworth Ave. Brack RG12 .... 27 D8
Kenilworth Ave. Oxsh KT11 .... 74 B5
Kenilworth Ave. Wimble SW19 .... 20 A4
Kenilworth Cl. Banstd SM7 .... 78 B3
Kenilworth Cl. Crawl RH11 .... 201 B2
Kenilworth Dr. Walt O T KT12 .... 54 D7
Kenilworth Gdns. Stain TW18 .... 13 C3
Kenilworth Rd.
  Ashf TW15 & TW19 .... 13 D5
Kenilworth Rd. Penge SE20 .... 43 D8
Kenilworth Rd. Stonel KT17 .... 58 A5
Kenilworth Rd. W Heath GU14 .... 84 C5
Kenilworth Terr. [3] Belm SM2 .... 59 A3
Kenley Cl. Cater CR3 .... 100 E7
Kenley Gdns. Thorn H CR7 .... 42 B5
Kenley House. [5] Penge SE20 .... 43 B8
Kenley La. Kenley CR8 .... 80 D3
Kenley Prim Sch. Kenley CR3 .... 80 E3
Kenley Rd. Head Dn GU35 .... 187 C5
Kenley Rd. King U T KT1 & KT3 .... 38 B7
Kenley Rd. Merton SW19 .... 40 A6
Kenley Rd. Twick TW1 .... 6 B1
Kenley Sta. Kenley CR8 .... 80 C5
Kenley Wlk. Cheam SM3 .... 58 D6
Kenlor Rd. Up Toot SW17 .... 20 D3
Kenmara Cl. Crawl RH10 .... 182 A1
Kenmara Ct. Crawl RH10 .... 182 A2
Kenmare Dr. Mitch CR4 .... 20 F1
Kenmare Rd. Thorn H CR7 .... 42 A3
Kenmore Cl. Friml GU16 .... 85 D8

Kenmore Cl. Rich TW9 .... 7 A7
Kenmore Cl. Rich TW9 .... 80 B5
Kennard Ct. For Row RH18 .... 206 E3
Kennedy Ave. E Grins RH19 .... 185 D3
Kennedy Ct. Ashf TW15 .... 14 C3
Kennedy Rd. Horsh RH13 .... 217 D1
Kennel Ave. N Asct SL5 .... 28 F8
Kennel Cl. Fetch KT22 & KT23 .... 94 C3
Kennel Cl. N Asct SL5 .... 8 F2
Kennel Gn. N Asct SL5 .... 28 E8
Kennel La. Fetch KT22 .... 94 C4
Kennel La. Frensh GU10 .... 146 C2
Kennel La. Hookw RH6 .... 160 D2
Kennel La. Windl GU20 .... 48 C5
Kennel Ride. N Asct SL5 .... 8 F1
Kennel Wood. N Asct SL5 .... 28 F8
Kennel Wood Cres.
  New Add CR0 .... 82 D8
Kennels La. Farnb GU14 .... 84 C2
Kennet Cl. Ash GU12 .... 106 A1
Kennet Cl. Crawl RH11 .... 200 F5
Kennet Cl. W Heath GU14 .... 84 E6
Kennet House. [6] Redh RH1 .... 118 F2
Kennet Rd. Islew TW7 .... 5 F4
Kennet Sq. Mitch CR4 .... 40 E8
Kenneth Rd. Woodm SM7 .... 78 D4
Kennoldes. Dulw SE21 .... 22 D6
Kenrick Sq. Bletch RH1 .... 120 E1
Kensington Ave. S Norw CR7 .... 42 A8
Kensington Avenue Inf Sch.
  S Norw CR7 .... 42 A8
Kensington Avenue Jun Sch.
  S Norw CR7 .... 42 A8
Kensington Rd. Crawl RH11 .... 201 C2
Kensington Terr. S Croy CR2 .... 61 D3
Kent Cl. Mitch CR4 & SW16 .... 41 E5
Kent Cl. Stain TW18 .... 13 D2
Kent Dr. Tedd TW11 .... 16 E3
Kent Gate Way. Add CR0 .... 63 B5
Kent Gate Way.
  New Add CR0 & CR2 .... 62 F4
Kent Hatch Rd.
  Limps RH8 & TN8 .... 123 D4
Kent Hatch Rd.
  The Char RH8 & TN8 .... 123 D4
Kent House La. Penge BR3 .... 23 E3
Kent House Rd.
  For Hil SE26 & BR3 .... 23 E2
Kent House Rd.
  Penge SE26 & BR3 .... 23 E2
Kent House Sta. Penge BR3 .... 43 E8
Kent Lodge. [9] Putney SW19 .... 19 D7
Kent Rd. E Mole KT8 .... 36 C5
Kent Rd. King U T KT1 .... 37 D6
Kent Rd. Mayb GU22 .... 70 C3
Kent Rd. Rich TW9 .... 7 A7
Kent Rd. W Wick BR4 .... 44 B1
Kent Rd. Windl GU20 .... 48 D5
Kent Tower. Penge SE20 .... 23 B1
Kent Way. Surb KT6 .... 56 F8
Kentigern Dr. Crowth RG11 .... 45 E5
Kenton Ave. Sunby TW16 .... 35 C7
Kenton Cl. Brack RG12 .... 27 D7
Kenton Cl. Friml GU16 .... 65 F1
Kenton Cl. For Hil SE26 .... 23 E4
Kenton Way. Woking GU21 .... 68 F2
Kentwyns Rise. S Nutf RH1 .... 140 F3
Kenwood Cl. Harm UB7 .... 3 A8
Kenwood Dr. Beck BR3 .... 44 C6
Kenwood Dr. Whit V KT12 .... 54 B5
Kenwood Pk. Whit V KT13 .... 53 D4
Kenwood Ridge. Kenley CR8 .... 80 B2
Kenwyn Rd. Wimble SW20 .... 39 C8
Kenya Ct. Horley RH6 .... 160 F4
Kenyngton Dr. Ashf TW16 .... 15 A3
Kenyngton Manor Prim Sch.
  Ashf TW16 .... 15 A2
Kenyons. W Hors KT24 .... 112 B7
Keogh Barracks. Ash GU16 .... 86 B1
Keogh Cl. Mytch GU16 .... 86 B2
Keppel Rd. Dork RH4 .... 115 B1
Keppel Spur. Old W SL4 .... 11 B8
Kepple Pl. Bagsh GU19 .... 47 F3
Kerdale Cl. Worth RH10 .... 202 C2
Kerria Way. W End GU24 .... 67 F6
Kerrill Ave. Coulsd CR5 .... 100 A8
Kerrsland Cotts. Shackl GU7 .... 149 F1
Kerry Terr. Woking GU21 .... 70 B3
Kersey Dr. Selsd CR2 .... 81 D7
Kershaw House. [7]
  W Norw SE27 .... 22 B5
Keston Ave. Coulsd CR5 & CR8 .... 100 B8
Keston Ave. Woodhm KT15 .... 71 A8
Keston Avenue Cty Prim Sch.
  Coulsd CR5 .... 100 A8
Keston Rd. Thorn H CR7 .... 42 A3
Kestrel Cl. Crawl RH11 .... 201 C8
Kestrel Cl. Crond GU10 .... 124 D7
Kestrel Cl. Horsh RH12 .... 217 E5
Kestrel Cl. Merrow GU4 .... 110 D3
Kestrel House. M Bourn GU9 .... 146 A8
Kestrel Rd. Farnb GU14 .... 85 B2
Kestrel Way. New Add CR0 .... 63 D2
Keswick Ave.
  King U T KT2 & SW15 .... 18 E3
Keswick Ave. Merton SW19 .... 40 A7
Keswick Ave. Up Hall TW17 .... 34 E6
Keswick Cl. Crawl RH11 .... 200 D4
Keswick Cl. Friml GU15 .... 66 D4
Keswick Cl. Sutton SM1 .... 59 C6
Keswick Dr. Lhtwat GU18 .... 67 B8
Keswick Rd. Fetch KT22 & KT23 .... 94 C3
Keswick Rd. Thor L TW20 .... 12 B1
Keswick Rd. Twick TW2 .... 5 C1
Keswick Rd. W Wick BR4 .... 63 E8
Keswick Rd. Witley GU8 .... 170 D6
Kettering Ct. S Norw CR7 .... 42 C5
Kettering St. Streat SW16 .... 21 C2
Kettlewell Cl. Horse GU21 .... 69 E4
Kettlewell Dr. Horse GU21 .... 69 E5

Kettlewell Hill. Horse GU21 .... 69 E4
Ketton Gn. Merst RH1 .... 119 D7
Kevan Dr. Send M GU23 .... 90 E2
Kevin Cl. Hounsl TW4 .... 4 D5
Kew Bridge Rd. Brent TW8 .... 6 F8
Kew Cres. Cheam SM3 .... 58 F7
Kew Foot Rd. Rich TW9 .... 6 E4
Kew Gardens Rd. Rich TW9 .... 7 A6
Kew Gardens Sta. Rich TW9 .... 7 A6
Kew Gn. Rich TW9 .... 6 F8
Kew Lodge. 10 Rich TW9 .... 6 F6
Kew Observatory. Rich TW9 .... 6 C4
Kew Rd. Rich TW9 & W4 .... 6 F5
Key Cross. Tilf GU10 .... 147 D5
Keymer Cl. Bigg H TN16 .... 83 D3
Keymer Rd. Crawl RH11 .... 201 D4
Keymer Rd. Streat SW2 .... 21 F6
Keynsham Rd. Cheam SM4 .... 40 B1
Keynsham Way. Sandh GU15 .... 45 D2
Keynsham Wlk. Cheam SM4 .... 40 B1
Keysham Ave. Cranf TW5 .... 4 A6
Keywood Dr. Ashf TW16 .... 15 A2
Khama Rd. Up Toot SW17 .... 20 E4
Khartoum Rd. Up Toot SW17 .... 20 D4
Khartoum Rd. Witley GU8 .... 170 E6
Kibble Gn. Easth RG12 .... 27 C3
Kidborough Down.
  G Book KT23 .... 114 A8
Kidborough Rd. Crawl RH11 .... 200 F4
  For Row RH18 .... 206 D1
Kidbrooke Park (Michael Hall Sch).
  For Row RH18 .... 206 E2
Kidbrooke Rise. For Row RH18 ..... 206 E2
Kidderminster Rd. Thorn H CR0 .... 42 C2
Kidmans Cl. Horsh RH12 .... 217 F5
Kidworth Cl. Horley RH6 .... 160 F5
Kielder Wlk. Friml GU15 .... 66 C4
Kier Pk. Ascot SL5 .... 29 C6
Kilberry Cl. Hounsl TW7 .... 5 D6
Kilcorral Cl. Ewell KT17 .... 77 A5
Killasser Ct. Tadw KT20 .... 97 C4
Killearn Rd. Catf SE6 .... 24 D7
Killester Gdns.
  N Cheam KT17 & KT4 .... 58 B6
Killick House. Sutton SM1 .... 59 B6
Killicks. Cran GU6 .... 174 F4
Killieser Ave. Streat SW2 .... 21 E6
Killigrew House. Charlt TW16 .... 14 E1
Killross Rd. E Bed TW14 .... 14 D7
Kilmarnock Pk. Reig RH2 .... 118 B2
Kilmartin Ave. Thorn H SW16 .... 42 A6
Kilmartin Gdns. Friml GU16 .... 65 F1
Kilmington Cl. Brack RG12 .... 27 E2
Kilmiston Ave. Shep TW17 .... 34 C3
Kilmiston House. Shep TW17 .... 34 C3
Kilmore Dr. Friml GU15 .... 66 B4
Kilmorey Gdns. Islew TW1 .... 6 B3
Kilmorey Rd. Islew TW1 .... 6 B3
Kilmorie Prim Sch. For Hil SE23 ... 23 E6
Kilmorie Rd. For Hil SE23 .... 23 E6
Kilmuir Cl. Sandh GU15 .... 64 D7
Kiln Cl. Harl UB3 .... 3 D8
Kiln Copse. Cran GU6 .... 174 E4
Kiln Fields. Haslem GU27 .... 208 C8
Kiln La. Brack RG12 .... 27 A7
Kiln La. Brock RH3 .... 116 C1
Kiln La. Ewell KT17 .... 76 E8
Kiln La. Horley RH6 .... 161 A5
Kiln La. M Bourn GU10 & GU9 .... 146 C6
Kiln La. Ripley GU23 .... 91 B3
Kiln La. Sunnin SL5 .... 30 A4
Kiln Meadows. Fairl GU3 .... 108 C5
Kiln Rd. Crawl D RH10 .... 204 B7
Kiln Way. Alder GU11 .... 126 B7
Kiln Way. Graysh GU26 .... 187 E5
Kiln Wlk. Earls RH1 .... 140 A4
Kilnfield Rd. Rudg RH12 .... 214 D8
Kilnmead. Crawl RH10 & RH11 ... 201 E7
Kilnmead Cl. Crawl RH10 .... 201 E7
Kilnside. Clayg KT10 .... 56 A3
Kilnwood La. Crawl RH12 .... 200 B3
Kilnwood La. Faygt RH12 .... 199 F3
Kilross Rd. E Bed TW14 .... 14 D7
Kilrue La. Whit V KT12 .... 53 F6
Kilrush Terr. Woking GU21 .... 70 A3
Kilsha Rd. Walt O T KT12 .... 35 C3
Kimber Ct. Merrow GU4 .... 110 D3
Kimber Ctr The. Wands SW18 ...... 20 A8
Kimber Rd. Wands SW18 .... 20 B8
Kimberley. Easth RG12 .... 27 C1
Kimberley Cl. Horley RH6 .... 160 E3
Kimberley Pl. 5 Purley CR8 .... 80 A8
Kimberley Rd. Crawl RH10 .... 202 B7
Kimberley Rd. Penge BR3 .... 43 D7
Kimberley Rd.
  Thorn H CR0 & CR7 .... 42 B3
Kimberley Rd. Cobham KT11 .... 74 B6
Kimberley Wlk. Walt O T KT12 ..... 35 B2
Kimbers La. Farnh GU9 .... 125 D3
Kimble Rd. Mitch SW17 & SW19 ... 20 D2
Kimbolton Cl. Lewish SE12 .... 24 F8
Kimmeridge. Brack RG12 .... 27 E3
Kimpton Bsns Ctr. Cheam SM3 .... 58 F8
Kimpton House. Rhampt SW15 ..... 19 A8
Kimpton Ind Est. Cheam SM3 ...... 58 F8
Kimpton Rd. Cheam SM3 .... 58 F8
Kinburn Dr. Eng Gn TW20 .... 11 E3
Kindell House. 4 Mortl SW14 .... 7 D4
Kindersley Cl. E Grins RH19 .... 186 B3
Kinfauns Rd. Streat SW2 .... 22 A6
King Acre Ct. Stain TW18 .... 12 E5
King Alfred Ave. Catf SE6 .... 24 A4
King Athelstan Prim Sch.
  King U T KT1 .... 37 F6
King Charles Cres. Surb KT5 .... 37 F2
King Charles' Rd.
  Surb KT5 & KT6 .... 37 F3
King Charles Wlk. 6
  Putney SW19 .... 19 E7
King Edward Dr. Chess KT6 .... 56 E7
King Edward VII (Old Windsor
  Unit). Old W SL4 .... 10 F8

King Edward's Gr. Tedd TW11 .... 17 C2
King Edward's Sch.
  Wormly GU8 .... 170 F1
King Edwards Rd. N Asct SL5 .... 28 E8
King Edwards Rise. N Asct SL5 ..... 28 E8
King Garth Mews. For Hil SE23 .... 23 C6
King Gdns. Croy CR0 .... 61 B5
King George Ave. E Grins RH19 185 C3
King George Ave. Walt O T KT12 35 D1
King George Cl. Ashf TW16 .... 14 E3
King George Sq. Rich TW10 .... 6 F1
King George V1 Ave.
  Bigg H TN16 .... 83 D3
King George VI Ave. Mitch CR4 .... 40 F5
King George's Cotts.
  Dunst GU8 .... 192 F6
King George's Dr.
  Woodhm KT15 .... 52 A1
King George's Lodge.
  Stough GU2 .... 109 A4
King George's Trad Est.
  Chess KT9 .... 57 A6
King Henry's Dr. New Add CR0 .... 82 E8
King Henry's Dr. W Wick CR0 ...... 82 E8
King Henry's Rd.
  King U T KT1 & KT3 .... 38 B6
King St. Chert KT16 .... 33 A1
King St. E Grins RH19 .... 185 E1
King St. Rich TW10 & TW9 .... 6 D2
King St. Twick TW1 .... 17 A7
King Street Par. 6 Twick TW1 ..... 17 A7
King William IV Gdns.
  Penge SE20 .... 23 C2
King's Ave. Ashf TW16 .... 14 F2
King's Ave. Hounsl TW3 & TW5 ..... 5 B6
King's Cl. Stain TW18 .... 13 D1
King's Cl. Thame D KT7 .... 37 A2
King's Coll Sch. Wimble SW19 .... 19 D2
King's Court Cty Fst Sch.
  Old W SL4 .... 11 B8
King's Ct. Alder GU10 & GU12 ... 126 E8
King's Ct. Beck BR3 .... 44 B6
King's Ct. Wimble SW19 .... 20 A2
King's Dr. Thame D KT7 .... 37 B2
King's Head La. Byfl KT14 .... 71 D8
King's House Jun Sch.
  Rich TW10 .... 6 F2
King's House Sch. Rich TW10 .... 6 F2
King's Keep. Sandh GU17 .... 45 B1
King's La. Carsh SM1 & SM2 .... 59 D5
King's Paddock. Hampt TW12 ...... 36 C8
King's Pas. King U T KT2 .... 37 D8
King's Rd. Alder GU11 .... 104 F1
King's Rd. Ascot SL5 .... 29 D4
King's Rd. Cran GU6 .... 174 F2
King's Rd. Crowth RG11 .... 45 C5
King's Rd. Croy SE25 .... 43 A6
King's Rd. Egham TW20 .... 12 A4
King's Rd. Farnc GU7 .... 150 F6
King's Rd. Haslem GU27 .... 208 A6
King's Rd. Horsh RH12 & RH13 ... 217 E3
King's Rd. King U T KT2 .... 18 E1
King's Rd. Long D KT6 .... 37 C1
King's Rd. Mortl SW14 .... 7 D4
King's Rd. Tedd TW11 & TW12 .... 16 D3
King's Rd. Twick TW1 .... 6 A3
King's Rd. Wimble SW19 .... 20 A2
King's Ride. Brack SL5 .... 28 D5
King's Ride. Camb GU15 .... 65 D7
King's Shade Wlk. 1
  Epsom KT18 .... 76 D6
King's Terr. 8 Islew TW7 .... 6 A4
King's Way. Pirb GU24 .... 87 D8
King's Wlk. Sandh GU15 .... 64 F6
Kingcup Cl. Croy CR0 .... 43 D1
Kingcup Dr. Bisley GU24 .... 68 A4
Kingfield Cl. Old Wok GU22 .... 89 F7
Kingfield Dr. Old Wok GU22 .... 89 F7
Kingfield Gdns. Old Wok GU22 ... 89 F7
Kingfield Rd. Old Wok GU22 .... 89 F7
Kingfield Sch. Old Wok GU22 ...... 90 A7
Kingfisher Cl. Crawl RH10 .... 182 E1
Kingfisher Cl. Hersh KT12 .... 54 E5
Kingfisher Cl. Putney SW19 .... 19 E6
Kingfisher Cl. W Heath GU14 ...... 84 D6
Kingfisher Ct. Dork RH4 .... 136 A8
Kingfisher Ct. E Mole KT8 .... 36 E5
Kingfisher Ct. Islew TW3 .... 5 B2
Kingfisher Ct. Sheer GU21 .... 70 C5
Kingfisher Dr. Merrow GU4 .... 110 C3
Kingfisher Dr. Redh RH1 .... 119 A3
Kingfisher Dr. Stain TW18 .... 12 F4
Kingfisher Dr. Tedd TW10 .... 17 B4
Kingfisher Gdns. Selsd CR2 .... 62 D1
Kingfisher Lodge. Tedd TW11 ...... 17 A4
Kingfisher Rise. E Grins RH19 ... 205 F8
Kingfisher Sports Ctr The. 12
  King U T KT1 .... 37 E7
Kingfisher Way. Beck CR0 .... 43 D4
Kingfisher Way. Horsh RH12 ...... 217 C5
Kingfisher Wlk. Alder GU12 .... 105 F2
Kingham Cl. Wands SW18 .... 20 C8
Kings Ave. Ash GU10 & GU12 ..... 126 E8
Kings Ave. Broml BR1 .... 24 F2
Kings Ave. Byfl KT14 .... 71 D7
Kings Ave. Earls RH1 .... 139 E7
Kings Ave. New Mal KT3 .... 38 F5
Kings Ave. Streat SW12 & SW4 ... 21 D8
Kings Ave. Wallin SM5 .... 59 F3
Kings Chase. E Mole KT8 .... 36 C6
Kings Cl. Walt O T KT12 .... 35 B1
Kings Copse. 9 E Grins RH19 .... 205 F8
Kings Cres. Camb GU15 .... 65 C8
Kings Cross La. S Nutf RH1 .... 140 E6
Kings Ct. Horsh RH13 .... 217 D3
Kings Ct. 16 Islew TW7 .... 5 F4
Kings Ct. 11 Rhampt SW15 .... 19 A8
Kings Ct. Tadw KT20 .... 97 C5
Kings Ct. 3 Wallin SM6 .... 60 B4
Kings Dr. Surb KT5 .... 38 A3
Kings Dr The. Whit V KT12 .... 53 F2

Kings Farm Ave. Rich TW10 .... 7 A3
Kings Gate. Farnc GU7 .... 150 F6
Kings Hall Rd. Penge BR3 .... 43 E8
Kings Keep. King U T KT6 .... 37 E5
Kings La. Eng Gn TW20 .... 11 A2
Kings La. Windl GU20 .... 48 C5
Kings La. Wreccl GU10 & GU9 ... 145 D1
Kings' Manor Sch. Stough GU2 ... 108 E1
Kings Mead. S Nutf RH1 .... 140 E7
Kings Mead. Smallf RH6 .... 162 B3
Kings Mead Pk. Clayg KT10 .... 55 E3
Kings Mill La. S Nutf RH1 .... 140 D5
Kings Mill La. Salfs RH1 .... 140 D5
Kings Rd. Belm SM2 .... 59 A1
Kings Rd. Bigg H TN16 .... 83 C2
Kings Rd. Felt TW13 .... 15 C7
Kings Rd. Horley RH6 .... 161 A3
Kings Rd. Mitch CR4 .... 41 A6
Kings Rd. Rich TW10 & TW9 .... 6 F2
Kings Rd. Shalf GU4 .... 130 E2
Kings Rd. W End GU24 .... 68 A6
Kings Rd. Walt O T KT12 .... 35 B1
Kings Rd. Woking GU21 .... 70 A3
Kings Rd. Woner GU5 .... 152 B8
Kings Rd. Woodhm KT15 .... 71 B8
Kings Way. Croy CR0 .... 60 F5
Kings Wlk. Hams Gn CR2 .... 81 B5
Kings's Rd. 2 Guild GU1 .... 109 D1
Kingsbridge House. 1
  Penge SE20 .... 43 B8
Kingsbridge Rd. W Barn SM4 .... 39 D2
Kingsbridge Rd. Walt O T KT12 ... 35 B2
Kingsbrook. Leahd KT22 .... 75 E1
Kingsbury Cres. Egham TW18 ...... 12 D4
Kingsbury Dr. Old W SL4 .... 11 B8
Kingsclear Pk. Camb GU15 .... 65 D4
Kingsclere Cl. Rhampt SW15 .... 19 A8
Kingscliffe Gdns. Wands SW19 .... 19 F7
Kingscote Hill. Crawl RH11 .... 201 B4
Kingscote Rd. Croy CR0 & CR9 ... 43 B2
Kingscote Rd. King U T KT3 .... 38 D6
Kingscote Sta. E Grins RH19 ..... 204 F4
Kingscourt Rd. Streat SW16 .... 21 E5
Kingscroft Cty Mid Sch.
  Stain TW18 .... 13 A2
Kingscroft La. New Gn RG12 & SL4 8 A6
Kingscroft Rd. Leahd KT22 .... 95 B7
Kingscroft Rd. Woodm SM7 .... 78 E4
Kingsdale Rd. Penge SE20 .... 23 E1
Kingsdale Sch. Dulw SE21 .... 22 E5
Kingsdene. Tadw KT20 .... 97 B5
Kingsdown. 1 Wimble SW19 .... 19 D1
Kingsdown Ave.
  S Croy CR2 & CR8 .... 61 C2
Kingsdown Rd. Cheam SM3 .... 58 E5
Kingsdown Rd. Ewell KT17 .... 77 A6
Kingsdowne Rd. Surb KT6 .... 37 F2
Kingsfield. Farl Gn GU5 .... 153 E7
Kingsfold Ct. Warn RH12 .... 198 B5
Kingsford Ave. Wallin SM6 .... 60 E3
Kingsgate Bsns Ctr.
  King U T KT2 .... 37 E8
Kingsgate Rd. King U T KT2 .... 37 E8
Kingshill Ave. New Mal KT4 .... 39 B2
Kingslake Ct. 2 Knaph GU21 .... 68 E1
Kingsland. Newd RH5 .... 158 A1
Kingslea. Horsh RH13 .... 217 E3
Kingslea. Leahd KT22 .... 95 A7
Kingslee Ct. 12 Sutton SM2 .... 59 B3
Kingsleigh Pl. Mitch CR4 .... 40 F6
Kingsleigh Wlk. Hayes BR2 .... 44 F5
Kingsley Ave. Banstd SM7 .... 78 A4
Kingsley Ave. Camb GU15 .... 65 D3
Kingsley Ave. Carsh SM1 .... 59 D6
Kingsley Ave. Eng Gn TW20 .... 11 B2
Kingsley Ave. Hounsl TW3 .... 5 C5
Kingsley Cl. Crowth RG11 .... 45 B3
Kingsley Cl. Hersh KT12 .... 160 F5
Kingsley Cl. Walt O T KT12 .... 54 A7
Kingsley Ct. Worc Pk KT4 .... 57 F8
Kingsley Dr. Worc Pk KT4 .... 57 F8
Kingsley Gr. Dovgn RH2 .... 139 B5
Kingsley House. 8 King U T KT6 39 E4
Kingsley Inf Sch. Thorn H CR9 .... 42 A1
Kingsley Jun Sch. Thorn H CR9 ... 42 A1
Kingsley Rd. Crawl RH11 .... 201 A3
Kingsley Rd. Horley RH6 .... 160 F5
Kingsley Rd. Hounsl TW3 .... 5 C5
Kingsley Rd. Thorn H CR0 .... 42 A1
Kingsley Rd. W Heath GU14 .... 84 F6
Kingsley Rd. Wimble SW19 .... 20 B3
Kingslyn Cres. S Norw SE19 .... 42 E8
Kingsmead. Bigg H TN16 .... 83 D3
Kingsmead. Cran GU6 .... 174 E3
Kingsmead. Farnb GU14 .... 85 B4
Kingsmead. Friml GU16 .... 85 E7
Kingsmead. Rich TW10 .... 6 F1
Kingsmead. Whit V KT12 .... 53 D4
Kingsmead Ave. Mitch CR4 .... 41 C6
Kingsmead Ave. N Cheam KT4 ..... 58 B7
Kingsmead Ave. Tolw KT6 .... 57 A8
Kingsmead Cl. Horsh RH12 .... 218 A6
Kingsmead Cl. Tedd TW11 .... 17 B1
Kingsmead Cl. W Ewell KT19 .... 57 D3
Kingsmead Cl. W Ewell KT19 .... 57 D3
Kingsmead Pl. Broad H RH12 .... 216 D3
Kingsmead Rd. Broad H RH12 ... 216 D3
Kingsmead Rd. Streat SW2 .... 22 A6
Kingsmead Sh Ctr. Farnb GU14 .. 85 B3
Kingsmere. Catf SE6 .... 24 B7
Kingsmere Rd. Brack RG12 .... 26 F3
Kingsmere Rd. Putney SW19 .... 19 D6
Kingsnympton Pk. King U T KT2 .. 18 B2
Kingsthorpe Rd. For Hil SE26 ...... 23 D4
Kingston Ave. Cheam SM3 .... 58 E7
Kingston Ave. E Hors KT24 .... 92 E1
Kingston Ave. Felt TW14 .... 3 F1

Kingston Ave. Leahd KT22 .... 95 B6
Kingston Bsns Ctr. Chess KT9 ..... 56 F7
Kingston By - Pass. Tolw KT6 .... 57 B8
Kingston By-Pass.
  Surb KT6 & KT7 & KT9 .... 56 C7
Kingston Cl. Tedd TW11 .... 17 B2
Kingston Coll of F Ed.
  King U T KT1 .... 37 D6
Kingston Coll of F Ed (M V Annex).
  King U T KT1 .... 37 E8
Kingston Cres. Beck BR3 .... 43 F8
Kingston Cres. Stain TW15 .... 13 C2
Kingston Gdns. Wallin CR0 .... 60 E7
Kingston Gram Sch.
  King U T KT2 .... 37 F7
Kingston Hall Rd. King U T KT1 .. 37 D6
Kingston Hill. King U T KT2 .... 18 C2
Kingston Hill Pl.
  King U T KT2 & TW10 .... 18 C4
Kingston Hospl. King U T KT2 ..... 38 B8
Kingston House Gdns.
  Leahd KT22 .... 95 B6
Kingston La. Tedd TW11 .... 17 C3
Kingston La. W Hors KT24 .... 112 A8
Kingston Lodge. 1
  New Mal KT3 .... 38 E5
Kingston Poly (Gipsy Hill Ctr).
  King U T KT2 .... 18 D3
Kingston Rd. Ashf TW15 & TW17 13 F2
Kingston Rd. Ashtd KT22 & KT9 ... 75 A3
Kingston Rd. Camb GU15 .... 47 A1
Kingston Rd. Ewell KT17 .... 57 D6
Kingston Rd. King U T KT1 & KT3 . 38 C5
Kingston Rd. Leahd KT22 .... 75 A1
Kingston Rd.
  Merton SW19 & SW20 .... 39 E7
Kingston Rd. New Mal KT3 .... 38 C5
Kingston Rd.
  Putney SW15 & SW19 .... 19 B7
Kingston Rd.
  Rhampt SW15 & SW19 .... 19 B7
Kingston Rd. Stain TW15 & TW18 13 B2
Kingston Rd. Tedd TW11 .... 17 B2
Kingston Rd.
  Tolw KT4 & KT5 & KT6 .... 57 C6
Kingston Rd. Worc Pk KT17 .... 57 D6
Kingston Rise. Woodhm KT15 ...... 52 A1
Kingston Sq. N Norw SE19 .... 22 D3
Kingston Sta. King U T KT2 .... 37 E8
Kingston Univ. King U T KT2 .... 18 D3
Kingston Univ. King U T KT1 .... 37 E6
Kingston Univ Annex.
  King U T KT1 .... 37 F7
Kingston Univ Roehampton
Vale Ctr. Rhampt SW15 .... 18 F5
Kingston Vale.
  King U T KT2 & SW15 .... 18 E4
Kingston Vale. King U T SW15 ..... 18 E4
Kingstons Ind Est. Alder GU12 .. 105 E2
Kingsway. Alder GU11 .... 104 E1
Kingsway. Blckw GU17 .... 64 E5
Kingsway. Coney H BR4 .... 63 F7
Kingsway. Mortl SW14 & TW9 .... 7 B4
Kingsway. Stan TW19 .... 13 E2
Kingsway. W Barn KT3 .... 39 C4
Kingsway. Woking GU21 .... 69 D1
Kingsway Ave. Selsd CR2 .... 62 D2
Kingsway Ave. Woking GU21 .... 69 D2
Kingsway Bsns Pk The.
  Hampt TW12 .... 35 F8
Kingsway Rd. Cheam SM3 .... 58 E3
Kingsway Terr. Whit V KT13 .... 53 A2
Kingsway The. Ewell KT17 .... 57 F1
Kingswear House. For Hil SE23 ... 23 C6
Kingswick Cl. Ascot SL5 .... 29 D5
Kingswick Dr. Ascot SL5 .... 29 D5
Kingswood Ave. Beck BR2 & BR3 44 E5
Kingswood Ave. Hampt TW12 ...... 16 B2
Kingswood Ave. Hams Gn CR2 .... 81 C4
Kingswood Ave.
  Hounsl TW3 & TW5 .... 4 F5
Kingswood Ave. Thorn H CR7 ...... 42 A4
Kingswood Cl. Eng Gn TW20 .... 11 D4
Kingswood Cl. Merrow GU1 .... 110 D2
Kingswood Cl. New Mal KT3 .... 38 F3
Kingswood Cl. Surb KT6 .... 37 E2
Kingswood Cl. Whit V KT13 .... 53 B3
Kingswood Ct. Horse GU21 .... 69 E3
Kingswood Ct. 6 Rich TW10 .... 6 F2
Kingswood Cty Fst Sch.
  L Kings KT20 .... 117 F7
Kingswood Dr. Belm SM2 .... 59 B2
Kingswood Dr. Carsh SM5 .... 40 F1
Kingswood Dr. Dulw SE19 & SE21 22 F4
Kingswood Firs. Graysh GU26 .... 188 C2
Kingswood Golf Course.
  Kings KT20 .... 98 A3
Kingswood Hall of Residence.
  Eng Gn TW20 .... 11 D4
Kingswood House. 3
  King U T KT2 .... 18 B2
Kingswood House Sch.
  Epsom KT18 .... 76 C6
Kingswood La. Warlgm CR6 .... 81 C4
Kingswood Prim Sch.
  W Norw SE27 .... 22 D3
Kingswood Rd. Beck BR2 .... 44 E6
Kingswood Rd. Merton SW19 .... 39 F8
Kingswood Rd. Penge SE20 .... 23 C2
Kingswood Rd. Streat SW2 .... 21 E8
Kingswood Rd. Tadw KT20 .... 97 C4
Kingswood Rise. Eng Gn TW20 .... 11 D4
Kingswood Sta. Kings KT20 .... 97 F6
Kingswood Way. Hams Gn CR2 .... 81 C6
Kingswood Way. Selsd CR2 .... 81 D7
Kingswood Way. Wallin SM6 .... 60 E5
Kingsworth Cl. Beck BR3 .... 43 E4
Kingsworthy Cl. King U T KT1 ...... 37 F6
Kinloss Rd. Carsh SM5 .... 40 C2
Kinnaird Ave. Broml BR1 .... 24 F2
Kinnaird Ave. Chisw W4 .... 7 C7

Kinnaird Cl. Broml BR1 .... 24 F2
Kinnear Ct. Wimble SW20 .... 39 D8
Kinnersley Wlk. Dovgn RH2 .... 139 B4
Kinnibrugh Dr. Dorman RH7 ...... 165 A1
Kinross Ave. Ascot SL5 .... 28 F4
Kinross Ave. Worc Pk KT4 .... 58 A8
Kinross Cl. Ashf TW16 .... 14 F3
Kinross Ct. Ascot SL5 .... 28 F4
Kinross Dr. Ashf TW16 .... 14 F3
Kinsey House. Dulw SE21 .... 22 E4
Kintyre Cl. Thorn H SW16 .... 41 F6
Kintyre Ct. 17 Streat SW2 .... 21 E8
Kinver Rd. For Hil SE26 .... 23 C4
Kipings. Tadw KT20 .... 97 D5
Kipling Cl. Crawl RH10 .... 202 C8
Kipling Ct. Horsh RH13 .... 218 A4
Kipling Dr. Mitch SW17 .... 20 D2
Kipling Way. E Grins RH19 .... 185 C1
Kirby Cl. Worc Pk KT19 .... 57 F5
Kirby Rd. Horse GU21 .... 69 D3
Kirby Way. Walt O T KT12 .... 35 C3
Kirdford Cl. Crawl RH11 .... 201 A8
Kirk Rise. Sutton SM1 .... 59 B7
Kirkby Ct. Friml GU16 .... 65 E1
Kirkdale. For Hil SE26 .... 23 B5
Kirkfield. Stough GU2 .... 109 A4
Kirkgate The. 2 Epsom KT17 .... 76 E6
Kirkham Cl. Sandh GU15 .... 45 D2
Kirkland Ave. Woking GU21 .... 68 F3
Kirkleas Rd. Surb KT6 .... 37 E1
Kirklees Rd. Thorn H CR7 .... 42 A4
Kirkley Rd. Merton SW19 .... 40 A8
Kirkly Cl. S Croy CR2 .... 61 E2
Kirkstall Gdns. Streat SW2 .... 21 E7
Kirkstall Rd. Streat SW2 .... 21 E7
Kirksted Rd. Cheam SM4 .... 40 B1
Kirkstone Cl. Friml GU15 .... 66 D4
Kirkstone Way. Catf BR1 .... 24 E1
Kirrane Cl. New Mal KT3 .... 39 A3
Kirriemuir Gdns. Normdy GU12 106 D3
Kirtley Rd. For Hil SE26 .... 23 E4
Kitchener Rd. S Norw CR7 .... 42 D6
Kitchener's Rd. Farnb GU11 ...... 105 D6
Kitchenride Cnr. Longc KT16 ...... 51 A6
Kites Cl. Crawl RH11 .... 201 C6
Kithurst Cl. Crawl RH11 .... 201 D4
Kitley Gdns. S Norw SE19 .... 42 F8
Kitsmead. Copth RH10 .... 183 A2
Kitsmead La. Longc KT16 .... 50 D8
Kittiwake Cl. Crawl RH11 .... 200 D4
Kittiwake Cl. Selsd CR0 & CR2 .... 62 E1
Klondyke Villas. Grays GU27 ...... 190 A1
Knaggs House. 1 Tedd TW11 .... 16 E3
Knapdale Cl. For Hil SE23 .... 23 B6
Knaphill Cty Jun Sch.
  Knaph GU21 .... 68 C1
Knaphill Lower Sch The.
  Knaph GU21 .... 68 B1
Knapmill Rd. Catf SE6 .... 24 B6
Knapmill Way. Catf SE6 .... 24 B6
Knapp Rd. Ashf TW15 .... 13 F4
Knapton Mews. Mitch SW17 .... 21 A2
Knaresborough Dr.
  Wands SW18 .... 20 B7
Kneller Gdns. Islew TW7 .... 5 D1
Kneller Rd. New Mal KT3 .... 38 E2
Kneller Rd. Twick TW2 .... 5 D1
Knepp Cl. Crawl RH10 .... 202 C6
Knight's Hill.
  W Norw SE19 & SE27 .... 22 B4
Knight's Hill Sq. W Norw SE27 .... 22 B4
Knight's Pk. King U T KT1 .... 37 E6
Knighton Cl. Crawl RH10 .... 182 D2
Knighton Cl. Croy CR2 .... 61 B2
Knighton Park Rd. For Hil SE26 .. 23 D3
Knighton Rd. Earls RH1 .... 140 A7
Knightons La. Dunsf GU8 .... 193 A2
Knights Cl. Egham TW20 .... 12 D2
Knights Ct. King U T KT1 .... 37 E6
Knights Ct. Penge BR3 .... 43 E8
Knights Rd. Heath E GU9 .... 125 E7
Knights Way. Friml GU15 .... 66 C4
Knightsbridge Cres. Stain TW18 13 B2
Knightsbridge Rd. Camb GU15 ... 65 E7
Knightswood. Easth RG12 .... 27 B1
Knightswood. Woking GU21 .... 69 C1
Knightwood Cl. Woodh RH2 .... 139 A7
Knightwood Cres. New Mal KT3 38 E3
Knipp Hill. Cobham KT11 .... 73 F6
Knob Hill. Warn RH12 .... 198 A1
Knobfield. Peasl GU5 .... 133 F1
Knobfield. Peasl GU5 .... 154 F8
Knole Cl. Crawl RH10 .... 202 D7
Knole Cl. Croy CR0 .... 43 C3
Knole Gr. E Grins RH19 .... 185 C3
Knole Wood. Sunnin SL5 .... 29 C1
Knoll Ct. Dulw SE19 .... 22 F3
Knoll Park Rd. Chert KT16 .... 32 F1
Knoll Quarry. Farnc GU7 .... 150 E6
Knoll Rd. Camb GU15 .... 65 D6
Knoll Rd. Dork RH4 .... 136 A5
Knoll Rd. Farnc GU7 .... 150 E6
Knoll The. Beck BR3 .... 44 B8
Knoll The. Cobham KT11 .... 74 A6
Knoll The. Leahd KT22 .... 95 A6
Knoll Wood. Farnc GU7 .... 150 D6
Knollmead. Tolw KT4 & KT5 .... 38 C1
Knollmead Prim Sch. Tolw KT4 ... 58 C1
Knolls Cl. N Cheam KT4 .... 58 B7
Knolls The. Nork KT17 .... 77 C3
Knolly's Cl. W Norw SE27 & SW16 22 A5
Knolly's Rd.
  W Norw SE27 & SW16 .... 22 A5
Knollys' Rd. Alder GU11 .... 104 F3
Knott Park House. Oxsh KT22 ...... 74 C4
Knowl Hill. Mayb GU22 .... 70 B1
Knowl Hill Sch The. Pirb GU24 ... 87 E5
Knowle Cl. Copth RH10 .... 183 C3

Knowle Dr. Copth RH10 .... 183 B3
Knowle Gdns. W Byfl KT14 .... 70 F6
Knowle Gn. Went GU25 .... 31 C2
Knowle Grove Cl. Went GU25 .... 31 C2
Knowle Hill. Went GU25 .... 31 C2
Knowle La. Cran GU6 & RH12 .... 194 D4
Knowle Lodge. Cater CR3 .... 101 A4
Knowle Park Ave. Stain TW18 ... 13 B3
Knowle Pk. Cobham KT11 .... 73 E4
Knowle Rd. Twick TW2 .... 16 F7
Knowlton Gn. Hayes BR2 .... 44 F4
Knox Rd. Stough GU2 .... 109 B6
Kohat Ct. Alder GU11 .... 104 F2
Kohat Rd. Wimble SW19 .... 20 B3
Kohima Cl. Alder GU11 .... 105 B3
Koonowla Cl. Bigg H TN16 .... 83 D4
Kooringa. Warlgm CR6 .... 101 B8
Korda Cl. Littlt TW17 .... 33 F6
Kreisel Wlk. Rich TW9 .... 6 F8
Kristina Ct. Belm SM2 .... 59 A4
Krooner Rd. Camb GU15 .... 65 B3
Kuala Gdns. S Norw SW16 .... 41 F8
Kyle Cl. Easth RG12 .... 27 B6
Kynaston Cres.
   Thorn H CR0 & CR7 .... 42 C4
Kynaston Ct. Cater CR3 .... 100 E2
Kynaston House. 7 Streat SW2 .. 21 F7
Kynaston Rd. Thorn H CR0 & CR7 42 C4
Kynersley Ct. Carsh SM5 .... 59 F7

La Retraite RC Girls Sch.
   Streat SW12 .... 21 C8
Laburnam Ct. 12 W Norw SW16 . 22 A3
Laburnam Ct. Chert KT16 .... 33 A1
Laburnam Ave. Carsh SM1 .... 59 E7
Laburnam Cl. Alder GU11 .... 105 A1
Laburnam Cl. Bellf GU1 .... 109 C4
Laburnum Cres. Sunby TW16 .... 35 B8
Laburnum Ct. Mitch CR4 .... 41 A7
Laburnum Gdns. Croy CR0 .... 43 D1
Laburnum Gr. Bra Hil SL3 .... 1 B8
Laburnum Gr. Hounsl TW3 .... 4 F3
Laburnum Gr. King U T KT3 ...... 38 D7
Laburnum Pas. Alder GU11 ...... 105 A1
Laburnum Rd. Alder GU11 .... 105 A2
Laburnum Rd. Epsom KT18 ...... 76 E6
Laburnum Rd. Heath E GU9 ...... 125 E2
Laburnum Rd. Merton SW19 ..... 20 C1
Laburnum Rd. Mitch CR4 .... 41 A7
Laburnum Rd. Woking GU22 ..... 89 D7
Laburnum Way. Stan TW19 .... 13 F7
Laburnums The. Blckw GU17 .... 64 B5
Lacey Ave. Couslsd CR5 .... 100 A4
Lacey Cl. Egham TW20 .... 12 D1
Lacey Dr. Couslsd CR5 .... 100 B7
Lacey Dr. Hampt TW12 .... 35 F8
Lackford Rd. Chips CR5 .... 78 F1
Lacock Cl. Wimble SW19 .... 20 C2
Lacy Gn. Couslsd CR5 .... 100 A7
Ladas Rd. W Norw SE27 .... 22 C3
Ladbroke Cotts. 2 Redh RH1 .... 119 A2
Ladbroke Ct. 7 Redh RH1 .... 119 A2
Ladbroke Gr. Redh RH1 .... 119 A2
Ladbroke Hurst. Dorman RH7 ... 165 A1
Ladbroke Rd. Epsom KT18 .... 76 D5
Ladbroke Rd. Horley RH6 .... 161 B5
Ladbroke Rd. Redh RH1 .... 119 A3
Ladbrook Rd. S Norw SE25 ...... 42 D5
Ladderstile Ride. King U T KT2 .. 18 C3
Ladderstile Ride.
   Rich KT2 & TW10 .... 18 B3
Ladlands. Dulw SE22 .... 23 A8
Lady Booth Rd. 7 King U T KT1 . 37 E7
Lady Eleanor Holles Sch The
   (Jun Girls). Hampt TW12 ..... 16 B3
Lady Eleanor Holles Sch The
   (Senior Girls). Hampt TW12 .. 16 B3
Lady Hay. New Mal KT4 .... 57 F8
Lady Margaret Rd. Crawl RH11 . 201 A7
Lady Margaret Rd. Sunnin SL5 .. 29 F2
Lady Margaret Wlk.
   Crawl RH11 .... 201 A7
Ladybank. Easth RG12 .... 27 B1
Ladycross. Milf GU8 .... 170 E8
Ladycross Mews. Milf GU8 ...... 170 E8
Ladygate Rd. Dork RH5 .... 136 D8
Ladygate Rd. Dork RH5 .... 136 D8
Ladygate Dr. Graysh GU26 .... 188 A3
Ladygrove. Selsd CR2 .... 62 D2
Ladygrove Dr. Burph GU4 .... 110 B6
Ladymead. Guild GU1 .... 109 C2
Ladymead Retail Ctr.
   Guild GU1 .... 109 E2
Ladythorpe Cl. Addl KT15 .... 52 B6
Ladywood Ave. W Heath GU14 .. 84 C4
Ladywood Rd. Tolw KT6 .... 57 A8
Laffan Track. Farnb GU11 .... 104 D6
Laffan's Rd. Farnb GU11 .... 104 E6
Lafone Ave. Felt TW13 .... 15 C6
Lafone House. 11 Streat SW2 ... 21 F8
Lagham Pk. S Godst RH9 .... 142 E6
Lagham Rd. S Godst RH9 .... 142 F5
Laglands Cl. Reig RH2 .... 118 C3
Laings Ave. Mitch CR4 .... 40 F7
Laings Cnr. Mitch CR4 .... 40 F8
Lainlock Pl. Hounsl TW3 .... 5 B6
Lainson St. Wands SW18 .... 20 A8
Laird Ct. Bagsh GU19 .... 47 E1
Lairdale Cl. W Norw SE21 .... 22 C8
Laitwood Rd. Balham SW12 ..... 21 B7
Lake Cl. Byfl KT14 .... 71 D7
Lake Cl. 6 Wimble SW19 .... 19 F3
Lake Cotts. Bowl Gn GU8 .... 169 F4
Lake End Way. Crowth RG11 .... 45 A4
Lake Gdns. Hackb SM6 .... 60 B7

Lake Gdns. Rich TW10 .... 17 B6
Lake House. 4 W Norw SW27 .... 22 C8
Lake La. Docken GU10 .... 166 E6
Lake Rd. Croy CR0 .... 62 F8
Lake Rd. Friml GU16 .... 86 B6
Lake Rd. Ockley RH5 .... 177 D6
Lake Rd. Vir W GU25 .... 31 B5
Lake Rd. Wimble SW19 .... 19 F3
Lake Side The. Blckw GU17 ...... 64 D4
Lake View. Dork RH5 .... 136 C4
Lake View Rd. Copth RH10 ...... 184 C4
Lake View Rd. Dome RH10 ...... 184 C4
Lake View Rd. Dorm Pk RH19 .. 185 F5
Lake View Rd. Dorman RH19 ... 185 F5
Lakehall Gdns. Thorn H CR7 .... 42 B4
Lakehall Rd. Thorn H CR7 .... 42 B4
Lakehurst Rd. W Ewell KT19 .... 57 E5
Lakehurst Rd. W Ewell KT19 .... 57 E5
Lakeland Dr. Friml GU16 .... 65 E1
Lakeman Ct. S Norw CR7 .... 42 C7
Lakers Lea. Loxwd RH14 .... 212 F1
Lakers Rise. Woodm SM7 .... 78 E3
Lakes Cl. Chil GU4 .... 131 B3
Lakeside. Beck BR3 .... 44 B6
Lakeside. 3 Brack RG12 .... 27 C8
Lakeside. Hackb SM6 .... 60 B6
Lakeside. Horsh RH12 .... 217 C5
Lakeside. 10 King U T KT2 .... 18 B1
Lakeside. Knaph GU21 .... 88 E8
Lakeside. Oat Pk KT13 .... 53 E8
Lakeside. Redh RH1 .... 119 A3
Lakeside. W Ewell KT19 .... 57 E4
Lakeside. W Norw SE27 .... 22 B3
Lakeside Cl. Ash V GU12 .... 105 F4
Lakeside Cl. Knaph GU21 .... 88 E8
Lakeside Cl. S Norw SE25 .... 43 A7
Lakeside Cty Prim Sch.
   Friml GU16 .... 65 F1
Lakeside Dr. Esher KT10 .... 55 C4
Lakeside Est. Harm SL3 .... 2 A8
Lakeside Gdns. W Heath GU14 . 84 D7
Lakeside Grange. Weyb KT13 ... 53 C7
Lakeside Mid Sch. Friml GU16 .. 65 F1
Lakeside Rd.
   Ash V GU11 & GU12 .... 105 F4
Lakeside Rd. Coln SL3 .... 1 F7
Lakeside Rd. Farnb GU11 .... 105 A7
Lakeview Rd. W Norw SE27 ..... 22 B3
Laleham C of E Prim Sch.
   Laleh TW18 .... 33 C7
Laleham Ct. Horse GU21 .... 69 E3
Laleham Lea Prep Sch.
   Purley CR8 .... 60 E1
Laleham Rd. Catf SE6 .... 24 C8
Laleham Rd. Lewish SE6 .... 24 C8
Laleham Rd. Shep SW17 .... 34 B3
Laleham Rd. Shep Gn TW17 .... 34 A4
Laleham Rd. Stain TW18 .... 12 F2
Lamb's Bsns Pk. S Godst RH9 .. 142 C5
Lamberhurst Wlk. Crawl RH10 . 202 A5
Lambert Ave. Mortl TW9 .... 7 B4
Lambert Cl. Bigg H TN16 .... 83 D3
Lambert Cotts. Bletch RH1 ...... 120 E2
Lambert Cres. Blckw GU17 ...... 64 C4
Lambert Rd. Banstd SM7 .... 78 B5
Lambert's Pl. Croy CR0 .... 42 D1
Lambert's Rd. King U T KT6 ..... 37 F4
Lambeth Cl. Crawl RH11 .... 201 B2
Lambeth Inst Strand Ctr.
   Streat SW2 .... 21 F8
Lambeth Prospect.
   W Norw SE19 .... 22 D2
Lambeth Rd. Thorn H CR0 .... 42 B1
Lambly Hill. Thorpe GU25 .... 31 E6
Lamborne Cl. Sandh GU17 ...... 45 A1
Lambourn Cl. E Grins RH19 ..... 185 E3
Lambourne Ave. Wimble SW19 . 19 F4
Lambourne Cl. Crawl RH10 ...... 201 F4
Lambourne Cres. Sheer GU21 .. 70 D6
Lambourne Dr. Bagsh GU19 .... 47 D2
Lambourne Dr. Cobham KT11 .. 73 D4
Lambourne Gr. Brack RG12 ..... 27 E7
Lambourne Gr. King U T KT1 ... 38 B7
Lambourne Way. Tongh GU10 .. 126 F7
Lambs Cres. Horsh RH12 .... 217 F5
Lambs Farm Cl. Horsh RH12 ... 218 A5
Lambs Farm Rd. Horsh RH12 ... 218 A6
Lambs Green Rd.
   Lamb Gn RH12 .... 199 F6
Lambton Rd. Wimble SW20 ..... 39 C8
Lambyn Croft. Horley RH6 .... 161 C4
Lamerock Rd. Catf BR1 .... 24 F4
Lammas Ave. Mitch CR4 .... 41 A7
Lammas Cl. Godal GU7 .... 151 A6
Lammas Ct. Farnc GU7 .... 150 E5
Lammas Ct. Stan TW19 .... 12 D5
Lammas Dr. Wray TW18 .... 11 D7
Lammas Gate. Farnc GU7 .... 150 F6
Lammas Hill. Esher KT10 .... 55 A5
Lammas La. Esher KT10 .... 55 A6
Lammas Rd. Godal GU7 .... 151 A5
Lammas Rd. Rich TW10 .... 17 C4
Lammermoor Rd. Balham SW12 21 B8
Lampard La. Churt GU10 .... 167 E2
Lampeter Cl. 4 Woking GU22 .. 69 E1
Lampton Ave. Hounsl TW5 ...... 5 B6
Lampton Cl. Hounsl TW5 .... 5 B6
Lampton House Cl. Wimble SW19 19 F4
Lampton Park Rd. Hounsl TW3 . 5 B5
Lampton Rd. Hounsl TW3 & TW5 5 B5
Lampton Sch. Hounsl TW5 ...... 5 A6
Lanain Ct. Lewish SE12 .... 24 F8
Lanark Cl. Friml GU16 .... 65 E2
Lanark Cl. Horsh RH13 .... 217 E2
Lancaster Ave. Mitch CR4 .... 41 E4
Lancaster Ave.
   W Norw SE21 & SE27 .... 22 C6

Lancaster Ave. Wimble SW19 ... 19 D3
Lancaster Cl. Beck BR2 .... 44 A8
Lancaster Cl. Crawl RH10 .... 182 D1
Lancaster Cl. Eng Gn TW20 ..... 11 D3
Lancaster Cl. King U T KT2 ...... 17 D3
Lancaster Cl. Stan TW19 .... 2 E1
Lancaster Cl. Woking GU21 ..... 70 A3
Lancaster Cotts. 1 Rich TW10 .. 6 E1
Lancaster Ct. 1 Belm SM2 ...... 59 A3
Lancaster Ct. 1 Nork SM7 .... 77 F5
Lancaster Ct. Stan TW19 .... 13 E7
Lancaster Ct. Walt O T KT12 ... 35 B2
Lancaster Dr. E Grins RH19 ..... 186 A3
Lancaster Gdns. King U T KT2 .. 17 D3
Lancaster Gdns. Wimble SW19 . 19 E3
Lancaster House. Easth RG12 .. 27 B4
Lancaster House. Wands SW18 . 20 B8
Lancaster Mews. 2 Rich TW10 . 6 E1
Lancaster Pk. Rich TW10 .... 6 E2
Lancaster Pl. Hounsl TW5 .... 4 D5
Lancaster Pl. Twick TW1 .... 17 A8
Lancaster Pl. Wimble SW19 ..... 19 D3
Lancaster Rd. Farnb GU14 ...... 85 B1
Lancaster Rd. S Norw SE25 ..... 43 A6
Lancaster Rd. Wimble SW19 ... 19 E3
Lancaster Way. Farnb GU14 .... 85 C7
Lancelot Cl. Crawl RH11 .... 200 E6
Lancer Ct. Alder GU11 .... 104 E2
Lanchester Dr. Crowth RG11 ... 45 C7
Lancing Cl. Crawl RH11 .... 201 A8
Lancing Ct. Horsh RH12 .... 218 A4
Lancing Rd. Felt TW13 .... 14 F6
Lancing Rd. Thorn H CR0 .... 41 F2
Landen Cl. Woki RG11 .... 25 B4
Landen Pk. Horley RH6 .... 160 E5
Landgrove Rd. Wimble SW19 ... 20 A3
Landon Way. Ashf TW15 .... 14 B2
Landscape Rd. Warlgm CR6 .... 101 B8
Landsdowne Cl. Tolw KT5 .... 57 B8
Landseer Cl. Mitch SW19 .... 40 D8
Landseer Cl. Sandh GU15 .... 64 E6
Landseer Rd. Cheam SM1 & SM2 59 A4
Landseer Rd. New Mal KT3 ..... 38 D2
Lane Cl. Addl KT15 .... 52 B5
Lane Ct. Balham SW11 .... 20 F8
Lane End. Epsom KT18 .... 76 B5
Lane End. Hambl GU8 .... 191 B8
Lane End Dr. Knaph GU21 .... 68 C2
Lane House. Horsh RH12 .... 217 D2
Lane The. Ifold RH14 .... 212 C4
Lane The. Thorpe GU25 .... 31 E6
Lane The. Thorpe TK16 .... 33 A6
Lane The. Thursl GU8 .... 169 C4
Lanercost Rd. Crawl RH11 ...... 201 C5
Lanercost Rd. Streat SW2 .... 22 A6
Lanesborough Prep Sch.
   Guild GU1 .... 109 F1
Lang Cl. Fetch KT23 .... 94 B4
Langaller La. Fetch KT22 .... 94 B6
Langbourne Prim Sch.
   Dulw SE21 .... 22 E5
Langbourne Way. Clayg KT10 .. 56 A4
Langcroft Cl. Carsh SM5 .... 59 F7
Langdale Ave. Mitch CR4 .... 40 F6
Langdale Cl. Farnb GU14 .... 84 E4
Langdale Cl. Horse GU21 .... 69 C3
Langdale Cl. Mortl SW14 .... 7 B3
Langdale Dr. N Asct SL5 .... 28 E7
Langdale Rd. Crawl RH11 .... 200 D4
Langdale Rd. Thorn H CR7 ...... 42 A5
Langdon Cl. Friml GU15 .... 66 C3
Langdon Pl. Mortl SW14 .... 7 C4
Langdon Rd. Morden SM4 ...... 40 C4
Langdon Wlk. Morden SM4 ..... 40 C4
Langham Cl. Godal GU7 .... 150 F4
Langham Cl. M Bourn GU9 ...... 146 C7
Langham Ct. 12 Twick TW1 ..... 6 C1
Langham Ct. Wimble SW20 ..... 39 C7
Langham Dene. Purley CR8 ..... 80 B4
Langham Gdns. Rich TW10 ..... 17 C4
Langham House Cl. Rich TW10 . 17 D4
Langham Pk. Godal GU7 .... 150 F4
Langham Pl. Chisw W4 .... 7 E8
Langham Pl. Egham TW20 ...... 11 F3
Langham Rd. Tedd TW11 .... 17 B2
Langham Rd. Wimble SW20 ..... 39 C8
Langholm Cl. Streat SW12 ...... 21 D8
Langhurst Cl. Fayg RH12 .... 198 E4
Langhurst La. Rusper RH12 ..... 200 A8
Langhurstwood Rd.
   Fayg RH12 .... 198 D3
Langland Gdns. Croy CR0 .... 62 F8
Langlands Rise. Epsom KT19 ... 76 C6
Langley Ave.
   N Cheam KT4 & SM3 .... 58 D8
Langley Ave. Surb KT6 .... 37 E1
Langley Cl. Guild GU1 .... 109 D2
Langley Cl. Lang V KT18 .... 96 D8
Langley Cres. Harl UB3 .... 3 F7
Langley Ct. Reig RH2 .... 118 B2
Langley Dr. Camb GU15 .... 65 D6
Langley Dr. Crawl RH11 .... 201 D8
Langley Gr. King U T KT3 .... 38 E7
Langley Green Cty Fst Sch.
   Crawl RH11 .... 181 D1
Langley Green Cty Mid Sch.
   Crawl RH11 .... 201 C8
Langley La. Crawl RH11 .... 201 A8
Langley Oaks Ave. S Croy CR2 . 62 A1
Langley Par. Crawl RH11 .... 181 C1
Langley Park Golf Course.
   W Wick BR3 .... 44 C2
Langley Park Rd.
   Sutton SM1 & SM2 .... 59 C3
Langley Park Sch for Boys.
   Beck BR3 .... 44 B3
Langley Park Sch for Girls.
   Beck BR3 .... 44 C3
Langley Pl. Crawl RH11 .... 181 C1
Langley Rd. Beck BR3 .... 43 E5

Langley Rd. Islew TW7 .... 5 F5
Langley Rd. Merton SW19 .... 40 A8
Langley Rd. Selsd CR2 .... 62 D2
Langley Rd. Stain TW18 .... 12 E2
Langley Rd. Surb KT6 .... 37 E2
Langley Vale Rd.
   Lang V KT18 & KT21 .... 76 E1
Langley Way. W Wick BR4 .... 44 E2
Langley Wlk. Crawl RH11 .... 181 B1
Langley Wlk. Woking GU22 ..... 89 E8
Langmans Way. Woking GU21 .. 68 E3
Langmead St. W Norw SE27 .... 22 C4
Langport Ct. Walt O T KT12 .... 35 C1
Langridge Dr. E Grins RH19 .... 205 E8
Langridge House. Horsh RH12 . 217 B2
Langridge Mews. Hampt TW12 . 15 F2
Langroyd Rd. Up Toot SW17 .... 20 F6
Langshott. Horley RH6 .... 161 D4
Langshott La. Horley RH6 .... 161 C4
Langshott Cl. Woodhm KT15 ... 70 F8
Langshott Sch. Horley RH6 ..... 161 C3
Langsmead. Blind H RH7 .... 163 E8
Langstone Cl. Worth RH10 ...... 202 C3
Langthorne Ct. Catf SE6 .... 24 C4
Langton Cl. Addl KT15 .... 52 B7
Langton Cl. Woking GU21 .... 68 F2
Langton Dr. Head Dn GU35 ..... 187 A7
Langton House. 5 Streat SW16 . 21 C4
Langton Rd. E Mole KT8 .... 36 C5
Langton Rise.
   For Hil SE22 & SE23 .... 23 B8
Langton Way. Egham TW20 .... 12 C2
Langton Way. S Croy CR0 .... 61 E6
Langwood Chase. Tedd TW11 .. 17 C2
Lanherne House. 5
   Wimble SW19 .... 19 D1
Lanigan Dr. Islew TW3 .... 5 B2
Lankton Cl. Beck BR3 .... 44 C8
Lansbury Ave. Felt TW14 .... 4 B1
Lansbury Rd. Crawl RH11 .... 201 B3
Lansdell Rd. Mitch CR4 .... 41 A7
Lansdown. Guild GU1 .... 110 A1
Lansdown Cl. Horsh RH12 .... 218 B6
Lansdown Cl. Knaph GU21 ...... 88 F8
Lansdown Cl. Walt O T KT12 ... 35 C1
Lansdowne Cl. Twick TW1 .... 16 F7
Lansdowne Cl. Wimble SW20 .. 19 D1
Lansdowne Ct. Worc Pk KT4 ... 58 A8
Lansdowne Hill. W Norw SE27 . 22 B5
Lansdowne Pl. S Norw SE19 ... 22 F1
Lansdowne Rd. Alder GU11 ..... 105 A1
Lansdowne Rd. Croy CR0 .... 42 D1
Lansdowne Rd. Friml GU16 ..... 86 A8
Lansdowne Rd. Hounsl TW3 .... 5 B4
Lansdowne Rd. Purley CR8 ..... 80 A7
Lansdowne Rd. Stain TW18 .... 13 B1
Lansdowne Rd. W Ewell KT19 . 57 D3
Lansdowne Rd. W Ewell KT19 . 57 D3
Lansdowne Rd.
   Wimble SW19 & SW20 .... 19 C1
Lansdowne Wood. 11
   N Norw SE27 .... 22 B5
Lantern Ct. Wimble SW20 .... 39 D8
Lanyon Cl. Horsh RH12 .... 218 A6
Lanyon Mews. Horsh RH12 ..... 218 A6
Lapwing Cl. Horsh RH13 .... 217 F3
Lapwing Cl. Selsd CR0 & CR2 .. 62 E1
Lapwing Ct. Tolw KT6 .... 57 B8
Lapwing Gr. Merrow GU4 .... 110 D3
Lara Cl. Chess KT9 .... 56 E3
Larbert Rd. Streat SW16 .... 21 C1
Larby Pl. Ewell KT17 .... 57 E1
Larch Ave. Ascot SL5 .... 29 E4
Larch Ave. Bellf GU1 .... 109 C4
Larch Ave. Woki RG11 .... 25 B3
Larch Cl. Camb GU15 .... 65 E8
Larch Cl. Kings SE20 .... 98 C6
Larch Cl. Up Toot SW12 .... 21 B6
Larch Cl. Warlgm CR6 .... 101 E8
Larch Cl. Woodh RH2 .... 139 C7
Larch Cres. W Ewell KT19 .... 57 B4
Larch Cres. W Ewell KT19 .... 57 B4
Larch End. Horsh RH12 .... 217 B4
Larch Rd. Head Dn GU35 .... 187 B6
Larch Tree Way. Croy CR0 ...... 63 A7
Larches Ave. Mortl SW14 .... 7 D3
Larches The. Horse GU21 .... 69 E3
Larches The. Horsh RH12 .... 218 C6
Larches Way. Blckw GU17 ...... 64 B5
Larches Way. Crawl RH10 .... 204 C8
Larchvale Ct. 4 Sutton SM2 .... 59 B3
Larchwood. 5 Brack RG12 ...... 27 F5
Larchwood Cl. Nork SM7 .... 77 E4
Larchwood Dr. Eng Gn TW20 .. 11 C2
Larchwood Glade. Camb GU15 . 66 A7
Larchwood Rd. Knaph GU21 ... 88 D8
Larcombe Cl. S Croy CR0 .... 61 F6
Larges Bridge Dr. Brack RG12 . 27 D6
Larges La. Brack RG12 .... 27 D7
Largewood Ave. Tolw KT6 ...... 57 A8
Lark Ave. Stain TW18 .... 12 F5
Lark Rise. Crawl RH11 .... 201 C6
Lark Rise. E Hors KT24 .... 112 A8
Larkbere Rd. For Hil SE26 ...... 23 E4
Larkfield. Cobham KT11 .... 73 A6
Larkfield Cl. Ewh GU6 .... 175 E4
Larkfield Cl. Coney H BR2 ...... 63 F8
Larkfield Cl. Farnh GU9 .... 124 F2
Larkfield Ct. Smallf RH6 .... 162 A3
Larkfield Rd. Farnh GU9 .... 124 F2
Larkfield Rd. Rich TW9 .... 6 E3
Larkhall Cl. Hersh KT12 .... 54 C6
Larkham Cl. Felt TW13 .... 14 E5
Larkin Cl. Couslsd CR5 .... 79 F2
Larkins Rd. Crawl RH6 .... 181 D7
Larks Way. Knaph GU21 .... 68 C3
Larksfield. Eng Gn TW20 .... 11 C1

Larkspur Cl. Alder GU11 .... 126 A7
Larkspur Ct. Wallin SM6 .... 60 B3
Larkspur Way. Dork RH5 .... 136 D4
Larkspur Way. W Ewell KT19 .. 57 C5
Larkspur Way. W Ewell KT19 .. 57 C5
Larkswood Cl. Sandh GU17 .... 45 A1
Larkswood Dr. Crowth RG11 ... 45 B5
Lashmere. Copth RH10 .... 183 D3
Lashmere. Cran GU6 .... 174 B3
Laski Ct. Crawl RH11 .... 201 B1
Latham Ave. Friml GU16 .... 65 E4
Latham Cl. Bigg H TN16 .... 83 C3
Latham Cl. 5 Twick TW1 .... 17 A8
Latham Rd. Twick TW1 .... 16 F8
Latham's Way. Croy CR0 .... 60 F8
Lathwood House. 6
   Penge SE26 .... 23 B3
Latimer. Easth RG12 .... 27 B1
Latimer Cl. Crawl RH11 .... 181 C1
Latimer Cl. Mayb GU22 .... 70 B3
Latimer Cl. N Cheam KT4 .... 58 B6
Latimer House. Godal GU7 ..... 150 E3
Latimer Rd. Croy CR0 & CR9 ... 61 B7
Latimer Rd. Godal GU7 .... 150 E4
Latimer Rd. Tedd TW11 .... 16 F3
Latimer Rd. Wimble SW19 ...... 20 B2
Latimer Rd. Woki RG11 .... 25 B5
Latton Cl. Esher KT10 .... 55 B6
Latton Cl. Walt O T KT12 .... 35 E2
Latymer Cl. Weyb KT13 .... 53 C6
Laud Dr. Worth RH10 .... 202 D5
Laud St. Croy CR0 & CR9 .... 61 C7
Laud Way. Woki RG11 .... 25 E6
Lauder Cl. Friml GU16 .... 65 E2
Lauderdale Dr. Rich TW10 ...... 17 D5
Lauderdale House. Stain TW18 . 12 F3
Laughton Rd. Horsh RH12 ...... 217 F5
Launceston Ct. Thorn H CR7 ... 42 A3
Laundry La. Sandh GU15 .... 64 E5
Laundry Rd. Guild GU1 .... 130 C8
Laundry Way. Capel RH5 .... 178 C5
Lauradale. Easth RG12 .... 27 A5
Laurel Ave. Eng Gn TW20 .... 11 B3
Laurel Ave. Twick TW1 .... 16 F7
Laurel Cl. Camb GU15 .... 65 D4
Laurel Cl. Crawl RH10 .... 202 A3
Laurel Cl. Farnb GU14 .... 84 C3
Laurel Cl. Poyle SL3 .... 1 E7
Laurel Cl. Up Toot SW17 .... 20 E3
Laurel Cres. Croy CR0 .... 63 A7
Laurel Cres. Sheer GU21 .... 70 D6
Laurel Ct. S Norw SE25 .... 42 E4
Laurel Dene. E Grins RH19 ..... 185 F1
Laurel Dr. Oxted RH8 .... 122 F4
Laurel Gdns. Hounsl TW4 .... 4 E3
Laurel Gr. For Hil SE26 .... 23 E4
Laurel Gr. Penge SE20 .... 23 C1
Laurel Gr. Rowl GU10 .... 145 F5
Laurel Gr. Wreccl GU10 .... 146 A5
Laurel House. Morden SM4 ..... 40 B4
Laurel Manor. Sutton SM2 ...... 59 C3
Laurel Rd. Tedd TW12 .... 16 D3
Laurel Rd. Wimble SW20 .... 39 B8
Laurel Wlk. Horsh RH13 .... 217 F1
Laurels The. Banstd SM7 .... 77 F2
Laurels The. Cobham KT11 ..... 73 E4
Laurels The. Crawl RH10 .... 182 A1
Laurels The. Heath E GU9 ...... 125 F7
Laurels The. 6 Oat Pk KT13 ... 53 D7
Laurier Rd. Croy CR0 .... 42 F2
Lauriston Cl. Knaph GU21 .... 68 D2
Lauriston Rd. Wimble SW19 ... 19 D2
Lauser Rd. Stan TW19 .... 13 C8
Laustan Cl. Merrow GU1 .... 110 C2
Lavant Cl. Crawl RH11 .... 200 F5
Lavender Ave. Mitch CR4 .... 40 F8
Lavender Ave.
   N Cheam KT4 & SM3 .... 58 C7
Lavender Cl. Cater CR3 .... 100 C2
Lavender Cl. Couslsd CR5 .... 99 C8
Lavender Cl. Earls RH1 .... 140 B4
Lavender Cl. Wallin SM5 .... 60 B6
Lavender Ct. E Mole KT8 .... 36 B6
Lavender Gr. Mitch CR4 .... 40 E8
Lavender La. Rowl GU10 .... 145 F4
Lavender Park Rd. W Byfl KT14 71 A6
Lavender Pk. Brack SL5 .... 28 C6
Lavender Rd. Carsh SM1 .... 59 D6
Lavender Rd. Mayb GU22 .... 70 B3
Lavender Rd. Thorn H CR0 ...... 41 F3
Lavender Rd. W Ewell KT19 .... 57 B4
Lavender Rd. W Ewell KT19 .... 57 B4
Lavender Rd. Wallin SM5 .... 60 A6
Lavender Vale. Wallin SM6 ..... 60 D4
Lavender Way. Croy CR0 .... 43 D3
Lavengro Rd. W Norw SE27 .... 22 C6
Laverock Sch. Oxted RH8 .... 122 F4
Laverstoke Gdns. Rhampt SW15 19 A8
Lavington Cl. Crawl RH11 .... 201 A7
Lavington Rd. Wallin CR0 .... 60 F6
Lavinia Ct. Broml BR1 .... 24 E1
Lawbrook La. Gomsh GU5 .... 154 C7
Lawbrook La. Peasl GU5 .... 154 C7
Lawday Link. Hale GU9 .... 125 A7
Lawday Pl. Hale GU9 .... 125 A7
Lawday Place La. Hale GU9 ..... 125 A7

Lawdon Gdns. Croy CR0 .... 61 B6
Lawford Cl. Wallin SM6 .... 60 E2
Lawford Gdns. Kenley CR8 .... 80 C3
Lawford Rd. Chisw W4 .... 7 C7
Lawford's Hill Cl. Pirb GU3 .... 88 C3
Lawford's Hill Rd. Pirb GU3 ...... 88 C3
Lawman Ct. 2 Rich TW9 .... 6 F6
Lawn Cl. King U T KT3 .... 38 E7
Lawn Cres. Rich TW9 .... 7 A5
Lawn Rd. Beck BR3 .... 23 F1
Lawn Rd. Guild GU2 .... 130 C6
Lawns Rd. Cran RH12 .... 195 A3
Lawns The. Belm SM2 .... 58 E3
Lawns The. Farnb GU14 .... 84 E3
Lawns The. Milf GU8 .... 149 F1
Lawns The. N Asct SL5 .... 28 D6
Lawns The. Purley CR8 .... 61 B1
Lawns The. S Norw SE19 .... 42 D8
Lawns The. 1 Wimble SW19 .... 19 F3
Lawnsmead Cotts. Woner GU5 .. 152 B7
Lawnwood Cl. Godal GU7 .... 151 A5
Lawrence Ave. New Mal KT3 ...... 38 E2
Lawrence Cl. Burph GU4 .... 110 B6
Lawrence Cl. Woki RG11 .... 25 D6
Lawrence Cres. Windl GU20 .... 48 D4
Lawrence Est. Hounsl TW4 .... 4 C3
Lawrence Gr. Binf RG12 .... 26 D8
Lawrence La. Buckl RH3 .... 117 B3
Lawrence Lodge. Camb GU15 ...... 65 D7
Lawrence Rd. Hampt TW12 .... 15 F1
Lawrence Rd. Hounsl TW4 .... 4 C3
Lawrence Rd. Rich TW10 .... 17 C4
Lawrence Rd. S Norw SE25 .... 42 F5
Lawrence Way. Camb GU15 .... 64 F4
Lawrence Weaver Cl.
 Morden SM4 .... 40 A3
Lawrie Park Ave. For Hil SE26 .... 23 B3
Lawrie Park Cres. Penge SE26 .... 23 B3
Lawrie Park Gdns. For Hil SE26 . 23 B3
Lawrie Park Rd.
 For Hil SE19 & SE26 .... 23 C3
Lawrie Park Rd.
 Penge SE19 & SE26 .... 23 C3
Laws Cl. Crawl RH11 .... 200 E5
Laws Terr. Alder GU11 .... 105 C3
Lawson Cl. Wimble SW19 .... 19 D5
Lawson Cl. 13 Surb KT6 .... 37 D2
Lawson Way. Sunnin SL5 .... 30 B3
Lawson-Hunt Ind Pk.
 Slinfd RH12 .... 216 C4
Laxton Ct. S Norw CR7 .... 42 C5
Laxton Gdns. Merst RH1 .... 119 D7
Layard Rd. S Norw CR7 .... 42 D7
Layburn Cres. Bra Hil SL3 .... 1 B8
Layhams Rd.
 Coney H BR2 & BR4 & CR6 ...... 63 F5
Layhams Rd. W Wick BR2 .... 63 B5
Layton Cres. Croy CR0 .... 61 B5
Layton Ct. Weyb KT13 .... 53 B6
Layton Rd. Hounsl TW3 .... 5 B3
Layton's La. Sunby TW16 .... 34 F7
Le Chateau. Croy CR0 .... 61 D7
Le Marchant Rd.
 Friml GU15 & GU16 .... 65 F3
Le May Cl. Horley RH6 .... 161 A4
Le Personne Rd. Cater CR3 ...... 100 D5
Lea Cl. Ash GU12 .... 106 A1
Lea Cl. Crawl RH11 .... 200 F5
Lea Cl. Farnh GU9 .... 126 A6
Lea Croft. Crowth RG11 .... 45 B6
Lea Rd. Beck BR3 .... 44 A7
Lea Rd. Camb GU15 .... 65 B2
Lea The. Thor L TW20 .... 12 C1
Lea Way. Alder GU12 .... 105 F3
Leach Gr. Leahd KT22 .... 95 C5
Leacroft. Stain TW18 .... 13 B4
Leacroft. Sunnin SL5 .... 30 A4
Leacroft Ave. Balham SW12 .... 20 F8
Leacroft Cl. Kenley CR8 .... 80 C3
Leacroft Cl. Stain TW18 .... 13 B4
Leaf Cl. Thame D KT7 & KT8 ...... 36 E4
Leaf Gr. W Norw SE27 & SW16 ... 22 A3
Leafield Cl. S Norw SW16 .... 22 B2
Leafield Copse. Brack RG12 .... 27 F5
Leafield Rd.
 Merton SW19 & SW20 .... 39 F6
Leafield Rd. Sutton SM1 .... 59 A8
Leafy Way. S Croy CR0 .... 61 F8
Leamington Ave. Merton SM4 ..... 39 F5
Leamington Cl. Islew TW3 .... 5 C2
Leamington Cl. 4 For Hil SE26 . 23 A5
Leander Ct. 5 Surb KT6 .... 37 D2
Leander Rd. 4 Streat SW2 .... 21 F8
Leander Rd. Thorn H CR7 .... 41 F5
Leapale La. Guild GU1 .... 130 D8
Leapale Rd. Guild GU1 .... 130 D8
Leas Cl. Chess KT9 .... 56 F3
Leas La. Warlgm CR6 .... 81 D1
Leas Rd. Guild GU1 .... 130 C8
Leas Rd. Warlgm CR6 .... 81 D1
Leaside. Fetch KT23 .... 94 A4
Leather Cl. Mitch CR4 .... 41 A7
Leatherhead By-Pass Rd.
 Leahd KT22 .... 95 D5
Leatherhead General Hospl.
 Leahd KT22 .... 95 C5
Leatherhead Golf Club.
 Ashtd KT21 .... 75 A3
Leatherhead Ind Est.
 Leahd KT22 .... 95 A6
Leatherhead Rd.
 Ashtd KT21 & KT22 .... 95 E7
Leatherhead Rd. Chess KT9 .... 75 C6
Leatherhead Rd.
 Fetch KT22 & KT23 .... 94 C2
Leatherhead Rd.
 G Book KT22 & KT23 .... 94 C2
Leatherhead Rd. Oxsh KT10 .... 74 D4
Leatherhead Sta. Leahd KT22 .... 95 A6

Leaveland Cl. Beck BR3 .... 44 A5
Leaves Gn. Brack RG12 .... 27 D3
Leaves Green Cres. Bigg H BR2 . 83 C8
Leaves Green Rd. Bigg H BR2 .... 83 C8
Leavesden Rd. Weyb KT13 .... 53 B5
Leazes Ave. Cater CR3 .... 100 A4
Lebanon Ave. Felt TW13 .... 15 D3
Lebanon Ct. 11 Twick TW1 .... 17 B8
Lebanon Dr. Cobham KT11 .... 74 A6
Lebanon Gdns. Bigg H TN16 ...... 83 D2
Lebanon Pk. Twick TW1 .... 17 B8
Lebanon Rd. Croy CR0 .... 42 E1
Lechford Rd. Horley RH6 .... 161 A1
Leckford Rd. Wands SW18 .... 20 C7
Leconfield Ave.
 Mortl SW13 & SW15 .... 7 F4
Ledbury Pl. Croy CR0 .... 61 C6
Ledbury Rd. Croy CR0 & CR9 ..... 61 D6
Ledbury Rd. Reig RH2 .... 118 A2
Ledger Cl. Merrow GU1 .... 110 B3
Ledger Dr. Row Tn KT15 .... 51 F4
Ledgers Rd. Chelsh CR6 .... 82 B1
Ledrington Rd. Penge SE19 .... 23 A2
Lee Ct. Alder GU11 .... 126 C8
Lee Hollow. Gomsh GU5 .... 133 C1
Lee Rd. Alder GU11 .... 104 E2
Lee Rd. Merton SW19 .... 40 B8
Lee St. Horley RH6 .... 160 E4
Leech La. Head KT18 & KT22 ...... 96 C1
Leechcroft Rd. Hackb SM6 .... 60 A7
Leechpool La.
 Horsh RH12 & RH13 .... 218 A4
Leechpool Lane Cty Prim Sch.
 Horsh RH13 .... 218 A4
Leeds Ct. Carsh SM5 .... 59 F7
Leeds Ct. Catf SE6 .... 24 B5
Leehurst. Milf GU8 .... 149 E1
Lees The. Croy CR0 .... 62 F8
Leeson House. 8 Twick TW1 .... 17 B8
Leeward Gdns. Wimble SW19 ..... 19 F2
Leewood Way. Effing KT24 .... 113 D8
Legge Cres. Alder GU11 .... 104 E1
Legion Ct. Morden SM4 .... 40 A3
Legrace Ave. Hounsl TW4 & TW5 . 4 D5
Legsheath La. For Row RH19 .... 205 D1
Leicester. Brack RG12 .... 27 E2
Leicester Ave. Mitch CR4 .... 41 E5
Leicester Cl. N Cheam KT4 .... 58 C6
Leicester House. 2
 Thame D KT7 .... 37 A2
Leicester Rd. 3 Croy CR0 .... 42 E1
Lewin Rd. Streat SW16 .... 21 E2
Lewin Rd. Mortl SW14 .... 7 D4
Lewin Rd. Streat SW16 .... 21 D2
Lewins Rd. Epsom KT18 .... 76 B5
Lewis Cl. Addl KT15 .... 52 C6
Lewis Rd. Mitch CR4 .... 40 E7
Lewis Rd. 18 Rich TW10 .... 6 D2
Lewis Rd. Sutton SM1 .... 59 B6
Lewis Sports & L Ctr.
 S Norw SE19 .... 42 F8
Lewisham Cl. Crawl RH11 .... 201 C2
Lewisham Coll. Beck SE6 .... 23 F3
Lewisham Coll Downham Branch.
 Catf BR1 .... 24 E3
Lewisham Way. Sandh GU15 ...... 45 D7
Lexden Rd. Mitch CR4 .... 41 D5
Lexington Ct. Purley CR8 .... 80 C8
Lexton Gdns. Streat SW12 .... 21 D7
Ley Rd. Farnb GU14 .... 85 A8
Leybone Pk. Rich TW9 .... 7 A6
Leyborne Cl. Byfl KT14 .... 71 F6
Leybourne Cl. Byfl KT14 .... 71 F6
Leybourne Cl. Crawl RH11 .... 201 C1
Leyburn Gdns. S Croy CR0 .... 61 E8
Leycester Cl. Windl GU20 .... 48 B6
Leyfield. New Mal KT3 .... 38 F1
Leyland Track. Farnb GU14 .... 104 B8
Leylands La. Stan TW19 .... 2 A2
Leylands Rd. Abin C RH5 .... 155 F5
Leylands Rd. Worth RH5 .... 156 A6
Leys Rd. Oxsh KT22 .... 74 D7
Leys The. Hersh KT12 .... 54 E6
Leyside. Crowth RG11 .... 45 A5
Leyton Rd. Merton SW19 .... 20 C1
Liberty Ave. Mitch SW19 .... 40 D8
Liberty Hall Rd. Addl KT15 .... 52 A5
Liberty La. Addl KT15 .... 52 B5
Liberty Mid Sch. Mitch CR4 .... 40 E7
Liberty Rise. Row Tn KT15 .... 52 A4
Library Rd. Farnb GU14 .... 85 B2
Licensed Victuallers Sch.
 Wink SL5 .... 28 C6
Lichfield Ct. King U T KT6 .... 37 E4
Lichfield Ct. Rich TW9 .... 6 E3
Lichfield Gdns. Rich TW10 & TW9 . 6 E2
Lichfield Rd. Hounsl TW4 .... 4 C4
Lichfield Rd. Rich TW9 .... 6 F6
Lichfield Terr. 1 Rich TW9 .... 6 E2
Lichfield Way. Selsd CR2 .... 62 D2
Lichfields. Brack RG12 .... 27 E7
Lickfolds Rd. Rowl GU10 .... 145 E3
Liddel Way. Ascot SL5 .... 28 F5
Liddell Ct. 3 Purley CR8 .... 80 A7
Liddington Hall Dr.
 Stough GU3 .... 108 E4
Liddington Hall Est.
 Stough GU3 .... 108 E4
Liddington New Rd.
 Stough GU3 .... 108 E4
Lidiard Rd. Wands SW18 .... 20 C6
Lido Rd. Guild GU1 .... 109 D7
Lidstone Cl. Woking GU21 .... 69 B2
Lightwater Meadow.
 Lhtwat GU18 .... 67 B8
Lightwater Rd. Lhtwat GU18 .... 67 C8
Lightwater Village Sch.
 Lhtwat GU18 .... 48 A1
Lightwood. Brack RG12 .... 27 D3
Lilac Ave. Woking GU22 .... 89 D7
Lilac Cl. Bellf GU1 .... 109 C5
Lilac Gdns. Croy CR0 .... 63 A7
Lilian Rd. Mitch CR4 & SW16 ..... 41 C8
Lilian Rolfe House. 5
 W Norw SE27 .... 22 D4

Leominster Wlk. Morden SM4 .... 40 C3
Leonard Ave. Morden SM4 .... 40 C4
Leonard Cl. Friml GU16 .... 85 D8
Leonard Rd. Mitch CR4 & SW16 . 41 C8
Leonardslee Ct. Crawl RH10 .... 202 B3
Leopold Ave. Farnb GU14 .... 85 B5
Leopold Ave. Wimble SW19 .... 19 F3
Leopold Rd. Crawl RH11 .... 201 C6
Leopold Rd. Wimble SW19 .... 19 F4
Leopold Terr. Wimble SW19 .... 20 A3
Leppington. Easth RG12 .... 27 B2
Leret Way. Leahd KT22 .... 95 B6
Lesbourne Rd. Reig RH2 .... 139 B8
Lescombe Cl. For Hil SE23 .... 23 E5
Lescombe Rd. For Hil SE23 & SE6 23 E5
Lesley Ct. 8 Wallin SM6 .... 60 B6
Leslie Gdns. Belm SM2 .... 59 A3
Leslie Gr. Croy CR0 .... 42 E1
Leslie Park Rd. Croy CR0 .... 42 E1
Leslie Rd. Chobh GU24 .... 49 E1
Leslie Rd. Pixham RH4 .... 115 D1
Lessing St. For Hil SE23 .... 23 E8
Lessingham Ave. Up Toot SW17 . 21 A4
Lessness Rd. Morden SM4 .... 40 C4
Letchworth Ave. E Bed TW14 ..... 14 F8
Letchworth Cl. Crawl RH11 ...... 200 E3
Letchworth St. Up Toot SW17 .... 20 F4
Letcombe Sq. Brack RG12 .... 27 F5
Levana Cl. Putney SW19 .... 19 E7
Levehurst House. W Norw SE27 . 22 C3
Levendale Rd. For Hil SE23 & SE6 23 F6
Leveret Cl. New Add CR0 .... 82 D8
Leveret La. Crawl RH11 .... 201 B8
Leverkusen Rd. Easth RG12 .... 27 B6
Levern Dr. Hale GU9 .... 125 C6
Leverson St. Streat SW16 .... 21 C2
Levett House. 8 Streat SW16 .... 21 C3
Levett Rd. Leahd KT22 .... 95 B7
Levylsdene. Merrow GU1 .... 110 D1
Lewes Cl. Crawl RH10 .... 202 C6
Lewes Ct. 3 Mitch CR4 .... 40 F6
Lewes House. Dovgn RH2 .... 139 B5
Lewes Rd. Ash W RH19 .... 206 C6
Lewes Rd. E Grins RH19 .... 206 C6
Lewes Rd. For Row RH18 .... 206 C6
Lewes Rd. For Row RH19 .... 206 C6
Lewesdon Cl. 13 Putney SW19 ... 19 D7
Lilleshall Rd. Morden SM4 .... 40 D3
Lilley Dr. Kgswd KT20 .... 98 B5
Lillie Rd. Bigg H TN16 .... 83 D1
Lilliput Childrens Ctr.
 Hersh KT12 .... 54 C5
Lily Hill Dr. Brack RG12 .... 27 E7
Lily Hill Rd. Brack RG12 .... 27 F7
Lilyfields Chase. Ewh GU6 .... 175 E4
Lime Ave. Camb GU15 .... 66 A6
Lime Ave. Horsh RH12 .... 218 A4
Lime Ave. Wink SL4 .... 9 F5
Lime Cl. Carsh SM5 .... 59 F8
Lime Cl. Copth RH10 .... 183 B3
Lime Cl. Crawl RH11 .... 181 C1
Lime Cl. W Clan GU4 .... 111 B7
Lime Cl. Woodh RH2 .... 139 B6
Lime Cres. Sunby TW16 .... 35 C7
Lime Ct. Mitch CR4 .... 40 D7
Lime Gr. Addl KT15 .... 52 A6
Lime Gr. King U T KT3 .... 38 E6
Lime Gr. Stough GU1 .... 109 B5
Lime Gr. Twick TW1 .... 6 A1
Lime Gr. W Clan GU4 .... 111 B7
Lime Gr. Warlgm CR6 .... 81 E1
Lime Gr. Westfd GU22 .... 89 E6
Lime Lodge. 3 Charlt TW16 .... 14 F1
Lime Meadow Ave. Sander CR2 . 81 B6
Lime St. Alder GU11 .... 104 F2
Lime Tree Ave.
 Thame D KT10 & KT7 .... 36 E1
Lime Tree Cl. Fetch KT23 .... 94 A3
Lime Tree Gr. Croy CR0 .... 62 F7
Lime Tree La. Crawl RH11 .... 201 B8
Lime Tree Rd. Hounsl TW5 .... 5 B6
Lime Tree Wlk. Coney H BR4 ...... 63 F6
Lime Tree Wlk. Thorpe GU25 ..... 31 E5
Lime Wlk. Brack RG12 .... 27 C5
Limebush Cl. New Haw KT15 ...... 52 C2
Limecroft Cl. W Ewell KT19 .... 57 D3
Limecroft Cl. W Ewell KT19 .... 57 D3
Limecroft Rd. Knaph GU21 .... 68 B2
Limerick Cl. Brack RG12 .... 27 A8
Limerick Cl. Streat SW12 .... 21 C8
Limerick Cl. 1 Streat SW12 .... 21 C8
Limerick House. Woking GU22 ... 70 A1
Limes Ave. Barnes SW13 .... 7 F5
Limes Ave. Carsh SM5 .... 40 F1
Limes Ave. Croy CR0 & CR9 .... 61 A7
Limes Ave. Horley RH6 .... 161 B3
Limes Ave. Penge SE20 .... 23 B1
Limes Cl. Ashf TW15 .... 14 A3
Limes Cl. Beck BR3 .... 44 B7
Limes Field Rd. Mortl SW14 .... 7 E4
Limes Rd. Beck BR3 .... 44 B7
Limes Rd. Egham TW20 .... 11 F3
Limes Rd. Thorn H CR0 .... 42 D2
Limes Rd. W Heath GU14 .... 84 C5
Limes Rd. Weyb KT13 .... 53 A6
Limes The. Belm SM2 .... 59 A4
Limes The. Dorm Pk RH19 .... 185 A5
Limes The. E Mole KT8 .... 36 B5
Limes The. Horse GU21 .... 69 D4
Limes The. Woking GU21 .... 70 A3
Limetree Cl. Streat SW2 .... 21 F7
Limetree Pl. Mitch CR4 .... 41 B8
Limetree Wlk. 2 Up Toot SW17 . 21 A3
Limeway Terr. Dork RH4 .... 115 A1
Limewood Cl. Knaph GU21 .... 68 F2
Limpsfield Ave. Putney SW19 ..... 19 D6
Limpsfield Ave. Thorn H CR7 ..... 41 F4
Limpsfield CE Inf Sch.
 Limps RH8 .... 123 C6
Limpsfield Chart Golf Club.
 Limps RH8 .... 123 C6
Limpsfield Grange Sch.
 Limps RH8 .... 123 A8
Limpsfield Rd.
 Hams Gn CR2 & CR6 .... 81 C3
Limpsfield Rd. Sander CR2 & CR6 81 C3
Limpsfield Rd.
 Warlgm CR2 & CR6 .... 81 C3
Linacre Dr. Cran GU6 & RH12 .. 195 C4
Linacre Dr. Cran GU6 & RH12 .. 195 C4
Lince La. Westc RH4 .... 135 D6
Linchmere Pl. Crawl RH11 .... 201 A7
Linchmere Rd. Lewish SE12 .... 24 F8
Linchmere Rd. Linch GU27 .... 207 C4
Linchmere Rd. Linch GU27 .... 207 D5
Lincoln Ave. Twick TW2 .... 16 C4
Lincoln Ave. Wimble SW19 .... 19 D5
Lincoln Cl. Crawl RH10 .... 201 E3
Lincoln Cl. Croy SE25 .... 43 B3
Lincoln Cl. Friml GU15 .... 66 B4
Lincoln Cl. Horley RH6 .... 161 A2
Lincoln Cl. Hampt TW12 .... 15 F3
Lincoln Dr. Pyrf GU22 .... 70 E3
Lincoln Lodge. Beck BR3 .... 44 B7
Lincoln Rd. Croy SE25 .... 43 B6
Lincoln Rd. Dork RH4 .... 115 C1
Lincoln Rd. Felt TW13 .... 15 F5
Lincoln Rd. King U T KT3 .... 38 C6
Lincoln Rd. Mitch CR4 .... 41 E4
Lincoln Rd. N Cheam KT4 .... 39 B1
Lincoln Rd. Stough GU2 .... 108 F3
Lincoln Terr. 4 Belm SM2 .... 59 A3
Lincoln Way. Charlt TW16 .... 34 E8
Lincoln Wlk. Epsom KT19 .... 57 D1
Lincolns Mead. Lingf RH7 .... 164 C6
Lincombe Rd. Catf BR1 .... 24 F5
Lind Rd. Sutton SM1 .... 59 C5
Linda Ct. Chess KT9 .... 56 D6
Lindale Cl. Went GU25 .... 30 F5
Lindbergh Rd. Wallin SM6 .... 60 E3
Linden. 3 Brack RG12 .... 27 F4
Linden Ave. E Grins RH19 .... 185 C2
Linden Ave. Hounsl TW3 .... 5 B2
Linden Ave. Thorn H CR7 .... 42 B5

Linden Bridge Sch The.
 Worc Pk KT4 .... 57 E7
Linden Cl. Crawl RH10 .... 202 A3
Linden Cl. Horsh RH12 .... 217 E4
Linden Cl. Tadw KT20 .... 97 D7
Linden Cl. Thame D KT7 .... 37 A2
Linden Cl. Woodhm KT15 .... 71 A8
Linden Cres. King U T KT1 .... 37 F7
Linden Ct. Beck BR3 .... 44 B6
Linden Ct. Camb GU15 .... 65 F7
Linden Ct. Eng Gn TW20 .... 11 B2
Linden Ct. Leahd KT22 .... 95 B6
Linden Ct. Penge SE20 .... 23 B1
Linden Dr. Cater CR3 .... 100 C3
Linden Gdns. Leahd KT22 .... 95 C6
Linden Gr. King U T KT3 .... 38 E6
Linden Gr. Penge SE20 .... 23 C2
Linden Gr. Tedd TW11 .... 16 F3
Linden Gr. Walt O T KT12 .... 53 F8
Linden Lea. Dork RH4 .... 136 C5
Linden Leas. S Wick BR4 .... 63 D8
Linden Lodge Sch. Putney SW19 19 E8
Linden Pit Path. Leahd KT22 ...... 95 B6
Linden Pl. Ewell KT17 .... 76 E7
Linden Pl. Mitch CR4 .... 40 E5
Linden Pl. Stain TW18 .... 13 A4
Linden Rd. Guild GU1 .... 109 D1
Linden Rd. Hampt TW12 .... 36 A8
Linden Rd. Head Dn GU35 .... 187 C5
Linden Rd. Leahd KT22 .... 95 B6
Linden Rd. Whit V KT13 .... 53 C2
Linden Way. Send GU23 .... 90 F3
Linden Way. Shep TW17 .... 34 C4
Linden Way. Wallin CR8 .... 60 C1
Linden Way. Westfd GU22 .... 89 F6
Lindenhill Rd. Brack RG12 .... 26 F8
Lindens Cl. Effing KT24 .... 113 E7
Lindens The. Chisw W4 .... 7 D6
Lindens The. Copth RH10 .... 183 B3
Lindens The. M Bourn GU9 .... 125 D1
Lindens The. New Add CR0 .... 63 C4
Lindfield Gdns. Guild GU1 .... 109 F2
Lindfield Rd. Croy CR0 .... 42 F3
Lindgren Wlk. Crawl RH11 .... 201 B1
Lindisfarne Rd. Wimble SW20 .... 19 A1
Lindley Ct. Tedd KT1 .... 37 C8
Lindley Ct. W Byfl KT14 .... 71 B7
Lindley Rd. Tyl Gn RH9 .... 121 C5
Lindley Rd. Walt O T KT12 .... 54 D2
Lindon Bennett Sch. Felt TW13 . 15 D3
Lindores Rd. Carsh SM5 .... 40 C1
Lindsay Cl. Chess KT9 .... 56 E3
Lindsay Cl. Epsom KT18 .... 76 C6
Lindsay Cl. Stan TW19 .... 2 D2
Lindsay Dr. Shep TW17 .... 34 D3
Lindsay Rd. Hampt TW12 .... 16 B4
Lindsay Rd. N Cheam KT4 .... 58 B8
Lindsay Rd. Woodhm KT15 .... 71 B8
Lindsey Cl. Mitch CR4 & SW16 ... 41 E5
Lindsey Gdns. E Bed TW14 .... 14 D8
Lindum Dene. Alder GU11 .... 105 A1
Lindum Rd. Tedd TW11 .... 17 C1
Lindums The. Beck BR3 .... 23 F2
Lindway. W Norw SE27 .... 22 B3
Linersh Dr. Bramly GU5 .... 152 A6
Linersh Wood Cl. Bramly GU5 .. 152 B5
Linersh Wood Rd. Bramly GU5 . 152 A6
Linfield Cl. Hersh KT12 .... 54 B5
Linford Ct. Mitch CR4 .... 40 E8
Ling Cres. Head Dn GU35 .... 187 B6
Ling Dr. Lhtwat GU18 .... 67 A8
Ling's Coppice. W Norw SE21 .... 22 D6
Lingfield Ave. King U T KT1 & KT5 37 F5
Lingfield Common Rd.
 Lingf RH7 .... 164 C6
Lingfield Ct. Wimble SW19 .... 19 D2
Lingfield Cty Mid Sch.
 Lingf RH7 .... 164 D4
Lingfield Dr. Crawl RH10 .... 202 E2
Lingfield Gdns. Coulsd CR5 ...... 100 B8
Lingfield Hospital Sch.
 Lingf RH7 .... 165 A4
Lingfield House. Penge SE26 ..... 23 B3
Lingfield Park Race Course.
 Felct RH7 .... 164 E2
Lingfield Prim Sch. Lingf RH7 ... 164 D4
Lingfield Rd. Dorm Pk RH19 ..... 185 D3
Lingfield Rd. E Grins RH19 .... 185 D3
Lingfield Rd. Eden TN8 .... 165 F8
Lingfield Rd. Haxted TN8 .... 165 F8
Lingfield Rd. N Cheam KT4 .... 58 C7
Lingfield Rd. Wimble SW19 .... 19 D2
Lingfield Sta. Lingf RH7 .... 164 E4
Lingwell Rd. Up Toot SW17 .... 20 E5
Lingwood. Easth RG12 .... 27 C3
Lingwood Gdns. Hounsl TW7 .... 5 E7
Link La. Wallin SM6 .... 60 E4
Link Prim Day Sch The.
 Wallin CR0 .... 60 E6
Link Rd. Addl KT15 .... 52 E6
Link Rd. Carsh CR4 & SM6 .... 41 A1
Link Rd. E Bed TW14 .... 14 F8
Link Rd. Farnb GU14 .... 84 D1
Link Sec Day Sch The.
 Wallin CR0 .... 60 E6
Link The. Crawl RH11 .... 201 D6
Link The. Tedd TW11 .... 16 F2
Link Way. Rich TW10 .... 17 B6
Link Way. Stain TW18 .... 13 B2
Link's Rd. Ewell KT17 .... 77 A5
Linkfield. E Mole KT8 .... 36 B6
Linkfield Cnr. Redh RH1 .... 118 E2
Linkfield Gdns. Redh RH1 .... 118 E1
Linkfield La. Redh RH1 .... 118 E3
Linkfield Rd. Islew TW7 .... 5 F5
Linkfield St. Redh RH1 .... 118 E1
Linklater's Cotts. Hawley GU14 . 84 B6

Links Ave. Morden SM4 .... 40 A5
Links Brow. Fetch KT22 .... 94 E4
Links Cl. Ashtd KT21 .... 75 C2
Links Cl. Ewh GU6 .... 175 E6
Links Green Way. Cobham KT11 74 A5
Links Gdns. S Norw SW16 .... 22 A1
Links Prim Sch. Mitch SW17 ...... 21 A2
Links Rd. Ashf TW15 .... 13 E3
Links Rd. Ashtd KT21 .... 75 C2
Links Rd. Bramly GU5 .... 151 E3
Links Rd. Mitch SW16 & SW17 ...... 21 A2
Links Rd. W Wick BR4 .... 44 C1
Links The. N Asct SL5 .... 28 E7
Links The. Walt O T KT12 .... 54 A8
Links View Ave.
  Brock RH3 & RH5 .... 116 A1
Links View Rd. Croy CR0 .... 63 A7
Links View Rd. Hampt TW12 ...... 16 C4
Links Way. Beck BR3 .... 44 A3
Links Way. Effing KT24 .... 113 E7
Links Way. Farnb GU14 .... 84 C3
Links Way. Mitch SW17 .... 21 A2
Linkscroft Ave. Ashf TW15 ...... 14 B2
Linkside. King U T KT3 .... 38 E7
Linkside E. Beac H GU26 .... 188 C7
Linkside N. Beac H GU26 .... 188 B7
Linkside S. Beac H GU26 .... 188 C6
Linkside W. Beac H GU26 .... 188 B6
Linkway. Camb GU15 .... 65 C4
Linkway. Crawl RH6 .... 182 C2
Linkway. Crowth RG11 .... 45 A5
Linkway. Mayb GU22 .... 70 C2
Linkway. Stough GU2 .... 108 F2
Linkway. W Barn SW20 .... 39 B5
Linkway. W Barn KT3 & SW20 ..... 39 B6
Linkway The. Sutton SM2 .... 59 C2
Linley Ct. ▓ Dulw SE21 .... 22 E4
Linley Ct. Sutton SM1 .... 59 C6
Linnell Rd. Earls RH1 .... 140 B8
Linnet Cl. Selsd CR2 .... 62 D1
Linnet Gr. Merrow GU4 .... 110 D3
Linnet Mews. Balham SW12 ...... 21 A8
Linsford Bsns Pk. Mytch GU16 ... 85 F3
Linsford La. Mytch GU16 .... 85 F3
Linslade Cl. Hounsl TW4 .... 4 E2
Linstead Rd. W Heath GU14 ...... 84 D4
Linstead Way.
  Putney SW18 & SW19 .... 19 E8
Linton Cl. Carsh CR4 & SM5 ...... 40 F2
Linton Glade. New Add CR0 ...... 62 E1
Linton Gr. W Norw SE27 .... 22 C3
Linton's La. Ewell KT17 .... 76 E7
Lintott Ct. Stan TW19 .... 2 D1
Lintott Gdns. Horsh RH13 ...... 217 E3
Lion and Lamb Way. ▓
  Farnh GU9 .... 125 B2
Lion and Lamb Yd. ▓
  Farnh GU9 .... 125 B2
Lion Ave. Twick TW1 .... 16 F7
Lion Cl. Littlt TW17 .... 33 E6
Lion Cl. Shottm GU27 .... 207 F7
Lion Ctr The. Felt TW13 .... 15 E5
Lion Gate Gdns. Rich TW9 ...... 6 F4
Lion Gn. Shottm GU27 .... 207 F6
Lion Green Rd. Coulsd CR5 ...... 79 D3
Lion La. Shottm GU27 .... 207 F7
Lion La. Turn H RH10 .... 204 A4
Lion Mead. Shottm GU27 .... 207 F6
Lion Park Ave. Chess KT9 ...... 57 A6
Lion Rd. Farnb GU14 .... 85 B2
Lion Rd. Thorn H CR0 .... 42 C4
Lion Rd. Twick TW1 & TW2 ...... 16 F7
Lion Way. Brent TW8 .... 6 D7
Lion Wharf Rd. Islew TW7 ...... 6 B4
Liphook Cres. For Hil SE23 ...... 23 C8
Liphook Rd. Linch GU27 .... 207 B4
Liphook Rd. Shottm GU27 ...... 207 F6
Lipsham Cl. Banstd SM7 .... 78 D6
Lisbon Ave. Twick TW2 .... 16 C6
Liscombe. Easth RG12 .... 27 B2
Liscombe House. Easth RG12 ..... 27 B2
Liskeard Dr. ▓ W Heath GU14 ... 85 A6
Lismore. ▓ Wimble SW19 ...... 19 F3
Lismore Cl. Islew TW7 .... 6 A5
Lismore Cres. Crawl RH11 ...... 201 B3
Lismore Rd. S Croy CR2 .... 61 E4
Lissoms Rd. Chips CR5 .... 79 A1
Lister Ave. E Grins RH19 ...... 205 F6
Lister Cl. Mitch SW19 .... 40 E8
Lister Ct. ▓ Purley CR8 .... 80 B7
Litchfield Ave. Morden SM4 ... 39 F2
Litchfield Rd. Sutton SM1 ...... 59 C6
Litchfield Way. Onsl V GU2 ...... 129 F7
Lithgow's Rd. Hatton TW14 & TW6 3 F3
Little Acre. Beck BR3 .... 44 A6
Little Austins Rd. M Bourn GU9 146 D8
Little Birch Cl. New Haw KT15 ... 52 D2
Little Bookham St. L Book KT23 93 F2
Little Bornes. Dulw SE21 .... 22 E4
Little Borough. Brock RH3 ...... 137 A8
Little Brownings. For Hil SE23 ... 23 B6
Little Browns La. Eden TN8 ...... 144 F4
Little Collins. Horl RH6 .... 162 B7
Little Common La. Bletch RH1 ... 120 C3
Little Comptons. Horsh RH13 ... 217 F2
Little Crabtree. Crawl RH11 ... 201 C7
Little Cranmere La.
  W Hors KT24 .... 112 C6
Little Ct. W Wick BR4 .... 63 E8
Little Dimocks. Up Toot SW12 ... 21 B6
Little Elms. Harl UB3 .... 3 D7
Little Ferry Rd. Twick TW1 ...... 17 B7
Little Gn. Elst GU8 .... 148 D4
Little Grebe. Horsh RH12 ...... 217 C5
Little Green La. Addl KT16 ...... 51 E2
Little Green La. Wrecl GU4 ..... 146 A6
Little Halliards. Walt O T KT12 ... 35 A3

Little Haven La. Horsh RH12 ... 217 F5
Little Heath La. Cobham KT11 ... 74 A5
Little Heath Rd. Burrh GU24 ... 49 E2
Little Hide. Merrow GU1 .... 110 B3
Little Holland Bglws.
  Cater CR3 .... 100 D4
Little Kiln. Farnc GU7 .... 150 E8
Little King St. E Grins RH19 ...... 185 E1
Little London. Shere GU5 ...... 132 F2
Little London. Witley GU8 ...... 170 E5
Little Lullenden. Lingf RH7 ..... 164 E5
Little Manor Gdns. Cran GU6 ... 174 E2
Little Mead. Woki RG11 .... 68 F3
Little Mead Ind Est. Cran GU6 . 174 B3
Little Moor. Sandh GU17 .... 45 C1
Little Orch. Horse GU21 .... 70 A5
Little Orch. Woodhm KT15 ...... 71 A8
Little Orchard Way. Shalf GU4 130 E1
Little Orchards. Epsom KT18 ... 76 E5
Little Paddock. Camb GU15 ...... 66 A8
Little Park Dr. Felt TW13 .... 15 E6
Little Park Enterprises.
  Rusper RH6 .... 180 E3
Little Platt. Stough GU2 .... 108 D2
Little Queens Rd. Tedd TW11 ... 16 F2
Little Ringdale. Brack RG12 ...... 27 E5
Little Roke Ave. Purley CR8 ...... 80 B5
Little Roke Rd. Purley CR8 ...... 80 C5
Little St. Stough GU2 .... 109 B5
Little St Leonards. Mortl SW14 ... 7 C4
Little Sutton La. Bra Hil SL3 ...... 1 B8
Little Tangley Flats.
  Woner GU5 .... 131 C1
Little Thatch. Farnc GU7 .... 150 F6
Little Thurbans Cl. Wrecl GU9 146 A6
Little Tumners Ct. Farnc GU7 ... 150 E6
Little Warren Cl. Merrow GU4 . 131 B7
Little Wellington St.
  Alder GU11 .... 105 A2
Little Wildwood. Cran GU6 ..... 174 F1
Little Woodcote La.
  Wallin CR8 & SM5 & SM6 ...... 79 B8
Littlebourne. ▓ Lewish SE13 ... 24 E8
Littlebrook Cl. Croy CR0 .... 43 D3
Littlecote Cl. Putney SW19 ...... 19 E8
Littlecroft Rd. Egham TW20 ...... 11 F3
Littledale Cl. Brack RG12 .... 27 E6
Littlefield Cl. Ash GU12 .... 106 A1
Littlefield Cl. Fairl GU3 .... 108 D5
Littlefield Cl. ▓ King U T KT1 ...... 37 E7
Littlefield Cotts. Worpl GU3 ... 108 B6
Littlefield Gdns. Ash GU12 ...... 106 A1
Littlefield Way. Fairl GU3 ...... 108 D5
Littleford La. Woner GU4 & GU5 152 F7
Littlehaven Sch. Horsh RH12 ... 217 F5
Littleheath Rd. S Croy CR2 ...... 62 B2
Littlemead. Esher KT10 .... 55 D6
Littlers Cl. Mitch SW19 .... 40 D8
Littlestone Cl. ▓ Shackl GU8 ... 24 A2
Littleton C of E Fst Sch.
  Littlt TW17 .... 34 A6
Littleton Cross. Arting GU3 ... 130 A4
Littleton House. ▓ Reig RH2 ... 118 A2
Littleton La. Arting GU3 .... 130 A3
Littleton La. Reig RH2 .... 138 E7
Littleton La.
  Shep Gn TW17 & TW18 .... 33 E4
Littleton Rd. Littlt TW15 & TW17 . 14 C1
Littleton St. Wands SW18 ...... 20 C6
Littlewick Cotts. Woking GU21 ... 68 F4
Littlewick Rd. Woking GU21 ... 68 E3
Littlewood. Cran GU6 .... 174 F1
Littlewood Ave. Esher KT10 ...... 55 D5
Littlewood House. Hams Gn CR2 81 B5
Littleworth Ave. Esher KT10 ..... 55 D5
Littleworth Common Rd.
  Esher KT10 .... 55 D7
Littleworth La. Esher KT10 ...... 55 D6
Littleworth Pl. Esher KT10 ...... 55 D6
Littleworth Rd. Hinch W KT10 ... 55 E6
Littleworth Rd.
  Putt GU10 & GU8 .... 148 C8
Littleworth Rd. The San GU10 . 126 F1
Liverpool Rd. King U T KT2 ..... 18 A1
Liverpool Rd. S Norw CR7 ...... 42 C6
Livesey Cl. King U T KT1 .... 37 F6
Livingstone Ct. Stan TW19 ...... 13 E7
Livingstone Rd. Cater CR3 ...... 100 D5
Livingstone Rd. Crawl RH10 ... 201 E4
Livingstone Rd. Horsh RH13 ... 217 D1
Livingstone Rd. Hounsl TW3 ...... 5 C3
Livingstone Rd. S Norw CR7 ... 42 D7
Llanaway Cl. Farnc GU7 .... 150 F6
Llanaway House. Farnc GU7 ... 150 F6
Llanaway Rd. Farnc GU7 .... 150 F6
Llangar Gr. Crowth RG11 .... 45 A5
Llanthony Rd. Morden SM4 ... 40 D4
Llanvair Cl. Ascot SL5 .... 29 A3
Llanvair Dr. Ascot SL5 .... 28 F3
Llewellyn Ct. Penge SE20 .... 43 C8
Lloyd Ave. Thorn H SW16 ...... 41 E8
Lloyd Ave. Wallin CR5 .... 79 B5
Lloyd Ct. ▓ W Norw SE27 ...... 22 B5
Lloyd House. Beck BR3 .... 24 B2
Lloyd Park Ave. S Croy CR0 ...... 61 F6
Lloyd Rd. N Cheam KT4 & SM3 ... 58 D7
Lloyds Ct. Crawl RH10 .... 181 E1
Lloyds Way. Beck BR3 .... 43 F4
Lobelia Rd. Bisley GU24 .... 68 A4
Lochinvar St. Balham SW12 ... 21 B8
Lochinver. Easth RG12 .... 27 B2
Lock Cl. Sheer GU23 & KT15 ...... 70 E2
Lock La.
  Ockham GU22 & GU23 & KT14 ... 71 C3
Lock Rd. Bellf GU1 .... 109 D4
Lock Rd. Farnb GU11 .... 105 D5
Lock Rd. Rich TW10 .... 17 C4
Lock's La. Mitch CR4 .... 41 A7
Locke King Rd. Whit V KT13 ... 53 A3
Locke-King Cl. Whit V KT13 ...... 53 A3
Lockesley Sq. Surb KT6 .... 37 D3

Lockfield Dr. Woking GU21 ...... 68 F2
Lockhart Rd. Cobham KT11 ...... 73 C6
Lockhursthatch La.
  Farl Gn GU5 .... 153 E6
Locks Meadow. Dorman RH7 ... 165 A1
Locks Ride. Windl SL5 .... 8 C2
Locksley Dr. Knaph GU21 ...... 68 F2
Locksmeade Rd. Rich TW10 ...... 17 C4
Lockswood. Brookw GU24 ...... 88 B7
Lockton Chase. N Asct SL5 ...... 28 D6
Lockton House. Woki RG11 ...... 25 C6
Lockwood Cl. For Hil SE26 ...... 23 D4
Lockwood Cl. Horsh RH12 ...... 218 A5
Lockwood Cl. W Heath GU14 ... 84 E8
Lockwood Ct. Crawl RH10 ...... 201 F8
Lockwood Path. Sheer GU21 ... 70 E6
Lockwood Way. Chess KT9 ...... 57 A5
Lodden Cl. Camb GU15 .... 66 A6
Loddon Rd. W Heath GU14 ...... 84 D6
Loddon Way. Ash GU12 .... 106 A1
Loder Cl. Sheer GU21 .... 70 D7
Lodge Ave. Croy CR0 & CR9 ...... 61 A7
Lodge Cl. Brent TW7 .... 6 B6
Lodge Cl. Carsh CR4 .... 41 A1
Lodge Cl. Crawl RH11 .... 201 C6
Lodge Cl. Dork RH5 .... 136 C3
Lodge Cl. E Ewell KT17 .... 58 C1
Lodge Cl. E Grins RH19 .... 185 D1
Lodge Cl. Eng Gn TW20 .... 11 D3
Lodge Cl. Fetch KT22 .... 94 D5
Lodge Cl. Stk D'A KT11 .... 73 F3
Lodge Gdns. Beck BR3 .... 43 F4
Lodge Hill. Purley CR8 .... 80 A4
Lodge Hill Cl. M Bourn GU10 ... 146 A6
Lodge Hill Rd. M Bourn GU10 . 146 A7
Lodge La. Beck BR3 .... 44 B5
Lodge La. New Add CR0 & CR9 ... 63 B3
Lodge La. S Croy CR0 .... 63 A4
Lodge La. Ś Holm RH5 .... 157 F8
Lodge La. Salfs RH1 .... 139 F1
Lodge Pl. Sutton SM1 .... 59 B5
Lodge Rd. Fetch KT22 .... 94 D5
Lodge Rd. Sutton SM1 .... 59 B5
Lodge Rd. Thorn H CR0 .... 42 B2
Lodge Rd. Wallin SM6 .... 60 C5
Lodge Way. Ashf TW15 .... 13 E6
Lodge Way. Charlt TW17 .... 34 C7
Lodgebottom Rd.
  Head KT22 & RH5 .... 116 A8
Logan Cl. Hounsl TW4 .... 4 F5
Logmore La. Westc RH4 & RH5 135 D3
Lois Dr. Shep TW17 .... 34 B4
Lollesworth La. W Hors KT24 ... 112 C4
Loman Rd. Mytch GU16 .... 86 A4
Lomas Cl. New Add CR0 ...... 63 C3
Lombard Bsns Pk. Merton SW19 40 B7
Lombard Bsns Pk. Thorn H CR9 . 41 F2
Lombard Rd. Merton SW19 ...... 40 B7
Lombard St. Shackl GU8 .... 149 B7
Lombardy Cl. Woking GU21 ...... 68 F2
Lomond Gdns. S Croy CR2 ...... 62 E3
Loncin Mead Ave.
  New Haw KT15 .... 52 C2
London Cross. E Hors KT24 ... 112 F4
London Fields House.
  Crawl RH11 .... 201 C2
London Inst The. Streat SW17 ... 21 B3
London La. Broml BR1 .... 24 F1
London La. Shere GU5 .... 133 A5
London Rd. Abbots GU1 & GU4 . 110 B8
London Rd. Ascot SL5 .... 29 D5
London Rd. Ashf
  TW15 & TW18 & TW19 & TW14 ... 13 D5
London Rd. Bagsh GU15 & GU19 . 47 C1
London Rd. Binf RG12 .... 26 B7
London Rd. Binf RG12 & RG11 ... 26 C7
London Rd. Blckw GU15 & GU17 . 64 E4
London Rd. Bra Hil SL3 .... 1 B8
London Rd. Brack RG12 & SL5 ... 28 C6
London Rd. Brent TW7 & TW8 ... 6 B6
London Rd. Broml BR1 .... 24 F1
London Rd. Burgh GU1 & GU4 ... 110 B4
London Rd. Camb GU15 .... 65 C6
London Rd. Cater CR3 .... 100 D4
London Rd. Cheam SM3 .... 58 C6
London Rd. Crawl RH11 .... 181 E3
London Rd. Dork RH4 .... 115 C3
London Rd. E Grins RH19 ...... 185 D1
London Rd. Eng Gn TW20 ...... 11 C1
London Rd. Ewell KT17 .... 58 C6
London Rd. For Hil SE22 & SE23 23 C7
London Rd. For Row RH18 ...... 206 E4
London Rd. Guild GU1 .... 109 F1
London Rd. Hackb SM6 & CR4 ... 60 B7
London Rd. Hind GU26 .... 188 F4
London Rd. Horsh RH12 .... 217 C2
London Rd.
  Hounsl TW3 & TW7 & TW1 & TW8 . 5 D5
London Rd. Islew TW7 & TW8 ... 6 B6
London Rd. King U T KT1 & KT2 ... 37 F7
London Rd. Mitch CR4 & SW17 ... 40 F6
London Rd. Morden SM4 .... 40 A5
London Rd.
  N Cheam KT4 & SM3 & SM4 ...... 58 C6
London Rd. Redh RH1 .... 119 A3
London Rd. Reig RH2 .... 117 D1
London Rd. Send M GU23 ...... 90 E1
London Rd.
  Stonel KT17 & KT4 & SM3 ...... 58 C6
London Rd. Sunnin SL5 .... 30 B6
London Rd. Sunnin SL5 .... 30 C4
London Rd.
  Thorn H CR0 & CR7 & SW16 ...... 42 A3
London Rd. Twick TW1 .... 17 A7
London Rd. Vir W GU25 .... 31 B7
London Rd. Went SL5 & GU25 ... 30 C4
London Rd. Westh RH4 .... 115 C3
London Rd. Windl GU19 & GU20 . 48 C7
London Rd. Woki RG11 & RG12 . 26 C7
London Rd N. Merst RH1 .... 99 B2

London Rd S. Merst RH1 .... 119 B6
London Rd S. Redh RH1 .... 119 B6
London Road Sta. Guild GU1 ... 109 E1
London St. Chert KT16 .... 33 A2
Lone Oak. Burst RH6 .... 162 B1
Loneacre. Windl GU20 .... 48 B5
Lonesome Fst Sch. Mitch CR4 ... 41 B7
Lonesome La.
  Dovgn RH1 & RH2 .... 139 D3
Lonesome La. Salfs RH1 & RH2 139 D3
Long Acre. Crawl D RH10 ...... 204 A8
Long Beech Dr. Farnb GU14 ... 84 C3
Long Bridge. Farnh GU9 .... 125 C2
Long Cl. Crawl RH10 .... 202 D6
Long Copse Cl. Fetch KT23 ...... 94 B4
Long Ditton Cty Inf Sch.
  Long D KT6 .... 37 C1
Long Dyke. Merrow GU1 .... 110 B3
Long Garden Mews. ▓
  Farnh GU9 .... 125 B2
Long Garden Way. Farnh GU9 . 125 B2
Long Garden Wlk. ▓
  Farnh GU9 .... 125 B2
Long Garden Wlk E. ▓
  Farnh GU9 .... 125 B2
Long Garden Wlk W. ▓
  Farnh GU9 .... 125 B2
Long Gore. Farnc GU7 .... 150 E8
Long Grove Rd. Epsom KT19 ... 57 B1
Long Hill. The San GU10 .... 126 E1
Long Hill. Wold CR3 .... 101 F6
Long Hill Dr. Wink RG12 & SL5 ... 28 A7
Long Houses. Pirb GU24 .... 87 D3
Long La. Croy CR0 .... 43 C3
Long La. Stan TW19 .... 13 F7
Long Lodge Dr. Walt O T KT12 ... 54 C7
Long Meadow Cl.
  W Wick BR3 & BR4 .... 44 C2
Long Mickle. Sandh GU17 ...... 45 B1
Long Rd The. Rowl GU10 ...... 146 A2
Long Reach. Ockham GU23 ...... 92 B3
Long Reach. W Hors KT24 ...... 92 B2
Long Shaw. Leahd KT22 .... 95 A7
Long Wlk. Burgh H KT20 .... 97 D8
Long Wlk. King U T KT3 .... 38 C6
Long Wlk The. Old W SL4 ...... 10 D7
Long's Way. Woki RG11 .... 25 E7
Longacre. Ash GU12 .... 106 A2
Longacre Pl. Wallin SM5 .... 60 A4
Longacre Sch. Sham Gn GU5 ... 152 D4
Longbourne Gn. Farnc GU7 ... 150 E8
Longbourne Way. Chert KT16 ... 32 F3
Longbridge Gate. Crawl RH6 ... 181 E8
Longbridge Rd. Crawl RH6 ...... 181 F8
Longbridge Rd. Horley RH6 ... 160 F1
Longbridge Rdbt. Hookw RH6 . 160 E2
Longbridge Wlk. Horley RH6 ... 160 F1
Longchamp Cl. Horley RH6 ... 161 C3
Longcroft Ave. Banstd SM7 ...... 78 C5
Longcross Rd.Longc KT16 & GU24 50 C7
Longcross Sta. Went GU24 ...... 30 F1
Longdene Rd. Haslem GU27 ... 208 B6
Longdown La N. Ewell KT17 ... 77 A6
Longdown La S.
  Epsom KT17 & KT18 .... 77 A4
Longdown Lodge. Sandh GU17 . 64 B8
Longdown Rd. Catf SE6 .... 24 A4
Longdown Rd. Ewell KT17 ...... 77 A6
Longdown Rd. M Bourn GU10 . 146 C6
Longdown Rd. Merrow GU4 ... 131 B6
Longdown Rd. Sandh GU17 ...... 45 B1
Longfellow Cl. Horsh RH12 ... 217 E7
Longfellow Rd. N Cheam KT4 ... 39 B1
Longfield. Broml BR1 .... 44 F8
Longfield Ave. Carsh CR4 & SM6 41 A1
Longfield Cl. Farnb GU14 ...... 85 B8
Longfield Cres. Burgh H KT20 ... 97 C7
Longfield Cres.
  For Hil SE23 & SE26 .... 23 C5
Longfield Dr. Mitch SW19 ...... 40 E8
Longfield Dr. Mortl SW14 ...... 7 B2
Longfield Rd. Ash GU12 .... 106 A2
Longfield Rd. Dork RH4 .... 135 F6
Longfield Rd. Horsh RH12 ...... 217 A1
Longfield St. Wands SW18 ...... 20 A8
Longfield Way. Stan TW19 ...... 13 E7
Longford Ave. Felt TW14 ...... 3 F1
Longford Cl. Camb GU15 ...... 65 D4
Longford Cl. Hampt TW12 ...... 16 A4
Longford Ct. E Ewell KT19 ...... 57 C6
Longford Ct. For Row RH18 ... 206 E4
Longford Gdns. Sutton SM1 ... 59 C8
Longford House. Catf BR1 ...... 24 D3
Longford House. Hampt TW12 ... 16 A4
Longford Ind Est. Hampt TW12 . 16 B2
Longford Rd. Twick TW2 .... 16 B7
Longford Sch. E Bed TW14 ...... 14 F8
Longford Way. Stan TW19 ...... 13 E7
Longford Wlk. ▓ Streat SW2 ... 22 A8
Longheath Dr. L Book KT23 ...... 93 E3
Longhedge Gdns. Croy CR0 ...... 43 C4
Longhedge House. For Hil SE26 23 A4
Longhill Rd. Catf SE6 .... 24 D5
Longhope Dr. Wrecl GU10 ...... 146 A6
Longhurst Rd. Crawl RH11 ... 201 A1
Longhurst Rd. Croy CR0 .... 43 C3
Longhurst Rd. E Hors KT24 ... 112 E6
Longlands Ave. Wallin CR5 ...... 79 A5
Longlands Cl. Mitch CR4 .... 41 A8
Longlands Ct. Mitch CR4 .... 41 A8
Longlands Way. Friml GU15 ... 66 D5
Longleat Sq. Farnb GU14 ...... 85 E3
Longleat Way. E Bed TW14 ...... 14 D8
Longley Rd. M Bourn GU9 ...... 125 D1
Longley Rd. Thorn H CR0 .... 42 B2
Longley Rd. Up Toot SW17 ...... 20 F2
Longmead. Merrow GU1 .... 110 C2
Longmead Bsns Ctr.
  Epsom KT19 .... 76 D8

Longmead Cl. Cater CR3 .... 100 E5
Longmead House. W Norw SE27 22 C3
Longmead Rd. Epsom KT19 ...... 57 E1
Longmead Rd. Thame D KT7 ...... 36 F2
Longmead Rd. Up Toot SW17 ... 20 F3
Longmeadow.
  Friml GU15 & GU16 .... 65 F3
Longmeadow. L Book KT23 ...... 93 F2
Longmere Gdns. Burgh H KT20 ... 97 C8
Longmere Rd. Crawl RH11 ...... 201 D8
Longmoors. Brack RG12 .... 26 E8
Longmore Rd. Hersh KT12 ...... 54 E6
Longpoles Rd. Cran GU6 .... 174 F2
Longridge Gr. Pyrf GU22 .... 70 E5
Longs Cl. Pyrf GU22 .... 71 A3
Longs Ct. ▓ Rich TW9 .... 6 F3
Longshot Ind Est. Binf RG12 ... 26 E7
Longshot La. Binf RG12 .... 26 E7
Longside Cl. Thorpe TW20 ...... 32 C8
Longstaff Cres. Wands SW18 ... 20 A8
Longstaff Rd. Wands SW17 ...... 21 B3
Longstone Rd. Streat SW17 ... 21 B3
Longthornton Rd. Mitch SW16 ... 41 D7
Longton Ave. For Hil SE26 ...... 23 A4
Longton Gr. For Hil SE26 .... 23 B4
Longwater Rd. Easth RG12 ...... 27 C3
Longwood Dr. Putney SW15 ... 19 B8
Longwood Rd. Kenley CR8 ...... 80 D3
Longwood View. Crawl RH10 ... 202 A3
Longyard House. Horley RH6 ... 161 B5
Lonsdale Gdns.
  Thorn H CR7 & SW16 .... 41 F5
Lonsdale Mews. ▓ Rich TW9 ... 7 A6
Lonsdale Rd. Barnes SW13 ...... 7 F7
Lonsdale Rd. Croy SE25 .... 43 B5
Lonsdale Rd. Dork RH4 .... 136 B8
Lonsdale Rd. Whit V KT13 ...... 53 A3
Look Out (Heritage Ctr) The.
  Crowth RG11 .... 27 D1
Loop Rd. Old Wok GU22 .... 89 F7
Loop Rd. Woodc KT18 .... 76 C3
Loppets Rd. Crawl RH10 .... 201 F3
Loraine Gdns. Ashtd KT21 ...... 75 E2
Loraine House. ▓ Wallin SM5 ... 60 B6
Loraine Rd. Chisw W4 .... 7 B8
Lord Chancellor Wlk.
  King U T KT2 .... 38 C8
Lord Knyvett Cl. Stan TW19 ...... 2 D1
Lordell Pl. Wimble SW19 ...... 19 C2
Lords Cl. Felt TW13 .... 15 E6
Lords Cl. W Norw SE27 .... 22 C6
Lordsbury Field. Wallin SM6 ... 60 C1
Lordsgrove Cl. Burgh H KT20 ... 97 B7
Lordshill Rd. Sham Gn GU5 ... 152 C5
Lordship La. Dulw SE21 & SE22 ... 23 A8
Loretto Cl. Cran GU6 .... 175 A3
Lorian Dr. Reig RH2 .... 118 C2
Loriners. Crawl RH10 .... 201 D3
Loring Rd. Islew TW7 .... 5 F5
Lorne Ave. Croy CR0 .... 43 D2
Lorne Gdns. Croy CR0 .... 43 D2
Lorne Rd. ▓ Rich TW10 .... 6 F2
Lorne The. G Book KT23 .... 94 A1
Lorraine Ct. Beck BR3 .... 44 C8
Lorraine Cty Fst Sch.
  Camb GU15 .... 65 F8
Lorraine Rd. Camb GU15 .... 65 F8
Lory Ridge. Bagsh GU19 .... 47 E4
Loseberry Rd. Esher KT10 ...... 55 D5
Loseley Rd. Farnc GU7 .... 150 E8
Lothian Rd. Pirb GU24 .... 87 A6
Lothian Wood. Tadw KT20 ...... 97 B5
Lotus Rd. Bigg H TN16 .... 83 F1
Loubet St. Up Toot SW17 ...... 20 F2
Loudwater Cl. Sunby TW16 ...... 35 A5
Loudwater Rd. Sunby TW16 ... 35 A5
Loughborough. Brack RG12 ...... 27 E3
Louis Fields. Fairl GU3 .... 108 C5
Louisa Ct. Twick TW2 .... 16 E6
Louisa House. Rhampt SW15 ... 7 F3
Louise Margaret Maternity Hospl.
  Alder GU11 .... 105 B3
Louise Margaret Rd.
  Alder GU11 .... 105 C3
Louisville Rd. Up Toot SW17 ... 21 A5
Lovat Wlk. Heston TW5 .... 4 E7
Love La. Cheam SM3 .... 58 E4
Love La. Croy SE25 .... 43 B6
Love La. Godst RH9 .... 121 C3
Love La. Long D KT6 .... 56 D8
Love La. Mitch CR4 .... 40 E6
Love La. Morden SM4 .... 40 B2
Love La. Sutton SM4 .... 40 B2
Love La. Walt o t h KT20 .... 97 A1
Loveday House. ▓ Streat SW2 ... 22 A7
Lovedean Ct. Brack RG12 ...... 27 E3
Lovekyn Cl. King U T KT2 .... 37 F7
Lovel La. Wink SL5 .... 9 B3
Lovel Rd. Wink SL5 .... 9 A4
Lovelace Cl. E Hors KT24 ...... 93 A4
Lovelace Dr. Pyrf GU22 .... 70 F3
Lovelace Dr. Pyrf GU22 .... 70 F4
Lovelace Gdns. Hersh KT12 ... 54 C5
Lovelace Gdns. Surb KT6 ...... 37 D2
Lovelace Prim Sch. Chess KT9 . 56 C5
Lovelace Rd. Easth RG12 ...... 26 E5
Lovelace Rd. Surb KT6 .... 37 D2
Lovelace Rd. W Norw SE21 ...... 22 C7
Lovelands La. L Kings KT20 ... 118 B8
Lovelands La. W End GU24 ...... 68 C6
Loveletts. Crawl RH11 .... 201 A5
Lovell House. ▓ Merton SW19 ... 40 C8
Lovell Rd. Rich TW10 .... 17 C5
Lovells Cl. Lhtwat GU18 .... 48 B1
Lovelock Cl. Kenley CR8 .... 80 C2
Lovers La. Frensh GU10 .... 167 C2
Lovett Dr. Carsh SM5 .... 40 D2
Lovett House. ▓ Farnh GU9 ... 125 B2
Lovett Rd. Egham TW20 .... 12 C4
Low Cross Wood La. Dulw SE21 22 F5
Low La. Farnh GU9 .... 126 B6

Lowbury. Brack RG12 .... 27 E5
Lowburys. Dork RH4 .... 136 B4
Lowdells Cl. E Grins RH19 ...... 185 C4
Lowdells Dr. E Grins RH19 ...... 185 C4
Lowdells La. E Grins RH19 ...... 185 D3
Lower Addiscombe Rd.
Croy CR0 .... 42 E1
Lower Barn Cl. Horsh RH12 ... 217 F5
Lower Barn Rd. Sander CR8 ...... 80 D6
Lower Breache Rd. Ewh GU6 ... 176 B4
Lower Bridge Rd. Redh RH1 .... 118 F1
Lower Broadmoor Rd.
Crowth RG11 .... 45 D4
Lower Charles St. Camb GU15 .. 65 C6
Lower Church La. 13
Farnh GU9 .... 125 B2
Lower Church St.
Croy CR0 & CR9 .... 61 B8
Lower Coombe St.
Croy CR0 & CR9 .... 61 C6
Lower Court Rd. Epsom KT19 ... 76 C8
Lower Ct. Epsom KT19 .... 76 D8
Lower Dene. E Grins RH19 ...... 186 A4
Lower Downs Rd. Wimble SW20 39 D8
Lower Dunnymans. 4
Banstd SM7 .... 77 F5
Lower Eashing. Shackl GU7 ... 149 F4
Lower Edgeborough Rd.
Guild GU1 .... 130 F8
Lower Farm Rd.
Effing KT23 & KT24 .... 93 C3
Lower Farnham Rd.
Alder GU11 & GU12 .... 126 C7
Lower Forecourt. Crawl RH6 ... 182 B7
Lower George St. 13 Rich TW10 . 6 D2
Lower Gn. Hersh KT12 .... 54 D5
Lower Gn W. Mitch CR4 .... 40 E6
Lower Green Rd. Esher KT10 .... 55 C8
Lower Green Rd. Thame D KT10 55 C8
Lower Grove Rd. Rich TW10 .... 6 F2
Lower Guildford Rd.
Knaph GU21 .... 68 D1
Lower Ham La. Elst GU8 .... 148 E4
Lower Ham Rd. King U T KT2 .... 17 D2
Lower Hampton Rd.
Sunby TW12 & TW16 .... 35 D7
Lower Hanger. Bramsh GU27 .. 207 C6
Lower Hanger. Shottm GU27 ... 207 D6
Lower Hill Rd. Epsom KT19 .... 76 C7
Lower House Rd. Bowl Gn GU8 169 F2
Lower Manor Rd. Farnc GU7 ... 150 F6
Lower Manor Rd. Milf GU8 ...... 149 E1
Lower Marsh La.
King U T KT1 & KT5 .... 38 A5
Lower Mere. E Grins RH19 ..... 205 F8
Lower Mill Field. Bagsh GU19 ... 47 D2
Lower Morden La. W Barn SM4 .. 39 E3
Lower Mortlake Rd. Rich TW9 ... 6 F4
Lower Moushill La. Milf GU8 .. 149 D1
Lower Nelson St. Alder GU11 .. 105 A2
Lower Northfield. 5
Banstd SM7 .... 77 F5
Lower Park Rd. Woodm CR5 .... 78 E1
Lower Peryers. E Hors KT24 ... 112 E7
Lower Pillory Down. Wallin SM5 79 B7
Lower Rd. Effing KT24 .... 113 D8
Lower Rd.
Fetch KT22 & KT23 & KT24 ...... 94 C3
Lower Rd. For Row RH18 .... 206 F3
Lower Rd.
G Book KT22 & KT23 & KT24 ... 94 C3
Lower Rd. Grays GU27 .... 189 F2
Lower Rd. Purley CR8 .... 80 B6
Lower Rd. Sutton SM1 .... 59 C6
Lower Rd. Woodh RH1 & RH2 .. 139 D7
Lower Richmond Rd.
Mortl SW14 & TW9 .... 7 B4
Lower Sandfields. Send GU23 .. 90 D3
Lower Sawleywood. 2
Banstd SM7 .... 77 F5
Lower Shott. G Book KT23 ...... 94 B1
Lower South St. Godal GU7 .... 150 C4
Lower South View. Farnh GU9 125 C3
Lower Sq. For Row RH18 .... 206 E3
Lower St. Haslem GU27 .... 208 C6
Lower St. Shere GU5 .... 133 A4
Lower Staithe. Chisw W4 .... 7 C6
Lower Sunbury Rd.
Hampt TW12 .... 36 A7
Lower Sydenham Sta. Beck SE6 23 F3
Lower Tanbridge Way.
Horsh RH12 .... 217 B2
Lower Teddington Rd.
Tedd KT1 .... 37 D8
Lower Terrace Rd. Farnb GU14 105 A8
Lower Village Rd. Ascot SL5 .... 29 C4
Lower Weybourne La.
Farnh GU9 .... 126 A6
Lower Weybourne La.
Heath E GU9 .... 125 F6
Lowestoft Wlk. Crawl RH10 .... 202 B4
Loweswater Wlk. Friml GU15 ... 66 D4
Lowfield Cl. Lhtwat GU18 .... 67 A8
Lowfield Heath Rd. Crawl RH6 180 F5
Lowfield Heath Rd. Crawl RH6 180 F5
Lowfield Rd. Slinfd RH13 ...... 215 D3
Lowfield Way. Crawl RH6 .... 181 C5
Lowicks Rd. Rushm GU10 ...... 168 C6
Lowlands Rd. Blckw GU17 .... 64 C4
Lowlands Rd. Stan TW19 .... 2 D2
Lowndes Bldgs. Farnh GU9 .... 125 B3
Lowood Ct. Dulw SE19 .... 22 F3
Lowry Cl. Sandh GU15 .... 64 D6
Lowry Cres. Mitch CR4 .... 40 E7
Lowther Hill. For Hil SE23 .... 23 E8
Lowther Rd. Barnes SW13 .... 7 F6
Lowther Rd. King U T KT2 .... 37 F8
Lowthorpe. 5 Woking GU21 .... 69 A1
Loxford Ct. Crawl GU6 .... 173 F2
Loxford Rd. Cater CR3 .... 100 F2

Loxford Way. Cater CR3 .... 100 F2
Loxley Cl. For Hil SE26 .... 23 D3
Loxley Rd. Hampt TW12 .... 15 F4
Loxley Rd. Wands SW18 .... 20 D7
Loxton Rd. For Hil SE23 .... 23 E7
Loxwood Cl. H Bed TW14 .... 14 E7
Loxwood Cty Prim Sch.
Loxwd RH14 .... 213 A4
Loxwood Rd. Alf Cr GU6 .... 193 F2
Loxwood Rd. Alfold GU6 .... 193 F2
Loxwood Rd. Buck Gn RH12 ... 214 A6
Loxwood Rd. Ifold RH14 .... 212 A2
Loxwood Rd.
Loxwd GU6 & RH14 .... 212 F8
Loxwood Rd.
Loxwd RH12 & RH14 .... 213 D4
Loxwood Rd. Plaist RH14 .... 212 A2
Loxwood Wlk. Crawl RH11 ...... 201 A8
Lucan Dr. Stain TW18 .... 13 D1
Lucas Cl. E Grins RH19 .... 186 A1
Lucas Ct. For Hil SE26 .... 23 E3
Lucas Field. Shottm GU27 ...... 207 E6
Lucas Green Rd. W End GU24 ... 67 E5
Lucas Rd. Penge SE20 .... 23 C2
Lucas Rd. Warn RH12 .... 216 F8
Lucerne Cl. Woking GU22 .... 89 E8
Lucerne Ct. 8 Beck BR3 .... 24 A1
Lucerne Rd. Thorn H CR7 .... 42 C5
Lucie Ave. Ashf TW15 .... 14 B2
Lucien Rd. Up Toot SW17 .... 21 A4
Lucien Rd. Wimble SW18 .... 20 B6
Lucille House. Penge SE26 .... 23 B2
Luckley Oakfield Sch.
Woki RG11 .... 25 B3
Luckley Path. Woki RG11 .... 25 C6
Luckley Rd. Woki RG11 .... 25 B3
Luckley Wood. Woki RG11 .... 25 B3
Lucraft House. 12 Streat SW2 .... 21 E8
Luddington Ave.
Thorpe GU25 & TW20 .... 31 F7
Ludford Cl. Croy CR0 .... 61 B6
Ludgrove Sch. Woki RG11 .... 25 D3
Ludlow. Easth RG12 .... 27 B2
Ludlow Cl. Friml GU16 .... 86 A7
Ludlow Rd. Felt TW13 .... 15 A4
Ludlow Rd. Guild GU1 .... 130 B8
Ludovick Wlk. Rhampt SW15 ...... 7 F3
Ludshott Gr. Head Dn GU35 ... 187 B5
Luke Rd. Alder GU11 .... 125 E8
Luke Rd E. Alder GU11 .... 125 F8
Lullarook Cl. Bigg H TN16 .... 83 C3
Lullington Rd. Penge SE20 .... 23 A1
Lulworth Ave. Hounsl TW5 & TW7 . 5 C7
Lulworth Cl. W Heath GU14 ...... 85 A7
Lulworth Cres. Mitch CR4 .... 40 E7
Lumley Cl. Horley RH6 .... 161 A4
Lumley Gdns. Cheam SM3 .... 58 E5
Lumley House. New Mal KT3 .... 38 D1
Lumley Rd. Cheam SM1 & SM3 .. 58 E5
Lumley Rd. Horley RH6 .... 161 A3
Luna Rd. S Norw CR7 .... 42 C6
Lunar Cl. Bigg H TN16 .... 83 D3
Lundy Cl. Crawl RH11 .... 201 C3
Lunghurst Rd. Wold CR3 .... 102 A5
Lunham Rd. W Norw SE19 .... 22 E2
Lupin Cl. Bagsh GU19 .... 47 C1
Lupin Cl. Croy CR0 .... 43 D1
Lupin Cl. Streat SW2 .... 22 B6
Lupin Ride. Crowth RG11 .... 45 B7
Lupus Ct. S Norw SE19 .... 42 D8
Luscombe Ct. Beck BR2 .... 44 F7
Lushington Dr. Cobham KT11 ... 73 B5
Lushington House.
Walt O T KT12 .... 35 C3
Lushington Rd. Catf SE6 .... 24 B3
Lusted Hall La. Bigg H TN16 ... 103 C7
Lusted Hall La. Tats TN16 ...... 103 C7
Lusteds Cl. Dork RH4 & RH5 ... 136 C4
Lutea House. Sutton SM2 .... 59 C3
Luther Rd. Tedd TW11 .... 17 A3
Lutwyche Rd. For Hil SE23 & SE6 23 F6
Lutyens Cl. Crawl RH11 .... 200 E4
Luxford Cl. Horsh RH12 .... 217 F5
Luxford's La. Ash W RH19 ...... 206 B6
Luxford's La. For Row RH19 ... 206 B6
Lyall Ave. Dulw SE21 .... 22 F4
Lyall Pl. Heath E GU9 .... 125 B7
Lycett House. 10 Streat SW2 .... 21 E8
Lych Way. Horse GU21 .... 69 D3
Lyconby Gdns. Croy CR0 .... 43 E2
Lydbury. Brack RG12 .... 27 F6
Lydden Gr. Wands SW18 .... 20 B8
Lydden Rd. Wands SW18 .... 20 B8
Lydele Cl. Horse GU21 .... 69 F4
Lydford Cl. Friml GU16 .... 86 A7
Lydford Cl. 2 W Heath GU14 ..... 85 A7
Lydhurst Ave. Streat SW2 .... 21 F6
Lydney. Easth RG12 .... 27 B2
Lydney Cl. Putney SW19 .... 19 E6
Lydon House. Crawl RH11 ...... 181 D1
Lye Copse Ave. Farnb GU14 ...... 85 B8
Lye The. Tadw KT20 .... 97 C5
Lye View Cotts. Woking GU21 ... 89 A8
Lyefield Cl. For Gn GU6 & RH5 . 176 C5
Lyfield. Oxsh KT11 & KT22 .... 74 B5
Lyford Rd. Wands SW18 .... 20 E7
Lyham Rd. Streat SW2 .... 21 E8
Lyle Cl. Carsh CR4 .... 41 A2
Lymbourne Cl. Belm SM2 .... 59 A1
Lymden Gdns. Woodh RH2 ...... 139 B7
Lyme Regis Rd. Banstd SM7 ..... 77 F2
Lymer Ave. Dulw SE19 .... 22 F3
Lymescote Gdns. Sutton SM1 .. 59 A8
Lyminge Gdns.
Wands SW17 & SW18 .... 20 E7
Lymington Cl. Mitch SW16 .... 41 D7
Lymington Cl. Sutton SM1 .... 59 C7
Lymington Gdns. Worc Pk KT19 . 57 F2
Lyn Ct. Guild GU1 .... 131 A8
Lynch Rd. M Bourn GU9 .... 125 E2
Lynchen Cl. Cranf TW5 .... 4 B6

Lynchford La.
Farnb GU11 & GU14 .... 105 E3
Lynchford Rd.
Farnb GU11 & GU14 .... 105 D8
Lyncroft Gdns. Ewell KT17 ...... 57 F2
Lyncroft Gdns. Islew TW3 .... 5 C2
Lyndale Ct. 3 Redh RH1 .... 119 A4
Lyndale Rd. Redh RH1 .... 119 A4
Lynde House. Walt O T KT12 ..... 35 C3
Lynden Gate. Putney SW15 .... 19 B8
Lynden Hurst. Croy CR0 .... 61 F8
Lyndhurst Ave. Alder GU11 .... 126 C6
Lyndhurst Ave. Blckw GU17 ...... 64 C6
Lyndhurst Ave. Mitch SW16 ...... 41 D7
Lyndhurst Ave. Sunby TW16 ...... 35 A6
Lyndhurst Ave. Tolw KT5 .... 38 B1
Lyndhurst Ave.
Twick TW2 & TW4 .... 16 A7
Lyndhurst Cl. Brack RG12 .... 28 A6
Lyndhurst Cl. Crawl RH11 ...... 201 D5
Lyndhurst Cl. Horse GU21 .... 69 D4
Lyndhurst Cl. S Croy CR0 .... 61 F7
Lyndhurst Ct. 7 Belm SM2 .... 59 A3
Lyndhurst Dr. New Mal KT3 ...... 38 F2
Lyndhurst Farm Cl. Felb RH19 184 D4
Lyndhurst House. 2
Rhampt SW15 .... 19 A8
Lyndhurst Rd. Ascot SL5 .... 29 A5
Lyndhurst Rd. Coulsd CR5 .... 79 A3
Lyndhurst Rd. Thorn H CR7 ...... 42 A5
Lyndhurst Rd. Woodh RH2 ..... 139 A6
Lyndhurst Sch. Camb GU15 .... 65 B5
Lyndhurst Way. Belm SM2 .... 59 A2
Lyndon Ave. Hackb SM6 .... 60 A7
Lyndon Yd. Wimble SW17 .... 20 B4
Lyndsey Cl. W Heath GU14 .... 84 B4
Lyne Cl. Longc GU25 .... 31 F3
Lyne Crossing Rd.
Chert KT16 & TW20 .... 32 B3
Lyne Ct. Longc GU25 .... 31 F2
Lyne La. Chert KT16 & TW20 .... 32 A3
Lyne La. Lyne KT16 .... 32 A2
Lyne & Longcross C of E Fst Sch.
Lyne KT16 .... 51 B8
Lyne Place Manor. Longc GU25 . 31 F2
Lyne Rd. Longc GU25 .... 31 E3
Lynegrove Ave. Ashf TW15 ...... 14 C3
Lyneham Rd. Crowth RG11 .... 45 B5
Lynfield Ct. For Hil SE23 .... 23 D8
Lynmouth Ave. W Barn SM4 ..... 39 D2
Lynmouth Gdns. Heston TW5 ..... 4 D6
Lynn Cl. Ashf TW15 .... 14 D3
Lynn Cl. Streat SW16 .... 21 D3
Lynn Ct. Whytlf CR3 .... 80 F1
Lynn Rd. Balham SW12 .... 21 B8
Lynn Way. W Heath GU14 .... 84 F7
Lynn Wlk. Dovgn RH2 .... 139 B6
Lynne Cl. Selsd CR2 .... 81 C8
Lynne Ct. For Hil SE23 .... 23 F8
Lynne Ct. Guild GU1 .... 130 F8
Lynne Ct. S Croy CR2 .... 61 E6
Lynne Ct. Wimble SW20 .... 39 B8
Lynne Wlk. Esher KT10 .... 55 C5
Lynscott Way. Croy CR2 .... 61 B2
Lynsted Ct. Penge BR3 .... 43 E7
Lynton. Thame D KT7 .... 37 A2
Lynton Cl. Chess KT9 .... 56 E6
Lynton Cl. E Grins RH19 .... 186 A2
Lynton Cl. Islew TW7 .... 5 F3
Lynton Ct. Sutton SM2 .... 59 B2
Lynton Park Ave. E Grins RH19 186 A3
Lynton Prep Sch. Ewell KT17 ... 76 F8
Lynton Rd. New Mal KT3 .... 38 D4
Lynton Rd. Thorn H CR0 & CR7 .. 42 A3
Lynwick St. Buck Gn RH12 ...... 214 C8
Lynwick St. Cox Gn RH12 .... 195 D1
Lynwick St. Rudg RH12 .... 214 C8
Lynwood. Guild GU2 .... 130 B8
Lynwood Ave. Egham TW20 ...... 11 E2
Lynwood Ave. Epsom KT17 ...... 76 F5
Lynwood Ave. Wallin CR5 .... 79 B4
Lynwood Chase. 1 Brack RG12 . 27 C8
Lynwood Cl. Sheer GU21 .... 70 D6
Lynwood Cres. Sunnin SL5 .... 29 E3
Lynwood Ct. Horsh RH12 .... 217 C3
Lynwood Dr. N Cheam KT4 .... 58 A8
Lynwood Flats. Ascot SL5 .... 29 E4
Lynwood Gdns. Croy CR0 .... 60 F6
Lynwood Rd. Epsom KT17 .... 76 F5
Lynwood Rd. Redh RH1 .... 119 A3
Lynwood Rd. Thame D KT7 .... 36 F1
Lynwood Rd. Up Toot SW17 ..... 20 F4
Lynx Hill. E Hors KT24 .... 112 F8
Lyon Ct. Horsh RH13 .... 217 E2
Lyon Rd. Crowth RG11 .... 45 C6
Lyon Rd. Merton SW19 .... 40 C8
Lyon Rd. Walt O T KT12 .... 54 E8
Lyon Way. Friml GU16 .... 65 C1
Lyon Way Ind Est. Friml GU16 .. 65 C1
Lyons Cl. Slinfd RH13 .... 215 D3
Lyons Ct. Dork RH4 .... 136 B7
Lyons Dr. Stough GU2 .... 109 A6
Lyons Rd. Slinfd RH13 .... 215 E3
Lyonsdene. L Kings KT20 .... 117 F8
Lyric Cl. Worth RH10 .... 202 D4
Lyric Rd. Barnes SW13 .... 7 F6
Lysander Rd. Wallin CR0 .... 60 F4
Lysander Way. Farnb GU14 ...... 85 B1
Lysias Rd. Balham SW12 .... 21 B8
Lyson's Rd. Alder GU11 .... 105 A1
Lysons Ave. Ash V GU12 .... 105 F8
Lytchet Minster Cl. 4
Brack RG12 .... 27 F4
Lytchgate Cl. S Croy CR2 .... 61 E3
Lytcott Dr. E Mole KT8 .... 35 F4
Lytham. Easth RG12 .... 26 E3
Lytham Ct. Ascot SL5 .... 29 C4
Lytton Dr. Crawl RH10 .... 202 D7
Lytton Gdns. Wallin SM6 .... 60 D6

Lytton House. 3 Hampt TW12 .. 16 B2
Lytton Rd. Mayb GU22 .... 70 A3
Lyveden Rd. Mitch SW17 & SW19 20 F2
Lywood Cl. Tadw KT20 .... 97 C5

Mabbotts. Tadw KT20 .... 97 D6
Mabel St. Woking GU21 .... 69 D2
Maberley Cres. Penge SE19 ..... 23 A1
Maberley Ct. Penge SE19 .... 23 A1
Maberley Rd. Penge SE19 .... 23 A1
Maberley Rd. Penge BR3 .... 43 D6
Macadam Ave. Crowth RG11 .... 45 C7
MacArthur House. 4 Streat SW2 21 E8
Macaulay Ave. Hinch W KT10 ... 55 E8
Macaulay Ct. Cater CR3 .... 100 E6
Macaulay Rd. Cater CR3 .... 100 E6
Macbeth Ct. Wink RG12 .... 27 E8
Macclesfield Rd. Croy CR0 & SE25 43 C4
Macdonald Ave. Hounsl TW3 ...... 5 C3
Macdonald Rd. Heath E GU9 .. 125 B7
Macdonald Rd. Lhtwat GU18 .... 67 A8
MacGregor House. Streat SW12 21 D7
Mackenzie Rd. Penge BR3 .... 43 D7
Mackie House. Streat SW2 .... 22 A8
Mackie Rd. 18 Streat SW2 .... 22 A8
Mackies Hill. Peasl GU5 .... 154 D7
Macklin House. For Hil SE23 ..... 23 B6
Mackrells. Woodh RH1 .... 139 C6
Macleod Rd. Horsh RH13 .... 217 F1
Macmillan House. Banstd SM7 .. 77 F4
Macphail Cl. Woki RG11 .... 25 E8
Maddison Cl. Tedd TW11 .... 16 F2
Maddox La. L Book KT23 .... 93 E3
Maddox Pk. L Book KT23 .... 93 E4
Madehurst Ct. Crawl RH11 ..... 200 F3
Madeira Ave. Broml BR1 .... 24 E1
Madeira Ave. W Byfl KT14 .... 70 A6
Madeira Cres. Byfl KT14 .... 70 A6
Madeira Rd. Mitch CR4 .... 40 F5
Madeira Rd. Streat SW16 .... 21 E3
Madeira Rd. W Byfl KT14 .... 70 A6
Madeira Wlk. Reig RH1 & RH2 . 118 D2
Madeline Rd. Penge SE20 .... 23 A1
Madgehole La. Sham Gn GU5 .. 153 B3
Madingley. Easth RG12 .... 27 B1
Madingley Ct. Twick TW1 .... 6 C2
Madison Gdns. Beck BR2 .... 44 F6
Madox Brown End. Sandh GU15 64 F6
Madrid Rd. Guild GU2 .... 130 B8
Maesmaur Rd. Tats TN16 .... 103 D6
Mafeking Ave. Brent TW8 .... 6 D8
Mafeking Rd. Wray TW19 .... 12 B6
Magazine Cotts. Chil GU4 ...... 131 C3
Magazine Pl. Leahd KT22 .... 95 B5
Magazine Rd. Cater CR3 .... 100 B5
Magazine Rd. Farnb GU14 ...... 104 D8
Magdala Rd. Islew TW7 .... 6 A4
Magdala Rd. S Croy CR2 .... 61 D3
Magdalen Cl. Byfl KT14 .... 71 E5
Magdalen Cres. Byfl KT14 .... 71 E5
Magdalen Ct. Croy SE25 .... 43 A4
Magdalen Rd. Wands SW18 ...... 20 D7
Magdalene Cl. Crawl RH10 .... 182 C1
Magdalene Rd. Littlt TW17 .... 33 F6
Magdalene Rd.
Sandh GU15 & RG11 .... 45 F2
Magellan Terr. Crawl RH10 .... 182 A2
Magna Carta La. Wray TW19 .... 11 E7
Magna Carta Sch The.
Egham TW20 .... 12 D2
Magna Rd. Eng Gn TW20 .... 11 B2
Magnolia Cl. King U T KT2 .... 18 B2
Magnolia Cl. Sandh GU15 .... 45 D1
Magnolia Ct. 3 Belm SM2 .... 59 B3
Magnolia Ct. Horley RH6 .... 161 A3
Magnolia Ct. Rich TW9 .... 7 B6
Magnolia Ct. Wallin SM6 .... 60 B5
Magnolia Dr. Bigg H TN16 .... 83 E3
Magnolia Way. Chisw W4 .... 7 B8
Magnolia Way. Dork RH5 .... 136 D4
Magnolia Way. W Ewell KT19 ... 57 C5
Magnolia Way. W Ewell KT19 ... 57 C5
Magnolia Wharf. Brent W4 .... 7 B8
Magpie Cl. Coulsd CR5 .... 79 C1
Magpie Cl. Crond GU10 .... 124 D8
Magpie Wlk. Crawl RH10 .... 201 F8
Maguire Dr. Friml GU16 .... 66 C3
Maguire Dr. Rich TW10 .... 17 C4
Mahonia Cl. W End GU24 .... 67 F6
Maida Rd. Alder GU11 .... 105 B4
Maiden La. Crawl RH11 .... 201 C8
Maiden's Gn. Wink SL4 .... 8 B6
Maidenbower Cty Fst Sch.
Worth RH10 .... 202 C4
Maidenbower Dr. Worth RH10 . 202 C4
Maidenbower La. Worth RH10 . 202 C4
Maidenshaw Rd. Epsom KT19 .. 76 D7
Maids of Honour Row. 4
Rich TW9 .... 6 D2
Maidstone Cres. Pirb GU24 ...... 87 D6
Main Dr. Wink RG12 & SL5 .... 28 B8
Main Dr. Wink RG12 & SL5 .... 28 B8
Main Gate Rd. Farnb GU14 ...... 85 B2
Main Rd. Bigg H TN16 .... 83 C5
Main St. Chert KT15 .... 52 E7
Main St. Felt TW13 .... 15 D3
Mainprize Rd. Brack RG12 .... 27 E7
Mainstone Cl. Friml GU16 .... 86 C7
Mainstone Rd. Bisley GU24 ...... 67 F3
Mainwaring Ct. Mitch CR4 .... 41 A7
Mais House. For Hil SE26 .... 23 B6
Maise Webster Cl. Stan TW19 ... 13 D8
Maisonettes The. Cheam SM1 .. 58 F5
Maitland Cl. Hounsl TW4 .... 4 F4
Maitland Cl. W Byfl KT14 .... 71 A6
Maitland Rd. Farnb GU14 .... 105 B8
Maitland Rd. Penge SE26 .... 23 D7
Maitlands Cl. Tongh GU10 ...... 126 F6
Maizecroft. Horley RH6 .... 161 C4

Majestic Way. Mitch CR4 .... 40 F7
Major's Farm Rd. Bra Hil SL3 ..... 1 A8
Major's Hill. Worth RH10 .... 203 C5
Malacca Farm. W Clan GU4 .... 111 B7
Malan Cl. Bigg H TN16 .... 83 E2
Malcolm Cl. Penge SE20 .... 23 C1
Malcolm Dr. Surb KT6 .... 37 E1
Malcolm Gdns. Hookw RH6 .... 160 D1
Malcolm Prim Sch. Penge SE20 23 C1
Malcolm Rd. Coulsd CR5 .... 79 D4
Malcolm Rd. Croy CR0 & SE25 . 43 A3
Malcolm Rd. Penge SE20 .... 23 C1
Malcolm Rd. Wimble SW19 .... 19 E2
Malden Ave. Croy SE25 .... 43 B6
Malden Ct. W Barn KT3 .... 39 B6
Malden Golf Course.
King U T KT3 .... 38 F7
Malden Green Ave.
New Mal KT4 .... 39 A1
Malden Hill. New Mal KT3 .... 38 F6
Malden Hill Gdns. New Mal KT3 38 F6
Malden Manor Prim Sch.
New Mal KT3 .... 38 E2
Malden Manor Sta.
New Mal KT3 .... 38 E2
Malden Parochial CE Prim Sch.
New Mal KT3 .... 38 E1
Malden Pk. New Mal KT3 .... 38 F3
Malden Rd. Cheam KT4 & SM3 . 58 D5
Malden Rd. New Mal KT3 & KT4 . 38 F2
Malden Rd. Old W SL4 .... 11 B8
Malden Way. W Barn KT3 .... 39 A5
Malden Way (Kingston By Pass).
New Mal KT3 & KT5 .... 38 E4
Maldon Rd. Wallin SM6 .... 60 C5
Maldon Rd. Wallin SM6 .... 60 B5
Malet Cl. Egham TW20 .... 12 D2
Maley Ave. W Norw SE27 .... 22 B6
Malham Fell. Easth RG12 .... 27 A5
Malham Rd. For Hil SE23 .... 23 D7
Malham Road Ind Est.
For Hil SE23 .... 23 D7
Mall The. Brent TW8 .... 6 D8
Mall The. Croy CR9 .... 61 C8
Mall The. Guild GU1 .... 130 C8
Mall The. Hersh KT12 .... 54 D5
Mall The. King U T KT6 .... 37 D4
Mall The. Mortl SW14 .... 7 C2
Mall The (Prep Sch).
Twick TW2 .... 16 D5
Mallard Cl. Alder GU12 .... 105 F2
Mallard Cl. Horsh RH12 .... 217 C5
Mallard Cl. Redh RH1 .... 119 A4
Mallard Cl. Shottm GU27 .... 207 E6
Mallard Cl. Twick TW4 .... 16 A8
Mallard Cl. Dork RH4 .... 136 A8
Mallard Ct. 6 Rich TW10 .... 6 D1
Mallard Pl. E Grins RH19 .... 205 F8
Mallard Pl. Twick TW1 .... 17 A5
Mallard Rd. Selsd CR2 .... 62 D1
Mallard Way. Wallin SM6 .... 60 C2
Mallard Wlk. Beck BR3 & CR0 ... 43 D4
Mallard's Reach. Oat Pk KT13 ... 53 D8
Mallards The. Laleh TW18 .... 33 B7
Mallards Way. Lhtwat GU18 ...... 67 A8
Malling Cl. Croy CR0 .... 43 C3
Malling Gdns. Morden SM4 ...... 40 C3
Malling House. 9 Beck BR3 .... 24 A1
Mallinson Rd. Wallin SM6 .... 60 D7
Mallinson Rd. Hayes BR2 .... 44 F2
Mallow Cl. Burgh H KT20 .... 97 B8
Mallow Cl. Croy CR0 .... 43 D1
Mallow Cl. Horsh RH12 .... 217 E6
Mallowdale Rd. Brack RG12 ..... 27 E2
Malloy Ct. Woking GU21 .... 70 A3
Malmains Cl. Beck BR3 .... 44 D5
Malmains Way. Beck BR3 .... 44 D5
Malmesbury Fst Sch.
Morden SM4 .... 40 C2
Malmesbury Mid Sch.
Morden SM4 .... 40 C3
Malmesbury Rd. Morden SM4 ... 40 C3
Malmstone Ave. Merst RH1 .... 119 D6
Malt Hill. Egham TW20 .... 11 E3
Malt House. Old W SL4 .... 11 B8
Malt House Cl. Old W SL4 .... 11 B8
Malta Rd. Friml GU16 .... 86 E8
Maltby Rd. Chess KT9 .... 57 A4
Malthouse Dr. Felt TW13 .... 15 D3
Malthouse La. Pirb GU24 & GU3 . 88 C2
Malthouse La. W End GU24 .... 67 F7
Malthouse Mead. Witley GU8 .. 170 F5
Malthouse Rd.
Crawl RH10 & RH11 .... 201 D4
Malthouses The. Cran GU6 ..... 174 E3
Maltings Cl. Barnes SW13 .... 7 E5
Maltings The. Byfl KT14 .... 71 F6
Maltings The. Oxted RH8 .... 122 F4
Maltings The. Stain TW18 .... 12 F4
Malthouse La. Hambl GU8 ...... 171 C1
Malton House. S Norw SE25 ..... 42 E5
Malus Cl. Row Tn KT15 .... 51 F3
Malus Dr. Row Tn KT15 .... 51 F3
Malvern Cl. Mitch CR4 .... 41 C6
Malvern Cl. Ottsh KT16 .... 51 C4
Malvern Cl. Penge SE20 .... 43 A7
Malvern Cl. Surb KT6 .... 37 E1
Malvern Cl. Belm SM2 .... 59 A3
Malvern Ct. Bra Hil SL3 .... 1 A1
Malvern Ct. 3 Surb KT6 .... 37 E1
Malvern Dr. Felt TW13 .... 15 D3
Malvern Rd. Crawl RH11 .... 201 C5
Malvern Rd. Hampt TW12 .... 16 A1
Malvern Rd. Harl UB3 .... 3 E7
Malvern Rd. Surb KT6 .... 37 E1
Malvern Rd. Thorn H CR7 .... 42 A5
Malvern Rd. W Heath GU14 ...... 84 D7
Malyons The. Shep TW17 .... 34 D3

Manchester Rd. S Norw CR7 42 C6
Mandeville Cl. Merton SW19 39 E8
Mandeville Cl. Stough GU2 109 A4
Mandeville Ct. Egham TW20 12 A4
Mandeville Dr. Surb KT6 37 D1
Mandeville Rd. Islew TW7 6 A5
Mandeville Rd. Shep Gn TW17 34 A4
Mandora Rd. Alder GU11 105 B4
Mandrake Rd. Up Toot SW17 20 F5
Manfield Cty Fst Sch. Ash GU12 106 B2
Manfield Pk. Rowly GU6 174 B5
Manfield Rd. Ash GU12 106 A2
Mangles Rd. Bellf GU1 109 D3
Manley Bridge Rd. Rowl GU10 145 E4
Manley Bridge Rd. Wreccl GU10 145 E4
Mann's Cl. Islew TW7 5 F2
Mannamead. Lang V KT18 96 E8
Mannamead Cl. Lang V KT18 96 E8
Manning Cl. E Grins RH19 185 D2
Manning Pl. Rich TW10 6 F1
Mannings Cl. Crawl RH10 182 D1
Manningtree Cl. Putney SW19 19 E7
Manoel Rd. Twick TW2 16 C6
Manor Ave. Cater CR3 100 E3
Manor Ave. Hounsl TW4 4 D5
Manor Chase. Weyb KT13 53 B5
Manor Cl. E Hors KT24 112 E7
Manor Cl. Horley RH6 160 F3
Manor Cl. New Mal KT4 38 E1
Manor Cl. Pyrf GU22 70 F3
Manor Cl. Shottm GU27 207 E6
Manor Cl. Tongh GU10 126 F7
Manor Cl. Warlgm CR6 81 E2
Manor Cotts. Woking GU21 68 E5
Manor Cres. Byfl KT14 71 F6
Manor Cres. Pirb GU24 87 D7
Manor Cres. Shottm GU27 207 E6
Manor Cres. Stough GU2 109 B3
Manor Cres. Surb KT5 38 A3
Manor Ct. Horsh RH12 218 A5
Manor Ct. King U T KT2 38 A8
Manor Ct. Streat SW16 21 E5
Manor Ct. Twick TW2 16 C6
Manor Ct. Weyb KT13 53 B6
Manor Dr. Felt TW13 15 D3
Manor Dr. Hinch W KT10 56 A7
Manor Dr. Horley RH6 160 F3
Manor Dr. Sunby TW16 35 A7
Manor Dr. Surb KT5 38 A3
Manor Dr. W Ewell KT19 57 E4
Manor Dr. W Ewell KT19 57 E4
Manor Dr. Woodhm KT15 52 A1
Manor Dr N. New Mal KT3 & KT4 38 D2
Manor Dr The. New Mal KT4 38 F1
Manor Farm Ave. Shep TW17 34 B3
Manor Farm Bsns Ctr. Tongh GU10 126 F5
Manor Farm Cl. Ash GU12 105 F1
Manor Farm Ct. Egham TW20 12 A3
Manor Farm La. Egham TW20 12 A3
Manor Farm Rd. S Norw CR7 & SW16 42 A7
Manor Fields. Horsh RH12 & RH13 218 A4
Manor Fields. Milf GU8 149 E2
Manor Fields. Seale GU10 127 B4
Manor Gdns. Effing KT24 113 D7
Manor Gdns. Farnc GU7 150 E7
Manor Gdns. Hampt TW12 16 C1
Manor Gdns. M Bourn GU10 146 D5
Manor Gdns. Merton SW19 & SW20 39 F7
Manor Gdns. Rich TW10 & TW9 6 F3
Manor Gdns. S Croy CR2 61 F4
Manor Gdns. Stough GU2 109 B3
Manor Gdns. Sunby TW16 35 A7
Manor Gn. Milf GU8 149 E1
Manor Gr. Beck BR3 44 B7
Manor Gr. Rich TW9 7 A4
Manor Green Rd. Epsom KT19 76 C7
Manor Hill. Woodm SM7 78 F4
Manor Hospl The. Epsom KT19 76 A7
Manor House. Wallin SM6 60 B5
Manor House Ct. Epsom KT18 76 C6
Manor House Dr. Ascot SL5 9 A1
Manor House Flats. Tongh GU10 126 F6
Manor House Sch The. Effing KT23 113 E8
Manor House The. Camb GU15 65 D6
Manor House Way. Islew TW7 6 B4
Manor La. Felt TW13 15 A6
Manor La. Harl UB3 3 D8
Manor La. L Kings KT20 118 A6
Manor La. Lewish SE12 24 F8
Manor La. Sham Gn GU5 152 E3
Manor La. Sunby TW16 35 B7
Manor La. Sutton SM1 59 C5
Manor Lea. Shottm GU27 207 E6
Manor Lea Cl. Milf GU8 149 E2
Manor Lea Rd. Milf GU8 149 E2
Manor Leaze. Egham TW20 12 B3
Manor Lodge. Stough GU2 109 B3
Manor Mead Sch. Shep TW17 34 B4
Manor Mount. For Hil SE23 23 C7
Manor Park Cl. W Wick BR4 44 B1
Manor Park Ctr (Coll of Tech). Alder GU11 105 B1
Manor Park Ind Est. Alder GU12 105 C1
Manor Park Prim Sch. Sutton SM1 59 C5
Manor Park Rd. Sutton SM1 59 C5
Manor Park Rd. W Wick BR4 44 B1
Manor Pk. Rich TW9 6 F3
Manor Pl. E Bed TW14 15 A7
Manor Pl. Mitch CR4 41 C6
Manor Pl. Stain TW18 13 B3
Manor Pl. Sutton SM1 59 B6
Manor Rd. Alder GU11 & GU12 126 A8
Manor Rd. Ash GU10 & GU12 126 F8
Manor Rd. Ashf TW15 14 A3
Manor Rd. Beck BR3 44 B7
Manor Rd. Belm SM2 58 F2
Manor Rd. Croy SE25 43 A6
Manor Rd. E Grins RH19 185 C2
Manor Rd. E Mole KT8 36 D5
Manor Rd. Farnb GU14 85 D3
Manor Rd. Farnh GU9 125 E4
Manor Rd. Horsh RH12 218 A5
Manor Rd. Merst RH1 119 C6
Manor Rd. Merton SW20 39 F7
Manor Rd. Mitch CR4 & SW16 41 C6
Manor Rd. Reig RH2 117 F3
Manor Rd. Rich TW10 & TW9 6 F3
Manor Rd. Rich TW11 17 B3
Manor Rd. Send M GU23 90 F4
Manor Rd. Stough GU2 109 B3
Manor Rd. Tats TN16 103 E7
Manor Rd. Twick TW2 16 D6
Manor Rd. W Wick BR4 63 B8
Manor Rd. Wallin SM5 & SM6 60 B5
Manor Rd. Walt O T KT12 34 F2
Manor Rd. Woki RG11 25 A2
Manor Rd N. Hackb SM5 & SM6 60 A6
Manor Rd N. Hinch W KT7 56 A8
Manor Rd S. Hinch W KT10 55 E6
Manor Royal. Crawl RH10 & RH11 181 E1
Manor Sch The. Byfl KT14 71 E5
Manor The. Milf GU8 149 F1
Manor Way. Bagsh GU19 47 F3
Manor Way. Beck BR3 44 A6
Manor Way. Egham TW20 12 A2
Manor Way. Mitch CR4 & SW16 41 C6
Manor Way. New Mal KT4 38 F1
Manor Way. Old Wok GU22 90 B6
Manor Way. Onsl V GU2 129 F6
Manor Way. Oxsh KT22 74 C3
Manor Way. Purley CR8 79 E7
Manor Way. S Croy CR2 61 F4
Manor Way. Woodm SM7 78 F3
Manor Way The. Wallin SM6 60 B6
Manor Wlk. Weyb KT13 53 B5
Manor Wood Rd. Purley CR8 79 E6
Manorcroft Sch. Egham TW20 12 A2
Manorcrofts Rd. Egham TW20 12 A2
Manordene Cl. Hinch W KT7 37 A1
Manorfields. Crawl RH11 200 D2
Manorgate Rd. King U T KT2 38 A8
Manorhouse La. Effing KT23 113 E8
Manorside Cl. Ash GU10 & GU12 126 F8
Mansard Beeches. Streat SW17 21 A3
Mansard Manor. Sutton SM2 59 C3
Manse Cl. Harl UB3 3 D8
Mansel Cl. Stough GU2 109 B6
Mansel Rd. Wimble SW19 19 F2
Mansell Way. Cater CR3 100 D5
Mansfield Cl. N Asct SL5 28 D7
Mansfield Cres. Easth RG12 27 B3
Mansfield Dr. Merst RH1 119 D6
Mansfield Pl. N Asct SL5 28 D8
Mansfield Rd. Chess KT9 56 D5
Mansfield Rd. S Croy CR2 61 D4
Mansfield Rd. Woki RG11 25 A5
Manship Rd. Mitch CR4 41 A8
Manston Cl. Penge SE20 43 C8
Manston Dr. Easth RG12 27 C3
Manston Gr. King U T KT2 17 D3
Manston Rd. Burph GU4 110 A5
Mantilla Rd. Up Toot SW17 21 A4
Mantlet Cl. Streat SW16 21 C1
Manville Ct. Shalf GU4 130 E1
Manville Gdns. Up Toot SW17 21 B5
Manville Rd. Up Toot SW17 21 B5
Many Gates. Up Toot SW12 21 B6
Manygate La. Shep TW17 34 C3
Maori Rd. Guild GU1 130 F8
Mapel Ct. 3 Brack RG12 27 F5
Maple Cl. Ash V GU12 106 A7
Maple Cl. Blckw GU17 64 C5
Maple Cl. Crawl RH11 181 C1
Maple Cl. Hampt TW12 15 F2
Maple Cl. Horsh RH12 218 A5
Maple Cl. Mitch CR4 41 B8
Maple Cl. Whytlf CR3 80 F2
Maple Ct. Catf SE6 24 B7
Maple Ct. 2 Croy CR0 61 C6
Maple Ct. Eng Gn TW20 11 B2
Maple Ct. Horse GU21 69 C3
Maple Ct. King U T KT3 38 D6
Maple Ct. 11 W Norw SW16 22 A3
Maple Dr. Crowth RG11 45 C7
Maple Dr. E Grins RH19 186 A1
Maple Dr. Lhtwat GU18 66 F8
Maple Dr. Lhtwat GU18 67 A8
Maple Gdns. Stan TW15 & TW19 13 E6
Maple Gr. Bellf GU1 109 D3
Maple Gr. Brent TW8 6 B7
Maple Gr. Westfd GU22 89 E6
Maple Gr Bsns Ctr. Hounsl TW4 4 C3
Maple House. 2 King U T KT6 37 E4
Maple Ind Est. Felt TW13 15 A5
Maple Inf Sch. King U T KT6 37 D4
Maple Leaf Cl. Bigg H TN16 83 D3
Maple Leaf Cl. Farnb GU14 84 F3
Maple Mews. Streat SW16 21 F3
Maple Pl. Nork KT17 77 D5
Maple Rd. Ashtd KT21 95 D8
Maple Rd. Earls RH1 139 F5
Maple Rd. King U T KT6 37 D4
Maple Rd. Penge SE20 43 C8
Maple Rd. Send M GU23 91 A3
Maple Rd. Whytlf CR3 80 F2
Maple Way. Felt TW13 15 B5
Maple Way. Head Dn GU35 187 B6
Maple Way. Hooley CR5 99 B6
Maple Wlk. Alder GU12 126 D8
Maple Wlk. Sutton SM2 59 B1
Mapledale Ave. S Croy CR0 62 B7
Mapledrakes Cl. Ewh GU6 175 E5
Mapledrakes Rd. Ewh GU6 175 E5
Maplehatch Cl. Godal GU7 150 E2
Maplehurst. Beck BR2 44 E7
Maplehurst. Fetch KT22 94 D4
Maplehurst Cl. King U T KT1 37 E5
Maples The. Banstd SM7 78 B5
Maples The. Ottsh KT16 51 C4
Maples The. 4 Tedd KT8 17 C1
Maplestead Rd. Streat SW2 21 F8
Maplethorpe Rd. Thorn H CR7 42 B5
Marble Hill Cl. Twick TW1 17 B8
Marble Hill Gdns. Twick TW1 17 B8
Marbles Way. Burgh H KT20 97 D8
March Rd. 6 Twick TW1 17 A8
March Rd. Weyb KT13 53 A5
Marcheria Cl. Easth RG12 27 B3
Marches Rd. Warn RH12 197 E4
Marchmont House. 10 Streat SW16 21 C3
Marchmont Rd. Rich TW10 6 F2
Marchmont Rd. Wallin SM6 60 C3
Marchside Cl. Heston TW5 4 D6
Marcus Ct. Brent TW8 6 E7
Mardale. Friml GU15 66 C4
Mardell Rd. Croy CR0 43 D4
Marden Ave. Hayes BR2 44 F3
Marden Cres. Thorn H CR0 41 F3
Marden Lodge Cty Prim Sch. Cater CR3 101 B6
Marden Rd. Thorn H CR0 41 F3
Mardens The. Crawl RH11 201 B7
Mare Hill. Witley GU8 170 E5
Mare Hill Cotts. Witley GU8 170 D4
Mare La. Hasc GU8 172 C4
Mares Field House. Merrow GU4 110 D2
Mareschal Rd. Guild GU2 130 C7
Maresfield. S Croy CR0 61 E7
Mareth Cl. Alder GU11 105 B2
Marfleet Cl. Carsh SM5 59 E8
Margaret Cl. Stain TW18 13 D2
Margaret Rd. Guild GU1 130 C8
Margaret Roper RC Prim Sch. Purley CR8 61 A1
Margaret Way. Coulsd CR8 100 B8
Margery Gr. L Kings KT20 117 E6
Margery La. L Kings KT20 & RH2 118 A6
Margin Dr. Wimble SW19 19 D4
Marham Gdns. Morden SM4 40 C3
Marham Gdns. Wands SW17 & SW18 20 E7
Maria Montessori Sch. Horne RH6 162 F5
Maria Theresa Cl. New Mal KT3 38 D4
Marian Ct. Sutton SM1 59 B5
Marian Rd. Mitch CR4 & SW16 41 C8
Marian Vian Prim Sch. Beck BR3 43 E4
Mariette Way. Wallin SM6 60 E2
Marigold Cl. Crowth RG11 45 A6
Marigold Ct. Bellf GU1 109 E4
Marigold Dr. Bisley GU24 68 A4
Marigold Way. Croy CR0 43 D1
Marina Ave. W Barn KT3 39 B4
Marina Way. Tedd TW11 17 D1
Mariner Gdns. Rich TW10 17 C5
Mariners Dr. Farnb GU14 85 C6
Mariners Dr. Normdy GU3 107 B4
Marion Ave. Shep TW17 34 B4
Marion Ct. Up Toot SW17 20 E3
Marion Rd. Crawl RH10 202 B3
Marion Rd. Thorn H CR0 42 D4
Marist RC Prim Sch. W Byfl KT14 70 F6
Marius Mansions. 3 Up Toot SW17 21 A6
Marius Rd. Up Toot SW17 21 A6
Marjoram Cl. Stough GU2 109 A5
Marjoram Cl. W Heath GU14 84 B4
Marjorie Fosters Way. Pirb GU24 87 D8
Marjory Kinnon Sch. Hatton TW14 3 E2
Mark Oak La. Fetch KT22 94 A6
Mark St. Reig RH2 118 B2
Mark Way. Farnc GU7 150 B8
Markedge La. L Kings CR5 & RH2 98 F2
Markenfield Rd. Guild GU1 109 D1
Markenhorn. Farnc GU7 150 D7
Market Par. Croy SE25 43 A5
Market Par. Felt TW13 15 E6
Market Pl. Brent TW8 6 C7
Market Pl. King U T KT1 37 D7
Market Pl. Woki RG11 25 C5
Market Rd. Mortl TW9 7 A4
Market Sq. Horsh RH12 217 C1
Market Sq. Reig RH2 118 A1
Market Sq. Stain TW18 12 E4
Market St. Brack RG12 27 B7
Market St. Guild GU1 130 D8
Market The. Carsh SM1 & SM4 & SM5 40 C1
Marketfield Way. Earls RH1 119 A1
Markfield. New Add CR0 81 F8
Markfield Rd. Cater CR3 101 B2
Markham House. 9 Dulw SE21 22 E4
Markham Mews. Woki RG11 25 C6
Markham Rd. Capel RH5 178 C5
Markhole Cl. Hampt TW12 15 F1
Marks Rd. Warlgm CR6 81 E1
Marks Rd. Woki RG11 25 A8
Marksbury Ave. Rich TW9 7 A4
Markville Gdns. Cater CR3 101 A2
Markway The. Sunby TW16 35 C7
Markwell Cl. For Hil SE26 23 B4
Markwick La. Hasc GU8 172 C2
Marlang Ct. Beck BR3 44 D8
Marlborogh Rd. Brent TW7 & TW8 6 B7
Marlborough. 11 Putney SW19 19 D7
Marlborough Cl. Crawl RH11 201 C2
Marlborough Cl. Hersh KT12 54 D7
Marlborough Cl. Horsh RH12 217 D5
Marlborough Cl. Mitch SW19 20 E2
Marlborough Ct. Dork RH4 136 B7
Marlborough Ct. Woki RG11 25 D7
Marlborough Cty Inf Sch. Farnb GU11 105 C7
Marlborough Dr. Weyb KT13 53 C7
Marlborough Gdns. Surb KT6 37 D2
Marlborough House. Wimble SW19 19 D5
Marlborough Jun & Inf Sch. Islew TW7 6 A6
Marlborough Rd. Ashf TW15 13 E3
Marlborough Rd. Dork RH4 136 B7
Marlborough Rd. Felt TW13 15 D6
Marlborough Rd. Hampt TW12 16 A2
Marlborough Rd. Mitch SW19 20 E2
Marlborough Rd. Rich TW10 6 F1
Marlborough Rd. S Croy CR2 61 C3
Marlborough Rd. Sutton SM1 59 A8
Marlborough Rd. Woking GU21 70 A3
Marlborough Rise. Camb GU15 65 E6
Marlborough Trad Est. Rich TW9 7 B6
Marlborough View. W Heath GU14 84 C5
Marld The. Ashtd KT21 75 F1
Marler Rd. For Hil SE23 23 F7
Marles La. Rudg RH14 214 C1
Marlesford Ct. Wallin SM6 60 C6
Marley Cl. Row Tn KT15 51 F4
Marley Combe Rd. King Gn GU27 207 F4
Marley Croft. Stain TW18 12 E5
Marley Hanger. King Gn GU27 208 A3
Marley La. Linch GU27 207 E4
Marley Rise. Dork RH4 136 A4
Marlfield Ct. New Mal KT3 38 F2
Marling Ct. Hampt TW12 15 F2
Marlingdene Cl. Hampt TW12 16 A2
Marlings Cl. Kenley CR3 80 E2
Marlins Cl. Sutton SM1 59 C5
Marlow Cl. Penge SE20 43 B6
Marlow Cres. Twick TW1 5 F1
Marlow Ct. Crawl RH10 & RH11 201 D7
Marlow Dr. Cheam SM3 58 D7
Marlow House. Tedd TW11 17 A4
Marlow Rd. Penge SE20 & SE25 43 B7
Marlowe Ct. Dulw SE19 22 F3
Marlowe Ct. 6 King U T KT2 17 D4
Marlowe House. King U T KT1 37 D5
Marlowe Lodge. Croy CR0 62 E8
Marlowe Sq. Mitch CR4 41 C5
Marlowe Way. Wallin CR0 60 E8
Marlpit Ave. Coulsd CR5 79 E2
Marlpit Cl. E Grins RH19 185 E4
Marlpit La. Coulsd CR5 79 E2
Marlyns Cl. Burph GU4 110 A4
Marlyns Dr. Burph GU1 & GU4 110 A4
Marmion House. 13 Balham SW12 21 B8
Marmot Rd. Hounsl TW4 4 D4
Marncrest Ct. Hersh KT12 54 B5
Marnell Way. Hounsl TW4 4 D4
Marneys Cl. Epsom KT18 76 A4
Maroons Way. Catf SE6 24 A3
Marqueen Towers. Streat SW16 21 F1
Marquis Ct. 1 King U T KT1 37 E5
Married Quarters. Cater CR3 100 C5
Marriott Cl. Hatton TW14 3 D1
Marriott House. Catf SE6 24 C4
Marriott Lodge Cl. Addl KT15 52 C6
Marrowbrook Cl. Farnb GU14 85 A4
Marrowbrook La. Farnb GU14 85 A3
Marrowells. Walt O T KT13 53 F7
Marryat Pl. Wimble SW19 19 E4
Marryat Rd. Wimble SW19 19 E3
Marsh Ave. Epsom KT19 57 E1
Marsh Ave. Mitch CR4 41 A7
Marsh Ct. Crawl RH11 201 B1
Marsh Ct. 3 Merton SW19 40 C8
Marsh Farm Rd. Twick TW2 16 F7
Marsh La. Addl KT15 52 B6
Marshall Cl. Friml GU16 66 D2
Marshall Cl. Hounsl TW4 4 F2
Marshall Cl. W Heath GU14 84 F7
Marshall House. 3 New Mal KT3 38 E5
Marshall Par. Pyrf GU22 70 F4
Marshall Pl. New Haw KT15 52 C2
Marshall Rd. Farnc GU7 150 E6
Marshall Rd. Sandh GU15 64 D6
Marshall Rd. Worth RH10 202 C4
Marshall's Rd. Sutton SM1 59 B6
Marshalls. M Bourn GU9 146 B8
Marshalls Cl. Epsom KT19 76 C6
Marsham Ct. 19 Putney SW19 19 D7
Marshfields C of E Fst Sch. Ottsh KT16 51 E4
Marshwood Rd. Lhtwat GU18 67 D8
Marston. Epsom KT19 76 C8
Marston Ave. Chess KT9 56 E4
Marston Ct. Walt O T KT12 35 C1
Marston Dr. Farnb GU14 85 B7
Marston Dr. Warlgm CR6 81 E1
Marston House. Redh RH1 118 F2
Marston Rd. Farnh GU9 124 F2
Marston Rd. Rich TW11 17 B3
Marston Rd. Woking GU21 69 B2
Marston Way. N Asct SL5 28 E7
Marston Way. S Norw SE19 22 C1
Martel Cl. Camb GU15 66 C7
Martell Rd. W Norw SE21 22 D5
Martens Pl. Farnc GU7 150 E6
Martin Cl. Crawl RH11 201 D8
Martin Cl. Selsd CR2 62 D1
Martin Cl. Warlgm CR6 81 B3
Martin Cres. Thorn H CR0 42 A1
Martin Ct. Merton SW19 20 A1
Martin Gr. Merton SM4 & SW19 40 A6
Martin House. 5 New Mal KT3 38 E5
Martin Rd. Stough GU2 109 A3
Martin Way. Friml GU16 65 E2
Martin Way. Merton SW19 & SW20 & SM4 39 E6
Martin Way. Woking GU21 69 A1
Martin's Heron Sta. Brack RG12 27 F5
Martin's Rd. Broml BR2 44 F7
Martindale. Mortl SW14 7 C2
Martindale Ave. Friml GU15 66 C4
Martindale Cl. Merrow GU4 110 D3
Martindale Rd. Balham SW12 21 B8
Martindale Rd. Hounsl TW4 4 E4
Martindale Rd. Woking GU21 69 A1
Martindale Sch. Hounsl TW4 4 E4
Martineau Cl. Esher KT10 55 D6
Martineau Dr. Dork RH4 136 B5
Martingale Cl. Sunby TW16 35 A5
Martingale Ct. Alder GU11 104 E2
Martingales Cl. Rich TW10 17 D5
Martins Cl. Blckw GU17 64 D4
Martins Cl. Merrow GU1 110 C2
Martins Cl. W Wick BR4 63 D8
Martins Dr. Woki RG11 25 B7
Martins La. Brack RG12 27 E6
Martins The. Crawl D RH10 204 C8
Martins The. For Hil SE26 23 B3
Martins Wood. Witley GU8 170 E7
Martinsyde. Mayb GU22 70 C2
Martlet Cnr. Rudg RH12 214 D7
Martlets Cl. Horsh RH12 217 C5
Martlets The. Crawl RH10 201 E6
Marton Cl. Catf SE6 24 A5
Marts The. Rudg RH12 214 D7
Martyns Pl. E Grins RH19 206 A8
Martyr Rd. Guild GU1 130 D8
Martyrs Ave. Crawl RH11 181 D1
Martyrs La. Sheer GU21 70 B7
Marvell Cl. Crawl RH10 202 C8
Marwell Cl. Coney H BR4 63 F8
Mary Adelaide Cl. King U T SW15 18 E5
Mary Rd. Guild GU1 130 C8
Mary Rose Cl. Hampt TW12 36 A8
Mary Rose Gdns. Chess KT9 56 E6
Mary Vale. Godal GU7 150 D2
Mary's Terr. Twick TW1 17 A8
Marygold House. Hounsl TW3 5 C6
Maryhill Cl. Kenley CR8 80 C2
Maryland Ct. King U T KT1 38 B7
Maryland Rd. S Norw CR7 42 B8
Maryland Way. Sunby TW16 35 A7
Marymount International Sch. King U T KT2 18 C1
Masefield Ct. 10 Surb KT6 37 D2
Masefield Rd. Crawl RH11 200 E3
Masefield Rd. Hampt TW13 15 F4
Masefield Way. Stan TW19 13 F7
Maskall Cl. Streat SW2 22 A7
Maskani Wlk. Streat SW16 21 C1
Maskell Rd. Wands SW17 20 C5
Maskell Way. Farnb GU14 84 D3
Mason Cl. E Grins RH19 185 E2
Mason Cl. Hampt TW12 35 F8
Mason Cl. Wimble SW20 39 D8
Mason Ct. 3 Penge SE19 22 F1
Mason Rd. Crawl RH10 201 E4
Mason Rd. W Heath GU14 84 E6
Mason Way. Alder GU11 126 B7
Mason's Ave. Croy CR0 & CR9 61 C7
Mason's Bridge Rd. Earls RH1 140 C3
Mason's Bridge Rd. Salfs RH1 140 C3
Mason's Pl. Mitch CR4 40 F8
Masonic Hall Rd. Chert KT16 32 F3
Masons Paddock. Dork RH4 115 A1
Massetts Rd. Horley RH6 161 A2
Master Cl. Oxted RH8 122 E6
Mastin House. Wands SW18 20 A7
Maswell Park Cres. Islew TW3 5 C2
Maswell Park Rd. Islew TW3 5 C3
Matham Rd. E Mole KT8 36 D4
Mathew Terr. Alder GU11 105 C2
Mathews Cl. Farnb GU14 105 E8
Mathias Cl. Epsom KT18 76 C6
Mathisen Way. Poyle SL3 1 E6
Mathon Ct. Guild GU1 109 F1
Matlock Cres. Cheam SM3 58 E6
Matlock Gdns. Cheam SM1 & SM3 58 E6
Matlock Pl. Cheam SM1 & SM3 58 E6
Matlock Rd. Cater CR3 100 E6
Matlock Way. King U T KT3 38 D8
Matthew Arnold Cl. Cobham KT11 73 A5
Matthew Arnold Sch The. Stain TW18 13 C2
Matthew Ct. Mitch CR4 41 D4
Matthew Rd. Alder GU9 125 E8
Matthew's Gdns. New Add CR0 82 D8
Matthew's St. Dovgn RH2 139 A5
Matthews Ct. Ascot SL5 29 D5
Matthews Dr. Worth RH10 202 C3
Matthews La. Stain TW18 12 F4
Matthews Rd. Camb GU15 65 C8
Matthewsgreen Rd. Woki RG11 25 A8
Matthey Pl. Crawl RH10 182 D1
Matthias Ct. 12 Rich TW10 6 E1
Maultway Cl. Camb GU15 66 B8
Maultway Cres. Camb GU15 66 B8
Maultway N. Camb GU15 47 B1
Maultway The. Camb GU15 & GU16 66 D6
Maultway The. Friml GU15 & GU16 66 D6
Maunsell Pk. Crawl RH10 202 B6
Maurice Ave. Cater CR3 100 D5
Maurice Ct. 3 Brent TW8 6 D7
Mavery Ct. Broml BR1 24 F1
Mavins Rd. M Bourn GU9 146 B8

Mavis Ave. Worc Pk KT19 ... 57 E5
Mavis Cl. Ottsh KT16 ... 51 D4
Mawbey Rd. Ottsh KT16 ... 51 D4
Mawson Cl. Merton SW20 ... 39 E7
Mawson La. Chisw W4 ... 7 F3
Maxine Cl. Sandh GU17 ... 45 B1
Maxton Wlk. Crawl RH11 ... 201 B2
Maxwell Cl. Croy CR0 ... 41 E1
Maxwell Ct. Dulw SE21 ... 23 A7
Maxwell Dr. W Byfl KT14 ... 71 C8
Maxwell Rd. Ashf TW15 ... 14 C2
Maxwell Way. Crawl RH10 ... 182 A1
May Cl. Chess KT9 ... 56 F4
May Cl. Ock Rid GU7 ... 150 B2
May Cl. 2 Sandh GU15 ... 64 D8
May Cotts. L Kings CR5 ... 98 B2
May Cres. Ash GU12 ... 105 E1
May Ct. 2 Merton SW19 ... 40 C8
May Rd. Twick TW2 ... 16 E7
May's Hill Rd. Beck BR2 ... 44 E6
Mayberry Pl. Surb KT5 ... 37 F2
Maybourne Grange. S Croy CR0 61 E8
Maybourne Rise. Westfd GU22 .. 89 D3
Maybury Cl. Burgh H KT20 ... 97 E8
Maybury Cl. Friml GU16 ... 85 D8
Maybury Ct. Mayb GU22 ... 70 B2
Maybury Cty Inf Sch.
  Woking GU21 ... 70 A3
Maybury Hill. Mayb GU21 & GU22 70 B2
Maybury Rd. Woking GU21 ... 70 A3
Maybury Rough. Mayb GU22 ... 70 B2
Maybury St. Up Toot SW17 ... 20 E3
Maycroft. Coney H BR2 ... 44 F1
Maycross Ave. Morden SM4 ... 40 A5
Mayday Hospl. Thorn H CR7 ... 42 B3
Mayday Rd. Thorn H CR0 & CR7 .. 42 B3
Maydwell Ave. Slinfd RH13 ... 215 C2
Mayefield Rd. Thorn H CR7 ... 41 F4
Mayell Cl. Leahd KT22 ... 95 C4
Mayes Cl. Warlgm CR6 ... 81 D1
Mayes La. Warn RH12 ... 197 F3
Mayfair Ave. New Mal KT4 ... 39 A1
Mayfair Ave. Twick TW2 ... 16 C8
Mayfair Cl. Beck BR3 ... 44 B8
Mayfair Cl. Surb KT6 ... 37 E1
Mayfair Ct. Beck BR3 ... 44 B8
Mayfair Ct. 4 S Croy CR0 ... 61 F8
Mayfield. Dorman RH7 ... 165 A1
Mayfield. Hersh KT12 ... 54 C6
Mayfield. Rowl GU10 ... 145 F3
Mayfield. Worth RH10 ... 202 D6
Mayfield Ave. Woodhm KT15 ... 52 C1
Mayfield Cl. Ashf TW15 ... 14 B2
Mayfield Cl. Earls RH1 ... 140 A3
Mayfield Cl. Farnh GU9 ... 126 B6
Mayfield Cl. Hersh KT12 ... 54 A6
Mayfield Cl. Hinch W KT7 ... 37 B1
Mayfield Cl. Penge SE20 ... 43 B8
Mayfield Cl. Weyb KT15 ... 52 C1
Mayfield Cres. Thorn H CR7 ... 41 F5
Mayfield Ct. Earls RH1 ... 139 F4
Mayfield Ct. Sutton SM2 ... 59 C3
Mayfield Cty Inf Sch.
  W Heath GU14 ... 85 B6
Mayfield Cty Jun Sch.
  W Heath GU14 ... 85 A6
Mayfield Gdns. Egham TW18 ... 12 F2
Mayfield Gdns. Walt O T KT12 ... 54 A6
Mayfield Rd. Camb GU15 ... 65 B1
Mayfield Rd. Hersh KT12 ... 54 A6
Mayfield Rd. Merton SW19 ... 39 F8
Mayfield Rd. S Croy CR2 ... 61 D2
Mayfield Rd. Sutton SM2 ... 59 D4
Mayfield Rd. W Heath GU14 ... 84 F7
Mayfield Rd. Wilts KT15 ... 52 F5
Mayflower Cl. Worth RH10 ... 202 D5
Mayford Cl. Balham SW12 ... 20 F8
Mayford Cl. Penge BR3 ... 43 D6
Mayford Cl. Westfd GU22 ... 89 D5
Mayford Rd. Balham SW12 ... 21 A8
Mayhurst Ave. Mayb GU22 ... 70 C3
Mayhurst Cl. Mayb GU22 ... 70 C3
Mayhurst Cres. Mayb GU22 ... 70 C3
Maynard Ct. Stain TW18 ... 13 A4
Maynooth Gdns. Carsh SM4 ... 40 F2
Mayo Rd. Thorn H CR0 ... 42 D4
Mayo Rd. Walt O T KT12 ... 35 A2
Mayow Rd. For Hil SE23 & SE26 .. 23 D4
Maypole Rd. Ash W RH19 ... 206 E6
Maypole Rd. E Grins RH19 ... 185 D2
Mayroyd Ave. Tolw KT6 ... 57 A8
Mays Cl. Whit V KT13 ... 52 F1
Mays Cnr. Send GU23 ... 90 D3
Mays Gr. Send GU23 ... 90 D4
Mays Rd. Tedd TW11 & TW12 ... 16 D3
Mays Rd. Woki RG11 ... 25 E6
Maysfield Rd. Send GU23 ... 90 D4
Maytree Cl. Belff GU1 ... 109 C5
Maytree Ct. Mitch CR4 ... 41 A6
Maytree Wlk. Streat SW2 ... 22 A6
Maytrees. Knaph GU21 ... 68 C2
Maywater Cl. S Croy CR2 ... 80 D8
Maywood Cl. Beck BR3 ... 24 B1
Maywood Dr. Camb GU15 ... 66 A7
Maze Rd. Rich TW9 ... 7 A7
McAlmont Ridge. Farnc GU7 ... 150 D7
McCarthy Rd. Felt TW13 ... 15 D3
McCormick House. 9
  Streat SW2 ... 22 A7
McDonald House. 1
  King U T KT1 ... 17 F1
McDonough Cl. Chess KT9 ... 56 E6
McDougall Ct. Rich TW9 ... 7 A5
McIndoe Rd. E Grins RH19 ... 185 D3
McIntosh Cl. Wallin SM6 ... 60 E3
McIver Cl. Felb RH19 ... 184 F4
McKay Cl. Alder GU11 ... 105 C3
McKay Rd. Wimble SW20 ... 19 C2
Mckay Trad Est. Poyle SL3 ... 1 E5
McKinlay Ct. Beck BR3 ... 43 F7

Mcleod Ct. Dulw SE21 ... 23 A7
McLeod House. For Hil SE23 ... 23 C6
McMillan Cl. Catf SE6 ... 24 F7
McNaughton Cl. Farnb GU14 ... 84 D3
McRae Cl. Carsh CR4 ... 40 F2
Meachen Cl. Woki RG11 ... 25 C6
Mead Ave. Salfs RH1 ... 140 A1
Mead Cl. Cran GU6 ... 174 E2
Mead Cl. Egham TW20 ... 12 B2
Mead Cl. Redh RH1 ... 119 A4
Mead Cres. Carsh SM1 ... 59 E6
Mead Cres. L Book KT23 ... 94 A2
Mead Ct. Woking GU21 ... 68 E3
Mead Dr. Coulsd CR5 ... 79 E5
Mead End. Ashtd KT21 ... 75 F3
Mead La. Chert KT16 ... 33 C1
Mead La. Farnh GU9 ... 125 B2
Mead Path. Mitch SW17 ... 20 D2
Mead Pl. Thorn H CR0 ... 42 C1
Mead Rd. Carter CR3 ... 100 F4
Mead Rd. Cran GU6 ... 174 E3
Mead Rd. Crawl RH10 ... 201 F7
Mead Rd. Hersh KT12 ... 54 E6
Mead Rd. Hind GU26 ... 188 F4
Mead Rd. Rich TW10 ... 17 C5
Mead The. Ashtd KT21 ... 95 E8
Mead The. Beck BR3 ... 44 C8
Mead The. Dork RH4 ... 136 C4
Mead The. Farnb GU14 ... 85 B4
Mead The. W Wick BR4 ... 44 D1
Mead The. Wallin SM6 ... 60 D4
Mead Way. Burph GU4 ... 110 C6
Mead Way. Coulsd CR5 ... 79 F1
Mead Way. Croy CR0 ... 62 E8
Mead Way. Hayes BR2 & BR4 ... 44 F3
Meadcroft House. 4
  New Mal KT3 ... 38 E2
Meade Cl. Brent W4 ... 7 A8
Meade Cl. Bagsh GU19 ... 47 F3
Meade Cl. Walt o t H KT20 ... 97 A3
Meades Cl. Dorman RH7 ... 165 B1
Meades The. Dorman RH7 ... 165 A1
Meadfoot Rd. Streat SW16 ... 41 C8
Meadhurst Rd. Chert KT16 ... 33 B1
Meadhurst Sports Club.
  Ashf TW16 ... 14 F3
Meadlands Dr. Rich TW10 ... 17 D6
Meadlands Prim Sch. Rich TW10 17 C4
Meadow App. Copth RH10 ... 183 A3
Meadow Ave. Croy CR0 ... 43 D3
Meadow Bank. E Hors KT24 ... 112 E8
Meadow Bglws. Chil GU4 ... 131 B3
Meadow Brook Ind Ctr.
  Crawl RH10 ... 182 A1
Meadow Cl. Ash V GU12 ... 85 F1
Meadow Cl. Catf SE6 ... 24 A3
Meadow Cl. Copth RH10 ... 183 A3
Meadow Cl. Farnc GU7 ... 150 E7
Meadow Cl. Hawley GU17 ... 64 D4
Meadow Cl. Hersh KT12 ... 54 F6
Meadow Cl. Hinch W KT10 ... 55 F7
Meadow Cl. Horsh RH12 ... 218 A5
Meadow Cl. Milf GU8 ... 150 A1
Meadow Cl. Purley CR8 ... 79 D6
Meadow Cl. Rich TW10 ... 17 E7
Meadow Cl. Sutton SM1 ... 59 C8
Meadow Cl. Twick TW4 ... 16 A8
Meadow Cl. W Barn SW20 ... 39 C5
Meadow Cotts. W End GU24 ... 67 F7
Meadow Croft Cl. Horley RH6 .. 182 C8
Meadow Ct. Epsom KT18 ... 76 C6
Meadow Ct. Farnb GU14 ... 84 F4
Meadow Ct. Stain TW18 ... 12 E5
Meadow Dr. Send M GU23 ... 90 F4
Meadow Farm La. Horsh RH12 217 F7
Meadow Gate Rd. Farnb GU14 .. 84 F1
Meadow Gdns. Egham TW18 ... 12 D3
Meadow Hill. Coulsd CR5 & CR8 . 79 C6
Meadow Hill. New Mal KT3 ... 38 E3
Meadow Hill. Purley CR5 & CR8 .. 79 C6
Meadow House. Merrow GU4 . 110 D2
Meadow La. Fetch KT22 ... 94 C5
Meadow Pl. Chisw W4 ... 7 E7
Meadow Rd. Ashf TW15 ... 14 D3
Meadow Rd. Ashtd KT21 ... 75 E2
Meadow Rd. Broml BR2 ... 44 E7
Meadow Rd. Burph GU4 ... 110 A5
Meadow Rd. Carsh SM1 ... 59 E5
Meadow Rd. Clayg KT10 ... 55 E4
Meadow Rd. Farnb GU14 ... 85 B7
Meadow Rd. Felt TW13 ... 15 E6
Meadow Rd. Merton SW20 ... 20 C1
Meadow Rd. Went GU25 & SL5 ... 30 E4
Meadow Rd. Woki RG11 ... 25 A5
Meadow Rise. Coulsd CR5 ... 79 D6
Meadow Rise. Knaph GU21 ... 68 D2
Meadow Stile. Croy CR0 & CR9 .. 61 C7
Meadow The. Copth RH10 ... 183 A3
Meadow Vale. Shottm GU27 ... 208 A6
Meadow Vale Cty Prim Sch.
  Brack RG12 ... 26 F8
Meadow View. Smallf RH6 ... 162 C3
Meadow View Rd. Thorn H CR7 . 42 B4
Meadow Waye. Addl KT15 ... 52 B6
Meadow Way. Blckw GU17 ... 64 C5
Meadow Way. Brack RG12 ... 27 A8
Meadow Way. Burgh H KT20 ... 77 E2
Meadow Way. Chess KT9 ... 56 E5
Meadow Way. Dovgn RG12 ... 139 B5
Meadow Way. Fetch KT23 ... 94 B4
Meadow Way. Rowl GU10 ... 145 F3
Meadow Way. W End GU24 ... 67 F6
Meadow Way. W Hors KT24 ... 92 D2
Meadow Way. Woki RG11 ... 25 A5
Meadow Wlk.
  W Ewell KT19 & KT19 ... 57 F3
Meadow Wlk. Walt o t H KT20 ... 97 B3
Meadow Wlk. Woki RG11 ... 25 A6

Meadowbank. Surb KT5 ... 37 F3
Meadowbank Gdns.
  Cranf TW4 & TW5 ... 4 B6
Meadowbank Rd. Lhtwat GU18 .. 48 C1
Meadowbrook. Oxted RH8 ... 122 D5
Meadowbrook Cl. Poyle SL3 ... 1 F6
Meadowbrook Rd. Dork RH4 ... 136 A7
Meadowcroft Cl. Crawl RH11 ... 200 F8
Meadowcroft Cl. E Grins RH19 . 185 C2
Meadowcroft Cty Sch.
  Addl KT16 ... 51 F7
Meadowlands. Cobham KT11 ... 73 A6
Meadowlands. Crawl RH10 ... 201 C6
Meadowlands. Oxted RH8 ... 123 A1
Meadowlands. W Clan GU4 ... 111 B5
Meadowlea Cl. Harm UB7 ... 2 D8
Meadows End. Sunby TW16 ... 35 A8
Meadows Leigh Cl. Weyb KT13 . 53 C7
Meadows The. Ash GU12 ... 106 B2
Meadows The. Churt GU10 ... 167 F1
Meadows The. Guild GU2 ... 130 C6
Meadows The. Sandh GU15 ... 64 E5
Meadows The. Warlgm GU6 ... 81 C3
Meadowside. Fetch KT23 ... 94 A4
Meadowside. Horley RH6 ... 161 B4
Meadowside. Walt O T KT12 ... 54 B8
Meadowside Rd. Belm SM2 ... 58 E2
Meadowview. Stan TW19 ... 1 A7
Meadowview Rd. Catf SE6 ... 24 A3
Meadowview Rd. W Ewell KT19 . 57 E2
Meadowview Rd. W Ewell KT19 . 57 E2
Meadrow. Farnc GU7 ... 150 F6
Meadrow Lock. Farnc GU7 ... 151 A6
Meads Cty Prim Sch The.
  E Grins RH19 ... 205 E7
Meads Rd. Merrow GU1 ... 110 B1
Meads The. Cheam SM3 ... 58 E2
Meads The. E Grins RH19 ... 205 E7
Meads The. Shottm GU27 ... 207 F6
Meads The. Whitt V KT13 ... 53 D4
Meadside. 4 Epsom KT18 ... 76 D6
Meadside. 7 Woking GU21 ... 69 F1
Meadsview Ct. 3 Farnb GU14 ... 85 B4
Meadvale. Horsh RH12 ... 216 F2
Meadvale Rd. Croy CR0 ... 43 A3
Meadway. Ashf TW15 ... 14 A4
Meadway. Beck BR3 ... 44 C8
Meadway. Effing KT24 ... 113 C7
Meadway. Epsom KT19 ... 76 C7
Meadway. Esher KT10 ... 55 B2
Meadway. Friml GU16 ... 65 F2
Meadway. Oxsh KT22 ... 74 E5
Meadway. Shottm GU27 ... 207 F6
Meadway. Stain TW18 ... 13 A1
Meadway. Tolw KT5 ... 38 C1
Meadway. Twick TW2 ... 16 D7
Meadway. W Barn SW20 ... 39 C5
Meadway. Warlgm CR6 ... 81 C3
Meadway Cl. Stain TW18 ... 13 A1
Meadway Dr. Hcrse GU21 ... 69 D4
Meadway Dr. New Haw KT15 ... 52 C3
Meadway The. Horley RH6 ... 161 C3
Meaford Way. Penge SE20 ... 23 B1
Meare Cl. Tadw KT20 ... 97 C4
Meath Green Ave. Horley RH6 . 160 F5
Meath Green Cty Fst Sch.
  Horley RH6 ... 160 F5
Meath Green Cty Inf Sch.
  Horley RH6 ... 161 A5
Meath Green Cty Jun Sch.
  Horley RH6 ... 160 F5
Meath Green La.
  Horley RH1 & RH6 ... 160 E6
Meath Green La.
  Salfs RH1 & RH6 ... 160 E6
Meath St. Ottsh RH11 ... 51 D3
Medawar Rd. Onsl V GU2 ... 129 D8
Mede Cl. Wray TW19 ... 11 D7
Mede Ct. Stain TW18 ... 12 E5
Mede Field. Fetch KT22 ... 94 D3
Medfield St. Putney SW15 ... 19 B8
Medhurst Cl. Chobh GU24 ... 49 F2
Medina Ave. Hinch W KT10 ... 55 E7
Medlake Rd. Egham TW20 ... 12 C2
Medland Cl. Burgh H KT20 ... 97 C7
Medland Gn. Burgh H KT20 ... 97 C7
Medland Rise.
  Burgh H KT18 & KT20 ... 97 C8
Medland Rise Cty Prim Schs.
  Burgh H KT20 ... 97 C8
Medway. Turn H RH10 ... 204 A5
Medway Cl. Croy CR0 ... 43 C3
Medway Cl. Horsh RH12 ... 218 B5
Medway Ct. S Norw SE25 ... 42 E4
Medway Dr. E Grins RH19 ... 205 D6
Medway Dr. For Row RH18 ... 206 F2
Medway Dr. W Heath GU14 ... 84 E7
Medway Rd. Crawl RH11 ... 200 F5
Medwyn Wlk. Horsh RH12 ... 217 C2
Melbourne Cl. Wallin SM6 ... 60 C5
Melbourne Ct. Penge SE20 ... 23 A1
Melbourne Ct. Twick TW2 ... 16 D7
Melbourne Mews. Lewish SE6 .. 24 C8
Melbourne Rd. Merton SW19 ... 40 A8
Melbourne Rd. Tedd TW11 ... 17 C2
Melbourne Rd. Wallin SM6 ... 60 C5
Melbourne Way. Horsh RH12 .. 217 F5
Melbury Cl. Chert KT16 ... 33 A2
Melbury Cl. Clayg KT10 ... 56 B4
Melbury Cl. W Byfl KT14 ... 71 A5
Melbury Gdns. Wimble SW20 ... 39 B8
Melbury House. Twick TW2 ... 16 D6
Meldon Cl. Wallin SM6 ... 60 E5
Meldone Cl. Tolw KT5 ... 38 B3
Meldrum Cl. Oxted RH8 ... 123 A4
Melfont Ave. Thorn H CR7 ... 42 B6
Melford Cl. Chess KT9 ... 56 F5
Melford Ct. Dulw SE22 ... 23 A8
Melford Ct. Sutton SM2 ... 59 C3

Melford Rd. Dulw SE21 & SE22 .. 23 A7
Melfort Rd. Thorn H CR7 & SW16 42 B6
Meliot Rd. Catf SE6 ... 24 D6
Melksham Cl. Horsh RH13 ... 217 E1
Meller Cl. Wallin SM6 ... 60 A5
Mellersh Hill Rd. Woner GU5 .. 152 C6
Mellish Ct. Surb KT6 ... 37 E3
Mellison Rd. Up Toot SW17 ... 20 E3
Mellor Cl. Walt O T KT12 ... 35 F2
Mellor Ct. 2 Merton SW19 ... 20 C1
Mellor House. 2 Dulw SE21 ... 22 E4
Mellow Cl. Banstd SM7 ... 78 C5
Mellows Rd. Wallin SM6 ... 60 D5
Melody Rd. Bigg H TN16 ... 83 C1
Melrose. Easth RG12 ... 27 B1
Melrose Ave. Mitch CR4 ... 21 B1
Melrose Ave. Thorn H SW16 ... 42 A6
Melrose Ave. Twick TW2 ... 16 B8
Melrose Ave. W Heath GU14 ... 84 E5
Melrose Gdns. Hersh KT12 ... 54 C5
Melrose Gdns. King U T KT3 ... 38 D6
Melrose Rd. Barnes SW13 ... 7 F5
Melrose Rd. Bigg H TN16 ... 83 C3
Melrose Rd. Coulsd CR5 ... 79 B4
Melrose Rd. Merton SW19 ... 40 A8
Melrose Rd. Weyb KT13 ... 53 A5
Melrose Sch. Mitch CR4 ... 40 E6
Melrose Tudor. Wallin SM6 ... 60 E5
Melsa Rd. Morden SM4 ... 40 C3
Melton Ct. 8 Croy CR0 ... 61 F8
Melton Ct. 2 Twick TW1 ... 17 B8
Melton Fields. Epsom KT19 ... 57 D2
Melton Pl. Epsom KT19 ... 57 D2
Melton Rd. Merst RH1 ... 119 C5
Melville Ave. Friml GU16 ... 65 F1
Melville Ave. S Croy CR0 & CR2 .. 61 F5
Melville Ave. Wimble SW20 ... 19 A1
Melvin Ct. 11 Rich TW9 ... 7 A6
Melvin Rd. Penge SE20 ... 43 C8
Melvinshaw. Leahd KT22 ... 95 C6
Membury Cl. Friml GU16 ... 86 A7
Membury Wlk. Brack RG12 ... 27 F5
Memorial Cl. Heston TW5 ... 4 F8
Memory Cotts. Burgh H KT20 ... 97 E8
Mendip Cl. For Hil SE26 ... 23 C4
Mendip Cl. Harl U83 ... 3 D7
Mendip Cl. N Cheam KT4 ... 58 C8
Mendip Rd. Brack RG12 ... 27 E4
Mendip Rd. W Heath GU14 ... 84 E7
Mendip Wlk. Crawl RH11 ... 201 B6
Menin Way. M Bourn GU9 ... 125 D1
Menlo Gdns. S Norw SE19 ... 22 D1
Meon Cl. Tadw KT20 ... 97 B5
Meon Ct. W Heath GU14 ... 84 D6
Meon Ct. Hounsl TW7 ... 5 E5
Meopham Rd. Mitch CR4 & SW16 41 E8
Merantum Way. Merton SW19 ... 40 C8
Merantum Way. Mitch SW19 ... 40 C8
Mercer Cl. Thame D KT7 ... 36 F2
Mercer Cl. Worth RH10 ... 202 C3
Mercer Rd. Faygt RH12 ... 217 C8
Merchiston Rd. Catf SE6 ... 24 D6
Mercia Wlk. 5 Woking GU21 ... 69 F2
Mercury Cl. Crawl RH11 ... 200 E3
Mercury Ctr. Felt TW14 ... 4 B2
Mere Cl. Putney SW15 & SW19 .. 19 D8
Mere Rd. Croy CR0 ... 43 D2
Mere Rd. Oat Pk KT13 ... 53 D7
Mere Rd. Shep TW17 ... 34 B3
Mere Rd. Tadw KT20 ... 97 B4
Mere Rd. Walt o t H KT20 ... 97 B4
Merebank La. Croy CR0 & SM6 .. 60 F5
Merefield Gdns. Burgh H KT20 . 97 D8
Meretune Ct. Morden SM4 ... 39 F6
Merevale Cres. Morden SM4 ... 40 C3
Mereway Industry. Twick TW2 .. 16 E7
Mereway Rd. Twick TW2 ... 16 E7
Mereworth Cl. Hayes BR2 ... 44 F4
Mereworth Dr. Crawl RH10 ... 202 D8
Meridian Ct. Catf SE6 ... 24 F7
Meridian Ct. Croy CR0 ... 61 A6
Meridian Ct. Sunnin SL5 ... 29 C1
Meridian Gr. Horley RH6 ... 161 C4
Meridian Way. E Grins RH19 ... 185 F3
Merland Cl. Burgh H KT20 ... 97 C7
Merland Gn. Burgh H KT20 ... 97 C7
Merle Common Rd. Limps RH8 144 B7
Merlewood. Brack RG12 ... 27 D4
Merlewood Cl. Cater CR3 ... 100 D7
Merlin Cl. Bra Hil SL3 ... 1 B8
Merlin Cl. Crawl RH11 ... 200 E6
Merlin Cl. Mitch CR4 ... 40 E6
Merlin Cl. S Croy CR0 ... 61 E6
Merlin Clove. Wink RG12 ... 8 B2
Merlin Ct. Beck BR2 ... 44 F5
Merlin Ct. Friml GU16 ... 65 D1
Merlin Ctr. Crawl RH11 ... 181 D2
Merlin Gr. Beck BR3 ... 44 A4
Merlin Rd. Farnb GU14 ... 85 B2
Merlin Way. E Grins RH19 ... 186 A3
Merlin Way. Farnb GU14 ... 84 D3
Merlins Cl. M Bourn GU9 ... 125 C1
Merrick House. Reig RH2 ... 118 C1
Merricks Rd. Mortl SW14 ... 7 B3
Merrilands Rd. N Cheam KT4 ... 39 C1
Merrilyn Cl. Clayg KT10 ... 56 A5
Merrist Wood Agricultural Coll
  Brewerstreet Farm Ctr.
  Bletch RH1 ... 120 C4
Merrist Wood Coll (Agricultural).
  Worpl GU3 ... 108 C7
Merritt Gdns. Chess KT9 ... 56 C4
Merrivale Gdns. Horse GU21 ... 69 C2
Merrow Bsns Ctr. Merrow GU4 110 D4

Merrow CE Inf Sch.
  Merrow GU4 ... 110 D3
Merrow Chase. Merrow GU1 ... 110 D1
Merrow Common Rd.
  Merrow GU4 ... 110 D4
Merrow Copse. Merrow GU1 ... 110 B2
Merrow Croft. Merrow GU1 ... 110 C2
Merrow Cross. Merrow GU1 ... 110 D1
Merrow Ct. Mitch CR4 ... 40 D7
Merrow La. Burph GU4 ... 110 C5
Merrow La. Merrow GU4 ... 110 C4
Merrow Rd. E Ewell SM2 ... 58 D2
Merrow St. Merrow GU1 & GU4 110 D2
Merrow Way. New Add CR0 ... 63 C4
Merrow Woods. Merrow GU1 ... 110 B3
Merryacres. Witley GU8 ... 170 E6
Merryfield Dr. Horsh RH12 ... 217 A3
Merryhill Rd. Brack RG12 ... 27 B8
Merryhills Cl. Bigg H TN16 ... 83 D3
Merryhills La. Loxwd RH14 ... 213 A5
Merrylands. Addl KT16 ... 51 E7
Merrylands Ct. L Book KT23 ... 93 F3
Merrylands Farm. Fetch KT23 ... 94 A3
Merrylands Rd. L Book KT23 ... 93 F3
Merryman Dr. Crowth RG11 ... 45 A7
Merrymeet. Woodm SM7 ... 78 F5
Merryweather Ct. 1
  New Mal KT3 ... 38 E4
Merrywood. Leahd KT22 ... 95 C6
Merrywood Gr. Reig KT20 ... 117 C5
Merrywood Pk. Friml GU15 ... 65 F4
Merrywood Pk. Reig RH2 ... 118 B3
Merryworth Cl. Ash GU12 ... 105 F1
Mersham Pl. Penge SE20 ... 43 B8
Mersham Pl. S Norw CR7 ... 42 D7
Mersham Rd. S Norw CR7 ... 42 D7
Merstham Cty Fst Sch.
  Merst RH1 ... 119 C6
Merstham Rd. Bletch RH1 ... 120 A5
Merstham Sta. Merst RH1 ... 119 C7
Merton Abbey Prim Sch.
  Merton SW19 ... 40 B8
Merton Cl. Sandh GU15 ... 45 F2
Merton Gdns. Burgh H KT20 ... 97 D8
Merton Hall Gdns. Merton SW20 39 E8
Merton Hall Rd.
  Merton SW19 & SW20 ... 39 E8
Merton High St. Merton SW19 ... 20 C1
Merton House. Wands SW18 ... 20 A7
Merton Ind Pk. Merton SW19 ... 40 C8
Merton Mansions. Merton SW20 39 D7
Merton Park Par. Merton SW19 39 F8
Merton Park Prim Sch.
  Merton SW19 ... 40 A7
Merton Park Sta. Merton SW19 . 40 A8
Merton Pl. 9 Merton SW19 ... 20 C1
Merton Rd. Beck BR3 ... 43 A4
Merton Rd. Merton SW19 ... 20 B1
Merton Rd. Wands SW18 ... 20 A7
Merton Sixth Form Coll.
  Morden SM4 ... 40 C4
Merton Tech Coll. Morden SM4 . 39 F4
Merton Tech Coll (Annexe).
  Merton SW19 ... 40 A8
Merton Way. E Mole KT8 ... 36 C6
Merton Way. Leahd KT22 ... 95 A8
Merton Wlk. Leahd KT22 ... 75 A1
Mervyn Rd. Shep TW17 ... 34 C2
Metcalf Rd. Ashf TW15 ... 14 B3
Metcalf Way. Crawl RH11 ... 181 D2
Metcalfe Wlk. Felt TW13 ... 15 E4
Meteor Rd. Farnb GU14 ... 85 A1
Meteor Way. Wallin SM6 ... 60 E3
Meteorological Off (HQ).
  Brack RG12 ... 27 D7
Metro Bsns Ctr The. Penge SE26 23 F3
Metro Ctr. W Barn SM4 ... 39 D2
Metro Ind Ctr. Hounsl TW7 ... 5 E5
Meudon Ave. Farnb GU14 ... 85 B3
Meudon Ct. King U T KT6 ... 37 D4
Meville Ct. Guild GU2 ... 130 C6
Mews Ct. E Grins RH19 ... 205 F6
Mews The. Banstd SM7 ... 78 B4
Mews The. Broad H RH12 ... 216 D4
Mews The. Dunsf GU8 ... 192 F5
Mews The. Guild GU8 ... 130 C8
Mewsend. Bigg H TN16 ... 83 D3
Meyer House. 1 Balham SW12 . 21 B8
Meyrick Cl. Woking GU21 ... 68 E3
Mezel Hill Cotts. Old W SL4 ... 10 C3
Miall Wlk. For Hil SE26 ... 23 E4
Michael Cres. Horley RH6 ... 161 A1
Michael Fields. For Row RH18 .. 206 E2
Michael Rd. S Norw SE25 ... 42 E5
Michaelson House. 4 Dulw SE21 22 E4
Michel's Row. 2 Rich TW9 ... 6 E3
Micheldever Way. Brack RG12 .. 27 F4
Michelet Cl. Lhtwat GU18 ... 48 B1
Michelham Gdns. Burgh H KT20 97 C7
Michelham Gdns. Twick TW1 ... 16 F5
Michell Cl. Horsh RH12 ... 217 A2
Michels Almshouses. 11
  Rich TW10 ... 6 E2
Mickle Hill. Sandh GU17 ... 45 A1
Micklefield Sch. Reig RH2 ... 118 A2
Mickleham Dr. Leahd KT22 & RH5 95 C1
Mickleham Gdns. Cheam SM3 .. 58 E4
Mickleham Hall. Mickle RH5 ... 115 C7
Mickleham Way. New Add CR0 .. 63 D3
Mid Holmwood La. Dork RH5 .. 136 B1
Mid St. Nutf RH1 ... 119 F1
Mid St. S Nutf RH1 ... 140 F7
Middle Ave. M Bourn GU9 ... 146 D8
Middle Bourne La.
  M Bourn GU10 & GU9 ... 146 C2
Middle Church La. 12
  Farnh GU9 ... 125 B2
Middle Cl. Coulsd CR5 ... 100 A7

262 Mid – Moo

Middle Cl. Ewell KT17 76 E7
Middle Cl. Friml GU15 66 C6
Middle Farm Cl. Effing KT24 113 D8
Middle Farm Pl. Effing KT24 113 D8
Middle Gn. Stain TW18 13 D1
Middle Gordon Rd. Camb GU15 65 D5
Middle Green Cl. 3 Surb KT5 37 F3
Middle Hill. Alder GU11 105 A3
Middle Hill. Eng Gn TW20 11 D3
Middle Hill. Frensh GU10 146 C1
Middle La. Ewell KT17 76 E7
Middle La. Tedd TW11 16 F2
Middle Old Pk. Farnh GU9 124 F4
Middle Rd. Leahd KT22 95 B6
Middle Rd. Mitch SW16 41 D7
Middle Row. 1 E Grins RH19 205 F8
Middle St. Brock RH3 137 C5
Middle St. Croy CR0 & CR9 61 C7
Middle St. Horsh RH12 217 C2
Middle St. Shere GU5 133 A4
Middle Way. Mitch SW16 41 D7
Middlefield. Horley RH6 161 C4
Middlefield. M Bourn GU9 146 A7
Middlefields. New Add CR0 62 E2
Middlemarch. Witley GU8 170 E5
Middlemead Cl. L Book KT23 94 A2
Middlemead Rd. L Book KT23 93 F2
Middlemoor Rd. Friml GU16 85 E8
Middlesex Ct. Addl KT15 52 C6
Middlesex House. 6 Penge SE20 23 C1
Middlesex Rd. Mitch CR4 41 E4
Middleton Gdns. W Heath GU14 84 E6
Middleton Rd. Camb GU15 65 F7
Middleton Rd. Carsh CR4 & SM5 40 D2
Middleton Rd. Downs KT11 93 C8
Middleton Rd. Epsom KT19 57 D1
Middleton Rd. Horsh RH12 217 A2
Middleton Rd. Morden SM4 40 D2
Middleton Way. Crawl RH11 200 E5
Midgarth Cl. Oxsh KT22 74 D6
Midgley Rd. Crawl RH10 201 F8
Midholm Rd. Croy CR0 62 E8
Midhope Cl. Woking GU22 89 E8
Midhope Gdns. Woking GU22 89 E8
Midhope Rd. Woking GU22 89 E8
Midhurst. Penge SE26 23 C2
Midhurst Ave. Thorn H CR0 42 A2
Midhurst Cl. Crawl RH11 201 A7
Midhurst Rd. Haslem GU27 208 B5
Midleton Cl. Milf GU8 149 F2
Midleton Industrial Estate Rd. Stough GU2 109 B2
Midleton Rd. Guild GU2 109 A2
Midleton Rd. King U T KT3 38 C7
Midleton Rd. Stough GU2 109 B2
Midmoor Rd. Streat SW12 21 C7
Midmoor Rd. Wimble SW19 39 E8
Midsummer Ave. Hounsl TW4 4 F3
Midsummer Wlk. Horse GU21 69 D3
Midway. Cheam SM3 & SM4 39 F2
Midway. Walt O T KT12 54 B8
Midway Ave. Egham TW20 32 B6
Midway Ave. Thorpe KT16 33 A6
Midway Ave. Thorpe KT16 33 B6
Miena Way. Ashtd KT21 75 D2
Mike Hawthorn Dr. Farnh GU9 125 C3
Milbanke Ct. Brack RG12 26 F7
Milbanke Way. Brack RG12 26 F7
Milborne Rd. Worth RH10 202 C2
Milborough Cres. Lewish SE12 24 E8
Milbourne La. Esher KT10 55 C5
Milbourne Lodge Jun Sch. Esher KT10 55 C4
Milbourne Lodge Sch. Esher KT10 55 D4
Milbrook. Esher KT10 55 C4
Milburn House. Wimble SW20 39 B7
Milburn Wlk. Epsom KT18 76 E4
Milden Cl. Friml GU16 86 A6
Milden Gdns. Friml GU16 85 F6
Mile Path. Woking GU22 89 B7
Mile Rd. Carsh CR4 & SM6 41 A1
Mile Rd. Wallin CR0 & CR4 & CR9 & SM6 41 C1
Miles Ct. Thorn H CR9 61 B8
Miles La. Cobham KT11 73 E6
Miles La. S Godst RH9 142 F7
Miles La. Tand RH8 & RH9 143 A7
Miles Pl. Lhtwat GU18 66 F7
Miles Rd. Ash GU12 106 B3
Miles Rd. Epsom KT19 76 D7
Miles Rd. Mitch CR4 40 E6
Miles's Hill. Hol St M RH5 155 C3
Miles's Hill. Peasl RH5 155 C3
Milestone Cl. Ripley GU23 91 B5
Milestone Cl. Sutton SM2 59 D3
Milestone Rd. Penge SE19 22 F2
Milford By Pass Rd. Milf GU8 149 D2
Milford Gr. Sutton SM1 59 C6
Milford Heath Rd. Milf GU8 170 E8
Milford Hospl. Godal GU7 171 C8
Milford Lodge. Milf GU8 170 F8
Milford Mews. Streat SW16 21 F5
Milford Rd. Elst GU8 148 E4
Milford Sta. Milf GU8 171 A7
Milking La. Bigg H BR2 83 D8
Milking La. Downe BR6 83 E7
Mill Bay La. Horsh RH12 217 B1
Mill Cl. Carsh SM5 60 A8
Mill Cl. E Grins RH19 205 E7
Mill Cl. Fetch KT23 94 A3
Mill Cl. Horley RH6 160 E4
Mill Cl. Shottm GU27 207 E6
Mill Cl. Woki RG11 25 A7
Mill Copse Rd. Fern GU27 208 B4
Mill Cotts. E Grins RH19 205 E7
Mill Cotts. Rudg RH12 214 D5
Mill Farm Ave. Charlt TW16 14 E1
Mill Farm Cres. Twick TW4 15 E7
Mill Farm Rd. Horsh RH13 218 A4
Mill Field. Bagsh GU19 47 D3
Mill Gdns. For Hil SE26 23 B5
Mill Gn. Carsh CR4 41 A2
Mill Green Bsns Pk. Carsh CR4 41 A2
Mill Green Rd. Carsh CR4 41 A2
Mill Hill. Brock RH3 137 B8
Mill Hill La. Brock RH3 116 B1
Mill House La. Egham KT16 32 B5
Mill La. Ascot SL5 30 A7
Mill La. Bramly GU5 151 F6
Mill La. Byfl KT14 71 F6
Mill La. Carsh SM5 60 A7
Mill La. Chidd GU8 191 B3
Mill La. Chil GU4 & GU5 131 F4
Mill La. Copth RH10 183 E3
Mill La. Crawl RH11 201 A8
Mill La. Croy CR0 60 F7
Mill La. Croy CR0 61 A7
Mill La. Dork RH4 136 B8
Mill La. Dunsf GU8 192 F4
Mill La. Easth RG12 26 F5
Mill La. Egham KT16 & TW20 32 C5
Mill La. Ewell KT17 57 F2
Mill La. Felb RH19 184 E5
Mill La. Felct RH7 164 F2
Mill La. Fern GU27 208 C3
Mill La. Fetch KT22 95 A5
Mill La. For Gn RH5 176 D7
Mill La. Frensh GU10 167 B7
Mill La. Godal GU7 150 D4
Mill La. Guild GU1 & GU2 130 D7
Mill La. Hookw RH6 160 D3
Mill La. Horton SL3 1 C4
Mill La. Merst RH1 119 D4
Mill La. Ockham GU23 91 D8
Mill La. Oxted RH8 122 F2
Mill La. Parkg RH5 158 D5
Mill La. Pirb GU24 87 E3
Mill La. Shalf GU3 130 C1
Mill La. The Char RH8 123 F4
Mill La. Witley GU8 170 F5
Mill Lane Trad Est. Croy CR0 60 F7
Mill Mead. Stain TW18 12 F4
Mill Pl. King U T KT1 37 F6
Mill Plat. Islew TW7 6 A5
Mill Plat. Islew TW7 6 B4
Mill Plat Ave. Islew TW7 6 A5
Mill Pond Rd. Windl GU20 48 B6
Mill Rd. Cobham KT11 73 C4
Mill Rd. Crawl RH10 202 B7
Mill Rd. Epsom KT17 76 F7
Mill Rd. Ewell KT17 76 F7
Mill Rd. Kings KT20 97 D4
Mill Rd. Merton SW19 20 C1
Mill Rd. S Holm RH5 157 D7
Mill Rd. Thame D KT10 55 A8
Mill Rd. Twick TW2 16 C6
Mill Ride. N Asct SL5 28 D8
Mill Shaw. Oxted RH8 122 F3
Mill St. Coln SL3 1 D7
Mill St. King U T KT1 37 E6
Mill St. Redh RH1 139 F8
Mill Stream. Heath E GU9 125 E6
Mill Vale. Broml BR2 44 F7
Mill View Cl. Ewell KT17 57 F3
Mill View Gdns. S Croy CR0 62 D7
Mill Way. E Grins RH19 205 E7
Mill Way. Felt TW14 4 B2
Mill Way. Head KT22 96 A2
Millais. Horsh RH13 218 A3
Millais Cl. Crawl RH11 200 F2
Millais Ct. Horsh RH13 218 A4
Millais Rd. New Mal KT3 38 E2
Millais Sch. Horsh RH13 217 F2
Millais Sch Lower Sch. Horsh RH13 217 F2
Millais Way. W Ewell KT19 57 C6
Millais Way. W Ewell KT19 57 C6
Millan Cl. Woodhm KT15 52 B1
Milland House. 11 Rhampt SW15 19 A7
Millbank. Wallin SM6 60 D5
Millbank The. Crawl RH11 200 F6
Millbourne Rd. Felt TW13 15 E4
Millbrook. Guild GU1 & GU2 130 D7
Millbrook. Oat Pk KT13 53 E6
Millbrook Way. Poyle SL3 1 E5
Millcombe Cl. 5 Woking GU21 69 B1
Millcroft House. Catf SE6 24 B4
Miller House. 9 Streat SW2 21 E8
Miller Rd. Merrow GU4 110 C4
Miller Rd. Mitch SW19 20 D2
Miller Rd. Thorn H CR0 42 A1
Miller's Ct. Egham TW20 12 D2
Miller's La. Outw RH1 162 C7
Millers Cl. Stain TW18 13 B3
Millers Copse. Lang V KT18 96 D8
Millers Copse. Outw RH1 162 B7
Millers Gate. Horsh RH12 217 D6
Millfarm Bsns Pk. Twick TW4 15 E8
Millfield. Charlt TW16 34 D8
Millfield. King U T KT1 37 F6
Millfield La. L Kings KT20 98 A2
Millfield Rd. Twick TW4 15 F7
Millford. Woking GU21 69 B2
Millford Cty Fst Sch. Milf GU8 149 F1
Millgate Ct. Farnh GU9 125 D3
Millhedge Cl. Cobham KT11 73 E3
Millholme Wlk. Friml GU15 66 C4
Millhouse Pl. W Norw SE27 22 B4
Millins Cl. Sandh GU15 45 E1
Millmead. Byfl KT14 71 F7
Millmead. Guild GU2 130 C7
Millmead. Woki RG11 25 A7
Millmead Terr. Guild GU2 130 C7
Millpond Cotts. Hasc GU8 172 D4
Millpond Ct. Addl KT15 52 E5
Mills Spur. Old W SL4 11 B8
Mills's Rd. Hersh KT12 54 C5
Millside. Carsh SM5 59 F8
Millside Ct. Fetch KT23 94 A2
Millside Pl. Islew TW7 6 B5
Millstream The. Linch GU27 207 E5
Millthorpe Rd. Horsh RH12 217 F4
Millview Cl. Redh RH1 118 D3
Millway. Reig RH2 118 D1
Millwood. Turn H RH19 204 E5
Millwood Rd. Islew TW3 & TW7 5 C2
Milman Cl. Brack RG12 28 A7
Milne Cl. Crawl RH11 200 E3
Milne Pk E. New Add CR0 82 D8
Milne Pk W. New Add CR0 82 D8
Milner App. Cater CR3 101 A6
Milner Cl. Cater CR3 101 A5
Milner Dr. Cobham KT11 73 F7
Milner Dr. Twick TW2 16 D8
Milner Rd. Cater CR3 101 A6
Milner Rd. King U T KT1 37 D6
Milner Rd. Merton SW19 40 B8
Milner Rd. Morden CR4 & SM4 40 D4
Milner Rd. S Norw CR7 42 D6
Milnthorpe Rd. Chisw W4 7 D8
Milnwood Rd. Horsh RH12 217 C3
Milstead Cl. Tadw KT20 97 B5
Milton Ave. Carsh SM1 59 E6
Milton Ave. Croy CR0 42 D2
Milton Ave. Westc RH4 135 D6
Milton Cl. Carsh SM1 59 D7
Milton Cl. Easth RG12 27 B3
Milton Cl. Horton SL3 1 A4
Milton Cres. E Grins RH19 205 C8
Milton Ct. King U T KT2 17 E4
Milton Ct. Twick TW2 16 E5
Milton Ct. Woki RG11 25 B7
Milton Dr. Shep Gn TW17 33 E5
Milton Dr. Woki RG11 25 B7
Milton Gdns. Epsom KT18 76 E5
Milton Gdns. Stan TW19 13 F7
Milton Gdns. Woki RG11 25 B6
Milton House. 12 Beck BR3 24 A1
Milton House. 5 King U T KT2 18 B2
Milton House. Sutton SM1 59 A7
Milton Lodge. Twick TW1 16 F8
Milton Mount. Crawl RH10 182 D1
Milton Mount Ave. Crawl RH10 202 D8
Milton Mount Fst & Mid Sch. Crawl RH10 202 C8
Milton Rd. Cater CR3 100 D6
Milton Rd. Crawl RH10 202 C7
Milton Rd. Croy CR0 42 D2
Milton Rd. Egham TW20 11 F3
Milton Rd. Hampt TW12 36 B8
Milton Rd. Horsh RH12 217 C3
Milton Rd. Mitch CR4 21 A1
Milton Rd. Mortl SW14 7 D4
Milton Rd. Row Tn KT15 52 A4
Milton Rd. Sutton SM1 59 A6
Milton Rd. Wallin SM6 60 D4
Milton Rd. Walt O T KT12 54 D7
Milton Rd. Wimble SW19 20 C2
Milton Rd. Woki RG11 25 B6
Milton St. Westc RH4 135 D6
Milton Way. Fetch KT23 94 C2
Miltoncourt La. Dork RH4 135 E7
Miltons Cres. Ock Rid GU7 150 B2
Milverton House. For Hil SE23 23 E5
Milward Gdns. Binf RG12 26 C7
Mina Rd. Merton SW19 40 A8
Minard Rd. Catf SE6 24 E7
Minchin Cl. Leahd KT22 95 A5
Mincing La. Burrh GU24 49 F2
Mincing La. Chobh GU24 49 F2
Minden Rd. Cheam SM3 58 F8
Minden Rd. Penge SE20 43 B8
Mindleheim Ave. E Grins RH19 186 B2
Minehead Rd. Streat SW16 21 F3
Minerva Cl. Stan TW19 2 A2
Minerva Rd. Farnb GU14 85 B1
Minerva Rd. King U T KT1 37 F7
Mink Ct. Hounsl TW4 4 C5
Minley Cl. W Heath GU14 84 E4
Minley Rd. Hawley GU14 84 A7
Minley Rd. W Heath GU14 84 D5
Minniedale. King U T KT5 37 F4
Minorca Ave. Friml GU16 66 E2
Minorca Rd. Friml GU16 66 E1
Minorca Rd. Weyb KT13 53 A6
Minshull Pl. 24 Beck BR3 24 A1
Minstead Cl. Brack RG12 27 F6
Minstead Gdns. Rhampt SW15 18 F8
Minstead Way. New Mal KT3 38 E3
Minster Ave. Sutton SM1 59 A8
Minster Ct. Camb GU15 64 F4
Minster Ct. Camb GU15 65 D7
Minster Dr. S Croy CR0 61 E6
Minster Gdns. E Mole KT8 35 F5
Minster Rd. Godal GU7 150 E1
Minsterley Ave. Up Hall TW16 & TW17 34 E5
Minstrel Gdns. King U T KT5 37 F5
Mint Gdns. Dork RH4 136 A8
Mint La. L Kings KT20 118 A6
Mint Rd. Wallin SM5 & SM6 60 B6
Mint Rd. Woodm SM7 78 C3
Mint St. Godal GU7 150 D4
Mint The. Godal GU7 150 D4
Mint Wlk. Croy CR0 & CR9 61 C7
Mint Wlk. Knaph GU21 68 E2
Mint Wlk. Warlgm CR6 81 D2
Miranda Wlk. Crawl RH11 200 E4
Mirfield Ct. Penge SE20 43 A7
Misbrooks Green Rd. Capel RH5 178 E8
Missenden Cl. E Bed TW14 14 F7
Missenden Gdns. Morden SM4 40 C3
Mission Sq. 13 Brent TW8 6 E8
Mistletoe Cl. Croy CR0 43 D1
Mistley Ct. 6 Epsom KT18 76 D6
Misty's Field. Walt O T KT12 35 C1
Mitcham Garden Village. Mitch CR4 41 A4
Mitcham Ind Est. Mitch CR4 41 A8
Mitcham Junc. Mitch CR4 41 A4
Mitcham La. Streat SW16 21 C3
Mitcham Pk. Mitch CR4 40 F5
Mitcham Rd. Camb GU15 47 A1
Mitcham Rd. Thorn H CR0 & CR9 41 F3
Mitcham Rd. Up Toot SW17 20 F3
Mitcham Sta. Mitch CR4 40 E5
Mitchell Gdns. Slinfd RH13 215 E3
Mitchell's Row. Shalf GU4 130 E2
Mitchells Cl. Shalf GU4 130 E3
Mitchells Cotts. Woner GU4 131 E1
Mitchells Rd. Crawl RH10 201 F6
Mitchley Ave. Sander CR2 & CR8 80 D6
Mitchley Gr. Sander CR2 81 A6
Mitchley Hill. Sander CR2 80 F6
Mitchley View. Sander CR2 81 A6
Mitford Wlk. 11 Crawl RH11 201 A3
Mitre Cl. Shep TW17 34 D3
Mitre Cl. Sutton SM2 59 D3
Mixbury Gr. Whit V KT13 53 D4
Mixnams La. Thorpe KT16 33 A6
Mizen Cl. Cobham KT11 73 D5
Mizen Way. Cobham KT11 73 D4
Moat Ct. Ashtd KT21 75 E2
Moat Ct. Ottsh KT16 51 C4
Moat Rd. E Grins RH19 185 E2
Moat Side. Felt TW13 15 C4
Moat The. King U T KT3 38 E8
Moat Wlk. Crawl RH10 202 C7
Moats La. S Nutf RH1 140 F3
Moberly Rd. Streat SW4 21 D8
Model Cotts. Mortl SW14 7 C4
Moffat Ct. Up Toot SW17 20 E4
Moffat Ct. Wimble SW19 20 A3
Moffat Rd. S Norw CR7 42 D7
Moffat Rd. Up Toot SW17 20 F4
Moffatts Cl. Sandh GU17 64 A8
Mogador Cotts. L Kings KT20 117 D7
Mogador Rd. L Kings KT20 117 E7
Mogden La. Islew TW7 5 F2
Moir Cl. S Croy CR2 62 A2
Moira Ct. Up Toot SW17 21 A6
Mole Abbey Gdns. E Mole KT8 36 A6
Mole Bsns Pk. Leahd KT22 95 A6
Mole Cl. Crawl RH11 201 B8
Mole Cl. W Heath GU14 84 D6
Mole Ct. W Ewell KT19 57 C6
Mole Ct. W Ewell KT19 57 C6
Mole House. Hersh KT12 54 E5
Mole Rd. Fetch KT22 94 D6
Mole Rd. Hersh KT12 54 D5
Mole St. Wall W RH5 177 B5
Mole Valley Pl. Ashtd KT21 95 D8
Molember Ct. E Mole KT7 36 E5
Molember Rd. Thame D KT8 36 E4
Moles Cl. Woki RG11 25 D5
Moles Hill. Oxsh KT22 74 D8
Molesey Ave. E Mole KT12 & KT8 35 F4
Molesey Cl. Hersh KT12 54 E6
Molesey Dr. Cheam SM3 58 E7
Molesey Hospl. E Mole KT8 36 A4
Molesey Park Ave. E Mole KT8 36 B4
Molesey Park Cl. E Mole KT8 36 C4
Molesey Park Rd. E Mole KT8 36 C4
Molesey Rd. E Mole KT12 35 E2
Molesey Rd. Hersh KT12 54 D5
Molesham Cl. E Mole KT8 36 B6
Molesham Way. E Mole KT8 36 B6
Molesley Rd. Hersh KT12 54 E8
Molesley Rd. Walt O T KT12 54 E8
Molesworth Rd. Cobham KT11 73 A6
Moliner Ct. 4 Beck BR3 24 A1
Molins Ct. 5 Crawl RH11 201 A3
Mollie Davis Ct. S Norw SE19 22 F2
Mollison Dr. Wallin SM6 60 E3
Molly Huggins Cl. Streat SW12 21 C8
Molly Millar Bridge. Woki RG11 25 B4
Molly Millar's La. Woki RG11 25 A4
Molyneux Rd. Farnc GU7 150 F7
Molyneux Rd. Weyb KT13 53 A5
Molyneux Rd. Windl GU20 48 D4
Monahan Ave. Purley CR8 79 F8
Monarch Cl. Coney H BR4 63 F6
Monarch Cl. Crawl RH11 201 A3
Monarch Cl. E Bed TW14 14 E8
Monarch Mews. W Norw SE27 & SW16 22 A3
Monarch Par. Mitch CR4 40 F7
Monaveen Gdns. E Mole KT8 36 B6
Monby Lodge Inf Sch. Whit V KT13 53 C5
Mondial Way. Harl UB7 3 C7
Money Ave. Cater CR3 100 E5
Money Rd. Cater CR3 100 D5
Monivea Rd. Beck BR3 23 F1
Monk's Wlk. M Bourn GU10 & GU9 146 F8
Monk's Wlk. Reig RH2 118 B1
Monkleigh Rd. Merton SM4 & SW20 39 E5
Monks Ave. E Mole KT8 35 F4
Monks Cl. Ascot SL5 29 B3
Monks Cl. Farnb GU14 85 C4
Monks Cres. Addl KT15 52 B5
Monks Cres. Walt O T KT12 35 B1
Monks Ct. Reig RH2 118 B1
Monks Dr. Ascot SL5 29 B3
Monks Gn. Fetch KT22 94 D6
Monks La. Limps RH8 & TN8 144 E6
Monks La. Rowhk RH5 196 F5
Monks Orchard Rd. Beck BR3 & CR0 44 A1
Monks Orchard Rd. Croy BR3 & CR0 44 A1
Monks Orchard Sch. Croy CR0 43 D4
Monks Rd. Banstd SM7 78 A3
Monks Rd. Vir W GU25 31 D5
Monks Way. Beck BR3 44 A3
Monks Way. Harm UB7 2 E8
Monks Way. Stain TW18 13 D1
Monks' Well. Farnh GU10 147 C8
Monks Wlk. Ascot SL5 29 B3
Monksdene Gdns. Sutton SM1 59 B7
Monksfield. Crawl RH10 201 F7
Monkshanger. M Bourn GU9 125 E2
Monkshood Cl. Woki RG11 25 E7
Monkswell La. L Kings CR5 98 B2
Monkton La. Farnh GU9 125 E5
Monkton Pk. Farnh GU9 125 F4
Monmouth Ave. Tedd KT1 17 C1
Monmouth Cl. Mitch CR4 & SW16 41 E5
Monro Dr. Stough GU2 109 B4
Monroe Dr. Mortl SW14 7 B2
Mons Cl. Farnb GU11 105 E7
Mons Wlk. Egham TW20 12 C3
Monsell Gdns. Egham TW18 12 E3
Monson Rd. Redh RH1 118 F4
Montacute Cl. Farnb GU14 85 D4
Montacute Rd. For Hil SE23 & SE6 23 F8
Montacute Rd. Morden SM4 40 D3
Montacute Rd. New Add CR0 63 C2
Montagu Gdns. Wallin SM6 60 C6
Montague Ave. Sander CR2 80 E7
Montague Cl. Camb GU15 65 B5
Montague Cl. Lhtwat GU18 48 A1
Montague Cl. Walt O T KT12 35 A2
Montague Dr. Cater CR3 100 C5
Montague House (Coll & Liby). Woki RG11 25 C6
Montague Rd. Hounsl TW3 5 B4
Montague Rd. Merton SW19 20 B1
Montague Rd. Rich TW10 6 E1
Montague Rd. Thorn H CR0 42 B1
Montana Cl. S Croy CR2 61 D1
Montana Rd. Up Toot SW17 21 A5
Montana Rd. Wimble SW20 39 C8
Montem Rd. For Hil SE23 23 F8
Montem Rd. New Mal KT3 38 E5
Montford Rd. Sunby TW16 35 A5
Montfort Pl. Putney SW19 19 D7
Montfort Rise. Salfs RH1 139 F1
Montgomerie Dr. Stough GU2 109 A6
Montgomery Ave. Hinch W KT10 55 E8
Montgomery Cl. Mitch CR4 41 E5
Montgomery Cl. Sandh GU17 64 B8
Montgomery Ct. Chisw W4 7 C8
Montgomery Ct. Leahd KT22 95 C7
Montgomery House. 5 Mortl SW14 7 D4
Montgomery Rd. Farnb GU14 84 F3
Montgomery Rd. 2 Woking GU22 69 E1
Montpelier Ct. Beck BR2 44 F5
Montpelier Rd. Purley CR2 & CR8 61 B1
Montpelier Rd. S Croy CR2 & CR8 61 B1
Montpelier Rd. Sutton SM1 59 C6
Montpelier Row. Twick TW1 17 C8
Montrave Rd. Penge SE20 23 C1
Montrell Rd. Streat SW2 21 E7
Montreux Ct. Crawl RH11 201 B6
Montrose Ave. Twick TW2 16 B8
Montrose Cl. Ashf TW15 14 C3
Montrose Cl. Friml GU16 65 E2
Montrose Gdns. Mitch CR4 40 F7
Montrose Gdns. Oxsh KT22 74 D7
Montrose Gdns. Sutton SM1 59 B8
Montrose Rd. E Bed TW14 3 D1
Montrose Way. For Hil SE23 23 D7
Montrose Wlk. Weyb KT13 53 B7
Montrouge Cres. Nork KT17 77 C3
Montserrat Cl. W Norw SE19 22 D3
Monument Bridge Ind Est W. Woking GU21 70 A4
Monument Hill. Weyb KT13 53 B6
Monument Hill Cty Prim Sch. Mayb GU22 70 C4
Monument Rd. Sheer GU21 70 B4
Monument Rd. Weyb KT13 53 B7
Monument Way E. Sheer GU21 70 B4
Monument Way W. Woking GU21 70 A4
Moon Ct. Fetch KT22 94 D6
Moon's La. Dorman RH19 & RH7 & TN8 186 E8
Moons Hill. M Bourn GU10 146 C2
Moons La. Horsh RH13 217 E1
Moor Cl. Sandh GU15 45 E1
Moor House Sch. Oxted RH8 122 F3
Moor La. Chess KT9 56 E5
Moor La. Harm UB7 2 C8
Moor La. Lingf RH7 & TN8 165 D3
Moor La. Stain TW18 12 D6
Moor La. Stan TW19 12 D6
Moor La. Westfd GU22 89 F5
Moor Lane Jun Sch. Chess KT9 56 F5
Moor Mead Rd. Twick TW1 6 A1
Moor Park Cres. Crawl RH11 200 D5
Moor Park Gdns. King U T KT2 18 E1
Moor Park House. Easth RG12 26 E3
Moor Park La. Farnh GU10 & GU9 126 A2
Moor Park Way. M Bourn GU9 125 F2
Moor Pl. E Grins RH19 185 D2
Moor Pl. Windl GU20 48 B5
Moor Rd. Farnb GU14 85 A8
Moor Rd. Friml GU16 85 F8
Moor Rd. Linch GU27 207 C5
Moor Rdbt. Harm UB7 2 B7
Moorcroft. Godst RH9 121 C3
Moorcroft Cl. Crawl RH11 201 B7
Moorcroft Rd. Streat SW16 21 E5
Moordale Ave. Brack RG12 26 E8
Moore Cl. Addl KT15 52 B5
Moore Cl. Mitch CR4 41 B7
Moore Cl. Mortl SW14 7 C4
Moore Cl. Wallin SM6 60 E3
Moore Ct. Horsh RH12 217 A1
Moore Grove Cres. Egham TW20 11 F1

Moore House. **1** W Norw SE27 . **22** C4
Moore Rd. Pirb GU24 .... **87** B6
Moore Rd. S Norw SE19 .... **22** C2
Moore Way. Belm SM2 .... **59** A2
Moore's Rd. Dork RH4 & RH5 ... **136** B8
Mooreland Rd. Broml BR1 .... **24** F1
Moores Gn. Woki RG11 .... **25** E8
Moorfield. King Go GU27 .... **207** F5
Moorfield Ctr The. Belff GU1 .... **109** D5
Moorfield Rd. Chess KT9 .... **56** E5
Moorfield Rd. Stough GU21 ...... **109** E5
Moorfields. Egham TW18 .... **32** E8
Moorfields Ct. **6** Streat SW16 .. **21** C4
Moorhayes Dr. Laleh TW18 ...... **33** C6
Moorhead Rd. Horsh RH12 .... **218** B5
Moorholme. Woking GU22 .... **89** E8
Moorhouse Rd. The Char RH8 . **123** F5
Moorhurst La. Coldh RH5 .... **157** B4
Moorland Cl. Twick TW4 .... **16** A8
Moorland Rd. Harm UB7 .... **2** C8
Moorlands. Walt O T KT12 .... **54** A7
Moorlands Cl. Hind GU26 .... **188** E4
Moorlands Pl. Camb GU15 .... **65** B5
Moorlands Rd. Camb GU15 .... **65** B4
Moorlands The. Westfd GU22 ... **89** F6
Moormead Dr. Worc Pk KT19 .... **57** E5
Moormede Cres. Stain TW18 .... **12** F4
Moors La. Elst GU8 .... **148** C3
Moors The. Tongh GU10 .... **126** F7
Moorside Cl. W Heath GU14 ...... **65** A1
Moorside Rd. Catf BR1 .... **24** F4
Moorsom Way. Coulsd CR5 .... **79** D2
Moray Ave. Sandh GU15 .... **64** D7
Moray House. **11** King U T KT6 ... **37** E4
Mordaunt Dr. Crowth RG11 .... **45** B3
Morden Cl. Brack RG12 .... **27** F5
Morden Cl. Burgh K KT20 .... **97** D7
Morden Court Par. Morden SM4 **40** A5
Morden Ct. Morden SM4 .... **40** B5
Morden Farm Mid Sch.
W Barn SM4 .... **39** E2
Morden Fst Sch. Morden SM4 ... **40** A4
Morden Gdns. Mitch CR4 .... **40** D5
Morden Hall Rd.
Morden SM4 & SW19 .... **40** C5
Morden House. Morden SM4 ..... **40** A5
Morden Park Sch Sports Ctr.
Morden SM4 .... **39** F4
Morden Rd. Merton SW19 .... **40** B7
Morden Rd.
Mitch CR4 & SM4 & SW19 ..... **40** D5
Morden Road Sta. Merton SW19 **40** B7
Morden South Sta. Morden SM4 **40** A4
Morden Sta. Merton SW19 .... **40** B6
Morden Way. Cheam SM3 .... **40** A2
Mordred Rd. Catf SE6 .... **24** E6
More Circ. Farnc GU7 .... **150** C2
More Cl. Purley CR8 .... **80** A8
More House Sch.
M Bourn GU10 .... **146** C2
More La. Esher KT10 .... **55** B7
More Rd. Farnc GU7 .... **150** E7
Morecambe Cl. Crawl RH11 .... **200** F4
Morecote Cl. Shalf GU4 .... **130** E2
Moreland Ave. Coln SL3 .... **1** C7
Moreland Cl. Coln SL3 .... **1** C7
Morella Cl. Vir W GU25 .... **31** D5
Morella Rd.Balham SW11 & SW12 **20** F8
Moremead Rd. Catf SE6 .... **24** A4
Morena St. Lewish SE6 .... **24** B8
Moresby Ave. Tolw KT5 .... **38** B2
Moreton Ave. Hounsl TW7 .... **5** E6
Moreton Cl. Churt GU10 .... **167** E1
Moreton Green Fst Sch.
Morden SM4 .... **40** D4
Moreton House. Up Toot SW17 . **20** D4
Moreton Rd. N Cheam KT4 .... **58** B8
Moreton Rd. S Croy CR2 .... **61** D5
Morgan Ct. Ashf TW15 .... **14** B3
Moring Rd. Up Toot SW17 .... **21** A4
Morkyns Wlk. Dulw SE21 .... **22** E5
Morland Ave. Croy CR0 .... **42** E1
Morland Cl. Hampt TW12 .... **15** F3
Morland Cl. Mitch CR4 .... **40** E6
Morland Rd. Alder GU11 .... **126** C6
Morland Rd. Croy CR0 .... **42** F2
Morland Rd. Penge SE20 .... **23** D2
Morland Rd. Sutton SM1 .... **59** C5
Morland's Rd. Farnb GU11 ...... **105** D5
Morley Ct. Beck BR3 .... **44** D8
Morley Ct. Beck BR3 .... **44** F5
Morley Ct. Sunnin SL5 .... **29** F3
Morley House. Streat SW2 .... **21** E8
Morley Rd. Cheam SM3 .... **39** F1
Morley Rd. M Bourn GU9 .... **125** D1
Morley Rd. S Croy CR2 .... **61** F1
Morley Rd. Twick TW1 .... **6** D1
Morningside Rd. N Cheam KT4 .. **58** C8
Mornington Cl. Bigg H TN16 .... **83** D3
Mornington Cres. Cranf TW5 ...... **4** B6
Mornington Rd. Ashf TW15 ...... **14** C3
Mornington Wlk. Rich TW10 ..... **17** C4
Morrell Ave. Horsh RH12 .... **217** F4
Morrell Ave. Horsh RH12 .... **218** A6
Morris Cl. Croy BR3 & CR0 .... **43** E4
Morris Gdns. Wands SW18 .... **20** A8
Morris Rd. Farnb GU14 .... **105** D8
Morris Rd. Islew TW7 .... **5** F4
Morris Rd. S Nutf RH1 .... **140** E7
Morrish Rd. Streat SW2 .... **21** E8
Morrison Ct. **5** Crawl RH11 .... **201** B1
Morrison House. Streat SW2 .... **22** A4
Morston Cl. Burgh K KT20 .... **97** B7
Mortaine Rd. Ashf TW15 .... **13** D5
Mortimer Cl. Streat SW16 .... **21** D6
Mortimer Rd. Worc Pk KT4 ...... **57** D7
Mortimer Lodge. **11**
Putney SW19 .... **19** E7

Mortimer Rd. Bigg H TN16 ...... **83** C7
Mortimer Rd. Capel RH5 .... **178** D6
Mortimer Rd. Mitch CR4 .... **40** F8
Mortimer Sch. Streat SW16 ...... **21** D6
Mortlake Cl. Wallin CR0 .... **60** E7
Mortlake Dr. Mitch CR4 .... **40** E8
Mortlake High St. Mortl SW14 .... **7** D4
Mortlake Rd. Rich SW14 & TW9 .. **7** A6
Mortlake Sta. Mortl SW14 .... **7** C4
Morton. Tadw KT20 .... **97** D6
Morton Cl. Friml GU16 .... **85** F7
Morton Cl. Horse GU21 .... **69** D4
Morton Gdns. Wallin SM6 .... **60** C5
Morton House. W Norw SE27 .... **22** D3
Morton Rd. E Grins RH19 .... **205** E7
Morton Rd. Horse GU21 .... **69** D4
Morton Rd. Morden CR4 & SM4 . **40** D4
Morval Cl. Farnb GU14 .... **84** E4
Morven Rd. Up Toot SW17 .... **20** F5
Moselle Cl. W Heath GU14 .... **84** B5
Moselle Rd. Bigg H TN16 .... **83** F1
Mosford Cl. Horl RH6 .... **160** F5
Mospey Cres. Epsom KT17 .... **76** F4
Moss Gdns. S Croy CR2 .... **62** D3
Moss La. Godal GU7 .... **150** D4
Moss Lane Cty Prim Sch.
Godal GU7 .... **150** D4
Mossfield. Cobham KT11 .... **73** A6
Mosslea Rd. Kenley CR3 .... **80** F2
Mosslea Rd. Penge SE20 .... **23** C2
Mossville Gdns.
Merton SM4 & SW20 .... **39** F5
Mostyn Rd. Merton SW19 .... **39** F3
Mostyn Terr. Earls RH1 .... **140** A8
Motspur Park Sta. W Barn KT3 . **39** B4
Motspur Rd. New Mal KT3 .... **39** B3
Motts Hill La. Tadw KT20 .... **97** A4
Motts Hill La. Walt o t H KT20 ... **97** A4
Mouchotte Cl. Bigg H TN16 ..... **83** C7
Moulton Ave. Hounsl TW3 & TW5 . **4** F5
Mount Adon Pk.
Dulw SE21 & SE22 .... **23** A8
Mount Angelus Rd.
Rhampt SW15 .... **18** F8
Mount Ararat Rd. Rich TW10 ...... **6** E2
Mount Arlington. Beck BR2 ...... **44** E7
Mount Ash Rd. For Hil SE26 ..... **23** B5
Mount Ave. Cater CR3 .... **100** C3
Mount Cl. Crawl RH10 .... **202** D7
Mount Cl. Ewh GU6 .... **175** E5
Mount Cl. Fetch KT22 .... **94** F4
Mount Cl. Kenley CR8 .... **80** D3
Mount Cl. Wallin SM5 .... **60** A2
Mount Cl. Woking GU22 .... **89** C6
Mount Cl The. Went GU25 .... **31** D4
Mount Ct. Guild GU2 .... **130** C2
Mount Ct. **6** King U T KT2 ...... **18** B1
Mount Ct. W Wick BR4 .... **63** E8
Mount Ephraim La. Streat SW16 **21** D5
Mount Ephraim Rd.
Streat SW16 .... **21** E5
Mount Felix. Walt O T KT12 ...... **34** F7
Mount Gdns. For Hil SE26 .... **23** B5
Mount Hermon Cl. Woking GU22 **69** E1
Mount Hermon Rd.
Woking GU22 .... **69** E1
Mount La. Brack RG12 .... **27** C1
Mount La. Turn H RH10 .... **204** A4
Mount Lee. Egham TW20 .... **11** F3
Mount Nod Rd.
Streat SW16 & SW2 .... **21** F5
Mount Park Ave. S Croy CR2 .... **61** B2
Mount Pk. Wallin SM5 .... **60** A2
Mount Pl. Guild GU1 .... **130** C2
Mount Pleasant. Bigg H TN16 ... **83** E2
Mount Pleasant. Brack RG12 .... **27** C6
Mount Pleasant. Effing KT24 ... **113** E7
Mount Pleasant. Ewell KT17 .... **57** F1
Mount Pleasant. Farnh GU9 ... **125** A1
Mount Pleasant. Guild GU2 .... **130** C2
Mount Pleasant. Sandh GU17 ... **45** A1
Mount Pleasant. W Hors KT24 . **112** B6
Mount Pleasant. Weyb KT13 .... **53** A7
Mount Pleasant. Woki RG11 ..... **25** A6
Mount Pleasant Cl. Lhtwat GU18 **48** A1
Mount Pleasant Rd.
Alder GU12 .... **105** C2
Mount Pleasant Rd. Cater CR3 **101** D4
Mount Pleasant Rd.King U T KT3 **38** C6
Mount Pleasant Rd. Lingf RH7 **164** C4
Mount Prim Sch The.
King U T KT3 .... **38** C6
Mount Rd. Chess KT9 .... **56** F5
Mount Rd. Chobh GU24 .... **69** B7
Mount Rd. Cran GU6 .... **174** E2
Mount Rd. Felt TW13 .... **15** E5
Mount Rd. King U T KT3 .... **38** D6
Mount Rd. S Norw SE19 .... **22** D2
Mount Rd. Wimble SW18 & SW19 **20** B6
Mount Rd. Woking GU22 .... **89** B6
Mount Rise. For Hil SE23 .... **23** C6
Mount Rise. Woodh RH1 .... **139** D7
Mount St. Dork RH4 .... **136** A7
Mount The. Cran GU6 .... **174** E2
Mount The. Esher KT10 .... **55** A4
Mount The. Ewell KT17 .... **57** F1
Mount The. Ewh GU6 .... **175** E5
Mount The. Fetch KT22 .... **94** E4
Mount The. Grays GU27 .... **189** F1
Mount The. Guild GU2 .... **130** C7
Mount The. Head Dn GU35 ..... **187** A6
Mount The. L Kings KT20 .... **97** F1
Mount The. N Cheam KT4 .... **58** B6
Mount The. New Mal KT3 .... **38** F6
Mount The. Oat Pk KT13 .... **53** E8
Mount The.
Rusper RH11 & RH12 .... **180** B1
Mount The. Rusper RH12 .... **200** B8

Mount The. Wallin CR5 .... **79** B5
Mount The. Went GU25 .... **31** D1
Mount The. Woking GU21 & GU22 **69** D1
Mount View. Alder GU11 .... **105** A1
Mount View Rd. Clayg KT10 ..... **56** B3
Mount Villas. W Norw SE27 ..... **22** B5
Mount Way. Wallin SM5 .... **60** C5
Mountacre Cl. For Hil SE26 ...... **23** A4
Mountbatten Cl. Crawl RH11 .. **201** C2
Mountbatten Cl. **6**
W Norw SE19 .... **22** E3
Mountbatten Gdns. Beck BR3 ... **43** E5
Mountbatten Rise. Sandh GU17 . **45** A1
Mountcombe Cl. Surb KT6 .... **37** E2
Mountearl Gdns.
Streat SW16 & SW2 .... **21** F5
Mounthurst Rd. Hayes BR2 ...... **44** F2
Mounts Hill. W Sla & SL5 .... **9** C3
Mountsfield Cl. Stan TW19 .... **2** A2
Mountside. Cater CR3 .... **100** F3
Mountside. Guild GU2 .... **130** C2
Mountview. **5** Streat SW16 ..... **21** F1
Mountview. Cl. Woodh RH1 ..... **139** E7
Mountview Dr. Earls RH1 .... **139** E7
Mountwood. E Mole KT8 .... **36** B6
Mountwood Cl. S Croy CR2 ...... **62** B1
Moushill La. Milf GU8 .... **170** E8
Mowat Ct. Worc Pk KT4 .... **57** F8
Mowbray Ave. Byfl KT14 .... **71** F6
Mowbray Cres. Egham TW20 .... **12** A3
Mowbray Ct. S Norw SE19 .... **42** F8
Mowbray Dr. Crawl RH11 ...... **200** F4
Mowbray Gdns. Dork RH4 ..... **115** B1
Mowbray Rd. Rich TW10 .... **17** C5
Mowbray Rd. S Norw SE19 .... **42** F8
Mower Cl. Woki RG11 .... **25** F7
Mower Pl. Cran GU6 .... **174** E4
Moyne Cl. **4** Knaph GU21 ...... **68** F1
Moyne Rd. Crawl RH11 .... **201** C2
Moyser Rd. Streat SW16 & SW17 **21** B3
Muchelney Rd. Morden SM4 ..... **40** C3
Muckhatch La. Thorpe TW20 .... **32** B7
Mudie House. **8** Streat SW2 .... **21** E8
Muggeridge's Hill.
Capel RH12 & RH5 .... **198** E8
Muggeridge's Hill.
Rusper RH12 & RH5 .... **198** E8
Muirdown Ave. Mortl SW14 .... **7** D3
Muirfield Cl. Crawl RH11 .... **200** D5
Muirfield House. Easth RG12 ... **26** E3
Muirfield Rd. Woking GU21 ...... **69** A1
Muirkirk Rd. Catf SE6 .... **24** C7
Mulberries The. Farnh GU9 ... **125** F4
Mulberry Ave. Stan TW19 .... **13** E7
Mulberry Bsns Pk. Woki RG11 .. **25** A4
Mulberry Cl. Ash GU12 .... **106** A4
Mulberry Cl. Crowth RG11 .... **45** C4
Mulberry Cl. Horse GU21 .... **69** E5
Mulberry Cl. Horsh RH12 ...... **217** C5
Mulberry Cl. **1** Sandh GU15 .... **64** D8
Mulberry Cl. Streat SW16 .... **21** C4
Mulberry Cl. Weyb KT13 .... **53** B7
Mulberry Cres. Brent TW8 .... **6** C7
Mulberry Ct. Ashtd KT21 .... **75** D1
Mulberry Ct. **1** Brack RG12 .... **27** F4
Mulberry Ct. Merrow GU4 ...... **110** D3
Mulberry Ct. **4** Surb KT6 .... **37** D2
Mulberry La. Twick TW1 .... **16** F5
Mulberry La. Woki RG11 .... **25** C6
Mulberry La. Croy CR0 .... **42** F1
Mulberry Mews. **2** Wallin SM6 . **60** C4
Mulberry Rd. Crawl RH11 ...... **181** B1
Mulberry Trees. Shep TW17 ..... **34** D2
Mulgrave Chambers.
Sutton SM2 .... **59** B4
Mulgrave Manor. Sutton SM2 ... **59** B4
Mulgrave Rd. Belm SM2 .... **59** A4
Mulgrave Rd. Croy CR0 & CR9 .. **61** D7
Mulgrave Rd. Friml GU16 .... **65** F2
Mulgrave Rd. Sutton SM2 .... **59** A4
Mulgrave Way. Knaph GU21 .... **68** E1
Mulholland Cl. Mitch CR4 .... **41** B7
Mullards Cl. Carsh CR4 .... **40** F1
Mullein Wlk. Crawl RH11 .... **201** A2
Mullens Rd. Egham TW20 .... **12** C3
Mullins Path. Mortl SW14 .... **7** D4
Mulroy Dr. Camb GU15 .... **66** A6
Multon Rd. Wands SW18 .... **20** D8
Muncaster Cl. Ashf TW15 .... **14** A4
Muncaster Rd. Ashf TW15 .... **14** B3
Muncies Mews. Catf SE6 .... **24** C6
Munday's Boro. Putt GU3 .... **128** A4
Munday's Boro Rd. Putt GU3 ... **128** A4
Munnings Dr. Sandh GU15 ...... **64** E6
Munnings Gdns. Islew TW7 .... **5** D2
Munroe House. Woodh RH1 ... **139** A6
Munstead Ct. Sutton SM2 .... **59** C3
Munstead Heath Rd.
Bramly GU5 & GU7 & GU8 ... **151** C3
Munstead Heath Rd.
Godal GU5 & GU7 & Gu8 ..... **151** C3
Munstead Pk. Bramly GU8 ..... **151** C2
Munstead View. Arting GU3 ... **130** C4
Munstead View Rd.
Bramly GU5 .... **151** D5
Munster Ave. Hounsl TW4 .... **4** E2
Munster Ct. Tedd TW11 .... **17** C2
Munster Rd. Tedd TW11 .... **17** C3
Murdoch Cl. Stain TW18 .... **13** A3
Murdoch Rd. Woki RG11 .... **25** D5
Murfett Cl. Putney SW19 .... **19** E6
Murray Ave. Hounsl TW3 .... **5** B2
Murray Ct. Ascot SL5 .... **29** C3
Murray Ct. Crawl RH11 .... **201** A1
Murray Ct. Horsh RH13 .... **218** B4
Murray Gn. Sheer GU21 .... **70** C5
Murray Rd. Ottsh KT15 & KT16 .. **51** D5
Murray Rd. Rich TW10 .... **17** C6
Murray Rd. Wimble SW19 .... **19** D2

Murray Rd. Woki RG11 .... **25** A6
Murray's La. Byfl KT14 .... **71** E5
Murray's Rd. Farnb GU11 ...... **105** D5
Murrell Rd. Ash GU12 .... **106** A3
Murrellhill La. Binf RG12 .... **26** C8
Murrells La. Camb GU15 .... **65** B3
Murrells Wlk. Fetch KT23 .... **94** A3
Murreys The. Ashtd KT21 .... **75** D1
Muschamp Inf Sch. Carsh SM5 . **59** E8
Muschamp Jun Sch. Carsh SM5 **59** E8
Muschamp Rd. Carsh SM1 & SM5 **59** E8
Museum Hill. Haslem GU27 .... **208** D6
Musgrave Ave. E Grins RH19 ... **205** E8
Musgrave Rd. Hounsl TW7 .... **5** F5
Mushroom Castle La. Wink RG12 **8** B2
Musquash Way. Hounsl TW4 ...... **4** C5
Mustard Mill Rd. Stain TW18 .... **12** E4
Mutton Hill. Dorman RH7 ...... **186** B7
Mutton Oaks. Binf RG12 .... **26** D8
Muybridge Rd. New Mal KT3 .... **38** C7
Mychell House. **8** Merton SW19 **20** C1
Mychett Cty Fst Sch.
Mytch GU16 .... **85** F4
Mychett Heath. Mytch GU16 ..... **86** A3
Myers Way. Friml GU16 .... **66** D2
Mylis Cl. For Hil SE26 .... **23** B4
Mylne Sq. Woki RG11 .... **25** D6
Mylor Cl. Horse GU21 .... **69** E5
Mynn's Cl. Epsom KT18 .... **76** B5
Mynterne Ct. **15** Putney SW19 .. **19** D7
Myrna Cl. Mitch SW19 .... **20** E1
Myrtle Ave. Hatton TW14 .... **3** E2
Myrtle Cl. Lhtwat GU18 .... **67** B8
Myrtle Cl. Poyle SL3 .... **1** E6
Myrtle Cl. Sand GU47 .... **64** D5
Myrtle Dr. Blckw GU17 .... **64** D5
Myrtle Gr. King U T KT3 .... **38** C7
Myrtle Rd. Croy CR0 .... **63** A7
Myrtle Rd. Dork RH4 .... **136** A8
Myrtle Rd. Hampt TW12 .... **16** C2
Myrtle Rd. Hounsl TW3 .... **5** C5
Myrtle Rd. Sutton SM1 .... **59** C5
Mytchett Lake Rd. Mytch GU16 . **86** A1
Mytchett Place Rd. Mytch GU16 **86** C1
Mytchett Place Rd.
Normdy GU12 & GU16 &GU24 **86** C1
Myton Rd. W Norw SE21 .... **22** C5

Naafi Rdbt. Alder GU11 .... **105** B2
Nadine Cl. Wallin SM6 .... **60** C2
Nailsworth Cres. Merst RH1 ... **119** D6
Nairn Cl. Friml GU16 .... **65** E2
Nairn Ct. **3** Wallin SM6 .... **60** C4
Nairn Ct. Wimble SW19 .... **20** B2
Naldrett Cl. Horsh RH12 .... **217** F4
Naldretts La. Rudg RH12 .... **214** D5
Nallhead Rd. Felt TW13 .... **15** C3
Namton Dr. Thorn H CR7 & SW16 **41** F5
Napier Cl. Crowth RG11 .... **45** D5
Napier Cl. Farnb GU11 .... **105** E7
Napier Cl. Cater CR3 .... **100** E5
Napier Cl. Horse GU21 .... **69** E3
Napier Cl. **10** Croy CR0 .... **61** F8
Napier Ct. Horse GU21 .... **69** E3
Napier Ct. Camb GU15 .... **66** A8
Napier Gdns. Merrow GU1 ..... **110** B2
Napier Lodge. Ashf TW15 .... **14** C2
Napier Rd. Ashf TW15 .... **14** C1
Napier Rd. Crowth RG11 .... **45** C4
Napier Rd. Croy SE25 .... **43** B5
Napier Rd. Harm TW6 .... **3** A3
Napier Rd. Islew TW7 .... **6** A3
Napier Rd. S Croy CR2 .... **61** D3
Napier Rd. W. Crawl RH10 ..... **182** A1
Napier Wlk. Ashf TW15 .... **14** C1
Napoleon Ave. Farnb GU14 ...... **85** B6
Napoleon Rd. Twick TW1 .... **17** B8
Napper Cl. N Asct SL5 .... **28** D7
Narrow La. Warlgm CR6 .... **101** B8
Naseby. Easth RG12 .... **27** B1
Naseby Cl. Hounsl TW7 .... **5** E6
Naseby Rd. S Norw SE19 .... **22** D2
Nash Cl. Farnb GU14 .... **84** F4
Nash Dr. **6** Redh RH1 .... **119** A3
Nash Cl. N Asct SL5 .... **28** E7
Nash Gdns. Redh RH1 .... **118** F3
Nash Rd. Crawl RH10 .... **201** E3
Nassau Rd. Barnes SW13 .... **7** F6
Nasturtium Dr. Bisley GU24 ..... **68** A4
Natal Rd. S Norw CR7 .... **42** D6
Natal Rd. Streat SW16 .... **21** D2
Natalie Cl. E Bed TW14 .... **14** D8
Natalie Mews. Twick TW2 .... **16** D5
National Physical Laboratory.
Tedd TW11 .... **16** E2
National Wks. Hounsl TW4 .... **4** F4
Nayland House. Catf SE6 .... **24** C4
Neale Cl. E Grins RH19 .... **185** B3
Neath Gdns. Morden SM4 .... **40** C3
Neb La. Oxted RH8 .... **122** D4
Needles Bank. Godst RH9 ...... **121** B4
Needles Cl. Horsh RH12 .... **217** B1
Neelem Cl. Farnb GU14 .... **85** C1
Neil Cl. Ashf TW15 .... **14** C3
Neil Wates Cres. **18**
Streat SW2 .... **22** A7
Nelgarde Rd. Catf SE6 .... **24** A8
Nelgarde Rd. Lewish SE6 .... **24** A8
Nell Ball. Plaist RH14 .... **211** E2
Nell Gwynn Ave. Shep TW17 .... **34** D3
Nell Gwynne Ave. Ascot SL5 .... **29** D5
Nell Gwynne Ave. Ascot SL5 .... **29** D5
Nello James Gdns.
W Norw SE27 .... **22** A4
Nelson Cl. Alder GU12 .... **105** D1
Nelson Cl. Bigg H TN16 .... **83** D3
Nelson Cl. Brack RG12 .... **27** A5
Nelson Cl. E Bed TW14 .... **14** F7
Nelson Cl. Heath E GU9 .... **125** D8
Nelson Cl. Thorn H CR0 .... **42** B1

Nelson Cl. Walt O T KT12 .... **35** B1
Nelson Cl. Worth RH10 .... **202** C5
Nelson Ct. Carsh SM5 .... **59** F7
Nelson Ct. Chert KT16 .... **33** A1
Nelson Gdns. Merrow GU1 .... **110** A2
Nelson Gdns. Twick TW3 & TW4 . **5** A1
Nelson Grove Rd. Merton SW19 **40** C8
Nelson Hospl. Merton SW20 .... **39** F7
Nelson Prim Sch. Twick TW2 ..... **5** B1
Nelson Rd. Ashf TW15 .... **13** E3
Nelson Rd. Cater CR3 .... **100** D4
Nelson Rd. Harm TW6 .... **2** F6
Nelson Rd. Heath E GU9 .... **125** D8
Nelson Rd. Horsh RH12 .... **217** C3
Nelson Rd. Merton SW19 .... **20** C1
Nelson Rd. New Mal KT3 .... **38** D4
Nelson Rd. Twick TW2 & TW4 ... **16** B8
Nelson St. Alder GU11 .... **105** A2
Nelson Way. Camb GU15 .... **64** F4
Nene Gdns. Felt TW13 .... **15** F6
Nene Rd. Harl TW6 & UB7 .... **3** B6
Nepean St. **4** Putney SW15 ..... **19** A8
Neptune Cl. Crawl RH11 .... **200** E4
Neptune Rd. Harl TW6 .... **3** C6
Nesbit Ct. Crawl RH11 .... **200** E3
Nesbitt Sq. S Norw SE19 .... **22** E1
NESCOT Epsom's Coll of FE & HE.
Ewell KT17 .... **77** A8
Nether Mount. Guild GU2 ...... **130** B7
Netheravon Rd S. Chisw W4 ...... **7** F8
Netherby Pk. Whit V KT13 .... **53** E5
Netherby Rd. For Hil SE23 .... **23** C8
Nethercote Ave. Woking GU21 .. **68** F3
Netherfield Rd. Up Toot SW17 .. **21** A5
Netherlands The. Coulsd CR5 ... **99** C8
Netherleigh Pk. S Nutf RH1 ... **140** E6
Nethern Court Rd. Wold CR3 .. **102** A4
Netherne Hospl. Hooley CR5 .... **99** D5
Netherne La. Hooley CR5 .... **99** C5
Netherton. Easth RG12 .... **27** A5
Netherton Rd. Twick TW1 .... **6** B2
Netherwood. Crawl RH11 ...... **201** B4
Netherwood Ct. Farnc GU7 ... **150** E5
Netley Cl. Cheam SM3 .... **58** D5
Netley Cl. New Add CR0 .... **63** C3
Netley Dr. Walt O T KT12 .... **35** F2
Netley Gdns. Morden SM4 .... **40** C2
Netley Rd. Brent TW8 .... **6** E8
Netley Rd. Harl TW6 .... **3** D6
Netley Rd. Morden SM4 .... **40** C2
Netley Rd (W). Harl TW6 .... **3** D6
Netley St. Farnb GU14 .... **105** C8
Nettlecombe. Brack RG12 .... **27** D3
Nettlecombe Cl. Sutton SM2 .... **59** B2
Nettlefold Pl. W Norw SE27 ..... **22** B5
Nettles Terr. **3** Guild GU1 ..... **109** D1
Nettlestead Cl. Beck BR3 .... **23** F1
Nettlestead Cl. Beck BR3 .... **44** A8
Nettleton Rd. Harl TW6 .... **3** B6
Nettlewood Rd. Streat SW16 .... **21** D1
Neuchatel Rd. For Hil SE6 .... **23** F6
Nevada Cl. Farnb GU14 .... **84** D3
Nevada Cl. King T KT3 .... **38** C5
Nevelle Pl. Binf RG12 .... **26** D8
Nevile Cl. Crawl RH11 .... **201** A3
Neville Ave. King U T KT3 .... **38** D8
Neville Cl. Banstd SM7 .... **78** B5
Neville Cl. Esher KT10 .... **54** F4
Neville Cl. Hounsl TW3 .... **5** B5
Neville Ct. **10** Streat SW12 ...... **21** C8
Neville Duke Rd. W Heath GU14 **84** F8
Neville Rd. Croy CR0 .... **42** D2
Neville Rd. King U T KT1 .... **38** A7
Neville Rd. Rich TW10 .... **17** C6
Neville Wlk. Carsh SM5 .... **40** E2
Nevis Rd. Up Toot SW17 .... **21** A6
New Barn La. Kenley CR3 .... **80** E3
New Barn La. Wall W RH5 ...... **177** A3
New Barns Ave. Mitch CR4 ...... **41** C5
New Beckenham Sta. Beck BR3 **23** F1
New Belmont House.
For HII SE23 .... **23** C7
New Berry La. Hersh KT12 .... **54** D5
New Chapel Sq. Felt TW13 ...... **15** B7
New Church Ct. **3** Penge SE19 . **23** A1
New Cl. Felt TW13 .... **15** E3
New Cl. Mitch SW19 .... **40** C6
New Colebrooke Ct. Wallin SM5 **60** A3
New Cotts. Betch RH3 .... **116** D4
New Cotts. Sidlow RH2 .... **138** F1
New Cotts. Turn H RH10 .... **204** A4
New Cross Rd. Stough GU2 ..... **109** B3
New Cswy. Dovgn RH1 & RH2 .. **139** C6
New Ct. Addl KT15 .... **52** C7
New Dawn Cl. Farnb GU14 ...... **84** D3
New Farthingdale.
Dorman RH7 .... **186** B8
New Forest Cotts. Old Wok GU22 **89** F7
New Forest Ride. Brack RG12 ... **27** F4
New Haw Cty Jun Sch.
Woodhm KT15 .... **52** A1
New Haw Rd. New Haw KT15 ... **52** C4
New Heston Rd. Heston TW5 ..... **4** F7
New House Farm La.
Wood S V GU3 .... **108** C2
New House La. Salfs RH1 .... **161** E8
New Inn La. Burph GU4 .... **110** B4
New Kelvin Ave. Tedd TW11 ..... **16** E2
New La. Westfd GU22 & GU4 .... **89** F3
New Life Sch. E Grins RH19 ... **185** D2
New Lodge Dr. Limps RH8 ..... **122** F7
New Malden Sta. New Mal KT3 . **38** E6
New Meadow. Ascot SL5 .... **28** C8
New Mile Rd. Ascot SL5 .... **29** C7
New Moorhead Dr.
Horsh RH12 .... **218** C6
New North Rd. Woodh RH2 .... **138** F6

New Par . Ashf TW15 .... 13 F4
New Park Ct. 26 Streat SW2 ...... 21 E8
New Park Par. 14 Streat SW2 ...... 21 E8
New Park Rd. Ashf TW15 .... 14 C3
New Park Rd. Cran GU6 .... 174 F2
New Park Rd.
  Streat SW12 & SW2 .... 21 E7
New Park Rd. Streat SW2 .... 21 E8
New Pl. Add CR0 .... 63 A4
New Pond Rd. Arting GU3 .... 129 E1
New Pond Rd. Compt GU3 .... 129 E1
New Poplars The. Ash GU12 ...... 106 A1
New Rd. Albury GU5 .... 132 D3
New Rd. Bagsh GU19 .... 47 F3
New Rd. Brack RG12 .... 27 D7
New Rd. Brent TW8 .... 6 D8
New Rd. Carsh CR4 .... 41 A1
New Rd. Chil GU4 .... 131 B3
New Rd. Crowth RG11 .... 45 C5
New Rd. E Bed TW14 .... 3 D1
New Rd. E Clan GU4 .... 111 E4
New Rd. E Mole KT8 .... 36 A6
New Rd. Egham TW18 .... 12 C4
New Rd. Esher KT10 .... 55 C6
New Rd. Felt TW14 .... 15 B7
New Rd. Felt TW13 .... 15 E3
New Rd. For Gn RH5 .... 176 E6
New Rd. Gomsh GU5 .... 133 C4
New Rd. Harl TW6 & UB7 .... 3 C7
New Rd. Hawley GU17 .... 64 E4
New Rd. Hounsl TW3 .... 5 B3
New Rd. Hyde GU8 .... 171 F5
New Rd. King U T KT2 .... 18 A1
New Rd. Limps RH8 .... 123 B5
New Rd. Linch GU27 .... 207 F5
New Rd. Littlt TW17 .... 34 B6
New Rd. Milf GU8 .... 170 E8
New Rd. N Asct SL5 .... 8 F1
New Rd. Oxsh KT10 & KT22 ...... 55 F1
New Rd. Oxsh KT10 & KT22 ...... 74 F8
New Rd. Rich TW10 .... 17 C4
New Rd. Sandh GU17 .... 64 A8
New Rd. Smallf RH6 .... 162 B3
New Rd. Tadw KT20 .... 97 C4
New Rd. Tand RH8 & RH9 .... 143 A7
New Rd. Tongh GU10 .... 126 F6
New Rd. Weyb KT13 .... 53 C5
New Rd. Windl GU19 & GU20 .... 48 A4
New Rd. Woner GU5 .... 152 B8
New Rd. Wormly GU8 .... 191 A8
New Rd Units. Hounsl TW3 .... 5 B3
New Residences. Addl KT16 ...... 51 C7
New Scotland Hill Cty Prim Sch.
  Sandh GU17 .... 45 A2
New Sq. E Bed TW14 .... 14 C7
New St. Crawl RH10 .... 202 A7
New St. Horsh RH13 .... 217 D2
New St. Stain TW18 .... 13 A4
New Town. Copth RH10 .... 183 B3
New Victoria Hospl The.
  King U T KT3 .... 38 E8
New Way. Ock Rid GU7 .... 150 C4
New Wickham La. Thor L TW2 .. 12 B1
New Wokingham Rd.
  Crowth RG11 .... 45 A6
New Woodlands Sch. Catf BR1 .. 24 E4
New Zealand Ave. Walt O T KT12 34 F1
Newall Rd. Harl TW6 .... 3 C6
Newark Cl. Burph GU4 .... 110 B6
Newark Cl. Ripley GU23 .... 91 A6
Newark Ct. Walt O T KT12 .... 35 C1
Newark La. Mayb GU22 .... 90 F8
Newark La. Ripley GU22 & GU23 .. 91 A6
Newark Rd. Crawl RH10 .... 201 F8
Newark Rd. S Croy CR2 .... 61 D4
Newark Rd. Windl GU20 .... 48 B6
Newbolt Ave. Cheam SM3 .... 58 D5
Newborough Gn. New Mal KT3 .. 38 D5
Newborough House.
  Mitch SW19 .... 20 D1
Newbridge Cl. Broad H RH12 .. 216 C3
Newbridge Ct. Cran GU6 .... 174 B3
Newbridge Ct. Up Toot SW17 .. 20 C4
Newbridge Point. 3
  For Hil SE23 .... 23 D5
Newbury Gdns. Worc Pk KT19 .. 57 F6
Newbury Rd. Harm TW6 .... 2 F6
Newchapel Rd. Lingf RH7 ...... 164 B3
Newchapel Rd. Newch RH7 .... 163 F2
Newcome Gdns. Streat SW16 .... 21 E4
Newcome Pl. Alder GU12 .... 126 D7
Newcome Rd. Heath E GU9 ...... 125 E6
Newdigate Endowed CE Inf Sch.
  Newd RH5 .... 158 B1
Newdigate House. 6
  King U T KT2 .... 18 B2
Newdigate Rd. Bear Gn RH5 .... 157 E2
Newdigate Rd. Rusper RH12 .... 199 C8
Newenham Rd. G Book KT23 .... 94 A1
Newent Cl. Carsh SM5 .... 40 F1
Newfield Ave. W Heath GU14 .... 84 E6
Newfield Cl. Hampt TW12 .... 36 A8
Newfield Rd. Ash V GU12 ...... 106 A6
Newfoundland Cl. Friml GU16 .. 86 D8
Newgate. Croy CR0 .... 42 C1
Newgate Cl. Felt TW13 .... 15 E5
Newhache. Dorman RH7 .... 165 A1
Newhaven Cres. Ashf TW15 ...... 14 D3
Newhaven Rd. S Norw SE25 .... 42 D4
Newhouse. 5 New Mal KT3 ...... 38 E2
Newhouse Cl. New Mal KT3 ...... 38 E2
Newhouse Wlk. Morden SM4 .... 40 C2
Newland House Sch. Tedd TW1 16 F4
Newland House Sch Annex.
  Tedd TW1 .... 16 F4
Newlands Ave. Thame D KT7 .... 36 E1
Newlands Ave. Westfd GU22 .... 89 F6
Newlands Cl. Hersh KT12 .... 54 E6

Newlands Cl. Horley RH6 .... 160 F5
Newlands Cl. Albury GU4 .... 132 A7
Newlands Cres. E Grins RH19 .. 185 D2
Newlands Croft. Penge SE20 .... 23 C2
Newlands Ct. Addl KT15 .... 52 B5
Newlands Ct. Cater CR3 .... 100 C6
Newlands Ct. Streat SW16 .... 21 E3
Newlands Dr. Ash GU12 .... 106 B4
Newlands Dr. Poyle SL3 .... 1 E4
Newlands Estate. Witley GU8 .. 170 F5
Newlands Flats. Guild GU1 ...... 109 F2
Newlands Pk. Copth RH10 ...... 183 E3
Newlands Pk.
  For Hil SE26 & SE26 .... 23 D3
Newlands Pk. Penge SE26 .... 23 D3
Newlands Pl. For Row RH18 .... 206 F3
Newlands Rd. Camb GU15 .... 65 B1
Newlands Rd. Crawl RH11 ...... 201 C5
Newlands Rd. Horsh RH12 ...... 217 C4
Newlands Rd. Thorn H SW16 .... 41 E7
Newlands The. Wallin SM6 .... 60 D3
Newlands Way. Chess KT9 .... 56 C5
Newlands Wood. New Add CR0 .. 62 F2
Newman Cl. Worth RH10 .... 202 C4
Newman Rd. Thorn H CR0 .... 41 F1
Newmans Ct. Hale GU9 .... 125 A7
Newmarket Rd. Crawl RH10 .... 202 A4
Newminster Rd. Morden SM4 .... 40 C3
Newnham Cl. S Norw CR7 .... 42 C7
Newnham House. Catf SE6 .... 24 C5
Newport Jun Sch. Alder GU12 .. 105 D1
Newport Rd. Alder GU12 .... 105 D1
Newport Rd. Harm TW6 .... 3 A6
Newquay Rd. Catf SE6 .... 24 C6
Newry Rd. Islew TW1 .... 6 A2
Newsham Rd. 1 Woking GU21 .. 68 F2
Newstead Cl. Farnc GU7 .... 150 D6
Newstead House. Cater CR3 .... 101 B1
Newstead Rd. Lewish SE12 ...... 24 F8
Newstead Rise. Cater CR3 ...... 101 B1
Newstead Way. Wimble SW19 .... 19 E4
Newstead Wlk.
  Carsh SM4 & SM5 .... 40 C2
Newton Ave. E Grins RH19 ...... 205 F6
Newton Rd. Crawl RH10 .... 181 F2
Newton Rd. Farnb GU14 .... 85 D6
Newton Rd. Harm TW6 .... 2 E6
Newton Rd. Islew TW7 .... 5 F5
Newton Rd. Merton SW19 .... 19 E1
Newton Rd. Purley CR8 .... 79 C7
Newton Way. Tongh GU10 ...... 126 F7
Newton Wood Rd. Ashtd KT21 .. 75 F3
Newtown Ct. Horsh RH13 ...... 217 E1
Newtown Rd. Sandh GU17 .... 64 B8
Nicholas Gdns. Pyrf GU22 .... 70 F3
Nicholas House. Penge SE26 .... 23 B2
Nicholas Lodge. Thame D KT10 .. 55 A8
Nicholass Ct. 7 Purley CR8 ...... 80 B7
Nicholes Rd. Hounsl TW3 .... 5 A3
Nicholsfield. Loxwd RH14 ...... 212 F4
Nicholson Rd. Croy CR0 .... 42 F1
Nicholson Wlk. 3 Egham TW20 12 A3
Nicol Cl. 6 Twick TW1 .... 6 B1
Nicola Cl. Croy CR2 .... 61 C4
Nicosia Rd. Wands SW18 .... 20 E8
Niederwald Rd. For Hil SE26 .... 23 E4
Nightingale Ave. W Hors KT24 .. 92 F2
Nightingale Cl. Carsh SM5 .... 60 A8
Nightingale Cl. Chisw W4 .... 7 C8
Nightingale Cl. Cobham SL1 ...... 73 D8
Nightingale Cl. Crawl RH11 .... 201 D5
Nightingale Cl. E Grins RH19 .. 205 D7
Nightingale Cl. W Heath GU14 .. 84 C6
Nightingale Cres. W Hors KT24 .. 92 A6
Nightingale Cl. 3 Knaph GU21 .. 68 F1
Nightingale Ct. Penge SE19 ...... 22 F2
Nightingale Ct. 8 Redh RH1 .... 119 A2
Nightingale Dr. Mytch GU16 .... 86 A3
Nightingale Dr. W Ewell KT19 .. 57 B4
Nightingale Dr. W Ewell KT19 .. 57 B4
Nightingale Gdns. Sandh GU17 .. 64 B8
Nightingale La.
  Balham SW11 & SW12 .... 20 F8
Nightingale La. Rich TW10 ...... 17 E8
Nightingale La. Ash GU12 ...... 106 C3
Nightingale La. Carsh SM5 .... 60 A8
Nightingale La. E Hors KT24 .... 92 F2
Nightingale La. E Mole KT8 ...... 36 B4
Nightingale Rd. Esher KT10 ...... 54 F4
Nightingale Rd. Farnc GU7 ...... 150 E6
Nightingale Rd. Guild GU1 ...... 109 E1
Nightingale Rd. Hampt TW12 .... 16 A2
Nightingale Rd. Horsh RH12 .... 217 D3
Nightingale Rd. Selsd CR2 ...... 62 D1
Nightingale Rd. Walt O T KT12 .. 35 B2
Nightingale Sq. Balham SW12 .... 21 A8
Nightingale Way. Bletch RH1 .. 120 E2
Nightingales. Cran GU6 .... 174 E1
Nightingales The. Stan TW19 .... 13 F7
Nightjar Cl. Crond GU10 .... 124 D8
Nimbus Rd. Epsom KT19 .... 57 D1
Nimrod Cl. Crawl RH10 .... 182 D1
Nimrod Rd. Harm TW6 .... 3 A6
Nimrod Rd. Streat SW16 & SW17 21 B3
Nimrod Way. Harm TW6 .... 3 A6
Nine Elms Cl. E Bed TW14 ...... 14 F7
Nine Mile Ride.
  Crowth RG12 & RG11 .... 26 F1
Nine Mile Ride.
  Easth RG12 & RG11 .... 26 F1
Nineacres Way. Coulsd CR5 ...... 79 E3
Ninehams Cl. Cater CR3 .... 100 D7
Ninehams Gdns. Cater CR3 .... 100 D7
Ninehams Rd. Cater CR3 .... 100 D6
Ninehams Rd. Tats TN16 .... 103 D6
Nineteenth Rd. Mitch CR4 .... 41 E5
Ninfield Ct. Crawl RH11 .... 200 F2
Niton Rd. Rich TW9 .... 7 A4
Niven Cl. Worth RH10 .... 202 D5

Nobel Dr. Harl TW6 .... 3 E7
Noble Cnr. Heston TW5 .... 5 A6
Noble Cl. Mitch CR4 .... 40 D7
Noble St. Walt O T KT12 .... 54 C7
Nobles Way. Egham TW20 .... 11 E2
Noel Dr. Hounsl TW4 .... 4 F4
Noel Terr. For Hil SE23 .... 23 C6
Noke Dr. Earls RH1 .... 119 A2
Nonsuch Court Ave. Ewell KT17 58 B1
Nonsuch Ct. Cheam SM3 .... 58 E4
Nonsuch High Sch for Girls.
  Cheam SM3 .... 58 D3
Nonsuch Ind Est. Ewell KT17 .. 76 E8
Nonsuch Prim Sch. Stonel KT17 58 B5
Nonsuch Wlk. E Ewell SM2 ...... 58 D1
Noons Corner Rd. Wotton RH5 156 A8
Norbiton Ave.
  King U T KT1 & KT2 .... 38 A7
Norbiton Common Rd.
  King U T KT1 & KT3 .... 38 B6
Norbiton Hall. King U T KT2 ...... 37 F7
Norbiton Sta. King U T KT1 ...... 38 A8
Norbury Ave. Islew TW3 .... 5 D3
Norbury Ave.
  S Norw CR7 & SW16 .... 42 B7
Norbury Cl. S Norw SW16 .... 42 B8
Norbury Court Rd.
  Thorn H SW16 .... 41 E7
Norbury Cres. Thorn H SW16 .... 42 A7
Norbury Cross. Thorn H SW16 .. 41 E6
Norbury Hill. S Norw SW16 ...... 22 B1
Norbury Manor High Sch for Girls.
  S Norw CR7 .... 42 A8
Norbury Rd. Reigh RH2 .... 117 F1
Norbury Rd. S Norw CR7 .... 42 C6
Norbury Rise. Thorn H SW16 .... 41 E6
Norbury Sta. S Norw SW16 ...... 41 F8
Norbury Trad Est.
  Thorn H SW16 .... 41 F7
Norbury Way. G Book KT23 ...... 94 C2
Norcroft Gdns. Dulw SE22 .... 23 A8
Norcutt Rd. Twick TW2 .... 16 F7
Norfolk Ave. S Croy CR2 .... 62 A1
Norfolk Cl. Crawl RH11 .... 200 E2
Norfolk Cl. Horley RH6 .... 161 A2
Norfolk Cl. 5 Twick TW1 .... 6 B1
Norfolk Cotts. S Nutf RH1 ...... 140 E7
Norfolk Cl. Dork RH5 .... 136 B3
Norfolk Cl. Clayg KT10 .... 55 E5
Norfolk Cl. Dork RH4 .... 136 A7
Norfolk Cl. Surb KT5 .... 37 F3
Norfolk Cl. S Holm RH5 .... 157 C6
Norfolk Farm Cl. Mayb GU22 .... 70 D3
Norfolk Farm Rd. Mayb GU22 .. 70 D3
Norfolk House. 2 Croy CR0 ...... 61 D8
Norfolk House. 11
  Merton SW19 .... 20 C1
Norfolk House. Penge SE20 ...... 43 C8
Norfolk House Rd. Streat SW16 21 E5
Norfolk La. Dork RH5 .... 136 B1
Norfolk Rd. Clayg KT10 .... 55 E5
Norfolk Rd. Dork RH4 .... 136 A7
Norfolk Rd. Felt TW13 .... 15 C7
Norfolk Rd. Horsh RH12 & RH13 217 D2
Norfolk Rd. Mitch SW19 .... 20 E2
Norfolk Rd. S Holm RH5 .... 157 C6
Norfolk Terr.
  Horsh RH12 & RH13 .... 217 D2
Norgrove St. Balham SW12 ...... 21 A8
Norheads La. Bigg H TN16 ...... 83 B2
Norheads La. Chelsh TN16 ...... 83 B2
Norheads La.
  Chelsh CR6 & TN16 .... 103 A8
Norhyrst Ave. S Norw SE25 ...... 42 F6
Nork Gdns. Nork SM7 .... 77 E5
Nork Rise. Nork SM7 .... 77 D3
Nork Way. Nork KT17 & SM7 .... 77 D4
Norlands La.
  Egham TW18 & TW20 .... 32 E7
Norlands La.
  Thorpe TW18 & TW20 .... 32 E7
Norley Vale. Rhampt SW15 ...... 19 A7
Norman Ave. Ewell KT17 .... 76 F7
Norman Ave. Felt TW13 .... 15 F6
Norman Ave. S Croy CR2 & CR8 .. 61 C1
Norman Ave. Twick TW1 .... 17 C8
Norman Colyer Court.
  Epsom KT19 .... 57 D1
Norman Cres. Heston TW5 .... 4 D7
Norman Ct. 9 Hampt TW12 ...... 36 A8
Norman Ct. M Bourn GU9 ...... 125 C1
Norman Ct. Streat SW16 .... 22 A3
Norman House. Felt TW13 .... 15 F6
Norman House. Lo Hall TW17 .... 34 A2
Norman House. Woodh RH2 .... 138 F6
Norman Rd. Ashf TW15 .... 14 D2
Norman Rd. Merton SW19 .... 20 C1
Norman Rd. Sutton SM1 .... 59 A5
Norman Rd. Thorn H CR7 .... 42 B7
Norman's Rd. Outw RH1 & RH6 162 C5
Normandy Horsh RH12 .... 217 C1
Normandy Cl. 7 E Grins RH19 .. 205 F8
Normandy Cl. Friml GU16 .... 86 E8
Normandy Cl. Worth RH10 ...... 202 C4
Normandy Gdns. Horsh RH12 .. 217 C1
Normandy Wlk. Egham TW20 .... 12 C3
Normanhurst. Ashf SW15 .... 14 A3
Normanhurst Cl. Crawl RH10 .. 201 F6
Normanhurst Dr. Twick TW1 ...... 6 B2
Normanhurst Rd. Streat SW2 .... 21 F6
Normanhurst Rd. Walt O T KT12 54 D8
Normans La. Haxted TN8 .... 165 E7
Normansfield Ave.
  Tedd KT1 & KT8 .... 17 C1
Normansfield Hospl. Tedd KT8 .. 17 C1
Normanton. Reig RH2 .... 117 D2
Normanton Ave.
  Wimble SW18 & SW19 .... 20 A6
Normanton Rd. S Croy CR2 ...... 61 E4
Normanton St. For Hil SE23 ...... 23 D6
Normington Cl. Streat SW16 .... 22 A3
Norrels Dr. E Hors KT24 .... 92 F1

Norrels Ride. E Hors KT24 .... 92 F2
Norreys Ave. Woki RG11 .... 25 D7
Norris Hill Rd.
  Chur C GU13 & GU14 .... 104 A8
Norris Rd. Stain TW18 .... 12 F4
Norstead Pl. Rhampt SW15 ...... 19 A6
North Acre. Banstd SM7 .... 77 F3
North Ash. Horsh RH12 .... 217 C4
North Ave. Heath E GU9 .... 125 D7
North Ave. 8 Rich TW9 .... 7 A6
North Ave. Wallin SM5 .... 60 A3
North Ave. Whit V KT12 .... 53 E2
North Beta Rd. Farnb GU14 ...... 85 B2
North Camp Sta. Ash V GU12 .. 105 F8
North Cl. Ash GU12 .... 105 E1
North Cl. Crawl RH10 .... 201 F7
North Cl. Dork RH5 .... 136 C3
North Cl. E Bed TW14 .... 3 D1
North Cl. Farnb GU14 .... 85 A8
North Cl. Merton SM4 .... 39 E5
North Comm. Weyb KT13 .... 53 C6
North Crofts. Dulw SE21 .... 23 B7
North Dene. Hounsl TW5 .... 5 B6
North Down. Sander CR2 .... 80 E7
North Downs Cres.
  New Add CR0 .... 63 B1
North Downs Golf Course.
  Wold RH9 .... 102 A2
North Downs Rd. New Add CR0 .. 63 C1
North Dr. Beck BR3 .... 44 B5
North Dr. Hounsl TW3 & TW7 .... 5 C5
North Dr. Pirb GU24 .... 87 C6
North Dr. Streat SW16 .... 21 C4
North Dr. Went GU25 .... 30 E4
North East Surrey Coll of Tech.
  Epsom KT19 .... 57 D1
North End. Croy CR0 & CR9 ...... 61 C8
North End La. Sunnin SL5 .... 30 E2
North Farm Rd. W Heath GU14 .. 84 F8
North Farnborough Cty Inf Sch.
  Farnb GU14 .... 85 D5
North Feltham Trad Est.
  Felt TW14 .... 4 B3
North Gate Rd. Farnb GU14 ...... 85 C2
North Gdns. Mitch SW19 .... 20 D1
North Gn. Brack RG12 .... 27 D8
North Gr. Chert KT16 .... 32 F3
North Hatton Rd. Harl TW6 .... 3 D6
North Heath Cl. Horsh RH12 .... 217 D5
North Heath Cty Prim Sch.
  Horsh RH12 .... 217 D5
North Heath Est. Horsh RH12 .. 217 D6
North Heath La. Horsh RH12 .... 217 E6
North Holmes Cl. Horsh RH12 .. 218 D5
North Hyde La. Heston TW5 ...... 4 F8
North La. Alder GU11 & GU12 .. 105 D2
North La. Tedd TW11 .... 16 F2
North Lodge Dr. N Asct SL5 ...... 28 C7
North Mead. Crawl RH10 .... 201 E8
North Mead. Redh RH1 .... 118 F4
North Minden House.
  Friml GU16 .... 86 D7
North Moors. Bellf GU1 .... 109 E6
North Munstead La.
  Godal GU7 .... 151 A1
North Par. Chess KT9 .... 56 F5
North Par. Horsh RH12 .... 217 C3
North Park La. Bletch RH9 ...... 121 A5
North Pl. Mitch SW19 .... 20 F1
North Pl. Tedd TW11 .... 16 F2
North Pole La. Coney H BR2 .... 63 F4
North Rd. Ash V GU12 .... 105 F4
North Rd. Brent TW8 .... 6 E8
North Rd. Crawl RH10 .... 202 A4
North Rd. E Bed TW14 .... 3 D1
North Rd. Farnb GU11 .... 105 D7
North Rd. Hersh KT12 .... 54 C5
North Rd. Heston TW5 .... 4 C8
North Rd. King U T KT6 .... 37 D3
North Rd. Mitch SW17 & SW19 .. 20 C2
North Rd. Rich TW9 .... 7 A5
North Rd. Stough GU2 .... 109 B4
North Rd. W Wick BR4 .... 44 B1
North Rd. Wimble SW17 & SW19 .. 20 C2
North Rd. Wink SL5 .... 28 B8
North Rd. Woking GU21 .... 70 A3
North Rd. Woodh RH2 .... 138 F6
North Sheen Sta. Rich TW10 .... 7 A3
North Side. Stough GU10 .... 126 F7
North St. Carsh SM5 .... 59 F6
North St. Dork RH4 .... 136 A7
North St. Egham TW20 .... 11 F2
North St. Farnc GU7 .... 150 E7
North St. Guild GU1 .... 130 D8
North St. Horsh RH12 & RH13 .. 217 D1
North St. Islew TW7 .... 6 A4
North St. Leahd KT22 .... 95 A6
North St. Redh RH1 .... 118 F2
North St. Turn H RH10 .... 204 A4
North St. Wink SL4 .... 9 A6
North Station App. S Nutf RH1 140 F7
North Terminal App.
  Crawl RH6 .... 181 F6
North View. Wimble SW19 .... 19 C3
North View Cres. Burgh H KT18 .. 77 C2
North Weald La. King U T KT2 .. 17 D3
North Weylands Ind Est.
  Walt O T KT12 .... 54 E8
North Wlk. New Add CR0 .... 63 C5
North Worple Way. Mortl SW14 .. 7 D4
Northampton Cl. Brack RG12 .... 27 E6
Northampton Rd.
  Croy CR0 & CR9 .... 62 A8
Northanger Rd. Streat SW16 .... 21 E2
Northborough Rd.
  Thorn H SW16 .... 41 E7
Northbourne. Farnc GU7 .... 150 F8
Northbrook Coll of Design & Tech.
  Horsh RH12 .... 217 C4
Northbrook Copse. Brack RG12 27 F3
Northbrook Rd. Alder GU11 .... 126 B8

Northbrook Rd. Thorn H CR0 .... 42 D4
Northcliffe Cl. Worc Pk KT4 ...... 57 E7
Northcote. Addl KT15 .... 52 D6
Northcote Ave. Islew TW7 .... 6 A2
Northcote Ave. Tolw KT5 .... 38 B2
Northcote Cl. W Hors KT24 ...... 92 C2
Northcote Cres. W Hors KT24 .. 92 C2
Northcote La. Sham Gn GU5 .. 152 E6
Northcote Pk. Oxsh KT22 .... 74 C4
Northcote Rd. Ash V GU12 ...... 106 A7
Northcote Rd. Islew TW1 & TW7 .. 6 A2
Northcote Rd. King U T KT3 ...... 38 D6
Northcote Rd. Thorn H CR0 ...... 42 D3
Northcote Rd. W Heath GU14 .... 84 F6
Northcote Rd. W Hors KT24 ...... 92 C2
Northcott. Easth RG12 .... 27 A1
Northcroft Cl. Eng Gn TW20 .... 11 B3
Northcroft Gdns. Eng Gn TW20 .. 11 B3
Northcroft Rd. Eng Gn TW20 .... 11 B3
Northcroft Rd. W Ewell KT19 .... 57 E3
Northcroft Villas. Eng Gn TW20 . 11 B3
Northdown Cl. Horsh RH12 .... 217 F4
Northdown Ct. Tyl Gn RH9 .... 121 C5
Northdown La. Guild GU1 ...... 130 E6
Northdown Rd. Belm SM2 .... 59 A1
Northdown Rd.
  Wold CR3 & RH9 .... 102 A2
Northdown Terr. E Grins RH19 185 D3
Northdowns. Cran GU6 .... 174 E1
Northend Ct. G Book KT23 .... 94 C1
Northern Perimeter Rd.
  Harl TW6 .... 3 E6
Northern Perimeter Rd.
  Hatton TW6 .... 3 E6
Northern Perimeter Road (W).
  Harm TW6 .... 2 D6
Northernhay Wlk. Merton SM4 .. 39 E5
Northey Ave. Belm SM2 .... 58 E1
Northey Ave. E Ewell SM2 .... 58 E1
Northfield. Lhtwat GU18 .... 67 B8
Northfield. Shalf GU4 .... 130 E1
Northfield. Witley GU8 .... 170 E4
Northfield Cl. Alder GU12 ...... 105 D1
Northfield Cres. Cheam SM3 .... 58 E6
Northfield Ct. Stain TW18 .... 33 B8
Northfield Hospl. Alder GU12 .. 105 D2
Northfield Pl. Whit V KT13 ...... 53 B3
Northfield Rd. Cobham KT11 .... 73 B6
Northfield Rd. Heston TW5 .... 4 D7
Northfield Rd. Stain TW18 .... 33 B8
Northfields. Ashtd KT21 .... 95 E8
Northgate Ave. Crawl RH10 .... 201 F7
Northgate Cty Fst Sch.
  Crawl RH10 .... 201 E7
Northgate Cty Mid Sch.
  Crawl RH10 .... 201 E7
Northgate Dr. Camb GU15 .... 66 A7
Northgate Pl. Crawl RH10 ...... 201 E7
Northgate Rd. Crawl RH6 .... 181 F8
Northgate Rd.
  Crawl RH10 & RH11 .... 201 D6
Northington Cl. Brack RG12 ...... 27 F3
Northlands Bglws. Newd RH5 .. 158 B1
Northlands Rd. Faygt RH12 .... 198 F2
Northlands Rd. Horsh RH12 .... 217 E7
Northlands Rd. Warn RH12 .... 197 D2
Northmead. Farnb GU14 .... 85 B4
Northmead Grant Maintained
  Jun Sch. Stough GU2 ...... 109 B4
Northmoor. 4 For Hil SE23 ...... 23 D5
Northolt Rd. Harm TW6 .... 2 E6
Northover. Catf BR1 .... 24 F5
Northrop Rd. Harl TW6 .... 3 E6
Northspur Rd. Sutton SM1 ...... 59 A7
Northstead Rd. Streat SW2 ...... 22 A6
Northumberland Ave.
  Hounsl TW7 .... 6 A7
Northumberland Cl. Stan TW19 .. 2 E1
Northumberland Cres. Felt TW14 3 E1
Northumberland Gdns.
  Hounsl TW7 .... 6 A7
Northumberland Gdns.
  Mitch CR4 .... 41 D4
Northumberland Pl. 26
  Rich TW10 .... 6 D2
Northway. Crawl RH6 .... 181 F8
Northway. Farnc GU7 .... 150 B7
Northway. Merton SM4 & SW20 .. 39 E5
Northway. Stough GU2 .... 109 A3
Northway. Wallin SM6 .... 60 C6
Northway Rd. Croy CR0 .... 42 F2
Northwood Ave. Knaph GU21 .... 68 D1
Northwood Ave. Purley CR8 ...... 80 B6
Northwood Pk. Crawl RH10 .... 182 A2
Northwood Rd. Harm TW6 .... 2 D6
Northwood Rd. S Norw CR7 ...... 42 C7
Northwood Rd. Wallin SM5 ...... 60 A4
Northway. 1 W Norw SE19 ..... 22 E2
Norton Ave. Tolw KT5 .... 38 B2
Norton Ct. Beck BR3 .... 43 F8
Norton Gdns. Thorn H SW16 .... 41 E7
Norton House. 4 New Mal KT3 .. 38 E5
Norton Pk. Ascot SL5 .... 29 C4
Norton Rd. Friml GU15 .... 66 C4
Norton Rd. Woki RG11 .... 25 C5
Norwich Ave. Camb GU15 .... 65 E3
Norwich Rd. Crawl RH10 .... 202 B5
Norwich Rd. S Norw CR7 .... 42 C6
Norwood Cl. Effing KT24 .... 113 C7
Norwood Cl. Twick TW2 .... 16 C6
Norwood Cres. Harl TW6 .... 3 C6
Norwood Farm La. Cater KT11 .. 73 B8
Norwood Heights Sh Ctr.
  S Norw SE19 .... 22 C2
Norwood High St. W Norw SE27 22 C4
Norwood Hill. Charl RH6 .... 159 D3
Norwood Hospl. S Norw SE19 .. 22 D2
Norwood Junction Sta.
  Croy SE25 .... 43 A5

Norwood Park Rd.
W Norw SE27 22 C3
Norwood Rd. Effing KT24 113 E7
Norwood Rd. Streat SE24 & SE27 22 B7
Norwood Rd. W Norw SE24 & SE27 22 B7
Norwood Sch. W Norw SE27 22 C3
Norwood Sch. W Norw SE27 22 C4
Norwoodhill Rd. Charl RH6 159 F2
Noseby Ct. Walt O T KT12 54 C8
Notley End. Eng Gn TW20 11 C1
Notre Dame Int Sch.
Crawl RH10 202 D6
Notre Dame Jun Sch.
Lingf RH7 164 F3
Notre Dame Sen Sch.
Lingf RH7 164 F3
Notson Rd. Croy SE25 43 B5
Nottingham Cl. Knaph GU21 68 F1
Nottingham Ct. 6 Knaph GU21 68 F1
Nottingham Rd. Croy CR2 61 C5
Nottingham Rd. Islew TW7 5 F5
Nottingham Rd. Up Toot SW17 20 F7
Nova Mews. W Barn SM4 39 E2
Nova Rd. Thorn H CR0 42 C2
Nower Lodge Sch. Dork RH4 136 A6
Nower Rd. Dork RH4 136 A6
Nowhurst La. Slinfd RH12 216 A5
Noyna Rd. Up Toot SW17 20 F5
Nuffield Dr. Sandh GU15 45 E1
Nugee Ct. Crowth RG11 45 B5
Nugent Ct. Stough GU2 109 B4
Nugent Ct. Streat SW16 21 C4
Nugent Rd. Onsl V GU2 129 D8
Nugent Rd. S Norw SE25 42 F6
Numa Ct. Brent TW8 6 D7
Nunappleton Way. Oxted RH8 123 A3
Nuneaton. Brack RG12 27 E3
Nuneham. Streat SW16 21 D4
Nuns Wlk. Vir W GU25 31 D4
Nuptown La. New Gn SL4 8 A8
Nursery Ave. Croy CR0 62 D8
Nursery Cl. Capel RH5 178 C5
Nursery Cl. Croy CR0 62 D8
Nursery Cl. Ewell KT17 57 E1
Nursery Cl. Felt TW14 15 B8
Nursery Cl. Friml GU16 85 F7
Nursery Cl. Horse GU21 69 C3
Nursery Cl. Walt o t H KT20 97 B2
Nursery Cl. Woodhm KT15 51 F1
Nursery Cotts. Woking GU21 88 F8
Nursery Gdns. Chil GU4 131 B3
Nursery Gdns. Stain TW18 13 B1
Nursery Gdns. Sunby TW16 34 F7
Nursery Hill. Sham Gn GU5 152 D5
Nursery La. Hookw RH6 160 D2
Nursery La. N Asct SL5 28 E8
Nursery Rd. Farnc GU7 150 F7
Nursery Rd. Knaph GU21 68 D2
Nursery Rd. Merton SW19 40 B7
Nursery Rd. Mitch CR4 40 E6
Nursery Rd. S Norw CR7 & SE25 42 D5
Nursery Rd. Sunby TW16 34 F7
Nursery Rd. Sutton SM1 59 C6
Nursery Rd. Walt o t H KT20 97 B2
Nursery Rd. Wimble SW19 19 E1
Nurserylands. Crawl RH11 201 A6
Nutborn House. Wimble SW19 19 D2
Nutbourne. Heath E GU9 125 E7
Nutbourne Cotts. Hambl GU8 191 E7
Nutbourne Ct. Stain TW18 12 F1
Nutcombe La. Dork RH4 135 F7
Nutcombe La.
Shottm GU26 & GU27 188 E1
Nutcroft Gr. Fetch KT22 94 E6
Nutfield Church Prim Sch.
S Nutf RH1 140 F8
Nutfield Cl. Carsh SM5 59 E7
Nutfield Ct. Camb GU15 65 D7
Nutfield Marsh Rd. Nutf RH1 119 E4
Nutfield Rd. Coulsd CR5 79 A3
Nutfield Rd. Earls RH1 119 C1
Nutfield Rd. Merst RH1 119 C5
Nutfield Rd. Nutf RH1 119 C1
Nutfield Rd. Thorn H CR7 42 B5
Nutfield Sta. S Nutf RH1 140 E7
Nuthatch Cl. Crond GU10 124 D7
Nuthatch Gdns. Dovgn RH2 139 C5
Nuthatch Way. Horsh RH12 217 D7
Nuthurst. Brack RG12 27 E4
Nuthurst Ave. Cran GU6 174 E3
Nuthurst Ave. Streat SW2 21 F6
Nuthurst Cl. Crawl RH11 201 A7
Nutley. Easth RG12 27 A1
Nutley Ct. Reig RH2 118 A1
Nutley La. Reig RH2 117 F2
Nutmeg Ct. W Heath GU14 84 C5
Nutshell La. Hale GU9 125 C6
Nutty La. Littlt TW17 34 C6
Nutwell St. Up Toot SW17 20 E3
Nutwood. Farnc GU7 150 D6
Nutwood Ave. Brock RH3 137 C8
Nutwood Cl. Brock RH3 137 C8
Nyefield Pk. Walt o t H KT20 97 A1
Nylands Ave. Rich TW9 7 A5
Nymans Cl. Horsh RH12 218 A7
Nymans Ct. Crawl RH10 202 B3
Nymans Gdns. W Barn SW20 39 B6
Nyon Gr. For Hil SE23 & SE6 23 F6

O'Connor Rd. Farnb GU11 105 E7
O'Gorman Ave. Farnb GU14 85 B2
Oak Ave. Croy CR0 63 B8
Oak Ave. Egham TW20 12 D1
Oak Ave. Hampt TW12 & TW13 15 E2
Oak Ave. Heston TW5 4 E7
Oak Ave. Sandh GU15 45 D1
Oak Bank. New Add CR0 63 C4
Oak Cl. Box H KT20 116 B5
Oak Cl. Chidd GU8 191 A4
Oak Cl. Copth RH10 183 A3
Oak Cl. Farnc GU7 150 E8
Oak Cnr. Bear Gn RH5 157 C4
Oak Cottage Cl. Catf SE6 24 F7
Oak Cottage Cl. Wood S V GU3 108 C2
Oak Cotts. Shottm GU27 207 E6
Oak Croft. E Grins RH19 206 A8
Oak Ct. M Bourn GU9 125 B1
Oak Dell. Crawl RH10 202 C7
Oak Dr. Box H KT20 116 B5
Oak End. Bear Gn RH5 157 C3
Oak End Way. Woodhm KT15 70 F7
Oak Farm Cl. Blckw GU17 64 C5
Oak Farm Cty Sec Sch.
W Heath GU14 84 F6
Oak Gdns. Croy CR0 63 A8
Oak Glade. Epsom KT19 76 A7
Oak Gr. Loxwd RH14 213 A4
Oak Gr. Sunby TW16 15 B1
Oak Gr. W Wick BR4 44 C1
Oak Grange Rd. W Clan GU4 111 B6
Oak Grove Cres. Sandh GU15 64 F6
Oak Grove Rd. Penge SE20 43 C7
Oak Hill. Burph GU4 110 C6
Oak Hill. Surb KT6 37 E2
Oak Hill. Wood S V GU3 108 B3
Oak Hill. Woodc KT18 76 D3
Oak Hill Cres. Surb KT6 37 E2
Oak Hill Gr. Surb KT6 37 E3
Oak Hill Rd. Surb KT6 37 E3
Oak House. Penge SE20 43 B7
Oak La. Broad H RH12 216 E3
Oak La. Eng Gn TW20 11 C5
Oak La. Islew TW7 5 E3
Oak La. Mayb GU22 70 B3
Oak La. Twick TW1 17 A8
Oak Leaf Cl. Epsom KT19 76 C7
Oak Lodge. 4 Charlt TW16 14 F1
Oak Lodge. Crowth RG11 45 C5
Oak Lodge Cl. Hersh KT12 54 C5
Oak Lodge Dr. Salfs RH1 140 A1
Oak Lodge Dr. W Wick BR4 44 B2
Oak Lodge Prim Sch.
W Wick BR4 44 B2
Oak Lodge Sch. Balham SW12 21 A8
Oak Mead. Farnc GU7 150 E8
Oak Park Gdns. Putney SW19 19 D7
Oak Pk. Sheer KT14 70 E6
Oak Rd. Cater CR3 100 E5
Oak Rd. Cobham KT11 73 E4
Oak Rd. Crawl RH11 201 C5
Oak Rd. Farnb GU14 85 C3
Oak Rd. King U T KT3 38 D7
Oak Rd. Leahd KT22 95 A8
Oak Rd. Reig RH2 118 B2
Oak Ridge. Dork RH4 136 B4
Oak Row. Mitch CR4 41 C7
Oak Tree Cl. Alder GU12 126 E8
Oak Tree Cl. Ash V GU12 85 F1
Oak Tree Cl. Bellf GU4 109 C6
Oak Tree Cl. Burph GU4 110 C6
Oak Tree Cl. Knaph GU21 68 B1
Oak Tree Cl. Went GU25 31 D3
Oak Tree Dr. Bellf GU1 109 C5
Oak Tree Dr. Eng Gn TW20 11 C3
Oak Tree La. Shottm GU27 207 D6
Oak Tree Rd. Knaph GU21 68 B1
Oak Tree Rd. Knaph GU21 88 B8
Oak Tree Rd. Milf GU8 149 F1
Oak Tree View. Heath E GU9 125 E6
Oak Tree Way. Horsh RH13 217 F4
Oak Way. Ashtd KT21 76 A3
Oak Way. Crawl RH10 201 E8
Oak Way. Croy CR0 43 D3
Oak Way. E Bed TW14 14 E7
Oak Way. Reig RH2 139 D8
Oak Wlk. Faygt RH12 199 F1
Oak's Rd. Woking GU21 69 E2
Oakapple Cl. Crawl RH11 201 B1
Oakapple Cl. Hams Gn CR2 81 B5
Oakbank. Fetch KT22 94 D4
Oakbank. Woking GU22 89 E8
Oakbank Ave. Walt O T KT12 35 F2
Oakbrook. Beck BR3 44 B7
Oakcombe Cl. King U T KT3 38 E8
Oakcroft Bsns Ctr. Chess KT9 56 F6
Oakcroft Cl. W Byfl KT14 70 F5
Oakcroft House. 3 New Mal KT3 38 E2
Oakcroft Rd. Chess KT9 56 F6
Oakcroft Rd. Pyrf KT14 70 F5
Oakcroft Villas. Chess KT9 56 F6
Oakdale. Beck BR3 44 C7
Oakdale. Brack RG12 27 D3
Oakdale Rd. Epsom KT19 57 D2
Oakdale Rd. Streat SW16 21 E3
Oakdale Rd. Weyb KT13 53 A7
Oakdale Way. Carsh CR4 41 A2
Oakdene. Chobh GU24 49 F1
Oakdene. Kings KT20 97 E7
Oakdene. Sunnin SL5 29 F3
Oakdene. 1 W Norw SE19 22 E3
Oakdene Ave. Thame D KT7 37 A1
Oakdene Cl. Brock RH3 137 C7
Oakdene Cl. G Book KT23 114 C8
Oakdene Ct. Walt O T KT12 54 B7
Oakdene Dr. Tolw KT5 38 C1
Oakdene Lodge. Penge SE20 23 B1
Oakdene Mews. Cheam SM3 39 F1
Oakdene Par. Cobham KT11 73 B5
Oakdene Rd. Brock RH3 137 C7
Oakdene Rd. Cobham KT11 73 B5
Oakdene Rd. Godal GU7 150 D3
Oakdene Rd. L Book KT23 93 F3
Oakdene Rd. Redh RH1 118 F1
Oakdene Rd. Shalf GU3 130 C1
Oaken Coppice. Ashtd KT21 96 A8
Oaken Copse Cres. Farnb GU14 85 B7
Oaken Dr. Clayg KT10 55 F4
Oaken La. Clayg KT10 55 E5
Oakengates. Easth RG12 27 A1
Oakenshaw Cl. Surb KT6 37 E2
Oakfield. Plaist RH14 211 E2
Oakfield. Woking GU21 68 E3
Oakfield Cl. New Mal KT3 38 F4
Oakfield Cl. Weyb KT13 53 C6
Oakfield Ct. Croy CR2 61 C4
Oakfield Ct. Woki RG11 25 A5
Oakfield Cty Jun Sch.
Fetch KT22 94 D4
Oakfield Dr. Reig RH2 118 B3
Oakfield Gdns. Beck BR3 44 A4
Oakfield Gdns. Carsh SM5 40 F1
Oakfield Gdns. 3 Dulw SE19 22 E3
Oakfield Glade. Weyb KT13 53 C6
Oakfield Rd. Ashf TW15 14 B3
Oakfield Rd. Ashtd KT21 75 E1
Oakfield Rd. Cobham KT11 73 B5
Oakfield Rd. Hawley GU17 64 F3
Oakfield Rd. Penge SE20 23 B1
Oakfield Rd. Thorn H CR0 42 C1
Oakfield Rd. Wimble SW19 19 D5
Oakfield Sch. Dulw SE21 22 D7
Oakfield Sch. Pyrf GU22 70 F4
Oakfield Way. E Grins RH19 185 F3
Oakfields. Camb GU15 65 B5
Oakfields. Crawl RH10 202 D7
Oakfields. Stough GU2 108 F3
Oakfields. W Byfl KT14 71 B5
Oakfields. Wall W RH5 196 D8
Oakfields. Walt O T KT12 35 A1
Oakhall Ct. Ashf TW16 14 F3
Oakhall Dr. Ashf TW16 14 F3
Oakham Cl. For Hil SE6 23 F6
Oakham Dr. Hayes BR2 44 F5
Oakhaven. Crawl RH10 & RH11 201 D4
Oakhill. Clayg KT10 56 A4
Oakhill Cl. Ashtd KT21 75 C1
Oakhill Ct. 8 Surb KT6 37 E3
Oakhill Ct. Wimble SW19 19 D1
Oakhill Gdns. Oat Pk KT13 53 E8
Oakhill Lodge. Purley CR8 80 A6
Oakhill Rd. Ashtd KT21 75 C1
Oakhill Rd. Beck BR3 44 C7
Oakhill Rd. Head Dn GU35 187 B5
Oakhill Rd. Horsh RH13 217 E2
Oakhill Rd. Reig RH2 139 B8
Oakhill Rd. Row Tn KT15 51 F4
Oakhill Rd. Sutton SM1 59 C7
Oakhill Rd. Thorn H SW16 41 F8
Oakhurst. Burrh GU24 49 E2
Oakhurst. Graysh GU26 188 D3
Oakhurst Cl. 4 Tedd TW11 16 E3
Oakhurst Gdns. E Grins RH19 185 C2
Oakhurst La. Loxwd RH14 212 E7
Oakhurst Rd. W Ewell KT19 57 D4
Oakhurst Rd. W Ewell KT19 57 D4
Oakhurst Rise. Sutton SM5 59 E1
Oakhyrst Grange Sch.
Cater CR3 100 D1
Oakington. 6 King U T KT1 38 A7
Oakington Dr. Sunby TW16 35 C7
Oakland Ave. Heath E GU9 125 E7
Oakland Way. W Ewell KT19 57 E4
Oakland Way. W Ewell KT19 57 E4
Oaklands. Croy CR0 61 B5
Oaklands. Fetch KT22 94 D3
Oaklands. Haslem GU27 208 C7
Oaklands. Horley RH6 161 C3
Oaklands. Horsh RH13 217 E2
Oaklands. Purley CR8 80 C5
Oaklands. S Godst RH9 142 E5
Oaklands. Twick TW2 16 C8
Oaklands Ave. Hounsl TW7 5 F8
Oaklands Ave. Thame D KT10 36 D1
Oaklands Ave. Thorn H CR7 42 A5
Oaklands Ave. W Wick BR4 63 B7
Oaklands Cl. Chess KT9 56 C6
Oaklands Cl. N Asct SL5 8 F1
Oaklands Cl. Shalf GU4 130 E1
Oaklands Ct. Addl KT15 52 B7
Oaklands Cty Jun Sch.
Crowth RG11 45 A6
Oaklands Dr. Earls RH1 140 B7
Oaklands Dr. N Asct SL5 8 F1
Oaklands Dr. Woki RG11 25 A5
Oaklands Gdns. Purley CR8 80 C5
Oaklands Inf Sch. Bigg H TN16 83 C3
Oaklands Inf Sch. Crowth RG11 45 A6
Oaklands Jun Sch. Bigg H TN16 83 C3
Oaklands La. Bigg H TN16 83 C5
Oaklands La. Crowth RG11 45 B7
Oaklands Pk. Woki RG11 25 A3
Oaklands Pk. Woki RG11 25 A4
Oaklands Rd. Broml BR1 24 E1
Oaklands Rd. Mortl SW14 7 D4
Oaklands Sch. Islew TW3 5 D4
Oaklands Way. Tadw KT20 97 C5
Oaklands Way. Wallin SM6 60 D3
Oaklawn Rd. Ashtd KT22 74 E2
Oaklawn Rd. Leahd KT22 74 E2
Oaklea. Ash V GU12 106 A5
Oaklea Ct. S Croy CR2 61 D2
Oakleigh. Epsom KT18 76 E5
Oakleigh. Lhtwat GU18 67 C8
Oakleigh Annexe (Queen Victoria
Hospl). Ash W RH19 206 C7
Oakleigh Ave. Tolw KT6 57 B8
Oakleigh Ct. Oxted RH8 122 E6
Oakleigh Ct. Penge SE20 23 B1
Oakleigh Rd. Horsh RH12 217 F4
Oakleigh Way. Mitch CR4 41 B8
Oakleigh Way. 1 Tolw KT6 38 B1
Oakley Ave. Wallin CR0 60 E6
Oakley Cl. Addl KT15 52 D6
Oakley Cl. E Grins RH19 206 B7
Oakley Cl. Hounsl TW7 5 D6
Oakley Cotts. Ash W RH19 206 C7
Oakley Ct. 15 Redh RH1 119 A2
Oakley Dell. Merrow GU4 110 C3
Oakley Gdns. Banstd SM7 78 B4
Oakley House. Farnc GU7 150 E8
Oakley Rd. Camb GU15 65 B4
Oakley Rd. Croy SE25 43 B4
Oakley Rd. Whytlf CR6 81 A1
Oakman House. 29
Putney SW19 19 D7
Oakmead Gn. Woodc KT18 76 C4
Oakmead Pl. Mitch CR4 40 E8
Oakmead Rd. Up Toot SW12 21 B7
Oakmead Rd. Wallin CR0 41 D3
Oakridge. W End GU24 67 F6
Oakridge Rd. Catf BR1 24 E4
Oaks Ave. Felt TW13 15 E6
Oaks Ave. N Cheam KT4 58 B6
Oaks Ave. W Norw SE19 & SE27 22 E3
Oaks Cl. Horsh RH12 218 B6
Oaks Cl. Leahd KT22 95 A6
Oaks Ct. Leahd KT22 95 A6
Oaks La. S Croy CR0 62 C7
Oaks La. S Holm RH5 157 B8
Oaks Rd. Purley CR8 80 B5
Oaks Rd. Reig RH2 118 D2
Oaks Rd. S Croy CR0 62 C6
Oaks Rd. Stan TW19 2 D1
Oaks Sports Ctr. Wallin SM5 78 F8
Oaks The. Brack RG12 27 D7
Oaks The. Dork RH4 136 B4
Oaks The. E Grins RH19 206 B8
Oaks The. Epsom KT18 76 F5
Oaks The. Farnb GU14 84 D3
Oaks The. Stain TW18 12 F4
Oaks The. W Byfl KT14 71 A5
Oaks The. Wimble SW19 19 E2
Oaks Track. Wallin SM5 & SM6 60 B1
Oaks Way. Burgh H KT18 97 B8
Oaks Way. Long D KT6 37 D1
Oaks Way. Purley CR8 80 C5
Oaks Way. Wallin SM5 59 F3
Oaksford Ave. For Hil SE26 23 B5
Oakshade Rd. Catf BR1 24 D4
Oakshade Rd. Oxsh KT22 74 C5
Oakshaw. Oxted RH8 122 D8
Oakshaw Rd. Wands SW18 20 B8
Oakside Ct. Horley RH6 161 C4
Oakside La. Horley RH6 161 C4
Oaktree Way. Sandh GU17 45 A1
Oaktrees. Ash GU12 105 F1
Oaktrees. Hale GU9 125 B6
Oakview. Woki RG11 25 B4
Oakview Gr. Croy CR0 43 E1
Oakview Rd. Catf SE6 24 B3
Oakway. Alder GU12 126 E8
Oakway. Beck BR2 44 D7
Oakway. Knaph GU21 88 E8
Oakway. W Barn SW20 39 C5
Oakway Dr. Friml GU16 65 E1
Oakwood. Stough GU2 109 A6
Oakwood. Wallin SM6 60 B2
Oakwood Ave. Beck BR2 & BR3 44 C7
Oakwood Ave. Mitch CR4 40 D7
Oakwood Ave. Purley CR8 80 C7
Oakwood Cl. E Hors KT24 112 E8
Oakwood Cl. Earls RH1 119 A1
Oakwood Cl. S Nutf RH1 140 F7
Oakwood Ct. Beck BR3 44 C7
Oakwood Ct. Bisley GU24 68 A3
Oakwood Dr. E Hors KT24 112 E8
Oakwood Dr. W Norw SE19 22 E2
Oakwood Gdns. Knaph GU21 68 B1
Oakwood Gdns. Sutton SM1 59 A8
Oakwood Ind Pk. Crawl RH10 182 A2
Oakwood Pk. For Row RH18 206 F2
Oakwood Pl. Thorn H CR0 42 A3
Oakwood Rd. Bletch RH1 120 A6
Oakwood Rd. Brack RG12 27 E7
Oakwood Rd. Horley RH6 161 B4
Oakwood Rd. Knaph GU21 88 E8
Oakwood Rd. Thorn H CR0 & CR7 42 A3
Oakwood Rd. Thorpe GU25 31 C4
Oakwood Rd. Wimble SW20 39 A8
Oakwood Rd. Windl GU20 48 E4
Oakwood Sch. Horley RH6 161 C3
Oareborough. Brack RG12 27 E4
Oast House Cl. Wray TW19 11 E8
Oast House Cres. Hale GU9 125 D6
Oast House La. Hale GU9 125 D6
Oast La. Alder GU11 126 B7
Oast Rd. Oxted RH8 122 F4
Oates Cl. Beck BR2 44 D6
Oates Wlk. Crawl RH10 201 F3
Oatfield Rd. Tadw KT20 97 B6
Oatlands. Crawl RH11 201 A5
Oatlands. Horley RH6 161 C4
Oatlands Ave. Oat Pk KT13 53 E6
Oatlands Ave. Weyb KT13 53 E6
Oatlands Chase.
Oat Pk KT12 & KT13 53 E7
Oatlands Cl. Weyb KT13 53 D6
Oatlands Ct. 3 Putney SW19 19 D7
Oatlands Cty Inf Sch.
Oat Pk KT13 53 D6
Oatlands Dr. Oat Pk KT13 & KT12 53 D7
Oatlands Dr. Weyb KT13 & KT12 53 D7
Oatlands Gn. Oat Pk KT13 53 D7
Oatlands Mere. Oat Pk KT13 53 D7
Oatlands Rd. Burgh H KT20 97 E8
Oban Rd. S Norw SE25 42 D5
Obelisk Way. Camb GU15 65 C6
Oberon Way. Crawl RH11 200 E3
Oberon Way. Littlt TW17 33 E6
Oberursel Way. Alder GU11 104 F2
Observatory Rd. Mortl SW14 7 C3
Observatory Wlk. 3 Redh RH1 118 F1
Occam Rd. Onsl V GU2 129 D8
Ockenden Cl. Woking GU22 69 F1
Ockenden Gdns. Woking GU22 69 F1
Ockenden Rd. Woking GU22 69 F1
Ockfields. Milf GU8 149 F1
Ockford Ct. Godal GU7 150 D4
Ockford Dr. Ock Rid GU7 150 C3
Ockford Rd. Godal GU7 150 D4
Ockford Ridge. Ock Rid GU7 150 B2
Ockham Dr. W Hors KT24 92 D3
Ockham La. Downs KT11 92 D7
Ockham La. Mart Gn GU23 92 D7
Ockham La. Ockham GU23 92 D7
Ockham Rd N. Ockham GU23 92 C3
Ockham Rd N. W Hors KT24 92 C3
Ockham Rd S. E Hors KT24 112 E7
Ockley CE (VA) Fst Sch.
Ockley RH5 177 D4
Ockley Ct. Burph GU4 110 B6
Ockley House. 8 King U T KT2 18 B2
Ockley Rd. Ewh GU6 175 F6
Ockley Rd. For Gn GU6 & RH5 176 C7
Ockley Rd. Ockley RH5 177 B7
Ockley Rd. Streat SW16 21 E5
Ockley Rd. Thorn H CR0 & CR9 41 F2
Ockley Rd. Wotton GU6 & RH5 176 C7
Ockley Sta. Ockley RH5 178 A5
Ockleys Mead. Tyl Gn RH9 121 C5
Octagon Rd. Whit V KT12 53 E1
Octavia. Easth RG12 27 A1
Octavia Cl. Mitch CR4 40 E4
Octavia Rd. Islew TW7 5 F4
Octavia Way. Stain TW18 13 A2
October Ct. Beck BR2 44 F6
Odard Rd. E Mole KT8 36 A5
Odette House. 6 W Norw SE27 22 D4
Odiham Rd. Crond GU9 & GU10 124 D7
Odiham Rd. Heath E GU10 & GU9 124 D7
Ogden House. Felt TW13 15 E4
Okeburn Rd. Up Toot SW17 21 A3
Okehurst Rd. Rudg RH14 214 C1
Okingham Cl. Sandh GU15 45 D1
Olaf Palme House. Felt TW13 15 B5
Old Acre. Pyrf KT14 71 A5
Old Ave. Sheer GU21 & KT14 70 E6
Old Ave. Whit V KT13 53 C3
Old Avenue Cl. Sheer KT14 70 E6
Old Barn Cl. Belm SM2 58 E3
Old Barn Dr. Capel RH5 178 D6
Old Barn La. Churt GU10 168 B1
Old Barn La. Kenley CR3 80 F3
Old Barn Rd. Woodc KT18 76 C2
Old Barn View. Godal GU7 150 C2
Old Bisley Rd. Friml GU16 66 C3
Old Bracknell Cl. Easth RG12 27 B6
Old Bracknell La E. Easth RG12 27 B6
Old Bracknell La W. Easth RG12 27 B6
Old Brickfield Rd. Alder GU11 126 B7
Old Bridge St. Tedd KT1 37 D7
Old Brighton Rd S.
Crawl RH11 & RH6 181 E5
Old Bromley Rd. Catf BR1 24 D3
Old Charlton Rd. Shep TW17 34 C4
Old Chertsey Rd. Chobh GU24 50 C1
Old Chestnut Ave. Esher KT10 55 B4
Old Church La. M Bourn GU9 146 D7
Old Church Path. Esher KT10 55 B6
Old Claygate La. Clayg KT10 56 A5
Old Common Rd. Esher KT11 73 B7
Old Compton La. M Bourn GU9 125 F2
Old Control Rd. Crawl RH6 181 D6
Old Convent The. E Grins RH19 185 E2
Old Cote Dr. Heston TW5 5 A8
Old Cotts. Shalf GU3 130 C2
Old Court Rd. Guild GU2 130 A8
Old Crawley Rd. Crawl RH12 218 C7
Old Cross Tree Way. Ash GU12 127 C8
Old Ct. Ashtd KT21 95 E8
Old Dean Rd. Camb GU15 65 D7
Old Deer Park Gdns. Rich TW9 6 E4
Old Denne Gdns. Horsh RH12 217 C1
Old Devonshire Rd.
Balham SW12 21 B8
Old Dock Cl. Rich TW9 7 A8
Old Elstead Rd. Milf GU8 149 E2
Old Esher Cl. Hersh KT12 54 D5
Old Esher Rd. Hersh KT12 54 E5
Old Farleigh Rd.
Farlgh CR0 & CR2 & CR6 81 E6
Old Farleigh Rd.
Selsd CR0 & CR6 & CR22 81 E6
Old Farm Cl. Hounsl TW4 4 F3
Old Farm Rd. Bellf GU1 109 D4
Old Farm Rd. Hampt TW12 15 F2
Old Farmhouse Dr. Oxsh KT22 74 D4
Old Farnham La. Bentl GU10 124 A1
Old Farnham La. M Bourn GU9 146 C8
Old Ford House. Wallin CR0 60 E7
Old Forge Cres. Shep TW17 34 B3
Old Fox Cl. Coulsd CR3 100 B6
Old Frensham Rd.
Frensh GU10 146 E4
Old Frensham Rd.
M Bourn GU10 146 E4
Old Green La. Camb GU15 65 C7
Old Guildford Rd.
Mytch GU12 & GU16 & GU24 86 C4
Old Guildford Rd. Warn RH12 216 E4
Old Haslemere Rd.
Haslem GU27 208 C5
Old Heath Way. Heath E GU9 125 C7
Old Hill. Woking GU22 89 D7
Old Horsham Rd. Crawl RH11 201 B4
Old Hospital Cl.
Up Toot SW12 & SW17 20 F7
Old House Cl. Ewell KT17 57 F1
Old House Cl. Wimble SW19 19 E3
Old House Gdns. 9 Twick TW1 6 C1
Old Kiln Cl. Churt GU10 167 F2
Old Kiln La. Brock RH3 137 C8
Old Kiln La. Churt GU10 167 F2
Old Kingston Rd. Tolw KT4 57 C7
Old La. Alder GU12 105 E3
Old La. Alder GU11 126 A7
Old La. Docken GU10 166 F4
Old La. E Hors KT11 93 A5
Old La. Mart Gn KT11 92 E7
Old La. Ockham GU23 & KT11 72 B1
Old La. Oxted RH8 122 F5
Old La. Tats TN16 103 D6

Old Lands Hill. Wink RG12 .... 27 D8
Old Lane Gdns. E Hors KT11 .... 93 A5
Old Lodge Cl. Ock Rid GU7 .... 150 B3
Old Lodge La. Purley CR8 .... 80 A3
Old Lodge Pl. **7** Twick TW1 .... 6 B1
Old London Rd.
Epsom KT17 & KT18 .... 77 A2
Old London Rd. Mickle RH5 .... 115 C8
Old Malden La. Worc Pk KT4 .... 57 E8
Old Malt Way. Horse GU21 .... 69 D2
Old Manor Cl. Crawl RH11 .... 201 A8
Old Manor Dr. Twick TW7 .... 5 C1
Old Manor Gdns. Chil GU4 .... 131 C3
Old Martyrs. Crawl RH11 .... 181 D1
Old Merrow St. Merrow GU4 .... 110 D3
Old Mill La. Merst RH1 .... 119 B7
Old Millmeads. Horsh RH12 .... 217 C5
Old Museum Ct. Haslem GU27 ..... 208 D6
Old Nursery Pl. Ashf TW15 .... 14 B3
Old Oak Ave. Chips CR5 .... 98 E8
Old Orch. Byfl KT14 .... 71 F7
Old Orch. Sunby TW16 .... 35 C2
Old Orchard The. M Bourn GU9 ... 146 A8
Old Palace La. Rich TW9 .... 6 C2
Old Palace Rd. Croy CR0 & CR9 .... 61 C7
Old Palace Rd. Guild GU2 .... 130 A8
Old Palace Rd. Weyb KT13 .... 53 B7
Old Palace Sch. Croy CR9 .... 61 B7
Old Palace Terr. **8** Rich TW9 .... 6 D2
Old Palace Yd. **2** Rich TW9 .... 6 D2
Old Park Cl. Hale GU9 .... 125 A6
Old Park La. Farnh GU9 .... 125 A6
Old Park La. Hale GU9 .... 124 F6
Old Park Mews. Heston TW5 .... 4 F7
Old Parvis Rd. W Byfl KT14 .... 71 C7
Old Pasture Rd.
Friml GU16 & GU15 .... 65 F3
Old Pharmacy Ct. Crowth RG11 ..... 45 C4
Old Pond Cl. Friml GU15 .... 65 C1
Old Portsmouth Rd.
Arting GU2 & GU3 & GU7 .... 130 C3
Old Portsmouth Rd. Friml GU15 66 A3
Old Portsmouth Rd.
Shalf GU2 & GU3 & GU7 .... 130 C3
Old Portsmouth Rd.
Thursl GU8 .... 169 D4
Old Pottery Cl. Woodh RH2 .... 139 B7
Old Quarry The. King Gn GU27 ... 207 F4
Old Rd. Buckl RH3 .... 116 F1
Old Rd. E Grins RH19 .... 185 F1
Old Rd. Row Tn KT15 .... 51 F3
Old Rectory Cl. Walt o t H KT20 .... 97 A3
Old Rectory Dr. Ash GU12 .... 106 B2
Old Rectory Gdns. Farnb GU14 ..... 85 D4
Old Rectory Gdns. Guild GU2 ..... 150 F2
Old Rectory La. E Hors KT24 .... 92 E1
Old Redstone Dr. Earls RH1 .... 140 A8
Old Reigate Rd. Brock RH3 .... 116 C1
Old Reigate Rd. Pixham RH4 ...... 115 F2
Old Sawmill La. Crowth RG11 ...... 45 C6
Old School Cl. Ash GU12 .... 106 A3
Old School Cl. Merton SW19 .... 40 A7
Old School Cl. Penge BR3 .... 43 E7
Old School Cl. Wray TW19 .... 11 E8
Old School La. Brock RH3 .... 137 A7
Old School La. Newd RH5 .... 158 B1
Old School Mews. Oat Pk KT13 .. 53 D6
Old School Sq. Thame D KT7 .... 36 F3
Old Schools La. Ewell KT17 .... 57 F2
Old Station App. Leahd KT22 .... 95 A6
Old Station Cl. Crawl D RH10 ..... 204 B7
Old Station Rd. Farnc GU7 .... 150 E6
Old Station Way. Farnc GU7 .... 150 E5
Old Swan Yd. Carsh SM5 .... 59 F6
Old Town. Croy CR0 & CR9 .... 61 B7
Old Tye Ave. Bigg H TN16 .... 83 E3
Old Westhall Cl. Warlgm CR6 ..... 101 C8
Old Wickhurst La.
Broad H RH12 .... 216 D2
Old Woking Rd. Mayb GU22 .... 90 A4
Old Woking Rd. Old Wok GU22 .. 90 C8
Old Woking Rd.
Pyrf GU22 & KT14 .... 70 D3
Old Woking Rd. W Byfl KT14 .... 71 A6
Old Wokingham Rd.
Crowth RG11 .... 45 C7
Old Wokingham Rd. Easth RG11 45 C7
Oldacre. W End GU24 .... 67 F7
Oldbury Cl. Friml GU16 .... 85 F8
Oldbury Rd. Chert KT16 .... 32 E2
Olde Farm Dr. Blckw GU17 .... 64 B5
Olden La. Purley CR8 .... 80 A7
Oldfield Gdns. Ashtd KT21 .... 95 D8
Oldfield House. Streat SW16 .... 21 B4
Oldfield House Sch.
Hampt TW12 .... 35 F8
Oldfield Rd. Hampt TW12 .... 35 F8
Oldfield Rd. Horley RH6 .... 160 F1
Oldfield Rd. Wimble SW19 .... 19 E2
Oldfields Rd. Sutton SM1 & SM3 . 59 A8
Oldfields Trad Est. Sutton SM1 .. 59 A7
Oldfieldwood. Mayb GU22 .... 70 B2
Oldham House. **10** Dulw SE21 .... 22 E4
Oldhouse La. Bisley GU24 .... 68 A5
Oldhouse La. W End GU24 .... 48 A5
Oldhouse La. Windl GU18 & GU24 48 C2
Olding House. **6** Streat SW12 .... 21 C8
Oldridge Rd. Balham SW12 .... 21 B8
Oldstead. Brack RG12 .... 27 D4
Oldstead Rd. Catf BR1 .... 24 D4
Oldwood Chase. Farnb GU14 .... 84 C3
Oleander Cl. Crowth RG11 .... 45 A7
Olive Rd. **3** Merton SW19 .... 20 C1
Oliver Ave. S Norw SE25 .... 42 F6
Oliver Cl. Addl KT15 .... 52 B6
Oliver Cl. Brent W4 .... 7 B8

Oliver Gr. S Norw SE25 .... 42 F5
Oliver Rd. Ascot SL5 .... 29 B5
Oliver Rd. Horsh RH12 .... 217 A1
Oliver Rd. King U T KT3 .... 38 C7
Oliver Rd. Sutton SM1 .... 59 D6
Olivier Rd. Worth RH10 .... 202 D5
Ollerton. East RG12 .... 27 A1
Olley Cl. Wallin SM6 .... 60 E4
Olveston Wlk. Carsh SM4 & SM5 . 40 D3
Olyffe Dr. Beck BR3 .... 44 C8
Omega Rd. Woking GU21 .... 70 A3
Omega Way. Thorpe TW20 .... 32 C8
One Tree Cnr. Merrow GU4 .... 131 B8
One Tree Hill Rd. Merrow GU4 ... 131 B7
Ongar Cl. Row Tn KT15 .... 51 F4
Ongar Hill. Row Tn KT15 .... 52 A4
Ongar Pl. Row Tn KT15 .... 52 A4
Ongar Place Inf Sch.
Row Tn KT15 .... 52 A4
Ongar Rd. Addl KT15 .... 52 A5
Onslow Ave. Belm SM2 .... 77 F8
Onslow Ave. Rich TW10 .... 6 E2
Onslow Avenue Mansions. **10**
Rich TW10 .... 6 E2
Onslow Cl. Thame D KT7 .... 36 E1
Onslow Cl. Woking GU22 .... 70 A2
Onslow Cres. Woking GU22 .... 70 A2
Onslow Cty Inf Sch.
Onsl V GU2 .... 129 F7
Onslow Dr. Ascot SL5 .... 9 A1
Onslow Gdns. Sander CR2 .... 81 A7
Onslow Gdns. Thame D KT7 .... 36 E1
Onslow Gdns. Wallin SM6 .... 60 C3
Onslow House. **1** Hale GU9 .... 125 C1
Onslow Lodge. Stain TW18 .... 12 F1
Onslow Mews. Chert KT16 .... 33 A3
Onslow Rd. Guild GU1 .... 109 D1
Onslow Rd. New Mal KT3 .... 39 A5
Onslow Rd. Rich TW10 .... 6 E1
Onslow Rd. Sunnin SL5 .... 30 B2
Onslow Rd. Thorn H CR0 .... 42 A1
Onslow Rd. Whit V KT12 .... 54 A5
Onslow St. Guild GU1 .... 130 C8
Onslow Way. Pyrf GU22 .... 70 F4
Onslow Way. Thame D KT7 .... 36 E1
Ontario Cl. Smallf RH6 .... 162 A2
Onyx House. New Mal KT4 .... 38 D1
Opal House. New Mal KT4 .... 38 D1
Openview. Wands SW17 & SW18 20 D6
Opladen Way. Brack RG12 .... 27 E4
Opossum Dr. Hounsl TW4 .... 4 C4
Opus Pk. Jacobs GU4 .... 109 D6
Oracle Ctr. Brack RG12 .... 27 C7
Orangery The. Rich TW10 .... 17 C6
Orchard Ave. Ashf TW15 .... 14 C2
Orchard Ave. Carsh CR4 .... 41 A1
Orchard Ave. Croy CR0 .... 43 E1
Orchard Ave. Hatton TW14 .... 3 D2
Orchard Ave. Heston TW5 .... 4 E7
Orchard Ave. Hinch W KT7 .... 56 A8
Orchard Ave. King U T KT3 .... 38 E6
Orchard Ave. Woodhm KT15 .... 70 F8
Orchard Bsns Ctr Sch.
Salfs RH1 .... 161 A8
Orchard Cl. Ash V GU12 .... 106 A5
Orchard Cl. Ashf TW15 .... 14 C2
Orchard Cl. Ashtd KT21 .... 95 D7
Orchard Cl. Banstd SM7 .... 78 B5
Orchard Cl. E Hors KT24 .... 92 F3
Orchard Cl. Farnh GU9 .... 126 A6
Orchard Cl. Fetch KT22 .... 94 D5
Orchard Cl. Flexf GU3 .... 107 B1
Orchard Cl. Horley RH6 .... 160 F4
Orchard Cl. Mayb GU22 .... 70 B3
Orchard Cl. Merrow GU1 .... 110 B1
Orchard Cl. W Barn SW20 .... 39 C5
Orchard Cl. W End GU24 .... 67 D6
Orchard Cl. W Ewell KT19 .... 57 B4
Orchard Cl. W Ewell KT19 .... 57 B4
Orchard Cl. W Heath GU14 .... 64 F1
Orchard Cl. Walt O T KT12 .... 35 B2
Orchard Cl. Woki RG11 .... 25 D6
Orchard Cotts. Charl RH6 .... 180 C7
Orchard Cotts. Lingf RH7 .... 165 B3
Orchard Ct. Barnes SW13 .... 7 F4
Orchard Ct. Brack RG12 .... 27 C7
Orchard Ct. Croy BR3 .... 44 A1
Orchard Ct. Harm UB7 .... 2 C1
Orchard Ct. Hounsl TW7 .... 5 D7
Orchard Ct. Wallin SM6 .... 60 B5
Orchard Ct. Walt O T KT12 .... 34 F1
Orchard Cty Fst Sch The.
E Mole RH12 .... 36 D5
Orchard Dene. W Byfl KT14 .... 71 A6
Orchard Dr. Horse GU21 .... 69 F4
Orchard Dr. Sunby TW17 .... 34 E6
Orchard End. Cater CR3 .... 100 E5
Orchard End. Fetch KT22 .... 94 C3
Orchard End. Oat Pk KT13 .... 53 E8
Orchard End. Rowl GU10 .... 145 F3
Orchard Gate. Sandh GU17 .... 64 B8
Orchard Gate. Thame D KT10 .... 36 D1
Orchard Gdns. Alder GU11 .... 126 C8
Orchard Gdns. Chess KT9 .... 56 E6
Orchard Gdns. Cran GU6 .... 174 F2
Orchard Gdns. Effing KT24 .... 113 E7
Orchard Gdns. Epsom KT18 .... 76 C4
Orchard Gdns. Sutton SM1 .... 59 A5
Orchard Gr. Croy CR0 .... 43 E2
Orchard Gr. Penge SE20 .... 23 A1
Orchard Hill. Rudg RH12 .... 214 C7
Orchard Hill. Windl GU20 .... 48 D3
Orchard House. Merrow GU4 .... 110 D2
Orchard House. Tongh GU10 .... 126 F7
Orchard House Cheyne Ctr
(Hospl). W Wick BR4 .... 63 C7
Orchard Jun & Inf Sch The.
Hounsl TW3 .... 5 A3
Orchard La. Thame D KT8 .... 36 D3
Orchard La. Wimble SW20 .... 39 B8

Orchard Lea Cl. Pyrf GU22 .... 70 E4
Orchard Mains. Woking GU22 ...... 89 C8
Orchard Rd. Woki RG11 .... 25 C6
Orchard Rd. Brent TW8 .... 6 C8
Orchard Rd. Burph GU4 .... 110 B5
Orchard Rd. Chess KT9 .... 56 E6
Orchard Rd. Dork RH4 .... 136 B6
Orchard Rd. Farnb GU14 .... 85 A4
Orchard Rd. Farnh GU9 .... 125 C1
Orchard Rd. Hampt TW12 .... 15 F1
Orchard Rd. Hams Gn CR2 .... 81 B5
Orchard Rd. Horsh RH13 .... 217 E2
Orchard Rd. Hounsl TW4 .... 5 A2
Orchard Rd. King U T KT1 .... 37 E7
Orchard Rd. Mortl TW9 .... 7 A4
Orchard Rd. Onsl V GU2 .... 129 F7
Orchard Rd. Reig RH2 .... 118 B1
Orchard Rd. Shalf GU4 .... 130 E3
Orchard Rd. Shere GU5 .... 133 A4
Orchard Rd. Smallf RH6 .... 162 C3
Orchard Rd. Sunby TW16 .... 15 B1
Orchard Rd. Sutton SM1 .... 59 A6
Orchard Rd. Twick TW1 .... 6 B2
Orchard Rise. Croy CR0 .... 43 F1
Orchard Rise. King U T KT2 .... 18 C1
Orchard Rise. Mortl TW10 .... 7 B3
Orchard School Sports Ctr.
Penge SE20 .... 43 A8
Orchard St. Crawl RH11 .... 201 D6
Orchard St. Thame D KT7 .... 37 B2
Orchard The. Banstd SM7 .... 78 A4
Orchard The. Dork RH5 .... 136 C3
Orchard The. Ewell KT17 .... 57 F1
Orchard The. Ewell KT17 & KT19 57 F2
Orchard The. Haslem GU27 .... 207 F5
Orchard The. Hounsl TW3 .... 5 C5
Orchard The. Lhtwat GU18 .... 67 B8
Orchard The. Thorpe GU25 .... 31 E4
Orchard The. Westfd GU22 .... 89 E5
Orchard The. Weyb KT13 .... 53 B6
Orchard Way. Addl KT15 .... 52 B4
Orchard Way. Alder GU11 &12 .. 126 C8
Orchard Way. Ashf TW15 .... 13 F6
Orchard Way. Beck BR3 & CR0 .... 43 E3
Orchard Way. Camb GU15 .... 65 B2
Orchard Way. Carsh SM1 .... 59 D6
Orchard Way. Croy BR3 & CR0 .... 43 E3
Orchard Way. Dork RH4 .... 136 B6
Orchard Way. Dovgn RH2 .... 139 B6
Orchard Way. E Grins RH19 .... 185 E1
Orchard Way. Esher KT10 .... 55 C4
Orchard Way. Flexf GU3 .... 107 B1
Orchard Way. L Kings KT20 .... 97 F1
Orchard Way. Oxted RH8 .... 123 A2
Orchard Way. Send GU23 .... 90 C2
Orchard Way Prim Sch.
Croy CR0 .... 43 E2
Orchardfield Rd. Farnc GU7 .... 150 F7
Orchardleigh. Leahd KT22 .... 95 B5
Orchards Cl. W Byfl KT14 .... 71 A5
Orchards The. Ashf TW15 .... 14 D3
Orchards The. **4** Crawl RH11 . 200 D5
Orchards The. Horsh RH12 .... 217 F5
Orchid Dr. Bisley GU24 .... 68 A4
Orde Cl. Crawl RH10 .... 182 D1
Ordnance Cl. Felt TW13 .... 15 A6
Ordnance Rd. Alder GU11 .... 105 C3
Ordnance Rdbt. Alder GU11 .... 105 B2
Oregano Way. Stough GU2 .... 109 A6
Oregon Cl. King U T KT3 .... 38 C5
Orestan La. Effing KT24 .... 113 C8
Orford Ct. S Norw SE27 .... 22 B6
Orford Ct. Wallin SM6 .... 60 C5
Orford Gdns. Twick TW1 .... 16 F6
Orford Rd. Catf SE6 .... 24 B5
Oriel Cl. Crawl RH10 .... 182 C1
Oriel Cl. Mitch CR4 .... 41 D6
Oriel Ct. **6** Croy CR0 .... 42 D1
Oriel Hill. Camb GU15 .... 65 D4
Oriel Jun & Inf Sch. Felt TW13 . 15 E5
Oriental Cl. Woking GU22 .... 70 A2
Oriental Rd. Ascot SL5 .... 29 D5
Oriental Rd. Woking GU22 .... 70 A3
Orion. Easth RG12 .... 27 A1
Orion Ct. Crawl RH11 .... 200 D4
Orion Ctr The. Wallin CR0 .... 60 E8
Orlando Gdns. Epsom KT19 .... 57 D1
Orlean Ct. Walt O T KT12 .... 54 C8
Orleans Cl. Esher KT10 .... 55 B8
Orleans Ct. Twick TW1 .... 17 B8
Orleans Inf Sch. Twick TW1 .... 17 B8
Orleans Park Sec Sch.
Twick TW1 .... 17 B8
Orleans Rd. S Norw SE19 .... 22 D2
Orleans Rd. **10** Twick TW1 .... 17 C8
Orltons La. Rusper RH12 .... 179 F2
Ormanton Rd. For Hil SE26 .... 23 A4
Orme Rd. King U T KT1 & KT3 .... 38 B7
Ormeley Rd. Balham SW12 .... 21 B7
Ormerod Gdns. Mitch CR4 .... 41 A8
Ormesby Wlk. Crawl RH10 .... 202 B4
Ormond Ave. Hampt TW12 .... 36 B8
Ormond Ave. **22** Rich TW10 .... 6 D2
Ormond Cres. Hampt TW12 .... 36 B8
Ormond Dr. Hampt TW12 .... 16 B1
Ormond Rd. Rich TW10 .... 6 D2
Ormonde Ave. Epsom KT19 .... 57 D1
Ormonde Lodge (West London
Inst of H Ed). Islew TW7 .... 6 B2
Ormonde Rd. Farnc GU7 .... 150 E6
Ormonde Rd. Horse GU21 .... 69 C3
Ormonde Rd. Mortl SW14 .... 7 C4
Ormonde Rd. Woki RG11 .... 25 A5
Ormsby. Sutton SM2 .... 59 B3
Ormside Way. Redh RH1 .... 119 B4
Ormuz Cotts. Lingf RH7 .... 164 C4
Orpin Rd. Merst RH1 .... 119 C5
Orpwood Cl. Hampt TW12 .... 15 F2
Orwell Cl. W Heath GU14 .... 84 E6
Orwell Gdns. Reig RH2 .... 139 B7
Orwell House. **7** Redh RH1 .... 118 F2

Osborn La. For Hil SE23 .... 23 E8
Osborn Rd. Farnh GU9 .... 125 D4
Osborne Ave. Stan TW19 .... 13 F7
Osborne Cl. Beck BR3 .... 43 E5
Osborne Cl. Felt TW13 .... 15 D3
Osborne Cl. Friml GU16 .... 85 F8
Osborne Ct. Crawl RH11 .... 201 B2
Osborne Ct. Farnb GU14 .... 105 C3
Osborne Ct. **10** Surb KT6 .... 37 E3
Osborne Dr. Lhtwat GU18 .... 67 A8
Osborne Gdns. S Norw CR7 .... 42 C7
Osborne Pl. Carsh SM1 .... 59 D5
Osborne Rd. Egham TW20 .... 11 F2
Osborne Rd. Farnb GU14 .... 105 C8
Osborne Rd. Hounsl TW3 & TW4 .. 4 F4
Osborne Rd. King U T KT2 .... 37 E8
Osborne Rd. Redh RH1 .... 119 A4
Osborne Rd. S Norw CR7 .... 42 C7
Osborne Rd. Walt O T KT12 .... 35 A1
Osborne Rd. Woki RG11 .... 25 C6
Osbourne Terr. **1**
Up Toot SW17 .... 21 A3
Osier Cl. Mitch CR4 .... 40 F4
Osier Way. Nork KT17 & SM7 .... 77 E5
Oslac Rd. Catf SE6 .... 24 B3
Oslo Ct. Mitch SW19 .... 20 D1
Osman's Cl. Wink RG12 .... 8 B1
Osmond Gdns. Wallin SM6 .... 60 C5
Osmund Cl. Worth RH10 .... 202 E6
Osmunda Bank. Dorm Pk RH19 . 185 E6
Osnaburgh Hill. Camb GU15 .... 65 B5
Osney Cl. Crawl RH11 .... 201 C5
Osney Wlk. Carsh SM4 & SM5 ...... 40 D3
Osprey Cl. Fetch KT22 .... 94 C5
Osprey Gdns. Selsd CR0 & CR2 ... 62 E1
Ospringe Cl. **9** Penge SE20 .... 23 C1
Ostade Rd. Streat SW2 .... 21 F8
Osterley Ave. Hounsl TW7 .... 5 D7
Osterley Cres. Hounsl TW7 .... 5 F6
Osterley Lodge. **1** Hounsl TW7 .. 5 E6
Osterley Rd. Hounsl TW7 .... 5 E6
Osterley Sta. Hounsl TW7 .... 5 D7
Osterly Gdns. S Norw CR7 .... 42 C7
Oswald Cl. Fetch KT22 .... 94 C5
Oswald Rd. Fetch KT22 .... 94 C5
Osward. New Add CR0 .... 62 F1
Osward Rd.
Up Toot SW12 & SW17 .... 20 F6
Otford Cl. Penge SE20 .... 43 C8
Othello Gr. Wink RG12 .... 27 E8
Otho Ct. **5** Brent TW8 .... 6 D7
Otter Cl. Crowth RG11 .... 45 A7
Otter Cl. Ottsh KT16 .... 51 B4
Otterbourne Rd. **1**
Croy CR0 & CR9 .... 61 C8
Otterburn Gdns. Hounsl TW7 .... 6 A7
Otterburn St. Up Toot SW17 .... 20 F2
Otterden St. Catf SE6 .... 24 A4
Ottermead La. Ottsh KT16 .... 51 C4
Ottershaw Hospl. Ottsh KT16 ..... 51 D4
Ottershaw House. Mitch CR4 .... 40 D7
Ottershaw Pk. Ottsh KT16 .... 51 A3
Ottways Ave. Ashtd KT21 .... 95 D8
Ottways La. Ashtd KT21 & KT22 .. 95 D8
Otway Cl. Crawl RH11 .... 200 F4
Oulton Wlk. Crawl RH10 .... 202 B4
Our Lady of the Rosary RC Sch.
Stain TW18 .... 13 A2
Our Lady Queen Of Heaven
RC (Aided) Sch. Crawl RH11 ... 201 B8
Our Lady Queen of Heaven
RC Prim Sch. Putney SW19 .... 19 D8
Our Lady & St Philip Neri Prim
Sch. For Hil SE26 .... 23 E4
Our Lady & St Philip Neri RC
Sch. For Hil SE23 .... 23 D5
Our Lady & St Philip Neri RC
Sch. For Hil SE23 .... 23 E4
Our Lady's Prep Sch.
Crowth RG11 .... 45 B5
Our Ladys RC First Sch.
Chert KT16 .... 33 A1
Ouseley Rd. Up Toot SW12 .... 20 F7
Ouseley Rd. Wray TW19 .... 11 D8
Outdowns. Effing KT24 .... 113 B5
Outram Pl. Whit V KT13 .... 53 C5
Outram Rd. Croy CR0 .... 61 F8
Outwood House. **6** Streat SW2 21 F8
Outwood La. Bletch RH1 .... 141 D7
Outwood La. Chips CR5 & KT20 ... 98 C6
Outwood La. Kings CR5 & KT20 ... 98 C6
Outwood La. Outw RH1 .... 141 D1
Oval Prim Sch. Croy CR0 .... 42 E1
Oval Rd. Croy CR0 .... 42 E1
Oval The. Banstd SM7 .... 78 A5
Oval The. Farnc GU7 .... 150 F7
Oval The. Guild GU2 .... 130 A8
Oval The. Wood S V GU3 .... 108 B2
Overbrae. Beck BR3 .... 23 A3
Overbrook. Godal GU7 .... 151 A5
Overbrook. W Horn KT24 .... 112 B6
Overbury Ave. Beck BR3 .... 44 C6
Overbury Cres. New Add CR0 ...... 63 C1
Overbury Ct. Beck BR3 .... 44 C6
Overdale. Ashtd KT21 .... 75 E3
Overdale. Bletch RH1 .... 120 C2
Overdale. Dork RH5 .... 136 D8
Overdale Ave. King U T KT3 .... 38 D7
Overdale Rise. Friml GU15 .... 65 E3
Overdene Dr. Crawl RH11 .... 201 A6
Overdown Rd. Catf SE6 .... 24 B4
Overford Cl. Cran GU6 .... 174 E2
Overford Dr. Cran GU6 .... 174 E2
Overhill. Warlgm CR6 .... 101 C8
Overhill Rd. Dulw SE22 & SE22 ... 23 A8
Overhill Rd. Wallin CR8 .... 61 A1
Overhill Way. Beck BR3 .... 44 D4
Overlord Cl. Camb GU15 .... 65 C8
Overstand Cl. Beck BR3 .... 44 A4

Overstone Gdns. Croy CR0 .... 43 F3
Overthorpe. Knaph GU21 .... 68 E2
Overton Cl. Alder GU11 .... 126 C6
Overton Cl. Islew TW7 .... 5 F6
Overton House. Rhampt SW15 ..... 18 F8
Overton Rd. Belm SM2 .... 59 A3
Overton Shaw. E Grins RH19 ...... 185 E4
Overton's Yd. Croy CR0 & CR9 .... 61 C7
Oveton Way. G Book KT23 .... 94 B1
Ovett Cl. S Norw SE19 .... 22 E2
Ovington Ct. Woking GU21 .... 68 F3
Ovington Pl. Thorn H CR0 .... 42 D3
Owen House. Felt TW14 .... 15 A8
Owen House. **6** Twick TW1 .... 17 B8
Owen Pl. Leahd KT22 .... 95 B5
Owen Rd. Farnc GU7 .... 150 F6
Owen Rd. Windl GU20 .... 48 D5
Owen Wlk. **6** Penge SE20 .... 23 A1
Owens Way. For Hil SE23 .... 23 E8
Owl Cl. Selsd CR2 .... 62 D1
Owlbeech Ct. Horsh RH13 .... 218 B4
Owlbeech Pl. Horsh RH13 .... 218 B4
Owlbeech Way. Horsh RH13 .... 218 B4
Owletts. Crawl RH10 .... 202 D7
Owlscastle Cl. Horsh RH12 .... 217 D5
Owlsmoor Cty Prim Sch.
Sandh GU15 .... 45 E1
Owlsmoor Rd. Sandh GU15 .... 45 D1
Ownstead Gdns. S Croy CR2 .... 80 F8
Ownsted Hill. New Add CR0 .... 63 D1
Oxdowne Cl. Oxsh KT11 .... 74 B5
Oxenden Cl. Alder GU10 .... 126 E8
Oxenden Rd. Ash GU10 & GU12 126 F8
Oxenhope. Easth RG12 .... 27 A5
Oxford Ave. Harl TW6 .... 3 F7
Oxford Ave. Heston TW5 .... 5 A8
Oxford Ave. Merton SW20 .... 39 E7
Oxford Cl. Littlt TW15 & TW17 ...... 14 C1
Oxford Cl. Mitch CR4 .... 41 C6
Oxford Cres. New Mal KT3 .... 38 D3
Oxford Ct. Epsom KT18 .... 76 E5
Oxford Ct. **17** King U T KT6 .... 37 E4
Oxford Gdns. Brent W4 .... 7 A8
Oxford Rd. Carsh SM2 & SM5 .... 59 E5
Oxford Rd. Crawl RH10 .... 201 F2
Oxford Rd. Farnb GU14 .... 85 C1
Oxford Rd. Guild GU1 .... 130 D7
Oxford Rd. Horsh RH13 .... 217 E2
Oxford Rd. Redh RH1 .... 118 E2
Oxford Rd. S Norw SE19 .... 22 D2
Oxford Rd. Tedd TW11 & TW12 ... 16 D3
Oxford Rd. Wallin SM6 .... 60 C5
Oxford Rd. Woki RG11 .... 25 A6
Oxford Terr. Guild GU1 .... 130 D7
Oxford Way. Felt TW13 .... 15 D4
Oxleigh Cl. New Mal KT3 .... 38 E4
Oxlip Cl. Croy CR0 .... 43 D1
Oxshott Cl. Ashtd KT22 .... 74 F3
Oxshott Rd. Leahd KT22 .... 75 A2
Oxshott Rise. Cobham KT11 .... 73 E5
Oxshott Sta. Oxsh KT22 .... 74 C6
Oxshott Way. Cobham KT11 .... 73 F4
Oxted Cl. Mitch CR4 .... 40 D6
Oxted Cty Sch. Limps RH8 .... 122 F7
Oxted Gn. Witley GU8 .... 170 F2
Oxted Hospl. Oxted RH8 .... 122 D7
Oxted Rd. Tand RH9 .... 121 D4
Oxted Rd. Tyl Gn RH9 .... 121 D4
Oxted Sta. Oxted RH8 .... 122 E6
Oxtoby Way. Mitch SW16 .... 41 D8
Oyster Ct. Byfl KT14 .... 71 E7

Pacific Cl. E Bed TW14 .... 14 F7
Packer Cl. E Grins RH19 .... 186 A3
Packham Ct. N Cheam KT4 .... 58 C7
Packway. M Bourn GU9 .... 146 A6
Padbrook. Limps RH8 .... 123 A6
Padbury Cl. E Bed TW14 .... 14 D7
Padbury Oaks. Harm UB7 .... 2 B6
Paddock Cl. Bear Gn RH5 .... 157 D4
Paddock Cl. Camb GU15 .... 66 A6
Paddock Cl. Cobham KT11 .... 73 C5
Paddock Cl. For Hil SE26 .... 23 D4
Paddock Cl. Hambl GU8 .... 171 C1
Paddock Cl. New Mal KT4 .... 38 E1
Paddock Cl. Oxted RH8 .... 122 F4
Paddock Cl. W Barn SW20 .... 39 C5
Paddock Gdns. E Grins RH19 ..... 205 E2
Paddock Gdns. S Norw SE19 .... 22 E2
Paddock Gr. Bear Gn RH5 .... 157 D4
Paddock House. Merrow GU4 ...... 110 D2
Paddock House. Rhampt SW15 ...... 7 F3
Paddock The. Add CR0 .... 63 A4
Paddock The. Brack RG12 .... 27 C6
Paddock The. Cran GU6 .... 174 D3
Paddock The. Crawl RH10 .... 202 D7
Paddock The. Crowth RG11 .... 45 A6
Paddock The. Ewh GU6 .... 175 E4
Paddock The. Godal GU7 .... 150 F3
Paddock The. Graysh GU26 .... 188 A4
Paddock The. Merrow GU1 .... 110 D2
Paddock The. Shottm GU27 .... 208 A8
Paddock The. Westc RH4 .... 135 C6
Paddock Way. Grays GU27 .... 190 A2
Paddock Way. Oxted RH8 .... 122 F4
Paddock Way. Sheer GU21 .... 70 B5
Paddock Wlk. Warlgm CR6 .... 101 B8
Paddockhurst Rd. Crawl RH11... 201 A5
Paddockhurst Rd. Worth RH10 .. 203 C2
Paddocks Cl. Ashtd KT21 .... 75 E1
Paddocks Mead. Woking GU21 ... 68 F3
Paddocks Rd. Burph GU4 .... 110 A5
Paddocks The. Flexf GU3 .... 107 C1
Paddocks The. G Book KT23 .... 94 B1
Paddocks The. Oat Pk KT13 .... 53 E7
Paddocks Way. Ashtd KT21 .... 75 E1
Paddocks Way. Chert KT16 .... 33 B1
Padstow Wlk. Crawl RH11 .... 200 F4
Padstow Wlk. E Bed TW14 .... 14 F7
Padua Rd. Penge SE20 .... 43 C8

Padwick Rd. Horsh RH13 .... 218 A2
Page Cl. Hampt TW12 .... 15 E2
Page Cres. Croy CR0 .... 61 B5
Page Croft. Chert KT15 .... 52 B8
Page Ct. Horsh RH13 .... 217 D1
Page Rd. E Bed TW14 .... 3 D1
Page's Croft. Woki RG11 .... 25 D5
Page's Yd. Chisw W4 .... 7 E8
Pageant Wlk. S Croy CR0 .... 61 E7
Pagehurst Rd. Croy CR0 .... 43 B2
Paget Ave. Carsh SM1 .... 59 D7
Paget Cl. Camb GU15 .... 66 B7
Paget Cl. Hampt TW12 .... 16 D4
Paget La. Islew TW7 .... 5 E4
Paget Pl. King U T KT2 .... 18 C2
Paget Pl. Thame D KT7 .... 36 F1
Pagoda Ave. Rich TW9 .... 6 F4
Paice Gn. Woki RG11 .... 25 D7
Pain's Cl. Mitch CR4 .... 41 B7
Paines Hill. Limps RH8 .... 123 C4
Paisley Rd. Carsh SM5 .... 40 D1
Pakenham Cl. Up Toot SW12 ...... 21 A7
Palace Ct. S Norw CR7 .... 42 D5
Palace Ct. Streat SW2 .... 22 A6
Palace Ct. Woking GU21 .... 70 A3
Palace Dr. Weyb KT13 .... 53 B7
Palace Gn. New Add CR0 .... 62 F3
Palace Gr. Penge SE19 .... 22 F1
Palace Rd. E Mole KT8 .... 36 D6
Palace Rd. King U T KT1 .... 37 D5
Palace Rd. Penge SE19 .... 22 F1
Palace Rd.
  Streat SE27 & SW16 & SW2 .... 22 A6
Palace Rd. Woodhm KT15 .... 52 B2
Palace Sq. Penge SE19 .... 22 F1
Palace View. Croy CR0 .... 62 F6
Palestine Gr. Mitch SW19 .... 40 D8
Palewell Common Dr.
  Mortl SW14 .... 7 D2
Palewell Pk. Mortl SW14 .... 7 D3
Palgrave House. 4 Twick TW2 ... 16 C8
Pallingham Dr. Worth RH10 .... 202 C3
Palm Cl. Beck BR3 .... 43 F6
Palm Gr. Bellf GU1 .... 109 C5
Palmer Ave. Cheam KT4 & SM3 ... 58 C6
Palmer C of E Jun Sch The.
  Woki RG11 .... 25 D7
Palmer Cl. Crowth RG11 .... 45 A8
Palmer Cl. Earls RH1 .... 140 A8
Palmer Cl. Heston TW5 .... 5 A6
Palmer Cl. Horley RH6 .... 160 F5
Palmer Cl. W Wick BR4 .... 63 D8
Palmer Cres. King U T KT1 .... 37 E6
Palmer Cres. Ottsh KT16 .... 51 D4
Palmer Rd. Worth RH10 .... 202 C3
Palmer School Rd. Woki RG11 ... 25 C6
Palmer's Lodge. Guild GU2 .... 130 B8
Palmers Gr. E Mole KT8 .... 36 A5
Palmers Rd. Mortl SW14 .... 7 C4
Palmers Rd. Thorn H SW16 .... 41 F7
Palmersfield Rd. Banstd SM7 .... 78 B5
Palmerston Cl. Horse GU21 .... 70 A5
Palmerston Cl. 9 Surb KT6 .... 37 D2
Palmerston Gr. 4 Merton SW19 . 20 A1
Palmerston House. Banstd SM7 . 77 F4
Palmerston Rd. Carsh SM5 .... 60 A6
Palmerston Rd. Merton SW19 .... 20 A1
Palmerston Rd. Mortl SW14 .... 7 C3
Palmerston Rd. Sutton SM1 .... 59 C5
Palmerston Rd. Thorn H CR0 ...... 42 D4
Palmerston Rd. Twick TW2 .... 5 E1
Pampisford Rd. Croy CR2 & CR8 . 61 B2
Pampisford Rd.
  Purley CR2 & CR8 .... 61 B2
Pams Way. W Ewell KT19 .... 57 D5
Pams Way. W Ewell KT19 .... 57 D5
Pan's Gdns. Friml GU15 .... 65 F4
Pandora Cl. 4 Surb KT6 .... 37 E3
Pangbourne Ct. Up Toot SW17 ... 20 C4
Pankhurst Ct. 11 Crawl RH11 .... 201 B1
Pankhurst Dr. Brack RG12 .... 27 D4
Pankhurst Rd. Walt O T KT12 ..... 35 C2
Panmuir Rd. Wimble SW20 .... 39 B8
Panmure Rd. For Hil SE26 .... 23 B5
Pannell Cl. E Grins RH19 .... 185 D1
Pannells. M Bourn GU10 .... 146 D5
Pannells Cl. Chert KT16 .... 32 F1
Pannells Ct. Guild GU1 .... 130 D8
Pantile Rd. Oat Pk KT13 .... 53 D6
Pantiles Cl. Woking GU21 .... 69 B1
Paper Mews. Dork RH4 .... 136 B8
Papercourt La. Ripley GU23 .... 90 F6
Papworth Way. Streat SW2 .... 22 A8
Parade Cl. Send GU23 .... 90 C4
Parade Mews.
  Streat SE27 & SW2 .... 22 B6
Parade The. Ash GU12 .... 106 A4
Parade The. Ashf TW16 .... 14 F1
Parade The. Burgh H KT20 .... 97 E8
Parade The. Clayg KT10 .... 55 E4
Parade The. Coulsd CR5 .... 80 A1
Parade The. Epsom KT18 .... 76 D6
Parade The. 2 King U T KT2 .... 37 E7
Parade The. Wallin SM6 .... 60 C6
Parade The. Went GU25 .... 31 D3
Paradise Rd. Rich TW10 .... 6 E2
Paragon Gr. Surb KT5 .... 37 F3
Parbury Rise. Chess KT9 .... 56 E4
Parchmore Rd. S Norw CR7 .... 42 C6
Parchmore Way. S Norw CR7 ..... 42 B7
Pares Cl. Woking GU21 .... 69 D3
Parfew Cl. Dulw SE22 .... 23 B6
Parfitts Cl. Farnh GU9 .... 125 A2
Parfour Dr. Kenley CR8 .... 80 C3
Parham Rd. Crawl RH11 .... 200 F7
Parish Church C of E Inf & Jun
  Schs. Croy CR0 .... 61 B7
Parish Cl. Ash GU12 .... 125 A6
Parish Cl. King U T KT6 .... 37 E3
Parish House. 6 Crawl RH11 ..... 201 D5

Parish La. Penge SE20 & SE26 .... 23 D1
Parish Rd. Farnb GU14 .... 105 B8
Park Ave. Broml BR1 .... 24 F2
Park Ave. Camb GU15 .... 65 D4
Park Ave. Cater CR3 .... 100 E3
Park Ave. Egham TW20 .... 12 C1
Park Ave. Islew TW3 .... 5 B1
Park Ave. Mitch CR4 .... 21 B1
Park Ave. Mortl SW14 .... 7 D3
Park Ave. P Harow GU8 .... 149 C5
Park Ave. Salfs RH1 .... 139 F1
Park Ave. Stain TW18 .... 13 A2
Park Ave. Up Hall TW17 .... 34 E6
Park Ave. W Wick BR4 .... 55 A6
Park Ave. Wallin SM6 .... 60 A4
Park Ave. Woki RG11 .... 25 B6
Park Ave E. Stonel KT17 .... 58 A4
Park Ave W. Stonel KT17 .... 58 A4
Park Barn Dr.
  Stough GU2 & GU3 .... 108 E2
Park Barn E. Stough GU2 .... 108 F2
Park Chase. Godal GU7 .... 150 E2
Park Chase. Guild GU1 .... 109 E1
Park Cl. Binst GU10 .... 145 A2
Park Cl. Brock RH3 .... 137 B4
Park Cl. Esher KT10 .... 55 A4
Park Cl. Fetch KT22 .... 94 D3
Park Cl. Grays GU1 .... 190 A1
Park Cl. Hampt TW12 .... 36 C8
Park Cl. Islew TW3 & TW7 .... 5 C2
Park Cl. Islew TW7 .... 6 B5
Park Cl. King U T KT2 .... 38 A8
Park Cl. Oat Pk KT13 .... 53 F8
Park Cl. Wallin SM5 .... 59 F4
Park Cl. Woodhm KT15 .... 52 C1
Park Close Cotts. Eng Gn TW20 . 10 F3
Park Copse. Dork RH5 .... 136 D7
Park Corner Dr. E Hors KT24 .... 112 E7
Park Cotts. 10 Twick TW1 .... 6 B1
Park Cres. Sunnin SL5 .... 29 F3
Park Cres. Twick TW2 .... 16 D7
Park Ct. Beck BR3 .... 44 B6
Park Ct. New Mal KT3 .... 38 D5
Park Ct. Tedd SE1 .... 37 C8
Park Ct. Up Toot SW12 .... 21 A7
Park Ct. W Norw SE21 .... 22 B5
Park Ct. Wallin SM6 .... 60 E5
Park Ct. Woking GU22 .... 69 F1
Park Dr. Bramly GU5 .... 151 F6
Park Dr. Cran GU6 .... 174 F3
Park Dr. Mortl SW14 .... 7 D3
Park Dr. Sunnin SL5 .... 29 F3
Park Dr. Weyb KT13 .... 53 B5
Park Dr. Woking GU22 .... 69 F1
Park End. Broml BR1 .... 44 F8
Park Farm Ind Est. Horsh RH12 . 217 D7
Park Farm Ind Est. Friml GU16 .. 65 C1
Park Farm Rd. Horsh RH12 .... 217 D7
Park Farm Rd. King U T KT2 ...... 17 E1
Park Gate Cotts. Cran GU6 .... 174 C3
Park Gate Ct. Tedd TW12 .... 16 C3
Park Gate Ct. 11 Woking GU22 .. 69 E1
Park Gdns. King U T KT2 .... 17 F3
Park Gn. Fetch KT22 .... 94 A3
Park Hall Rd. Dulw SE21 .... 22 D5
Park Hall Rd. Reig RH2 .... 118 A3
Park Hall Rd. W Norw SE21 .... 22 D5
Park Hall Road Trad Est.
  W Norw SE27 .... 22 D5
Park Hill. For Hil SE23 .... 23 C7
Park Hill. Rich TW10 .... 6 F1
Park Hill. Wallin SM5 .... 59 F4
Park Hill Cl. Carsh SM5 .... 59 E5
Park Hill Ct. S Croy CR0 .... 61 E8
Park Hill Ct. Up Toot SW17 .... 20 F5
Park Hill Inf Sch. S Croy CR0 .... 61 E7
Park Hill Jun Sch. S Croy CR0 ... 61 E7
Park Hill Rd. Beck BR2 .... 44 E7
Park Hill Rd. Ewell KT17 .... 76 F8
Park Hill Rd. S Croy CR0 & CR2 . 61 E7
Park Hill Rd. Wallin SM6 .... 60 B3
Park Hill Rise. S Croy CR0 .... 61 E8
Park Hill Sch. King U T KT2 .... 18 A1
Park Horsley. E Hors KT24 .... 113 A6
Park House. Penge SE26 .... 23 A3
Park House. Woodh RH2 .... 138 F7
Park House Cotts. Cran GU6 ...... 174 F3
Park House Dr. Woodh RH2 .... 138 F7
Park House Gdns. Twick TW1 .... 6 C2
Park House Mid Sch.
  Wimble SW19 .... 19 F4
Park La. Ash W RH19 .... 206 D6
Park La. Ashtd KT21 .... 96 A8
Park La. Camb GU15 .... 65 C5
Park La. Cheam SM3 .... 58 E4
Park La. Cranf TW5 .... 4 A7
Park La. Croy CR0 & CR9 .... 61 D7
Park La. Hooley CR5 .... 99 D6
Park La. Horton SL3 .... 1 A4
Park La. Lingf RH7 .... 164 F5
Park La. Merrow GU4 .... 110 D3
Park La. Ockley RH5 .... 177 F7
Park La. Reig RH2 .... 138 E8
Park La. Rich TW9 .... 6 D3
Park La. Tedd TW11 .... 16 F2
Park La. Wallin SM5 & SM6 .... 60 A5
Park La. Wink SL4 .... 9 B7
Park La E. Reig RH2 .... 139 A7
Park La E. Woodh RH2 .... 139 A7
Park Lawn. S Norw CR7 .... 42 C7
Park Lawn Rd. Weyb KT13 .... 53 B6
Park Ley Rd. Wold CR3 .... 101 D6
Park Mansions. Ashtd KT21 ...... 95 E8
Park Mead Grant Maintd Jun Sch.
  Cran GU6 .... 175 A3
Park Mead Inf Sch. Cran GU6 .... 175 A3
Park Mews. Stan TW19 .... 13 F8
Park Pl. Hampt TW12 .... 16 C2
Park Pl. Horsh RH12 .... 217 C1
Park Pl. 4 Horsh RH12 .... 217 C1
Park Prim Sch. Alder GU11 .... 126 C7
Park Rd. Albury GU5 .... 132 E2

Park Rd. Alder GU11 .... 126 B8
Park Rd. Ashf TW15 .... 14 B3
Park Rd. Ashtd KT21 .... 75 E1
Park Rd. Banstd SM7 .... 78 C3
Park Rd. Beck BR3 .... 23 F1
Park Rd. Brack RG12 .... 27 D8
Park Rd. Burst RH6 .... 162 C1
Park Rd. Camb GU15 .... 65 C4
Park Rd. Cater CR3 .... 100 E4
Park Rd. Cheam SM3 .... 58 E4
Park Rd. Chisw W4 .... 7 D8
Park Rd. Crow RH7 .... 143 E2
Park Rd. Dorm Pk RH19 .... 185 F6
Park Rd. E Grins RH19 .... 185 D1
Park Rd. E Mole KT8 .... 36 C5
Park Rd. Egham TW20 .... 12 A4
Park Rd. Esher KT10 .... 55 B6
Park Rd. Farnb GU11 & GU14 .... 105 E8
Park Rd. Farnh GU9 .... 125 D4
Park Rd. Faygt RH12 .... 199 F1
Park Rd. Felt TW13 .... 15 D4
Park Rd. Fickl CR6 .... 82 E5
Park Rd. For Row RH18 .... 206 F2
Park Rd. Godal GU7 .... 150 E2
Park Rd. Guild GU1 .... 109 D1
Park Rd. Hackb SM6 .... 60 B8
Park Rd. Hampt TW12 .... 16 C3
Park Rd. Haslem GU27 .... 208 C5
Park Rd. Islew TW3 & TW7 .... 5 C2
Park Rd. Islew TW7 .... 6 B5
Park Rd. Kenley CR8 .... 80 C4
Park Rd. King U T KT2 & TW10 .. 18 A4
Park Rd. Limps RH8 .... 122 F1
Park Rd. Lo Hall TW17 .... 34 A1
Park Rd. Mayb GU22 .... 70 B2
Park Rd. Mitch SW19 .... 20 C2
Park Rd. New Mal KT3 .... 38 D5
Park Rd. Redh RH1 .... 118 F3
Park Rd. Rich TW10 .... 6 F1
Park Rd. S Norw SE25 .... 42 E5
Park Rd. Sandh GU47 .... 64 C8
Park Rd. Slinfd RH13 .... 215 D3
Park Rd. Stan TW19 .... 2 C1
Park Rd. Sunby TW16 .... 15 B1
Park Rd. Surb KT5 .... 37 C8
Park Rd. Tedd TW11 .... 16 F2
Park Rd. Tedd KT1 .... 37 C8
Park Rd. Twick TW1 .... 6 C1
Park Rd. Wallin SM6 .... 60 B5
Park Rd. Woki RG11 .... 25 B6
Park Rd. Woking GU22 .... 70 A2
Park Rd.
  Woodm CR5 & KT20 & SM7 .... 78 C3
Park Rise. For Hil SE23 .... 23 E7
Park Rise. Horsh RH12 .... 217 B4
Park Rise. Leahd KT22 .... 95 B6
Park Rise Cl. Leahd KT22 .... 95 B6
Park Rise Rd. For Hil SE23 .... 23 E7
Park Road House. 3
  King U T KT2 .... 18 A1
Park Row. Farnh GU9 .... 125 B3
Park Sch The. Woking GU22 ...... 70 A2
Park Sheen. Mortl SW14 .... 7 B3
Park Side. Woodhm KT15 .... 52 C1
Park Sq. 1 Esher KT10 .... 55 B6
Park St. Bagsh GU19 .... 47 E3
Park St. Camb GU15 .... 65 C5
Park St. Croy CR0 & CR9 .... 61 C8
Park St. Guild GU1 & GU2 .... 130 C7
Park St. Horsh RH12 .... 217 D2
Park St. Poyle SL3 .... 1 D6
Park St. Slinfd RH13 .... 215 C3
Park St. Tedd TW11 .... 16 E2
Park Terr. Carsh SM5 .... 59 E7
Park Terr. New Mal KT4 .... 39 A1
Park Terr E. Horsh RH13 .... 217 D1
Park Terr W. Horsh RH13 .... 217 D1
Park The. Fetch KT23 .... 94 A3
Park The. For Hil SE23 .... 23 C7
Park The. Wallin SM5 .... 59 F5
Park View. Bagsh GU19 .... 47 D3
Park View. Fetch KT23 .... 94 A2
Park View. Horley RH6 .... 161 A3
Park View. New Mal KT3 .... 38 F6
Park View. Purley CR8 .... 80 B8
Park View. Tand RH8 .... 143 B5
Park View Ct. Woking GU22 .... 89 F8
Park View Rd. Wold CR3 .... 101 F5
Park Way. Crawl RH10 .... 202 C7
Park Way. E Mole KT8 .... 36 B6
Park Way. Felt TW14 .... 15 B8
Park Way. Fetch KT23 .... 94 A4
Park Way. Horsh RH12 .... 217 C2
Park Wood Cl. Nork SM7 .... 77 D4
Park Wood Rd. Nork SM7 .... 77 D4
Park Wood View. Nork SM7 .... 77 D4
Park Works Rd. Nutf RH1 .... 119 E2
Parkcroft Rd. Lewish SE12 .... 24 F8
Parkdale Cres. Worc Pk KT4 ...... 57 D7
Parke Rd. Sunby TW16 .... 35 A5
Parker Cl. Worth RH10 .... 202 D5
Parker Ct. Wimble SW19 .... 19 E1
Parker Rd. Croy CR0 & CR9 .... 61 C6
Parkers Cl. Ashtd KT21 .... 95 E8
Parker's Hill. Ashtd KT21 .... 95 E8
Parker's La. Ashtd KT21 .... 95 F8
Parker's La. Wok RG12 & SL4 .... 8 B5
Parkfield. Godal GU7 .... 150 E2
Parkfield. Horsh RH12 .... 217 C3
Parkfield. 3 Hounsl TW7 .... 5 E6
Parkfield Ave. For Hil SE23 .... 15 A5
Parkfield Ave. Mortl SW14 .... 7 E3
Parkfield Cl. Crawl RH11 .... 200 F6
Parkfield Cres. Felt TW13 .... 15 A5
Parkfield Par. Felt TW13 .... 15 A5
Parkfield Rd. Felt TW13 .... 15 A5
Parkfields. Croy CR0 .... 43 F1
Parkfields. Oxsh KT22 .... 74 D8

Parkfields Ave. Wimble SW20 .... 39 B7
Parkfields Cl. Hackb SM5 .... 60 A6
Parkfields Rd. King U T TW10 .... 17 F3
Parkgate Cl. King U T KT2 .... 18 B2
Parkgate Gdns. Mortl SW14 ...... 7 D2
Parkgate Cl. Newd RH5 .... 158 C3
Parkgate Cl. Parkg RH5 .... 158 C3
Parkgate Rd. Reig RH2 .... 139 B8
Parkgate Rd. Wallin SM5 & SM6 . 60 B5
Parkham Ct. Beck BR2 .... 44 E7
Parkhill Cl. Blckw GU17 .... 64 D4
Parkhill Rd. Blckw GU17 .... 64 D4
Parkhurst. Epsom KT19 .... 57 C1
Parkhurst Cotts. Churt GU10 .... 187 F8
Parkhurst Fields. Churt GU10 ... 167 F1
Parkhurst Gr. Horley RH6 .... 160 E4
Parkhurst Rd. Carsh SM1 .... 59 D6
Parkhurst Rd. Horley RH6 .... 160 E4
Parkhurst Rd. Stough GU2 .... 109 B2
Parkin House. Penge SE20 .... 23 D1
Parkland Dr. Brack RG12 .... 27 E8
Parkland Gdns. 12
  Putney SW19 .... 19 D7
Parkland Gr. Ashf TW15 .... 14 A4
Parkland Gr. Heath E GU9 .... 125 E7
Parkland Rd. Ashf TW15 .... 14 A4
Parklands. Addl KT15 .... 52 C5
Parklands. Dork RH5 .... 136 B3
Parklands. Fetch KT23 .... 94 A4
Parklands. King U T KT5 .... 37 F4
Parklands. Oxted RH8 .... 122 E4
Parklands. Redh RH1 .... 119 A3
Parklands Cl. Mortl SW14 .... 7 C2
Parklands Ct. Heston TW5 .... 4 B8
Parklands Pl. Merrow GU4 .... 110 B1
Parklands Rd.
  Streat SW16 & SW17 .... 21 B3
Parklawn Ave. Epsom KT18 .... 76 B6
Parklawn Ave. Horley RH6 .... 160 F5
Parkleigh Ct. Merton SW19 .... 40 B7
Parkleys. King U T KT2 & TW10 . 17 D4
Parkleys. Rich KT2 & TW10 .... 17 D4
Parkpale La. Betch RH3 .... 137 A4
Parkshot. Rich TW9 .... 6 E3
Parkside. Beck BR3 .... 44 B7
Parkside. Cheam SM3 .... 58 E4
Parkside. Crawl RH10 .... 201 E6
Parkside. E Grins RH19 .... 185 C1
Parkside. Hale GU9 .... 125 C6
Parkside. Tedd TW13 .... 16 C3
Parkside. Wimble SW19 .... 19 D4
Parkside Ave. Wimble SW19 ..... 19 D3
Parkside Cl. E Hors KT24 .... 92 F2
Parkside Cl. Penge SE19 .... 22 F2
Parkside Cl. S Croy WK13 .... 53 A6
Parkside Gdns. Coulsd CR5 ...... 79 B2
Parkside Gdns. Wimble SW19 ... 19 D4
Parkside Hosp. Wimble SW19 ... 19 D5
Parkside Mews. Horsh RH12 ..... 217 D2
Parkside Pl. E Hors KT24 .... 92 F2
Parkside Rd. Hounsl TW3 .... 5 B2
Parkside Sch. Stk D'A KT11 ...... 74 A1
Parkstone Dr. Camb GU15 .... 65 C8
Parkthorne Rd. Streat SW12 ..... 21 D8
Parkview Lodge. Beck BR3 .... 44 B6
Parkview Rd. Croy CR0 & CR9 ... 43 A1
Parkview Vale. Merrow GU4 ...... 110 C3
Parkway. Camb GU15 .... 65 C3
Parkway. Crowth RG11 .... 45 A5
Parkway. Dork RH4 .... 136 A8
Parkway. Guild GU1 .... 109 E2
Parkway. Horley RH6 .... 161 A3
Parkway. New Add CR0 & CR9 .. 63 C1
Parkway. Oat Pk KT13 .... 53 D6
Parkway. W Barn SM4 & SW20 .. 39 D5
Parkway Sch The. Cranf TW5 .... 4 A7
Parkway The. Cranf TW5 .... 4 B7
Parkway Trad Est. Heston TW5 .. 4 C8
Parkwood. Beck BR3 .... 24 A1
Parkwood Ave. Thame D KT10 .. 36 C1
Parkwood Gr. Sunby TW16 .... 35 A6
Parkwood Rd. Bigg H TN16 .... 103 F6
Parkwood Rd. Hounsl TW7 .... 5 F6
Parkwood Rd. Nutf RH1 .... 119 E2
Parkwood Rd. Wimble SW19 ..... 19 F3
Parley Dr. Woking GU21 .... 69 C1
Parliament Mews. Mortl SW14 .. 7 C5
Parliamentary Rd. Pirb GU24 .... 87 A6
Parnall House. 11 Dulw SE19 .... 22 E4
Parnham Ave. Lhtwat GU18 ...... 67 B8
Parr Ave. Ewell KT17 .... 58 B2
Parr Cl. Leahd KT22 .... 94 F7
Parr Ct. Felt TW13 .... 15 C4
Parris Croft. Dork RH5 .... 136 C4
Parrs Cl. S Croy CR2 .... 61 D2
Parry Cl. Stonel KT17 .... 58 A3
Parry Dr. Whit V KT13 .... 53 A1
Parry Rd. S Norw SE25 .... 42 E6
Parsley Gdns. Croy CR0 .... 43 D1
Parson's Mead. Thorn H CR0 .... 42 B1
Parson's Mead Sch. Ashtd KT21 95 E8
Parson's Pightle. Coulsd CR5 ... 100 A7
Parsonage Bsns Pk.
  Horsh RH12 .... 217 E4
Parsonage Cl. Warlgm CR6 .... 81 F3
Parsonage Cl. Westc RH4 .... 135 C5
Parsonage Farm Cty Inf Sch.
  W Heath GU9 .... 84 C5
Parsonage La. Westc RH4 .... 135 C6
Parsonage La. Cran GU6 .... 174 D3
Parsonage Rd. Eng Gn TW20 .... 11 D3
Parsonage Rd.
  Horsh RH12 & RH13 .... 217 E4
Parsonage Sq. Dork RH4 .... 136 A8
Parsonage Way. Friml GU16 ..... 65 D1
Parsonage Way. Horsh RH12 .... 217 E4

Parsons Cl. Haslem GU27 .... 208 C8
Parsons Cl. Horley RH6 .... 160 E4
Parsons Field. Sandh GU17 .... 64 B8
Parsons Gn. Haslem GU27 .... 208 C8
Parsons Green Ct. Bellf GU1 ..... 109 D3
Parsons House. 21
  Streat SW12 .... 21 E8
Parsons La. Beac H GU26 .... 188 D6
Parsons Mead. E Mole KT8 .... 36 C6
Parsonsfield Cl. Nork SM7 .... 77 B4
Parsonsfield Rd. Nork SM7 .... 77 D4
Parthia Cl. Burgh H KT20 .... 97 B8
Partridge Cl. Crond GU10 .... 124 D8
Partridge Cl. Friml GU16 .... 65 E1
Partridge Knoll. Purley CR8 ...... 80 B6
Partridge La. Parkg RH5 .... 158 C6
Partridge Mead. Nork SM7 .... 77 C4
Partridge Rd. 8 Hampt TW12 ... 16 A2
Partridge Way. Merrow GU4 ..... 110 D3
Parvis Rd. Byfl KT14 .... 71 D7
Parvis Rd. W Byfl KT14 .... 71 D7
Parvis Rd. W Byfl KT14 .... 71 F7
Paschal Rd. Camb GU15 .... 65 F8
Passfields. Catf SE6 .... 24 C2
Passingham House. Heston TW5 . 5 A8
Pastens Rd. Limps RH8 .... 123 C4
Pasture Rd. Catf SE6 .... 24 F7
Pasture The. Crawl RH10 .... 202 C6
Pasture Wood Rd. Abin C RH5 .. 155 D6
Patching Cl. Crawl RH11 .... 200 F7
Patchings. Horsh RH13 .... 217 F3
Paterson Cl. Friml GU16 .... 66 C3
Pates Manor Dr. E Bed TW14 .... 14 D8
Path Link. Crawl RH10 .... 201 E7
Path The. Merton SW19 .... 40 B8
Pathfield. Chidd GU8 .... 191 B4
Pathfield Cl. Chidd GU8 .... 191 B4
Pathfield Cl. Rudg RH12 .... 214 D7
Pathfield Rd. Rudg RH12 .... 214 D7
Pathfield Rd. Streat SW16 .... 21 D2
Pathfields. Shere GU5 .... 133 A4
Pathfields Cl. Haslem GU27 ...... 208 D7
Pathfinders The. Farnb GU14 .... 84 C3
Pathway The. Send W GU23 ...... 90 F2
Patmore La. Whit V KT12 .... 53 F4
Patmore La. Lingf RH7 .... 164 E5
Paton Cl. Alder GU11 .... 125 E8
Patricia Gdns. Belm SM2 .... 78 A8
Patrington Cl. Crawl RH11 .... 201 A3
Patten Ash Dr. Woki RG11 .... 25 E7
Patten Rd. Wands SW18 .... 20 E8
Pattenden Rd. For Hil SE23 & SE6 23 F7
Patterdale Cl. Catf BR1 .... 24 E2
Patterdale Cl. Crawl RH11 .... 201 C4
Patterson Ct. Penge SE19 .... 22 F2
Patterson Rd. Penge SE19 .... 22 F2
Paul Cl. Alder GU11 .... 125 E8
Paul Gdns. S Croy CR0 .... 61 F8
Paul Vanson Ct. Hersh KT12 ..... 54 D4
Paul's Pl. Ashtd KT21 .... 96 B8
Pauline Cres. Twick TW2 .... 16 C7
Pauls Mead. Lingf RH7 .... 164 E5
Paved Ct. 9 Rich TW9 .... 6 D2
Pavement The. 11
  W Norw SE27 .... 22 C4
Pavilion Gdns. Stain TW18 .... 13 B1
Pavilion Rd. Alder GU11 .... 104 E1
Pavilion Rd. Farnb GU11 .... 104 D6
Pavilion Way. E Grins RH19 ...... 205 E8
Pavilions End. Camb GU15 .... 65 D3
Paviors. Farnh GU9 .... 125 C3
Pawleyne Cl. Penge SE20 .... 23 C1
Pawson's Rd. Thorn H CR0 .... 42 C4
Pax Cl. Crawl RH11 .... 200 E4
Paxton Cl. Rich TW9 .... 6 F5
Paxton Cl. Walt O T KT12 .... 35 C2
Paxton Ct. For Hil SE26 .... 23 E4
Paxton Ct. Mitch CR4 .... 40 F7
Paxton Gdns. Sheer GU21 .... 70 E7
Paxton Pl. W Norw SE19 .... 22 E2
Paxton Rd. For Hil SE23 .... 23 E5
Paxton Prim Sch. W Norw SE19 . 22 E2
Payley Dr. Woki RG11 .... 25 E8
Payne Cl. Crawl RH10 .... 202 D8
Paynesfield Ave. Mortl SW14 .... 7 D4
Paynesfield Rd. Tats TN16 .... 103 D7
Paynesfield Rd. Tats TN16 .... 103 D8
Peabody Est. Streat SE24 .... 22 C8
Peabody Hill. W Norw SE21 ...... 22 C7
Peabody Rd.
  Farnb GU11 & GU14 .... 105 D8
Peacemaker Cl. Crawl RH11 ..... 200 E4
Peach St. Woki RG11 .... 25 C2
Peach Tree Cl. W Heath GU14 ... 85 A7
Peaches Cl. Belm SM2 .... 58 E3
Peacock Ave. E Bed TW14 .... 14 D7
Peacock Cotts. Easth RG12 .... 26 C5
Peacock Gdns. Selsd CR0 & CR2 62 F1
Peacock La. Woki RG12 .... 26 D6
Peacock Wlk. 9 Crawl RH11 ...... 201 A3
Peacocks Sh Ctr The.
  Woking GU21 .... 69 E2
Peak Hill. For Hil SE26 .... 23 C4
Peak Hill Ave. For Hil SE26 .... 23 C4
Peak Hill Gdns. For Hil SE26 ..... 23 C4
Peak Rd. Stough GU2 .... 109 A4
Peak The. For Hil SE26 .... 23 C5
Peakfield. Frensh GU10 .... 167 C7
Peaks Hill. Purley CR8 .... 60 E1
Peaks Hill Rise. Purley CR8 .... 60 E1
Peall Rd. Thorn H CR0 .... 41 F3
Pear Ave. Up Hall TW17 .... 34 E6
Pear Tree Cl. Addl KT15 .... 52 A5
Pear Tree Cl. Mitch CR4 .... 40 E7
Pear Tree Ct. Camb GU15 .... 66 B8
Pear Tree Hill. Salfs RH1 .... 161 A8
Pear Tree La. Rowl GU10 .... 145 F3
Pear Tree Rd. Ashf TW15 .... 14 C3
Pearce House. 7 Streat SW2 ..... 21 E8

Pearcefield Ave. For Hil SE23	23	C7
Pearfield Rd. For Hil SE23	23	E5
Pearl Ct. Woking GU21	68	E3
Pearmain Cl. Shep TW17	34	B4
Pears Rd. Hounsl TW3	5	C4
Pearson Ct. Morden SM4	40	B4
Pearson Rd. Crawl RH10	202	C6
Peartree Ave. Wands SW17	20	C5
Peartree Cl. Hams Gn CR2	81	B5
Peary Cl. Horsh RH12	217	D6
Peaslake C of E Fst Sch.		
Peasl GU5	154	E7
Peaslake La. Peasl GU5	154	D6
Peat Comm. Elst GU8	148	C2
Peatmore Ave. Pyrf GU22	71	A3
Peatmore Cl. Pyrf GU22	71	A3
Peatmore Dr. Pirb GU24	87	C6
Pebble Cl. Box H KT20	116	E6
Pebble Hill. W Hors KT24	112	C2
Pebble Hill Cotts. Limps RH8	123	B6
Pebble La. Ashtd KT18 & KT21	96	A5
Pebblehill Rd.		
Betch KT20 & RH3	116	E5
Pebblehill Rd.		
Box H KT20 & RH3	116	E5
Pebworth Ct. 8 Redh RH1	119	A3
Pebworth Lodge. S Norw SE25	42	F5
Peckarmans Wood.		
Dulw SE21 & SE26	23	A5
Peek Cres. Wimble SW19	19	D3
Peeks Brook La. Crawl RH6	182	E7
Peeks Brook La. Horley RH6	161	F2
Peel Ave. Frml GU16	86	A7
Peel Ct. Farnb GU14	105	C8
Peel Ctr The. Brack RG12	27	B7
Pegasus Ave. Alder GU12	105	E2
Pegasus Cl. Linch GU27	207	D5
Pegasus Ct. Crawl RH11	200	E4
Pegasus Ct. Farnb GU14	85	E1
Pegasus Ct. King U T KT1	37	D6
Pegasus Rd. Croy CR0 & CR9	61	A4
Pegasus Rd. 3 Farnb GU14	85	B2
Pegasus Rd. W Heath GU14	84	F7
Pegasus Way. E Grins RH19	186	B3
Pegg Rd. Heston TW5	4	D7
Peggotty Pl. Sandh GU15	45	E2
Pegwell Cl. Crawl RH11	200	F4
Peket Cl. Egham TW18	32	E8
Peldon Ct. Rich TW10	6	F2
Pelham Cl. Crawl RH11	201	B2
Pelham Ct. G Book KT23	94	C1
Pelham Ct. Horsh RH12	217	B2
Pelham Ct. Stain TW18	13	B3
Pelham Dr. Crawl RH11	201	A2
Pelham House. Cater CR3	100	F3
Pelham Pl. Crawl RH11	201	B2
Pelham Prim Sch. Merton SW19	20	A1
Pelham Rd. Merton SW19	20	A1
Pelham Rd. Penge BR3 & SE20	43	C7
Pelham Way. G Book KT23	94	C1
Pelhams Cl. Esher KT10	55	A6
Pelhams Wlk. Esher KT10	55	A6
Pelinore Rd. Catf SE6	24	E6
Pelling Hill. Old W SL4	11	B7
Pelton Ave. Sutton SM2	59	B1
Pelton Ct. S Croy CR2	61	C4
Pemberton House. For Hil SE26	23	A4
Pemberton Pl. Esher KT10	55	C7
Pemberton Rd. E Mole KT8	36	C5
Pembley Gn. Copth RH10	183	E3
Pembridge Ave. Twick TW4	15	F7
Pembroke Ave. Easth RG12	27	A1
Pembroke Ave. Hersh KT12	54	D6
Pembroke Ave. Surb KT5	38	B4
Pembroke Broadway.		
Camb GU15	65	C5
Pembroke Cl. Ascot SL5	29	D4
Pembroke Cl. Banstd SM7	78	B2
Pembroke Gdns. Woking GU22	70	A1
Pembroke Mews. Ascot SL5	29	D4
Pembroke Pl. Hounsl TW7	5	E5
Pembroke Rd. Crawl RH10	182	C1
Pembroke Rd. Mitch CR4	41	A7
Pembroke Rd. S Norw SE25	42	E5
Pembroke Rd. Woking GU22	70	A2
Pembroke Villas. Rich TW9	6	D3
Pembroke Lodge. 2		
Streat SW16	21	F5
Pembury Ave. N Cheam KT4	39	A2
Pembury Ave. New Mal KT4	39	A2
Pembury Cl. Hayes BR2	44	F2
Pembury Cl. Wallin CR5	79	A5
Pembury Ct. Harl UB3	3	D8
Pembury Pl. Alder GU12	105	C1
Pembury Rd. Croy SE25	43	A5
Pemdevon Rd. Thorn H CR0	42	A2
Penarth Ct. Sutton SM2	59	C3
Penates. Esher KT10	55	D6
Penberth Rd. Catf SE6	24	C7
Penceat Ct. Penge SE20	43	C7
Pendarves Rd. Wimble SW20	39	C8
Pendell Ave. Harl UB3	3	F7
Pendell Rd. Bletch RH1	120	B4
Pendennis Cl. W Byfl KT14	71	A5
Pendennis Rd. Streat SW16	21	E4
Pendennis Rd. Hounsl TW3	5	A4
Penderry Rise. Catf SE6	24	D6
Pendine House. 13 For Hil SE26	23	A5
Pendle Rd. Streat SW16	21	B3
Pendlebury. Easth RG12	27	A2
Pendleton Cl. Earls RH1	139	F7
Pendleton Rd. Woodh RH1	139	E6
Pendragon Rd. Catf BR1	24	F5
Pendragon Way. Frml GU15	66	D3
Penerley Rd. Catf SE6	24	B7
Penfold Cl. Croy CR0 & CR9	61	A7
Penfold Croft. Farnh GU9	125	F4
Penfold Ct. Mitch CR4	41	A7
Penfold Rd. Crawl RH10	202	B2
Penge East Sta.		
Penge SE20	23	C2
Penge La. Penge SE20	23	D1
Penge Rd. Croy SE20 & SE25	43	A6
Penge West Sta. Penge SE20	23	B2
Penhurst. Horse GU21	69	F5
Penistone Rd. Streat SW16	21	E1
Penn Cl. Crawl RH11	181	D1
Pennards The. Sunby TW16	35	C6
Pennefather's Rd. Alder GU11	104	F3
Penner Cl. Putney SW19	19	E6
Pennine Cl. Crawl RH11	201	B6
Pennine Way. Harl UB7	3	D7
Pennine Way. W Heath GU14	84	F7
Pennings Ave.		
Stough GU2 & GU3	108	F3
Pennington Cl. 10		
W Norw SE27	22	D4
Pennington Dr. Oat Pk KT13	53	E7
Pennington Lodge. 18		
King U T KT5	37	E4
Penns Wood. Farnb GU14	85	D1
Penny Dr. Wood S V GU3	108	B2
Penny La. Oat Pk TW17	34	E2
Penny Royal. Wallin SM6	60	D4
Pennycroft. New Add CR0	62	E2
Pennyfield. Cobham KT11	73	A6
Pennymead Dr. E Hors KT24	112	F8
Pennymead Rise. E Hors KT24	112	F8
Pennypot La. Chobh GU24	68	C7
Penrhyn Cl. Alder GU11	105	B1
Penrhyn Cres. Mortl SW14	7	C3
Penrhyn Gdns. King U T KT1	37	D5
Penrhyn Rd. King U T KT1	37	E6
Penrith Cl. Beck BR3	44	B8
Penrith Cl. Redh RH1	118	E2
Penrith Pl. W Norw SE27	22	B6
Penrith Rd. New Mal KT3	38	D5
Penrith Rd. S Norw CR7	42	C7
Penrith St. Streat SW16	21	C2
Penrose Ct. Eng Gn TW20	11	C2
Penrose Rd. Fetch KT22	94	C5
Penryn Dr. Head Dn GU35	187	C5
Penry House. 5 Redh RH1	119	A3
Pensfold La. Rudg RH12 & RH13	214	E5
Pensford Ave. Rich TW9	7	A5
Pensford Cl. Crowth RG11	45	B7
Penshurst Gn. Hayes BR2	44	F4
Penshurst Rd. Thorn H CR7	42	B4
Penshurst Rise. Frml GU16	85	F8
Penshurst Wlk. Hayes BR2	44	F4
Pentelow Gdns. Felt TW14	4	A1
Penthorpe Sch. Rudg RH12	214	C7
Pentland Ave. Shep Gn TW17	34	A4
Pentland Pl. W Heath GU14	84	E7
Pentlands. Beck BR3	44	C8
Pentlands Cl. Mitch CR4	41	B6
Pentney Rd. Streat SW12	21	C7
Pentney Rd.		
Wimble SW19 & SW20	39	E8
Penton Ave. Stain TW18	32	F8
Penton Ct. Stain TW18	12	F2
Penton Hall. Stain TW18	33	A8
Penton Hall Dr. Stain TW18	33	A8
Penton Hook Marina.		
Egham TW18	32	F7
Penton Hook Marina.		
Thorpe KT16	33	A6
Penton Hook Rd. Stain TW18	33	A8
Penton House. Sutton SM2	59	C3
Penton Rd. Stain TW18	12	F1
Pentreath Ave. Onsl V GU2	129	F8
Penwerris Ave.		
Hounsl TW5 & TW7	5	C7
Penwerris Ct. Hounsl TW7	5	C7
Penwith Dr. Linch GU27	207	E5
Penwith Rd. Wands SW18	20	B6
Penwith Wlk. Woking GU22	89	D8
Penwood End. Woking GU22	89	B6
Penwood Gdns.		
Easth RG11 & RG12	26	D3
Penwood House. Rhampt SW15	7	F1
Penwortham Prim Sch.		
Streat SW17	21	B2
Penwortham Rd. S Croy CR2	61	D1
Penwortham Rd. Streat SW16	21	C2
Peper Harow La. P Harow GU8	149	C6
Peperham House.		
Haslem GU27	208	C7
Peperham Rd. Haslem GU27	208	C8
Peperharow Rd. Farnc GU7	150	C6
Pepper Cl. Cater CR3	100	E2
Pepperbox La. Crawl GU5	173	E4
Peppermint Cl. Croy CR0	41	E2
Pepys Cl. Ashtd KT21	76	A2
Pepys Cl. Bra Hil SL3	1	B8
Pepys Rd. Wimble SW20	39	C8
Perak Ct. Tolw KT5	38	C2
Percheron Cl. Islew TW7	5	F4
Percival Rd. Felt TW13	14	F6
Percival Rd. Mortl SW14	7	C3
Percival Way. W Ewell KT19	57	D6
Percival Way. W Ewell KT19	57	D6
Percy Ave. Ashf TW15	14	A3
Percy Bilton Ct. Heston TW5	5	B6
Percy Bryant Rd. Charlt TW16	14	E1
Percy Ct. 1 Surb KT5	37	F3
Percy Gdns. 3 Islew TW7	6	A4
Percy Gdns. New Mal KT4	38	E1
Percy House. 4 Streat SW16	21	C4
Percy Rd. Carsh SM5	40	E1
Percy Rd. Croy SE25	43	A4
Percy Rd. Hampt TW12	16	A1
Percy Rd. Horsh RH12	217	B3
Percy Rd. Islew TW7	6	A3
Percy Rd. Penge SE20	43	D8
Percy Rd. Stough GU2	109	B3
Percy Rd. Twick TW2	16	C7
Percy Way. Twick TW2	16	C7
Peregrine Cl. Cran GU6	174	E4
Peregrine Cl. Easth RG12	27	B4
Peregrine Gdns. Croy CR0	62	E8
Peregrine Rd. Sunby TW16	34	F7
Peregrine Way.		
Wimble SW19 & SW20	19	C1
Performing Arts & Tech Sch.		
Thorn H SE25	42	D3
Perifield. W Norw SE21	22	C7
Perimeter Rd E. Crawl RH6	182	B6
Perimeter Rd N. Crawl RH6	160	F1
Perimeter Rd N. Crawl RH6	181	D7
Perimeter Rd N. Crawl RH6	182	A8
Perimeter Rd S. Crawl RH6	181	E5
Perkins Ct. Ashf TW15	13	F3
Perkins Way. Woki RG11	25	A5
Perkstead Ct. 7 Crawl RH11	201	A3
Perleybrooke La. Woking GU21	69	A2
Perowne St. Alder GU11	104	F2
Perram Wks. Merrow GU4	110	C4
Perran Rd. Streat SE24 & SW2	22	B6
Perran Wlk. 16 Brent TW8	6	E8
Perrin Cl. Ashf TW15	13	F3
Perrin Ct. Sheer GU21	70	B4
Perring Ave. W Heath GU14	84	F8
Perring Rd. Farnb GU14	85	A2
Perrior Rd. Farnc GU7	150	E7
Perry Ave. E Grins RH19	185	E3
Perry Cl. Godal GU7	151	B5
Perry Hill. For Hil SE23 & SE6	23	F5
Perry House. 24 Streat SW2	21	E8
Perry How. New Mal KT4	38	F1
Perry Oaks. Brack RG12	27	E7
Perry Oaks Dr. Harm TW6 & UB7	2	C5
Perry Rise. For Hil SE23 & SE6	23	E5
Perry Vale. For Hil SE23	23	D6
Perry Way. Brack RG12	27	E7
Perry Way. Lhtwat GU18	66	F7
Perryfield House. 7		
Crawl RH11	201	D5
Perryfield Rd. Crawl RH11	201	D5
Perryfield Way. Rich TW10	17	B6
Perrylands. Charl RH6	180	F7
Perrylands La. Smallf RH6	162	A2
Perrymount Prim Sch.		
For Hil SE23	23	D6
Perryn Ct. 2 Twick TW1	17	A8
Perrywood Bsns Pk. Salfs RH1	140	B1
Persant Rd. Catf SE6	24	E6
Perseverance Cotts.		
Ripley GU23	91	C6
Persfield Mews. Ewell KT17	57	F1
Persfield Rd. Ewell KT17	58	A1
Pershore Gr. Carsh SM5	40	D3
Perth Cl. Crawl RH11	181	D1
Perth Cl. Wimble SW20	39	A7
Perth Rd. Beck BR3	44	C7
Perth Way. Horsh RH12	217	F4
Perystreete. For Hil SE23	23	C6
Petauel Rd. Tedd TW11	16	E3
Petavel Rd. Tedd TW11	16	E2
Peter Ave. Oxted RH8	122	D6
Peter Kennedy Ct. Croy CR0	43	F3
Peter's Path. For Hil SE26	23	B4
Peterborough Rd.		
Carsh CR4 & SM4 & SM5	40	E3
Peterborough Rd. Crawl RH10	201	E2
Peterborough Rd. Stough GU2	108	F3
Peterhouse Cl. Sandh GU47	45	F2
Peterhouse Par. Crawl RH10	182	C1
Peterlee Wlk. Crawl RH11	200	E4
Petersfield Ave.		
Stain TW15 & TW18	13	C2
Petersfield Cres. Coulsd CR5	79	E4
Petersfield Rd. Stain TW18	13	C3
Petersfield Rise. Rhampt SW15	19	B7
Petersham Ave. Byfl KT14	71	E7
Petersham Cl. Byfl KT14	71	E7
Petersham Cl. Cheam SM1	59	A5
Petersham Cl. Rich TW10	17	C6
Petersham Rd. Rich TW10	17	E7
Peterstow Cl. Putney SW19	19	E6
Peterwood Pk. Croy CR0	60	F8
Peterwood Way. Croy CR0	60	F8
Petrel Ct. 7 S Norw SE21	22	D6
Petridge Rd. Earls RH1	139	F4
Petters Rd. Ashtd KT21	75	F3
Petts La. Shep Gn TW17	34	A5
Petworth Cl. Coulsd CR5	99	C8
Petworth Cl. Frml GU16	85	F8
Petworth Ct. Crawl RH11	200	D3
Petworth Ct. Haslem GU27	208	D6
Petworth Dr. Horsh RH12	217	F7
Petworth Gdns. W Barn SW20	39	B6
Petworth Rd.		
Chidd GU27 & GU8	209	C5
Petworth Rd. Witley GU8	170	F5
Petworth Rd. Wormly GU8	170	F5
Pevensey Cl. Crawl RH10	202	C5
Pevensey Cl. Hounsl TW7	5	C7
Pevensey Ct. S Norw SW16	22	A5
Pevensey House. Dovgn RH2	139	B5
Pevensey Rd. Felt TW13	15	E7
Pevensey Rd. Up Toot SW17	20	D4
Pevensey Way. Frml GU16	86	A8
Peverel Rd. Crawl RH11	200	E5
Peveril Dr. Tedd TW11	16	D3
Pewley Bank. Guild GU1	130	E7
Pewley Down Inf Sch.		
Guild GU1	130	E7
Pewley Hill. Guild GU1	130	E7
Pewley Point. Guild GU1	130	E7
Pewley Way. Guild GU1	130	E7
Pewsey Vale. Brack RG12	27	F4
Peyton's Cotts. Nutf RH1	119	F3
Pharaoh Cl. Carsh CR4	40	F2
Pheasant Cl. Purley CR8	80	B6
Philanthropic Rd. Earls RH1	140	B8
Philip Gdns. Croy CR0	62	F8
Philip Rd. Stain TW18	13	D2
Philip Southcote Sch.		
Chert KT15	52	C8
Philips House. Graysh GU26	188	B3
Phillips Cl. Godal GU7	150	D2
Phillips Cotts. Ock Rid GU7	150	B4
Phillips Hatch. Woner GU5	152	C8
Philpot La. Chobh GU24	69	C7
Phipp's Bridge Rd.		
Mitch CR4 & SW19	40	D6
Phoenix Bsns Pk. Binf RG12	26	C7
Phoenix Cl. W Wick BR4	63	E8
Phoenix Ct. Alder GU11	105	A2
Phoenix Ct. Croy SE25	43	A4
Phoenix Ct. Guild GU1	130	D7
Phoenix La. Ash V GU35	168	A2
Phoenix Pl. Stain TW18	13	A3
Phoenix Rd. Penge SE20	23	C2
Phoenix Way. Heston TW5	4	D8
Phyllis Ave. W Barn KT3	39	B4
Phyllis House. Croy CR0	61	B6
Piccards The. Guild GU2	130	C5
Pickering. Easth RG12	27	A5
Pickering Gdns. Croy SE25	42	F3
Picket Post Cl. Brack RG12	27	F6
Pickets Hill. Head Dn GU35	166	C1
Pickets La. Salfs RH1	161	C8
Pickford St. Alder GU11	105	B2
Pickhurst Gn. Hayes BR2	44	F3
Pickhurst Inf Sch. Hayes BR2	44	F3
Pickhurst Jun Sch. Hayes BR2	44	F3
Pickhurst La.		
Hayes BR2 & BR3 & BR4	44	E2
Pickhurst Mead. Hayes BR2	44	F2
Pickhurst Pk. Hayes BR2	44	F4
Pickhurst Rise. Chidd GU8	191	C3
Pickins Piece. Horton SL3	1	A5
Pickwick Cl. Hounsl TW4	4	E2
Pickwick Rd. Dulw SE21	22	E8
Picquets Way.		
Burgh H KT20 & SM7	77	F2
Picton Cl. Camb GU15	66	B7
Picton House. 1 Streat SW4	21	E8
Pier Rd. Felt TW14	4	B2
Pierrefondes Ave. Farnb GU14	85	B5
Pierrepoint. S Norw SE25	42	E6
Pierrepont Sch. Frensh GU10	146	E1
Pierson House. 12 Dulw SE19	22	E4
Pigbush La. Loxwd RH14	213	A7
Pigeon La. Hampt TW12	16	A4
Pigeonhouse La. Kings CR5	98	C3
Pigeonhouse La. Wink SL4 & SL5	8	E4
Piggott Ct. Horsh RH13	217	E1
Pigott Ct. Woki RG11	25	D6
Pigott Rd. Woki RG11	25	E8
Pike Cl. Alder GU11	105	C2
Pikes Hill. Epsom KT17	76	E6
Pikes La. Crow RH7	143	E2
Pikethorne. For Hil SE23	23	D6
Pilgrim Cl. Morden SM4	40	B2
Pilgrim Hill. W Norw SE27	22	C4
Pilgrim House. Guild GU1	130	D7
Pilgrim's Way. S Croy CR2	61	F5
Pilgrims Cl. M Bourn GU9	146	A8
Pilgrims Cl. Shere GU5	133	A4
Pilgrims Cl. Westh RH5	115	B4
Pilgrims La. Cater CR3	100	B1
Pilgrims La. Tats TN16	103	D3
Pilgrims La. Titsey RH8 & TN16	103	D3
Pilgrims Pl. Reig RH2	118	A3
Pilgrims View. Ash GU12	127	C8
Pilgrims Way. Bisley GU24	68	A3
Pilgrims' Way. Guild GU1	130	E5
Pilgrims' Way. Reig RH2	118	A3
Pilgrims Way. Shere GU5	133	A4
Pilgrims Way. Westh RH5	115	B4
Pilgrims Way Cotts. Betch RH3	116	C2
Pilgrims Way Cty Sch The.		
M Bourn GU9	146	B8
Pilsden Cl. Putney SW19	19	D7
Pilton Est The. Thorn H CR9	61	B8
Pimms Cl. Burgh GU4	110	A5
Pinckards. Chidd GU8	191	B5
Pincott La. W Hors KT24	112	B6
Pincott Rd. Merton SW19	40	C8
Pine Ave. Camb GU15	65	D3
Pine Ave. W Wick BR4	44	B1
Pine Bank. Hindh GU26	188	E4
Pine Cl. Ash V GU12	106	A6
Pine Cl. Crawl RH11	181	C1
Pine Cl. Horse GU21	69	C3
Pine Cl. Kenley CR8	80	D2
Pine Cl. Penge SE20	43	C8
Pine Cl. Sandh GU15	64	E7
Pine Cl. Woodhm KT15	71	B8
Pine Coombe. S Croy CR0	62	D6
Pine Cres. Sutton SM5	78	D8
Pine Croft Rd. Woki RG11	25	A2
Pine Ct. Brack RG12	27	E5
Pine Ct. 2 Whit V KT13	53	C5
Pine Dean. G Book KT23	94	B2
Pine Dr. Hawley GU17	64	E3
Pine Gdns. Horley RH6	161	A2
Pine Gdns. Surb KT5	38	A3
Pine Gr. E Grins RH19	185	B3
Pine Gr. M Bourn GU10	146	E6
Pine Gr. Weyb KT13	53	C5
Pine Gr. Wimble SW19	19	F3
Pine Gr. Windl GU20	48	D4
Pine Grove Mews. 3		
Whit V KT13	53	C5
Pine Hill. Woodc KT18	76	D4
Pine Mount Rd. Camb GU15	65	D4
Pine Pl. Nork KT17	77	D5
Pine Rd. Woking GU22	89	C7
Pine Ridge. Wallin SM5	60	A2
Pine Ridge Cty Inf Sch.		
Camb GU15	47	A1
Pine Ridge Dr. M Bourn GU10	146	C5
Pine Ridge Golf Ctr. Frml GU16	66	D2
Pine Shaw. Crawl RH10	202	D2
Pine Tree Cl. Cranf TW5	4	B6
Pine Tree Hill. Mayb GU22	70	D3
Pine Trees Bsns Pk.		
Egham TW18	12	E3
Pine View. Head Dn GU35	187	C6
Pine View Cl. Chil GU4	131	F5
Pine View Cl. Farnh GU9	126	A5
Pine View Cl. Haslem GU27	208	C8
Pine Way. Eng Gn TW20	11	B2
Pine Way Cl. E Grins RH19	205	E3
Pine Wlk. Cater CR3	100	F5
Pine Wlk. Cobham KT11	73	D5
Pine Wlk. E Hors KT24	112	F7
Pine Wlk. Kings KT23	94	B2
Pine Wlk. Surb KT5	38	A3
Pine Wlk. Sutton SM5	59	D1
Pine Wlk. Woodm CR5 & SM7	78	F2
Pine Wood. Sunby TW16	35	A8
Pineacre Ct. Mayb GU22	70	B2
Pinecote Dr. Sunnin SL5	29	F2
Pinefields. Addl KT15	52	B6
Pinefields Cl. Crowth RG11	45	B4
Pinehill Rd. Crowth RG11	45	C3
Pinehill Rise. Sandh GU17	64	C8
Pinehurst. Ascot SL5	29	D4
Pinehurst. Horsh RH12	217	C4
Pinehurst. 8 Woking GU22	69	F1
Pinehurst Ave. Farnb GU14	85	B3
Pinehurst Cl. Kings KT20	98	A5
Pinehurst Cotts. Farnb GU14	85	B2
Pines Ct. 14 Putney SW19	19	D7
Pines Cty Inf Sch The.		
Easth GU35	27	A2
Pines Cty Jun Sch The.		
Easth GU35	27	A2
Pines The. Camb GU15	65	F7
Pines The. Dork RH4	136	B6
Pines The. Horsh RH12	218	C5
Pines The. Purley CR8	80	C6
Pines The. S Norw SE19 & SW16	22	B2
Pines The. Stough GU3	108	E3
Pines The. Sunby TW16	35	A6
Pinetrees Cl. Copth RH10	183	B3
Pinewood Ave. Crowth RG11	45	C6
Pinewood Ave. Woodhm KT15	52	C1
Pinewood Cl. Broad H RH12	216	D3
Pinewood Cl. Horse GU21	70	A4
Pinewood Cl. S Croy CR0	62	E7
Pinewood Cres. W Heath GU14	84	C5
Pinewood Ct. Addl KT15	52	B6
Pinewood Ct. Woking GU21	70	A3
Pinewood Cty Inf Sch.		
W Heath GU14	84	D7
Pinewood Dr. Stain TW18	13	A3
Pinewood Gdns. Bagsh GU19	47	C3
Pinewood Gr. Woodhm KT15	52	B1
Pinewood Mews. Stan TW19	2	D1
Pinewood Pk. W Heath GU14	84	C7
Pinewood Pk. Woodhm KT15	71	B8
Pinewood Pl. W Ewell KT19	57	D6
Pinewood Pl. W Ewell KT19	57	D6
Pinewood Rd. Felt TW13	15	B5
Pinewood Rd. Normdy GU12	106	D3
Pinewood Rd. Went GU25	31	A5
Pinfold Rd. Streat SW16	21	E4
Pinglestone Cl. Harm TW6 & UB7	2	E7
Pinkcoat Cl. Felt TW13	15	B5
Pinkerton Pl. Streat SW16	21	D4
Pinkhurst La. Slinfd RH13	216	A2
Pioneers Ind Pk. Wallin CR9	41	E1
Piper Rd. King U T KT1	38	A6
Piper's End. Vir W GU25	31	D6
Pipers Cl. Cobham KT11	73	D3
Pipers End. Slinfd RH13	215	E3
Pipers Gdns. Croy CR0	43	E2
Pipers Patch. 1 Farnb GU14	85	B4
Pipewell Rd. Carsh SM5	40	E3
Pippbrook Gdns. Dork RH4	136	B8
Pippin Cl. Croy CR0	43	F1
Pippins Ct. Ashf TW15	14	B2
Piquet Rd. Penge BR3 & SE20	43	C7
Pirbright Cres. New Add CR0	63	C4
Pirbright Cty Prim Sch.		
Pirb GU24	87	E5
Pirbright House. 11		
King U T KT2	18	B2
Pirbright Rd. Farnb GU14	85	C3
Pirbright Rd. Normdy GU3	107	B6
Pirbright Rd. Wands SW18	20	A7
Pirbright Terr. Pirb GU24	87	F4
Pirles Pl. Horsh RH12	217	C2
Pisley La. Wall W RH5	177	A4
Pit Farm Rd. Guild GU1	110	A1
Pit Wood Gn. Burgh H KT20	97	C7
Pitcairn Rd. Mitch CR4	20	F1
Pitchfont La. Limps CR6 & RH8	102	F2
Pitfold Ave. Shottm GU27	207	D6
Pitfold Cl. Shottm GU27	207	D6
Pitlake. Thorn H CR0 & CR9	61	B8
Pitland St. Hol St M RH5	155	C5
Pitman's Coll. Wimble SW19	19	F3
Pitson Cl. Addl KT15	52	D6
Pitt Cres. Wimble SW19	20	B4
Pitt Pl. Epsom KT17	76	E5
Pitt Rd. Epsom KT17	76	E5
Pitt Rd. Thorn H CR0 & CR7	42	C4
Pitt Way. W Heath GU14	84	F5
Pittville Gdns. S Norw SE25	43	A6
Pixfield Ct. Broml BR2	44	F7
Pixham Firs. Pixham RH4	115	C2
Pixham La. Pixham RH4	115	C3
Pixholme Ct. Pixham RH4	115	C2
Pixholme Gr. Pixham RH4	115	C1
Pixton Way. New Add CR0 & CR2	62	E2
Place Ct. Alder GU11	126	D2
Place Farm Rd. Bletch RH1	120	D4
Placehouse La. Coulsd CR5	80	A1
Plaistow Cty Inf Sch.		
Plaist RH14	211	F3

Plaistow Rd. Dunsf GU8 .... 192 D2
Plaistow Rd. Ifold RH14 .... 212 D1
Plaistow Rd. Loxwd RH14 .... 212 D1
Plaistow St. Lingf RH7 .... 164 D4
Plane St. For Hil SE26 .... 23 B5
Plane Tree Cres. Felt TW13 ... 15 B5
Plane Tree Wlk. 4

W Norw SE19 .... 22 E2
Planes The. Chert KT16 .... 33 C2
Plantagenet Cl. Worc Pk KT19 .... 57 D6
Plantain Cres. Crawl RH11 ..... 201 A2
Plantation La. Warlgm CR6 .... 101 E8
Plantation Row. Camb GU15 ...... 65 B5
Plassy Rd. Catf SE6 .... 24 B8
Plat The. Horsh RH12 .... 217 A3
Platt Meadow. Merrow GU4 .... 110 D3
Platt The. Dorman RH7 .... 186 A8
Platt's Eyot. Hampt TW12 .... 36 A7
Plaws Hill. Peasl GU5 .... 154 D6
Plawsfield Rd. Penge BR3 .... 43 D8
Playden Ct. 4 Crawl RH11 ...... 201 A3
Playgreen Way. Catf SE6 .... 24 A4
Playground Rd. Penge BR3 .... 43 D7
Pleasant Gr. Croy CR0 .... 62 F7
Pleasant Pl. Hersh KT12 .... 54 D4
Pleasure Pit Rd. Ashtd KT21 .... 76 B1
Plesman Way. Wallin SM6 .... 60 D7
Plevna Rd. Hampt TW12 .... 36 B8
Pleydell Ave. Penge SE19 .... 22 F1
Plough Cl. Crawl RH11 .... 200 F8
Plough Ind Est. Leahd KT22 ..... 95 A7
Plough La. Downs KT11 .... 73 A2
Plough La. Ewh GU6 .... 176 A5
Plough La. Horsh RH12 .... 217 C5
Plough La.

Purley CR0 & CR8 & SM6 .... 60 F1
Plough La. Wallin CR0 & SM6 ..... 60 E5
Plough La. Wallin SM6 .... 60 E5
Plough La. Wimble SW17 & SW19 20 C4
Plough La. Woki RG11 .... 25 F6
Plough Lane Cl.

Wallin CR0 & SM6 .... 60 E5
Plough Rd. Dorman RH7 .... 165 A2
Plough Rd. Smallf RH6 .... 162 C3
Plough Rd. W Ewell KT19 .... 57 D3
Plough Rd. W Ewell KT19 .... 57 D3
Ploughlands. Brack RG12 .... 26 F8
Ploughmans End. Islew TW7 ...... 5 D2
Plover Cl. Crawl RH11 .... 201 C8
Plover Cl. Stain TW18 .... 12 F5
Plovers Rd. Horsh RH13 .... 217 F3
Plovers Rise. Pirb GU24 .... 87 E7
Plowman House. Putney SW19 ... 19 D6
Plummer La. Mitch CR4 .... 40 F7
Plummer Rd. Streat SW4 .... 21 D8
Plumpton Way. Carsh SM5 .... 59 E7
Plumtree Cl. Wallin SM6 .... 60 D3
Pocklington Ct. Rhampt SW15 ... 19 A7
Point (L Ctr) The. Brack RG12 ... 27 B7
Point Royal. Easth RG12 .... 27 B4
Pointers Hill. Westc RH4 .... 135 C5
Pointers Rd. Downs KT11 .... 72 E2
Pointers The. Ashtd KT21 .... 95 E7
Polden Cl. W Heath GU14 .... 84 E7
Polecroft La. For Hil SE6 .... 23 F6
Poles La. Rusper RH11 & RH6 .. 181 C3
Polesden Gdns. W Barn SW20 ... 39 B7
Polesden La. Ripley GU23 .... 91 A6
Polesden La. Send M GU23 .... 90 F5
Polesden Rd. G Book KT23 .... 114 B6
Polesden View. G Book KT23 .... 114 B8
Polesteeple Hill. Bigg H TN16 ... 83 D2
Police Station Rd. Hersh KT12 ... 54 C4
Pollard Gr. Friml GU15 .... 66 C4
Pollard Rd. Cheam KT4 .... 58 C6
Pollard Rd. Mayb GU22 .... 70 B3
Pollard Rd. Morden SM4 .... 40 D4
Pollardrow Ave. Brack RG12 ..... 26 F8
Pollards. Crawl RH11 .... 201 A5
Pollards Cres. Thorn H SW16 .... 41 F6
Pollards Dr. Horsh RH13 .... 217 F2
Pollards Hill E. Thorn H SW16 ... 41 F6
Pollards Hill N. Thorn H SW16 ... 41 F6
Pollards Hill S. Thorn H SW16 ... 41 F6
Pollards Hill W. Thorn H SW16 ... 41 F6
Pollards Oak Cres. Oxted RH8 . 123 A3
Pollards Oak Rd. Oxted RH8 .... 123 A3
Pollards Wood Hill. Limps RH8 123 B5
Pollards Wood Rd. Limps RH8 123 B4
Pollards Wood Rd.

Thorn H SW16 .... 41 E6
Polsted La. Compt GU3 .... 129 C3
Polsted Rd. For Hil SE6 .... 23 F8
Poltimore Rd. Guild GU2 .... 130 B7
Polworth Rd. Streat SW16 .... 21 E3
Polyanthus Way. Crowth RG11 ... 45 B8
Pond Cl. Loxwd RH14 .... 212 D4
Pond Cl. Whit V KT12 .... 54 A4
Pond Copse La. Loxwd RH14 ... 212 F7
Pond Cottage La.

Croy BR3 & BR4 .... 44 A1
Pond Cotts. Dulw SE21 .... 22 E7
Pond Head La. For Gn RH5 ...... 176 E5
Pond Head La. Wall W RH5 ..... 176 D3
Pond Hill Gdns. Cheam SM3 ...... 58 E4
Pond House. Merrow GU4 .... 110 D2
Pond La. Frensh GU10 .... 167 C5
Pond La. Peasl GU5 .... 154 D7
Pond Meadow. Stough GU2 ..... 108 E2
Pond Meadow Sch.

Stough GU2 .... 108 E2
Pond Moor Rd. Easth RG12 .... 27 B4
Pond Piece. Oxsh KT22 .... 74 B6
Pond Rd. Egham TW20 .... 12 C2
Pond Rd. Farnb GU14 .... 85 B2
Pond Rd. Head Dn GU35 .... 187 B4
Pond Rd. Woking GU22 .... 89 B7
Pond Way. E Grins RH19 .... 186 B1
Pond Way. Tedd TW11 .... 17 F1
Pond Wood Rd. Crawl RH10 .... 202 A8
Pondfield House. W Norw SE27 . 22 C3

Pondfield Rd. Farnc GU7 .... 150 F7
Pondfield Rd. Kenley CR8 .... 80 B3
Pondfield Rd. Rudg RH12 .... 214 D8
Pondfield Rd. W Wick BR2 .... 44 E1
Pondpenny La. Farnb GU14 .... 84 A1
Ponds La. Farl Gn GU5 .... 153 F8
Ponds The. Whit V KT13 .... 53 E4
Pondside Cl. Harl UB3 .... 3 D7
Pondtail Cl. Horsh RH12 .... 217 D6
Pondtail Dr. Horsh RH12 .... 217 B5
Pondtail Rd. Horsh RH12 .... 217 C5
Ponsonby Rd. Putney SW15 .... 19 B8
Pontefract Rd. Broml BR1 .... 24 F3
Ponton House. Streat SW2 .... 22 A7
Pony Chase. Cobham KT11 .... 73 F6
Pool Cl. Beck BR3 .... 24 A3
Pool Cl. Catf SE6 .... 24 A6
Pool End Cl. Shep Gn TW17 .... 34 A4
Pool Rd. Alder GU11 .... 126 C7
Pool Rd. E Mole KT12 & KT8 .... 35 F4
Poole Court Rd. Hounsl TW5 .... 4 E5
Poole Ct. Hounsl TW5 .... 4 E5
Poole Rd. W Ewell KT19 .... 57 D4
Poole Rd. W Ewell KT19 .... 57 D4
Poole Rd. Woking GU21 .... 69 E3
Pooley Ave. Egham TW20 .... 12 B3
Pooley Green Cl. Egham TW20 .. 12 C3
Pooley Green Rd. Egham TW20 . 12 C3
Pope Cl. E Bed TW14 .... 14 F7
Pope Cl. Mitch SW17 & SW19 ..... 20 D2
Pope Ct. 10 King U T KT2 .... 17 F4
Pope's Ave. Twick TW2 .... 16 E6
Pope's Gr. Twick TW1 & TW2 ...... 16 F6
Popes Cl. Coln SL3 .... 1 C7
Popes Gr. Croy CR0 .... 62 F7
Popes La. Oxted RH8 .... 143 F8
Popes Mead. Haslem GU27 ..... 208 C7
Popeswood Rd. Binf RG12 .... 26 D8
Popham Cl. Brack RG12 .... 27 F4
Popham Ct. Felt TW13 .... 15 F5
Popham Gdns. Rich TW9 .... 7 B4
Poplar Ave. Leahd KT22 .... 95 C5
Poplar Ave. Mitch CR4 .... 40 F8
Poplar Ave. Windl GU20 .... 48 B6
Poplar Cl. Crawl RH11 .... 181 C1
Poplar Cl. Mytch GU16 .... 86 A3
Poplar Cl. Poyle SL3 .... 1 E6
Poplar Cotts. Stough GU3 .... 108 E4
Poplar Cres. W Ewell KT19 .... 57 C4
Poplar Cres. W Ewell KT19 .... 57 C4
Poplar Ct. 4 Streat SW16 .... 21 F5
Poplar Ct. 13 Twick TW1 .... 6 C1
Poplar Ct. Wimble SW19 .... 20 A3
Poplar Dr. Nork KT17 & SM7 ...... 77 D5
Poplar Farm Cl. W Ewell KT19 ... 57 C4
Poplar Farm Cl. W Ewell KT19 ... 57 C4
Poplar Fst Sch. Merton SW19 .... 40 A6
Poplar Gdns. King U T KT3 .... 38 D6
Poplar Gr. King U T KT3 .... 38 D6
Poplar Gr. Woking GU22 .... 89 E8
Poplar La. Beck BR3 .... 44 B4
Poplar Rd. Ashf TW15 .... 14 C3
Poplar Rd. Cheam SM3 .... 39 F1
Poplar Rd. Merton SW19 .... 40 A7
Poplar Rd. Shalf GU4 .... 130 E2
Poplar Rd S.

Merton SM4 & SW19 .... 40 A6
Poplar Road C of E Prim Sch.

Leahd KT22 .... 95 B5
Poplar Way. Felt TW13 .... 15 B5
Poplar Wlk. Cater CR3 .... 100 E4
Poplar Wlk. Croy CR0 .... 42 C1
Poplar Wlk. Heath E GU7 .... 125 D7
Poplars Cl. W Heath GU14 .... 84 C5
Poplars The. Ascot SL5 .... 29 A4
Poplars The. Horsh RH13 .... 217 E3
Poppy La. Croy CR0 & CR9 .... 43 C1
Poppy Pl. Woki RG11 .... 25 B6
Poppyhills Rd. Camb GU15 .... 65 F5
Porchester. Ascot SL5 .... 29 A5
Porchester Mead. Beck BR3 ...... 24 B2
Porchester Rd. King U T KT1 ..... 38 B7
Porchfield Cl. Sutton SM2 .... 59 B1
Porlock House. 5 For Hil SE26 .. 23 C5
Porridge Pot Alley. Guild GU2 . 130 C7
Port Way. Bisley GU24 .... 68 A3
Portal Cl. W Norw SE27 .... 22 A5
Porteridges. Dork RH4 .... 136 C4
Portesbery Hill Dr. Camb GU15 . 65 E6
Portesbery Rd. Camb GU15 ...... 65 E6
Portesbery Sch. Camb GU15 ..... 65 D6
Porthcawe Rd. For Hil SE26 .... 23 F4
Portia Gr. Wink RG12 .... 27 E8
Portland Ave. New Mal KT3 .... 38 F2
Portland Cotts. Wallin CR0 .... 41 D2
Portland Cres.

Felt TW13 & TW15 .... 14 D4
Portland Dr. Merst RH1 .... 119 D6
Portland House. 5

E Grins RH19 .... 205 F8
Portland House. Merst RH1 ..... 119 D6
Portland House. 20

Streat SW2 .... 22 A7
Portland House Mews.

Epsom KT18 .... 76 D5
Portland Pl. Croy SE25 .... 43 A5
Portland Pl. Ewell KT17 .... 76 E7
Portland Rd. Ashf TW15 .... 13 E5
Portland Rd. Croy SE25 .... 43 B4
Portland Rd. Dork RH4 .... 136 A8
Portland Rd. E Grins RH19 ...... 205 F8
Portland Rd. King U T KT1 .... 37 F6
Portland Rd. Mitch CR4 .... 40 E7
Portland Terr. Rich TW9 .... 6 D3
Portley La. Cater CR3 .... 100 E6
Portley Wood Rd. Whytlf CR3 .. 101 A7
Portman Ave. Mortl SW14 .... 7 D4
Portman Cl. 5 Brack RG12 .... 27 A8
Portman Rd. King U T KT1 .... 37 F7
Portmore Park Rd. Weyb KT13 . 53 A7

Portmore Quays. Weyb KT13 ..... 52 F6
Portmore Way. Weyb KT13 .... 53 A7
Portnall Dr. Went GU25 .... 30 F4
Portnall Rd. Went GU25 .... 30 F4
Portnall Rise. Went GU25 .... 30 F4
Portnalls Cl. Coulsd CR5 .... 79 B3
Portnalls Rd. Coulsd CR5 .... 79 B2
Portnalls Rise. Coulsd CR5 .... 79 C3
Portobello House. 6

W Norw SE27 .... 22 B3
Porton Ct. King U T KT6 .... 37 C3
Portsea House. 3 Rhampt SW15 19 B7
Portsmouth Ave. Thame D KT7 .. 37 A2
Portsmouth Rd. Bramsh GU26 .. 187 A2
Portsmouth Rd. Camb GU15 ..... 66 A7
Portsmouth Rd.

Cobham KT10 & KT11 .... 73 C7
Portsmouth Rd. Esher KT10 ...... 55 A4
Portsmouth Rd. Esher KT10 ...... 55 A4
Portsmouth Rd. Guild GU2 ...... 130 C6
Portsmouth Rd.

Hinch W KT10 & KT7 .... 55 E8
Portsmouth Rd. Hind GU26 ..... 188 E2
Portsmouth Rd.

King U T KT1 & KT6 .... 37 C3
Portsmouth Rd. Milf GU8 .... 149 E1
Portsmouth Rd.

Ock Rid GU7 & GU8 .... 150 B2
Portsmouth Rd. Ockham GU23 .. 91 B4
Portsmouth Rd. Putney SW15 ... 19 C8
Portsmouth Rd. Ripley GU23 ..... 91 B4
Portsmouth Rd. Send M GU23 ... 91 B4
Portsmouth Rd. Shottm GU26 .. 188 E2
Portsmouth Rd.

Thame D KT6 & KT7 .... 37 C3
Portsmouth Rd. Thursl GU8 ..... 169 E8
Portsmouth Rd. Whit V KT11 ..... 72 F6
Portsmouth Rd.

Wisley GU23 & KT11 .... 72 C3
Portsmouth Rd. Witley GU8 ..... 170 B6
Portswood Pl. Rhampt SW15 ...... 7 F1
Portugal Gdns. Twick TW2 .... 16 C6
Portugal Rd. Woking GU21 .... 69 F3
Portway. Ewell KT17 .... 58 A2
Portway Cres. Ewell KT17 .... 58 A2
Post House La. L Book KT23 ...... 94 A2
Post La. Twick TW2 .... 16 E7
Postford Mill Cotts. Chil GU4 .. 131 F5
Postmill Cl. Croy CR0 & CR9 ..... 62 D7
Potley Hill Cty Prim Sch.

Yatly GU17 .... 64 A5
Potley Hill Rd. Yatly GU17 .... 64 A5
Potter Cl. Mitch CR4 .... 41 B7
Potter's La. Streat SW16 .... 21 D2
Potterhill Rd. Tedd TW11 .... 17 B1
Potteries La. Mytch GU16 .... 86 A3
Potteries The. W Heath GU14 ... 84 D6
Potterne Cl. 5

Putney SW15 & SW19 .... 19 D8
Potters Cl. Croy CR0 .... 43 E1
Potters Cl. Milf GU8 .... 149 F2
Potters Cres. Ash GU12 .... 106 B2
Potters Croft. Horsh RH13 ...... 217 E2
Potters Gate. Farnh GU9 .... 125 A2
Potters Gate CE Prim Sch.

Farnh GU9 .... 125 A2
Potters Gr. New Mal KT3 .... 38 C5
Potters La. Send GU23 .... 90 B2
Potters Way. Dovgn RH2 .... 139 C5
Pottersfield. Crawl RH10 .... 201 D7
Pottery Ct. Wreccl GU10 .... 145 F6
Pottery La. Wreccl GU10 .... 145 F6
Pottery Rd. Brent TW8 .... 6 E8
Poulett Gdns. Twick TW1 .... 17 A7
Poullett House. Streat SW2 .... 22 B7
Poulton Ave. Carsh SM1 & SM5 .. 59 D7
Pound Cl. Godal GU7 .... 150 E4
Pound Cl. Long D KT6 .... 37 C1
Pound Cl. Loxwd RH14 .... 212 F5
Pound Cres. Fetch KT22 .... 94 D6
Pound Ct. Ashtd KT21 .... 75 F1
Pound Ct. Wood S V GU3 .... 108 B2
Pound Farm La. Normdy GU12 106 D1
Pound Field. Guild GU1 .... 109 D1
Pound Hill. Wood S V GU3 ...... 108 B2
Pound Hill Cty Fst & Mid Schs.

Crawl RH10 .... 202 C7
Pound Hill Par. Crawl RH10 .... 202 C6
Pound Hill Pl. Crawl RH10 ...... 202 C6
Pound La. Epsom KT18 .... 76 D8
Pound La. Godal GU7 .... 150 E4
Pound La. Windl GU20 .... 48 C4
Pound La. Wood S V GU3 .... 108 B2
Pound Pl. Shalf GU4 .... 130 F3
Pound Place Cl. Shalf GU4 ...... 130 F3
Pound Rd. Alder GU12 .... 105 C1
Pound Rd. Banstd SM7 .... 78 A2
Pound Rd. Chert KT16 .... 33 B2
Pound St. Wallin SM5 .... 59 F5
Poundfield Gdns. Old Wok GU22 90 C7
Poundfield La. Ifold RH14 .... 212 B3
Povey Cross Rd. Hookw RH6 ... 160 E1
Powder Mill La.

Twick TW2 & TW4 .... 16 A7
Powderham Ct. Knaph GU21 ..... 68 E1
Powell Cl. Horley RH6 .... 160 E4
Powell Cl. Onsl V GU2 .... 129 F7
Powell Cl. Wallin SM6 .... 60 E5
Powell Corderoy Prim Sch.

Dork RH4 .... 135 F6
Powell Ct. Croy CR0 .... 61 C6
Powell's Wlk. Chisw W4 .... 7 F8
Powells Cl. Dork RH5 .... 136 C4
Powers Ct. Twick TW1 .... 17 D8
Pownall Gdns. Hounsl TW3 .... 5 B3
Pownall Rd. Hounsl TW3 .... 5 B3
Poyle 14 Trad Est. Poyle SL3 ...... 1 E4
Poyle Cty Fst Sch. Poyle SL3 ..... 1 F6
Poyle Gdns. Wink RG12 .... 27 D8
Poyle House. Merrow GU4 ...... 110 D2
Poyle New Cotts. Poyle SL3 .... 1 F5

Poyle Rd. Guild GU1 .... 130 E7
Poyle Rd. Poyle SL3 .... 1 E5
Poyle Rd. Tongh GU10 .... 127 B7
Poyle Tech Ctr The. Poyle SL3 .... 1 E5
Poynders Gdns. Streat SW12 .... 21 C8
Poynders Rd.

Streat SW12 & SW4 .... 21 D8
Poynes Rd. Horley RH6 .... 160 E5
Poynings Rd. Crawl RH11 .... 200 E5
Prairie Cl. Addl KT15 .... 52 B7
Prairie Rd. Addl KT15 .... 52 B7
Pratts Corner. Dunsf GU8 .... 193 A8
Pratts La. Hersh KT12 .... 54 D6
Precinct The. Cran GU6 .... 174 E4
Precinct The. E Mole KT8 .... 36 B6
Precinct The. Egham TW20 .... 12 A3
Precincts The. Morden SM4 .... 40 A3
Prendergast House. 7

Streat SW4 .... 21 D8
Prentice Cl. Farnb GU14 .... 85 B8
Prentice Ct. 2 Wimble SW19 .... 19 F3
Prentis Rd. Streat SW16 .... 21 D4
Presburg Rd. New Mal KT3 .... 38 E4
Presbury Ct. Woking GU21 .... 69 A1
Prescott. Easth RG12 .... 26 F2
Prescott Rd. Poyle SL3 .... 1 E5
Presentation Mews. Streat SW2 21 F7
Prestbury Cres. Woodm SM7 .... 78 F3
Preston Cl. Twick TW2 .... 16 E5
Preston Ct. Walt O T KT12 .... 35 C1
Preston Dr. W Ewell KT19 .... 57 F4
Preston Dr. W Ewell KT19 .... 57 F4
Preston Gr. Ashtd KT21 .... 75 C2
Preston La. Burgh H KT20 .... 97 C7
Preston Pl. Rich TW10 .... 6 E2
Preston Rd. S Norw SE19 .... 22 B2
Preston Rd. Shep Gn TW17 .... 34 A4
Preston Rd. Wimble SW20 .... 18 F1
Prestwick Cl. Crawl RH11 .... 200 D5
Prestwick La. Chidd GU27 .... 190 B2
Prestwick La. Grays GU27 .... 190 B2
Prestwood Cl. Crawl RH11 ...... 181 B1
Prestwood Cl. Thorn H CR0 .... 42 C2
Prestwood La.

Rusper RH11 & RH12 & RH6 .... 180 C3
Pretoria Ct. Chert KT16 .... 32 F1
Pretoria Rd. Streat SW16 .... 21 C3
Pretty La. Hooley CR5 .... 99 C6
Prey Heath Cl. Woking GU22 ..... 89 C3
Prey Heath Rd. Woking GU22 ... 89 B3
Preymead Ind Est. Alder GU9 .. 126 B7
Price Cl. Up Toot SW17 .... 20 F5
Price Rd. Croy CR0 .... 61 B5
Price Way. Hampt TW12 .... 15 E2
Prices La. Woodh RH2 .... 139 B6
Prickley Wood. Coney H BR2 .... 44 F1
Priddy's Yd. 4 Croy CR9 .... 61 C8
Prides Crossing. Ascot SL5 .... 9 A1
Pridham Rd. S Norw CR7 .... 42 D5
Priest Ave. Woki RG11 .... 25 F5
Priest Croft Cl. Crawl RH11 ..... 201 A6
Priest Hill. Eng Gn TW19 & TW20 11 C6
Priest Hill. Limps RH8 .... 123 B6
Priest Hill Sch Sports Ctr.

Ewell KT17 .... 77 B8
Priest La. W End GU24 .... 67 C5
Priestfield Rd. For Hil SE23 .... 23 E5
Priestley Gdns. Old Wok GU22 .. 90 A7
Priestley Rd. Mitch CR4 .... 41 A7
Priestley Rd. Onsl V GU2 .... 129 D8
Priestley Way. Crawl RH10 ...... 182 A3
Priests Bridge.

Mortl SW14 & SW15 .... 7 E4
Priestwood Ave. Brack RG12 .... 26 F8
Priestwood Court Rd.

Brack RG12 .... 27 A8
Priestwood Sq. 1 Brack RG12 .. 27 A8
Prim Sch of Our Lady Immaculate.

Tolw KT6 .... 38 B1
Primrose Ave. Horley RH6 .... 161 B3
Primrose Cl. Carsh CR4 .... 41 B1
Primrose Cl. Catf SE6 .... 24 C3
Primrose Cl. Crawl RH11 .... 201 B2
Primrose Ct. New Mal KT4 .... 39 A2
Primrose Ct. 11 Streat SW16 ..... 21 D8
Primrose Dr. Bisley GU24 .... 68 A4
Primrose Gdns. Farnb GU14 ..... 84 E3
Primrose House. 1 Rich TW9 ..... 6 F6
Primrose La. Croy CR0 .... 43 D1
Primrose Rd. Hersh KT12 .... 54 C5
Primrose Ridge. Gd Rur GU7 .. 150 B2
Primrose Way. Bramly GU5 ..... 151 D5
Primrose Way. Sandh GU17 ...... 45 B1
Primrose Wlk. Brack RG12 .... 27 C4
Primrose Wlk. Ewell KT17 .... 57 F3
Prince Albert Dr. Brack RG12 .... 28 D4
Prince Albert Sq. Earls RH1 .... 140 A4
Prince Andrew Way. N Asct SL5 28 D7
Prince Charles Cres.

Farnb GU14 .... 85 C8
Prince Charles Way. Hackb SM6 60 B7
Prince Consort Dr. Ascot SL5 .... 28 E4
Prince Consort's Dr. Old W SL4 . 10 A6
Prince Consort's Dr. Wink SL4 .... 9 F4
Prince Dr. Sandh GU17 .... 45 A1
Prince George's Ave.

Merton SW20 .... 39 C7
Prince Georges Rd. Mitch SW19 40 D8
Prince Of Wales' Rd. Carsh SM1 59 D8
Prince Of Wales Rd.

S Norw SE25 .... 141 A2
Prince of Wales Wlk. 1

Camb GU15 .... 65 C6
Prince Rd. S Norw SE25 .... 42 E4
Prince Regent Rd. Hounsl TW3 ... 5 C4
Prince William Ct. Ashf TW15 ... 13 F1
Prince's Ave. Farnb GU11 .... 105 C5
Prince's Ave. Farnc GU7 .... 150 F7
Prince's Cl. Tedd TW11 & TW12 . 16 A4
Prince's Dr. Oxsh KT22 .... 74 D7

Prince's Rd. Earls RH1 .... 139 F7
Prince's Rd. Mortl SW14 .... 7 D4
Prince's Rd. Tedd TW11 & TW12 16 D4
Prince's Rd. Weyb KT13 .... 53 C5
Prince's Rd. Rich TW10 & TW9 ... 6 F2
Prince's Rd. Wimble SW19 .... 20 A2
Princes Ave. Hams Gn CR2 .... 81 B4
Princes Ave. Tolw KT6 .... 57 A8
Princes Ave. Wallin SM5 .... 59 F2
Princes Cl. Bagsh GU19 .... 47 E1
Princes Cl. Hams Gn CR2 .... 81 B4
Princes Ct. New Mal KT3 .... 38 F6
Princes Ct. Weyb KT13 .... 53 B5
Princes Gdns. Worpl GU3 .... 108 E8
Princes Mead. Farnb GU14 .... 85 B3
Princes Rd. Ashf TW15 .... 13 F3
Princes Rd. Egham TW20 .... 11 F2
Princes Rd. Felt TW13 .... 14 F5
Princes Rd. King U T KT2 .... 18 A1
Princes Rd. Penge SE20 .... 23 D2
Princes Rd. Rich TW10 .... 6 F2
Princes Rd. Rich TW9 .... 6 F2
Princes St. Sutton SM1 .... 59 D6
Princes Way. Alder GU11 .... 105 A2
Princes Way. Coney H BR4 .... 63 F7
Princes Way. Croy CR0 .... 60 F5
Princes Way.

Putney SW15 & SW19 .... 19 E7
Princess Anne Rd. Rudg RH12 . 214 D7
Princess Ct. 9 Wimble SW19 .... 19 D1
Princess Gdns. Mayb GU22 .... 70 B3
Princess House. 1 Redh RH1 . 119 A2
Princess Margaret Rd.

Rudg RH12 .... 214 D7
Princess Mary's Rd. Addl KT15 . 52 C6
Princess Rd. Crawl RH11 .... 201 C6
Princess Rd. Mayb GU22 .... 70 C3
Princess Rd. Thorn H CR0 .... 42 C3
Princess Sq. Brack RG12 .... 27 B7
Princess Way. Camb GU15 .... 65 C5
Princess Way. Redh RH1 .... 119 A2
Princethorpe Rd. For Hil SE26 .. 23 D4
Princeton Mews. 3

King U T KT2 .... 38 A8
Pringle Gdns. Purley CR8 .... 60 F1
Pringle Gdns. Streat SW16 .... 21 C4
Prior Ave. Sutton SM2 & SM5 .... 59 E3
Prior Croft Cl. Friml GU15 .... 66 A4
Prior End. Friml GU15 .... 66 A5
Prior Heath Cty Inf Sch.

Friml GU15 .... 66 A5
Prior Rd. Friml GU15 .... 66 A5
Prior's La. Yatly GU17 .... 64 A5
Prioress Rd. W Norw SE27 .... 22 B5
Priors Cl. Farnb GU14 .... 85 B8
Priors Cl. Ash GU12 .... 105 E1
Priors Ct. Woking GU21 .... 69 A1
Priors Field Sch. Compt GU7 ... 129 A1
Priors Hatch La. Compt GU7 .... 128 F1
Priors Lodge. 4 Rich TW10 .... 6 E1
Priors Mews. Fetch KT23 .... 94 C2
Priors The. Ashtd KT21 .... 95 D8
Priors Wlk. Crawl RH10 .... 201 F6
Priors Wood. Shottm GU27 ...... 207 F6
Priorsfield Rd. Compt GU7 .... 129 A1
Priorswood. Compt GU7 .... 128 F2
Priory Ave. Cheam SM3 .... 58 D6
Priory C of E Mid Sch.

Wimble SW19 .... 20 B3
Priory Cl. Beck BR3 .... 43 E6
Priory Cl. Dork RH4 .... 136 A5
Priory Cl. Hampt TW12 .... 35 F8
Priory Cl. Horley RH6 .... 160 F4
Priory Cl. 3 Merton SW19 .... 40 B8
Priory Cl. Sheer GU21 .... 70 C3
Priory Cl. Sunby TW16 .... 15 A1
Priory Cl. Sunnin SL5 .... 30 A2
Priory Cl. Walt O T KT12 .... 54 A7
Priory Cres. Cheam SM3 .... 58 D6
Priory Cres. S Norw SE19 .... 22 C1
Priory Ct. Camb GU15 .... 64 F5
Priory Ct. Cheam SM3 .... 58 E6
Priory Ct. Egham TW20 .... 12 C2
Priory Ct. Hounsl TW3 .... 5 B4
Priory Ct. Rhampt SW15 .... 7 F3
Priory Dr. Woodh RH2 .... 139 A7
Priory Gdns. Hampt TW12 .... 35 F8
Priory Gdns. Mortl SW13 .... 7 F4
Priory Gn. Stain TW18 .... 13 B3
Priory Hospl The. Rhampt SW15 . 7 F3
Priory House Sch. Catf SE6 .... 24 B7
Priory La. E Mole KT8 .... 36 B5
Priory La. Frensh GU10 .... 167 E8
Priory La. Rhampt SW15 .... 7 F2
Priory Lodge. Coney H BR4 .... 63 E7
Priory Mews. Stain TW18 .... 13 B3
Priory Pl. Walt O T KT12 .... 54 A7
Priory Rd. Cheam SM3 .... 58 D6
Priory Rd. Chess KT9 .... 56 E7
Priory Rd. For Row RH18 .... 206 D2
Priory Rd. Hampt TW12 .... 16 A1
Priory Rd. Islew TW3 .... 5 C2
Priory Rd. Mitch SW19 .... 20 D1
Priory Rd. Rich TW9 .... 7 A7
Priory Rd. Sunnin SL5 .... 30 A2
Priory Rd. Thorn H CR0 .... 42 A2
Priory Rd. Wink SL5 .... 28 A6
Priory Rd. Woodh RH2 .... 139 A6
Priory Sch. S Norw SE25 .... 42 F5
Priory Sch The. Banstd SM7 ...... 78 A4
Priory St. Farnb GU14 .... 85 D4
Priory The. Croy CR0 .... 61 A7
Priory The. Godst RH9 .... 121 B3
Priory The. 21 King U T KT6 .... 37 E4
Priory Way. Harl UB3 .... 3 D8
Priory Wlk. Brack RG12 .... 27 F5
Priscilla House. 8 Charlt TW16 . 14 F1

Probyn Rd. Streat SW2 .... 22 B6
Proctor Gdns. G Book KT23 ...... 94 B2
Proctors Cl. E Bed TW14 .... 15 A7
Proctors Rd. Woki RG11 .... 25 F6
Profumo Rd. Hersh KT12 .... 54 D5
Progress Bsns Pk. Croy CR9 ...... 60 F8
Progress Way. Croy CR0 .... 60 F8
Promenade Approach Rd.
 Chisw W4 .... 7 E7
Promenade De Verdun.
 Purley CR8 .... 79 D8
Promenade The. Chisw W4 .... 7 E6
Propeller Rd. Farnb GU14 .... 85 B2
Prospect Ave. Farnb GU14 .... 85 B6
Prospect Cl. For Hil SE26 .... 23 B4
Prospect Cl. Hounsl TW5 .... 4 F6
Prospect Cotts. Binf RG12 .... 26 D8
Prospect Cres. Twick TW2 .... 5 C1
Prospect La. Eng Gn TW20 .... 11 A3
Prospect Pl. Crawl RH11 .... 201 C6
Prospect Pl. Ewell KT17 .... 76 E5
Prospect Pl. Stain TW18 .... 12 F3
Prospect Rd. Ash GU12 .... 106 A5
Prospect Rd. Rowl GU10 .... 145 E3
Prospect Rd. Thame D KT6 .... 37 C3
Prospect Rd. W Heath GU14 ..... 85 A5
Prossers. Tadw KT20 .... 97 D6
Providence House. Bagsh GU19 47 E3
Providence La. Harl UB3 .... 3 D7
Providence Pl. Ewell KT17 .... 76 E5
Providence Pl. Farnb GU14 ..... 125 C2
Provincial Terr. Penge SE20 ...... 23 D1
Prune Hill. Egham TW20 .... 11 E1
Prunus Cl. W End GU24 .... 67 E6
Public Record Office. Rich TW9 ... 7 B7
Puckridge Gate Rd.
 Farnb GU11 .... 104 E6
Puckridge Hill Rd. Alder GU11 104 E6
Puckshill. Knaph GU21 .... 68 D2
Puckshott Way. Haslem GU27 . 208 D8
Pudding La. Charl RH6 .... 180 E7
Puddenhole Cotts. Brock RH4 . 116 A3
Puffin Cl. Beck BR3 & CR0 .... 43 D4
Puffin Rd. Farnb GU14 .... 200 D5
Pulborough Way. Hounsl TW4 .... 4 C3
Pullman Ct. Streat SW2 .... 21 F7
Pullman La. Godal GU7 .... 150 C2
Pump Alley. ⑧ Brent TW8 .... 6 D7
Pump La. Ascot SL5 .... 29 E8
Pump Pail N. Croy CR0 & CR9 ... 61 C7
Pump Pail S. Croy CR0 & CR9 ... 61 C7
Pumping Station Rd. Chisw W4 .. 7 E8
Punch Copse Rd. Crawl RH10 .. 201 F7
Punchbowl La.
 Dork RH4 & RH5 .... 136 D6
Punnetts Ct. Crawl RH11 .... 200 F3
Purbeck Ave. New Mal KT3 .... 38 F3
Purbeck Cl. Merst RH1 .... 119 D7
Purbeck Ct. ④ Stough GU2 ..... 108 C1
Purbeck Dr. Horse GU21 .... 69 F5
Purberry Gr. Ewell KT17 .... 57 F1
Purberry Shot. Ewell KT17 .... 57 F1
Purbrook Ct. Brack RG12 .... 27 E3
Purbrook House. ②
 Rhampt SW15 .... 19 B7
Purcell House. Twick TW2 .... 5 D1
Purcell Rd. Crawl RH11 .... 200 F3
Purcell Rd. Crowth RG11 .... 45 B7
Purcell's Cl. Ashtd KT21 .... 75 F1
Purdey Ct. ③ Worc Pk KT4 .... 39 A1
Purley Bury Ave. Purley CR8 ...... 80 C8
Purley Bury Cl. Purley CR8 .... 80 C8
Purley Cl. Purley CR8 .... 61 B1
Purley Downs Rd. S Croy CR2 ... 80 E8
Purley High Sch For Boys.
 Coulsd CR5 .... 100 A8
Purley Hill. Purley CR8 .... 80 B7
Purley Hospl. Purley CR8 .... 80 A8
Purley Knoll. Purley CR8 .... 80 A8
Purley Oaks Prim Sch.
 S Croy CR2 .... 61 D3
Purley Oaks Rd. S Croy CR2 ...... 61 D1
Purley Oaks Sta. S Croy CR2 .... 61 D2
Purley Par. ② Purley CR8 .... 80 A8
Purley Park Rd. Purley CR8 .... 61 B1
Purley Rd. Purley CR8 .... 80 A8
Purley Rd. S Croy CR2 .... 61 D3
Purley Rise. Purley CR8 .... 79 F7
Purley Sta. Purley CR8 .... 80 A7
Purley Vale. Purley CR8 .... 80 B6
Purley View Terr. S Croy CR2 .... 61 D3
Purley Way. Friml GU16 .... 85 E8
Purley Way. Purley CR8 .... 80 A8
Purley Way. Thorn H CR0 & CR9 . 41 F1
Purmerend Cl. W Heath GU14 ... 84 C5
Pursers Hollow. Peasl GU5 ...... 154 D8
Pursers La. Peasl GU5 .... 154 D8
Purslane. Woki RG11 .... 25 D5
Purton Rd. Horsh RH12 .... 217 B4
Putney Heath. Putney SW15 .... 19 B8
Putney Hill. Putney SW15 .... 19 D8
Puttenham Heath Rd. Putt GU3 128 E3
Puttenham Heath Rd.
 Wanb GU3 .... 128 E3
Puttenham Hill. Wanb GU3 ..... 128 C5
Puttenham La.
 Shackl GU3 & GU8 .... 128 C1
Puttenham Rd. Seale GU10 ..... 127 C4
Puttenham Sch CE (VA).
 Putt GU3 .... 128 C4
Puttock Cl. Linch GU27 .... 207 D5
Pyecombe Ct. ④ Crawl RH11 .. 200 F3
Pyegrove Chase. Brack RG12 ... 27 E2
Pyestock Cres. W Heath GU14 ... 84 C4
Pylbrook Rd. Sutton SM1 .... 59 B7
Pyle Hill. Westfd GU22 & GU4 ... 89 D3
Pymers Mead. Dulw SE21 .... 22 C7

Pymers Mead. W Norw SE21 .... 22 C7
Pyne Rd. Tolw KT6 .... 38 A1
Pyrcroft Cty Fst Sch. Chert KT16 32 E2
Pyrcroft Grange Prim Sch.
 Chert KT16 .... 32 E3
Pyrcroft La. Weyb KT13 .... 53 B5
Pyrcroft Rd. Chert KT16 .... 32 E2
Pyrford Common Rd.
 Mayb GU22 .... 70 E2
Pyrford Cty Prim Sch.
 Pyrf GU22 .... 70 F3
Pyrford Heath. Pyrf GU22 .... 70 F3
Pyrford Prim Sch. Pyrf GU22 ... 71 A3
Pyrford Rd. Mayb GU22 & KT14 71 A4
Pyrford Rd. Pyrf GU22 & KT14 .. 71 A4
Pyrford Rd. W Byfl GU22 & KT14 71 A4
Pyrford Woods Cl. Pyrf GU22 ... 70 F4
Pyrford Woods Rd. Pyrf GU22 .. 70 F4
Pyrland Rd. Rich TW10 .... 6 F1
Pyrmont Gr. W Norw SE27 .... 22 B5
Pyrmont Rd. Brent W4 .... 7 A8
Pytchley Cres. S Norw SE19 ..... 22 C2

Quadrangle Lodge.
 Wimble SW19 .... 20 A2
Quadrangle The. Guild GU2 .... 130 A8
Quadrant Ct. Brack RG12 .... 27 E6
Quadrant Rd. Rich TW9 .... 6 D3
Quadrant Rd. Thorn H CR7 .... 42 B5
Quadrant The. Ash V GU12 .... 106 A4
Quadrant The. Merton SW20 .... 39 E8
Quadrant The. Rich TW9 .... 6 E3
Quadrant The. Sutton SM2 .... 59 C4
Quail Cl. Horsh RH12 .... 217 D7
Quail Gdns. Selsd CR2 .... 62 E1
Quakers Way. Fairl GU3 .... 108 C5
Qualitas. Brack RG12 .... 26 F1
Quality St. Merst RH1 .... 119 B7
Quantock Cl. Crawl RH11 .... 201 B6
Quantock Cl. Harl UB3 .... 3 D7
Quantock Dr. N Cheam KT4 ...... 58 C8
Quarr Rd. Carsh SM5 .... 40 E3
Quarry Bank. Lhtwat GU18 .... 67 A8
Quarry Cl. Crawl RH11 .... 201 B6
Quarry Cl. Oxted RH8 .... 122 E5
Quarry Hill. Ock Rid GU7 .... 150 B3
Quarry Hill Pk. Reig RH2 .... 118 C4
Quarry Park Rd. Cheam SM1 .... 58 F4
Quarry Rd. Oxted RH8 .... 122 E5
Quarry Rd. Shackl GU7 .... 150 A7
Quarry Rd. Wold RH9 .... 121 C7
Quarry Rise. Cheam SM1 .... 58 F4
Quarry Rise. E Grins RH19 ...... 186 A3
Quarry St. Guild GU1 & GU2 .... 130 D7
Quarry The. Betch RH3 .... 116 D3
Quarter Mile Rd. Godal GU7 ... 150 E2
Quarterbrass Farm Rd.
 Horsh RH12 .... 217 D7
Quartermaine Ave. Westfd GU22 89 F5
Quartermaine Sch.
 Shottm GU27 .... 189 B2
Quarters Rd. Farnb GU14 .... 85 C2
Quay West. Rich TW9 .... 17 B3
Quebec Cl. Smallf RH6 .... 162 A3
Quebec Gdns. Hawley GU17 ..... 64 D4
Queen Adelaide Ct. Penge SE20 23 C2
Queen Adelaide Rd. Penge SE20 23 C1
Queen Alexandra's Ct. ⑤
 Wimble SW19 .... 19 F3
Queen Anne Ave. Beck BR2 ...... 44 F6
Queen Anne Dr. Clayg KT10 ...... 55 E3
Queen Anne's Cl. Old W SL4 ..... 10 B5
Queen Anne's Gdns. Leahd KT22 95 B6
Queen Anne's Gdns. Mitch CR4 .. 40 F6
Queen Anne's Terr. Leahd KT22 95 B6
Queen Annes Cl. Twick TW2 ..... 16 D5
Queen Annes Ct. Leahd KT22 .... 95 B6
Queen Eleanor's C of E Mid Sch.
 Onsl GU2 .... 130 A8
Queen Eleanor's Rd.
 Onsl GU2 .... 129 F8
Queen Elizabeth Dr.
 Alder GU11 .... 104 F2
Queen Elizabeth Gdns.
 Morden SM4 .... 40 A5
Queen Elizabeth Hospl.
 Woodm SM7 .... 78 C1
Queen Elizabeth II Jubilee Sch The.
 Horsh RH13 .... 217 F1
Queen Elizabeth Rd.Camb GU15 46 D1
Queen Elizabeth Rd.
 King U T KT2 .... 37 F7
Queen Elizabeth Rd.
 Rudg RH12 .... 214 D7
Queen Elizabeth Way.
 Old Wok GU22 .... 90 A8
Queen Elizabeth's Dr.
 New Add CR0 .... 63 D1
Queen Elizabeth's Gdns.
 New Add CR0 .... 63 D1
Queen Elizabeth's Training Coll.
 Ashtd KT2 .... 74 D2
Queen Elizabeth's Wlk
 Wallin SM6 .... 60 D6
Queen Mary Ave. Camb GU15 ... 65 A5
Queen Mary Ave. W Barn SM4 .. 39 D4
Queen Mary Ave.
 W Barn SM4 & SW20 .... 39 D4
Queen Mary Cl. Mayb GU22 ..... 70 D3
Queen Mary Rd. Charlt TW7 ..... 34 C7
Queen Mary Rd. S Norw SE19 .. 22 B2
Queen Mary's Ave. Wallin SM5 . 59 F3
Queen Mary's Dr. Woodhm KT15 52 A1
Queen St. Alder GU12 .... 105 D2
Queen St. Chert KT16 .... 33 A1
Queen St. Croy CR0 & CR9 ...... 61 C6
Queen St. Godal GU7 .... 150 E4
Queen St. Gomsh GU5 .... 133 C4
Queen St. Horsh RH13 .... 217 D1
Queen Victoria Cross Roads.
 Sandh GU15 .... 65 A6

Queen Victoria Hospl The.
 E Grins RH19 .... 185 F3
Queen Victoria Way. Pirb GU24 87 D8
Queen's Ave. Alder GU11 .... 105 B5
Queen's Ave. Farnb GU14 .... 105 B5
Queen's C of E Jun Mix Sch The.
 Rich TW9 .... 7 A7
Queen's C of E Jun Sch The.
 Rich TW9 .... 7 A7
Queen's Cl. Farnb GU14 .... 105 B8
Queen's Cl. N Asct SL5 .... 28 E8
Queen's Cl. Wallin SM6 .... 60 B5
Queen's Ct. Beck BR3 .... 44 A8
Queen's Ct. Croy CR2 .... 61 C5
Queen's Ct. Farnb GU14 .... 105 C8
Queen's Ct. ⑥ King U T KT2 ... 18 A1
Queen's Ct. ⑤ Rich TW10 .... 6 F1
Queen's Ct. Stain TW18 .... 13 D2
Queen's Ct. Thorn H CR7 .... 42 A4
Queen's Dr. Farnc GU7 .... 150 C7
Queen's Dr. Stough GU2 .... 109 A4
Queen's Dr. Thame D KT7 .... 37 A3
Queen's Gate Rd. Farnb GU14 . 105 B8
Queen's Gdns. Heston TW5 .... 4 E6
Queen's Hospl. Thorn H CR0 ... 42 C3
Queen's Mead. Chidd GU8 ...... 191 B4
Queen's Mead Rd. Broml BR2 ... 44 F7
Queen's Park Rd. Cater CR3 .... 100 E4
Queen's Pl. Ascot SL5 .... 29 A6
Queen's Pl. Morden SM4 .... 40 A5
Queen's Rd. Alder GU11 .... 104 F2
Queen's Rd. Ascot SL5 .... 29 A4
Queen's Rd. Beck BR3 .... 43 E7
Queen's Rd. E Grins RH19 ...... 185 E1
Queen's Rd. Egham TW20 .... 11 F2
Queen's Rd. Farnb GU14 .... 105 D8
Queen's Rd. Felt TW13 & TW14 . 15 B7
Queen's Rd. Guild GU1 .... 109 D1
Queen's Rd. Hampt TW12 .... 16 B4
Queen's Rd. Horley RH6 .... 161 A3
Queen's Rd. Hounsl TW3 .... 5 B4
Queen's Rd. King U T KT2 .... 18 A1
Queen's Rd. Knaph GU21 .... 68 D1
Queen's Rd. Mitch CR4 .... 40 D6
Queen's Rd. Mortl SW14 .... 7 D4
Queen's Rd. New Mal KT3 .... 38 F4
Queen's Rd. Rich TW10 .... 6 F1
Queen's Rd. Rich KT2 & TW10 .. 18 A3
Queen's Rd. Tedd TW11 .... 16 F2
Queen's Rd. Thame D KT7 .... 36 F4
Queen's Rd. Thorn H CR0 .... 42 C3
Queen's Rd. Wallin SM6 .... 60 B5
Queen's Rd. Wimble SW19 .... 20 A2
Queen's Rdbt. Farnb GU11 ...... 105 B7
Queen's Rise. Rich TW10 .... 6 F1
Queen's Terr. Islew TW7 .... 6 A3
Queen's Way. Pirb GU24 .... 87 D8
Queendale Ave. Woking GU21 ... 68 F3
Queenhill Rd. S Croy CR2 .... 62 B1
Queenhythe Rd. Jacobs GU4 ... 109 D7
Queens Acre.
 Cheam SM2 & SM3 .... 58 E3
Queens Ave. Byfl KT14 .... 71 D7
Queens Cl. Felt TW13 .... 15 C4
Queens Cl. Bisley GU24 .... 68 A3
Queens Cl. Walt o t H KT20 .... 97 A3
Queens Court Ride.
 Cobham KT11 .... 73 A6
Queens Cres. Rich TW10 .... 6 F2
Queens Ct. ③ Redh RH1 .... 119 A2
Queens Ct. Whit V KT13 .... 53 E4
Queens Dr. Oxsh KT22 .... 74 C8
Queens Dr. Surb KT5 .... 38 A3
Queens Gate. Crawl RH6 .... 182 A8
Queens Hill Rise. Ascot SL5 ..... 29 C6
Queens Keep. Camb GU15 .... 65 D5
Queens Keep. ⑩ Twick TW1 ...... 6 C1
Queens La. Heath E GU9 .... 125 D2
Queens Park Gdns. Felt TW13 ... 14 F5
Queens Pine. Brack RG12 .... 27 E3
Queens Pl. Whit V KT12 & KT13 . 53 E5
Queens Rd. Belm SM2 .... 78 A8
Queens Rd. Bisley GU24 .... 67 F1
Queens Rd. Camb GU15 .... 65 B3
Queens Rd. Hale GU9 .... 125 C6
Queens Rd. Hersh KT12 .... 54 A6
Queens Rd. Morden SM4 .... 40 A5
Queens Rd. Twick TW1 .... 17 A7
Queens Rd. Weyb KT13 .... 53 C5
Queens Rd. Whit V KT13 .... 53 C5
Queens Reach. E Mole KT8 .... 36 E5
Queens Sq. Crawl RH10 .... 201 D6
Queens Way. Croy CR0 .... 60 F5
Queens Way. Felt TW13 .... 15 C4
Queens Wlk. Ashf TW15 .... 13 F8
Queensberry House. ⑥ Rich TW9 6 D2
Queensbridge Pk. Islew TW7 ...... 5 E2
Queensbury Ct. S Norw CR7 ..... 42 C7
Queensbury Pl. Hawley GU17 ... 64 C3
Queensfield Ct. Cheam SM3 ..... 58 C6
Queensgate. Cobham KT11 .... 73 D7
Queenshill Lodge. Ascot SL5 .... 29 B6
Queensland Ave. Merton SW19 . 40 B8
Queensmead. Farnb GU14 .... 85 B1
Queensmead Ave. E Ewell KT17 . 58 B1
Queensmere Cl. Putney SW19 .. 19 D6
Queensmere Rd. Putney SW19 . 19 D6
Queensmere (Southlands Coll).
 Putney SW19 .... 19 D6
Queensthorpe Rd. For Hil SE26 . 23 D4
Queensville Rd.
 Streat SW12 & SW4 .... 21 D8
Queensway. Coney H BR4 .... 63 F6
Queensway. Cran GU6 .... 174 F2
Queensway. Crawl RH10 .... 201 E6
Queensway. E Grins RH19 ...... 185 E1
Queensway. Friml GU16 .... 86 A7
Queensway. Hersh KT12 .... 54 B5
Queensway. Redh RH1 .... 118 F2

Queensway. Sunby TW16 .... 35 B7
Queensway N. Hersh KT12 .... 54 D6
Queensway S. Hersh KT12 .... 54 C5
Queenswood Ave. Hampt TW12 . 16 B2
Queenswood Ave.
 Hounsl TW3 & TW5 .... 4 F5
Queenswood Ave. Thorn H CR7 . 42 A4
Queenswood Ave.
 Wallin CR0 & SM6 .... 60 D6
Queenswood Ct. ⑪
 W Norw SE27 .... 22 D4
Queenswood Rd. For Hil SE23 ... 23 E5
Queenswood Rd. Knaph GU21 ... 88 D8
Quennel House. ⑦ Streat SW12 21 F8
Quennell Cl. Ashtd KT21 .... 95 F8
Quennells Hill. Wreccl GU10 ... 145 E6
Quentin Way. Vir W GU25 .... 31 B5
Quicks Rd. Merton SW19 .... 20 B1
Quiet Cl. Addl KT15 .... 52 A6
Quillot The. Whit V KT12 .... 53 F5
Quince Cl. Ascot SL5 .... 29 D5
Quince Dr. Bisley GU21 & GU24 . 68 B4
Quincy Rd. Egham TW20 .... 12 A3
Quinneys. Farnb GU14 .... 85 D1
Quintilis. Easth RG12 .... 27 A1
Quintin Ave. Merton SW20 .... 39 F8
Quintin Ct. Chisw W4 .... 7 C7
Quintock House. ② Rich TW9 .... 7 A6
Quinton Cl. Beck BR3 .... 44 C6
Quinton Cl. Hackb SM6 .... 60 B6
Quinton Cl. Heston TW5 .... 4 B7
Quinton Rd. Thame D KT7 .... 37 A1
Quinton St. Wands SW18 .... 20 C6
Quintrell Cl. Woking GU21 .... 69 B2

Rabbit La. Whit V KT12 .... 54 B3
Rabies Heath Rd. Bletch RH1 .. 120 F2
Rabies Heath Rd.
 Godst RH1 & RH9 .... 121 B1
Raby Rd. New Mal KT3 .... 38 D5
Raccoon Way. Hounsl TW4 .... 4 C5
Racecourse Rd. Crawl RH6 ..... 181 F8
Racecourse Rd. Dorman RH7 ... 165 A2
Racecourse Rd. Lingf RH7 .... 164 F3
Racecourse Way. Crawl RH6 ... 181 F8
Rachel Ct. Sutton SM2 .... 59 D3
Rackfield. Shottm GU27 .... 207 D7
Rackham Cl. Crawl RH11 .... 201 D4
Rackham Mews. Streat SW16 ... 21 C2
Racks Ct. Guild GU1 .... 130 D7
Rackstraw Rd.
 Sandh GU15 & GU11 .... 45 D2
Racquets Court Hill.
 Farnc GU7 .... 150 C6
Rad La. Peasl GU5 .... 133 D1
Rad La. Peasl GU5 .... 133 E1
Radar Rd. Farnb GU14 .... 84 D1
Radbourne Rd. Streat SW12 ..... 21 D7
Radcliff Mews. Hampt TW12 ..... 16 C3
Radcliffe Cl. Friml GU16 .... 86 A7
Radcliffe Gdns. Sutton SM5 ...... 59 E3
Radcliffe Rd. S Croy CR0 .... 61 F7
Radcliffe Way. Binf RG12 .... 26 E8
Radcot Point. ② For Hil SE23 ... 23 D5
Radford Cl. Hale GU9 .... 125 E5
Radford Rd. Crawl RH10 & RH6 . 182 C4
Radius Pk. Hatton TW6 .... 3 F3
Radlet Ave. For Hil SE23 .... 23 B6
Radley Cl. E Bed TW14 .... 14 F7
Radley Ct. Catf BR1 .... 24 C4
Radley Lodge. ㉚ Putney SW19 . 19 D7
Radnor Cl. Mitch CR4 .... 41 E5
Radnor Ct. ⑥ For Hil SE23 .... 23 D5
Radnor Ct. Redh RH1 .... 118 E1
Radnor Gdns. Twick TW1 .... 16 F6
Radnor La. Abing C RH5 .... 155 B2
Radnor La. Ewh GU6 .... 155 A2
Radnor Rd. Brack RG12 .... 27 F6
Radnor Rd. Peasl GU5 & GU6 .. 154 E4
Radnor Rd. Twick TW1 .... 16 F6
Radnor Rd. Weyb KT13 .... 53 A7
Radnor Wlk. Croy CR0 .... 43 E3
Radolphs. Tadw KT20 .... 97 D5
Radstock Way. Merst RH1 .... 119 C7
Radstone Ct. ① Woking GU22 .. 69 F1
Rae Rd. Farnb GU14 .... 85 B1
Raeburn Ave. Surb KT3 .... 38 B3
Raeburn Ave. Tolw KT5 & KT6 .. 38 B3
Raeburn Cl. Tedd KT1 .... 17 D1
Raeburn Ct. Woking GU21 .... 89 A8
Raeburn Way. Sandh GU15 ...... 64 D6
Raf Gate Rd. Farnb GU14 .... 85 B1
RAF Staff Coll. Brack RG12 .... 27 E7
Rag Hill. Tats TN16 .... 103 E6
Rag Hill Cl. Tats TN16 .... 103 E6
Rag Hill Rd. Tats TN16 .... 103 E6
Raglan Cl. Alder GU12 .... 105 C1
Raglan Cl. Farnb GU14 .... 86 A8
Raglan Cl. Hounsl TW4 .... 4 F2
Raglan Cl. Reig RH2 .... 118 D3
Raglan Ct. Croy CR0 & CR2 ...... 61 B5
Raglan Prec The. Cater CR3 ..... 100 E5
Raglan Rd. Knaph GU21 .... 68 E1
Raglan Rd. Reig RH2 .... 118 C3
Raglans House. Reig RH2 .... 118 B4
Ragwort Cl. ① For Hil SE26 ...... 23 B3
Raikes La. Abing C RH5 .... 134 B2
Railey Rd. Crawl RH10 .... 201 E7
Railshead Rd. Islew TW1 & TW7 .. 6 B3
Railton Rd. Stough GU2 .... 109 B5
Railway App. Chert KT16 .... 32 F1
Railway App. E Grins RH19 ..... 185 E1
Railway App. ⑩ Twick TW1 ...... 17 A8
Railway App. Wallin SM6 .... 60 B5
Railway Cotts. Purley CR8 .... 79 F6
Railway Rd. Tedd TW11 .... 16 F4
Railway Side. Mortl SW13 & SW14 7 E4
Railway Terr. Egham TW18 .... 12 D3
Railway Terr. Felt TW13 & TW14 . 15 A7
Railway Terr. Hersh KT12 .... 54 B5
Rainbow Ct. Woking GU21 .... 68 E3
Rainbow Ctr The. Ewell KT17 ... 76 E7
Rake La. Milf GU8 .... 171 A7
Rake La. Witley GU8 .... 170 F7
Rakers Ridge. Horsh RH12 ...... 217 D5
Raleigh Ave. Wallin SM6 .... 60 D6
Raleigh Ct. Beck BR3 .... 44 B8
Raleigh Ct. Crawl RH10 .... 182 A3
Raleigh Ct. Dulw SE19 .... 22 F3
Raleigh Ct. Stain TW18 .... 13 A4
Raleigh Ct. Wallin SM6 .... 60 B4
Raleigh Dr. Esher KT10 .... 55 D5
Raleigh Dr. Smallf RH6 .... 162 A3
Raleigh Dr. Tolw KT5 .... 38 C1
Raleigh Gdns. Mitch CR4 .... 40 F6
Raleigh House. ① Thame D KT7 37 A2
Raleigh Rd. Felt TW13 & TW14 .. 14 F6
Raleigh Rd. Penge SE20 .... 23 D1
Raleigh Rd. Rich TW9 .... 6 F4
Raleigh Sch The. W Hors KT24 .. 92 C2
Raleigh Way. Felt TW13 .... 15 C3
Raleigh Wlk. Friml GU15 & GU16 65 F3
Raleigh Wlk. Crawl RH10 .... 201 E4
Ralliwood Rd. Ashtd KT21 .... 96 A8
Ralph Perring Ct. Beck BR3 ...... 44 A5
Ralphs Ride. Brack RG12 .... 27 E6
Rambler Cl. Streat SW16 .... 21 C4
Ramblers Way. ⑫
 Crawl RH11 .... 201 B1
Rame Cl. Up Toot SW17 .... 21 A3
Ramillies Pk. Farnb GU11 .... 105 E7
Ramillis Cl. Farnb GU11 .... 105 E7
Ramin Ct. Bellf GU1 .... 109 C4
Ramornie Cl. Hersh KT12 .... 54 F6
Rams La. Dunsf GU8 .... 193 B3
Ramsay Rd. Windl GU20 .... 48 E5
Ramsbury Cl. Easth RG12 .... 26 E1
Ramsdale Rd. Streat SW17 .... 21 A3
Ramsdean House. ①
 Rhampt SW15 .... 19 B7
Ramsden Rd. Balham SW12 ..... 21 A8
Ramsden Rd. Godal GU7 .... 150 D3
Ramsey Cl. Camb GU15 .... 66 B8
Ramsey Cl. Horley RH6 .... 160 F3
Ramsey Cl. Horsh RH12 .... 217 D5
Ramsey Ct. ⑱ Crawl RH11 ...... 201 B1
Ramsey Ct. Croy CR9 .... 61 B8
Ramsey House. Merton SW19 ... 40 B8
Ramsey Rd. Thorn H CR7 .... 41 F3
Ramslade Rd. Brack RG12 .... 27 D5
Rances La. Woki RG11 .... 25 E5
Randal Cres. Woodh RH2 .... 139 A7
Randall Schofield Ct.
 Crawl RH10 .... 202 A7
Randalls Cotts. Cobham KT11 ... 73 B7
Randalls Cres. Leahd KT22 .... 95 A3
Randalls Park Ave. Leahd KT22 . 95 A7
Randalls Rd. Leahd KT22 .... 94 E7
Randalls Way. Leahd KT22 .... 95 A7
Randell Cl. W Heath GU14 .... 64 E1
Randisbourne Gdns. Catf SE6 .. 24 B5
Randle Rd. Rich TW10 .... 17 C4
Randlesdown Rd. Catf SE6 .... 24 B5
Randmore Ct. ⑥ Beck BR3 ...... 44 A1
Randolph Cl. King U T KT2 .... 18 C3
Randolph Cl. Knaph GU21 .... 68 E2
Randolph Cl. Oxsh KT11 .... 74 A4
Randolph Dr. Farnb GU14 .... 84 C3
Randolph Rd. Epsom KT17 .... 76 F5
Ranelagh Cotts. Smallf RH6 ... 162 A3
Ranelagh Cres. N Asct SL5 .... 28 E8
Ranelagh Dr. Brack RG12 .... 27 C6
Ranelagh Dr. Islew TW1 .... 6 B2
Ranelagh Gdns. Chisw W4 .... 7 C7
Ranelagh Pl. New Mal KT3 .... 38 E4
Ranelagh Rd. Redh RH1 .... 118 E1
Ranelagh Sch. Brack RG12 .... 27 C6
Ranfurly Rd. Sutton SM1 .... 59 A8
Range Rd. Farnb GU14 .... 84 D1
Range Ride. Sandh GU15 .... 64 F7
Range The. Bramly GU5 .... 152 A4
Range View. Sandh GU15 .... 64 E8
Range Villas. Lo Hall TW17 .... 33 E2
Range Way. Lo Hall TW17 .... 34 A2
Rangefield Prim Sch. Catf BR1 . 24 E3
Rangefield Rd. Broml BR1 .... 24 F3
Rangefield Rd. Catf BR1 .... 24 F3
Rankine Cl. Farnh GU9 .... 126 A6
Ranmere St. Balham SW12 .... 21 B7
Ranmore Ave. S Croy CR0 .... 61 F7
Ranmore Cl. Redh RH1 .... 119 A4
Ranmore Common Rd.
 Wotton RH5 .... 114 D2
Ranmore Ct. King U T KT6 .... 37 D4
Ranmore Ct. Wimble SW20 .... 39 D8
Ranmore Pl. Weyb KT13 .... 53 C5
Ranmore Rd. Dork RH4 .... 136 A8
Ranmore Rd. E Ewell SM2 .... 58 D2
Ranmore Rd.
 Wotton RH4 & RH5 .... 114 E1
Rann House. Mortl SW14 .... 7 D4
Rannoch Ct. ⑨ King U T KT6 .... 37 E4
Ransford House. ⑯ Dulw SE21 . 22 E4
Ransome Cl. Crawl RH11 .... 200 E3
Ranyard Cl. Chess KT9 .... 56 F7
Rapallo Cl. Farnb GU14 .... 85 C4
Rapley Cl. Camb GU15 .... 65 F8
Rapley Gn. Easth RG12 .... 27 C4
Rapley's Field. Pirb GU24 .... 87 E4
Rapsley La. Knaph GU21 .... 68 B1
Rastell Ave. Streat SW12 .... 21 D7
Ratcliffe Rd. Farnb GU14 .... 85 A8
Rathbone House. Crawl RH11 . 201 B1
Rathbone House. ⑧
 Wimble SW19 .... 19 D1
Rathfern Prim Sch. For Hil SE23 23 F7
Rathfern Rd. For Hil SE23 & SE6 . 23 F7
Rathgar Cl. Earls RH1 .... 140 A4
Rathlin Rd. Crawl RH11 .... 201 B3
Raven Cl. Horsh RH12 .... 217 E6
Raven La. Crawl RH11 .... 201 C8

Ravendale Rd. Sunby TW16 .... 34 F7
Ravendene Ct. **3** Crawl RH11 . 201 D5
Ravenfield Rd. Up Toot SW17 ... 20 F5
Ravens Cl. Broml BR2 .... 44 F7
Ravens Cl. Knaph GU21 .... 68 C3
Ravens Cl. Redh RH1 .... 118 F2
Ravens Wold. Kenley CR8 .... 80 C4
Ravensbourne. **3** Twick TW1 ... 6 C1
Ravensbourne Ave.
Broml BR2 & BR3 .... 44 E8
Ravensbourne Ave. Catf BR2 ... 24 D1
Ravensbourne Ave. Stan TW19 . 13 E7
Ravensbourne Ct. For Hil SE6 ... 24 A8
Ravensbourne House.
Catf BR1 .... 24 D3
Ravensbourne Park Cres.
For Hil SE6 .... 23 F8
Ravensbourne Pk.
For Hil SE4 & SE6 .... 24 A8
Ravensbourne Rd. For Hil SE23 . 23 F7
Ravensbourne Rd. Twick TW1 ... 6 C1
Ravensbourne Sta. Catf BR3 ..... 24 D1
Ravensbury Ave. Morden SM4 ... 40 C4
Ravensbury Ct. Mitch CR4 .... 40 D5
Ravensbury Gr. Mitch CR4 .... 40 D5
Ravensbury Rd. Mitch CR4 .... 40 D5
Ravensbury Rd. Wands SW18 .... 20 B6
Ravensbury Terr. Wands SW18 .. 20 B6
Ravenscar Lodge. **11** 19 D1
Wimble SW19 .... 19 D1
Ravenscar Rd. Catf BR1 .... 24 E4
Ravenscar Rd. Surb KT6 .... 56 F8
Ravenscote Jun Sch.
Friml GU16 .... 66 A3
Ravenscourt. Sunby TW16 .... 34 F8
Ravenscroft Cl. Ash GU12 .... 106 C3
Ravenscroft Rd. Horsh RH12 ... 217 C3
Ravenscroft Rd. Penge BR3 ...... 43 D7
Ravenscroft Rd. Whit V KT13 ... 72 C8
Ravensdale Gdns. S Norw SE19 . 22 D1
Ravensdale Rd. Ascot SL5 .... 29 A4
Ravensdale Rd. Hounsl TW4 ..... 4 E4
Ravensfield. Eng Gn TW20 .... 11 C2
Ravensfield Gdns. Worc Pk KT19 57 E6
Ravenshead Cl. Selsd CR2 .... 81 C8
Ravenside. King U T KT6 .... 37 D4
Ravenslea Rd.
Balham SW11 & SW12 .... 20 F8
Ravensmead Rd. Broml BR2 ..... 24 D1
Ravensroost. S Norw SE19 .... 42 D8
Ravenstone Jun & Inf Schs.
Up Toot SW12 .... 21 A6
Ravenstone Rd. Friml GU15 ..... 66 D5
Ravenstone St. Up Toot SW12 .. 21 A7
Ravensview Ct. King U T KT6 .... 37 D4
Ravenswood Ave. Tolw KT6 ...... 57 A8
Ravenswood Ave. W Wick BR4 .. 44 C1
Ravenswood Cl. Cobham KT11 .. 73 D4
Ravenswood Cres. W Wick BR4 . 44 C1
Ravenswood Ct. Woking GU22 .. 69 F1
Ravenswood Dr. Friml GU15 ..... 66 A5
Ravenswood Gdns. Hounsl TW7 .. 5 E6
Ravenswood Rd. Balham SW12 .. 21 B8
Ravenswood Rd. Croy CR0 & CR9 61 B7
Rawlins Cl. S Croy CR2 .... 62 F3
Rawlinson Rd. Sandh GU15 ...... 64 F6
Rawnsley Ave. Mitch CR4 .... 40 E4
Raworth Cl. Worth RH10 .... 202 C4
Ray Cl. Lingf RH7 .... 164 C5
Ray Cnr. Lingf RH7 .... 164 B6
Ray La. Blind H RH7 .... 163 F7
Ray La. Lingf RH7 .... 164 B5
Ray La. Tand RH7 .... 164 B6
Ray Rd. E Mole KT8 .... 36 B4
Raybell Ct. Islew TW7 .... 5 F5
Rayford Ave. Lewish SE12 .... 24 F8
Rayleigh Ave. Tedd TW11 .... 16 E2
Rayleigh Cl. **2** King U T KT1 ... 37 F7
Rayleigh Rd. Merton SW19 .... 39 F8
Rayleigh Rise. S Croy CR2 .... 61 E4
Raymead Ave. Thorn H CR7 ...... 42 A4
Raymead Rd. Fetch KT22 .... 94 F5
Raymead Way. Fetch KT22 .... 94 F5
Raymer Wlk. Horley RH6 .... 161 C4
Raymond Cl. For Hil SE26 .... 23 C3
Raymond Cl. Poyle SL3 .... 1 E6
Raymond Cres. Onsl V GU2 ..... 129 F8
Raymond Rd. Beck BR3 .... 43 E5
Raymond Rd. Wimble SW19 ..... 19 E2
Raymond Way. Clayg KT10 .... 56 A4
Raynald House. **15** 21 E5
Streat SW16 .... 21 E5
Rayners Cl. Coln SL3 .... 1 C7
Raynes Park High Sch.
W Barn KT3 .... 39 B6
Raynes Park Sta. W Barn SW20 . 39 C7
Raynesfield. W Barn SW20 .... 39 C6
Rays Rd. W Wick BR4 .... 44 C2
Raywood Cl. Harl UB7 .... 3 C7
Read Rd. Ashtd KT21 .... 75 D2
Readens The. Woodm SM7 .... 78 F3
Reading Arch Rd. Redh RH1 .... 118 F1
Reading Rd. Blckw GU17 .... 64 B4
Reading Rd. Farnb GU14 .... 85 D1
Reading Rd. Sutton SM1 .... 59 C5
Reading Rd. Woki RG11 .... 25 A7
Reading Rd. Yatly GU17 .... 64 B4
Readman Ct. **9** Penge SE20 .. 43 B8
Reads Rest La. Banstd KT20 ..... 98 A7
Reapers Cl. Horsh RH12 .... 217 D5
Reapers Way. Islew TW7 .... 5 D2
Rebecca Ct. Beck BR3 .... 44 A8
Recovery St. Up Toot SW17 ...... 20 E3
Recreation Rd. Broml BR2 .... 44 F7
Recreation Rd. For Hil SE26 .... 23 D4
Recreation Rd. Guild GU1 ...... 109 D1
Recreation Rd. Rowl GU10 ..... 145 E3
Recreation Way.
Mitch CR4 & SW16 .... 41 E6
Rectory Cl. Ashtd KT21 .... 95 F8
Rectory Cl. Bramly GU5 .... 151 F6
Rectory Cl. Byfl KT14 .... 71 E6

Rectory Cl. Easth RG12 .... 27 C5
Rectory Cl. Ewh GU6 .... 175 E5
Rectory Cl. Godal GU7 .... 150 F2
Rectory Cl. Littlt TW17 .... 34 A6
Rectory Cl. Long D KT6 .... 37 C1
Rectory Cl. Merrow GU4 .... 110 D3
Rectory Cl. Ockley RH5 .... 177 C3
Rectory Cl. W Barn SW20 .... 39 C6
Rectory Cl. Woki RG11 .... 25 C6
Rectory Ct. Cranf TW5 .... 4 C5
Rectory Ct. Felt TW13 .... 15 C4
Rectory Ct. Sander CR2 .... 80 F7
Rectory Ct. Wallin SM6 .... 60 C6
Rectory Gdns. Beck BR3 .... 44 A8
Rectory Gn. Beck BR3 .... 43 F8
Rectory Gr. Croy CR0 & CR9 .... 61 B8
Rectory Gr. Hampt TW12 & TW13 15 F4
Rectory Green La. Buckl RH3 .. 116 F3
Rectory La. Ashtd KT21 .... 95 F8
Rectory La. Byfl KT14 .... 71 E6
Rectory La. Charl RH6 .... 180 D7
Rectory La. Crawl RH11 .... 200 F8
Rectory La. Easth RG12 .... 27 B5
Rectory La. G Book KT23 .... 113 F8
Rectory La. Long D KT6 .... 37 C1
Rectory La. Shere GU5 .... 133 A4
Rectory La. Streat SW17 .... 21 A3
Rectory La. Titsey TN16 .... 103 E4
Rectory La. Wallin SM6 .... 60 C6
Rectory La. Windl GU20 .... 48 C4
Rectory La. Woodm CR5 & SM7 .. 78 F3
Rectory Orch. Wimble SW19 .... 19 E4
Rectory Pk. Sander CR2 .... 80 F7
Rectory Rd. Beck BR3 .... 44 A8
Rectory Rd. Cranf TW5 .... 4 C5
Rectory Rd. Farnb GU14 .... 85 D4
Rectory Rd. L Kings GR5 .... 98 D2
Rectory Rd. Sutton SM1 .... 59 B7
Rectory Rd. Woki RG11 .... 25 C6
Rectory Row. Easth RG12 .... 27 B5
Rectory Sch. Hampt TW12 .... 16 A3
Red Admiral St. Horsh RH12 ... 217 C5
Red Deer Cl. Horsh RH13 .... 218 B4
Red Gables Dr. S Croy CR2 .... 61 D1
Red House La. Elst GU8 .... 148 C2
Red House La. Walt O T KT12 ... 54 B8
Red House Rd. Wallin CR0 & CR9 41 D3
Red House Sch. Kings KT20 ...... 97 E6
Red La. Clayg KT10 .... 56 A4
Red La. Head Dn GU35 .... 187 B7
Red La. Limps RH8 .... 144 B7
Red La. S Holm RH5 & RH3 .... 136 F1
Red Lion Bsns Ctr. Surb KT6 ... 56 F7
Red Lion La. Burrh GU24 .... 49 E2
Red Lion La. Farnh GU9 .... 125 B1
Red Lion Rd. Burrh GU24 .... 49 E2
Red Lion Rd. Surb KT6 .... 57 A8
Red Lion St. Rich TW10 .... 6 D2
Red Lodge. W Wick BR4 .... 44 C2
Red Lodge Rd.
W Wick BR3 & BR4 .... 44 D2
Red Rd.
W End GU18 & GU24 & GU15 .. 67 C7
Red River Ct. Horsh RH12 ...... 217 B5
Redan Gdns. Alder GU12 .... 105 C2
Redan Hill Est. Alder GU11 ..... 105 C2
Redan Rd. Alder GU12 .... 105 C2
Redbarn Cl. Purley CR8 .... 80 B7
Redberry Gr. For Hil SE23 & SE26 23 C5
Redcar House. Penge SE26 .... 23 B2
Redcliffe Missionary Training Coll.
Chisw W4 .... 7 B7
Redclose Ave. Morden SM4 ...... 40 A4
Redclyffe Terr. **2** Belm SM2 .. 59 A3
Redcote. Pixham RH4 .... 115 D1
Redcourt. Mayb GU22 .... 70 D4
Redcourt. Pyrf GU22 .... 70 E4
Redcrest Gdns. Camb GU15 ..... 65 F5
Redcroft Wlk. Cran GU6 .... 174 E2
Redding Way. Knaph GU21 ...... 68 C1
Reddington Cl. S Croy CR2 ...... 61 D2
Redditch. Brack RG12 .... 27 D2
Redditch Cl. Crawl RH11 .... 200 E2
Reddons Rd. Penge BR3 .... 23 E1
Reddown Rd. Coulsd CR5 .... 79 D2
Rede Ct. Weyb KT13 .... 53 B7
Redehall Prep Sch. Smallf RH6 162 B2
Redehall Rd. Burst RH6 .... 183 C8
Redehall Rd. Smallf RH6 .... 162 B2
Redesdale Gdns. Hounsl TW7 .... 6 A7
Redfern Ave. Twick TW2 & TW4 .. 16 A8
Redfern Rd. Lewish SE6 .... 24 C8
Redford Ave. Horsh RH12 .... 217 B4
Redford Ave. Thorn H CR7 .... 41 F5
Redford Ave. Wallin SM6 .... 60 E4
Redford Ave. Wallin CR5 .... 79 B4
Redford Cl. Felt TW13 .... 14 F6
Redgarth Ct. E Grins RH19 ..... 185 B3
Redgrave Dr. Worth RH10 .... 202 D5
Redgrove Ct. Alder GU12 .... 105 F2
Redhall Cl. Cater CR3 .... 100 D4
Redhearne Fields. Churt GU10 167 C2
Redhill Coll. Earls RH1 .... 140 B8
Redhill Ct. Streat SW2 .... 22 A4
Redhill Distribution Ctr.
Salfs RH1 .... 161 A8
Redhill Rd. Whit V KT11 .... 72 B5
Redhill Sta. Redh RH1 .... 119 A2
Redhouse Rd. Tats TN16 .... 103 C6
Redkiln Cl. Horsh RH13 .... 217 F4
Redkiln Way.
Horsh RH12 & RH13 .... 217 F3
Redknap House. Rich TW10 ..... 17 C5
Redlake La. Woki RG11 .... 25 F2
Redland Gdns. E Mole KT8 ...... 35 F5
Redlands. Coulsd CR5 .... 79 E3
Redlands The. Dork RH4 .... 17 A2
Redlands CE Fst Sch The.
Dork RH4 .... 136 B4
Redlands Cotts. Dork RH5 ...... 136 B1

Redlands Ct. Broml BR1 .... 24 F1
Redlands Cty Jun Sch The.
Dork RH4 .... 136 B4
Redlands La. Crond GU10 ...... 124 B7
Redlands La. Dork RH5 .... 136 A1
Redlands The. Beck BR3 .... 44 A8
Redlands Way. Streat SW2 .... 21 F8
Redlane Cotts. Oxted RH8 ...... 123 B2
Redleaves Ave. Ashf TW15 ...... 14 B2
Redlees Cl. Islew TW7 .... 6 A3
Redlin Ct. Redh RH1 .... 118 F3
Redmayne. Friml GU15 .... 66 C4
Redroofs Cl. Beck BR3 .... 44 B8
Redruth House. Sutton SM2 ..... 59 B3
Redshank Ct. **5** Crawl RH11 .. 200 D5
Redstart Cl. New Add CR0 & CR9 . 63 D1
Redstone Hill. Earls RH1 .... 119 A1
Redstone Hollow. Earls RH1 ... 140 A8
Redstone Manor. Earls RH1 .... 119 A1
Redstone Pk. Earls RH1 .... 119 B1
Redstone Rd. Earls RH1 .... 140 A8
Redvers Buller Rd.
Farnb GU11 .... 105 D7
Redvers Ct. Warlgm CR6 .... 81 C1
Redvers Rd. Easth RG12 .... 27 B4
Redvers Rd. Warlgm CR6 .... 81 C1
Redway Cotts. Woking GU21 ..... 88 F8
Redway Dr. Twick TW2 .... 16 C8
Redwing Ave. Farnc GU7 .... 150 E8
Redwing Cl. Horsh RH13 .... 217 F3
Redwing Cl. Selsd CR2 .... 81 D8
Redwing Rise. Merrow GU4 .... 110 D3
Redwood. Egham TW20 .... 32 E7
Redwood Cl. Crawl RH10 .... 201 E8
Redwood Cl. Kenley CR8 .... 80 C5
Redwood Cl. **10** Surb KT6 ... 37 D2
Redwood Dr. Friml GU15 .... 66 D4
Redwood Dr. Sunnin SL5 .... 30 B3
Redwood Est. Heston TW5 .... 4 B8
Redwood Gr. Chil GU4 .... 131 C3
Redwood Manor. Haslem GU27 208 C7
Redwood Mount. Reig RH2 .... 118 A4
Redwood Wlk. Surb KT6 .... 37 D1
Redwoods. Rhampt SW15 .... 19 A7
Reed Cl. Farnb GU11 .... 105 D5
Reed Pl. Sheer GU21 & KT14 .... 70 E6
Reed Place Bsns Park.
Lo Hall TW17 .... 33 F1
Reed's Hill. Easth RG12 .... 27 B4
Reed's Sch. Cobham KT11 .... 74 A7
Reedham Dr. Purley CR8 .... 79 F6
Reedham Dr. Purley CR8 .... 80 A6
Reedham Park Ave. Purley CR8 80 A3
Reedham Sta. Purley CR8 .... 79 F6
Reedings. Crawl RH11 .... 200 D4
Reeds Rd The. Frensh GU10 ... 146 E2
Reeds Rd The. Tilf GU10 .... 147 A3
Reedsfield Cl. Ashf TW15 .... 14 B5
Reedsfield Rd. Ashf TW15 .... 14 B4
Rees Gdns. Croy CR0 .... 42 F3
Reeve Ct. Stough GU2 .... 109 A5
Reeve Rd. Dovgn RH1 .... 139 C5
Reeves Cnr. Croy CR0 & CR9 .... 61 B8
Reeves Rd. Alder GU12 .... 105 C1
Reeves Way. Woki RG11 .... 25 A4
Regal Cres. Hackb SM6 .... 60 B7
Regal Ct. **1** Guild GU1 ...... 109 D1
Regal Ct. **2** Mitch CR4 .... 40 F6
Regal Dr. **10** E Grins RH19 . 205 F8
Regalfield Cl. Stough GU2 ..... 109 A5
Regan Cl. Stough GU2 .... 109 B6
Regency Cl. Hampt TW12 .... 15 F3
Regency Ct. **4** Penge SE19 . 23 A1
Regency Ct. **4** Surb KT5 ...... 37 F4
Regency Ct. Sutton SM1 .... 59 B6
Regency Dr. W Byfl KT14 .... 70 F6
Regency Gdns. Walt O T KT12 ... 35 D1
Regency Lodge. Oat Pk KT13 ... 53 E7
Regency Mews. Beck BR3 .... 44 C8
Regency Mews. Islew TW7 .... 5 E2
Regency Wlk. Croy CR0 .... 43 F3
Regency Wlk. **8** Rich TW10 .... 6 E2
Regent Cl. Cranf TW5 .... 4 B6
Regent Cl. New Haw KT15 .... 52 D2
Regent Cres. Redh RH1 .... 118 F3
Regent Ct. Bagsh GU19 .... 47 F2
Regent Ct. Stough GU2 .... 109 B3
Regent Lodge. **9** Streat SW2 . 21 F7
Regent Pk. Leahd KT22 .... 75 A1
Regent Pl. Croy CR0 .... 42 F1
Regent Pl. Wimble SW19 .... 20 C3
Regent Rd. Surb KT5 .... 38 A4
Regent St. Brent W4 .... 7 A8
Regent Way. Friml GU16 .... 66 A1
Regents Cl. Crawl RH11 .... 201 C2
Regents Cl. S Croy CR2 .... 61 E4
Regents Cl. Whytlf CR3 .... 80 F1
Regents Ct. **23** Beck BR3 .... 24 A1
Regents Ct. Broml BR1 .... 24 F1
Regents Ct. Whit V KT13 .... 53 B4
Regents Pl. Sandh GU17 .... 64 C8
Regents Wlk. Sunnin SL5 .... 29 C2
Regiment Cl. Farnb GU14 .... 84 C3
Regina Coeli RC Prim Sch.
Croy CR2 .... 61 B3
Regina Rd. Croy SE25 .... 43 A6
Reginald Ct. Beck BR3 .... 44 C8
Regis Ct. E Bed TW14 .... 3 D1
Regis Ct. Mitch SW19 .... 40 E8
Regnolruf Ct. Walt O T KT12 .... 35 A2
Reid Ave. Cater CR3 .... 100 D6
Reid Ct. Mortl SW14 .... 7 C5
Reidonhill Cotts. Bisley GU21 ... 68 B1
Reigate Ave. Cheam SM3 & SM4 . 40 B1
Reigate Cl. Crawl RH10 .... 182 D1
Reigate Coll. Reig RH2 .... 118 B1
Reigate Day Hospl.
Woodh RH2 .... 139 A7
Reigate Gram Sch. Reig RH1 .. 118 C1
Reigate Heath Cotts. Reig RH2 117 E1
Reigate Hill. Reig RH2 .... 118 B4

Reigate Hill Cl. Reig RH2 .... 118 B4
Reigate Priory Prim Sch.
Reig RH2 .... 118 A1
Reigate Rd.
Betch RH3 & RH4 & RH2 & RH5 . 116 D2
Reigate Rd.
Brock RH3 & RH4 & RH2 & RH5 . 116 D2
Reigate Rd. Burgh H KT18 .... 77 C4
Reigate Rd. Catf BR1 .... 24 F5
Reigate Rd. Dork RH4 & RH5 .. 136 C8
Reigate Rd. Ewell KT17 .... 77 C4
Reigate Rd. Hookw RH6 .... 160 C4
Reigate Rd. Leahd KT22 .... 95 D4
Reigate Rd. Nork KT17 .... 77 C4
Reigate Rd. Pixham RH4 .... 115 C1
Reigate Rd. Reig RH2 .... 118 C1
Reigate Rd. Sidlow RH2 & RH6 160 C4
Reigate Sch. Woodh RH1 .... 139 C6
Reigate Sch of Art & Design.
Reig RH2 .... 118 B1
Reigate Sta. Reig RH2 .... 118 A2
Reigate St Mary's Prep Sch.
Reig RH2 .... 118 B1
Reigate Way. Wallin SM6 .... 60 E5
Reindorp Cl. Guild GU2 .... 130 A8
Relko Ct. Epsom KT19 .... 76 D8
Relko Gdns. Carsh SM1 .... 59 D5
Rembrandt Way. Walt O T KT12 . 54 B8
Rendle Cl. Croy CR0 & SE25 .... 43 A4
Renfree Way. Shep TW17 .... 34 A2
Renfrew Ct. Hounsl TW5 .... 4 E5
Renfrew Rd. Hounsl TW5 .... 4 E5
Renfrew Rd. King U T KT2 .... 18 C1
Renmans The. Ashtd KT21 .... 75 F3
Renmuir St. Up Toot SW17 ...... 20 F2
Rennie Cl. Ashf TW15 .... 13 D5
Rennie Terr. Earls RH1 .... 140 A8
Renown Cl. Thorn H CR0 .... 42 B1
Renshaw House. **11** 22 B3
W Norw SW27 .... 22 B3
Replingham Rd. Wands SW18 ... 20 A7
Repton Cl. Carsh SM3 & SM5 ... 59 E5
Repton Ct. Beck BR3 .... 44 B8
Reservoir Rd. Farnb GU14 .... 84 D1
Restmor Way. Hackb SM5 & SM6 60 A8
Restormel Cl. Hounsl TW3 .... 5 A2
Restwell Ave. Rowly GU6 .... 174 B6
Retreat The. Eng Gn TW20 ...... 11 E3
Retreat The. Mortl SW14 .... 7 E4
Retreat The. N Cheam KT4 .... 58 B8
Retreat The. S Norw CR7 .... 42 D5
Retreat The. Surb KT5 .... 37 F3
Revell Cl. Fetch KT22 .... 94 B5
Revell Dr. Fetch KT22 .... 94 B5
Revell Rd. Cheam SM1 .... 58 F4
Revell Rd. King U T KT1 .... 38 B8
Revelstoke Ave. Farnb GU14 .... 85 B6
Revelstoke Rd.
Wands SW18 & SW19 .... 20 A6
Revesby Cl. W End GU24 .... 67 D6
Revesby Rd. Carsh SM5 .... 40 E3
Rewley Rd. Carsh SM4 .... 40 D3
Rex Ave. Ashf TW15 .... 14 A3
Rex House. Felt TW13 .... 15 E5
Reynard Cl. Horsh RH12 .... 218 B5
Reynard Dr. S Norw SE19 .... 22 F1
Reynolds Ave. Chess KT9 .... 56 E3
Reynolds Cl. Carsh CR4 & SM5 .. 40 F1
Reynolds Cl. Mitch CR4 & SW19 . 40 D8
Reynolds Gn. Sandh GU15 ...... 64 B4
Reynolds Pl. **12** Rich TW10 ... 6 F1
Reynolds Rd. Crawl RH11 ...... 201 C7
Reynolds Rd. Farnb GU14 ..... 104 B8
Reynolds Rd. New Mal KT3 ...... 38 D2
Reynolds Way. S Croy CR0 .... 61 E6
Rheingold Way. Wallin SM6 ..... 60 E2
Rhine Banks. W Heath GU14 .... 84 D5
Rhodes Cl. Egham TW20 .... 12 C3
Rhodes Ct. Egham TW20 .... 12 C3
Rhodes Way. Crawl RH10 ...... 201 F3
Rhodes-Moorhouse Ct.
Morden SM4 .... 40 A3
Rhododendron Cl. N Asct SL5 ... 8 E1
Rhododendron Rd. Friml GU16 .. 86 B8
Rhododendron Ride.
Eng Gn SL4 & TW20 .... 10 F3
Rhododendron Wlk. N Asct SL5 .. 8 E1
Rhodrons Ave. Chess KT9 .... 56 E5
Rialto Rd. Mitch CR4 .... 41 A7
Ribble Pl. W Heath GU14 .... 84 E7
Ribblesdale. Dork RH4 .... 136 A5
Ribblesdale Rd. Streat SW16 ... 21 B3
Ricardo Ct. Bramly GU5 .... 151 F5
Ricards Lodge High Sch.
Wimble SW19 .... 19 F3
Ricards Rd. Wimble SW19 .... 19 F3
Rice's Cnr. Chil GU4 .... 131 A2
Rices Hill. E Grins RH19 .... 185 E1
Richard Atkins Prim Sch.
Streat SW2 .... 21 E8
Richard Challoner Sch.
New Mal KT3 .... 38 C2
Richard Thornton House.
Merton SW19 .... 40 A7
Richards Cl. Ash GU12 .... 106 A5
Richards Cl. Harl UB3 .... 3 D8
Richards Ct. Penge BR3 .... 43 D8
Richards Field. Epsom KT19 ..... 57 D2
Richards Rd. Oxsh KT11 .... 74 A5
Richardson Ct. **17**
Crawl RH11 .... 201 B1
Richardson's Lawn Cotts.
Old W SL4 .... 10 B5
Richbell Cl. Ashtd KT21 .... 75 D1
Richfield Ct. Beck BR3 .... 43 F8
Richland Ave. Wallin CR5 .... 79 A5
Richlands Ave. Worc Pk KT17 ... 58 A6
Richmond Adult Coll. Rich TW9 . 6 D3
Richmond Athletic Gd. Rich TW9 6 D3

Richmond Ave. Felt TW14 .... 3 E7
Richmond Ave. Merton SW20 ... 39 E8
Richmond Bridge. Twick TW1 .... 6 D1
Richmond Bridge Mansions. **1**
Twick TW1 .... 6 D1
Richmond Cl. Bigg H TN16 ..... 103 B8
Richmond Cl. Epsom KT18 .... 76 E5
Richmond Cl. Fetch KT23 .... 94 C3
Richmond Cl. Friml GU16 .... 65 F1
Richmond Coll. Rich TW10 .... 17 E2
Richmond Cres. Stain TW18 ..... 12 F3
Richmond Ct. **12** King U T KT2 . 18 A1
Richmond Ct. Mitch CR4 .... 40 D6
Richmond Ct. Wimble SW20 ..... 39 F7
Richmond Dr. Shep TW17 .... 34 D3
Richmond Gn. Wallin CR0 .... 60 E7
Richmond Hill. Rich TW10 .... 6 E1
Richmond Hill Ct. **5** Rich TW10 .. 6 E1
Richmond House. **12**
For Hil SE6 .... 23 A5
Richmond House. (Sandh GU15 .. 64 E7
of Rectory Sch). Hampt TW12 . 15 F3
Richmond Mansions. **5**
Twick TW1 .... 6 D1
Richmond Park Rd.
King U T KT2 .... 17 E1
Richmond Park Rd. Mortl SW14 . 7 D3
Richmond Rd. Coulsd CR5 .... 79 B4
Richmond Rd. Farnc GU7 .... 150 E6
Richmond Rd. Horsh RH12 ..... 217 D4
Richmond Rd. Islew TW7 .... 6 A4
Richmond Rd. King U T KT2 ..... 17 E2
Richmond Rd. Sandh GU15 ..... 64 E8
Richmond Rd. Stain TW18 .... 12 F3
Richmond Rd. Thorn H CR7 ..... 42 B5
Richmond Rd. Twick TW1 .... 6 D2
Richmond Rd. Wallin CR0 .... 60 E7
Richmond Rd. Wimble SW20 ... 39 E8
Richmond Sq. E Grins RH19 ... 185 D2
Richmond Sta. Rich TW9 .... 6 E3
Richmond Upon Thames Coll.
Twick TW2 .... 6 D1
Richmond Way. E Grins RH19 .. 205 F8
Richmond Way. Fetch KT23 ...... 94 C3
Richmondwood. Sunnin SL5 ..... 30 B1
Rickard Cl. Streat SW2 .... 22 A7
Rickards Cl. Surb KT6 .... 56 E8
Ricketts Hill Rd. Tats TN16 .... 103 E7
Rickfield. Crawl RH11 .... 201 A5
Rickford Hill. Worpl GU3 .... 88 D1
Rickman Cl. Easth RG12 .... 27 C3
Rickman Cres. Addl KT15 .... 52 B7
Rickman Ct. Addl KT15 .... 52 B7
Rickman Hill. Coulsd CR5 .... 79 B2
Rickman Hill Rd. Chips CR5 ..... 79 B1
Rickman's La. Plaist RH14 ..... 211 F2
Ricksons La. W Hors KT24 ...... 112 B8
Rickwood. Horley RH6 .... 161 B4
Rickyard. Stough GU2 .... 108 D1
Riddens The. Buck Gn RH12 ... 214 A6
Riddings The. Cater CR3 .... 100 F2
Riddlesdown Ave. Purley CR8 ... 80 C7
Riddlesdown High Sch.
Sander CR2 .... 80 E5
Riddlesdown Rd.
Purley CR3 & CR8 .... 80 D5
Riddlesdown Sta. Sander CR8 ... 80 D6
Ride La. Farl Gn GU5 .... 153 D7
Ride The. Ifold RH14 .... 212 C2
Ride Way. Ewh GU5 & GU6 ..... 154 C1
Riders Way. Tyl Gn RH9 .... 121 C4
Rideway Cl. Camb GU15 .... 65 B4
Ridge Cl. Brock RH3 .... 137 B5
Ridge Cl. Woking GU22 .... 89 B6
Ridge Ct. Warlgm CR6 .... 81 A1
Ridge Gn. S Nutf RH1 .... 140 E6
Ridge Green Cl. S Nutf RH1 .... 140 E6
Ridge House. **4** King U T KT2 . 18 B1
Ridge Langley. S Croy CR2 .... 62 A2
Ridge Moor Cl. Beac H GU26 .. 188 C6
Ridge Mount Rd. Sunnin SL5 ... 30 A1
Ridge Pk. Wallin CR8 & SM6 .... 60 D7
Ridge Prim Sch. Cheam SM3 .... 39 E1
Ridge Rd. Cheam SM3 & SM4 .. 39 F1
Ridge Rd. Mitch CR4 .... 21 B1
Ridge The. Coulsd CR5 .... 79 E5
Ridge The. Fetch KT22 .... 94 D3
Ridge The. Limps CR3 & CR6 .. 102 D2
Ridge The. Mayb GU22 .... 70 B2
Ridge The. Surb KT5 .... 38 A4
Ridge The. Twick TW2 .... 16 D8
Ridge The. Wallin CR8 .... 60 D1
Ridge The. Wold CR3 & RH9 ... 102 D2
Ridge The. Woodk KT18 & KT21 . 76 C1
Ridge Way. Felt TW13 .... 15 E5
Ridge Way The. S Croy CR2 ...... 61 E1
Ridgedale. Crawl RH10 .... 204 B8
Ridgegate Cl. Reig RH2 .... 118 D3
Ridgehurst Dr. Horsh RH12 .... 216 F1
Ridgelands. Fetch KT22 .... 94 D3
Ridgemead Rd. Eng Gn TW20 ... 11 B5
Ridgemount. Guild GU2 .... 130 B8
Ridgemount. Oat Pk KT13 .... 53 E7
Ridgemount Ave. Coulsd CR5 ... 79 B2
Ridgemount Ave. Croy CR0 ...... 62 D8
Ridgemount Cl. Penge SE20 ..... 23 B1
Ridgemount Est. Friml GU16 .... 86 C2
Ridges The. Arting GU3 .... 130 C4
Ridgeside. Crawl RH10 .... 201 F6
Ridgeway. E Grins RH19 .... 205 E7
Ridgeway. Epsom KT19 .... 76 C7
Ridgeway. Horse GU21 .... 69 D4
Ridgeway. Pyrf GU22 .... 71 A4
Ridgeway. **11** Rich TW9 .... 6 E1
Ridgeway. Walt O T KT12 .... 34 F1
Ridgeway. Wimble SW19 & SW20 19 D2
Ridgeway Cl. Cran GU6 .... 175 A3

Ridgeway Cl. Dork RH4 .... 136 A5
Ridgeway Cl. Horse GU21 .... 69 D4
Ridgeway Cl. Lhtwat GU18 .... 67 A8
Ridgeway Cl. Oxsh KT22 .... 74 C5
Ridgeway Cl. Redh RH1 .... 118 F1
Ridgeway Dr. Dork RH4 .... 136 A4
Ridgeway Gdns. Horse GU21 .... 69 D4
Ridgeway Hill Rd.
 M Bourn GU9 .... 146 C8
Ridgeway Inf Sch. S Croy CR2 ... 61 E1
Ridgeway Jun Sch. S Croy CR2 .. 61 E1
Ridgeway Rd. Dork RH4 .... 136 A5
Ridgeway Rd. Hounsl TW7 .... 5 E6
Ridgeway Rd. M Bourn GU9 .... 146 C8
Ridgeway Rd. Redh RH1 .... 118 F1
Ridgeway Rd N. Hounsl TW7 .... 5 E7
Ridgeway Sch The.
 M Bourn GU9 .... 146 C7
Ridgeway The. Brack RG12 .... 27 C6
Ridgeway The. Brookw GU24 .... 88 A7
Ridgeway The. Cran GU6 .... 174 F3
Ridgeway The. Croy CR0 .... 60 F7
Ridgeway The. Fetch KT22 .... 94 D3
Ridgeway The. Guild GU1 .... 131 A8
Ridgeway The. Horley RH6 .... 161 A1
Ridgeway The. Horsh RH12 .... 217 B4
Ridgeway The. Lhtwat GU18 .... 48 B1
Ridgeway The. Oxsh KT22 .... 75 C5
Ridgewood Ctr (Hospl).
 Friml GU16 .... 66 C3
Ridgley Rd. Chidd GU8 .... 191 B4
Ridgway Ct. Wimble SW19 .... 19 D2
Ridgway Gdns. Wimble SW19 .... 19 D1
Ridgway Pl. Wimble SW19 .... 19 E2
Ridgway Rd. Pyrf GU22 .... 70 F4
Ridgway The. Sutton SM2 .... 59 D4
Riding Hill. Sander CR2 .... 81 A6
Riding The. Cran GU6 .... 174 F4
Riding The. Sheer GU21 .... 70 A4
Ridings The. Ashtd KT21 .... 75 D2
Ridings The. Bigg H TN16 .... 83 E2
Ridings The. Cobham KT11 .... 74 A7
Ridings The. Crawl RH10 .... 202 D7
Ridings The. E Hors KT24 .... 92 F2
Ridings The. Epsom KT18 .... 76 F4
Ridings The. Ewell KT17 .... 57 F2
Ridings The. Friml GU16 .... 66 B3
Ridings The. Kings KT20 .... 97 F7
Ridings The. Redh RH1 .... 118 D3
Ridings The. Row Tn KT15 .... 51 E4
Ridings The. Send M GU23 .... 91 A4
Ridings The. Sunby TW16 .... 35 A8
Ridings The. Surb KT5 .... 38 A4
Ridlands Gr. The Char RH8 .... 123 E5
Ridlands La. The Char RH8 .... 123 E5
Ridlands Rise. The Char RH8 ...... 123 E4
Ridley Ct. Streat SW16 .... 21 E2
Ridley Rd. Broml BR2 .... 44 F6
Ridley Rd. Merton SW19 .... 20 B1
Ridley Rd. Warlgm CR6 .... 81 D1
Ridsdale Rd. Penge SE20 .... 43 B8
Ridsdale Rd. Woking GU21 .... 69 B2
Riesco Dr. S Croy CR0 .... 62 C4
Rifle Way. Farnb GU14 .... 84 C3
Rigby Cl. Croy CR0 & CR9 .... 61 A7
Rigg House. 2 Streat SW4 .... 21 D8
Riggindale Rd. Streat SW16 .... 21 D4
Rikkyo Sch in England.
 Buck Gn RH14 .... 213 D8
Riley House. 1 Streat SW4 .... 21 D8
Rill Wlk. E Grins RH19 .... 186 B1
Rillside. Crawl RH10 .... 202 A3
Rimbault Cl. Farnb GU11 .... 105 E7
Rinaldo Rd. Balham SW12 .... 21 B8
Ring Rd N. Horley RH6 .... 182 C8
Ring Rd S. Crawl RH6 .... 182 C7
Ring The. Brack RG12 .... 27 C7
Ringley Ave. Horley RH6 .... 161 A2
Ringley Oak. Horsh RH12 .... 217 F4
Ringley Park Ave. Reig RH2 .... 139 D8
Ringley Park Rd. Reig RH2 .... 118 C1
Ringley Rd. Horsh RH12 .... 217 E4
Ringmead. Easth RG12 .... 26 E4
Ringmead. Easth RG12 .... 27 B2
Ringmore Dr. Merrow GU4 .... 110 C4
Ringmore Rd. Walt O T KT12 .... 54 C7
Ringmore Rise. For Hil SE23 .... 23 B8
Ringstead Rd. Carsh SM1 .... 59 D5
Ringstead Rd. Lewish SE6 .... 24 B8
Ringwold Cl. Penge BR3 .... 23 E1
Ringwood. Easth RG12 .... 26 F2
Ringwood Ave. Redh RH1 .... 118 F4
Ringwood Ave.
 Thorn H CR0 & CR9 .... 41 E2
Ringwood Cl. Ascot SL5 .... 29 B5
Ringwood Cl. Crawl RH10 .... 201 E4
Ringwood Gdns. Rhampt SW15 ..... 19 A7
Ringwood Lodge. 1 Redh RH1 .... 119 A4
Ringwood Rd. Blckw GU17 .... 64 C6
Ringwood Rd. Farnb GU14 .... 85 C7
Ringwood Way. Hampt TW12 .... 16 A4
Ripley Ave. Egham TW20 .... 11 E2
Ripley By-Pass. Ockham GU23 ...... 91 C4
Ripley By-Pass. Ripley GU23 .... 91 C4
Ripley C of E Inf Sch.
 Ripley GU23 .... 91 B6
Ripley Cl. New Add CR0 .... 63 C4
Ripley Court Sch. Ripley GU23 ... 91 C6
Ripley Ct. Mitch CR4 .... 40 D7
Ripley Gdns. Mortl SW14 .... 7 D4
Ripley Gdns. Sutton SM1 .... 59 C6
Ripley House. 13 King U T KT2 ..... 18 B2
Ripley House. Mortl SW14 .... 7 E4
Ripley House. 5 Penge SE26 .... 23 B3
Ripley La. Ripley GU23 .... 91 F3
Ripley La. W Hors KT24 & GU23 .. 112 A7
Ripley Rd. E Clan GU4 .... 111 D6
Ripley Rd. Hampt TW12 .... 16 A1

Ripley Rd. Ripley GU23 & GU4 ... 111 D7
Riplington Ct. Putney SW15 .... 19 B8
Ripon Cl. Friml GU15 .... 66 D3
Ripon Cl. Stough GU2 .... 108 F3
Ripon Gdns. Chess KT9 .... 56 D5
Ripon Rd. Hawley GU14 .... 84 A7
Ripplesmere. Brack RG12 .... 27 D5
Ripplesmore Cl. Sandh GU17 .... 64 B8
Ripston Rd. Ashf TW15 .... 14 D3
Rise The. Sunnin SL5 .... 29 F3
Rise The. Crawl RH10 .... 202 D6
Rise The. Crowth RG11 .... 45 A5
Rise The. E Grins RH19 .... 205 F8
Rise The. E Hors KT24 .... 92 E1
Rise The. Ewell KT17 .... 57 F1
Rise The. S Croy CR2 .... 62 C2
Rise The. Tadw KT20 .... 97 C6
Rise The. Woki RG11 .... 25 A7
Ritchie Rd. Croy CR0 .... 43 B6
Ritherdon Rd. Up Toot SW17 .... 21 B6
River Ave. Thame D KT7 .... 37 A2
River Bank. Thame D KT7 .... 36 F4
River Crane Way. Felt TW13 .... 15 F6
River Ct. King U T KT6 .... 37 D4
River Ct. Sheer GU21 .... 70 C5
River Gdns. Carsh SM5 .... 60 A7
River Gdns. Felt TW14 .... 4 B2
River Gdns Bsns Ctr. Felt TW14 .... 4 B3
River Grove Pk. Beck BR3 .... 43 F8
River Hill. Cobham KT11 .... 73 B4
River House. For Hil SE26 .... 23 B5
River House. Mortl SW13 .... 7 E5
River Island Cl. Fetch KT22 .... 94 D7
River La. Cobham KT11 .... 73 E3
River La. Farnh GU10 & GU9 .... 145 C2
River La. Fetch KT22 .... 94 D6
River La. Leahd KT22 .... 94 E7
River La. Rich TW10 .... 17 D7
River La. Wreccl GU10 & GU9 .... 145 C2
River Mead. Crawl RH11 .... 181 A1
River Mead. Horsh RH12 .... 217 B1
River Meads Ave.
 Twick TW13 & TW2 .... 16 B5
River Mount. Walt O T KT12 .... 34 F2
River Mount Gdns. Guild GU2 .... 130 C6
River Park Ave. Egham TW18 .... 12 D4
River Rd. Stain TW18 .... 32 F8
River Reach. Tedd TW11 .... 17 C3
River View. Addl KT15 .... 52 C5
River View Gdns. Twick TW1 .... 16 F6
River Way. Twick TW3 & TW2 .... 16 B6
River Way. W Ewell KT19 .... 57 E5
River Way. W Ewell KT19 .... 57 E5
River Wlk. Sunby TW16 .... 34 F5
River Wlk. Walt O T KT12 .... 35 A3
Riverbank. E Mole KT8 .... 36 E5
Riverbank. Stain TW18 .... 12 F2
Riverbank Way. Brent TW8 .... 6 C8
Riverdale. Pixham RH4 .... 115 C3
Riverdale. Wreccl GU10 .... 145 E7
Riverdale Dr. Wands SW18 .... 20 B7
Riverdale Dr. Westfd GU22 .... 89 F6
Riverdale Gdns. Twick TW1 .... 6 C2
Riverdale Rd. Felt TW13 .... 15 F4
Riverdale Rd. Twick TW1 .... 6 C2
Riverdene Ind Est. Hersh KT12 ... 54 D5
Riverfield Rd. Stain TW18 .... 12 F2
Riverhead Dr. Belm SM2 .... 59 B1
Riverholme Dr. W Ewell KT19 .... 57 E2
Riverholme Dr. W Ewell KT19 .... 57 E2
Rivermead. Byfl KT14 .... 71 F6
Rivermead. E Mole KT8 .... 36 A6
Rivermead. King U T KT6 .... 37 D4
Rivermead Cl. New Haw KT15 .... 52 C3
Rivermead Cl. Rich TW11 .... 17 B3
Rivermead House. Sunby TW16 .... 35 C6
Rivermead Rd. Camb GU15 .... 65 B2
Rivernook Cl. Walt O T KT12 .... 35 C4
Riverpark Gdns. Catf BR2 .... 24 C5
Rivers Cl. Farnb GU14 .... 85 E1
Riversdale Prim Sch.
 Wands SW18 .... 20 A7
Riversdale Rd. Thame D KT7 .... 37 A3
Riversdell Cl. Chert KT16 .... 32 F2
Riverside. Bellf GU1 .... 109 D3
Riverside. Catf SE6 .... 23 F4
Riverside. For Row RH18 .... 206 E3
Riverside. Horley RH6 .... 161 A1
Riverside. Horsh RH12 .... 217 A2
Riverside. Oat Pk TW17 .... 34 E2
Riverside. Pixham RH4 .... 115 D1
Riverside. Sunby TW16 .... 35 D7
Riverside. Twick TW1 .... 6 C2
Riverside. Wray TW19 .... 11 C8
Riverside Ave. E Mole KT8 .... 36 D4
Riverside Ave. W Molit SE N 67 C8
Riverside Bsns Ctr.
 Wands SW18 .... 20 B7
Riverside Bsns Pk.
 Merton SW19 .... 40 C8
Riverside Cl. Brookw GU24 .... 87 F7
Riverside Cl. Hackb SM6 .... 60 B7
Riverside Cl. King U T KT1 .... 37 D5
Riverside Cl. Stain TW18 .... 32 F8
Riverside Cl. W Heath GU14 .... 84 F5
Riverside Cl. Pixham RH4 .... 115 D1
Riverside Ct. Tedd TW11 .... 17 C3
Riverside Dr. Bramly GU5 .... 152 A7
Riverside Dr. Chisw W4 .... 7 E6
Riverside Dr. Egham TW18 .... 12 A3
Riverside Dr. Esher KT10 .... 55 A6
Riverside Dr. Mitch CR4 .... 40 E4
Riverside Dr. Rich TW10 .... 17 B5
Riverside Dr. Stain TW18 .... 32 F8
Riverside Gdns. Old Wok GU22 ..... 90 B6
Riverside House. Morden SW19 .... 40 C5
Riverside L Ctr. Chisw W4 .... 7 E6
Riverside Pk. Farnb GU14 .... 125 D3

Riverside Pl. Stan TW19 .... 2 D1
Riverside Rd. Hersh KT12 .... 54 E6
Riverside Rd. Stain TW18 .... 12 F1
Riverside Rd. Stan TW19 .... 2 E1
Riverside Rd.
 Wands SW17 & SW19 .... 20 C5
Riverside The. E Mole KT8 .... 36 D6
Riverside Way. Camb GU15 .... 65 A3
Riverside Wlk. Islew TW7 .... 5 E4
Riverside Wlk. W Wick BR4 .... 44 B1
Riverstone Cl. King U T KT2 .... 37 F8
Riverview. Shep TW17 .... 34 D2
Riverview Cty Fst Sch.
 W Ewell KT19 .... 57 D6
Riverview Cty Fst Sch.
 W Ewell KT19 .... 57 D6
Riverview Gr. Chisw W4 .... 7 B8
Riverview Pk. For Hil SE6 .... 24 A6
Riverview Rd. Chisw W4 .... 7 B8
Riverview Rd. W Ewell KT19 .... 57 D5
Riverview Rd. W Ewell KT19 .... 57 D5
Riverview Rd. W Ewell KT19 .... 57 D6
Riverway. Stain TW18 .... 33 B8
Riverway Est. Shalf GU7 .... 151 C8
Riverwood Ct. Bellf GU1 .... 109 A3
Rivett-Drake Rd. Stough GU2 ...... 109 A5
Rivey Cl. Pyrf KT14 .... 70 F5
Road House Est. Old Wok GU22 ... 90 A7
Roakes Ave. Chert KT15 .... 52 B8
Robert Cl. Hersh KT12 .... 54 B5
Robert Gerard House. 7
 W Norw SE27 .... 22 D4
Robert May Cty Fst Sch The.
 Crawl RH10 .... 201 F4
Robert St. Croy CR0 & CR9 .... 61 C7
Robert Way. Horsh RH12 .... 217 F7
Robert Way. Mytch GU16 .... 85 F3
Roberts Cl. Cheam SM3 .... 58 D3
Roberts Cl. Stan TW19 .... 2 C1
Roberts Ct. Penge SE20 .... 43 C8
Roberts House. 5 W Norw SE27 .. 22 B5
Roberts Rd. Alder GU12 .... 105 C3
Roberts Rd. Sandh GU15 .... 65 A6
Roberts Way. Eng Gn TW20 .... 11 C1
Robertsbridge Rd. Carsh SM5 ...... 40 D2
Robertson Ct. 5 Knaph GU21 .... 68 E1
Robertson House. Up Toot SW17 .. 20 E3
Robertson Way. Ash GU12 .... 105 F1
Robin Cl. Addl KT15 .... 52 D5
Robin Cl. Ash V GU12 .... 106 A6
Robin Cl. Crawl RH11 .... 201 C8
Robin Cl. E Grins RH19 .... 185 F2
Robin Cl. Hampt TW12 .... 15 E3
Robin Ct. Wallin SM6 .... 60 C4
Robin Gdns. Redh RH1 .... 119 A3
Robin Gr. Brent TW8 .... 6 C8
Robin Hill. Farnc GU7 .... 150 D7
Robin Hill Dr. Friml GU15 .... 66 A3
Robin Hood Cl. Knaph GU21 .... 68 F1
Robin Hood Cl. W Heath GU14 ..... 85 A7
Robin Hood Cres. Knaph GU21 .... 68 E2
Robin Hood Ct. Sutton SM1 .... 59 B5
Robin Hood Inf Sch. Sutton SM1 .. 59 A5
Robin Hood Jun Sch.
 Sutton SM1 .... 59 B5
Robin Hood La. King U T SW15 ..... 18 E4
Robin Hood La. Sutton SM1 .... 59 B5
Robin Hood La. Warn RH12 .... 216 F5
Robin Hood La. Westfd GU4 .... 89 F3
Robin Hood Prim Sch.
 King U T SW15 .... 18 E3
Robin Hood Rd. Knaph GU21 .... 68 E2
Robin Hood Rd. Knaph GU21 .... 68 F1
Robin Hood Rd.
 Wimble SW15 & SW19 .... 18 F3
Robin Hood Rdbt.
 King U T SW15 .... 18 E5
Robin Hood Way (Kingston By-
Pass). King U T
 KT2 & SW15 & SW20 .... 18 E3
Robin Hood Works. Knaph GU21 . 68 E1
Robin La. Sandh GU47 .... 45 C1
Robin Way. Stain TW18 .... 12 F5
Robin Way. Stough GU2 .... 109 B5
Robin's Bow. Camb GU15 .... 65 B4
Robin's Ct. Beck BR3 .... 44 D7
Robinhood Cl. Mitch CR4 .... 41 C6
Robinhood La. Mitch CR4 .... 41 C6
Robins Ct. Rich TW10 .... 6 E1
Robins Dale. Knaph GU21 .... 68 C2
Robinson Ct. 4 Rich TW9 .... 6 F3
Robinson Rd. Crawl RH11 .... 201 D5
Robinson Rd. Mitch CR4 .... 20 E2
Robinsway. Hersh KT12 .... 54 C6
Robinswood Ct. Horsh RH12 .... 217 F4
Robinwood Pl. King U T SW15 ...... 18 D4
Robson Rd. W Norw SE21 & SE27 22 C5
Rochdale. 7 S Norw SE19 .... 22 E2
Roche Rd. Thorn H SW16 .... 41 F8
Roche Wlk. Carsh SM4 & SM5 ...... 40 D3
Rochelle Ct. Beck BR3 .... 24 B1
Rochester Ave. Felt TW13 .... 14 F6
Rochester Cl. Streat SW16 .... 21 E1
Rochester Ct. S Norw SE25 .... 43 A7
Rochester Gdns. Cater CR3 .... 100 E5
Rochester Gdns. S Croy CR0 .... 61 E7
Rochester Par. Felt TW13 .... 15 A5
Rochester Rd. Carsh SM5 .... 59 F6
Rochester Rd. Egham TW20 .... 12 D2
Rochester Wlk. Dovgn RH2 .... 139 B5
Rochford Way. Thorn H CR0 .... 41 E3
Rock Ave. 13 Mortl SW14 .... 7 D4
Rock Gdns. Alder GU11 .... 104 F1
Rock Hill. Dulw SE19 .... 22 F4
Rock La. Rowl GU10 .... 146 E5
Rockbourne Rd. For Hil SE23 .... 23 D7
Rockdale Dr. Graysh GU26 .... 188 D3
Rockery The. Farnb GU14 .... 84 E3
Rocket Rd. Farnb GU14 .... 84 D1
Rockfield Cl. Oxted RH8 .... 122 F4

Rockfield Rd. Oxted RH8 .... 122 F5
Rockfield Way. 4 Sandh GU15 ..... 64 D8
Rockhampton Cl. 4
 W Norw SE27 .... 22 A4
Rockhampton Rd. S Croy CR2 ...... 61 E4
Rockhampton Rd.
 W Norw SE27 & SW16 .... 22 A4
Rockingham Cl. Rhampt SW15 .... 7 F3
Rockingham Ct. 20 Beck BR3 ...... 24 A1
Rockmount Jun Mix & Inf Lower
 Schs. S Norw SE19 .... 22 D2
Rockmount Jun Mix & Inf Upper
 Schs. S Norw SE19 .... 22 D2
Rockmount Rd. S Norw SE19 .... 22 D2
Rocks The. Ash W RH19 .... 206 D6
Rockshaw Rd. Cater RH1 .... 119 D6
Rockshaw Rd. Merstt RH1 .... 119 E8
Rockwell Gdns. Dulw SE19 .... 22 E4
Rocky La. Gatton RH1 & RH2 ..... 119 A6
Rocombe Cres. For Hil SE23 .... 23 C8
Rodborough Cty Sec Sch.
 Witley GU8 .... 170 F7
Rodd Est. Shep TW17 .... 34 D4
Roden Gdns. Thorn H CR0 & SE25 42 E3
Rodenhurst Rd. Streat SW4 .... 21 D8
Rodgers House. 4 Streat SW4 ..... 21 D8
Roding Cl. Crawl GU6 .... 173 F2
Rodmill La. Streat SW2 .... 21 E8
Rodney Cl. New Mal KT3 .... 38 E4
Rodney Cl. Thorn H CR0 .... 42 B1
Rodney Cl. Walt O T KT12 .... 35 C1
Rodney Gn. 2 Walt O T KT12 .... 54 C8
Rodney Pl. Merton SW19 .... 40 C8
Rodney Rd. Mitch CR4 .... 40 E6
Rodney Rd. New Mal KT3 .... 38 E4
Rodney Rd. Twick TW4 .... 16 A8
Rodney Rd. Walt O T KT12 .... 35 C1
Rodney Way. Guild GU1 .... 109 D4
Rodney Way. Merrow GU1 .... 110 A2
Rodney Way. Poyle SL3 .... 1 E6
Rodona Rd. Whit V KT13 .... 72 D8
Rodway Rd. Rhampt SW15 .... 19 A8
Rodwell Cl. Addl KT15 .... 52 C6
Rodwell Ct. Walt O T KT12 .... 54 B7
Roe Way. Wallin SM6 .... 60 E4
Roebuck Cl. Ashtd KT21 .... 95 E7
Roebuck Cl. Felt TW13 .... 15 B4
Roebuck Cl. Horsh RH13 .... 218 B4
Roebuck Cl. Reig RH2 .... 118 A1
Roebuck Ct. 2 New Mal KT3 .... 38 E4
Roebuck Rd. Chess KT9 .... 57 A5
Roedean Cres. Rhampt SW15 .... 7 E2
Roedeer Copse. Shottm GU27 .... 207 E6
Roehampton CE Prim Sch.
 Rhampt SW15 .... 19 B8
Roehampton Club Golf Course.
 Rhampt SW15 .... 7 F2
Roehampton Gate. Rhampt SW15 . 7 E1
Roehampton Gate Cty Prim Sch.
 Rhampt SW15 .... 7 E1
Roehampton High St.
 Putney SW15 .... 19 A8
Roehampton La.
 Putney SW15 & SW19 .... 19 A8
Roehampton La.
 Rhampt SW15 & SW19 .... 19 A8
Roehampton Vale.
 Rhampt SW15 .... 18 F5
Roehampton Vale.
 Rhampt SW15 .... 18 F6
Roffes La. Cater CR3 .... 100 D2
Roffey Cl. Horley RH6 .... 160 F3
Roffey Cl. Purley CR8 .... 80 B3
Roffey Cnr. Horsh RH12 .... 218 B4
Roffey's Cl. Copth RH10 .... 183 A4
Roffords. Woking GU21 .... 69 B2
Roger Simmons Ct. L Book KT23 94 A3
Rogers Cl. Cater CR3 .... 101 B5
Rogers Cl. Coulsd CR5 & CR8 .... 80 B1
Rogers La. Chelsh CR6 .... 81 F1
Rogers Mead. Godst RH9 .... 121 B3
Rogers Rd. Up Toot SW17 .... 20 E4
Rogosa Rd. W End GU24 .... 67 E6
Rojack Rd. For Hil SE23 .... 23 D7
Roke Cl. Purley CR8 .... 80 C5
Roke Cl. Witley GU8 .... 170 F5
Roke La. Witley GU8 .... 170 F5
Roke Lane Cotts. Witley GU8 ...... 170 F5
Roke Lodge Rd. Purley CR8 .... 80 B6
Roke Prim Sch. Purley CR8 .... 80 B5
Roke Rd. Purley CR8 .... 80 C5
Rokeby Cl. Brack RG12 .... 27 D6
Rokeby Ct. Knaph GU21 .... 68 D2
Rokeby House. 9 Balham SW12 .. 21 B8
Rokeby Pl. Wimble SW20 .... 19 B1
Rokeby Sch. King U T KT2 .... 18 C1
Rokell House. Catf BR3 .... 24 B3
Rokers La. Shackl GU8 .... 149 D7
Roland Ct. S Norw SE19 .... 42 F8
Roland Way. Worc Pk KT4 .... 57 F8
Rollesby Rd. Chess KT19 & KT9 ... 57 A4
Rolleston Rd. S Croy CR2 .... 61 D3
Rollit Cres. Hounsl TW3 .... 5 A2
Roman Cl. Felt TW14 .... 4 C2
Roman House. Woodh RH2 .... 138 C7
Roman Ind Est. Croy CR0 .... 42 E2
Roman Rd. Dork RH4 .... 136 B5
Roman Rise. S Norw SE19 .... 22 D2
Roman Way. Croy CR0 .... 61 B8
Roman Way. Farnh GU9 .... 125 C4
Roman Way. Thorn H CR9 .... 61 B8
Roman Way. Wink RG12 .... 27 F8
Romana Ct. Stain TW18 .... 13 A4
Romanby Ct. 1 Redh RH1 .... 139 F8
Romanhurst Ave. Beck BR2 .... 44 E5
Romanhurst Gdns.
 Beck BR2 & BR3 .... 44 E5
Romans Way. Pyrf GU22 .... 71 A4
Romany Gdns. Cheam SM3 .... 40 A2
Romany Prospect. W Norw SE19 22 D2
Romany The. Farnb GU14 .... 84 A1

Romayne Cl. W Heath GU14 .... 85 A5
Romberg Rd. Up Toot SW17 .... 21 A5
Romeo Hill. Wink RG12 .... 27 F8
Romeyn Rd. Streat SW16 .... 21 F5
Romley Ct. M Bourn GU9 .... 125 D1
Rommany Ct. W Norw SE27 .... 22 D4
Rommany Rd. W Norw SE27 .... 22 D4
Romney Cl. Ashf TW15 .... 14 C3
Romney Cl. Chess KT9 .... 56 E6
Romney House. Brack RG12 .... 27 E5
Romney Rd. Farnb GU14 .... 84 E1
Romney Rd. New Mal KT3 .... 38 D3
Romola Rd. Streat SE24 & SW2 .... 22 B7
Romsey Cl. Alder GU11 .... 126 C6
Romsey Cl. Blckw GU17 .... 64 C6
Romulus Ct. 6 Brent TW8 .... 6 D7
Rona Cl. Crawl RH11 .... 201 B3
Ronald Ross Prim Sch.
 Putney SW19 .... 19 E8
Ronelane Rd. Surb KT6 .... 56 F7
Ronneby Cl. Oat Pk KT13 .... 53 E7
Ronson Way. Leahd KT22 .... 95 A6
Ronver Rd. Lewish SE12 .... 24 F7
Rook La. Cater CR3 .... 100 B3
Rook Way. Horsh RH12 .... 217 F6
Rookeries Cl. Felt TW13 .... 15 C5
Rookery Cl. Fetch KT22 .... 94 E3
Rookery Dr. Westc RH4 .... 135 A5
Rookery Hill. Ashtd KT21 .... 76 A1
Rookery Hill. Outw RH1 & RH6 .. 162 B6
Rookery Rd. Stain TW18 .... 13 B3
Rookery The. Westc RH4 .... 135 A5
Rookery Way. L Kings KT20 .... 117 F8
Rookley Cl. Sutton SM2 .... 59 B2
Rooks Hill. Bramly GU5 .... 152 C2
Rooksmead Rd. Sunby TW16 .... 34 F7
Rookstone Rd. Up Toot SW17 .... 20 F3
Rookwood Ave. Sandh GU15 .... 45 E2
Rookwood Ave. N Barn KT3 .... 39 A5
Rookwood Ave. Wallin SM6 .... 60 D6
Rookwood Cl. Merst RH1 .... 119 B6
Rookwood Ct. Guild GU2 .... 130 C6
Rookwood Pk. Horsh RH12 .... 216 F3
Roothill La. Betch RH3 .... 137 A3
Roper House. 13
 Dulw SE19 & SE27 .... 22 E4
Roper Way. Mitch CR4 .... 41 A7
Ropers Wlk. 13 Streat SE24 .... 22 A8
Rorkes Drift. Mytch GU16 .... 86 A4
Rosa Ave. Ashf TW15 .... 14 A4
Rosalind Franklin Cl.
 Onsl V GU2 .... 129 E8
Rosamond St. For Hil SE26 .... 23 B5
Rosamund Cl. S Croy CR2 .... 61 D6
Rosamund Rd. Crawl RH10 .... 202 B3
Rosary Cl. Hounsl TW3 & TW5 .... 4 E5
Rosary Gdns. Ashf TW15 .... 14 A4
Rosary RC Inf Sch. Heston TW5 .... 5 A8
Rosary RC Jun Sch. Heston TW5 .. 5 A8
Rose Ave. Mitch CR4 .... 40 F8
Rose Ave. Morden SM4 .... 40 C4
Rose Bank Cotts. Westfd GU22 .... 89 E3
Rose Bushes. Nork KT17 .... 77 C3
Rose Cotts. Ent Gn GU8 .... 171 A2
Rose Cotts. Esher KT10 .... 55 D5
Rose Ct. 10 Wimble SW19 .... 19 F3
Rose Ct. Woki RG11 .... 25 C6
Rose End. N Cheam KT4 .... 39 D1
Rose Gdns. Farnb GU14 .... 84 E3
Rose Gdns. Felt TW13 .... 15 A6
Rose Gdns. Stan TW19 .... 13 D8
Rose Hill. Dork RH4 .... 136 B7
Rose Hill. Sutton SM1 & SM4 .... 40 B1
Rose Hill Pk W. Sutton SM1 .... 59 C8
Rose La. Ripley GU23 .... 91 B5
Rose St. Woki RG11 .... 25 C6
Rose View. Addl KT15 .... 52 C5
Rose Wlk. Purley CR8 .... 79 D8
Rose Wlk. Surb KT5 .... 38 B4
Rose Wlk. W Wick BR4 .... 63 D8
Rose Wood. Woking GU22 .... 90 A8
Roseacre. Oxted RH8 .... 123 A1
Roseacre Cl. Shep Gn TW17 .... 34 A4
Roseacre Gdns. Chil GU4 .... 131 F3
Rosebank. Epsom KT18 .... 76 C5
Rosebank. Penge SE20 .... 23 B1
Rosebank Cl. Tedd TW11 .... 17 A2
Rosebay. Woki RG11 .... 25 E8
Roseberry Pl.
 Lang V KT18 & KT21 .... 96 F5
Rosebery Ave. Epsom KT17 .... 76 E5
Rosebery Ave. King U T KT3 .... 38 F6
Rosebery Ave. S Norw CR7 .... 42 C7
Rosebery Cl. W Barn SM4 .... 39 D3
Rosebery Cres. Old Wok GU22 ..... 89 F7
Rosebery Gdns. Sutton SM1 .... 59 B6
Rosebery Rd. Cheam SM1 & SM2 . 58 F4
Rosebery Rd. Islew TW3 & TW7 ..... 5 C2
Rosebery Rd. King U T KT1 .... 38 B7
Rosebery Sch. Epsom KT18 .... 76 C5
Rosebery Sq. King U T KT1 .... 38 B7
Rosebine Ave. Twick TW2 .... 16 D8
Rosebriar Cl. Pyrf GU22 .... 71 A3
Rosebriars. Cater CR3 .... 100 E7
Rosebriars. Esher KT10 .... 55 C5
Rosebury Dr. Bisley GU24 .... 68 A4
Rosecourt Rd. Thorn H CR0 .... 41 F3
Rosecroft Cl. Bigg H TN16 .... 83 F1
Rosecroft Gdns. Twick TW2 .... 16 D7
Rosedale. Alder GU12 .... 105 C2
Rosedale. Ashtd KT21 .... 75 C1
Rosedale. Cater CR3 .... 100 E4
Rosedale Cl. Crawl RH11 .... 201 A4
Rosedale Gdns. Easth RG12 .... 27 A4
Rosedale Rd. N Cheam KT17 .... 58 E5
Rosedale Rd. Rich TW9 .... 6 E3
Rosedale Rd. Stonel KT17 .... 58 A5
Rosedene Ave. Morden SM4 .... 40 A4
Rosedene Ave. Streat SW16 .... 21 F5
Rosedene Ave. Thorn H CR0 .... 41 E2

Rosedene La. Sandh GU15 ...... 64 D7
Rosefield Cl. Carsh SM5 .... 59 E5
Rosefield Gdns. Ottsh KT16 ..... 51 D4
Rosefield Rd. Stain TW18 .... 13 A4
Roseheath Rd. Hounsl TW4 .... 4 F2
Rosehill. Clayg KT10 .... 56 A4
Rosehill. Hampt TW12 .... 36 A8
Rosehill Ave. Carsh SM1 and SM5 .. 40 C1
Rosehill Ave. Horse GU21 .... 69 C3
Rosehill Farm Meadow.
  Banstd SM7 .... 78 B4
Rosehill Gdns. Sutton SM1 .... 59 C8
Rosehill Rd. Bigg H TN16 .... 83 C2
Roseleigh Cl. 3 Twick TW1 .... 6 D1
Rosemary Ave. Ash V GU12 ...... 106 A8
Rosemary Ave. E Mole KT8 .... 36 A5
Rosemary Ave. Hounsl TW4 .... 4 D5
Rosemary Cl. Oxted RH8 .... 123 A2
Rosemary Cl. W Heath GU14 ...... 84 D4
Rosemary Cotts. Wimble SW19 .. 19 C1
Rosemary Cres. Stough GU2 ..... 109 A5
Rosemary Ct. Haslem GU27 ..... 208 C7
Rosemary Ct. Horley RH6 .... 160 E4
Rosemary Gdns. Blckw GU17 .... 64 D5
Rosemary Gdns. Mortl SW14 ...... 7 C4
Rosemary La. Alfold GU6 .... 212 E8
Rosemary La. Blckw GU17 .... 64 D5
Rosemary La. Charl RH6 .... 180 E7
Rosemary La. Egham TW20 .... 32 B6
Rosemary La. Horley RH6 .... 161 B3
Rosemary La. Mortl SW14 .... 7 C4
Rosemary Rd. Rowl GU10 .... 145 E4
Rosemary Rd. Wands SW17 ...... 20 C5
Rosemead. Chert KT16 .... 33 B2
Rosemead Ave. Felt TW13 .... 14 F6
Rosemead Ave.
  Mitch CR4 & SW16 .... 41 C7
Rosemead Cl. Woodh RH1 .... 139 D7
Rosemead Sch. W Norw SE27 .... 22 C6
Rosemont Rd. King U T KT3 ...... 38 C6
Rosemont Rd. Rich TW10 .... 6 E1
Rosemount. 5 Wallin SM6 .... 60 C4
Rosemount Par. W Byfl KT14 ..... 71 A6
Rosemount Par. W Byfl KT14 ..... 71 A6
Rosemount Point. 10
  For Hil SE23 .... 23 D5
Rosendale Infs Sch.
  W Norw SE21 .... 22 C8
Rosendale Jun Sch.
  W Norw SE21 .... 22 C8
Rosendale Rd.
  Streat SE21 & SE24 .... 22 C7
Rosendale Rd.
  W Norw SE21 & SE24 .... 22 C7
Roseneath Ct. Cater CR3 .... 101 A2
Roseneath Dr. Chidd GU8 .... 191 B4
Rosery The. Croy CR0 .... 43 D3
Roses Cotts. Dork RH4 .... 136 A7
Rosethorn Cl. Streat SW12 .... 21 D8
Rosetrees. Guild GU1 .... 131 A8
Rosetta Ct. S Norw SE19 .... 22 E1
Roseville Ave. Hounsl TW3 & TW4 . 5 A2
Rosevine Rd. Wimble SW20 ...... 39 C8
Rosewarne Cl. Woking GU21 ..... 69 A1
Rosewood Ct. King U T KT2 .... 18 A1
Rosewood Dr. Shep Gn TW17 .... 33 F4
Rosewood Gr. Sutton SM1 .... 59 C8
Rosewood Way. W End GU24 ...... 67 E6
Roskeen Ct. Wimble SW19 .... 19 C1
Roslan Ct. Horley RH6 .... 161 B2
Roslyn Cl. Mitch CR4 .... 40 D7
Ross Cl. Crawl RH10 .... 201 F3
Ross Ct. Croy CR2 .... 61 C4
Ross Ct. 4 Putney SW15 .... 19 D8
Ross House. Twick TW2 .... 16 B6
Ross Par. Wallin SM6 .... 60 B4
Ross Rd. Cobham KT11 .... 73 C6
Ross Rd. S Norw SE25 .... 42 E6
Ross Rd. Twick TW2 .... 16 C7
Ross Rd. Wallin SM6 .... 60 B4
Rossal Ct. Penge SE20 .... 23 B1
Rossdale. Carsh SM1 .... 59 E5
Rossendon Ct. 1 Wallin SM6 ..... 60 C4
Rossett Cl. Easth RG12 .... 27 B5
Rossetti Gdns. Coulsd CR5 .... 79 F1
Rossignol Gdns. Carsh SM5 ...... 60 A8
Rossindel Rd. Hounsl TW3 .... 5 A2
Rossiter Lodge. Guild GU1 ...... 131 A8
Rossiter Rd. Balham SW12 .... 21 B7
Rosslyn Ave. Felt TW14 .... 4 A1
Rosslyn Ave. Mortl SW13 & SW14 . 7 F4
Rosslyn Cl. Ashf TW16 .... 14 E2
Rosslyn Cl. Coney H BR4 .... 63 F7
Rosslyn House. 8 Rich TW9 .... 6 F6
Rosslyn Pk. Oat Pk KT13 .... 53 D6
Rosslyn Rd. Twick TW1 .... 6 C1
Rossmore Ct. Crawl RH10 .... 182 D2
Rossmore Gdns. Alder GU11 .... 104 F1
Rosswood Gdns. Wallin SM6 ..... 60 C4
Rostella Rd. Up Toot SW17 .... 20 D4
Rostrevor Rd. Wimble SW19 ...... 20 A3
Rothbury Gdns. Hounsl TW7 .... 6 A7
Rothbury Wlk. Friml GU15 .... 66 C4
Rother Cl. Sandh GU17 .... 64 C8
Rother Cres. Crawl RH11 .... 200 F5
Rother House. 4 Redh RH1 ...... 118 F2
Rother Rd. W Heath GU14 .... 84 E7
Rotherfield Ave. Woki RG11 ...... 25 A7
Rotherfield Rd. Wallin SM5 .... 60 A5
Rotherhill Ave. Streat SW16 ..... 21 D2
Rothermere Rd. Croy CR0 .... 60 F5
Rothervale. Horley RH6 .... 160 F5
Rotherwick Ct. Farnb GU14 ..... 105 C8
Rotherwood Cl.
  Wimble SW19 & SW20 .... 39 E8
Rothes Rd. Dork RH4 .... 136 B8
Rothesay Ave. Merton SW20 ..... 39 E7
Rothesay Ave. Mortl SW14 & TW10 7 B3
Rothesay Rd. S Norw SE25 .... 42 E5
Rothschild St. W Norw SE27 ...... 22 C4
Rothwell House. Crowth RG11 .... 45 C4

Rothwell House. Heston TW5 .... 5 A8
Rotunda Est The. Alder GU11 ... 105 B2
Rougemont Ave. Morden SM4 .... 40 A3
Rough Field. E Grins RH19 .... 185 D4
Rough Rd. Woking GU22 .... 88 C5
Rough Rew. Dork RH4 & RH5 .... 136 A4
Rough Way. Horsh RH12 .... 217 F5
Roughets La. Bletch RH1 .... 120 E6
Roughlands. Pyrf GU22 .... 70 E4
Round Gr. Croy CR0 .... 43 D2
Round Hill. For Hil SE23 .... 23 C5
Round Oak Rd. Wey KT13 .... 52 F6
Roundabout Cotts. Rudg RH12 .. 214 C5
Roundacre. Putney SW19 .... 19 D6
Roundals La. Hambl GU8 .... 191 E8
Roundell House. 14
  Dulw SE19 & SE21 .... 22 E4
Roundhay Cl. For Hil SE23 .... 23 D6
Roundhill. Mayb GU22 .... 90 B8
Roundhill Dr. Mayb GU22 .... 70 B1
Roundhill Way. Oxsh KT11 .... 74 B7
Roundhill Way. Stough GU2 ..... 108 F1
Roundshaw Ctr. Wallin SM6 ...... 60 E3
Roundtable Rd. Catf BR1 .... 24 F5
Roundthorn Way. Woking GU21 .. 68 F3
Roundway. Bigg H TN16 .... 83 D4
Roundway. Egham TW20 .... 12 C3
Roundway. Friml GU15 .... 66 C6
Roundway Cl. Friml GU15 .... 66 C6
Roundway Ct. Crawl RH11 .... 201 D8
Roundway The. Clayg KT10 .... 55 F4
Roundwood View. Nork SM7 ..... 77 D4
Roundwood Way. Nork SM7 ...... 77 D4
Roupell House. 1 King U T KT2 .. 17 F1
Roupell Rd. Streat SW2 .... 21 F7
Rouse Gdns. Dulw SE21 .... 22 E4
Routh Ct. E Bed TW14 .... 14 D7
Routh Rd. Wands SW18 .... 20 E8
Row Hill. Row Tn KT15 .... 51 F4
Row La. Farl Gn GU5 .... 153 E5
Row The. Lingf RH7 .... 164 D4
Row Town. Row Tn KT15 .... 51 F3
Rowallan Ct. Catf SE6 .... 24 F7
Rowan. 2 Brack RG12 .... 27 F4
Rowan Ave. Egham TW20 .... 12 C3
Rowan Chase. Rowl GU10 .... 146 A5
Rowan Cl. Bellf GU1 .... 109 C4
Rowan Cl. Camb GU15 .... 65 F8
Rowan Cl. Crawl RH10 .... 201 F6
Rowan Cl. Horsh RH12 .... 218 B5
Rowan Cl. King U T KT3 .... 38 E7
Rowan Cl. Mitch SW16 .... 41 C8
Rowan Cl. Woodh RH2 .... 139 C7
Rowan Cres. Mitch SW16 .... 41 C8
Rowan Ct. For Hil SE26 .... 23 C4
Rowan Ct. 11 King U T KT2 .... 18 A1
Rowan Ct. Wimble SW20 .... 39 B7
Rowan Dr. Crowth RG11 .... 45 C6
Rowan Gdns. S Croy CR0 .... 61 F7
Rowan Gn. Oat Pk KT13 .... 53 D6
Rowan Gr. Hooley CR5 .... 99 B6
Rowan High Sch. Mitch SW16 ... 41 C7
Rowan Prep Sch. Clayg KT10 .... 55 F3
Rowan Rd. Brent TW8 .... 6 B7
Rowan Rd. Mitch SW16 .... 41 C7
Rowan Way. Horsh RH12 .... 218 C5
Rowans Cl. W Heath GU14 .... 64 E1
Rowans Cl. W Heath GU14 .... 84 E8
Rowans The. Ashf TW16 .... 14 F3
Rowans The. Graysh GU26 ...... 188 D2
Rowans The. 3 Woking GU22 ..... 69 E1
Rowanside Cl. Head Dn GU35 ... 187 C4
Rowbarns Way. E Hors KT24 .... 112 F5
Rowbury. Farnc GU7 .... 151 A7
Rowcroft. Ash V GU12 .... 106 A6
Rowden Rd. Penge BR3 .... 43 F8
Rowden Rd. W Ewell KT19 .... 57 C6
Rowden Rd. W Ewell KT19 .... 57 C6
Rowdown Cres. New Add CR0 .... 63 E2
Rowdown Inf & Jun Schs.
  New Add CR0 .... 63 D1
Rowe La. Pirb GU24 .... 88 A3
Rowena House. Crawl RH11 ..... 181 D1
Rowfant Bsns Ctr. Worth RH10 . 203 E6
Rowfant Rd.
  Up Toot SW12 & SW17 .... 21 A6
Rowhill Ave. Alder GU11 .... 125 F8
Rowhill Cres. Alder GU11 .... 125 F8
Rowhills. Heath E GU9 .... 125 E8
Rowhills Cl. Heath E GU9 .... 125 F7
Rowhook Hill. Warn RH12 .... 215 F8
Rowhook Rd. Rowhk RH12 ...... 196 E1
Rowhook Rd. Slinfd RH12 .... 216 A8
Rowhurst Ave. Addl KT15 .... 52 B4
Rowland Cl. Burst RH10 .... 183 E5
Rowland Gr. For Hil SE26 .... 23 B5
Rowland Hill Almshouses.
  Ashf TW15 .... 14 A3
Rowland Rd. Cran GU6 .... 174 D3
Rowland Way. Littlt TW15 .... 14 D1
Rowland Way. Merton SW19 ..... 40 B8
Rowlands Rd. Horsh RH12 ...... 218 A6
Rowledge CE (VC) Prim Sch.
  Binst GU10 .... 145 E3
Rowley Cl. Brack RG12 .... 27 E6
Rowley Cl. Pyrf GU22 .... 71 B3
Rowley Ct. Cater CR3 .... 100 C5
Rowlls Rd. King U T KT1 .... 37 F6
Rowly Dr. Rowly GU6 .... 174 A6
Rowly Edge. Rowly GU6 .... 174 A6
Rowntree Rd. Twick TW2 .... 16 E7
Rowplatt La. Felb RH19 .... 184 E4
Roxbee Cox Rd. Farnb GU14 .... 84 A1
Roxborough Ave. Hounsl TW7 ... 5 F7
Roxburgh Cl. Friml GU15 .... 66 C4
Roxburgh Rd. W Norw SE27 ..... 22 B3
Roxeth Ct. Ashf TW15 .... 14 A3
Roxford Cl. Up Hall TW17 .... 34 E4
Roxton Gdns. Add CR0 .... 63 A5
Roy Gr. Hampt TW12 .... 16 B2

Royal Alexandra & Albert Sch The.
  Gatton RH2 .... 118 E6
Royal Ascot Golf Club.
  Ascot SL5 .... 29 B7
Royal Ave. Worc Pk KT4 .... 57 E8
Royal Cir. W Norw SE27 .... 22 B5
Royal Cl. Worc Pk KT4 .... 57 E8
Royal Cl. 9 King U T KT2 .... 18 B1
Royal Dr. Burgh H KT18 .... 77 B1
Royal Dr. Burgh H KT18 & KT20 .. 97 B8
Royal Earlswood Hospl.
  Earls RH1 .... 140 A6
Royal Grammar Sch.
  Guild GU1 .... 130 D8
Royal Holloway Univ of London.
  Eng Gn TW20 .... 11 D2
Royal Horticultural Society Cotts.
  Wisley GU23 & KT14 .... 71 E3
Royal Horticultural Society's
  Garden. Wisley GU23 .... 71 E1
Royal Hospl. Putney SW19 .... 19 E8
Royal Hospl. Rich TW10 .... 17 C7
Royal Kent Sch The. Oxsh KT22 74 C5
Royal Marsden Hospl (Surrey
  Branch) The. Sutton SM2 .... 59 C1
Royal Mews. Hampt KT8 .... 36 E6
Royal Mid-Surrey Golf Club.
  Rich TW9 .... 6 D4
Royal Military Acad.
  Sandh GU15 .... 64 F6
Royal Military Acad Hospl.
  Sandh GU15 .... 65 A8
Royal Military Sch of Music
  (Kneller Hall). Twick TW2 .... 5 D1
Royal Naval Sch. Shottm GU27 . 189 A2
Royal Oak Ctr The. S Croy CR2 .. 61 C1
Royal Oak Hse. Crawl D RH10 .. 204 B7
Royal Oak Rd. Woking GU21 ..... 69 D1
Royal Orchard Ct. Putney SW18 . 19 E8
Royal Rd. Tedd TW11 .... 16 D3
Royal Russell Sch (Ballards).
  S Croy CR0 .... 62 B5
Royal Sch for the Blind.
  Leahd KT22 .... 95 C5
Royal School. Old W SL4 .... 10 C4
Royal Surrey Cty Hospl.
  Onsl V GU2 .... 129 E8
Royal Surrey Cty Hospl.
  Stough GU2 .... 108 E1
Royal Victoria Gdns. Ascot SL5 . 29 A4
Royal Way The. Friml GU16 .... 86 D7
Royal Wimbledon Golf Course.
  Wimble SW19 .... 19 B2
Royal Wlk. Hackb SM6 .... 60 B7
Royale Cl. Alder GU11 .... 126 C8
Royals The. Guild GU1 .... 130 E8
Royce Rd. Crawl RH10 .... 182 A3
Roycroft Cl. Streat SW2 .... 22 A7
Roydon Ct. Hersh KT12 .... 54 A6
Roydon Lodge. Addl KT15 .... 52 D7
Roymount Ct. Twick TW2 .... 16 E5
Royston Ave. Byfl KT14 .... 71 E7
Royston Ave. Carsh SM1 .... 59 D7
Royston Ave. Wallin SM6 .... 60 D6
Royston Cl. Cranf TW5 .... 4 B6
Royston Cl. Crawl RH10 .... 182 A2
Royston Cl. Walt O T KT12 .... 35 A1
Royston Ct. 3 Rich TW9 .... 6 F6
Royston Ct. Tolw KT5 .... 38 B4
Royston Prim Sch. Penge SE20 . 43 D8
Royston Rd. Byfl KT14 .... 71 E7
Royston Rd. Penge BR3 & SE20 .. 43 D8
Royston Rd. Rich TW10 .... 6 E2
Roystons The. Surb KT5 .... 38 B4
Rozeldene. Hind GU26 .... 188 E3
Rubens St. For Hil SE6 .... 23 F6
Rubus Cl. W End GU24 .... 67 E6
Ruckmans La. Ockley RH5 ...... 197 B7
Rudd Hall Rise. Camb GU15 ...... 65 E4
Ruden Way. Nork KT17 .... 77 B4
Rudge Rise. Row Tn KT15 .... 51 F5
Rudgwick Cty Prim Sch.
  Rudg RH12 .... 214 D7
Rudgwick Rd. Crawl RH11 ...... 200 F7
Rudloe Rd. Streat SW12 .... 21 C8
Rudolph Ct. Dulw SE22 .... 23 B8
Rudsworth Cl. Coln SL3 .... 1 D7
Ruffetts Cl. S Croy CR2 .... 62 B3
Ruffetts The. S Croy CR2 .... 62 B3
Ruffetts Way. Burgh H KT20 ...... 77 E1
Rufus Bsns Ctr. Wimble SW18 .. 20 B6
Rufwood. Crawl D RH10 .... 204 A8
Rugby Cl. Sandh GU15 .... 45 E1
Rugby La. E Ewell SM2 .... 58 D2
Rugby Rd.
  Twick TW1 & TW2 & TW7 .... 5 E1
Ruggles-Brise Rd. Ashf TW15 ... 13 D3
Ruislip St. Up Toot SW17 .... 20 F4
Rumsey Cl. Hampt TW12 .... 15 F2
Runcorn Cl. Crawl RH11 .... 200 E2
Runes Cl. Mitch CR4 .... 40 E5
Runnemede Rd. Egham TW20 ... 12 A4
Running Horse Yd. 12
  Brent TW8 .... 6 E8
Runnymede Ctr The.
  Chert KT15 .... 52 B8
Runnymede. Mitch SW19 .... 40 D8
Runnymede Cl. Twick TW2 .... 16 B8
Runnymede Cotts. Poyle TW19 . 12 D7
Runnymede Cres. Streat SW16 .. 41 E8
Runnymede Ct. Egham TW20 ... 12 A4
Runnymede Ct. W Heath GU14 .. 85 A7
Runnymede Ct. 1 Wallin SM6 .... 60 B4
Runnymede Gdns. Twick TW2 ... 16 B8
Runnymede Hospl The.
  Addl KT16 .... 51 D7
Runnymede Rd. Twick TW2 .... 5 B1
Runnymede Rdbt. Egham TW20 . 12 B4
Runshooke Ct. 10 Crawl RH11 . 201 A3
Runtley Wood La. Westfd GU4 ... 89 F2
Runwick La. Farnh GU10 .... 124 C1

Rupert Rd. Guild GU2 .... 130 E7
Rural Life Centre. Tilf GU10 .... 146 F3
Rural Way. Earls RH1 .... 119 A1
Rural Way. Mitch SW16 .... 21 B1
Ruscoe Dr. Woking GU22 .... 70 A2
Ruscoe House. 12
  W Norw SW27 .... 22 B3
Ruscombe Way. E Bed TW14 .... 14 F8
Rush Croft. Farnc GU7 .... 151 A8
Rush The. Merton SW20 .... 39 F8
Rusham Park Ave. Egham TW20 12 A2
Rusham Rd. Balham SW12 .... 20 F8
Rusham Rd. Egham TW20 .... 11 F2
Rushams Rd. Horsh RH12 .... 217 B3
Rushbury Ct. 6 Hampt TW12 ..... 36 A8
Rushden Cl. S Norw SE19 .... 22 D1
Rushden Way. Heath E GU9 .... 125 D7
Rushdene Wlk. Bigg H TN16 ..... 83 D2
Rushen Wlk. Carsh SM5 .... 40 D1
Rushett Cl. Thame D KT7 .... 37 B1
Rushett Dr. Dork RH4 .... 136 C4
Rushett La. Chess KT9 .... 75 D7
Rushett Rd. Thame D KT7 .... 37 B2
Rushetts Pl. Crawl RH11 .... 181 C1
Rushetts Rd. Crawl RH11 .... 181 B1
Rushetts Rd. Dovgn RH1 & RH2 . 139 C5
Rushey Cl. New Mal KT3 .... 38 D5
Rushey Gn. Lewish SE6 .... 24 B8
Rushey Green Prim Sch.
  Catf SE6 .... 24 B7
Rushfords. Lingf RH7 .... 164 E5
Rushmead. Rich TW10 .... 17 B5
Rushmead Cl. S Croy CR0 .... 61 F6
Rushmere Cl. Worc Pk KT4 .... 58 A8
Rushmere House. 2
  Rhampt SW15 .... 19 A7
Rushmere Pl. Wimble SW19 ..... 19 D3
Rushmon Gdns. Walt O T KT12 .. 54 B7
Rushmon Pl. Cheam SM3 .... 58 E4
Rushmoor Cl. Stough GU2 ..... 108 F5
Rushmoor Independant Sch.
  Farnb GU14 .... 85 C1
Rushmoor Rd. Alder GU11 ...... 104 E4
Rusholme Gr. S Norw SE19 ...... 22 E3
Rushton Ave. S Godst RH9 ...... 142 D5
Rushworth Rd. Reig RH2 .... 118 B2
Rushy House. Brack RG12 .... 27 E5
Rushy Meadow La. Carsh SM5 .. 59 E7
Rushy Meadow Prim Sch.
  Carsh SM5 .... 59 E7
Ruskin Ave. Felt TW14 .... 3 F1
Ruskin Ave. Rich TW9 .... 7 A7
Ruskin Cl. Crawl RH10 .... 182 C1
Ruskin Dr. N Cheam KT4 .... 58 C8
Ruskin Par. Croy CR0 .... 61 D5
Ruskin Rd. Croy CR0 & CR9 ...... 61 B8
Ruskin Rd. Isiew TW7 .... 5 F4
Ruskin Rd. Stain TW18 .... 12 F2
Ruskin Rd. Wallin SM5 .... 60 A5
Ruskin Way. Mitch SW19 .... 40 D8
Rusper Cl. Coulsd CR5 .... 79 D3
Rusper Cty Prim Sch.
  Rusper RH12 .... 199 C7
Rusper Rd. Capel RH5 .... 178 D2
Rusper Rd. Crawl RH11 .... 200 E6
Rusper Rd. Faygt RH12 .... 199 A1
Rusper Rd. Horsh RH12 .... 217 F6
Rusper Rd. Lamb Gn RH11 ...... 200 D7
Rusper Rd. Newd RH12 & RH5 .. 179 C4
Rusper Rd.
  Rusper RH11 & RH12 .... 200 D7
Ruspers Keep. Crawl RH11 ...... 200 F7
Russ Hill. Charl RH5 & RH6 ..... 180 C5
Russel Cl. Beck BR3 .... 44 C6
Russell Cl. Hounsl TW4 .... 4 C3
Russell Cl. Walt o t h KT20 .... 97 A2
Russell Ct. Bellf GU1 .... 109 C4
Russell Ct. Blckw GU17 .... 64 D5
Russell Ct. Broml BR1 .... 24 F1
Russell Ct. Hind GU26 .... 188 F4
Russell Ct. Leahd KT22 .... 95 B5
Russell Ct. Streat SW16 .... 21 F3
Russell Ct. Surb KT6 .... 37 E2
Russell Ct. Wallin SM6 .... 60 C5
Russell Dr. Stan TW19 .... 2 D1
Russell Gdns. Harm UB7 .... 3 A8
Russell Gdns. Rich TW10 .... 17 C6
Russell Green Cl. Purley CR8 .... 61 A1
Russell Hill. Wallin CR8 .... 60 F1
Russell Hill Par. 4 Purley CR8 .. 80 A8
Russell Hill Pl. Purley CR8 .... 80 A8
Russell Hill Rd. Purley CR8 .... 80 A8
Russell Kerr Cl. Chisw W4 .... 7 C7
Russell Par. 3 Purley CR8 .... 80 A8
Russell Prim Sch The.
  Rich TW10 .... 17 D7
Russell Rd. Horse GU21 .... 69 C4
Russell Rd. Lo Hall TW17 .... 34 C2
Russell Rd. Merton SW19 .... 20 A1
Russell Rd. Mitch CR4 .... 40 E6
Russell Rd. Twick TW1 & TW2 ... 35 A3
Russell Sch The. Rich TW10 ..... 17 D6
Russell Way. Crawl RH10 .... 202 A5
Russell Way. Sutton SM1 .... 59 B5
Russell Wlk. 4 Rich TW10 .... 6 F1
Russells. Tadw KT20 .... 97 D5
Russells Cres. Horley RH6 ...... 161 A2
Russet Ave. Sunby TW16 & TW17 34 E6
Russet Cl. Hersh KT12 .... 54 E7
Russet Cl. Horley RH6 .... 161 C3
Russet Cl. Stan TW19 .... 1 F1
Russet Cl. Tongh GU10 .... 126 E7
Russet Dr. Croy CR0 .... 43 E1
Russet Gdns. Camb GU15 .... 65 D3
Russet Glade. Alder GU11 ...... 125 E8
Russet Way. Dork RH5 .... 136 D4
Russets. Tadw KT20 .... 97 C4
Russett Ct. Cater CR3 .... 101 A2
Russetts Cl. Horse GU21 .... 69 F4
Russington Rd. Shep TW17 ...... 34 D3

Russley Gn. Woki RG11 .... 25 A1
Rusthall Cl. Croy CR0 .... 43 C3
Rustic Ave. Mitch SW16 .... 21 B1
Rustington Wlk. Morden SM4 ... 39 F2
Ruston Ave. Tolw KT5 .... 38 B2
Ruston Way. N Asct SL5 .... 28 E7
Rutford Rd. Streat SW16 .... 21 E3
Ruth Cl. W Heath GU14 .... 84 C5
Ruthen Cl. Epsom KT18 .... 76 B5
Rutherford Cl. Sutton SM2 .... 59 D4
Rutherford Way. Crawl RH10 ... 182 A3
Rutherwick Cl. Horley RH6 ...... 160 F3
Rutherwick Rise. Coulsd CR5 ... 79 E3
Rutherwyke Cl. Chert KT16 ...... 32 E2
Rutherwyke Cl. Stonel KT17 ..... 58 A4
Rutland Cl. Alder GU11 .... 105 A3
Rutland Cl. Epsom KT19 .... 57 D1
Rutland Cl. Mitch SW19 .... 20 E1
Rutland Cl. Mortl SW14 .... 7 C4
Rutland Cl. Redh RH1 .... 118 F2
Rutland Dr. Morden SM4 .... 40 A2
Rutland Dr. Rich TW10 .... 17 E7
Rutland Gate. Hayes BR2 .... 44 F5
Rutland Gdns. S Croy CR0 .... 61 E6
Rutland Lodge. For Hil SE6 .... 23 F6
Rutland Pk. For Hil SE6 .... 23 F6
Rutland Rd. Mitch SW19 .... 20 E1
Rutland Rd. Twick TW2 .... 16 D6
Rutland Terr. Alder GU11 .... 105 A3
Rutland Wlk. For Hil SE6 .... 23 F6
Rutlish Rd. Merton SW19 .... 40 A8
Rutlish Sch (Boys).
  Merton SW20 .... 39 F7
Rutson Rd. Byfl KT14 .... 71 F5
Rutter Gdns. Mitch CR4 & SW19 . 40 D5
Rutton Hill Rd. Bowl Gn GU8 ... 189 E8
Ruxbury Ct. Ashf TW15 .... 13 E5
Ruxbury Rd. Chert KT16 .... 32 D3
Ruxley Cl. W Ewell KT19 .... 57 B5
Ruxley Cl. W Ewell KT19 .... 57 B5
Ruxley Cres. Clayg KT10 .... 56 B3
Ruxley Ct. W Ewell KT19 .... 57 C5
Ruxley Ct. W Ewell KT19 .... 57 C5
Ruxley La. W Ewell KT19 .... 57 C5
Ruxley La. W Ewell KT19 .... 57 C5
Ruxley Mews. W Ewell KT19 ..... 57 B5
Ruxley Mews. W Ewell KT19 ..... 57 B5
Ruxley Ridge. Clayg KT10 .... 56 A3
Ryan Ct. Streat SW16 .... 21 E1
Ryan Dr. Brent TW8 .... 6 A8
Ryan Mount. Sandh GU17 .... 64 A8
Rycott Path. Dulw SE22 .... 23 A8
Rydal Cl. Crawl RH11 .... 200 D4
Rydal Cl. Farnb GU14 .... 84 D3
Rydal Cl. Friml GU15 .... 66 D5
Rydal Cl. Sander CR8 .... 80 D6
Rydal Dr. W Wick BR4 .... 63 E8
Rydal Gdns. King U T SW15 .... 18 E3
Rydal Gdns. Twick SW2 & TW3 .... 5 B1
Rydal Pl. Lhtwat GU18 .... 67 B8
Rydal Rd. Streat SW16 .... 21 D4
Rydal Way. Thor L TW20 .... 12 B1
Ryde Cl. Ripley GU23 .... 91 C6
Ryde Ct. Alder GU12 .... 105 C1
Ryde Heron. Knaph GU21 .... 68 E2
Ryde Lands. Cran GU6 .... 174 F4
Ryde Pl. Twick TW1 .... 6 D1
Ryde The. Stain TW18 .... 33 B8
Ryde Vale Rd. Up Toot SW12 .... 21 C6
Ryde's Hill Cres.
  Stough GU2 & GU3 .... 108 F5
Ryde's Hill Rd.
  Stough GU2 & GU3 .... 108 F4
Rydens Ave. Walt O T KT12 .... 54 C8
Rydens Cl. Walt O T KT12 .... 54 C8
Rydens Gr. Hersh KT12 .... 54 D6
Rydens Pk. Walt O T KT12 .... 54 D8
Rydens Rd. Walt O T KT12 .... 54 C8
Rydens Sch. Hersh KT12 .... 54 C6
Rydens Way. Old Wok GU22 ..... 90 A7
Ryder House. 5 Merton SW19 ... 40 B8
Ryders Way. Horsh RH12 .... 217 F7
Rydes Ave. Stough GU2 .... 108 F4
Rydes Hill Prep Sch.
  Stough GU2 .... 108 F3
Rydon's La. Coulsd CR3 & CR5 . 100 C7
Rydon's Wood Cl.
  Coulsd CR3 & CR5 .... 100 C7
Rye Ash. Crawl RH10 .... 202 A7
Rye Brook Rd. Leahd KT22 .... 75 A1
Rye Cl. Stough GU2 .... 108 E3
Rye Cl. W Heath GU14 .... 84 E7
Rye Cl. Wink RG12 .... 27 D8
Rye Ct. Beck BR3 .... 43 F8
Rye Gr. Windl GU24 .... 48 F2
Ryebridge Cl. Leahd KT22 .... 75 A1
Ryebrook Bsns Pk. Leahd KT22 . 95 A7
Ryecotes Mead. Dulw SE21 ...... 22 E7
Ryecroft Ave. Twick TW2 .... 16 B7
Ryecroft Dr. Horsh RH12 .... 217 A3
Ryecroft Gdns. Blckw GU17 ..... 64 E4
Ryecroft Rd. S Norw SW16 .... 22 A2
Ryedale Ct. 8 Hampt TW12 .... 36 A8
Ryefield Path. 7 Rhampt SW15 . 19 A7
Ryefield Rd. S Norw SE19 .... 22 C2
Ryehill Ct. New Mal KT3 .... 38 F2
Ryelands. Crawl RH11 .... 201 A5
Ryelands. Horley RH6 .... 161 C4
Ryelands Cl. Cater CR3 .... 100 E6
Ryelands Ct. Leahd KT22 .... 75 A1
Ryelands Inf Sch. S Croy SE25 .. 43 B4
Ryelands Pl. Oat Pk KT13 .... 53 E7
Ryemead La. Wink RG12 & SL4 .... 8 B7
Ryersh La. Bear Gn RH5 .... 178 C8
Ryfold Rd. Wimble SW19 .... 20 A5
Ryland Cl. Felt TW13 .... 14 F4
Ryland House. 11 Streat SW16 .. 21 C3
Rylandes Rd. S Croy CR2 .... 62 B1

Ryle Rd. M Bourn GU9 146 B8
Rylton House. Walt O T KT12 35 A1
Rymer Rd. Croy CR0 42 E2
Rythe Ct. Thame D KT7 37 A2
Rythe House. Catf BR1 24 D3
Rythe Rd. Esher KT10 55 E5

Sabah Ct. Ashf TW15 14 A4
Sable Cl. Hounsl TW4 4 C4
Sable Ct. 3 New Mal KT3 38 E4
Sabre Ct. Alder GU11 104 E2
Sachel Court Rd. Alfold GU6 & GU8 193 D3
Sackville Cl. E Grins RH19 185 C3
Sackville Coll. E Grins RH19 185 F1
Sackville Cotts. Bletch RH1 120 D1
Sackville Ct. 3 E Grins RH19 205 F8
Sackville Gdns. E Grins RH19 185 C3
Sackville House. 16 Streat SW16 21 E5
Sackville La. E Grins RH19 185 C3
Sackville Rd. Belm SM2 59 A3
Sackville Sch. E Grins RH19 186 A1
Sacred Heart Catholic Prim Sch. W Barn KT3 39 A5
Sacred Heart Coll. Sunnin SL5 30 C3
Sacred Heart RC Prim Sch. Tedd TW11 17 B1
Saddleback Rd. Camb GU15 65 E8
Saddlebrook Pk. Ashf TW16 14 E1
Saddler Row. Crawl RH10 201 D3
Saddlers Cl. Merrow GU1 110 D2
Saddlers Scarp. Graysh GU26 188 A4
Saddlers Way. Lang V KT18 96 D8
Saddlewood. Camb GU15 65 C4
Sadler Cl. Mitch CR4 40 F7
Sadlers Ride. E Mole KT8 36 C7
Saffron Cl. Crawl RH11 201 A3
Saffron Ct. W Heath GU14 84 C4
Saffron Platt. Stough GU2 109 A5
Saffron Rd. Easth RG12 27 B5
Saffron Way. Surb KT6 37 D1
Sailors La. Thursl GU8 169 A2
Sainfoin Rd. Up Toot SW17 21 A6
Sainsbury Ctr The. Chert KT16 33 A2
Sainsbury Rd. W Norw SE19 22 E3
Saint Hill Rd. E Grins RH19 205 C5
Saints Cl. W Norw SE27 22 B4
SS Peter & Paul's RC Prim Sch. Mitch CR4 40 F5
St Agatha's Dr. King U T KT2 17 F2
St Agatha's Gr. Carsh CR4 & SM5 40 F1
St Agatha's RC Prim Sch. King U T KT2 17 F2
St Agatha's RC Sch. King U T KT2 17 F1
St Agnes Rd. E Grins RH19 185 E2
St Aidan's RC Prim Sch. Coulsd CR5 79 C3
St Alban's Gdns. Tedd TW11 17 A3
St Alban's Gr. Carsh SM5 40 E2
St Alban's RC Prim Sch. E Mole KT8 36 C4
St Alban's Rd. Reig RH2 118 A3
St Alban's Rdbt. Farnb GU14 105 C7
St Albans Ave. Felt TW13 15 D3
St Albans Ave. Weyb KT13 53 A7
St Albans Cl. Wood S V GU3 108 B2
St Albans House. 2 Streat SW16 22 A4
St Albans Rd. Cheam SM1 58 F6
St Albans Rd. King U T KT2 17 E2
St Amunds Cl. Catf SE6 24 A4
St Andrew's C of E Fst & Mid Sch. Crawl RH10 202 A4
St Andrew's C of E Sec Sch. Cobham KT11 73 C6
St Andrew's C of E Sec Sch. Croy CR0 61 B6
St Andrew's CE (VC) Inf Sch. Farnh GU9 125 B2
St Andrew's Cl. 2 Hounsl TW7 5 E6
St Andrew's Cl. Reig RH2 139 B8
St Andrew's Cl. Up Hall TW17 34 D5
St Andrew's Cl. Wray TW19 11 E8
St Andrew's Ct. Wands SW18 20 C6
St Andrew's RC Sch. Ashtd KT22 95 D7
St Andrew's RC Sch The Grange. Ashtd KT22 95 D7
St Andrew's Rd. Coulsd CR5 79 B4
St Andrew's Rd. 3 Croy CR0 & CR9 61 C6
St Andrew's Rd. King U T KT6 37 D3
St Andrew's Sch. Horse GU21 69 D3
St Andrew's Sq. King U T KT6 37 D3
St Andrew's & St Mark's Sch. King U T KT6 37 D4
St Andrew's Way. Friml GU16 85 F7
St Andrew's Wlk. Cobham KT11 73 B4
St Andrews. Cran GU6 174 B4
St Andrews. Easth RG12 26 E3
St Andrews Cl. Horse GU21 69 C2
St Andrews Ct. Ascot SL5 29 C4
St Andrews Ct. Chisw W4 7 C6
St Andrews RC Prim Sch. Streat SW16 21 E3
St Andrews Rd. Carsh SM5 59 E7
St Andrews Rd. Crawl RH11 200 D5
St Andrews Way. The Char RH8 123 F4
St Ann's Cl. Chert KT16 32 F3
St Ann's Heath Cty Mid Sch. Thorpe GU25 31 E4
St Ann's Hill. Wands SW18 20 C8
St Ann's Hill Rd. Chert KT16 32 D3
St Ann's Rd. Chert KT16 32 F3
St Ann's Sch. Morden SM4 40 B4
St Ann's Way. Croy CR2 61 B4
St Anne's Ave. Stan TW19 13 D8
St Anne's Dr. Redh RH1 119 A2
St Anne's Prim Sch. Stan TW19 13 E8
St Anne's RC Prim Sch. Chert KT16 33 A1
St Anne's RC (VA) Prim Sch. Banstd SM7 78 A3
St Anne's Rd. Crawl RH10 182 C2
St Anne's Rd. Godal GU7 151 A5
St Annes Glade. Bagsh GU19 47 D3
St Annes Mount. 7 Redh RH1 119 A2
St Annes Rise. Redh RH1 119 A2
St Annes Way. 5 Redh RH1 119 A2
St Anns Rd. Barnes SW13 7 F6
St Anselm's Ct. Streat SW16 21 E3
St Anselm's RC Prim Sch. Up Toot SW17 21 A5
St Anthony's Ct. 1 Balham SW12 21 A8
St Anthony's Ct. Up Toot SW17 21 A6
St Anthony's Hospl. N Cheam KT4 39 D1
St Anthony's Way. Hatton TW14 3 F3
St Anthonys Cl. Brack RG12 27 A8
St Anthonys Cl. Up Toot SW17 20 E6
St Antony's RC Prim Sch. Penge SE20 43 B8
St Arvans Cl. S Croy CR0 61 E7
St Aubin Cl. Crawl RH11 200 F2
St Aubyn's Ave. Hounsl TW3 & TW4 5 A2
St Aubyn's Ave. Wimble SW19 19 F3
St Aubyn's Ct. Wimble SW19 19 E2
St Aubyn's Rd. S Norw SE19 22 F2
St Augustine's Ave. Croy CR2 61 C3
St Augustine's Ave. S Croy CR2 61 C3
St Augustine's Cl. Alder GU12 105 D1
St Augustines Ct. Penge BR3 43 E7
St Augustines's RC Prim Sch. Catf SE6 24 C3
St Austins. Graysh GU26 188 D3
St Barnabas Cl. Beck BR3 44 C7
St Barnabas Ct. Crawl RH10 202 C7
St Barnabas' Gdns. E Mole KT8 36 A4
St Barnabas Rd. Mitch CR4 21 A1
St Barnabas Rd. Sutton SM1 59 D5
St Bartholomew CE Fst Sch. Haslem GU27 208 C7
St Bartholomew CE Prim Sch. Haslem GU27 208 C7
St Bartholomew's Cl. For Hil SE26 23 C4
St Bartholomew's Prim Sch. For Hil SE26 23 C4
St Bede's C of E Jun Sch. Send GU23 90 D3
St Bede's RC Inf Sch. Streat SW12 21 D7
St Bede's Sch. Redh RH2 118 E4
St Benedict's Cl. Alder GU11 105 A1
St Benedict's Cl. Up Toot SW17 21 A3
St Benet's Gr. Carsh SM4 & SM5 40 C2
St Benets Cl. Up Toot SW17 20 E6
St Bernadette RC Jun Mix Sch. Streat SW12 21 C8
St Bernadette's RC Prim Sch. W Heath GU14 85 A5
St Bernards. S Croy CR0 61 E7
St Bernards Cl. 8 W Norw SE27 22 D4
St Boniface Catholic Prim Sch. Up Toot SW17 20 F3
St Brelades Cl. Dork RH4 136 A5
St Brelades Rd. Crawl RH11 200 F2
St Catherine's Convent Girls Prep & Senior Schs. Twick TW1 17 A6
St Catherine's Cross. Bletch RH1 120 E2
St Catherine's Dr. Arting GU2 130 B5
St Catherine's Hill. Arting GU2 130 C5
St Catherine's RC Mid Sch. W Barn KT3 39 C4
St Catherine's Sch. Bramly GU5 151 F7
St Catherine's Sch. Camb GU15 65 D4
St Catherines. Weyb KT13 53 B7
St Catherines. Woking GU22 89 C8
St Catherines Cl. Up Toot SW17 20 E6
St Catherines Ct. Felt TW13 15 A7
St Catherines Fst & Mid Schs. Bletch RH1 120 E2
St Catherines Rd. Crawl RH10 182 D1
St Catherines Rd. Friml GU16 86 A8
St Cecilia's RC Prim Sch. N Cheam SM3 58 D8
St Chad's RC Prim Sch. S Norw SE25 42 E4
St Chads Cl. Long D KT6 37 C2
St Charles Borromeo RC Prim Sch. Weyb KT13 53 A7
St Charles Pl. Weyb KT13 53 A5
St Christopher's. Lingf RH7 164 D4
St Christopher's Cl. Hounsl TW7 5 E6
St Christopher's Cl. Shottm GU27 208 A6
St Christopher's Ct. 3 Walt O T KT12 54 C8
St Christopher's Gn. Shottm GU27 208 A6
St Christopher's Hospice. Penge SE26 23 C3
St Christopher's Mews. Wallin SM6 60 C5
St Christopher's Rd. 2 Farnb GU14 85 A3
St Christopher's Rd. Shottm GU27 208 A6
St Christopher's Sch. Beck BR3 44 C7
St Christopher's Sch. Epsom KT18 76 E5
St Christophers Cl. Horsh RH12 217 D4
St Christophers Day Hospl. Horsh RH12 217 D3
St Christophers Gdns. N Asct SL5 28 D8
St Christophers Gdns. Thorn H CR7 42 A6
St Christophers Pl. 1 Farnb GU14 85 A3
St Clair Cl. Oxted RH8 122 D5
St Clair Cl. Reig RH2 118 C1
St Clair Dr. N Cheam KT4 58 B6
St Clair's Rd. S Croy CR0 61 E8
St Claire Cotts. Dorman RH7 165 B1
St Clare Bsns Pk. Hampt TW12 16 C2
St Clement Rd. Crawl RH11 200 F2
St Clements Ct. Farnb GU14 85 B7
St Clements RC Prim Sch. Ewell KT17 57 F2
St Cloud Rd. W Norw SE27 22 D4
St Crispin's Sch. Woki RG11 25 E6
St Crispins Way. Ottsh KT16 51 C2
St Cross Rd. Farnh GU9 125 C3
St Cross Rd. Friml GU16 86 B7
St Cuthbert Mayne RC Fst Sch. Cran GU6 174 E3
St Cuthbert's Cl. Eng Gn TW20 11 D2
St Cuthbert's RC Prim Sch. Eng Gn TW20 11 C1
St Cyprian's St. Up Toot SW17 20 F4
St David's. Coulsd CR5 79 F2
St David's Cl. Heath E GU9 125 E7
St David's Cl. Reig RH2 118 C2
St David's Cl. W Heath GU14 84 F8
St David's Cl. W Wick BR3 & BR4 44 B2
St David's Coll. W Wick BR4 44 B2
St David's Jun Sch. Ashf TW15 13 F5
St Denis Rd. W Norw SE27 22 D4
St Deny's Cl. Knaph GU21 68 D1
St Dominic's Sch. Hambl GU8 171 C1
St Dunstan's C of E Prim Sch. Belm SM3 58 E3
St Dunstan's Cl. For Hil SE6 24 A7
St Dunstan's Hill. Cheam SM1 & SM3 58 E5
St Dunstan's La. Beck BR3 44 C4
St Dunstan's RC Prim Sch. Woking GU22 70 A2
St Dunstan's Rd. Cranf TW5 4 B5
St Dunstan's Rd. Cranf TW5 4 C5
St Dunstan's Rd. Felt TW13 14 F5
St Dunstan's Rd. S Norw SE25 42 F5
St Ebba's Hospl. Epsom KT19 57 C2
St Edmund Cl. Crawl RH11 181 D1
St Edmund's Catholic Prim Sch. Twick TW2 16 B8
St Edmund's La. Twick TW2 16 B8
St Edmund's RC Prim Sch. Godal GU7 150 F2
St Edmunds Cl. Up Toot SW17 20 E6
St Edmunds Sch. Graysh GU26 188 D3
St Edward's Cl. E Grins RH19 185 C1
St Edwards Cl. New Add CR0 82 D8
St Elizabeth's RC Prim Sch. Rich TW10 6 F1
St Elphege's RC Prim Sch. Wallin SM6 60 E4
St Faith's Rd. Streat SE24 22 B7
St Fillans. Mayb GU22 70 B3
St Fillans Rd. Catf SE6 24 C8
St Francis of Assisi RC (Aided) Sch. Crawl RH10 201 E4
St Francis RC Fst Sch. Woking GU22 70 A2
St Francis RC Prim Sch. Whytlf CR3 100 F6
St Francis RC Sch. Ascot SL5 29 A3
St Francis Wlk. Crawl RH11 200 E4
St George's Ave. Whit V KT13 53 C4
St George's Bsns Ctr. Whit V KT13 53 A2
St George's Cl. Farnh GU9 126 B6
St George's Cl. Whit V KT13 53 C5
St George's Coll. Chert KT15 52 D7
St George's Gdns. Epsom KT17 76 F5
St George's Gdns. Horsh RH13 217 E4
St George's Gdns. Tolw KT6 57 B8
St George's Gr. Wands SW17 20 D5
St George's Hill Artisan Golf Club. Whit V KT13 53 C2
St George's Hill Golf Course. Whit V KT13 72 B8
St George's Hospl. Up Toot SW17 20 D3
St George's Ind Est. King U T KT2 17 D3
St George's La. Ascot SL5 29 B5
St George's Lodge. Whit V KT13 53 D5
St George's Rd. Alder GU11 & GU12 105 B1
St George's Rd. Beck BR3 44 B8
St George's Rd. Camb GU15 65 D6
St George's Rd. Felt TW13 15 D4
St George's Rd. Islew TW1 6 B2
St George's Rd. 2 King U T KT2 18 A1
St George's Rd. M Bourn GU9 125 D1
St George's Rd. Mitch CR4 41 B6
St George's Rd. Rich TW9 6 F4
St George's Rd. S Nutf RH1 140 E1
St George's Rd. Wallin SM6 60 B5
St George's Rd. Whit V KT13 53 D4
St George's Rd. Wimble SW19 19 F2
St George's Rd E. Alder GU12 105 B1
St George's Sch. Ascot SL5 29 B6
St George's Sch. Farnh GU9 125 B2
St George's Sq. New Mal KT3 38 E6
St George's Wlk. Croy CR0 & CR9 61 C7
St Georges Cl. Horley RH6 161 B3
St Georges Cotts. Crow RH7 143 E4
St Georges Ct. Addl KT15 52 C6
St Georges Ct. Crawl RH11 201 D8
St Georges Ct. E Grins RH19 185 C3
St Georges Ct. Penge SE20 43 B8
St Georges Rd. Addl KT15 52 C6
St Georges Rd. Farnh GU10 126 B4
St German's Rd. For Hil SE23 23 E7
St Giles C of E Inf Sch. Ashtd KT21 75 F1
St Giles' Sch. Croy CR2 61 B4
St Gothard Rd. W Norw SE21 & SE27 22 D4
St Gregory's RC Inf Sch. Camb GU15 65 B6
St Helen's Cres. Thorn H SW16 41 F8
St Helen's Rd. Thorn H SW16 41 F8
St Helena Terr. 23 Rich TW9 6 D2
St Helens. Thame D KT7 36 F2
St Helens Cres. Sandh GU17 64 B8
St Helier Ave. Morden SM4 40 C3
St Helier Cl. Crawl RH11 201 A2
St Helier Cl. Woki RG11 25 B3
St Helier Hospl. Carsh SM5 40 C1
St Helier Sta. Morden SM4 40 A3
St Heliers Ave. Hounsl TW3 & TW4 5 A2
St Hilary's Sch. Godal GU7 150 D3
St Hilda's Ave. Ashf TW15 13 E3
St Hilda's Cl. Crawl RH10 182 C1
St Hilda's Cl. Horley RH6 161 B3
St Hilda's Cl. Knaph GU21 68 D2
St Hildas Cl. Up Toot SW17 20 E6
St Hugh of Lincoln RC Prim Sch. Knaph GU21 88 D8
St Hugh's Cl. Crawl RH10 182 C1
St Hugh's Rd. Penge SE20 23 B1
St Hughes Cl. Up Toot SW17 20 E6
St Ignatius RC Fst & Mid Sch. Sunby TW16 35 A8
St Ives. Crawl RH10 202 C7
St Ives Sch. Haslem GU27 208 E8
St James Ave. Ewell KT17 77 A8
St James' Ave. Farnh GU9 125 D3
St James Ave. Sutton SM1 59 A5
St James C of E Prim Sch. Elst GU8 148 C3
St James C of E Prim Sch. Weyb KT13 53 C7
St James Cl. Epsom KT18 76 E5
St James' Cl. New Mal KT3 38 F4
St James Cl. Woking GU21 69 A1
St James Ct. Ashtd KT21 75 D2
St James Ct. Farnh GU9 125 C3
St James' Ct. 7 King U T KT1 37 E6
St James Ct. Thorn H CR0 42 B2
St James Mews. Weyb KT13 53 B6
St James Rd. Carsh SM5 59 E7
St James' Rd. King U T KT6 37 D3
St James' Rd. Mitch CR4 21 A1
St James' Rd. Purley CR8 80 C6
St James Rd. Sutton SM1 & SM2 59 A5
St James' Terr. Farnh GU9 125 C3
St James The Great RC (Aided) Sch. S Norw CR7 42 B7
St James Wlk. Crawl RH11 201 C2
St James's Ave. Beck BR3 43 E6
St James's Ave. Hampt TW12 16 C3
St James's Cl. Up Toot SW17 20 F6
St James's Cotts. 14 Rich TW10 6 D2
St James's Dr. Balham SW12 & SW17 20 F8
St James's Dr. Up Toot SW17 20 F7
St James's Lodge. 4 Croy CR0 42 E1
St James's Pk. Thorn H CR0 42 C2
St James's Pl. Cran GU6 174 C3
St James's Rd. Croy CR0 42 D2
St James's Rd. E Grins RH19 185 D1
St James's Rd. Hampt TW12 16 B3
St James's Rd. King U T KT1 37 D7
St James's Rd. Thorn H CR0 42 D2
St James's Sch. Twick TW2 16 E5
St James's Terr. 3 Up Toot SW12 21 A7
St Joan Cl. Crawl RH11 181 D1
St John Baptist C of E Prim Sch. Catf BR1 24 C4
St John Cl. Horsh RH13 217 E1
St John Fisher RC Prim Sch. W Barn KT3 39 D4
St John Rigby RC Coll. Coney H BR4 63 D6
St John The Bapist Sch. Old Wok GU22 90 A8
St John the Baptist C of E Jun Sch. Tedd KT1 17 D1
St John's. Dork RH5 136 C3
St John's Ave. Leahd KT22 95 B6
St John's Beamont Prep Sch. Eng Gn TW20 11 B6
St John's Beamont Sch. Eng Gn TW19 11 B6
St John's C of E Prim Sch. Churt GU10 167 E1
St John's C of E Prim Sch. Penge SE20 23 C1
St John's CE Jun Sch. Cater CR3 101 B2
St John's CE Prim Sch. King U T KT1 37 E6
St John's CE (VA) Inf Sch. Cater CR3 101 B2
St John's Cl. E Grins RH19 185 E2
St John's Cl. Leahd KT22 95 C7
St John's Cl. Onsl V GU2 130 A8
St John's Cotts. 2 Penge SE20 23 C1
St John's Court. King U T KT1 37 E5
St John's Cres. Broad H RH12 216 E3
St John's Ct. Brookw GU24 87 F7
St John's Ct. Islew TW7 5 F5
St John's Ct. W Heath GU14 84 D5
St John's Cty Prim Sch. Knaph GU21 68 E1
St John's Dr. Wands SW18 20 B7
St John's Fst Sch. Dork RH4 136 B3
St John's Gr. Barnes SW13 7 F5
St John's Gr. 1 Rich TW9 6 E3
St John's Hill. Purley CR8 80 A2
St John's Hill Rd. Woking GU21 & GU22 89 B8
St John's Hospl. Twick TW1 17 A8
St John's Lye. Woking GU21 88 F8
St John's Lye (Festival Path). Woking GU21 88 F8
St John's Meadow. Blind H RH7 163 E8
St John's RC Prim Sch. Horsh RH12 217 A1
St John's Rd. Carsh SM5 59 E7
St John's Rd. Crawl RH11 201 C6
St John's Rd. Croy CR0 & CR9 61 B7
St John's Rd. E Grins RH19 185 E2
St John's Rd. E Mole KT8 36 D5
St John's Rd. Earls RH1 139 F7
St John's Rd. Felt TW13 15 F4
St John's Rd. Islew TW7 5 F5
St John's Rd. Leahd KT22 95 C6
St John's Rd. M Bourn GU9 146 B8
St John's Rd. N Asct SL5 8 F1
St John's Rd. Onsl V GU2 130 A8
St John's Rd. Penge SE20 23 C2
St John's Rd. Rich TW9 6 E3
St John's Rd. Sandh GU17 64 C7
St John's Rd. Sutton SM1 59 B8
St John's Rd. Tedd KT1 37 C7
St John's Rd. W Heath GU14 84 E5
St John's Rd. Westc RH4 135 C6
St John's Rd. Wimble SW19 19 E2
St John's Rd. Woking GU21 69 B2
St John's Rise. Woking GU21 89 B8
St John's Sch. Leahd KT22 95 B6
St John's (Shirley) C of E Prim Sch. Croy CR0 62 D7
St John's St. Farnc GU7 150 F6
St John's Terrace Rd. Earls RH1 139 F7
St Johns Ave. Ewell KT17 77 A7
St Johns Ct. Egham TW20 12 A3
St Johns Ct. S Godst RH9 142 F5
St Johns Ct. Woking GU21 89 A8
St Johns Cty Prim Sch. Earls RH1 139 E7
St Johns Dr. Walt O T KT12 35 C1
St Johns Gr. M Bourn GU9 146 B8
St Johns Mews. Woking GU21 89 A8
St Johns Rd. King U T KT1 38 C6
St Joseph's Convent Prep Sch. E Mole KT8 36 C4
St Joseph's RC Coll. S Norw SW16 22 B2
St Joseph's RC Inf Sch. S Norw SE19 22 C2
St Joseph's RC Jun Sch. S Norw SE19 22 C2
St Joseph's RC Prim Sch. Brack RG12 27 D7
St Joseph's RC Prim Sch. Dork RH4 136 A7
St Joseph's RC Prim Sch. Epsom KT18 76 C5
St Joseph's RC Prim Sch. King U T KT1 37 F7
St Joseph's RC Prim Sch. Redh RH1 118 E2
St Joseph's RC (VA) Jun Sch. Stough GU2 108 F3
St Joseph's Rd. Alder GU11 & GU12 105 A1
St Joseph's Sch. Cran GU6 174 F6
St Josephs RC Prim Sch. Alder GU11 126 A8
St Jude's C of E Sch. Eng Gn TW20 11 C2
St Jude's Cl. Eng Gn TW20 11 C3
St Jude's Cotts. Eng Gn TW20 11 C3
St Jude's Rd. Eng Gn TW20 11 C3
St Julian's Cl. W Norw SE27 & SW16 22 A4
St Julian's Farm Rd. W Norw SE27 & SW16 22 B4
St Katharines Rd. Cater CR3 101 A2
St Kitts Terr. W Norw SE19 22 E3
St Lawrence C of E (Aided) Fst & Mid Sch. Chobh GU24 68 E8
St Lawrence C of E Mid Sch. E Mole KT8 36 D5
St Lawrence Ct. Chobh GU24 68 E8
St Lawrence Prim Sch. Effing KT24 113 D8
St Lawrence RC Sch. Felt TW13 15 B6
St Lawrence's Hospl. Cater CR3 100 D4
St Lawrences Sch. Cater CR3 100 D4
St Lawrences Way. Reig RH2 118 A1
St Leonard's Gdns. Heston TW5 4 E6
St Leonard's Rd. Clayg KT10 55 F4
St Leonard's Rd. Croy CR0 & CR9 61 B7
St Leonard's Rd. King U T KT6 37 D4
St Leonard's Rd. Thame D KT7 37 A2
St Leonard's Rd. Wind SL4 9 D8
St Leonard's Sq. King U T KT6 37 D4
St Leonard's Wlk. Streat SW16 21 F1
St Leonards C of E Prim Sch. Streat SW16 21 D3
St Leonards Ct. Mortl SW14 7 C4
St Leonards Cty Inf Sch. Horsh RH13 217 E2
St Leonards Dr. Crawl RH10 202 A4
St Leonards Pk. E Grins RH19 185 E1
St Leonards Rd. Burgh H KT20 97 C8
St Leonards Rd. Horsh RH13 218 A1
St Leonards Rd. Mortl SW14 7 C4
St Louis Rd. W Norw SE27 22 D4
St Luke's C of E Prim Sch. King U T KT2 37 F8
St Luke's C of E Prim Sch. Rich TW9 7 A6
St Luke's C of E Prim Sch. W Norw SE27 22 C3

St Luke's Cl. Croy SE25 .... 43 B3
St Luke's Hospl. Guild GU1 ...... 130 F7
St Luke's Rd. Whytlf CR3 .... 80 F1
St Margaret Clitherow RC Prim
  Sch. Easth RG12 .... 26 F2
St Margaret's. Guild GU1 .... 109 F1
St Margaret's Ave. Cheam SM3 . 58 F2
St Margaret's Ave.
  Dorm Pk RH19 .... 185 F6
St Margaret's CE (Aided) Sch.
  Crawl RH11 .... 201 B7
St Margaret's Ct. Twick TW1 ... 6 B1
St Margaret's Dr. Islew TW1 .... 6 B2
St Margaret's Gr. Twick TW1 ...... 6 A1
St Margaret's Rd. E Grins RH19 185 F3
St Margaret's Rd. Hooley CR5 .... 99 B6
St Margaret's Rd. Islew TW1 .... 6 B2
St Margaret's Rd. Twick TW1 ...... 6 B2
St Margaret's Sta. Twick TW1 ... 6 B1
St Margarets Ave. Ashf TW15 .... 14 B3
St Margarets Bsns Ctr.
  Twick TW1 .... 6 B1
St Margarets Ct. Warn RH12 ... 216 F7
St Mark's C of E Prim Sch.
  Croy SE25 .... 43 A5
St Mark's C of E Prim Sch.
  Farnb GU14 .... 105 D8
St Mark's Catholic Sch.
  Hounsl TW3 .... 5 A4
St Mark's CE Prim Sch.
  Beck BR2 .... 44 F6
St Mark's CE (VA) Prim Sch.
  Ock Rid GU7 .... 150 B3
St Mark's Fst Sch. Mitch CR4 .... 40 F7
St Mark's Hill. King U T KT6 ...... 37 E3
St Mark's La. Horsh RH12 .... 217 E6
St Mark's Pl. Wimble SW19 .... 19 F2
St Mark's Rd. Binf RG12 .... 26 C8
St Mark's Rd. Tedd TW11 .... 17 B1
St Marks Cl. Farnb GU14 .... 85 C1
St Marks Pl. Heath E GU9 .... 125 B7
St Marks Rd.
  Burgh H KT18 & KT20 .... 77 C1
St Martha's Ave. Peasl GU5 ..... 154 E8
St Martha's Ct. Chil GU4 .... 131 B3
St Martin's Ave. Epsom KT18 .... 76 E5
St Martin's C of E Inf Sch.
  Woodc KT18 .... 76 D4
St Martin's C of E Jun Sch.
  Woodc KT18 .... 76 D4
St Martin's C of E Prim Sch.
  Dork RH4 .... 136 A8
St Martin's C of E Sch.
  Pixham RH4 .... 115 C1
St Martin's CE Prim Sch.
  Dork RH4 .... 136 A7
St Martin's Cl. Epsom KT17 .... 76 E6
St Martin's Ct. Stain TW15 .... 13 C3
St Martin's Ct. W Norw SE27 .... 22 B6
St Martin's Way. Wands SW17 ... 20 C5
St Martin's Wlk. Dork RH4 ...... 136 B8
St Martin-in-the-Fields High Sch.
  Streat SW2 .... 22 A7
St Martins Cl. E Hors KT24 ...... 112 E6
St Martins Ct. E Hors KT24 ...... 112 E6
St Martins Dr. Walt O T KT12 .... 54 C7
St Mary Ave. Hackb SM6 .... 60 B7
St Mary Magdalene C of E Sec Sch.
  Rich TW9 .... 7 A2
St Mary's. Oat Pk KT13 .... 53 D7
St Mary's Ave. Beck BR2 .... 44 E6
St Mary's Ave. Stan TW19 .... 13 D8
St Mary's Ave. Tedd TW11 .... 16 F2
St Mary's C of E Inf Sch.
  Leahd KT22 .... 95 C5
St Mary's C of E Prim Sch.
  Buckl RH3 .... 117 A2
St Mary's C of E Prim Sch.
  Chess KT9 .... 56 F4
St Mary's C of E Prim Sch.
  Long D KT7 .... 37 B1
St Mary's C of E Prim Sch.
  Wink RG12 .... 8 B2
St Mary's C of E Sch. Stan TW19 13 E8
St Mary's CE (Aided) Sch.
  E Grins RH19 .... 185 D2
St Mary's CE Jun Sch.
  Oxted RH8 .... 122 E7
St Mary's CE Prim Sch.
  Byfl KT14 .... 71 E6
St Mary's Church Sch.
  Twick TW1 .... 17 A8
St Mary's Cl. Chess KT9 .... 56 F3
St Mary's Cl. Ewell KT17 .... 57 F2
St Mary's Cl. Fetch KT22 .... 94 D4
St Mary's Cl. Oxted RH8 .... 122 E6
St Mary's Cl. Stan TW19 .... 13 D8
St Mary's Cl. Sunby TW16 .... 35 A5
St Mary's Cottage Hospl.
  Hampt TW12 .... 35 F8
St Mary's Cres. Hounsl TW7 ...... 5 E7
St Mary's Cres. Stan TW19 .... 13 D8
St Mary's Ct. King U T KT3 .... 38 E6
St Mary's Ct. Wallin SM6 .... 60 C6
St Mary's Dr. Crawl RH10 .... 202 B8
St Mary's Dr. E Bed TW14 .... 14 C8
St Mary's Gdns. Bagsh GU19 .... 47 E3
St Mary's Gdns. Horsh RH12 ... 217 C1
St Mary's Gn. Bigg H TN16 .... 83 C1
St Mary's Gr. Bigg H TN16 .... 83 C1
St Mary's Gr. Chisw W4 .... 7 B8
St Mary's Gr. Rich TW10 & TW9 ... 6 F3
St Mary's High Sch. Thorn H CR0 42 C1
St Mary's Hill. Ascot SL5 .... 29 C4
St Mary's House. Horsh RH12 ... 217 C1
St Mary's Pl. Farnh GU9 .... 125 C3
St Mary's RC Inf Sch. Croy CR0 42 D1
St Mary's RC Inf Sch.
  Stough GU3 .... 108 E3

St Mary's RC Jun Sch.
  Carsh SM5 .... 59 F5
St Mary's RC Jun Sch. Croy CR0 42 D1
St Mary's RC Prim Sch.
  Beck BR3 .... 24 C1
St Mary's RC Prim Sch.
  Chisw W4 .... 7 E8
St Mary's RC Prim Sch.
  Islew TW7 .... 6 A4
St Mary's RC Prim Sch.
  Merton SW19 .... 20 A1
St Mary's RC Sch. Islew TW7 ... 6 A4
St Mary's Rd. Ascot SL5 .... 29 B3
St Mary's Rd. Ash V GU12 ...... 106 A5
St Mary's Rd. Camb GU15 .... 65 C6
St Mary's Rd. E Mole KT8 .... 36 D4
St Mary's Rd. Horse GU21 .... 69 C2
St Mary's Rd. King U T KT6 .... 37 D3
St Mary's Rd. Long D KT6 .... 37 C1
St Mary's Rd. Oat Pk KT13 .... 53 D6
St Mary's Rd. Reig RH2 .... 139 B8
St Mary's Rd. S Croy CR2 .... 61 D2
St Mary's Rd. S Norw SE25 .... 42 E6
St Mary's Rd. Wimble SW19 ...... 19 F3
St Mary's Rd. Worc Pk KT4 .... 57 E8
St Mary's RC Inf Sch. Carsh SM5 59 F6
St Mary's Sch. Ascot SL5 .... 29 B2
St Mary's Sch. Horsh RH12 ..... 217 C1
St Mary's & St Peter's Prim Sch.
  Tedd TW11 .... 16 F3
St Mary's Univ Coll. Twick TW1 16 F5
St Marys CE (VA) Prim Sch.
  Chidd GU8 .... 191 C4
St Marys Cl. Sandh GU17 .... 64 C8
St Marys La. Wink SL4 .... 8 D5
St Marys Rd. Leahd KT22 .... 95 B4
St Matthew's Ave. Surb KT6 ...... 37 F1
St Matthew's C of E Prim Sch.
  Redh RH1 .... 118 F3
St Matthew's CE Prim Sch.
  Surb KT6 .... 37 E2
St Matthew's Ct. Ashf TW15 ..... 14 A3
St Matthew's Rd. Redh RH1 ... 118 F2
St Matthews (C of E) Sch.
  Downs KT11 .... 73 B1
St Merryn Ct. Beck BR3 .... 24 A1
St Michael's Ave. Fairl GU3 .... 108 C6
St Michael's C of E Prim Sch.
  Easth RG12 .... 27 A4
St Michael's CE (VA) Fst Sch.
  Mickle RH5 .... 115 C8
St Michael's Cl. Walt O T KT12 .. 54 C8
St Michael's Prim Sch.
  For Hil SE26 .... 23 E4
St Michael's Prim Sch.
  Wands SW18 .... 19 F8
St Michael's RC Prim Sch.
  Ashf TW15 .... 14 A3
St Michael's Rd.
  Alder GU11 & GU12 .... 105 B1
St Michael's Rd. Croy CR0 .... 42 C1
St Michael's Rd. Farnb GU14 .... 85 B6
St Michael's Rd. Sheer GU21 .... 70 D5
St Michael's Rd. Wallin SM6 ..... 60 C4
St Michael's Sch. Limps RH8 ... 123 A6
St Michael's & St Martin's RC Prim
  Sch. Hounsl TW4 .... 4 F4
St Michaels C of E Inf Sch.
  Alder GU11 .... 126 B8
St Michaels C of E Jun Sch.
  Alder GU11 .... 126 C8
St Michaels Cl. Worc Pk KT4 .... 57 F8
St Michaels Cotts. Crowth RG11 45 C8
St Michaels Ct. Whit V KT13 . 53 C5
St Michaels Rd. Ashf TW15 ...... 14 A3
St Michaels Rd. Camb GU15 ..... 65 B5
St Michaels Rd. Cater CR3 ...... 100 D5
St Michaels Rd. E Grins RH19 . 185 E2
St Micheal's C of E Sch.
  Ascot SL5 .... 29 D4
St Mildred's Rd. Guild GU1 .... 109 F2
St Mildreds Rd.
  Lewish SE12 & SE6 .... 24 F8
St Monica's Rd. Kings KT20 ...... 97 F6
St Nazaire Cl. Egham TW20 ...... 12 C1
St Nicholas Ave. Fetch KT23 ..... 94 B2
St Nicholas C of E Prim Sch.
  Shep TW17 .... 34 B3
St Nicholas C of E Sch.
  Cran GU6 .... 174 D3
St Nicholas Ct. Crawl RH10 .... 202 C7
St Nicholas Ctr. Sutton SM1 ..... 59 B5
St Nicholas Dr. Lo Hall TW17 .... 34 A2
St Nicholas Glebe.
  Up Toot SW17 .... 21 A2
St Nicholas Hill. Leahd KT22 .... 95 B5
St Nicholas Rd. Sutton SM1 ...... 59 B5
St Nicholas Rd. Thame D KT7 .... 36 F3
St Nicholas Sch. Merst RH1 .... 119 D6
St Nicholas Sch. Purley CR8 ..... 80 A6
St Nicholas Way. Sutton SM1 .... 59 B5
St Nicolas Ave. Cran GU6 ...... 174 E3
St Nicolas CE Inf Sch.
  Guild GU2 .... 130 C7
St Nicolas Cl. Cran GU6 .... 174 E3
St Normans Way. Ewell KT17 .... 58 A1
St Olave's Cl. Stain TW18 .... 12 F1
St Olave's Wlk. Mitch SW16 ...... 41 D7
St Omer Rd. Guild GU1 .... 131 A8
St Omer Ridge. Guild GU1 ...... 131 A8
St Osmund's RC Prim Sch.
  Barnes SW13 .... 7 F6
St Oswald's Rd. S Norw SW16 ... 42 B8
St Paul's C of E Jun Sch.
  King U T KT2 .... 18 A1
St Paul's C of E Prim Sch.
  Woki RG11 .... 25 A6
St Paul's Catholic Sch.
  Sunby TW16 .... 35 A8
St Paul's CE Inf Sch.
  Tongh GU10 .... 127 A7

St Paul's CE Prim Sch.
  Addl KT15 .... 52 A6
St Paul's CE Prim Sch.
  Chess KT9 .... 56 E6
St Paul's CE (VA) Prim Sch.
  Dork RH4 .... 136 B6
St Paul's Cl. Addl KT15 .... 52 A5
St Paul's Cl. Ashf TW15 .... 14 C3
St Paul's Cl. Carsh SM5 .... 40 E1
St Paul's Cl. Chess KT9 .... 56 E6
St Paul's Cl. Hounsl TW3 & TW4 ... 4 E5
St Paul's Cl. Hounsl TW4 .... 4 E4
St Paul's Gate. Woki RG11 .... 25 A6
St Paul's RC Prim Sch.
  Thame D KT7 .... 36 E2
St Paul's Rd. Brent TW8 .... 6 D8
St Paul's Rd. Egham TW18 .... 12 D2
St Paul's Rd. S Norw SE27 .... 42 C6
St Paul's Rd E. Dork RH4 & RH5 136 B7
St Paul's Rd W. Dork RH4 ...... 136 B6
St Pauls C of E Prim Sch.
  Brent TW8 .... 6 D8
St Pauls' CE Fst Sch.
  Tongh GU10 .... 126 F6
St Pauls Rd. Mayb GU22 .... 70 B2
St Pauls Rd. Rich TW9 .... 6 F4
St Peter & St Paul CE Prim Sch.
  Cater CR3 .... 100 A2
St Peter's Cl. Old Wok GU22 ..... 90 C7
St Peter's Cl. Stain TW18 .... 12 F2
St Peter's Gdns. Ashf TW15 ..... 22 A5
St Peter's Gdns. Wreccl GU10 . 145 F6
St Peter's Hospl. Addl KT16 ...... 51 D7
St Peter's Jun Sch. Farnb GU14 85 C4
St Peter's Prim Sch. S Croy CR2 61 E4
St Peter's RC (Aided) Sch.
  E Grins RH19 .... 185 C1
St Peter's RC Comp Sch.
  Merrow GU1 .... 110 C2
St Peter's Rd. Crawl RH11 ...... 201 C6
St Peter's Rd. Croy CR0 & CR2 ... 61 D6
St Peter's Rd. E Mole KT8 .... 36 A5
St Peter's Rd. Islew TW1 .... 6 B2
St Peter's Rd. Old Wok GU22 .... 90 B7
St Peter's St. Croy CR0 & CR2 .. 61 D5
St Peter's Way. Addl KT15 .... 51 F6
St Peter's Way.
  Addl KT15 & KT16 .... 51 F7
St Peter's Way. Chert KT15 ...... 52 B8
St Peter's Way. Friml GU16 ...... 85 F7
St Peters CE Inf Sch.
  Tand RH8 .... 122 A2
St Peters CE Prim Sch.
  Wreccl GU9 .... 146 A7
St Peters Cl. Up Toot SW17 ...... 20 E6
St Peters Ct. E Molle KT8 .... 36 A5
St Peters Mead. Ash GU12 ..... 106 B2
St Peters Pk. Alder GU11 & GU9 125 E8
St Peters Rd. King U T KT1 .... 38 A7
St Peters Way. Harl UB3 .... 3 D8
St Philip's Ave. N Cheam KT4 .... 58 B8
St Philip's Sch. King U T KT6 .... 37 D3
St Philips Sch. Chess KT9 .... 56 D4
St Philomena's Sch. Carsh SM5 59 E5
St Pier's La. Lingf RH7 & TN8 ... 165 B5
St Pinnock Ave. Stain TW18 ..... 33 A8
St Polycarp's RC Prim Sch.
  M Bourn GU9 .... 125 D1
St Richard's with St Andrew's
  CE Prim Sch. Rich TW10 .... 17 B5
St Richards Ct. Rich TW10 .... 17 B5
St Robert Southwell RC Sch.
  Horsh RH12 .... 218 A6
St Sampson Rd. Crawl RH11 ... 200 F2
St Saviour's Coll. W Norw SE27 . 22 D4
St Saviour's Pl. Guild GU1 ...... 109 C1
St Saviour's Rd. Thorn H CR0 ... 42 C3
St Stephen's C of E Jun Sch.
  Twick TW1 .... 6 B1
St Stephen's CE Prim Sch.
  S Godst RH9 .... 142 F6
St Stephen's Cl. Shottm GU27 . 207 F6
St Stephen's Cres. Thorn H CR7 42 A6
St Stephen's Gdns. Twick TW1 ... 6 C1
St Stephen's Rd.
  Hounsl TW3 & TW4 .... 5 A2
St Stephens Ave. Ashtd KT21 ... 75 E3
St Stephens Cl. Haslem GU27 . 208 C7
St Swithun's Cl. E Grins RH19 . 185 F1
St Tarsisius RC Jun Sch.
  Camb GU15 .... 65 D6
St Teresa's Prep Sch
  (Grove House). Effing KT24 ...... 113 D7
St Teresa's RC Prim Sch.
  Morden SM4 .... 40 D3
St Theresa's RC Prim Sch.
  Woki RG11 .... 25 D5
St Theresa's Rd. Hatton TW14 .... 3 F3
St Thomas Cl. Horse GU21 .... 69 C2
St Thomas' Cl. Surb KT6 .... 37 F1
St Thomas More RC Sch.
  E Mole KT8 .... 36 C4
St Thomas of Canterbur RC Mid
  Sch. Mitch CR4 .... 41 A0
St Thomas of Canterbury Sch.
  Merrow GU1 .... 110 B1
St Thomas' Rd. Chisw W4 .... 7 C8
St Thomas Wlk. Coln SL3 .... 1 D7
St Thomas's Dr. E Clan GU4 .... 111 E4
St Vincent Cl. W Norw SE27 ..... 22 B3
St Vincent Cl. Worth RH10 ...... 202 D5
St Vincent Rd. Twick TW2 .... 5 C1
St Vincent Rd. Walt O T KT12 ... 54 B7
St Wilfrid's RC (Aided) Sch.
  Crawl RH11 .... 201 B5
St William of York RC Prim Sch.
  For Hil SE23 .... 23 E7
St Winifred's RC Prim Sch.
  Lewish SE12 .... 24 F8

St Winifred's Rd. Bigg H TN16 ... 83 F1
St Winifred's Rd. Tedd TW11 .... 17 B2
St Winifreds. Kenley CR8 .... 80 C4
Salamanca Pk. Alder GU11 .... 104 F3
Salamander Quay. Tedd KT1 .... 37 D8
Salbrook Rd. Salfs RH1 .... 140 A1
Salcombe Dr. W Barn SM4 .... 39 D1
Salcombe House. For Hil SE23 .. 23 C6
Salcombe Rd. Ashf TW15 .... 13 E5
Salcot Cres. New Add CR0 .... 63 C1
Salcott Rd. Wallin CR0 .... 60 F6
Sale Garden Cotts. Woki RG11 .. 25 C5
Salehurst Rd. Worth RH10 ...... 202 E6
Salem Pl. Croy CR0 & CR9 .... 61 C7
Salerno Cl. Alder GU11 .... 105 A2
Salesian Catholic Comp Sch.
  Addl KT16 .... 51 E8
Salesian Coll. Farnb GU14 .... 85 D1
Salesian Sch. Chert KT16 .... 33 A1
Salesian View. Farnb GU14 .... 105 E8
Salford Rd. Streat SW12 & SW2 .. 21 D7
Salfords Cty Prim Sch.
  Earls RH1 .... 140 A3
Salfords Sta. Salfs RH1 .... 140 B1
Salfords Way. Salfs RH1 .... 140 A1
Salisbury Ave. Cheam SM1 & SM2 58 F4
Salisbury Cl. Woki RG11 .... 25 A2
Salisbury Cl. Worc Pk KT4 .... 57 F7
Salisbury Gdns. Wimble SW19 .. 19 E1
Salisbury Gr. Mytch GU16 .... 86 A3
Salisbury House. Wimble SW19 . 19 D5
Salisbury Pl. W Byfl KT14 .... 71 C8
Salisbury Rd. Ash GU12 .... 106 A3
Salisbury Rd. Banstd SM7 .... 78 B5
Salisbury Rd. Blckw GU17 .... 64 C5
Salisbury Rd. Crawl RH10 ...... 201 F2
Salisbury Rd. Croy CR0 & SE25 ... 43 A3
Salisbury Rd. Farnb GU14 .... 85 C3
Salisbury Rd. Felt TW13 .... 15 C7
Salisbury Rd. Harl TW6 .... 3 C1
Salisbury Rd. Hounsl TW4 .... 4 C4
Salisbury Rd. King U T KT3 .... 38 D6
Salisbury Rd. Rich TW9 .... 6 E3
Salisbury Rd. Tyl Gn RH9 .... 121 C4
Salisbury Rd. Wallin SM5 .... 59 F4
Salisbury Rd. Wimble SW19 ...... 19 E1
Salisbury Rd. Woking GU22 ...... 89 E8
Salisbury Rd.
  Worc Pk KT19 & KT4 .... 57 E7
Salisbury Terr. Mytch GU16 ...... 86 A3
Salix Cl. Sunby TW16 .... 15 B1
Salliesfield. Twick TW2 .... 5 D1
Salmons La. Whytlf CR3 .... 100 F7
Salmons La W. Cater CR3 .... 100 F7
Salmons Rd. Chess KT9 .... 56 E4
Salmons Rd. Effing KT24 .... 113 C6
Salt Box Rd. Jacobs GU3 & GU4 109 B6
Salt Box Rd. Worpl GU3 & GU4 . 109 B6
Salt La. Hyde GU8 .... 171 E5
Saltash Cl. Cheam SM1 .... 58 F6
Saltbox Hill. Bigg H TN16 .... 83 B6
Saltdean Cl.
  Crawl RH10 & RH11 .... 201 D3
Salter House. Streat SW16 ..... 21 C4
Salter's Hill.
  W Norw SE19 & SE27 .... 22 D3
Salterford Rd. Streat SW17 ...... 21 A2
Salterns Rd. Worth RH10 .... 202 C3
Saltire Gdns. Brack RG12 ...... 27 A8
Saltram Rd. Farnb GU14 .... 85 E2
Salvador. Up Toot SW17 .... 20 F3
Salvation Pl. Fetch KT22 .... 95 A3
Salvington Rd. Crawl RH11 .... 200 F3
Salwey Cl. Easth RG12 .... 27 B3
Samaritan Cl. Crawl RH11 ...... 200 E4
Samarkand Cl. Friml GU15 .... 66 B4
Samos Rd. Penge SE20 .... 43 B7
Samphire Cl. Crawl RH11 .... 201 A3
Sampleoak La. Chil GU4 .... 131 E2
Sampleoak La. Woner GU4 ..... 131 E2
Sampson Ct. Shep TW17 .... 34 C4
Sampson Pk. Binf RG12 .... 26 D8
Samuel Cody Sch The.
  Farnb GU11 .... 105 B7
Samuel Ct. Beck BR3 .... 44 B6
Samuel Johnson Cl.
  Streat SW16 .... 21 F4
San Carlos App. Alder GU11 ... 105 C2
San Feliu Ct. E Grins RH19 .... 186 B2
Sanctuary Rd. Harm TW19 & TW6 . 3 A1
Sanctuary The. Morden SM4 ..... 40 A3
Sand Hill. Farnb GU14 .... 85 B7
Sand Hill Ct. Farnb GU14 .... 85 B7
Sandal Rd. New Mal KT3 .... 38 E5
Sandalwood. Guild GU2 .... 130 B8
Sandalwood Ave. Addl KT16 ..... 51 E7
Sandalwood Rd. Felt TW13 .... 15 B5
Sandbourne Ave. Merton SW19 . 40 B7
Sandcross La. Dovgn RH2 ...... 139 A5
Sandcross Sch. Woodh RH2 ... 138 F5
Sandell's Ave. Ashf TW15 .... 14 C3
Sanders Cl. Hampt TW12 .... 16 C3
Sanders House. Streat SW16 ... 21 E2
Sandersfield Rd. Banstd SM7 .. 78 B4
Sanderstead Cl. Streat SW12 ... 21 C8
Sanderstead Court Ave.
  Sander CR2 .... 81 A6
Sanderstead Ct. Sander CR2 .... 81 A7
Sanderstead Hill. S Croy CR2 ... 80 F8
Sanderstead Hts. S Croy CR2 ... 81 A8
Sanderstead Rd. S Croy CR2 .... 61 D2
Sanderstead Sta. S Croy CR2 ... 61 D2
Sandes Pl. Leahd KT22 .... 75 A1
Sandfield Cty Prim Sch.
  Guild GU1 .... 130 D8
Sandfield Gdns. S Norw CR7 .... 42 B6
Sandfield Pl. S Norw CR7 .... 42 C6
Sandfield Rd. S Norw CR7 .... 42 B6
Sandfield Terr. Guild GU1 .... 130 D8
Sandfields. Send GU23 .... 90 A3
Sandford Ct. Alder GU11 .... 104 F1

Sandford Down. Brack RG12 ..... 27 F4
Sandford Rd. Alder GU11 .... 104 F1
Sandford Rd. Heath E GU9 ..... 125 B7
Sandgate House. Beck BR3 ... 24 A1
Sandgate La.
  Wands SW17 & SW18 .... 20 E7
Sandhawes Hill. E Grins RH19 . 186 A4
Sandheath Rd. Beac H GU26 .. 188 C7
Sandhill La. Crawl D RH10 ..... 204 B7
Sandhills. Wallin CR0 & SM6 .... 60 D6
Sandhills Ct. Thorpe GU25 .... 31 E4
Sandhills La.
  Thorpe GU25 & TW20 .... 31 F4
Sandhills Meadow.
  Lo Hall TW17 .... 34 C2
Sandhills Rd. Reig RH2 .... 139 A7
Sandhurst Ave. Tolw KT5 .... 38 B2
Sandhurst Cl. S Croy CR2 .... 61 E2
Sandhurst La. Blckw GU17 .... 64 A5
Sandhurst Prim Sch. Catf SE6 .. 24 E7
Sandhurst Rd. Catf SE6 .... 24 D7
Sandhurst Rd. Crowth RG11 ..... 45 B3
Sandhurst Rd. Woki RG11 .... 25 A1
Sandhurst Sch. Sandh GU15 .... 45 D1
Sandhurst Sta. Sandh GU17 ..... 64 A8
Sandhurst Way. S Croy CR2 ..... 61 E3
Sandiford House. Cater CR3 ... 100 E3
Sandiford Rd. Cheam SM3 .... 58 F8
Sandiland Cres. Coney H BR2 .. 63 F8
Sandilands. S Croy CR0 .... 62 A7
Sandlands Gr. Walt o t H KT20 .. 97 A4
Sandlands Rd. Walt o t H KT20 .. 97 A3
Sandon Cl. Thame D KT10 .... 36 D1
Sandon House. Streat SW2 ... 21 E8
Sandown Ave. Esher KT10 .... 55 C5
Sandown Cl. Blckw GU17 .... 64 D5
Sandown Cl. Cranf TW5 .... 4 A6
Sandown Cres. Alder GU11 ..... 126 B7
Sandown Ct. Belm SM2 .... 59 B3
Sandown Dr. Friml GU16 .... 65 E2
Sandown Dr. Wallin SM5 .... 60 A2
Sandown Gate. Esher KT10 ...... 55 D7
Sandown House. Penge SE26 ... 23 B2
Sandown Ind Pk. Thame D KT10 55 A8
Sandown Lodge. Woodc KT18 .. 76 D5
Sandown Park. Esher KT10 ...... 55 C8
Sandown Rd. Coulsd CR5 .... 79 A3
Sandown Rd. Croy SE25 .... 43 B4
Sandown Rd. Esher KT10 .... 55 C6
Sandpiper Cl. Crawl RH11 ...... 200 D4
Sandpiper Rd. Selsd CR2 .... 81 D8
Sandpit Hall Rd. Chobh GU24 ... 69 A7
Sandpit Heath. Fairl GU3 .... 108 D5
Sandpit Rd. Catf BR1 .... 24 E3
Sandpit Rd. Redh RH1 .... 139 F8
Sandpits Rd. Rich TW10 .... 17 D6
Sandpits Rd. S Croy CR0 .... 62 D6
Sandra Cl. Islew TW3 .... 5 B2
Sandra House. E Mole KT8 .... 36 D4
Sandringham Ave. Merton SW20 39 E7
Sandringham Cl. E Grins RH19 206 A8
Sandringham Cl. Farnb GU14 .. 105 B8
Sandringham Cl.
  Putney SW19 .... 19 D7
Sandringham Cl. Pyrf GU22 ...... 71 A3
Sandringham Ct. Beck BR3 ...... 44 C8
Sandringham Ct. Belm SM2 ..... 59 A2
Sandringham Cty Inf Sch.
  Friml GU16 .... 85 F7
Sandringham Dr. Ashf TW15 .... 13 C4
Sandringham Gdns. Cranf TW5 . 4 A6
Sandringham Rd. Crawl RH11 . 201 B2
Sandringham Rd. N Cheam KT4 . 58 A7
Sandringham Rd.
  Stan TW19 & TW6 .... 2 E2
Sandringham Rd. Thorn H CR0 .. 42 C4
Sandringham Way. Friml GU16 . 85 F8
Sandrock. Haslem GU27 .... 208 C6
Sandrock Hill Rd. Rowl GU10 .. 146 A5
Sandrock Hill Rd. Wreccl GU10 146 A5
Sandrock Pl. S Croy CR0 .... 62 D6
Sandrock Rd. Westc RH4 .... 135 B5
Sandroyd Way. Cobham KT11 ... 74 A6
Sands Cl. The San GU10 .... 126 D2
Sands Rd. Farnh GU10 .... 126 D2
Sands Rd. The San GU10 .... 126 D2
Sandstone. Rich TW9 .... 7 A7
Sandways. Rich TW9 .... 7 A6
Sandy Cl. Mayb GU22 .... 70 C2
Sandy Croft. E Ewell KT17 .... 58 C1
Sandy Cross. The San GU10 ... 126 F4
Sandy Dr. Cobham KT11 .... 73 F6
Sandy Dr. Cobham KT11 .... 74 A8
Sandy Hill Rd. Heath E GU9 ... 125 B7
Sandy Hill Rd. Wallin SM6 .... 60 C2
Sandy Holt. Cobham KT11 .... 73 F6
Sandy La. Albury GU5 .... 132 C2
Sandy La. Arting GU2 & GU3 ... 130 B5
Sandy La. Belm SM2 .... 58 E2
Sandy La. Betch RH3 .... 116 E1
Sandy La. Bletch RH1 .... 120 C3
Sandy La. Brack RG12 .... 27 C8
Sandy La. Burrh GU24 .... 49 E2
Sandy La. Camb GU15 .... 65 E6
Sandy La. Cobham KT11 & KT22 .. 74 B7
Sandy La. Crawl D RH10 .... 204 A8
Sandy La. E Grins RH19 .... 185 F1
Sandy La. Farnc GU7 .... 150 D6
Sandy La. Grays GU27 .... 189 E1
Sandy La. Kings KT20 .... 98 A4
Sandy La. Limps RH8 .... 123 B7
Sandy La. Mayb GU22 .... 70 C2
Sandy La. Mitch CR4 .... 41 A8
Sandy La. N Asct SL5 .... 28 C8
Sandy La. Normdy GU3 .... 107 D4
Sandy La. Nutf RH1 .... 119 E1
Sandy La. Oxted RH8 .... 122 C6

Sandy La. Pyrf GU22 .... 71 A3
Sandy La. Reig RH2 .... 138 B8
Sandy La. Rich TW10 .... 17 D6
Sandy La. Rushm GU10 .... 168 B5
Sandy La. S Nutf RH1 .... 119 E1
Sandy La. Sandh GU17 .... 45 A2
Sandy La. Send GU23 .... 90 C4
Sandy La. Shere GU5 .... 133 A3
Sandy La. Shottm GU26 .... 188 F2
Sandy La. Shottm GU26 & GU27 . 207 C7
Sandy La. Sunnin SL5 .... 30 A4
Sandy La. Tedd KT8 & TW11 ...... 17 B1
Sandy La. Thorpe GU25 .... 31 E5
Sandy La. W Heath GU14 .... 84 D7
Sandy La. Walt O T KT12 .... 35 C3
Sandy La. Wallin SM6 .... 60 D5
Sandy La S. Wallin SM6 .... 60 C3
Sandy Lane Cty Jun Sch.
  Brack RG12 .... 27 C8
Sandy Rd. Row Tn KT15 .... 52 A4
Sandy Ride. Ascot SL5 .... 29 E5
Sandy Way. Cobham KT11 .... 74 A7
Sandy Way. Croy CR0 .... 62 F7
Sandy Way. Mayb GU22 .... 70 C2
Sandy Way. Walt O T KT12 .... 34 F1
Sandycombe Rd. E Bed TW14 ..... 15 A7
Sandycombe Rd. Rich TW9 .... 7 A5
Sandycoombe Rd. Twick TW1 .... 6 C1
Sanger Ave. Chess KT9 .... 56 F6
Sanger Dr. Send GU23 .... 90 C4
Sangers Cty Jun Sch.
  Horley RH6 .... 160 F3
Sangers Dr. Horley RH6 .... 160 F3
Sangley Rd. Catf SE6 .... 24 C7
Sangley Rd. S Norw SE25 .... 42 E5
Santina Cl. Heath E GU9 .... 125 D8
Sanway Cl. Byfl KT14 .... 71 E5
Sanway Rd. Byfl KT14 .... 71 E5
Sappho Ct. Woking GU21 .... 68 E3
Sapte Cl. Cran GU6 .... 175 A3
Saracen Cl. Thorn H CR0 .... 42 D3
Sarah House. Rhampt SW15 .... 7 F3
Sarah Way. Farnb GU14 .... 85 B4
Sardeson House. **13**
  W Norw SW27 .... 22 B3
Sarel Way. Horley RH6 .... 161 B5
Sargent Cl. Crawl RH10 .... 201 F2
Sarjant Path. Putney SW19 .... 19 D6
Sark Cl. Crawl RH11 .... 201 A2
Sark Cl. Heston TW5 .... 5 A7
Sarsby Dr. Wray TW19 .... 12 A6
Sarsen Ave. Hounsl TW3 .... 5 A5
Sarsfield Rd.
  Up Toot SW12 & SW17 .... 20 F7
Sarum. Easth RG12 .... 26 F1
Sarum Cres. Woki GU11 .... 25 D7
Sarum Gn. Oat Pk KT13 .... 53 E7
Satellite Bsns Village The.
  Crawl RH10 .... 181 E2
Satis Rd. Ewell KT17 .... 76 F8
Saturn Cl. Crawl RH11 .... 200 E4
Saturn Croft. Wink RG12 .... 8 B2
Saunders Cl. Crawl RH10 .... 202 B7
Saunders Copse. Woking GU22 ... 89 B5
Saunders House. **11**
  Streat SW2 .... 22 A7
Saunders La. Woking GU22 .... 89 B5
Saundersfield House.
  Banstd SM7 .... 78 B5
Saunton Ave. Harl UB3 .... 3 F7
Saunton Gdns. **1** W Heath GU14 85 A6
Savernake Way. Brack RG12 .... 27 F4
Savernake Wlk. Crawl RH10 ...... 201 F1
Savile Cl. New Mal KT3 .... 38 E4
Savile Gdns. W Barn SW20 .... 39 A6
Saville Cres. Ashf TW15 .... 14 D2
Saville Gdns. Friml GU15 .... 66 B5
Saville Rd. Twick TW1 .... 16 F7
Saville Row. Coney H BR2 .... 44 F1
Savin Lodge. Sutton SM2 .... 59 C3
Savona Cl. **12** Wimble SW19 ...... 19 D1
Savona Ct. Wimble SW20 .... 39 D8
Savoy Gr. Hawley GU17 .... 64 D3
Sawkins Cl. Putney SW19 .... 19 E6
Sawtry Cl. Carsh SM5 .... 40 E2
Sawyer House. **15** Dulw SE21 ..... 22 E4
Sawyer's Hill. Rich TW10 .... 17 F8
Saxby Rd. Streat SW2 .... 21 E8
Saxby's La. Lingf RH7 .... 164 D5
Saxley. Horley RH6 .... 161 C4
Saxon Ave. Felt TW13 .... 15 F6
Saxon Bsns Ctr. Merton SW19 ..... 40 C8
Saxon Cl. Surb KT6 .... 37 D3
Saxon Cres. Horsh RH12 .... 217 B4
Saxon Croft. Farnh GU9 .... 125 C1
Saxon Cty Jun Sch.
  Shep GU TW17 .... 34 A4
Saxon Dr. Wink RG12 .... 27 E8
Saxon House. Felt TW13 .... 15 F6
Saxon House. Woodh RH2 .... 138 F6
Saxon House. Woodh RH2 .... 139 A6
Saxon Rd. Ashf TW15 .... 14 D2
Saxon Rd. Broml BR1 .... 24 F1
Saxon Rd. Thorn H CR0 & SE25 ... 42 D4
Saxon Rd. Walt O T KT12 .... 54 D7
Saxon Rd. Worth RH10 .... 202 E5
Saxon Way. Harm UB7 .... 2 C8
Saxon Way. Reig RH2 .... 117 F2
Saxonbury Ave. Sunby TW16 ...... 35 B7
Saxonbury Cl. Mitch CR4 .... 40 D6
Saxonbury Gdns. Long D KT6 ...... 37 C1
Saxons. Tadwrth KT20 .... 97 D6
Sayer Ct. **4** Knaph GU21 .... 68 E1
Sayer's Wlk. Rich TW10 .... 17 F8
Sayers Cl. Fetch KT22 .... 94 C4
Sayers Cl. Friml GU16 .... 85 E7
Sayers The. **5** E Grins RH19 .... 185 C1

Sayes Court Cty Jun Sch.
  Addl KT15 .... 52 B5
Sayes Court Farm Dr. Addl KT15 52 B5
Sayes Ct. Addl KT15 .... 52 C5
Sbac Track. Farnb GU11 .... 104 E6
Scaitcliffe Sch. Eng Gn TW20 ..... 11 A5
Scallops Cl. Crawl RH10 .... 202 A7
Scallows Rd. Crawl RH10 .... 202 A7
Scampton Rd. Stan TW6 .... 2 F1
Scania Wlk. Wink RG12 .... 8 B2
Scarborough Cl. Belm SM2 .... 77 F8
Scarborough Cl. Bigg H TN16 ..... 83 C1
Scarborough Rd. Harl TW6 .... 3 C1
Scarbrook Rd. Croy CR0 & CR9 ... 61 C7
Scarlet Oaks. Friml GU15 .... 65 E3
Scarlet Rd. Catf SE6 .... 24 E5
Scarlett Cl. Knaph GU21 .... 68 F1
Scarlett's La. Alder GU11 .... 105 A3
Scarlette Manor Wlk. **10**
  Streat SE24 .... 22 A8
Scarth Rd. Barnes SW13 .... 7 F4
Schiller International Univ.
  Coney H BR4 .... 63 D6
Scholars Ct. Crawl D RH10 .... 204 A8
Scholars Rd. Streat SW12 .... 21 C7
School Cl. Bellf GU1 .... 109 D3
School Cl. Bisley GU24 .... 68 A4
School Cl. Horsh RH12 .... 218 A6
School Cotts. Woking GU22 .... 89 C5
School Hill. Crowth RG45 .... 45 D4
School Hill. Merst RH1 .... 119 C7
School Hill. Sandh GU17 .... 45 A1
School Hill. Seale GU10 .... 127 B4
School Hill. Warn RH12 .... 216 F8
School Hill. Wreccl GU10 .... 145 F6
School House La. Tedd TW11 .... 17 C1
School Houses. Hasc GU8 .... 172 E4
School La. Addl KT15 .... 52 A6
School La. Ash W RH19 .... 206 E6
School La. Bagsh GU19 .... 47 E2
School La. Crond GU10 .... 124 D8
School La. E Clan GU4 .... 111 E4
School La. Egham TW20 .... 12 A3
School La. Fetch KT22 .... 94 D5
School La. Lo Hall TW17 .... 34 B2
School La. M Bourn GU10 .... 146 D6
School La. Mickle RH5 .... 115 C8
School La. Ockham GU23 .... 92 B5
School La. Pirb GU24 .... 87 E5
School La. Putt GU3 .... 128 C4
School La. Shackl GU8 .... 149 E6
School La. Surb KT6 .... 38 A1
School La. Tedd KT1 .... 37 C8
School La. W Hors KT24 .... 112 B6
School La. Walt o t H KT20 .... 97 A2
School La. Westc RH4 .... 135 D6
School La. Windl GU20 .... 48 D4
School of Art Pewley Annexe.
  Guild GU1 .... 130 E7
School Pas. **3** King U T KT1 ...... 37 F7
School Rd. Ascot SL5 .... 29 D4
School Rd. Ashf TW15 .... 14 B2
School Rd. Binst GU10 .... 145 E3
School Rd. E Mole KT8 .... 36 D5
School Rd. Graysh GU26 .... 188 B4
School Rd. Hampt TW12 .... 16 C2
School Rd. Harm UB7 .... 2 D8
School Rd. Hasc GU8 .... 172 E4
School Rd. Hounsl TW3 .... 5 C4
School Rd. Linch GU27 .... 207 F5
School Rd. Tedd KT1 .... 37 C8
School Rd. Windl GU20 .... 48 B5
School Rd. Woki RG11 .... 25 D6
School Road Ave. Hampt TW12 ... 16 C2
School Wlk. Shep TW16 .... 35 A6
Schroder Ct. Eng Gn TW20 .... 11 B3
Scillonian Rd. Guild GU2 .... 130 B7
Scilly Isles. Hinch W KT10 .... 55 E8
Scizdons Climb. Godal GU7 .... 150 F4
Scoles Cres. Streat SW2 .... 22 A7
Scoresdale. S Norw SE19 .... 42 E8
Scory Cl. Crawl RH11 .... 201 A3
Scotland Bridge Rd.
  Woodhm KT15 .... 71 A8
Scotland Cl. Ash V GU12 .... 106 A5
Scotland Farm Rd. Ash V GU12 106 A5
Scotland Hill. Sandh GU17 .... 45 A1
Scotland Hill. Sandh GU17 .... 64 A8
Scotlands Cl. Haslem GU27 ...... 208 D5
Scotlands Dr. Haslem GU27 ...... 208 C5
Scots Cl. Stan TW19 .... 13 D7
Scotsdale Cl. Cheam SM2 .... 58 E3
Scotshall La. Farlgh CR6 .... 82 C4
Scott Cl. Stough GU2 .... 109 A3
Scott Cl. Thorn H SW16 .... 41 F8
Scott Cl. W Ewell KT19 .... 57 C5
Scott Cl. W Ewell KT19 .... 57 C5
Scott Farm Cl. Hinch W KT7 .... 37 B1
Scott Gdns. Heston TW5 .... 4 D7
Scott House. Rich TW10 .... 17 C6
Scott Rd. Crawl RH10 .... 201 F3
Scott Terr. Brack RG12 .... 27 E8
Scott's Ave. Ashf TW16 .... 14 E1
Scott's Ave. Beck BR2 .... 44 D7
Scott's Cl. Farnb GU14 .... 85 B7
Scott's Grove Cl. W End GU24 .... 68 D6
Scott's Grove Rd. W End GU24 ... 68 C6
Scott's Hill. Outw RH1 & RH6 .... 162 D5
Scott's La. Beck BR2 & BR3 .... 44 D7
Scott's Way. Ashf TW16 .... 14 E1
Scotts Dr. Hampt TW12 .... 16 B1
Scotts Farm Rd. W Ewell KT19 ... 57 C4
Scotts Farm Rd. W Ewell KT19 ... 57 C4
Screw Corner Rd.
  Bowl Gn GU8 .... 170 A1
Scrooby St. **3** Lewish SE6 ...... 24 B8
Scrutton Cl. Streat SW12 .... 21 D8
Scylla Cres. E Bed TW6 .... 3 B1
Scylla Cres. E Bed TW6&TW14 .... 14 B8
Scylla Pl. Woking GU21 .... 89 A8

Scylla Rd. E Bed TW14 & TW6 .... 3 B1
Seabrook Dr. W Wick BR4 .... 63 E8
Seafire Way.
  Farnb GU11 & GU14 .... 104 E7
Seaford Rd. Crawl RH11 .... 201 A2
Seaford Rd. Stan TW19 & TW6 ..... 2 D2
Seaford Rd. Woki RG11 .... 25 D6
Seaforth Gdns. Worc Pk KT19 ..... 57 F5
Seaforth Lodge. Barnes SW13 ...... 7 F5
Sealand Rd. Harm TW6 .... 3 A1
Seale La. The San GU10 & GU3 .. 126 E4
Seale Rd. Elst GU8 .... 148 B7
Seale Rd. The San GU8 .... 148 B7
Seaman's Gn. Bear Gn RH5 .... 178 D8
Searchwood Rd. Warlgm CR6 ..... 81 B1
Searle Ct. Mitch CR4 .... 40 E8
Searle Hill. Woodh RH2 .... 139 A7
Searle Rd. M Bourn GU9 .... 146 C8
Searle's View. Horsh RH12 .... 217 E5
Seath House. **4** Penge SE26 ..... 23 B3
Seaton Cl. Putney SW15 .... 19 B8
Seaton Dr. Ashf TW15 .... 13 E6
Seaton Rd. Camb GU15 .... 65 B5
Seaton Rd. Mitch CR4 .... 40 E7
Seaton Rd. Twick TW2 .... 5 C1
Sebastopol Rd. Alder GU11 .... 105 B2
Second Ave. Mortl SW14 .... 7 E4
Second Ave. Walt O T KT12 .... 35 B3
Second Ave. Woodhm KT15 .... 52 B2
Second Cl. E Mole KT8 .... 36 C5
Second Cross Rd. Twick TW2 ...... 16 E6
Seddon Ct. Crawl RH11 .... 201 B1
Seddon Rd. Morden SM4 .... 40 D4
Sedgefield Cl. Crawl RH10 .... 202 E7
Sedgehill Rd. Catf SE6 .... 24 B3
Sedgehill Sch. Catf SE6 .... 24 B3
Sedgemoor. Farnb GU14 .... 85 B7
Sedgeway. Catf SE6 .... 24 F7
Sedgewick Cl. Crawl RH10 .... 202 C6
Sedgewick House. Putney SW19 19 D6
Sedgewood Cl. Hayes BR2 .... 44 F2
Sedley Ct. For Hil SE23 .... 23 B6
Seebys Oak. Sandh GU15 .... 64 E6
Seeley Dr. Dulw SE21 .... 22 E4
Seely Rd. Mitch SW17 .... 21 A2
Seething Wells Halls Of Residence.
  King U T KT6 .... 37 C3
Seething Wells La. King U T KT6 .. 37 C3
Sefton Cl. W End GU24 .... 67 F6
Sefton Ct. Hounsl TW5 .... 5 B6
Sefton Lodge. **2** Twick TW1 .... 6 C1
Sefton Rd. Croy CR0 .... 43 A1
Sefton Rd. Epsom KT19 .... 57 D1
Segal Cl. For Hil SE23 .... 23 E8
Segrave Cl. Whit V KT13 .... 53 A3
Segsbury Gr. Brack RG12 .... 27 F5
Sekhon Terr. Felt TW13 .... 16 A5
Selborne Ave. Alder GU11 .... 126 C6
Selborne Rd. Blckw GU17 .... 64 C6
Selborne Rd. S Croy CR2 .... 61 F7
Selbourne Ave. Woodhm KT15 ... 52 B2
Selbourne Cl. Crawl RH10 .... 182 D2
Selbourne Cl. Woodhm KT15 ...... 52 B1
Selbourne Rd. Burph GU1 .... 110 A4
Selbourne Sq. Tyl Gn RH9 .... 121 C5
Selby Cl. Chess KT9 .... 56 E3
Selby Ct. Twick TW2 .... 16 D6
Selby Gn. Carsh SM5 .... 40 E2
Selby Rd. Ashf TW15 .... 14 C2
Selby Rd. Carsh SM5 .... 40 E2
Selby Rd. Penge SE20 .... 43 A7
Selby Wlk. **1** Woking GU21 ...... 69 B1
Selbys. Lingf RH7 .... 164 E5
Selcroft Rd. Purley CR8 .... 80 B7
Selham Cl. Crawl RH11 .... 201 A7
Selhurst Cl. Horse GU21 .... 69 F4
Selhurst Cl. Putney SW19 .... 19 D7
Selhurst New Ct. Thorn H SE25 ... 42 E3
Selhurst New Rd. Thorn H SE25 .. 42 E3
Selhurst Park. S Norw SE25 .... 42 E5
Selhurst Pl. Thorn H CR0 & SE25 . 42 E3
Selhurst Rd. S Norw CR0 & SE25 . 42 E4
Selhurst Rd. Thorn H CR0 & SE25 42 E4
Selhurst Sta. S Norw SE25 .... 42 F4
Selkirk Rd. Twick TW2 .... 16 C7
Selkirk Rd. Up Toot SW17 .... 20 E4
Sellar's Hill. Farnc GU7 .... 150 D7
Sellincourt Inf Sch.
  Up Toot SW17 .... 20 E2
Sellincourt Jun Sch.
  Up Toot SW17 .... 20 E2
Sellincourt Rd. Up Toot SW17 .... 20 E2
Sellindge Cl. Beck BR3 .... 23 F1
Selsdon Ave. S Croy CR2 .... 61 D4
Selsdon Cl. King U T KT6 .... 37 E4
Selsdon Cres. S Croy CR2 .... 62 C1
Selsdon High Sch. S Croy CR2 ... 62 D3
Selsdon Park Golf Course.
  Sander CR2 .... 81 B7
Selsdon Park Rd.
  New Add CR0 & CR2 .... 62 E2
Selsdon Park Rd.
  S Croy CR0 or CR2 .... 62 E2
Selsdon Park Rd.
  Selsd CR0 or CR2 .... 62 E2
Selsdon Prim Sch. S Croy CR2 ... 62 C2
Selsdon Rd. Croy CR2 .... 61 D4
Selsdon Rd. N Worw SE27 .... 22 B4
Selsdon Rd. Woodhm KT15 .... 71 A8
Selsdon Road Ind Est.
  S Croy CR2 .... 61 D4
Selsey Ct. **3** Crawl RH11 .... 201 B2
Selsey Rd. Crawl RH11 .... 201 A2
Selsfield Rd.
  Turn H RH10 & RH19 .... 204 A2
Selsfield Rd. W Hoath RH19 ...... 204 B1
Seltops Cl. Cran GU6 .... 174 F2
Selwood Cl. Stan TW19 .... 2 C1

Selwood Gdns. Stan TW19 .... 2 C1
Selwood Rd. Cheam SM3 .... 39 F1
Selwood Rd. Chess KT9 .... 56 D6
Selwood Rd. Croy CR0 .... 43 B1
Selwood Rd. Old Wok GU22 .... 90 B7
Selworthy Rd. For Hil SE23 & SE6 23 F5
Selwyn Ave. Rich TW9 .... 6 F4
Selwyn Cl. Crawl RH10 .... 182 C1
Selwyn Cl. Hounsl TW4 .... 4 E3
Selwyn Ct. **7** Rich TW10 .... 6 F2
Selwyn Rd. New Mal KT3 .... 38 D4
Semaphore Rd. Guild GU1 .... 130 E7
Semley Rd. Thorn H SW16 .... 41 E7
Semper Cl. Knaph GU21 .... 68 E2
Send Barns La. Send GU23 .... 90 E2
Send Barns La. Send M GU23 ...... 90 E2
Send C of E Grant Maintained Sch.
  Send GU23 .... 90 E3
Send Cl. Send GU23 .... 90 C4
Send Hill. Send GU23 .... 90 C3
Send Marsh Rd. Send GU23 .... 90 E4
Send Marsh Rd. Send M GU23 ..... 90 E4
Send Rd. Send GU23 .... 90 C4
Seneca Rd. Thorn H CR7 .... 42 C5
Senga Rd. Carsh CR4 .... 41 A1
Senhouse Rd. Cheam SM3 .... 58 D7
Sequoia Pk. Crawl RH11 .... 201 D4
Serpentine Gn. Merst RH1 .... 119 D6
Serrin Way. Horsh RH12 .... 217 E5
Service Rd. Crawl RH6 .... 181 F8
Service Rd. Crawl RH6 .... 182 B7
Servite House. Beck BR3 .... 43 F8
Servite House. Dork RH4 .... 136 A5
Servite House. Knaph GU21 .... 68 D2
Servius Ct. **2** Brent TW8 .... 6 D7
Setley Way. Brack RG12 .... 27 F6
Seven Acres. Carsh SM5 .... 59 E8
Seven Arches App. Whit V KT13 ... 53 A3
Seven Hills Cl.
  Whit V KT12 & KT13 .... 53 E2
Seven Hills Rd.
  Whit V KT12 & KT13 .... 53 E3
Seven Hills Rd (South).
  Whit V KT11 .... 72 E6
Sevenoaks Cl. Belm SM2 .... 59 B1
Severn Cl. Sandh GU17 .... 64 C8
Severn Cres. Bra Hil SL3 .... 1 B8
Severn Dr. Hinch W KT10 .... 56 A8
Severn Dr. Walt O T KT12 .... 35 C2
Severn Rd. W Heath GU14 .... 84 E6
Severn Rd. Worth RH10 .... 202 C3
Seward Rd. Penge BR3 .... 43 D7
Sewell Ave. Woki RG11 .... 25 A8
Sewer's Farm Rd. Abin C RH5 ... 155 F6
Sewill Cl. Charl RH6 .... 180 F7
Seychelle Ct. Beck BR3 .... 24 B1
Seymour Ave. Cater CR3 .... 100 C4
Seymour Ave. Ewell KT17 .... 58 B2
Seymour Ave. W Barn SM4 .... 39 D2
Seymour Ct. E Mole KT8 .... 36 C4
Seymour Ct. Camb GU15 .... 66 B7
Seymour Gdns. Felt TW13 .... 15 C4
Seymour Gdns. King U T KT5 ...... 37 F4
Seymour Gdns. Twick TW1 .... 17 B8
Seymour Pl. Croy SE25 .... 43 B5
Seymour Rd. Carsh CR4 .... 41 A2
Seymour Rd. Crawl RH11 .... 201 B2
Seymour Rd. E Mole KT8 .... 36 C4
Seymour Rd. Hampt TW12 .... 16 C3
Seymour Rd. Head Dn GU35 ...... 187 C4
Seymour Rd. Ock Rid GU7 .... 150 D2
Seymour Rd. Tedd KT1 .... 37 D8
Seymour Rd. Wallin SM5 .... 60 A5
Seymour Rd. Wands SW18 .... 19 F8
Seymour Rd. Wimble SW19 .... 19 D5
Seymour Terr. Penge SE20 .... 43 B8
Seymour Villas. Penge SE20 .... 43 A8
Seymour Way. Ashf TW16 .... 14 A3
Shabden Cotts. Chips CR5 .... 98 F6
Shabden Park. Kings CR5 .... 98 E5
Shabden Park Hospl. Kings CR5 . 98 E5
Shackleford Rd. Old Wok GU22 ... 90 A7
Shackleford Rd. Shackl GU8 ..... 149 E6
Shackleford St Mary's Fst Sch.
  Shackl GU8 .... 149 E6
Shacklegate La. Tedd TW11 .... 16 E4
Shackleton Cl. For Hil SE23 .... 23 B6
Shackleton Ct. **2** Dulw SE21 .... 22 D6
Shackleton Ct. **6** Stan TW19 .... 2 E1
Shackleton Rd. Crawl RH10 ...... 201 F3
Shackstead La. Godal GU7 .... 150 C3
Shackster La. Godal GU7 .... 150 C3
Shadbolt Cl. Worc Pk KT4 .... 57 F8
Shady Nook. Hale GU9 .... 125 B6
Shadyhanger. Farnc GU7 .... 150 E6
Shaef Way. Tedd TW11 .... 17 A1
Shaftesbury Ave. Felt TW14 .... 4 A1
Shaftesbury Cl. Brack RG12 .... 27 D4
Shaftesbury Cres. Stain TW18 ..... 13 D1
Shaftesbury Ct. Farnb GU14 ...... 105 C8
Shaftesbury Ct. Woki RG11 .... 25 D7
Shaftesbury House. Croy SE25 .... 43 A3
Shaftesbury Independent Sch.
  Purley CR8 .... 80 B6
Shaftesbury Mount.
  Hawley GU17 .... 64 D3
Shaftesbury Rd. Beck BR3 .... 43 F7
Shaftesbury Rd. Bisley GU24 ...... 67 F3
Shaftesbury Rd. Carsh SM5 .... 40 E2
Shaftesbury Rd. Mayb GU22 .... 70 B2
Shaftesbury Rd. Rich TW9 .... 6 E3
Shaftesbury Rd. Worth RH10 .... 202 D4
Shaftesbury Way. Twick TW2 ...... 16 D5
Shaftewood Ct. Up Toot SW17 .... 20 F5
Shagbrook. Buckl RH2 .... 117 C2
Shakespeare Ave. Felt TW14 .... 4 A1
Shakespeare Gdns.
  W Heath GU14 .... 84 D5
Shakespeare Rd. Addl KT15 .... 52 D6
Shakespeare Way. Felt TW13 ...... 15 C4
Shakespeare Way. Wink RG12 ..... 27 E8

Shalbourne Rise. Camb GU15 ..... 65 D5
Shalden House. Rhampt SW15 ...... 7 F1
Shalden Rd. Alder GU12 .... 126 D5
Shaldon Dr. Merton SM4 .... 39 E4
Shaldon Way. Walt O T KT12 .... 54 C7
Shale Gn. Merst RH1 .... 119 D6
Shalesbrook La. For Row RH18 .. 206 F1
Shalford Cty Inf Sch.
  Shalf GU4 .... 130 E3
Shalford La. **7** Shalf GU4 .... 130 E4
Shalford Rd. Guild GU1 & GU4 ... 130 D5
Shalford Sta. Shalf GU4 .... 130 E3
Shalston Villas. Surb KT5 & KT6 .. 37 F3
Shalstone Rd. Mortl SW14 & TW9 . 7 B4
Shambles The. Guild GU1 .... 130 D7
Shamrock Cl. Fetch KT22 .... 94 D6
Shamrock Cl. Friml GU16 .... 85 D8
Shamrock House. For Hil SE26 .... 23 A4
Shamrock Rd. Thorn H CR0 .... 41 F3
Shandys Cl. Horsh RH12 .... 217 A1
Shanklin Ct. Alder GU12 .... 105 C1
Shannon Commercial Ctr.
  W Barn KT3 .... 39 A5
Shannon Corner. W Barn KT3 ...... 39 A5
Shannon Ct. Croy CR0 .... 42 C1
Shannon Way. Beck BR3 .... 24 B2
Shap Cres. Carsh SM5 .... 40 F1
Sharon Cl. Crawl RH10 .... 202 A4
Sharon Cl. Epsom KT19 .... 76 C6
Sharon Cl. Fetch KT23 .... 94 A3
Sharon Cl. Long D KT6 .... 37 C1
Sharonelle Ct. Woki RG11 .... 25 B6
Sharpthorne Cl. Crawl RH11 ..... 200 F6
Shaw Cl. Ewell KT17 .... 76 F8
Shaw Cl. Ottsh KT16 .... 51 C4
Shaw Cl. Sander CR2 .... 80 F7
Shaw Cres. Sander CR2 .... 80 F7
Shaw Ct. Cater CR3 .... 100 D6
Shaw Dr. Walt O T KT12 .... 35 C2
Shaw Path. Catf BR1 .... 24 F5
Shaw Pk. Crowth RG11 .... 45 B3
Shaw Rd. Catf BR1 .... 24 F5
Shaw Rd. Tats TN16 .... 103 C7
Shaw Way. Wallin SM6 .... 60 E3
Shawfield Cty Fst Sch.
  Ash GU12 .... 106 A3
Shawfield La. Alder GU12 .... 105 F2
Shawfield Rd. Ash GU12 .... 106 A3
Shawford Ct. **9** Rhampt SW15 ... 19 A8
Shawford Rd. Epsom KT19 .... 57 D4
Shawford Rd. W Ewell KT19 .... 57 D4
Shawley Cres. Burgh H KT18 ...... 77 D1
Shawley Cty Fst & Mid Schs.
  Burgh H KT18 .... 77 C1
Shawley Way. Burgh H KT18 .... 77 C1
Shaws Rd. Crawl RH10 .... 201 F7
Shaxton Cres. New Add CR0 .... 63 C2
Shearing Dr. Carsh SM4 .... 40 C2
Shears Ct. Charlt TW16 .... 14 E1
Shearwater Ct. **6** Crawl RH11 . 200 D5
Sheath's La. Oxsh KT22 .... 74 C6
Sheen Common Dr.
  Rich SW14 & TW10 .... 7 A2
Sheen Court Rd. Mortl TW10 .... 7 A3
Sheen Gate Gdns. Mortl SW14 ..... 7 C3
Sheen La. Mortl SW14 .... 7 C3
Sheen Mount Jun Mix & Inf Sch.
  Mortl SW14 .... 7 B2
Sheen Pk. Rich TW10 & TW9 .... 6 F3
Sheen Rd. Rich TW10 & TW9 .... 6 F3
Sheen Way. Wallin SM6 .... 60 F5
Sheen Wood. Mortl SW14 .... 7 C2
Sheendale Rd. Rich TW9 .... 6 F3
Sheenewood. For Hil SE26 .... 23 B4
Sheep Walk Mews.
  Wimble SW19 .... 19 E2
Sheep Wlk. Lang V KT18 .... 96 D6
Sheep Wlk. Reig RH2 .... 117 E6
Sheepbarn La. W Wick CR6 .... 82 F7
Sheepcote Cl. Cranf TW5 .... 4 A7
Sheepfold Rd. Stough GU2 .... 108 F4
Sheephatch La. Tilf GU10 .... 146 C6
Sheephouse. M Bourn GU9 .... 146 C8
Sheephouse Gn. Wotton RH5 .... 134 F3
Sheephouse La. Wotton RH4 ..... 135 A4
Sheephouse Way. New Mal KT3 ... 38 E2
Sheeplands Ave. Merrow GU1 .... 110 C3
Sheeps Ditch Cl. Stain TW18 ...... 13 A1
Sheepwalk. Shep TW17 ± 33 F3
Sheepwalk. Shep Gn TW17 .... 34 A3
Sheepwalk La. Abing H GU5 ...... 113 A1
Sheerwater Ave. Woodhm KT15 . 70 F7
Sheerwater Bsns Ctr.
  Sheer GU21 .... 70 C4
Sheerwater Cotts. W Byfl KT14 ... 70 F6
Sheerwater Rd.
  Sheer KT14 & KT15 .... 70 F6
Sheet Street Rd. Old W SL4 .... 10 A7
Sheet Street Rd. Wind SL4 .... 10 A7
Sheet's Heath La. Brookw GU24 .. 88 A7
Sheffield Cl. Crawl RH10 .... 202 B4
Sheffield Cl. Farnb GU14 .... 84 F4
Sheffield Rd. Harl TW14 & TW6 ..... 3 C1
Sheffield Way. Harl TW14 & TW6 ... 3 D2
Shefford Cres. Woki RG11 .... 25 D8
Shelburne House. **9**
  Streat SW16 .... 21 C3
Sheldon Cl. Penge SE20 .... 43 B8
Sheldon Cl. Reig RH2 .... 139 B8
Sheldon Cl. Worth RH10 .... 202 D5
Sheldon Ct. Guild GU1 .... 130 F8
Sheldon House. Tedd TW11 .... 17 A2
Sheldon St. Croy CR0 & CR9 .... 61 C7
Sheldrick Cl. Mitch CR4 .... 40 D7
Shelford. **9** King U T KT1 .... 38 A7
Shelford Rise. S Norw SE19 .... 22 F1
Shelley Ave. Brack RG12 .... 27 E7
Shelley Cl. Coulsd CR5 .... 79 F2
Shelley Cl. Crawl RH10 .... 202 C8
Shelley Cres. Heston TW5 .... 4 D6
Shelley Ct. Camb GU15 .... 65 C5

Shelley Ct. **9** King U T KT2 .... 17 D4
Shelley Ct. W Barn KT3 .... 39 A4
Shelley Dr. Broad H RH12 .... 216 D3
Shelley Rd. E Grins RH19 .... 185 D1
Shelley Rd. Horsh RH12 .... 217 B3
Shelley Way. Mitch SW17 .... 20 D2
Shellwood Dr. Dork RH5 .... 136 C3
Shellwood Rd.
 Leigh RH2 & RH3 .... 137 D1
Shelly Cl. Nork SM7 .... 77 E4
Shelly Cty Prim Sch.
 Broad H RH12 .... 216 E3
Shellys Ct. Horsh RH13 .... 218 A3
Shelson Ave. Felt TW13 .... 14 F4
Shelton Ave. Warlgm CR6 .... 81 C2
Shelton Cl. Stough GU2 .... 109 A6
Shelton Cl. Warlgm CR6 .... 81 C2
Shelton Rd. Merton SW19 .... 40 A8
Shelvers Gn. Tadw KT20 .... 97 C6
Shelvers Hill. Tadw KT20 .... 97 B6
Shelvers Spur. Tadw KT20 .... 97 C6
Shelvers Way. Tadw KT20 .... 97 C6
Shene Sec Sch. Mortl SW14 .... 7 E3
Shenley Rd. Heston TW5 .... 4 E6
Shenstone House. Streat SW16 ... 21 C3
Shenstone Pk. Ascot SL5 .... 29 E5
Shepherd Cl. Crawl RH10 .... 201 C3
Shepherd's Hill. Haslem GU27 ... 208 C6
Shepherd's Hill. Merst RH1 .... 99 C1
Shepherd's Hill. Stough GU2 ..... 109 A3
Shepherd's Hill Bglws.
 Haslem GU27 .... 208 C6
Shepherd's La. Stough GU2 .... 108 F4
Shepherd's Way. Guild GU4 ...... 130 E5
Shepherds Chase. Bagsh GU19 .. 47 E2
Shepherds Hill. Brack RG12 .... 27 C8
Shepherds La. Burrh GU20 .... 49 A6
Shepherds Way. Horsh RH12 ..... 218 A5
Shepherds Way. S Croy CR2 ...... 62 B3
Shepherds Way. Tilf GU10 .... 147 D4
Shepherds' Wlk.
 Ashtd KT18 & KT21 .... 96 B7
Shepherds Wlk. W Heath GU14 ... 84 E7
Shepherdsgrove La.
 Dorman RH19 .... 186 F5
Shepley Cl. Carsh SM5 .... 60 A7
Shepley Ct. Streat SW16 .... 21 C4
Shepley Dr. Went SL5 .... 30 D3
Shepley End. Went SL5 .... 30 D3
Sheppard Cl. King U T KT6 .... 37 E5
Sheppard House. **8** Streat SW2 22 A7
Shepperton Bsns Park.
 Shep TW17 .... 34 C4
Shepperton Court Dr.
 Shep TW17 .... 34 B4
Shepperton Ct. Shep TW17 .... 34 B3
Shepperton Rd.
 Laleh TW17 & TW18 .... 33 D5
Shepperton Sta. Shep TW17 .... 34 C4
Shepperton Studios. Littlt TW17 33 F6
Sheppey Cl. Crawl RH11 .... 201 C3
Sheraton Cl. Hawley GU17 .... 64 E4
Sheraton Dr. Epsom KT19 .... 76 C6
Sheraton The. **22** King U T KT6 .. 37 E4
Sheraton Wlk. **13** Crawl RH11 .. 201 B1
Sherborne Cl. Burgh H KT18 .... 77 C2
Sherborne Cl. Poyle SL3 .... 1 E6
Sherborne Cres. Carsh SM5 .... 40 E2
Sherborne Ct. Guild GU2 .... 130 C7
Sherborne Ct. Penge SE20 .... 43 C7
Sherborne Rd. Cheam SM3 .... 40 A1
Sherborne Rd. Chess KT9 .... 56 E5
Sherborne Rd. E Bed TW14 .... 14 D7
Sherborne Rd. Farnb GU14 .... 85 D1
Sherbourne. Albury GU5 .... 132 D5
Sherbourne Ct. **2** Hampt TW12 36 A8
Sherbourne Dr. Went GU25 .... 30 D4
Sherbourne Gdns. Oat Pk TW17 .. 34 E2
Shere Ave. E Ewell KT17 & SM2 ... 58 C1
Shere CE Inf Sch. Shere GU5 ..... 133 A4
Shere Cl. Chess KT9 .... 56 D5
Shere Cl. Dork RH5 .... 136 C3
Shere Ct. Shere GU5 .... 133 B2
Shere La. Shere GU5 .... 133 A4
Shere Rd. Albury GU4 & GU5 ..... 132 C6
Shere Rd. Ewh GU6 .... 175 D7
Shere Rd. Shere GU5 .... 133 B5
Shere Rd. W Clan GU4 & KT24 ... 111 B1
Shere Rd. W Hors KT24 .... 112 C4
Sherfield Gdns. Rhampt SW15 ..... 7 F1
Sheridan Cl. E Grins RH19 .... 185 C1
Sheridan Ct. Hounsl TW4 .... 4 E2
Sheridan Dr. Reig RH2 .... 118 B3
Sheridan Pl. Hampt TW12 .... 36 C8
Sheridan Pl. Mortl SW13 .... 7 F4
Sheridan Rd. Friml GU16 .... 85 D3
Sheridan Rd. Merton SW19 .... 39 F8
Sheridan Rd. Rich TW10 .... 17 C5
Sheridan Way. Beck BR3 .... 43 F8
Sheridans Rd. G Book KT23 .... 94 C1
Sheringham Ave. Twick TW2 .... 16 A7
Sheringham Prim Sch.
 Wands SW18 .... 19 F7
Sheringham Rd. Penge SE20 ...... 43 C6
Sherland Rd. Twick TW1 .... 16 F7
Shermanbury Ct. Horsh RH12 .... 217 B3
Sherrindon. Cran GU6 .... 174 F4
Sherrydon. Cran GU6 .... 174 F4
Sherwin Cres. Farnb GU14 .... 85 C7
Sherwood. Long D KT6 .... 56 D8
Sherwood Ave. Streat SW16 .... 41 D8
Sherwood Cl. Brack RG12 .... 28 A7
Sherwood Cl. Fetch KT22 .... 94 C4
Sherwood Cl. Knaph GU21 .... 68 E2
Sherwood Cres. Dovgn RH2 ...... 117 F8
Sherwood Ct. W Wick BR4 .... 44 B1
Sherwood Park Rd. Mitch CR4 .... 41 D5
Sherwood Park Rd. Sutton SM1 .. 59 A5
Sherwood Park Sch.
 Wallin SM6 .... 60 D7

Sherwood Prim Sch. Mitch CR4 41 C5
Sherwood Rd. Coulsd CR5 .... 79 C3
Sherwood Rd. Croy CR0 & CR9 .... 43 B1
Sherwood Rd. Hampt TW12 .... 16 C3
Sherwood Rd. Merton SW19 .... 19 F1
Sherwood Way. W Wick BR4 .... 63 C8
Sherwood Wlk. Crawl RH10 ...... 201 B1
Shetland Cl. Burgh GU4 .... 110 B6
Shetland Cl. Crawl RH10 .... 202 E7
Shewens Rd. Oat Pk KT13 .... 53 D6
Shey Copse. Mayb GU22 .... 70 C2
Shield Dr. Brent TW8 .... 6 A8
Shield Rd. Felt TW15 .... 14 D4
Shifford Path. For Hil SE23 .... 23 D5
Shilburn Way. Woking GU21 .... 69 A1
Shildon Cl. Friml GU15 .... 66 D3
Shillinglee Park Golf Course.
 Plaist GU8 .... 210 D6
Shimmings The. Guild GU1 .... 110 A2
Shinners Cl. Croy SE25 .... 43 A4
Shinwell Wlk. **3** Crawl RH11 ... 201 B1
Ship Alley. Farnb GU14 .... 85 C6
Ship Field Cl. Tats TN16 .... 103 C6
Ship Hill. Tats TN16 .... 103 D6
Ship La. Farnb GU14 .... 85 C6
Ship La. Mortl SW14 .... 7 C5
Ship St. E Grins RH19 .... 205 B8
Ship Yd. Weyb KT13 .... 53 B7
Shipka Rd. Balham SW12 .... 21 B7
Shiplake Ct. Up Toot SW17 .... 20 D4
Shiplake House. Brack RG12 .... 27 E3
Shipley Bridge La. Copth RH10 183 A3
Shipley Ct. Penge SE20 .... 43 A7
Shipley Rd. Crawl RH11 .... 201 A6
Shipleybridge La.
 Burst RH8 & RH6 .... 182 F4
Shipman Par. For Hil SE23 .... 23 E6
Shipman Rd. For Hil SE23 .... 23 D6
Shirburn Cl. For Hil SE23 .... 23 C8
Shire Cl. Bagsh GU19 .... 47 E2
Shire Ct. Alder GU11 .... 104 C2
Shire Ct. Ewell KT17 .... 57 F3
Shire Par. Crawl RH10 .... 202 D7
Shires Cl. Ashtd KT21 .... 95 D8
Shires House. Byfl KT14 .... 71 E6
Shires The. Rich TW10 .... 17 E4
Shirley Ave. Belm SM2 .... 58 F1
Shirley Ave. Carsh SM1 .... 59 E6
Shirley Ave. Coulsd CR5 & CR8 .. 100 B8
Shirley Ave. Croy CR0 & CR9 .... 43 C1
Shirley Ave. Earls RH1 .... 139 F4
Shirley Church Rd. Add CR0 .... 62 E7
Shirley Church Rd. Croy CR0 ...... 62 E7
Shirley Cl. Crawl RH11 .... 200 E2
Shirley Cl. Islew TW3 .... 5 C2
Shirley Cres. Beck BR3 .... 43 E5
Shirley Ct. Guild GU1 .... 130 D8
Shirley Ct. Thorn H SW16 .... 41 F6
Shirley Dr. Islew TW3 .... 5 C2
Shirley High Sch. S Croy CR0 ..... 62 F7
Shirley Hills Rd. S Croy CR0 .... 62 D5
Shirley Hts. Wallin SM6 .... 60 C2
Shirley Hyrst. Whit V KT13 .... 53 D4
Shirley Lodge. For Hil SE26 .... 23 E4
Shirley Oaks Hospl. Croy CR0 .... 43 C2
Shirley Oaks Rd. Croy CR0 & CR9 62 C8
Shirley Park Golf Course.
 S Croy CR0 .... 62 C7
Shirley Park Rd. Croy CR0 .... 43 C1
Shirley Pl. Knaph GU21 .... 68 C2
Shirley Rd. Croy CR0 & CR9 .... 43 A1
Shirley Rd. Wallin SM6 .... 60 C2
Shirley Way. Croy CR0 .... 62 F7
Shoe La. Farnb GU11 .... 105 A6
Sholto Rd. Stan TW6 .... 2 F2
Shop Cl. Rich TW10 .... 17 D5
Shophouse La. Farl Gn GU5 ...... 153 E7
Shord Hill. Kenley CR8 .... 80 D3
Shore Cl. Felt TW14 .... 15 A8
Shore Cl. Hampt TW12 .... 15 E3
Shore Gr. Felt TW13 .... 16 A4
Shore's Rd. Horse GU21 .... 69 F5
Shoreham Cl. Croy CR0 .... 43 C3
Shoreham Rd. Worth RH10 .... 202 C3
Shoreham Rd (E). Stan TW6 .... 2 E2
Shoreham Rd (W). Stan TW6 .... 2 E2
Shorndean St. Catf SE6 .... 24 C7
Short Cl. Crawl RH10 .... 201 D8
Short Dale Rd. Alder GU11 .... 126 C6
Short Gallop. Crawl RH10 .... 202 D7
Short La. Limps RH8 .... 123 B3
Short La. Stan TW15 & TW19 ...... 13 F7
Short Rd. Chisw W4 .... 7 E8
Short Rd. Stan TW19 .... 2 E1
Short St. Alder GU11 .... 105 A2
Short Way. Twick TW2 .... 16 C8
Shortcroft Rd. Ewell KT17 .... 57 F3
Shortfield Rd. Frensh GU10 .... 146 C1
Shortheath Crest. Wreccl GU9 .. 145 F6
Shortheath Rd.
 M Dourn GU9 & GU10 .... 146 A7
Shortheath Rd.
 Wreccl GU9 & GU10 .... 146 A7
Shortlands. Harl UB3 .... 3 D8
Shortlands Gdns.
 Broml BR1 & BR2 .... 44 E7
Shortlands Gr. Beck BR2 .... 44 D6
Shortlands Rd. Beck BR2 & BR3 .. 44 E6
Shortlands Rd. King U T KT2 .... 17 F1
Shortlands Sta. Beck BR2 .... 44 E7
Shorts Rd. Carsh SM5 .... 59 E5
Shortsfield Cl. Horsh RH12 .... 217 C5
Shortwood Ave. Ashf TW18 .... 13 B5
Shortwood Cty Inf Sch.
 Stan TW18 .... 13 B5
Shotfield. Wallin SM6 .... 60 B4
Shott Cl. Sutton SM1 .... 59 C5
Shottermill. Horsh RH12 .... 218 A4
Shottermill Cty Fst Sch.
 Shottm GU27 .... 207 F4

Shottermill Cty Jun Sch.
 Shottm GU27 .... 207 F7
Shottfield Ave. Mortl SW14 .... 7 E3
Shovelstrode La.Hammer RH19 206 D8
Shrewsbury Ave. Mortl SW14 ...... 7 D3
Shrewsbury Cl. Surb KT6 .... 56 E8
Shrewsbury Hse Sch.Long D KT6 56 D8
Shrewsbury Rd. Beck BR3 .... 43 E6
Shrewsbury Rd. Carsh SM5 .... 40 E2
Shrewsbury Rd. Harl TW14 & TW6 3 D1
Shrewsbury Rd. Redh RH1 .... 118 E1
Shrewsbury Wlk. **7** Islew TW7 .... 6 A4
Shrewton Rd. Mitch SW17 .... 20 F1
Shrivenham Cl. **3** Sandh GU15 .. 64 D8
Shroffold Rd. Catf BR1 .... 24 E4
Shropshire Cl. Mitch CR4 .... 41 E5
Shrubbery Rd. Streat SW16 .... 21 E4
Shrubbery The. Farnb GU14 .... 84 D3
Shrubbery The. **2** Surb KT6 ...... 37 E1
Shrubbs Hill. Burrh GU24 .... 49 C2
Shrubbs Hill La. Sunnin SL5 .... 30 C3
Shrubbs La. Rowl GU10 .... 145 F4
Shrubland Ct. Banstd SM7 .... 77 F3
Shrubland Gr. N Cheam KT4 .... 58 C7
Shrubland Rd. Banstd SM7 .... 78 A3
Shrublands Ave. Croy CR0 .... 63 A6
Shrublands Cl. For Hil SE26 .... 23 C5
Shrublands Dr. Lhtwat GU18 .... 67 B8
Shute End. Woki RG11 .... 25 B6
Sibthorp Rd. Mitch CR4 .... 40 F7
Sibton Rd. Carsh SM5 .... 40 E2
Sickle Rd. Haslem GU27 .... 208 A5
Sidbury Cl. Sunnin SL5 .... 30 A4
Siddons Rd. Croy CR0 & CR9 ...... 61 B7
Siddons Rd. For Hil SE23 .... 23 E6
Sidestrand Rd. Farnb GU11 .... 104 E7
Sidings The. Alder GU11 .... 105 C3
Sidings The. Rudge RH12 .... 214 D7
Sidings The. Stain TW18 .... 13 B4
Sidlaws Rd. W Heath GU14 .... 84 D6
Sidmouth Ave. Hounsl TW7 .... 5 E5
Sidney Gdns. Brent TW8 .... 6 D8
Sidney Rd. Croy SE25 .... 43 A4
Sidney Rd. Penge BR3 .... 43 E7
Sidney Rd. Stain TW18 .... 13 A4
Sidney Rd. Twick TW1 .... 6 B1
Sidney Rd. Walt O T KT12 .... 35 B1
Signal Ct. Lingf RH7 .... 164 E5
Silbury Ave. Mitch CR4 .... 40 E8
Silbury House. **9** For Hil SE26 ... 23 A5
Silchester Ct. Thorn H CR7 .... 42 A5
Silchester Dr. Crawl RH11 .... 201 B4
Silkham Rd. Oxted RH8 .... 122 E8
Silkin Wlk. **8** Crawl RH11 .... 201 B1
Silkmore La. W Hors KT24 .... 92 A2
Silkmore La. W Hors KT24 .... 112 B7
Silo Cl. Farnc GU7 .... 150 E8
Silo Dr. Farnc GU7 .... 150 F8
Silo Rd. Farnc GU7 .... 150 F8
Silver Birch Cl. Woodhm KT15 .... 70 E7
Silver Birches Way. Elst GU8 .... 148 E3
Silver Blades Ice Rink.
 Streat SW16 .... 21 D3
Silver Cl. Kings KT20 .... 97 E3
Silver Cl. Friml GU15 & GU16 ...... 66 C3
Silver Hill. Sandh GU15 .... 64 E8
Silver Jubilee Way. Cranf TW4 ..... 4 B5
Silver La. Purley CR8 .... 79 E7
Silver La. W Wick BR4 .... 63 D8
Silver Tree Cl. Walt O T KT12 ...... 54 A6
Silverdale. For Hil SE23 & SE26 ... 23 C4
Silverdale Ave. Oxsh KT22 .... 74 C5
Silverdale Ave.
 Walt O T KT12 .... 53 F7
Silverdale Cl. Brock RH3 .... 137 B5
Silverdale Cl. Cheam SM1 .... 58 F6
Silverdale Cl. Sunby TW16 .... 35 B7
Silverglade. Chess KT9 .... 75 C7
Silverhall St. Islew TW7 .... 6 A4
Silverlea Gdns. Horley RH6 .... 161 C2
Silverleigh Rd. Thorn H CR7 .... 42 A4
Silvermere Ct. Cater CR3 .... 100 F3
Silvermere Rd. **1** Lewish SE6 ... 24 B8
Silversmiths Way. Woking GU21 69 C1
Silverstone Cl. Redh RH1 .... 118 F3
Silverton Lodge. S Norw SE19 .... 22 E1
Silverwood Cl. Beck BR3 .... 24 A1
Silverwood Cl. New Add CR0 ...... 63 A2
Silverwood Dr. Camb GU15 .... 66 A7
Silwood. Easth RG12 .... 26 E1
Silwood Cl. Ascot SL5 .... 29 D7
Silwood Park (Imperial Coll).
 Ascot SL5 .... 29 F6
Silwood Rd. Ascot SL5 .... 29 F5
Silwood Rd. Sunnin SL5 .... 29 F5
Sim's Cotts. Clayg KT10 .... 55 F4
Simkins Cl. Wink RG12 .... 8 B2
Simmil Rd. Clayg KT10 .... 55 E5
Simmonds Cl. Binf RG12 .... 26 E8
Simmonds Cotts. Ock Rid GU7 . 150 B4
Simmondstone La. Churt GU10 162 F7
Simmons Pl. Egham TW18 .... 12 E3
Simms Cl. Carsh SM5 .... 59 E8
Simon Lodge. **31** Putney SW19 .. 19 D7
Simons Cl. Ottsh KT16 .... 51 C4
Simons Wlk. Eng Gn TW20 .... 11 C1
Simplemarsh Ct. Addl KT15 .... 52 B6
Simplemarsh Rd. Addl KT15 .... 52 B6
Simpson Rd. Rich TW10 .... 17 C4
Simpson Rd. Twick TW4 .... 4 F1
Sinclair Cl. Worth RH10 .... 202 C4
Sinclair Ct. **22** Beck BR3 .... 24 A1
Sinclair Cl. **2** Croy CR0 .... 61 F8
Sinclair Dr. Belm SM2 .... 59 B2
Sinclair House. Streat SW12 .... 21 D7
Sincots Rd. Redh RH1 .... 118 F1
Sine Cl. Farnb GU14 .... 85 B8
Singleton Prim Sch.
 Mitch SW19 .... 20 D1

Singleton Cl.
 Mitch SW17 & SW19 .... 20 E1
Singleton Cl. Thorn H CR0 .... 42 C2
Singleton Rd. Broad H RH12 ...... 216 D3
Sinhurst Rd. Camb GU15 .... 65 B4
Sion Cl. Twick TW1 .... 17 B7
Sion Rd. Twick TW1 .... 17 B7
Sipson Cl. Harm UB7 .... 3 A8
Sipson La. Harl UB7 .... 3 B8
Sipson La. Harl UB7 .... 3 A7
Sipson Rd. Harm UB7 .... 3 A7
Sipson Way. Harm UB7 .... 3 A7
Sir Cyril Black Way. **2**
 Merton SW19 .... 20 A1
Sir William Perkin's Ind Sch for
 Girls. Chert KT16 .... 32 F1
Sirdar Rd. Mitch CR4 .... 21 A2
Sirl Cotts. Ascot SL5 .... 29 C5
Siskin Cl. Horsh RH12 .... 217 E5
Sissinghurst Cl. Crawl RH10 ..... 202 D7
Sissinghurst Rd. Croy CR0 .... 43 A2
Sistova Rd. Balham SW12 .... 21 B7
Siward Rd. Wands SW17 .... 20 C5
Six Cross-Roads. Horse GU21 ... 70 A5
Sixth Cross Rd. Twick TW2 .... 16 C5
Skeena Mill.
 Putney SW18 & SW19 .... 19 E8
Skelbrook St. Wands SW18 .... 20 C6
Skelmersdale Wlk. Crawl RH11 200 E2
Skerne Rd. King U T KT2 .... 37 D8
Skid Hill La. Bigg H CR6 .... 82 F5
Skid Hill La. Fickl CR6 .... 82 F5
Skiff La. Loxwd RH14 .... 213 A1
Skiffington Cl. Streat SW2 .... 22 A7
Skimmington Cotts. Reig RH2 ... 138 D8
Skimpedhill La. Brack RG12 .... 27 B7
Skinners La. Ashtd KT21 .... 75 D1
Skinners La. Chidd GU8 .... 191 D5
Skinners La. Heston TW5 .... 5 B6
Skipton Way. Horley RH6 .... 161 B5
Sky Bsns Pk. Thorpe TW20 .... 32 C8
Skyes Dr. Stain TW18 .... 13 B3
Skylark View. Horsh RH12 .... 217 D7
Skyport Dr. Harm UB7 .... 3 A7
Skyway 14 Trad Est. Poyle SL3 ..... 1 F4
Slade Cl. Ottsh KT16 .... 51 D4
Slade House. Twick TW4 .... 4 F1
Slade Rd. Ottsh KT16 .... 51 D4
Slade Rd. Pirb GU24 .... 87 D7
Slaidburn Gn. Brack RG12 .... 27 E2
Slattery Rd. Felt TW13 .... 15 C7
Slaugham Ct. Crawl RH11 .... 200 F3
Sledmere Ct. E Bed TW14 .... 14 E7
Sleets Rd. Broad H RH12 .... 216 E3
Slim Cl. Farnb GU14 .... 105 E7
Slim Rd. Camb GU15 .... 65 C7
Slines New Rd.
 Wold CR3 & CR6 .... 101 E7
Slines Oak Rd. Wold CR3 & CR6 102 B6
Slinfold CE (Controlled) Sch.
 Slinfd RH12 .... 215 D4
Slinfold Park (Golf & Ctry Pk).
 Slinfd RH12 .... 215 A2
Slinfold Wlk. Crawl RH11 .... 201 A6
Slip Of Wood. Cran GU6 .... 174 F4
Slipshatch Rd. Dovgn RH2 .... 138 E5
Slipshoe St. Reig RH2 .... 118 A1
Sloane Hospl. Beck BR3 .... 44 D8
Sloane Wlk. Croy CR0 .... 43 F3
Slocock Hill. Horse GU21 .... 69 C2
Slough La. Buckl RH3 .... 117 A3
Slough La. Head KT18 .... 96 C2
Sloughbrook Cl. Horsh RH12 .... 217 F6
Slyfield Ct. Belif GU1 .... 109 E4
Slyfield Gn. Stough GU1 .... 109 E5
Slyfield Ind Est. Stough GU4 ..... 109 E5
Small's La. Crawl RH11 .... 201 C6
Smallberry Ave. Islew TW7 .... 5 F5
Smallfield Rd. Horley RH6 .... 161 C3
Smallfield Rd. Horne RH6 .... 162 E3
Smallmead. Horley RH6 .... 161 B3
Smallwood Jun & Inf Schs.
 Up Toot SW17 .... 20 D4
Smallwood Rd. Up Toot SW17 .... 20 D4
Smart's Heath La. Woking GU22 89 A4
Smart's Heath Rd. Woking GU22 89 B5
Smeaton Rd. Wands SW18 .... 20 A8
Smith Cl. Crawl RH10 .... 201 D1
Smith Ct. Sheer GU21 .... 70 D6
Smith Rd. Woodh RH2 .... 138 F6
Smith Sq. Brack RG12 .... 27 D7
Smith St. Surb KT5 .... 37 F3
Smith's Yd. Wands SW18 .... 20 C6
Smitham Bottom La.
 Purley CR5 & CR8 .... 79 D7
Smitham Cty Prim Sch.
 Coulsd CR5 .... 79 D4
Smitham Downs Rd.
 Purley CR5 & CR8 .... 79 E6
Smitham Prim Sch. Coulsd CR5 79 C3
Smitham Sta. Coulsd CR5 .... 79 E4
Smithbarn. Horsh RH13 .... 218 A2
Smithbarn Cl. Horley RH6 .... 161 B4
Smithers Cotts. Rudge RH12 .... 214 F7
Smithers House. Penge SE20 ...... 23 D1
Smithers The. Brock RH3 .... 137 B5
Smithfield La. Head Dn GU35 .... 167 A1
Smithwood Ave. Rowly GU6 ...... 174 B7
Smithwood Cl. Putney SW19 ...... 19 E6
Smithwood Common Rd.
 Rowly GU5 & GU6 .... 174 B7
Smithy Cl. L Kings KT20 .... 97 F1
Smithy La.
 Head Dn GU10 & GU35 .... 166 E2

Smithy La. L Kings KT20 .... 97 F1
Smithy's Gn. Windl GU20 .... 48 D4
Smock Wlk. Thorn H CR0 .... 42 C3
Smoke La. Reig RH2 .... 139 B7
Smokejack Hill. Wall W RH5 ..... 196 D7
Smolletts. E Grins RH19 .... 205 C8
Smoothfield. Hounsl TW3 .... 5 A3
Smugglers' La.
 Ockley RH12 & RH5 .... 197 E7
Smugglers' Way. The San GU10 126 E1
Snailslynch. Farnh GU9 .... 125 D2
Snatts Hill. Limps RH8 .... 122 F6
Snelgate Cotts. E Clan GU4 .... 111 D4
Snell Hatch. Crawl RH11 .... 201 B6
Snellings Rd. Hersh KT12 .... 54 C5
Snipe La. Marl Ht GU27 .... 208 A1
Snow Hill. Copth RH10 .... 183 F3
Snow Hill. Copth RH10 .... 184 A4
Snow Hill. Dome RH10 .... 183 F5
Snow Hill Bsns Ctr.
 Dome RH10 .... 184 A4
Snow House. W Norw SE27 .... 22 B5
Snowdenham La. Bramly GU5 .. 151 E5
Snowdenham Links Rd.
 Bramly GU5 .... 151 D6
Snowdon Rd. Harl TW6 .... 3 C1
Snowdon Rd. W Heath GU14 ...... 84 E7
Snowdown Cl. Penge SE20 .... 43 D8
Snowdrop Cl. Crawl RH11 .... 201 A2
Snowdrop Cl. **2** Hampt TW12 ... 16 A2
Snowdrop Way. Bisley GU24 .... 68 A2
Snowerhill Rd.
 Betch RH2 & RH3 .... 137 F6
Snowhill La. Dome RH10 .... 183 F5
Snows Paddock. Windl GU20 ...... 48 B7
Snows Ride. Windl GU20 .... 48 B6
Snowy Fielder Waye. Islew TW7 .. 6 B5
Snoxhall Field. Cran GU6 .... 174 D2
Soames Wlk. King U T KT3 .... 38 E8
Soane Cl. Crawl RH11 .... 200 E4
Soho Mills. Hackb SM6 .... 41 B1
Sol-y-vista. Farnc GU7 .... 150 D6
Solartron Rd. Farnb GU14 .... 85 B3
Sole Farm Ave. L Book KT23 ...... 93 F2
Sole Farm Cl. L Book KT23 .... 93 F3
Sole Farm Rd. L Book KT23 .... 93 F2
Solecote. L Book KT23 .... 94 A3
Solent Rd. Stan TW6 .... 2 F1
Soloms Court Rd.
 Woodm CR5 & SM7 .... 78 E2
Solway Cl. Hounsl TW4 .... 4 E4
Somborne House. Rhampt SW15 19 A8
Somerfield Cl. Burgh H KT20 ...... 97 E8
Somergate. Horsh RH12 .... 216 F2
Somers Cl. Reig RH2 .... 118 A2
Somers Pl. **1** Reig RH2 .... 118 A2
Somers Pl. Streat SW2 .... 21 F8
Somers Rd. Reig RH2 .... 118 A2
Somers Rd. **2** Streat SW2 .... 21 F8
Somersbury La.
 Ell Gu GU6 & RH12 .... 195 F7
Somersby Est. Penge SE20 .... 23 C1
Somerset Ave. Chess KT9 .... 56 D6
Somerset Ave. Wimble SW20 ...... 39 B7
Somerset Cl. Epsom KT19 .... 57 E2
Somerset Cl. Hersh KT12 .... 54 B5
Somerset Cl. New Mal KT3 .... 38 E4
Somerset Ct. **3** Hampt TW12 .... 36 A8
Somerset Gdns. Tedd TW11 .... 16 E3
Somerset Gdns. Thorn H SW16 .. 41 F6
Somerset House. Wimble SW19 .. 19 E5
Somerset Rd. Brent TW8 .... 6 C8
Somerset Rd. Farnb GU14 .... 85 C1
Somerset Rd. King U T KT1 .... 37 F7
Somerset Rd. Tedd TW11 .... 16 E3
Somerset Rd. Wimble SW19 .... 19 D5
Somerset Rd.
 Woodh RH1 & RH2 .... 139 D4
Somerset Waye. Heston TW5 .... 4 E7
Somersey. Shalf GU4 .... 130 E1
Somerton Ave. Mortl TW9 .... 7 B4
Somerton Cl. Purley CR8 .... 80 A3
Somertons Cl. Stough GU2 .... 109 A4
Somerville Ct. Streat SW16 .... 21 D2
Somerville Dr. Crawl RH10 .... 182 C1
Somerville Rd. Cobham KT11 ...... 74 A5
Somerville Rd.Penge BR3 & SE20 23 D1
Sondes Farm. Dork RH4 .... 135 F7
Sondes Place Dr. Dork RH4 ...... 135 F7
Sondes Place Sch. Dork RH4 .... 135 F6
Sonia Gdns. Heston TW5 .... 5 A7
Sonnet Wlk. Bigg H TN16 .... 83 C1
Sonning Ct. Croy CR0 .... 62 A8
Sonning Gdns. Hampt TW12 .... 15 C2
Sonning Rd. Croy CR0 .... 43 A3
Sonninge Cl. Sandh GU15 .... 64 D8
Sopwith Ave. Chess KT9 .... 56 E5
Sopwith Cl. Rich TW10 .... 17 F3
Sopwith Dr. Byfl KT13 & KT14 ..... 71 F7
Sopwith Rd. Heston TW5 .... 4 C7
Sopwith Way. King U T KT2 .... 37 E8
Sorbie Cl. Whit V KT13 .... 53 D4
Sorrel Bank. New Add CR0 .... 62 E2
Sorrel Cl. W Heath GU14 .... 84 C5
Sorrel Cl. Woki RG11 .... 25 C5
Sorrel Dr. Lhtwat GU18 .... 66 F7
Sorrel House. Hounsl TW3 .... 5 C6
Sorrel Rd. Horsh RH12 .... 217 E5
Sorrento Rd. Sutton SM1 .... 59 B7
South Albert Rd. Reig RH2 .... 117 F2
South Ash Cty Prim Sch.
 Ash GU12 .... 106 B2
South Atlantic Dr. Alder GU11 .. 105 C3
South Ave. Egham TW20 .... 12 C2
South Ave. Heath E GU9 .... 125 D6
South Ave. Rich TW9 .... 7 A5

South Ave. Wallin SM5 .... 60 A3
South Ave. Whit V KT12 .... 53 E1
South Bank. Surb KT6 .... 37 E3
South Bank Lodge. **2** Surb KT6 .. 37 E3
South Bank Terr. Surb KT6 .... 37 E3
South Beta Rd. Farnb GU14 ..... 85 B2
South Bookham Sch.
    G Book KT23 .... 114 C8
South Border The. Purley CR8 .. 79 E8
South Cl. Crawl RH10 .... 201 F7
South Cl. Horse GU21 .... 69 C3
South Cl. Morden SM4 .... 40 A3
South Cl. Twick TW13 .... 16 A5
South Cl. Woki RG11 .... 25 D4
South Close Gn.
    Merst RH1 & RH2 .... 119 B6
South Croxted Rd.
    W Norw SE21 .... 22 D4
South Croydon Sta. S Croy CR2 . 61 D5
South Dr. Banstd SM7 .... 78 E6
South Dr. Beck BR3 .... 44 C4
South Dr. Belm SM2 .... 58 E2
South Dr. Coulsd CR5 .... 79 D4
South Dr. Dork RH5 .... 136 C7
South Dr. Pirb GU24 .... 87 C6
South Dr. Went GU25 .... 31 A2
South Dr. Woki RG11 .... 25 C5
South Eden Park Rd. Beck BR3 . 44 B4
South Eden Park Rd.
    W Wick BR3 .... 44 B2
South End. Croy CR0 & CR9 ..... 61 C6
South End. G Book KT23 .... 94 B1
South Farm La. Windl GU19 ..... 48 A2
South Farnborough Cty Inf Sch.
    Farnb GU14 .... 105 D8
South Farnborough Cty Jun Sch.
    Farnb GU14 .... 85 D2
South Farnham Sch.
    M Bourn GU9 .... 125 D1
South Gate Ave. Felt TW13 ..... 14 D4
South Gdns. Mitch SW19 .... 20 D1
South Gr. Chert KT16 .... 32 F3
South Gr. Horsh RH13 .... 217 D1
South Hill. Godal GU7 .... 150 F4
South Hill. Guild GU1 .... 130 D7
South Hill Park. Farnb GU12 ..... 27 C2
South Hill Rd. Beck BR2 .... 44 E5
South Hill Rd. Easth RG12 .... 27 B3
South Holmes Rd. Horsh RH13 218 B4
South La. Ash GU12 .... 106 B1
South La. King U T KT1 .... 37 D6
South La. New Mal KT3 .... 38 D3
South La W. New Mal KT3 .... 38 D5
South Lawn Ct. Twick TW2 ..... 5 C1
South Lodge Ave.
    Mitch CR4 & CR7 & SW16 ..... 41 E5
South Lodge Rd. Whit V KT12 .. 54 B2
South London Coll.
    W Norw SE27 .... 22 B4
South Lynn Cres. Easth RG12 .... 27 B4
South Mead. Redh RH1 .... 118 F4
South Mead. W Ewell KT19 .... 57 F3
South Mead. W Ewell KT19 .... 57 F3
South Mead Rd. Alder GU11 .. 126 B8
South Meadow. Crowth RG11 ... 45 D1
South Merton Sta. Merton SW20 39 F6
South Munstead La.
    Godal GU8 .... 172 B7
South Norwood High Sch.
    Croy SE25 .... 43 B4
South Norwood Hill.
    S Norw SE25 & SE25 .... 42 F7
South Norwood Prim Sch.
    Croy SE25 .... 43 A5
South Oak Rd. Streat SW16 ..... 21 F4
South Par. Horley RH6 .... 160 F4
South Park Cres. Catf SE6 .... 24 F7
South Park Ct. **25** Beck BR3 ..... 24 A1
South Park Cty Inf Sch.
    Woodh RH2 .... 139 A6
South Park Gr. New Mal KT3 ..... 38 C5
South Park Hill Rd. S Croy CR2 . 61 D6
South Park La. Bletch RH1 ..... 142 A7
South Park Rd. Wimble SW19 ... 20 B2
South Pier Rd. Crawl RH6 ..... 182 B7
South Pl. Surb KT5 .... 37 F2
South Pl. Woki RG11 .... 25 C6
South Rd. Ash V GU12 .... 106 A4
South Rd. Bisley GU24 .... 67 F3
South Rd. Crowth RG11 .... 45 E3
South Rd. Easth RG11 & RG12 ... 26 E1
South Rd. Eng Gn TW20 .... 11 D2
South Rd. Felt TW13 .... 15 D3
South Rd. For Hil SE23 .... 23 D6
South Rd. Hampt TW12 .... 15 F2
South Rd. Horse GU21 .... 69 C4
South Rd. Merton SW19 .... 20 D2
South Rd. Mitch SW19 .... 20 D2
South Rd. Reig RH2 .... 139 B8
South Rd. Stough GU2 .... 109 B3
South Rd. Twick TW2 .... 16 D5
South Rd. Weyb KT13 .... 53 C5
South Rd. Whit V KT13 .... 53 B2
South Ridge. Whit V KT13 ..... 72 B8
South Rise. Wallin SM5 .... 59 E2
South Side. Tongh GU10 ..... 126 F7
South St. Dork RH4 .... 136 A7
South St. Epsom KT18 .... 76 D5
South St. Farnb GU14 .... 85 E1
South St. Farnh GU9 .... 125 C2
South St. Godal GU7 .... 150 D4
South St. Horsh RH12 .... 217 C2
South St. Islew TW7 .... 6 A4
South St. Stan TW18 .... 12 E2
South Station App. S Nutf RH1 140 F7
South Terr. Dork RH4 .... 136 B6
South Terr. Surb KT6 .... 37 E3

South Vale. S Norw SE19 .... 22 E2
South Vale Rd. **4** Surb KT6 ..... 56 E8
South View. Copth RH10 .... 183 E3
South View. Wimble SW19 .... 19 D2
South View Ct. S Norw SE19 ..... 22 C1
South View Rd. Ashtd KT21 ..... 95 D8
South Way. Croy CR0 .... 62 E7
South Way. Sutton SM5 .... 59 D1
South Way. Sutton SM5 .... 78 D8
South West London Coll.
    Streat SW16 .... 21 D5
South West London Coll.
    Up Toot SW17 .... 20 E3
South Western Rd. Twick TW1 ... 6 B1
South Wimbledon Sta.
    Merton SW18 .... 20 B1
South Wlk. Alder GU12 .... 105 D2
South Wlk. Coney H BR4 .... 63 E7
South Wlk. Reig RH2 .... 118 B1
South Worple Way. Mortl SW14 . 7 D4
Southall La. Heston TW5 .... 4 B8
Southam House. Addl KT15 ..... 52 B5
Southampton Cl. Blckw GU17 ... 64 C6
Southampton Gdns. Mitch CR4 . 41 E4
Southampton Rd.
    Stan TW19 & TW6 .... 2 F1
Southampton St. Farnb GU14 .. 105 B8
Southampton Way.
    Stan TW19 & TW6 .... 2 E1
Southbank. Thame D KT7 ..... 37 B2
Southborough Cl. Surb KT6 .... 37 D1
Southborough Rd. Surb KT6 .... 37 E1
Southbrook. Crawl RH11 .... 201 C1
Southbrook Rd. Streat SW16 .... 41 E8
Southbury. Guild GU2 .... 130 C7
Southcote. Horse GU21 .... 69 D3
Southcote Ave. Felt TW13 .... 15 A6
Southcote Ave. Tolw KT5 .... 38 B2
Southcote Dr. Friml GU15 .... 66 A5
Southcote Rd. S Croy CR2 ..... 61 F1
Southcote Rd. Merst RH1 ..... 119 C6
Southcote Rd. S Croy CR2 ..... 61 F1
Southdean Gdns. Putney SW19 . 19 F6
Southdown Cl. Horsh RH12 .... 218 A5
Southdown Dr. Wimble SW20 ... 19 D1
Southdown Rd. Hersh KT12 .... 54 E6
Southdown Rd. Wallin SM5 .... 60 A2
Southdown Rd. Wimble SW20 ... 39 D8
Southdown Rd. Wold CR3 ..... 101 F5
Southend La. Catf SE6 .... 24 B4
Southend La. For Hil SE26 & SE6 23 F4
Southend Rd. Beck BR3 .... 44 A8
Sutherland Cl. Weyb KT13 ..... 53 C6
Southern Ave. E Bed TW14 ..... 15 A7
Southern Ave. S Norw SE25 ..... 42 F6
Southern Ave. Salfs RH1 .... 140 A1
Southern Bglws. Chil GU4 ..... 131 B2
Southern Cotts. Stan TW19 ..... 2 A3
Southern Ind Area. Easth RG12 . 26 F6
Southern Perimeter Rd.
    E Bed TW6 .... 3 B1
Southern Perimeter Rd.
    Felt TW14 & TW6 .... 3 D2
Southern Perimeter Rd.
    Harl TW14 & TW6 .... 3 D2
Southern Perimeter Rd.
    Stan TW19 & TW6 .... 2 D2
Southern Rd. Camb GU15 .... 65 C6
Southern Way. Farnh GU9 ..... 84 E3
Southern Way. M Bourn GU9 .... 125 C1
Southerns La. L Kings CR5 ..... 98 C3
Southey Ct. Fetch KT23 .... 94 B3
Southey Rd. Merton SW19 ..... 20 A1
Southey St. Penge SE20 .... 23 D1
Southfield Gdns.
    Tedd TW1 & TW2 .... 16 F4
Southfield Pl. Whit V KT13 ..... 53 B3
Southfield Sta. Wands SW18 ... 19 F7
Southfields. Thame D KT8 ..... 36 E3
Southfields Ave. Ashf TW15 .... 14 B2
Southfields Ct. Sutton SM3 .... 59 A8
Southfields Rd.
    Wold CR3 & RH9 .... 102 B3
Southfields Sch. Wands SW18 .. 20 A7
Southfields Special Sch.
    Woki RG11 .... 25 D5
Southgate Ave.
    Crawl RH10 & RH11 .... 201 E4
Southgate Cty Fst & Mid Sch.
    Crawl RH10 .... 201 D4
Southgate Cty West Fst & Mid Sch.
    Crawl RH11 .... 201 C4
Southgate Dr.
    Crawl RH10 & RH11 .... 201 E4
Southgate Par. Crawl RH10 .... 201 D4
Southgate Rd.
    Crawl RH10 & RH11 .... 201 D4
Southholme Cl. S Norw SE19 .... 42 E8
Southland Way. Islew TW7 .... 5 D2
Southlands. E Grins RH19 ..... 205 E2
Southlands. Horley RH6 ..... 160 F3
Southlands Ave. Horley RH6 ... 161 A4
Southlands Cl. Ash GU12 .... 106 A1
Southlands Cl. Coulsd CR5 ..... 79 F2
Southlands Cl. Woki RG11 .... 25 D5
Southlands Coll. Putney SW19 .. 19 D6
Southlands La. Tand RH8 ..... 122 C1
Southlands Rd. Ash GU12 ..... 106 A1
Southlands Rd. Woki RG11 ..... 25 D4
Southmead Jun & Inf Sch.
    Putney SW19 .... 19 E7
Southmead Rd. Putney SW19 .. 19 E7
Southmont Rd. Hinch W KT10 .. 55 F7
Southridge Pl. Wimble SW20 ... 19 D1
Southsea Rd. King U T KT1 .... 37 E5

Southside Comm. Wimble SW19 19 D2
Southview Cl. Up Toot SW17 ..... 21 A3
Southview Cotts. Frensh GU10 146 D1
Southview Ct. **14** Woking GU22 .. 69 E1
Southview Gdns. Wallin SM6 ... 60 C3
Southview Rd. Catf BR1 .... 24 D4
Southview Rd. Head Dn GU35 .. 187 B5
Southview Rd. Warlgm CR6 ..... 101 A8
Southview Rd. Wold CR3 .... 102 B3
Southviews. Selsd CR2 .... 62 D2
Southville Cl. E Bed TW14 ..... 14 E7
Southville Cl. W Ewell KT19 .... 57 D2
Southville Cl. W Ewell KT19 .... 57 D2
Southville Cres. E Bed TW14 .... 14 E7
Southville Jun & Inf Schs.
    E Bed TW14 .... 14 F7
Southville Rd. E Bed TW14 ..... 14 E8
Southville Rd. Thame D KT7 .... 37 B2
Southwark Cl. Crawl RH11 .... 201 B2
Southwater Cl. Beck BR3 .... 24 B1
Southway. Camb GU15 .... 65 B4
Southway. Stough GU2 .... 108 F1
Southway. W Barn SW20 .... 39 D5
Southway. Wallin SM6 .... 60 C6
Southway. Stough GU2 .... 108 E1
Southways Pk. Crawl RH11 ... 181 D3
Southwell Park Rd. Camb GU15 65 C5
Southwell Rd.
    Thorn H CR0 & CR7 .... 42 A3
Southwick Cl. E Grins RH19 ... 185 D2
Southwick Cl. Brack RG12 ..... 27 E3
Southwick House.
    E Grins RH19 .... 185 D2
Southwold. Easth RG12 .... 26 E1
Southwood. Woki RG11 .... 25 D4
Southwood Ave.
    King U T KT2 & KT3 .... 38 C8
Southwood Ave. Knaph GU21 .. 68 D1
Southwood Ave. Ottsh KT16 .... 51 C3
Southwood Bsns Pk.
    Farnb GU14 .... 84 D4
Southwood Chase. Cran GU6 .. 174 F1
Southwood Cl. N Cheam KT4 .... 39 D1
Southwood Cres The.
    Farnb GU14 .... 84 D3
Southwood Ct. Weyb KT13 ..... 53 B5
Southwood Dr. Tolw KT5 .... 38 C1
Southwood Gdns. Hinch W KT10 56 A7
Southwood Golf Course.
    Farnb GU14 .... 84 E3
Southwood Inf Sch. Farnb GU14 84 D3
Southwood La. Farnb GU14 ..... 84 A3
Southwood La. Farnb GU14 ..... 84 D3
Southwood Rd. Farnb GU14 .... 84 E4
Sovereign Ct. E Mole KT8 .... 35 F5
Sovereign Ct. **3** Rich TW9 ..... 6 F3
Sovereign Dr. Camb GU15 .... 66 B7
Sovereign House. Ashf TW15 .. 13 E4
Sovereign House. Wimble SW19 19 E2
Spa Cl. S Norw SE19 .... 42 E8
Spa Dr. Epsom KT18 .... 76 A5
Spa Hill. S Norw CR7 & SE19 ... 42 D8
Spa View. **6** Streat SW16 ..... 21 F5
Space Waye. Felt TW14 .... 4 B2
Spalding Rd. Streat SW17 ..... 21 B3
Sparks Cl. Hampt TW12 .... 15 E2
Sparrow Cl. Hampt TW12 .... 15 E2
Sparrow Farm Dr. Felt TW14 ... 15 D8
Sparrow Farm Inf Sch.
    Felt TW14 .... 15 C8
Sparrow Farm Jun Sch.
    Felt TW14 .... 15 C8
Sparrow Farm Rd.
    N Cheam KT17 & KT4 .... 58 B6
Sparrow Row. Burrh GU24 ..... 49 B4
Sparrowhawk Cl. Crond GU10 . 124 D8
Sparrows Mead. Redh RH1 ..... 119 A4
Sparvell Rd. Knaph GU21 .... 88 B8
Sparvell Way. Camb GU15 .... 65 C6
Spats La. Head Dn GU35 .... 187 A8
Speaker's Ct. **3** Croy CR0 ..... 42 D1
Speart La. Heston TW5 .... 4 E7
Speedwell Cl. Merrow GU4 ..... 110 C4
Speedwell House. **5**
    Redh RH1 .... 119 A4
Speedwell Way. Horsh RH12 ... 217 E5
Speer Rd. Thame D KT7 .... 36 F3
Speirs Cl. New Mal KT3 .... 38 F3
Speke Rd. S Norw CR7 .... 42 D7
Speldhurst Cl. Hayes BR2 ..... 44 F4
Spelthorne Coll. Ashf TW15 ... 13 F4
Spelthorne Cty Inf Sch.
    Ashf TW15 .... 14 E2
Spelthorne Gr. Charlt TW16 ... 14 F1
Spelthorne Sports Club.
    Ashf TW15 .... 14 D1
Spence Ave. Byfl KT14 .... 71 F5
Spencer Cl. Friml GU16 .... 85 E6
Spencer Cl. Lang V KT18 ..... 96 E8
Spencer Cl. Sheer GU21 .... 70 D5
Spencer Ct. Leahd KT22 .... 95 C4
Spencer Gdns. Eng Gn TW20 ... 11 D3
Spencer Hill. Wimble SW19 ... 19 E1
Spencer Hill Rd. Wimble SW19 . 19 E1
Spencer House. **24**
    Putney SW19 .... 19 D7
Spencer House. Wimble SW19 .. 19 D5
Spencer Mews. Dulw SE21 ..... 22 D7
Spencer Pl. Croy CR0 .... 42 D2
Spencer Rd. Brack RG12 ..... 26 F8
Spencer Rd. Broml BR1 .... 24 F1
Spencer Rd. Carsh CR4 .... 41 A2
Spencer Rd. Cater CR3 .... 100 D6
Spencer Rd. Chisw W4 .... 7 C7
Spencer Rd. Cobham KT11 ..... 73 B4

Spencer Rd. E Mole KT8 .... 36 C4
Spencer Rd.
    Hounsl TW3 & TW5 & TW7 ..... 5 C6
Spencer Rd. Mitch CR4 .... 41 A6
Spencer Rd. S Croy CR2 .... 61 E5
Spencer Rd. Twick TW2 .... 16 E6
Spencer Rd. Wimble SW20 ..... 39 B8
Spencer Way. Earls RH1 .... 140 A4
Spencer's Rd. Horsh RH12 .... 217 B3
Spencers La. Charl RH6 .... 159 F2
Spencers Pl. Horsh RH12 .... 217 B4
Spencers Rd. Crawl RH11 .... 201 D5
Spenser Ave. Whit V KT13 .... 53 A2
Spenser Ct. **5** Rich TW10 .... 17 D4
Spiceall. Compt GU3 .... 129 B3
Spicer Cl. Walt O T KT12 .... 35 C3
Spicers Field. Oxsh KT22 .... 74 E6
Spices Yd. Croy CR0 .... 61 C6
Spiers Way. Horley RH6 .... 161 B1
Spindle Way. Crawl RH10 .... 201 F5
Spindlewood Gdns.
    S Croy CR0 & CR2 .... 61 E6
Spindlewoods. Tadw KT20 ..... 97 B4
Spinis. Easth RG12 .... 26 F1
Spinnaker Ct. **2** Tedd KT1 .... 37 D8
Spinner Gn. Easth RG12 ..... 27 B4
Spinney Cl. Cobham KT11 ..... 74 A8
Spinney Cl. Crawl D RH10 ..... 204 C8
Spinney Cl. Horsh RH12 .... 218 B6
Spinney Cl. New Mal KT3 .... 38 E4
Spinney Dr. E Bed TW14 .... 14 C8
Spinney Gdns. Dulw SE19 ..... 22 F3
Spinney Hill. Row Tn KT15 .... 51 F5
Spinney La. Wink SL4 .... 9 B7
Spinney The. Ascot SL5 .... 29 E4
Spinney The.
    Burgh H KT18 & KT20 .... 97 B8
Spinney The. Cheam SM3 .... 58 C6
Spinney The. Crawl RH11 .... 201 B4
Spinney The. Fetch KT23 ..... 94 B3
Spinney The. Friml GU15 .... 66 C6
Spinney The. Graysh GU26 ..... 188 A4
Spinney The. Haslem GU27 .... 208 C8
Spinney The. Horley RH6 .... 161 A5
Spinney The. Oxsh KT22 .... 74 C7
Spinney The. Purley CR8 .... 80 B8
Spinney The. Ripley GU23 .... 111 C8
Spinney The. Streat SW16 .... 21 D5
Spinney The. Sunby TW16 .... 35 A8
Spinneycroft. Oxsh KT22 .... 74 D4
Spinning Wlk The. Shere GU5 . 133 A4
Spire Ct. **10** Rich TW10 .... 6 E1
Spital Heath. Dork RH4 & RH5 . 136 C8
Spitfire Way. Farnb GU14 .... 104 E7
Spoil La. Tongh GU10 .... 126 F7
Spokane Cl. Alder GU11 .... 125 F8
Spook Hill. Dork RH5 .... 136 B3
Spooner House. Heston TW5 .... 5 A8
Spooner Wlk. Wallin SM6 .... 60 D5
Spooners Rd. Horsh RH12 .... 218 A4
Sportsbank St. Catf SE6 .... 24 C8
Spout Hill. Add CR0 .... 63 A5
Spout Hill. Stan TW19 .... 2 A3
Spout La N. Harm TW19 .... 2 B3
Spratts Alley. Ottsh KT16 .... 51 E4
Spratts La. Ottsh KT15 .... 51 E4
Spread Eagle Wlk. **2**
    Epsom KT18 .... 76 D6
Spreighton Rd. E Mole KT8 .... 36 B5
Spring Ave. Egham TW20 ..... 11 F2
Spring Bottom La. Cater RH1 .. 120 C8
Spring Cnr. Felt TW13 .... 14 F5
Spring Copse. Copth RH10 .... 183 C3
Spring Copse. E Grins RH19 ... 185 D3
Spring Cotts. King U T KT6 .... 37 D4
Spring Ct. Ewell KT17 .... 57 F2
Spring Ct. Stough GU2 .... 109 A5
Spring Gdns. Ascot SL5 .... 29 B5
Spring Gdns. Bigg H TN16 .... 83 C1
Spring Gdns. Copth RH10 .... 183 C3
Spring Gdns. Dork RH4 .... 136 A8
Spring Gdns. E Mole KT8 .... 36 C5
Spring Gdns. Friml GU15 .... 66 A5
Spring Gdns. W Heath GU14 .... 85 A7
Spring Gdns. Wallin SM6 .... 60 C5
Spring Gr. Brent W4 .... 7 A8
Spring Gr. Farnc GU7 .... 150 E8
Spring Gr. Fetch KT22 & KT23 ... 94 B4
Spring Gr. Hampt TW12 .... 36 B8
Spring Gr. Mitch CR4 .... 41 A8
Spring Grove Cres.
    Hounsl TW3 & TW5 .... 5 C6
Spring Grove Jun & Inf Sch.
    Hounsl TW7 .... 5 D5
Spring Grove Rd.
    Hounsl TW3 & TW5 & TW7 ..... 5 C6
Spring Grove Rd. Rich TW10 .... 6 F2
Spring Hill. For Hil SE26 ..... 23 C4
Spring Hill Wildfowl Park.
    For Row RH18 .... 206 A1
Spring House. Merton SW19 .... 39 F8
Spring La. Croy CR0 & SE25 .... 43 B3
Spring La. Hale GU9 .... 125 A7
Spring La. Oxted RH8 .... 122 D4
Spring La. Slinfd RH13 .... 215 C3
Spring La W. Hale GU9 .... 125 A6
Spring Meadow. Brack RG12 ... 27 D8
Spring Meadow. For Row RH18 206 F1
Spring Park Ave. Croy CR0 .... 62 D8
Spring Park Inf Sch. Croy CR0 . 63 A7
Spring Park Jun Sch. Croy CR0 63 A7
Spring Park Rd. S Croy CR0 .... 62 D8
Spring Plat. Crawl RH10 .... 202 C6
Spring Plat Ct. Crawl RH10 ... 202 C6
Spring Rd. Felt TW13 .... 14 F5
Spring Rise. Egham TW20 ..... 11 E2
Spring St. Ewell KT17 .... 57 F2
Spring Terr. Rich TW10 .... 6 E2
Spring Way. E Grins RH19 ..... 186 A4
Spring Woods. Sandh GU17 .... 45 C1
Spring Woods. Vir W GU25 .... 31 B5

Springbank Rd. Lewish SE13 ... 24 E8
Springbourne Ct. Beck BR3 ... 44 C8
Springclose La. Cheam SM3 ... 58 E4
Springcopse Rd. Reig RH2 .... 139 C7
Springfarm Rd. Linch GU27 .... 207 E5
Springfield. E Grins RH19 ..... 185 D4
Springfield. Elst GU8 .... 148 D3
Springfield. Lhtwat GU18 .... 67 D8
Springfield. Oxted RH8 .... 122 D5
Springfield. S Norw SE25 .... 43 A6
Springfield Ave. Hampt TW12 .. 16 B2
Springfield Ave. Merton SW20 . 39 F6
Springfield Cl. Knaph GU21 .... 68 E1
Springfield Cres. Horsh RH12 . 217 B2
Springfield Ct. Horsh RH12 .... 217 C2
Springfield Ct. **9** King U T KT1 . 37 E6
Springfield Ct. Wallin SM6 .... 60 B5
Springfield Cty Fst & Mid Schs.
    Sunby TW16 .... 34 F7
Springfield Gdns. W Wick BR4 .. 63 B8
Springfield Gr. Sunby TW16 ... 35 A8
Springfield Hospl.
    Up Toot SW17 .... 20 E5
Springfield La. Weyb KT13 .... 53 B6
Springfield Meadows.
    Weyb KT13 .... 53 B6
Springfield Pk Rd. Horsh RH12 217 B2
Springfield Pl. King U T KT3 .... 38 C5
Springfield Rd. Ash GU12 ..... 106 A5
Springfield Rd. Ashf TW15 .... 13 F3
Springfield Rd. Binf RG12 ..... 26 C8
Springfield Rd. Bra Hil SL3 .... 1 B7
Springfield Rd. Crawl RH11 .... 201 D5
Springfield Rd. E Ewell KT17 ... 58 C1
Springfield Rd. Friml GU15 .... 66 B5
Springfield Rd. Guild GU1 ..... 109 E1
Springfield Rd. Horsh RH12 .... 217 C2
Springfield Rd. King U T KT1 ... 37 E6
Springfield Rd. Penge SE26 ... 23 B3
Springfield Rd. S Norw CR7 .... 42 C8
Springfield Rd. **6** Tedd TW11 .. 17 A3
Springfield Rd. Twick TW2 .... 16 A7
Springfield Rd. Wallin SM6 .... 60 B5
Springfield Rd. Westc RH4 .... 135 C6
Springfield Rd. Wimble SW19 ... 20 A3
Springfield Rise. For Hil SE26 ... 23 B5
Springfield Terr. Bramly GU5 .. 151 F6
Springfield Way. Elst GU8 .... 148 E3
Springfields Cl. Chert KT16 .... 33 B1
Springfields Cl. Chert KT16 .... 33 B1
Springfields. Easth RG12 ..... 27 B5
Springhaven Cl. Guild GU1 ... 110 A1
Springhill. Elst GU8 .... 148 E3
Springhill Cl. Bigg H TN16 .... 83 C1
Springhurst Cl. Croy CR0 .... 62 F6
Springlakes Est. Alder GU12 ... 105 E3
Springmead Ct. Sandh GU15 ... 45 E1
Springpark Dr. Beck BR3 .... 44 C6
Springwell Cl. Streat SW16 .... 21 F4
Springwell Ct. Hounsl TW5 .... 4 D5
Springwell Jun & Inf Schs.
    Heston TW5 .... 4 E7
Springwell Rd. Bear Gn RH5 ... 157 D3
Springwell Rd. Heston TW5 .... 4 D6
Springwell Rd. Streat SW16 ... 22 A3
Springwood. Milf GU8 .... 150 A1
Springwood Ct. S Croy CR2 .... 61 E6
Sprint Ind Est. Byfl KT14 .... 71 D8
Spruce Dr. Lhtwat GU18 .... 67 A7
Spruce Pk. Beck BR2 .... 44 F5
Spruce Rd. Bigg H TN16 .... 83 D3
Sprucedale Gdns. S Croy CR0 . 62 D6
Sprucedale Gdns. Wallin CR8 . 60 E2
Spur Rd. Brent TW7 .... 6 B7
Spur Rd. Felt TW14 .... 4 B3
Spur The. Knaph GU21 .... 68 B1
Spurfield. E Mole KT8 .... 36 B6
Spurgeon Ave. S Norw SE19 ... 42 D8
Spurgeon Cl. Crawl RH11 ..... 201 C7
Spurgeon Rd. S Norw SE19 .... 22 D1
Spurgeon's Coll. S Norw SE25 .. 42 E7
Spurs Ct. Alder GU11 .... 104 E2
Spy La. Loxwd RH14 .... 213 A4
Square Dr. Marl Ht GU27 .... 208 B1
Square The. Bagsh GU19 .... 47 E3
Square The. Brack RG12 .... 27 C5
Square The. Crawl RH11 .... 201 D6
Square The. Harm TW6 .... 2 B6
Square The. Lhtwat GU18 ..... 48 C1
Square The. Lingf RH7 .... 164 C4
Square The. Onsl V GU2 .... 129 F7
Square The. Rowl GU10 .... 145 E3
Square The. Tats TN16 .... 103 C7
Square The. Wallin SM5 .... 60 A5
Square The. Weyb KT13 .... 53 C5
Square The. Wisley GU23 & KT14 71 E3
Squarey St. Wands SW17 ..... 20 C5
Squire Ct. **2** Croy CR0 .... 42 E1
Squire's Bridge Rd. Littlt TW17 . 34 A5
Squire's Rd. Shep Gn TW17 ... 34 A5
Squires Bridge Rd.
    Shep Gn KT17 .... 33 F5
Squires Cl. Crawl D RH10 ..... 204 A8
Squires Ct. Chert KT16 .... 33 B1
Squires Ct. Wimble SW19 .... 20 A4
Squires Hill La. Tilf GU10 .... 147 C4
Squires Wlk. Ashf TW15 .... 14 D1
Squirrel Cl. Crawl RH11 ..... 181 B1
Squirrel Cl. Hounsl TW4 .... 4 C4
Squirrel Cl. Sandh GU17 .... 64 B8
Squirrel Dr. Wink SL4 .... 9 B7
Squirrel Wood. Woodc KT18 ... 76 D4
Squirrels Cl. Farnc GU7 .... 129 D1
Squirrels Ct. Worc Pk KT4 .... 57 F8
Squirrels Gn. Fetch KT23 ..... 94 A4
Squirrels Gn. **12** Redh RH1 .... 118 F2
Squirrels Gn. Worc Pk KT4 .... 58 A8
Stable Croft. Bagsh GU19 .... 47 D2

Stable Ct. Cater CR3 ...... 101 A5
Stable Mews. W Norw SE27 ...... 22 C3
Stables The. Bellf GU1 ...... 109 D4
Stables The. Cobham KT11 ...... 73 F5
Stace Way. Crawl RH10 ...... 202 E8
Stacey Ct. Merst RH1 ...... 119 C6
Stacey's Farm Rd. Elst GU8 ...... 148 D4
Stack House. Oxted RH8 ...... 122 E5
Stackfield Rd. Crawl RH11 ...... 200 E5
Staddon Ct. Beck BR3 ...... 43 E5
Staff Coll. Camb GU15 ...... 65 C7
Staff College Rd. Camb GU15 ...... 65 B6
Staff Rd. Alder GU12 ...... 105 C2
Staffhurst Wood Rd.
  Limps RH8 ...... 144 C6
Stafford Cl. Cater CR3 ...... 100 F4
Stafford Cl. Cheam SM3 ...... 58 E4
Stafford Gdns. Croy CR0 ...... 60 F5
Stafford Lake.
  Bisley GU21 & GU24 ...... 68 A1
Stafford Pl. Rich TW10 ...... 17 F8
Stafford Rd. Cater CR3 ...... 101 A6
Stafford Rd. Crawl RH11 ...... 181 B1
Stafford Rd. Croy CR0 ...... 61 A6
Stafford Rd. King U T KT3 ...... 38 C6
Stafford Rd. Wallin CR0 & SM6 ...... 60 E4
Stafford Sq. 2 Oat Pk KT13 ...... 53 D6
Staffords Pl. Horley RH6 ...... 161 B2
Stag Hill. Guild GU2 ...... 130 A8
Stag Leys. Ashtd KT21 ...... 95 E7
Stag Leys Cl. Woodm SM7 ...... 78 E4
Stagbury Ave. Chips CR5 ...... 78 E1
Stagbury Cl. Chips CR5 ...... 98 E8
Stagbury House. Chips CR5 ...... 98 E8
Stagelands. Crawl RH11 ...... 201 C8
Stagelands Ct. Crawl RH11 ...... 201 C8
Stags Way. Hounsl TW7 ...... 5 F8
Stainash Cres. Stain TW18 ...... 13 B3
Stainash Par. Stain TW18 ...... 13 B3
Stainbank Rd. Mitch CR4 ...... 41 B6
Staines Ave. Cheam SM3 ...... 58 D8
Staines By-Pass.
  Stain TW15 & TW18 ...... 13 C3
Staines Central Trad Est.
  Stain TW18 ...... 12 E4
Staines La. Chert TW16 ...... 33 A3
Staines Lane Cl. Chert KT16 ...... 32 F4
Staines Prep Sch The.
  Stain TW18 ...... 13 A3
Staines Rd. Chert KT16 ...... 32 F3
Staines Rd. E Bed TW14 ...... 14 D8
Staines Rd.
  Felt TW14 & TW3 & TW4 ...... 4 D2
Staines Rd.
  Hounsl TW14 & TW3 & TW4 ...... 4 D2
Staines Rd. Laleh TW18 ...... 33 B7
Staines Rd. Stain TW18 ...... 33 B7
Staines Rd. Thorpe KT16 ...... 33 A5
Staines Rd. Twick TW13 & TW2 ...... 16 C6
Staines Rd. Wray TW19 ...... 11 F7
Staines Rd E.
  Sunby TW12 & TW16 ...... 35 C8
Staines Rd W. Ashf TW15 ...... 14 D1
Staines Sta. Stain TW18 ...... 13 A3
Stainford Cl. Ashf TW15 ...... 14 D3
Stainton Rd. Lewish SE13 ...... 24 D8
Stainton Wlk. Woking GU21 ...... 69 C1
Staiths Way. Burgh H KT20 ...... 97 B7
Stake La. Farnb GU14 ...... 85 A4
Stakescorner Rd. Arting GU3 ...... 130 A2
Stambourne Way. S Norw SE19 ...... 22 F1
Stambourne Way. W Wick BR4 ...... 63 C7
Stamford Ave. Friml GU16 ...... 65 F1
Stamford Dr. Hayes BR2 ...... 44 F5
Stamford Green Cty Fst & Mid
  Sch. Epsom KT19 ...... 76 B7
Stamford Green Rd.
  Epsom KT18 ...... 76 B6
Stamford Rd. Walt O T KT12 ...... 54 D7
Stan Hill. Charl RH6 ...... 180 D4
Stanborough Cl. Hampt TW12 ...... 15 F2
Stanborough Rd.
  Hounsl TW3 & TW7 ...... 5 D4
Stanbridge Cl. Crawl RH11 ...... 200 E6
Standard Rd. Hounsl TW4 ...... 4 E4
Standen Cl. E Grins RH19 ...... 185 A4
Standen (National Trust).
  E Grins RH19 ...... 205 D4
Standen Pl. Horsh RH12 ...... 218 A4
Standen Rd. Wands SW18 ...... 20 A8
Standinghall La. Worth RH10 ...... 203 B3
Standon La. Wall W RH5 ...... 176 F2
Standlake Point. 1 For Hil SE23 ...... 23 D5
Stane Cl. Merton SW19 ...... 20 B1
Stane House. Dork RH4 ...... 136 B8
Stane St. Ockley RH5 ...... 177 D4
Stane St. Slinfd RH12 & RH13 ...... 215 C4
Stane Way. Ewell KT17 ...... 58 A1
Stanedge Ct. Streat SW16 ...... 21 E3
Stanford Cl. Hampt TW12 ...... 15 F2
Stanford Cotts. Pirb GU24 ...... 87 E1
Stanford Mid Sch. Mitch SW16 ...... 41 D8
Stanford Orch. Warn RH12 ...... 216 F8
Stanford Pl. Lingf RH7 ...... 164 D3
Stanford Rd. Thorn H SW16 ...... 41 E7
Stanford Way. Broad H RH12 ...... 216 D3
Stanford Way. Mitch SW16 ...... 41 D7
Stanfords The. Ewell KT17 ...... 76 F7
Stangate Mansions. Twick TW1 ...... 16 F5
Stanger Rd. Croy SE25 ...... 43 A5
Stangrave Hall. Godst RH9 ...... 121 B3
Stanhope Ave. Hayes BR2 ...... 44 F1
Stanhope Cotts. Lingf RH7 ...... 164 F3
Stanhope Gr. Beck BR3 ...... 43 F5
Stanhope Heath. Stan TW19 ...... 2 C1
Stanhope Rd. Camb GU15 ...... 64 F4
Stanhope Rd. S Croy CR0 ...... 61 E7
Stanhope Rd. Wallin SM5 ...... 60 A3
Stanhope Way. Stan TW19 ...... 2 C1
Stanhopes. Limps RH8 ...... 123 B7

Stanier Cl. Worth RH10 ...... 202 B5
Staniland Dr. Wit V KT13 ...... 52 F1
Stanley Ave. Beck BR2 & BR3 ...... 44 C6
Stanley Ave. W Barn KT3 ...... 39 A4
Stanley Cl. Coulsd CR5 ...... 79 F2
Stanley Cl. Crawl RH11 ...... 201 E4
Stanley Cotts. Knaph GU21 ...... 68 D2
Stanley Ct. Belm SM2 ...... 59 B3
Stanley Ct. Wallin SM5 ...... 60 A3
Stanley Ctr. Crawl RH10 ...... 181 F2
Stanley Cty Inf Sch. Tedd TW12 ...... 16 E4
Stanley Cty Jun Sch. Tedd TW12 ...... 16 E4
Stanley Dr. Farnb GU14 ...... 84 C3
Stanley Gardens Rd. Tedd TW11 ...... 16 E3
Stanley Gdns. Hersh KT12 ...... 54 E6
Stanley Gdns. Mitch CR4 ...... 21 A2
Stanley Gdns. Sander CR2 ...... 81 A7
Stanley Gdns. Wallin SM6 ...... 60 C4
Stanley Gr. Thorn H CR0 & CR7 ...... 42 A3
Stanley Hill. Pirb GU24 ...... 87 C5
Stanley Mansions. Up Toot SW17 ...... 20 F6
Stanley Park High Sch.
  Wallin SM5 ...... 60 A4
Stanley Park Inf Sch.
  Wallin SM5 ...... 59 F3
Stanley Park Jun Sch.
  Wallin SM5 ...... 59 F3
Stanley Park Rd.
  Wallin SM5 & SM6 ...... 60 A3
Stanley Rd. Ashf TW15 ...... 13 E3
Stanley Rd. Hounsl TW3 ...... 5 C3
Stanley Rd. Mitch CR4 ...... 21 A1
Stanley Rd. Morden SM4 ...... 40 A5
Stanley Rd. Mortl SW14 ...... 7 B3
Stanley Rd. Sutton SM2 ...... 59 B3
Stanley Rd. Tedd TW11 & TW2 ...... 16 E3
Stanley Rd. Thorn H CR0 & CR7 ...... 42 A3
Stanley Rd. Twick TW2 ...... 16 D5
Stanley Rd. Wallin SM5 ...... 60 A3
Stanley Rd. Wimble SW19 ...... 20 A2
Stanley Rd. Woki RG11 ...... 25 E6
Stanley Rd. Woking GU21 ...... 69 F2
Stanley Sq. Wallin SM5 ...... 59 F2
Stanley St. Cater CR3 ...... 100 C5
Stanley Tech High Sch.
  S Norw SE25 ...... 42 F6
Stanley Wlk. Horsh RH13 ...... 217 D2
Stanleycroft Cl. Hounsl TW7 ...... 5 E6
Stanmore Cl. Ascot SL5 ...... 29 A5
Stanmore Gdns. Rich TW9 ...... 6 F4
Stanmore Gdns. Sutton SM1 ...... 59 C7
Stanmore Rd. Rich TW9 ...... 6 F4
Stanmore Terr. Beck BR3 ...... 44 A7
Stannet Way. Wallin SM6 ...... 60 C6
Stansfield Rd. Crawl TW4 & TW5 ...... 4 B5
Stanstead Gr. For Hil SE23 ...... 23 F7
Stanstead Manor. Sutton SM1 ...... 59 A3
Stanstead Rd. Cater CR3 & RH1 ...... 100 E2
Stanstead Rd. For Hil SE23 & SE6 ...... 23 F7
Stansted Rd. Stan TW6 ...... 2 F1
Stanthorpe Cl. Streat SW16 ...... 21 E3
Stanthorpe Rd. Streat SW16 ...... 21 E3
Stanthorpe Rd. Streat SW16 ...... 21 E4
Stanton Ave. Tedd TW11 ...... 16 E2
Stanton Cl. Cran GU6 ...... 174 A3
Stanton Cl. N Cheam KT4 ...... 39 D1
Stanton Cl. W Ewell KT19 ...... 57 B5
Stanton Cl. W Ewell KT19 ...... 57 B5
Stanton Rd. Barnes SW13 ...... 7 F5
Stanton Rd. Thorn H CR0 ...... 42 C2
Stanton Rd. Wimble SW20 ...... 39 D8
Stanton Sq. For Hil SE26 ...... 23 F4
Stanton Way. For Hil SE26 & SE6 ...... 23 F4
Stanway Sch. Dork RH4 ...... 115 B1
Stanwell Cl. Stan TW19 ...... 2 D1
Stanwell Gdns. Stan TW19 ...... 2 D1
Stanwell Moor Rd.
  Harm TW19 & TW6 & UB7 ...... 2 B4
Stanwell Moor Rd. Stan TW19 ...... 2 B4
Stanwell New Rd.
  Stan TW18 & TW19 ...... 13 B5
Stanwell Rd. Ashf TW15 ...... 13 E4
Stanwell Rd.
  E Bed TW14 & TW19 & TW6 ...... 14 B8
Stanwell Rd. Horton SL3 & TW19 ...... 1 C4
Stanworth Ct. Heston TW5 ...... 5 A7
Stanyhurst. For Hil SE23 ...... 23 E7
Staple Hill. Burgh H GU24 & KT16 ...... 49 E6
Staple La. E Clan GU4 ...... 111 C2
Staple La. Albury GU4 ...... 132 F8
Staplecross Rd. 1 Crawl RH11 ...... 201 A3
Staplefield Cl. 3 Streat SW2 ...... 21 E7
Stapleford Cl. King U T KT1 ...... 38 A6
Stapleford Cl. Putney SW19 ...... 19 E8
Staplehurst. Easth RG12 ...... 26 E2
Staplehurst Cl. Dovgn RH1 ...... 139 C5
Staplehurst Rd. Dovgn RH1 ...... 139 C5
Staplehurst Rd. Sutton SM5 ...... 59 E3
Stapleton Gdns. Croy CR0 ...... 61 A5
Stapleton Rd. Up Toot SW17 ...... 21 A5
Star and Garter Hill. Rich TW10 ...... 17 E8
Star Hill. Churt GU10 ...... 167 D2
Star Hill. Woking GU22 ...... 89 D8
Star Hill Dr. Churt GU10 ...... 167 D2
Star La. Alder GU12 ...... 105 F2
Star La. Hooley CR5 ...... 99 A6
Star La. King U T KT4 ...... 71 C8
Star Post Rd. Camb GU15 ...... 65 F8
Star Rd. Hounsl TW7 ...... 5 D5
Starborough Cotts.
  Dorman RH7 ...... 185 F7
Starborough Rd. Lingf TN8 ...... 165 E5
Starhurst Sch. Dork RH5 ...... 136 C5
Starling Way. Hampt TW12 ...... 15 E3
Starmead Dr. Woki RG11 ...... 25 E5
Starrock La. Chips CR5 ...... 99 A4
Starrock Rd. Coulsd CR5 ...... 99 C8
Starwood Cl. W Byfl KT14 ...... 71 C8
Staten Gdns. Twick TW1 ...... 16 F7
Statham Ct. Binf RG12 ...... 26 E8
Station App. Ash V GU12 ...... 106 A7

Station App. Ashf TW15 ...... 13 F4
Station App. Beck SE6 ...... 23 F3
Station App. Beck BR3 ...... 44 A8
Station App. Belm SM2 ...... 58 E3
Station App. Chips CR5 ...... 78 F1
Station App. Coulsd CR5 ...... 79 D4
Station App. 3 Croy CR0 ...... 61 D8
Station App. Dork RH4 ...... 115 C1
Station App. E Hors KT24 ...... 92 E1
Station App. Epsom KT17 & KT19 ...... 76 D6
Station App. Godal GU7 ...... 150 D4
Station App. Guild GU1 ...... 130 E8
Station App. Hampt TW12 ...... 36 A8
Station App. Haslem GU27 ...... 208 B6
Station App. Hinch W KT10 ...... 55 F7
Station App. Horley RH6 ...... 161 B2
Station App. 4
  King U T KT1 & KT2 ...... 38 A8
Station App. Leahd KT22 ...... 95 A6
Station App. 6 New Mal KT4 ...... 39 A1
Station App. Oxted RH8 ...... 122 E6
Station App. Purley CR8 ...... 80 A8
Station App. Rich TW9 ...... 7 A6
Station App. S Croy CR2 ...... 61 D2
Station App. Shep TW17 ...... 34 C4
Station App. Stain TW18 ...... 13 A3
Station App. Streat SW16 ...... 21 D3
Station App. Sunby TW16 ...... 35 A8
Station App. 1 Sunb SK16 ...... 37 D3
Station App. Sutton SM2 ...... 59 B1
Station App. Sutton SM2 ...... 97 C4
Station App. Vir W GU25 ...... 31 D5
Station App. W Byfl KT14 ...... 71 A7
Station App. Weyb KT13 ...... 53 A4
Station App. Whytif CR3 ...... 81 A1
Station App. Woking GU22 ...... 69 F2
Station App. Worc Pk KT19 ...... 58 A5
Station App E. Earls RH1 ...... 139 F7
Station App W. Earls RH1 ...... 139 F7
Station Approach Rd.
  Coulsd CR5 ...... 79 D4
Station Approach Rd.
  Crawl RH6 ...... 182 B7
Station Ave. Cater CR3 ...... 101 A3
Station Ave. King U T KT3 ...... 38 E6
Station Ave. W Ewell KT19 ...... 57 E2
Station Ave. W Ewell KT19 ...... 57 E2
Station Ave. Walt O T KT12 ...... 54 A6
Station Bldgs. Wimble SW20 ...... 39 C7
Station Cl. Hampt TW12 ...... 36 B8
Station Cl. Horsh RH13 ...... 217 D1
Station Cres. Ashf TW15 ...... 13 E4
Station Est. Beck BR3 ...... 43 D5
Station Estate Rd. Felt TW14 ...... 15 B7
Station Flats. Sunnin SL5 ...... 30 B2
Station Gdns. Chisw W4 ...... 7 C7
Station Hill. Ascot SL5 ...... 29 A5
Station Hill. Crawl RH10 ...... 202 B7
Station Hill. Hayes BR2 ...... 44 F4
Station Ind Est. Woki RG11 ...... 25 B6
Station La. Ent Gn GU8 ...... 171 A7
Station La. Milf GU8 ...... 171 A7
Station Par. Ashf TW15 ...... 13 E4
Station Par. Chips CR5 ...... 78 F1
Station Par. E Hors KT24 ...... 92 E1
Station Par. Felt TW14 ...... 15 B8
Station Par. Rich TW9 ...... 7 A6
Station Par. Vir W GU25 ...... 31 E4
Station Par. 5 Up Toot SW12 ...... 21 A7
Station Path. Stain TW18 ...... 12 F4
Station Rd. Addl KT15 ...... 52 D6
Station Rd. Alder GU11 ...... 105 B2
Station Rd. Ashf TW15 ...... 13 F4
Station Rd. Bagsh GU19 ...... 47 E4
Station Rd. Belm SM2 ...... 59 A1
Station Rd. Betch RH3 ...... 116 E3
Station Rd. Brack RG12 ...... 27 B7
Station Rd. Bramly GU5 ...... 152 A7
Station Rd. Broml BR2 ...... 44 F7
Station Rd. Carsh SM5 ...... 59 F6
Station Rd. Chert KT16 ...... 33 A1
Station Rd. Chess KT9 ...... 56 E5
Station Rd. Chobh GU24 ...... 69 B6
Station Rd. Crawl D RH10 ...... 204 B8
Station Rd. Croy CR0 ...... 42 C1
Station Rd. Dork RH4 ...... 136 A8
Station Rd. E Grins RH19 ...... 185 D1
Station Rd. Egham TW20 ...... 12 A3
Station Rd. Esher KT10 ...... 55 D8
Station Rd. Esher KT10 ...... 55 E5
Station Rd. Farnb GU14 ...... 85 B4
Station Rd. Farnc GU7 ...... 150 F7
Station Rd. For Row RH18 ...... 206 F3
Station Rd. Godal GU7 ...... 150 D4
Station Rd. Gomsh GU5 ...... 133 D4
Station Rd. Hampt TW12 ...... 36 B8
Station Rd. Horley RH6 ...... 161 B3
Station Rd. Horsh RH13 ...... 217 D2
Station Rd. Hounsl TW3 ...... 5 B3
Station Rd. Hyde GU8 ...... 171 D6
Station Rd. Kenley CR8 ...... 80 C5
Station Rd. Mitch SW16 ...... 41 C8
Station Rd. Worth RH10 ...... 202 C5
Station Rd. Lingf RH7 ...... 164 E4
Station Rd. Loxwd RH14 ...... 213 A3
Station Rd. Merst RH1 ...... 119 C7
Station Rd. Merton SW19 ...... 40 C8
Station Rd. Penge SE20 ...... 23 C2
Station Rd. Redh RH1 ...... 118 F2
Station Rd. Rudg RH12 ...... 214 D7
Station Rd. S Godst RH9 ...... 142 E5
Station Rd. S Norw SE25 ...... 42 F5
Station Rd. Shalf GU4 ...... 130 E3
Station Rd. Shep TW17 ...... 34 C4
Station Rd. Stk D'A KT11 ...... 73 E3
Station Rd. Sunby TW16 ...... 15 A1

Station Rd. Sunnin SL5 ...... 30 A4
Station Rd. Tedd TW11 ...... 17 A2
Station Rd. Tedd KT1 ...... 37 D8
Station Rd. Thame D K7 ...... 36 F2
Station Rd. Thame D KT10 ...... 55 D8
Station Rd. Twick TW1 ...... 16 F8
Station Rd. W Barn KT3 ...... 39 B4
Station Rd. W Wick BR4 ...... 44 C1
Station Rd. Warn RH12 ...... 217 B8
Station Rd. Whytlf CR3 ...... 80 F1
Station Rd. Woki RG11 ...... 25 B6
Station Rd. Wold CR3 ...... 101 F5
Station Rd. Wray TW19 ...... 1 A1
Station Rd E. Ash V GU12 ...... 106 A7
Station Rd E. Oxted RH8 ...... 122 E6
Station Rd N. Egham TW20 ...... 11 F3
Station Rd S. Merst RH1 ...... 119 C7
Station Rd W. Ash V GU12 ...... 105 F8
Station Rd W. Oxted RH8 ...... 122 E6
Station Rise. Streat SE27 ...... 22 B6
Station Row. Shalf GU4 ...... 130 E3
Station Terr. Dork RH4 ...... 136 A8
Station View. Ash V GU12 ...... 106 A8
Station Way. Cheam SM2 & SM3 ...... 58 E3
Station Way.
  Crawl RH10 & RH11 ...... 201 D5
Station Yd. Twick TW1 ...... 17 A8
Staunton Rd. King U T KT2 ...... 17 F1
Staveley Gdns. Chisw W4 ...... 7 D6
Staveley Rd. Ashf TW15 ...... 14 D2
Staveley Rd. Chisw W4 ...... 7 D7
Staveley Way. Knaph GU21 ...... 68 D3
Staverton Cl. Woki RG11 ...... 25 F6
Stavordale Rd. Carsh SM4 & SM5 ...... 40 C2
Stayne End. Went GU25 ...... 31 A5
Stayton Rd. Sutton SM1 ...... 59 A7
Steadfast Rd. King U T KT1 ...... 37 D8
Steam Farm La. Hatton TW14 ...... 3 F3
Steel's La. Oxsh KT11 & KT22 ...... 74 C5
Steele Rd. Islew TW7 ...... 6 A3
Steele's Rd. Alder GU11 ...... 105 B4
Steep Hill. Burrh GU24 ...... 49 C3
Steep Hill. S Croy CR0 ...... 61 E6
Steep Hill. Streat SW16 ...... 21 D5
Steeple Cl. Wimble SW19 ...... 19 E4
Steeple Heights Dr.
  Bigg H TN16 ...... 83 D2
Steepways. Beac H GU26 ...... 188 B6
Steeres Hill. Rusper RH12 ...... 199 C6
Steerforth Copse. Sandh GU15 ...... 45 E2
Steerforth St. Wands SW18 ...... 20 C6
Steers La. Crawl RH10 ...... 182 C4
Steers Mead. Mitch CR4 ...... 40 F8
Steetley Cl. Sutton SM2 ...... 59 C3
Stella Rd. Up Toot SW17 ...... 20 F2
Stembridge Rd. Penge SE20 ...... 43 B7
Stenning Ct. Leahd KT22 ...... 95 B5
Stepgates. Chert KT16 ...... 33 B2
Stepgates Cl. Chert KT16 ...... 33 B2
Stepgates Com Prim Sch. Chert KT16 ...... 33 B2
Stephanie Chase Ct. Woki RG11 ...... 25 D7
Stephen Cl. Crawl RH11 ...... 181 D1
Stephen Cl. Egham TW20 ...... 12 C2
Stephen Cl. 18 Putney SW19 ...... 19 D7
Stephendale Rd. Farnh GU9 ...... 125 D4
Stephenson Ct. Belm SM2 ...... 58 F3
Stephenson Dr. E Grins RH19 ...... 205 F7
Stephenson Pl. Crawl RH10 ...... 202 B6
Stephenson Way. Twick TW4 ...... 16 A8
Stepney Cl. Worth RH10 ...... 202 B6
Sterling Ave. Up Hall TW17 ...... 34 E6
Sterling Bldgs. Horsh RH12 ...... 217 C2
Sternhold Ave.
  Streat SW12 & SW2 ...... 21 D6
Sternhold Ave. Streat SW2 ...... 21 E6
Sterry Dr. Thame D K7 ...... 36 E3
Sterry Dr. Worc Pk KT19 ...... 57 E6
Steucers La. For Hil SE23 ...... 23 E7
Steve Biko La. Catf SE6 ...... 24 A4
Steve Biko Way. Hounsl TW3 ...... 5 A4
Stevenage Rd. Crawl RH11 ...... 200 E3
Stevens Cl. Beck BR3 ...... 24 A2
Stevens Cl. Epsom KT17 ...... 76 E6
Stevens Cl. Hampt TW12 ...... 15 E2
Stevens Cl. Beck BR3 ...... 24 A2
Stevens' La. Clayg KT10 ...... 56 A4
Stewart. Tadw KT20 ...... 97 D6
Stewart Ave. Shep Gn TW17 ...... 34 A5
Stewart Cl. Hampt TW12 ...... 15 E2
Stewart Cl. Woking GU21 ...... 68 F2
Stewart Fleming Prim Sch.
  Penge SE20 ...... 43 C6
Steyning Cl. Crawl RH10 ...... 201 E8
Steyning Cl. Purley CR8 ...... 80 B3
Steyning Way. Hounsl TW4 ...... 4 C3
Sthrathbrook Rd. Streat SW16 ...... 21 F1
Stile Gdns. Shottm GU27 ...... 207 F6
Stile House. Merrow GU4 ...... 110 D2
Stile Path. Sunby TW16 ...... 35 A6
Stirling Cl. Banstd SM7 ...... 77 F2
Stirling Cl. Farnb GU14 ...... 85 A3
Stirling Cl. Friml GU16 ...... 65 F2
Stirling Cl. Mitch SW16 ...... 41 C8
Stirling Cl. Worth RH10 ...... 202 C5
Stirling Gr. Hounsl TW3 ...... 5 C5
Stirling House. 9 Redh RH1 ...... 118 F1
Stirling Rd. Stan TW19 & TW6 ...... 2 F1
Stirling Rd. Stough GU2 ...... 108 L1
Stirling Rd. Twick TW2 ...... 16 B8
Stirling Way. E Grins RH19 ...... 186 B3
Stirling Way. Farnb GU14 ...... 104 B8
Stirling Way. Horsh RH13 ...... 217 C3
Stirrup Way. Crawl RH10 ...... 202 D7
Stites Hill Rd.
  Coulsd CR & CR5 ...... 100 C4
Stoatley Hollow. Shottm GU27 ...... 208 A8
Stoatley House. 10
  Rhampt SW15 ...... 19 A7

Stoatley Rise. Shottm GU27 ...... 208 A8
Stoats Nest Rd. Coulsd CR5 ...... 79 E5
Stoats Nest Village. Coulsd CR5 ...... 79 E4
Stock Hill. Bigg H TN16 ...... 83 D2
Stockbridge Dr. Alder GU11 ...... 126 C6
Stockbury Rd. Croy CR0 ...... 43 C3
Stockfield. Horley RH6 ...... 161 B4
Stockfield Rd. Clayg KT10 ...... 55 E5
Stockfield Rd. Streat SW16 ...... 21 F5
Stockhams Cl. S Croy CR2 ...... 61 D1
Stocklund Sq. Cran GU6 ...... 174 D3
Stockport Rd. Streat SW16 ...... 41 D8
Stocks Cl. Horley RH6 ...... 161 B2
Stockton Rd. Woodh RH2 ...... 139 A6
Stockwell Rd. E Grins RH19 ...... 205 E6
Stockwell Wks. Crawl RH10 ...... 202 A6
Stockwood Rise. Camb GU15 ...... 65 F3
Stockwood Way. Heath E GU9 ...... 125 F7
Stocton Cl. Guild GU1 ...... 109 C2
Stocton Rd. Guild GU1 ...... 109 D2
Stodart Rd. Penge SE20 ...... 43 C8
Stoford Cl. Putney SW19 ...... 19 E8
Stoke Brunswick Sch.
  Hammer RH19 ...... 206 E7
Stoke Cl. Stk D'A KT11 ...... 73 F3
Stoke Fields. 8 Guild GU1 ...... 109 D1
Stoke Gr. Guild GU1 ...... 109 D1
Stoke Hill Cty Prim Sch.
  Bellf GU1 ...... 109 C4
Stoke Hills. Farnh GU9 ...... 125 C3
Stoke Hosp (Almshouses). 6
  Guild GU1 ...... 109 D1
Stoke Park Ct. 5 Guild GU1 ...... 109 D1
Stoke Rd. Guild GU1 ...... 109 D1
Stoke Rd. King U T KT2 ...... 18 C1
Stoke Rd. Stk D'A KT11 ...... 73 E3
Stoke Rd. Walt O T KT12 ...... 54 C7
Stoke Rd Cotts. Fetch KT22 ...... 94 D6
Stokeford Cl. 5 Brack RG12 ...... 27 F4
Stokes Rd. Croy CR0 ...... 43 D3
Stokes Ridings. Tadw KT20 ...... 97 D4
Stokesby Rd. Chess KT9 ...... 56 F4
Stokesheath Rd. Oxsh KT22 ...... 74 C8
Stompond La. Walt O T KT12 ...... 54 A8
Stoms Path. Catf SE6 ...... 24 A3
Stonards Brow. Sham Gn GU5 ...... 152 D4
Stondon Pk. For Hil SE23 ...... 23 E8
Stone Cres. E Bed TW14 ...... 14 F8
Stone Hatch. Alf Cr GU6 ...... 194 A3
Stone House Gdns. Cater CR3 ...... 100 E2
Stone Park Ave. Beck BR3 ...... 44 B5
Stone Pl. Worc Pk KT4 ...... 58 A8
Stone Rd. Hayes BR2 ...... 44 F4
Stone St. Alder GU12 ...... 126 D8
Stone St. Croy CR0 & CR9 ...... 61 A5
Stone's Rd. Ewell KT17 ...... 76 E7
Stonebanks. Walt O T KT12 ...... 35 A2
Stonebridge Ct. Crawl RH11 ...... 201 C2
Stonebridge Ct. Horsh RH12 ...... 217 A2
Stonebridge Fields. Shalf GU4 ...... 130 D6
Stonebridge Wharf. Shalf GU4 ...... 130 D6
Stonecot Cl. Cheam SM3 & SM4 ...... 39 E1
Stonecot Hill. Cheam SM4 ...... 39 E1
Stonecourt Cl. Horley RH6 ...... 161 C3
Stonecrop Cl. Crawl RH11 ...... 201 B3
Stonecrop Rd.
  Merrow GU1 & GU4 ...... 110 C3
Stonedene Cl. Head Dn GU35 ...... 187 B4
Stonefield Cl.
  Crawl RH10 & RH11 ...... 201 D5
Stonegate. Friml GU15 ...... 66 C6
Stonehaven. Beck BR3 ...... 44 B7
Stonehill Cl. L Book KT23 ...... 94 A2
Stonehill Cl. Mortl SW14 ...... 7 D2
Stonehill Cres. Longc KT16 ...... 50 E4
Stonehill Pk. Head Dn GU35 ...... 187 C4
Stonehill Rd. Chobh GU24 & KT16 ...... 50 D3
Stonehill Rd. Head Dn GU35 ...... 187 C4
Stonehill Rd. Lhtwat GU18 ...... 48 A1
Stonehill Rd. Mortl SW14 ...... 7 D2
Stonehill Rd. Ottsh GU24 & KT16 ...... 50 D3
Stonehill's Mansions. 3
  Streat SW16 ...... 21 E6
Stonehills Ct. Dulw SE21 ...... 22 E5
Stonehouse Rise. Friml GU16 ...... 65 E1
Stoneleigh Ave.
  N Cheam KT17 & KT4 ...... 58 A7
Stoneleigh Cl. E Grins RH19 ...... 185 D1
Stoneleigh Cres. Worc Pk KT19 ...... 57 F5
Stoneleigh Ct. Friml GU16 ...... 65 F1
Stoneleigh Fst Grant Maintd Sch.
  N Cheam KT4 ...... 58 B6
Stoneleigh Lodge. 12 Rich TW9 ...... 6 F6
Stoneleigh Park Ave. Croy CR0 ...... 43 D3
Stoneleigh Park Rd.
  Worc Pk KT19 & KT4 ...... 58 A5
Stoneleigh Pk. Whit V KT13 ...... 53 C4
Stoneleigh Rd. Carsh SM5 ...... 40 E2
Stoneleigh Rd. The Char RH8 ...... 123 E5
Stoneleigh Sta. Stonel KT19 ...... 58 A5
Stonepit Cl. Ock Rid GU7 ...... 150 C4
Stoners Cl. Crawl RH6 ...... 181 E7
Stones La. Westc RH4 ...... 135 C6
Stoneswood Rd. Limps RH8 ...... 123 B5
Stoneworth Ct. Croy SE25 ...... 43 A3
Stoney Bottom. Graysh GU26 ...... 188 C3
Stoney Brook. Guild GU2 ...... 108 E2
Stoney Deep. Tedd TW11 ...... 17 A4
Stoney La. S Norw SE19 ...... 22 F2
Stoney Rd. Brack RG12 ...... 27 A8
Stoneybrook. Horsh RH12 ...... 216 F1
Stoneycroft Cl. Lewish SE12 ...... 24 F8
Stoneycroft Wlk. 3
  Crawl RH11 ...... 200 D5
Stoneyfield Rd. Coulsd CR5 ...... 79 F3
Stoneyland Ct. Egham TW20 ...... 11 F3
Stoneylands Rd. Egham TW20 ...... 11 F3

Stonny Croft. Ashtd KT21 .... 75 F2
Stony Hill. Esher KT10 .... 54 F1
Stoop Ct. W Byfl KT14 .... 71 B7
Stopham Rd. Worth RH10 .... 202 C3
Stormont Way. Chess KT9 .... 56 C5
Storrington Rd. Croy CR0 .... 42 F1
Stoughton Ave. Cheam SM3 .... 58 E5
Stoughton Cl. Rhampt SW15 .... 19 A7
Stoughton Grange Cty Jun Sch.
   Stough GU2 .... 109 B4
Stoughton Inf Sch. Stough GU2 109 B4
Stoughton Rd. Bellf GU1 & GU2 109 B3
Stoughton Rd.
   Stough GU1 & GU2 .... 109 B3
Stourhead Cl. Farnb GU14 .... 85 D4
Stourhead Cl. 6 Putney SW19 .. 19 D8
Stourhead Gdns. W Barn SW20 . 39 A6
Stourton Way. Felt TW13 .... 15 F4
Stovold's Way. Alder GU11 ...... 125 F8
Stovolds Hill. Alfold GU6 & GU8 193 D7
Stowell Ave. New Add CR0 ...... 63 D2
Stowford Coll. Sutton SM2 ...... 59 C3
Strachan Pl.
   Wimble SW19 & SW20 .... 19 C2
Strachey Ct. 1 Crawl RH11 ...... 201 B1
Strafford Rd. Hounsl TW3 .... 4 F4
Strafford Rd. Twick TW1 .... 17 A8
Straight Rd. Old W SL4 & TW19 .. 11 C8
Strand Cl. Lang V KT18 .... 96 D8
Strand Cl. Worth RH10 .... 202 D4
Strand on the Green Inf Sch.
   Brent W4 .... 7 A8
Strand on the Green Jun Sch.
   Brent W4 .... 7 A8
Strand-on-the-Green. Brent W4 7 A8
Stranraer Cl. Stan TW6 .... 2 E1
Stranraer Way. 1 Stan TW6 ...... 2 E1
Stratfield. Easth RG12 .... 26 E1
Stratfield House. Alder GU11 ... 105 A2
Stratford Cl. Farnb GU14 .... 85 C4
Stratford Ct. M Bourn GU9 ...... 125 C1
Stratford Ct. New Mal KT3 ...... 38 D5
Stratford Rd. Harl TW6 .... 3 C2
Stratford Rd. Thorn H CR7 ...... 42 B6
Strathavon Cl. Rowly GU6 ...... 174 B7
Strathcona Ave. Wallin SM6 ...... 60 D2
Strathdale. Street SW16 .... 21 F3
Strathdon Dr. Wands SW17 ...... 20 D5
Strathearn Ave. Harl UB3 .... 3 F7
Strathearn Ave. Twick TW2 ...... 16 C7
Strathearn Rd. Sutton SM1 ...... 59 A5
Strathearn Rd. Wimble SW19 .. 20 A4
Strathmore Cl. Cater CR3 ...... 100 E6
Strathmore Rd. Crawl RH11 .... 181 A1
Strathmore Rd.
   Tedd TW11 & TW2 .... 16 E4
Strathmore Rd. Thorn H CR0 .. 42 D2
Strathmore Rd. Wimble SW19 .. 20 A5
Strathmore Sch. Rich TW10 .... 17 D6
Strathville Rd. Wands SW18 .... 20 B6
Strathyre Ave.
   Thorn H CR7 & SW16 .... 42 A6
Stratton Ave. Wallin SM6 ...... 60 D2
Stratton Cl. Heston TW5 .... 5 A6
Stratton Cl. Merton SW19 ...... 40 A7
Stratton Cl. Walt O T KT12 ...... 35 C1
Stratton Ct. 10 King U T KT6 .... 37 E4
Stratton Rd. Merton SW19 ...... 40 A7
Stratton Rd. Sunby TW16 ...... 34 F7
Stratton Wlk. W Heath GU14 .... 85 A5
Strawberry Cl. Pirb GU24 .... 87 D7
Strawberry Fields. Bisley GU24 . 68 A4
Strawberry Hill Cl. Twick TW1 .. 16 F5
Strawberry Hill Golf Course.
   Twick TW2 .... 16 E5
Strawberry Hill Rd. Twick TW1 . 16 F5
Strawberry Hill Sta. Twick TW2 16 F5
Strawberry La. Carsh SM5 ...... 60 A7
Strawberry Rise. Bisley GU24 ... 68 A4
Strawberry Vale. Twick TW1 .... 17 A5
Stream Cl. Byfl KT14 .... 71 E7
Stream Farm Cl.
   M Bourn GU10 & GU9 . 146 D7
Stream Pk. E Grins RH19 ...... 185 A3
Stream Valley Rd.
   M Bourn GU10 .... 146 C6
Streatham Cl. Street SW16 ...... 21 E6
Streatham Comm N.
   Street SW16 .... 21 F3
Streatham Comm S.
   Street SW16 .... 21 F2
Streatham Common Sta.
   Street SW16 .... 21 D1
Streatham Ct. Street SW16 ...... 21 E5
Streatham High Rd.
   Street SW16 & SW2 .... 21 E3
Streatham Hill. Street SW2 ...... 21 E8
Streatham Hill & Clapham High
   Sch. Street SW2 .... 21 F7
Streatham Hill Sta. Street SW2 . 21 E6
Streatham Pl. Street SW2 ...... 21 E8
Streatham Rd. Mitch CR4 & SW16 21 B1
Streatham Rd. Mitch CR4 .... 41 A8
Streatham Sta. Street SW16 .... 21 D3
Streatham & Tooting Adult Inst.
   Street SW16 .... 21 F6
Streatham Vale. Street SW16 .. 21 D1
Streatleigh Par. 4 Street SW16 21 E6
Street The. Ashtd KT21 .... 75 F1
Street The. Betch RH3 .... 116 E1
Street The. Capel RH5 .... 178 D6
Street The. Charl RH6 .... 180 E7
Street The. Compt GU3 .... 129 B2

Street The. Docken GU10 ...... 166 E6
Street The. E Clan GU4 .... 111 E4
Street The. Effing KT24 .... 113 D8
Street The. Ewh GU6 .... 175 E5
Street The. Fetch KT22 .... 94 D5
Street The. Frensh GU10 ...... 167 C7
Street The. Plaist RH14 .... 211 E2
Street The. Putt GU3 .... 128 C4
Street The. Shackl GU8 .... 149 C8
Street The. Shalf GU4 .... 130 E3
Street The. Slinfd RH13 .... 215 D4
Street The. Thursl GU8 .... 169 C4
Street The. Tongh GU10 .... 126 F6
Street The. W Clan GU4 .... 111 B5
Street The. W Hors KT24 ...... 112 B7
Street The. Woner GU5 .... 152 A7
Street The. Wreccl GU10 ...... 145 F6
Streete Court Sch. Tyl Gn RH9 121 C5
Streeters Cl. Godal GU7 .... 151 A6
Streeters La. Wallin SM6 ...... 60 D7
Streetfield. Thursl GU8 .... 169 C4
Streetfield Rd. Slinfd RH13 .... 215 E3
Streets Heath. W End GU24 .... 67 F7
Stretton Rd. Croy CR0 .... 42 E2
Stretton Rd. Rich TW10 .... 17 C6
Strickland Cl. Crawl RH11 ...... 200 A5
Strickland Row. Wands SW18 .. 20 D8
Stringer's Ave. Jacobs GU4 .... 109 D7
Stringhams Copse.
   Send M GU23 .... 91 A3
Strode House. 3 Street SW2 .... 22 A7
Strode St. Egham TW20 .... 12 A4
Strode's Coll. Egham TW20 ...... 11 F3
Strode's Cres. Stain TW18 ...... 13 C3
Strodes College La.
   Egham TW20 .... 11 F3
Strood House. 12 Penge SE20 .. 23 C1
Strood La. Warn RH12 .... 216 C7
Strood La. Wink SL5 .... 9 C2
Stroud Cres. Rhampt SW15 .... 19 A5
Stroud Green Gdns. Croy CR0 .. 43 C2
Stroud Green Way. Croy CR0 ... 43 C3
Stroud La. Sham Gn GU5 ...... 153 A3
Stroud Rd. Croy SE25 .... 43 A3
Stroud Rd. Wimble SW19 ...... 20 A5
Stroud Way. Ashf TW15 .... 14 B2
Stroude Rd. Egham TW20 ...... 12 A1
Stroude Rd. Thorpe GU25 & TW20 31 E6
Stroudes Cl. New Mal KT4 ...... 38 F2
Stroudley Cl. Worth RH10 ...... 202 B5
Stroudwater Pk. Whit V KT13 .. 53 C4
Strudgate Cl. Crawl RH10 ...... 202 B4
Strudwicks Field. Cran GU6 ... 174 F4
Stuart Ave. Walt O T KT12 ...... 35 C1
Stuart Cl. W Heath GU14 ...... 85 A5
Stuart Cl. Worth RH10 .... 202 D5
Stuart Cres. Croy CR0 .... 62 F7
Stuart Cres. Woodh RH2 .... 139 A6
Stuart Ct. Godal GU7 .... 150 E4
Stuart Ct. 16 Redh RH1 .... 119 A2
Stuart Gr. Tedd TW11 .... 16 E3
Stuart House. 7 Brack RG12 ... 26 F8
Stuart Lodge. 7 Epsom KT18 .. 76 D6
Stuart Lodge. S Norw SE25 .... 42 E7
Stuart Pl. Mitch CR4 .... 40 F8
Stuart Rd. Rich TW10 .... 17 B5
Stuart Rd. S Norw SE27 .... 42 E7
Stuart Rd. Warlgm CR3 & CR6 .. 101 C7
Stuart Rd. Wimble SW19 ...... 20 A5
Stuart Rd. Woodh RH2 .... 139 A6
Stuart Way. E Grins RH19 ...... 205 F7
Stuart Way. Stain TW18 ...... 13 B2
Stuart Way. Vir W GU25 ...... 31 A5
Stubbington House Sch.
   Sunnin SL5 .... 29 B1
Stubbs Folly. Sandh GU15 ...... 64 D7
Stubbs La. L Kings KT20 ...... 118 A4
Stubbs Moor Rd. W Heath GU14 84 F5
Stubbs Way. Mitch SW19 ...... 40 D8
Stubfield. Horsh RH12 .... 217 A3
Stubpond La. Felb RH19 & RH7 184 D7
Stubs Cl. Dork RH4 .... 136 C5
Stubs Hill. Dork RH4 & RH5 .... 136 C4
Stubs Ind Site. Farnb GU12 .... 105 E5
Stucley Rd. Hounsl TW5 & TW7 .. 5 C7
Studios Rd. Littlt TW17 .... 33 F6
Studland Rd. Byfl KT14 .... 71 F6
Studland Rd. King U T KT2 ...... 17 E2
Studland Rd. Penge SE26 ...... 23 D3
Study Prep Sch The.
   Wimble SW19 .... 19 C3
Stumblets. Crawl RH10 .... 202 C7
Stumps Hill La. Beck BR3 ...... 24 A2
Sturdee Cl. Friml GU16 .... 65 E1
Sturges Rd. Woki RG11 .... 25 D5
Sturt Ave. King Gn GU27 ...... 207 F5
Sturt Ct. Merrow GU4 .... 110 C3
Sturt Rd. Friml GU16 .... 85 F5
Sturt Rd. Haslem GU27 .... 207 F5
Sturt Rd. Heath E GU9 .... 125 B7
Sturt Rd. Shottm GU27 .... 207 F5
Sturt's La. Walt o t h KT20 .... 117 A8
Stychens Cl. Bletch RH1 ...... 120 C2
Stychens La. Bletch RH1 ...... 120 C2
Styles End. G Book KT23 ...... 114 B8
Styles Way. Beck BR3 .... 44 C5
Styventon Pl. Chert KT16 ...... 32 F2
Succomb's Hill.
   Whytf CR3 & CR6 .... 101 B7
Succombs Pl. Warlgm CR6 ...... 101 B7
Sudbrook Gdns. Rich TW10 ...... 17 E5
Sudbrook La. Rich TW10 .... 17 E6
Sudbrook Pk (Richmond Golf Club).
   Rich TW10 .... 17 E6
Sudbury Gdns. S Croy CR0 ...... 61 E6
Suffield Cl. Selsd CR2 .... 81 D7
Suffield La.
   Putt GU3 & GU10 & GU8 .. 128 B2
Suffield Rd. Penge SE20 ...... 43 C7
Suffolk Cl. Bagsh GU19 .... 47 E2
Suffolk Cl. Horley RH6 .... 161 A2

Suffolk Ct. 3 Streat SW16 ...... 22 A4
Suffolk Dr. Burgh GU4 .... 110 B6
Suffolk House. 4 Croy CR0 ...... 61 D8
Suffolk House. Penge SE20 .... 43 C8
Suffolk Rd. Barnes SW13 .... 7 F7
Suffolk Rd. S Norw SE25 .... 42 F5
Suffolk Rd. Worc Pk KT19 ...... 57 E8
Sugden Rd. Hinch W KT7 ...... 37 B1
Sulina Rd. Streat SW2 .... 21 E8
Sullington Hill. Crawl RH11 .... 201 D4
Sullington Mead.
   Broad H RH12 .... 216 E3
Sullivan Cl. E Mole KT8 .... 36 B6
Sullivan Cl. Farnb GU14 .... 85 A4
Sullivan Ct. 4 Croy CR0 .... 43 A1
Sullivan Dr. Crawl RH11 .... 200 E3
Sullivan House. Kenley CR8 .... 80 C5
Sullivan House. Twick TW2 ...... 5 D1
Sullivan Rd. Camb GU15 .... 65 A5
Sullivans Reach. Walt O T KT12 . 35 A2
Sultan St. Penge BR3 .... 43 D7
Summer Ave. Thame D KT8 ...... 36 B6
Summer Gdns. Friml GU15 ...... 66 C5
Summer Rd. E Mole KT8 .... 36 B6
Summer Rd. Thame D KT7 & KT8 36 F4
Summer Trees. Sunby TW16 .... 35 B8
Summer's Rd. Farnc GU3 & GU7 151 A8
Summerene Cl. Streat SW16 .... 21 C1
Summerfield. Ashtd KT21 ...... 95 D8
Summerfield La. Long D KT6 .... 56 D8
Summerfield La. Rowl GU10 .. 146 B2
Summerfield St. Lewish SE12 .. 24 F8
Summerfields Cl. Row Tn RH15 . 51 F5
Summerhayes Cl. Horse GU21 .. 69 E5
Summerhill. Farnc GU7 .... 150 D5
Summerhill Way. Mitch CR4 .... 41 A8
Summerhouse Ave. Heston TW5 .. 4 E6
Summerhouse Rd. Godal GU7 . 150 D4
Summerhouse Ct.
   Graysh GU26 .... 188 D3
Summerlands La. Harm UB7 .... 2 D8
Summerlay Cl. Kings KT20 ...... 97 E7
Summerleigh. 8 Whit V KT13 .. 53 D4
Summerley St. Wands SW18 .... 20 B6
Summerly Ave. Reig RH2 ...... 118 A2
Summers Cl. Belm SM2 .... 59 A3
Summers Cl. Whit V KT13 ...... 72 A8
Summers La. Compt GU7 ...... 150 A8
Summersbury Dr. Shalf GU4 .. 130 E1
Summersbury Hall. Shalf GU4 130 E1
Summersby Cl. Farnc GU7 .... 150 F7
Summersell House.
   W Norw SE27 .... 22 D3
Summerstown. Wands SW17 .. 20 C4
Summersvere Cl. Crawl RH10 .. 182 A1
Summerswood Cl. Kenley CR8 .. 80 D3
Summerville Gdns. Cheam SM1 58 F4
Summerwood Rd.
   Islew TW1 & TW7 .... 5 F1
Summit Ave. Farnb GU14 ...... 84 C3
Summit Ctr. Harm UB7 .... 2 D7
Summit Pl. Whit V KT13 .... 53 A3
Summit The. Sunby TW16 ...... 15 A1
Summit Way. S Norw SE19 .... 22 C1
Sumner Cl. Fetch KT22 .... 94 D3
Sumner Gdns. Thorn H CR0 .... 42 A1
Sumner Pl. Addl KT15 .... 52 A5
Sumner Rd. Farnh GU9 .... 125 C3
Sumner Rd. Thorn H CR0 ...... 42 B1
Sumner Rd S. Thorn H CR0 ...... 42 A1
Sun Alley. 5 Rich TW9 .... 6 E3
Sun Brow. Haslem GU27 ...... 208 A5
Sun Hill. Woking GU22 .... 89 A6
Sun Inn Rd. Dunsf GU8 .... 192 F5
Sun Life Trad Est. Hatton TW14 . 4 A4
Sun Ray Est. Sandh GU47 ...... 64 A8
Sunbury Ave. Mortl SW14 ...... 7 D3
Sunbury Court Island.
   Sunby TW16 .... 35 D6
Sunbury Court Rd. Sunby TW16 35 C7
Sunbury Cres. Felt TW13 ...... 14 F4
Sunbury Cross Centre. 9
   Charlt TW16 .... 14 F1
Sunbury Ct. Sunby TW16 ...... 35 D7
Sunbury Ct (Con Ctr).
   Sunby TW16 .... 35 D7
Sunbury Int Bsns Ctr.
   Charlt TW16 .... 34 E8
Sunbury La. Walt O T KT12 .... 35 A3
Sunbury Manor Sch.
   Sunby TW16 .... 34 F8
Sunbury Rd. Cheam SM3 .... 58 E7
Sunbury Rd. Felt TW13 .... 14 F4
Sunbury Sta. Sunby TW16 ...... 35 A8
Sunbury Way. Felt TW13 ...... 15 C3
Suncroft Pl. For Hil SE26 ...... 23 C5
Sundale Ave. Selsd CR2 .... 62 C1
Sunderland Ct. Dulw SE22 ...... 23 A8
Sunderland Ct. 11 Stan TW19 .. 2 E1
Sunderland Mount. For Hil SE23 23 D6
Sunderland Rd. For Hil SE23 .. 23 D6
Sundew Cl. Crawl RH11 .... 201 A2
Sundew Cl. Lhtwat GU18 .... 67 D8
Sundew Cl. Woki RG11 .... 25 E7
Sundial Ave. S Norw SE25 ...... 42 F6
Sundial Cl. Tolw KT5 .... 57 B8
Sundon Cres. Went GU25 ...... 31 C4
Sundown Ave. S Croy CR2 ...... 80 F8
Sundown Rd. Ashf TW15 ...... 14 C3
Sundridge Cl. Crawl RH11 ...... 201 A2
Sundridge Rd. Old Wok GU22 .. 90 A7
Sunkist Way. Wallin SM6 ...... 60 E2
Sunmead Cl. Fetch KT22 .... 94 F5
Sunmead Rd. Sunby TW16 .... 35 A6
Sunna Gdns. Sunby TW16 ...... 35 B7
Sunniholme Ct. Croy CR2 ...... 61 C5

Sunning Ave. Sunnin SL5 ...... 29 E2
Sunning House. Ascot SL5 ...... 29 D5
Sunning House. Windl GU20 .. 48 F8
Sunningdale Ave. Felt TW13 .. 15 E6
Sunningdale Cl. 2 Surb KT6 ... 56 E8
Sunningdale Ct. Crawl RH11 .. 201 D4
Sunningdale Ct. 13
   King U T KT2 .... 18 A1
Sunningdale House. Mitch CR4 . 40 D7
Sunningdale Park (Civil Service
   Coll). Sunnin SL5 .... 29 F3
Sunningdale Rd. Cheam SM1 .. 58 F6
Sunningdale Sch. Sunnin SL5 .. 29 F3
Sunningdale Sta. Sunnin SL5 .. 30 A2
Sunninghill Cl. Ascot SL5 ...... 29 D5
Sunninghill Ct. Ascot SL5 ...... 29 C5
Sunninghill Lodge. Ascot SL5 .. 29 C7
Sunninghill Rd. Ascot SL5 ...... 29 D5
Sunninghill Rd. Windl GU20 .. 48 A7
Sunninghill Rd. Wink SL4 & SL5 .. 9 E2
Sunningvale Ave. Bigg H TN16 83 D3
Sunningvale Cl. Bigg H TN16 .. 83 D3
Sunny Ave. Crawl D RH10 ...... 204 A8
Sunny Bank. Croy SE25 .... 43 A6
Sunny Bank. Warlgm CR6 ...... 81 E2
Sunny Bank. Woodc KT18 ...... 76 C3
Sunny Down. Witley GU8 ...... 170 E5
Sunny Hill. Witley GU8 .... 170 E6
Sunny Hill Rd. Alder GU11 ...... 104 D2
Sunny Nook Gdns. Croy CR2 .. 61 D4
Sunny Rise. Cater CR3 .... 100 D3
Sunny View Cl. Alder GU12 .... 105 C1
Sunnybank Mews. Ash GU12 .. 106 B3
Sunnybank Rd. W Heath GU14 84 D6
Sunnybank Rd. W Heath GU14 84 E6
Sunnybank Villas. Bletch RH1 120 F3
Sunnycroft Rd. Croy SE25 ...... 43 A6
Sunnycroft Rd. Hounsl TW3 ...... 5 B5
Sunnydell La.
   Wreccl GU10 & GU9 .... 146 A6
Sunnydene Rd. Purley CR8 .... 80 B6
Sunnydene St. For Hil SE26 .... 23 E4
Sunnydown Boys' Sch.
   Whytf CR3 .... 100 F6
Sunnyhill Cl. Crawl D RH10 .... 204 A8
Sunnyhill Prim Sch.
   Streat SW16 .... 21 F4
Sunnyhill Rd. Streat SW16 ...... 21 E4
Sunnyhurst Cl. Sutton SM1 .... 59 B7
Sunnymead. Crawl RH11 ...... 201 D6
Sunnymead. Crawl D RH10 .... 204 B8
Sunnymead Ave.
   Mitch CR4 & SW16 .... 41 D6
Sunnymede Ave. Sutton SM5 .. 78 D8
Sunnymede Ave. W Ewell KT19 . 57 E3
Sunnymede Ave. W Ewell KT19 . 57 E3
Sunnyside. Knaph GU21 .... 88 B8
Sunnyside. Walt O T KT12 ...... 35 C4
Sunnyside. Wimble SW19 ...... 19 E2
Sunnyside Pl. Wimble SW19 .. 19 E2
Sunnyside Rd. Head Dn GU35 . 187 C4
Sunnyside Rd. Tedd TW11 ...... 16 D4
Sunray Ave. Tolw KT5 .... 57 B8
Sunrise Cl. Felt TW13 .... 15 F5
Sunset Cl. S Norw SE25 .... 42 F7
Sunset Rd. Wimble SW19 ...... 19 B3
Sunshine Way. Mitch CR4 ...... 40 F7
Sunstone Gr. Merst RH1 ...... 119 E6
Sunvale Ave. Shottm GU27 .... 207 D6
Sunvale Cl. Shottm GU27 ...... 207 D6
Surbiton Cres.
   King U T KT1 & KT6 .... 37 E5
Surbiton Ct. King U T KT6 ...... 37 D3
Surbiton Hall Cl. King U T KT1 . 37 E5
Surbiton High Sch. King U T KT1 37 E5
Surbiton High Sch Jun Sch for Girls.
   King U T KT1 .... 37 E5
Surbiton Hill Pk. Surb KT5 ...... 38 A4
Surbiton Hill Rd. King U T KT6 .. 37 E5
Surbiton Hospl. Surb KT6 ...... 37 E3
Surbiton Prep Sch. King U T KT6 37 E4
Surbiton Rd. Camb GU15 ...... 47 A1
Surbiton Rd. King U T KT1 ...... 37 E5
Surbiton Sta. Surb KT6 .... 37 E3
Surrey Ave. Camb GU15 .... 65 A4
Surrey Bsns Pk. Ewell KT17 .... 76 E8
Surrey Gr. Carsh SM1 .... 59 D7
Surrey Hills Ave. Box H KT20 . 116 C4
Surrey Hills Way. Box H KT20 116 C4
Surrey Inst of Art & Design The.
   Farnh GU9 .... 125 B2
Surrey Mews. W Norw SE27 .. 22 E4
Surrey Rd. W Wick BR4 .... 44 B1
Surrey Research Pk The.
   Onsl V GU2 .... 129 D3
Surrey St. Croy CR0 & CR9 ...... 61 C7
Surrey Tower. 5 Penge SE20 .. 23 C1
Surrey Towers. Addl KT15 ...... 52 C5
Surridge Ct. Bagsh GU19 ...... 47 E2
Surridge Gdns. S Norw SE19 .. 22 D2
Sussex Ave. Islew TW7 .... 5 E4
Sussex Cl. Knaph GU21 .... 68 C1
Sussex Cl. New Mal KT3 .... 38 E5
Sussex Cl. Reig RH2 .... 139 D8
Sussex Cl. 4 Twick TW1 .... 6 B1
Sussex Ct. Addl KT15 .... 52 C5
Sussex Ct. Barnes SW13 .... 7 F5
Sussex Gdns. Chess KT9 ...... 56 D5
Sussex Ho. Rich TW9 .... 6 F5
Sussex Lodge. Horsh RH12 .... 217 C4
Sussex Manor Bsns Pk.
   Crawl RH10 .... 182 A2
Sussex Rd. New Mal KT3 ...... 38 E5
Sussex Rd. Croy CR2 .... 61 D4
Sussex Rd. Mitch CR4 .... 41 E4
Sussex Rd. New Mal KT3 ...... 38 E5
Sussex Rd. S Croy CR2 .... 61 D4

Sussex Rd. W Wick BR4 .... 44 B1
Sussex Rd. Wallin SM6 .... 59 F4
Sutherland Ave. Bigg H TN16 .. 83 E1
Sutherland Ave. Jacobs GU4 .. 109 E7
Sutherland Ave. Sunby TW16 .. 34 F7
Sutherland Chase. N Asct SL5 .. 28 E7
Sutherland Dr.
   Burph GU1 & GU4 .... 110 A4
Sutherland Dr. Mitch SW19 .... 40 D8
Sutherland Gdns. Mortl SW14 .. 7 E4
Sutherland Gdns. N Cheam KT4 . 39 B1
Sutherland Gdns. Sunby TW16 .. 34 F7
Sutherland Gr.
   Putney SW18 & SW19 .... 19 F8
Sutherland Gr. Tedd TW11 ...... 16 E3
Sutherland House. Rich TW10 .. 17 C6
Sutherland Rd. Chisw W4 .... 7 E8
Sutherland Rd. Thorn H CR0 .. 42 A2
Sutton Arc. Sutton SM1 .... 59 B5
Sutton Ave. Knaph GU21 ...... 88 E8
Sutton Cl. Beck BR3 .... 44 B8
Sutton Common Rd.
   Cheam SM3 .... 40 A1
Sutton Common Rd.
   Sutton SM1 & SM3 .... 59 B8
Sutton Common Sta.
   Sutton SM1 .... 59 B8
Sutton Court Rd. Chisw W4 ...... 7 C8
Sutton Court Rd.
   Sutton SM1 & SM2 .... 59 C4
Sutton Courtenay House.
   Up Toot SW17 .... 20 D4
Sutton Ct. Chisw W4 .... 7 C8
Sutton Ct. E Mole KT8 .... 35 F4
Sutton Ct. Penge SE19 .... 22 F1
Sutton Ct. Sutton SM2 .... 59 C4
Sutton Dene. Hounsl TW3 ...... 5 B6
Sutton Gdns. Croy CR0 & SE25 .. 42 F4
Sutton Gdns. Merst RH1 ...... 119 D6
Sutton Gr. Carsh SM1 .... 59 D5
Sutton Gram Sch For Boys.
   Sutton SM1 .... 59 C5
Sutton Green Rd. Westfd GU4 .. 89 F1
Sutton Hall. Heston TW5 .... 5 A7
Sutton High Sch For Girls.
   Sutton SM1 .... 59 B4
Sutton Hospl. Sutton SM2 ...... 59 B1
Sutton La. Abin C RH5 ...... 155 C8
Sutton La. Banstd SM2 & SM7 .. 78 B6
Sutton La. Bra Hil SL3 .... 1 B8
Sutton La.
   Hounsl TW3 & TW4 & TW5 .. 4 F5
Sutton La S. Chisw W4 .... 7 C8
Sutton Lodge. Guild GU1 ...... 109 E1
Sutton Park Rd.
   Sutton SM1 & SM2 .... 59 B4
Sutton Pl. Bra Hil SL3 .... 1 B8
Sutton Pl. Peasl GU5 .... 154 F8
Sutton Rd. Camb GU15 .... 47 A1
Sutton Rd. Heston TW5 .... 5 A6
Sutton Sq. Heston TW5 .... 4 F6
Sutton Sta. Sutton SM2 .... 59 C4
Sutton Way. Heston TW5 .... 5 A6
Swaby Rd. Wands SW17 & SW18 20 C6
Swaffield Prim Sch.
   Wands SW18 .... 20 C8
Swaffield Rd. Wands SW18 .... 20 C8
Swail House. 8 Epsom KT18 .. 76 D6
Swain Cl. Streat SW16 & SW17 . 21 B2
Swain Rd. Thorn H CR7 .... 42 C4
Swains Rd.
   Mitch CR4 & SW17 & SW19 .. 20 F1
Swale House. 2 Redh RH1 .... 119 A3
Swale Rd. W Heath GU14 ...... 84 E6
Swaledale. Easth RG12 .... 27 A4
Swaledale Cl. Crawl RH11 ...... 201 C3
Swallands Rd. Catf SE6 ...... 24 A5
Swallow Cl. Stain TW18 .... 12 F4
Swallow Cl. Witley GU8 ...... 170 E7
Swallow La. Dork RH5 .... 136 B1
Swallow Pk. Surb KT6 .... 56 F7
Swallow Rd. Crawl RH11 ...... 201 C8
Swallow Rise. Knaph GU21 .... 68 C2
Swallowdale. New Add CR2 .... 62 D2
Swallowdale. Selsd CR2 .... 62 D2
Swallowfield. Dorman RH7 .... 165 A2
Swallowfield. Eng Gn TW20 .... 11 B2
Swallows Ct. Penge SE20 ...... 23 D1
Swallowtail Rd. Horsh RH12 .. 217 E6
Swan Barn Cl. Haslem GU27 .. 208 D6
Swan Cl. Croy CR0 .... 42 E2
Swan Cl. Felt TW13 .... 15 E4
Swan Cl. Bellf GU1 .... 109 D3
Swan Ct. Leahd KT22 .... 95 B5
Swan Ctr. Wands SW17 .... 20 C5
Swan House. Sandh GU17 ...... 64 B7
Swan La. Charl RH6 .... 180 F7
Swan La. Guild GU1 .... 130 D7
Swan La. Sandh GU47 .... 64 B7
Swan Mill Gdns. Pixham RH4 .. 115 D1
Swan Pl. Barnes SW13 .... 7 F5
Swan Rd. Felt TW13 .... 15 E4
Swan Sq. Horsh RH12 .... 217 C2
Swan St. Islew TW7 .... 6 B4
Swan Wlk. Horsh RH12 .... 217 C2
Swan Wlk. Oat Pk TW17 .... 34 E2
Swancote Gn. Easth RG12 ...... 27 B4
Swandrift. Stain TW18 .... 12 F1
Swann Ct. 6 Islew TW7 .... 6 A4
Swann Way. Broad H RH12 .... 216 D3
Swanns Meadow. G Book KT23 .. 94 A1
Swans Ghyll. For Row RH18 .... 206 E3
Swansea Rd. Harl TW14 & TW6 .. 3 D1
Swansmere Sch. Walt O T KT12 . 35 C1
Swanton Gdns. Putney SW19 .. 19 D7
Swanwick Cl. Rhampt SW15 .. 18 F8
Swanworth La. Mickle RH5 .... 115 B7
Swayne's La. Merrow GU1 .... 110 E1
Swaynesland Rd. Limps RH8 .. 123 F1
Swaythling House. Rhampt SW15 19 F1
Swedish Sch. Barnes SW13 ...... 7 F8

Sweeps Ditch Cl. Stain TW18 ... 13 B1
Sweeps La. Egham TW20 ... 11 F3
Sweet La. Peasl GU5 ... 154 E6
Sweetbriar. Crowth RG11 ... 45 A7
Sweetwater Cl. Sham Gn GU5 ... 152 D4
Sweetwater La. Ent Gn GU8 ... 171 B2
Sweetwater La. Sham Gn GU5 ... 152 D4
Swievelands Rd. Bigg H TN16 ... 83 C1
Swift Ct. Sutton SM2 ... 59 B3
Swift La. Crawl RH11 ... 201 C8
Swift La. Windl GU19 ... 47 F3
Swift Rd. Felt TW13 ... 15 E4
Swift Rd. Heath E GU9 ... 125 C7
Swift's Cl. Farnh GU10 ... 126 B1
Swiftsden Way. Catf BR1 ... 24 E2
Swinburne Cres. Croy CR0 ... 43 C3
Swindon Rd. Harl TW6 ... 3 C2
Swindon Rd. Horsh RH12 ... 217 B4
Swinfield Cl. Felt TW13 ... 15 E4
Swingate Rd. M Bourn GU9 ... 146 D8
Swinley County Prim Sch. Ascot SL5 ... 29 A4
Swinley Forest Golf Club. Brack SL5 ... 28 F2
Swinley Rd. Brack SL5 ... 28 C4
Swiss Cl. Rowl GU10 ... 146 A4
Swissland Hill. Dorm Pk RH19 & RH7 ... 185 E7
Switchback La. Rowl GU10 ... 145 F4
Switchback La. Rowl GU10 ... 146 A3
Swordfish Way. Farnb GU14 ... 104 F7
Sycamore Ave. Horsh RH12 ... 218 C6
Sycamore Cl. Carsh SM5 ... 59 F6
Sycamore Cl. Crawl RH11 ... 181 C1
Sycamore Cl. Felt TW13 ... 15 A5
Sycamore Cl. Fetch KT22 ... 94 F5
Sycamore Cl. Friml GU16 ... 65 E1
Sycamore Cl. Sandh GU17 ... 64 B8
Sycamore Ct. Farnc GU7 ... 150 E8
Sycamore Ct. For Hil SE26 ... 23 C4
Sycamore Ct. Hounsl TW4 ... 4 E3
Sycamore Ct. Ottsh KT16 ... 51 C5
Sycamore Ct. 10 W Norw SW16 ... 22 A3
Sycamore Ct. Walt O T KT13 ... 53 F7
Sycamore Dr. Ash V GU12 ... 106 A7
Sycamore Dr. E Grins RH19 ... 186 A1
Sycamore Dr. Friml GU16 ... 65 E1
Sycamore Dr. Wreccl GU10 ... 146 A6
Sycamore Gdns. Mitch CR4 ... 40 D7
Sycamore Gr. King U T KT3 ... 38 E6
Sycamore Gr. Penge SE20 ... 43 A8
Sycamore Lodge. 7 Charlt TW16 ... 14 F1
Sycamore Rd. Farnb GU14 ... 85 D2
Sycamore Rd. Guild GU1 ... 109 D1
Sycamore Rd. Wimble SW19 & SW20 ... 19 C2
Sycamore Rise. Brack RG12 ... 27 D6
Sycamore Rise. Nork KT17 & SM7 ... 77 D5
Sycamore Way. Tedd TW11 ... 17 C2
Sycamore Wlk. Eng Gn TW20 ... 11 B2
Sycamore Wlk. Woodh RH2 ... 139 C6
Sycamores The. Blckw GU17 ... 64 B5
Sycamores The. Farnb GU14 ... 85 D3
Sydenham Ave. Penge SE26 ... 23 B3
Sydenham High Sch For Girls. For Hil SE26 ... 23 B4
Sydenham Hill. For Hil SE26 ... 23 B5
Sydenham Hill Sta. Dulw SE21 ... 22 F5
Sydenham House. 16 Surb KT6 ... 37 D2
Sydenham Ind Est. Penge SE26 ... 23 F3
Sydenham Park Mansions. For Hil SE26 ... 23 C5
Sydenham Park Rd. For Hil SE23 & SE26 ... 23 C5
Sydenham Pk. For Hil SE26 ... 23 C5
Sydenham Rd. Croy CR0 ... 42 D2
Sydenham Rd. For Hil SE26 & SE6 ... 23 D3
Sydenham Rd. Guild GU1 ... 130 E8
Sydenham Rd. Thorn H CR0 ... 42 D2
Sydenham Rise. For Hil SE23 ... 23 B6
Sydenham Sch. For Hil SE26 ... 23 B5
Sydenham Sec Sch. For Hil SE26 ... 23 B5
Sydenham Sta. For Hil SE26 ... 23 C4
Sydenham Station App. For Hil SE26 ... 23 C4
Sydmons Ct. For Hil SE23 ... 23 C8
Sydney Ave. Purley CR8 ... 79 F7
Sydney Cl. Crowth RG11 ... 45 C7
Sydney Cotts. Clayg KT10 ... 55 F4
Sydney Cres. Ashf TW15 ... 14 B2
Sydney Pl. Guild GU1 ... 130 F8
Sydney Rd. E Bed TW14 ... 15 A7
Sydney Rd. Guild GU1 ... 130 F8
Sydney Rd. Merton SW20 ... 39 D7
Sydney Rd. Rich TW10 & TW9 ... 6 E3
Sydney Rd. Sutton SM1 ... 59 A6
Sydney Rd. Tedd TW11 ... 16 F3
Sydney Smith Ave. Farnb GU14 ... 85 B1
Sydney Terr. Clayg KT10 ... 55 F4
Sylva Ct. 3 Putney SW15 ... 19 D8
Sylvan Cl. Limps RH8 ... 123 B6
Sylvan Cl. Mayb GU22 ... 70 B2
Sylvan Cl. S Croy CR2 ... 62 B1
Sylvan Gdns. Surb KT6 ... 37 D2
Sylvan Hill. S Norw SE19 ... 42 E8
Sylvan Rd. Crawl RH10 ... 202 A4
Sylvan Rd. S Norw SE19 ... 42 F8
Sylvan Ridge. Sandh GU17 ... 45 A1
Sylvan Way. Coney H BR4 ... 63 E6
Sylvan Way. Earls RH1 ... 140 A8
Sylvanus. Easth RG12 ... 26 F2
Sylvaways Cl. Cran GU6 ... 175 A3
Sylverdale Rd. Croy CR0 & CR9 ... 61 B7
Sylverdale Rd. Purley CR8 ... 80 B6
Sylvia Cl. Bisley GU24 ... 68 A4
Syon Gate Way. Brent TW8 ... 6 B7
Syon Gate Way. Hounsl TW7 & TW8 ... 6 A7
Syon Ho. Brent TW8 ... 6 C6
Syon La. Brent TW7 ... 6 A7
Syon La. Brent TW7 & TW8 ... 6 B7
Syon La. Hounsl TW7 ... 6 A7
Syon Lane Sta. Brent TW7 ... 6 A7
Syon Lane Sta. Hounsl TW7 ... 6 A7
Syon Park Cotts. Brent TW8 ... 6 C6
Syon Park Gdns. Hounsl TW7 ... 5 F7
Syon Pl. Farnb GU14 ... 85 D4
Sythwood. Woking GU21 ... 69 B2
Sythwood Cty Fst & Mid Sch. Woking GU21 ... 69 B3
Szabo Cres. Flexf GU3 ... 107 B1

Tabard House. Tedd KT1 ... 37 C8
Tabarin Way. Nork KT17 ... 77 C3
Tabor Ct. Cheam SM3 ... 58 E4
Tabor Gdns. Cheam SM2 & SM3 ... 58 F3
Tabor Gr. Wimble SW19 ... 19 F1
Tachbrook Rd. E Bed TW14 ... 14 F8
Tadlow. King U T KT1 ... 38 A6
Tadmor Cl. Lo Hall TW16 ... 34 F5
Tadorne Rd. Tadw KT20 ... 97 C5
Tadworth Ave. New Mal KT3 ... 38 F4
Tadworth Cl. Tadw KT20 ... 97 D5
Tadworth Court Hospl. Tadw KT20 ... 97 D6
Tadworth Cty Fst & Mid Sch. Tadw KT20 ... 97 D5
Tadworth St. Tadw KT20 ... 97 C5
Tadworth Sta. Tadw KT20 ... 97 C5
Taffy's How. Mitch CR4 ... 40 E6
Tait Rd. Croy CR0 & SE25 ... 42 E2
Talavera Cty Inf Sch. Alder GU11 ... 105 B3
Talavera Cty Jun Sch. Alder GU11 ... 105 B3
Talbot Cl. Mytch GU16 ... 86 A4
Talbot Cl. Reig RH2 ... 139 B8
Talbot La. Horsh RH12 ... 217 C1
Talbot Lodge. Esher KT10 ... 55 A5
Talbot Pl. Bagsh GU19 ... 47 E4
Talbot Rd. Ashf TW15 ... 13 E3
Talbot Rd. Islew TW1 & TW7 ... 6 A3
Talbot Rd. Lingf RH7 ... 164 D4
Talbot Rd. M Bourn GU9 ... 146 B8
Talbot Rd. S Norw CR7 ... 42 D5
Talbot Rd. Twick TW2 ... 16 F7
Talbot Rd. Wallin SM5 ... 60 A5
Talcott Path. 12 Streat SW2 ... 22 A7
Taleworth Cl. Ashtd KT21 ... 95 D7
Taleworth Pk. Ashtd KT21 ... 95 D7
Taleworth Rd. Ashtd KT21 ... 95 E7
Talgarth Dr. Farnb GU14 ... 85 D2
Taliesin Hts. Farnc GU7 ... 150 D6
Talisman Sq. For Hil SE26 ... 23 A4
Talisman Way. Nork KT17 ... 77 C3
Tall Elms Cl. Hayes BR2 ... 44 F4
Tall Trees. Poyle SL3 ... 1 E6
Tall Trees. Thorn H SW16 ... 41 F6
Tallis Cl. Crawl RH11 ... 200 F3
Tally Rd. The Char RH8 ... 123 E4
Talma Gdns. Twick TW2 ... 16 E8
Talmage Cl. For Hil SE23 ... 23 C8
Talman Cl. Crawl RH11 ... 200 E5
Tamar Cl. Worth RH10 ... 202 C5
Tamarind Cl. Stough GU2 ... 109 A6
Tamarind Ct. 3 Egham TW20 ... 11 F3
Tamarisk Rise. Woki RG11 ... 25 C7
Tamerton Sq. Woking GU22 ... 89 E8
Tamesa House. Lo Hall TW17 ... 34 A2
Tamesis Gdns. New Mal KT4 ... 57 E8
Tamian Ind Est. Hounsl TW4 ... 4 C3
Tamian Way. Hounsl TW4 ... 4 C3
Tamworth. Brack RG12 ... 27 D2
Tamworth La. Mitch CR4 ... 41 B6
Tamworth Manor High Sch. Mitch CR4 ... 41 D6
Tamworth Pk. Mitch CR4 ... 41 B6
Tamworth Pl. 3 Croy CR0 & CR9 ... 61 C8
Tamworth Rd. Croy CR0 & CR9 ... 61 C8
Tanbridge House Sch. Horsh RH12 ... 216 F2
Tanbridge Pk. Horsh RH12 ... 217 B1
Tanbridge Pl. Horsh RH12 ... 217 B1
Tandridge Ct. Cater CR3 ... 101 A5
Tandridge Ct. Sutton SM2 ... 59 B4
Tandridge Gdns. Sander CR2 ... 81 A6
Tandridge Golf Course. Tand RH9 ... 122 B4
Tandridge La. Tand RH7 & RH8 & RH9 ... 143 B4
Tandridge Rd. Warlgm CR6 ... 101 D8
Tandridgehill La. Tand RH9 ... 121 F6
Tandridgehill La. Wold RH9 ... 121 F6
Tanfield Ct. Horsh RH12 ... 217 B2
Tanfield Rd. Croy CR0 & CR9 ... 61 C6
Tangier Ct. Alder GU11 ... 104 F2
Tangier Rd. Guild GU1 ... 131 A8
Tangier Rd. Mortl TW10 ... 7 B4
Tangier Way. Burgh H KT20 ... 77 E1
Tangier Wood. Burgh H KT20 ... 77 E1
Tangle Oak. Felb RH19 ... 184 E4
Tanglewood Cl. Longc KT16 ... 50 B7
Tanglewood Cl. Mayb GU22 ... 70 D3
Tanglewood Cl. S Croy CR0 ... 62 C7
Tanglewood Ride. W End GU24 ... 67 D7
Tanglewood Way. Felt TW13 ... 15 B5
Tangley Dr. Woki RG11 ... 25 B4
Tangley Gr. Rhampt SW15 ... 18 F8
Tangley La. Worpl GU3 ... 108 F6
Tangley Park Rd. Hampt TW12 ... 15 F3
Tanglyn Ave. Shep Gn TW17 ... 34 B4
Tangmere Gr. King U T KT2 ... 17 D3
Tangmere Rd. Crawl RH11 ... 200 F6
Tanhouse La. Woki RG11 ... 25 A5
Tanhouse Rd. Oxted RH8 ... 122 E3
Tanhurst House. 27 Streat SW2 ... 21 E8
Tanhurst La. Wotton RH5 ... 155 E2
Tank Rd. Sandh GU15 ... 64 F5
Tanker Rd. Farnb GU14 ... 85 B1
Tankerton Rd. Surb KT6 ... 56 F8
Tankerton Terr. Thorn H CR0 ... 41 F3
Tankerville Rd. Streat SW16 ... 21 E1
Tanner House. 1 Merton SW19 ... 40 C8
Tanner's Ct. Brock RH3 ... 137 C5
Tanner's Hill. Brock RH3 ... 137 B8
Tanners Cl. Walt O T KT12 ... 35 B3
Tanners Dean. Leahd KT22 ... 95 D5
Tanners La. Haslem GU27 ... 208 C7
Tanners Meadow. Brock RH3 ... 137 B5
Tanners Yd. Bagsh GU19 ... 47 E3
Tannersfield. Shalf GU4 ... 130 E1
Tannery Cl. Beck BR3 & CR0 ... 43 D4
Tannery Cl. Slinfd RH13 ... 215 D3
Tannery Cotts. Gomsh GU5 ... 133 C4
Tannery La. Send GU23 ... 90 E5
Tannery La. Send M GU23 ... 90 E5
Tannery The. Redh RH1 ... 118 F1
Tannsfeld Rd. For Hil SE26 ... 23 D3
Tansy Cl. Merrow GU4 ... 110 C3
Tantallon Rd. Balham SW12 ... 21 A7
Tanyard Ave. E Grins RH19 ... 206 A8
Tanyard Cl. Horsh RH13 ... 217 E1
Tanyard La. Bramly GU5 ... 151 F8
Tanyard Way. Horley RH6 ... 161 B4
Tapestry Cl. Sutton SM2 ... 59 B3
Taplow Ct. Mitch CR4 ... 40 E5
Tapner's Rd. Leigh RH2 ... 137 F3
Tapping Cl. 5 King U T KT2 ... 18 A1
Tara Ct. Beck BR3 ... 44 B7
Tara Pk. Chips CR5 ... 98 F7
Taragon Ct. Stough GU2 ... 109 A5
Tarbat Ct. 6 Sandh GU15 ... 64 D8
Target Cl. Felt TW14 ... 3 E1
Tarham Cl. Horley RH6 ... 160 E5
Tarleton Gdns. For Hil SE23 ... 23 B7
Tarmac Way. Harm UB7 ... 2 B7
Tarn Rd. Hind GU26 ... 188 E3
Tarnbrook Way. Brack RG12 ... 27 E2
Tarquin House. For Hil SE26 ... 23 A4
Tarragon Cl. W Heath GU14 ... 84 C4
Tarragon Dr. Stough GU2 ... 109 A5
Tarragon Gr. Penge SE26 ... 23 D2
Tarrington Cl. Streat SW16 ... 21 D5
Tartar Hill. Cobham KT11 ... 73 B6
Tartar Rd. Cobham KT11 ... 73 C6
Tasker Cl. Harl UB7 ... 3 C7
Tasman Ct. Ashf TW16 ... 14 E1
Tatchbury House. Rhampt SW15 ... 7 F1
Tate Cl. Leahd KT22 ... 95 C4
Tate Rd. Cheam SM1 ... 59 A5
Tate's Way. Rudg RH12 ... 214 D7
Tatham Ct. Crawl RH11 ... 201 B1
Tatsfield Cty Prim Sch. Tats TN16 ... 103 D6
Tatsfield La. Bigg H TN16 ... 103 F6
Tattenham Cnr. Epsom KT18 ... 77 A1
Tattenham Corner Rd. Lang V KT18 ... 77 A1
Tattenham Corner Sta. Burgh H KT18 ... 77 B1
Tattenham Cres. Burgh H KT18 ... 77 B1
Tattenham Gr. Burgh H KT18 & KT20 ... 97 B8
Tattenham Way. Burgh H KT18 & KT20 ... 77 E2
Tattersall Cl. Woki RG11 ... 25 E5
Taunton Ave. Cater CR3 ... 100 F4
Taunton Ave. Hounsl TW3 ... 5 C5
Taunton Ave. Wimble SW20 ... 39 B7
Taunton Cl. Cheam SM3 ... 40 A1
Taunton La. Coulsd CR5 ... 100 B8
Taunton Manor High Sch. Coulsd CR5 ... 100 B7
Tavistock Cl. Stain TW18 ... 13 D1
Tavistock Cres. Mitch CR4 ... 41 E5
Tavistock Ct. 1 Croy CR0 ... 42 D1
Tavistock Gdns. Farnb GU14 ... 85 B7
Tavistock Gr. Croy CR0 ... 42 D2
Tavistock Rd. Beck BR2 ... 44 F5
Tavistock Rd. Carsh SM5 ... 40 D1
Tavistock Rd. Croy CR0 ... 42 D1
Tavistock Wlk. Carsh SM5 ... 40 D1
Tavy House. 3 Redh RH1 ... 118 F2
Tawfield. Easth RG12 ... 26 E2
Tawny Cl. Felt TW13 ... 15 A5
Tay Cl. W Heath GU14 ... 84 E6
Tayben Ave. Twick TW2 ... 5 E1
Tayles Hill. Ewell KT17 ... 57 F1
Taylor Ave. Rich TW9 ... 7 B5
Taylor Cl. Hampt TW12 ... 16 C3
Taylor Cl. Hounsl TW3 ... 5 C6
Taylor Ct. Penge SE20 ... 43 C7
Taylor House. 10 Streat SW2 ... 22 A7
Taylor Rd. Ashtd KT21 ... 75 D2
Taylor Rd. Mitch CR4 & SW19 ... 20 E1
Taylor Rd. Wallin SM6 ... 60 B5
Taylor Wlk. Crawl RH11 ... 201 C6
Taylor's La. For Hil SE26 ... 23 B4
Taylors Cres. Cran GU6 ... 174 F3
Taylors Ct. Felt TW13 ... 15 A6
Taymount Grange. For Hil SE23 ... 23 C6
Taymount Rise. For Hil SE23 ... 23 C6
Taynton Dr. Merst RH1 ... 119 D6
Teal Cl. Horsh RH12 ... 217 C5
Teal Cl. Selsd CR2 ... 81 D8
Teal Ct. Dork RH4 ... 136 A8
Teal Ct. Wallin SM6 ... 60 C5
Tealing Dr. W Ewell KT19 ... 57 D6
Tealing Dr. W Ewell KT19 ... 57 D6
Teasel Cl. Crawl RH11 ... 201 B3
Teasel Cl. Croy CR0 ... 43 D1
Teazlewood Pk. Leahd KT22 ... 75 A1
Tebbit Cl. Brack RG12 ... 27 D7
Tebbs House. 14 Streat SW2 ... 22 A8
Tedder Cl. Chess KT9 ... 56 C5
Tedder Rd. S Croy CR2 ... 62 D2
Teddington Cl. Epsom KT19 ... 57 D1
Teddington Memorial Hospl. Tedd TW11 ... 16 E2
Teddington Park Rd. Tedd TW11 ... 16 F4
Teddington Pk. Tedd TW11 ... 16 F3
Teddington Sch. Tedd TW11 ... 17 C2
Teddington Sta. Tedd TW11 ... 17 A2
Tedham La. Horne RH9 ... 163 B7
Tees Cl. W Heath GU14 ... 84 E6
Teesdale. Crawl RH11 ... 201 C3
Teesdale Ave. Islew TW7 ... 6 A6
Teesdale Gdns. Islew TW7 ... 6 A6
Teesdale Gdns. S Norw SE25 ... 42 E7
Teevan Cl. Croy CR0 ... 43 A2
Teevan Rd. Croy CR0 & CR9 ... 43 A2
Tegg's La. Pyrf GU22 ... 70 F3
Tekels Ave. Camb GU15 ... 65 D4
Tekels Ct. Camb GU15 ... 65 E4
Tekels Way. Friml GU15 ... 65 F3
Telconia Cl. Head Dn GU35 ... 187 C4
Telegraph La. Clayg KT10 ... 55 F5
Telegraph Rd. Putney SW15 ... 19 C8
Telegraph Track. Wallin SM5 & SM6 ... 60 A1
Telfei House. 8 Dulw SE21 ... 22 E4
Telferscot Jun Mix & Inf Sch. Streat SW12 ... 21 D7
Telferscot Rd. Streat SW12 ... 21 D7
Telford Ave. Crowth RG11 ... 45 C8
Telford Ave. Streat SW12 & SW2 ... 21 E7
Telford Avenue Mansions. 7 Streat SW2 ... 21 E7
Telford Cl. S Norw SE19 ... 22 F2
Telford Ct. Guild GU1 ... 130 F8
Telford Dr. Walt O T KT12 ... 35 C2
Telford Parade Mansions. 8 Streat SW2 ... 21 E7
Telford Pl. Crawl RH10 ... 201 E5
Telford Rd. Twick TW4 ... 16 A8
Telham Ct. 5 Crawl RH11 ... 200 F3
Tellisford. Esher KT10 ... 55 B6
Temperley Rd. Balham SW12 ... 21 A8
Tempest Rd. Egham TW20 ... 12 C2
Templar Cl. Sandh GU17 ... 64 A8
Templar Ct. New Add CR0 ... 62 E2
Templar Pl. Hampt TW12 ... 16 A1
Temple Ave. Croy CR0 ... 62 F7
Temple Bar Rd. Knaph GU21 ... 88 F8
Temple Cl. Worth RH10 ... 202 D5
Temple Ct. 9 Rich TW10 ... 6 E2
Temple Field Cl. Addl KT15 ... 52 B4
Temple Gdns. Egham TW18 ... 32 F8
Temple La. Capel RH5 ... 178 F5
Temple Market. Weyb KT13 ... 53 B6
Temple Rd. Bigg H TN16 ... 83 D2
Temple Rd. Croy CR0 ... 61 D6
Temple Rd. Epsom KT19 ... 76 D7
Temple Rd. Hounsl TW3 ... 5 C3
Temple Rd. Rich TW9 ... 6 F5
Temple Sheen. Mortl SW14 ... 7 C2
Temple Sheen Rd. Mortl SW14 ... 7 C3
Temple Way. Binf RG12 ... 26 E8
Temple Way. Carsh SM1 ... 59 D7
Temple Wood Dr. Redh RH1 ... 118 F4
Temple's Cl. Farnh GU10 ... 126 C1
Templecombe Mews. Mayb GU22 ... 70 B3
Templecombe Way. Merton SM4 ... 39 E4
Templecroft. Ashf TW15 ... 14 D2
Templedene. Beck BR2 ... 44 D7
Templedene Ave. Stain TW18 ... 13 C2
Templeman Cl. Purley CR8 ... 80 B3
Templemere. Oat Pk KT13 ... 53 D7
Templeton Cl. S Norw CR7 & SE19 ... 42 D8
Templewood House. Redh RH1 ... 118 F4
Ten Acre. Woking GU21 ... 69 A1
Ten Acre La. Thorpe TW20 ... 32 C7
Ten Acres. Fetch KT22 ... 94 D3
Ten Acres Cl. Fetch KT22 ... 94 D3
Tenbury Ct. Streat SW12 ... 21 D7
Tenby Dr. Ascot SL5 ... 29 D4
Tenby Rd. Friml GU16 ... 86 A8
Tenchley's La. Limps RH8 ... 123 D4
Tenchley's La. The Char RH8 ... 123 E2
Tenham Ave. Streat SW2 ... 21 D6
Tennison Cl. Coulsd CR5 ... 100 B7
Tennison Rd. Croy SE25 ... 42 F4
Tennison Rd. S Norw SE25 ... 42 F4
Tennyson Ave. Twick TW1 ... 16 F7
Tennyson Ave. W Barn KT3 ... 39 B4
Tennyson Cl. Crawl RH10 ... 202 B8
Tennyson Cl. Felt TW14 ... 4 A1
Tennyson Cl. Horsh RH12 ... 217 E6
Tennyson Ct. 3 Rich TW10 ... 17 D4
Tennyson Rd. Addl KT15 ... 52 E6
Tennyson Rd. Ashf TW15 ... 13 E3
Tennyson Rd. Hounsl TW3 ... 5 C5
Tennyson Rd. Penge SE20 ... 23 D1
Tennyson Rd. Wimble SW19 ... 20 C2
Tennyson Rise. E Grins RH19 ... 205 C8
Tennyson's La. Haslem GU27 ... 208 E4
Tennyson's La. Lurg GU27 ... 209 A2
Tennysons. Haslem GU27 ... 208 E4
Tensing Ct. Stan TW19 ... 13 E7
Tenterden Gdns. Croy CR0 ... 43 A2
Tenterden Rd. Croy CR0 ... 43 A2
Tern Rd. Crawl RH11 ... 200 D5
Terra Cotta Rd. S Godst RH9 ... 142 C5
Terrace Gdns. Barnes SW13 ... 7 F5
Terrace La. Rich TW10 ... 6 E1
Terrace Rd. Walt O T KT12 ... 35 B3
Terrace The. Addl KT15 ... 52 E5
Terrace The. Ascot SL5 ... 29 D4
Terrace The. Barnes SW13 & SW14 ... 7 E5
Terrace The. Camb GU15 ... 65 A5
Terrace The. Crowth RG11 ... 45 D5
Terrace The. Mortl SW13 & SW14 ... 7 E5
Terrace The. Old Wok GU22 ... 90 A6
Terrace The. Woki RG11 ... 25 B6
Terrapin Ct. Up Toot SW17 ... 21 B5
Terrapin Rd. Up Toot SW17 ... 21 B5
Terrapins. Surb KT6 ... 37 D2
Terry House. Streat SW2 ... 22 A7
Terry Rd. Crawl RH11 ... 201 B1
Testard Rd. Guild GU2 ... 130 C7
Testers Cl. Oxted RH8 ... 123 B3
Teviot Cl. Stough GU2 ... 109 A4
Tewkesbury Ave. For Hil SE23 ... 23 B8
Tewkesbury Cl. Byfl KT14 ... 71 D8
Tewkesbury Rd. Carsh SM5 ... 40 D1
Thackeray Cl. Wimble SW19 ... 19 D1
Thackeray Manor. Sutton SM1 ... 59 C5
Thackery Lodge. E Bed TW14 ... 3 D1
Thakeham Cl. For Hil SE26 ... 23 B3
Thames Ave. Thorpe KT16 ... 33 A6
Thames Bank. Mortl SW14 ... 7 C5
Thames Cl. Chert KT16 ... 33 C2
Thames Cl. E Mole TW12 ... 36 B7
Thames Cl. W Heath GU14 ... 84 E6
Thames Ct. E Mole KT8 ... 36 B7
Thames Ditton Cty Fst Sch. Thame D KT7 ... 36 F3
Thames Ditton & Esher Golf Club. Esher KT10 ... 55 D8
Thames Ditton Hospl. Thame D KT7 ... 36 F2
Thames Ditton Island. Thame D KT7 ... 37 A4
Thames Ditton Jun Sch. Thame D KT7 ... 36 F2
Thames Ditton Sta. Thame D KT7 ... 36 F2
Thames Eyot. 7 Twick TW1 ... 17 A7
Thames Haven. King U T KT6 ... 37 D4
Thames Link House. 6 Rich TW9 ... 6 E3
Thames Mead. Walt O T KT12 ... 35 A2
Thames Meadow. E Mole KT8 ... 36 A6
Thames Meadow. Lo Hall KT12 & TW17 ... 34 E1
Thames Rd. Brent W4 ... 7 B8
Thames Rd. Chisw W4 ... 7 B8
Thames Side. King U T KT1 ... 37 D8
Thames Side. Laleh KT16 & TW18 ... 33 C5
Thames Side. Stain TW18 ... 12 F2
Thames Side. Thame D KT7 ... 37 B3
Thames St. E Mole TW12 ... 36 B7
Thames St. King U T KT1 & KT2 ... 37 D7
Thames St. Stain TW18 ... 12 F3
Thames St. Sunby TW16 ... 35 B6
Thames St. Walt O T KT12 ... 34 F2
Thames St. Weyb KT13 ... 53 B7
Thames View House. Walt O T TW12 ... 35 A3
Thames Village. Chisw W4 ... 7 C6
Thamesfield Ct. Shep TW17 ... 34 C2
Thamesgate Cl. Tedd TW10 ... 17 B4
Thameside. Tedd TW11 ... 17 D1
Thamesmead Sch. Shep TW17 ... 34 D3
Thamespoint. Tedd TW11 ... 17 D1
Thamesvale Cl. Hounsl TW3 ... 5 A5
Thanescroft Gdns. S Croy CR0 ... 61 E7
Thanet House. 1 W Norw SE27 ... 22 B5
Thanet Pl. Croy CR0 ... 61 C6
Tharp Rd. Wallin SM6 ... 60 D5
Thatcher Cl. Crawl RH10 ... 201 D3
Thatchers Cl. Horley RH6 ... 161 B5
Thatchers Cl. Horsh RH12 ... 217 E4
Thatchers La. Worpl GU3 ... 108 E8
Thatchers Way. Islew TW7 ... 5 D2
Thaxted Pl. 7 Wimble SW20 ... 19 D1
Thayers Farm Rd. Penge BR3 ... 43 E8
Theal Cl. Sandh GU15 ... 64 D8
Theatre Rd. Farnb GU14 ... 105 B8
Thelma Gr. Tedd TW11 ... 17 A2
Thelton Ave. Broad H RH12 ... 216 D3
Theobald Rd. Thorn H CR0 & CR9 ... 61 B8
Theobalds Way. Friml GU16 ... 66 C3
Thepps Cl. S Nutf RH1 ... 140 F6
Therapia La. Thorn H CR0 ... 41 E3
Therapia La. Wallin CR0 & CR4 ... 41 D2
Therapia La. Wallin CR0 ... 41 E2
Theresa's Wlk. S Croy CR2 ... 61 D2
Therfield Sch. Leahd KT22 ... 95 A8
Thesiger Rd. Penge BR3 & SE20 ... 23 D1
Thetford Ct. Dulw SE21 ... 23 B6
Thetford Rd. Ashf TW15 ... 13 E5
Thetford Rd. New Mal KT3 ... 38 E4
Thetis Terr. Rich TW9 ... 7 A8
Theydon Cl. Crawl RH10 ... 202 A4
Thibet Rd. Sandh GU17 ... 64 C8
Thicket Cres. Sutton SM1 ... 59 C6
Thicket Gr. Penge SE20 ... 23 A1
Thicket Rd. Penge SE19 & SE20 ... 23 B1
Thicket Rd. Sutton SM1 ... 59 C6
Thickthorne La. Stain TW18 ... 13 C1
Third Cl. E Mole KT8 ... 36 C5
Third Cross Rd. Twick TW2 ... 16 D6
Thirlmere Cl. Farnb GU14 ... 84 E4
Thirlmere Cl. Thor L TW20 ... 12 B1
Thirlmere House. Islew TW1 ... 5 F2
Thirlmere Rd. Crawl RH11 ... 200 D4
Thirlmere Rd. Streat SW16 ... 21 D4
Thirlmere Rise. Broml BR1 ... 24 F2
Thirlmere Wlk. Friml GU15 ... 66 D4
Thirsk Rd. Mitch CR4 ... 21 A1
Thirsk Rd. S Norw SE25 ... 42 D5
Thistle Way. Smallf RH6 ... 162 C3
Thistlecroft Rd. Hersh KT12 ... 54 C6
Thistledene. Thame D KT7 ... 36 E3
Thistledene. W Byfl KT14 ... 70 F6
Thistlewood Cres. New Add CR0 ... 82 D7
Thistleworth Cl. Hounsl TW7 ... 5 D7
Thistley La. Cran GU6 ... 174 E4
Thomas Ave. Cater CR3 ... 100 C6

Thomas Becket Jun Mix & Inf Sch. Croy SE25 43 A3
Thomas Bennett Comm Coll. Crawl RH10 201 D3
Thomas Bennett Comm Sch. Crawl RH10 201 E2
Thomas' La. Catf SE6 24 A8
Thomas Moore House. Reig RH2 118 C1
Thomas More RC High Sch. Purley CR8 61 A1
Thomas Pooley Ct. Surb KT6 37 E2
Thomas Wall Cl. Sutton SM1 59 B5
Thompson Ave. Rich TW9 7 A4
Thompson Ct. 16 Crawl RH11 201 B1
Thompson's La. Burrh GU24 49 D2
Thompsons Cl. Pirb GU24 87 D4
Thomson Cres. Thorn H CR0 42 A1
Thorburn Chase. Sandh GU15 64 E6
Thorburn Way. Mitch SW19 40 D8
Thorkhill Gdns. Thame D KT7 37 B1
Thorkhill Rd. Thame D KT7 37 B2
Thorley Cl. Pyrf KT14 71 A5
Thorley Gdns. Pyrf KT14 71 A5
Thorn Bank. Onsl V GU2 130 A7
Thorn Cl. Rowl GU10 145 F4
Thorn Rd. Rowl GU10 146 A5
Thornash Cl. Horse GU21 69 C4
Thornash Rd. Horse GU21 69 C4
Thornash Way. Horse GU21 69 C4
Thornbank Cl. Stan TW19 2 A2
Thornbury Ave. Hounsl TW7 5 D7
Thornbury Cl. Crowth RG11 45 B5
Thornbury Ct. Hounsl TW7 5 E7
Thornbury Ct. Whytlf CR3 100 F7
Thornbury Rd. Hounsl TW7 5 D6
Thorncombe St. Bramly GU5 & GU8 151 E2
Thorncroft. Eng Gn TW20 11 C1
Thorncroft Cl. Coulsd CR5 100 A8
Thorncroft Rd. Sutton SM1 59 B6
Thorndean St. Wands SW18 20 C6
Thorndon Gdns. Worc Pk KT19 57 E6
Thorndown La. Windl GU20 48 D3
Thorndyke Cl. Worth RH10 202 D5
Thorne Cl. Crowth RG11 45 A7
Thorne Cl. Littlt TW15 14 C1
Thorne St. Mortl SW13 & SW14 7 E4
Thorne's Cl. Beck BR3 44 C6
Thorneloe Gdns. Croy CR0 & CR9 61 B5
Thorneycroft Cl. Walt O T KT12 35 C3
Thornfield Gn. Hawley GU17 64 F3
Thornfield Rd. Banstd SM7 78 A2
Thornhill. Brack RG12 27 E5
Thornhill Ave. Surb KT6 56 E8
Thornhill Rd. Alder GU11 105 D4
Thornhill Rd. Surb KT6 56 F8
Thornhill Rd. Thorn H CR0 42 C2
Thornhill Way. Shep Gn TW17 34 A4
Thornlaw Rd. W Norw SE27 22 B4
Thornleas Pl. E Hors KT24 92 E1
Thornsbeach Rd. Catf SE6 24 C6
Thornsett Pl. Penge SE20 43 B7
Thornsett Rd. Penge SE20 43 B7
Thornsett Rd. Wands SW18 20 B7
Thornsett Terr. Penge SE20 43 B7
Thornton Ave. Streat SW2 21 D7
Thornton Ave. Thorn H CR0 41 F3
Thornton Cl. Horley RH6 160 E3
Thornton Cl. Stough GU2 109 A4
Thornton Cres. Coulsd CR5 100 A8
Thornton Ct. W Barn SW20 39 D4
Thornton Dene. Beck BR3 44 A7
Thornton Gdns. Streat SW12 21 D7
Thornton Heath Sta. Thorn H CR7 42 C5
Thornton Hill. Wimble SW19 19 E1
Thornton Pl. Horley RH6 160 F3
Thornton Rd. Carsh SM5 40 D1
Thornton Rd. Mortl SW14 7 D4
Thornton Rd. Streat SW12 & SW2 21 D7
Thornton Rd. Thorn H CR0 & CR7 & CR9 41 F3
Thornton Rd. Wimble SW19 19 D1
Thornton Rd E. Wimble SW19 19 D2
Thornton Row. Thorn H CR7 42 A4
Thornycroft Ct. Rich TW9 6 F5
Thornyhurst Rd. Mytch GU16 86 A4
Thorold Cl. Selsd CR0 & CR2 62 D1
Thorold House. 6 Streat SW2 21 E8
Thorold Rd. Farnb GU9 125 C3
Thoroughfare The. Walt o t H KT20 97 A3
Thorpe By-Pass. Egham KT16 & TW20 32 B6
Thorpe C of E Fst Sch. Egham TW20 32 B6
Thorpe Cl. For Hil SE26 23 D4
Thorpe Cl. New Add CR0 82 C8
Thorpe Cl. Woki RG11 25 A3
Thorpe Ind Est. Thorpe TW20 32 C8
Thorpe Ind Pk. Thorpe TW20 32 C8
Thorpe Lea Prim Sch. Egham TW20 12 D2
Thorpe Lea Rd. Egham TW20 12 C2
Thorpe Lea Rd. Thor L TW20 12 C2
Thorpe Park. Thorpe TW20 32 E5
Thorpe Rd. Chert KT16 32 D4
Thorpe Rd. Egham TW18 & TW20 12 D3
Thorpe Rd. King U T KT2 17 E1
Thorpes Cl. Stough GU2 109 A4
Thorpeside Cl. Egham TW18 & TW20 32 E7
Thorpewood Ave. For Hil SE23 & SE26 23 B6
Thorsden Cl. Woking GU22 89 E8
Thorsden Ct. 10 Woking GU22 69 E1
Thorsden Way. 2 W Norw SE19 22 E3
Thrale Almhouses. Streat SW16 21 E3
Thrale Rd. Streat SW16 21 C3
Three Acres. Horsh RH12 217 A1
Three Arch Rd. Earls RH1 140 A5
Three Bridges Cty Fst Sch. Crawl RH10 202 A7
Three Bridges Cty Mid Sch. Crawl RH10 201 F6
Three Bridges Rd. Crawl RH10 202 A6
Three Bridges Sta. Crawl RH10 202 B6
Three Gates. Merrow GU1 110 C3
Three Gates La. Haslem GU27 208 E8
Three Mile Rd. Ewh GU6 & RH5 155 A2
Three Pears Rd. Merrow GU1 110 E1
Three Stiles Rd. Farnb GU9 124 F3
Three Ways. Binst GU10 166 D6
Threestile Rd. Warn RH12 197 F1
Threshfield. Easth RG12 27 A4
Thriffwood. For Hil SE23 & SE26 23 D5
Thrift Vale. Merrow GU4 110 D4
Thrigby Rd. Chess KT9 56 F4
Throat Handpost Cnr The. Woki RG11 25 A1
Throwley Rd. Sutton SM1 59 B5
Throwley Way. Sutton SM1 59 B5
Thrupp Cl. Mitch CR4 41 B7
Thrupps Ave. Hersh KT12 54 D5
Thrupps La. Hersh KT12 54 D5
Thundery Hill. The San GU10 126 F4
Thurbans Rd. M Bourn GU9 146 A7
Thurbarn Rd. Catf SE6 24 B3
Thurbarns Hill. Bear Gn RH5 157 E1
Thurlby Rd. W Norw SE27 22 A4
Thurleigh Rd. Balham SW11 & SW12 20 F8
Thurleston Ave. Merton SM4 39 E4
Thurlestone Cl. Shep TW17 34 C3
Thurlestone Par. Shep TW17 34 C3
Thurlestone Rd. W Norw SE27 22 A4
Thurlow Hill. W Norw SE21 22 C6
Thurlow House. 17 Streat SW16 21 E5
Thurlow Park Rd. Dulw SE21 & SE24 22 C6
Thurlow Park Rd. W Norw SE21 & SE24 22 C6
Thurlow Park Sch. W Norw SE27 22 B6
Thurlow Towers. W Norw SE27 22 A5
Thurlow Wlk. Cran GU6 174 E1
Thurlton Ct. Horse GU21 69 E3
Thurnby Ct. Twick TW2 16 E5
Thurne Way. Rudg RH12 214 D7
Thurnham Way. Tadw KT20 97 D7
Thursby Rd. Woking GU21 69 A1
Thursley Cres. New Add CR0 63 D3
Thursley Gdns. Putney SW19 19 D6
Thursley House. 3 King U T KT2 18 B1
Thursley House. 13 Streat SW2 21 F8
Thursley Rd. Churt GU10 & GU8 168 C3
Thursley Rd. Thursl GU8 & GU10 169 B6
Thurso St. Up Toot SW17 20 D4
Thurstan Rd. Wimble SW20 19 B1
Thurston House. Beck BR3 24 B2
Thurza Ct. Hounsl TW7 5 F5
Thyme Ct. W Heath GU14 84 C5
Tibbet's Cnr. Putney SW19 19 D8
Tibbet's Ride. Putney SW19 19 D8
Tibbets Cl. Putney SW19 19 D7
Ticehurst Cl. Worth RH10 202 E6
Ticehurst Rd. For Hil SE23 23 E6
Tichborne Cl. Blckw GU17 64 D5
Tichborne Pl. Alder GU12 126 D8
Tichbourne Cl. Friml GU16 65 F3
Tichmarsh. Epsom KT19 57 C1
Tidenham Gdns. S Croy CR0 61 E7
Tideswell Rd. Croy CR0 63 A7
Tideway Cl. Rich TW10 17 C4
Tideway Yd. Mortl SW13 7 E5
Tidwells Lea. Wink RG12 27 E8
Tiepigs La. Coney H BR2 & BR4 44 F1
Tiepigs La. Hayes BR2 & BR4 44 F1
Tierney Ct. 1 Croy CR0 61 F8
Tierney Rd. Streat SW2 21 E7
Tierney Terr. Streat SW2 21 E7
Tiffin Girls' Sch. King U T KT2 17 E2
Tiffin Sch. King U T KT2 37 F7
Tilburstow Cotts. Godst RH9 121 C3
Tilburstow Hill Rd. Blind H RH9 142 D5
Tilburstow Hill Rd. S Godst RH9 142 D5
Tile Barn Cl. W Heath GU14 85 A5
Tilehouse Rd. Guild GU4 130 E5
Tilehurst La. Betch RH3 & RH5 136 F5
Tilehurst La. Dork RH3 & RH5 136 F5
Tilehurst Rd. Cheam SM3 58 E5
Tilehurst Rd. Wands SW17 & SW18 20 D7
Tiler's Way. Dovgn RH1 139 C5
Tilford Ave. New Add CR0 63 C2
Tilford Gdns. Putney SW19 19 D7
Tilford House. 11 Streat SW2 21 F8
Tilford Rd. Beac H GU10 & GU26 188 E6
Tilford Rd. Hind GU10 & GU26 188 E6
Tilford Rd. M Bourn GU10 & GU9 146 F7
Tilford Rd. Rushm GU10 168 C4
Tilford Rd. Tilf GU10 147 C4
Tilford St. Tilf GU10 147 D5
Tilgate Comm. Bletch RH1 120 C2
Tilgate Dr. Crawl RH10 & RH11 201 E2
Tilgate Forest Bsns Ctr. Crawl RH11 201 D1
Tilgate Forest Golf Course. Crawl RH10 202 A2
Tilgate Forest Recn Ctr. Crawl RH10 201 D1
Tilgate Par. Crawl RH10 201 E3
Tilgate Pl. Crawl RH10 201 E3
Tilgate Way. Crawl RH10 201 E3
Tilgates Cotts. Bletch RH1 120 C3
Tilletts La. Warn RH12 216 E8
Tilley La. Head KT18 96 C4
Tillingbourne Cty Jun Sch. Chil GU4 131 B2
Tillingbourne Rd. Shalf GU4 130 E3
Tillingdown Hill. Cater CR3 101 A5
Tillingdown La. Cater CR3 101 B2
Tillingdown La. Wold CR3 101 B3
Tillman House. 8 Streat SW2 21 F7
Tillotson Cl. Worth RH10 202 D5
Tilly's La. Stain TW18 12 F4
Tilney Ct. King U T KT6 37 D4
Tilson Gdns. Streat SW2 & SW4 21 E8
Tilson House. Streat SW2 21 E8
Tilt Cl. Stk D'A KT11 73 E3
Tilt Meadow. Cobham KT11 73 E3
Tilt Rd. Cobham KT11 73 D3
Tilthams Corner Rd. Shalf GU7 & GU7 151 C8
Tilthams Gn. Shalf GU7 151 B8
Tiltview. Cobham KT11 73 C4
Tiltwood Dr. Crawl D RH10 204 C8
Timber Bank. Friml GU16 86 A6
Timber Cl. G Book KT23 114 C8
Timber Cl. Pyrf GU22 70 F5
Timber Ct. Horsh RH12 217 C3
Timber Hill. Ashtd KT21 95 E8
Timber Hill Rd. Cater CR3 101 A3
Timber La. Cater CR3 101 A3
Timbercroft. Worc Pk KT19 57 E6
Timberham Farm Rd. Hookw RH6 181 D8
Timberham Link. Crawl RH6 181 E8
Timberham Way. Crawl RH6 181 E8
Timberlands. 14 Crawl RH11 201 B1
Timberling Gdns. S Croy CR2 61 D1
Timbermill Ct. Shottm GU27 207 F6
Timberslip Dr. Wallin SM6 60 D2
Timbertop Rd. Bigg H TN16 83 C1
Times Sq. Sutton SM1 59 B5
Timline Gn. Brack RG12 27 F7
Timperley Ct. Redh RH1 118 E3
Timperley Gdns. Redh RH1 118 E3
Timsbury Wlk. 5 Rhampt SW15 19 A7
Timsway. Egham TW18 12 F3
Tina Ct. W Norw SW16 22 A5
Tindale Cl. S Croy CR2 80 D8
Tinsey Cl. Egham TW20 12 B3
Tinsley Gn. Crawl RH10 182 B4
Tinsley La. Crawl RH10 182 A1
Tinsley La N. Crawl RH10 182 B3
Tinsley La S. Crawl RH10 202 A8
Tintagel Cl. Epsom KT17 76 F5
Tintagel Ct. Horsh RH13 217 D1
Tintagel Dr. Friml GU16 65 F1
Tintagel Way. Woking GU22 70 A3
Tintells La. W Hors KT24 112 B7
Tintern Cl. Merton SW19 20 C2
Tintern Rd. Carsh SM5 40 D1
Tintern Rd. Crawl RH11 201 A4
Tippits Mead. Binf RG12 26 D8
Tipton Dr. S Croy CR0 61 E6
Tiree Path. Crawl RH11 201 B3
Tirlemont Rd. Croy CR2 61 C3
Tirrell Rd. Thorn H CR0 42 C3
Tisbury Rd. Thorn H SW16 41 E7
Titchfield Rd. Carsh SM5 40 D1
Titchfield Wlk. Carsh SM5 40 D2
Titchwell Rd. Wands SW18 20 D7
Tite Hill. Eng Gn TW20 11 D3
Tithe Barn Cl. King U T KT2 37 F8
Tithe Barn The. E Clan GU4 111 D4
Tithe La. Wray TW19 1 A1
Tithe Meadows. Went GU25 31 D3
Tithe Orch. Felb RH19 184 E4
Tithepit Shaw La. Warlgm CR2 & CR6 81 B3
Titlarks Hill Rd. Sunnin SL5 30 B1
Titmus Dr. Crawl RH10 201 F2
Titsey Cnr. Limps RH8 123 B7
Titsey Hill. Titsey CR6 & RH8 103 B4
Titsey Rd. Limps RH8 123 B8
Titsey Rd. Titsey RH8 103 B1
Tiverton Rd. Hounsl TW3 5 C5
Tiverton Way. Chess KT9 56 D5
Tiverton Way. Friml GU16 65 F1
Tivoli Rd. Hounsl TW4 4 E3
Tivoli Rd. W Norw SE19 & SE27 22 C3
Toad La. Hawley GU17 64 E4
Tobias Sch of Art. E Grins RH19 205 E6
Toby Way. Tolw KT5 & KT6 57 B8
Todds Cl. Horley RH6 160 E5
Toftwood Cl. Crawl RH10 202 C5
Toll Bar Ct. Sutton SM2 59 B2
Toll Gdns. Brack RG12 27 F6
Tolldene Cl. Knaph GU21 68 E2
Tollers La. Coulsd CR5 99 F8
Tollgate. Merrow GU1 110 D1
Tollgate Ave. Earls RH1 139 F4
Tollgate Ct. Earls RH1 139 F4
Tollgate Dr. Dulw SE21 22 E6
Tollgate Hill. Crawl RH11 201 C1
Tollgate Jun Mix & Inf Sch. Croy CR0 43 C3
Tollgate Rd. Dork RH4 136 B4
Tollhouse La. Wallin SM6 60 C2
Tolson Ho. 2 Islew TW7 6 A4
Tolson Rd. Islew TW7 6 A4
Tolvaddon. Woking GU21 69 A2
Tolverne Rd. Wimble SW20 39 C8
Tolworth Cl. Tolw KT6 38 B1
Tolworth Girls' Sch. Surb KT6 56 F7
Tolworth Hospl. Tolw KT6 57 A8
Tolworth Inf Sch. Surb KT6 37 F1
Tolworth Jun Sch. Surb KT6 37 F1
Tolworth Park Rd. Surb KT6 56 F8
Tolworth Rd. Surb KT6 56 E8
Tolworth Rise N. Tolw KT5 38 B1
Tolworth Rise S. Tolw KT5 38 B1
Tolworth Sta. Tolw KT5 57 B8
Tolworth Underpass. Tolw KT5 & KT6 57 B8
Tomlin Cl. Epsom KT19 76 D8
Tomlin Ct. Epsom KT19 76 D8
Tomlins Ave. Friml GU16 65 F2
Tomlinscote Sch. Friml GU16 66 A1
Tomlinscote Way. Friml GU16 66 A2
Tompset's Bank. For Row RH18 206 F1
Tonbridge Cl. Woodm SM7 78 F5
Tonbridge Rd. E Mole KT12 & KT8 35 F5
Tonfield Rd. Cheam SM3 39 F1
Tonge Cl. Beck BR3 44 A4
Tongham Meadows. Tongh GU10 126 F7
Tongham Rd. Alder GU12 126 D8
Tongham Rd. Farnb GU10 126 C4
Tonstall Rd. Epsom KT19 76 D8
Tonstall Rd. Mitch CR4 41 A7
Tooting Bec Gdns. Streat SW16 21 D4
Tooting Bec Hospl. Up Toot SW17 21 B4
Tooting Bec Rd. Streat SW16 21 B4
Tooting Bec Rd. Up Toot SW17 21 B4
Tooting Bec Sta. Up Toot SW17 21 A5
Tooting Broadway. Up Toot SW17 20 F3
Tooting Broadway Sta. Up Toot SW17 20 E3
Tooting Gr. Up Toot SW17 20 E3
Tooting High St. Up Toot SW17 & SW19 20 E3
Tooting Mkt. Up Toot SW17 20 F4
Tooting Sta. Mitch SW17 20 F2
Tootswood Rd. Beck BR2 & BR3 44 E5
Top Pk. Beck BR3 44 E4
Top Terrace Rd. Farnb GU14 105 A8
Topaz House. New Mal KT4 38 D1
Topiary Sq. Rich TW9 6 F4
Topiary The. Ashtd KT21 95 E7
Topiary The. Farnb GU14 84 E3
Toplady Pl. Heath E GU9 125 C7
Topsham Rd. Up Toot SW17 21 A4
Tor La. Whit V KT13 72 D8
Tor Rd. Farnh GU9 124 F2
Torcross Dr. For Hil SE23 23 C6
Torin Ct. Eng Gn TW20 11 C3
Torland Dr. Oxsh KT22 74 D6
Tormead Cl. Sutton SM1 59 A4
Tormead Rd. Guild GU1 109 F1
Tormead Sch. Guild GU1 109 F1
Toronto Dr. Smallf RH6 162 A3
Torr Rd. Penge SE20 23 D1
Torre Wlk. Carsh SM5 40 E1
Torridge Rd. Bra Hil SL3 1 B8
Torridge Rd. Thorn H CR7 42 B4
Torridon Cl. Woking GU21 69 B2
Torridon Inf Sch. Catf SE6 24 D6
Torridon Jun Sch. Catf SE6 24 D6
Torridon Rd. Catf SE13 & SE6 24 D7
Torrington Cl. Clayg KT10 55 E4
Torrington Ct. Penge SE26 23 A3
Torrington Rd. Clayg KT10 55 E4
Torrington Sq. Croy CR0 42 D2
Torrington Way. Morden SM4 40 A3
Torwood La. Whytlf CR3 100 F8
Totford La. Putt GU10 127 E4
Totham Lodge. Wimble SW20 39 B8
Totland Cl. W Heath GU14 85 A6
Tottenham Rd. Farnc GU7 150 E6
Tottenham Wlk. Sandh GU15 45 D1
Totterdown St. Up Toot SW17 20 F3
Totton Rd. Thorn H CR7 42 A6
Tournai Cl. Farnb GU11 105 E7
Toutley Rd. Woki RG11 25 A8
Tovil Cl. Penge SE20 43 B7
Tower Cl. E Grins RH19 185 E2
Tower Cl. Hind GU26 188 E4
Tower Cl. Horley RH6 160 F3
Tower Cl. Horse GU21 69 D2
Tower Cl. Penge SE20 23 B1
Tower Cotts. Esher KT10 54 F1
Tower Ct. E Grins RH19 185 E2
Tower Gr. Oat Pk KT13 53 E8
Tower Hill. Dork RH4 136 B5
Tower Hill. Farnb GU14 85 A3
Tower Hill Cty Prim Sch. Farnb GU14 84 F3
Tower Hill Rd. Dork RH4 136 B5
Tower Hill Rise. Gomsh GU5 133 C3
Tower Rd. Crawl RH12 218 F8
Tower Rd. Hind GU26 188 E4
Tower Rd. Tadw KT20 97 C4
Tower Rd. Twick TW1 & TW2 16 F5
Tower Rise. Rich TW9 6 E4
Tower View. Croy CR0 43 E2
Towerhill. Gomsh GU5 133 C3
Towers Dr. Crowth RG11 45 B4
Towers Pl. Rich TW10 6 E2
Towers The. Kenley CR8 80 C4
Towers The. 1 Rich TW9 6 F3
Towers Wlk. Whit V KT13 53 B4
Towfield Ct. Felt TW13 15 F6
Towfield Rd. Felt TW13 15 F6
Town Barn Rd. Crawl RH11 201 C7
Town End Cl. Cater CR3 100 E5
Town End Cl. Godal GU7 150 E4
Town End St. Godal GU7 150 E4
Town Farm Cty Prim Sch. Stan TW19 13 D8
Town Farm Way. Stan TW19 13 D8
Town Hill. Lingf RH7 164 E4
Town La. Stan TW19 13 D7
Town Mead. Bletch RH1 120 D2
Town Mead. Crawl RH11 201 D7
Town Meadow. Brent TW8 6 D7
Town Quay. Laleh TW18 33 C6
Town Sq. Brack RG12 27 C7
Town Sq. Camb GU15 65 C6
Town Sq. 3 Woking GU21 69 F2
Town Tree Rd. Ashf TW15 14 A3
Townend. Cater CR3 100 E5
Townend Ct. Broml BR1 44 F8
Townfield Ct. Dork RH4 136 A6
Townfield Rd. Dork RH4 136 A6
Towngate. Cobham KT11 73 E4
Townmead Rd. Rich TW9 7 B5
Townsend Cl. Brack RG12 27 E4
Townsend La. Old Wok GU22 90 B6
Townsend Rd. Ashf TW15 13 E3
Townshend Rd. Rich TW9 6 F3
Townshend Terr. Rich TW9 6 F3
Townshott Cl. G Book KT23 94 A1
Towpath Way. Croy CR0 & SE25 42 F4
Towton Rd. W Norw SE27 22 C6
Toynbee Rd. Merton SW19 & SW20 39 E8
Toynbee Rd. Wimble SW19 & SW20 39 E8
Tracery The. Banstd SM7 78 B4
Tracious Cl. Horse GU21 69 B3
Traemore Ct. W Norw SW16 22 A5
Trafalgar Ave. N Cheam KT4 & SM3 & SM4 39 D1
Trafalgar Ct. Cobham KT11 73 A6
Trafalgar Ct. Farnh GU9 125 C1
Trafalgar Ct. Hounsl TW3 4 F4
Trafalgar Ct. W Barn KT3 39 B6
Trafalgar Cty Inf Prim Sch. Horsh RH12 217 B4
Trafalgar Dr. Walt O T KT12 54 B7
Trafalgar Inf Sch. Twick TW2 16 D6
Trafalgar Jun Sch. Twick TW2 16 D6
Trafalgar Rd. Horsh RH12 217 C4
Trafalgar Rd. Merton SW19 20 C1
Trafalgar Rd. Twick TW2 16 D6
Trafalgar Way. Camb GU15 64 F4
Trafalgar Way. Croy CR0 & CR9 61 A8
Trafford Rd. Friml GU16 85 D8
Trafford Rd. Thorn H CR7 41 F4
Traherne Lodge. 3 Tedd TW11 16 F3
Tramway Path. Mitch CR4 40 E5
Tranmere Ct. Sutton SM2 59 C3
Tranmere Rd. Twick TW2 16 B8
Tranmere Rd. Wands SW17 & SW18 20 C6
Tranquil Dale. Buckl RH3 116 F3
Transport Ave. Brent TW8 6 B8
Transport Rd. Farnb GU14 85 B1
Transport & Road Research Laboratory. Crowth RG11 45 C7
Trap La. Wall W RH5 176 F2
Traps La. King U T KT2 & KT3 38 E8
Trasher Mead. Dork RH4 & RH5 136 C4
Travellers Way. Cranf TW5 4 C5
Travis La. Sandh GU17 64 C7
Treadcroft Dr. Horsh RH12 217 E5
Treadwell Rd. Epsom KT18 76 F4
Treaty Ctr. Hounsl TW3 5 B4
Trebor Ave. M Bourn GU9 146 D8
Tredenham Cl. Farnb GU14 105 C8
Tredown Rd. For Hil SE26 23 C3
Tredwell Rd. W Norw SE27 22 B4
Tree Ave. Shottm GU27 207 F8
Tree Cl. Rich TW10 17 D7
Tree Tops. Whytlf CR6 81 A1
Tree Tops Ave. Camb GU15 66 B8
Tree View Cl. S Norw SE19 42 E8
Treebourne Rd. Bigg H TN16 83 C1
Treebys Ave. Jacobs GU4 109 D7
Treelands. Dork RH5 136 C4
Treemount Ct. Epsom KT17 76 E6
Treen Ave. Mortl SW13 & SW14 7 F4
Trees Sch The. Mayb GU22 90 B8
Treeside Dr. Heath E GU9 125 E7
Treetops. S Godst RH9 142 E6
Treetops Ct. Thorn H CR7 42 C4
Treeview. Crawl RH11 201 C1
Treeview Ct. 3 Reig RH2 118 D1
Treeway. Reig RH2 118 B4
Trefoil Cl. Horsh RH12 217 E5
Trefoil Cl. Woki RG11 25 E7
Trefoil Cres. Crawl RH11 201 A2
Trefusis Ct. Cranf TW5 4 B6
Tregaron Gdns. New Mal KT3 38 E5
Tregarth Pl. Woking GU21 68 F2
Tregarthen Pl. Leahd KT22 95 C6
Treglos Ct. Oat Pk KT13 53 E8
Tregolls Dr. Farnb GU14 85 D3
Trehaven Par. Woodh RH2 139 B6
Trehern Rd. 12 Mortl SW14 7 D4
Treherne Ct. Up Toot SW17 21 A4
Trelawn Cl. Ottsh KT16 51 C3
Trelawne Dr. Cran GU6 174 E2
Trelawney Gr. Weyb KT13 53 A4
Treloar Gdns. S Norw SE19 22 D2
Tremaine Rd. Penge SE20 43 B7
Trematon Pl. Tedd TW11 17 C1
Tremayne Wlk. Friml GU15 66 C4
Trenance. Woking GU21 69 A2
Trenchard Cl. Hersh KT12 54 C5
Trenchard Ct. Morden SM4 40 A3
Trenear Cl. Horsh RH13 217 E2
Trenham Dr. Warlgm CR6 81 C3
Trenholme Cl. Penge SE20 23 B1
Trenholme Ct. Cater CR3 101 A4
Trenholme Rd. Penge SE20 23 B1
Trenholme Terr. Penge SE20 23 B1
Trent Cl. Crawl RH11 200 F4
Trent Cl. W Heath GU14 84 E6
Trent Rd. Bra Hil SL3 1 B8
Trent Way. N Cheam KT4 58 C7
Trentham Cres. Old Wok GU22 90 A6
Trentham Rd. Earls RH1 140 A7
Trentham St. Wands SW18 20 A7
Trenton Cl. Friml GU16 66 A1
Treport St. Wands SW18 20 A8
Treryn Hts. Farnc GU7 150 D6
Tresco Cl. Catf BR1 24 E2
Tresidder House. 10 Streat SW4 21 D8

Tresillian Way. Woking GU21 ... 69 B2
Tresta Wlk. Woking GU21 ... 69 A3
Trevanne Plat. Crawl RH10 ... 202 D7
Trevelayan Rd. Up Toot SW17 ... 20 F7
Trevelyan. Easth RG12 ... 26 E2
Trevelyan Ct. S New Mal KT3 ... 38 F2
Trevelyan House. 6 Twick TW1 ... 6 C1
Trevenna House. 13
  For Hil SE23 ... 23 D5
Trevereux Hill. The Char RH8 ... 123 F4
Treversh Ct. Broml BR1 ... 44 F8
Treville St. Putney SW15 ... 19 B8
Treviso Rd. For Hil SE23 ... 23 D6
Trevithick Cl. E Bed TW14 ... 14 F7
Trevor Cl. Hayes BR2 ... 44 F2
Trevor Cl. Islew TW7 ... 5 F2
Trevor Rd. Merton SW19 ... 19 E1
Trevose Ave. W Byfl KT14 ... 70 F5
Trewenna Dr. Chess KT9 ... 56 D5
Trewince Rd. Wimble SW20 ... 39 C8
Trewint St. Wands SW18 ... 20 C6
Trewsbury Rd. For Hil SE26 ... 23 D3
Treyford Cl. Crawl RH11 ... 200 F6
Triangle The. King U T KT3 ... 38 E7
Triangle The. Woking GU21 ... 69 C1
Trickett House. Sutton SM1 ... 59 B2
Trident Ind Est. Poyle SL3 ... 1 E4
Trig St. Newd RH5 ... 178 F8
Trigg's Cl. Woking GU22 ... 89 D8
Trigg's La. Woking GU21 & GU22 ... 89 D8
Trigo Ct. Epsom KT19 ... 76 D8
Trilby Rd. For Hil SE23 ... 23 D6
Trimmer Wlk. 11 Brent TW8 ... 6 E8
Trimmers Cl. Heath E GU9 ... 125 C7
Trimmers Field. M Bourn GU9 ... 125 E1
Trimmers Wood. Beac H GU26 ... 188 E6
Trindles Rd. S Nutf RH1 ... 140 F7
Tring Ct. Tedd TW1 ... 17 A4
Tringham Cl. Ottsh KT16 ... 51 C5
Trinity. Sandh GU15 ... 65 B4
Trinity C of E Sch. Esher KT10 ... 55 A7
Trinity Cl. Crawl RH10 ... 202 C8
Trinity Cl. Hounsl TW4 ... 4 E3
Trinity Cl. S Croy CR2 ... 61 E2
Trinity Cl. Stan TW19 ... 2 C1
Trinity Cotts. Rich TW9 ... 6 F6
Trinity Cres. Up Toot SW17 ... 21 A6
Trinity Ct. Croy CR0 ... 61 C8
Trinity Ct. For Hil SE23 ... 23 C5
Trinity Ct. Thorn H SE25 ... 42 E3
Trinity Ct. Twick TW2 ... 16 E6
Trinity Fields. Hale GU9 ... 125 A6
Trinity Hill. Hale GU9 ... 125 A6
Trinity Mews. Penge SE20 ... 43 B8
Trinity Par. Hounsl TW3 ... 5 B4
Trinity Rd. Knaph GU21 ... 68 B1
Trinity Rd. Rich TW9 ... 6 F4
Trinity Rd. Up Toot SW17 & SW18 ... 20 E7
Trinity Rd. Wands SW17 & SW18 ... 20 E7
Trinity Rd. Wimble SW19 ... 20 A2
Trinity Rise. Streat SE24 & SW2 ... 22 B8
Trinity St. Croy CR9 ... 62 C8
Trinity St Mary's (C of E) Prim Sch.
  Up Toot SW17 ... 21 A7
Tristram Rd. Catf BR1 ... 24 F4
Tritton Ave. Wallin CR0 ... 60 E6
Tritton Rd. W Norw SE21 & SE27 ... 22 D5
Trittons. Tadw KT20 ... 97 D6
Triumph Cl. Harl UB7 ... 3 C6
Trodd's La. Merrow GU1 & GU4 ... 110 E1
Trojan Way. Croy CR0 ... 60 F7
Troon Cl. Crawl RH11 ... 200 D5
Troon Ct. Ascot SL5 ... 29 C4
Troston Ct. Stain TW18 ... 12 F3
Trotsworth Ave. Vir W GU25 ... 31 E5
Trotsworth Ct. Vir W GU25 ... 31 D5
Trotters La. Chobh GU24 ... 51 A8
Trotwood Cl. Sandh GU15 ... 45 E2
Trout Rd. Shottm GU27 ... 207 E6
Troutbeck Wlk. Friml GU15 ... 66 D3
Trowers Way. Redh RH1 ... 119 B4
Trowlock Ave. Tedd TW11 ... 17 C2
Trowlock Way. Tedd TW11 ... 17 D2
Troy La. Eden TN8 ... 144 F4
Troy Rd. S Norw SE19 ... 22 D2
Trumpeters Inn. Rich TW9 ... 6 C2
Trumpetshill Rd. Reig RH2 ... 138 B7
Trumps Green Cl. Thorpe GU25 ... 31 E4
Trumps Green Cty Fst Sch.
  Went GU25 ... 31 D3
Trumps Mill La. Longc GU25 ... 31 F4
Trumps Mill La. Thorpe GU25 ... 31 F4
Trumpsgreen Ave. Went GU25 ... 31 D3
Trumpsgreen Rd. Vir W GU25 ... 31 D3
Trundle Mead. Horsh RH12 ... 217 C5
Trunk Rd. W Heath GU14 ... 84 C5
Trunley Heath Rd. Shalf GU5 ... 151 C8
Truslove Rd. W Norw SE27 ... 22 B3
Truss Hill Rd. Ascot SL5 ... 29 C4
Trust Wlk. Streat SE21 ... 22 B7
Trys Hill. Longc KT16 ... 51 A8
Trystings Cl. Clayg KT10 ... 56 A4
Tucker Rd. Ottsh KT16 ... 51 D4
Tuckers Dr. Cran GU6 ... 174 B3
Tuckey Gr. Send M GU23 ... 90 F3
Tudor Ave. Hampt TW12 ... 16 A1
Tudor Ave. N Cheam KT4 ... 58 B6
Tudor Circ. Farnc GU7 ... 150 E7
Tudor Cl. Ashf TW15 ... 13 E4
Tudor Cl. Cheam SM3 ... 58 E4
Tudor Cl. Chess KT9 ... 56 E5
Tudor Cl. Cobham KT11 ... 73 F6
Tudor Cl. Coulsd CR5 ... 80 A1
Tudor Cl. E Grins RH19 ... 205 F8
Tudor Cl. Graysh GU26 ... 188 D2
Tudor Cl. Hampt TW12 ... 16 C3
Tudor Cl. Hams Gn GU22 ... 81 B4
Tudor Cl. L Book KT23 ... 94 A3
Tudor Cl. Nork SM7 ... 77 E4
Tudor Cl. Smallf RH6 ... 162 B3

Tudor Cl. Wallin SM6 ... 60 C3
Tudor Cl. Woki RG11 ... 25 F5
Tudor Cl. Woking GU22 ... 70 A2
Tudor Cl. Worth RH10 ... 202 D5
Tudor Ct. Farnc GU7 ... 150 E5
Tudor Ct. Felt TW13 ... 15 C4
Tudor Ct. 12 Redh RH1 ... 119 A2
Tudor Ct. Stan TW19 ... 2 E1
Tudor Ct. Tedd TW11 ... 16 F2
Tudor Dr. King U T KT2 ... 17 E3
Tudor Dr. W Barn SM4 ... 39 E3
Tudor Dr. Walt O T KT12 ... 35 D1
Tudor Gdns. Mortl SW13 & SW14 ... 7 E4
Tudor Gdns. Twick TW1 ... 16 F2
Tudor Gdns. W Wick BR4 ... 63 C7
Tudor House. Easth RG12 ... 27 B4
Tudor House. Horsh RH13 ... 217 E1
Tudor House. Weyb KT13 ... 53 A4
Tudor La. Old W SL4 ... 11 C8
Tudor Par. Hounsl TW3 ... 5 D5
Tudor Pl. Mitch SW19 ... 20 E1
Tudor Prim Sch. W Barn SM4 ... 39 D2
Tudor Rd. Ashf TW15 ... 14 D2
Tudor Rd. Beck BR3 ... 44 C6
Tudor Rd. Croy CR0 & SE25 ... 43 B4
Tudor Rd. Farnc GU7 ... 150 E5
Tudor Rd. Hampt TW12 ... 16 A1
Tudor Rd. Islew TW3 ... 5 D3
Tudor Rd. King U T KT2 ... 18 A1
Tudor Rd. Penge SE19 ... 22 F1
Tudor Wlk. Leahd KT22 ... 94 F7
Tudor Wlk. 3 Weyb KT13 ... 53 B7
Tudors The. Beck BR3 ... 44 B7
Tuesley Cnr. Godal GU7 ... 150 D3
Tuesley La. Godal GU7 & GU8 ... 150 D1
Tuesley La. Milf GU7 ... 171 C7
Tufton Gdns. E Mole KT8 ... 36 B7
Tugela Rd. Thorn H CR0 ... 42 D3
Tugela St. For Hil SE6 ... 23 F6
Tuggles Plat. Warn RH12 ... 216 E1
Tulip Cl. Croy CR0 ... 43 D1
Tulip Cl. Hampt TW12 ... 15 F2
Tulip Ct. Horsh RH12 ... 217 C4
Tull St. Carsh CR4 ... 40 F7
Tullett Rd. Crawl RH10 ... 202 B2
Tulse Cl. Beck BR3 ... 44 C6
Tulse Hill. Streat SW2 & SE24 ... 22 A8
Tulse Hill Sta. W Norw SE27 ... 22 B6
Tulsemere Rd.
  W Norw SE21 & SE27 ... 22 C6
Tulyar Cl. Burgh K KT20 ... 97 B7
Tumber St. Head KT18 & KT22 ... 96 C2
Tumblewood Rd. Nork SM7 ... 77 E3
Tumbling Bay. Walt O T KT12 ... 35 A3
Tummons Gdns. S Norw SE25 ... 42 E7
Tunbridge Ct. 1 For Hil SE26 ... 23 A5
Tunley Rd. Up Toot SW12 & SW17 ... 21 A6
Tunnel Link Rd. Harm TW6 ... 3 A2
Tunnel Rd. Farnb GU14 ... 84 E1
Tunnel Rd E. Harl TW6 ... 3 B6
Tunnel Rd W. Harm TW6 ... 3 B6
Tunnmeade. Crawl RH11 ... 200 E5
Tunsgate. Guild GU1 ... 130 D7
Tunsgate Sq. Guild GU1 ... 130 D7
Tunstall Cl. 13 Redh TW9 ... 6 F1
Tunstall Rd. Croy CR0 ... 42 E1
Tunstall Wlk. 10 Brent TW8 ... 6 E8
Tunworth Cres. Rhampt SW15 ... 7 F1
Tupwood La. Cater CR3 ... 101 A1
Tupwood Scrubbs Rd.
  Cater CR3 & RH9 ... 121 A8
Turf Hill Rd. Camb GU15 ... 65 F8
Turfhouse La. Burrh GU24 ... 49 E2
Turkey Oak Cl. S Norw SE19 ... 42 E8
Turle Rd. Thorn H SW16 ... 41 E7
Turnberry. Easth RG12 ... 26 E2
Turner Ave. Mitch CR4 ... 40 F8
Turner Ave. Twick TW2 ... 16 C5
Turner Cl. Bigg H TN16 ... 83 C7
Turner Ct. E Grins RH19 ... 186 A3
Turner Ct. Godal GU7 ... 150 E4
Turner House. Bear Gn RH5 ... 157 C4
Turner Lodge. 10 Putney SW19 ... 19 D7
Turner Pl. Sandh GU15 ... 64 D6
Turner Rd. New Mal KT3 ... 38 D2
Turner's Hill Rd. E Grins RH19 ... 205 B6
Turners Cl. Stain TW18 ... 13 B3
Turners Hill CE (Controlled) Sch.
  Turn H RH10 ... 204 A3
Turners Hill Rd. Copth RH10 ... 183 F2
Turners Hill Rd. Crawl D RH10 ... 204 A7
Turners Hill Rd. Turn H RH10 ... 203 F5
Turners Hill Rd. Worth RH10 ... 203 D5
Turners La. Whit V KT12 ... 54 B3
Turners Mead. Chidd GU8 ... 191 C3
Turners Meadow Way. Beck BR3 ... 43 F8
Turners Way. Croy CR0 & CR9 ... 61 A8
Turney Rd. Dulw SE21 ... 22 D8
Turney Sch. W Norw SE21 ... 22 D8
Turnham Cl. Guild GU2 ... 130 C5
Turnoak Ave. Woking GU22 ... 89 E7
Turnoak Cnr. Woking GU22 ... 89 E8
Turnoak La. Woking GU22 ... 89 E8
Turnpike La. Sutton SM1 ... 59 C5
Turnpike Link. S Croy CR0 ... 61 E8
Turnpike Pl. Crawl RH11 ... 201 D8
Turnpike Rd. Binf RG12 ... 26 D7
Turnstone Cl. Selsd CR0 & CR2 ... 62 E1
Turnville Rd. Lhtwat GU18 ... 48 A1
Turpin Rd. Felt TW14 ... 3 F1
Turpin Way. Wallin SM6 ... 60 B3
Turpins Rise. Windl GU20 ... 48 B6
Turret Ct. E Grins RH19 ... 185 C3
Turret House. King U T KT2 ... 17 E2
Turville Ct. G Book KT23 ... 94 B3
Tuscam Way. Camb GU15 ... 64 F4
Tushmore Ave.
  Crawl RH10 & RH11 ... 181 E1
Tushmore La.
  Crawl RH10 & RH11 ... 201 E8

Tushmore Rdbt. Crawl RH11 ... 201 D8
Tussock Cl. Crawl RH11 ... 201 A4
Tweed Cl. W Heath GU14 ... 84 E6
Tweed La. Brock RH3 ... 137 B5
Tweed La. Rusper RH11 ... 180 F1
Tweed Rd. Bra Hil SL3 ... 1 B8
Tweeddale Inf Sch. Carsh SM5 ... 40 D2
Tweeddale Jun Sch. Carsh SM5 ... 40 D2
Tweeddale Rd. Carsh SM5 ... 40 D1
Tweedsmuir Cl. Farnb GU14 ... 84 D3
Tweedy Rd. Broml BR1 ... 44 F1
Twelve Acre Cl. L Book KT23 ... 93 F3
Twelve Acre Cres. W Heath GU14 ... 84 E4
Twickenham Bridge. Twick TW9 ... 6 C2
Twickenham Cl. Wallin CR0 ... 60 F7
Twickenham Golf Course.
  Hampt TW12 ... 16 B4
Twickenham Rd. Felt TW13 ... 15 E5
Twickenham Rd. Islew TW1 & TW7 ... 6 A4
Twickenham Rd. Rich TW1 & TW9 ... 6 C3
Twickenham Rd. Tedd TW11 ... 17 A4
Twickenham Rugby Football Union
  Gd. Twick TW2 ... 5 E1
Twickenham Sta. Twick TW1 ... 16 F8
Twickenham Trad Ctr. Islew TW1 ... 5 F1
Twilley St. Wands SW18 ... 20 B8
Twining Ave. Twick TW2 ... 16 C5
Twinoaks. Cobham KT11 ... 74 A6
Twitten La. Felb RH19 ... 184 E4
Two Oaks. Weyb KT13 ... 53 B6
Two Ways. Loxwd RH14 ... 213 A4
Twycross Rd. Farnc GU7 ... 150 D7
Twyford La. Wreccl GU10 ... 146 B6
Twyford Par. Tolw KT6 ... 38 A1
Twyford Rd. Carsh SM5 ... 40 D1
Twyford Rd. Woki RG11 ... 25 B8
Twyne Cl. Crawl RH11 ... 200 F4
Twyner Cl. Horley RH6 ... 161 D4
Tybenham Rd. Merton SW19 ... 40 A6
Tychbourne Dr. Merrow GU4 ... 110 C4
Tydcombe Rd. Warlgm CR6 ... 101 D8
Tyers House. 1 Streat SW16 ... 21 C3
Tylden Way. Horsh RH12 ... 217 F6
Tylecroft Rd. Thorn H SW16 ... 41 E7
Tylehost. Stough GU2 ... 109 A5
Tyler Gdns. Addl KT15 ... 52 C6
Tyler Rd. Crawl RH10 ... 201 D3
Tylers Cl. Tyl Gn RH9 ... 121 B5
Tylers Path. Carsh SM5 ... 59 F6
Tylney Ave. Dulw SE19 ... 22 F3
Tymperley Ct. Horsh RH13 ... 217 E3
Tynamara. King U T KT1 ... 37 D5
Tynan Cl. E Bed TW14 ... 15 A7
Tyndalls Estate. Hind GU26 ... 188 F4
Tyne Cl. W Heath GU14 ... 84 E6
Tyne Cl. Worth RH10 ... 202 C5
Tynedale Rd. Brock RH3 ... 137 B5
Tynemouth Rd. Mitch CR4 ... 21 A1
Tynley Gr. Jacobs GU4 ... 109 D7
Tynwald House. 14
  For Hil SE26 ... 23 A5
Tyrell Cl. Carsh SM5 ... 59 F6
Tyrolean Ct. Banstd SM7 ... 78 B4
Tyrrell House. Catf BR3 ... 24 B3
Tyrrell Sq. Mitch CR4 ... 40 E8
Tyrrell's Wood Golf Course.
  Head KT22 ... 95 F2
Tyrwhitt Ave. Stough GU2 ... 109 B5
Tyson Rd. For Hil SE23 ... 23 C8
Tythebarn Cl. Burph GU4 ... 110 B6
Tythebarns La. Ripley GU23 ... 91 B1
Tythebarns La. Send M GU23 ... 91 B1
Tytherton. Brack RG12 ... 27 C7

Uckfield Rd. Mitch CR4 ... 41 A8
Udney Park Rd. Tedd TW11 ... 17 A2
Uffington Dr. Brack RG12 ... 27 E5
Uffington Rd. W Norw SE27 ... 22 A4
Ujima Ct. Streat SW16 ... 21 E4
Ujima House. Streat SW16 ... 21 E4
Ullathorne Rd. Streat SW16 ... 21 C4
Ullswater. Brack RG12 ... 26 F2
Ullswater Ave. Farnb GU14 ... 84 E3
Ullswater Cl. Broml BR1 ... 24 E1
Ullswater Cl. Hale GU9 ... 125 A6
Ullswater Cl.
  King U T KT2 & SW15 ... 18 D4
Ullswater Cres. Coulsd CR5 ... 79 E3
Ullswater Cres. King U T SW15 ... 18 D4
Ullswater Rd. Lhtwat GU18 ... 48 B1
Ullswater Rd.
  W Norw SE21 & SW16 ... 22 B6
Ulstan Cl. Wold CR3 ... 102 A4
Ulster Ct. King U T KT2 ... 17 D2
Ulverstone Rd. W Norw SE27 ... 22 B6
Ulwyn Ave. Byfl KT14 ... 71 E5
Underhill Cl. Godal GU7 ... 150 E3
Underhill La.
  M Bourn GU10 & GU9 ... 146 B7
Underhill Park Rd. Reig RH2 ... 118 A4
Underhill Rd. Dulw SE21 & SE22 ... 23 B8
Underhill Rd. Newd RH5 ... 158 B1
Undershaw Rd. Catf BR1 ... 24 F5
Underwood. Easth RG12 ... 26 E3
Underwood. New Add CR0 ... 63 C5
Underwood Ave. Ash GU12 ... 105 F1
Underwood Cl. Crawl D RH10 ... 204 B8
Underwood Cl. Cater CR3 ... 100 F2
Underwood Cl. Cater CR3 ... 100 F2
Underwood Rd. Shottm GU27 ... 207 F7
Undine St. Up Toot SW17 ... 20 F3
Unicorn Sch. Rich TW9 ... 6 F6
Union Cl. Sandh GU15 ... 45 E2
Union Ct. 2 Rich TW10 ... 6 E2
Union Rd. Farnh GU9 ... 125 C2
Union Rd. Friml GU16 ... 86 D8
Union Rd. Thorn H CR0 ... 42 C2
Union St. Alder GU11 ... 105 A2
Union St. Farnb GU14 ... 85 B4
Union St. King U T KT1 ... 37 D7

Union St. Pirb GU24 ... 87 A6
Unity Cl. New Add CR0 ... 63 B2
Unity Cl. W Norw SE19 & SE27 ... 22 C3
Univ of Greenwich The.
  Rhampt SW15 ... 19 A8
University Rd. Mitch SW19 ... 20 D2
Unstead La. Shalf GU5 ... 151 C7
Unstead Wood. Shalf GU3 ... 130 C1
Unwin Ave. Hatton TW14 ... 3 D2
Unwin Rd. Islew TW7 ... 5 E4
Upavon Gdns. Brack RG12 ... 27 F4
Upchurch Cl. Penge SE20 ... 23 B1
Updown Hill. Windl GU20 ... 48 D4
Upfield. Horley RH6 ... 161 A1
Upfield. S Croy CR0 & CR9 ... 62 B7
Upfield Cl. Horley RH6 ... 161 A1
Upfold Cl. Cran GU6 ... 174 B5
Upfold La. Cran GU6 ... 174 C5
Upfolds Gn. Burph GU4 ... 110 C5
Upgrove Manor Way. 12
  Streat SE24 ... 22 A8
Upland Ct. For Hil SE23 ... 23 C6
Upland Rd. Camb GU15 ... 65 D7
Upland Rd. S Croy CR2 ... 61 D5
Upland Rd. Dulw SE21 & SE22 ... 23 A8
Upland Rd. Sutton SM2 ... 59 D3
Upland Rd. Wold CR3 ... 102 B7
Upland Way. Burgh KT18 ... 77 C1
Uplands. Ashtd KT21 & KT22 ... 95 D7
Uplands. Beck BR3 ... 44 A7
Uplands. Warlgm CR6 ... 81 F1
Uplands Cl. Haslem GU27 ... 208 D8
Uplands Cl. Mortl SW14 ... 7 B2
Uplands Cl. Sandh GU17 ... 64 B8
Uplands Dr. Oxsh KT22 ... 74 D7
Uplands Prim Sch. Sandh GU17 ... 64 B8
Uplands Rd. Kenley CR8 ... 80 C2
Uplands Rd. M Bourn GU9 ... 125 E1
Uppark Gdns. Horsh RH12 ... 217 F6
Upper Beulah Hill. S Norw SE19 ... 42 E8
Upper Bourne La. Rowl GU10 ... 146 B5
Upper Bourne Vale.
  Rowl GU10 ... 146 A5
Upper Bridge Rd. Redh RH1 ... 118 F1
Upper Brighton Rd. Surb KT6 ... 37 E2
Upper Broadmoor Rd.
  Crowth RG11 ... 45 D5
Upper Butts. Brent TW8 ... 6 C8
Upper Charles St. Camb GU15 ... 65 C6
Upper Chobham Rd.
  Friml GU15 & GU16 ... 66 B4
Upper Church La. 11
  Farnh GU9 ... 125 B2
Upper Cl. For Row RH18 ... 206 F2
Upper College Rd. Camb GU15 ... 65 E8
Upper Court Rd. Epsom KT19 ... 76 C8
Upper Court Rd. Wold CR3 ... 102 A3
Upper Dr. Bigg H TN16 ... 83 C1
Upper Dunnymans. 6
  Banstd SM7 ... 77 F5
Upper Edgeborough Rd.
  Guild GU1 ... 130 F8
Upper Elmers End Rd.
  Beck BR3 ... 43 E4
Upper Elms Rd. Alder GU11 ... 105 A1
Upper Fairfield Rd. Leahd KT22 ... 95 B6
Upper Farm L Pk. Box H KT20 ... 115 F3
Upper Farm Rd. E Mole KT8 ... 35 F5
Upper Forecourt. Crawl RH6 ... 182 B7
Upper Gn E. Mitch CR4 ... 40 F6
Upper Gn E. Mitch CR4 ... 41 A6
Upper Gn W. Mitch CR4 ... 40 F7
Upper Gordon Rd. Camb GU15 ... 65 D5
Upper Gr. S Norw SE25 ... 42 F5
Upper Grotto Rd. Twick TW1 ... 16 F6
Upper Guildown Rd.
  Guild GU2 ... 130 C6
Upper Hale Rd. Hale GU9 ... 125 C6
Upper Halliford Halt.
  Up Hall TW17 ... 34 E7
Upper Halliford Rd.
  Up Hall TW17 ... 34 E6
Upper Ham Rd. Rich KT2 & TW10 ... 17 D4
Upper Harestone. Cater CR3 ... 121 A8
Upper High St. Epsom KT17 ... 76 E6
Upper House La. Sham Gn GU5 ... 152 F1
Upper Manor Rd. Farnc GU7 ... 150 E6
Upper Manor Rd. Milf GU8 ... 149 F1
Upper Mount. Grays GU27 ... 208 C6
Upper Mulgrave Rd. Belm SM2 ... 58 E3
Upper Nursery. Sunnin SL5 ... 30 A4
Upper Old Park La. Hale GU9 ... 125 A5
Upper Park Rd. Camb GU15 ... 65 E6
Upper Park Rd. King U T KT2 ... 18 A2
Upper Pillory Down. Wallin SM5 ... 79 A7
Upper Pinewood Rd.
  Normdy GU12 ... 106 D3
Upper Rd. Wallin SM6 ... 60 E5
Upper Richmond Rd. Mortl SW15 ... 7 F3
Upper Richmond Rd W.
  Mortl TW10 & SW14 & SW15 ... 7 C3
Upper Rose Hill. Dork RH4 ... 136 B6
Upper Sawleywood. 3
  Banstd SM7 ... 77 F5
Upper Selsdon Rd. S Croy CR2 ... 62 A2
Upper Shirley Rd.
  S Croy CR0 & CR9 ... 62 D7
Upper South View. Farnh GU9 ... 125 C3
Upper Springfield. East GU8 ... 148 B3
Upper Sq. For Row RH18 ... 206 E3
Upper Sq. Islew TW7 ... 6 A4
Upper St. Shere GU5 ... 133 A4
Upper St Michael's Rd.
  Alder GU11 ... 126 B8
Upper Staithe. Chisw W4 ... 7 C6
Upper Stanford Rd. Pirb GU24 ... 87 F1
Upper Sunbury Rd.
  Hampt TW12 ... 36 A8
Upper Sutton La. Heston TW5 ... 5 A6
Upper Teddington Rd.
  Tedd KT1 & KT8 ... 37 C8

Upper Terrace Rd. Farnb GU14 ... 105 A8
Upper Tooting Independent High
  Sch. Up Toot SW17 ... 20 F6
Upper Tooting Park Mansions. 1
  Up Toot SW17 ... 21 A6
Upper Tooting Pk.
  Up Toot SW17 ... 20 F6
Upper Tooting Rd.
  Up Toot SW17 ... 20 F5
Upper Tulse Hill. Streat SW2 ... 21 F8
Upper Union St. Alder GU11 ... 105 A2
Upper Union Terr. Alder GU11 ... 105 A2
Upper Vann La. Hambl GU8 ... 172 A1
Upper Vernon Rd. Carsh SM1 ... 59 D5
Upper Verran Rd. Camb GU15 ... 65 D3
Upper Village Rd. Ascot SL5 ... 29 D4
Upper Warlingham Sta.
  Warlgm CR6 ... 81 A1
Upper Way. M Bourn GU9 ... 146 B8
Upper West St. Reig RH2 ... 117 F1
Upper Weybourne La.
  Heath E GU9 ... 125 E7
Upper Wlk. Thorpe GU25 ... 31 E5
Upper Woodcote Village.
  Purley CR8 ... 79 D7
Upperton Rd. Guild GU2 ... 130 C7
Upshire Gdns. Brack RG12 ... 27 F5
Upshott La. Mayb GU22 ... 70 F2
Upton. Woking GU21 ... 69 B2
Upton Cl. Farnb GU14 ... 85 D3
Upton Ct. Penge SE20 ... 23 C1
Upton Ct. 4 Wimble SW19 ... 19 D1
Upton Dene. Belm SM2 ... 59 B3
Upton Rd. Hounsl TW3 ... 5 A4
Upton Rd. S Norw CR7 ... 42 D7
Upwood Rd. Thorn H SW16 ... 41 E8
Urmston Dr. Putney SW19 ... 19 E7
Urquhart Ct. Beck BR3 ... 23 F1
Ursuline Convent Prep Sch.
  Wimble SW19 ... 19 D1
Ursuline Convent Sch.
  Wimble SW20 ... 39 D8
Usherwood Cl. Box H KT20 ... 116 C4
Uvedale Cl. New Add CR0 ... 82 D8
Uvedale Cres. New Add CR0 ... 82 E8
Uvedale Rd. Limps RH8 ... 122 F5
Uxbridge Rd. Felt TW13 ... 15 D6
Uxbridge Rd.
  Hampt TW12 & TW13 ... 16 B3
Uxbridge Rd. King U T KT1 & KT6 ... 37 D4

Vachery La. Cran GU6 ... 194 E7
Vaillant Rd. Weyb KT13 ... 53 C6
Valan Leas. Beck BR2 ... 44 E6
Vale Cl. Coulsd CR5 ... 79 E5
Vale Cl. Horse GU21 ... 69 E3
Vale Cl. M Bourn GU10 ... 146 C4
Vale Cl. Oat Pk KT13 ... 53 D7
Vale Cl. Twick TW1 ... 17 A5
Vale Cres. King U T SW15 ... 18 E4
Vale Croft. Clayg KT10 ... 55 F2
Vale Ct. Oat Pk KT13 ... 53 D7
Vale Dr. Horsh RH12 ... 217 B3
Vale Farm Rd. Woking GU21 ... 69 E2
Vale House. Woking GU21 ... 69 E2
Vale Lodge. For Hil SE23 ... 23 C6
Vale Rd. Ash V GU12 ... 106 A5
Vale Rd. Camb GU15 ... 65 A4
Vale Rd. Clayg KT10 ... 55 F3
Vale Rd. Mitch CR4 ... 41 D5
Vale Rd. Oat Pk KT13 ... 53 D7
Vale Rd. Sutton SM1 ... 59 B6
Vale Rd. Worc Pk KT19 & KT4 ... 57 F7
Vale Rd N. Surb KT6 ... 56 E8
Vale Rd S. Ashf TW16 ... 15 A2
Vale The. Coulsd CR5 & CR8 ... 79 E5
Vale The. Croy CR0 ... 62 D8
Vale The. Felt TW14 ... 4 B1
Vale The. Heston TW5 ... 4 E8
Vale Wood Dr. M Bourn GU10 ... 146 C4
Vale Wood La. Graysh GU26 ... 188 C4
Valens House. 1 Streat SW2 ... 22 A7
Valentine Ct. For Hil SE23 ... 23 D6
Valentyne Cl. New Add CR0 ... 82 E8
Valerie Ct. Sutton SM2 ... 59 B3
Valeswood Rd. Catf BR1 ... 24 F3
Valewood Rd. Fern GU27 ... 208 C4
Valiant Way. Farnb GU14 ... 104 D8
Valley Cres. Woki RG11 ... 25 A8
Valley Ct. Cater CR3 ... 101 A3
Valley End C of E Inf Sch.
  Burrh GU24 ... 49 A4
Valley End Rd. Burrh GU24 ... 49 B4
Valley Gdns. Mitch SW19 ... 20 D1
Valley La. M Bourn GU9 ... 146 C2
Valley Mews. Twick TW1 ... 17 A6
Valley Pl. Surb KT6 ... 37 E3
Valley Prim Sch. Broml BR2 ... 44 F7
Valley Prospect. 3
  W Norw SE19 ... 22 E2
Valley Rd. Beck BR2 ... 44 E7
Valley Rd. Friml GU16 ... 86 B8
Valley Rd. Kenley CR3 & CR8 ... 80 D4
Valley Rd. Streat SW16 ... 21 F4
Valley The. Guild GU2 ... 130 C5
Valley View. Bigg H TN16 ... 83 D1
Valley View. Godal GU7 ... 150 D4
Valley View Gdns. Kenley CR8 ... 80 E4
Valley Wlk. Croy CR0 ... 62 C8
Valleyfield Rd. Streat SW16 ... 21 F3
Vallis Way. Chess KT9 ... 56 D6
Valnay St. Up Toot SW17 ... 20 F3
Valornus. Merst RH1 ... 119 B5
Valroy Cl. Camb GU15 ... 65 D6
Van Dyck Ave. New Mal KT3 ... 38 D2
Vanborough Ct. Sutton SM2 ... 59 C4
Vanbrugh Cl. Crawl RH11 ... 200 E3

Vanbrugh Dr. Walt O T KT12 ...... 35 C3
Vancouver Cl. Epsom KT19 ...... 76 C3
Vancouver Ct. Smallf RH6 ...... 162 A3
Vancouver Dr. Crawl RH11 ...... 181 D1
Vancouver Rd. For Hil SE23 ...... 23 E6
Vancouver Rd. Rich TW10 ...... 17 C4
Vanderbilt Rd. Wands SW18 ...... 20 C7
Vandyke. Easth RG12 ...... 26 E3
Vandyke Cl. Redh RH1 ...... 118 F3
Vandyke Cl. Putney SW15 ...... 19 D8
Vanfame Ct. New Mal KT3 ...... 38 F6
Vanguard Cl. Thorn H CR0 ...... 42 B1
Vanguard House. [7]
  Merton SW19 ...... 20 C1
Vanguard House. [5] Stan TW19 .. 2 E1
Vanguard Way. Wallin SM6 ...... 60 E3
Vann Farm Rd. Ockley RH5 ...... 177 E4
Vann La. Chidd GU8 ...... 191 E4
Vann La. Hambl GU8 ...... 171 D1
Vann Lake. Ockley RH5 ...... 177 F3
Vann Lake Rd. Ockley RH5 ...... 178 A4
Vanners. Crawl RH10 ...... 201 E7
Vant Rd. Up Toot SW17 ...... 20 F3
Vapery La. Pirb GU24 ...... 87 D6
Varley Way. Mitch CR4 ...... 40 D7
Varna Rd. Hampt TW12 ...... 36 B8
Varney Cl. W Heath GU14 ...... 84 E5
Varsity Dr. Islew TW1 & TW7 ...... 5 F1
Varsity Row. Mortl SW14 ...... 7 C5
Varsity Track. Farnb GU11 ...... 104 C7
Vaughan Almshouses.
  Ashf TW15 ...... 14 B3
Vaughan Rd. Thame D KT7 ...... 37 B2
Vaughan Way. Dork RH4 ...... 136 A7
Vaux Cres. Hersh KT12 ...... 54 B4
Vauxhall Gdns. Croy CR2 ...... 61 C4
Veals Mead. Mitch CR4 ...... 40 E8
Vectis Gdns. Mitch SW17 ...... 21 B2
Vectis Rd. Mitch SW17 ...... 21 B2
Vegal Cres. Eng Gn TW20 ...... 11 C3
Vellum Dr. Hackb SM5 ...... 60 A7
Venita Manor. W Norw SE27 ...... 22 A3
Venner Rd. For Hil SE20 & SE26 .. 23 C3
Venner Rd. Penge SE20 & SE26 .. 23 C3
Ventnor Rd. Sutton SM2 ...... 59 B3
Ventnor Terr. Alder GU12 ...... 105 C1
Venton Cl. Woking GU21 ...... 69 B2
Verbania Way. E Grins RH19 .. 186 B1
Verdant Ct. [3] Catf SE6 ...... 24 E8
Verdant La. Catf SE6 ...... 24 E7
Verdayne Ave. Croy CR0 & CR9 .. 62 D8
Verdayne Gdns. Warlgm CR6 ..... 81 C3
Vere Bank. Wands SW19 ...... 19 F7
Vereker Dr. Sunby TW16 ...... 35 A6
Vermont Rd. S Norw SE19 ...... 22 E2
Vermont Rd. Sutton SM1 ...... 59 B7
Verney House. Hounsl TW3 ...... 5 C3
Vernon Ave. Merton SW20 ...... 39 D7
Vernon Cl. Horsh RH12 ...... 218 A4
Vernon Cl. Ottsh KT16 ...... 51 D4
Vernon Cl. W Ewell KT19 ...... 57 C4
Vernon Cl. W Ewell KT19 ...... 57 C4
Vernon Ct. Farnh GU9 ...... 125 A2
Vernon Dr. Cater CR3 ...... 100 C5
Vernon Dr. N Asct SL5 ...... 28 E7
Vernon Rd. Felt TW13 ...... 14 F6
Vernon Rd. Mortl SW14 ...... 7 D4
Vernon Rd. Sutton SM1 ...... 59 D5
Vernon Way. Stough GU2 ...... 108 F2
Vernon Wlk. Tadw KT20 ...... 97 D7
Verona Dr. Surb KT6 ...... 56 E8
Veronica Gdns.
  Mitch CR4 & SW16 ...... 41 C8
Veronica Rd. Up Toot SW17 ...... 21 B6
Verralls. Mayb GU22 ...... 70 B2
Verran Rd. Balham SW12 ...... 21 B8
Verran Rd. Camb GU15 ...... 65 D3
Versailles Rd. Penge SE20 ...... 23 A1
Verulam Ave. Purley CR8 ...... 79 C7
Veryan. Woking GU21 ...... 69 A2
Vesey Cl. W Heath GU14 ...... 85 A5
Vestris Rd. For Hil SE23 ...... 23 D6
Vevers Rd. Dovgn RH2 ...... 139 C6
Vevey St. For Hil SE23 & SE6 ...... 23 F6
Vibart Gdns. Streat SW2 ...... 21 F8
Viburnum Ct. W End GU24 ...... 67 E6
Vicarage Ave. Egham TW20 ...... 12 B3
Vicarage Cl. Kings KT20 ...... 97 E3
Vicarage Cl. L Book KT23 ...... 94 A2
Vicarage Cl. Lingf RH7 ...... 164 D4
Vicarage Cl. M Bourn GU9 ...... 146 D7
Vicarage Cres. Egham TW20 ...... 12 B3
Vicarage Ct. Beck BR3 ...... 43 E6
Vicarage Ct. E Bed TW14 ...... 14 C8
Vicarage Ct. Egham TW20 ...... 12 B2
Vicarage Ct. [8] Rhampt SW15 ... 19 A8
Vicarage Dr. Beck BR3 ...... 44 A8
Vicarage Dr. Mortl SW14 ...... 7 D2
Vicarage Farm Ct. Heston TW5 .... 4 F7
Vicarage Farm Rd.
  Heston TW3 & TW4 & TW5 ...... 4 E6
Vicarage Farm Rd.
  Hounsl TW3 & TW4 & TW5 ...... 4 E6
Vicarage Fields. Walt O T KT12 .. 35 C3
Vicarage Gate. Onsl V GU2 ...... 130 A7
Vicarage Gdns. Ascot SL5 ...... 29 A4
Vicarage Gdns. Graysh GU26 .. 188 C3
Vicarage Gdns. Mitch CR4 ...... 40 E6
Vicarage Gdns. Mortl SW14 ...... 7 D2
Vicarage Hill.
  M Bourn GU8 & GU9 ...... 146 D7
Vicarage House. [1] King U T KT1 37 F7
Vicarage La. Capel RH5 ...... 178 D6
Vicarage La. Farnh GU9 ...... 125 B2
Vicarage La. Heath E GU9 ...... 125 C7
Vicarage La. Horley RH6 ...... 160 F4
Vicarage La. Laleh TW18 ...... 33 C6

Vicarage La. Leahd KT22 ...... 95 B5
Vicarage La. M Bourn GU9 ...... 146 D7
Vicarage La. Send GU23 ...... 90 D1
Vicarage La. Shottm GU27 ...... 207 F6
Vicarage La. Wray TW19 ...... 11 F7
Vicarage Rd. Ashf TW16 ...... 14 F2
Vicarage Rd. Bagsh GU19 & GU20 47 C3
Vicarage Rd. Chobh GU24 ...... 68 E3
Vicarage Rd. Crawl D RH10 ...... 204 A8
Vicarage Rd. Croy CR0 & CR9 .... 61 A7
Vicarage Rd. Egham TW20 ...... 12 B3
Vicarage Rd. Hawley GU17 ...... 64 E4
Vicarage Rd. King U T KT1 & KT2 37 D7
Vicarage Rd. Lingf RH7 ...... 164 D4
Vicarage Rd. Mortl SW14 ...... 7 D2
Vicarage Rd. Stain TW18 ...... 12 E5
Vicarage Rd. Sutton SM1 ...... 59 B7
Vicarage Rd. Tedd TW11 ...... 17 A3
Vicarage Rd. Tedd KT1 & KT8 .... 37 C8
Vicarage Rd. Twick TW2 ...... 5 C1
Vicarage Rd. Twick TW2 ...... 16 E6
Vicarage Rd. Westfd GU22 ...... 89 F6
Vicarage Way. Coln SL3 ...... 1 D7
Vicars Oak Rd. W Norw SE19 .... 22 E2
Viceroy Ct. [5] Croy CR0 ...... 42 D1
Viceroy Lodge. [6] King U T KT6 . 37 E4
Vickers Ct. [9] Stan TW19 ...... 2 E1
Vickers Dr N. Byfl KT13 ...... 52 E1
Vickers Dr S. Byfl KT13 ...... 71 E8
Victor Ct. Crawl RH10 ...... 182 D1
Victor Rd. Penge SE20 ...... 23 D1
Victor Rd. Tedd TW11 ...... 16 E4
Victor Seymour Inf Sch.
  Carsh SM5 ...... 59 F6
Victor Way. Farnb GU14 ...... 104 D8
Victoria Almshouses. [4]
  Redh RH1 ...... 119 A4
Victoria Almshouses. [1]
  Reig RH2 ...... 118 C1
Victoria Ave. Camb GU15 ...... 65 A5
Victoria Ave. E Mole KT8 ...... 36 B6
Victoria Ave. Hackb SM5 & SM6 .. 60 A7
Victoria Ave. Hounsl TW3 & TW4 .. 5 A2
Victoria Ave. King U T KT1 ...... 37 D3
Victoria Ave. S Croy CR2 ...... 61 C1
Victoria Cl. E Mole KT8 ...... 36 A6
Victoria Cl. Horley RH6 ...... 161 A3
Victoria Cl. Oat Pk KT13 ...... 53 D7
Victoria Cotts. [7] Rich TW9 ...... 7 A6
Victoria Cres. Merton SW19 ...... 19 F1
Victoria Cres. S Norw SE19 ...... 22 E2
Victoria Ct. Bagsh GU19 ...... 47 E1
Victoria Ct. Guild GU1 ...... 130 D8
Victoria Ct. Horsh RH13 ...... 217 D2
Victoria Ct. Penge SE26 ...... 23 C2
Victoria Dr. Blckw GU17 ...... 64 C4
Victoria Dr.
  Putney SW15 & SW19 ...... 19 D7
Victoria Entertainments Ctr The.
  Woking GU21 ...... 69 E2
Victoria Gdns. Bigg H TN16 ...... 83 C4
Victoria Gdns. Heston TW5 ...... 4 E6
Victoria Jun Sch The.
  Felt TW13 ...... 15 B7
Victoria La. Harl UB7 ...... 3 D8
Victoria Lodge. Wimble SW19 ... 19 C1
Victoria Pl. [5] Esher KT10 ...... 55 B6
Victoria Pl. Ewell KT17 ...... 76 E7
Victoria Pl. [16] Rich TW10 ...... 6 D2
Victoria Rd. Addl KT15 ...... 52 D6
Victoria Rd. Alder GU11 ...... 105 A2
Victoria Rd. Ascot SL5 ...... 29 A4
Victoria Rd. Coulsd CR5 ...... 79 D4
Victoria Rd. Cran GU6 ...... 174 D3
Victoria Rd. Crawl RH11 ...... 201 C6
Victoria Rd. Earls RH1 ...... 140 A8
Victoria Rd. Farnb GU14 ...... 85 B4
Victoria Rd. Farnh GU9 ...... 125 C2
Victoria Rd. Felt TW13 ...... 15 B6
Victoria Rd. Godal GU7 ...... 150 E4
Victoria Rd. Guild GU1 ...... 109 E1
Victoria Rd. Horley RH6 ...... 161 B2
Victoria Rd. King U T KT6 ...... 37 D3
Victoria Rd. King U T KT1 ...... 37 F7
Victoria Rd. Knaph GU21 ...... 68 E1
Victoria Rd. Mitch CR4 & SW19 .. 20 F1
Victoria Rd. Mortl SW14 ...... 7 D4
Victoria Rd. Oat Pk KT13 ...... 53 D7
Victoria Rd. Sandh GU15 ...... 65 A5
Victoria Rd. Stain TW18 ...... 12 E5
Victoria Rd. Sutton SM1 ...... 59 D5
Victoria Rd. Tedd TW11 ...... 17 A2
Victoria Rd. Twick TW1 ...... 17 B8
Victoria Rd. Woking GU22 ...... 69 F2
Victoria St. Eng Gn TW20 ...... 11 C2
Victoria St. Horsh RH13 ...... 217 D2
Victoria Terr. Dork RH4 ...... 136 A7
Victoria Track. Farnb GU11 ...... 104 E7
Victoria Villas. Rich TW9 ...... 6 F3
Victoria Way. E Grins RH19 ...... 205 F7
Victoria Way. Oat Pk KT13 ...... 53 D7
Victoria Way.
  Woking GU21 & GU22 ...... 69 E2
Victors Dr. Hampt TW12 ...... 15 E2
Victory Ave. Morden SM4 ...... 40 C4
Victory Bsns Ctr The. Islew TW7 . 5 F3
Victory Cotts. Effing KT24 ...... 113 E7
Victory Park Rd. Addl KT15 ...... 52 C6
Victory Pl. S Norw SE19 ...... 22 D2
Victory Rd. Chert KT16 ...... 33 A1
Victory Rd. Horsh RH12 ...... 217 B3
Victory Rd. Merton SW19 ...... 20 C1
Victory Road Mews. [5]
  Merton SW19 ...... 20 C1
Vienna Ct. W Heath GU14 ...... 85 A6
View Cl. Bigg H TN16 ...... 83 C3
View Terr. Dorman RH7 ...... 165 A1
Viewfield Rd. Wands SW18 ...... 19 F8
Viggory La. Horse GU21 ...... 69 C4
Vigilant Cl. For Hil SE26 ...... 23 A4
Viking. Easth RG12 ...... 26 E4

Viking Ct. Hampt TW12 ...... 36 B8
Village Cl. [3] Oat Pk KT13 ...... 53 D7
Village Cl. Ascot SL5 ...... 29 C4
Village Gate. Ewell KT17 ...... 57 F1
Village Gdns. Ewell KT17 ...... 57 F1
Village Green Ave. Bigg H TN16 83 E2
Village Green Way. Bigg H TN16 83 E2
Village Rd. Egham TW20 ...... 32 C6
Village Row. Belm SM2 ...... 59 A3
Village The. Old W SL4 ...... 10 B5
Village The. Ashf TW15 ...... 14 A4
Village Way. Beck BR3 ...... 44 A6
Village Way. Sander CR2 ...... 81 A6
Villas The. Blind H RH7 ...... 163 E8
Villiers Ave. King U T KT5 ...... 37 F5
Villiers Ave. Twick TW2 ...... 15 F7
Villiers Cl. King U T KT5 ...... 37 F5
Villiers Gr. E Ewell SM2 ...... 58 D2
Villiers Mead. Woki RG11 ...... 25 A6
Villiers Rd. Hounsl TW7 ...... 5 E5
Villiers Rd. King U T KT1 ...... 37 F6
Villiers Rd. Penge BR3 ...... 43 D7
Villiers The. Whit V KT13 ...... 53 D4
Vinall Gdns. Broad H RH12 ...... 216 D4
Vincam Cl. Twick TW2 ...... 16 A8
Vincent Ave. Sutton SM5 ...... 78 D8
Vincent Ave. [3] Tolw KT5 ...... 38 B1
Vincent Cl. Chert KT16 ...... 32 E2
Vincent Cl. Esher KT10 ...... 55 B7
Vincent Cl. Harm UB7 ...... 3 A8
Vincent Cl. Horsh RH13 ...... 217 F2
Vincent Dr. Dork RH4 ...... 136 A6
Vincent Dr. Up Hall TW17 ...... 34 E6
Vincent La. Dork RH4 ...... 136 A7
Vincent Rd. Chert KT16 ...... 32 E2
Vincent Rd. Coulsd CR5 ...... 79 C3
Vincent Rd. Croy CR0 ...... 42 E2
Vincent Rd. Dork RH4 ...... 136 A7
Vincent Rd. Hounsl TW4 ...... 4 D4
Vincent Rd. Hounsl TW7 ...... 5 D6
Vincent Rd. New Mal KT3 ...... 38 F5
Vincent Rise. Brack RG12 ...... 27 E6
Vincent Row. Hampt TW12 ...... 16 C3
Vincent Sq. Bigg H TN16 ...... 83 C6
Vincents Cl. Chips CR5 ...... 98 F7
Vine Cl. Farnb GU11 ...... 105 A6
Vine Cl. Rowl GU10 ...... 146 A4
Vine Cl. Stan TW19 ...... 2 A2
Vine Cl. Surb KT5 ...... 37 F3
Vine Cl. Sutton SM1 ...... 59 C7
Vine Cotts. Cran GU6 ...... 174 B3
Vine Ct. Hersh KT12 ...... 54 C4
Vine House Cl. Mytch GU16 ...... 86 A3
Vine La. Rowl GU10 ...... 146 A5
Vine Pl. Hounsl TW3 ...... 5 B3
Vine Rd. Barnes SW13 & SW15 .... 7 F4
Vine Rd. E Mole KT8 ...... 36 C5
Vine Rd. Mortl SW13 & SW15 ...... 7 F4
Vine St. Alder GU11 ...... 105 A1
Vine Way. Rowl GU10 ...... 146 A5
Vineries Cl. Harm UB7 ...... 3 A8
Viners Cl. Walt O T KT12 ...... 35 C3
Viney Bank. New Add CR0 ...... 62 F2
Vineyard Cl. For Hil SE6 ...... 24 A7
Vineyard Cl. King U T KT1 ...... 37 F6
Vineyard Hill Rd. Wimble SW19 . 20 A4
Vineyard Path. Mortl SW14 ...... 7 D4
Vineyard Row. Tedd KT1 & KT8 .. 37 C8
Vineyard Sch The. Rich TW10 .... 6 E1
Vineyard The. Rich TW10 ...... 6 E2
Vineyards The. Felt TW13 ...... 15 A5
Vinter Ct. Shep Gn SW17 ...... 34 A4
Viola Ave. Felt TW14 ...... 4 C1
Viola Ave. Stan TW19 ...... 13 E7
Viola Croft. Wink RG12 ...... 27 F8
Violet Cl. Carsh CR4 ...... 41 A1
Violet Gdns. Croy CR0 ...... 61 B5
Violet La. Croy CR0 ...... 61 B5
Violette Szabo House. [4]
  W Norw SE27 ...... 22 D4
Virginia Ave. Vir W GU25 ...... 31 C4
Virginia Beeches. Vir W GU25 .. 31 C6
Virginia Cl. Ashtd KT21 ...... 75 D1
Virginia Cl. King U T KT3 ...... 38 C5
Virginia Cl. Laleh TW18 ...... 33 C6
Virginia Cl. Whit V KT13 ...... 53 C4
Virginia Ct. Vir W GU25 ...... 31 D5
Virginia Dr. Vir W GU25 ...... 31 C5
Virginia Gdns. Farnb GU14 ...... 85 C2
Virginia Gdns. W Byfl KT14 ...... 71 B7
Virginia Rd. S Norw CR7 ...... 42 B8
Virginia Water Prep Sch.
  Vir W GU25 ...... 31 E4
Virginia Water Sta. Vir W GU25 31 E4
Viscount Gdns. Byfl KT14 ...... 71 E7
Viscount Ind Est. Poyle SL3 ...... 1 E4
Viscount Rd. Stan TW19 ...... 13 E7
Viscount Way. Harlton TW6 ...... 3 E3
Vivien Cl. Chess KT9 ...... 56 E3
Vivienne Cl. Crawl RH11 ...... 181 D1
Vivienne Cl. Twick TW1 ...... 6 D1
Vivienne House. Stain TW18 ...... 13 A3
Vixen Track. Farnb GU14 ...... 104 C8
Voewood Cl. New Mal KT3 ...... 38 F3
Vogan Cl. Woodh RH2 ...... 139 B6
Volta Way. Croy CR0 & CR9 ...... 41 F1
Voltaire. [14] Rich TW9 ...... 6 F6
Voss Ct. Streat SW16 ...... 21 E2
Vowels La. W Hoath RH19 ...... 204 E2
Vulcan Bsns Ctr. New Add CR9 .. 63 E2
Vulcan Cl. Crawl RH11 ...... 201 C2
Vulcan Cl. Sandh GU17 ...... 64 A7
Vulcan Cl. Wallin SM6 ...... 60 F3
Vulcan Way. Sandh GU17 ...... 64 B7
Vulcan Way. New Add CR0 & CR9 63 E1
Vulcan Way. Sandh GU17 ...... 64 B7

Waddington Ave.
  Coulsd CR5 & CR8 ...... 100 B8
Waddington Cl. Coulsd CR5 ...... 100 B8
Waddington Cl. Crawl RH11 ...... 201 A3
Waddington Way.
  S Norw CR7 & SE19 ...... 42 D8
Waddon Cl. Croy CR0 & CR9 ...... 61 A7
Waddon Court Rd.
  Croy CR0 & CR9 ...... 61 A7
Waddon Inf Sch. Croy CR9 ...... 61 A5
Waddon Marsh Sta. Croy CR0 .... 41 F1
Waddon Marsh Way.
  Croy CR0 & CR9 ...... 41 F1
Waddon New Rd.
  Croy CR0 & CR9 ...... 61 B8
Waddon Park Ave.
  Croy CR0 & CR9 ...... 61 A7
Waddon Rd. Croy CR0 & CR9 .... 61 A7
Waddon Sta. Croy CR0 ...... 61 A6
Waddon Way.
  Croy CR0 & CR2 & CR9 ...... 61 B4
Wade's La. Tedd TW11 ...... 17 A3
Wadham. Sandh GU15 ...... 45 F1
Wadham Cl. Crawl RH10 ...... 182 C1
Wadham Cl. Shep SW17 ...... 34 C2
Wadhurst Cl. Penge SE20 ...... 43 B7
Wadlands Brook Rd.
  Dorm Pk RH19 ...... 185 D5
Wagbullock Rise. Easth RG12 .... 27 C3
Wagg Cl. E Grins RH19 ...... 186 A1
Waggon Cl. Stough GU2 ...... 108 E2
Waggoners Hollow. Bagsh GU19 47 E2
Waggoners Way. Graysh GU26 . 188 A4
Waggoners Wells Rd.
  Graysh GU26 ...... 188 A2
Wagtail Cl. Horsh RH12 ...... 217 D7
Wagtail Gdns. Selsd CR2 ...... 62 E1
Waights Ct. King U T KT2 ...... 37 E8
Wain End. Horsh RH12 ...... 217 D5
Wainford Cl. Putney SW19 ...... 19 D7
Wainwright Gr. Islew TW7 ...... 5 D3
Wainwrights. Crawl RH11 ...... 201 D3
Waite Davies Rd. Lewish SE12 .. 24 F8
Wakefield Cl. Byfl KT14 ...... 71 E7
Wakefield Gdns. S Norw SE19 .... 22 E1
Wakefield House. Dulw SE22 .... 23 B7
Wakefield Rd. Rich TW10 ...... 6 D2
Wakefield Rd. [19]
  Crawl RH10 ...... 182 D1
Wakehams Green Dr.
  Crawl RH10 ...... 182 D1
Wakehurst Dr.
  Crawl RH10 & RH11 ...... 201 D3
Wakehurst Mews. Horsh RH12 216 F1
Wakehurst Path. Sheer GU21 .... 70 C5
Wakelin House. For Hil SE23 .... 23 E8
Wakeling House. [8]
  W Norw SE27 ...... 22 B5
Wakely Cl. Bigg H TN16 ...... 83 C1
Walburton Rd. Purley CR8 ...... 79 C7
Walbury. Brack RG12 ...... 27 E5
Waldby Ct. Crawl RH11 ...... 201 A3
Waldeck Gr. W Norw SE27 ...... 22 B5
Waldeck Rd. Brent W4 ...... 7 A8
Waldeck Rd. Mortl SW14 ...... 7 C4
Waldeck Terr. Mortl SW14 ...... 7 C4
Waldegrave Ct. [1] Tedd TW11 .. 16 F3
Waldegrave Gdns. Twick TW1 .. 16 F5
Waldegrave Pk. Tedd TW11 ...... 16 F3
Waldegrave Rd. Penge SE19 .... 22 F1
Waldegrave Rd. Tedd TW11 ...... 16 F4
Waldegrave Sch for Girls.
  Twick TW2 ...... 16 D5
Waldegrove. S Croy CR0 ...... 61 F7
Waldemar Rd. Wimble SW19 .... 20 A3
Walden Cotts. Normdy GU3 .... 107 A3
Walden Gdns.
  Thorn H CR7 & SW16 ...... 41 F5
Waldens Park Rd. Horse GU21 .. 69 C3
Waldens Rd. Woking GU21 ...... 69 C2
Waldenshaw Rd. For Hil SE23 .. 23 C7
Waldo Pl. Mitch SW19 ...... 20 E1
Waldorf Cl. Croy CR2 ...... 61 B2
Waldorf Hts. Hawley GU17 ...... 64 D3
Waldram Cres. For Hil SE23 .... 23 C7
Waldram Park Rd. For Hil SE23 . 23 C7
Waldram Pl. For Hil SE23 ...... 23 C7
Waldron Gdns. Beck BR2 ...... 44 D6
Waldron Hill. Brack RG12 ...... 27 F8
Waldron Rd.
  Wands SW17 & SW18 ...... 20 C6
Waldronhyrst. Croy CR0 ...... 61 B6
Waldrons The. Croy CR0 ...... 61 C6
Waldrons The. Oxted RH8 ...... 122 F4
Waldy Rise. Cran GU6 ...... 174 E4
Wales Ave. Carsh SM5 ...... 59 E5
Walesbeech. Crawl RH10 ...... 202 A5
Waleton Acres. Wallin SM6 ...... 60 C4
Waley's La. Ockley RH5 ...... 177 C1
Walford Rd. Dork RH5 ...... 136 C3
Walham Rise. Wimble SW19 ...... 19 E2
Walk The. Ashf TW16 ...... 14 F1
Walk The. Ranstn RH8 ...... 122 A2
Walkden Hall (Hall of Residence).
  King U T KT2 ...... 18 D4
Walker Cl. E Bed TW14 ...... 14 F8
Walker Cl. Hampt TW12 ...... 15 F2
Walker Rd. Worth RH10 ...... 202 C4
Walker's Ridge. Camb GU15 .... 65 E5
Walkerscroft Mead.
  W Norw SE21 ...... 22 C7
Wakfield Dr. Brack H RH18 ...... 77 B2
Walking Bottom. Peasl GU5 .. 154 C6
Wall Hill Rd.
  For Row RH18 & RH19 ...... 206 E5
Wallace Cl. Guild GU3 ...... 108 C4
Wallace Cl. Up Hall TW17 ...... 34 D5
Wallace Cres. Carsh SM5 ...... 59 F5
Wallace Fields. Ewell KT17 ...... 77 A6
Wallace Fields Cty Inf Sch.
  Ewell KT17 ...... 77 A6
Wallace Fields Cty Jun Sch.
  Ewell KT17 ...... 77 A7

Wallace Wlk. Addl KT15 ...... 52 C6
Wallage La. Worth RH10 ...... 203 D6
Wallage La. Worth RH10 ...... 203 D6
Wallbrook Bsns Ctr. Hounsl TW4 . 4 B4
Walled Garden The.
  Loxwd RH14 ...... 212 F7
Walled Garden The. Tadw RH20 97 D5
Walled Gdn The. Betch RH3 .... 137 D8
Waller La. Cater CR3 ...... 100 F4
Wallingford Cl. Brack RG12 ...... 27 E5
Wallington Ct. [10] Wallin SM6 .. 60 B4
Wallington High Sch for Boys.
  Wallin SM6 ...... 60 B6
Wallington High Sch for Girls.
  Wallin SM6 ...... 60 B2
Wallington Rd. Camb GU15 ...... 47 A1
Wallington Sq. [4] Wallin SM6 .. 60 C4
Wallington Sta. Wallin SM6 ...... 60 B4
Wallis Ct. Crawl RH10 ...... 181 D2
Wallis House. E Grins RH19 ...... 185 E1
Wallis Mews. Fetch KT22 ...... 95 A5
Wallis Way. Horsh RH13 ...... 218 A4
Wallner Way. Woki RG11 ...... 25 E5
Wallop Sch. Weyb KT13 ...... 53 B5
Wallorton Gdns. Mortl SW14 .... 7 D3
Walmer Cl. Crowth RG11 ...... 45 C5
Walmer Cl. Friml GU16 ...... 86 A7
Walmer House. [11] Penge SE20 . 23 C1
Walmsley House. [1]
  Streat SW16 ...... 21 C4
Walnut Cl. Alder GU11 ...... 126 A8
Walnut Cl. Carsh SM5 ...... 59 F5
Walnut Cl. Epsom KT18 ...... 76 F4
Walnut Cl. Horsh RH13 ...... 217 E1
Walnut Dr. Kings KT20 ...... 97 E3
Walnut Gr. Nork SM7 ...... 77 D5
Walnut House. Woodh RH2 .... 139 C7
Walnut La. Crawl RH11 ...... 181 B1
Walnut Mews. Sutton SM2 ...... 59 C3
Walnut Tree Ave. Mitch CR4 ...... 40 E6
Walnut Tree Cl. Barnes SW13 ...... 7 F6
Walnut Tree Cl. Belm SM7 ...... 77 F2
Walnut Tree Cl. Guild GU1 ...... 130 C8
Walnut Tree Gdns. Farnc GU7 . 150 E7
Walnut Tree La. Byfl KT14 ...... 71 D7
Walnut Tree Rd. Brent TW8 ...... 6 E8
Walnut Tree Rd. Charlt TW17 .... 34 C7
Walnut Tree Rd. Heston TW5 .... 4 F8
Walpole Ave. Chips CR5 ...... 98 F8
Walpole Ave. Rich TW9 ...... 6 F5
Walpole Cres. [7] Tedd TW11 .... 16 F3
Walpole Ct. Twick TW2 ...... 16 E6
Walpole Ct. Twick TW2 ...... 16 E5
Walpole Pl. [6] Tedd TW11 ...... 16 F3
Walpole Rd. Croy CR0 & CR9 .... 61 D8
Walpole Rd. Mitch SW19 ...... 20 D2
Walpole Rd. Old W SL4 ...... 11 B8
Walpole Rd. Surb KT6 ...... 37 E3
Walpole Rd. Tedd TW11 ...... 16 F3
Walpole Rd. Twick TW2 ...... 16 E6
Walrus Rd. Farnb GU14 ...... 104 D8
Walsh Cres. New Add CR0 ...... 82 E7
Walsh Meml C of E Mid Sch.
  Ash GU12 ...... 106 A1
Walsh Memorial C of E Fst Sch.
  Ash GU12 ...... 105 F1
Walsham Rd. Felt TW14 ...... 15 B8
Walsingham Gdns.
  Worc Pk KT19 ...... 57 F5
Walsingham Rd. Mitch CR4 ...... 40 F4
Walsingham Rd. New Add CR0 .. 63 C1
Walstead House. [2]
  Crawl RH10 ...... 201 D5
Walter Cty Inf Sch. Woki RG11 .. 25 A6
Walter St. [1] King U T KT2 ...... 37 E8
Walter's Mead. Ashtd KT21 ...... 75 E2
Walter's Rd. S Norw SE25 ...... 42 E5
Waltham Ave. Stough GU2 ...... 109 B5
Waltham Cl. Sandh GU15 ...... 45 D1
Waltham Rd. Carsh SM5 ...... 40 E1
Waltham Rd. Cater CR3 ...... 101 B5
Walton Ave. Cheam SM3 ...... 58 F7
Walton Ave. New Mal KT3 ...... 38 F5
Walton Bridge Rd.
  Oat Pk KT12 & TW17 ...... 34 E2
Walton Comm Hospl.
  Walt O T KT12 ...... 54 C8
Walton Ct. Woking GU21 ...... 70 A3
Walton Dr. N Asct SL5 ...... 28 F8
Walton Gdns. Felt TW13 ...... 14 F4
Walton Gn. New Add CR0 ...... 63 C3
Walton Heath. Crawl RH10 ...... 202 D8
Walton La. Lo Hall TW17 ...... 34 D2
Walton La. Oat Pk KT12 ...... 34 E1
Walton La. Weyb KT12 & KT13 .. 53 C8
Walton Leigh Special Training Sch.
  Walt O T KT12 ...... 53 F6
Walton on the Hill C of E Jun Sch.
  Walt o t H KT20 ...... 97 A2
Walton on the Hill Cty Prim Sch.
  Walt o t H KT20 ...... 97 B3
Walton Park La. Walt O T KT12 .. 54 D8
Walton Pk. Walt O T KT12 ...... 54 D8
Walton Rd. Ashtd KT18 ...... 96 C6
Walton Rd. E Mole KT8 & KT12 .. 35 E4
Walton Rd. Woking GU21 ...... 70 A3
Walton St. Walt o t H KT20 ...... 97 B3
Walton Terr. Woking GU21 ...... 70 B4
Walton Way. Mitch CR4 ...... 41 C5
Wanborough Dr. Rhampt SW15 . 19 B7
Wanborough Hill. Wanb GU3 .. 128 C6
Wanborough La. Cran GU6 .... 175 A3
Wanborough Sta. Flexf GU3 .... 107 C1
Wandle Bank. Merton SW19 .... 20 D1
Wandle Bank. Wallin CR0 ...... 60 E7
Wandle Cl. Ash GU12 ...... 106 A1
Wandle Cl. Worth RH10 ...... 202 C5
Wandle Court Gdns. Wallin CR0 60 E7
Wandle Ct. W Ewell KT19 ...... 57 C6

Wandle Ct. Wallin CR0 .... 60 E7
Wandle House. Catf BR1 .... 24 D3
Wandle House. ⁵ Redh RH1 ... 118 F2
Wandle House. Wands SW18 ...... 20 B8
Wandle Lodge. Wallin CR0 .... 60 E7
Wandle Prim Sch. Wands SW18 20 B7
Wandle Rd. Croy CR0 & CR9 .... 61 C7
Wandle Rd. Hackbr SM6 .... 60 B8
Wandle Rd.
   Morden CR4 & SM4 & SW19 ... 40 D4
Wandle Rd. Up Toot SW17 .... 20 E6
Wandle Rd. Wallin CR0 .... 60 E7
Wandle Side. Croy CR0 .... 60 F7
Wandle Side. Hackbr SM6 .... 60 F7
Wandle Tech Pk. Carsh CR4 .... 40 F2
Wandle Trad Est. Carsh CR4 .... 40 F2
Wandle Valley Sch. Carsh SM5 . 40 E2
Wandle Way. Mitch CR4 .... 40 F4
Wandle Way. Wands SW18 .... 20 B7
Wandsdyke Cl. Friml GU16 .... 85 F8
Wandsworth Common Sta.
   Balham SW12 .... 20 F8
Wandsworth Sch. Putney SW18 19 F8
Wansford Gn. ³ Woking GU21 ... 68 F2
Wanstraw Gr. Brack RG12 .... 27 E2
Wantage Cl. Brack RG12 .... 27 E4
Wantage Rd. Sandh GU15 .... 64 D8
Wapiti Way. Farnb GU14 .... 104 D8
Waplings The. Walt o t H KT20 ... 97 B3
Wapshott Rd. Egham TW18 .... 12 E3
War Coppice Rd. Cater RH1 ... 120 D7
War Memorial Homes.
   Chisw W4 .... 7 D7
War Memorial Hospl.
   Wallin SM5 .... 59 F4
Warbank Cl. New Add CR0 .... 63 E1
Warbank Cres. New Add CR0 ...... 63 E1
Warbank La. W Norw SE21 .... 18 F1
Warblers Gn. Cobham KT11 .... 73 F5
Warbleton House. ⁶
   Crawl RH11 .... 200 F3
Warboys App. King U T KT2 .... 18 B2
Warboys Rd. King U T KT2 .... 18 B2
Warburton Cl. E Grins RH19 ..... 206 A8
Warburton Rd. Twick TW2 .... 16 B7
Warbury La. Knaph GU21 .... 68 C3
Ward Cl. Woki RG11 .... 25 D8
Ward La. Warlgm CR6 .... 81 D2
Ward St. Guild GU1 .... 130 D8
Wardle Cl. Bagsh GU19 .... 47 E3
Wardley St. Wands SW18 .... 20 B8
Wardrobe The. ³ Rich TW9 .... 6 D2
Wards Stone Pk. Brack RG12 ..... 27 E2
Ware Ct. Cheam SM1 .... 58 F6
Wareham Cl. Hounsl TW3 .... 5 B3
Wareham Rd. Brack RG12 .... 27 F4
Warenne Rd. Fetch KT22 .... 94 C5
Warfield Rd. Brack RG12 .... 27 C8
Warfield Rd. E Bed TW14 .... 14 E8
Warfield Rd. Hampt TW12 .... 36 B8
Wargrove Dr. Sandh GU15 .... 64 D8
Warham Rd. Croy CR0 & CR2 ..... 61 C5
Waring St. W Norw SE27 .... 22 C4
Warkworth Gdns. Hounsl TW7 ..... 6 A7
Warlingham Cty Sec Sch.
   Warlgm CR6 .... 81 A3
Warlingham Park Hospl.
   Chelsh CR6 .... 82 A4
Warlingham Park Sch.
   Chelsh CR6 .... 82 A3
Warlingham Rd. Thorn H CR7 ..... 42 B5
Warltersville Way. Horley RH6 161 C4
Warminster Gdns. S Norw SE25 43 A7
Warminster Rd. S Norw SE25 ..... 43 A7
Warminster Sq. S Norw SE25 ..... 43 A7
Warminster Way. Mitch CR4 .... 41 B7
Warner Ave. Cheam SM3 .... 58 E8
Warner Cl. Harl UB3 .... 3 D7
Warner Cl. Cheam SM3 .... 58 E8
Warner House. Beck BR3 .... 24 B2
Warner Rd. Broml BR1 .... 24 F1
Warners La. Albury GU5 .... 132 E2
Warnford House. Rhampt SW15 ... 7 E1
Warnham CE (Controlled) Sch.
   Warn RH12 .... 216 D1
Warnham Court Rd. Wallin SM5 59 F3
Warnham Ct. Horsh RH12 .... 216 F7
Warnham House. ⁹ Streat SW2 21 F8
Warnham Nature Reserve.
   Horsh RH12 .... 217 B6
Warnham Rd. Broad H RH12 .... 216 D4
Warnham Rd. Crawl RH10 .... 202 A6
Warnham Rd. Horsh RH12 .... 217 B5
Warnham Sta. Faygt RH12 ...... 217 C8
Warpole Pk. Whit V KT13 .... 53 A3
Warramill Rd. Godal GU7 .... 151 A5
Warren Ave. Belm SM2 .... 58 F1
Warren Ave. Broml BR1 .... 24 E1
Warren Ave. Mortl SW14 & TW10 .. 7 B3
Warren Ave. S Croy CR2 .... 62 D3
Warren Cl. Esher KT10 .... 55 B6
Warren Cl. Felb RH19 .... 184 E3
Warren Cl. Sandh GU17 .... 64 A8
Warren Cl. W Norw SE21 .... 22 C8
Warren Cnr. Crond GU10 .... 124 C7
Warren Ct. ¹⁸ Beck BR3 .... 24 A1
Warren Ct. ⁶ Croy CR0 .... 42 E1
Warren Ct. Weyb KT13 .... 53 A5
Warren Cutting. King U T KT2 ..... 18 D1
Warren Down. Brack RG12 .... 26 E8
Warren Dr. Crawl RH11 .... 201 A4
Warren Dr. Kings KT20 .... 98 A4
Warren Dr N. Tolw KT5 & KT6 .... 38 B1
Warren Dr S. Tolw KT5 .... 38 C1
Warren Farm Mobile Home Pk.
   Mayb GU23 .... 91 B8
Warren Hill. Woodc KT18 .... 76 D3
Warren House Rd. Woki RG11 ... 25 D8
Warren La. Mayb GU22 & GU23 .. 71 B1
Warren La. Oxsh KT22 .... 74 C7
Warren La. Oxted RH8 .... 123 A1

Warren Lodge. Kings KT20 .... 97 E3
Warren Lodge Dr. Kings KT20 .... 97 E3
Warren Mead. Nork SM7 .... 77 C4
Warren Mead Cty Inf Sch.
   Nork SM7 .... 77 D4
Warren Mead Cty Jun Sch.
   Nork SM7 .... 77 D4
Warren Park Rd.
   Carsh SM1 & SM2 .... 59 E4
Warren Pk. King U T KT2 .... 18 C2
Warren Pk. Warlgm CR6 .... 81 D1
Warren Rd. Ashf TW15 .... 14 E1
Warren Rd. Croy CR0 .... 42 F1
Warren Rd. Farnc GU7 .... 150 E7
Warren Rd. Guild GU1 & GU4 ... 131 A8
Warren Rd. King U T KT2 .... 18 C2
Warren Rd. Mitch SW19 .... 20 E2
Warren Rd. Nork KT17 & SM7 ..... 77 D5
Warren Rd. Purley CR8 .... 80 B8
Warren Rd. Reig RH2 .... 118 B2
Warren Rise. Friml GU16 .... 65 F3
Warren Rise. King U T KT3 .... 38 D8
Warren Row. N Asct SL5 .... 28 D7
Warren The. Alder GU11 .... 104 F1
Warren The. Ashtd KT21 .... 95 F7
Warren The. E Hors KT24 .... 112 F5
Warren The. Heath E GU9 .... 125 E8
Warren The. Heston TW5 .... 4 F7
Warren The. Kings KT20 .... 97 E6
Warren The. Oxsh KT22 .... 74 D6
Warren The. Sutton SM2 & SM5 .. 59 E2
Warren The. Worc Pk KT19 & KT4 57 D7
Warren Track. Farnb GU14 .... 104 D7
Warren Way. Whit V KT13 .... 53 C4
Warren Wood Cl. Coney H BR2 .. 63 F8
Warreners La. Whit V KT13 .... 53 D3
Warrenhyrst. Guild GU1 .... 131 A8
Warrenne Rd. Brock RH3 .... 137 C7
Warrington Cl. Crawl RH11 .... 200 E2
Warrington Mews. Alder GU11 ... 68 B2
Warrington Rd. Croy CR0 & CR9 . 61 B7
Warrington Rd. ²¹ Rich TW10 .... 6 D2
Warrington Spur. Old W SL4 .... 11 B8
Warwick. Brack RG12 .... 27 E3
Warwick Ave. Stain TW18 .... 13 C2
Warwick Ave. Thor L TW20 .... 32 C8
Warwick Cl. Alder GU11 .... 126 C8
Warwick Cl. Friml GU15 .... 66 B3
Warwick Cl. Hampt TW12 .... 16 C1
Warwick Cl. S Holm RH5 .... 157 B7
Warwick Ct. Beck BR2 .... 44 F7
Warwick Ct. Weyb KT13 .... 53 A5
Warwick Gr. Surb KT5 .... 37 F2
Warwick House. ⁴ King U T KT2 37 E8
Warwick La. Woking GU21 .... 89 A8
Warwick Lodge. Cheam SM1 ...... 58 F6
Warwick Rd. Ash V GU12 .... 106 A8
Warwick Rd. Ashf TW15 .... 13 E8
Warwick Rd. Coulsd CR5 .... 79 D5
Warwick Rd. Farnb GU14 .... 104 D8
Warwick Rd. Hounsl TW4 .... 4 B4
Warwick Rd. King U T KT3 .... 38 C6
Warwick Rd. Penge SE20 .... 43 B6
Warwick Rd. Redh RH1 .... 118 F2
Warwick Rd. S Holm RH5 .... 157 C7
Warwick Rd. Sutton SM1 .... 59 C5
Warwick Rd. Tedd KT1 .... 37 C8
Warwick Rd. Thame D KT7 .... 36 F4
Warwick Rd. Thorn H CR7 .... 42 A6
Warwick Rd. Twick TW2 .... 16 E7
Warwick Sch The. Redh RH1 .... 119 A2
Warwick Villas. Thor L TW20 ...... 32 C8
Warwick Wold Rd. Bletch RH1 .. 120 A7
Warwick Wold Rd. Cater RH1 ... 120 A7
Warwick's Bench Rd.
   Guild GU1 .... 130 E6
Warwicks Bench. Guild GU1 ..... 130 D6
Wasdale Cl. Sandh GU15 .... 45 D2
Washington Cl. Reig RH2 .... 118 A3
Washington Ct. Up Toot SW17 ... 20 F2
Washington Rd. Crawl RH11 ..... 200 E3
Washington Rd. King U T KT1 ..... 38 A7
Washington Rd. N Cheam KT4 ... 39 B1
Washpond La. Chelsh CR6 .... 82 C1
Wasp Green La. Outw RH1 .... 162 C8
Wassand Cl. Crawl RH10 .... 202 A6
Wastdale Rd. For Hil SE23 .... 23 D7
Watchetts Cty Jun Sch.
   Camb GU15 .... 65 B2
Watchetts Dr. Camb GU15 .... 65 C2
Watchetts Lake Cl. Camb GU15 . 65 D3
Watchetts Rd. Camb GU15 .... 65 B4
Watchmoor Rd. Camb GU15 .... 65 A4
Watchmoor Trade Ctr.
   Camb GU15 .... 65 A3
Watcombe Cotts. Rich TW9 .... 7 A8
Wattendon Rd. Croy SE25 .... 43 B4
Water La. Abin C RH5 .... 155 B8
Water La. Bisley GU24 .... 87 E8
Water La. Cobham KT11 .... 73 F5
Water La. Ent Gn GU8 .... 171 B4
Water La. Farnh GU9 .... 125 F4
Water La. King U T KT1 .... 37 D8
Water La. L Book KT23 & KT24 ... 93 E1
Water La. Limps RH8 .... 123 A8
Water La. Lingf TN8 .... 165 D7
Water La. Oxted RH8 .... 123 A1
Water La. S Godst RH9 .... 142 D5
Water La. Twick TW1 .... 17 A7
Water La. W Heath GU14 .... 85 A7
Water La. Wormly GU8 .... 171 B4
Water Mill Way. Felt TW13 .... 16 A6
Water Splash La. Ascot SL5 .... 29 E8

Water Tower Hill.
   S Croy CR0 & CR2 .... 61 D6
Water View. Horley RH6 .... 161 C3
Waterbank Rd. Catf SE6 .... 24 C4
Watercress Way. Woking GU21 .. 69 B2
Waterden Cl. Guild GU1 .... 130 F8
Waterden Rd. Guild GU1 .... 130 E8
Waterer Gdns. Burgh H KT20 ..... 77 E1
Waterer House. Catf SE6 .... 24 C4
Waterer Rise. Wallin SM6 .... 60 D4
Waterers Rise. Knaph GU21 .... 68 D2
Waterfall Cl. Vir W GU25 .... 31 A6
Waterfall Cotts. Mitch SW19 ...... 20 D2
Waterfall Rd. Mitch SW19 .... 20 D2
Waterfall Terr. Up Toot SW17 ..... 20 E2
Waterfield. H KT20 .... 97 B7
Waterfield Cty Fst Sch.
   Crawl RH11 .... 200 E4
Waterfield Dr. Warlgm CR6 .... 101 C8
Waterfield Gdns. Crawl RH11 ... 200 E4
Waterfield Gdns. S Norw SE25 ... 42 E4
Waterfield Gn. Burgh H KT20 ..... 97 B7
Waterfields. Leahd KT22 .... 95 B8
Waterford Way. Woki RG11 .... 25 C6
Watergardens The. King U T KT2 18 C2
Waterham Rd. Easth RG12 .... 27 B3
Waterhouse Ct. ⁵ Tedd TW11 .... 16 F3
Waterhouse La. Bletch RH1 ..... 121 A3
Waterhouse La. Coulsd CR8 .... 100 C8
Waterhouse La. Kings KT20 .... 97 E6
Waterhouse Mead. Sandh GU15 64 D7
Waterlands La. Rowhk RH12 .... 196 E1
Waterloo Cl. Camb GU15 .... 66 B7
Waterloo Cl. E Bed TW14 .... 14 F7
Waterloo Cres. Woki RG11 .... 25 E4
Waterloo Pl. Rich TW9 .... 7 A8
Waterloo Rd. Alder GU12 .... 105 C1
Waterloo Rd. Carsh SM1 .... 59 D5
Waterloo Rd. Crowth RG11 .... 45 B4
Waterloo Rd.
   Epsom KT17 & KT19 .... 76 D6
Waterloo Rd. Woki RG11 .... 25 F5
Waterlow Rd. Reig RH2 .... 139 D8
Watermans Bsns Pk The.
   Egham TW18 .... 12 E4
Watermans Cl. ¹² Brent TW8 .... 6 D8
Watermans Ct. ² Brent TW8 .... 6 E8
Watermead. E Bed TW14 .... 14 F7
Watermead. Tadw KT20 .... 97 B6
Watermead. Woking GU21 .... 69 B1
Watermead La. Carsh CR4 .... 40 F2
Watermead Rd. Catf SE6 .... 24 C4
Watermeads High Sch.
   Morden SM4 .... 40 D3
Watermen's Sq. ¹ Penge SE20 .. 23 C1
Watermill Cl. Rich TW10 .... 17 C5
Watermill Way. Merton SW19 ..... 40 D8
Waterperry La. Chobh GU24 .... 49 F1
Waters Dr. Stain TW18 .... 12 F4
Waters Rd. King U T KT1 .... 38 B7
Waters Sq. King U T KT1 .... 38 B6
Watersedge. W Ewell KT19 .... 57 C6
Watersedge. W Ewell KT19 .... 57 C6
Waterside. Beck BR3 .... 44 A8
Waterside. E Grins RH19 .... 186 B1
Waterside. Horley RH6 .... 161 A5
Waterside. Crawl RH11 .... 200 E4
Waterside Cl. Godal GU7 .... 151 A5
Waterside Cl. Surb KT6 .... 56 E8
Waterside La. Godal GU7 .... 150 C3
Waterside Mews. Belif GU1 ...... 109 C3
Waterside Rd. Belif GU1 .... 109 C3
Waterside Trad Est. Addl KT15 .. 52 E6
Waterside Way. ² Woking GU21 69 B1
Waterslade. Redh RH1 .... 118 C1
Watersmeet Cl. Burph GU4 ...... 110 A6
Watersplash Cl. King U T KT1 ..... 37 E6
Watersplash Rd. Shep Gn TW17 . 34 A5
Waterway Rd. Fetch KT22 .... 95 A5
Waterway Rd. Leahd KT22 .... 95 A5
Watery La. Chobh GU24 .... 49 D1
Watery La. Merton SW19 & SW20 39 F7
Wates Way. Mitch CR4 .... 40 F3
Watford Cl. Guild GU1 .... 109 F1
Wathen Rd. Dork RH4 .... 136 B8
Watlings Cl. Croy CR0 .... 43 E3
Watlington Gr. For Hil SE26 .... 23 E3
Watney Cotts. Mortl SW14 .... 7 C4
Watney Rd. Mortl SW14 .... 7 C4
Watneys Rd. Mitch CR4 .... 41 D4
Watson Ave. Cheam SM3 .... 58 E8
Watson Cl. Mitch SW19 .... 20 E1
Watson House. ³ Streat SW2 ..... 21 E8
Watson Rd. Westc RH4 .... 135 C6
Watt's La. Tadw KT20 .... 97 B6
Watt's La. Tedd TW11 .... 17 A3
Watt's Mead. Tadw KT20 .... 97 C5

Waverley Cl. Friml GU15 .... 65 F4
Waverley Cl. Horsh RH12 .... 217 B2
Waverley Ct. ¹ Woking GU22 ..... 69 E1
Waverley Dr. Addl KT16 .... 51 D7
Waverley Dr. Ash V GU12 .... 106 A6
Waverley Dr. Camb GU15 .... 66 B3
Waverley Dr. Vir W GU25 .... 31 A5
Waverley La. Farnh GU10 & GU9 147 C8
Waverley Gdns. Ash V GU12 .... 106 A6
Waverley La. M Bourn GU9 ...... 125 E1
Waverley Pl. Leahd KT22 .... 95 B5
Waverley Rd. Bagsh GU19 .... 47 E3
Waverley Rd. Croy SE25 .... 43 B6
Waverley Rd. Farnb GU14 .... 85 D3
Waverley Rd. Oxsh KT11 & KT22 . 74 B5
Waverley Rd. Stonel KT17 & KT4 . 58 B5
Waverley Rd. Weyb KT13 .... 53 A5
Waverley Way.
   Sutton SM2 & SM5 .... 59 E4
Waverton Rd. Wands SW18 .... 20 C8
Wavertree Ct. ⁹ Streat SW2 .... 21 E7
Wavertree Rd. Streat SW2 .... 21 E7
Way The. Reig RH2 .... 118 D2
Waye Ave. Cranf TW5 .... 4 A6
Wayland Cl. Brack RG12 .... 27 F5
Waylands Mead. Beck BR3 .... 44 B8
Waylett Pl. W Norw SE27 .... 22 B5
Wayman Rd. W Heath GU14 .... 84 E8
Wayneflete Tower Ave.
   Esher KT10 .... 55 A7
Waynflete Ave. Croy CR0 & CR9 . 61 B7
Waynflete La. Farnh GU9 .... 124 F2
Waynflete St. Wands SW18 .... 20 C6
Ways End. Camb GU15 .... 65 C4
Wayside. Capel RH5 .... 178 D6
Wayside. Crawl RH11 .... 200 A3
Wayside. Mortl SW14 .... 7 C2
Wayside. New Add CR0 .... 63 B4
Wayside. Hounsl TW7 .... 5 E5
Wayside Ct. Twick TW1 .... 6 C1
Wayside Ct. Woking GU21 .... 68 C3
W.C. Lee's Resthouses.
   Windl GU20 .... 48 D4
Weald CE Prim Sch The.
   Bear Gn RH5 .... 157 D3
Weald Cl. Shalf GU4 .... 130 E3
Weald Day Hospl The.
   Crawl RH11 .... 201 C6
Weald Dr. Crawl RH10 .... 202 A4
Weald The. E Grins RH19 .... 185 F4
Weald View Cotts. Coldh RH5 .. 126 D3
Weald Way. Cater CR3 & RH1 ... 100 E4
Weald Way. Dovgn RH2 .... 139 C5
Wealdon Ct. ² Stough GU2 ...... 108 F1
Wealdstone Rd. Cheam SM3 ..... 58 F8
Weapon Rd. Farnb GU14 .... 85 B2
Weare St. Capel RH5 .... 178 B4
Weare St. Ockley RH5 .... 177 F1
Weasdale Ct. Woking GU21 .... 68 F3
Weatherall Cl. Addl KT15 .... 52 B5
Weatherhill Cl. Horley RH6 ...... 161 F3
Weatherhill Cotts. Smallf RH6 .. 162 A3
Weatherill Ct. Croy SE25 .... 43 B4
Weaver Cl. Crawl RH11 .... 200 E5
Weaver Wlk. W Norw SE27 .... 22 B4
Weavers Ct. Islew TW7 .... 5 E3
Weavers Gdns.
   Wreccl GU10 & GU9 .... 145 F7
Webb Cl. Bagsh GU19 .... 47 E1
Webb Cl. Crawl RH11 .... 201 B1
Webb Ct. Woki RG11 .... 25 E8
Webb House. Felt TW13 .... 15 E5
Webster Cl. Oxsh KT11 & KT22 .. 74 B5
Websters Cl. Woking GU22 .... 89 B7
Weddell Rd. Crawl RH10 .... 201 F3
Wedgewood Cl. Beck BR2 .... 44 F5
Wedgewood Way. S Norw SE19 . 22 C1
Wedgwoods. Tats TN16 .... 103 C6
Weeks House. Rich TW10 .... 17 C4
Weighbridge Rd. Woodhm KT15 52 B2
Weighton Rd. Penge SE20 .... 43 B7
Weihurst Ct. Carsh SM1 .... 59 E5
Weihurst Gdns. Carsh SM1 .... 59 D5
Weir Ave. Farnb GU14 .... 85 A3
Weir Cl. Farnb GU14 .... 85 A3
Weir House. ⁸ Streat SW12 .... 21 C8
Weir Pl. Egham TW18 .... 32 E8
Weir Rd. Chert KT16 .... 33 B2
Weir Rd. Farnb GU4 .... 84 A2
Weir Rd. Streat SW12 .... 21 C8
Weir Rd. Walt O T KT12 .... 35 A3
Weir Rd. Wimble SW18 & SW19 .. 20 B5
Weirbrook. Crawl RH10 .... 202 A3
Welbeck. Easth RG12 .... 26 E4
Welbeck Cl. Ewell KT17 .... 58 A3
Welbeck Cl. Farnb GU14 .... 85 B1
Welbeck Cl. New Mal KT3 .... 38 F4
Welbeck Rd. Carsh SM3 & SM5 .. 59 D8
Welbeck Wlk. Carsh SM5 .... 40 D1
Welcome Cotts. Wold CR3 .... 102 A4
Welcome Terr. Whytlf CR3 .... 80 F3
Welcomes Rd. Kenley CR8 .... 80 C3
Weldon Cl. Thorn H CR7 .... 42 A4
Weldon Dr. E Mole KT8 .... 35 F5
Weldon Way. Merst RH1 .... 119 D6
Welford Pl. Wimble SW19 .... 19 E4
Welham Rd. Streat SW16 & SW17 21 B2
Welhouse Rd. Carsh SM5 .... 59 B8
Well Cl. Camb GU15 .... 66 A5
Well Cl. Horse GU21 .... 69 C2
Well Cl. Streat SW16 .... 21 F4
Well Farm Rd.
   Whytlf CR3 & CR6 .... 101 A8
Well House. Banstd SM7 .... 78 B4
Well La. Haslem GU27 .... 208 D6
Well La. Horse GU21 .... 69 C2
Well La. Mortl SW14 .... 7 C2
Well Path. Horse GU21 .... 69 C2
Well Way. Epsom KT18 .... 76 A5

Welland Cl. Bra Hil SL3 .... 1 B8
Wellburn Cl. Sandh GU17 .... 64 B7
Weller Cl. Worth RH10 .... 202 D5
Weller Dr. Camb GU15 .... 65 C3
Wellesford Cl. Banstd SM7 .... 77 F2
Wellesley Cl. Ash V GU12 .... 105 F7
Wellesley Cl. Bagsh GU19 .... 47 C3
Wellesley Court Rd. ¹
   Croy CR0 & CR9 .... 61 D8
Wellesley Cres. Twick TW2 .... 16 E5
Wellesley Ct. Cheam SM3 .... 39 E1
Wellesley Ct. Twick TW2 .... 16 E5
Wellesley Garden.
   Heath E GU9 .... 125 C7
Wellesley Gate. Alder GU12 ..... 105 B1
Wellesley Gr. Croy CR0 & CR9 ... 61 D8
Wellesley Rd. Alder GU11 .... 104 E2
Wellesley Rd. Croy CR0 .... 42 C1
Wellesley Rd. Farnb GU14 .... 104 D8
Wellesley Rd. Rushm GU10 ...... 168 C6
Wellesley Rd. Sutton SM2 .... 59 C4
Wellesley Rd. Twick TW2 .... 16 E5
Wellfield. Ash W RH19 .... 206 C7
Wellfield Rd. Streat SW16 .... 21 F4
Wellhouse Rd. Beck BR3 .... 44 A5
Wellhouse Rd. Betch RH3 .... 137 D6
Wellington Ave.
   Hounsl TW3 & TW4 .... 5 A2
Wellington Ave. N Cheam KT4 ... 58 C7
Wellington Ave. Vir W GU25 .... 31 B4
Wellington Ave. Went GU25 .... 31 B4
Wellington Cl. Crawl RH10 .... 182 E1
Wellington Cl. Sandh GU17 .... 64 C8
Wellington Cl. Walt O T KT12 ..... 34 F1
Wellington Coll. Crowth RG11 .... 45 A3
Wellington Cotts. E Hors KT24 .. 112 E6
Wellington Cres. King U T KT3 ... 38 C6
Wellington Ct. Stan TW19 .... 13 E8
Wellington Ct. ⁵ Surb KT6 .... 37 E3
Wellington Ct. Tedd TW12 .... 16 E8
Wellington Ctr. Alder GU11 ...... 105 A2
Wellington Dr. Brack RG12 .... 27 E4
Wellington Dr. Wallin CR8 .... 60 F1
Wellington Gdns. Alder GU11 ... 104 F1
Wellington Gdns.
   Tedd TW12 & TW2 .... 16 D4
Wellington La. Heath E GU9 ..... 125 D7
Wellington Prim Sch.
   Hounsl TW3 .... 4 F5
Wellington Rd. Ashf TW15 .... 13 E3
Wellington Rd. Cater CR3 .... 100 D5
Wellington Rd. Crowth RG11 ...... 45 C4
Wellington Rd. Hatton TW14 .... 3 E2
Wellington Rd.
   Horsh RH12 & RH13 .... 217 D2
Wellington Rd.
   Sandh GU15 & GU17 .... 64 C8
Wellington Rd.
   Tedd TW12 & TW2 .... 16 D4
Wellington Rd. Thorn H CR0 .... 42 B2
Wellington Rd. Wimble SW19 ..... 20 A6
Wellington Rd. Woki RG11 .... 25 B5
Wellington Rd N. Hounsl TW4 ...... 4 F4
Wellington Rd S. Hounsl TW4 ...... 4 F3
Wellington St. Alder GU11 .... 105 A2
Wellington Terr. ⁶ Knaph GU21 68 E1
Wellington Terr. Sandh GU15 ..... 64 C8
Wellington Town Rd.
   E Grins RH19 .... 185 D2
Wellington Way. Byfl KT13 .... 52 E1
Wellington Way. Farnb GU14 .... 104 D7
Wellington Way. Horley RH6 ..... 160 F5
Wellington Way. Whit V KT13 ..... 52 F1
Wellingtonia House. Addl KT15 .. 52 A5
Wellmeadow Rd.
   Catf SE21 & SE6 .... 24 E7
Wellow Wlk. Carsh SM5 .... 40 D1
Wells Cl. Fetch KT23 .... 94 C3
Wells Cl. Horsh RH12 .... 216 F2
Wells Cotts. Wreccl GU9 .... 146 A7
Wells La. Ascot SL5 .... 29 B5
Wells Lea. Normdy GU3 .... 107 C4
Wells Lea. E Grins RH19 .... 185 D3
Wells Meadow. E Grins RH19 ... 185 D3
Wells Park Ct. For Hil SE26 .... 23 B4
Wells Park Rd.
   For Hil SE21 & SE26 .... 23 B4
Wells Pl. Merst RH1 .... 119 B6
Wells Rd. Crawl RH10 .... 201 E2
Wells Rd. Epsom KT18 .... 76 B4
Wells Rd. Merrow GU4 .... 110 C4
Wells The. Haslem GU27 .... 208 C6
Wellside Gdns. Mortl SW14 .... 7 C2
Wellwood Cl. Coulsd CR5 & CR8 . 79 E5
Wellwood Rd. Horsh RH12 .... 218 B4
Wellwynds Rd. Cran GU6 .... 174 E2
Welwyn Ave. Felt TW14 .... 3 F1
Welwyn Cl. Crawl RH11 .... 200 E2
Wembley Rd. Hampt TW12 .... 36 A8
Wembury Pk. Newch RH7 .... 163 E1
Wend The. Coulsd CR5 .... 79 D5
Wendela Cl. Woking GU22 .... 69 F1
Wendley Dr. Woodhm KT15 .... 51 F3
Wendling Rd. Carsh SM1 & SM5 . 59 D8
Wendover Dr. Friml GU16 .... 66 D3
Wendover Dr. New Mal KT3 .... 38 F3
Wendover Pl. Egham TW18 .... 12 D3
Wendover Rd.
   Egham TW18 & TW20 .... 12 D3
Wendron Cl. ² Woking GU21 ...... 69 A1
Wendy Cres. Guild GU2 .... 109 A3
Wenlock Cl. Crawl RH11 .... 201 A4
Wenlock Edge. Dork RH4 .... 136 C5
Wensleydale. Crawl RH11 .... 200 D5
Wensleydale Dr. Friml GU15 ...... 66 D5
Wensleydale Gdns. Hampt TW12 16 B1
Wensleydale Rd. Hampt TW12 ... 16 B1

Wentland Cl. Catf SE6 .... 24 D6
Wentland Rd. Catf SE6 .... 24 D6
Wentworth Ave. N Asct SL5 .... 28 C7
Wentworth Cl. Ash V GU12 ...... 106 A7
Wentworth Cl. Ashf TW15 ...... 14 B4
Wentworth Cl. Heath E GU9 ...... 125 F6
Wentworth Cl. Long D KT6 ...... 56 D8
Wentworth Cl. Morden SM4 ...... 40 A2
Wentworth Cl. Ripley GU23 ...... 91 B6
Wentworth Club. Ash V GU25 .... 31 A4
Wentworth Cres. Ash V GU12 ... 106 A6
Wentworth Ct. King U T KT6 .. 37 E4
Wentworth Ct. Twick TW2 ...... 16 E5
Wentworth Dr. Crawl RH10 ...... 202 D7
Wentworth Dr. Went GU25 ...... 30 F5
Wentworth House. Addl KT15 .... 52 B6
Wentworth Rd. Thorn H CR0 ...... 42 A2
Wentworth Way. Hams Gn CR2 .. 81 A4
Wentworth Way. N Asct SL5 ...... 28 C7
Werndee Rd. Croy SE25 .... 43 A5
Wesco Cl. Woking GU21 .... 70 A3
Wescott Cty Inf Sch. Woki RG11 25 D6
Wescott Rd. Woki RG11 .... 25 D6
Wesley Ave. Hounsl TW3 .... 4 F5
Wesley Cl. Crawl RH11 .... 200 E3
Wesley Cl. Horley RH6 .... 161 A5
Wesley Cl. Reig RH2 .... 138 F8
Wesley Dr. Egham TW20 .... 12 A2
Wesley Pl. Wink SL4 .... 9 B6
Wessels. Tadw KT20 .... 97 D6
Wessex Ave. Merton SW19 ...... 40 A6
Wessex Cl. King U T KT1 & KT2 .. 38 B8
Wessex Cl. 4 Stan TW19 .... 2 E1
Wessex Pl. M Bourn GU9 ...... 125 C1
Wessex Rd. Farnb GU14 .... 84 F2
Wessex Rd. Harm TW19 & TW6 .. 2 E4
Wesson House. 3 Croy CR0 ...... 43 A1
West Ashtead Cty Prim Sch.
  Ashtd KT21 .... 95 E7
West Ave. Crawl RH10 .... 202 A8
West Ave. Earls RH1 .... 140 A3
West Ave. Heath E GU9 .... 125 D7
West Ave. Wallin CR0 & SM6 .... 60 E5
West Ave. Whit V KT12 & KT13 ... 53 E2
West Bank. Dork RH4 .... 136 A6
West Barnes La.
  W Barn KT3 & SW20 .... 39 B6
West Barnes La.
  Wimble KT3 & SW20 .... 39 E4
West Byfleet Cty Inf Sch.
  W Byfl KT14 .... 71 B7
West Byfleet Cty Jun Sch.
  W Byfl KT14 .... 71 B7
West Cl. Ashf TW15 .... 13 E4
West Cl. Heath E GU9 .... 125 D7
West Cross Ctr. Brent TW8 ...... 6 B8
West Cross Way. Brent TW8 ...... 6 B8
West Croydon Sta. Thorn H CR9 42 C1
West Ct. Burgh GU4 .... 110 B5
West Ct. Hounsl TW7 .... 5 C7
West Down. G Book KT23 ...... 114 B8
West Dr. Belm SM2 .... 58 E2
West Dr. Burgh H KT20 .... 77 D1
West Dr. Streat SW16 & SW17 ... 21 C4
West Dr. Sutton SM5 .... 59 D1
West Dr.
  Went GU24 & GU25 & SL5 .... 30 E2
West Dr. Woodhm KT15 .... 52 B2
West Dulwich Sta. Dulw SE21 .. 22 D7
West End Cty Inf Sch.
  Alder GU11 .... 104 F2
West End Gdns. Esher KT10 .... 54 F5
West End Gr. Farnh GU9 ...... 125 A2
West End La. Esher KT10 ...... 54 F4
West End La. Harl UB7 .... 3 C7
West Ewell Cty Inf Sch.
  W Ewell KT19 .... 57 D5
West Ewell Cty Inf Sch.
  W Ewell KT19 .... 57 D5
West Ewell Cty Jun Sch.
  W Ewell KT19 .... 57 D5
West Ewell Cty Jun Sch.
  W Ewell KT19 .... 57 D5
West Farm Ave. Ashtd KT21 .... 95 D8
West Farm Dr. Ashtd KT21 ...... 95 C8
West Farm Dr. Ashtd KT21 ...... 95 D8
West Flexford La. Wanb GU3 .. 128 E8
West Gdns. Ewell KT17 .... 57 F1
West Gdns. Mitch SW19 .... 20 E2
West Gr. Hersh KT12 .... 54 B6
West Green Cty Fst Sch.
  Crawl RH11 .... 201 C7
West Green Dr. Crawl RH11 .... 201 C6
West Hall Rd. Rich TW9 .... 7 B6
West Heath. Pirb GU24 .... 87 D4
West Heath Rd. W Heath GU14 .. 84 F4
West Hill. Dorm Pk RH19 ...... 185 E6
West Hill. Downe BR6 .... 83 F7
West Hill. E Grins RH19 ...... 205 D8
West Hill. Elst GU8 .... 148 C3
West Hill. Epsom KT18 & KT19 .. 76 C6
West Hill. Oxted RH8 .... 122 D5
West Hill. Putney SW15 .... 19 D8
West Hill. S Croy CR2 .... 61 E2
West Hill. Woking GU22 .... 89 E8
West Hill Ave. Epsom KT19 .... 76 C7
West Hill Bank. Oxted RH8 .... 122 C5
West Hill Cl. Brookw GU24 .... 88 B7
West Hill Cl. Elst GU8 .... 148 C3
West Hill Rd. Wands SW18 .... 20 A8
West Hill Rd. Woking GU22 .... 89 E8
West Hill Sch. Leahd KT22 .... 75 A1
West Hoathly Rd. E Grins RH19 205 D4
West House. Penge SE20 .... 23 D1
West House. 9 Streat SW16 .... 21 C8
West House La. Putney SW19 .. 19 E7
West La. E Grins RH19 .... 205 D8
West La. Wotton RH5 .... 134 D4

West Leigh. E Grins RH19 ...... 205 E7
West Mead. W Ewell KT19 ...... 57 E4
West Mead. W Ewell KT19 ...... 57 E4
West Mead Sch. Woki RG11 .... 25 E6
West Meads. Onsl V GU2 ...... 129 F8
West Middlesex Univ Hospl.
  Islew TW7 .... 6 A5
West Mount. Guild GU2 .... 130 C7
West Norwood Sta.
  W Norw SE27 .... 22 B5
West Oak. Beck BR3 .... 44 C8
West Palace Gdns. Weyb KT13 .. 53 B7
West Par. Horsh RH12 .... 217 C4
West Park Ave. Rich TW9 ...... 7 B6
West Park Cl. Heston TW5 ...... 4 F8
West Park Hospl. Epsom KT19 .. 75 E7
West Park Rd. Dome RH10 ...... 183 F5
West Park Rd. Epsom KT19 .... 75 F7
West Park Rd.
  Horne RH7 & RH10 .... 184 B7
West Park Rd. Rich TW9 .... 7 A6
West Pl. Wimble SW19 .... 19 C3
West Ramp. Harm TW6 .... 3 A6
West Rd. Camb GU15 .... 65 D5
West Rd. Chess KT9 .... 75 C8
West Rd. E Bed TW14 .... 14 D8
West Rd. Easth RG11 & RG12 ... 26 D2
West Rd. Farnb GU14 .... 85 B8
West Rd. Guild GU1 .... 130 E8
West Rd. King U T KT2 & KT3 .. 38 C3
West Rd. Reig RH2 .... 139 B8
West Rd. Whit V KT13 .... 53 B3
West Ring. Tongh GU10 ...... 126 F7
West Sheen Vale. Rich TW9 .... 6 F3
West Side Comm. Wimble SW19 19 C3
West St. Carsh SM5 .... 59 F5
West St. Crawl RH11 .... 201 D5
West St. Croy CR0 & CR9 ...... 61 C6
West St. Dork RH4 .... 136 A7
West St. Dorman RH7 .... 165 A1
West St. E Grins RH19 .... 205 E8
West St. Epsom KT18 & KT19 .. 76 C6
West St. Ewell KT17 .... 57 F1
West St. Farnh GU9 .... 125 A2
West St. Haslem GU27 ...... 208 C6
West St. Horsh RH12 .... 217 C2
West St. Reig RH2 .... 117 F1
West St. Sutton SM1 .... 59 B5
West St. Woking GU21 .... 69 F2
West Street La. Carsh SM5 .... 59 F6
West Street Pl. 1
  Croy CR0 & CR9 .... 61 C6
West Surrey Estates.
  Littlt TW5 .... 34 C8
West Sutton Sta. Sutton SM1 .. 59 A6
West Temple Sheen. Mortl SW14 7 B2
West Thames Coll. Hounsl TW7 .. 5 E6
West Thornton Prim Sch.
  Thorn H CR0 .... 41 F3
West View Ave. E Bed TW14 .... 14 C8
West View Ave. Whytlf CR3 .... 80 F1
West View Gdns. E Grins RH19 205 E8
West View Rd. Head Dn GU35 .. 187 C4
West View Rd. Warlgm CR6 .... 101 B8
West Way. Crawl RH10 .... 202 A7
West Way. Croy CR0 .... 62 E7
West Way. Heston TW5 .... 4 D6
West Way. Shep TW17 .... 34 D3
West Way. Slinfd RH13 .... 215 D3
West Way. Sutton SM2 & SM5 .. 59 D1
West Way. W Wick BR4 .... 44 E3
West Way Gdns. Croy CR0 .... 62 D8
West Wickham Sta. W Wick BR3 44 C2
Westacres. Esher KT10 .... 54 F3
Westbank Rd. Hampt TW12 .... 16 C2
Westborough Cty State Prim Sch.
  Stough GU2 .... 108 F2
Westbourne Ave. Cheam SM3 .. 58 E8
Westbourne Dr. For Hil SE23 .. 23 D6
Westbourne House. Heston TW5 . 5 A8
Westbourne House. 9
  Twick TW1 .... 17 B8
Westbourne Prim Sch.
  Sutton SM1 .... 59 A7
Westbourne Rd. Croy CR0 ...... 42 F3
Westbourne Rd. Felt TW13 .... 14 F5
Westbourne Rd. Penge SE26 ... 23 D2
Westbourne Rd. Sandh GU15 .. 64 E7
Westbourne Rd. Stain TW18 .... 13 B1
Westbrook. For Row RH18 ...... 206 E3
Westbrook Ave. Hampt TW12 .. 15 F1
Westbrook Gdns. Brack RG12 .. 27 D8
Westbrook Hill. Elst GU8 ...... 148 C3
Westbrook Rd. Heston TW5 .... 4 F7
Westbrook Rd. Ock Rid GU7 .. 150 C5
Westbrook Rd. S Norw CR7 .... 42 D7
Westbrook Rd. Stain TW18 .... 12 F3
Westbury Ave. Clayg KT10 .... 55 F4
Westbury Cl. Crowth RG11 .... 45 B6
Westbury Cl. Shep TW17 ...... 34 B3
Westbury Cl. Whytlf CR3 ...... 80 F1
Westbury Ct. Beck BR3 .... 44 B8
Westbury House Sch.
  New Mal KT3 .... 38 D4
Westbury Pl. 2 Brent TW8 ...... 6 D8
Westbury Rd. Beck BR3 .... 43 E6
Westbury Rd. Felt TW13 .... 15 D6
Westbury Rd. New Mal KT3 .... 38 D4
Westbury Rd. Penge SE20 ...... 43 D8
Westbury Rd. Thorn H CR0 .... 42 D3
Westcar La. Hersh KT12 .... 54 B5
Westcombe Ave. Thorn H CR0 .. 41 F2
Westcombe Ave. Wimble SW20 38 F8
Westcote Rd. Streat SW16 ...... 21 C3
Westcott C of E Fst Sch.
  Westc RH4 .... 135 D5
Westcott Rd. New Add CR0 .... 63 B2
Westcott Rd. Dork RH4 .... 135 F7
Westcott St. Westc RH4 .... 135 B6
Westcott Way. E Ewell SM2 .... 58 C1

Westcroft Gdns.
  Merton SM4 & SW20 .... 39 F5
Westcroft Rd. Hackb SM5 & SM6 60 A6
Westdene. Godal GU7 .... 150 E3
Westdene Meadows.
  Cran GU6 .... 174 A3
Westdown Rd.
  For Hil SE13 & SE6 .... 24 A8
Westende. Woki RG11 .... 25 D6
Westende Cty Jun Sch.
  Woki RG11 .... 25 D6
Westerdale Rd. Friml GU16 .... 66 B3
Westerfolds Cl. Mayb GU22 .... 70 C2
Westerham. 13 King U T KT6 .. 37 E4
Westerham Cl. Belm SM2 ...... 59 A1
Westerham Cl. New Haw KT15 .. 52 C4
Westerham Lodge. 10
  Beck BR3 .... 24 A1
Westerham Rd.
  Limps RH8 & TN16 .... 123 C6
Westerley Cres.
  For Hil SE26 & SE6 .... 23 F3
Westermain. Woodhm KT15 .... 52 C1
Western Apron Rd. Crawl RH6 181 F8
Western Ave. Egham TW20 ...... 32 B6
Western Ave. Thorpe KT16 ...... 33 A6
Western Cl. Thorpe KT16 ...... 33 A6
Western Ctr The. Brack RG12 ... 26 F7
Western Dr. Shep TW17 .... 34 D3
Western Ind Area. Brack RG12 .. 27 A7
Western La. Balham SW12 ...... 21 A8
Western Perimeter Rd.
  Harm TW19 & TW6 & UB7 ... 2 B5
Western Rd. Alder GU11 ...... 104 E1
Western Rd. Brack RG12 .... 26 F7
Western Rd. Mitch CR4 & SW19 .. 40 E7
Western Rd. Sutton SM1 ...... 59 A5
Westfield. Ashtd KT21 .... 75 F1
Westfield. Peasl GU5 .... 154 E8
Westfield. Reig RH2 .... 118 B4
Westfield Ave. Sander CR2 & CR8 80 E6
Westfield Ave. Westfd GU22 .. 89 E7
Westfield Cl. Cheam SM1 ...... 58 F6
Westfield Comm. Westfd GU22 . 89 E5
Westfield Ct. King U T KT6 .... 37 D4
Westfield Ct. New Haw KT15 ... 52 D1
Westfield Dr. Fetch KT23 ...... 94 B5
Westfield Gr. Westfd GU22 .... 89 E7
Westfield Rd. Wreccl GU10 ... 145 E6
Westfield Par. New Haw KT15 .. 52 D1
Westfield Prim Sch.
  Westfd GU22 .... 89 F6
Westfield Rd. Beck BR3 .... 43 F7
Westfield Rd. Camb GU15 ...... 65 B2
Westfield Rd. Cheam SM1 ...... 58 F6
Westfield Rd. Crawl RH11 ...... 201 B6
Westfield Rd. King U T KT6 .... 37 D4
Westfield Rd. Stough GU1 ...... 109 B5
Westfield Rd. Thorn H CR0 & CR9 61 B8
Westfield Rd. Walt O T KT12 ... 35 E2
Westfield Rd. Westfd GU22 .... 89 E5
Westfield Way. Westfd GU22 .. 89 F5
Westfields. Mortl SW13 .... 7 F4
Westfields Ave.
  Mortl SW13 & SW14 .... 7 E4
Westfields Sch. Mortl SW13 .... 7 F4
Westgate. Beck BR3 .... 44 C8
Westgate Rd. Croy SE25 .... 43 B5
Westglade. Farnb GU14 .... 84 D4
Westhall Pk. Warlgm CR6 ...... 101 C8
Westhall Rd. Warlgm CR6 ...... 101 B8
Westhay Gdns. Mortl SW14 .... 7 B2
Westhumble St. Westh RH5 .... 115 B4
Westland Cl. Stain TW19 .... 2 E1
Westland Dr. Coney H BR2 & BR4 63 F8
Westlands. Horsh RH13 .... 217 E3
Westlands Cl. E Mole KT8 ...... 36 E5
Westlands Ct. Epsom KT18 .... 76 C4
Westlands Way. Oxted RH8 ... 122 D8
Westleas. Horley RH6 .... 160 E5
Westlees Cl. Dork RH5 .... 136 D4
Westleigh Ave. Coulsd CR5 .... 79 B3
Westmacott Dr. E Bed TW14 .. 14 F7
Westmark Point. 13
  Rhampt SW15 .... 19 B7
Westmead. Farnb GU14 .... 85 B3
Westmead. 8 Farnh GU9 ...... 125 B2
Westmead. Putney SW15 ...... 19 B8
Westmead. Woking GU21 ...... 69 B2
Westmead Dr. Salfs RH1 ...... 140 A1
Westmead Rd. Carsh SM1 ...... 59 D6
Westminster Ave. S Norw CR7 . 42 B7
Westminster Cl. E Bed TW14 ... 15 A7
Westminster Cl. Teddl TW11 .... 17 A3
Westminster Cl. Old Wok GU22 . 90 B6
Westminster Rd.
  Carsh SM1 & SM5 .... 59 D8
Westminster Rd. Worth RH10 .. 202 C5
Westmoat Cl. Beck BR3 .... 24 C1
Westmont Rd. Hinch W KT10 ... 55 E8
Westmore Rd. Tats TN16 ...... 103 C7
Westmoreland Dr. Sutton SM2 .. 59 B2
Westmoreland Rd. Barnes SW13 .. 7 F6
Westmoreland Rd.
  Beck BR2 & BR3 .... 44 F5
Westmorland Cl. Epsom KT19 .. 57 E2
Westmorland Ct. 3 Twick TW1 .. 6 B1
Westmorland Ct. 12 Surb KT6 .. 37 D2
Westmorland Dr.
  Friml GU15 & GU16 .... 66 B3
Westmorland Sq. Mitch CR4 .. 41 E4
Westmorland Way. Mitch CR4 .. 41 E5
Weston Ave. Addl KT15 .... 52 B6
Weston Ave. E Mole KT8 ...... 35 F5
Weston Ave.
  Thame D KT10 & KT7 .... 36 E2
Weston Cl. Coulsd CR5 .... 99 F7
Weston Cl. Farnc GU7 .... 150 E6

Weston Ct. Farnc GU7 .... 150 E6
Weston Ct. 3 King U T KT1 ... 37 E6
Weston Fields. Albury GU5 .... 132 C4
Weston Gdns. Hounsl TW7 ...... 5 E6
Weston Gn. Thame D KT7 ...... 36 E1
Weston Gr. Bagsh GU19 .... 47 F2
Weston Gr. Broml BR1 .... 44 F8
Weston Green Prep Sch.
  Thame D KT7 .... 36 E1
Weston Green Rd. Thame D KT7 36 E2
Weston Lea. W Hors KT24 ...... 92 D2
Weston Park. Thame D KT7 .... 36 E1
Weston Pk. King U T KT1 ...... 37 E7
Weston Pk. Thame D KT10 & KT7 36 E1
Weston Rd. Broml BR1 .... 24 F1
Weston Rd. Ewell KT17 .... 76 E8
Weston Rd. Stough GU2 ...... 109 A2
Weston Rd. Thame D KT7 ...... 36 E1
Weston Way. Pyrf GU22 .... 70 F3
Westons Cl. Sutton SM2 ...... 59 B2
Westover Cl. Sutton SM2 ...... 59 B2
Westover Rd. Wands SW18 .... 20 C8
Westow Hill. S Norw SE19 .... 22 F2
Westow St. S Norw SE19 ...... 22 E2
Westpoint. Beck BR2 .... 44 D6
Westview. 5 Woking GU22 .... 69 F1
Westview Cl. Earls RH1 .... 139 E6
Westville Rd. Thame D KT7 .... 37 A2
Westward Ho. Abbots GU1 .... 109 F3
Westwates Cl. Wink RG12 ...... 27 E8
Westway. Cater CR3 .... 100 D5
Westway. Copth RH10 .... 183 A3
Westway. Crawl RH6 .... 182 B7
Westway. W Barn KT3 & SW20 .. 39 C5
Westway. W Barn SW20 .... 39 B6
Westway Ct. Cater CR3 .... 100 D4
Westway Gdns. Redh RH1 ...... 119 A4
Westways. Worc Pk KT19 ...... 57 F6
Westwell Rd. Streat SW16 ...... 21 E2
Westwell Road App.
  Streat SW16 .... 21 E2
Westwick Gdns. Cranf TW4 & TW5 4 B5
Westwood Ave. S Norw SE19 .. 42 C8
Westwood Ave. Woodhm KT15 .. 70 F7
Westwood Cl. Esher KT10 ...... 55 C7
Westwood Ct. For Hil SE23 .... 23 C7
Westwood Ct. Stough GU2 .... 108 F2
Westwood Ct. 7 Wimble SW19 . 19 F3
Westwood Gdns. Mortl SW13 .. 7 F4
Westwood Hill.
  For Hil SE19 & SE26 .... 23 B4
Westwood La. Flexf GU3 ...... 107 A2
Westwood La. Normdy GU3 .... 107 A2
Westwood La. Wanb GU3 ...... 128 B7
Westwood Park Prim Sch.
  Stough GU2 .... 108 E1
Westwood Pk. For Hil SE23 .... 23 B8
Westwood Rd. Coulsd CR5 .... 79 D1
Westwood Rd.
  Mortl SW13 & SW15 .... 7 F4
Westwood Rd. Windl GU20 .... 48 E6
Westwood Sch. S Norw SE19 .. 22 D1
Wetheral Cl. Up Toot SW17 .... 20 D4
Wetherby Ct. S Norw SE25 .... 42 E7
Wetherby Gdns. 2 Farnb GU14 85 C1
Wetherby House. Camb GU15 .. 65 D7
Wetherby Way. Chess KT9 .... 56 E3
Wettern Cl. S Croy CR2 .... 61 E1
Wetton Pl. Egham TW20 .... 11 F3
Wexfenne Gdns. Pyrf GU22 ... 71 B3
Wexford Rd. Balham SW12 .... 20 F8
Wey Ave. Thorpe KT16 .... 33 A6
Wey Cl. Ash GU12 .... 106 A1
Wey Cl. Camb GU15 .... 65 B5
Wey Cl. W Byfl KT14 .... 71 B6
Wey Ct. Farnc GU7 .... 151 A6
Wey Ct. New Haw KT15 .... 52 D2
Wey Ct. W Ewell KT19 .... 57 C6
Wey Ct. W Ewell KT19 .... 57 C6
Wey Hill. Shottm GU27 ...... 208 A6
Wey House Sch. Shalf GU5 ... 151 E8
Wey Manor Rd. New Haw KT15 .. 52 D2
Wey Rd. Godal GU7 .... 151 A5
Wey Rd. Weyb KT13 .... 52 F7
Weybank. Wisley GU23 .... 71 E3
Weybank Cl. Farnh GU9 ...... 125 C3
Weybarton. Byfl KT14 .... 71 F6
Weybourne Cty Inf Sch.
  Heath E GU9 .... 125 E6
Weybourne Pl. S Croy CR2 .... 61 D1
Weybourne Rd.
  Heath E GU11 & GU9 .... 125 E6
Weybourne St. Wands SW18 .. 20 C6
Weybridge Bsns Pk. Addl KT15 . 52 E6
Weybridge Hospl. Weyb KT13 .. 53 A6
Weybridge House. Whit V KT13 . 53 D5
Weybridge Pk. Weyb KT13 ...... 53 B5
Weybridge Rd. Addl KT15 & KT13 52 E6
Weybridge Rd. Thorn H CR7 .. 42 A5
Weybridge Rd.
  Weyb KT13 & KT15 .... 52 E6
Weybridge Sta. Weyb KT13 .... 53 A4
Weybridge Trad Est. Addl KT15 52 D6
Weybrook Dr. Burgh GU4 ...... 110 B6
Weycombe Rd. Haslem GU27 .. 208 C8
Weydon Hill Cl. M Bourn GU9 . 146 B8
Weydon Hill Rd. M Bourn GU9 . 146 C8
Weydon La. M Bourn GU9 ...... 146 A8
Weydon La. Wreccl GU9 ...... 145 F8
Weydon Mill La. Farnh GU9 .. 125 B1
Weydon Sch. Wreccl GU9 ...... 145 F7
Weydown Cl. Putney SW19 .... 19 E7
Weydown Cl. Stough GU2 ...... 109 A6
Weydown Ct. Haslem GU27 ... 208 B7
Weydown La. Stough GU2 ...... 109 A6
Weydown Rd. Haslem GU27 ... 208 B7
Weyfield Prim Sch. Bellf GU1 . 109 D4
Weylands Pk. Whit V KT13 .... 53 D4
Weylea Ave. Burph GU1 & GU4 .. 110 A4

Weymead Cl. Chert KT16 ...... 33 C1
Weymede. Byfl KT14 .... 71 F7
Weymouth Ct. Belm SM2 ...... 59 A3
Weymouth Ct. 18 Streat SW2 .. 21 F8
Weyside. Farnh GU9 .... 125 C2
Weyside Cl. Byfl KT14 .... 71 F7
Weyside Gdns. Bellf GU1 ...... 109 C3
Weyside Rd. Bellf GU1 .... 109 B3
Weysprings. Shottm GU27 .... 208 A6
Weyvern Pk. Shalf GU3 .... 130 B1
Weywood Cl. Heath E GU9 .... 125 F7
Weywood La. Heath E GU9 .... 125 E7
Whaley Rd. Woki RG11 .... 25 D8
Wharf Bridge Rd. Islew TW7 .. 6 B4
Wharf La. Send GU23 .... 90 C4
Wharf La. Twick TW1 .... 17 A7
Wharf Rd. Ash GU12 .... 106 A4
Wharf Rd. Friml GU16 .... 86 A6
Wharf Rd. Guild GU1 .... 109 C1
Wharf Rd. Wray TW19 .... 11 D8
Wharf St. Godal GU7 .... 150 E4
Wharf Way. Friml GU16 .... 86 A6
Wharfedale Gdns.
  Thorn H CR7 & SW16 .... 41 F6
Wharfenden Way. Friml GU16 .. 85 F6
Wharncliffe Gdns. S Norw SE25 42 E7
Wharncliffe Rd. S Norw SE25 ... 42 E7
Whateley Rd. Penge SE20 ...... 23 D1
Whateley Rd. Stough GU2 .... 109 B5
Whatley Ave. Merton SW20 .... 39 E6
Whatley Gn. Easth RG12 ...... 27 B3
Whatman Rd. For Hil SE23 .... 23 D8
Whatmore Cl. Stan TW19 ...... 2 A1
Wheat Knoll. Kenley CR8 ...... 80 C5
Wheatash Rd. Chert KT15 .... 33 B1
Wheatash Rd. Chert KT15 .... 52 B8
Wheatfield Way. Horley RH6 .. 161 C4
Wheatfield Way. King U T KT1 .. 37 E7
Wheathill House. Penge SE20 .. 43 B7
Wheathill Rd. Penge SE20 ...... 43 B6
Wheatlands. Heston TW5 ...... 5 A8
Wheatlands Rd. Up Toot SW17 .. 21 A5
Wheatley. Easth SW20 .... 26 E4
Wheatley House. 3
  Rhampt SW15 .... 19 A8
Wheatley Rd. Islew TW7 .... 5 F4
Wheatley's Ait. Lo Hall TW16 .. 35 A4
Wheatley's Ait. Sunby TW16 ... 35 A4
Wheatsheaf Cl. Horsh RH12 ... 217 E5
Wheatsheaf Cl. Ottsh KT16 .... 51 D4
Wheatsheaf Cl. Woking GU21 .. 69 F3
Wheatsheaf La. Stain TW18 .... 12 F1
Wheatstone Cl. Crawl RH10 .. 182 B3
Wheatstone Cl. Mitch SW19 .... 40 E8
Wheeler Ave. Oxted RH8 ...... 122 D6
Wheeler La. Witley GU8 ...... 170 E6
Wheeler Rd. Worth RH10 ...... 202 B4
Wheelers La. Brock RH3 ...... 137 C7
Wheelers La. Epsom KT18 .... 76 C5
Wheelers La. Smallf RH6 ...... 162 B3
Wheelers Way. Felb RH19 ...... 184 E3
Wheelwrights La. Graysh GU26 188 A4
Wheelwrights Pl. Coln SL3 .... 1 C7
Whelan Way. Wallin SM6 ...... 60 D7
Wherwell Lodge. Guild GU2 .. 130 C7
Wherwell Rd. Guild GU2 ...... 130 C7
Whetstone Rd. W Heath GU14 . 84 C4
Whimbrel Cl. S Croy CR2 & CR8 . 80 D8
Whinfell Cl. Streat SW16 ...... 21 D3
Whins Cl. Camb GU15 .... 65 B4
Whins Dr. Camb GU15 .... 65 B4
Whinshill Ct. Sunnin SL5 ...... 30 A1
Whipley Cl. Burph GU4 .... 110 B6
Whirlwind Track. Farnb GU14 . 104 D7
Whistler Cl. Crawl RH10 ...... 201 F3
Whistler Gr. Sandh GU15 ...... 64 D6
Whistley Cl. Brack RG12 ...... 27 E6
Whitby Cl. Bigg H TN16 .... 83 B1
Whitby Gdns. Carsh SM1 & SM5 .. 59 D8
Whitby Rd. Carsh SM1 & SM5 .. 59 D8
Whitchurch Cl. Alder GU11 ... 126 D6
Whitchurch Ct. Up Toot SW17 . 20 D4
Whitchurch House. Catf SE6 .. 24 C5
White Acres Rd. Mytch GU16 .. 85 F4
White Beam Way. Tadw KT20 .. 97 A6
White Bridge Cl. Felt TW14 .... 3 F1
White Bushes. Earls RH1 ...... 140 A4
White City. Crowth RG11 ...... 45 D5
White Cottage Cl. Heath E GU9 125 D6
White Ct. Stough GU2 .... 109 A4
White Hart Ct. Horsh RH12 ... 217 C4
White Hart Ct. Ripley GU23 .... 91 C6
White Hart Ind Est. Blckw GU17 64 E4
White Hart La. Mortl SW14 ...... 7 E4
White Hart La. Wood S V GU3 .. 108 A2
White Hart Lodge.
  Wimble SW19 .... 20 C2
White Hart Meadows.
  Ripley GU23 .... 91 C6
White Hart Row. Chert KT16 .. 33 A2
White Heron Mews. Tedd TW11 16 F2
White Hill. Kings CR5 .... 98 D4
White Hill. S Croy CR2 .... 61 D1
White Hill. Windl GU20 .... 48 B6
White Horse Dr. Epsom KT18 .. 76 C5
White Horse La. Ripley GU23 .. 91 C6
White House. 3 Streat SW4 .... 21 D8
White House La. Beck BR3 .... 44 C8
White House La. Jacobs GU4 .. 109 D6
White House Prep Sch.
  Woki RG11 .... 25 A3
White House Wlk.
  Heath E GU9 .... 125 D7
White Knights Rd. Whit V KT13 . 53 C3
White Knobs Way. Cater CR3 .. 101 A2
White La. Ash GU10 & GU12 ... 127 C7
White La. Merrow GU4 .... 131 D7
White La. Titsey RH8 & TN16 .. 103 B3
White La. Tongh GU10 & GU12 . 127 C7
White Lodge. Ashtd KT21 ...... 95 E7
White Lodge. S Norw SE19 .... 22 B1

White Lodge Cl. Sutton SM2 59 C3
White Lodge Gdns. Salfs RH1 140 A1
White Lodge The Royal Ballet Sch. Rich TW10 18 D7
White Oak Dr. Beck BR3 44 D7
White Post La. Rowl GU10 146 A4
White Rd. Sandh GU15 64 F6
White Rose La. M Bourn GU9 146 B7
White Rose La. Mayb GU22 90 A8
White Rose La. Woking GU22 69 F1
White Way. G Book KT23 94 B1
Whitebeam Dr. Woodh RH2 139 B6
Whitebeams Gdns. Farnb GU14 84 C3
Whiteberry Rd. Wotton RH5 156 B7
Whitebines. Farnh GU9 125 D2
Whitecroft Cl. Beck BR3 44 D5
Whitecroft Way. Beck BR3 44 D5
Whitefield Ave. Purley CR8 80 B3
Whitefield House. Purley CR8 80 B3
Whitefoot La. Catf BR1 & SE6 24 D5
Whitefoot Terr. Catf BR1 24 F5
Whitegate Way. Burgh H KT20 97 B7
Whitegates. Old Wok GU22 89 F7
Whitegates. Whytlf CR3 101 A8
Whitehall Cres. Chess KT9 56 D5
Whitehall Dr. Crawl RH11 200 E6
Whitehall Farm La. Thorpe GU25 31 E6
Whitehall Gdns. Chisw W4 7 B8
Whitehall La. Egham TW20 11 F1
Whitehall La. Horton TW19 1 A1
Whitehall La. Woodh RH2 138 F6
Whitehall Park Rd. Chisw W4 7 B8
Whitehall Pl. Wallin SM5 60 B6
Whitehall Rd. Thorn H CR7 42 A4
Whitehead Cl. Wands SW18 20 C8
Whitehill Cl. Camb GU15 65 D7
Whitehill La. Bletch RH1 120 D6
Whitehill La. Mart Gn GU23 92 C4
Whitehill Pl. Thorpe GU25 31 E4
Whitehorse La. S Norw SE25 42 E5
Whitehorse Manor Inf Sch. S Norw CR7 42 D5
Whitehorse Manor Jun Sch. S Norw CR7 42 D5
Whitehorse Rd. Horsh RH12 218 B6
Whitehorse Rd. S Norw CR0 & CR7 & SE25 42 D3
Whitehorse Rd. Thorn H CR0 & CR7 & SE25 42 D3
Whitehouse Dr. Merrow GU1 110 B1
Whitelands Coll. Putney SW18 19 E8
Whitelands Dr. N Asct SL5 28 D8
Whiteley House. 9 Streat SW4 21 D8
Whiteley House & Hospl. Whit V KT12 53 F2
Whiteley Rd. W Norw SE19 22 D3
Whiteleys House. Felt TW13 16 A5
Whiteleys Way. Felt TW13 16 A5
Whitelocke Cty Inf Sch. Woki RG11 25 D7
Whitely Hill. Worth RH10 202 F1
Whitely Way. Farnb GU14 84 E1
Whitemore Rd. Bellf GU1 109 D5
Whiteoak House. S Norw SE19 22 C1
Whiteoaks. Banstd SM7 78 B6
Whitepost Hill. Redh RH1 118 E1
Whitepost House. Redh RH1 118 E1
Whites Dr. Hayes BR2 44 F2
Whites Rd. Farnb GU14 85 E1
Whitethorn Ave. Wallin CR5 79 B4
Whitethorn Cotts. Rowly GU6 174 B6
Whitethorn Gdns. Croy CR0 62 B8
Whiteways Ct. Stain TW18 13 B1
Whiteways End. Farnh GU10 126 D4
Whitewood Cotts. Tats TN16 103 C7
Whitewood La. Horne RH9 163 B7
Whitfield Cl. Haslem GU27 189 C1
Whitfield Cl. Stough GU2 109 A4
Whitfield Ct. 3 Dulw SE21 22 E4
Whitfield Rd. Haslem GU27 189 C1
Whitford Gdns. Mitch CR4 40 F6
Whitgift Ave. Croy CR2 61 C5
Whitgift Ctr. Croy CR9 61 C8
Whitgift House. Croy CR2 61 C5
Whitgift Sch. Croy CR2 61 C5
Whitgift St. Croy CR0 & CR9 61 C7
Whitgift Wlk. Crawl RH10 201 D3
Whitland Rd. Carsh SM5 40 D1
Whitley Cl. Stan TW19 2 E1
Whitlock Dr. Putney SW19 19 E7
Whitmead Cl. S Croy CR2 61 E4
Whitmead La. Tilf GU10 147 E4
Whitmoor La. Westfd GU4 89 D1
Whitmoor Rd. Bagsh GU19 47 F2
Whitmoor Vale Rd. Beac H GU26 188 A5
Whitmore Cl. Sandh GU15 45 D1
Whitmore Gn. Heath E GU9 125 E6
Whitmore La. Sunnin SL5 30 A5
Whitmore Rd. Beck BR3 43 F6
Whitmore Vale. Graysh GU26 187 F6
Whitmore Vale. Head Dn GU26 187 F6
Whitmore Vale Rd. Graysh GU26 188 A4
Whitmore Vale Rd. Head Dn GU10 & GU26 187 E7
Whitmore Way. Horley RH6 160 E3
Whitmores Cl. Woodc KT18 76 C4
Whitstable Cl. Beck BR3 43 F8
Whittaker Ave. Rich TW10 & TW9 6 D2
Whittaker Ct. Ashtd KT21 75 D2
Whittaker Pl. 24 Rich TW10 6 D2
Whittaker Rd. Cheam SM3 58 F7
Whittam House. W Norw SE27 22 C3
Whittell Gdns. For Hil SE26 23 C5
Whittingham Ct. Chisw W4 7 E7
Whittington Coll. Felb RH19 185 A4
Whittington Ct. Penge SE20 43 B7
Whittington Rd. Crawl RH10 201 E3
Whittle Cl. Sandh GU17 45 A1
Whittle Cres. W Heath GU14 84 F7
Whittle Rd. Heston TW5 4 C7
Whittle Way. Crawl RH10 182 A3
Whittlebury Cl. Wallin SM5 59 F2
Whitton Dene. Islew TW2 & TW3 & TW7 5 D2
Whitton Dene. Twick TW2 & TW7 5 D1
Whitton Manor Rd. Islew TW7 5 C1
Whitton Rd. Brack RG12 27 F6
Whitton Rd. Hounsl TW3 5 B2
Whitton Rd. Islew TW3 5 B2
Whitton Rd. Twick TW1 17 A8
Whitton Sch. Twick TW2 16 B6
Whitton Sta. Twick TW2 16 C8
Whitton Waye. Twick TW2 & TW3 5 A1
Whitworth Rd. Crawl RH11 181 D2
Whitworth Rd. S Norw SE25 42 F5
Whopshott Ave. Horse GU21 69 C3
Whopshott Cl. Horse GU21 69 C3
Whopshott Dr. Horse GU21 69 C3
Whynstones Rd. Ascot SL5 29 A4
Whyte Ave. Alder GU12 126 D7
Whyteacre. Whytlf CR3 101 B7
Whytebeam View. Whytlf CR3 80 F1
Whytecliffe Rd N. Purley CR8 80 B8
Whytecliffe Rd S. Purley CR8 80 B8
Whytecroft. Heston TW5 4 D7
Whyteleafe Bsns Village. Whytlf CR3 80 F2
Whyteleafe Hill. Whytlf CR3 80 F1
Whyteleafe Rd. Cater CR3 100 F6
Whyteleafe Rd. Whytlf CR3 100 F6
Whyteleafe Sch. Whytlf CR3 80 F1
Whyteleafe South Sta. Whytlf CR3 101 A8
Whyteleafe Sta. Whytlf CR3 80 F2
Wick House. 1 Tedd KT1 37 D8
Wick La. Eng Gn TW20 10 F3
Wick Rd. Eng Gn TW20 11 B1
Wick Rd. Tedd TW11 17 C1
Wicket Hill. Wreccl GU10 & GU9 146 A6
Wicket The. Add CR0 63 A5
Wickets The. Ashf TW15 13 E4
Wickham Ave. Cheam KT4 & SM3 58 C5
Wickham Ave. Croy CR0 43 E1
Wickham Chase. W Wick BR4 44 E2
Wickham Cl. Horley RH6 160 F4
Wickham Cl. New Mal KT3 38 F4
Wickham Court Rd. W Wick BR4 63 C8
Wickham Cres. W Wick BR4 63 C8
Wickham La. Thor L TW20 12 A1
Wickham Rd. Beck BR3 44 B6
Wickham Rd. Camb GU15 65 E8
Wickham Rd. Croy CR0 & CR9 62 E8
Wickham Vale. Easth RG11 & RG12 26 E3
Wickham Way. Beck BR3 44 C4
Wickhurst Gdns. Broad H RH12 216 E3
Wickhurst La. Broad H RH12 216 E3
Wickland Ct. Crawl RH10 201 D3
Wicklow Ct. Penge SE26 23 C3
Wide Way. Mitch CR4 & SW16 41 D6
Widgeon Way. Horsh RH12 217 C5
Widmen Ct. Hounsl TW5 4 E5
Wigan Rd. Farnb GU14 104 D8
Wiggie La. Redh RH1 119 A3
Wigley Rd. Felt TW13 15 D7
Wigmore La. Bear Gn RH5 157 C1
Wigmore Rd. Carsh SM5 40 E1
Wigmore Wlk. Carsh SM5 59 D8
Wilberforce Ct. Epsom KT18 76 D5
Wilberforce Way. Brack RG12 27 D4
Wilberforce Way. Wimble SW19 19 D2
Wilbury Ave. Belm SM2 58 F1
Wilbury Rd. Woking GU21 69 D2
Wilcot Cl. Bisley GU24 68 A3
Wilcot Gdns. Bisley GU24 68 A3
Wilcox Gdns. Littlt TW17 33 F6
Wilcox Rd. Sutton SM1 59 B6
Wilcox Rd. Tedd TW11 16 D4
Wild Acres. W Byfl KT14 71 C8
Wildacre Cl. Ifold RH14 212 D3
Wildbank Ct. 2 Woking GU22 69 F1
Wildcroft Dr. Dork RH5 136 D4
Wildcroft Dr. Woki RG11 25 A1
Wildcroft Manor. Putney SW15 19 C8
Wildcroft Rd. Putney SW15 19 C8
Wildcroft Wood. Witley GU8 170 D6
Wilde Theatre. Easth RG12 27 C2
Wilderness Ct. Onsl V GU2 129 F7
Wilderness Rd. Friml GU16 65 E2
Wilderness Rd. Onsl V GU2 129 F7
Wilderness Rd. Oxted RH8 122 E5
Wilderness Rise. Dorman RH19 186 A6
Wilderness The. E Mole KT8 36 C4
Wilderness The. Hampt TW12 16 B4
Wilders Cl. Friml GU15 65 E3
Wilders Cl. Woking GU21 69 C1
Wilderwick Rd. Dorman RH19 & RH7 186 A5
Wildfell Rd. Lewish SE6 24 B8
Wildfield Cl. Wood S V GU3 108 B2
Wildgoose Dr. Horsh RH12 216 F3
Wildridings Cty Prim Sch. Easth RG12 27 A5
Wildridings Rd. Easth RG12 27 A5
Wildridings Sq. Easth RG12 27 A5
Wildwood Cl. E Hors KT24 92 F2
Wildwood Cl. Lewish SE12 24 F8
Wildwood Cl. Pyrf GU22 70 F4
Wildwood Ct. Kenley CR8 80 D4
Wildwood La. Alf Cr GU6 194 C5
Wilford Rd. Thorn H CR0 42 C2
Wilfred Owen Cl. Wimble SW19 20 C2
Wilfred St. Woking GU21 69 D1
Wilhelmina Ave. Coulsd CR5 99 C8
Wilkes Rd. 3 Brent TW8 6 E8
Wilkins Cl. Mitch CR4 40 E8
Wilkinson Ct. 4 Crawl RH11 201 B1
Wilkinson Ct. Up Toot SW17 20 D4
Wilks Gdns. Croy CR0 43 E1
Will Miles Ct. 6 Merton SW19 20 C1
Willats Cl. Chert KT16 33 A3
Willcocks Cl. Chess KT9 56 E7
Willems Ave. Alder GU11 104 F2
Willerton Lodge. 1 Whit V KT13 53 D4
Willett Pl. Thorn H CR7 42 A4
Willett Rd. Thorn H CR7 42 A4
Willetts. Dork RH4 136 C4
Willey Broom La. Cater CR3 100 A2
Willey Farm La. Cater CR3 100 C1
Willey La. Cater CR3 100 D2
William Booth Rd. Penge SE20 43 A8
William Brown Ct. W Norw SE27 22 B6
William Byrd Sch. Harl UB7 3 D8
William Cobbett Cty Jun Sch. Heath E GU9 125 E6
William Ellis Sch. For Gn RH5 176 E8
William Evelyn Ct. Wotton RH5 134 F4
William Farthing Cl. Alder GU11 105 A2
William Harvey House. 1 Putney SW19 19 E7
William Lilly House. Hersh KT12 54 C5
William Morris Mid Sch. Mitch CR4 41 D6
William Morris Way. Crawl RH11 201 C1
William Rd. Cater CR3 100 D5
William Rd. Guild GU1 109 C1
William Rd. Merton SW19 19 E1
William Rd. Sutton SM1 59 C5
William Russell Ct. 3 Knaph GU21 68 E1
William Sim Wood. Wink RG12 8 B2
William St. Carsh SM5 59 F7
William Wood House. For Hil SE26 23 C5
Williams Cl. Addl KT15 52 B5
Williams Cl. Ewh GU6 175 E5
Williams House. 14 Streat SW2 22 A7
Williams La. Morden SM4 40 C4
Williams La. Mortl SW14 7 C5
Williams Terr. Croy CR0 61 A4
Williams Way. Crawl RH10 202 B5
Williamson Cl. Grays GU27 189 F2
Willingham Way. King U T KT1 38 A7
Willington Cl. Camb GU15 65 B6
Willis Ave. Sutton SM2 59 E4
Willis Cl. Epsom KT18 76 B5
Willis Rd. Thorn H CR0 42 C2
Willlows The. Croy CR0 62 E8
Willmore End. Merton SW19 40 B7
Willoughby Ave. Wallin CR0 60 F6
Willoughby Rd. Easth RG12 26 F6
Willoughby Rd. King U T KT2 37 F8
Willoughby Rd. Twick TW1 6 D2
Willoughbys The. Mortl SW15 7 E3
Willow Ave. Barnes SW13 7 F5
Willow Bank. Westfd GU22 89 F6
Willow Brean. Horley RH6 160 E5
Willow Cl. Bear Gn RH5 157 C4
Willow Cl. Brent TW8 6 C8
Willow Cl. Catf SE6 24 F7
Willow Cl. Coln SL3 1 C7
Willow Cl. Crawl RH10 201 E8
Willow Cl. E Grins RH19 185 D3
Willow Cl. Mytch GU16 85 E4
Willow Cl. Woodhm KT15 70 F8
Willow Cnr. Charl RH6 180 F7
Willow Cotts. Carsh CR4 40 F2
Willow Cotts. Rich TW9 7 A8
Willow Cres. Farnb GU14 85 B7
Willow Ct. Ash V GU12 106 A7
Willow Ct. Friml GU16 65 D1
Willow Ct. Horley RH6 161 B6
Willow Ct. 3 Streat SW16 21 F5
Willow Ct. Thorn H CR7 42 D4
Willow Ct. Woki RG11 25 B6
Willow Ctr The. Mitch CR4 40 F3
Willow Dr. Brack RG12 27 C8
Willow Dr. Flexf GU3 107 C1
Willow Dr. Send M GU23 91 A3
Willow End. Surb KT6 37 E1
Willow Gdns. Hounsl TW5 5 A6
Willow Glade. Woodh RH2 139 B6
Willow Gn. W End GU24 68 A6
Willow House. Felt TW14 4 B2
Willow La. Guild GU1 110 A2
Willow La. Hawley GU17 64 D4
Willow La. Mitch CR4 40 F3
Willow Lodge. 6 Charlt TW16 14 F1
Willow Manor. Cheam SM1 58 F6
Willow Mead. Dork RH4 136 A8
Willow Mead. 8 E Grins RH19 205 F8
Willow Mead. Witley GU8 170 E5
Willow Mount. S Croy CR0 61 E7
Willow Pk. Alder GU12 105 F2
Willow Rd. Farnc GU7 150 F8
Willow Rd. Horsh RH12 218 B5
Willow Rd. King U T KT3 38 C5
Willow Rd. Poyle SL3 1 E5
Willow Rd. Wallin SM6 60 B3
Willow Rd. Woodh RH1 & RH2 139 C6
Willow Ridge. Turn H RH10 204 A3
Willow Tree Cl. Wands SW18 20 B7
Willow Vale. Fetch KT23 94 B4
Willow View. Mitch SW19 40 D8
Willow Way. Alder GU12 126 E8
Willow Way. For Hil SE26 23 C5
Willow Way. Godst RH9 121 B3
Willow Way. Heath E GU9 125 D6
Willow Way. Stough GU1 109 B5
Willow Way. Sunby TW16 35 A5
Willow Way. Twick TW2 16 B6
Willow Way. W Byfl KT14 71 C8
Willow Way. W Ewell KT19 57 D4
Willow Way. W Ewell KT19 57 D4
Willow Way. Woking GU22 89 E7
Willow Wlk. Box H KT20 116 B5
Willow Wlk. Cheam SM1 & SM3 58 F7
Willow Wlk. Earls RH1 140 B7
Willow Wlk. Eng Gn TW20 11 C3
Willow Wood Cres. Thorn H SE25 42 E3
Willowbrook Rd. Stan TW19 13 E6
Willowdene Cl. Twick TW2 16 C8
Willowfield. 4 Crawl RH11 201 D5
Willowhayne Dr. Walt O T KT12 35 B2
Willowhayne Gdns. N Cheam KT4 58 C6
Willowherb Cl. Woki RG11 25 E7
Willowmead. Stain TW18 33 B8
Willowmead Cl. Woking GU21 69 A3
Willowmere. Esher KT10 55 C6
Willows Ave. Morden SM4 40 B4
Willows End. Sandh GU17 64 B8
Willows Path. Epsom KT18 76 B5
Willows The. Beck BR3 44 A8
Willows The. 1 Brack RG12 27 F5
Willows The. Byfl KT14 71 E6
Willows The. Chidd GU8 191 A4
Willows The. Clayg KT10 55 E4
Willows The. Farnh GU10 126 C4
Willows The. Horsh RH12 217 D5
Willows The. Lhtwat GU18 48 C1
Willows The. Merrow GU4 110 D3
Willows The. 2 Redh RH1 139 F8
Willows The. Stough GU2 108 F6
Willows The. Weyb KT13 53 A7
Wills Cres. Twick TW3 5 B1
Willson Rd. Eng Gn TW20 11 B3
Wilmar Gdns. W Wick BR4 44 B1
Wilmer Cl. King U T TW10 17 F3
Wilmer Cres. King U T KT2 & TW10 17 F3
Wilmerhatch La. Woodc KT18 & KT21 76 B2
Wilmington Ave. Chisw W4 7 D7
Wilmington Cl. Crawl RH11 201 C1
Wilmington Ct. Streat SW16 21 E1
Wilmot Rd. Purley CR8 80 A7
Wilmot Rd. Wallin SM5 59 F5
Wilmot Way. Banstd SM7 78 A5
Wilmot Way. Friml GU15 65 F3
Wilmot's La. Horne RH1 & RH6 162 E5
Wilmots Cl. Reig RH2 118 C2
Wilna Rd. Wands SW18 20 C8
Wilson Ave. Mitch CR4 & SW19 40 E8
Wilson Cl. Croy CR0 61 D5
Wilson Dr. Ottsh KT16 51 B5
Wilson Hospl. Mitch CR4 40 F5
Wilson Rd. Alder GU12 105 D1
Wilson Rd. Chess KT9 56 F4
Wilson Rd. Farnb GU14 84 F3
Wilson Way. Horse GU21 69 D3
Wilson's Sch. Wallin SM6 60 E4
Wilsons. Tadw KT20 97 D6
Wilsons Rd. Head Dn GU35 187 B5
Wilton Cl. Harm UB7 2 D8
Wilton Cres. Merton SW19 39 F8
Wilton Ct. Farnb GU14 85 D3
Wilton Ct. 4 Rich TW10 6 E2
Wilton Gdns. E Mole KT8 36 A6
Wilton Gdns. Walt O T KT12 35 D1
Wilton Gr. Merton SW19 39 F8
Wilton Gr. New Mal KT3 38 F3
Wilton Par. Felt TW13 15 B6
Wilton Pl. Beck BR3 44 C6
Wilton Pl. New Haw KT15 52 D2
Wilton Rd. Camb GU15 65 B3
Wilton Rd. Hounsl TW4 4 D4
Wilton Rd. Mitch SW19 20 E1
Wilton Rd. Redh RH1 139 F8
Wiltshire Ave. Crowth RG11 45 B5
Wiltshire Dr. Woki RG11 25 D7
Wiltshire Gdns. Twick TW2 16 C7
Wiltshire Rd. Thorn H CR7 42 A6
Wiltshire Rd. Woki RG11 25 C7
Wilverley Cres. New Mal KT3 38 E3
Wilwood Rd. Brack RG12 26 E8
Wimbart Rd. Streat SW2 21 F8
Wimbledon Bridge. Wimble SW19 19 F2
Wimbledon Chase Mid Sch. Merton SW20 39 E8
Wimbledon Chase Sta. Merton SW20 39 E7
Wimbledon Cl. Camb GU15 46 F1
Wimbledon Cl. 2 Wimble SW20 19 D1
Wimbledon Coll. Wimble SW19 19 D1
Wimbledon Common Prep Sch. Wimble SW19 19 D1
Wimbledon High Sch. Wimble SW19 19 E2
Wimbledon Hill Rd. Wimble SW19 19 F2
Wimbledon House Sch. Merton SW19 40 A8
Wimbledon Lawn Tennis Mus. Wimble SW19 19 E5
Wimbledon Park Ct. Putney SW19 19 F7
Wimbledon Park Prim Sch. Wimble SW19 20 B6
Wimbledon Park Rd. Putney SW18 & SW19 19 F7
Wimbledon Park Rd. Wands SW18 & SW19 19 F7
Wimbledon Park Side. Putney SW19 19 D7
Wimbledon Park Sta. Wimble SW19 20 A5
Wimbledon Rd. Camb GU15 46 F1
Wimbledon Rd. Wands SW17 20 C4
Wimbledon Sch of Art. Merton SW19 39 E8
Wimbledon Sch of Art Annexe. Merton SW19 20 A1
Wimbledon Sta. Wimble SW19 19 F2
Wimbledon Stadium. Wimble SW17 20 C4
Wimblehurst Ct. Horsh RH12 217 C4
Wimblehurst Rd. Horsh RH12 217 C4
Wimborne Ave. Earls RH1 139 F4
Wimborne Ave. Earls RH1 140 A4
Wimborne Cl. Epsom KT17 76 E6
Wimborne Cl. N Cheam KT4 39 C1
Wimborne House. Croy CR0 43 C4
Wimborne House. Up Toot SW12 21 C5
Wimborne Way. Beck BR3 43 E5
Wimbourne Ct. Mitch SW19 20 D1
Wimbourne Ct. S Croy CR2 61 E4
Wimland Hill. Faygt RH12 199 D2
Wimland Rd. Faygt RH12 199 D1
Wimland Rd. Rusper RH12 199 C4
Wimlands La. Rusper RH12 199 E3
Wimpole Cl. 1 King U T KT1 38 A7
Wimshurst Cl. Croy CR0 41 E1
Wincanton Rd. Wands SW18 19 F8
Winchcombe Rd. Carsh SM5 40 E1
Winchelsey Rise. S Croy CR2 61 F4
Winchendon Rd. Tedd TW11 & TW12 16 D4
Winchester Ave. Heston TW5 4 F8
Winchester Cl. Beck BR2 44 F6
Winchester Cl. Esher KT10 55 A7
Winchester Cl. King U T KT2 18 B1
Winchester Cl. Poyle SL3 1 E6
Winchester Pk. Beck BR2 44 F6
Winchester Rd. Ash GU12 106 A3
Winchester Rd. Beck BR2 44 F6
Winchester Rd. Crawl RH10 201 E2
Winchester Rd. Felt TW13 15 F5
Winchester Rd. Harl UB3 3 E7
Winchester Rd. Rushm GU10 168 B7
Winchester Rd. Twick TW1 6 B1
Winchester Rd. Walt O T KT12 35 A1
Winchester St. Farnb GU14 105 C8
Winchester Way. Blckw GU17 64 C6
Winchet Wlk. Croy CR0 43 C3
Winchfield House. Rhampt SW15 7 F1
Winchfield Rd. For Hil SE26 23 E3
Winchilsea Cres. E Mole KT8 36 C7
Winchstone Cl. Shep Gn TW17 33 F5
Windborough Rd. Wallin SM5 60 A3
Windermere Ave. Merton SM4 & SW19 40 B6
Windermere Cl. E Bed TW14 14 F7
Windermere Cl. Farnb GU14 84 E3
Windermere Cl. Stan TW19 13 D6
Windermere Cl. Thor L TW20 12 B1
Windermere Ct. Barnes SW13 7 F8
Windermere Ct. Purley CR8 80 B4
Windermere House. Islew TW1 5 F2
Windermere Rd. Coulsd CR5 79 E4
Windermere Rd. Croy CR0 42 F1
Windermere Rd. King U T SW15 18 E3
Windermere Rd. Lhtwat GU18 48 B1
Windermere Rd. Mitch SW16 41 D7
Windermere Rd. W Wick BR4 63 E8
Windermere Way. Hale GU9 125 A6
Windermere Way. Redh RH1 118 E2
Windermere Wlk. Friml GU15 66 D5
Windfield. Leahd KT22 95 B5
Windfield Cl. For Hil SE26 23 D4
Windgates. Merrow GU4 110 C4
Windham Ave. New Add CR0 63 D1
Windham Rd. Rich TW9 6 F4
Winding Wood Dr. Friml GU15 & GU16 66 B3
Windings The. S Croy CR2 80 F8
Windle Cl. Windl GU20 48 D4
Windlebrook Gn. 3 Brack RG12 27 A8
Windlemere Golf Ctr. W End GU24 67 E8
Windlesham Ct. Windl GU20 48 C6
Windlesham Gr. Putney SW19 19 D7
Windlesham House. Mitch CR4 40 D7
Windlesham Rd. Brack RG12 26 F8
Windlesham Rd. Burrh GU24 49 C3
Windlesham Rd. W End GU24 67 F7
Windlesham Village Cty Inf Sch. Windl GU20 48 B6
Windley Cl. For Hil SE23 23 C6
Windmill Ave. Ewell KT17 76 F8
Windmill Bridge House. 1 Croy CR0 42 E1
Windmill Bsns Village. Charlt TW16 34 E8
Windmill Cl. Cater CR3 100 C6
Windmill Cl. Charlt TW16 14 E1
Windmill Cl. Ewell KT17 76 F7
Windmill Cl. Horley RH6 161 B3
Windmill Cl. Horsh RH13 218 A4
Windmill Cl. Long D KT6 37 C2
Windmill Ct. Crawl RH11 201 D8
Windmill Dr. Head Dn GU35 187 B6
Windmill Dr. Leahd KT22 95 C4
Windmill Dr. Redh RH1 118 E3
Windmill End. Ewell KT17 76 F7
Windmill Field. Windl GU20 48 D4
Windmill Gr. Thorn H CR0 42 C3
Windmill La. Ash W RH19 206 C7
Windmill La. E Grins RH19 185 D3
Windmill La. Ewell KT17 76 F7
Windmill La. Thame D KT7 37 B2
Windmill Lodge. Charlt TW16 34 E8
Windmill Rd. Alder GU12 105 C1
Windmill Rd. Brack RG12 27 A8
Windmill Rd. Brent TW8 6 D8
Windmill Rd. Charlt TW16 34 E8
Windmill Rd. Hampt TW12 16 C3
Windmill Rd. Mitch CR4 41 C5
Windmill Rd. Rhampt SW19 19 B5
Windmill Rd. Thorn H CR0 42 C2
Windmill Rd W. Charlt TW16 34 E8
Windmill Rise. King U T KT2 18 B1
Windmill Terr. Lo Hall TW17 34 E2

Windmill Trad Est. Charlt TW16 ...... 34 E8
Windmill Way. Redh RH1 .... 118 D3
Windrush Cl. Bramly GU5 .... 151 F6
Windrush Cl. Chisw W4 .... 7 C7
Windrush Cl. Crawl RH11 .... 200 F4
Windrush House. 8 Redh RH1 ...... 118 F2
Windrush La. For Hil SE23 .... 23 D5
Winds Ridge. Send GU23 .... 90 C2
Windsor Ave. Cheam SM3 .... 58 E7
Windsor Ave. E Mole KT8 .... 36 A6
Windsor Ave. Merton SW19 .... 40 C8
Windsor Ave. New Mal KT3 .... 38 C4
Windsor Cl. Crawl RH11 .... 201 C2
Windsor Cl. Onsl V GU2 .... 129 F7
Windsor Cl. W Norw SE27 .... 22 C4
Windsor Cres. Hale GU9 .... 125 B6
Windsor Ct. Ashf TW16 .... 15 A1
Windsor Ct. Burrh GU24 .... 49 E2
Windsor Ct. Horsh RH13 .... 217 F3
Windsor Ct. S Norw SE19 .... 42 E8
Windsor Dr. Ashf TW15 .... 13 D4
Windsor Gdns. Ash GU12 .... 105 F1
Windsor Gdns. Wisbeach CR0 .... 60 E7
Windsor Gr. W Norw SE27 .... 22 C4
Windsor House. Dovgn RH2 .... 139 B4
Windsor Mews. For Hil SE23 .... 23 E7
Windsor Park Rd. Harl UB3 .... 3 F7
Windsor Pk. Merton SW19 .... 40 C8
Windsor Pl. Chert KT16 .... 33 A3
Windsor Pl. E Grins RH19 .... 206 A8
Windsor Rd. Ashf TW16 .... 15 A2
Windsor Rd. Burrh GU24 .... 49 D3
Windsor Rd. Cranf TW4 & TW5 .... 4 C5
Windsor Rd.
 Eng Gn TW19 & TW20 .... 11 E6
Windsor Rd. Farnb GU14 .... 85 D1
Windsor Rd. Farnb GU14 .... 104 D8
Windsor Rd. King U T KT2 .... 17 E1
Windsor Rd. N Asct SL5 .... 29 A8
Windsor Rd. Rich TW9 .... 6 F5
Windsor Rd. S Norw CR7 .... 42 B7
Windsor Rd. Tedd TW11 .... 16 D3
Windsor Rd. Worc Pk KT4 .... 58 A8
Windsor Ride. Brack SL5 .... 28 C4
Windsor Ride. Sandh GU15 .... 65 A8
Windsor St. Chert KT16 .... 33 A3
Windsor Way. Alder GU11 .... 105 B2
Windsor Way. Friml GU16 .... 85 F8
Windsor Way. Magd GU2 .... 70 C3
Windsor Wlk. Walt O T KT12 .... 35 D1
Windsor Wlk. Weyb KT13 .... 53 B5
Windways. Dunsf GU8 .... 192 F7
Windy Ridge Cl. Wimble SW19 ...... 19 D3
Windy Wood. Godal GU7 .... 150 C3
Windycroft Cl. Coulsd CR5 & CR8 ... 79 D4
Windyridge. Crawl RH11 .... 201 A5
Winern Glebe. Byfl KT14 .... 71 D6
Winery La. King U T KT1 .... 37 F6
Winfield Ct. Newd RH5 .... 158 B1
Winfield Gr. Newd RH5 .... 158 B1
Winfrith Rd. Wands SW18 .... 20 C7
Wingate Cres. Thorn H CR0 .... 41 E3
Wingfield Cl. Woodhm KT15 .... 52 B1
Wingfield Rd. King U T KT2 .... 18 A2
Wingham House. 3 Penge SE26 ... 23 B3
Wingrove Rd. Catf SE6 .... 24 E6
Wings Cl. Hale GU9 .... 125 B6
Wings Cl. Sutton SM1 .... 59 A6
Wings Rd. Hale GU9 .... 125 B6
Winifred Rd. Coulsd CR5 .... 79 B4
Winifred Rd. Hampt TW12 .... 16 A4
Winifred Rd. Merton SW19 .... 40 A8
Winkfield Cl. Woki RG11 .... 25 B3
Winkfield La. Wink SL4 .... 8 D7
Winkfield Plain. Wink SL4 .... 9 B8
Winkfield Rd. Ascot SL5 .... 29 B7
Winkfield Rd. Wind SL4 .... 9 C8
Winkfield Row. Wink RG12 .... 8 B3
Winkfield St. Wink SL4 .... 8 C6
Winkworth Pl. Banstd SM7 .... 78 A5
Winkworth Rd. Banstd SM7 .... 78 A5
Winlaton Rd. Catf BR1 & SE6 .... 24 D4
Winner Way. Crawl RH6 .... 181 D6
Winnington Way. Woking GU21 ..... 69 C1
Winscombe. Easth RG12 .... 26 E4
Winsford Rd. For Hil SE6 .... 23 F5
Winslade Way. Catf SE6 .... 24 B8
Winslow Way. Felt TW13 .... 15 E5
Winslow Way. Walt O T KT12 .... 54 C7
Winstanley Cl. Cobham KT11 .... 73 B5
Winstanley Wlk. Cobham KT11 ..... 73 B5
Winston Churchill Sch The.
 Knaph GU21 .... 68 F1
Winston Cl. Friml GU16 .... 85 F8
Winston Dr. Stk D'A KT11 .... 73 E3
Winston Way. Old Wok GU22 .... 90 B7
Winston Wlk. M Bourn GU10 ...... 146 C6
Winter Box Wlk. Rich TW10 .... 6 F2
Winterbourne. Horsh RH12 .... 217 F7
Winterbourne Ct. Brack RG12 ...... 27 D7
Winterbourne Gr. Whit V KT13 ...... 53 C4
Winterbourne Inf Sch.
 Thorn H CR7 .... 42 A5
Winterbourne Jun Boys' Sch.
 Thorn H CR7 .... 42 A5
Winterbourne Jun Girls' Sch.
 Thorn H CR7 .... 42 A5
Winterbourne Rd.
 For Hil SE23 & SE6 .... 23 F7
Winterbourne Rd. Thorn H CR7 ... 42 A5
Winterbourne Wlk. Friml GU16 ..... 85 F8
Winterdown Gdns. Esher KT10 ..... 54 F4
Winterdown Rd. Esher KT10 .... 54 F4
Winterfold. Crawl RH10 .... 202 A3
Winterfold Cl. Putney SW19 .... 19 E6
Winterfold La. Farl Gn GU5 .... 153 E6

Winterhill Way. Burph GU4 .... 110 B5
Winters Rd. Thame D KT7 .... 37 B2
Wintersells Ind Est. Byfl KT14 ...... 52 D1
Wintersells Rd. Byfl KT13 & KT14 .. 52 E1
Winterstoke Rd.
 For Hil SE23 & SE6 .... 23 F7
Winterton Ct. Horsh RH13 .... 217 D3
Winton Ct. 15 Surb KT6 .... 37 D2
Winton House. Purley CR8 .... 80 A3
Winton House Sch. Croy CR0 ...... 61 F8
Winton Rd. Alder GU11 .... 105 A1
Winton Rd. Farnh GU9 .... 125 D4
Winton Rd. W Norw SW16 .... 22 A3
Wire Mill La. Newch RH7 .... 184 F8
Wirrall House. 15 For Hil SE26 ... 23 A5
Wisbeach Rd. Thorn H CR0 .... 42 D4
Wisborough Ct. Crawl RH11 .... 200 F3
Wisborough Rd. S Croy CR2 .... 61 F2
Wisdom Ct. 5 Islew TW7 .... 6 A4
Wiseman Rd. 12 E Norw SE19 ...... 22 E3
Wiseton Rd. Up Toot SW17 .... 20 F7
Wishanger La.
 Head Dn GU10 & GU35 .... 167 B3
Wishbone Way. Woking GU21 ...... 68 F3
Wishford Ct. Ashtd KT21 .... 75 F1
Wishmoor Cl. Camb GU15 .... 65 E8
Wishmoor Rd. Camb GU15 .... 65 E8
Wishmore Cross Sch.
 Chobh GU24 .... 49 F1
Wisley La. Wisley GU23 & KT14 .... 71 E3
Wispers Sch. Haslem GU27 .... 189 C1
Wiston Ct. Crawl RH11 .... 200 F3
Witham Rd. Hounsl TW7 .... 5 D6
Witham Rd. Penge BR3 & SE20 .... 43 C6
Wither Dale. Ashf RH6 .... 160 E4
Witherby Cl. S Croy CR0 & CR2 .... 61 E4
Witherslack Cl. Head Dn GU35 .... 187 C4
Withey Brook. Hookw RH6 .... 160 D1
Withey Meadows. Hookw RH6 ... 160 D1
Witheygate Ave. Stain TW18 .... 13 B2
Withies La. Compt GU3 .... 129 C2
Withies The. Knaph GU21 .... 68 E2
Withies The. Leahd KT22 .... 95 B6
Withy Cl. Lhtwat GU18 .... 48 C1
Withybed Cnr. Tadw KT20 .... 97 B4
Withypitts. Turn H RH10 .... 204 A3
Withypitts E. Turn H RH10 .... 204 A3
Witley CE Inf Sch. Witley GU8 .... 170 F4
Witley Cres. Pyrwd GU6 .... 63 C4
Witley House. 5 Streat SW2 .... 21 F8
Witley Point. 8 Rhampt SW15 ...... 19 B7
Witley Sta. Wormly GU8 .... 190 F8
Witney Path. For Hil SE23 .... 23 D5
Witten House. New Mal KT3 .... 38 D1
Wittenham Rd. Brack RG12 .... 27 F8
Wittering Ct. King U T KT2 .... 17 D3
Wittersham Rd. Catf BR1 .... 24 F3
Wittmead Rd. Mytch GU16 .... 85 F4
Wivenhoe Ct. Hounsl TW4 .... 4 F3
Wiverton Rd. Penge SE20 & SE26 .. 23 C3
Wix Hill. W Hors KT24 .... 112 B4
Woburn Ave. Farnb GU14 .... 85 D3
Woburn Ave. Purley CR8 .... 80 A8
Woburn Cl. Friml GU16 .... 66 A1
Woburn Cl. Merton SW19 .... 20 C2
Woburn Ct. Croy CR0 .... 42 C1
Woburn Ct. Rich TW9 .... 6 F4
Woburn Hill. Addl KT15 .... 52 D7
Woburn Hill Pk. Chert KT15 .... 52 D8
Woburn Hill Sch. Chert KT15 ...... 52 D7
Woburn Rd. Carsh SM5 .... 40 E1
Woburn Rd. Crawl RH11 .... 201 A4
Woburn Rd. Croy CR0 .... 42 C1
Wodeland Ave. Guild GU2 .... 130 B7
Woffington Cl. Tedd KT1 & KT8 .... 37 C8
Woking Bsns Pk. Sheer GU21 ...... 70 B4
Woking Cl. Rhampt SW15 .... 7 F3
Woking Coll. Old Wok GU22 .... 90 A7
Woking Comm Hospl.
 Woking GU22 .... 69 F1
Woking Nuffield Hospl The.
 Horse GU21 .... 69 E5
Woking Rd. Bellf GU1 & GU4 ...... 109 D5
Woking Rd. Jacobs GU1 & GU4 ... 109 D5
Woking Sta. Woking GU22 .... 69 F2
Wokingham Hospl. Woki RG11 .... 25 A6
Wokingham Rd. Brack RG12 .... 26 F8
Wokingham Sta. Woki RG11 .... 25 B6
Wokingham Theatre.
 Woki RG11 .... 25 B8
Wold Cl. Crawl RH11 .... 200 F4
Wold The. Wold CR3 .... 102 A5
Woldhurstlea Cl. Crawl RH11 ...... 201 A4
Woldingham Sch The.
 Warlgm CR3 & CR6 .... 101 C7
Woldingham Sta. Wold CR3 ...... 101 D5
Wolf's Cnr. Limps RH8 .... 123 A5
Wolf's Hill. Limps RH8 .... 123 A4
Wolf's Rd. Limps RH8 .... 123 B5
Wolfe Rd. Alder GU12 .... 105 C1
Wolfington Rd. W Norw SE27 ...... 22 B4
Wolfs Wood. Oxted RH8 .... 123 A3
Wolseley Ave.
 Wimble SW18 & SW19 .... 20 A6
Wolseley Gdns. Chisw W4 .... 7 B8
Wolseley Rd. Alder GU11 .... 105 A1
Wolseley Rd. Carsh CR4 .... 41 A2
Wolseley Rd. Farnc GU7 .... 150 F6
Wolsey Cl. Islew TW3 .... 5 C3
Wolsey Cl. King U T KT2 .... 38 B8
Wolsey Cl. Wimble SW20 .... 19 B1
Wolsey Cl. Worc Pk KT19 & KT4 ... 58 A6
Wolsey Cres. New Add CR0 .... 63 C2
Wolsey Cres. W Barn SM4 .... 39 F2
Wolsey Ct. Broml BR1 .... 24 F1
Wolsey Dr. King U T KT2 .... 17 E2
Wolsey Dr. Walt O T KT12 .... 35 D1
Wolsey Gr. 2 Esher KT10 .... 55 B6
Wolsey House. 2 Hampt TW12 ... 16 B2

Wolsey Inf & Jun Schs.
 New Add CR0 .... 63 D3
Wolsey Pl Sh Ctr. Woking GU22 .. 69 E2
Wolsey Rd. Ashf TW15 .... 13 F4
Wolsey Rd. Ashf TW16 .... 14 F2
Wolsey Rd. E Mole KT8 .... 36 D5
Wolsey Rd. Esher KT10 .... 55 B6
Wolsey Rd. Hampt TW12 .... 16 C2
Wolsey Spring. S Norw SE25 .... 57 A5
Wolsey Wlk. 4 Woking GU21 .... 69 F2
Wolstonbury Ct. Crawl RH11 ..... 201 C4
Wolvens La. Coldh RH5 .... 156 E5
Wolvens La. Westc RH4 & RH5 .... 135 B2
Wolverton Ave. King U T KT2 ...... 38 A8
Wolverton Rd. Horley RH6 .... 160 F1
Wolverton Gdns. Horley RH6 ...... 160 F2
Wolves Hill. Capel RH5 .... 178 C4
Wonersh & Shamley Green CE Prim
 Sch. Sham Gn GU5 .... 152 D5
Wonersh Way. E Ewell SM2 .... 58 D2
Wonford Cl. King U T KT2 & KT3 .. 38 E8
Wonford Cl. Walt o t h KT20 .... 97 A1
Wonham La. Betch RH3 & RH2 ... 137 F8
Wonham Way. Gomsh GU5 .... 133 D3
Wonham Way. Peasl GU5 .... 133 D1
Wontford Rd. Purley CR8 .... 80 B4
Wontner Rd.
 Up Toot SW12 & SW17 .... 20 F6
Wood Cl. Salfs RH1 .... 161 A8
Wood Cl. Stough GU2 .... 109 B2
Wood End. Horsh RH12 .... 218 C5
Wood End The. Wallin SM6 .... 60 B2
Wood La. Banstd KT20 .... 77 F2
Wood La. Binf RG12 .... 26 E8
Wood La. Cater CR3 .... 100 D3
Wood La. Farnb GU14 .... 85 A3
Wood La. Hounsl TW7 .... 5 F7
Wood La. Knaph GU21 .... 68 D1
Wood La. Seale GU10 .... 127 B5
Wood La. Whit V KT13 .... 53 C2
Wood Lodge La. W Wick BR4 .... 63 C7
Wood Rd. Beac H GU26 .... 188 D6
Wood Rd. Bigg H TN16 .... 83 C1
Wood Rd. Camb GU15 .... 65 B1
Wood Rd. Farnc GU7 .... 150 F7
Wood Rd. Heath E GU9 .... 125 C7
Wood Rd. Shep Gn TW17 .... 34 A5
Wood Riding. Pyrf GU22 .... 70 E4
Wood Rise. Stough GU3 .... 108 E3
Wood St. Ash V GU12 .... 106 A6
Wood St. Carsh CR4 .... 41 A2
Wood St. E Grins RH19 .... 185 D1
Wood St. King U T KT2 .... 37 E8
Wood St. Merst RH1 .... 119 C7
Wood Street Inf Sch.
 Wood S V GU3 .... 108 C3
Wood Vale. For Hil SE22 .... 23 B8
Woodbank Rd. Catf BR1 .... 24 F5
Woodbastwick Rd. Penge SE26 .. 23 E3
Woodberry Cl. Ashf TW16 .... 15 A2
Woodberry Cl. Chidd GU8 .... 191 A5
Woodbine Cl. Sandh GU17 .... 64 C7
Woodbine Cotts. Shalf GU4 ...... 130 E2
Woodbine Gr. Penge SE20 .... 23 B1
Woodbine La. N Cheam KT4 .... 58 C7
Woodbines Ave. King U T KT1 ...... 37 D6
Woodbourne. Heath E GU9 .... 125 E7
Woodbourne Ave. Streat SW16 .. 21 D5
Woodbourne Cl. Streat SW16 ...... 21 E5
Woodbourne Dr. Clayg KT10 .... 55 F4
Woodbourne Gdns. Wallin SM6 .. 60 B3
Woodbridge Ave. Leahd KT22 ...... 75 A1
Woodbridge Ct. Horsh RH12 ...... 218 A5
Woodbridge Dr. Camb GU15 .... 65 D7
Woodbridge Gr. Leahd KT22 .... 75 A1
Woodbridge Hill. Stough GU2 ... 109 B2
Woodbridge Hill Gdns.
 Stough GU2 .... 109 A2
Woodbridge Meadows.
 Guild GU1 .... 109 C2
Woodbridge Pk Est. Guild GU1 .. 109 C2
Woodbridge Rd. Blckw GU17 ...... 64 B5
Woodbridge Rd.
 Guild GU1 & GU2 .... 109 C2
Woodbrook Sch. Beck BR3 .... 43 F8
Woodbury Ave. E Grins RH19 .... 186 B1
Woodbury Cl. Bigg H TN16 .... 83 F1
Woodbury Cl. E Grins RH19 ...... 206 B8
Woodbury Cl. S Croy CR0 .... 61 F8
Woodbury Dr. Sutton SM2 .... 59 C1
Woodbury House. For Hil SE26 ... 23 B5
Woodbury St. Up Toot SW17 .... 20 E3
Woodby Dr. Sunnin SL5 .... 29 F2
Woodcock Dr. Burrh GU24 .... 49 C3
Woodcock Hill.
 Felb RH19 & RH7 .... 184 F6
Woodcock La. Burrh GU24 .... 49 B3
Woodcombe Cres. For Hil SE23 .. 23 C7
Woodcot Gdns. W Heath GU14 .... 84 D4
Woodcote. Arting GU2 & GU3 .... 130 B5
Woodcote. Cran GU6 .... 174 B4
Woodcote. Farnc GU7 .... 150 D6
Woodcote. Horley RH6 .... 161 C4
Woodcote Ave. Thorn H CR7 .... 42 B5
Woodcote Ave. Wallin SM6 .... 60 B2
Woodcote Cl. Epsom KT18 .... 76 D5
Woodcote Cl. King U T KT2 .... 17 F3
Woodcote Dr. Purley CR8 .... 60 D1
Woodcote End. Woodc KT18 .... 76 D4
Woodcote Gn. Wallin SM6 .... 60 C2
Woodcote Green Rd.
 Woodc KT18 .... 76 C4
Woodcote Grove Rd.
 Coulsd CR5 .... 79 D5
Woodcote Hall. Epsom KT18 ...... 76 D5
Woodcote Hall. Wallin SM6 .... 60 B2
Woodcote High Sch.
 Coulsd CR5 .... 79 D6
Woodcote House. Woodc KT18 .. 76 D4

Woodcote House Ct.
 Woodc KT18 .... 76 D4
Woodcote House (Sch).
 Windl GU20 .... 48 B5
Woodcote Hurst. Woodc KT18 .... 76 C3
Woodcote Inf Sch. Coulsd CR5 ... 79 D5
Woodcote Jun Sch. Coulsd CR5 . 79 D5
Woodcote La. Purley CR8 .... 79 D7
Woodcote Mews. Wallin SM6 ...... 60 B4
Woodcote Park Ave.
 Purley CR5 & CR8 .... 79 C7
Woodcote Park Golf Club.
 Wallin CR5 .... 79 B5
Woodcote Park Golf Course.
 Woodc KT18 .... 76 D2
Woodcote Park Rd.
 Woodc KT18 .... 76 C4
Woodcote Pl. 1 W Norw SE27 .... 22 B3
Woodcote Rd. Epsom KT18 .... 76 D5
Woodcote Rd. For Row RH18 .... 206 F2
Woodcote Rd. Wallin CR8 & SM6 60 C2
Woodcote Rd. Woodc KT18 .... 76 D5
Woodcote Side. Woodc KT18 ...... 76 B4
Woodcote Valley Rd.
 Purley CR8 & CR8 .... 79 E7
Woodcott House. 1
 Rhampt SW15 .... 19 A8
Woodcott Terr. Alder GU12 .... 126 D8
Woodcourt. Crawl RH11 .... 201 C1
Woodcrest Rd. Purley CR8 .... 79 E6
Woodcroft Rd. Crawl RH11 .... 200 D4
Woodcroft Rd.
 Thorn H CR0 & CR7 .... 42 B3
Woodend. Farnb GU14 .... 85 D3
Woodend. Leahd KT22 .... 95 C2
Woodend. S Norw SE19 .... 22 C2
Woodend. Sutton SM1 .... 59 C8
Woodend. Thame D KT10 .... 55 C8
Woodend Cl. Crawl RH10 .... 202 A8
Woodend Cl. N Asct SL5 .... 28 E8
Woodend Cl. Woking GU21 .... 89 A8
Woodend Dr. Ascot SL5 .... 29 A4
Woodend Pk. Cobham KT11 .... 73 D4
Woodend Rd. For Hil GU16 .... 86 C7
Woodenhill. Easth RG12 .... 26 E1
Woodenhill Cty Prim Sch.
 Easth RG12 .... 26 E2
Wooderson Cl. S Norw SE25 .... 42 E5
Woodfield. Ashtd KT21 .... 75 D2
Woodfield Ave. Streat SW16 .... 21 D5
Woodfield Cl. Ashtd KT21 .... 75 D2
Woodfield Cl. Coulsd CR5 .... 99 C8
Woodfield Cl. Crawl RH10 .... 201 E7
Woodfield Cl. Redh RH1 .... 118 E3
Woodfield Cl. S Norw SE19 .... 22 C1
Woodfield Gdns. New Mal KT3 .... 38 F4
Woodfield Gr. Streat SW16 .... 21 D5
Woodfield Hill. Coulsd CR5 .... 99 B8
Woodfield House. 11
 For Hil SE23 .... 23 D5
Woodfield House. New Mal KT3 .. 38 F4
Woodfield La. Ashtd KT21 .... 75 E2
Woodfield Rd. Ashtd KT21 .... 75 D2
Woodfield Rd. Cranf TW4 & TW5 .. 4 B5
Woodfield Rd. Crawl RH10 .... 201 F7
Woodfield Rd.
 Hinch W KT10 & KT7 .... 55 F8
Woodfield Rd. Rudg RH12 .... 214 D7
Woodfield Way. Redh RH1 .... 118 E3
Woodfields The. S Croy CR2 .... 80 F8
Woodfields. Sutton SM1 .... 59 C7
Woodford Gn. Brack RG12 .... 27 F5
Woodgate Ave. Chess KT9 .... 56 D5
Woodgates Cl. Horsh RH13 ...... 217 F3
Woodgavil. Nork SM7 .... 77 F3
Wooder Cl.
 Merrow GU1 & GU4 .... 110 C3
Woodgrange Cl. Coney H BR2 .... 44 F1
Woodhall Ave. Dulw SE21 .... 22 F5
Woodhall Dr. Dulw SE21 .... 22 F5
Woodhall La. Windl GU20 .... 48 E8
Woodham La. New Haw KT15 ...... 52 B1
Woodham La.
 Sheer GU21 & KT15 .... 70 D7
Woodham La. Woodhm KT15 ...... 52 B1
Woodham Park Rd.
 Woodhm KT15 .... 70 F8
Woodham Park Way.
 Woodhm KT15 .... 70 F8
Woodham Rd. Catf SE6 .... 24 C5
Woodham Rd. Horse GU21 .... 69 F4
Woodham Rise. Horse GU21 .... 70 A4
Woodham Waye. Sheer GU21 ...... 70 B5
Woodhatch Rd.
 Dovgn RH1 & RH2 .... 139 E5
Woodhatch Rd.
 Earls RH1 & RH2 .... 139 E5
Woodhatch Spinney.
 Coulsd CR5 .... 79 E3
Woodhaw. Egham TW20 .... 12 B4
Woodhayes. Horley RH6 .... 161 C4
Woodhayes Rd.
 Wimble SW19 & SW20 .... 19 C2
Woodhill. Send GU23 .... 90 D2
Woodhill La. Sham Gn GU5 ...... 152 F4
Woodhouse La.
 Peasl GU5 & RH5 .... 155 A8
Woodhouse St. Binf RG12 .... 26 E8
Woodhurst La. Oxted RH8 .... 122 E4
Woodhurst Pk. Oxted RH8 .... 122 E5
Woodhyrst Gdns. Purley CR8 ...... 80 B4
Wooding Gr. 15 Crawl RH11 ...... 201 B1
Woodland Ave. Cran GU6 .... 174 F3
Woodland Cl. E Hors KT24 .... 112 F8
Woodland Cl. Horsh RH13 .... 218 B4
Woodland Cl. W Ewell KT19 .... 57 E4
Woodland Cl. W Ewell KT19 .... 57 E4

Woodland Cl. W Norw SE19 .... 22 E2
Woodland Ct. Cheam SM1 .... 59 A4
Woodland Ct. Ewell KT17 .... 76 F7
Woodland Dr. E Hors KT24 .... 112 E7
Woodland Dr. Crawl D RH10 ...... 204 B8
Woodland Dr. M Bourn GU10 .... 146 B6
Woodland Dr. Ockley RH5 .... 178 A5
Woodland Gdns. Islew TW7 .... 5 E4
Woodland Gdns. Selsd CR2 .... 81 C8
Woodland Gr. Weyb KT13 .... 53 D6
Woodland Hill. W Norw SE19 ...... 22 E2
Woodland Rd. Thorn H CR7 .... 42 A5
Woodland Rd. W Norw SE19 .... 22 F2
Woodland Rise. Oxted RH8 .... 122 E5
Woodland View. Farnc GU7 .... 129 E1
Woodland Way. Cater RH1 .... 120 E8
Woodland Way. Croy CR0 & CR9 .. 43 E1
Woodland Way. Horsh RH13 ...... 218 B4
Woodland Way. Kings KT20 .... 97 E4
Woodland Way. Merton SM4 .... 39 F5
Woodland Way. Mitch CR4 .... 21 A1
Woodland Way. Purley CR8 .... 80 A6
Woodland Way. Tolw KT5 .... 57 B8
Woodland Way. W Wick BR4 .... 63 C7
Woodland Way. Whit V KT13 .... 53 D5
Woodlands. Beck BR3 .... 24 B1
Woodlands. Chert KT15 .... 52 E7
Woodlands. Crawl RH10 .... 202 D8
Woodlands. Horley RH6 .... 161 C4
Woodlands. Send M GU23 .... 90 F2
Woodlands. W Barn SW20 .... 39 D5
Woodlands Ave. Earls RH1 .... 139 F8
Woodlands Ave. Heath E GU9 .... 125 F7
Woodlands Ave. King U T KT3 ...... 38 D8
Woodlands Ave. W Byfl KT14 ...... 70 F7
Woodlands Ave.
 W Byfl KT14 & KT15 .... 71 A7
Woodlands Ave. Worc Pk KT4 ...... 58 A8
Woodlands Cl. Ascot SL5 .... 28 F3
Woodlands Cl. Ash GU12 .... 106 A5
Woodlands Cl. Clayg KT10 .... 55 F3
Woodlands Cl. Cran GU6 .... 174 F2
Woodlands Cl. Crawl D RH10 .... 204 B7
Woodlands Cl. Ottsh KT16 .... 51 B1
Woodlands Cl. W Heath GU14 ...... 64 E1
Woodlands Cl. Broml BR1 .... 44 F8
Woodlands Cl. Dulw SE22 .... 23 B8
Woodlands Cl. Sandh GU15 .... 65 A5
Woodlands Cl. 7 Woking GU21 ... 69 A1
Woodlands Copse. Ashtd KT21 ... 75 D3
Woodlands Ct. Woking GU22 .... 89 E8
Woodlands Dr. S Godst RH9 ...... 142 E4
Woodlands Dr. Sunby TW16 .... 35 C7
Woodlands Gr. Coulsd CR5 .... 79 B2
Woodlands Gr. Islew TW7 .... 5 E5
Woodlands House. Sheer GU21 ... 70 C5
Woodlands La.
 Shottm GU27 .... 207 F3
Woodlands La. Stk D'A KT11 .... 74 B2
Woodlands La.
 Windl GU20 & GU24 .... 48 E3
Woodlands Par. Ashf TW15 .... 14 C2
Woodlands Pk. Box H KT20 .... 116 B4
Woodlands Pk. Merrow GU1 ...... 110 B2
Woodlands Pk. Row Tn KT15 .... 51 F5
Woodlands Pk. Sheer GU21 .... 70 C5
Woodlands Rd.
 Ashtd KT11 & KT22 .... 74 D1
Woodlands Rd. Bellf GU1 .... 109 D5
Woodlands Rd. Camb GU15 .... 65 B5
Woodlands Rd. E Grins RH19 .... 186 A4
Woodlands Rd. Earls RH1 .... 139 F7
Woodlands Rd.
 Effing KT23 & KT24 .... 113 F6
Woodlands Rd. Epsom KT18 .... 76 A4
Woodlands Rd. Hambl GU8 ...... 171 D1
Woodlands Rd. Islew TW7 .... 5 D5
Woodlands Rd.
 Leahd KT11 & KT22 .... 74 D1
Woodlands Rd. Mortl SW13 .... 7 F4
Woodlands Rd. Pyrf KT14 .... 70 F5
Woodlands Rd. Surb KT6 .... 37 D2
Woodlands Rd. Vir W GU25 .... 31 C5
Woodlands Rd. W Heath GU14 .... 84 D6
Woodlands Rd E. Vir W GU25 ...... 31 C5
Woodlands Rd W. Vir W GU25 .... 31 C5
Woodlands Ride. Ascot SL5 .... 29 A3
Woodlands Sch. Leahd KT22 ...... 95 C5
Woodlands St. Lewish SE13 .... 24 D8
Woodlands The. Islew TW7 .... 5 F5
Woodlands The. Lewish SE13 ...... 24 D8
Woodlands The. Mitch CR4 .... 41 A6
Woodlands The. S Norw SE19 ...... 22 C1
Woodlands The. Smallf RH6 ...... 162 B3
Woodlands The. Thame D KT10 ... 55 C8
Woodlands The. Wallin SM6 .... 60 B2
Woodlands Way. Box H KT20 .... 116 C5
Woodlands Wlk. W Heath GU14 .. 64 E1
Woodlawn Cres. Twick TW2 .... 16 B6
Woodlawn Dr. Felt TW13 .... 15 D6
Woodlawn Gr. Horse GU21 .... 69 F4
Woodlea Cty Prim Sch.
 Wold CR3 .... 101 F5
Woodlea Dr. Hayes BR2 .... 44 E4
Woodlee Cl. Vir W GU25 .... 31 C7
Woodleigh. 1 Surb KT5 .... 37 F4
Woodleigh Gdns. Streat SW16 .... 21 E5
Woodley Cl. Mitch SW17 .... 20 F1
Woodley House. Farnc GU7 ...... 150 E8
Woodley La. Carsh SM1 & SM5 .... 59 E7
Woodlodge. Ashtd KT21 .... 75 E2
Woodlodge. 4 Wimble SW19 ...... 19 F3
Woodman Rd. Coulsd CR5 .... 79 D4
Woodmancote Gdns.
 W Byfl KT14 .... 71 A6
Woodmancott Cl. Brack RG12 ...... 27 F3
Woodmans Hill. Crawl GU7 .... 150 C8
Woodmans Hill. Crawl RH11 ...... 201 C2
Woodmansterne Cty Prim Sch.
 Woodm SM7 .... 78 F5

Woodmansterne La.
Banstd SM7 .... 78 D4
Woodmansterne La.
Wallin SM5 & SM6 .... 79 A7
Woodmansterne La.
Woodm SM7 .... 78 D4
Woodmansterne Prim Sch.
Streat SW16 .... 41 D8
Woodmansterne Rd.
Coulsd CR5 .... 79 C4
Woodmansterne Rd.
Streat SW16 .... 41 D8
Woodmansterne Rd.
Sutton SM5 & SM2 .... 59 E2
Woodmansterne St.
Woodm SM7 .... 78 E4
Woodmansterne Sta.
Coulsd CR5 .... 79 B3
Woodmere. Brack RG12 ...... 27 E5
Woodmere Ave. Croy CR0 .... 43 D2
Woodmere Cl. Croy CR0 ...... 43 D2
Woodmere Gdns. Croy CR0 .. 43 D2
Woodmere Way. Beck BR3 ... 44 D4
Woodnook Rd. Streat SW16 ... 21 B3
Woodpecker Cl. Cobham KT11 ... 73 E7
Woodpecker Cl. Crond GU10 ... 124 D8
Woodpecker La. Newd RH5 ... 158 C2
Woodpecker Mount.
New Add CR0 .... 62 F2
Woodpecker Way. Westfd GU22 89 D3
Woodpeckers. Easth RG12 ..... 27 B5
Woodpeckers. Witley GU8 ... 170 E7
Woodplace Cl. Coulsd CR5 .... 79 C1
Woodplace La. Coulsd CR5 .... 99 C7
Woodplace La. Hooley CR5 .... 99 C7
Woodridge Cl. Brack RG12 .... 27 C6
Woodrough Copse.
Bramly GU5 .... 152 A5
Woodrow Dr. Woki RG11 ...... 25 F6
Woodroyd Ave. Horley RH6 ... 160 F2
Woodroyd Gdns. Horley RH6 .. 160 F1
Woodruff Ave. Burph GU1 ... 110 B4
Woods Hill Cl. Ash W RH19 ... 206 D6
Woods Hill La. Ash W RH19 ... 206 D6
Woodshore Cl. Went GU25 .... 31 B3
Woodside. **1** Farnb GU14 ...... 85 B7
Woodside. Fetch KT22 .... 94 B5
Woodside. Hawley GU17 .... 64 C3
Woodside. Horsh RH13 .... 218 B4
Woodside. Hyde GU8 .... 171 E5
Woodside. L Kings KT20 ...... 117 F7
Woodside. Sandh GU15 .... 64 F7
Woodside. W Hors KT24 .... 92 C1
Woodside. Wimble SW19 .... 19 F3
Woodside Ave. Croy SE25 ..... 43 B4
Woodside Ave. Hersh KT12 ... 54 B6
Woodside Ave. Thame D KT10 ... 36 E2
Woodside Cl. Cater CR3 ..... 100 E3
Woodside Cl. Chidd GU8 ..... 191 B4
Woodside Cl. Knaph GU21 ..... 68 D2
Woodside Cl. Tolw KT5 .... 38 C2
Woodside Cotts. Elst GU8 .... 148 C3
Woodside Court Rd.
Croy CR0 .... 43 A2
Woodside Cres. Smallf RH6 ... 162 A3
Woodside Gn. Croy CR0 & SE25 .. 43 A3
Woodside House. Wimble SW19 19 F2
Woodside Jun & Inf Sch.
Croy CR0 .... 43 A2
Woodside La. Wink SL4 & SL5 .... 9 C3
Woodside Pk Est. Godal GU7 .. 150 F4
Woodside Pk. Croy SE25 ...... 43 B3
Woodside Rd. Bear Gn RH5 ... 157 D3
Woodside Rd. Chidd GU8 ..... 191 B5
Woodside Rd. Cobham KT11 ... 74 A6
Woodside Rd. Crawl RH10 ... 201 F8
Woodside Rd. Croy SE25 ...... 43 B3
Woodside Rd. Farnb GU11 ... 104 F7
Woodside Rd. Heath E GU9 ... 125 E7
Woodside Rd. King U T KT2 ... 17 E1
Woodside Rd. King U T KT3 ... 38 E7
Woodside Rd. Purley CR8 ..... 79 E6
Woodside Rd. Stough GU2 ... 108 F2
Woodside Rd. Sutton SM1 ..... 59 C7
Woodside Sta. Croy CR0 ...... 43 B3
Woodside Way. Croy CR0 ..... 43 C3
Woodside Way. Earls RH1 ... 140 A3
Woodside Way. Earls RH1 ... 140 A8
Woodside Way. Streat CR4 .... 41 C8
Woodside Way. Vir W GU25 .... 31 B6
Woodsome Lodge. Whit V KT13 53 C4
Woodspring Rd. Putney SW19 ... 19 E6
Woodstock. E Grins RH19 .... 185 C2
Woodstock. W Clan GU4 ...... 111 B7
Woodstock. Woki RG11 .... 25 C6
Woodstock Ave.
Cheam SM3 & SM4 .... 39 F2
Woodstock Ave. Islew TW7 .... 6 A2
Woodstock Cl. Cran GU6 .... 174 F3
Woodstock Cl. Horse GU21 .... 69 E3
Woodstock Cl. Horsh RH12 ... 217 D5
Woodstock Coll. Long D KT6 .. 56 C8
Woodstock Ct. Ewell KT17 ..... 76 D7
Woodstock Gdns. Beck BR3 ... 24 B1
Woodstock Gr. Farnc GU7 ... 150 E7

Woodstock La N. Long D KT6 .. 56 C8
Woodstock La S.
Clayg KT10 & KT6 .... 56 C6
Woodstock Rd. Coulsd CR5 ... 79 B3
Woodstock Rd. Croy CR0 & CR9 . 61 D7
Woodstock Rd.
Wallin SM5 & SM6 .... 60 A5
Woodstock Rise. Cheam SM3 ... 39 F2
Woodstock Way. Mitch CR4 ... 41 C7
Woodstocks. Farnb GU14 ...... 85 D6
Woodstone Ave.
Stonel KT17 & KT4 .... 58 A5
Woodsway. Oxsh KT22 .... 74 E5
Woodsyre. Dulw SE19 & SE26 .. 22 F4
Woodthorpe Rd. Ashf TW15 ... 13 D4
Woodthorpe Rd. Stain TW15 ... 13 D4
Woodvale Ave. S Norw SE25 ... 42 F7
Woodvale Ct. S Norw SE25 ..... 42 F6
Woodview. Chess KT9 .... 75 C8
Woodview Cl. Hams Gn CR2 ... 81 B5
Woodview Cl. King U T SW15 ... 18 D4
Woodview Ct. Weyb KT13 ...... 53 C5
Woodville Cl. Blckw GU17 ..... 64 B5
Woodville Cl. Tedd TW11 ...... 17 A4
Woodville Gdns. Surb KT6 .... 37 D2
Woodville Pl. Cater CR3 ..... 100 C5
Woodville Rd. Leahd KT22 ..... 95 B7
Woodville Rd. Merton SM4 .... 40 A5
Woodville Rd. Rich TW10 ...... 17 C5
Woodville Rd. S Norw CR7 .... 42 C4
Woodville Sch The. Leahd KT22 95 B7
Woodward Cl. Clayg KT10 ..... 55 F4
Woodwarde Rd. Dulw SE22 ... 22 F8
Woodwards. Crawl RH11 ..... 201 C1
Woodway. Camb GU15 .... 65 B5
Woodway. Merrow GU1 .... 110 B2
Woodyard La. Dulw SE21 ...... 22 E8
Woodyers Cl. Woner GU5 ..... 152 B7
Wool Rd. Wimble SW20 .... 39 C7
Woolborough Cl. Crawl RH10 .. 201 E7
Woolborough La. Crawl RH10 .. 181 F1
Woolborough La. Crawl RH10 .. 202 A8
Woolborough La. S Nutf RH1 .. 161 F8
Woolborough Rd. Crawl RH10 .. 201 E7
Woolford Cl. Wink RG12 .... 8 C1
Woolfords La. Elst GU8 .... 169 B7
Woolhampton Way. Brack RG12 27 D4
Woolhams. Cater CR3 .... 101 A1
Woollards Rd. Ash GU12 ..... 106 B4
Woolmead Rd. Farnh GU9 ... 125 C3
Woolmead The. Farnh GU9 ... 125 C3
Woolmer Hill Rd.
Shottm GU26 & GU27 ..... 207 D7
Woolmer Hill Sch.
Shottm GU27 .... 207 D7
Woolmer View. Graysh GU26 .. 188 D3
Woolsack Way. Godal GU7 ... 150 F4
Woolstone Rd.
For Hil SE23 & SE6 .... 23 E6
Wooshill La. Woki RG11 ...... 25 A5
Wootton Cl. Epsom KT18 ...... 76 F3
Wootton Grange. Woking GU22 . 89 E8
Worbeck Rd. Penge SE20 ...... 43 B7
Worcester Cl. Croy CR0 .... 63 A8
Worcester Cl. Farnb GU14 ..... 85 B7
Worcester Cl. Mitch CR4 ...... 41 A7
Worcester Ct. Ashf TW15 ...... 14 B3
Worcester Ct. Walt O T KT12 ... 35 C1
Worcester Ct. Worc Pk KT4 .... 57 E7
Worcester Dr. Ashf TW15 ...... 14 B3
Worcester Gdns. Worc Pk KT4 .. 57 E7
Worcester Park Rd.
Worc Pk KT4 .... 57 D7
Worcester Park Sta.
New Mal KT4 .... 39 A1
Worcester Rd. Belm SM2 ...... 59 B3
Worcester Rd. Crawl RH10 ... 201 E2
Worcester Rd. Reig RH2 ..... 118 A2
Worcester Rd. Stough GU2 ... 108 F3
Worcester Rd. Sutton SM2 .... 59 B3
Worcester Rd. **1**
Wimble SW19 .... 19 F3
Wordsworth. Easth RG12 ...... 26 F4
Wordsworth Ave. Kenley CR8 ... 80 D4
Wordsworth Cl. Crawl RH10 ... 202 B8
Wordsworth Dr.
Cheam KT4 & SM3 .... 58 C6
Wordsworth Mead. Redh RH1 .. 119 B3
Wordsworth Pl. Horsh RH12 ... 217 E7
Wordsworth Rd. Addl KT15 .... 52 D6
Wordsworth Rd.
Hampt TW12 & TW13 ...... 15 F4
Wordsworth Rd. Penge SE20 ... 23 D1
Wordsworth Rd. Wallin SM6 ... 60 D4
Wordsworth Rise. **6**
E Grins RH19 .... 185 C1
Works Rd. Woodhm KT15 ...... 52 B2
World of Adventures.
Chess KT9 .... 56 C1
Worlds End Hill. Brack RG12 ... 27 F3
Worple Ave. Islew TW7 .... 6 A2
Worple Ave. Stain TW18 .... 13 B2
Worple Ave. Wimble SW19 ..... 19 D1
Worple Ct. Wimble SW19 .... 19 E2
Worple Prim Sch. Islew TW7 ... 6 A3

Worple Rd. Epsom KT18 .... 76 E5
Worple Rd. Islew TW7 .... 6 A3
Worple Rd. Leahd KT22 .... 95 B4
Worple Rd. Stain TW18 .... 13 B1
Worple Rd.
Wimble SW19 & SW20 ...... 39 D8
Worple Rd. Woodc KT18 .... 76 D4
Worple Road Mews.
Wimble SW19 .... 19 F2
Worple St. Mortl SW14 .... 7 D4
Worple Way. Rich TW10 .... 6 E3
Worplesdon Cty Prim Sch.
Fairl GU3 .... 108 D4
Worplesdon Golf Course.
Woking GU22 .... 88 D4
Worplesdon Hill. Woking GU22 .. 88 D5
Worplesdon Rd. Stough GU2 ... 109 A4
Worplesdon Sta. Woking GU22 . 89 B3
Worslade Rd. Up Toot SW17 ... 20 D4
Worsley Bridge Jun Sch.
Beck BR3 .... 24 A1
Worsley Bridge Rd.
Beck BR3 & SE6 .... 24 A2
Worsley Bridge Rd. Catf SE6 ... 23 F3
Worsley House. For Hil SE23 ... 23 B6
Worsley Rd. Friml GU16 .... 85 F7
Worsted Gn. Merst RH1 ...... 119 D6
Worsted La. E Grins RH19 ... 206 B8
Worth Abbey & Sch.
Worth RH10 .... 203 B1
Worth Park Ave. Crawl RH10 ... 202 C7
Worth Rd. Crawl RH10 .... 202 C6
Worth Way. Worth RH10 ...... 202 C6
Worthfield Cl. W Ewell KT19 ... 57 D3
Worthfield Cl. W Ewell KT19 ... 57 D3
Worthing Rd. Heston TW5 .... 4 F8
Worthing Rd. Horsh RH12 ... 217 B1
Worthington Cl. Mitch CR4 .... 41 B6
Worthington House. **16**
Streat SW2 .... 21 F8
Worthington Rd. Surb KT6 ..... 37 F1
Wortley Rd. Thorn H CR0 ...... 42 A2
Worton Ct. Islew TW7 .... 5 E3
Worton Gdns. Hounsl TW7 .... 5 D3
Worton Hall Est. Islew TW7 ...... 5 E3
Worton Rd. Islew TW7 .... 5 E3
Worton Way. Hounsl TW3 & TW7 . 5 D5
Wotton Dr. Wotton RH5 .... 134 E3
Wotton Way. E Ewell SM2 ..... 58 C1
Wrabness Way. Stain TW18 .... 33 B8
Wray Cl. Ash W RH19 .... 206 D6
Wray Common Cty Prim Sch.
Reig RH2 .... 118 D2
Wray Common Rd. Reig RH2 ... 118 C2
Wray House. **11** Streat SW2 ... 21 E7
Wray La. Reig RH2 .... 118 D4
Wray Mill House. Redh RH1 ... 118 E3
Wray Mill Pk. Redh RH1 ...... 118 E3
Wray Park Rd. Reig RH2 ..... 118 C2
Wray Rd. Belm SM2 .... 58 F2
Wrayfield Ave. Reig RH2 ..... 118 C2
Wrayfield Rd. Cheam SM3 .... 58 D7
Wraylands Dr. Redh RH1 & RH2 118 E3
Wraymead Pl. Reig RH2 ...... 118 B2
Wraymill Ct. **4** Reig RH2 ... 118 D1
Wraysbury Cl. Hounsl TW4 .... 4 E2
Wraysbury Rd. Stain TW18 .... 12 C5
Wraysbury Rd. Wray TW19 .... 12 C5
Wraysbury Sta. Wray TW19 ..... 1 A1
Wrecclesham Hill.
Wrecc GU10 .... 145 E5
Wrecclesham Rd.
Farnh GU9 & GU9 .... 145 F8
Wrecclesham Rd.
Wrecc GU10 & GU9 .... 145 F8
Wren Cl. Horsh RH12 .... 217 D7
Wren Cl. Selsd CR2 .... 62 D2
Wren Cres. Addl KT15 .... 52 D5
Wren Ct. Ash GU12 .... 106 A3
Wren Ct. Crawl RH10 .... 201 E3
Wren Ct. S Croy CR0 .... 61 D6
Wren House. **4** Hampt TW12 .. 16 B2
Wren Way. W Heath GU14 ..... 84 F7
Wren's Ave. Ashf TW15 .... 14 C4
Wren's Hill. Oxsh KT22 .... 74 C4
Wrenthorpe Rd. Catf BR1 ..... 24 E4
Wright Rd. Heston TW5 .... 4 C7
Wright's Row. Wallin SM5 ..... 60 B6
Wrighton Ct. Cheam SM1 ..... 58 F4
Wrights Rd. S Norw SE25 ..... 42 E6
Wrotham Hill. Dunsf GU8 ..... 192 E3
Wrotham House. Beck BR3 .... 23 F1
Wroxam. Easth RG12 .... 26 F4
Wroxham Wlk. Crawl RH10 ... 202 B4
Wrythe Gn. Carsh SM5 .... 59 F7
Wrythe Green Rd. Carsh SM5 .. 59 F7
Wrythe La.
Carsh SM1 & SM5 & SM4 ... 59 E7
Wyatt Cl. Felt TW13 .... 15 D7
Wyatt Park Mansions. **1**
Streat SW2 .... 21 E6
Wyatt Park Rd. Streat SW2 ... 21 F6
Wyatt Rd. Stain TW18 .... 13 A3
Wyatt's Almshouses.
Farnc GU7 .... 151 A6
Wyatt's Cl. Farnc GU7 .... 151 A6

Wych Elm Rise. Guild GU1 ... 130 E6
Wych Hill. Woking GU22 .... 89 C8
Wych Hill La. Woking GU22 .... 89 E8
Wych Hill Pk. Woking GU22 ... 89 C8
Wych Hill Rise. Woking GU22 .. 89 E8
Wych Hill Way. Woking GU22 .. 89 D8
Wyche Gr. S Croy CR2 .... 61 D2
Wychelm Rd. Lhtwat GU18 ..... 67 C8
Wychwood Ave. Brack RG12 ... 27 E5
Wychwood Ave. S Norw CR7 ... 42 C6
Wychwood Cl. Alder GU12 ... 105 F2
Wychwood Cl. Ashf TW16 ...... 15 A2
Wychwood Pl. Camb GU15 ..... 66 B8
Wychwood Way. W Norw SE19 .. 22 C2
Wycliffe Bldgs. Guild GU2 ... 130 C7
Wycliffe Ct. Crawl RH11 ...... 200 E3
Wycliffe Rd. Merton SW19 ..... 20 B2
Wycliffe Rd. Wimble SW19 .... 20 B2
Wycombe Pl. Wands SW18 .... 20 C1
Wydell Cl. W Barn SM4 .... 39 D3
Wydenhurst Rd. Croy CR0 & CR9 43 B2
Wye Cl. Ashf TW15 .... 14 B4
Wyecliffe Gdns. Merst RH1 ... 119 C5
Wyeth's Mews. Epsom KT17 ... 76 F6
Wyeth's Rd. Epsom KT17 ...... 76 F6
Wyke Ave. Normdy GU12 ..... 106 E3
Wyke Bglws. Normdy GU12 ... 106 D3
Wyke Cl. Hounsl TW7 .... 5 F8
Wyke Cty Prim Sch The.
Normdy GU3 .... 106 F4
Wyke Green Golf Course.
Hounsl TW7 .... 5 E6
Wyke La. Normdy GU12 ...... 106 D2
Wyke Rd. Wimble SW20 .... 39 C7
Wykeham Cl. Harm UB7 .... 3 C1
Wykeham House. Farnb GU14 .. 105 C8
Wykeham House. Merton SW19 40 B1
Wykeham Rd. Farnh GU9 ..... 125 C3
Wykeham Rd. Merrow GU1 ... 110 D2
Wylam. Easth RG12 .... 26 F4
Wyleu St. For Hil SE23 .... 23 E8
Wymering Ct. Farnb GU14 ..... 85 D3
Wynash Gdns. Carsh SM5 ..... 59 E5
Wynbourne Ct. Penge SE20 ... 43 B7
Wyncote Way. Selsd CR2 ..... 62 D2
Wyndham Ave. Cobham KT11 .. 73 A6
Wyndham Cl. Belm SM2 .... 59 A3
Wyndham Cres. Cran GU6 ... 174 A3
Wyndham Cres. Twick TW4 ..... 5 A1
Wyndham Rd. King U T KT2 ... 17 F1
Wyndham Rd. Woking GU21 ... 69 B1
Wyndham St. Alder GU12 ..... 105 C1
Wynell Rd. For Hil SE23 .... 23 D5
Wynfields. Mytch GU16 .... 85 F3
Wynlea Cl. Crawl D RH10 ..... 204 A8
Wynne Ct. **4** Islew TW7 .... 6 A4
Wynnstow Pk. Oxted RH8 ... 122 F4
Wynsham Way. Windl GU20 ... 48 B6
Wynton Gdns. S Norw SE25 ... 42 E4
Wynton Gr. Walt O T KT12 ..... 54 A7
Wyphurst Rd. Cran GU6 ..... 174 E4
Wyresdale. Brack RG12 .... 27 F2
Wysemead. Horley RH6 ...... 161 C4
Wythegate. Stain TW18 .... 12 F1
Wyvern Cl. Easth RG12 .... 26 F4
Wyvern Est The. W Barn KT3 .. 39 A5
Wyvern Pl. Addl KT15 .... 52 B6
Wyvern Rd. Purley CR8 .... 61 B1

Yaffle Rd. Whit V KT13 .... 53 C1
Yale Cl. Hounsl TW4 .... 4 F2
Yale Cl. Sandh GU15 .... 45 F2
Yarborough Rd. Mitch SW19 ... 40 D8
Yarbridge Cl. Sutton SM2 ..... 59 B1
Yard Mead. Egham TW20 ...... 12 A5
Yardley. Easth RG12 .... 26 F4
Yardley Cl. Reig RH2 .... 118 B3
Yardley Ct. Cheam SM3 .... 58 C6
Yarm Cl. Leahd KT22 .... 95 C4
Yarm Court Rd. Leahd KT22 ... 95 C4
Yarm Way. Leahd KT22 .... 95 D4
Yarmouth Cl. Crawl RH10 .... 202 A4
Yarnold Cl. Woki RG11 .... 25 F7
Yarrow Cl. Horsh RH12 ...... 217 E5
Yateley Ct. Purley CR8 .... 80 C5
Yatesbury Cl. Farnh GU9 ..... 145 C7
Yattendon Rd. Horley RH6 ... 161 B3
Yattendon Sch. Horley RH6 ... 161 A4
Yaverland Dr. Bagsh GU19 ... 47 D2
Ye Market. Croy CR0 .... 61 D5
Yeats Cl. Woodh RH1 .... 139 C6
Yehudi Menuhin Sch.
Fetch KT11 .... 94 A8
Yellowcress Dr. Bisley GU24 ... 68 A3
Yelverton Ct. G Book KT23 .... 94 A1
Yelverton Lodge. Twick TW1 ... 17 C8
Yenston Cl. Morden SM4 ...... 40 A3
Yeoman Cl. W Norw SE27 ..... 22 B5
Yeoman Way. Earls RH1 ..... 140 B4
Yeomanry Cl. Ewell KT17 ..... 76 F7
Yeomans Cl. Ash GU10 & GU12 . 126 F8
Yeomans Cl. W Heath GU14 ... 85 A5
Yeomans Mews. Islew TW7 ..... 5 D2
Yeomans Way. Camb GU15 ... 65 E5
Yeoveney Cl. Stan TW19 ...... 12 D6
Yeovil Cl. Farnb GU14 .... 85 D1
Yeovil Rd. Farnb GU14 .... 85 E1

Yeovil Rd. Sandh GU15 .... 45 E1
Yetminster Rd. Farnb GU14 ... 85 D1
Yew La. E Grins RH19 .... 185 B3
Yew Pl. Walt O T KT13 .... 53 F7
Yew Tree Bottom Rd.
Nork KT17 & KT18 .... 77 C2
Yew Tree Cl. Chips CR5 .... 98 F8
Yew Tree Cl. Farnb GU14 ...... 84 C3
Yew Tree Cl. Horley RH6 ...... 161 A4
Yew Tree Cl. New Mal KT4 .... 38 C1
Yew Tree Cotts. Esher KT10 ... 55 D8
Yew Tree Ct. Sutton SM2 .... 59 C3
Yew Tree Dr. Bellf GU1 .... 109 C6
Yew Tree Dr. Cater CR3 ...... 100 F2
Yew Tree Gdns. Woodc KT18 .. 76 C4
Yew Tree House. New Mal KT4 .. 38 E1
Yew Tree La. Reig RH2 .... 118 B4
Yew Tree Rd. Charl RH6 ..... 180 E7
Yew Tree Rd. Dork RH4 ...... 115 A1
Yew Tree Rd. Witley GU8 ..... 170 D6
Yew Tree Wlk. Effing KT24 ... 113 D8
Yew Tree Wlk. Friml GU16 ..... 65 F1
Yew Tree Wlk. Hounsl TW4 ..... 4 F2
Yew Tree Wlk. S Croy CR2 ..... 61 C1
Yew Trees. Shep Gn TW17 ..... 33 F5
Yewbank Cl. Kenley CR8 .... 80 D4
Yewdale Cl. Catf BR1 .... 24 E2
Yewens. Chidd GU8 .... 191 B5
Yewlands Cl. Banstd SM7 ..... 78 C4
Yewlands Wlk. Crawl RH11 ... 200 D4
Yews The. Ashf TW15 .... 14 B4
Yewtree Rd. Beck BR3 .... 43 F6
Yewtrees. Egham TW20 .... 32 C6
Yockley Cl. Friml GU15 .... 66 D3
Yolland Cl. Heath E GU9 ..... 125 C7
York Ave. E Grins RH19 ...... 206 A8
York Ave. Mortl SW14 .... 7 C2
York Cl. Byfl KT14 .... 71 E7
York Cl. Horsh RH13 .... 217 F3
York Cl. Morden SM4 .... 40 B5
York Cres. Alder GU11 .... 104 F1
York Ct. Beck BR3 .... 44 D8
York Ct. King U T KT2 .... 17 D2
York Ct. Wallin SM6 .... 60 C4
York Gdns. Walt O T KT12 .... 54 D8
York Hill. W Norw SE27 & SW16 .. 22 B5
York House. Brack RG12 .... 26 F8
York House. For Hil SE26 ...... 23 C3
York House. **4** King U T KT2 ... 17 F1
York House. Rich TW9 .... 7 A6
York House. S Norw SE25 ..... 42 E5
York Rd. Alder GU11 .... 104 F1
York Rd. Ash GU12 .... 106 A3
York Rd. Belm SM1 & SM2 .... 59 A3
York Rd. Bigg H TN16 .... 103 B8
York Rd. Byfl KT14 .... 71 E7
York Rd. Camb GU15 .... 65 D7
York Rd. Crawl RH10 .... 201 E2
York Rd. Farnb GU14 .... 85 C1
York Rd. Farnb GU14 .... 104 E8
York Rd. Guild GU1 .... 130 D8
York Rd. Hounsl TW3 .... 5 B4
York Rd. King U T KT2 .... 17 F1
York Rd. M Bourn GU9 .... 125 C1
York Rd. **3** Rich TW10 .... 6 F2
York Rd. Selsd CR2 .... 62 D1
York Rd. Tedd TW11 .... 16 E4
York Rd. Thorn H CR0 .... 42 A2
York Rd. Weyb KT13 .... 53 C6
York Rd. Wimble SW19 .... 20 C2
York Rd. Woking GU22 .... 69 E1
York St. Carsh CR4 .... 41 A2
York St. Twick TW1 .... 17 A7
York Town Ind Est. Camb GU15 65 A5
York Way. Chess KT9 .... 56 E3
York Way. Felt TW13 .... 15 F5
York Way. Sandh GU47 .... 64 B8
Yorke Gate Rd. Cater CR3 .... 100 D5
Yorke Gdns. Reig RH2 .... 118 A2
Yorke Rd. Reig RH2 .... 118 A2
Yorkshire Rd. Mitch CR4 ...... 41 E5
Yorktown Rd.
Sandh GU15 & GU17 .... 64 C7
Yorktown Rd. Sandh GU15 .... 64 E7
Youlden Cl. Friml GU15 .... 66 A5
Youlden Dr. Friml GU15 .... 66 B6
Young St. Fetch KT22 .... 94 F3
Young St. Leahd KT22 .... 95 A3
Youngman. Lingf RH7 .... 165 B4
Youngs Dr. Alder GU12 .... 105 F2
Youngstroat La. Chobh GU24 ... 50 E7
Yukon Rd. Balham SW12 .... 21 B8
s
Zealand Ave. Harm UB7 .... 2 E7
Zennor Rd. Streat SW12 .... 21 C7
Zermatt Rd. Thorn H CR7 ...... 42 C5
Zig Zag Rd. Kenley CR8 .... 80 C3
Zig Zag Rd.
Mickle KT20 & RH4 & RH5 .. 115 D4
Zinnia Dr. Bisley GU24 .... 68 A3
Zion Pl. S Norw CR7 .... 42 D5
Zion Rd. S Norw CR7 & SE25 .. 42 D5
Zodiac Ct. Thorn H CR0 .... 42 B1

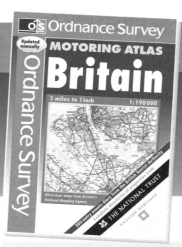

The   .nual of

Calorie
Counting

First published by Parragon in 2010

Parragon

Queen Street House

4 Queen Street

Bath BA1 1HE, UK

Page layout by Stonecastle Graphics

ISBN 978-1-4075-9362-3

Printed in China

The Mini Manual of
Calorie
Counting

Bath • New York • Singapore • Hong Kong • Cologne • Delhi • Melbourne

CONTENTS

INTRODUCTION

The aim of this book is to give you a greater understanding of food. We are all familiar with the term 'calories' and have some understanding of fat and its role in health. Because we eat food, we have a natural interest in it. However, we are often very confused about many issues surrounding food and diet. We are told one thing one day and, lo and behold, the next day it seems it is completely different. Who do you believe, who is telling the truth? It is all too easy to become over-anxious about food, whether about becoming too fat or simply eating the wrong things.

This book begins by describing the different nutrients found in food. It gives you an idea of what these nutrients do, together with information on the amount that a healthy person needs. It then describes the important role that food plays in normal health. However, when we select food to eat, our personal preferences rather than the benefits of the nutrients tend to dictate choice. This book will help us to select certain foods because we know that they are a good source of a certain valuable nutrient.

We next learn a little more about the importance of nutrition and are guided on how to choose a balanced diet, with practical advice as to how to create a healthy diet while still keeping our enjoyment of food alive.

WHY A FAT, CARBOHYDRATE & FIBRE COUNTER?

Balancing the amounts of fat, carbohydrate and fibre we consume daily is vital to good health. Your diet should provide all the energy, protein, vitamins and minerals you need to stay healthy and active every day, so enabling you to enjoy life to the full.

In our affluent Western society, however, it is very easy to choose a diet that is too high in fat, sugar and salt and too low in fibre, especially as our busy lifestyles often mean that we eat takeaway meals or ready-prepared foods. It is well known that a high-fat, high-sugar, high-salt diet may be harmful, leading to increased risk of coronary heart disease, high blood pressure and certain forms of cancer.

Choosing to eat sensibly is clearly vital to good health. Although there are no single 'good' or 'bad' foods, the key to better health is to select a balanced range of nutritious foods every day, and indulge in fattening or less nutritious 'treats' less often.

The Mini Manual of Calorie Counting is designed to help you achieve this. It will enable you to understand the composition of a wide range of available foods and give you the knowledge to select and balance your daily nutritional requirements and those of your family.

Dietary energy is measured in kilocalories (kcal) or kilojoules (kJ), which comes from three major food

sources: protein, fat and carbohydrate. The daily number of calories (as they are more usually known) needed depends on your sex, age, weight and activity level.

While protein is essential for the growth and maintenance of body tissues, most adults eat more than enough. High-fibre foods, such as bread and pulses, also provide useful amounts of protein, so achieving your daily fibre target can mean that you also obtain your protein requirements.

The A–Z food listing focuses on counting three essential nutrition elements in the foods you choose: fat, carbohydrate and fibre. (Although fibre is not a nutrient, it has a vital role in keeping the gut active and healthy.)

If you follow the recommendations for your daily intake, you will also obtain the optimum protein, vitamins and minerals essential for good health. The most useful foods are highest in carbohydrate and fibre – so aim to limit the fats and choose starchy, not sugary (low-fibre), carbohydrates.

Your diet need not meet strict daily targets. Balance too much fat one day with less the next. Overall, try to achieve a healthy diet and remember that eating should be enjoyed!

THE FOOD PYRAMID

This diagram shows the recommended balance of the five different food groups in your daily diet. The largest group is the starchy carbohydrates, followed by fruit and vegetables. Protein and dairy foods are next, with the smallest group containing the fatty and sugary foods. Around half the total calories you need should come from the starchy carbohydrates and 33–35 per cent from fats.

Foods containing fat, foods containing sugar
Eat only small amounts of these foods

Milk and dairy foods
Consume in moderation

Meat, fish and alternatives
Limit to 15–20 per cent
of daily energy

Fruit and vegetables
(high in fibre, low
in calories). Aim
for five helpings
a day

Starchy carbohydrates – bread, other cereals and potatoes
Should provide 45–50 per cent of daily energy

Similar to the food pyramid, the 'eatwell plate' was created in the UK by The Food Standards Agency as a simple pictorial guide to healthy eating. Further information is available at www.eatwell.gov.uk.

BREAD, OTHER CEREALS AND POTATOES

This group includes all the low-fat, starchy carbohydrate foods, such as bread, rolls, chapatis, breakfast cereals, oats, pasta, noodles, rice, beans, lentils, plantain, green bananas and dishes made from maize, millet and polenta.

Most of these foods are good sources of dietary fibre and contain other vital nutrients. For good health the aim should be to derive 45–50 per cent of your daily energy (calories) intake from this food group.

FRUIT AND VEGETABLES

This includes all fresh, frozen and canned fruit and vegetables, salad vegetables, beans and lentils and can also include some dried fruit and fruit juice. Try to choose a wide variety of fruit and vegetables – at least five portions every day – to get the vital vitamins, minerals and antioxidants they provide.

MILK AND DAIRY FOODS

The dairy foods (milk, cheese, yogurt, fromage frais) are all good sources of protein and minerals, especially calcium. Low-fat dairy products retain the calcium

content of full-fat kinds. If avoiding dairy products, choose alternatives fortified with calcium.

MEAT, FISH AND ALTERNATIVES
This group includes red meats, such as beef, pork, bacon, lamb and meat products (e.g. sausages, beefburgers), also poultry, fish, fish products (e.g. fish fingers, fish cakes), offal (liver, kidney, heart), eggs, beans and lentils, nuts and nut products, textured vegetable protein and other meat alternatives. Only small amounts of these high-protein foods are needed.

FOODS CONTAINING FAT, FOODS CONTAINING SUGAR
This includes butter, margarine, low-fat spreads, cooking oils, mayonnaise and oily salad dressings, biscuits, cakes, puddings, ice cream, chocolate, sweets, crisps, sugar and sweetened drinks. Try to limit your intake of fatty and sugary foods. The natural sugar in fruit, vegetables and milk is not harmful to health – but the aim is to limit added sugar.

SO WHAT IS A BALANCED DIET?

When faced with the enormous choice of food that we have today, it seems almost impossible to try and work out what a balanced diet is. Indeed, everyone seems to have their own ideas about what they think is good and what is not. Some people feel that the more food costs then the better it is for you. This is by no means the case. Others feel that if they manage to fulfil their quota of five portions of fruit and vegetables each day, then they have done enough to eat a good diet. For some it is eating a cooked meal every day.

Many people, if they are honest, are not really sure what a balanced diet is. Are they eating the right sorts of foods? Is it enough? Sometimes the messages are confusing, but there are a few simple rules:

EAT THREE MEALS A DAY

They need not be the traditional meals, but aim for three separate eating occasions. Space them out so that there are no really long gaps between eating (apart from sleeping). The traditional breakfast, lunch and evening meal is great if you follow a traditional life pattern. But for many, shifts and odd working hours are the norm, so just rearrange your meals accordingly and, if necessary, use a little ingenuity.

EAT THREE TYPES OF FOOD AT EACH MEAL

Choose something from the protein group (e.g. milk, meat, eggs, cheese, fish, pulses or nuts), then select something from the fruit and vegetable group and finally, but very importantly, something from the carbohydrate group, such as potatoes, cereals, breads, rice, pasta or chapatis (e.g. starchy foods).

EAT A VARIETY OF FOOD

The greater the variety of foods, the better the chance of getting a wide variety of vitamins. With fruit and vegetables, the more different colours they are, the better they are for you nutritionally.

AND FINALLY …

Think SAS as your rescue service. These products are OK to consume in sensible amounts:

Spreading fats

Low-fat spreads, butter and cooking oils for example. Use in small amounts as they are great for providing fat-soluble vitamins and essential fatty acid.

Alcohol

Drink modestly and wisely.

Sugar and sugar-containing foods

The odd treat now and then is acceptable, especially if you need to keep your calories up, if you are prone to be underweight or if you exercise a lot.

Take a look at the recipe ideas later in the book for some simple ideas showing how it all fits together.

NUTRIENTS AT RISK

There are some nutrients that are vital for health and which need special mention. They are:

Iron

Iron-deficiency anaemia is a relatively common deficiency. It is most commonly found in teenage girls and women. High menstrual blood loss and a poor diet cause anaemia, especially if iron-rich foods are not often eaten. Typical symptoms are fatigue, and the sufferer can be paler in skin colour, although this symptom is not always easy to spot.

Iron-deficiency anaemia is far more common than it used to be as there has been a shift away from eating red meat to choosing chicken or even vegetarian options. Vegetable-based diets need not be low in iron if carefully balanced. There is an increasing trend towards snacking during the day and eating fewer meals, so though not every choice has to be perfect, eating too many foods that are not ideal is unwise.

Avoid becoming anaemic by eating some lean red meat each week. If you favour a vegetarian diet, choose eggs, which are rich in iron, for one or two meals a week. Pulses, e.g. beans of all kinds, peas and lentils, are very good sources of iron. Always include plenty of fruit and vegetables with your meals as they increase the amount of iron that the body absorbs from food. Breakfast cereals are usually fortified with iron

equivalent to 25–33 per cent of the daily requirement for adult females. You need not have them at breakfast; eat them as a snack during the day or at bedtime.

Calcium

Bones constantly repair themselves throughout life. Bone growth is greatest during childhood, and relative to their size children's need for calcium is high. There is a constant cycle of bone growth, repair and bone loss, but bone density tends to decline after the age of thirty-five. Therefore dietary calcium intake is more important after that age to maintain good bone strength. There is considerable debate over the amount of calcium that is required by adults. Research suggests that the official recommended daily allowance is set too low, and we should be consuming more than 1000 mg daily.

Osteoporosis results from a person having a low bone-mineral content, causing bones to fracture easily. It is commonly found in women after their menopause, as the hormones responsible for regular menstruation also play a role in maintaining bone strength. Men have bigger skeletons than women, but they are not immune from osteoporosis, though it takes a little longer for them to reach the critical level at which osteoporosis becomes a problem.

Osteoporosis can become a problem in people who don't get enough calcium. There are many individuals

who choose to drop milk from their diet, commonly because they wish to lose weight. However, there are also people who may be allergic or intolerant to milk and are not taking corrective steps to ensure they are getting enough calcium. Because milk is such a valuable source of calcium, it is unwise to omit it from the diet without good reason. Lower-fat varieties of milk are just as good sources of calcium as full-fat milk, and if allergy or intolerance appears to be a problem, then get your diet checked out by a dietician. They can suggest ways of increasing the levels if they are low.

Finally, we know that exercise is good as it strengthens bones. However, avoid smoking and excessive alcohol as this weakens the bones.

Folic Acid/Folate

Deficiency of folic acid or folate is not a recognized medical condition. However, it is considered prudent for women who are planning to have a baby to take folic acid supplements as this will help reduce the risk of neural tube defects such as spina bifida. It is also thought that diets high in folic acid may help to reduce the risk of heart disease. One of the richest sources of this vitamin is fruit and vegetables. We also know that fruit and vegetables may have other heart-protective factors.

DO I NEED VITAMIN AND MINERAL SUPPLEMENTS?

The simple answer is no, as long as you are following the guidelines on foods set out in this book. However, if you feel that you would like a little reassurance, then choose a multivitamin and mineral preparation. There are many inexpensive ones available at the chemists or in supermarkets and either taking one every other day or even taking half a tablet each day is sufficient.

FUNCTIONAL FOODS

These are defined as foods that have health-giving properties over and above their nutritional value. Those presently available are the new margarines enriched with 'stanols' or 'sterols' that could help to lower cholesterol levels, and, for women, breads with phytoestrogens added by enriching the bread with soya and linseed. This bread has been recommended for women who wish to avoid using synthetic hormones to help to reduce some of the problems associated with the menopause.

Other interesting foods in this group are the new range of fermented milks and yogurts with live (probiotic) bacteria that can survive in the gut. These foods have been used to grow beneficial bacteria in the intestines. They are specifically useful in individuals who have had food poisoning or have been taking antibiotics.

ENERGY & BODY WEIGHT

Are you the right weight for your height? There are charts available for you to check or you can work out your body mass index (BMI).

To do this, divide your weight (in kg) by your height (in metres squared). Alternatively, divide your weight (in pounds) by your height (in inches squared) and multiply the figure by 703:

HOW YOU SHAPE UP

BMI (BODY MASS INDEX) =

$$\frac{\text{weight in kilograms}}{\text{(height in metres)} \times \text{(height in metres)}}$$

OR

$$\frac{\text{weight in pounds}}{\text{(height in inches)} \times \text{(height in inches)}} \times 703$$

For example, a person who weighs 65 kg and is 1.7 m tall has a BMI of 22.5

$$\frac{65\ \text{kg}}{(1.7\ \text{m}) \times (1.7\ \text{m})}$$

Below 18.5	underweight (may harm your health)
18.5–24.9	normal weight range (within the healthy range)
25.0–29.9	overweight (losing weight is recommended)
Over 30	obese (may harm your health)

(Calculation of BMI source: Centers for Disease Control and Prevention, 2008)

WAIST CIRCUMFERENCE

MEN
Waist circumference over 94 cm (37 in) indicates a **slight** health risk

Waist circumference over 102 cm (40 in) indicates a **substantial** health risk

WOMEN
Waist circumference over 80 cm (31½ in) indicates a **slight** health risk

Waist circumference over 88 cm (34½ in) indicates a **substantial** health risk

How much food energy you need each day varies according to your sex, age, weight and activity level. The following equations will give an estimate of your energy requirement, but remember, these are very general calculations.

1. Use the equation for your sex and age, and factor in your weight in kg:

MEN
Age 18–29: [(0.063 × weight) + 2.896] × 239
Age 30–60: [(0.048 × weight) + 3.653] × 239
Age over 60: [(0.049 × weight) + 2.459] × 239

WOMEN
Age 19–29: [(0.062 × weight) + 2.036] × 239
Age 30–60: [(0.034 × weight) + 3.538] × 239
Age over 60: [(0.038 × weight) + 2.755] × 239

2. Although this gives you the basic calories you require, it does not take account of activity, so multiply the answer to equation 1 by your activity level (see page 20).
First select the activity level for your job. A desk job will be 'light', but a more active job such as nursing will be at least 'moderate'. If you exercise regularly you will be moderately active, but if you exercise rarely your leisure activity level will be 'non-active'.

LEISURE ACTIVITY	OCCUPATIONAL ACTIVITY					
	light		moderate		moderate/ heavy	
	M	F	M	F	M	F
Non-active	1.4	1.4	1.6	1.5	1.7	1.5
Moderately active	1.5	1.5	1.7	1.6	1.8	1.6
Very active	1.6	1.6	1.8	1.7	1.9	1.7

To lose weight, subtract about 500 calories from your daily requirement and use the calorie counter to check your intake. Very low-calorie diets are not a good way to lose weight. By making a smaller adjustment you will lose weight more slowly, but have a better chance of long-term success.

Note: These guidelines are for adults only – children need a proportionately higher calorie intake.

LOSING WEIGHT SAFELY

If you're trying to lose weight, you're not alone. Over 61 per cent of adults in the USA were classified as overweight (BMI over 25) or obese (BMI over 30). The number of obese people in the USA has doubled in the last two decades.

Many nutritionists believe that the reason for this alarming rise is due not to our eating more, but to our doing less. Modern technology and labour-saving devices mean that we're much less active than we used to be. Our weight is a reflection of the balance between the energy (calories) we consume and the energy we use. Our energy intake is determined by the amount and type of food we eat. Our energy expenditure is determined by a combination of our resting metabolic rate and the amount of calories we burn in day-to-day activities.

The resting metabolic rate is the amount of energy our body needs during rest or sleep. This is similar to the fuel used by a car when the engine is idling but the car is stationary. If our energy intake equals our energy expenditure, our body weight will remain the same, but if our intake exceeds our expenditure, the excess energy is stored in the body as fat (see page 22).

THE SEE-SAW EFFECT

Weight gain
If energy intake is greater than energy expenditure, the see-saw will tip at an angle, e.g. weight gain.

Weight loss
If energy expenditure is greater than energy intake, the see-saw will tip in the opposite direction, e.g. weight loss.

Weight maintenance
If energy expenditure equals energy intake, the see-saw will be flat, e.g. weight maintenance.

energy intake, e.g. calories consumed

energy expenditure, e.g. a combination of metabolic rate and physical activities

THE IDEAL RATE OF WEIGHT LOSS

Experts agree the best and safest way to lose weight is slowly and steadily between 0.5–1 kg (1–2 lb) a week is the ideal rate. If you lose too much weight too quickly, there is a danger of losing lean muscle tissue as well as fat. Since our basal metabolic rate (the number of calories the body needs to function) is related to the amount of lean muscle tissue we have, it's a good idea to do whatever we can to preserve it.

HOW LOW SHOULD YOU GO?

The total number of calories we need to eat each day varies, depending on a number of factors, including age, weight, sex, activity levels, body composition and metabolic rate. As a general guide, women need around 2000 calories a day and men need 2500. To lose 0.5 kg (1 lb) a week, you need to reduce your calorie intake by 500 calories a day. Diets that restrict calories too severely (fewer than 1200 calories a day) are not recommended.

HOW YOU SHAPE UP

Although most of us can get a pretty good idea of whether we need to lose weight or not just by looking in the mirror, you can get a more accurate assessment by calculating your Body Mass Index or measuring your waist circumference (see panel on page 18).

THE THREE MAIN REASONS THAT DIETS FAIL

Setting unrealistic goals
If you set unrealistic goals, you're more likely to become disheartened and give up. Aim for a slow but steady weight loss of 0.5–1 kg (1–2 lb) a week. If you lose too much weight too quickly, there's a danger of losing lean muscle tissue as well as fat.

Following the wrong sort of diet
However tempting they may seem, crash diets just don't work. Although you may lose weight initially, you'll find that you will end up putting on not just the weight you originally lost but even more.

Not eating enough
A mistake people often make is to reduce their calorie intake too severely. Overly strict diets are difficult to stick to in the long run, they're not necessary and they're not healthy. If you restrict your calories too severely, the chances are that you'll end up missing out on important nutrients.

UNDERSTANDING YOUR RELATIONSHIP WITH FOOD

Often we eat out of habit or to satisfy emotional needs rather than because we are hungry. We use food to celebrate, to relieve boredom or to make us feel better when we're unhappy or lonely. Certain people, places, moods and situations can also prompt us to eat.

Keeping a food diary will help you to identify these external cues. Buy a notebook and divide the pages into columns. Keep a record of everything you eat and drink and how you feel for two weeks.

FOOD DIARY

Date	Monday	Tuesday
Time	3.30pm	10.30am
Where were you?	At home	At work
What were you doing?	Nothing	Trying to meet a deadline
Who were you with?	No-one	Work colleagues
How did you feel?	Bored	Stressed
What did you eat?	Packet of crisps	Chocolate bar
How hungry were you? (On a scale of 1–5)	5	4

1 = hungry, 5 = not hungry

At the end of two weeks, review your diary and make a list of all the triggers that prompt you to eat when you're not really hungry.

Once you have identified these trigger factors, you can start to think about solutions and ways to avoid those situations in future. Work out strategies that will help avoid or change the way you behave when faced with these triggers. If, for instance, you find you get home after work so hungry that you end up eating a family-size package of cheesy snacks while preparing the evening meal, plan ahead. Have a healthy snack, such as a banana or yogurt, before you leave the office so you won't feel so hungry when you get home.

If your diary reveals that you use food as a way of making yourself feel better when you're unhappy or depressed, make a list of non-food-related activities that will help to lift your spirits when you're feeling low. Rent a video, have a manicure or take a long leisurely bath rather than reaching for a chocolate bar.

KEEPING THE FAT DOWN

Choose lower-fat milks. Milk is good for you and your bones so don't give it up, just choose semi-skimmed or skimmed milks.

Use a lower-fat spread on breads

Don't give up spreads altogether as they provide useful fat-soluble vitamins.

Keep fried foods to the minimum

Cooking in oil, even if it is polyunsaturated, still adds calories. Grill or oven-bake instead.

Trim visible fat from meats and avoid large helpings

Meat is not bad for you if eaten wisely. It provides useful vitamins and minerals.

Cut out baked goods

Cakes, biscuits and pies are usually high in fat.

Avoid mayonnaise

Often used in sandwiches or on salads, it is high in fat and can easily be avoided.

If you are a cheese lover, ration it

Just eat a small piece for each meal, and grate it so it looks like more. Some lower-fat cheeses can make good substitutes, but sometimes at the expense of flavour.

KEEPING THE CALORIES DOWN

Use artificial sweeteners instead of sugar – you can save as much as 20 calories per teaspoon.

Choose diet soft drinks

Avoid the ordinary variety. Check out the differences and you will be amazed at how many calories you can save.

Avoid desserts

Choose fresh fruit or a yogurt, which have much fewer calories (a really tempting dessert can easily set you back 500 calories). Desserts read 'stressed' backwards!

Try to avoid snacks between meals

The extra calories soon add up. If you enjoy snacks, then make sure you don't over-indulge at mealtimes.

Keep an eye on your 'portion control'

Does your plate look really full, or are you going back for seconds?

Don't miss meals

Skip a meal and you are more likely to snack or over-eat on the next occasion.

MAKING DIETS WORK FOR YOU

Tackling dieting on your own can be tough. If you can, seek help from a sympathetic and good friend. You must also help yourself by not becoming a diet bore. Diet bores are their own worst enemy. They think and talk about their diet all the time, a good way to lose friends and support! Try being diplomatic – you may not mention you are on a diet to your friends. Some may not notice, especially if you are not making too many changes to your usual eating pattern.

If you are trying to lose weight, it can sometimes take a little while for people to notice a weight change and by that time you can be well on your way to losing 'real' weight. If you are simply trying to improve your eating habits, then gradual changes are the best and are far more successful in the long term. Remember, Rome was not built in a day.

THINGS TO DO

If you feel like eating something, then maybe you should have a list of handy distractions. The list can be anything from reading a book, tidying out that drawer, getting out an address book and phoning a friend, or enjoying some aromatherapy treatment. These may just help you from straying from your good intentions.

MOTIVATIONAL TIPS

Try making a list of motivational tips to help you with your diet. Here are some ideas to begin with.

Choose wisely

One bad meal choice or mistake doesn't make a bad diet. Likewise, watch out for the 'all or nothing situation'. If you have eaten a piece of chocolate, you don't have to eat the rest of the bar or box.

Take your time

It takes 15–20 minutes for the body to register satisfaction, so wait before you decide whether you are really hungry and need a second helping or not.

Don't become afraid of food

Food is to be enjoyed, so learn to enjoy and take pleasure from foods that you know are better for your health.

Enjoy your diet

If there is a food on your diet that you are supposed to eat but you don't like it, find a good substitute. If you don't enjoy your diet you won't keep to it.

Never make your target for weight-loss unrealistic

Aim for a small loss, achieve that and then go on to lose more if you want to. Remember, you did not get fat overnight so you won't lose weight overnight either.

Be proud of small achievements
If weight-loss was easy nobody would be fat, so if you have achieved a loss, no matter how small, you are quite remarkable and should be proud of your efforts.

Feel good about yourself
You have made a conscious effort to make a change, so pat yourself on the back. Take one day at a time and congratulate yourself for what you have achieved on that day.

No excuses
Don't use your 'heavy' bones or build as a reason for being big; it is only you that you are kidding.

Shopping list
When shopping, use a list and keep to those foods you know you need. Don't buy something you know you will regret. Avoid shopping when you're hungry – you may buy more than you really need.

Be shop-wise
Don't be tempted by special offers on foods you don't need – the supermarkets are interested in profits, not your waistline.

FOOD LABELLING

To find out what is in a food before we buy, we look at the label. But almost without exception people find food labels very confusing. Food labels are supposed to provide information to allow you to make a sensible choice and to compare different foods.

HOW TO READ FOOD LABELS

So what do you need to look for? The label should describe the food and not misrepresent its contents, e.g. if it is described as 'meat and potato', then there should be more meat than potato. You will be able to see this by looking at the ingredients.

The contents list

Contents should be listed in quantity order. Therefore, the food in the largest amount should be listed first, with the smallest quantity of an ingredient listed last. If a food states 'no added sugar' then that is what it means. However, problems often occur with foods such as 'no added sugar' yogurts.

A quick glance down the nutrition information list shows that sugar is in fact contained and panic thus sets in. Sugar content needs to be checked more closely because with milk and fruit there are complications.

When foods are analysed for sugars, the total sugar content includes milk sugars (lactose) and fruit sugars (fructose) as well as the familiar sugar (sucrose). Typically, an individual pot of yogurt with sugar added will have approximately 20 g of sugar per serving (10 g of that is added sugar); if no sugar is added then the sugar content will be 10 g, this 10 g coming from milk and fruit sugars. Milk and fruit sugars are used in the body in a slightly different way to ordinary sugar and should not be of concern to people with diabetes.

Where to start

We read the nutrition label first. There is plenty of nutrition information but we are really only interested in calories and fat, which is why some manufacturers include a special panel for calories and fat only. The separate panel also states the typical calories and fat that adult females and males should consume.

Nutritional information is given per 100 g and/or per suggested portion size so you can work out how much you are eating. You can work out how much fat you are eating as a percentage of the food's total calories. It is very simple and all you need to know is the amount of calories and fat in any food and the calorie value of fat: 1 g of fat provides 9 calories (1 g of protein provides 4 calories, and 1 g of carbohydrate provides 4 calories). The rest is simple mathematics …

The information

For carbohydrates, the first figure given is the total amount of carbohydrate in the product. Giving information on sugars helps in choosing items with a lower sugar content.

Fats are presented as total fat in the product, and may also state how much is saturated. Information on saturates is helpful, because any fat that is not saturated will be mono- or polyunsaturated.

The basic nutritional information found on all food labels in the UK:

Energy as kcal and kJ
protein g
carbohydrate g
fat g

Although not mandatory, many foods are labelled more fully:

energy as kcal/kJ
protein g
carbohydrate g, of which
     sugars g
     starch g
fat g, of which
     saturates g
     monounsaturates g
     polyunsaturates g
     fibre g
     salt g
     sodium g

USING THE COUNTER

The A–Z food counter in this book lists the carbohydrate, fibre and fat content in grams per weight/average serving of food. If the food has no typical serving, a 100 g amount is given.

Everyone's fat and carbohydrate requirements differ slightly depending on their individual daily energy (calorie) needs. A normal-weight female aged 19–50 needs around 1900 calories per day, while a normal-weight male of 19–50 needs around 2500 calories. Follow these guides or estimate your own daily calorie count using the calculation on page 19.

FAT

Fat is regarded as the long-term energy source. After digestion, it is broken down and stored in the body. When the body requires more fuel to maintain its normal functions, then it draws upon its fat stores to provide itself with energy. Important fat-soluble vitamins and essential fatty acids are only found in foods containing fat.

Fat is classified as either saturated, monounsaturated or polyunsaturated. Saturated fats are usually solid at room temperature (e.g. butter), while the others are liquid and are more commonly known as oils. Typical sources are butter, margarine, lards, oils, cream, mayonnaise, fried foods, pastry goods and

nuts. Animal-origin fats are saturated, olive and groundnut (peanut) oils are monounsaturated oils, while sunflower and corn oils are good examples of polyunsaturated oils.

All fats contain a mixture of fatty acids: saturated, monounsaturated and polyunsaturated. While the kind of fat we eat can make a difference, all types are equally high in calories. Fat in food may be visible (e.g. butter, oil) or invisible (e.g. cheese, meat).

Dietary fat raises cholesterol in the bloodstream. High blood cholesterol increases the risk of coronary heart disease and other medical conditions. Current advice states that the total daily fat intake should provide 33 per cent of the daily calories, of which no more than 10 per cent should come from saturated fats.

Saturated fats are believed to raise the level of the harmful LDL (low density lipoprotein) cholesterol connected to heart disease.

Polyunsaturated fats reduce both HDL (high density lipoprotein) and LDL cholesterol. The omega-3 fatty acids (found in oily fish) may help to prevent unwanted clotting and reduce the risk of heart disease.

Monounsaturated fats raise the ratio of beneficial HDL to LDL cholesterol and may also have a protective role in the prevention of coronary heart disease.

COUNTING FAT

A woman who needs 1900 calories a day will require about 630 calories (33 per cent) to come from fats. If 1 gram fat = 9 calories, the desired fat intake would be 70 g/day. A man using a base figure of 2500 calories needs no more than 95 g fat.

CARBOHYDRATE

Carbohydrate is the body's instant-energy fuel. That which is not immediately required is stored as fat. The digestion of carbohydrates provides glucose, which is the preferred fuel of the body.

Carbohydrates comprise starchy and sugary foods. Staple foods worldwide, such as bread, rice, potatoes, millet, pasta, cassava, yam, plantains and green bananas, are starchy carbohydrates. High-protein beans, lentils, seeds and nuts also contain starchy carbohydrates.

Natural sugars are present in milk and many plant foods, especially fruit. Concentrated or pure sugars, occurring in honey and cane/beet sugars are high in calories, but of little nutritional value.

Note: Although sugar provides a quicker supply of glucose than starchy foods, excess sugar (extrinsic sugars) can lead to dental decay and obesity.

COUNTING CARBOHYDRATES

A recommended 50 per cent of daily energy should come from carbohydrates (with the least from pure sugars) but 45 per cent is acceptable. At a rate of 4 kcal/g this works out at 215 g daily (based on 1900 calories) or 280 g daily (based on 2500 calories).

FIBRE

Vital for the bowel to function normally, fibre is also known to help lower blood fats (lipids), helping to reduce the risk of heart disease. This is the fibrous part of plant foods (cereals, fruit, vegetables, pulses, nuts, seeds) that remains in the intestine after digestion. Fibre helps to prevent constipation, coronary heart disease, gall bladder disease and some cancers.

The recommended intake of dietary fibre is an average of 18 g/day. To achieve this, eat plenty of bread, cereals and potatoes, as well as five portions of fruit and vegetables.

Note: Too much fibre can reduce the absorption of some minerals. It is also important to drink plenty of fluids. Aim for a minimum of 2 litres per day/approx. 3 1/2 pints.

VITAMINS & MINERALS

Some vitamins are soluble in fat and hence known as fat-soluble vitamins (and are only found in fat-containing foods), while others are water-soluble. Excess fat-soluble vitamins are normally stored in the liver, while excess water-soluble vitamins are excreted. It is difficult to have an overdose of water-soluble vitamins, but 'mega' dosing on vitamins is not generally regarded to be wise. There is very little scientific data to prove that it has any health benefits. Vitamins and minerals work together. It can be harmful to take large doses of one nutrient as it may affect the action of another.

Some vitamins are known as antioxidants. These have a very important role in the body by helping to protect against molecular damage caused by 'free radicals'. Free radicals, which are harmful, can accumulate in the body as the result of exposure to car exhaust fumes, the sun's ultraviolet rays, cigarette smoke and excess alcohol.

ESSENTIAL VITAMINS & MINERALS

These are the main vitamins and minerals you need. A good varied diet should contain these and other vitamins and minerals required in much smaller amounts.

VITAMIN A (Retinol)

FUNCTION	Helps vision in dim light and to maintain healthy skin and surface tissues.
	In excess it can be poisonous. Supplements should not be taken in pregnancy.
TO BE FOUND IN	Liver, fish oils, dairy produce and egg yolks.

VITAMIN B1 THIAMIN

FUNCTION	All B vitamins are essential for enzyme systems and metabolism.
TO BE FOUND IN	Animal and vegetable foods, such as milk, offal, pork, eggs, vegetables, fruit, wholegrain cereals and fortified breakfast cereals. In the UK all flour except wholemeal is fortified with thiamin.

VITAMIN B2 RIBOFLAVIN

FUNCTION	All B vitamins are essential for enzyme systems and metabolism.
TO BE FOUND IN	In foods, especially of animal origin. Milk is a particularly important source for many people.

VITAMIN B3 NIACIN

FUNCTION	All B vitamins are essential for enzyme systems and metabolism.
TO BE FOUND IN	Widely distributed. Found in cereals, meat, fish, dairy products.

VITAMIN C (Ascorbic acid)

FUNCTION	Essential for healthy connective tissue. Deficiency results in bleeding gums etc.
TO BE FOUND IN	Vegetables and fruit, especially citrus fruits, guavas and blackcurrants.

VITAMIN D (Cholecalciferol)

FUNCTION	Needed for the absorption of calcium into the blood and maintenance of bones. In children deficiency of vitamin D leads to rickets, and in adults to osteomalacia.
TO BE FOUND IN	Main source is the action of sunlight on the skin and most people require no more than this. Natural dietary sources are all of animal origin, such as fish and animal livers and oils, fatty fish, butter, milk and eggs. It may be added to some foods as a supplement.

FOLATE (Folic acid)

FUNCTION	Essential for cell growth, especially in pregnancy. Deficiency may lead to a form of anaemia.
TO BE FOUND IN	Offal, yeast extract, green leafy vegetables

CALCIUM

FUNCTION	Essential for the maintenance of bones and connective tissue. Deficiency may accelerate osteoporosis.
TO BE FOUND IN	Milk, cheese and yogurt are best sources. Also occurs in fruits, vegetables and seeds. May be added to bread and flour.

IRON

FUNCTION	Essential for the prevention of anaemia.
TO BE FOUND IN	Present in a wide range of foods, especially proteins – meat and dairy foods.

ZINC

FUNCTION	Helps wound healing and enzyme activity.
TO BE FOUND IN	Present in a wide range of foods, especially proteins – meat and dairy foods.

VITAMINS IN DETAIL

VITAMIN A
(retinol: fat-soluble; carotenes: water-soluble)
Average requirement: Women and men 600 mcg per day (more if pregnant or breastfeeding).

Vitamin A is important for cell growth and development, and for the formation of visual pigments in the eye. Carotenes are an important antioxidant. There are several, of which beta-carotene is the best known. Good sources: retinol is found in liver, meat and meat products, whole milk and its products, e.g. cheese and butter, and eggs. Beta-carotene is found in red and yellow fruits and vegetables, e.g. carrots, peppers, mangoes and apricots.

Note: If taking a supplement, ensure that it is no more than 100 per cent RDA. Women who are pregnant should avoid Vitamin A supplements and liver or liver products, since it is known that excess intakes of the vitamin may cause birth defects.

VITAMIN B1
(thiamin: water-soluble)
Average requirement: Women and men 1 mg per day.

Important to enable the release of energy from carbohydrate-containing foods. Good sources include

yeast and yeast products, bread, fortified breakfast cereals and potatoes.

Note: The amount of thiamin required is directly linked to the amount of carbohydrate eaten in the diet. Thiamin deficiency is very unlikely except where alcohol is a major part of the diet.

VITAMIN B2
(riboflavin: water-soluble)
Average requirement: Women and men 1.3 mg per day (more if pregnant or breastfeeding).

Important for metabolism of carbohydrates, proteins and fats to produce energy. Good sources are meat, yeast extracts, fortified breakfast cereals, milk, milk products.

Note: Riboflavin in milk is easily destroyed by exposure to sunlight, so keep milk out of the sunlight!

VITAMIN B3
(niacin: water-soluble)
Average requirement: Women and men 18 mg per day.

Required for the metabolism of food into energy. Good sources are milk and milk products, fortified breakfast cereals, pulses, meat, poultry and eggs.

Note: It is uncommon to have a dietary deficiency of this vitamin.

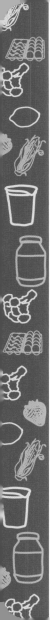

VITAMIN B5
(pantothenic acid: water-soluble)
Average requirement: Women and men 3–7 mg per day.

Important for metabolism of food into energy. Good sources: most foods, especially fortified breakfast cereals, wholegrain bread and dairy products.

Note: There has been no evidence of deficiency of this vitamin as it is found in so many foods.

VITAMIN B6
(pyridoxine: water-soluble)
Average requirement: Women and men 1.5 mg per day.

Important for metabolism of protein and fat. It may also be involved with the regulation of sex hormones. Good sources are liver, fish, pork, soya beans and peanuts.

Note: Drugs containing penicillin or oestrogen may increase the need for B6. It is also thought to help some women who suffer from PMT. Regular high doses have been known to cause some peripheral nerve damage.

VITAMIN B12
(cyanocobalamin: water-soluble)
Average requirement: Women and men 1.5 mgc per day (more if pregnant or breastfeeding).

Important for production of red blood cells and DNA and vital for growth and the nervous system. Good sources are meat, fish, eggs, poultry and milk. There are no plant sources of this vitamin.

Note: Supplements are recommended for vegans. The metabolic functions are closely associated with those of folic acid.

FOLIC ACID, FOLATE
(B vitamin: water-soluble)
Average requirement: Women and men 200 mcg per day (more if pregnant or breastfeeding).

Folic acid is important for protein metabolism, and in the development of the neural tube in the foetus during the early stages of pregnancy. Good sources are wholegrain cereals, fortified breakfast cereals, green leafy vegetables, oranges and liver.

Note: It is recommended to take a daily supplement of 400 mcg of folic acid prior to conception and during the first 13 weeks of pregnancy. It is also thought that folic acid may play a role in helping to prevent heart disease.

BIOTIN
(B group: water-soluble)
Average requirement: Women and men 0.15 mg per day.

Important for the metabolism of fatty acids. Good sources are liver, kidney, eggs and nuts. Micro-organisms also manufacture this vitamin in the gut.

Note: A protein found in raw egg binds with the biotin to make it unavailable and prevents the body utilizing it.

VITAMIN C
(ascorbic acid: water-soluble)
Average requirement: Women and men 60 mg per day.

Important for wound-healing and the formation of collagen as it is a major component of skin, muscle and bone. Also an important antioxidant. Good sources are citrus fruits, soft summer fruits, vegetables and potatoes.

Note: It is thought that high doses (1000 mg/1 g) help reduce the severity of the common cold. However at those levels it may irritate the stomach lining, causing diarrhoea or renal stones.

VITAMIN D
(cholecalciferol and ergocalciferol: fat-soluble)
Average requirement: Women and men 5 mcg per day.

Important for absorption and handling of calcium to help build bone strength. Good sources are oily fish, eggs, full-fat milk and milk products, margarine. The manufacture of vitamin D just under the skin is very important.

Note: Elderly, housebound people and those who are covered up even in sunny weather may need supplements to obtain the recommended amounts.

VITAMIN E
(tocopherol: fat-soluble)
Average requirement: Women and men 10 mg per day.

Important as an antioxidant, helping to protect cell membranes from damage. Good sources are vegetable oils, margarine, seeds, nuts and green vegetables.

Note: High doses of this vitamin have not been shown to cause any health problems, even though it is a fat-soluble vitamin.

MINERALS IN DETAIL

Like vitamins, minerals are required in small amounts but are essential to good health.

CALCIUM

Average requirement: Women and men 800 mg per day (more if breastfeeding).

Important for healthy bones and teeth, nerve transmission, muscle contraction, blood clotting and hormone function. Good sources are dairy products, small fish bones, nuts, pulses, fortified white flours and bread, green leafy vegetables.

Note: People who have low-calcium intakes and do little exercise are at risk of osteoporosis later in life. This applies especially to women who have passed the menopause. Abnormal deposits of calcium can occur if the diet is very high in vitamin D.

IRON

Average requirement: Women 14.8 mg per day.
Men 8.7mg per day.

Iron is a key building block of haemoglobin, which carries oxygen around the body and is therefore vital for normal growth and development. Good sources are liver, corned beef, red meat, fortified breakfast cereals,

pulses, green leafy vegetables, egg yolk, cocoa and cocoa products.

Note: Eating foods rich in vitamin C helps improve iron absorption from vegetable-based foods.

MAGNESIUM

Average requirement: Women and men 300 mg per day.

Important for the efficient functioning of metabolic enzymes, development of the skeleton and nerve/muscle transmission. Good sources are nuts, green vegetables, meat, cereals, milk and yogurt.

Note: Women with PMT may benefit from extra magnesium.

ZINC

Average requirement: Women and men 15 mg per day.

Important for metabolism and for healing wounds. A deficiency is thought to be related to male infertility, as quite high levels are found in the prostate gland. Good sources are liver, meat, pulses, wholegrain cereals, nuts and oysters.

Note: Low zinc intakes may result in a poor sense of taste; prolonged high doses may cause copper deficiency.

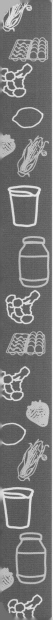

IODINE
Average requirement: Women and men 140 mcg
per day.

Important for the manufacture of thyroid hormones
and for normal development. Good sources are
seafood, seaweed, milk and dairy products.
    Note: The absorption of iodine may be reduced by
foods that contain goitrogens. These are found in foods
such as peaches, almonds, soya beans and cassava.
Dietary deficiencies are rare in the UK.

SELENIUM
Average requirement: Women and men 75 mcg per day.

Important antioxidant mineral that forms part of an
enzyme system found in red blood cells. Good sources
are liver, kidney, meat, eggs, cereals, nuts and dairy
products.
    Note: Supplements with more than 100 mcg should
be avoided as they can cause toxicity.

POTASSIUM
Average requirement: Women and men 3500 mg per day

Important for the normal transmission of nerve–
muscle signals. Good sources are fruit, vegetables, milk
and bread.

Note: Diets high in potassium may protect against high blood pressure.

SODIUM
Average requirement: Women and men 1600 mg per day.

Important in helping to control body fluid and balance, and involved in muscle and nerve function. All foods are good sources, but processed, pickled and salted foods are the richest sources.

Note: Many people consume more salt than is required, so it is best to avoid foods known to be salty. Adding salt to food at the table is not advisable.

TRACE ELEMENTS
These are a group of nutrients that are essential to health but only required in very small amounts. It is quite difficult to establish how much the body needs and indeed if the body needs them every day. It is most likely that a healthy diet will provide all the trace elements that a typical body needs.

PHYTONUTRIENTS

In recent years there has been a considerable amount of interest and research into a group of nutrients often known as phytonutrients – 'phyto' means 'plant'. It is thought that there are a number of exciting new chemicals that are found only in plants that may be beneficial to health. An example is the recent research into a substance called lycopene, which is found in tomatoes. This nutrient may have a role in helping to prevent prostate cancer. Similarly, oestrogens found in some foods, especially soya, may help to prevent some of the symptoms of the menopause. Much of this research is still in the early stages; suffice to say that it suggests we should be eating more fruit and vegetables.

OMEGA OILS

There is increasing evidence that a diet including omega oils is good for health, benefiting people with heart disease and arthritis. They are found in oily fish, such as herring, mackerel, salmon, sardines, pilchards and trout. Fish such as cod, plaice, haddock and even tuna have relatively low levels of omega oils. For those people who do not like oily fish, a fish oil supplement may be preferable and if you eat oily fish only once a week, then take a supplement every other day.

RAW VERSUS COOKED VEGETABLES

Cooking is known to destroy water-soluble vitamins, but by eating raw vegetables are you getting more vitamins? The simple answer is no. Scientific studies have shown that cooking helps break down the cell walls to allow vitamins and minerals to be absorbed more easily by the digestive system. We would have to do a lot of chewing to break down the cell walls so easily. But keep cooking to a minimum to maximize the uptake of vitamins.

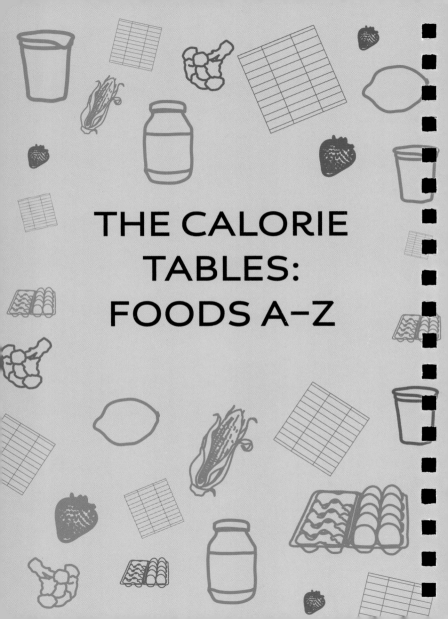

THE CALORIE TABLES: FOODS A–Z

FOOD	FAT g	FIBRE g	CARB g	ENERGY kcal	kJ
++ known to be present but unmeasured					
0+ trace only present					

A

ALCOHOL

BEER

FOOD	FAT g	FIBRE g	CARB g	ENERGY kcal	kJ
bitter, draught, 1 pint, 574 ml	0	0	13	172	712
bitter, low-alcohol, 333 ml	0	0	7	43	180
brown ale, bottled, 1 pint, 574 ml	0	0	17	172	723
lager, alcohol-free, canned, 333 ml	0	0	5	23	103
lager, canned, 333 ml	0	0	0+	97	403
lager, low-alcohol, canned, 333 ml	0	0	5	33	137
lager, premium, canned, 333 ml	0	0	8	196	813
pale ale, draught, 1 pint, 574 ml	0	0	12	161	677
shandy, canned, 333 ml	0	0	10	37	160
stout, canned, 333 ml	0	0	5	100	420
stout, strong, canned, 333 ml	0	0	15	120	509
strong ale/barley wine, 1 pint, 574 ml	0	0	35	379	1579

CIDER

FOOD	FAT g	FIBRE g	CARB g	ENERGY kcal	kJ
dry, draught, 1 pint, 574 ml	0	0	15	207	872
low alcohol, canned, 333 ml	0	0	12	57	246
sweet, draught, 1 pint, 574 ml	0	0	25	241	1010

LIQUEURS

FOOD	FAT g	FIBRE g	CARB g	ENERGY kcal	kJ
cream-based, 25 ml	4	0	6	81	338
egg-based, 25 ml	2	0	7	65	273
higher strength, (Curaçao, Drambuie), 25 ml	0	0	6	79	328
lower strength, (cherry brandy, coffee) 25 ml	0	0	8	66	275

SPIRITS

FOOD	FAT g	FIBRE g	CARB g	ENERGY kcal	kJ
brandy, gin, rum, whisky					
alcohol 40% 25 ml	0	0	0	56	230

FOOD	FAT g	FIBRE g	CARB g	ENERGY kcal	ENERGY kJ
alcohol 37.5%	0	0	0	52	215
WINES					
champagne, dry, 125 ml	0	0	2	95	394
port, 125 ml	0	0	15	196	819
red, dry, 125 ml	0	0	0.3	85	354
rosé, 125 ml	0	0	3	89	368
sherry, dry, 50 ml	0	0	1	58	241
sherry, medium, 50 ml	0	0	3	58	241
sherry, sweet, 50 ml	0	0	4	68	284
tonic wine, 100 ml	0	0	12	127	532
vermouth, dry, 1 measure, 48 ml	0	0	1	52	217
vermouth, sweet, 1 measure, 48 ml	0	0	8	72	303
white, dry, 125 ml	0	0	1	83	344
white, medium, 125 ml	0	0	4	93	385
white, sparkling, sweet, 125 ml	0	0	6	93	384
white, sweet, 125 ml	0	0	7	118	493
APPLE					
cooking, baked with sugar, 1, 150 g	0	4	29	111	477
cooking, baked (flesh only), no sugar, 100 g	0.1	2.2	11	43	183
cooking, raw, peeled, 1, 100 g	0.1	2.2	9	34	150
cooking, raw, with skin & core, 100 g	0.1	1.6	6	27	109
cooking, cooked with sugar, 100 g	0	1.8	19	74	314
cooking, cooked without sugar, 100 g	0	2.0	8	33	138
eating, dried, 100 g	0.5	10	60	238	1014
eating, raw, peeled, 1 av.	0	1.8	11	45	190
eating, raw, unpeeled, 1 av.	0	2.4	14	56	239
juice, 100 ml	0	0+	10	38	164
APRICOT					
canned in juice, 140 g	0	1.7	12	48	206

FOOD	FAT g	FIBRE g	CARB g	ENERGY kcal	kJ
canned in syrup, 140 g	0	1.7	23	88	375
dried, 100 g	0.7	22	43	188	802
dried, cooked with sugar, 100 g	0.3	8.5	22	92	393
dried, cooked without sugar, 100 g	0.3	8.9	18	77	328
raw, 3, 120 g	0	2.3	9	37	160
ready-to-eat, 100 g	0.6	18	37	158	674
cooked with sugar, 100 g (including stones)	0.1	1.7	17	67	88
cooked without sugar, 100 g (inc. stones)	0.1	1.5	6	25	108
ARTICHOKE					
globe, boiled, 220 g	0	++	3	18	75
Jerusalem, peeled, boiled, 100 g	0	++	11	41	207
ASPARAGUS					
boiled, 120 g	0.5	0.8	1	16	64
canned, 100 g	0.5	2.9	2	24	100
AUBERGINE					
raw, 100 g	0.4	2.3	2	15	64
fried in oil, 100g	32	3	3	302	1262
AVOCADO					
raw, 1 av., 145 g	2.8	++	3	276	1137

B

BABY FOODS (Retail)

apple & apricot cereal, dried, organic, 100 g	5.8	4.6	70	384	1840
apple & banana, jar, 100 g	0.2	1.5	14	60	256
apple & raspberry, dried, 100 g	4.5	5.6	70	374	1586
banana & apple purée, jar, 100 g	0.2	1.5	14	60	256
carrot & lamb, jar, 100 g	2.4	0.8	8	63	264
carrot & potato, organic, jar, 100 g	0.1	2.7	6	26	111

FOOD	FAT g	FIBRE g	CARB g	ENERGY kcal	ENERGY kJ
cheese & tomato bake, dried, 100 g	11.6	2.2	64	411	1718
cottage pie, jar, 100 g	2.8	1.0	8	68	284
fruit & yogurt, dried, 100 g	3.8	1.9	77	386	1637
mixed fruit, jar, 100 g	0.2	1.4	15	64	270
pasta bolognese, jar, 100 g	1.6	0.5	9	65	274
porridge, creamed, jar, 100 g	2.5	0.4	12	80	338
rice, baby, dried, 100 g	1.7	2.0	86	391	1658
rice pudding, jar, 100 g	3.3	0.1	13	92	387
roast pork & apple, dried, 100 g	10	2.2	66	404	1687
rusk, 1, 17 g	1.2	0.4	13	69	290
rusk, reduced sugar, 1, 17 g	1.5	0.5	13	70	293
seasonal vegetable & chicken, dried, reconstituted, 100 g	1.4	1	17	93	391
strawberry cheesecake, jar, 100 g	2.8	0.3	12	81	342
vegetables, beans & bacon, jar, 100 g	3	1.6	7	69	290
vegetables, cheese & pasta, organic, jar, 100 g	2.2	0.9	10	71	299
vegetables, pasta & pork, jar, 100 g	2.7	1.5	7	65	270
BACON					
gammon rasher, grilled, 170 g	21	0	0	388	1620
rasher, back, grilled, 1, 25 g	8	0	0	101	420
rasher, back, microwaved, 1, 25 g	6	0	0	77	319
rasher, middle, grilled, 1, 40 g	14	0	0	166	689
rasher, streaky, grilled, 1, 20 g	7	0	0	84	350
BAMBOO SHOOTS					
canned, drained, 140 g	0.3	++	1	15	63
BANANAS					
green, raw, peeled, 100 g	++	2.2	22	89	379
plantain, boiled, 200 g	0.4	4.4	57	224	954

FOOD	FAT g	FIBRE g	CARB g	ENERGY kcal	ENERGY kJ
plantain, raw, 100 g	0.3	2.3	29	117	500
raw, peeled, 100 g	0.3	3.1	23	95	403
BEANS					
adzuki, dried, boiled, 120 g	0.2	++	27	148	630
baked, in tomato sauce, 100 g	0.6	6.9	15	84	355
baked, in tomato sauce, reduced sugar, 100 g	0.4	3.7	13	75	320
beansprouts, mung, raw, 1 tbsp, 20 g	0.1	1.1	1	6	26
black-eyed, dried, boiled, 100 g	0.7	++	20	116	494
broad, boiled, 100 g	0.6	++	12	81	344
butter, canned, drained, 100 g	0.5	++	13	77	327
French, raw, 100 g	0.5	3	3	24	99
red kidney, canned, 100 g	0.6	8.5	18	100	424
runner, boiled, 90 g	0.4	2.8	2	16	68
soya, dried, boiled, 100 g	7	++	5	141	590
BEEF					
corned, canned, 1 slice, 38 g	5	0	0	82	344
fillet steak, lean, grilled, 120 g	10	0	0	226	949
flank, lean, pot-roasted, 2 slices, 90 g	13	0	0	228	953
minced, extra lean, casseroled, 100 g	7	0.2	3	121	504
pastrami, 100 g	1	1	0.1	95	402
rump steak, lean, grilled, 150 g	9	0	0	252	1062
sirloin steak, grilled, 180 g	23	0	0	383	1598
stewing steak, lean, 100 g	6	0	0	185	777
topside, lean, roast, 90 g	4	0	0	140	593
BEETROOT					
boiled, peeled, 1, 35 g	0	0.8	3	16	68
pickled, 5 slices, 50 g	0	1.3	3	14	59

FOOD	FAT g	FIBRE g	CARB g	ENERGY kcal	kJ
BEVERAGES (Hot)					
cappuccino coffee, retail, 450 ml					
- full-fat milk	9	0	15	180	752
- semi-skimmed milk	5	0	15	140	585
- skimmed milk	0	0	15	110	46
chocolate, instant, low-calorie, sachet, 28 g	0.9	++	4	35	140
chocolate, instant, regular, sachet, 28 g	4	++	18	120	505
cocoa, full-fat milk, 1 tsp sugar, 200 ml	8	0.4	14	152	640
cocoa, semi-skimmed milk, 1 tsp sugar, 200 ml	4	0.2	14	114	486
coffee, full-fat milk, 225 ml	0.9	0	1	16	70
coffee, semi-skimmed milk, 225 ml	0.5	0	2	16	65
coffee, skimmed milk, 225 ml	0	0	2	11	46
latte coffee, retail, 450 ml					
- full-fat milk	14	0	22	270	1129
- semi-skimmed milk	7	0	22	220	920
- skimmed milk	1	0	22	160	669
iced coffee latte, retail, 450 ml					
- full-fat milk	8	0	13	160	669
- semi-skimmed milk	5	0	14	130	543
- skimmed milk	0	0	14	100	418
latte tea, retail, full-fat milk, 450 ml	5	0	52	320	1338
malted milk, powder, 1 cup, 20 g	1	0.8	15	76	322
malted milk, powder, low-fat, 20 g	1.2	0.6	13	72	303
mocha coffee, retail, large, 450 ml					
- full-fat milk	21	2	40	370	1547
- semi-skimmed milk	16	2	40	340	1421
- skimmed milk	11	2	40	290	1212
tea, black, 250 ml	0	0	0	0	0
tea, full-fat milk, 250 ml	1.0	0	1	20	80

FOOD	FAT g	FIBRE g	CARB g	ENERGY kcal	kJ
tea, herbal, infusion, 250 ml	0	0	0.5	3	33
tea, semi-skimmed milk, 250 ml	0.5	0	2	18	70
tea, skimmed milk, 250 ml	0	0	2	14	59

BISCUITS

FOOD	FAT g	FIBRE g	CARB g	ENERGY kcal	kJ
chocolate chip, 1 small, 8 g	2	0.1	5	39	163
chocolate, full-coated, 1, 25 g	7	0.7	17	131	549
crackers, low-fat, 2, 10 g	0.1	++	8	36	152
cream crackers, 2, 14 g	2	0.9	10	62	260
digestive, chocolate, 1, 17 g	4	0.5	11	84	352
digestive, plain, 1, 13 g	3	0.6	9	61	257
fruit shortcake, 1, 8 g	1.6	0.2	6	38	161
gingernuts, 1 small, 10 g	1.5	0.2	8	46	192
oatmeal, 1, 14 g	3	0.7	9	69	289
sandwich, 1, 10 g	3	0.1	7	51	215
semi-sweet (rich tea, petit-beurre), 1, 15 g	2.5	0.3	11	69	289
water, 2, 14 g	1.8	0.9	11	62	260

BLACKBERRIES

FOOD	FAT g	FIBRE g	CARB g	ENERGY kcal	kJ
cooked with sugar, 100 g	0.2	5	14	56	239
cooked without sugar, 100 g	0.2	6	4	21	88
cooked with sugar, and apple, 100 g	0.1	3.6	18	70	300
raw, 100 g	0.2	6.6	5	25	104

BLACKCURRANTS

FOOD	FAT g	FIBRE g	CARB g	ENERGY kcal	kJ
canned in juice, 140 g	0	6	11	43	189
canned in syrup, 140 g	0	5	26	101	428
raw, 100 g	0	7.8	7	28	121
cooked with sugar, 140 g	0	9	21	81	353

BLUEBERRIES

FOOD	FAT g	FIBRE g	CARB g	ENERGY kcal	kJ
raw, 100 g	0.2	2.5	7	30	128

BRAN (see Cereals)

FOOD	FAT g	FIBRE g	CARB g	ENERGY kcal	kJ
BREAD					
bagel, plain, 1	1.4	3.1	42	216	916
bagel, sweet, 1	2	2.3	44	266	1129
beefburger bun, 1, 85 g	4	3.4	42	224	953
breadsticks, 1	0.6	++	5	27	116
brown bread, 1 large slice, 38 g	0.8	2.2	17	83	352
brown roll, crusty, 1, 48 g	1.3	3.4	24	122	521
brown roll, soft, 1, 48 g	1.8	3.1	25	129	547
chapati, made with fat, 1, 60 g	7.8	4.2	29	197	830
chapati, made without fat, 1, 55 g	0.6	3.5	24	111	473
ciabatta, 100 g	5	4.2	52	280	1184
croissant. 1, 60 g	12	1.5	23	216	903
crumpet, toasted, 1, 40 g	0.4	1.2	17	80	338
currant loaf, 1 small slice, 25 g	1.9	0.9	13	72	305
focaccia, 50 g	5	1.1	23	145	610
French, half baguette, 120 g	3	6.1	67	324	1379
gluten-free rice, 1 slice, 38 g	3	2.0	14	86	360
granary, 1 large slice, 38 g	1	2.5	18	89	380
muffin, English, 1	1	1.8	27	144	611
malt, 1 small slice, 35 g	0.8	2.3	20	94	399
milk, 1 small slice, 35 g	3	0.9	17	104	437
naan, 160g	20	3.5	80	538	2264
pitta, white, 1, 60 g	0.8	2.1	29	147	624
pitta, wholemeal, 1, 60 g	0.9	3.1	27	146	618
poppadums, fried, 1, 13 g	2	1.2	5	48	201
rye, 1 small slice, 25 g	0.4	1.5	11	55	233
soda, 1 large slice, 38 g	0.9	0.9	21	98	416
tortilla, wheat flour, 1, 30 g	0.3	0.8	18	79	334
white, 1 large slice, 35 g	0.7	1.3	17	82	351

FOOD	FAT g	FIBRE g	CARB g	ENERGY kcal	ENERGY kJ
white, reduced starch, 1 large slice, 20 g	0.4	0.6	9	46	197
wholemeal, 1 large slice, 38 g	0.9	2.8	16	82	347
wholemeal, reduced starch, 1 large slice, 20 g	0.6	1.4	7	43	183
wholemeal roll, 1, 48 g	1.4	4.2	23	116	492
BROCCOLI					
green, boiled, 100 g	0.8	++	1	24	100
green, raw, 100 g	0.9	++	2	33	138
BRUSSELS SPROUTS					
boiled, 100 g	1.3	2.6	4	35	153
raw, 100 g	1.4	3.8	4	42	177
BUCKWHEAT KERNELS					
boiled, 100 g	2.5	2.1	73	334	1400
BULGAR (cracked wheat)					
cooked, 100 g	2.5	++	69	319	1340
BUTTER					
10 g	8	0	0	74	303
ghee, av. portion, 10 g	10	0	0	90	369
spreadable, 10 g	8.3	0	0	75	306

C

CABBAGE					
Chinese, raw, 40 g	0.1	++	1	5	20
green, boiled, 100 g	0.5	2.6	2	17	372
green, raw, 100 g	0.4	2.9	4	26	109
red, boiled, 60 g	0.2	1.5	1.4	9	37
red, raw, 100 g	0.3	3.1	4	21	89
white, raw, 100 g	0.2	2.4	5	21	113

FOOD	FAT g	FIBRE g	CARB g	ENERGY kcal	kJ
CAKES/PASTRIES/BUNS					
Bakewell tart, iced individual, 1	8	0.6	27	190	796
Battenburg, 1 slice, 32 g	6	0.5	16	118	496
bran loaf, 1 slice, 30 g	0.5	1.6	18	76	324
carrot cake, soft cheese topping, 100 g	15	0.9	49	343	1440
cheesecake, American-style, individual, 100 g	21	0.9	36	347	1449
cheesecake, frozen, 100 g	11	0.9	33	241	1013
Chelsea bun, 1, 78 g	11	1.7	44	285	1203
chocolate, sponge, 1 slice, 60 g	16	2.3	30	274	1145
chocolate marshmallow teacake, 1, 18 g	3	0.2	12	75	320
chocolate, with butter icing, 1 slice, 100 g	30	3	51	481	2009
crispie cake (chocolate & cereal), 1, 25 g	5	0.2	18	116	488
currant bun/teacake, 1, 60 g	5	1.1	32	176	750
Danish pastry, 1, 110 g	19	3.0	56	411	1728
éclair, cream-filled, frozen, 1, 35 g	11	0.5	9	139	576
fruitcake, plain, 1 slice, 60 g	8	1.5	35	212	894
fruitcake, rich, 1 slice, 70 g	8	2.2	42	239	1007
gâteau, 1 slice, 85 g	14	0.4	37	286	1201
gingerbread, 1 slice, 50 g	6	0.7	32	190	799
Greek pastry (baklava), 100 g	17	1.9	40	322	1349
hot cross bun, 1, 50 g	3	1.1	29	155	657
iced fancy, 1, 30 g	5	0.7	21	122	515
jam tart, 1, 34 g	4	0.9	22	125	525
Madeira, 1 slice, 40 g	7	0.5	23	157	661
muffin, blueberry, 1, 85 g	14	1.5	37	277	1158
muffin, chocolate chip, 1, 85 g	13	0.8	38	280	1170
sponge, butter icing, 1 slice, 60 g	18	0.4	31	294	1228
sponge, fatless, 1 slice, 58 g	4	0.6	31	171	1152
sponge, jam-filled, 1 slice, 60 g	3	0.7	39	181	768

FOOD	FAT g	FIBRE g	CARB g	ENERGY kcal	ENERGY kJ
Swiss roll, chocolate individual, 1, 25 g	3	0.6	15	84	355
vanilla slice, individual, 1, 60 g	11	0.5	24	198	830
Welsh cake, 1, 30 g	6	0.5	19	129	542
CAROB					
powder, 40 g	0	++	15	64	272
CARROT					
canned, 100g	0.3	++	4	20	87
juice, 125 ml	0.1	++	7	30	129
old, boiled, 70 g	0.3	2.0	3	17	70
young, raw, 50 g	0.3	1.3	3	15	63
CASSAVA					
boiled, 100 g	0.2	1.5	34	130	552
raw, 100 g	0.2	1.7	37	142	607
CAULIFLOWER					
baked with cheese, 200 g	14	2.8	10	210	876
boiled, 100 g	0.9	1.6	2	28	117
raw, 50 g	0.4	0.9	2	17	71
CELERIAC					
boiled, 120 g	0.6	5.3	2	18	74
raw, 120 g	0.5	6.1	3	22	88
CELERY					
boiled, 50 g	0.2	1.0	0.4	4	17
raw, 1 stick, 30 g	0.1	0.5	0.3	2	10
CEREALS (Bars)					
apple & blackberry with yogurt, 29 g	3.2	++	21	121	510
fruit & fibre, 28 g	2.5	1.0	18	96	404
fruit & nut, with milk chocolate, 29 g	4.2	++	20	125	525
hazelnut, organic, 33 g	7.2	2.6	19	151	634
strawberry, with cereal mix, 37 g	3.5	1.0	26	140	550

FOOD	FAT g	FIBRE g	CARB g	ENERGY kcal	ENERGY kJ
CEREALS (Breakfast)					
bran, natural wheat, 1 tsp. 7 g	0.4	2.8	2	14	61
bran flakes, 30 g	0.6	5.2	21	95	406
bran flakes, oat, 30 g	1.2	++	22	107	456
bran strands, 30 g	0.9	8.5	16	82	349
bran, whole 30 g	1	9.0	14	78	333
chocolate flavoured rice pops, 30 g	0.3	0.3	28	115	491
corn flakes, 30 g	0.2	1.0	26	107	455
corn flakes with nuts, 30 g	1.0	0.5	27	119	507
fruit & fibre flakes, 30 g	1.4	3.0	22	106	449
grapenuts, 30 g	0.2	1.9	24	104	443
muesli, 100 g	7	8	66	365	1542
muesli, crunchy, 100 g	13	5.0	66	410	1727
porridge, with water, 160 g	2	1.3	14	78	334
porridge, with milk, 160 g	8.1	1.3	22	93	400
puffed wheat, 20 g	0.3	1.8	14	64	273
puffed rice, 30 g	0.2	0.3	29	115	490
quick-cook oatmeal, with milk, 180 g	14	12.2	125	700	2961
rice-based crispies, 30 g	0.3	0.3	27	111	472
shredded wheat biscuits, 2, 44 g	1.0	4.4	30	143	609
sugar-coated puffed rice, 30 g	0.3	1.4	25	97	414
sultana bran flakes, 50 g	0.8	7.8	34	151	644
waffles, pre-cooked with jam, 1, 50 g	5	0.7	35	195	825
wholewheat biscuits, large, 40 g	0.8	4.6	30	137	582
wholewheat biscuits, small, 45 g	0.7	4.9	33	149	635
CHARD					
boiled, 100 g	0.1	++	3	20	84
raw, 100 g	0.2	++	3	19	81

FOOD	FAT g	FIBRE g	CARB g	ENERGY kcal	ENERGY kJ
CHEESE					
Brie, 40 g	11	0	0	128	529
Camembert, 40 g	10	0	0	119	493
Cheddar type, 40 g	14	0	0	165	683
cottage, plain reduced fat, carton 112 g	1.6	0	4	87	371
cottage, with extras, carton, 112 g	4.3	++	3	106	448
cream, full-fat, 30 g	14	0	0	132	542
Danish blue, 30 g	9	0	0	104	431
double Gloucester, 30 g	10	0	0	122	503
Edam, 40 g	10	0	0	133	553
Edam-type, reduced fat, 40 g	4	0	0	92	383
Emmenthal, 40 g	12	0	0	153	635
feta, 40 g	8	0	0	98	407
goat, soft, 30 g	5	0	0.3	59	247
Gouda, 40 g	12	0	0	150	622
Gruyère, 40 g	13	0	0	164	678
halloumi, 40 g	9	0	0.6	116	486
Jarlsberg, 40 g	11	0	0	144	600
Lancashire, 40 g	12	0	0	149	665
Leicester, 40 g	14	0	0	160	665
mozzarella, 30 g	6	0	0	87	361
Parmesan, 30 g	10	0	0	136	564
processed, plain, 1 slice, 20 g	5	0	0.2	66	273
quark, 30 g	0+	0	1.2	22	94
ricotta, 30 g	3	0	0.6	43	180
Roquefort, 40 g	13	0	0	150	621
soft, full-fat, 30 g	9	0	0	94	388
soya, 40 g	11	0	0+	128	528
spread, low-fat, with chives, 100 g	16	0.3	3	185	760

FOOD	FAT g	FIBRE g	CARB g	ENERGY kcal	kJ
spread, very low-fat, plain, 100 g	6	0	4	128	537
Stilton, blue, 35 g	12	0	0	144	595
vegetarian, Cheddar-type, 100 g	36	0	0	425	1759
Wensleydale, 40 g	13	0	0	151	625
CHERRIES					
canned in syrup, 100 g	0	0.7	19	71	305
glacé, 6, 30 g	0	0.4	20	75	321
raw, 100 g (weight with stones)	0.1	1.2	10	39	168
CHICKEN					
breast, grilled, with skin 100 g	6	0	0	173	728
breast, grilled, without skin 100 g	3	0	0	148	626
breast strips, stir-fried, 100 g	5	0	0	161	677
dark meat, roasted, 100 g	11	0	0	196	820
drumstick, casseroled, with skin & bone 90 g	8	0	0	127	528
drumstick, casseroled, meat only, 50 g	5	0	0	93	386
light meat, roasted, 100 g	4	0	0	154	646
portion, fried, meat, skin & bone, 1, 70 g	8	0	0	125	677
quarter, roast, without skin, with bone,190 g	5	0	0	140	590
CHICKPEAS					
canned, 100 g	3	++	16	115	487
CHICORY					
boiled, 100 g	0.3	++	2	7	31
raw, 100 g	0.6	++	3	11	45
CHILLI					
green, raw, 1, 20 g	0.1	++	0.1	4	17
powder, 1 tsp, 3 g	0.8	0+	0+	0+	0+
red, raw, 1, 20 g	0.3	++	2	23	97
CHINESE CABBAGE					
(see Cabbage)					

FOOD	FAT g	FIBRE g	CARB g	ENERGY kcal	kJ
CHIVES					
fresh, 2 tbsp, 40 g	0.2	++	0.7	9	39
CHOCOLATE					
buttons, 33 g	10	0	19	173	724
coated biscuit fingers, 4-finger bar, 48 g	13	++	29	247	1032
coated caramel bar, 1, 50 g	11	++	32	240	1005
coated coconut bar, 1, 57 g	15	++	32	268	1122
coated malt balls, 37 g	9	++	23	177	740
coated nougat & toffee bar, 54 g	9	++	37	243	1020
dark, 100 g	26	++	61	500	2080
fruit & nut, dark, 100 g	28	6.4	55	494	2066
fruit & nut, milk, 100 g	26	++	56	490	2060
flake, 1 stick, 32 g	10	0	19	180	755
in crisp sugar shells, 1 tube, 37 g	7	0.3	31	195	820
milk, 7-square bar, 49 g	15	0	28	260	1065
powder, drinking, 18 g	1	0+	14	66	280
spread, chocolate nut, 8 g	3	0.1	5	44	184
white, 1 square, 7 g	2	0	4	37	155
CHUTNEY, PICKLES & RELISHES					
brinjal (aubergine) pickle, 30 g	7	0.3	10	110	458
mango chutney, oily, 20 g	2	0.3	10	57	240
mango chutney, sweet, 20 g	0	++	10	38	161
tomato chutney, 20 g	0	++	6	26	108
vegetable pickle, sweet, 30 g	0.1	0.4	10	42	182
CLEMENTINES					
(see Mandarin Oranges)					
COCOA					
powder, 1 heaped tsp, 6 g	1.3	++	0.7	19	79
CORDIALS (see Soft Drinks)					

FOOD	FAT g	FIBRE g	CARB g	ENERGY kcal	kJ
CORN					
baby, canned, 100 g	0.4	++	2	23	96
cob, whole, boiled. 100 g	1.4	2.5	12	66	280
corn, baby, raw, 100 g	0.4	2.2	7	30	130
kernels, canned, 30 g	0.4	1.2	8	37	156
COURGETTE					
boiled, 90 g	0.4	++	2	17	73
raw, 1, 90 g	0.4	++	4	23	95
COUSCOUS					
cooked, 100 g	0.4	0+	24	107	449
CRANBERRY					
raw, 100 g	0.1	3.8	3	15	65
juice, 250 ml	0	0	29	123	518
sauce, 25 g	0	++	10	38	162
CREAM					
buttermilk & oil, full-fat, 100g	36	0.3	4	349	1435
buttermilk & oil, single, 100g	10	0.3	6	124	513
clotted, 100 g	64	0	2	586	2413
crème fraîche, 100g	40	0	3	380	1567
double, 100 g	48	0	3	449	1849
half, 100 g	13	0	4	148	613
single, 100 g	19	0	4	198	817
soured, 100 g	20	0	4	205	845
UHT spray can, 10 g	3	0	0.3	31	127
whipping, 100 g	39	0	3	373	1539
CRISPBREAD					
crackerbread, 1 slice, 5 g	0.2	0.2	4	19	81
crisp rounds, 1, 7 g	0.3	0.3	6	31	130
multigrain, 1 slice, 11 g	0.7	1.9	6	37	155

FOOD	FAT g	FIBRE g	CARB g	ENERGY kcal	kJ
rye, 1 slice, 9 g	0.1	1.5	6	28	120
sesame seed, 1 slice, 9 g	0.6	1.5	5	30	128
toasts, 1, 10 g	0.8	0.4	7	41	170
CROISSANT					
plain, 1, 60 g	12	1.5	23	216	903
chocolate-filled, 1, 60 g	14	1.9	25	240	1006
CRUMPET					
1, toasted, 40 g	0.4	1.2	17	80	338
CUCUMBER					
raw, 5 slices, 30 g	0	0.2	0.4	3	12
CURRANTS (see Dried Fruit)					
CURRY PASTE					
ready-made, 25 g	5	++	2	59	244
powder, 1 tsp, 3g	0.3	++	1	7	29
CUSTARD					
egg, baked, 100 g	6	0	11	118	494
powder, with full-fat milk, 100 g	5	0	17	117	495
powder, with semi-skimmed milk, 100 g	2	0	17	94	403
ready-made, 100 g	3	0	16	100	420
CUSTARD APPLE					
bullock's heart, raw, 100 g	0.4	++	16	70	298
sugar apple, raw, 100 g	0.3	++	16	69	296

D

DAMSONS (see Plums)					
DATES					
dried, 100 g	0.2	7.8	68	270	1151

FOOD	FAT g	FIBRE g	CARB g	ENERGY kcal	kJ
dried, 100 g (weight with stones)	0.2	6.5	57	227	969
fresh, 100 g (weighed with stones)	0.1	3.1	27	107	456

DESSERTS & PUDDINGS

FOOD	FAT g	FIBRE g	CARB g	ENERGY kcal	kJ
apple pie, 100 g	13	2.1	36	266	1115
apple pie, wholemeal pastry, 100 g	14	3.5	32	257	1079
apple sponge, 150 g	20	2.6	43	362	1514
banana split, with ice cream, 200 g	22	2.8	39	364	1522
banoffee cream pie, 70 g	15	2.7	24	239	1500
blackcurrant pie, retail, 110 g	15	5.3	38	288	1209
bread pudding, 190 g	18	5.7	94	564	2379
chocolate mousse, 100 g	5	0	20	139	586
chocolate mousse, rich, 100 g	7	0	26	178	751
chocolate pudding with sauce, canned, 78 g	7	1.1	38	227	954
Christmas pudding, retail, 100 g	12	3.4	56	329	1388
crème caramel, 90 g	2	0	19	98	416
crumble, apple, 100 g	7	2.1	37	207	1388
crumble, fruit, 170 g	12	3.7	58	337	1420
crumble, fruit, wholemeal, 170 g	12	5.1	54	328	1382
frozen mousse, fruit, 100 g	7	0.3	21	157	658
fruit pie, individual, 110 g	15	2.4	37	286	1198
ice-cream sponge roll, 50 g	3	0.4	17	100	424
instant dessert, with full-fat milk, 120 g	8	0.2	18	132	558
instant dessert, with skimmed milk, 120 g	4	0.2	18	100	425
jam sponge, canned, 82 g	7	0.5	42	237	999
jelly, with full-fat milk, 200 g	3	0	33	176	746
jelly, with water, 200 g	0	0	30	122	520
lemon meringue pie, 190 g	27	1.5	87	606	2550
rice/tapioca (milk) pudding, full-fat, 200 g	9	0.4	39	256	1080
rice/tapioca (milk), skimmed, 200 g	0.4	0.4	40	184	790

FOOD	FAT g	FIBRE g	CARB g	ENERGY kcal	kJ
sponge pudding, with dried fruit, 110 g	16	1.8	53	364	1531
sponge pudding, with jam or treacle, 120 g	17	1.3	58	400	1678
sticky toffee pudding, canned, 77 g	9	0.6	36	239	1003
tiramisù, retail, chilled, 100 g	11	++	39	286	1200
treacle tart, 100 g	14	1.4	60	368	1550
trifle, 113 g	7	0.5	25	181	762

DIPS

FOOD	FAT g	FIBRE g	CARB g	ENERGY kcal	kJ
cheese & chive, 100 g	22	0.1	7	245	1005
guacamole (avocado), 100 g	13	2.6	2	126	530
hummus, 30 g	4	1.0	4	56	234
mayonnaise with garlic, 100 g	50	0.1	5	480	1975
spicy tomato salsa, 100 g	1.3	0.9	8	50	205
taramasalata, 100 g	49	0.7	6	480	1980
tzatziki, 100 g	3	0.5	6	79	333

DOUGHNUTS

FOOD	FAT g	FIBRE g	CARB g	ENERGY kcal	kJ
jam, 1, 75 g	11	1.9	37	252	1061
ring, 1, 60 g	13	1.9	28	238	997
ring, iced, 1, 80 g	14	1.9	44	306	1288

DRESSINGS (see also Mayonnaise)

FOOD	FAT g	FIBRE g	CARB g	ENERGY kcal	kJ
blue cheese, 1 tbsp, 15 g	7	0	1.3	69	283
caesar (oil/vinegar/cheese), 100 g	4	0.3	4	498	2052
fat-free, any, 1 tbsp, 15 g	0.2	0	2.1	10	42
Italian (oil/vinegar/lemon juice), 100 g	1	0	0.6	545	2250
low-fat, any, 1 tbsp, 15 g	0.5	0	1.4	11	45
oil & lemon, 1 tbsp, 15 g	11	0	0.4	97	399
thousand island, 1 tbsp, 15 g	4.5	++	1.9	48	200
thousand island, reduced-calorie, 1 tbsp, 15 g	2.3	++	2	29	122
vinaigrette (balsamic or wine vinegar), 100 g	35	0	4	333	1370
yogurt-based, 1 tbsp, 15 g	4	++	1.4	44	181

FOOD	FAT g	FIBRE g	CARB g	ENERGY kcal	kJ
DRIED FRUIT					
currants, 25 g	0.1	1.5	17	67	285
mixed fruit, 100 g	0.4	5.6	68	268	1144
mixed peel, 25 g	0.2	++	15	58	246
raisins, 1 tbsp, 30 g	0.1	1.8	21	82	348
sultanas, 1 tbsp, 30 g	0.1	1.9	21	83	351
DUCK					
roasted, meat only, 100 g	10	0	0	189	789
roasted, with fat & skin, 100 g	38	0	0	423	1750

E

FOOD	FAT g	FIBRE g	CARB g	ENERGY kcal	kJ
EGGS					
duck, boiled, 1, 65 g	10	0	0	129	534
hen, boiled or poached, 1 medium, 50 g	5	0	0	74	306
hen, fried, 1, 60 g	8	0	0	107	447
hen, scrambled with milk, 2, 120 g	27	0	0.7	296	1230
hen, yolk only, raw, 18 g	6	0	0	61	252
hen, white only, raw, 32 g	0	0	0.7	12	49
omelette, 2-egg plain, 120 g	20	0	0	229	950
quail, 1, raw, 10 g	1	0	0	15	63
ELDERBERRIES					
raw, 100 g	0.5	++	7	35	149
ENDIVE					
raw, 60 g	0	102	0.6	8	32

FOOD	FAT g	FIBRE g	CARB g	ENERGY kcal	kJ

FALAFEL

deep-fried, retail, 60 g	7	2.6	9	107	450

FAST FOOD/TAKEAWAY

beefburger, 160 g	16	++	36	357	1496
beefburger, with cheese, 195 g	26	++	42	500	2105
chicken, deep-fried, 2 pieces, 200 g	14	++	16	266	1114
chicken nuggets, deep-fried, 6	17	++	19	276	1160
chips (thick), 100 g	26	6	64	502	2102
doner kebab, lamb, with pitta/salad, 230 g	37	2.8	32	587	2450
fish (e.g. cod) in batter, deep-fried, 180 g	28	0.9	21	445	1856
frankfurter in bun, with ketchup & onions, 150 g	15	4	39	327	1371
french fries, medium, 110 g	17	3.4	37	308	1291
milkshake (thick), 1, 300 g	10	0	61	374	1569

FATS & OILS

(see also Margarines)

beef dripping, 15 g	15	0	0	134	549
cocoa butter, 15 g	15	0	0	134	552
lard, 15 g	15	0	0	134	549
low-fat spread, 15 g	6	0	0	58	241
oil, any (e.g. vegetable, corn, olive), 1 tbsp, 20ml	11	0	0	99	407
suet, beef, shredded, 100 g	87	0.6	12	826	3402
suet, vegetable, 100 g	88	0	10	836	3444
very low-fat spread, 15 g	4	0	0	41	169

FENNEL

boiled, 1, 150 g	0.3	++	2.3	17	71

FIGS

dried, 100 g	1.6	12.4	53	227	967

FOOD	FAT g	FIBRE g	CARB g	ENERGY kcal	ENERGY kJ
dried, cooked with sugar, 100 g	0.8	6.5	34	143	612
raw, 1, 40 g	0.1	0.9	4	17	74
ready-to-eat, 1, 55 g	0.8	6.3	27	115	489
FISH					
anchovies, 3, 9 g	2	0	0	25	105
bass, 100 g	2.5	0	0	100	421
bloater, grilled, 100 g	17	0	0	251	1043
bream, 100 g	3	0	0	96	405
carp, raw, 100 g	4.7	0	0	112	471
clams, canned, 100 g	0.6	0	2	77	325
cod fillet, baked, 100 g	1.2	0	0	96	408
cod fillet, poached/steamed, 100 g	1	0	0	94	396
cod, deep-fried in batter, 180 g	28	0.9	21	445	1856
cod, in parsley sauce, 170 g	5	0.2	5	143	402
cod, smoked, poached, 100 g	1.6	0	0+	101	426
cod, smoked, raw, 100 g	0.6	0	0	79	333
coley, raw fillet, 100 g	1.0	0	0	82	348
coley, steamed, 100 g	1.3	0	0	105	444
conger eel, grilled, 100 g	5.5	0	0	137	478
conger eel, raw, 100 g	4.6	0	0	114	478
crabmeat, boiled, 40 g	2.2	0	0	51	214
crabmeat, canned, 85 g	0.4	0	0	65	277
crab stick, 1, 17 g	0	0	1	12	49
crayfish, raw, meat only, 100 g	0.8	0	0	67	283
cuttlefish, raw, 100 g	1	0	0	71	300
dab, raw, 100 g	1.2	0	0	74	311
Dover sole, raw, 100 g	1.8	0	0	89	374
eel, jellied, 100 g	7	0	0	98	406
eel, raw, 100 g	11	0	0	98	700

FOOD	FAT g	FIBRE g	CARB g	ENERGY kcal	kJ
eel, smoked, 100 g	13	0	1	167	700
flounder, raw, 100 g	1.8	0	0	82	345
flounder, steamed, 100 g	2.2	0	0	101	427
flying fish, raw, 100 g	0.3	0	0	86	366
goujons, white fish, fried, 100 g	29	0.9	14	374	1553
haddock fillet, grilled, 100 g	0.8	0	0	104	442
haddock fillet, in crumbs, fried, 100 g	8	0.5	10	157	657
haddock fillet, raw, 100 g	0.6	0	0	81	345
haddock, poached in milk, 100 g	4	0	0	113	47
haddock, smoked, steamed, 100 g	0.9	0	0	101	429
hake, fillet, grilled, 100 g	2.7	0	0	113	310
hake, fillet, raw, 100 g	2.2	0	0	92	387
halibut, grilled, 100 g	2.2	0	0	121	345
halibut, poached in milk, 100 g	5.7	0	1	154	648
halibut, raw, 100 g	1.9	0	0	103	436
herring, canned in tomato sauce, 100 g	14	0	3	193	802
herring, dried, salted, 100 g	7	0	0	168	704
herring fillet, grilled, 100 g	11	0	0	181	756
herring fillet, raw, 1, 119 g	16	0	0	226	941
herring, pickled, 100 g	11	0	10	209	877
hilsa, raw, 100 g	19	0	0	262	1088
hoki, grilled, 100 g	2.7	0	0	121	510
hoki, raw, 100 g	1.9	0	0	85	358
jackfish, raw, 100 g	2	0	0	108	458
John Dory, raw, 100 g	1.9	0	0	89	375
kipper, boiled in the bag, 100 g	17	0	0	237	984
kipper fillet, grilled, 100 g	19	0	0	255	1060
kipper, grilled, 100 g (weight with bones)	12	0	0	161	667
kipper, raw, 100 g	18	0	0	229	952

FOOD	FAT g	FIBRE g	CARB g	ENERGY kcal	kJ
lemon sole, grilled, 100 g	1.7	0	0	97	408
lemon sole, grilled, with bones & skin, 100 g	1.1	0	0	62	261
lemon sole, raw, 100 g	1.5	0	0	83	351
lemon sole, steamed, 100 g	0.9	0	0	91	384
lemon sole, steamed, with bones & skin, 100 g	0.6	0	0	64	272
ling, raw, 100 g	0.7	0	0	82	346
lobster, meat, boiled, 85 g	1.4	0	0	88	370
lobster, whole, 500 g (weight with shell)	3	0	0	185	785
mackerel, canned in brine, drained, 100 g	18	0	0	237	985
mackerel, canned in tomato sauce, 100 g	15	0	1	206	856
mackerel, grilled, 100 g	17	0	0	239	994
mackerel, raw, 100 g	16	0	0	220	914
mackerel, smoked, 100 g	31	0	0	354	1465
monkfish, grilled, 100 g	0.6	0	0	96	314
monkfish, raw, 100 g	0.4	0	0	66	282
mullet, grey, grilled, 100 g	5.2	0	0	150	629
mullet, grey, raw, 100 g	5	0	0	150	629
mullet, red, grilled, 100 g	4.4	0	0	121	510
mullet, red, raw, 100 g	4	0	0	121	510
mussels, boiled, without shells, 40 g	1	0	0	42	176
octopus, raw, 100 g	1.3	0	0	83	352
orange roughy, raw, 100 g	7	0	0	126	527
oysters, raw, 6, 60 g	0.8	0	2	39	165
parrot fish, raw, 100 g	0.4	0	0	83	353
pilchards, canned in tomato sauce, 1, 55 g	4.5	0	0.6	79	331
plaice fillet, grilled, 100 g	1.7	0	0	96	404
plaice, in batter, deep-fried, 200 g	34	1	24	514	2144
plaice, in breadcrumbs, fried, 150 g	21	0.6	13	342	1427
plaice fillet, raw, 100 g	1.4	0	0	79	336

FOOD	FAT g	FIBRE g	CARB g	ENERGY kcal	ENERGY kJ
plaice fillet, steamed, 100 g	1.5	0	0	92	389
pollack, Alaskan, raw, 100 g	0.6	0	0	72	304
pomfret, black, raw, 100 g	2.6	0	0	99	416
pomfret, white, raw, 100 g	2.1	0	0	92	389
prawns, boiled, 60 g	0.5	0	0	59	251
red snapper fillet, fried, 100 g	3.1	0	0	126	531
red snapper, raw, 100 g	1.3	0	0	90	381
redfish, raw, 100 g	2.7	0	0	98	413
rock salmon, in batter, deep-fried, 200 g	44	1	21	590	245
rohu, raw, 100 g	1.4	0	0	79	334
salmon, canned, meat only, 100 g	7	0	0	153	644
salmon, grilled, 100 g	13	0	0	215	896
salmon, raw, 100 g	12	0	0	182	757
salmon, smoked, 56 g	2.5	0	0	80	335
salmon, steamed, 100 g	12	0	0	194	812
sardines, canned in brine, 1, 25 g	2.4	0	0	43	180
sardines, canned in oil, 1, 25 g	3.5	0	0	55	230
sardines, canned in tomato sauce, 1, 25 g	2.5	0	0.3	41	170
sardines, grilled, 100 g	10	0	0	165	815
sardines, raw, 100 g	9	0	0	165	691
scallops, steamed, 100 g	1.4	0	3	118	501
scampi, in breadcrumbs, fried, 170 g	23	1.9	35	403	1685
shark, raw, 100 g	1.1	0	0	102	432
skate, fillet, grilled, 100 g	0.5	0	0	79	337
skate, in batter, fried, 200 g	20	0.4	10	336	1404
sprats, fried, meat only, 100 g	35	0	0	415	1718
squid, in batter, fried, 100 g	10	0.6	16	195	815
squid, raw, 100 g	1.7	0	1	81	344
swordfish, grilled, 100 g	5	0	0	139	583

FOOD	FAT g	FIBRE g	CARB g	ENERGY kcal	ENERGY kJ
swordfish, raw, 100 g	4	0	0	109	458
trout, brown, raw, 100 g	4	0	0	112	470
trout, rainbow, raw, 100 g	5	0	0	125	565
tuna, canned in brine, 100 g	0.6	0	0	99	422
tuna, canned in oil, 100 g	9	0	0	189	794
tuna, grilled, 100 g	7	0	0	166	714
tuna, raw, 100 g	5	0	0	136	573
turbot, grilled, 100 g	3.5	0	0	122	514
turbot, raw, 100 g	3	0	0	95	401
whitebait, in flour, deep-fried, 80 g	38	0.2	4	420	1739
whiting, raw, 100 g	0.7	0	0	81	344
whiting, steamed, 85 g	0.8	0	0	78	331

FLOUR

FOOD	FAT g	FIBRE g	CARB g	ENERGY kcal	ENERGY kJ
arrowroot, 100 g	0.1	++	94	355	1515
buckwheat, 100 g	1.5	++	85	364	1522
carob, 100 g	0.7	++	89	180	753
chapati, brown, 100 g	1.2	10.3	74	333	1419
chapati, white, 100 g	0.5	4.1	78	335	1426
chickpea, 100 g	5	13.5	50	313	1328
cornflour, 100 g	0.7	++	92	354	1508
maize, 100 g	1	++	78	362	1515
millet, 100 g	1.7	++	75	354	1481
potato, 100 g	0.9	7	76	328	1398
rice, 100 g	0.8	++	80	366	1531
rye, whole, 100 g	2	++	76	335	1428
semolina, raw, 100 g	2	4	78	350	1489
soya, full-fat, 100 g	24	10.7	24	447	1871
soya, low-fat, 100 g	7	13.3	28	352	1488
wheat, brown, 100 g	2	7	69	323	1377

FOOD	FAT g	FIBRE g	CARB g	ENERGY kcal	kJ
wheat, white, breadmaking, 100 g	1.4	3.7	75	341	1451
wheat, white, plain, 100 g	1.3	3.6	78	341	1450
wheat, wholemeal, 100 g	2	8.6	64	310	1318
FRANKFURTER					
cooked, 1, 46 g	12	0	1	129	533
FROMAGE FRAIS					
fruit, small carton, 1, 60 g	4	0	8	79	331
plain, small carton, 1, 60 g	4	0	3	68	281
very low-fat, small carton, 1, 60 g	0.1	0	4	35	148
FRUIT SALAD/COCKTAIL					
canned in juice, 100 g	0	1	7	29	122
canned in syrup, 100 g	0	1	15	57	244

G

FOOD	FAT g	FIBRE g	CARB g	ENERGY kcal	kJ
GARLIC					
fresh, 2 peeled cloves, 6 g	0	++	1	6	25
powder, 1 tbsp, 10 g	0	++	4	25	105
GELATINE					
powder, sachet, 15 g	0	0	0	51	215
GHERKINS					
pickled, 1 large, 36 g	0	0.4	1	5	22
GINGER					
glacé, 2 tbsp, 25 g	0.1	0.5	21	83	354
ground, 1 tbsp, 10 g	0.3	++	6	15	110
root, raw, 1 tbsp, 10 g	0.1	++	1	5	19
stem, in syrup, drained, 100 g	0.1	1.4	6.7	271	1151
GOLDEN SYRUP					
1 tbsp, 25 g	0	0	20	75	317

FOOD	FAT g	FIBRE g	CARB g	ENERGY kcal	kJ
GOOSE					
roast, meat only, 100 g	22	0	0	319	1327
GOOSEBERRIES					
cooking, cooked with sugar, 100 g	0.3	2.3	13	54	229
cooking, cooked without sugar, 100 g	0.3	2.4	3	16	66
dessert, canned in syrup, 100 g	0.2	1.7	19	73	310
dessert, raw, 100 g	0.3	3.1	9	40	170
GRAPEFRUIT					
canned in juice, 100 g	0	0.8	7	30	120
canned in syrup, 100 g	0	0.9	16	60	257
juice, concentrate, unsweetened, 100 ml	0.5	0	41	166	709
juice, unsweetened, 100 ml	0.1	0	8	33	140
raw, I, 160 g	0.2	2.6	11	48	202
GRAPES					
raw, 100 g	0.1	0.8	15	60	257
GRAVY					
instant granules, 2 tsp, 8g	3	0	4	46	193
instant granules, mixed with water, 100 g	2	0	3	33	139
GREENGAGES					
cooked, with sugar, 100 g	0.1	2.1	21	81	347
cooked, without sugar, 100 g	0.1	2.1	9	36	155
raw, 100 g	0.1	2.3	10	41	173
raw, 100 g (weight with stones)	0.1	2.2	9	38	163
GRENADILLAS					
raw, 100 g	0.3	14	8	42	179
GUACAMOLE (see Dips)					
GUAVA					
canned in syrup, 100 g	0	3.2	16	60	258
raw, 100 g	0.5	4.7	5	26	112

FOOD	FAT g	FIBRE g	CARB g	ENERGY kcal	kJ

H

HAGGIS

FOOD	FAT g	FIBRE g	CARB g	ENERGY kcal	kJ
boiled, 100 g	22	++	19	310	1292

HALVA

carrot, 30 g	7	0.9	13	106	445
retail, 30 g	12	++	16	185	771

HAM

canned, 1 slice, 35 g	2	0	0	42	176
dry-cured, breaded, 100 g	2	0	7	151	633
dry-cured prosciutto, 100g	12	0	0	220	918
ham & pork, chopped, canned, 50 g	12	0.2	0.7	138	570
honey roast, 100g	5	0	1	147	617
joint, boiled, lean, 100 g	12	0	0	204	851
joint, roasted, smoked/unsmoked, 100g	12	0	0	202	844
oak smoked, 100g	3	0	1	121	510
Parma, 50 g	6	0	0	112	466

HEART

beef, ox, casseroled, 100 g	6	0	0	179	752
beef, ox, raw, 100 g	4	0	0	108	455

HONEY

honeycomb, 30 g	4	0	22	84	360
strained, jar, 15 g	0	0	12	43	184

HORSERADISH

raw, 1 tsp	0	0.4	1	3	13
sauce, retail, 15 g	1.3	++	3	23	96

HUMMUS (see Dips)

FOOD	FAT g	FIBRE g	CARB g	ENERGY kcal	kJ

I

ICE CREAM

FOOD	FAT g	FIBRE g	CARB g	ENERGY kcal	kJ
caramel with toffee & chocolate, 100g	12	0.3	27	222	929
chocolate covered bar, 1, 50 g	12	++	12	160	666
cone, chocolate & hazelnut, 1, 80g	10	0.3	24	194	812
cone, vanilla & toffee	7	0.1	26	180	754
dairy, block, flavoured, 75 g	6	0	19	134	563
dairy, block, vanilla, 75 g	7	0	18	146	611
lolly, caramel with chocolate, 1, 75ml	14	++	26	244	1018
non-dairy, reduced-calorie, 75 g	5	0	10	89	374
soft scoop, vanilla, 100 g	8	0.2	22	170	695
soft scoop, vanilla, cherry & chocolate chip	8	0	14	133	929

J

JAM

FOOD	FAT g	FIBRE g	CARB g	ENERGY kcal	kJ
apricot, 1 tsp, 15g	0	0.1	9	38	161
blackcurrant conserve, high fruit, 1 tsp, 15g	0.1	0.2	7	29	121
blackcurrant, reduced sugar, 1 tsp, 15g	0.1	0.1	10	40	169
fruit marmalade, 1 tsp, 8 g	0	0	6	21	89
reduced sugar, 1 tsp, 8 g	0	++	3	10	42

JELLY (see Desserts)

K

KALE

FOOD	FAT g	FIBRE g	CARB g	ENERGY kcal	kJ
curly, boiled, 100 g	1	2.6	1	24	100
curly, raw, 100 g	2	3.3	1	33	140

FOOD	FAT g	FIBRE g	CARB g	ENERGY kcal	kJ
KIDNEY					
beef, ox, raw, 100 g	8	0	0	86	363
lamb, raw, 100 g	3	0	0	91	385
pig, raw, 100 g	3	0	0	90	377
KIWI FRUIT					
raw, 1 medium, without peel, 60 g	0.3	++	6	29	124
raw, with peel, 60 g	0.2	++	6	25	106
KOHL RABI					
boiled, 100 g	0.2	++	3	18	77
raw, 100 g	0.2	++	4	23	95
KUMQUAT					
raw, 1, 20 g	0.1	++	2	9	37

L

FOOD	FAT g	FIBRE g	CARB g	ENERGY kcal	kJ
LAMB					
breast, lean, roast, 75 g	13	0	0	189	787
chump chops, lean, fried in oil, 100g	11	0	0	213	892
chump chops, lean & fat, fried in oil, 100g	23	0	0	308	1278
cutlets, best end, lean, barbecued, 100g	14	0	0	236	985
cutlets, best end, lean & fat, barbecued, 100g	27	0	0	342	1420
leg, roast, lean, 150 g	12	0	0	287	1200
leg steak, lean, grilled, 9	9	0	0	198	829
loin chop, grilled, lean, 70 g	9	0	0	155	650
loin chop, grilled, lean/fat/bone, 120 g	27	0	0	332	1376
minced, casseroled, 100g	12	0	0	208	870
shoulder, roasted, lean, 75 g	8	0	0	147	614
stewing, lean, casseroled, 100 g	15	0	0	240	1000
stewing, lean & fat, casseroled, 100 g	20	0	0	279	1159

FOOD	FAT g	FIBRE g	CARB g	ENERGY kcal	kJ
LARD (see Fats & Oils))					
LASAGNE					
(see Pasta/Ready Meals)					
LEEKS					
boiled, 160 g	1	3.8	4	34	139
boiled, cheese sauce, full-fat milk, 100 g	7	1.5	5	99	412
boiled, cheese sauce, semi-skimmed milk,100 g	6	1.5	5	92	384
raw, 100 g	0.5	2.8	3	22	93
LEMON					
curd, retail, 1 tsp, 15 g	0.8	0.1	9	42	177
juice, fresh, 100 ml	0	0	2	7	31
raw, with peel, no pips, 100g	0.3	4.7	3	19	79
sorbet, 2 scoops, 60 g	0	0	21	79	337
LENTILS					
dahl curry, black gram, 100 g	3.4	1.9	7	74	310
green & brown, dried, boiled, 40 g	0.3	++	7	42	178
red, split, boiled, 40 g	0.2	1.3	7	40	170
yellow split peas, boiled, dried, 100g	0.9	4.6	23	126	538
yellow split peas, raw, dried, 100g	2.4	11	58	328	1396
LETTUCE					
cos, 100 g	0.6	1.3	2	16	65
iceberg, 100 g	0.3	1.3	2	13	53
mixed salad leaves 100 g	0.2	1.6	1	13	57
raddicchio, 100 g	0.2	++	2	14	58
LIME					
juice, fresh, 100 g	0.1	0.1	2	9	36
pickle, oily, 25 g	4	1.4	2	45	185
raw, without peel, 50 g	0.2	++	0.4	5	38
LINGUINE (see Pasta)					

FOOD	FAT g	FIBRE g	CARB g	ENERGY kcal	ENERGY kJ
LIVER					
calf, fried, 40 g	5	0.1	3	102	425
chicken, fried, 40 g	4	0.1	1	78	324
lamb, fried, 100 g	14	0	4	232	970
ox, casseroled, 100 g	10	0	4	198	831
pig, casseroled, 100 g	8	0	4	189	793
LOGANBERRIES					
canned in juice, 100 g	0	3	26	101	429
cooked with sugar, 100 g	0	4.4	13	50	214
cooked without sugar, 100 g	0	4.8	3	14	62
raw, 100 g	0	5.6	3	17	73
LOQUATS					
canned in syrup, 100 g	0.1	++	22	84	351
raw, 100 g	0.2	++	6	28	351
LOTUS					
tuber, canned, 100 g	0	++	3	51	63
LYCHEES					
canned in syrup, 100 g	0	0.7	18	68	290
raw, 100 g	0.1	1.5	14	58	248

M

FOOD	FAT g	FIBRE g	CARB g	ENERGY kcal	ENERGY kJ
MACARONI (see Pasta)					
MANDARIN ORANGES (Loose-skinned)					
clementine, raw, 1, 40 g	0.1	0.7	3	15	63
mandarin segments, canned in juice, 100 g	0	0.3	8	32	135
mandarin segments, canned in syrup, 100 g	0	0.3	13	52	223
ortanique, raw, 100 g	0.2	1.8	12	49	205

FOOD	FAT g	FIBRE g	CARB g	ENERGY kcal	ENERGY kJ
satsuma, raw, peeled, 1 av., 50 g	0.1	0.9	4	18	78
tangerine, raw, peeled, 1 av., 70 g	0.1	1.2	6	25	103
MANGETOUT					
mangetout, boiled, 100 g	0.1	4.0	3	26	111
mangetout, raw, 100 g	0.2	4.2	4	32	136
MANGO					
canned in syrup, 100 g	0	0.9	21	81	347
chutney, sweet, 1 tbsp, 25 g	0	0+	12	47	202
juice, 100 g	0.2	0+	10	39	166
raw, 150 g	0.3	4.4	21	86	368
MANGOSTEEN					
raw, 100 g	0.5	1.3	16	73	307
MAPLE SYRUP					
100 g	0	0	66	264	1122
MARGARINE					
(see also Fats & Oils)					
buttermilk & vegetable oil spread, 100 g	69	0	1	627	2578
dairy-free, with vegetable oil, 100 g	58	1.4	0	525	2159
hard, vegetable oil, 100 g	82	0	0	740	3040
hard, vegetable oil, 11 g	9	0	0	81	334
low-fat spread, 11 g	5	0	0.1	43	177
olive oil spread, (vegetable/olive oil), 100 g	59	0	1	536	2203
polyunsaturated, 11 g	9	0	0	81	334
soft, saturated, 11 g	9	0	0	81	335
MARMALADE (see Jam)					
MARROW					
boiled, 100 g	0.2	1.0	1.6	9	38
raw, 100 g	0.2	1.1	2	12	51

FOOD	FAT g	FIBRE g	CARB g	ENERGY kcal	ENERGY kJ
MARZIPAN					
home-made, 1 tbsp, 20 g	5	1.2	10	92	387
retail, 1 tbsp, 20 g	3	0.6	14	81	341
MATZOS					
square, 1 large, 22 g	0.3	0.6	18	79	334
tea, round, 1, 5 g	0.1	0.2	4	18	76
tea, wheaten, round, 1, 5 g	0.1	0.4	4	18	76
MAYONNAISE					
home-made, 30 g	26	0	0	237	974
retail, 30 g	23	0	1	207	853
retail, reduced calorie, 30 g	8	0	3	86	356
MEAT SUBSTITUTE					
mycoprotein, 100 g	4	++	2	86	360
mycoprotein mince, 100 g	2	6	5	94	397
MELON					
cantaloupe-type, 150 g	0.2	1.3	6	29	122
galia, 150 g	0.2	1.3	8	36	153
honeydew, 150 g	0.2	1.2	10	42	179
watermelon, 200 g	0.6	0.6	14	62	266
MERINGUE					
shell with cream, 28 g	7	0	11	105	440
shell without cream, 8 g	0	0	8	30	129
MILK					
buttermilk, 100 g	0.5	0	5	37	157
calcium-fortified, 100 g	0.5	0	6	44	186
condensed, full-fat, sweetened, 100 g	10	0	56	333	1406
condensed, skimmed, sweetened, 100 g	0.2	0	60	267	1137
dried skimmed, powder/granules, 100 g	0.6	0	53	348	1482
dried skimmed, with vegetable fat, 100 g	26	0	43	487	2038

FOOD	FAT g	FIBRE g	CARB g	ENERGY kcal	kJ
evaporated, full-fat, 100 g	16	0	14	257	1069
flavoured, 100 g	1.5	0	11	68	287
full-fat, 100 g	4	0	5	66	275
goat, 100 g	3.5	0	4	60	253
semi-skimmed, 100 g	1.6	0	5	46	195
skimmed, 100 g	0.1	0	5	33	140
soya, flavoured, 100 g	1.7	0	4	40	168
soya, plain, 100 g	1.9	0	1	32	132
MILKSHAKE					
powder, any flavour, 15 g	0.1	0	15	59	251
retail, 500 ml container					
- banana, 100 g	0.8	0	10	61	259
- raspberry, 100 g	2.1	0	11	79	333
- syrup, any flavour, 20 ml	0.1	0	6	25	108
- syrup & full-fat milk, 220 ml	8	0	16	157	658
MISO					
1 heaped tbsp, 25 g	1.5	++	6	51	214
MIXED PEEL (see Dried Fruit)					
MIXED VEGETABLES					
frozen, boiled, 100 g	0.5	++	7	42	180
MOLASSES					
1 tbsp	0	0	10	40	167
MULBERRIES					
cooked with sugar, 100 g	0	1.2	16	65	276
cooked without sugar, 100 g	0	1.3	7	30	129
raw, 100 g	0	1.5	8	36	152
MUSHROOMS					
Chinese, dried, raw, 25 g	0.4	++	15	71	297
closed/open cup, boiled, 100 g	0.3	2.3	0.4	11	48

FOOD	FAT g	FIBRE g	CARB g	ENERGY kcal	kJ
closed/open cup, fried, 50 g	8	1.5	0	79	323
closed/open cup, raw, 100 g	0.5	2.3	0.4	13	55
oyster, raw, 100 g	0.2	++	0	8	35
straw, canned, 100 g	0.2	++	1.2	15	62
MUSTARD					
American, 1 tsp, 5 g	0.2	++	0.1	3	12
English, powder, 1 tsp	0.9	++	1	14	57
English, powder, made up, heaped tsp, 8g	1.4	++	1	23	94
French, 1 tsp, 5 g	0.2	++	0.2	4	16
wholegrain, retail, 14 g	1.4	++	1	20	82
MUSTARD & CRESS					
raw, 5 g portion	0	0.2	0	1	3

N

NASHI PEAR					
1 raw, 130 g	0.1	++	9	38	159
NECTARINE					
raw, 1, 150 g (weight with stone)	0.2	3.3	14	60	257
NOODLES					
egg, boiled, 100 g	0.5	1.0	13	62	264
noodles, fried, 100 g	12	0.9	11	153	638
plain, boiled, 100 g	0.4	1.2	13	62	264
plain, dried, 100 g	6	5.2	76	388	1646
rice, cooked, 100 g	1.9	1.1	18	95	405
rice, dried, 100 g	0.1	++	82	360	1506
NUTS					
almonds, shelled, 2, 13 g	7	1.7	1	80	329
Brazil, shelled, 3, 10 g	7	0.8	0.3	68	281

FOOD	FAT g	FIBRE g	CARB g	ENERGY kcal	kJ
cashews, roasted/salted, 10, 10 g	5	++	2	61	253
chestnut purée, 100 g	2	3	27	133	560
chestnuts, peeled, 5, 50 g	1.4	3.0	18	85	360
cob (hazel) shelled, 10, 10 g	6	0.6	0.6	65	269
peanuts, dry roasted, 25 g	12	1.9	3	147	610
peanuts, roasted & salted, 25 g	13	1.7	2	151	623
pecans, shelled, 5, 30 g	21	++	2	207	853
pistachios, roasted/salted, 10 kernels, 10 g	6	++	1	60	249
pistachios, with shells, 25 g	8	++	1	83	343
walnuts, shelled, 6 halves, 20 g	14	1.2	1	138	567

OILS (see Fats & Oils)

OKRA

boiled, 50 g	0.4	2.0	1	14	60
canned, 50 g	++	1.4	1	8	32
raw, 100 g	1	4.5	3	31	130

OLIVES

in brine, without stones, 50 g	6	2.0	0	52	211
in brine, 50 g (weight with stones)	4	1.6	0	41	169

ONIONS

boiled, 100 g	0.1	0.7	3.7	17	73
fried, 40 g	5	1.3	6	66	274
pickled, 1, 15 g	0	0.2	1	4	15
raw, 1 medium, 150 g	0.3	2.3	12	54	225

ORANGES

juice, fresh squeezed, 100 g	0	0.1	8	33	140
juice, unsweetened, 100 g	0.1	0.1	9	36	153

FOOD	FAT g	FIBRE g	CARB g	ENERGY kcal	kJ
raw, 1 medium, peeled, 120 g	0.1	2.2	10	44	190

ORTANIQUE

(see Mandarin Oranges)

OXTAIL

casseroled, meat only, 100 g	13	0	0	243	1014
casseroled, with fat & bones, 100 g	5	0	0	92	386

P

PANCAKES/CREPES

savoury, made with full-fat milk, 1, 60 g	11	0.6	14	164	683
savoury, made with skimmed milk, 1, 60 g	9	0.6	15	149	623
sweet, made with full-fat milk, 1, 60 g	10	0.5	21	181	756
sweet, made with skimmed milk, 1, 60 g	8	0.5	21	168	705

PAPADUM

fried, 1, 13 g	2	1.2	5	48	201
raw, 1, 13 g	0.2	1.5	6	35	150

PARSNIP

boiled, 65 g	1	2.9	8	43	181
raw, 100g	1	4.3	13	64	271

PASSION FRUIT

raw, 1, 15 g	0.1	++	1	5	23

PASTA

buckwheat pasta, dried, 100 g	2	4.8	74	352	1484
cappelletiti, prosciutto-filled, fresh,					
boiled, 150g	50	4	8	354	1492
corn pasta, dried, 100 g	2	3.2	82	367	1549
fusilli, tricolore, fresh, boiled, 210g	59	4	5	363	1536
lasagne, fresh, 100 g	1.4	1.8	28	147	624

FOOD	FAT g	FIBRE g	CARB g	ENERGY kcal	kJ
linguine, dried, boiled, 210 g	1.5	2.3	66	321	1363
macaroni, boiled, 150 g	0.8	2.3	28	129	548
macaroni, canned in cheese sauce, 335 g	22	2.7	55	462	1940
macaroni cheese bake, 300 g	32	2.4	41	534	2229
penne, fresh, 100 g	1.6	2.1	30	159	675
potato gnocchi, fresh, 100 g	0.3	0.4	37	170	724
ravioli, fresh, mushroom & ricotta, 100 g	7	1.8	26	194	81
spaghetti, white, 100 g	2	5.1	74	342	1456
spaghetti, white, boiled, 220 g	2	4.0	49	229	972
spaghetti, wholemeal, boiled, 220 g	2	8.8	51	249	1067
tagliatelli, fresh, with sun-dried tomato, 100 g	1.4	1.4	24	125	531
tortellini, spinach & ricotta, fresh, boiled 150g	47	6	8	323	1361
PASTA SAUCES					
bacon & tomato (amatriciana), fresh, 100 g	5	1.4	7	90	374
bolognese, fresh, 100 g	7.2	1.6	6	119	498
carbonara, fresh, 100 g	12	0	9	175	729
carbonara, jar, 100 g	13	0	3	145	599
four cheese, fresh, 100 g	11	0.5	6	149	62
four cheese, low-fat, fresh, 100 g	4	0.2	6	80	335
pesto, green, jar, 100 g	44	2	4	430	1770
pesto, red, jar, 100 g	32	2	5	321	1325
smoky bacon, long-life, 100 g	13	++	7	165	685
spicy pepperoni, long-life, 100 g	12	++	8	147	608
tomato & basil, rich, jar, 100 g	6	0.8	8	90	373
tomato & mascarpone, fresh, 100 g	8	0.4	9	118	491
tomato & olive (puttanesca), jar, 100g	6	0.9	7	90	375
PASTRY					
choux, cooked, 100 g	20	1.4	30	325	1355
filo, raw, 10 sheets, 100 g	4	0.8	62	315	1317

FOOD	FAT g	FIBRE g	CARB g	ENERGY kcal	kJ
flaky, cooked, 100 g	41	2.1	46	560	2332
shortcrust, cooked, 100 g	32	2.5	54	521	2174
wholemeal, cooked, 100 g	33	6.0	45	499	2080
PATE					
liver, 50 g	14	0	0.5	158	654
liver, low-fat, 50 g	6	0	1	96	398
smoked mackerel, 50 g	17	0	0.6	184	761
tuna, 50 g	9	0	0.2	118	491
vegetable, 50 g	7	++	3	87	359
PEACHES					
canned in juice, 120 g	0	1.1	12	47	198
canned in syrup, 120 g	0	1.1	17	66	280
dried, 100 g	0.8	13	53	219	936
dried, cooked with sugar, 100 g	0.3	5.1	26	104	446
dried, cooked without sugar, 100 g	0.3	5.3	22	89	383
raw, with skin, 1 medium, 110 g	0.1	2.5	8	36	156
PEARS					
canned in juice, 135 g	0	2.0	12	45	190
canned in syrup, 135 g	0	2.0	18	68	290
cooked with sugar, 100 g	0.1	1.6	22	89	152
cooked without sugar, 100 g	0.1	1.8	9	35	152
dried, 100 g	0.5	11	52	207	884
raw, with peel, 1, 150 g	1.5	4.7	11	83	344
PEAS					
frozen, boiled, 70 g	0.6	5.1	7	48	204
mushy, canned, 80 g	0.6	++	11	65	276
raw, shelled, 100 g	1.5	4.7	11	83	344
split, dried, boiled, 100 g	1	4.6	23	126	538

FOOD	FAT g	FIBRE g	CARB g	ENERGY kcal	kJ
PEPPERS					
green, raw, 1, 160 g	0.5	3	4	24	104
red, raw, 1, 160 g	0.6	3	10	51	214
yellow, raw, 1, 160 g	0.3	3.2	9	42	181
PHEASANT					
roast, meat only, 100 g	9	0	0	213	892
PIGEON					
roast, meat only, 1, 115 g	15	0	0	265	1105
PINEAPPLE					
canned in juice, 1 ring/6 chunks, 40 g	0	0.3	5	19	80
canned in syrup, 1 ring/ 6 chunks, 40 g	0	0.3	7	26	109
dried, 100 g	1.3	8.8	68	276	2190
raw, 1 slice, without skin, 80 g	0.2	1	8	33	141
PLANTAIN (see Banana)					
PLUMS					
canned in juice, with stones, 200 g	0	2	21	80	336
canned in syrup, with stones, 200 g	0	2	31	118	506
damson, raw, 100 g	0	3.7	10	38	16
damson, cooked with sugar, 100 g	0	3.0	19	74	316
damson, cooked without sugar, 100 g	0	3.4	9	34	147
raw, without stones, 55 g	0.1	1.2	5	19	80
raw, 100 g (weight with stones)	0.1	2.2	8	34	145
POMEGRANATE					
flesh only, raw, 100 g	0.6	++	17	72	301
PORK					
crackling, cooked, 25 g	11	0	0	138	570
fillet, sliced, lean only, grilled, 100 g	4	0	0	170	719
leg, roasted, lean only, 90 g	6	0	0	167	699
loin chop, grilled, lean only, 100 g	11	0	0	226	945

FOOD	FAT g	FIBRE g	CARB g	ENERGY kcal	kJ
POTATOES					
baked, flesh/skin, 1, 180 g	0.4	++	57	245	1046
boiled, 1, 60 g	0.1	0.8	10	43	184
chips, oven, baked, 10 chips, 100 g	4	2.8	30	162	687
chips, thin fries, takeaway, 110 g	17	3.4	37	308	1291
chips, thick, takeaway, 10 chips, 100 g	12	3	31	239	1001
mashed, with butter/milk, 175 g	8	2.3	27	182	767
new, boiled, with skin, 1, 40 g	0.1	0.6	6	26	112
new, boiled, without skin, 1, 40 g	0.1	0.5	7	30	128
roasted, 1, 85 g	4	2	22	127	536
PRUNES					
canned in juice, without stones, 100 g	0.2	++	20	79	335
canned in syrup, with stones, 100 g	0.2	++	23	90	386
cooked with sugar, 100 g	0.2	7	26	103	439
cooked with sugar, with stones, 100 g	0.2	6.3	24	95	405
cooked without sugar, 100 g	0.3	7.4	20	81	346
cooked without sugar, with stones, 100 g	0.2	6.7	18	74	314
ready-to-eat, 100 g	0.3	11	29	121	514
PUMPKIN					
boiled, 100 g	0.3	0.5	2	13	56
raw, 100 g	0.2	0.5	2	13	55
QUICHE					
Lorraine, (cream, bacon, cheese), 100 g	28	0.8	20	390	1629
Lorraine, wholemeal pastry, 100 g	28	2.0	17	384	1599
mushroom, 100 g	20	1.2	18	284	1185
mushroom, wholemeal pastry, 100 g	20	2.3	15	277	1156

FOOD	FAT g	FIBRE g	CARB g	ENERGY kcal	kJ

R

RABBIT

FOOD	FAT g	FIBRE g	CARB g	ENERGY kcal	kJ
casseroled, meat only, 100 g	8	0	0	179	749

RADISH

FOOD	FAT g	FIBRE g	CARB g	ENERGY kcal	kJ
red, raw, 3, 24 g	0	0.2	0.5	3	12
white (mooli), raw, 100 g	0.1	++	4	24	100

RAISINS (see Dried Fruit)

RASPBERRIES

FOOD	FAT g	FIBRE g	CARB g	ENERGY kcal	kJ
canned in syrup, 90 g	0.1	4	20	79	337
cooked with sugar, 100 g	0.3	6	15	63	271
cooked without sugar, 100 g	0.3	6.5	4	24	105
frozen, raw 100 g	0.3	7	5	26	110
raw, 60 g	0.2	4	3	15	65

READY MEALS (Prepared Foods)

FOOD	FAT g	FIBRE g	CARB g	ENERGY kcal	kJ
beef casserole, canned, 200 g	5	1.6	13	146	614
bhaji, onion, 1, 140 g	30	10	31	435	1814
bhaji, vegetable, 1, 140 g	21	6.3	30	329	1365
burger, spicy bean, 1, cooked, quarter-pounder	13	3.4	27	241	1010
burger, vegetarian, 1, 47 g	4	0.9	12	95	400
cannelloni, spinach & ricotta, 450 g	35	2.3	58	662	2768
cashew nut roast mix, 100 g	32	++	26	480	2000
chicken chow mein, 340 g	7	6.5	49	353	1493
chicken kiev, 1, 140 g	35	1.3	14	427	1769
chicken kiev, reduced fat, 1, 140 g	20	1.7	16	319	1330
chicken pie, individual, baked, 130 g	23	3	32	374	1563
chicken & turkey satay, 1 stick, 30 g	3	0.4	0.8	45	188
chilli con carne, 220 g	19	7	18	332	1390
chow mein, 100 g	3.4	0.6	16	119	503

FOOD	FAT g	FIBRE g	CARB g	ENERGY kcal	ENERGY kJ
cod fillet, breaded, 1 fillet, 170 g	13	3	24	304	1280
cod fish cake, 1, 90 g	8	0.7	15	168	703
cod mornay, with cheese sauce, 180 g	14	1.4	3	236	987
corned beef hash, canned, 200 g	18	++	12	328	6871
cottage pie, 350 g	14	3.5	35	315	1322
egg fried rice, 100 g	2.2	1.1	25	149	682
falafel, 6, 85 g	7	7	16	200	829
fish pie, 100 g	4	0.9	9	93	389
garlic bread, half baguette, 90 g	16	2.0	41	342	1434
garlic bread, half baguette, reduced-fat, 90 g	8	1.8	41	263	1109
gefilte fish balls, 6, 100 g	3.9	1.0	12	140	585
hash browns, 100 g	7.3	++	24	174	729
Lancashire hotpot, 450 g	16	5.4	46	424	1784
lasagne, meat, 100 g	9	1.4	10	161	675
lasagne, spinach, wholemeal, 100 g	3	3	13	193	395
lasagne, vegetable, 100 g	5	0.5	14	212	517
macaroni cheese, canned, 200 g	9.5	0.6	20	191	799
noodle/pasta savoury pots, dry weight					
- chicken curry, 87 g	14	3.2	56	384	1610
- chilli, 71 g	14	1.7	47	337	1409
- korma, 75 g	3	1.1	52	273	1148
- mushroom & chicken, 68 g	8	2.7	43	269	1133
- spicy curry, 119 g	20	4.4	77	530	2229
noodle, Thai-style, 100 g	6	0.8	16	142	598
nut roast, dry mix, 100 g	30	7.0	23	482	2011
pasta shapes in tomato sauce, can, 205 g	0.8	1.2	26	128	542
pasta shapes with sausage, can, 213 g	11	0.4	26	230	967
pasty, cheese & onion, 1, 150 g	33	1.5	35	477	1988
pasty, meat & potato (Cornish), 1, 227 g	36	2.5	43	567	2367

FOOD	FAT g	FIBRE g	CARB g	ENERGY kcal	kJ
pizza, deep-pan, pepperoni, 190 g	21	5.6	45	453	1900
pizza, thin & crispy, four cheese, 145 g	13	4.3	40	343	1443
pizza, thin & crispy, ham/mushroom, 160 g	11	7.6	30	288	1211
potato, jacket, cheese & beans, 340 g	7	7.5	47	305	1286
potato, jacket, chilli con carne, 340 g	12	4.1	35	319	1341
potato, jacket, tuna & sweetcorn, 340 g	13	3.4	43	333	1398
potato skins					
- cheese & bacon, 140 g	22	3.5	24	349	1445
- spicy with salsa, 205 g	8	0.8	47	290	165
prawn cocktail, prawns & mayonnaise, 100 g	35	0.5	3	353	1457
prawn cocktail, reduced-fat, 100 g	13	0.5	3	160	662
raita, yogurt, cucumber & mint, 65 g	1.2	++	6	41	180
ravioli, meat, canned in tomato sauce, 200 g	2.3	1.1	26	145	613
salmon fish cakes, oven-baked, 2, 140 g	15	2.2	26	306	1280
samosa, meat, 1 large, 140 g	79	3.4	25	830	3430
samosa, vegetable, 1 large, 140 g	59	3.4	31	660	2736
sauce, cooking					
- black bean, 100 g	0.6	0.8	18	80	340
- hoisin, 100 g	2	0.7	37	175	740
- korma, 100 g	14	1	11	180	740
- madras, 100 g	8	2	10	115	480
- red wine, 100 g	0.6	0+	10	46	195
sauce, cooking for chicken					
- extra creamy mushroom, 100 g	7	0.5	9	87	362
- honey & mustard, 100 g	5	0.6	15	106	443
sauce, stir-fry sachet					
- black bean, 100 g	11	1.5	17	185	765
- green Thai, 100 g	32	2.1	12	345	1415
- oyster & spring onion, 100 g	0.7	1.1	20	92	391

FOOD	FAT g	FIBRE g	CARB g	ENERGY kcal	ENERGY kJ
sausage roll, flaky pastry, 1 medium, 60 g	22	0.7	19	286	1191
sausage roll, shortcrust pastry, 1, 60 g	19	0.8	23	275	1149
sausage roll, vegetarian, 1 roll, 50 g	8	0.8	12	267	1115
Scotch egg, retail, 1, 120 g	21	1.9	16	301	1255
shepherd's pie, 100 g	4	1	10	90	378
spaghetti bolognese, can, 200 g	2.7	1.0	26	149	692
spaghetti rings in tomato sauce, can, 200 g	0.4	1.1	23	111	472
spaghetti with sausages, can in tomato sauce, 200 g	5.2	1.0	22	165	694
spring roll, vegetable, 1, 140 g	9	2.3	37	250	1055
steak & kidney pie, puff pastry, 150 g	24	1.4	40	423	1769
steak & kidney pie, shortcrust pastry, 240 g	42	3.4	55	715	2986
sweet & sour pork, canned, 200 g	2.6	2.0	28	206	868
tortellini, fresh, meat, 100 g	6	1.4	21	170	710
tortellini, fresh, spinach & ricotta, 100 g	4.8	2.4	24	169	712
vegetarian fillets, mycoprotein, 1, 100 g	1.8	4.7	6	90	381
vegetarian fillets, mycoprotein, garlic & herb, 1, 100 g	10	4.1	17	198	828
vine leaves, stuffed, vegetarian, 1, 30 g	1.5	++	7	44	184
REDCURRANTS					
jelly, 1 tsp, 9 g	0	0	6	22	92
raw, 100 g	0	++	4	21	89
cooked with sugar, 100 g	0	5.8	13	53	227
cooked without sugar, 100 g	0	6.3	4	17	76
RHUBARB					
canned in syrup, 100 g	0	1.3	8	31	130
cooked with sugar, 140 g	0.1	2.8	16	67	284
cooked without sugar, 140 g	0.1	2.1	0.7	7	30
raw, 100 g	0.1	2.3	0.8	7	32

FOOD	FAT g	FIBRE g	CARB g	ENERGY kcal	kJ
RICE					
arborio, raw, 100 g	0.5	0.5	79	349	1481
basmati, boiled, 100 g	0.3	0.8	30	123	522
brown, boiled, 180 g	2.0	2.7	58	254	1075
red (wild), raw, 100 g	2.7	2.5	73	343	1453
white, easy-cook, boiled, 180 g	2	1.8	56	248	1057
white, polished, boiled, 180 g	0.5	1.4	53	221	940
RICE CAKES					
plain, 1 slice	0.2	0.1	6	28	120
rice & maize, with cheese, 1, 10 g	0.3	0.1	8	38	160

S

FOOD	FAT g	FIBRE g	CARB g	ENERGY kcal	kJ
SALSIFY					
boiled, 100 g	0.4	++	9	23	99
SATSUMA					
(see Mandarin Oranges)					
SAUCES/SAVOURY					
bread, semi-skimmed milk, 45 g	1.4	0.3	6	42	177
bread, full-fat milk, 45 g	2.3	0.3	6	50	208
brown, bottled, 20 g	0	++	5	20	84
cheese, semi-skimmed milk, 100 g	13	0.2	9	179	750
cheese, full-fat milk, 100 g	15	0.2	9	197	819
hollandaise, 50 g	38	++	0	358	1456
horseradish, 20 g	1.7	++	4	31	128
tartare, jar, 20 g	4	0.2	4	58	242
tomato ketchup, bottled, 20 g	0	++	5	20	84
white, semi-skimmed,100 g	11	0.3	8	128	539

FOOD	FAT g	FIBRE g	CARB g	ENERGY kcal	ENERGY kJ
white, full-fat milk, 100 g	11	0.3	10	150	624
Worcestershire, 15 g	0	0	2	10	41
SAUSAGE					
beef, fried or grilled, 1, 40 g	7	0.3	6	108	450
black pudding, dry-fried, 1 slice, 30 g	6	0.2	5	89	371
black pudding, fried in oil, 1 slice, 30 g	7	0.5	4	310	381
bratwurst, 1, 75 g	16	++	2	195	811
chicken frankfurters, 3, 100 g	21	0	6	243	1007
chorizo, 1, 60 g	15	0	1	182	757
liver sausage, 100 g	17	0.5	6	226	942
mortadella, 100 g	30	++	1	331	1368
pork, fried, 1, 40 g	10	0.3	4	128	527
pork, grilled, 1, 40 g	13	0.4	6	165	686
salami, 1 slice, 20 g	9	0	0.4	98	406
salami stick, 1, 25 g	12	0	0.4	132	547
vegetarian, raw, 1, 35 g	5	0.4	3	88	366
SEEDS					
melon, 15 g	7	++	3	87	365
poppy, 15 g	4	++	2	46	195
pumpkin, 15 g	7	++	2	85	354
sesame, 15 g	9	++	0.1	90	371
sunflower, 15 g	7	++	3	87	362
sunflower, toasted, 15 g	7	++	3	90	375
SHARON FRUIT					
raw, 100 g	0	++	19	73	311
SNACKS					
bacon-flavoured maize snacks, 25 g	6	1.2	12	117	490
banana chips, 25 g	8	1.2	15	128	534
Bombay mix, 100 g	34	6	51	546	2278

FOOD	FAT g	FIBRE g	CARB g	ENERGY kcal	kJ
cheese-flavoured biscuits, 50 g	14	1.3	27	257	1074
corn chips (tortilla), 100 g	19	4	68	461	1935
croûtons, flavoured, 50 g	15	1.3	26	260	1083
fruit & nut mix with coconut, 100 g	15	++	54	374	1572
peanuts & raisins, 25 g	7	1.7	9	109	455
potato chips (matchstick-style), 50 g	17	1.9	27	264	1102
potato crisps, bag, 34.5 g	12	1.4	17	183	759
potato crisps, low-fat, 28 g	6	1.4	17	130	543
potato rings, 25 g	5	0.8	17	117	492
prawn crackers, 100 g	31	0.4	60	534	2231
pretzels, 50 g	2	1.7	41	200	850
spicy rice cracker mix, 100 g	0.1	1.6	83	360	1525
vegetable (not potato) crisps, 100 g	27	6	37	407	1691

SOFT DRINKS

FOOD	FAT g	FIBRE g	CARB g	ENERGY kcal	kJ
blackcurrant cordial, diluted, 250 ml	0	0	20	75	323
blackcurrant cordial, low sugar, diluted, 250 ml	0	0	1	8	35
elderflower, concentrated, 10 ml	0	0	6	24	102
fruit drink/squash, concentrated, 50 ml	0	0	12	47	200
fruit squash, diluted, 250 ml	0	0	1.3	8	35
fruit squash, no added sugar, diluted, 250 ml	0	0	0.1	4	16
lime juice, undiluted, 45ml	0	0	13	50	216
cola type, canned, 333 ml	0	0	35	133	559
diet (light) cola, canned, 333 ml	0	0	1	1	4
diet (light) lemonade, canned, 333 ml	0	0	1	4	13
ginger beer, canned, 333 ml	0	0	25	110	462
lemonade, canned, 333 ml	0	0	36	141	595
orangeade, canned, 333 ml	0	0	43	172	724

SOUPS

FOOD	FAT g	FIBRE g	CARB g	ENERGY kcal	kJ
carrot & coriander, ready-made, 300 ml	4	1.8	10	105	441

FOOD	FAT g	FIBRE g	CARB g	ENERGY kcal	kJ
condensed, chicken, undiluted, 150 g	11	++	9	147	611
condensed, tomato, undiluted, 150 g	10	++	22	185	771
corn chowder, ready-made, 300 ml	7	4	25	183	771
cream of chicken, canned, 150 g	6	++	7	87	363
cream of mushroom, ready-made, 150 g	6	++	6	80	333
cream of tomato, ready-made, 150 g	5	++	9	83	345
lentil soup, canned, 100 g	0.2	++	7	39	164
mushroom, ready-made, 300 ml	9	0.9	11	153	633
powder, reduced-calorie, rehydrated to 250 ml	2	0.3	9	59	248
powder, rehydrated, 200 ml	3.4	++	16	96	408
reduced-calorie soup, canned, 150 g	0.3	++	6	30	131
SPINACH					
fresh, boiled, 90 g	0.7	3	1	17	71
frozen, boiled, 90 g	0.7	3	0.4	19	81
raw, 100 g	0.8	4	2	25	103
SPREADS (Savoury)					
barbecued bean paste, 100 g	0.4	++	20	106	449
chicken & mushroom, 100 g	11	++	5	187	782
peanut butter, on bread, 16 g	9	1.1	2	100	413
salmon, 100 g	10	++	5	172	720
sandwich spread, 1 tbsp, 16 g	2	++	4	30	124
soya with herbs & chives, 100 g	28	++	6	290	1210
SPRING GREENS					
boiled, 100 g	0.7	3.4	2	20	82
raw, 100 g	1.0	6.1	3	33	136
SPRING ONIONS					
raw, 1, 10 g	0.1	++	0.3	2	10
SPROUTING BEANS					
alfalfa, raw, 100 g	1	++	0.4	24	100

FOOD	FAT g	FIBRE g	CARB g	ENERGY kcal	kJ
mung bean, 100 g	0.2	++	6	35	146
SQUASH					
acorn, baked, 70 g	0.1	++	9	39	164
butternut, baked, 70 g	0.1	++	5	22	96
spaghetti, baked, 70 g	0.2	++	3	16	67
STAR FRUIT (Carambola)					
raw, 100 g	0.3	1.7	7	32	136
STOCK CUBES					
any, 1 cube, 5 g	0.8	0	0.5	12	52
STRAWBERRIES					
canned in juice, 100 g	0	1.0	12	50	211
canned in syrup, 100 g	0	0.9	17	65	279
raw, 100 g	0.1	2	6	27	113
STUFFING					
sage & onion, 50 g	7	1.2	10	116	481
SUET (see Fats and Oils)					
SUGAR					
any, 1 tsp, 5g	0	0	5	20	84
SUGAR SNAP PEAS					
boiled, 100 g	0.3	++	5	33	139
raw, 100 g	0.2	++	5	34	145
SULTANAS (see Dried Fruit)					
SWEDE					
boiled, 60 g	0.1	0.7	1	7	28
raw, 100 g	0.3	2.4	5	24	101
SWEETCORN (see Corn)					
SWEET POTATO					
boiled, 65 g	0.2	1.4	13	55	233
raw, 100 g	0.3	2.3	21	87	372

FOOD	FAT g	FIBRE g	CARB g	ENERGY kcal	kJ
T					
TAHINI					
1 heaped tbsp, 19 g	11	++	0.2	115	477
TAMARILLOS (Tree Tomato)					
raw, 90 g	0.3	++	4	25	108
TANGERINES					
(see Mandarin Oranges)					
TAPIOCA					
raw, 100 g	0.1	++	95	359	1531
boiled in water, 265g	0	0.3	19	75	315
TARAMASALATA (see Dips)					
TOFU					
canned, braised 100 g	19	0.1	7	247	1033
canned, fried, 100 g	25	++	4	302	1264
organic, 100 g	5	++	1	98	409
smoked, 100 g	7	++	2	127	530
steamed, 100 g	4	0.3	0.7	73	304
TOMATO					
cherry, raw, 100 g	0.4	1.3	3	18	76
juice, large glass, 250 ml	0	++	8	35	155
peeled, whole, canned, 400 g	0.4	3.2	12	64	276
purée, 1 heaped tbsp, 25 g	0.1	++	3	17	73
raw, 1, 85 g	0.3	1.1	3	14	62
sun-dried, 1, 10 g	5	++	0.5	50	204
sun-dried in oil, 100 g	51	0.8	4	93	2040
TORTILLAS					
wheat flour, 1, 50 g	0.5	1.4	30	131	557

FOOD	FAT g	FIBRE g	CARB g	ENERGY kcal	kJ
TURKEY					
breast fillet, grilled, 100 g	2	0	0	155	658
drumstick, roasted, with skin & bone, 180 g	11	0	0	241	1010
minced, casseroled, 100 g	7	0	0	176	739
roasted, dark meat, no skin, 100 g	4	0	0	148	624
roasted, light meat, no skin, 100 g	1.4	0	0	132	558
roll, 1 slice, 19 g	2	0	1	32	132
smoked, 100 g	1.3	0	0	107	447
strips, stir-fried, 100 g	4.5	0	0	164	692
thigh, casseroled, 100 g	8	0	0	181	760
TURNIP					
boiled, 1 medium, 60 g	0.1	1.2	1	7	31
raw, 100 g	0.3	2.5	5	23	98
TZATZIKI (see Dips)					
V					
VEAL					
escalope/cutlet, in breadcrumbs, fried, 150 g	12	0.5	7	323	1356
escalope, meat, no coating, fried, 100 g	7	0	0	196	825
fillet, roast, 100 g	12	0	0	230	963
VENISON					
roast, 120 g	3	0	0	198	838
VINEGAR					
all varieties, 1tbsp, 15 ml	0	0	0	4	16
VINE LEAVES					
in brine, 100 g	0	4.5	0.2	15	64

FOOD	FAT g	FIBRE g	CARB g	ENERGY kcal	kJ
W					
WAFFLES					
plain, 1, 35 g	6	0.7	14	117	490
potato, frozen, cooked, 1	4	++	14	117	379
WATER CHESTNUTS					
canned, 40 g	0	++	5	20	82
raw, 50 g	0.1	++	5	23	99
WATERCRESS					
fresh, 20 g	0.2	0.6	0	4	19
Y					
YAM					
baked, 100 g	0.4	4.9	38	153	651
boiled, 130 g	0.4	5	43	173	738
raw, 100 g	0.3	3.7	28	114	488
YEAST					
bakers, compressed, 15 g	0.1	0.9	0	7	34
dried, sachet, 7 g	0.1	1.4	0	12	50
YEAST EXTRACT					
vegetable extract, 4 g	0	0.1	0.8	9	37
YOGURT					
drinking yogurt					
- peach & mango, low-fat,100 g	0.1	0	14	58	241
- strawberry, 100 g	1.2	0	15	81	342
live fermented skimmed milk drink, 65 ml	0.1	0	12	50	209
full-fat milk, fruit, 125 g	4	++	20	131	551
full-fat milk, plain, 125 g	4	++	10	99	416

FOOD	FAT g	FIBRE g	CARB g	ENERGY kcal	kJ
goat's, full-fat milk, 125 g	5	0	5	79	329
Greek-style, cow, 125 g	11	0	3	144	596
Greek-style, sheep, 125 g	9	0	7	133	553
low-fat, flavoured, 125 g	1	++	22	113	480
low-fat, fruit, 125 g	1	++	22	113	478
low-fat, muesli/nut, 125 g	3	++	24	140	593
low-fat, plain, 125 g	1	0	9	70	295
thick & creamy, 150 g	8	0	28	206	864

YORKSHIRE PUDDING

	FAT g	FIBRE g	CARB g	ENERGY kcal	kJ
1, 50 g	5	0.5	12	104	437

RECIPES:
DELICIOUS BREAKFASTS, LUNCHES, DINNERS AND DESSERTS

GREEK YOGURT WITH HONEY, NUTS & BLUEBERRIES

Serves 4

Ingredients
3 tbsp clear honey
100 g/3 1/2 oz mixed unsalted nuts
8 tbsp Greek yogurt
200 g/7 oz fresh blueberries

Nutritional Fact
Excellent for balancing blood sugar, blueberries are, therefore, a good food with which to begin the day.

Serving Analysis
- Calories 239
- Protein 4.3 g
- Carbohydrate 24 g
- Sugars 19.4 g
- Fat 15.6 g
- Saturates 2.7 g

1 Heat the honey in a small saucepan over a medium heat, add the nuts and stir until they are well coated. Remove from the heat and leave to cool slightly.

2 Divide the yogurt between four serving bowls, then spoon over the nut mixture and blueberries.

MEXICAN EGGS

Serves 4

Ingredients
8 large eggs
2 tbsp milk
pepper
1 tsp olive oil
1 red pepper, deseeded and thinly sliced
1/2 fresh red chilli
1 fresh chorizo sausage, skinned and sliced
4 tbsp chopped fresh coriander
To serve
4 slices toasted wholemeal bread

Nutritional Fact
A good protein breakfast helps to sustain good blood-sugar levels throughout the day.

Serving Analysis
• Calories 279
• Protein 15.8 g
• Carbohydrate 4.9 g
• Sugars 3.9 g
• Fat 21.8 g
• Saturates 6.3 g

1 Beat the eggs, milk and pepper to taste in a large bowl. Set aside.

2 Heat the oil in a non-stick frying pan over a medium heat, add the red pepper and chilli and cook, stirring frequently, for 5 minutes, or until the red pepper is soft and browned in places. Add the chorizo and cook until just browned. Transfer to a warmed plate and set aside.

3 Return the pan to the heat, add the egg mixture and cook to a soft scramble. Add the chorizo mixture, stir to combine and scatter over the coriander. Serve immediately on toasted wholemeal bread.

BIRCHER MUESLI

Serves 4

Ingredients

150 g/5^1/2 oz rolled oats
225 ml/8 fl oz apple juice
1 apple, grated
125 ml/4 fl oz natural yogurt
150 g/5^1/2 oz blackberries
2 plums, stoned and sliced
2 tbsp clear honey

Nutritional Fact

Oats release their sugars very slowly, making them a good breakfast food.

Serving Analysis

- Calories 285
- Protein 8.4 g
- Carbohydrate 56 g
- Sugars 25.5 g
- Fat 4.2 g
- Saturates 1.1 g

1 Put the oats and apple juice into a mixing bowl and combine well. Cover and refrigerate overnight.

2 To serve, stir the apple and yogurt into the soaked oats and divide between four serving bowls. Top with the blackberries and plums and drizzle with the honey.

BAKED MUSHROOMS

Serves 4

Ingredients
2 tbsp olive oil
8 field mushrooms
55 g/2 oz button mushrooms, finely chopped
2 garlic cloves, crushed
4 slices lean cooked ham, finely chopped
2 tbsp finely chopped fresh parsley
pepper
To serve
4 slices rye bread

Nutritional Fact
Parsley is a good stress tonic that helps to keep blood-sugar levels manageable.

Serving Analysis
• Calories 124
• Protein 6.6 g
• Carbohydrate 4 g
• Sugars 1.2 g
• Fat 9.7 g
• Saturates 0.8 g

1 Preheat the oven to 190°C/375°F/Gas Mark 5. Brush a baking tray with a little of the oil. Arrange the field mushrooms, cup-side up, on the baking tray.

2 Mix the button mushrooms, garlic, ham and parsley together in a bowl.

3 Divide the ham mixture between the field mushroom cups. Drizzle with the remaining oil and season to taste with pepper.

4 Bake in the preheated oven for 10 minutes, then serve immediately with rye bread.

WINTER WARMER RED LENTIL SOUP

Serves 6

Ingredients

225 g/8 oz dried red split lentils
1 red onion, diced
2 large carrots, sliced
1 celery stick, sliced
1 parsnip, diced
1 garlic clove, crushed
1.2 litres/2 pints vegetable stock
2 tsp paprika
freshly ground black pepper
1 tbsp snipped fresh chives, to garnish

To serve
6 tbsp low-fat natural fromage frais (optional)
crusty wholemeal or white bread

Nutritional Fact

Lentils contain good levels of B vitamins, which are thought to stop the build-up of a substance called homocysteine that can build up in the body and cause damage to the heart.

Serving Analysis
• Calories 87
• Protein 4.4 g
• Carbohydrate 18 g
• Sugars 5 g
• Fat 0.4 g
• Saturates 0.07 g

1 Put the lentils, onion, vegetables, garlic, stock and paprika into a large saucepan. Bring to the boil and boil rapidly for 10 minutes. Reduce the heat, cover and simmer for 20 minutes, or until the lentils and vegetables are tender.

2 Leave the soup to cool slightly, then purée in small batches in a food processor or blender. Process until the mixture is smooth.

3 Return the soup to the saucepan and heat through thoroughly. Season to taste with pepper.

4 To serve, ladle the soup into warmed bowls and swirl in a tablespoonful of fromage frais, if desired. Sprinkle the chives over the soup to garnish and serve immediately with crusty bread.

SPEEDY BROCCOLI SOUP

Serves 6

Ingredients
350 g/12 oz broccoli
1 leek, sliced
1 celery stick, sliced
1 garlic clove, crushed
350 g/12 oz potato, diced
1 litre/1³/4 pints vegetable stock
1 bay leaf
freshly ground black pepper
To serve
crusty bread or toasted croûtons,

Nutritional Fact
Broccoli is a source of vitamins B3 and B5, both of which are thought to raise good cholesterol levels in the blood, and therefore help to balance good and bad cholesterol levels.

Serving Analysis
• Calories 140
• Protein 5.6 g
• Carbohydrate 29 g
• Sugars 3.6 g
• Fat 1.3 g
• Saturates 0.27 g

1 Cut the broccoli into florets and set aside. Cut the thicker broccoli stalks into 1-cm/¹/2-inch dice and put into a large saucepan with the leek, celery, garlic, potato, stock and bay leaf. Bring to the boil, then reduce the heat, cover and simmer for 15 minutes

2 Add the broccoli florets to the soup and return to the boil. Reduce the heat, cover and simmer for a further 3–5 minutes, or until the potato and broccoli stalks are tender.

3 Remove from the heat and leave the soup to cool slightly. Remove and discard the bay leaf. Purée the soup, in small batches, in a food processor or blender until smooth.

4 Return the soup to the saucepan and heat through thoroughly. Season to taste with pepper. Ladle the soup into warmed bowls and serve immediately with crusty bread or toasted croûtons.

BAKED LEMON COD

Serves 4

Ingredients
4 oz/115 g cucumber
2 celery sticks
4 thick cod fillets, about 5 oz/140 g each
1 tbsp chopped fresh parsley
grated rind and juice of 1 lemon
freshly ground black pepper

To serve
lemon wedges
boiled new potatoes, lightly cooked
seasonal vegetables, or salads

Nutritional Fact
White fish, such as cod and flounder, is low in saturated fat and high in protein that is essential for healthy building and repair of the body's cells.

Serving Analysis
• Calories 121
• Protein 25 g
• Carbohydrate 2.6 g
• Sugars 1.2 g
• Fat 1.3 g
• Saturates 0.02 g

1 Preheat the oven to 200°C/ 400°F/Gas Mark 6. Cut the cucumber and celery into long fine sticks and sprinkle over the base of an ovenproof dish that is large enough to fit the cod fillets in a single layer.

2 Arrange the cod fillets on the cucumber and celery and sprinkle the parsley, lemon rind and juice over the fillets. Season with pepper. Cover the dish with an ovenproof lid or foil and bake in the preheated oven for about 20 minutes, depending on the thickness of the fillets, until the flesh turns white and flakes easily.

3 Transfer the fish to a warmed serving plate with the cucumber and celery and spoon over the cooking juices. Garnish with lemon wedges and serve at once with boiled new potatoes, seasonal vegetables, or salads.

BEEF BOURGUIGNON

Serves 4

Ingredients

400 g/14 oz lean beef
2 low-salt lean smoked back bacon
rashers
12 shallots, peeled
1 garlic clove, crushed
225 g/8 oz closed-cup mushrooms,
sliced
300 ml/10 fl oz red wine
425 ml/15 fl oz beef stock
2 bay leaves
2 tbsp chopped fresh thyme
55 g/2 oz cornflour
100 ml/3¹/₂ fl oz cold water
freshly ground black pepper

To serve

boiled brown or white rice
lightly cooked seasonal vegetables

Nutritional Fact

Choosing brown rice instead of white
can help to increase your intake of
insoluble fibre and B vitamins and
clean toxins out of your system.

Serving Analysis

- Calories 376
- Protein 35 g
- Carbohydrate 20 g
- Sugars 1.6 g
- Fat 11 g
- Saturates 4.1g

1 Trim any visible fat from the beef and bacon and cut the meat into
bite-sized pieces. Put the meat into a large saucepan with the shallots,
garlic, mushrooms, wine, stock, bay leaves and 1 tablespoon of the
thyme. Bring to the boil, then reduce the heat, cover and simmer for
50 minutes, or until the meat and shallots are tender.

2 Blend the cornflour with the water in a small bowl and stir into
the casserole. Return to the boil, stirring constantly, and cook until
the casserole thickens. Reduce the heat and simmer for a further
5 minutes. Season to taste with pepper.

3 Remove and discard the bay leaves.Transfer the beef bourguignon
to a warmed casserole dish and sprinkle over the remaining thyme.
Serve with boiled rice and seasonal vegetables.

STICKY LIME CHICKEN

Serves 4

Ingredients

4 part-boned, skinless chicken breasts, about 140 g/5 oz each
grated rind and juice of 1 lime
1 tbsp clear honey
1 tbsp olive oil
1 garlic clove, chopped (optional)
1 tbsp chopped fresh thyme
freshly ground black pepper

To serve

boiled new potatoes
lightly cooked seasonal vegetables

Nutritional Fact

Removing the skin from the chicken gets rid of most of the saturated fat.

Serving Analysis

• Calories 203
• Protein 32.5 g
• Carbohydrate 5.3 g
• Sugars 4.4 g
• Fat 5.3 g
• Saturates 1 g

1 Preheat the oven to 190°C/375°F/Gas Mark 5. Arrange the chicken breasts in a shallow roasting tin.

2 Put the lime rind and juice, honey, oil, garlic, if using, and thyme in a small bowl and combine thoroughly. Spoon the mixture evenly over the chicken breasts and season with pepper.

3 Roast the chicken in the preheated oven, basting every 10 minutes, for 35–40 minutes, or until the chicken is tender and the juices run clear when a skewer is inserted into the thickest part of the meat. If the juices still run pink, return the chicken to the oven and cook for a further 5 minutes, then re-test. As the chicken cooks, the liquid in the pan thickens to give the tasty sticky coating.

4 Serve with boiled new potatoes and seasonal vegetables.

TUNA & AVOCADO SALAD

Serves 4

Ingredients
2 avocados, stoned, peeled and cubed
250 g/9 oz cherry tomatoes, halved
2 red peppers, deseeded and chopped
1 bunch fresh flat-leaved parsley, chopped
2 garlic cloves, crushed
1 fresh red chilli, deseeded and finely chopped
juice of $1/2$ lemon
6 tbsp olive oil
pepper
3 tbsp sesame seeds
4 fresh tuna steaks, about 150 g/ $5^1/2$ oz each

To serve
8 cooked new potatoes, cubed
rocket leaves

Nutritional Fact
Avocados are rich in nutrients that can help to protect the eyes against diabetes-related damage.

Serving Analysis
• Calories 785
• Protein 44 g
• Carbohydrate 57 g
• Sugars 7.1 g
• Fat 46 g
• Saturates 3 g

1 Toss the avocados, tomatoes, red peppers, parsley, garlic, chilli, lemon juice and 2 tablespoons of the oil together in a large bowl. Season to taste with pepper, cover and chill in the refrigerator for 30 minutes. Lightly crush the sesame seeds in a mortar with a pestle. Tip the crushed seeds on to a plate and spread out. Press each tuna steak in turn into the crushed seeds to coat on both sides.

2 Heat 2 tablespoons of the remaining oil in a frying pan, add the potatoes and cook, stirring frequently, for 5–8 minutes, or until crisp and brown. Remove from the pan and drain on kitchen paper.

3 Wipe out the pan, add the remaining oil and heat over a high heat. Add the tuna steaks and cook for 3–4 minutes on each side. Divide the avocado salad between 4 serving plates and top each with a tuna steak, then sprinkle over the potatoes and a handful of rocket leaves.

TOASTED PINE KERNEL & VEGETABLE COUSCOUS

Serves 4

Ingredients
115 g/4 oz dried green lentils
55 g/2 oz pine kernels
1 tbsp olive oil
1 onion, diced
2 garlic cloves, crushed
280 g/10 oz courgettes, sliced
250 g/9 oz tomatoes, chopped
400 g/14 oz canned artichoke hearts, drained and cut in half lengthways
250 g/9 oz couscous
450 ml/16 fl oz vegetable stock
3 tbsp torn fresh basil leaves, plus extra leaves to garnish
freshly ground black pepper

Nutritional Fact
Pine kernels have beneficial omega-3 oils and polyunsaturated fats. They also contain plant sterols, which are thought to help to regulate cholesterol.

Serving Analysis
• Calories 600
• Protein 17 g
• Carbohydrate 71 g
• Sugars 7.9 g
• Fat 28 g
• Saturates 4 g

1 Put the lentils into a saucepan with plenty of cold water and boil rapidly for 10 minutes. Reduce the heat, cover and simmer for a further 15 minutes, or until tender. Meanwhile, preheat the grill to medium. Spread the pine kernels out in a single layer on a baking tray and toast under the grill, turning to brown evenly – watch constantly as they brown quickly. Tip the pine kernels into a small dish and set aside.

2 Heat the oil in a frying pan over a medium heat, add the onion, garlic and courgettes and cook, stirring frequently, for 8–10 minutes. Add the tomatoes and artichoke halves and cook for 5 minutes, or until heated through. Meanwhile, put the couscous into a heatproof bowl. Bring the stock to the boil in a saucepan and pour over the couscous, cover and leave for 10 minutes until the couscous absorbs the stock and is tender.

3 Drain the lentils and stir into the couscous. Stir in the torn basil leaves and season well with pepper. Transfer the couscous to a warmed serving dish and spoon over the cooked vegetables. Sprinkle the pine kernels over the top, garnish with basil leaves and serve immediately.

WARM RED LENTIL SALAD WITH GOAT'S CHEESE

Serves 4

Ingredients

2 tbsp olive oil
2 tsp cumin seeds
2 garlic cloves, crushed
2 tsp grated fresh root ginger
300 g/10^1/$_2$ oz split red lentils
700 ml/1^1/$_4$ pints vegetable stock
2 tbsp chopped fresh mint
2 tbsp chopped fresh coriander
2 red onions, thinly sliced
200 g/7 oz baby spinach leaves
1 tsp hazelnut oil
150 g/5^1/$_2$ oz soft goat's cheese
4 tbsp Greek yogurt
pepper

To serve

1 lemon, cut into quarters, to garnish
toasted rye bread

Nutritional Fact

Lentils and spinach contain B vitamins and iron. These are important for energy production and controlling sugar cravings.

Serving Analysis

• Calories 310
• Protein 16g
• Carbohydrate 24 g
• Sugars 6 g
• Fat 17 g
• Saturates 5.9 g

1 Heat half the olive oil in a large saucepan over a medium heat, add the cumin seeds, garlic and ginger and cook for 2 minutes, stirring constantly. Stir in the lentils, then add the stock, a ladleful at a time, until it is all absorbed, stirring constantly – this will take about 20 minutes. Remove from the heat and stir in the herbs.

2 Meanwhile, heat the remaining olive oil in a frying pan over a medium heat, add the onions and cook, stirring frequently, for 10 minutes, or until soft and lightly browned.

3 Toss the spinach in the oil, then divide between 4 serving plates. Mash the goat's cheese with the yogurt and season with pepper.

4 Divide the lentils between the serving plates and top with the onions and goat's cheese mixture. Garnish with lemon quarters and serve with toasted rye bread.

BLUEBERRY FROZEN YOGURT

Serves 4

Ingredients
175 g/6 oz fresh blueberries
finely grated rind and juice of 1 orange
3 tbsp maple syrup
500 g/1 lb 2 oz natural low-fat yogurt

Nutritional Fact
Blueberries may increase sensitivity to insulin and help to control Type II diabetes.

Serving Analysis
- Calories 157
- Protein 7 g
- Carbohydrate 29 g
- Sugars 26 g
- Fat 2 g
- Saturates 1.1 g

1 Put the blueberries and orange juice into a food processor or blender and process to a purée. Strain through a nylon sieve into a bowl or jug.

2 Stir the maple syrup and yogurt together in a large mixing bowl, then fold in the fruit purée.

3 Churn the mixture in an ice-cream machine, following the manufacturer's instructions, then freeze for 5–6 hours. If you don't have an ice-cream machine, transfer the mixture to a freezer-proof container and freeze for 2 hours. Remove from the freezer, turn out into a bowl and beat until smooth. Return to the freezer and freeze until firm.

LITTLE DARK CHOCOLATE MOUSSE POTS WITH POACHED BERRIES

Serves 4

Ingredients

100 g/3^1/2 oz plain dark chocolate, minimum 70 per cent cocoa solids
25 g/1 oz unsalted butter
2 eggs, separated
1 tbsp maple syrup
100 g/3^1/2 oz mixed dark berries, such as blackberries, blackcurrants and blueberries
1 tbsp crème de cassis
fresh mint leaves, to decorate

Nutritional Fact

Dark chocolate is lower in sugar than milk chocolate and can be an occasional treat if eaten in small amounts, such as in this recipe.

Serving Analysis

• Calories 241
• Protein 4.4 g
• Carbohydrate 24 g
• Sugars 20 g
• Fat 16 g
• Saturates 8.7 g

1 Break the chocolate into pieces, put into a heatproof bowl with the butter and place over a saucepan of simmering water. Leave to melt, then allow to cool slightly. Stir in the egg yolks and maple syrup.

2 Whisk the egg whites in a large bowl until stiff, then fold into the cooled chocolate mixture. Divide between 4 ramekins and chill in the refrigerator for 3 hours.

3 Meanwhile, put the berries into a small saucepan with the crème de cassis over a low heat and cook for 5–10 minutes, or until the berries are glossy and soft. Leave to cool.

4 To serve, spoon the berries on top of the chocolate mousse and decorate with mint leaves.

INDEX

Pages marked * denote Calorie Tables: Foods A-Z

alcohol 13, 16, 39, 43, *55-6
anaemia, iron-deficiency 14-15, 41
antioxidants 9, 39, 42, 46, 47, 50
apple *56
apricot *56-7
artichoke *57
artificial sweetener 28
ascorbic acid see vitamin C
asparagus *57
aubergine *57
avocado *57

baby foods *57-8
bacon *58
balanced diet, explanation of 11-12
bamboo shoots *58
bananas *58-9
beans *59
beef *59
beer *55
beetroot *59
beverages *59-61
beta-carotene 42
biotin 46
biscuits *61
blackberries *61
blackcurrants *61
blueberries *61
body mass index (BMI) 18, 21, 23
bread 8, 9, *61-3
broccoli *63
Brussels sprouts *63
buckwheat kernels *63
bulgar *63
buns see cakes/pastries/buns
butter 35, 36, *63

cabbage *63
cakes/pastries/buns *63-4
calcium 9, 15, 16, 41, 48
for healthy bones 15
calories 6-7, 21, 23, 33, 36
daily requirement calculation 19, 23, 33
tips to reduce calorie intake 28

carbohydrates 6, 7, 12, 33, 34, 35, 37, 38
counting 38
starchy 8, 9, 37
carob *65
carotenes 42
carrot *65
cassava *65
cauliflower *65
celery *65
celeriac *65
cereals 8, 9, *65-6
chard *66
cheese 27, 36, *66-7
cherries *68
chicken *68
chickpeas *68
chicory *68
chilli *68
chives *68
chocolate *68-9
cholecalciferol see vitamin D
cholesterol 36
    HDL (high density lipoprotein) 36
    LDL (low density lipoprotein) 36
chutney, pickles and relishes *69
cider *55
clementines see mandarin oranges
cocoa *69
collagen 46
cordials see soft drinks
corn *69-70
courgette *70
couscous *70
cranberry *70
cream *70
crispbread *70-1
croissant *71
crumpet *71
cucumber *71
currants see dried fruit
curry paste *71
custard *71
custard apple *71
cyanocobalamin see vitamin B12
daily calorie requirement 23, 35
damsons see plums

dates *71
desserts and puddings *72-3
diabetes 33
diet guidance for weight loss 20-1
    reasons for diet failure 24
    tips to help with dieting 29, 30-1
dips *73
doughnuts *73
dressings *73
dried fruit *74
duck *74

eggs 14, *74
elderberries *74
endive *74
energy balance (intake/expenditure) 21, 22
ergocalciferol see vitamin D

falafel *75
fast food/takeaway *75
fats 6, 7, 33, 34, 35, 35, 36
    counting fat intake 37
    monounsaturated 34, 35
    polyunsaturated 34, 35
    reducing fat intake 27
    saturated 34, 35, 36
fats and oils *75
fatty acids 35, 36
    omega-3 36
fennel *75
fibre 6, 7, 35, 38
    dietary benefits of 38
figs *75
fish *76-80
fish oil supplements 52
flour *80-1
folate see folic acid
folic acid 16, 41, 45
    supplements 16
food, personal relationship with 25,
food counter, how to use 35,
food diary 25, 26,
food labels, how to read 32-4
food pyramid 8

foods containing fat and sugar, food group 8, 10
frankfurter *81
free radicals 39

fromage frais *81
fructose 33

fruit and vegetables, food
    group 8, 9, 12
fruit, as source of sugars 37
fruit salad *81
fruit sugars see fructose

garlic *81
gelatine *81
gherkins *81
ginger *81
glucose 37
goitrogens 50
golden syrup *81
goose *82
gooseberries *82
grapefruit *82
grapes *82
gravy *82
greengages *82
grenadillas *82
guacamole see dips
guava *82

haemoglobin 48
haggis *83
halva *83
ham *83
HDL (high density lipoprotein)
    see cholesterol
health and diet 5, 6, 7
heart *83
heart disease
    benefits of eating fibre 38
    benefits of eating
    omega-3 fatty acids 36
    cholesterol-related 36
high blood pressure
    (hypertension) 51
honey 37, *83
horseradish *83
hummus see dips

ice cream *84
infertility, male 49
iodine 50
iron 14, 41, 48-9
    deficiency in 14

jam *84
jelly see desserts

kale *84
kidney *85

kilocalories (kcal) 6
kilojoules (kJ) 6
kiwi fruit *85
kohl rabi *85
kumquat *85

labels, food see food labels
lactose 33
lamb *85
lard see fats and oils
lasagne see pasta/ready
    meals
LDL (low density lipoprotein)
    see cholesterol
leeks *86
lemon *86
lentils *86
lettuce *86
lime *86
linguine see pasta
lipids 38
liqueurs *55
liver *87
loganberries *87
loquats *87
lotus *87
lychees *87
lycopene 52

macaroni see pasta
magnesium 49
mandarin oranges *87-8
mangetout *88
mango *88
mangosteen *88
maple syrup *88
margarine 35, *88
    with stanols or sterols 17
marmalade see jam
marrow *88
marzipan *89
matzos *89
mayonnaise 27, 35, *89
meat 36
meat, fish and alternatives,
    food group 8, 10
meat substitute *89
melon *89
menopause 52
meringue *89
metabolic rate 21, 23
milk 16, 27, 37, 43, *89-90
milk and dairy foods, food
    group 8, 9
milk sugars see lactose
milkshake *90

minerals 9, 39, 48-51
    chart of essential 40-1
    supplements 17
miso *90
mixed vegetables *90
molasses *90
monounsaturated fats see
    fats
motivational tips for dieters
    30-1
mulberries *90
mushrooms *90-1
mustard *91
mustard and cress *91

nashi pear *91
nectarine *91
noodles *91
nuts *91-2
nutritional information, on
    food labels 34

obesity 18, 37
oils 35, 36, 52 see also fats
    and oils
oily fish, benefits of eating
    52,
okra *92
olives *92
omega oils 52
omega-3 fatty acids 36
onions *92
oranges *92-3
osteoporosis 15, 48
oxtail *93

pancakes/crepes *93
pantothenic acid see vitamin
    B5
papadum *93
parsnip *93
passion fruit *93
pasta *93-4
pasta sauces *94
pastries see cakes/pastries/
    buns
pastry *94-5
pâté *95
peaches *95
pears *95
peas *95
peppers *96
pheasant *96
phytoestrogens 17
phytonutrients 52

pickles see chutney, pickles and relishes
pigeon *96
pineapple *96
plants, sources of phytonutrients 52
plums *96
PMT (pre-menstrual tension) 44, 49
pomegranate *96
polyunsaturated fats see fats
pork *96
potassium 50
potatoes 8, 9, *97
pregnancy, effect of folic acid on 45
probiotic yogurts 17
prostate gland 49, 52
protein 6, 7, 12, 33
prunes *97
puddings see desserts
pulses 14
pumpkin *97
pyridoxine see vitamin B6

quiche *97

rabbit *98
radish *98
raisins see dried fruit
raspberries *98
ready meals *98-101
recipes
    baked lemon cod 118
    baked mushrooms 115
    beef bourguignon 119
    bircher muesli 114
    blueberry frozen yogurt 124
    Greek yogurt with honey, nuts and blueberries 112
    little dark chocolate mousse pots with poached berries 125
    Mexican eggs 113
    speedy broccoli soup 117
    sticky lime chicken 120
    toasted pine kernel and vegetable couscous 122
    tuna and avocado salad 121
    warm red lentil salad with goat's cheese 123
    winter warmer red lentil soup 116
redcurrants *101

relishes see chutney, pickles and relishes
retinol see vitamin A
rhubarb *101
rice *102
rice cakes *102

salsify *102
salt 6, 51
satsuma see mandarin oranges
saturated fats see fats
sauces/savoury *102-3
sausage *103
seeds *103
selenium 50
sharon fruit *103
snacks *103-4
sodium 51
soft drinks 28, *104
soups *104-5
spinach *105
spirits *55
spreading fats 13
spreads (savoury) *105
spring greens *105
spring onions *105
sprouting beans *105-6
squash *106
starchy carbohydrates, food group 8, 9, 37
star fruit *106
stock cubes *106
strawberries *106
stuffing *106
sucrose see sugar
suet see fats and oils
sugar 6, 7, 13, 28, 32, 33, 34, 37, *106
    specified on food labels 32-3
sugary foods 37
sugar snap peas *106
sultanas see dried fruit
swede *106
sweet potato *106

tahini *107
tamarillos *107
tangerines see mandarin oranges
tapioca *107
taramasalata see dips
thyroid hormones 50
tocopherol see vitamin E

tofu *107
tomato *107
tortillas *107
trace elements 51
trigger factors for eating 26
turkey *108
turnip *108
tzatziki see dips

veal *108
vegetables, raw or cooked 53
vegetarian diet 14
venison *108
vinegar *108
vine leaves *108
vitamin A (retinol) 40, 42
vitamin B1 thiamin 40, 42-3
vitamin B2 riboflavin 40, 43
vitamin B3 niacin 40, 43
vitamin B5 (pantothenic acid) 44
vitamin B6 (pyridoxine) 44
vitamin C (ascorbic acid) 40, 46, 49
vitamin B12 (cyanocobalamin) 45
vitamin D (cholecalciferol) 41, 47, 48
vitamin E (tocopherol) 47
vitamins 6, 7, 9, 12, 39, 42-5
    chart of essential 40-1
    fat-soluble 35, 39
    supplements 17
    water-soluble 39

waffles *109
waist measurement, indicator of health risk 18, 23
water chestnuts *109
watercress *109
weight loss 21, 22
    ideal rate of 23
    motivational dieting tips 30-1
    reasons for diet failure 24
Western diet, health risks of 6
wines *56

yam *109
yeast *109
yeast extract *109
yogurt *109-10
Yorkshire pudding *110

zinc 41, 49

NOTES

....

....

....

....

....

....

....

....

....

....

....

....

....